New Zealand's North Island

Brett

Sarah Bennett, Peter Dragi   y

CAPE REINGA (p172)
Experience the mysterious beauty of Maoridom's most sacred site and watch an ocean and sea collide

AUCKLAND (p86)
Alternate volcano- and island-hopping with culture and culinary stops in NZ's biggest city

RAGLAN (p214)
Ease into the chilled vibe of this laid-back surf town

WHITIANGA (p194)
Splash in the clear waters off sandy beaches or paddle around the craggy limestone coast

ROTORUA (p303)
Kia ora and *haere mai*; meet Maori face-to-face and get all steamed up at this cultural and geothermal hot spot

To Tokelau

To Kermadec Islands

SOUTH PACIFIC OCEAN

Cape Reinga
Wahii Landing
North Cape
Ninety Mile Beach
Great Exhibition Bay
Karikari Peninsula
Kaitaia
Kaikohe
Kerikeri
Opononi
Pahia
Russell
Cape Brett
Bay of Islands
Hokianga Harbour
Dargaville
Poor Knights Islands
Whangarei
Hen & Chicken Islands
Goat Is
Wellsford
Warkworth
Little Barrier Is
Great Barrier Island
Helensville
Takapuna
Kaipara Harbour
AUCKLAND
Manukau Harbour
Hauraki Gulf
Cape Colville
Coromandel Peninsula
Papakura
Thames
Whitianga
Raglan
Ngaruawahia
Huntly
Hamilton
Cambridge
Paeroa
Waihi
Kawhia
Tauranga
Mt Maunganui
Mayor Island
Bay of Plenty
Whakaari (White Island)
Whakatane
Cape Runaway
East Cape
Hicks Bay
35

TASMAN SEA

2

TONGARIRO NATIONAL PARK (p288)
Explore the volcanic wonderland on one of the world's best day walks or a challenging mountain bike ride

WHANGANUI NATIONAL PARK (p260)
Canoe or kayak down the history-rich Whanganui River, or take a drive along the Whanganui River Rd

WELLINGTON (p379)
Windy Welly isn't all politics: revel in NZ's best nightlife and caffeine-scene along Cuba St and Courtenay Pl

NAPIER (p362)
Sip on a Syrah amid the art deco ambience of the Hawke's Bay wine region

To Chatham Islands

ELEVATION
3000m
2000m
1000m
500m
200m
0

LEGEND
Primary Road
Secondary Road
Tertiary Road

100 km
60 miles

On the Road

BRETT ATKINSON
Coordinating Author
From Auckland, I can be across on Waiheke Island (p123) in just 30 minutes, or exploring the vineyards and surf beaches on Kumeu (p136) in a similar time. The cafes and restaurants of buzzy Wellington (p379) are a preferred weekend break, and I'm always up for a road-trip from Auckland to funky Raglan (p214) or art deco Napier (p362).

PETER DRAGICEVICH
Matakana (p140), north of Auckland, may be well and truly gentrified (would you believe that these hard-nosed giantesses adorn the new public toilets), but if you're a lover of wine, food and beaches – and I'm guilty on all counts – it's a great stop. Just beware the terminal *hongi* (traditional Maori greeting).

SARAH BENNETT
I said I'd never, ever do it. Ever. Not in a million years. But, somehow, things felt different on this beautiful, breathless, blue-sky day in Taupo (p273). If ever I was going to leap out of a plane at 15,000ft, the moment had surely arrived. I committed myself to enjoying every minute.

CHARLES RAWLINGS-WAY
New Zealand is so flush with swoon-worthy vistas, empty swathes of coastline and rampant, snowcapped mountain ranges that the locals are often blasé about the smaller stuff. This isn't to say that it's any less beautiful, it's just less big! Wairere Falls (p335), a picture-perfect little waterfall tumbling down a cliff behind Whakatane's main street, goes almost unheralded.

For full author biographies see p455.

NORTH ISLAND INTENSIVE

More than three-quarters of New Zealand's population live in the North Island, and the qualities that make it a great place to live also make it a superb travel destination. Auckland and Wellington hum with a restless, cosmopolitan energy, with excellent vineyards just a short drive away. The scenery challenges anything further south, with kayaking, mountain biking and hiking options for an energetic exploration of alpine vistas, island labyrinths and dense forests. NZ's indigenous Maori culture is at its most robust, especially amid the geothermal landscapes around Rotorua, and the 'take it easy' ambience of the isolated East Cape.

Action Plus

Kilometres of rugged coastline, tumbling rivers and waterfalls, and only-in-Auckland big-city thrills conspire to make the North Island an essential destination for adventure seekers. With alpine thrills in winter and surfing in summer, the North Island effortlessly maintains NZ's reputation as the planet's adventure capital.

① Diving the Poor Knights Islands
The Poor Knights Islands (p151) bathe in a warm subtropical current from the Coral Sea. Underwater cliffs up to 60m high drop away amid a labyrinth of caves, canyons and tunnels dotted with tropical and sub-tropical fish.

② Surfing Raglan
The laid-back bohemia of Raglan (p214) is more than just a surfing mecca. After testing yourself on the world-renowned breaks, kick back in cool cafes and look forward to regular summertime gigs from NZ's best bands.

③ Canyoning in Auckland's Waitakere Ranges
Ready? One, two, three…jump! That's the usual command as adventure buffs negotiate a thrilling path down the bush-clad waterfalls and canyons of Auckland's Waitakere Ranges (p134). Also look forward to abseiling down a few moss-covered cascades.

④ Match Racing on Auckland Harbour
Don your boat shoes and recreate NZ's proud history in the America's Cup. After you've gone head to head with another yacht used in NZ's successful 1995 Cup challenge (p101), recharge with a gin and tonic at Auckland's Viaduct Harbour.

⑤ Auckland's Sky Walk & Sky Jump
Walking hands-free 192m above Auckland is loads of fun, once you get over the shock of your bright orange jumpsuit. After carefully negotiating the slim halo on the Sky Tower, take a controlled jump to the camera-wielding tourists below (p101).

⑥ Skiing Mt Ruapehu
The North Island's premier winter sports destination features runs for skiers and snowboarders of all levels on the expansive slopes of Mt Ruapehu (p290).

⑦ Fishing Lake Taupo
Formed by one of the world's biggest-ever eruptions, Lake Taupo and its surrounding rivers are great places to land a plump trout (p285). Wily locals can tutor you on the finer points of fly-fishing amid glorious scenery.

⑧ Mountain Biking around Rotorua
Take to two knobbly wheels in the Whakarewarewa Forest near Rotorua. More than 100km of tracks criss-cross the forest (p309), a network that's been used for the UCI Mountain Bike World Cup.

⑨ Kayaking the Whanganui River
Here's where your expectations of atmospheric back-country landscapes come alive. The languidly flowing Whanganui River is safe for beginner kayakers, while the occasional burst of minirapids attracts the more experienced (p262).

⑩ White-water Rafting the Kaituna River
Don't expect any dull days on the Kaituna River (p310). This is a waterway with a type-A, 'look at me' personality. Look forward to an exciting Grade V experience, either in an inflatable raft or on a personal white-water sledge (body board).

3

The Great Outdoors

Scenic diversity is the North Island's trump card, and perhaps nowhere else in the world delivers so many different landscapes in such a small area. NZ's volcanic genesis bubbles away in the island's heart, while the coastline is trimmed with stunningly isolated beaches and dramatic natural formations.

4

❶ Waitomo Caves

One of the North Island's first tourist attractions is still one of its best. Travellers have marvelled at Waitomo's underground wonders (p227) for more than a century, and nowadays you can even drift along inky subterranean rivers on inflatable tyres.

❷ Bay of Islands

OK, it's not the most creative place name in the country, but it's certainly an accurate description of Northland's most popular destination (p153). There are myriad ways to explore the islands, ranging from swimming with dolphins to sea kayaking and sailing.

❸ Wai-O-Tapu Thermal Wonderland

In an area crammed full of bubbling, belching thermal sights, Wai-O-Tapu (p321) effortlessly earns its 'wonderland' tag, with a memory card full of attractions tucked into a small area. The highlight is the multihued Champagne Pool.

❹ Cathedral Cove

Summer weekends can get crowded at the glorious limestone arch at Cathedral Cove (p197), but even if there's an impromptu game of beach cricket on, it's still an impressive sight, especially if you explore the cove by kayak.

❺ Whakaari (White Island)

It's not just the North Island mainland that exhibits the restless drama and energy of NZ's thermal activity. The country's most active volcano (p339) lies 49km off the coast, and punctuates the Pacific's deep blue with a steaming, sulphurous intensity.

❻ Art Deco Napier

Rising confidently from the 1931 earthquake, Napier (p362) is now studded with pristine examples of art deco design and architecture. Visit during the annual art deco weekend for Gatsbyesque grand balls and dance bands. BYO straw boater hat.

❼ Waiheke Island

Not so long ago, Waiheke Island (p123) was a boho enclave of Birkenstock-wearing alternative lifestylers. Waiheke's individual spirit definitely lingers, but its rugged scenery is now complemented by sophisticated restaurants, galleries and vineyards.

❽ East Cape

Keep heading alongside the Pacific Ocean. That's all you need to know to negotiate East Cape's stunning SH35 (p345). Along the highway's coast-hugging, meandering way, you'll pass desolate beaches, Maori *marae* (meeting houses) and sleepy country pubs.

❾ Cape Reinga

Cape Reinga (p172) is the ultimate meeting of the waters, with the Tasman Sea fronting up gamely to the Pacific Ocean. Nearby, Spirits Bay is revered by Maori as the place where the spirits of the dead begin their journey to the afterlife.

❿ Tongariro Alpine Crossing

Reckon you can find a spare day in your itinerary? That's all you need to take on the Tongariro Alpine Crossing (p292). Look forward to skirting the conical perfection of Mt Ngauruhoe, aka Mordor's Mt Doom from a certain cult movie.

2

Maoritanga

Interactive and tour-based Maori tourism is booming across Aotearoa. On the North Island you can help to paddle a *waka* (war canoe), hear ancient Maori legends in primeval forests, and be welcomed onto a *marae* (meeting house) in *Whale Rider* country.

3

❶ Te Papa
Kiwis are justifiably proud of their national museum in Wellington, known colloquially as 'Our Place'. Te Papa (p387) houses a huge Maori collection, including its own *marae*, showcases superb examples of *pounamu* (greenstone), and is an essential guide to understanding NZ's indigenous culture.

❷ Ohinemutu
Often overlooked by visitors to Rotorua, the lakeside village of Ohinemutu (p309) is a fascinating mix of Maori and European influences. The stained-glass window at St Faith's Anglican Church features Christ appearing to walk on the waters of Lake Rotorua.

❸ Footprints Waipoua
Listen to Maori legends on a twilight journey into the mystical Waipoua Kauri Forest with Footprints Waipoua (p178). Be astounded by the immense size of Tane Mahuta, NZ's grandest and most revered tree.

❹ *Wakas* in Waitangi
Join Waka Tai-a-Mai (p162) for a paddle in a traditional *waka* on the waterways of Waitangi. After a thrilling paddle to the Haruru Falls, the journey continues for storytelling at a replica Maori village.

❺ Waitangi Treaty Grounds
Signed in 1840 between Maori tribal chiefs and the British Crown, the Treaty of Waitangi remains an integral part of NZ society. Visit the Treaty House (p160) and the *whare runanga*, a wonderfully-carved meeting house, to learn about the historic agreement.

❻ Potiki Tours
Much-acclaimed Potiki Tours (p104) offers both traditional and contemporary perspectives on 'Urban Maori' tours of Auckland. Itineraries include visits to West Coast beaches, Maori arts and crafts, and historic *pa* (Maori fortified village) sites.

❼ East Cape
Maori traditions remain strong in the proud communities around East Cape (p345). You're likely to hear Maori spoken in the streets, see full-face *moko* (tattoos), stay in authentic accommodation and experience Maori-run cultural tours.

❽ Kawhia Kai Festival
Kai (food) is the focal point on Kawhia's biggest day of the year (p224). Every February, the sleepy fishing town comes alive with traditional Maori food – including loads of *kai moana* (seafood) – and cultural performances.

❾ Whakarewarewa Thermal Village
The vibrant Whakarewarewa Thermal Village (p306) in Rotorua is home to proud locals who love demonstrating traditional crafts including weaving, carving, and *ta moko* (tattooing).

❿ Mokoia Island
Lake Rotorua's Mokoia Island (p308) holds a special place in Maori history, and the romantic legend of Hinemoa and Tutanekai is celebrated on island excursions by Mokoia Island Wai Ora Experiences. Tours include the opportunity to try traditional Maori food.

5 JENNY & TONY ENDERBY; 6 MARTIN ROBINSON

Food & Drink

New Zealanders take their eating and drinking very seriously. The dark days of British-style 'meat and three veg' have been washed away with world-renowned wines, surprising craft beers, and an eclectic approach to incorporating European, Asian and Pacific flavours. Dig in.

❶ Zest Food Tours

Wellington's compact downtown area makes it perfect for informative and interesting walking tours. Take a spin around the harbour city with Zest Food Tours (p390) to discover coffee, chocolate, wine and beer. Just as well you're getting some exercise, eh?

❷ Hawke's Bay Food Trail

If you fancy yourself as a dedicated foodie traveller, then the bountiful plains and valleys of Hawke's Bay are an ideal destination. Navigate with the *Hawkes Bay Food Trail* brochure (p370) to discover everything from organic cheese to artisan chutneys.

❸ Cycling Martinborough

Sure, everyone's heard of Kiwi sauvignon blanc, but New Zealand's latest wine superstars are the smoky, peppery pinot noir wines from Martinborough (p407). Most winemaking is on small, boutique vineyards, and the flat landscape can be negotiated perfectly by bicycle.

❹ Hallertau

West Auckland's is well-known for winemaking, but Hallertau's microbrewery/restaurant (p136) is another essential reason to visit, especially on a hot summer's day after visiting nearby beaches. Limited-edition seasonal brews ensures there's always something new and exciting on tap.

❺ Matakana Farmers Market

Organic coffee, artisan breads, and ice cream made with fresh blueberries are all pretty fine reasons to visit the Matakana Farmers Market (p140). When you've finished your culinary grazing, pop into the area's up and coming boutique wineries.

❻ Auckland's Restaurant Scene

The country's biggest city is easily its most cosmopolitan. Fuelled by influences from Auckland's diverse immigrant groups, the city's chefs shine in the restaurants of heritage suburbs such as Ponsonby, Mt Eden and Kingsland (p110).

Contents

Regional Map Contents

Destination North Island

The buzzing cities, arcing beaches and scenic beauty of New Zealand's North Island make the country's smaller, but more populated island, an essential stand-alone destination for intrepid travellers.

The island is punctuated north and south by NZ's two most energetic cities. With a population now edging above one million, Auckland is the country's closest thing to an international city. The 'City of Sails' is home to immigrants from around the world, especially Asia, and is justly proud of its position as the planet's biggest Polynesian urban hub. But despite Auckland's increasing size and cosmopolitan makeup, it remains laidback and quintessentially Kiwi. An Aucklander's typical summer weekend might entail kicking back at nearby vineyards, or taking to the waters of the Hauraki Gulf for yachting, cruising or fishing. At the opposite end of the island, Wellington is the nation's capital, but any excess of political hot air is quickly dispersed by coffee, cocktails and conversation in the city's cafes, bars and restaurants.

The North Island is also the heartland of NZ's indigenous Maori culture. In Rotorua it shares the stage with the restless steaming, belching and bubbling of spectacular geothermal activity, and in Northland and around the East Cape, tribal-based tours are informed with a fascinating dash of local tradition and centuries-old storytelling. The influence of more recent settlers is expressed in the wine regions of the North Island, with a unique background of art deco design and architecture in Hawke's Bay, and the pride of Croatian families in West Auckland. An internationally renowned wine scene deserves an equal focus on food, and across the North Island travellers are guaranteed an increasing range of artisan food producers and organic farmers markets.

The undoubted attractions of gourmet travel demand a balance of healthy exercise, and there are many opportunities to get active against idiosyncratic only-in-NZ scenic backdrops. Skirting the looming volcanic cones of the Tongariro National Park, the Tongariro Alpine Crossing is renowned as one of the planet's great one-day walks, and the slopes of Mt Ruapehu are a downhill haven for skiers and snowboarders. Immersion in the outdoors and great food are the natural outcomes of trout fishing in the waters of nearby Lake Taupo.

The country is slowly shrugging off the global economic gloom that had pushed the economy into recession and sent unemployment soaring. It's a challenge faced by the National Party, NZ's first centre-right government for several years. It was elected in late 2008 following nine years under Helen Clark's centre-left Labour Party; Clark went on to accept the third-highest job at the United Nations as Head of the UN Development Program. At the time of writing, prime minister John Keys was surfing a wave of popularity due in large part to his image as a thoroughly likeable Kiwi bloke. He's the guy pictured, beer in hand, hosting a barbecue for NZ's future king, Prince William. He's the guy doing an awkward dance with a couple of drag queens at a gay and lesbian festival in Auckland. He's the goofy guy slipping down the stairs and breaking his arm at a Chinese New Year celebration. Sure, he's a self-made millionaire after years working as a currency trader in London and New York, but his easy-going and likeable manner continues to strike a chord with Kiwis, especially after Helen Clark's sometimes severe and intellectual demeanour.

Conversation-wise, the discourse you're likely to hear in the cafes, pubs and bars of the North Island varies by location. In bustling, cosmopolitan Auckland, the issues often concern the effect the city's kinetic growth has

FAST FACTS

Population: NZ 4.4 million; North Island 3.4 million

Area: NZ 268,680 sq km; North Island 113,729 sq km

NZ GDP growth: -1% (2009)

NZ inflation: 2%

NZ unemployment: 6.5%

NZ life expectancy: men 78, women 82, tuatara (native lizards) 100+, kauri trees 2000+

Number of international visitors to NZ: 2.4 million in 2009

Area of Lake Taupo: 616 sq km

Actual Length of Ninety Mile Beach: 55 miles (88 km)

Height of Mt Ruapehu: 2797m (9177ft)

on its infrastructure. What's being done to ease the city's expanding rush hour? When will the city get a comprehensive plan for the downtown wharf area? Down in arty, political Wellington, don't be too surprised to hear important government issues occasionally being discussed over coffee in the funky cafes of Cuba St.

In provincial areas of the North Island, the balance between economic growth and green issues is of importance in regions like the Coromandel Peninsula. In 2010 John Key's centre-right government floated the idea of allowing mining in some areas of the country currently under Department of Conservation (DOC) protection. Tourism operators will be against any increase in mining, but for other locals the promise of steady employment is a compelling argument.

Sport is another shared conversational touchstone for many Kiwis. In Auckland, the 'on again/off again' performances of the Warriors rugby league team are always worth a few well-considered remarks. Wellington is the heartland of football (soccer) with the Wellington Phoenix regularly filling Westpac Stadium (known locally as the 'Cake Tin'). An essential Wellington experience is meeting supporters in the bars and pubs of Courtenay Place after a big match.

Of course, many Kiwis are also interested in the rugby. In September and October 2011, NZ will host the Rugby World Cup and chances are, whether you travel before, during or after the tournament, you'll be thoroughly sick of hearing about rugby by the end of your stay.

Rugby plays a special part in the nation's consciousness, partly because it was one of the first things in which NZ truly excelled. The All Blacks are the most successful rugby team in history (with a 74% winning record) but they've only snagged the Cup once. After yet another dazzling failure in France in 2007, the All Blacks are determined to redeem themselves on home soil.

With NZ's next general election scheduled for November 2011, the tournament finale at Auckland's Eden Park on October 23 promises to be more than just a rugby match. More than one political pundit has opined – and not entirely in jest – that an All Blacks victory or defeat could influence the decision-making of voters on election day. Watch this space.

> An essential Wellington experience is meeting supporters in the bars and pubs of Courtenay Place after a big match.

Getting Started

By world standards, New Zealand is an easy, accessible place to visit. Amiable locals, a moderate climate, good personal security, brilliant roads, well-organised activities and the fantastic i-SITE visitor information centre network (see p428) make travelling here a breeze! There's also a network of around 30 Department of Conservation (DOC) visitor centres around NZ – a handy resource for planning activities in parks, and for natural and cultural features. There are eating and accommodation options for all budgets, from a felafel and a dorm bunk to a crayfish dinner and a spa suite.

If you're scuttling between cities pursuing urban virtues, you won't need to do much forward planning, but if you're tramping into the wilderness or devising a cycling epic, do some research on equipment, accommodation, track and hut passes, and weather, and book what you need to well in advance.

WHEN TO GO

The warmer high-season months (November to April) are ripe for outdoor exploration. Summer (December to February) is also when Kiwis crank up the food and wine festivals, concerts and sports events. December in the far north can be rainy, however. If you're a snow bunny, visit when the powder is thickest – June to August is skiing high season. Remember, though, that in winter, warm-weather beach towns might be half asleep.

See Climate Charts (p419) for more information.

If you want a *real* holiday, staying and eating in your venues of choice, avoid school holidays (particularly late December to early February) and public holidays (p422). In the less touristed 'shoulder' period from late February to April, the weather is at its best (less chance of rain), the kids are back at school, and the ocean is still warm(ish) – a much better time to travel.

NZ is smack-bang in the middle of the Roaring Forties; these prevailing west-to-east winds buffet the country year-round, ranging from gentle breezes to tempestuous gales. On both islands it's drier in the east than in the west, where mountain ranges snare moisture-laden winds from the Tasman Sea. It's usually a few degrees cooler on the South Island than the North Island. Wherever you are, remember that NZ has a maritime climate – the weather changes rapidly. Anyone tramping at any time of year needs to be well prepared for all weather conditions. The **New Zealand Mountain Safety Council** (☎ 04-385 7162; www.mountainsafety.org.nz) has the information you need – available from DOC visitor centres nationwide.

DON'T LEAVE HOME WITHOUT...

- Double-checking the visa situation (see p429)
- A travel-insurance policy covering you for high-risk activities (see p422)
- Insect repellent to keep the sandflies at bay (see p420)
- The ability to get excited over a game of rugby (p42)
- Your driver's licence – the best way to see NZ's nooks and crannies is at your own speed (p439)
- A bottomless appetite for Kiwi food and wine (p58)
- A mobile phone (p427) for booking restaurants and accommodation on the hop
- An open ear and a notepad to jot down the NZ bands you're going to download when you get home (see www.amplifier.co.nz)

COSTS & MONEY

In recent years burgeoning tourism in NZ has seen prices rise with demand. However, if you're visiting from Europe or North America, it's still a fairly economical destination, unless you're throwing yourself out of a plane or jetboating every day. Activities like these generally top expense lists – think carefully about what you'll spend your money on.

Gastronomes will find food to be surprisingly pricey – cooked breakfasts at snazzy cafes average around $16, while main courses at top-end restaurants cost $30 and beyond. Food in remote areas also costs more, without necessarily being of better quality.

If you do some sightseeing, eat out once or twice a day and stay in cheap motels or B&Bs, budget on at least $150 per day (per person, travelling as a pair), not including car hire or activities. Packing kids into your suitcases obviously means greater expense, but museums, cinemas, and tour and activity organisers usually offer discounts for youngsters, and there are plenty of open-air attractions available for free!

At the low-cost end, if you camp or stay in hostels, cook your own meals, repress the urge to drink beer, tackle attractions independently and travel on a bus pass, you could probably eke out an existence on $80 per day. But if you want to enjoy the occasional restaurant meal and glass of wine, then $100 per day is more realistic.

TRAVELLING RESPONSIBLY

Since our inception in 1973, Lonely Planet has encouraged readers to tread lightly, travel responsibly and enjoy the magic that independent travel affords. International travel is growing at a jaw-dropping rate, and we still firmly believe in the benefits it can bring – but, as always, we encourage you to consider the impact your visit will have on both the global environment and the local economies, cultures and ecosystems.

It's not hard to make your NZ trip ecosavvy. For starters, check out our GreenDex (p474), which lists ecofriendly operators. Volunteer some of your time to a local environmental program. Consider carbon-offsetting your flights. If you're taking a tour, ask about the company's environmental policies: are they NZ-owned? Sensitive to indigenous culture? How do they dispose of rubbish? Support NZ businesses rather than multinational chains and eat at local restaurants and buy from farmers markets that sell locally sourced produce. Instead of car hire, consider car-pooling to travel from town to town; check hostel noticeboards to find a ride. Stay at hotels and hostels that actively engage in recycling and waste reduction. If you're tramping into the forests or along the coast, carry out your rubbish, travel in small groups, camp on durable surfaces, and don't wash in or near water sources.

HOW MUCH?

Cup of decent coffee $4

Movie ticket $14

Dorm bed $25-35

Motel room $100-160

Magnificent scenery $0

DIY NZ

At Lonely Planet we love travel (no kidding…), and we reckon part of the adventure is to fly by the seat of your pants. We're dedicated to bringing you comprehensive in-depth destination coverage, but we also encourage you to ditch your guidebook. Really! Go AWOL for a day or a week and explore NZ beyond the pages of a book.

Low population density = empty spaces – it's easy to get off the beaten track. Buy a detailed road map, pick a little town down a little road and go for it – you can't really lose when the scenery is so great. Scan the bulletin boards at local cafes for performances that night or swap a yarn or two with locals at a country pub. Kiwis are famously friendly – ask them about their favourite places to eat, hang out or blow off steam.

After your trip, drop us a line and tell us what you discovered: www.lonelyplanet.com/contact.

TOP 10

MANDATORY MOVIES

Spending an evening or three watching classic NZ movies makes a great intro to the country's much-publicised scenery, and will help you get under the national skin. Captured on celluloid, wry humour and an often-bleak mysticism await. See p45 for reviews of these and other locally produced films.

1 *Once Were Warriors* (1994) Director: Lee Tamahori

2 *The Lord of the Rings* trilogy (2001–03) Director: Peter Jackson

3 *Whale Rider* (2002) Director: Niki Caro

4 *Rain* (2001) Director: Christine Jeffs

5 *The Piano* (1993) Director: Jane Campion

6 *In My Father's Den* (2004) Director: Brad McGann

7 *Kaikohe Demolition* (2004) Director: Florian Harbicht

8 *Boy* (2010) Director: Taika Waititi

9 *Out of the Blue* (2006) Director: Robert Sarkies

10 *Sione's Wedding* (2006) Director: Chris Graham

BRILLIANT BOOKS

Escapist plots, multilayered fiction, reinvented realities and character-driven social commentary: Kiwi literature presents an opportunity to learn much about the country, drawing on NZ's unsettled history, burgeoning cultural awareness and the physical power of the landscape. See p45 for more on NZ literature.

1 *The Bone People* (1988) Keri Hulme

2 *Mister Pip* (2007) Lloyd Jones

3 *The Carpathians* (1988) Janet Frame

4 *Potiki* (1986) Patricia Grace

5 *Bulibasha: King of the Gypsies* (1994) Witi Ihimaera

6 *Live Bodies* (1998) Maurice Gee

7 *The 10pm Question* (2009) Kate de Goldi

8 *The Vintner's Luck* (2000) Elizabeth Knox

9 *Opportunity* (2007) Charlotte Grimshaw

10 *Hibiscus Coast* (2005) Paula Morris

FESTIVAL FRENZY

Kiwis love to party, and many travellers plan their journeys around food, wine and arts fiestas. Following are some of our favourite excuses to get festive. For other events in the North Island and further suggestions, see p421 and the Festivals & Events sections in destination chapters.

1 **Harvest Hawke's Bay** (www.harvesthawkesbay.co.nz) Hawke's Bay, late January (p371)

2 **Parihaka** (www.parihaka.com) Taranaki, January (see boxed text, p250)

3 **Art Deco Weekend** (www.artdeconapier.com) Napier & Hastings, February (p365)

4 **Fringe NZ** (www.fringe.org.nz) Wellington, February/March (p390)

5 **Pasifika Festival** (www.aucklandcity.govt.nz/whatson/events/pasifika) Auckland, March (p105)

6 **Cuba St Carnival** (www.cubacarnival.org.nz) Wellington, February (p390)

7 **WOMAD** (World Music Arts & Dance) (www.womad.co.nz) New Plymouth, March (p241)

8 **Toast Martinborough** (toastmartinborough.co.nz) Martinborough, November (p408)

9 **Rhythm & Vines** (www.rhythmandvines.co.nz) Gisborne, late December (p354)

10 **Opotiki Rodeo** (opotikirodeonz) Opotiki, December (p341)

For more tips online:

Department of Conservation (DOC; www.doc.govt.nz/getting-involved) Conservation events and programs that visitors can engage with.

Leave No Trace (www.lnt.org) Low-impact camping and tramping tips.

Lonely Planet (www.lonelyplanet.com/responsibletravel) Tips on sustainable travel.

Organic Explorer (www.organicexplorer.co.nz) Comprehensive guide to ecofriendly places to eat, stay and explore throughout NZ.

TRAVEL LITERATURE

Given NZ's starring role on the world tourism stage, the current bloom in dedicated NZ travel literature isn't surprising.

Bob Moore, a Wellington-based Englishman, traversed every kilometre of State Hwy 1 (NZ's national drag) then wrote *The 1 Thing: A Small Epic Journey Down New Zealand's Mother Road* (2006). Lyttelton-based Joe Bennett, another Englishman-in-NZ, wrote *A Land of Two Halves* (2004), a tale of hitchhiking around the country.

If you're into cycling, pick up *Long Cloud Ride* by Josie Dew (2007). Dew – a roaming Brit cyclist – chronicles her nine-month, 10,000km NZ journey. Through wind and rain, she gets close to the Kiwi psyche.

Liberal-minded travellers who don't mind the odd tree-hug will love *Slipping into Paradise: Why I Live in New Zealand* by Jeffrey Moussaieff Masson (2004), a gushing sonnet to NZ from a relative newcomer to the country.

How to Watch a Game of Rugby by Spiro Zavos (2004) is a brilliant insight into the national preoccupation by a respected sports journalist, and will ensure you don't ask stupid questions when you're watching the All Blacks at the pub. In the same series, astronomer Richard Hall helps you find the Southern Cross in *How to Gaze at the Southern Stars* (2005).

They're not technically travel lit, but fans of Kiwi films will enjoy Hamish McDouall's *100 Essential New Zealand Films* (2009), and history buffs will be engrossed by the comprehensive *Penguin History of New Zealand* (2003) by Michael King.

INTERNET RESOURCES

100% Pure New Zealand (www.newzealand.com) NZ's official tourism site, with comprehensive visitor info.

Department of Conservation (DOC; www.doc.govt.nz) Indispensable DOC parks, recreation and conservation info across NZ.

Destination New Zealand (www.destination-nz.com) Travel guide with excellent website listings.

DineOut (www.dineout.co.nz) Restaurant reviews and info across the nation.

Living Landscapes (www.livinglandscapes.co.nz) Maori tourism operators across NZ.

Lonely Planet (www.lonelyplanet.com) Get started with NZ summaries and travellers trading info on the Thorn Tree.

Muzic.net (www.muzic.net.nz) Gigs, reviews, bios, charts — Wellington rock to Dunedin dub.

New Zealand Tourism Online (www.tourism.net.nz) Commercial site with 10,000-plus listings and plenty of useful info.

Stuff (www.stuff.co.nz, www.stuff.co.nz/blogs) NZ news (sourced from Fairfax New Zealand publications) and an array of blogs.

Te Ara (www.teara.govt.nz) An online encyclopaedia of NZ.

Itineraries
SHORT BREAKS

AUCKLAND ENCOUNTER

Four to Seven Days / Auckland to Auckland

Bounce around Auckland's stellar bars and restaurants, museums, islands and beaches – multicultural New Zealand at its most engaging.

Check out the Maori gallery at the **Auckland Museum** (p90), then cross the Domain to **K Rd** (p111) for lunch. Take our architectural **walking tour** (p103), stopping at **Auckland Art Gallery** (p95) and the impossible-to-miss **Sky Tower** (p95). **Ponsonby** (p112) awaits for dinner and drinks.

Ferry over to **Rangitoto Island** (p121) for walking or to **Devonport** (p113) for good shopping and city views. Explore the **Waitakere Ranges Regional Park** (p133), **Karekare** (p134) and **Piha** (p134), and while you're 'out west', stop at **Kumeu** (p136) for excellent craft beers at Hallertau. Back in town hit the bars and restaurants of **Kingsland** (p112), before recharging with breakfast in **Mt Eden** (p112), and a brisk climb of **Maungawhau** (p112). Head downtown to catch a ferry to **Waiheke Island** (p123) for excellent wineries and beaches.

Near Auckland, you can snorkel at **Goat Island Marine Reserve** (p142), explore the legendary **Bay of Islands** (p153), ocean-gaze at **Cape Reinga** (p172), ogle the giant trees at **Waipoua Kauri Forest** (p179), explore the **Waitomo Caves** (p226), surf at **Raglan** (p214) or beach yourself at **Whitianga** (p194).

Some say Auckland is just Sydney for beginners. We think not. Sydney doesn't have access to two oceans, nor does it have the amazing melange of Polynesian culture on offer in the 'City of Sails'. Enjoy the big smoke, then explore some local highlights with this 450km to 900km itinerary.

TRAVEL FURTHER

CLASSIC NORTH ISLAND   Two to Three Weeks / Auckland to Wellington

Cruise the harbours, cafes and beaches of **Auckland** (p86) before heading north up SH1 for dolphin swimming, colonial history, and stunning scenery in the winterless **Bay of Islands** (p153). Return to Auckland and detour east to the rugged **Coromandel Peninsula** (p183); time to get active with bushwalking and sea-kayaking. Continue south to **Rotorua** (p303) for the town's classic mix of bubbling thermal activity and vibrant Maori culture. Thrillseekers can sign up here for white-water sledging or rafting on the Grade V **Kaituna River** (p310). More outdoor action awaits with trout fishing in **Taupo** (p273), and tramping (or skiing in winter) in the **Tongariro National Park** (p288). The Tongariro Alpine Crossing has been judged one of the best one-day walks on the planet. After all this exercise, the wineries and artisan organic food scene of **Hawke's Bay** (p357) provide a tasty reward. Between cycling around the region's vineyards and taking loads of oh-so-arty pics of the glorious art deco architecture in **Napier** (p362), the busy, busy gannets at **Cape Kidnappers** (p375) are another essential visit. Continue to point the car or campervan south to **Martinborough** (p407), where your newly-expanded knowledge of Kiwi wine will come in handy. Take time to discover NZ's best pinot noir in Martinborough's compact, boutique vineyards. The **Toast Martinborough festival** (p408) in November sees locals and visitors alike getting pleasantly raucous with a combination of food, wine and music. A final push across the dramatic Rimutaka Ranges leads to **Wellington** (p379), with NZ's energetic, compact capital offering world-class museums and galleries, and the country's best cafe, restaurant and bar scene.

This 1500km trip showcases the North Island, with attractions including beaches, islands, river rafting and tramping. You also get to touch down in the country's two most exciting cities.

OFF THE BEATEN TRAIL   Two to Three Weeks / Auckland to Wellington

Discover your own relaxed Kiwi havens in this itinerary for repeat visitors or the curious first-time NZ traveller. Maximise your time in energetic **Auckland** (p86), then head north to sleepy **Tutukaka** (p151) for diving around the Poor Knights Islands. Kayaking and snorkelling is also available for non-scuba-certified travellers. Further north, there are sailing and dolphin swimming trips at **Doubtless Bay** (p170), and perhaps the world's best fish and chips in Mangonui. Continue to windswept **Cape Reinga** (p172) on the North Island's northern tip, and post a letter (remember them?) home from NZ's most remote mailbox. Venture south skirting the windswept expanses of Ninety Mile Beach, before settling in at **Ahipara** (p174) for a few days. Explore massive sand dunes on sandboards, sand yachts or quad bikes, or just chill with a good book and ocean views. Next stop is **Hokianga** (p175), studded with colonial history. Head south through Auckland – avoiding rush hour on the city's motorways – to **Whakatane** (p335) on the eastern edge of the Bay of Plenty. Take a boat or helicopter out to **Whakaari** (White Island; p339), NZ's most active volcano, and a sulphurous South Pacific version of hell. Meander on SH35 around the stunning **East Cape** (p345). This is *Whale Rider* country, and the film's traditional Maori culture is showcased by locally-owned tourism ventures. In **Gisborne** (p349 there's excellent wine and craft beers. Follow SH2 south into the **Wairarapa region** (p406) and negotiate wiggly Akatarawa Rd to the deserted beaches of the **Kapiti Coast** (p403). Wellington is just down SH1, but at the nature reserve on **Kapiti Island** (p405), the bohemian cafes of Cuba St are a world away.

Probably none of these destinations figured at all in your pre-trip planning. That's possibly a big mistake, because a combination of friendly locals, stunning coastal scenery and unique off-shore islands means this 2200km North Island spin gets you to the very heart of NZ.

TAILORED TRIPS

FOOD & DRINK

The North Island's best festivals if you're hungry and thirsty: **Gisborne Food & Wine Festival** (p354), **Whitianga Scallop Festival** (p195), **Kawhia Kai Festival** (p224), **Harvest Hawke's Bay** (p371), and **Toast Martinborough** (p408).

Explore the best dining-out precincts in the North Island's two biggest cities. In Auckland **Mt Eden** (p112), **Ponsonby** (p112), and **Kingsland** (p112) have everything from French crêperies and Thai Isaan food, to Pacific Rim bistros and cool neighbourhood bars perfect for watching people, sport, or both at the same time. Wellington's vibrant cafe scene is centred on cosmopolitan **Cuba St** (p395), and around Courtenay Place you can imbibe craft beers from around the country at the **Malthouse** (p396), and dive into NZ's most authentic Asian food.

NZ has recently gone crazy for farmers markets. Search out the best of organic produce and artisan foodie goodies at the **Hawke's Bay Farmers Market** (p374) in Hastings, the **Matakana Farmers Market** (p140) and Auckland's **La Cigale market** (p113). If you're travelling in summer elsewhere in the North Island, ask at visitor information centres if any farmers markets are being held locally. Most towns and cities now hold at least one on a regular basis.

DISCOVERING MAORI

Auckland has the world's biggest population of Pacific Islanders, but it's also the ideal place to begin exploring Maori culture. Maori collection highlights at **Auckland Museum** (p90) include a 25m *waka* (war canoe) and a carved meeting house. The team at **Potiki Tours** (p104) run excellent tours of Auckland, underpinned with traditional and contemporary Maori culture. From Auckland, travel north to Waitangi and paddle a 50ft *waka* with the local Ngapuhi tribe and **Waka Tai-a-Mai** (p162).

Return south via the North Island's west coast, joining a walking tour with **Footprints Waipoua** (p178) in the **Waipoua Kauri Forest** (p179). Continue to **Rotorua** (p303) for slickly-rehearsed but moving performances of Maori song and dance. Most performances also include the opportunity to try food cooked in a *hangi* (traditional earth oven).

Venture to the **East Cape** (p345), probably the most traditional area for Maori in NZ. Several locally-owned tour companies explore the area's distinct and proud Maori culture. Continue southwest to Taupo to link up with **pureORAwalks** (p278). Guided walks showcase Maori storytelling and demonstrate how Maori utilised the natural resources of the forest. Finish your journey at another urban museum, this time with the hugely impressive Maori collection at Wellington's **Te Papa** (p387).

History James Belich

New Zealand's history is not long, but it is fast. In less than a thousand years these islands have produced two new peoples: the Polynesian Maori and European New Zealanders. The latter are often known by their Maori name, 'Pakeha' (though not all like the term). NZ shares some of its history with the rest of Polynesia, and with other European settler societies, but has unique features as well. It is the similarities that make the differences so interesting, and vice versa.

One of NZ's foremost modern historians, James Belich has written a number of books on NZ history and hosted the TV documentary series *NZ Wars*.

MAKING MAORI

Despite persistent myths (see the boxed text, p30), there is no doubt that the first settlers of NZ were the Polynesian forebears of today's Maori. Beyond that, there are a lot of question marks. Exactly where in east Polynesia did they come from – the Cook Islands, Tahiti, the Marquesas? When did they arrive? Did the first settlers come in one group or several? Some evidence, such as the diverse DNA of the Polynesian rats that accompanied the first settlers, suggests multiple founding voyages. On the other hand, only rats and dogs brought by the founders have survived, not the more valuable pigs and chickens. The survival of these cherished animals would have had high priority, and their failure to be successfully introduced suggests fewer voyages. See Kawhia (p224) and the boxed text on p338 for the tales of just two of the great migratory canoes that made the voyage.

For more about Maui and other mythological figures, Maori tribal structure and performing arts, see Maori Culture, p51.

NZ seems small compared to Australia, but it is bigger than Britain, and very much bigger than other Polynesian islands. Its regions vary wildly in environment and climate. Prime sites for first settlement were warm coastal gardens for the food plants brought from Polynesia (kumara or sweet potato, gourd, yam and taro); sources of workable stone for knives and adzes; and areas with abundant big game. NZ has no native land mammals apart from a few species of bat, but 'big game' is no exaggeration: the islands were home to a dozen species of moa (a large flightless bird), the largest of which weighed up to 240kg, about twice the size of an ostrich. There were also other species of flightless bird and large sea mammals such as fur seals, all unaccustomed to being hunted. For people from small Pacific islands, this was like hitting the jackpot. The first settlers spread far and fast, from the top of the North Island to the bottom of the South Island within the first 100 years. High-protein diets are likely to have boosted population growth.

Similarities in language between Maori and Tahitian indicate close contact in historical times. Maori is about as similar to Tahitian as Spanish is to French, despite the 4294km separating these island groups.

By about 1400, however, with big-game supply dwindling, Maori economics turned from big game to small game – forest birds and rats – and from hunting to gardening and fishing. A good living could still be made, but it required detailed local knowledge, steady effort and complex communal

TIMELINE

AD 1000–1200	1642	1769
Possible date of the arrival of Maori in NZ. Solid archaeological evidence points to about AD 1200, but much earlier dates have been suggested for the first human impact on the environment.	First European contact: Abel Tasman arrives on an expedition from the Dutch East Indies (Indonesia) to find the 'Great South Land'. The party leaves without landing after a sea skirmish with Maori, but its legacy remains in the country's name.	European contact recommences with visits by James Cook and Jean de Surville. Despite some violence, both managed to communicate with Maori, and this time NZ's link with the outside world proved permanent.

THE MORIORI & THEIR MYTH

One of NZ's most persistent legends is that Maori found mainland NZ already occupied by a more peaceful and racially distinct Melanesian people, known as the Moriori, whom they exterminated. This myth has been regularly debunked by scholars since the 1920s, but somehow hangs on.

To complicate matters, there were real 'Moriori', and Maori did treat them badly. The real Moriori were the people of the Chatham Islands, a windswept group about 900km east of the mainland. They were, however, fully Polynesian, and descended from Maori – 'Moriori' was their version of the same word. Mainland Maori arrived in the Chathams in 1835, as a spin-off of the Musket Wars, killing some Moriori and enslaving the rest. But they did not exterminate them. The mainland Moriori remain a myth.

---

organisation, hence the rise of the Maori tribes. Competition for resources increased, conflict did likewise, and this led to the building of increasingly sophisticated fortifications, known as *pa*. Vestiges of *pa* earthworks can still be seen around the country, on the hilltops of Auckland for example.

The Maori had no metals and no written language (and no alcoholic drinks or drugs). But their culture and spiritual life was rich and distinctive. Below Ranginui (sky father) and Papatuanuku (earth mother) were various gods of land, forest and sea, joined by deified ancestors over time. The mischievous demigod Maui was particularly important. In legend, he vanquished the sun and fished up the North Island before meeting his death between the thighs of the goddess Hine-nui-te-po in an attempt to conquer the human mortality embodied in her. Maori traditional performance art, the group singing and dancing known as *kapa haka,* has real power, even for modern audiences. Visual art, notably woodcarving, is something special – 'like nothing but itself', in the words of 18th-century explorer-scientist Joseph Banks.

Abel Tasman named NZ Statenland, assuming it was connected to Staten Island near Argentina. It was subsequently named after the province of Zeeland in Tasman's Holland.

ENTER EUROPE

NZ became an official British colony in 1840, but the first authenticated contact between Maori and the outside world took place almost two centuries earlier in 1642, in Golden Bay at the top of the South Island. Two Dutch ships sailed from Indonesia, to search for southern land and anything valuable it might contain. The commander, Abel Tasman, was instructed to pretend to any natives he might meet 'that you are by no means eager for precious metals, so as to leave them ignorant of the value of the same'.

When Tasman's ships anchored in the bay, local Maori came out in their canoes to make the traditional challenge: friends or foes? Misunderstanding this, the Dutch challenged back, by blowing trumpets. When a boat was lowered to take a party between the two ships, it was attacked. Four crewmen were killed. Tasman sailed away and did not come back; nor did any other European for 127 years. But the Dutch did leave a name: 'Nieuw Zeeland' or 'New Sealand'.

1790s	1818–36	1840
Whaling ships and sealing gangs arrive in the country. Relations are established with Maori, with Europeans depending on the contact for essentials such as food, water and protection.	Intertribal Maori 'Musket Wars' take place: tribes acquire muskets and win bloody victories against tribes without them. The war tapers off in 1836, probably as a result of the equal distribution of weapons.	On 6 February, the Treaty of Waitangi is signed by 40 chiefs in a sovereignty settlement presented by William Hobson. Copies of the treaty are circulated countrywide to collect signatures. NZ becomes a nominal British colony.

Contact between Maori and Europeans was renewed in 1769, when English and French explorers arrived, under James Cook (see the boxed text, p30) and Jean de Surville. Relations were more sympathetic, and exploration continued, motivated by science, profit and great power rivalry. Cook made two more visits between 1773 and 1777, and there were further French expeditions.

Unofficial visits, by whaling ships in the north and sealing gangs in the south, began in the 1790s. The first mission station was founded in 1814, in the Bay of Islands, and was followed by dozens of others: Anglican, Methodist and Catholic. Trade in flax and timber generated small European-Maori settlements by the 1820s. Surprisingly, the most numerous category of European visitor was probably American. New England whaling ships favoured the Bay of Islands for rest and recreation; 271 called there between 1833 and 1839 alone. To whalers, 'rest and recreation' meant sex and drink. Their favourite haunt, the little town of Kororareka (now Russell) was known to the missionaries as 'the hellhole of the Pacific'. New England visitors today might well have distant relatives among the local Maori.

One or two dozen bloody clashes dot the history of Maori-European contact before 1840 but, given the number of visits, inter-racial conflict was modest. Europeans needed Maori protection, food and labour, and Maori came to need European articles, especially muskets. Whaling stations and mission stations were linked to local Maori groups by intermarriage, which helped keep the peace. Most warfare was between Maori and Maori: the terrible intertribal 'Musket Wars' of 1818–36. Because Northland had the majority of early contact with Europe, its Ngapuhi tribe acquired muskets first. Under their great general Hongi Hika, Ngapuhi then raided south, winning bloody victories against tribes without muskets. Once they acquired muskets, these tribes saw off Ngapuhi, but also raided further south in their turn. The domino effect continued to the far south of the South Island in 1836. The missionaries claimed that the Musket Wars then tapered off through their influence, but the restoration of the balance of power through the equal distribution of muskets was probably more important.

Europe brought such things as pigs (at last) and potatoes, which benefited Maori, while muskets and diseases had the opposite effect. The negative effects have been exaggerated, however. Europeans expected peoples like the Maori to simply fade away at contact, and some early estimates of Maori population were overly high – up to one million. Current estimates are between 85,000 and 110,000 for 1769. The Musket Wars killed perhaps 20,000, and new diseases did considerable damage too (although NZ had the natural quarantine of distance: infected Europeans usually recovered or died during the long voyage, and smallpox, for example, which devastated native Americans, did not make it here). By 1840, the Maori had been reduced to about 70,000, a decline of at least 20%. Maori bent under the weight of European contact, but they certainly did not break.

Rumours of late survivals of the giant moa bird abound, but none have been authenticated. So if you see a moa in your travels, photograph it – you have just made the greatest zoological discovery of the last 100 years.

Scottish influence can still be felt in NZ, particularly in the south of the South Island. NZ has more Scottish pipe bands per capita than Scotland itself.

For a thorough overview of NZ history from Gondwanaland to today, visit http://history-nz.org.

1844	1853–56	1860–61
Young Ngapuhi chief, Hone Heke, challenges British sovereignty, first by cutting down the British flag at Russell, and then by sacking the town itself. The ensuing Northland War continues till 1846.	Provincial and central elected governments established. In 1853 the first elections are held for the New Zealand parliament; votes are restricted to adult, male, British subjects, and Maori votes are limited due to property-right rules.	First Taranaki war. Starting with the controversial swindling of Maori land by the government at Waitara, the war involves many military participants from the Waikato tribes (despite being traditional enemies of the Taranaki Maori).

CAPTAIN JAMES COOK *Tony Horwitz*

If aliens ever visit earth, they may wonder what to make of the countless obelisks, faded plaques and graffiti-covered statues of a stiff, wigged figure gazing out to sea from Alaska to Australia, from NZ to North Yorkshire, from Siberia to the South Pacific. James Cook (1728–79) explored more of the earth's surface than anyone in history, and it's impossible to travel the Pacific without encountering the captain's image and his controversial legacy in the lands he opened to the West.

For a man who travelled so widely, and rose to such fame, Cook came from an extremely pinched and provincial background. The son of a day labourer in rural Yorkshire, he was born in a mud cottage, had little schooling, and seemed destined for farm work – and for his family's grave plot in a village churchyard. Instead, Cook went to sea as a teenager, worked his way up from coal-ship servant to naval officer, and attracted notice for his exceptional charts of Canada. But Cook remained a little-known second lieutenant until, in 1768, the Royal Navy chose him to command a daring voyage to the South Seas.

In a converted coal ship called *Endeavour*, Cook sailed to Tahiti, and then became the first European to land at NZ and the east coast of Australia. Though the ship almost sank after striking the Great Barrier Reef, and 40% of the crew died from disease and accidents, the *Endeavour* limped home in 1771. On a return voyage (1772–75), Cook became the first navigator to pierce the Antarctic Circle and circled the globe near its southernmost latitude, demolishing the ancient myth that a vast, populous and fertile continent surrounded the South Pole. Cook also crisscrossed the Pacific from Easter Island to Melanesia, charting dozens of islands between. Though Maori killed and cooked 10 sailors, the captain remained strikingly sympathetic to islanders. 'Notwithstanding they are cannibals,' he wrote, 'they are naturally of a good disposition'.

On Cook's final voyage (1776–79), in search of a northwest passage between the Atlantic and Pacific, he became the first European to visit Hawaii, and coasted America from Oregon to Alaska. Forced back by Arctic pack ice, Cook returned to Hawaii, where he was killed during a skirmish with islanders who had initially greeted him as a Polynesian god. In a single decade of discovery, Cook had filled in the map of the Pacific and, as one French navigator put it, 'left his successors with little to do but admire his exploits'.

But Cook's travels also spurred colonisation of the Pacific, and within a few decades of his death, missionaries, whalers, traders and settlers began transforming (and often devastating) island cultures. As a result, many indigenous people now revile Cook as an imperialist villain who introduced disease, dispossession and other ills to the Pacific (hence the frequent vandalising of Cook monuments). However, as islanders revive traditional crafts and practices, from tattooing to *tapa,* they have turned to the art and writing of Cook and his men as a resource for cultural renewal. For good and ill, a Yorkshire farm boy remains the single most significant figure in the shaping of the modern Pacific.

Tony Horwitz is a Pulitzer-winning reporter and nonfiction author. In researching Blue Latitudes (or Into the Blue), Tony travelled the Pacific – 'boldly going where Captain Cook has gone before'.

1861	1868–72	1882
Gold discovered in Otago by Gabriel Read, an Australian prospector. As a result, the population of Otago climbs from less than 13,000 to over 30,000 in six months.	East Coast war. Te Kooti, having led an escape from his prison on the Chatham Islands, leads a holy guerrilla war in the Urewera region. He finally retreats to establish the Ringatu Church.	First refrigerated cargo to Britain. Exports to Britain had been dominated by the wool trade, but this development allows diversification into meat and dairy, and establishes NZ's early lead in the industry.

MAKING PAKEHA

By 1840, Maori tribes described local Europeans as 'their Pakeha', and valued the profit and prestige they brought. Maori wanted more of both, and concluded that accepting nominal British authority was the way to get them. At the same time, the British government was overcoming its reluctance to undertake potentially expensive intervention in NZ. It too was influenced by profit and prestige, but also by humanitarian considerations. It believed, wrongly but sincerely, that Maori could not handle the increasing scale of unofficial European contact. In 1840, the two peoples struck a deal, symbolised by the treaty first signed at Waitangi on 6 February that year. The Treaty of Waitangi now has a standing not dissimilar to that of the Constitution in the US, but is even more contested. The original problem was a discrepancy between British and Maori understandings of it. The English version promised Maori full equality as British subjects in return for complete rights of government. The Maori version also promised that Maori would retain their chieftainship, which implied local rights of government. The problem was not great at first, because the Maori version applied outside the small European settlements. But as those settlements grew, conflict brewed.

In 1840, there were only about 2000 Europeans in NZ, with the shanty town of Kororareka (now Russell) as the capital and biggest settlement. By 1850, six new settlements had been formed with 22,000 settlers between them. About half of these had arrived under the auspices of the New Zealand Company and its associates. The company was the brainchild of Edward Gibbon Wakefield, who also influenced the settlement of South Australia. Wakefield hoped to short-circuit the barbarous frontier phase of settlement with 'instant civilisation', but his success was limited. From the 1850s, his settlers, who included a high proportion of upper-middle-class gentlefolk, were swamped by succeeding waves of immigrants that continued to wash in until the 1880s. These people were part of the great British and Irish diaspora that also populated Australia and much of North America, but the NZ mix was distinctive. Lowland Scots settlers were more prominent in NZ than elsewhere, for example, with the possible exception of parts of Canada. NZ's Irish, even the Catholics, tended to come from the north of Ireland. NZ's English tended to come from the counties close to London. Small groups of Germans, Scandinavians and Chinese made their way in, though the last faced increasing racial prejudice from the 1880s, when the Pakeha population reached half a million.

Much of the mass immigration from the 1850s to the 1870s was assisted by the provincial and central governments, which also mounted large-scale public works schemes, especially in the 1870s under Julius Vogel. In 1876, Vogel abolished the provinces on the grounds that they were hampering his development efforts. The last imperial governor with substantial power was the talented but Machiavellian George Grey, who ended his second

The Waitangi Treaty Grounds (p160), where the Treaty of Waitangi was first signed in 1840, is now a tourist attraction for Kiwis and non-Kiwis alike. Each year on 6 February, Waitangi hosts treaty commemorations and protests.

'I believe we were all glad to leave New Zealand. It is not a pleasant place. Amongst the natives there is absent that charming simplicity... and the greater part of the English are the very refuse of society.' Charles Darwin, referring to Kororareka (Russell), in 1860.

1890–1912	1893	1914–18
The Liberal government is in power over an economy recovering from depression. Their major leader is Richard John Seddon, 'King Dick, as I am usually known'.	Votes for women granted, following a campaign led by Kate Sheppard, who had been petitioning the government for years. NZ becomes the first country in the world to grant the vote to women.	NZ's contribution to WWI is quite staggering for a country of just over one million people: about 100,000 NZ men serve overseas, and close on 60,000 became casualties, mostly on the Western Front in France.

Maurice Shadbolt's *Season of the Jew* (1987) is a semifictionalised story of bloody campaigns led by warrior Te Kooti against the British in Poverty Bay in the 1860s. Te Kooti and his followers compared themselves to the Israelites who were cast out of Egypt.

governorship in 1868. Thereafter, the governors (governors-general from 1917) were largely just nominal heads of state; the head of government, the premier or prime minister, had more power. The central government, originally weaker than the provincial governments, the imperial governor and the Maori tribes, eventually exceeded the power of all three.

The Maori tribes did not go down without a fight, however. Indeed, their resistance was one of the most formidable ever mounted against European expansion, comparable to that of the Sioux and Seminole in the US. The first clash took place in 1843 in the Wairau Valley, now a wine-growing district. A posse of settlers set out to enforce the myth of British control, but encountered the reality of Maori control. Twenty-two settlers were killed, including Wakefield's brother, Arthur, along with about six Maori. In 1845, more serious fighting broke out in the Bay of Islands, when Hone Heke sacked a British settlement. Heke and his ally Kawiti baffled three British punitive expeditions, using a modern variant of the traditional *pa* fortification. Vestiges of these innovative earthworks can still be seen at Ruapekapeka (south of Kawakawa). Governor Grey claimed victory in the north, but few were convinced at the time. Grey had more success in the south, where he arrested the formidable Ngati Toa chief Te Rauparaha, who until then wielded great influence on both sides of Cook Strait. Pakeha were able to swamp the few Maori living in the South Island, but the fighting of the 1840s confirmed that the North Island at that time comprised a European fringe around an independent Maori heartland.

In the 1850s, settler population and aspirations grew, and fighting broke out again in 1860. The wars burned on sporadically until 1872 over much of the North Island. In the early years, a Maori nationalist organisation, the King Movement (see the boxed text, p209), was the backbone of resistance. In later years, some remarkable prophet-generals, notably Titokowaru and Te Kooti (see the boxed text, p352), took over. Most wars were small-scale, but the Waikato War of 1863–64 was not. This conflict, fought at the same time as the American Civil War, involved armoured steamships, ultramodern heavy artillery, telegraph and 10 proud British regular regiments. Despite the odds, the Maori won several battles, such as that at Gate Pa, near Tauranga, in 1864. But in the end they were ground down by European numbers and resources. Maori political, though not cultural, independence ebbed away in the last decades of the 19th century. It finally expired when police invaded its last sanctuary, the Urewera Mountains, in 1916.

'Kaore e mau te rongo – ake, ake!' (Peace never shall be made – never, never!) War chief Rewi Maniapoto in response to government troops at the battle of Orakau, 1864

WELFARE & WARFARE

From the 1850s to the 1880s, despite conflict with Maori, the Pakeha economy boomed on the back of wool exports, gold rushes and massive overseas borrowing for development. The crash came in the 1880s, when NZ experienced its Long Depression. In 1890, the Liberals came to power, and stayed there until 1912, helped by a recovering economy. The Liberals were NZ's first

1935–49	1939–45	1974
First Labour government in power, under Michael Savage. This government creates NZ's pioneering version of the welfare state, and also takes some independent initiatives in foreign policy.	NZ troops back Britain and the Allied war effort during WWII, while a hundred thousand or so Americans arrive from 1942 to protect NZ from the Japanese.	Pacific Island migrants who have outstayed visas (dubbed 'overstayers') subjected to Dawn Raids (crackdowns by immigration police) under Robert Muldoon and the National government. These raids continue till the early 1980s.

organised political party, and the first of several governments to give NZ a reputation as 'the world's social laboratory'. NZ became the first country in the world to give women the vote in 1893, and introduced old-age pensions in 1898. The Liberals also introduced a long-lasting system of industrial arbitration, but this was not enough to prevent bitter industrial unrest in 1912–13. This happened under the conservative 'Reform' government, which had replaced the Liberals in 1912. Reform remained in power until 1928, and later transformed itself into the National Party. Renewed depression struck in 1929, and the NZ experience of it was as grim as any. The derelict little farmhouses still seen in rural areas often date from this era.

To find out more about the New Zealand Wars, visit www.newzealand wars.co.nz.

In 1935, a second reforming government took office: the First Labour government, led by Michael Joseph Savage, easily NZ's favourite Australian. For a time, the Labour government was considered the most socialist government outside Soviet Russia. But, when the chips were down in Europe in 1939, Labour had little hesitation in backing Britain.

NZ had also backed Britain in the Boer War (1899–1902) and WWI (1914–18), with dramatic losses in WWI in particular. You can count the cost

---

LAND WARS *Errol Hunt*

Five separate major conflicts made up what are now collectively known as the New Zealand Wars (also referred to as the Land Wars or Maori Wars). Starting in Northland and moving throughout the North Island, the wars had many complex causes, but *whenua* (land) was the one common factor. In all five wars, Maori fought both for and against the government, on whose side stood the Imperial British Army, Australians and NZ's own Armed Constabulary. Land confiscations imposed on the Maori as punishment for involvement in these wars are still the source of conflict today, with the government struggling to finance compensation for what are now acknowledged to have been illegal seizures.

Northland war (1844–46) 'Hone Heke's War' began with the famous chopping of the flagpole at Kororareka (now Russell, p157) and 'ended' at Ruapekapeka (south of Kawakawa). In many ways, this was almost a civil war between rival Ngapuhi factions, with the government taking one side against the other.

First Taranaki war (1860–61) Starting in Waitara, the first Taranaki war inflamed the passions of Maori across the North Island.

Waikato war (1863–64) The largest of the five wars. Predominantly involving Kingitanga (see the boxed text, p209), the Waikato war was caused in part by what the government saw as a challenge to sovereignty. However, it was land, again, that was the real reason for friction. Following defeats such as Rangiriri (p208), the Waikato people were pushed entirely from their own lands, south into what became known as the King Country.

Second Taranaki war (1865–69) Caused by Maori resistance to land confiscations stemming from the first Taranaki war, this was perhaps the war in which the Maori came closest to victory, under the brilliant, one-eyed prophet-general Titokowaru. However, once he lost the respect of his warriors (probably through an indiscretion with the wife of one of his warriors), the war too was lost.

East Coast war (1868–72) Te Kooti's holy guerrilla war; see the boxed text, p352.

1975	1981	1984
Waitangi Tribunal set up to investigate grievances of Maori people in relation to the Treaty of Waitangi. The tribunal's power is later extended to allow investigations of Crown confiscations as far back as 1840.	Springbok rugby tour divides the nation. Many New Zealanders show a strong anti-apartheid stance by protesting the games. Other Kiwis feel that sport and politics should not mix, and support the South African tour going ahead.	Fourth Labour government elected, adopting an anti-nuclear foreign policy, and a more-market economic policy. Social restrictions are removed almost as fast as economic ones – the pubs still close at six, but am, not pm.

in almost any little NZ town. A central square or park will contain a memorial lined with names – more for WWI than WWII. Even in WWII, however, NZ did its share of fighting: a hundred thousand or so New Zealanders fought in Europe and the Middle East. NZ, a peaceful-seeming country, has spent much of its history at war. In the 19th century it fought at home; in the 20th, overseas.

BETTER BRITONS?

British visitors have long found NZ hauntingly familiar. This is not simply a matter of the British and Irish origin of most Pakeha. It also stems from the tightening of NZ links with Britain from 1882, when refrigerated cargoes of food were first shipped to London. By the 1930s, giant ships carried frozen meat, cheese and butter, as well as wool, on regular voyages taking about five weeks one way. The NZ economy adapted to the feeding of London, and cultural links were also enhanced. NZ children studied British history and literature, not their own. NZ's leading scientists and writers, such as Ernest Rutherford and Katherine Mansfield (see the boxed text, p388), gravitated to Britain. This tight relationship has been described as 'recolonial', but it is a mistake to see NZ as an exploited colony. Average living standards in NZ were normally better than in Britain, as were the welfare and lower-level education systems. New Zealanders had access to British markets and culture, and they contributed their share to the latter as equals. The list of 'British' writers, academics, scientists, military leaders, publishers and the like who were actually New Zealanders is long. Indeed, New Zealanders, especially in war and sport, sometimes saw themselves as a superior version of the British – the Better Britons of the south. The NZ-London relationship was rather like that of the American Midwest and New York.

'Recolonial' NZ prided itself, with some justice, on its affluence, equality and social harmony. But it was also conformist, even puritanical. Until the 1950s, it was technically illegal for farmers to allow their cattle to mate in fields fronting public roads, for moral reasons. The 1953 American movie, *The Wild One*, was banned until 1977. Sunday newspapers were illegal until 1969, and full Sunday trading was not allowed until 1989. Licensed restaurants hardly existed in 1960, nor did supermarkets or TV. Notoriously, from 1917 to 1967, pubs were obliged to shut at 6pm. Yet the puritanical society of Better Britons was never the whole story. Opposition to Sunday trading stemmed, not so much from belief in the sanctity of the Sabbath, but from the belief that workers should have weekends too. Six o'clock closing was a standing joke in rural areas, notably the marvellously idiosyncratic region of South Island's west coast. There was always something of a Kiwi counterculture, even before imported countercultures took root from the 1960s.

There were also developments in cultural nationalism, beginning in the 1930s but really flowering from the 1970s. Writers, artists and film-makers were by no means the only people who 'came out' in that era.

'God's own country, but the devil's own mess.' Prime Minister Richard (King Dick) Seddon, speaking on the source of NZ's self-proclaimed nickname 'Godzone'.

Wellington-born Nancy Wake (codenamed 'The White Mouse') led a guerrilla attack against the Nazis with a 7000-strong army. She had the multiple honours of being the Gestapo's most-wanted person and being the most decorated Allied servicewoman of WWII.

1985	1987	1992
Rainbow Warrior sunk in Auckland Harbour by French government agents to prevent the Greenpeace protest ship from making its intended voyage to Mururoa, where the French government is conducting a nuclear-testing program.	The international stock market crash known as 'Black Monday' hits the NZ economy particularly hard, following optimistic financial investment in the free-market atmosphere. The economy takes years to recover.	Government begins reparations for land confiscated in the Land Wars, and confirms Maori fishing rights in the 'Sealord deal'. Major settlements of historical confiscation follow including, in 1995, reparations for the Waikato land confiscations.

COMING IN, COMING OUT

The 'recolonial' system was shaken several times after 1935, but managed to survive until 1973, when Mother England ran off and joined the Franco-German commune now known as the EU. NZ was beginning to develop alternative markets to Britain, and alternative exports to wool, meat and dairy products. Wide-bodied jet aircraft were allowing the world and NZ to visit each other on an increasing scale. NZ had only 36,000 tourists in 1960, compared with more than two million a year now. Women were beginning to penetrate first the upper reaches of the workforce and then the political sphere. Gay people came out of the closet, despite vigorous efforts by moral conservatives to push them back in. University-educated youths were becoming more numerous and more assertive.

From 1945, Maori experienced both a population explosion and massive urbanisation. In 1936, Maori were 17% urban and 83% rural. Fifty years later, these proportions had reversed. The immigration gates, which until 1960 were pretty much labelled 'whites only', widened, first to allow in Pacific Islanders for their labour, and then to allow in (East) Asians for their money. These transitions would have generated major socioeconomic change whatever happened in politics. But most New Zealanders associate the country's recent 'Big Shift' with the politics of 1984.

In 1984, NZ's third great reforming government was elected – the Fourth Labour government, led nominally by David Lange and in fact by Roger Douglas, the Minister of Finance. This government adopted an antinuclear foreign policy, delighting the left, and a more-market economic policy, delighting the right. NZ's numerous economic controls were dismantled with breakneck speed. Middle NZ was uneasy about the antinuclear policy, which threatened NZ's ANZUS alliance with Australia and the US. But in 1985, French spies sank the antinuclear protest ship *Rainbow Warrior* (see the boxed text, p169) in Auckland Harbour, killing one crewman. The lukewarm American condemnation of the French act brought middle NZ in behind the antinuclear policy, which became associated with national independence. Other New Zealanders were uneasy about the more-market economic policy, but failed to come up with a convincing alternative. Revelling in their new freedom, NZ investors engaged in a frenzy of speculation, and suffered even more than the rest of the world from the economic crash of 1987.

The early 21st century is an interesting time for NZ. Like NZ food and wine, film and literature are flowering as never before, and the new ethnic mix is creating something very special in popular music. There are continuities, however – the pub, the sportsground, the quarter-acre section, the bush, the beach and the bach – and they too are part of the reason people like to come here. Realising that NZ has a great culture, and an intriguing history, as well as a great natural environment, will double the bang for your buck.

The Ministry for Culture & Heritage's history website (www.nzhistory.net.nz) is an excellent source of info on NZ history.

The Six o'clock Swill referred to the frantic after-work drinking at pubs when men tried to drink as much as possible from 5.05pm until strict closing time at 6pm.

NZ's staunch antinuclear stance earned it the nickname 'The Mouse that Roared'.

1996	2004	2008
NZ changes from a two-party 'first past the post' (FPP) electoral system to Mixed Member Proportional (MMP) representation, allowing minority parties such as the Greens to take a representative role in government.	Maori TV begins broadcasting – for the first time, a channel committed to NZ content and the revitalisation of Maori language and culture hits the small screen.	An election replaces nine-year Labour prime minister Helen Clark with a National (conservative) government under John Key.

The Culture

THE NATIONAL PSYCHE

New Zealand is like that little guy at school when they're picking rugby teams – quietly waiting to be noticed, desperately wanting to be liked. Then, when he does get the nod, his sheer determination to prove himself propels him to score a completely unexpected try. When his team-mates come to congratulate him he stares at the ground and mumbles, 'It was nothing, ay'.

While a proud little nation, Kiwis traditionally don't have time for show-offs. Jingoistic flag-waving is generally frowned upon. People who make an impression on the international stage are respected and admired, but flashy tall poppies have traditionally had their heads lopped off. This is perhaps a legacy of NZ's early egalitarian ideals – the ones that sought to avoid the worst injustices of the 'mother country' (Britain) by breaking up large land holdings and enthusiastically adopting a 'cradle to grave' welfare state. 'Just because someone's got a bigger car than me, or bigger guns, doesn't make them better' is the general Kiwi attitude.

NZ has rarely let its size get in the way of making a point on the international stage. A founding member of the League of Nations (the precursor to the UN), it ruffled feathers between the world wars by failing to blindly follow Britain's position. It was in the 1980s, however, that things got really interesting.

Modern Kiwi culture pivots on that decade. Firstly, the unquestioned primacy of rugby union as a source of social cohesion (which rivalled the country's commitment to the two world wars as a foundation of nation-building) was stripped away when tens of thousands of New Zealanders took to the streets to protest a tour by the South African rugby side in 1981. They held that the politics of apartheid not only had a place in sport, they trumped it. The country was starkly divided; there were riots in paradise. The scar is still strong enough that most New Zealanders over 35 will recognise the simple phrase 'The Tour' as referring to those events.

The tour protests both harnessed and nourished a political and cultural renaissance among Maori which had already been rolling for a decade. Three years later, that renaissance found its mark when a reforming Labour government gave statutory teeth to the Waitangi Tribunal, an agency that has since guided a process of land return, compensation for past wrongs and interpretation of the Treaty of Waitangi – the 1840 pact between Maori and the Crown – as a living document.

At the same time antinuclear protests that had been rumbling for years gained momentum, with mass blockades of visiting US naval ships. In 1984 Prime Minister David Lange barred nuclear-powered or armed ships from entering NZ waters. The mouse had roared. As a result the US threw NZ out of ANZUS, the country's main strategic military alliance, which also included Australia, declaring NZ 'a friend but not an ally'.

The following year an event happened that would completely change the way NZ related to the world when French government agents launched an attack in Auckland Harbour, sinking Greenpeace's antinuclear flagship *Rainbow Warrior* and killing one of its crew. Being bombed by a country that NZ had fought two world wars with and the muted or nonexistent condemnation by other allies left an indelible mark. It strengthened NZ's resolve to follow its own conscience in foreign policy and in 1987 the NZ Nuclear Free Zone, Disarmament & Arms Control Act became law.

For many, Sir Edmund Hillary, the first person to climb Mt Everest, was the consummate New Zealander: humble, practical and concerned for social justice. A public outpouring of grief followed his death in 2008.

Ironically, the person responsible for the nuclear age was a New Zealander. In 1917 Ernest Rutherford was the first to split the nucleus of an atom. His face appears on the $100 note.

From the Boer to the Vietnam War, NZ had blithely trotted off at the behest of the UK or US. Not anymore, as is demonstrated by its lack of involvement in the invasion of Iraq. That's not to say that the country shirks its international obligations. NZ troops continue to be deployed in peacekeeping capacities throughout the world and are currently active in Afghanistan.

If that wasn't enough upheaval for one decade, 1986 saw another bitter battle split the community – this time over the decriminalisation of homosexuality. The debate was particularly rancorous, but the law that previously incarcerated consenting gay adults was repealed – paving the way for the generally accepting society that NZ is today. Just 13 years later Georgina Beyer, an openly transsexual former prostitute, would win a once safe rural seat off a conservative incumbent – an unthinkable achievement in most of the world.

Yet while the 1980s saw the country jump to the left on social issues, simultaneously economic reforms were carried out that were an extreme step to the right (to paraphrase one-time Hamiltonian Richard O'Brien's song *The Time Warp*). The bloated public sector was slashed, any state assets that weren't bolted to the floor were sold off, regulation was removed from many sectors, trade barriers dismantled and the power of the unions greatly diminished.

If there is broad agreement that the economy had to be restructured, the reforms carried a heavy price. The old social guarantees are not as sure. New Zealanders work long hours for lower wages than their Australian cousins would ever tolerate. Compared with other Organisation for Economic Co-operation and Development (OECD) nations, family incomes are low, child poverty rates are high and the gap between rich and poor is widening.

Yet there is a dynamism about NZ that was rare in the 'golden weather' years before the reforms. NZ farmers take on the world without the massive subsidies of yore, and Wellington's inner city – once virtually closed after dark by oppressive licensing laws – now thrives with great bars and restaurants.

As with the economic reforms, the 'Treaty process' of redress and reconciliation with Maori makes some New Zealanders uneasy, more in their uncertainty about its extent than that it has happened at all. A court decision suggesting that some Maori might have unforeseen rights to stretches of the country's seabed and foreshore (not the beaches themselves, but the area from the high tide outwards) hit a raw nerve among some. The assumption had long been that access to the beach was a NZ birthright, although its basis in law proved to be shaky. The conservative National Party, then ailing in opposition, tapped into public unease over this new and unexpected dimension to the Treaty process, claiming the country was moving towards 'separatism' – and shot up in the opinion polls. The Labour government, spooked by the public response, passed a law that confirmed the seabed and foreshore in Crown (public) ownership but offered Maori groups the chance to explore their 'customary rights' to places they had traditionally used.

Many Maori, feeling they had been denied due process, were angry, and a *hikoi* (march) of 15,000 protested at parliament, amid speculation that political allegiances were being re-drawn. The speculation was well founded: the momentum generated by the *hikoi* led directly to the formation of the Maori Party, which now holds five of the seven electorates reserved for Maori (unseating a Labour MP in each). The Maori Party currently has a 'confidence and supply' agreement with the National-led government and, at the time of research, it seems likely that they will win some concessions on the foreshore and seabed issue from their former foes.

'...a sordid act of international state-backed terrorism...' Prime Minister David Lange, describing the bombing of the *Rainbow Warrior* (1986)

For the younger generation, for whom the 1980s are prehistory, political apathy is the norm. Perhaps it's because a decade of progressive government has given them little to kick against – unlike those politicised by the anti–Iraq War movements in the UK, US and Australia. Ironically, as NZ has finally achieved its own interesting, independent cultural sensibility, the country's youth seem more obsessed by US culture than ever.

In 2009 NZ topped the Global Peace Index earning the distinction of being rated the world's most peaceful country.

This is particularly true within the hip-hop scene where a farcical identification with American gangsta culture has developed into a worrying youth gang problem. Even more ridiculous is the epidemic of boy racers, pulling burnouts and street-racing in souped-up V8s.

Despite all the change, key elements of the NZ identity are an unbroken thread, and fortune is still a matter of economics rather than class. If you are well served in a restaurant or shop, it will be out of politeness or pride in the job, rather than servility.

In country areas and on bush walks don't be surprised if you're given a cheery greeting from passers-by, especially in the South Island. In a legacy of the British past, politeness is generally regarded as one of the highest virtues. A 'please' and 'thank you' will get you a long way. The three great exceptions to this rule are: a) on the road, where genteel Dr Jekylls become raging Mr Hydes, especially if you have the misfortune of needing to change lanes; b) if you don't speak English very well; and c) if you are Australian.

NZ is defined as a state in the Australian constitution. At the time of Australia's federation into one country it was hoped that NZ would join. On this side of the Tasman that idea proved as unpopular then as it does now.

The latter two traits are the product of insularity and a smallness of world view that tends to disappear among Kiwis who have travelled (and luckily many do). The NZ/Australian rivalry is taken much more seriously on this side of the Tasman Sea. Although it's very unlikely that Kiwis will be rude outright, visiting Aussies must get pretty sick of the constant ribbing, much of it surprisingly ill-humoured. It's a sad truth that while most Australians would cheer on a NZ sports team if they were playing anyone other than their own, the opposite is true in NZ.

You might on your travels hear the phrase 'number-eight wire' and wonder what on earth it means. It's a catchphrase New Zealanders still repeat to themselves to encapsulate a national myth: that NZ's isolation and its pioneer stock created a culture in which ingenuity allowed problems to be solved and tools to be built from scratch. A NZ farmer, it was said, could solve pretty much any problem with a piece of number-eight wire (the gauge used for fencing on farms).

Kiwi inventions include the disposable syringe, nonshortable electric fence, Navman GPS and the child-proof top for pill bottles.

It's actually largely true – NZ farms are full of NZ inventions. One reason big offshore film and TV producers bring their projects here – apart from the low wages and huge variety of locations – is that they like the can-do attitude and ability to work to a goal of NZ technical crews. Many more New Zealanders have worked as managers, roadies or chefs for famous recording artists (everyone from Led Zeppelin and U2 to Madonna) than have enjoyed the spotlight themselves. Which just goes to show that New Zealanders operate best at the intersection of practicality and creativity, with an endearing (and sometimes infuriating) humility to boot.

LIFESTYLE

Living on an island has its perks, especially in summer. By the middle of the week your average Kiwi office worker is keeping a nervous watch on the weather, praying that the rain will hold off for the weekend so that they can head to the beach, maybe start working on the garden or at least get the kids out of the house for a few hours. Of course, the more gung-ho are already making the most of the long summer evenings – there's Carmen the teacher taking the kayak out fishing after school; and Steven the quantity surveyor with the surfboard in the car, itching to hit the breaks during the last few hours of daylight.

For all the stereotypes of the active healthy Kiwi, other clichés are just as real. Susan's working late at the office. Again. (New Zealanders have among the longest working hours in the developed world.) She'll probably grab some fast food on her way home and, yes, she does want fries with that. (A quarter of NZ adults are obese.) Then there's Dean, hanging around on the street with his other teenage mates, trying to look staunch while sweating into his hoodie. The fact is, there is no one NZ lifestyle.

> No matter where you are in NZ, you're never more than 128km from the sea.

Most Kiwis (except perhaps the farmers) would probably wish it rained a little less and they got paid a little more, but it sometimes takes a few years travelling on their 'Big OE' (Overseas Experience – a traditional right of passage) before they realise how good they've got it. In a 2009 study of the quality of life in the world's major cities, Auckland was rated fourth-equal and Wellington 12th.

For most of its history, NZ's small population and plentiful land has seen its people live in stand-alone houses on large, green sections. And while that's still the norm, for a number of reasons it has started to change.

In Auckland, concern about suburban sprawl and poor public transport, and the gentrification of once-poor inner-city suburbs, has seen a boom in

---

'SO, WHAT DO YOU THINK OF NEW ZEALAND?' *Russell Brown*

That, by tradition, is the question that visitors, especially important ones, are asked within an hour of disembarking in NZ. Sometimes they might be granted an entire day's research before being asked to pronounce, but asked they are. The question – composed equally of great pride and creeping doubt – is symbolic of the national consciousness.

When George Bernard Shaw visited for four weeks in 1934, he was deluged with what-do-you-think-of questions from newspaper reporters the length of the country. Although he never saw fit to write a word about NZ, his answers to those newspaper questions were collected and reprinted as *What I Saw in New Zealand: the Newspaper Utterances of George Bernard Shaw in New Zealand*. Yes, people really were that keen for vindication.

Other visitors were willing to pronounce in print, including the British Liberal MP, David Goldblatt, who came to NZ to convalesce from a heart attack in 1955, became fascinated with the place and wrote an intriguing and prescient little book called *Democracy At Ease: a New Zealand Profile*.

Goldblatt found New Zealanders a blithe people; kind, prosperous, fond of machines, frequently devoid of theory. In 'a land in which the practice of neighbourliness is most strongly developed' no one went wanting, yet few seemed to aspire. He admired the country's education system and its newspapers, despaired of its tariffs and barriers and wondered at laws that amounted to 'the complete control of the individual by the government'.

He was far from the first visitor to muse about NZ's contradictions – the American academic Leslie Lipson, who weathered the WWII years at Wellington's Victoria University, admired NZ's 'passion for social justice' but fretted about its 'restraint on talent' and 'lack of cultural achievement'.

For the *bon vivant* Goldblatt, the attitude towards food and drink was all too telling. Apart from one visit to a clandestine European-style restaurant in Auckland, where the bottles were hidden under tables, he found only 'the plain fare and even plainer fetch and carry of the normal feeding machine of this country' and shops catering 'in the same pedestrian fashion for a people never fastidious – the same again is the order of the day'.

Thus, a people with access to some of the best fresh ingredients on earth tended to boil everything to death. A nation strewn almost its entire length with excellent microclimates for viticulture produced only fortified plonk. Material comfort was valued, but was a plain thing indeed.

It took New Zealanders a quarter of a century more to shuck 'the same dull sandwiches', and embrace a national awareness – and, as Goldblatt correctly anticipated, it took 'hazards and misfortunes' to spur the 'divine discontent' for change.

But when it did happen, it *really* happened.

Russell Brown is a journalist and manager of the popular Public Address blog site (www.publicaddress.net).

terraced housing and apartments, either in the central city or on its fringes. As immigration-fuelled population growth continues to put pressure on space and prices, more Auckland citizens are learning to do without the birthright of owning their own home – let alone one with a backyard.

'How do you feel about your life as a whole?' In 2009, 86% responded 'satisfied' or 'very satisfied' to a Statistics NZ poll.

Wellington's inner-city boom is slightly different. As the public service has shrunk and large companies have moved their head offices away, old office buildings and warehouses have been converted for apartment living.

At the same time, a parallel trend has seen a rush to the coastlines, and to beautiful areas such as Nelson, at the top of the South Island, where property values have rocketed and orchards have been ploughed under to make way for more housing. In the process, an icon of the Kiwi lifestyle, the bach (pronounced 'batch') – a rough beach house, often passed down through families – has begun to disappear. Many New Zealanders feel this as a loss, especially when the land goes to foreign buyers, and the fear that coastal land is getting beyond the reach of ordinary families is a significant political issue.

The growth in economic inequality in recent decades is a serious problem. In a few poor urban areas such as South Auckland, two or three families may share a single house, with attendant public health problems. A partial return to the public housing policies that created a chunk of the country's current housing stock aims to address this problem.

According to a 2009 survey, the happiest women in the country live in the Bay of Plenty, while the happiest men live in Nelson/Marlborough. Wellingtonians were the least happy.

Family trends, meanwhile, are similar to those in other Western countries: New Zealanders are marrying later (the median age for marriage has increased from just over 20 to over 30 years of age in the last 20 years) or not marrying at all. For those under 25 years of age, de facto unions are now more common than formal marriage, and about a third of all people between the ages of 15 and 44 who are living in partnerships are not legally married. About 21,000 couples still get married every year, and half that many get divorced.

The law extends matrimonial property principles to unmarried couples, including same-sex couples. Despite the obligatory outrage from conservatives, civil unions were introduced in 2005 – creating a new category of union similar to but separate from marriage – with the support of the majority of the population.

ECONOMY

NZ may be a long way away from just about everywhere but it is not immune to the vagaries of the global economy. In the quarter to June 2009 it just edged out of its worst recession in 30 years, following six quarters of negative growth. At the time of research it was uncertain as to whether the recovery would hold.

NZ escaped the worst of the global financial crisis due in part to the strength of its banking sector, which was never exposed to the subprime mortgage crisis that triggered the problem. NZ's Gross Domestic Product (GDP) currently stands at around $128 billion per annum. Unemployment has risen to 6.5% – a nine-year high.

The median annual income is $24,400, and wealth is far less evenly spread than it was 25 years ago – 18% earn more than double that, while 43% survive on less than $20,000. The wealthiest region is Wellington, where one in 20 adults reaps more than $100,000 per annum.

With regards to wealth, NZ sits 22nd among the 30 OECD countries on a measure of GDP per head in terms of 'purchasing power parity', indicating that its people are nearly a quarter less affluent than those of Australia, or roughly as wealthy as the average South Korean.

NZ now has the sixth worst gap between rich and poor in the developed world, according to a 2009 UN report.

Back in the heady post-WWII days, NZ was towards the top of the list, buoyed by strong demand for wool, meat and dairy products. Things changed for the worse in 1973 when the country's preferential arrangements with

Britain ceased after the UK joined the European Economic Community (later the European Union). NZ was forced to find new markets, and now it exports mainly to Australia, the US, Japan and China. The main commodities exported (in order of value) are dairy products, meat, wood, fish and machinery. The country imports a great deal more than it exports (especially consumer and other manufactured goods) leading to a problematic balance of payments.

POPULATION & MULTICULTURALISM

There are an estimated 4.4 million resident New Zealanders, and almost one in three of them live in the largest city, Auckland, where growth has been fuelled both by a long-term drift north and more recent waves of immigration. The general drift to the cities means that urban areas now account for about 86% of the population.

The Maori population was somewhere between 100,000 and 200,000 at the time of first European contact 200 years ago. Disease and warfare subsequently brought the population near to collapse, but a high birth rate now sees about 15% of New Zealanders (565,000 people) identify as Maori, and that proportion is likely to grow.

The implication of the Treaty of Waitangi is one of partnership between Maori and the Crown (representing the New Zealanders who are 'Pakeha', or of British heritage), together forging a bicultural nation. After decades of attempted cultural assimilation it's now accepted in most quarters that the indigenous culture has a special and separate status within the country's ethnic mix. For example, Maori is an official language and there is a separate electoral role granting Maori guaranteed parliamentary seats.

NZ's population would hit 11 million if it were to take in all the people that wanted to settle there, according to Gallup, who rated it third in its 2009 Potential Net Migration Index.

Yet room has had to be found for the many New Zealanders of neither British nor Maori heritage. In each new wave of immigration there has been an unfortunate tendency to demonise before gradually accepting and celebrating what the new cultures have to offer. This happened with the Chinese in the mid-19th century, Croatians at the beginning of the 20th, Pacific Islanders in the 1970s and most recently the Chinese again in the 1990s. That said, NZ society is more integrated and accepting than most. People of all races are represented in all levels of society and race isn't an obstacle to achievement.

Auckland has been the prime destination for ethnic Chinese since immigration rules were relaxed in 1987. While many Asian immigrants have chosen to cluster in Auckland's eastern suburbs, visitors are often surprised by the 'Asianisation' of its central city, where thousands of East Asian students reside, either studying at Auckland University, learning English, or both.

Occasional incidents involving Asians – including some high-profile Asian-on-Asian crimes – have added to disquiet about Asian immigration in some parts of society. But opinion polls indicate that most Aucklanders tend to value the contribution of new migrants. Today, 13% of Aucklanders are of Asian extraction and it's estimated that numbers will reach 400,000 within seven years.

People born in other countries make up 23% of NZ residents. Of these, the main regions of origin are the UK and Ireland (29%), the Pacific Islands (15%), Northeast Asia (15%) and Australia (7%).

About 20% of Auckland Chinese were born in NZ, but considerable attention has been focused on the so-called '1.5 generation': young Chinese born overseas but socialised (and sometimes educated) in NZ. The traditionally quiescent culture of Chinese New Zealanders has been challenged in recent years, and a dynamic group of young ethnic Asians is emerging into leadership roles not only within their own community, but in wider NZ society.

Auckland is easily the most multicultural centre in NZ, with only slightly over half of the population of European descent (as opposed to around 80% in most of the South Island). It is effectively the capital of the South Pacific, with nearly 177,000 people of Pacific Island heritage living there. Pacific Islanders make up about 7% of the nation's population but 14% of Auckland's.

NZ never had an official 'white' immigration policy as Australia did, but for decades it tended to regard itself as an outpost of Britain. Now it is other influences – NZ's role in the Pacific, its burgeoning economic links to Asia, its offering of sanctuary to refugees – that will continue to shape what it is to be a New Zealander.

In percentage terms, Auckland is the seventh largest city for people of Chinese origin outside of China.

SPORT

The arena where Kiwis have most sated their desperation for recognition on the world stage is sport. For most of the 20th century, NZ's All Blacks dominated international rugby union, with one squad even dubbed 'The Invincibles'. Taking over this pastime of the British upper class did wonders for national identity and the game is now interwoven with NZ's history and culture. So when the All Blacks dip out of the Rugby World Cup at semifinal stage (as they have done no fewer than four times in recent tournaments), there is national mourning. Few seem to take solace in (or barely notice) the success of the NZ women's team, the Black Ferns, who have won the last three Women's Rugby World Cups. Below top international level, the Super 14 competition (with teams from Australia and South Africa) offers the world's best rugby, although local purists still prefer the National Provincial Championship (NPC).

For all rugby's influence on the culture, don't go to a game expecting to be caught up in an orgy of noise and cheering. Rugby crowds at Auckland's Eden Park (p116) are as restrained as their teams are cavalier, but they get noisier as you head south. Fans at Canterbury's excellent AMI Stadium are reputed to be the most one-eyed in the land.

In contrast, a home game for the NZ Warriors rugby league team at Auckland's Mt Smart Stadium (p116) is a thrilling spectacle, especially when the Polynesian drummers kick in. The Warriors are the only NZ team in the Australian NRL (National Rugby League) competition. Rugby League has traditionally been considered the working-class sport and support is strongest from Auckland's Maori, Polynesian and other immigrant communities.

RUGBY WORLD CUP 2011

On September 9, 2011 a burly bunch of men in black jerseys will start slapping their meaty thighs, rolling their eyes back in their heads, poking out their tongues and hurtling a bloodthirsty chant at their opposition. Such is NZ's rugby tradition. An overwhelming majority of the crowd packed into Auckland's Eden Park for the match against Tonga that marks the start of the 7th Rugby World Cup will be hoping and praying that the same ritual will be repeated here on October 23 at the final.

In the interim, 20 teams (divided into four pools of five) will be competing in games held all over the country, from Whangarei in the north to Invercargill in the south. The quarter finals are scheduled for the weekend of October 8 and 9 (in Wellington and Christchurch), with the semifinals in Auckland the following weekend. Expect accommodation to be scarce at these times.

Tickets go on sale to the public in late 2010, with a ballot for tickets for the finals held in early 2011 (see www.rugbyworldcup.com for details). Prices range from as little as $30 (children $15), for pool games featuring the minnows, up to $450 for top seats at All Blacks pool matches. Quarter finals tickets start at $190 and finals from $390.

If you can't nab (or can't afford) a ticket, the main centres are planning public events with big screens to follow the proceedings, particularly Auckland which is considering turning Princes Wharf into 'party central' for the duration. Whether you find yourself cheering on Namibia at a match or you watch all the action from a small-town pub, it's guaranteed to be a fascinating time to visit.

NZ are the current rugby league world champions, taking the trophy from Australia (in Australia) in 2008. Defeating the neighbours in their favourite game brought a smile to the faces of even the strongest supporters of the rival rugby code.

By the time this book is published the All Whites, NZ's national soccer (football) squad will have competed in the 2010 FIFA World Cup, qualifying for the second time in history. Nobody expects them to do as well as the rugby league boys but getting there is a huge achievement for such a rugby-mad nation. Scoring a few goals or (gasp!) winning a game would be the icing on the cake.

Netball is the leading sport for women and the one in which the national team, the Silver Ferns, perpetually vies for world supremacy with the Australians – one or other of the countries has taken the world championship at every contest (except for a tie in 1979). The rivalry has intensified since 2008 when both countries disbanded their national club leagues to start a new trans-Tasman competition featuring five teams from each country.

Cricket is the established summer team sport, and the State Shield (one-day) and State Championship provincial competitions take place alongside international matches involving the national side, the Black Caps, through the summer months. Wellington's Basin Reserve is the last sole-use test cricket venue in the main centres (and only a few minutes' walk from the bars and restaurants of Courtenay Pl) while New Plymouth's Pukekura Park (p239) is simply one of the prettiest cricket grounds in the world.

Other sports in which NZ pushes above its weight include sailing, rowing, canoeing, equestrian and triathlon. The most Olympic medals NZ has won have been in athletics, particularly in track and field events.

New Zealanders not only watch sport, they play it. Many workplaces have social teams or groups of mates get together for a friendly match. The most popular sports for men to participate in are (in order) golf, cricket, tennis, touch football and rugby union. For women it's netball, tennis, golf, touch football and skiing. Other popular active pursuits include kayaking, mountain biking, walking and running.

The first referee in the world to use a whistle to halt a game was William Atack of Christchurch. He thought of this now seemingly obvious and ubiquitous refereeing tool in 1884.

MEDIA

Almost all NZ cities have their own morning newspapers, sometimes coexisting with the Auckland-based *New Zealand Herald* (www.nzherald.co.nz).

The magazine market is more varied, and dominated by independent publishers. The *Listener* (like the *Herald,* owned by Australian company APN) is published weekly and offers TV and radio listings. Auckland's own magazine, *Metro,* is a good-looking guide to the style of the city. *Cuisine* is a sleek, popular and authoritative guide to food and wine.

Free-to-air TV is dominated by the two publicly owned TV New Zealand channels (TV One and TV2), versus the Australian-owned TV3 and its sibling music channel C4. Maori TV is a great source of locally produced programming as well as screening some interesting foreign documentaries and films. Much of it is broadcast in Maori, although subtitles are often added.

Radio Sport carries one of the sounds of the NZ summer: cricket commentaries. The public broadcaster, Radio New Zealand, is based in Wellington: its flagship, National Radio, offers strong news and feature programming and is available nationwide. The network of student stations, the bNet, offers an engaging and adventurous alternative (they're also the best place to hear about local gigs), and the most sophisticated of the stations, Auckland's 95bFM, is influential in its advocacy of new alternative music.

There is also a nationwide network of *iwi* (tribal) stations, some of which, including Waikato's Radio Tainui, offer welcome respite from the commercial networks – others, such as Auckland's Mai FM, take on the commercial broadcasters at their own game. Also worth noting are the national Pacific Island station Niu FM and the dance station George FM, which started from a bedroom in Auckland's Grey Lynn and can now be heard in 16 towns.

For interesting analysis of the issues of the day and the buzz on the streets check out the excellent *Public Address* blog site (www.publicaddress.net). Wellington is well serviced by the *Wellingtonista* (www.wellingtonista.com), which serves up 'random stuff about NZ's capital city'.

RELIGION

Although the national anthem, 'God Defend New Zealand', is an appeal to the Almighty, and parliament begins every day with prayers, New Zealanders are not a particularly pious people – far less so, according to polls, than Australians. A New Zealander is more likely to be spiritually fulfilled in the outdoors than in church. The land and sea were spiritual constants in pre-European Maori culture and they are scarcely less so today.

NZ is predominantly a Christian country (56%), although over a third of the population claim no religious affiliation at all. The number of people identifying as Christian has been falling – by 5% between the 2001 and 2006 censuses – although religion remains strong in the Pacific Island community, where 80% are members of that faith.

Reflecting its English heritage, NZ is nominally Anglican; where religion has a place in public affairs it will be of that flavour. Yet the Catholic Church is gaining ground, increasing its numbers by 5% in recent years. Catholicism now has 508,000 adherents to Anglicanism's 555,000.

Maori spirituality has been fused with Christianity since colonisation in movements such as Ratana and Ringatu, but is increasingly expressed in its own right.

Immigrants have brought their faiths with them, but religions such as Islam, Hinduism, Sikhism, Judaism and Buddhism in total account for less than 4% of the population.

WOMEN IN NEW ZEALAND

NZ is justifiably proud of being the first country in the world to give women the vote (in 1893). Kate Sheppard, the hero of the women's suffrage movement, even features on the $10 bill.

Despite that early achievement, the real role for women in public life was modest for many years. That can hardly be said now. The country has had two female prime ministers and for a time in 2000 every key constitutional position was held by a woman, including the attorney general, chief justice, governor general and head of state – although New Zealanders can't take credit for choosing Betty Windsor for that role. At the same time a Maori queen headed the Kingitanga (see the boxed text, p209) and a woman led NZ's biggest listed corporation.

Yet, even with the presence of a Ministry of Women's Affairs, some benefits have been slow to come to ordinary NZ women: paid parental leave was only instituted in 2002, for example. As in most other countries, women's wages tend to be lower than men's, although the gap is closing. Women are nearly twice as likely to work more than one job and there are three times more men in the top earnings decile (over $67,000 per annum) than women.

When NZ women complain that there aren't enough decent men to go around, they've got a point: there are 104 women for every 100 men. The man shortage is particularly acute for straight women in their 30s, an age at which Kiwi blokes are more likely to be living overseas than their

Glamorous Rotorua-born Jean Batten, known as Hine-o-te-Rangi (Daughter of the Skies), was a famous pilot and the most famous New Zealander of the 1930s. During a glittering career, she broke several records for long-distance solo flights.

countrywomen. If they do snag a keeper, chances are he'll be older – the median age for brides is 30, while its 33 for bridegrooms.

On the plus side, women live longer: the average life expectancy for women is 82, as opposed to 78 for men.

NZ has shamefully high rates of domestic and child abuse. A 2007 study suggested that as many as a quarter of NZ women had suffered some form of sexual abuse by the time they were 15. The figures were higher for rural women.

ARTS
Literature
A nationalist movement arose in literature in the 1930s, challenging the notion of NZ being an annex of the 'mother country' and striving for an independent identity. Some writers who appeared then – especially the poets Allen Curnow, Denis Glover, ARD Fairburn and RAK Mason – became commanding figures in the definition of a new culture, and were still around in the 1950s to be part of what prominent historian Keith Sinclair (himself a poet) called the time 'when the NZ intellect and imagination came alive'.

Katherine Mansfield's work began a NZ tradition in short fiction, and for years the standard was carried by novelist Janet Frame, whose dramatic life was depicted in Jane Campion's film of her autobiography, *An Angel at My Table*. Her novel *The Carpathians* (1989) won the Commonwealth Writers' Prize. A new era of international recognition began in 1985 when Keri Hulme's haunting *The Bone People* won the Booker Prize (the world is still waiting for the follow-up, *Bait*).

It wasn't until 2007 that another Kiwi looked likely to snag the Booker. Lloyd Jones' *Mister Pip* was pipped at the post, but the nomination rocketed his book up literature charts the world over.

Less recognised internationally, Maurice 'gee-I've-won-a-lot-of-awards' Gee has gained the nation's annual top fiction gong for *Blindsight* (2005), *Live Bodies* (1998), *Going West* (1992), *The Burning Boy* (1990), *Plumb* (1978) and *A Glorious Morning Comrade* (1975). His much-loved children's novel *Under The Mountain* (1979) was made into a seminal NZ TV series in 1981 and then a major motion picture in 2009. In 2004 the adaptation of another of his novels, *In My Father's Den* (1972), won major awards at international film festivals and is one of the country's highest grossing films. His latest novel is *Access Road* (2009).

Some of the most interesting and enjoyable NZ fiction voices belong to Maori writers. Witi Ihimaera's novels give a wonderful insight into small-town Maori life on the East Coast – especially *Bulibasha* (1994) and *The Whale Rider* (1987), which was made into an acclaimed film – while *Nights In The Gardens Of Spain* (1996) casts a similar light on Auckland's gay scene. His most recent novel is *The Trowenna Sea* (2009). Patricia Grace's work is similarly filled with exquisitely told stories of rural *marae*-centred life: try *Mutuwhenua* (1978), *Potiki* (1986) or *Tu* (2004).

Also worth checking out are Elizabeth Knox (*The Vintner's Luck*, 1998; *The Angel's Cut*, 2009), Charlotte Grimshaw (*Opportunity*, 2007) and Emily Perkins (*Novel About My Wife*, 2008).

Cinema & TV
If you first got interested in NZ by watching it on the silver screen, you're in good company. Peter Jackson's NZ-made *Lord of the Rings* (*LOTR*) trilogy was the best thing to happen to NZ tourism since Captain Cook.

Yet NZ cinema is hardly ever easy-going. In his BBC-funded documentary, *Cinema of Unease*, NZ actor Sam Neill described the country's film industry

In 1989 when Penny Jamieson was consecrated as the Bishop of Dunedin she became the world's second ever female Anglican bishop and the first to lead a diocese in her own right.

Witi Ihimaera wrote his novel *The Whale Rider* in a three-week burst in 1987, inspired by his daughters' complaints that he took them to movies with only male heroes.

NEW ZEALAND'S LORD OF THE REELS Errol Hunt

Peter Jackson was already a hero to NZ's small film industry before he directed his career-defining *Lord of the Rings* (*LOTR*) trilogy. From his very first film, *Bad Taste* (vomit-eating aliens and exploding sheep; 1987), it was obvious that he was a unique talent. It was followed by *Meet the Feebles* (muppets on acid; 1989) and an even gorier zombie movie, *Braindead* ('I kick ass for the Lord'; 1992). Two slightly-less-bloodstained films – *Heavenly Creatures* (1994) and *The Frighteners* (1996) – preceded the *LOTR* films, while *King Kong* (2005) and *The Lovely Bones* (2009) have followed in the tiny hobbits' giant footsteps.

The effect of the three *LOTR* films on NZ was unparalleled: the country embraced Jackson and his trilogy with a passion. Wellington was renamed Middle-earth for the week of the first film's release in late 2001, a Minister for the *LOTR* was named in the NZ government and Jackson was made a Companion of the New Zealand Order of Merit for his services in the film industry. The frenzy only increased for the second and third films, especially when the world premiere (*world* premiere!) of *The Return of the King* was held in Wellington in December 2003, and of course went on to win a record 11 Oscars.

For rainy-weekend viewing, hit the Jackson DVD back-catalogue and look for the man himself. He stars as both the chainsaw-wielding Derek and Robert the Alien in *Bad Taste*, and has cameos as the undertaker's assistant in *Braindead*, a hobo outside a cinema in *Heavenly Creatures* and a clumsy, chain-wearing biker in *The Frighteners*. In the *LOTR* films, Jackson appears as a belching hobbit outside a pub in *The Fellowship of the Ring*, a stone-throwing Helms Deep defender in *The Two Towers* and a captain of the Corsairs in *The Return of the King*. In *King Kong*, a slimmed-down Jackson plays a biplane machine gunner, while in *The Lovely Bones* he's a customer in the camera store.

---

as 'uniquely strange and dark', producing bleak, haunted work. One need only watch Lee Tamahore's harrowing *Once Were Warriors* (1994) to see what he means.

The *Listener*'s film critic, Philip Matthews, makes a slightly more upbeat observation: 'Between (Niki Caro's) *Whale Rider*, (Christine Jeffs') *Rain* and *Lord of the Rings*, you can extract the qualities that our best films possess. Beyond slick technical accomplishment, all share a kind of land-mysticism, an innately supernatural sensibility'.

You could add to this list Jane Campion's *The Piano* (1993), Brad McGann's *In My Father's Den* (2004), James Napier-Roberston's *I'm Not Harry Jenson* (2009) and Jackson's *Heavenly Creatures* (1994) – all of which use magically lush scenery to couch disturbing violence. It's a land-mysticism constantly bordering on the creepy.

Even when Kiwis do humour it's as resolutely black as their rugby jerseys. Check out Jackson's early splatter-fests (see the boxed text, above), Taika Cohen's oddball loser-palooza *Eagle vs Shark* (2007) and Jonathan King's sickly hilarious *Black Sheep* (2006) – 'get ready for the violence of the lambs'. Exporting NZ comedy hasn't been easy, yet the HBO-produced TV musical parody *Flight of the Conchords* – featuring a mumbling, bumbling Kiwi folk-singing duo trying to get a break in New York – has found surprising international success, particularly in the supposed irony-free zone that is the US.

New Zealanders have gone from never seeing themselves in international cinema to having whole cloned armies of Temuera Morrisons invading the universe in *Star Wars*. Familiar faces such as Cliff Curtis and Karl Urban seem to constantly pop up playing Mexican or Russian gangsters in action movies. Many of them got their start in long-running soap opera *Shortland St* (7pm weekdays, TV2).

Other local shows worth catching are *Outrageous Fortune*, a rough-edged comedy-drama set in West Auckland, and *bro'Town*, a better-drawn

Other than 2003's winner *Return of the King, The Piano* is the only NZ movie to be nominated for a Best Picture Oscar. Jane Campion was the first Kiwi nominated as Best Director and Peter Jackson the first to win it.

The only Kiwi actors to have won an Oscar are Anna Paquin (for *The Piano*) and Russell Crowe (for *Gladiator*). Paquin was born in Canada but moved to NZ when she was four, while Crowe moved from NZ to Australia at the same age.

Polynesian version of *South Park*. It's the Polynesian giggle-factor that seems likeliest to break down the bleak house of NZ cinema. The *bro'Town* boys (who also do stand-up comedy as the Naked Samoans) hit the big screen with the feel-good-through-and-through *Sione's Wedding* in 2006 – with the second-biggest local takings of any NZ film.

While another *LOTR*-style blockbuster has proved illusive, the NZ film industry has quietly continued producing well-crafted, affecting movies such as *Dean Spanley* (2008), *The Strength Of Water* (2009), *The Topp Twins: Untouchable Girls* (people's choice documentary winner at the Toronto and Melbourne film festivals, 2009) and *The Lovely Bones* (2009).

Music   Gareth Shute

New Zealand music began with the early forms of *waiata* (singing) developed by Maori following their arrival in the country. The main musical instruments were wind instruments made of bone or wood, the most well-known of which is the *nguru* (commonly known as the 'nose flute'), while percussion was provided by chest- and thigh-slapping. These days, the liveliest place to see Maori music being performed is at Kapa Haka competitions (see p258), in which groups compete with their own routines of traditional song and dance. In a similar vein is the Pasifika Festival (p114) in Auckland, which has sections that represent each of the Pacific Islands. It is a great place to see both traditional and modern forms of Polynesian music, whether that means modern hip-hop beats or throbbing Cook Island drums, or island-style guitar, ukulele, and slide guitar.

European music first arrived in New Zealand with immigrants from Europe, and steadily developed local variants over the early 1900s. In the 1950s Douglas Lilburn became one of the first internationally recognised NZ classical composers. More recently the country has produced a number of world-renowned musicians in this field, including opera singer Dame Kiri Te Kanawa, million-selling pop diva Hayley Westenra, composer John Psathas (who composed music for the 2004 Olympic Games) and composer/percussionist Gareth Farr (who also performs in drag under the name, Lilith). Each of the main universities in New Zealand runs its own music school and these often have free concerts which visitors can attend. More large scale performances are held at various venues within the Edge conglomerate of venues in Auckland (p116), the Town Hall/Michael Fowler Centre in Wellington (p398), and the Town Hall in Christchurch.

New Zealand also has a strong rock music scene, its most acclaimed exports being the revered indie label Flying Nun and the music of the Finn Brothers (p48). In 1981 Flying Nun was started by Christchurch record store owner, Roger Shepherd. Many of the early groups came from Dunedin, where local

> Gareth Shute is the author of four books, including *Hip Hop Music In Aotearoa* and *NZ Rock 1987–2007*. He is also a musician and has toured the UK, Europe, and Australia as a member of The Ruby Suns and The Brunettes. He now plays in The Conjurors and The Cosbys.

> A wide range of cultural events are listed on www.nzlive.com – this is a good place to find out about Kapa Haka performances.

MIDDLE-EARTH TOURISM

If you are one of those travellers inspired to come down under by the scenery of the *LOTR* movies, you won't be disappointed. Jackson's decision to film in NZ wasn't mere patriotism. Nowhere else on earth will you find such wildly varied, unspoiled landscapes.

You will doubtless recognise some places from the films. For example, Hobbiton (near Matamata; p222), Mt Doom (instantly recognisable as towering Ngauruhoe; p291) or the Misty Mountains (the South Island's Southern Alps). The visitor information centres in Wellington, Twizel or Queenstown should be able to direct you to local *LOTR* sites of interest. If you're serious about finding the exact spots where scenes were filmed, buy a copy of Ian Brodie's nerdtastic *The Lord of the Rings: Location Guidebook*, which includes instructions, and even GPS coordinates, for finding all the important scenes.

Concerts and classical music recitals can be found at www.event finder.co.nz. For more specific information on the NZ classical music scene, see: www.sounz .org.nz.

musicians took the do-it-yourself attitude of punk but used it to produce a lo-fi indie-pop which received rave reviews from the likes of *NME* in the UK and *Rolling Stone* magazine in the US. *Billboard* even claimed in 1989: 'There doesn't seem to be anything on Flying Nun Records that is less than excellent.' Many of the musicians from the Flying Nun scene still perform live to this day, including David Kilgour (from The Clean), Martin Phillipps (from The Chills), and Shayne Carter (from the Straitjacket Fits, now fronting Dimmer). Chick's Hotel in Port Chalmers (near Dunedin) and the Dux De Lux in Christchurch (and during the winter, its sister bar in Queenstown – see continue to be home to a flourishing indie-rock scene. Also recommended is Wunderbar in Lyttelton (near Christchurch) which is a rustic venue with a fantastic hillside view of the harbour below.

Flying Nun was recently bought back by its original owner, Roger Shepherd, and continues to release exciting new acts such as The Mint Chicks. Other young indie labels have also sprung up in the meantime including Lil Chief Records and Arch Hill Recordings. For more adventurous listeners, Bruce Russell continues to play in influential underground group The Dead C, and releases music through his Corpus Hermeticum label.

One of the most complete listings of NZ bands that have existed over the last couple of decades is available at www .muzic.net.nz. A thriving community of bloggers also discuss local music at www.nzmusic.com.

Since the new millennium, the NZ music scene has developed a new vitality after the government convinced commercial radio stations in the country to adopt a voluntary quota of 20% local music. This has enabled the more commercially orientated musicians to have solid careers. Rock groups such as Shihad, The Feelers, and Op-shop have thrived in this environment, as have a set of soulful female solo artists (who all happen to have Maori heritage): Bic Runga, Anika Moa, and Brooke Fraser (daughter of All Black, Bernie Fraser).

However, the genres of music that have been adopted most enthusiastically by Maori and Polynesian New Zealanders have been reggae (in the 1970s) and hip hop (in 1980s), which has led to distinct local variants of these musical styles. In Wellington, a thriving jazz scene took on a reggae influence to create a host of groups that blend dub, roots, and funky jazz – most notably Fat Freddy's Drop. Most of the venues for this music can be found

---

THE BROTHERS FINN

There are certain tunes that all Kiwis can sing along to, given a beer and the opportunity. The music of Tim and Neil Finn makes up a good proportion of these, and many of their songs have gone on to be international hits.

Tim Finn first came to prominence in late-70s group, Split Enz. When their original guitarist quit, Neil flew over to join the band in the UK despite being only 15 at the time. Split Enz amassed a solid following in Australia, New Zealand, and Canada before disbanding in 1985. Neil then formed Crowded House with two Australian musicians (Paul Hester and Nick Seymour) and one of their early singles, 'Don't Dream It's Over' went on to hit number two on the US charts. Tim later did a brief spell in the band, during which the brothers wrote 'Weather With You' – a song which reached number seven on the UK charts, pushing their album *Woodface* to gold sales. The original line-up of Crowded House played their final show in 1996, in front of 100,000 people on the steps of the Sydney Opera House (though Finn and Seymour reformed the group briefly in 2007 and continue to tour and record occasionally). Tim and Neil have both released a number of solo albums, as well as combining for the occasional album as the Finn Brothers.

More recently, Tim's solo career was reinvigorated when one of his songs was picked up for the movie *The Chronicles of Narnia: The Lion, the Witch & the Wardrobe*. Neil has also remained busy, organising a set of shows/releases under the name Seven Worlds Collide, which is a collaboration with well-known overseas musicians, including Jeff Tweedy (Wilco), Johnny Marr (The Smiths), and members of Radiohead. Both Tim and Neil were born in the small town of Te Awamutu and the local museum has a collection that documents their work (p217).

ICONIC NEW ZEALAND SONGS

Listed below are 20 songs that any self-respecting Kiwi is bound to know. If you'd like a local soundtrack for your NZ visit, then you might consider downloading the following 20 songs (legally of course) to your MP3 player either via i-Tunes or through www.amplifier.co.nz, which specialises in NZ music downloads. Alternatively, you may wish to search out the collection, *The Great New Zealand Songbook,* or the series of *Nature's Best* compilations.

Bic Runga (1997) Sway	**Hello Sailor** (1977) Blue Lady
Che Fu and DLT (1996) Chains	**John Rowles** (1970) Cheryl Moana Marie
The Chills (1991) Heavenly Pop Hit	**Kiri Te Kanawa** (this version, 1999) Pokarekare Ana
Chris Knox (1990) Not Given Lightly	**Ladyhawke** (2009) Magic
The Clean (1981) Tally Ho	**Savage** (2008) Swing
Crowded House (1986) Don't Dream it's Over	**Scribe** (2003) Not Many
David Dobbyn with Herbs (1986) Slice of Heaven	**Shihad** (1997) Home Again
Dragon (1978) April Sun in Cuba	**Split Enz** (1982) Six Months in a Leaky Boat
The Exponents (1991) Why Does Love Do This to Me?	**Straitjacket Fits** (1987) She Speeds
Fourmyula (1969) Nature	**The Swingers** (1981) Counting the Beat

along Courtenay Place or between the shops on Cuba Mall (see p397). The national public holiday, Waitangi Day, on February 6th also happens to fall on the birthday of Bob Marley and yearly reggae concerts are held on this day in Auckland and Wellington.

The local hip-hop scene has its heart in the suburbs of South Auckland, which have a high concentration of Maori and Pacific Island residents. This area is home to one of New Zealand's foremost hip-hop labels, Dawn Raid, which takes its name from the infamous early-morning house raids of the 1970s that police performed on Pacific Islanders who outstayed their visas. Dawn Raid's most successful artist is Savage, who sold a million copies of his single 'Swing' after it was featured in the movie, *Knocked Up.* Within New Zealand, the most well-known hip-hop acts are Scribe, Che Fu, and Smashproof (who broke the record for the longest running single at number one). Hip-hop shows in Auckland are held at a wide range of venues, though popular favourites are Rising Sun and 4:20 (p116) and funk-fuelled club, Khuja Lounge (p116).

Early in the new millennium, New Zealand became known as a home for garage rock after the international rise of two local acts: the Datsuns and the D4. In Auckland the main venues for rock music are the Kings Arms Taven (p115) and Cassette Number Nine (p116), though two joint venues in St Kevins Arcade (off Karangahape Rd) are also popular – the Wine Cellar/Whammy Bar (p115). Wellington is also rife with live music venues from Mighty Mighty (p396), to the San Francisco Bath House (p398), to Bodega (p398).

Dance music had its strongest following in Christchurch in the 1990s, when it gave rise to the popular dub/electronica outfit, Salmonella Dub. Drum 'n' bass remains popular locally and has spawned internationally successful acts such as Concord Dawn and Shapeshifter.

In summer, many of the beachfront towns throughout the country are visited by touring bands (winery shows are also popular). One venue of note in this respect is the Leigh Sawmill Café (p142) in Leigh (85km from Auckland), which also offers accommodation and is located near the popular scuba-diving/snorkelling spot at Goat Island.

A number of festivals also take place over the summer months, including the local leg of the Big Day Out (p104), new year's celebration Rhythm & Vines

An up-to-date list of gigs in the main centres is listed at www.groove guide.co.nz. For those interested in indie rock, a great source of information is www.cheese ontoast.co.nz, which lists gigs and has interviews/photographs of bands (both local and international).

The TV show, *Popstars,* originated in New Zealand though the resulting group, True Bliss, was short-lived. The series concept was then picked up in Australia, the UK, and the US, before inspiring the *Idol* series.

How Bizarre was a massive hit in Europe, the UK, the US, and Australia during 1996. The song was by OMC – an acronym for 'Otara Millionaire's Club', which made light of OMC's poverty-stricken home suburb of Otara.

(p354), and the Christian-rock festival, Parachute (www.parachutemusic.com), in January (held near Wellington). Also recommended is the underground festival held early each year by A Low Hum (www.alowhum.com). Lovers of world music may enjoy the local version of Womad (p241), which is held in New Plymouth and features both local and overseas acts that draw from traditional music forms.

Visual Arts

The NZ 'can do' attitude extends to the visual arts. If you're visiting a local's home don't be surprised to find one of the owner's paintings on the wall or one of their mate's sculptures in the back garden, pieced together out of bits of shell, driftwood and a length of the magical 'number-eight wire'.

This is symptomatic of a flourishing local art and crafts scene cultivated by lively tertiary courses churning out traditional carvers and weavers, jewellery makers, multimedia boffins, and moulders of metal and glass. The larger cities have excellent dealer galleries representing interesting local artists working across all mediums.

Not all the best galleries are in Auckland or Wellington. The energetic Govett-Brewster Art Gallery (p238) – home to the legacy of sculptor and film-maker Len Lye – is worth a visit to New Plymouth in itself, and Gore's Eastern Southland Gallery has an important and growing collection of works by Ralph Hotere, Rita Angus and others.

Traditional Maori art has a distinctive visual style with well-developed motifs that have been embraced by NZ artists of every race. In the painting medium, these include the cool modernism of the work of Gordon Walters and the more controversial pop-art approach of Dick Frizzell's *Tiki* series. Likewise, Pacific Island themes are common, particularly in Auckland. An example is the work of Niuean-born Auckland-raised John Pule, who is also a poet and novelist.

It should not be surprising that in a nation so defined by its natural environment, landscape painting constituted the first post-European body of art. John Gully and Petrus van der Velden were among those to arrive and paint memorable (if sometimes overdramatised) depictions of the land.

Rita Angus' 1936 work *Cass* was voted the country's greatest painting in a 2006 poll. It hangs at the Christchurch Art Gallery.

A little later, Charles Frederick Goldie painted a series of compelling, realist portraits of Maori, who were feared to be a dying race. Debate over the political propriety of Goldie's work raged for years, but its value is widely accepted now: not least because Maori themselves generally acknowledge and value them as ancestral representations.

From the 1930s NZ art took a more modern direction and produced some of the country's most celebrated artists including Rita Angus, Toss Woollaston and Colin McCahon. McCahon is widely regarded to have been the country's most important artist. His paintings might seem inscrutable, even forbidding, but, even where McCahon lurched into Catholic mysticism or quoted screeds from the Bible, his spirituality was rooted in geography. His bleak, brooding landscapes evoke the sheer power of NZ's terrain. The influence of his dramatic, simple canvasses can be seen in the work of celebrated current artists, such as Ralph Hotere and Shane Cotton.

Maori Culture John Huria

'Maori' once just meant 'common' or 'everyday', but now it means...let's just begin this chapter by saying that there is a lot of 'then' and a lot of 'now' in the Maori world. Sometimes the cultural present follows on from the past quite seamlessly; sometimes things have changed hugely; sometimes we just want to look to the future.

Maori today are a diverse people. Some are engaged with traditional cultural networks and pursuits; others are occupied with adapting tradition and placing it into a dialogue with globalising culture. The Maori concept of *whanaungatanga* – family relationships – is important to the culture. And families spread out from the *whanau* (extended family) to the *hapu* (subtribe) and *iwi* (tribe) and even, in a sense, beyond the human world and into the natural and spiritual worlds.

Maori are New Zealand's *tangata whenua* (people of the land), and the Maori relationship with the land has developed over hundreds of years of occupation. Once a predominantly rural people, many Maori now live in urban centres, away from their traditional home base. But it's still common practice in formal settings to introduce oneself by referring to home: an ancestral mountain, river, sea or lake, or an ancestor. There's no place like home, but it's good to be away as well.

If you're looking for a Maori experience in NZ you'll find it – in performance, in conversation, in an art gallery, on a tour...

MAORI THEN

Some three millennia ago people began moving eastwards into the Pacific, sailing against the prevailing winds and currents (hard to go out, easier to return safely). Some stopped at Tonga and Samoa, and others settled the small central East Polynesian tropical islands.

The Maori colonisation of Aotearoa began from an original homeland known to Maori as Hawaiki. Skilled navigators and sailors travelled across the Pacific, using many navigational tools – currents, winds, stars, birds and wave patterns – to guide their large, double-hulled ocean-going craft to a new land. The first of many was the great navigator Kupe who arrived, the story goes, chasing an octopus named Muturangi. But the distinction of giving NZ its well-known Maori name – Aotearoa – goes to his wife, Kuramarotini, who cried out, '*He ao, he ao tea, he ao tea roa!*' (A cloud, a white cloud, a long white cloud!).

Kupe and his crew journeyed around the land, and many places around Cook Strait (between the North and South Islands) and the Hokianga in Northland still bear the names that they gave them and the marks of his passage. Kupe returned to Hawaiki, leaving from (and naming) Northland's Hokianga. He gave other seafarers valuable navigational information. And then the great *waka* (ocean-going craft) began to arrive.

The *waka* that the first setters arrived on, and their landing places, are immortalised in tribal histories. Well-known *waka* include *Takitimu*, *Kurahaupo*, *Te Arawa*, *Mataatua*, *Tainui*, *Aotea* and *Tokomaru*. There are many others. Maori trace their genealogies back to those who arrived on the *waka* (and further back as well).

What would it have been like making the transition from small tropical islands to a much larger, cooler land mass? Goodbye breadfruit, coconuts, paper mulberry; hello moa, fernroot, flax – and immense space (relatively speaking). NZ has over 15,000km of coastline. Rarotonga, by way of contrast,

John Huria (Ngai Tahu, Muaupoko) has an editorial, research and writing background with a focus on Maori writing and culture. He was senior editor for Maori publishing company Huia (NZ) and now runs an editorial and publishing services company, Ahi Text Solutions Ltd (www.ahitextsolutions.co.nz).

Kupe's passage is marked around NZ: he left his sails (Nga Ra o Kupe) near Cape Palliser as triangular landforms; he named the two islands in Wellington Harbour Matiu and Makoro after his daughters; his blood stains the red rocks of Wellington's south coast.

Arriving for the first time in NZ, two crew members of *Tainui* saw the red flowers of the pohutu-kawa tree, and they cast away their prized red feather ornaments, thinking that there were plenty to be had on shore.

has a little over 30. There was land, lots of it, and a flora and fauna that had
developed more or less separately from the rest of the world for 80 million
years. There was an untouched, massive fishery. There were great seaside
mammalian convenience stores – seals and sea lions – as well as a fabulous
array of birds.

The early settlers went on the move, pulled by love, by trade opportunities and greater resources; pushed by disputes and threats to security. When
they settled, Maori established *mana whenua* (regional authority), whether
by military campaigns, or by the peaceful methods of intermarriage and
diplomacy. Looking over tribal history it's possible to see the many alliances,
absorptions and extinctions that went on.

Histories were carried by the voice, in stories, songs and chants. Great stress
was placed on accurate learning – after all, in an oral culture where people
are the libraries, the past is always a generation or two away from oblivion.

Maori lived in *kainga*, small villages, which often had associated gardens.
Housing was quite cosy by modern standards – often it was hard to stand
upright while inside. From time to time people would leave their home base
and go to harvest seasonal foods. When peaceful life was interrupted by
conflict, the people would withdraw to *pa*, fortified dwelling places.

And then Europeans began to arrive (see p28).

MAORI TODAY

Today's culture is marked by new developments in the arts, business, sport and
politics. Many historical grievances still stand, but some *iwi* (Ngai Tahu and
Tainui, for example) have settled historical grievances and are major forces
in the NZ economy. Maori have also addressed the decline in Maori language
use by establishing *kohanga reo*, *kura kaupapa Maori* and *wananga* (Maori-
medium preschools, schools and universities). There is now a generation
of people who speak Maori as a first language. There is a network of Maori
radio stations, and Maori TV is attracting a committed viewership. A recently

Maori legends are all around you as you tour NZ: Maui's waka became today's Southern Alps; a taniwha formed Lake Waikaremoana in its death throes; and a rejected Mt Taranaki walked into exile from the central North Island mountain group, carving the Whanganui River.

HOW THE WORLD BEGAN

In the Maori story of creation, first there was the void, then the night, then Rangi-nui and Papa-
tu-a-nuku (sky father and earth mother) came into being, embracing with their children nurtured
between them. But nurturing became something else. Their children were stifled in the darkness
of their embrace. Unable to stretch out to their full dimensions and struggling to see clearly
in the darkness, their children tried to separate them. Tawhiri-matea, the god of winds, raged
against them; Tu-mata-uenga, the god of war, assaulted them. Each god child in turn tried to
separate them, but still Rangi and Papa pressed against each other. And then Tane-mahuta, god
of the great forests and of humanity, placed his feet against his father and his back against his
mother and slowly, inexorably, began to move them apart. Then came the world of light, of
demigods and humanity.

In this world of light Maui, the demigod ancestor, was cast out to sea at birth and was found
floating in his mother's topknot. He was a shape-shifter, becoming a pigeon or a dog or an eel if
it suited his purposes. He stole fire from the gods. Using his grandmother's jawbone, he bashed
the sun so that it could only limp slowly across the sky, so that people would have enough time
during the day to get things done (if only he would do it again!). Using the South Island as a
canoe, he used the jawbone as a hook to fish up Te Ika a Maui (the fish of Maui) – the North
Island. And, finally, he met his end trying to defeat death itself. The goddess of death, Hine Nui
Te Po, had obsidian teeth in her vagina (obsidian is a volcanic glass that takes a razor edge when
chipped). Maui attempted to reverse birth (and hence defeat death) by crawling into her birth
canal to reach her heart as she slept. A small bird – a fantail – laughed at the absurd sight. Hine
Nui Te Po awoke, and crushed Maui between her thighs. Death one, humanity nil.

revived Maori event is becoming more and more prominent – Matariki, or Maori New Year. The constellation Matariki is also known as the Pleiades. It begins to rise above the horizon in late May or early June and its appearance traditionally signals a time for learning, planning and preparing as well as singing, dancing and celebrating. Watch out for talks and lectures, concerts, dinners, and even formal balls.

RELIGION

Christian churches and denominations are important in the Maori world: televangelists, mainstream churches for regular and occasional worship, and two major Maori churches (Ringatu and Ratana) – we've got it all.

But in the (non-Judaeo Christian) beginning there were the *atua Maori*, the Maori gods, and for many Maori the gods are a vital and relevant force still. It is common to greet the earth mother and sky father when speaking formally at a *marae*. The gods are represented in art and carving, sung of in *waiata* (songs), invoked through *karakia* (prayer and incantation) when a meeting house is opened, when a *waka* is launched, even (more simply) when a meal is served. They are spoken of on the *marae* and in wider Maori contexts. The traditional Maori creation story is well known and widely celebrated (see the boxed text, opposite).

You can check out a map that shows *iwi* distribution and a good list of *iwi* websites on Wikipedia (www.wikipedia.org).

THE ARTS

There are many collections of Maori *taonga* (treasures) around the country. Some of the largest and most comprehensive are at Wellington's Te Papa Museum (p387) and the Auckland Museum (p90). Canterbury Museum in Christchurch also has a good collection, and Hokitika's West Coast Historical Museum has an exhibition showing the story of *pounamu* (nephrite jade, or greenstone).

You can stay up to date with what is happening in the Maori arts by reading *Mana* magazine (available from most newsagents), listening to *iwi* stations (www.irirangi.net) or weekly podcasts from Radio New Zealand (www.radionz.co.nz/genre/maori,pacific). Maori TV also has regular features on the Maori arts – check out www.maoritelevision.com.

Maori TV went to air in 2004, an emotional time for many Maori who could at last see their culture, their concerns and their language in a mass medium. Over 90% of content is NZ made, and programs are in both Maori and English: they're subtitled and accessible to everyone. If you want to really get a feel for the rhythm and metre of spoken Maori from the comfort of your own chair, switch to Te Reo, a Maori-language-only channel.

Depending on area, the *powhiri* has gender roles: women *karanga* (call), men *whaikorero* (orate); women lead the way on to the *marae*, men sit on the *paepae* (the speakers' bench at the front). In a modern context, the debate around these roles continues.

Ta Moko

Ta moko is the Maori art of tattoo, traditionally worn by men on their faces, thighs and buttocks, and by women on their chins and lips. *Moko* were permanent grooves tapped into the skin using pigment (made from burnt caterpillar or kauri gum soot), and bone chisels: fine, sharp combs for broad work, and straight blades for detailed work. Museums in the major centres – Auckland, Wellington and Christchurch – all display traditional implements for *ta moko*.

The modern tattooist's gun is common now, but bone chisels are coming back into use for Maori who want to reconnect with tradition. Since the general renaissance in Maori culture in the 1960s, many artists have taken up *ta moko* and now many Maori wear *moko* with quiet pride and humility.

Can visitors get involved, or even get some work done? The term *kirituhi* (skin inscriptions) has arisen to describe Maori motif-inspired modern tattoos that non-Maori can wear. If you'd like to experience *ta moko*, or even

See Ngahuia Te Awekotuku's *Mau Moko: The World of Maori Tattoo* (2007) for the big picture, with powerful, beautiful images and an incisive commentary.

get *kirituhi,* your first stop is www.tamoko.org.nz. This website has articles, galleries and links to artists within NZ.

Carving

Traditional Maori carving, with its intricate detailing and curved lines, can transport the viewer. It's quite amazing to consider that it was done with stone tools, themselves painstakingly made, until the advent of iron (nails suddenly became very popular).

Some major traditional forms are *waka* (canoes), *pataka* (storage buildings), and *wharenui* (meeting houses). You can see sublime examples of traditional carving at Te Papa (p387) in Wellington, and at the following:

Auckland Museum (p90) Maori Court.

Hell's Gate (p320) Carver in action every day; near Rotorua

Otago Museum Nice old *waka* and *whare runanga* (meeting house) carvings, Dunedin.

Parihaka (p250) Historic site on Surf Highway 45, Taranaki.

Putiki Church (p255) Interior covered in carvings and *tukutuku* (wall panels), Whanganui.

Taupo Museum & Art Gallery (p275) Carved meeting house.

Te Manawa (p265) Museum with a Maori focus, Palmerston North.

Waikato Museum (p209) Beautifully carved *waka taua* (war canoe), Hamilton.

Wairakei Terraces Taupo (p283) Carved meeting house.

Waitangi Treaty Grounds (p160) *Whare runanga* and *waka taua.*

Whakarewarewa Thermal Village (p306) The 'living village' – carving, other arts, meeting house and performance, Rotorua.

Whanganui Regional Museum (p255) Wonderful carved *waka,* Whanganui.

The apex of carving today is the *whare whakairo* (carved meeting house). A commissioning group relates its history and ancestral stories to a carver, who then draws (sometimes quite loosely) on traditional motifs to interpret or embody the stories and ancestors in wood or composite fibreboard.

Rongomaraeroa Marae, by artist Cliff Whiting, at Te Papa in Wellington is a colourful example of a contemporary re-imagining of a traditional art form. The biggest change in carving (as with most traditional arts) has been in the use of new mediums and tools. Rangi Kipa uses a synthetic polymer called Corian to make his *hei tiki,* the same stuff that is used to make kitchen benchtops. You can check out his gallery at www.rangikipa.com.

Weaving

For information on Maori arts today, check out Toi Maori www.maoriart. org.nz.

Weaving was an essential art that provided clothing, nets and cordage, footwear for rough country travel, mats to cover earthen floors, and *kete* (bags) to carry stuff in. Many woven items are beautiful as well as practical. Some were major works – *korowai* (cloaks) could take years to finish. Woven predominantly with flax and bird feathers, they are worn now on ceremonial occasions, a stunning sight.

Working with natural materials for the greater good of the people involved getting things right by maintaining the supply of raw material and ensuring that it worked as it was meant to. Protocols were necessary, and women were dedicated to weaving under the aegis of the gods. Today, tradition is greatly respected, but not all traditions are necessarily followed.

CONNECTION WITH THE LAND

The best way to learn about the relationship between the land and the *tangata whenua* is to get out there and start talking with Maori. See the Maori New Zealand boxed texts in individual chapters for recommendations on Maori experiences in each area.

Flax was (and still is) the preferred medium for weaving. To get a strong fibre from flax leaves, weavers scraped away the leaves' flesh with a mussel shell, then pounded until it was soft, dyed it, then dried it. But contemporary weavers are using everything in their work: raffia, copper wire, rubber – even polar fleece and garden hoses!

The best place to experience weaving is to contact one of the many weavers running workshops. By learning the art, you'll appreciate the examples of weaving in museums even more. And if you want your own? Woven *kete* and backpacks have become fashion accessories and are on sale in most cities. Weaving is also found in dealer art galleries around the country.

Haka

Experiencing *haka* can get the adrenaline flowing, as it did for one Pakeha observer in 1929 who thought of dark Satanic mills: 'They looked like fiends from hell wound up by machinery'. *Haka* can be awe-inspiring; it can also be uplifting. The *haka* is not only a war dance – it is used to welcome visitors, honour achievement, express identity or to put forth very strong opinions.

Haka involves chanted words, vigorous body movements, and *pukana* (when performers distort their faces, eyes bulging with the whites showing, perhaps with tongue extended).

The well-known *haka* 'Ka Mate', performed by the All Blacks before rugby test matches, is credited to the cunning fighting chief Te Rauparaha. It celebrates his escape from death. Chased by enemies, he hid himself in a food pit. After they had left, a friendly chief named Te Whareangi (the 'hairy man' referred to in the *haka*), let him out; he climbed out into the sunshine and performed 'Ka Mate'.

You can experience *haka* at various cultural performances including at Mitai Maori Village (p307), Tamaki Maori Village (p307), Te Puia (p305) and Whakarewarewa Thermal Village (p306) in Rotorua; Katoro Waka Heritage Tours and Ko Tane in Christchurch; Maori Tours in Kaikoura; and Myths & Legends Eco-tours in Picton.

But the best displays of *haka* are at the national Te Matatini National Kapa Haka Festival (www.tematatini.org.nz), when NZ's top groups compete. It is held every two years, with the next festival in February 2011 in Gisborne.

Contemporary Visual Art

A distinctive feature of Maori visual art is the tension between traditional Maori ideas and modern artistic mediums and trends. Shane Cotton produced a series of works that conversed with 19th-century painted meeting houses, which themselves departed from Maori carved houses. Kelcy Taratoa uses toys, superheroes and pop urban imagery alongside weaving and carving design.

Of course not all Maori artists use Maori motifs. Ralph Hotere is a major NZ artist who 'happens to be Maori' (his words), and his career-long exploration of black speaks more to modernism than the traditional *marae* context.

Contemporary Maori art is by no means only about painting. Many other artists use installations as the preferred medium – look out for work by Jacqueline Fraser and Peter Robinson.

There are some great permanent exhibitions of Maori visual arts in the major centres. Both the Auckland and Christchurch Art Galleries hold strong collections, as does Wellington's Te Papa.

Contemporary Theatre

The 1970s saw the emergence of many Maori playwrights and plays, and theatre is a strong area of the Maori arts today. Maori theatre drew heavily on

Before you go touring NZ, pick up a Manaaki Card. This little beauty of a card will get you discounts at most Maori-operated tourist attractions. It also doubles as a phone card. See www.manaaki.co.nz.

See Hirini Moko Mead's *Tikanga Maori*, Pat and Hiwi Tauroa's *Visiting a Marae*, and Anne Salmond's *Hui* for detailed information on Maori customs.

the traditions of the *marae*. Instead of dimming the lights and immediately beginning the performance, many Maori theatre groups began with a stylised *powhiri* (see above), had space for audience members to respond to the play, and ended with a *karakia* (blessing or prayer) or a farewell.

Taki Rua is an independent producer of Maori work for both children and adults and has been in existence for over 25 years. As well as staging its shows in the major centres, it also tours most of its work – check out its website (www.takirua.co.nz) for the current offerings. Maori drama is also often showcased at the professional theatres in the main centres as well as the biennial New Zealand International Festival. Hone Kouka and Briar

---

VISITING MARAE

As you travel around NZ, you will see many *marae* complexes. Often *marae* are owned by a descent group. They are also owned by urban Maori groups, schools, universities and church groups, and they should only be visited by arrangement with the owners. Some *marae* that may be visited include: Huria Marae (p324) in Tauranga; Koriniti Marae on the Whanganui River Rd (p264); Pipitea Marae in Wellington (p383); and Te Papa Museum Marae in Wellington (p387).

Marae complexes include a *wharenui* (meeting house), which often embodies an ancestor. Its ridge is the backbone, the rafters are ribs, and it shelters the descendants. There is a clear space in front of the *wharenui* (ie the *marae atea*). Sometimes there are other buildings: a *wharekai* (dining hall); a toilet and shower block; perhaps even classrooms, play equipment and the like.

Hui (gatherings) are held at *marae*. Issues are discussed, classes conducted, milestones celebrated and the dead farewelled. Te reo Maori (the Maori language) is prominent, sometimes exclusively so.

Visitors sleep in the meeting house if a *hui* goes on for longer than a day. Mattresses are placed on the floor, someone may bring a guitar, and stories and jokes always go down well as the evening stretches out...

The Powhiri

If you visit a *marae* as part of an organised group, you'll be welcomed in a *powhiri*. The more common ones are outlined here.

There may be a *wero* (challenge). Using *taiaha* (quarter-staff) moves a warrior will approach the visitors and place a baton on the ground for a visitor to pick up.

There is a *karanga* (ceremonial call). A woman from the host group calls to the visitors and a woman from the visitors responds. Their long, high, falling calls begin to overlap and interweave and the visiting group walks on to the *marae atea*. It is then time for *whaikorero* (speechmaking). The hosts welcome the visitors, the visitors respond. Speeches are capped off by a *waiata* (song), and the visitors' speaker places *koha* (gift, usually an envelope of cash) on the *marae*. The hosts then invite the visitors to *hariru* (shake hands) and *hongi* (see below). Visitors and hosts are now united and will share light refreshments or a meal.

The Hongi

Press forehead and nose together firmly, shake hands, and perhaps offer a greeting such as 'Kia ora' or 'Tena koe'. Some prefer one press (for two or three seconds, or longer), others prefer two shorter (press, release, press). Men and women sometimes kiss on one cheek. Some people mistakenly think the *hongi* is a pressing of noses only (awkward to aim!) or the rubbing of noses (even more awkward).

Tapu

Tapu (spiritual restrictions) and *mana* (power and prestige) are taken seriously in the Maori world. Sit on chairs or seating provided (never on tables), and walk around people, not over them. The *powhiri* is *tapu*, and mixing food and *tapu* is right up there on the offence-o-meter. Do eat and drink when invited to do so by your hosts. You needn't worry about starvation: an important Maori value is *manaakitanga* (kindness).

Grace-Smith (both have published playscripts available) have toured their works around NZ and to festivals in the UK.

Contemporary Dance

Contemporary Maori dance often takes its inspiration from *kapa haka* and traditional Maori imagery. The exploration of pre-European life also provides inspiration. For example a Maori choreographer, Moss Patterson, used *kokowai* (a body-adorning paste made from reddish clay and shark oil) as the basis of his most recent piece of the same name.

NZ's leading specifically Maori dance company is the Atamira Dance Collective (www.atamiradance.co.nz). They have been producing critically acclaimed, beautiful and challenging work since 2000. If that sounds too earnest, another choreographer to watch out for is Mika Torotoro, who happily blends *kapa haka,* drag, opera, ballet and disco into his work. You can check out clips of his work at www.mika.co.nz.

Music plays an important role in traditional and contemporary Maori culture: see p47 for more details.

Maori Film-making

Although there had already been successful Maori documentaries (*Patu!* and the *Tangata Whenua* series are brilliant, and available from some urban video stores), it wasn't until 1987 that NZ had its first fiction feature-length movie by a Maori director with Barry Barclay's *Ngati*. Mereta Mita was the first Maori woman to direct a fiction feature with *Mauri* (1988). Both Mita and Barclay had highly political aims and ways of working, which involved a lengthy pre-production phase, during which they would consult with and seek direction from their *kaumatua* (elders). Films with significant Maori participation or control include the harrowing *Once Were Warriors* and the uplifting *Whale Rider*. Oscar-shortlisted Taika Waititi, of Te Whanau-a-Apanui descent, wrote and directed *Eagle vs Shark*.

The New Zealand Film Archive (www.filmarchive.org.nz) is a great place to experience Maori film, with most showings being either free or relatively inexpensive. It has offices in Auckland (p117) and Wellington (p384).

The first NZ hip-hop song to become a hit was Dalvanius Prime's 'Poi E', which was sung entirely in Maori by the Patea Maori Club. It was the highest-selling single of 1984 in NZ, outselling all international artists.

Maori Writing

There are many novels and collections of short stories by Maori writers, and personal taste will govern your choices. How about approaching Maori writing regionally? Read Patricia Grace (*Potiki, Cousins, Dogside Story, Tu*) around Wellington, and maybe Witi Ihimaera (*Pounamu, Pounamu, The Matriarch, Bulibasha, The Whale Rider*) on the North Island's East Coast. Keri Hulme (*The Bone People, Stonefish*) and the South Island go together like a mass of whitebait bound in a frying pan by a single egg (ie very well). Read Alan Duff (*Once Were Warriors*) anywhere, but only if you want to be saddened, even shocked. Definitely take James George (*Hummingbird, Ocean Roads*) with you to Auckland's West Coast beaches and Northland's Ninety Mile Beach. Paula Morris (*Queen of Beauty, Hibiscus Coast, Trendy but Casual*) and Kelly Ana Morey (*Bloom, Grace is Gone*) – hmm, Auckland and beyond? If poetry appeals you can't go past the giant of Maori poetry in English, the late, lamented Hone Tuwhare (*Deep River Talk: Collected Poems*). Famously sounding like he's at church and in the pub at the same time, you *can* take him anywhere.

Food & Drink Lauraine Jacobs

Lauraine Jacobs is an award-winning food writer, and food editor of *Cuisine* magazine. Passionate about NZ's wine and food, she travels the country extensively seeking out the best culinary experiences and new and exciting wines and food products.

New Zealand's international reputation as a clean, green producer of food products is well earned: its temperate climate, fertile soil and balance of sunshine and rainfall allows farmers to grow an abundance of produce for local and export markets; and there is an emphasis throughout the country on fresh, natural production.

With good advice on where to eat, and regional and seasonal specialities and the local wines to match them with, travelling in NZ can be a culinary adventure not to be missed.

FROM THE HANGI TO INTERNATIONAL-FUSION CUISINE

Before European settlement, Maori people ate a diet predominantly made up of fish, bird and root vegetables such as kumara (sweet potatoes brought from Polynesia and cultivated in NZ). They often cooked their food in an underground pit known as a *hangi*.

The first European settlers (most of whom were British) introduced beef, sheep and pigs to the country, and for more than a century thereafter the Kiwi diet was a stolid fare similar to the prewar food served up throughout the UK. There was lots of bread and potatoes, and plain cooking – with roasting and boiling as the predominant culinary techniques. Bland meat (mutton and beef) with three vegetables was served up throughout the nation each night for dinner.

For an authoritative guide to food and wine, visit www.cuisine.co.nz.

For some, that style of cooking continues today, often supplemented by the international fast-food brands found throughout the country. However, over the past 30 years there has been a massive shift towards a more varied, internationally inspired diet. NZ has embraced Asia and the Pacific Islands, and immigration from those regions has brought new flavours and cooking styles to NZ kitchens. At the same time, young New Zealanders have set off on overseas experiences and returned home with a keen appetite for lighter, fresher fare and a fusion of the culinary delights experienced in the Mediterranean and the East, or the 'new' British cuisine they have learnt about working in kitchens and pubs in the UK. The main style of cuisine now found in NZ cafes and restaurants is best described as Pacific Rim fusion, incorporating elements and ingredients from the countries of Southeast Asia, India and the Pacific.

Some farmers have also moved to diversify from traditional pastoral farming and ventured into vines, olives and kiwifruit. Wine and kiwifruit

---

ORGANIC NEW ZEALAND

No one is more aware of the importance of sustainability of the land than the farmers of NZ. With the country's economy, past and future, dependent on agricultural and pastoral industries, maintaining clean, unpolluted soil, water and air is a constant consideration.

Organic production and awareness is growing rapidly – many New Zealanders embrace the idea of organic food, convinced of the health benefits, and actively seek certified organic produce – and organic stores can be found in every major city throughout the country. In farmers markets and supermarkets organically grown and produced food will be proudly displayed and labelled as such.

However, in a country that produces more food than it could possibly consume, many food products are still imported. To really taste the goodness of NZ it is necessary to check that the meat, poultry, vegetables and fruit on menus and in stores has been grown in NZ.

POLYNESIAN SPECIALITIES

Some foods are highly prized by the Maori and Pacific Island population, but won't be found on many menus.

Mutton bird is not for everyone, as it is very fatty and has a fishy taste, but is a must for travellers who venture to Stewart Island. Equally fatty is *palusami*, traditionally a favourite with Pacific Islanders. Taro leaves or spinach are slow-cooked with coconut and corned beef to make this rich tasty meal.

Puha (prickly sow thistle) is a popular feature of Maori cooking, found growing wild in backyards and farms across the country. These leafy greens are boiled up with pork, mussels or mutton bones.

Kina and paua (abalone) are two types of shellfish to seek out. Kina is a sea urchin found among rocks on the coastline, with roe that is eaten raw from within the spiny shell. Paua has dark black meat and can be grilled or minced for fritters; it's very expensive and has a meaty savoury flavour.

Recently chefs have become interested in a range of local herbs and spices, which they add to meat and fish dishes. Peppery horopito (a bush pepper), scented kawakawa (bush basil) and kelp salt (from the seaweed plant) can be found on menus and in packets in speciality food stores.

particularly – industries hardly dreamed of 35 years ago – have grown from boutique operations to huge export earners.

STAPLES & SPECIALITIES
Meat
One of the joys of NZ fare is grass-fed meat. Cattle, sheep and venison munch on lush pastures year-round, enjoying the freedom of the outdoors and producing meat that's lean, tasty and sustainably grown.

Lamb is a must for any meat-eating visitor, whether it's taken as marinated chops sizzling on the barbecue, a roast leg with traditional mint sauce enjoyed around the farm table or a stylish dish in a top restaurant. The perfect ac-companiments are roasted potatoes, chunks of kumara and fresh green vegies.

New Zealanders also love their steak, and restaurants often list at least one fine-grained beef dish. Following hard on the heels of the sauvignon-blanc phenomenon, local red wines have garnered international attention, and both pinot noir and syrah varietals make a fine accompaniment to any red-meat meal.

Seafood
With more than 19,000km of pristine coastline and the largest fishing grounds of any country on earth, seafood is also a must-try on any culinary tour of NZ. Shellfish abound in coastal waters; the highly rated Bluff oysters are first choice with locals. It's rare, however, to find an oyster freshly shucked to order in NZ. Fish shops, supermarkets and markets sell fresh oysters, sometimes in the shell, but most often already shucked and packed in sea water in small plastic containers.

Seafood specialities include Greenshell mussels (which are tasty and often far larger than those served in other parts of the world), cockles, clams and scallops. Crayfish (a rock lobster) is rich and sweet, but expensive. Whitebait are much prized tiny threadlike fish that are most commonly served in frit-ters, and can be tracked down on the west coasts of both islands during the months of September through December. Getting takeaway fish and chips, a popular meal that is good value and in plentiful supply throughout NZ, is a common Friday-night family ritual.

Apart from large-scale salmon, oyster and mussel farming, NZ's aquacul-ture industry is still in its infancy. Keen fishermen will find plenty of places to catch their own rainbow or brown trout in the many lakes and rivers of

Bluff oysters are a wild species unique to NZ dredged from the deep waters near Bluff from mid-April until the strictly administered quota catch is filled.

TOP NZ EATING EXPERIENCES

Just as the climate changes from south to north, so do the local speciality foods of each region. In more upmarket restaurants, menus often reflect pride in the regional produce. Chefs carefully seek the very best, and celebrate fresh locally grown fruit, vegetables, olive oils and meat and locally caught fish, and often credit their suppliers on their menus. Cafes also occasionally pay homage to local producers.

Some specialities to look for on menus in the far north and the Auckland region are avocados, nuts, citrus fruits and Asian vegetables, as the subtropical climate allows them to flourish. North Island fish differ from the catch of more southern fishermen: fresh snapper, hapuku, tarakihi and flounder are common in the north; in the colder south there's more emphasis on groper, sole, brill, blue cod and turbot.

High-quality local lamb and beef can be found in Hawke's Bay, Taranaki, Wairarapa, Canterbury and Southland, and cervena venison (a low-fat, healthy red meat) is mostly raised in these regions, too.

A variety of fruits thrive in most of NZ's grape-growing districts, and travellers will also find some great local food matches with the speciality wines of each region. Farmers market stall holders will willingly point travellers in the direction of restaurants and cafes that champion and use local produce.

Our authors' favourite NZ eating experiences:

- Mt Maunganui's shiny new food haven, **Providores Urban Food Store** (p331), maintains a beachy, raffish charm while delivering a serious dose of culinary quality. Surf videos flickered across the walls as I tried to choose between buttery fresh-baked pastries, home-smoked meats and cheeses, sticky organic jams and killer coffee (…or all of the above). Further east around the Bay of Plenty, lonesome Maketu has seen better days, but it's worth a detour if only to visit legendary **Maketu Pies** (p334). I snaffled a mint-and-lamb special from the factory-shop pie warmer and wolfed it down on the foreshore, pastry flakes flying on the salty breeze. *Charles Rawlings-Way*

- It's not often that you get to sample every single item on a menu, but a friend's Hen's Party lunch at **Clooney** (p111) gave me just that opportunity (I was the bridesman – it was a very modern wedding). Every single dish was a winner – interesting, deftly executed and delicious. One wit quipped, 'Great, the strippers have arrived', just as two well-known middle-

NZ, and will be the only visitors to enjoy these treats as trout cannot be sold lawfully.

Fresh Produce

Fresh local produce can be found everywhere from farmers markets to local supermarkets, specialty food stores and road-side stalls. In the North, look for citrus fruit at farm stands around Kerikeri, avocados and kiwifruit near Tauranga and apples and stone fruit in Hawke's Bay. In the South, there are fruit and vegetable stalls throughout Nelson and Marlborough; freshly dug potatoes can be bought directly from farmers near Oamaru; and some excellent dried fruit can be sampled at several stops around Cromwell in Central Otago.

The furry-skinned kiwifruit with an emerald green, vitamin C–rich interior has become the champion of pastry chefs worldwide. Its sister, known as Gold, has a smoother skin and pale yellow interior that's even higher in vitamin C.

Sweets & Desserts

Visitors should also look for uniquely NZ foods such as pavlova (an indulgent cream-and-fruit-topped meringue cake) and hokey pokey ice cream (a vanilla ice cream filled with nuggets of crunchy golden toffee). Those with a sweet tooth will fall in love with the range of varietal honeys with the aromas of the specific vegetation of the region in which they are made – especially Manuka honey, which has extraordinary healthful and healing properties.

aged conservative politicians sat down at the next table. It's that kind of place. **Mangonui Fish Shop** (p171) is a very different kind of place. A stingray swam past while I was polishing off my fish and chips. Magic! *Peter Dragicevich*

■ It's official: Stewart Island's **Kai Kart** is NZ's southernmost eatery, and I reckon you could travel the length of the country without finding better fish and chips. The wee caravan turns out incredibly fresh blue cod and delicious battered mussels or oysters. Order up large, wrap up warm, and eat alfresco with the southern ocean winds whipping up in your face. Don't forget to grab a bottle of satay sauce to go with the mussels. In the Catlins, I may have been slightly underwhelmed by NZ's own, more subtle version of Niagara Falls, but the nearby **Niagara Falls Café** left me with no feelings of disappointment. Housed in a restored 19th-century schoolhouse, the cafe and art gallery is definitely worth a stop. My first visit was for South Island's best coffee and cheesecake, and I returned a few days later with my wife and enjoyed wonderful parmesan-baked blue cod. Beers from the Invercargill Brewery, and Central Otago wines, are also pretty compelling reasons to drop by. *Brett Atkinson*

■ Nowhere on my travels did I find the Kiwi home-baking tradition in finer fettle than at the **Wakamarinian Café** in Havelock. To quote the owner of the Havelock Garden Motel, 'If you don't love the raspberry-and-white-chocolate shortcake, there must be something wrong with you'. Too true! But there's more to life than pastry. There's paua ravioli, signature dish of **Logan-Brown** (p395). Housed in a grand 1920s banking chamber on groovy Cuba St, this is Wellington's – and NZ's – best. *Sarah Bennett*

■ Eating in Queenstown is an under-rated pleasure. If you're in the mood for some quick eats you can't go past **Fergburger**. This perennial favourite has become an essential Queenstown experience. Ferg's so sewn into the collective dining fabric that it has become a must for all Queenie visitors – backpacker or billionaire. Rightfully so – the burgers are *that* good. Those wanting to eat indoors, or at least without thumping drum 'n' bass, should look no further then around the corner at **Solero Vino**. This fine-dining French restaurant is the bee's knees for the cultured culinary crowd. Delicate flavours, amazing wine and awesome service – *bon appetit*! *Scott Kennedy*

The Dairy
Owner-operated stores, known locally as the 'dairy', are ubiquitous in small towns and city suburbs. All manner of food items, from ice creams rolled to order, bread and milk to newspapers and almost every staple need are stocked.

DRINKS
After work, around the barbecue, at the beach and in cafes up and down the country, beer, wine and cocktails are part of the social culture.

The zingy Marlborough sauvignon blanc – with fresh, fruity, almost herbal aromas that leap out of the glass – holds a unique position in the wine world, and is sought after all over the globe. Walk into any restaurant, and almost every table will be graced with a bottle or two of opened wine to accompany the meal. All supermarkets sell local wines, often at bargain prices, but the very best NZ wines are mainly sold in specialist wine stores or found on the wine lists of the better restaurants.

Beer, too, has long been part of the Kiwi culture, and boutique hand-crafted beers abound. Nelson – the region where hops, an essential ingredient in beer, are grown – has become a treasure trove of boutique beers and visitors can call in to several operations to pick up 'a dozen' or two to take to the beach.

For years only recognised for high-quality cheddar cheese, many small producers are now making artisan cheeses from cow's, sheep and goat's milk. All NZ cheese is made (by law) from pasteurised milk.

WINE TOURING

Visitors to NZ who have a real passion for food and wine can follow a wine trail right through the country from north to south, rather than following traditional tourist routes. Tour options include cycling or guided tours in minivans, organised by wine experts. Where good wines are created, there's usually good local food too.

Within each wine region there are numerous wineries that welcome visits at the cellar door, and many have good restaurants with food matched to the wines grown and produced on the estate.

As most international visitors arrive through the airport of Auckland, a great place to start is with a day visit to Matakana (p140) for its pinot gris, or to Waiheke Island (p123), a 45-minute ferry ride from Auckland's downtown, to taste the island's intense red wines and local chardonnays.

To take in the major wine-making areas, first head south from Auckland to Hawke's Bay (p357) for chardonnays and syrahs. This is a vast area so careful planning of a trail is essential to avoid endless criss-crossing. Next it's off through extensive sheep country to the Wairarapa to try the renowned pinot noirs of Martinborough (p407). From there an exhilarating drive over the Rimutaka hills will get you to Wellington, from where you can cross Cook Strait to Marlborough by ferry or air.

Marlborough's sauvignon blancs have made their mark internationally and firmly established NZ's credibility in the world of wine. (A side trip to experience the aromatic white wines of Nelson is also suggested.)

The wine tourist can then hit the trail through Waipara and North Canterbury for rieslings and pinot noirs, and finish in the scenic Central Otago region where wine tourism is a popular addition to the area's famous adventure tourism. The pinot noirs of Otago exhibit all the characteristics of the wild thyme- and heather-clad hills throughout the region.

Another speciality drink to look for is the internationally acclaimed 42Below vodka, a great example of Kiwi ingenuity. Innovator Geoff Ross produced uniquely NZ flavoured vodkas (kiwifruit, Manuka honey, feijoa and more), presented them in elegant bottles and then sold his company to Bacardi for many millions. He's been retained by Bacardi to oversee and guard the standards.

Coffee drinking has also become an important part of NZ culture, coinciding with the rise and rise of the cafe. To find the best coffee, follow the tried and tested rule of joining the crowd at the busiest spot in town.

CELEBRATIONS

During the harvest period in late summer (February to April) wine and food is celebrated in many of the wine regions with local festivals. Wine flows freely, there's no shortage of food stalls with local specialities, and it's all terrific fun, especially as the day lengthens and the wine kicks in.

Some visitors may be fortunate enough to attend a Maori *hangi,* a feature of almost any gathering, occasion or funeral at the *marae* (Maori meeting house). A pit is dug, a fire lit and stones placed in it. When the set-up is finally deemed hot enough, chicken, lamb, pork, kumara, potatoes, corn, pumpkin and other vegetables are covered with sacks and placed over the hot stones. The pit is covered with earth and the food steamed for an hour or two before being lifted out and carried to the table. The flavour of the food, which is usually not seasoned with spices or herbs, is earthy and tender. A great deal of associated drinking, chatter and comradeship are very much part of a *hangi.*

Smoking is banned in the workplace and any public place where food or drink is served, and it is considered very bad manners to smoke indoors or without requesting permission.

As NZ has evolved into a more multicultural society, many different ethnic groups have introduced their own celebrations. Pasifika, a festival celebrating Polynesian culture, takes place in Auckland over a weekend in February. It's two days of eating Island foods such as Pacific fruits and vegetables, sticky coconut buns, suckling pig, baked spinach or taro leaves with coconut and much more. Island sports, singing and cultural dancing take place.

The Diwali celebration of the Indian community has also become part of the Auckland calendar and many tiny food stalls are set up near the harbour in October for a weekend celebration. Spicy aromas waft through the air, and the vast array of savoury snacks and jewel-like sweets are irresistible.

In rural areas, agricultural and pastoral associations host annual showcases of farming practices and animal displays at local showgrounds. These fun days are full of competitions and events; food tends to be hearty, but hardly gourmet, including basic pies, hamburgers, barbecued sausages and hot dogs.

WHERE TO EAT & DRINK

The main cities are remarkably well served with a range of eating choices, from restaurants where the food is stylish and imaginative to small places where the ambience is simple, but the food authentic and prepared with love. Cafes are found everywhere, particularly in towns along the main touring routes, and usually serve hearty country fare. Many cafes open at 7am but close around 4pm or 5pm and don't serve dinner. For pub and restaurant opening hours see p418.

B&Bs in the more remote regions will often cook dinner, but usually only by request well ahead of arrival. Country-style pubs can be found in most places, and although very few offer a 'gastro' experience, they serve up a basic menu to accompany a frothy cold beer.

Farmers markets are generally held on Saturday or Sunday mornings, and all are great places to explore local food culture, meet local food producers and taste some terrific fresh food. Most have a mobile coffee stand, and usually there will be an entrepreneur serving a 'breakfast roll' bun stuffed with fried eggs and bacon.

Check out what Auckland and Wellington restaurants have to offer at www.menus.co.nz or www.dineout.co.nz.

The restaurant industry is NZ's largest private-sector employer, with nearly 4% of the total workforce.

TOP 10 NZ MICROBREWERIES

New Zealanders sure can brew up a storm! Here are our picks for the best Kiwi microbreweries you're likely to find:

Brew Moon Brewery The roadside Brew Moon Brewery in Amberley lures visitors in with three different beers on tap and an excellent cafe. Try the chocolatey Brew Moon Dark Side Stout. Amberley is just before the Waipara Valley wine region in North Canterbury.

Croucher Brewing Co (p316; www.croucherbrewing.co.nz) Croucher's crafty pale ale and pilsner rule the roost at Rotorua's boozy Underground Bar.

Emerson's Brewery (www.emersons.co.nz) Dunedin is full of students, and students like beer – and how blessed they are to drink Emerson's! Wheat beers, pilsners, porters, and bitter ales heavy on the malt and spice.

Founders Brewery (www.biobrew.co.nz) NZ's first certified organic brewery is in Nelson. Take a behind-the-scenes tour and sip the immaculate product.

Hallertau (p136; www.hallertau.co.nz) Auckland beer boffins are big fans of this microbrewery, where sexy packaging and barrel-aged beers collide (its 'Porter Noir' does time in old pinot barrels!). The pale ale is hoppy heaven.

Moa Beer (www.moabeer.co.nz) Winemaker's son Josh Scott produces a range of excellent bottle-fermented beers at his tasting room–bar in the thick of Marlborough's vineyards.

Renaissance Brewing Co (www.renaissancebrewing.co.nz) Seriously good ales with the medals to prove it. A fantastic use for a former ice-cream factory in Blenheim.

Three Boys Brewery (www.threeboysbrewery.co.nz) Three Boys IPA is available at discerning bars and restaurants in Christchurch. Packed with hops, it's an authentic version of the Indian Pale Ales originally crafted to last the long sea journey to colonial India.

Wanaka Beerworks (www.wanakabeerworks.co.nz) Look for this brewery's beers in restaurants around Queenstown and Wanaka. The Brewski pilsner is packed with floral, hoppy flavours and is an excellent rendition of a Czech-style lager.

White Cliffs Organic Brewery (p245; www.organicbeer.co.nz) White Cliffs enjoys a reputation far beyond Taranaki, particularly for Mike's Mild – an amber ale with notes of fruit and roasted nuts: a real connoisseur's drop.

TO MARKET, TO MARKET

Farmers markets are a relatively new introduction to the shopping options in NZ. In the past five years there has been extraordinary growth and from one market in 2001 (at Whangarei, in the north), the number has steadily increased each year to more than 50 throughout the country.

Most are held on weekend mornings and are happy local affairs where visitors will meet local producers and find fresh produce. It's a great way to find out just what food is the speciality of the region. Mobile coffee carts are usually present, and tastings are often offered by enterprising and innovative stall holders selling value-added food products.

Always take a bag to carry purchases in as many of the sustainable-minded markets ban the use of plastic bags. Arrive as early as possible – the best produce always sells out very quickly.

Look at www.farmersmarkets.org.nz to find dates and times of farmers markets throughout NZ.

VEGETARIANS & VEGANS

Vegetarians need not worry that they will not find suitable food around NZ. There isn't a great range of vegetarian restaurants, but almost all restaurants and cafes offer vegetarian choices on their menus (although sometimes only one or two). Many cafes also provide gluten-free and vegan options. Always check that the stocks and sauces are vegetarian, as chefs who have not traditionally cooked for those with strict vegetarian diets tend to think of vegetarian cooking as simply omitting the main serving of meat or fish from a meal.

It always pays to mention any dietary requirement when making a reservation at a restaurant or B&B, and it's essential in this meat-loving country to mention it to the host when invited to a private home.

Environment Vaughan Yarwood

THE LAND

New Zealand is a young country – its present shape is less than 10,000 years old. Having broken away from the supercontinent of Gondwanaland (which included Africa, Australia, Antarctica and South America) in a stately geological dance some 130 million years ago, it endured aeons of uplift and erosion, buckling and tearing, and the slow fall and rise of the sea as ice ages came and went. Straddling the boundary of two great colliding slabs of the earth's crust – the Pacific plate and the Indian/Australian plate – to this day NZ remains the plaything of nature's strongest forces.

The result is one of the most varied and spectacular series of landscapes in the world, ranging from snow-dusted mountains and drowned glacial valleys to rainforests, dunelands and an otherworldly volcanic plateau. It is a diversity of landforms you would expect to find across an entire continent rather than a small archipelago in the South Pacific.

Evidence of NZ's tumultuous past is everywhere. The South Island's mountainous spine – the 650km-long ranges of the Southern Alps – is a product of the clash of the two plates; the result of a process of rapid lifting that, if anything, is accelerating. Despite NZ's highest peak, Aoraki/Mt Cook, losing 10m from its summit overnight in a 1991 landslide, the Alps are on an express elevator that, without erosion and landslides, would see them 10 times their present height within a few million years.

On the North Island, the most impressive changes have been wrought by volcanoes. Auckland is built on an isthmus peppered by scoria cones, on many of which you can still see the earthworks of *pa* (fortified villages) built by early Maori. The city's biggest and most recent volcano, 600-year-old Rangitoto Island (p121), is just a short ferry ride from the downtown wharves. Some 300km further south, the classically shaped cone of snowcapped Mt Taranaki/Egmont (p245) overlooks tranquil dairy pastures.

But the real volcanic heartland runs through the centre of the North Island, from the restless bulk of Mt Ruapehu in Tongariro National Park (p288) northeast through the Rotorua lake district (p308) out to NZ's most

Vaughan Yarwood is a historian and travel writer who is widely published in NZ and internationally. His most recent book is *The History Makers: Adventures in New Zealand Biography*.

RESPONSIBLE TRAVEL

Toitu te whenua – care for the land. Help protect the environment by following these guidelines:

- Treat NZ's forests and native wildlife with respect. Damaging or taking plants is illegal in most parts of the country.

- Remove rubbish. Litter is unsightly and can encourage vermin and disease. Rather than burying or burning, carry out what you carry in.

- In areas without toilet facilities bury toilet waste in a shallow hole away from tracks, huts, campsites and waterways.

- Keep streams and lakes pure by cleaning away from water sources. Drain waste water into the soil to filter out soaps and detergent. If you suspect contamination, boil water for three minutes, filter, or chemically treat it before use.

- Where possible use portable fuel stoves. Keep open fires small, use only dead wood and make sure the fire is out by dousing it with water and checking the ashes before leaving.

- Keep to tracks where possible. Get permission before crossing private land and move carefully around livestock.

ENVIRONMENTAL ISSUES IN AOTEAROA NEW ZEALAND *Nandor Tanczos*

Most people think of Aotearoa New Zealand as clean and green, a place that respects the environment. We have the NZ Forest Accord to protect native forests, national parks and reserves now cover a third of the country, marine reserves continue to pop up around the coast, and our antinuclear legislation seems unassailable. A closer look, however, reveals a dirtier picture.

New Zealand has one of the highest per capita rates of greenhouse-gas emissions in the world. We are one of the most inefficient users of energy in the developed world. Public transport is negligible in most places and ecological values play little part in urban planning or building design. Add to that the ongoing battle being fought in many communities over the disposal of sewage and toxic waste into waterways, a conflict often spearheaded by *tangata whenua* (local Maori people), and the 'clean and green' label begins to look seriously compromised.

Our biggest polluting sector is pastoral farming, responsible for half of our greenhouse-gas emissions. The importation of European sheep and cattle-grazing systems has left many hillsides with marginal productivity, bare of trees and prone to erosion. Grazing threatens many waterways, with stock causing damage to stream and lake margins and run-off causing nutrient overload leading to eutrophication and algal blooms. Dairy farming, the worst culprit due to its intensity, is expanding into areas often poorly suited to this kind of land use, relying on a massive increase in the use of irrigation. Over-allocation of water has become a problem in many areas as a result. Regional councils and farming groups are fencing and planting stream banks to protect water quality, but their efforts are outstripped by the sheer growth in dairying.

The election of the centre-right National Government in 2008 has led to the unravelling of a number of important environmental protections. They have gutted the already inadequate Emissions Trading Scheme. The world-leading Resource Management Act has been significantly weakened, and the Government is proposing to open up Department of Conservation and other

active volcano, White Island (p339), in the Bay of Plenty. Called the Taupo Volcanic Zone, this great 250km-long rift valley – part of a volcano chain known as the 'Pacific Ring of Fire' – has been the seat of massive eruptions that have left their mark on the country physically and culturally.

Most spectacular were the eruptions from the volcano that created Lake Taupo (p273). Considered the world's most productive volcano in terms of the amount of material ejected, Taupo last erupted 1800 years ago in a display that was the most violent anywhere on the planet within the past 5000 years.

You can experience the aftermath of volcanic destruction on a smaller scale at Te Wairoa (the Buried Village; p321), near Rotorua on the shores of Lake Tarawera. Here, partly excavated and open to the public, lie the remains of a 19th-century Maori village overwhelmed when nearby Mt Tarawera erupted without warning. The famous Pink and White Terraces (one of several claimants to the popular title 'eighth wonder of the world') were destroyed overnight by the same upheaval.

The GreenDex (p474) at the end of this book lists ecofriendly places to explore, stay or dine throughout NZ. Discover more about ecotourism across the country with Leonie Johnsen's *Organic Explorer New Zealand* (www.organicexplorer. co.nz).

But when nature sweeps the board clean with one hand she often rebuilds with the other: Waimangu Valley (p321), born of all that geothermal violence, is the place to go to experience the hot earth up close and personal amid geysers, silica pans, bubbling mud pools, and the world's biggest hot spring. Or you can wander around Rotorua's Whakarewarewa Thermal Village (p306), where descendants of Maori displaced by the eruption live in the middle of steaming vents and prepare food for visitors in boiling pools.

A second by-product of movement along the tectonic plate boundary is seismic activity – earthquakes. Not for nothing has NZ been called 'the Shaky Isles'. Most quakes only rattle the glassware, but one was indirectly responsible for creating an internationally celebrated tourist attraction...

In 1931, an earthquake measuring 7.9 on the Richter scale levelled the Hawke's Bay city of Napier (p362) causing huge damage and loss of life.

protected land for mining. Local communities in places like the Coromandel Peninsula are now gearing up for a rerun of the fierce environmental battles of the 1970s and '80s, which ended with the Coromandel being declared off limits to mining.

Despite these things, New Zealand has some advantages. A relatively high proportion of our energy comes from renewable hydro-generation. Farm animals, except for pigs and chickens, are almost all grass fed and free range. We are starting to get serious about waste minimisation and resource recovery. But our biggest saving grace is our small population. As a result, Aotearoa is a place well worth visiting. This is a beautiful land with enormous geographical and ecological diversity. Our forests are unique and magnificent, and the bird species that evolved in response to an almost total lack of mammalian life are spectacular, although now reduced in numbers due to introduced predators such as rats, stoats and hedgehogs.

The responsibility of New Zealanders is to make change for ecological sustainability, not just at a personal level, but at an institutional and infrastructural level. The responsibility of visitors to Aotearoa New Zealand is to respect our unique biodiversity, and to query and question: every time you ask where the recycling centre is; every time you express surprise at the levels of energy use, car use and water use; every time you request organic food at a cafe or restaurant; you affect the person you talk to.

Aotearoa New Zealand has the potential to be a world leader in ecological wisdom. We have a strong tradition to draw from – the careful relationship of reciprocity that Maori developed with the natural world over the course of many, many generations. We live at the edge of the Pacific, on the Rim of Fire, a remnant of the ancient forests of Gondwanaland. We welcome conscious travellers.

Nandor Tanczos is an activist, researcher and educator based in Ngaruawahia. He was a Member of Parliament for the Green Party until 2008.

Napier was rebuilt almost entirely in the then-fashionable art-deco architectural style, and walking its streets today you can relive its brash exuberance in what has become a mecca for lovers of art deco (p362).

Travellers to the South Island can also see some evidence of volcanism – if the remains of the old volcanoes of Banks Peninsula weren't there to repel the sea, the vast Canterbury Plains, built from alpine sediment washed down the rivers from the Alps, would have eroded away long ago.

But in the south it is the Southern Alps themselves that dominate, dictating settlement patterns, throwing down engineering challenges and offering outstanding recreational opportunities. The island's mountainous backbone also helps shape the weather, as it stands in the path of the prevailing westerly winds which roll in, moisture-laden, from the Tasman Sea. As a result bush-clad lower slopes of the western Southern Alps are among the wettest places on earth, with an annual precipitation of some 15,000mm. Having lost its moisture, the wind then blows dry across the eastern plains towards the Pacific coast.

The North Island has a more even rainfall and is spared the temperature extremes of the South – which can plunge when a wind blows in from Antarctica. The important thing to remember, especially if you are tramping at high altitude, is that NZ has a maritime climate. This means weather can change with lightning speed, catching out the unprepared.

NZ is one of the most spectacular places in the world to see geysers. Rotorua's short-lived Waimangu geyser, formed after the Mt Tarawera eruption, was once the world's largest, often gushing to a dizzying height of 400m.

WILDLIFE

NZ may be relatively young, geologically speaking, but its plants and animals go back a long way. The tuatara, for instance, an ancient reptile unique to these islands, is a Gondwanaland survivor closely related to the dinosaurs, while many of the distinctive flightless birds (ratites) have distant African and South American cousins.

Due to its long isolation, the country is a veritable warehouse of unique and varied plants, most of which are found nowhere else. And with separation of the landmass occurring before mammals appeared on the scene, birds and insects have evolved in spectacular ways to fill the gaps.

The now extinct flightless moa, the largest of which grew to 3.5m tall and weighed over 200kg, browsed open grasslands much as cattle do today (skeletons can be seen at Auckland Museum, p90), while the smaller kiwi still ekes out a nocturnal living rummaging among forest leaf litter for insects and worms much as small mammals do elsewhere. One of the country's most ferocious-looking insects, the mouse-sized giant weta, meanwhile, has taken on a scavenging role elsewhere filled by rodents.

As one of the last places on earth to be colonised by humans, NZ was for millennia a safe laboratory for such risky evolutionary strategies, but with the arrival first of Maori and soon after of Europeans, things went downhill fast.

Many endemic creatures, including moa and the huia, an exquisite songbird, were driven to extinction, and the vast forests were cleared for their timber and to make way for agriculture. Destruction of habitat and the introduction of exotic animals and plants have taken a terrible environmental toll and New Zealanders are now fighting a rearguard battle to save what remains.

Birds & Animals

The first Polynesian settlers found little in the way of land mammals – just two species of bat – but forests, plains and coasts are alive with birds. Largely lacking the bright plumage found elsewhere, NZ's birds – like its endemic plants – have an understated beauty which does not shout for attention.

Among the most musical is the bellbird, common in both native and exotic forests everywhere except Northland, though like many birds it is more likely to be heard than seen. Its call is a series of liquid bell notes, most often sounded at dawn or dusk.

B Heather and H Robertson's *Field Guide to the Birds of New Zealand* is a comprehensive guide for birdwatchers and a model of helpfulness for anyone even casually interested in the country's remarkable bird life.

The tui, another nectar eater and the country's most beautiful songbird, is a great mimic, with an inventive repertoire that includes clicks, grunts and chuckles. Notable for the white throat feathers which stand out against its dark plumage, the tui often feeds on flax flowers in suburban gardens but is most at home in densely tangled forest ('bush' to New Zealanders).

Fantails are commonly encountered on forest trails, swooping and jinking to catch insects stirred up by passing hikers, while pukeko, elegant swamp-hens with blue plumage and bright red beaks, are readily seen along wetland margins and even on the sides of roads nearby – be warned, they have little road sense.

If you spend any time in the South Island high country, you are likely to come up against the fearless and inquisitive kea – an uncharacteristically drab green parrot with bright red underwings. Kea are common in the car parks of the Fox and Franz Josef Glaciers, where they hang out for food scraps or tear rubber from car windscreens.

Then there is the takahe, a rare flightless bird thought extinct until a small colony was discovered in 1948, and the equally flightless kiwi, NZ's national emblem and the nickname for New Zealanders themselves.

The kiwi has a round body covered in coarse feathers, strong legs and a long, distinctive bill with nostrils at the tip for sniffing out food. It is not easy to find them in the wild, but they can be seen in simulated environments at excellent nocturnal houses. One of the best is the Otorohanga Kiwi House (p225), which also has other birds, including native falcons, moreporks (owls) and weka.

To get a feel for what the bush used to be like, take a trip to Tiritiri Matangi Island (p127). This regenerating island is an open sanctuary and one of the country's most successful exercises in community-assisted conservation.

BIRDWATCHING

The flightless kiwi is the species most sought after by birdwatchers. Sightings of the Stewart Island subspecies are common at all times of the year. Elsewhere, wild sightings of this increasingly rare nocturnal species are difficult, apart from in enclosures. Other birds that twitchers like to sight are the royal albatross, white heron, Fiordland crested penguin, yellow-eyed penguin, Australasian gannet and wrybill.

On the Coromandel Peninsula, the Firth of Thames (particularly Miranda) is a haven for migrating birds, while the Wharekawa Wildlife Refuge at Opoutere Beach is a breeding ground of the endangered NZ dotterel. There's also a very accessible Australasian gannet colony at Muriwai, west of Auckland, and one in Hawke's Bay. There are popular trips to observe pelagic birds out of Kaikoura, and royal albatross viewing on the Otago Peninsula.

Two good guides are the newly revised *Field Guide to the Birds of New Zealand*, by Barrie Heather and Hugh Robertson, and *Birds of New Zealand: Locality Guide* by Stuart Chambers.

MARINE MAMMAL–WATCHING

Kaikoura, on the northeast coast of the South Island, is NZ's nexus of marine mammal-watching. The main attraction here is whale-watching, but this is dependent on weather conditions, so don't expect to just be able to rock up and head straight out on a boat for a dream encounter. The sperm whale, the largest toothed whale, is pretty much a year-round resident, and depending on the season you may also see migrating humpback whales, pilot whales, blue whales and southern right whales. Other mammals – including fur seals and dusky dolphins – are seen year-round.

Kaikoura is also an outstanding place to swim with dolphins. Pods of up to 500 playful dusky dolphins can be seen on any given day. Dolphin swimming is common elsewhere in NZ, with the animals gathering off the North Island near Whakatane, Paihia, Tauranga, and in the Hauraki Gulf, and off

---

KIWI SPOTTING

The kiwi is a threatened species, and with the additional difficulty of them being nocturnal, it's only on Stewart Island that you might easily see one in the wild. They can, however, be observed in many artificially dark 'kiwi houses':

- Auckland Zoo (p91)
- Otorohanga Kiwi House Native Bird Park (p225)
- National Aquarium of New Zealand, Napier (p364)
- Nga Manu Nature Reserve, Waikanae (p406)
- Pukaha Mt Bruce National Wildlife Centre, near Masterton (p411)
- Wellington Zoo (p387)
- Southern Encounter Aquarium & Kiwi House, Christchurch
- Orana Wildlife Park, Christchurch
- Willowbank Wildlife Reserve, Christchurch
- Kiwi Birdlife Park, Queenstown

Akaroa on the South Island's Banks Peninsula. Seal swimming is possible in Kaikoura and in the Abel Tasman National Park.

Swimming with sharks is also possible, though with a protective cage as a chaperone; you can do it in Tutukaka and Gisborne.

Trees

No visitor to NZ (particularly Australians!) will go for long without hearing about the damage done to the bush by that bad-mannered Australian import, the brush-tailed possum. The long list of mammal pests introduced to NZ accidentally or for a variety of misguided reasons includes deer, rabbits, stoats, pigs and goats. But the most destructive by far is the possum, 70 million of which now chew through millions of tonnes of foliage a year despite the best efforts of the Department of Conservation (DOC) to control them.

Among favoured possum food are NZ's most colourful trees: the kowhai, a small-leaved tree growing to 11m, that in spring has drooping clusters of bright yellow flowers (NZ's national flower); the pohutukawa, a beautiful coastal tree of the northern North Island which bursts into vivid red flower in December, earning the nickname 'Christmas tree'; and a similar crimson-flowered tree, the rata. Rata species are found on both islands; the northern rata starts life as a climber on a host tree (that it eventually chokes).

The few remaining pockets of mature centuries-old kauri are stately emblems of former days. Their vast hammered trunks and towering, epiphyte-festooned limbs, which dwarf every other tree in the forest, are reminders of why they were sought after in colonial days for spars and building timber. The best place to see the remaining giants is Northland's Waipoua Kauri Forest (p179), home to three-quarters of the country's surviving kauri.

Now the pressure has been taken off kauri and other timber trees, including the distinctive rimu (red pine) and the long-lived totara (favoured for Maori war canoes), by one of the country's most successful imports – *Pinus radiata*. Pine was found to thrive in NZ, growing to maturity in just 35 years, and plantation forests are now widespread through the central North Island – the southern hemisphere's biggest, Kaingaroa Forest, lies southeast of Rotorua.

You won't get far into the bush without coming across one of its most prominent features – tree ferns. NZ is a land of ferns (more than 80 species) and most easily recognised are the mamaku (black tree fern) – which grows to 20m and can be seen in damp gullies throughout the country – and the 10m-high ponga (silver tree fern) with its distinctive white underside. The silver fern is equally at home as part of corporate logos and on the clothing of many of the country's top sportspeople.

NATIONAL PARKS

A third of the country – more than five million hectares – is protected in environmentally important parks and reserves that embrace almost every conceivable landscape: from mangrove-fringed inlets in the north to the snow-topped volcanoes of the Central Plateau, and from the forested fastness

Lifestyles of New Zealand Forest Plants, by J Dawson and R Lucas, is a beautifully photographed foray into the world of NZ's forests. Far from being drab and colourless, these lush treasure houses are home to ancient species dating from the time of the dinosaurs. This guidebook will have you reaching for your boots.

TOWERING KAURI

When Chaucer was born this was a sturdy young tree. When Shakespeare was born it was 300 years old. It predates most of the great cathedrals of Europe. Its trunk is sky-rocket straight and sky-rocket bulky, limbless for half its height. Ferns sprout from its crevices. Its crown is an asymmetric mess, like an inverted root system. I lean against it, give it a slap. It's like slapping a building. This is a tree out of Tolkien. It's a kauri.

Joe Bennett (A Land of Two Halves) referring to the McKinney kauri in Northland.

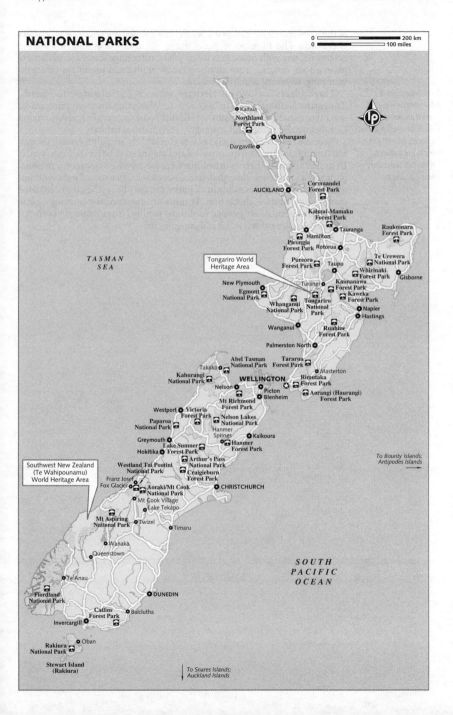

NATIONAL PARKS

0 — 200 km
0 — 100 miles

Kaitaia
Northland
Forest Park
Whangarei
Dargaville

*TASMAN
SEA*

Coromandel
Forest Park
AUCKLAND

Kaimai-Mamaku
Forest Park
Tauranga
Hamilton
Pirongia
Forest Park Rotorua
Pureora
Forest Park Taupo
New Plymouth
Egmont
National Park Turangi
Whanganui
National Park Tongariro
National Park
Wanganui

Raukumara
Forest Park
Te Urewera
National Park
Whirinaki
Forest Park
Gisborne
Kaimanawa
Forest Park
Kaweka
Forest Park
Napier
Hastings
Ruahine
Forest Park
Palmerston North

Tongariro World
Heritage Area

Takaka
Abel Tasman
National Park Tararua
Forest Park
Kahurangi
National Park WELLINGTON
Nelson Rimutaka
Picton Forest Park
Mt Richmond Blenheim
Forest Park Aorangi (Haurangi)
Forest Park
Westport Victoria
Forest Park
Paparoa Nelson Lakes
National Park National Park
Greymouth Hanmer
Lake Sumner Springs Kaikoura
Hokitika Forest Park
Hanmer
Westland Tai Poutini Arthur's Pass Forest Park
National Park National Park
Craigieburn
Franz Josef Forest Park
Fox Glacier Aoraki/Mt Cook CHRISTCHURCH
National Park
Mt Cook Village
Lake Tekapo
Mt Aspiring
National Park Twizel
Wanaka Timaru
Queenstown

Masterton

Southwest New Zealand
(Te Wahipounamu)
World Heritage Area

*SOUTH
PACIFIC
OCEAN*

To Bounty Islands;
Antipodes Islands →

Te Anau
Fiordland
National Park
Catlins DUNEDIN
Forest Park Balclutha
Invercargill
Rakiura Oban
National Park
Stewart Island
(Rakiura)

To Snares Islands;
Auckland Islands

of the Ureweras in the east to the Southern Alps' majestic mountains, glaciers and fiords. The 14 national parks, three maritime parks and two marine reserves, along with numerous forest parks, offer huge scope for wilderness experiences, ranging from climbing, snow skiing and mountain biking to tramping, kayaking and trout fishing.

Three places are World Heritage areas: NZ's Subantarctic Islands, Tongariro National Park (p288) and Te Wahipounamu, an amalgam of several national parks in southwest NZ that boast the world's finest surviving Gondwanaland plants and animals in their natural habitats.

Access to the country's wild places is relatively straightforward, though huts on walking tracks require passes and may need to be booked in advance. In practical terms, there is little difference for travellers between a national park and a forest park, though dogs are not allowed in national parks without a permit. Camping is possible in all parks, but may be restricted to dedicated camping grounds – check first. Permits are required for hunting (game birds), and licences are needed for inland fishing (trout, salmon); both can be bought online at www.fishandgame.org.nz.

The Department of Conservation website (www.doc.govt.nz) has useful information on the country's national parks, tracks and walkways. It also lists backcountry huts and campsites.

Active North Island

The North Island's astounding natural assets encourage even the laziest lounge lizards to drag themselves outside. Many travellers come here for the sole purpose of getting active, but the great outdoors aren't just the domain of thrill-seeking tourists – outdoor culture is ingrained in Kiwi life. From family camping holidays to exploring pristine coastal tracks, wandering into the wilderness and experiencing NZ's unpeopled majesty is the national habit.

It will come as no surprise then to learn that outdoor activities across the nation are accessible and supremely well organised. Commercial operators can hook you up with whatever kind of experience floats your boat – from bungy jumping off a canyon to sea kayaking around a national park – but the beauty of NZ is that you can do a lot of stuff under your own steam, without tagging along on a tour. This is still a wild frontier – don't miss the chance to engage with nature one on one, a million miles from home, just you and the great void.

See p417 for tips on less active sports like aerial sightseeing, fishing, sailing and golf; and p69 for the low-down on bird- and marine mammal-watching.

Adrenaline-pumping activities obviously have an element of risk – particularly white-water rafting, kayaking and anything that involves falling from a great height – but the perception of danger is part of the thrill. Despite some recent mishaps, chances of an accident remain negligible, but make sure you have travel insurance that fully covers you for any planned activities (for more info see p422).

TRAMPING

Tramping (aka bushwalking, hiking or trekking) is the perfect vehicle for a close encounter with the North Island's natural beauty. There are thousands of kilometres of tracks – some well marked, some barely a line on a map – plus an excellent network of huts enabling trampers to avoid lugging tents and (in some cases) cooking gear. Before plodding off into the forest, get up-to-date information from the appropriate authority – usually the **Department of Conservation** (DOC; www.doc.govt.nz) or regional i-SITE visitor information centres.

If you're planning your first walk, check out www.tramper.co.nz, a fantastic website with track descriptions and track ratings.

On the North Island, the most popular tracks are the Tongariro Northern Circuit (and the one-day Tongariro Alpine Crossing) and the Lake Waikaremoana Track. If you've got your heart set on a Great Walk in summer, check out the booking requirements and get in early. If you want to avoid the crowds, go in the shoulder season. DOC staff can help plan tramps on lesser-known tracks; see the DOC website for details.

When to Go

Tramping high season is during the school summer holidays, from two weeks before Christmas until the end of January – avoid it if you can. The best weather is from January to March, though most nonalpine tracks can be walked enjoy-

---

VOLUNTOURISM

NZ presents a swathe of active, outdoorsy opportunities for travellers to get some dirt under their fingernails and participate in conservation programs. Programs can include anything from tree-planting and weed removal to track construction, habitat conservation and fencing. Ask about local opportunities at any regional i-SITE visitor information centre, or check out www.conservationvolunteers.org.nz and www.doc.govt.nz/getting-involved, both of which allow you to browse for opportunities by region. See also WWOOFing (p415).

ably at any time from about October through to April. Winter (June to August) is not the time to be out in the wild, especially at altitude or on the Tongariro Alpine Crossing or Lake Waikaremoana track. Summer can be hot and exposed on the Tongariro Alpine Crossing, so cover up and carry lots of water.

What to Bring

For a primo tramp, the primary considerations are your feet and shoulders. Make sure your footwear is tough as old boots, and that your pack isn't too heavy. Adequate wet-weather gear is essential. If you're camping or staying in huts without stoves (eg on the Lake Waikaremoana Track), bring a camping stove. And don't forget your scroggin – a mixture of dried fruit and nuts (and sometimes chocolate) for munching en route.

Books

DOC publishes detailed books on the flora and fauna, geology and history of NZ's national parks, plus leaflets (50c to $2) detailing hundreds of walking tracks across NZ.

Lonely Planet's *Tramping in New Zealand* describes around 50 walks of various lengths and degrees of difficulty. Mark Pickering and Rodney Smith's *101 Great Tramps* has suggestions for two- to six-day tramps around the country. The companion guide, *202 Great Walks: the Best Day Walks in New Zealand*, by Mark Pickering, is handy for shorter, family-friendly excursions.

New trampers should check out *Don't Forget Your Scroggin* by Sarah Bennett and Lee Slater – all about being safe and happy on the track. The *Birdseye Tramping Guides* from Craig Potton Publishing have fab topographical maps, and there are countless books covering tramps and short urban walks around NZ – scan the bookshops.

Maps

The topographical maps produced by **Land Information New Zealand** (LINZ; www.linz.govt.nz) are a safe bet. Bookshops don't often have a good selection of these, but LINZ has map-sales offices in major cities and towns, and DOC offices often sell LINZ maps for local tracks. Outdoor stores also stock them (see the boxed text, p78). LINZ's map series includes park maps (national, state and forest parks), dedicated walking-track maps, and highly detailed 'Topomaps' (you may need two or three of these for one track).

If you don't want to be itching and scratching for weeks, bring some insect repellent on your tramp to keep the sandflies at bay (see p420).

Track Classification

Tracks are classified according to various features, including level of difficulty. In this chapter we loosely refer to the level of difficulty as easy, medium, hard or difficult. The widely used track classification system is as follows:

Short Walk Well formed; allows for wheelchair access or constructed to 'shoe' standard (ie walking boots not required). Suitable for people of all ages and fitness levels.

Walking Track Easy and well-formed longer walks; constructed to 'shoe' standard. Suitable for people of most ages and fitness levels.

Easy Tramping Track or Great Walk Well formed; major water crossings have bridges and track junctions have signs. Light walking boots required.

Tramping Track Requires skill and experience; constructed to 'boot' standard. Suitable for people of average physical fitness. Water crossings may not have bridges.

Route Requires a high degree of skill, experience and navigation skills. Well-equipped trampers only.

Track Safety

Thousands of people tramp across the North Island without incident, but every year a few folks meet their maker in the mountains. Some trails are only for the experienced, fit and well-equipped – don't attempt these if you don't fit the bill. NZ's climatic changeability subjects high-altitude walks to snow and ice, even in summer, so always check weather and track conditions before setting off. Consult a DOC visitor centre and leave your intentions with a responsible person before starting longer walks. See also www. mountainsafety.org.nz.

The Great Walks

NZ's nine official 'Great Walks' (one of which is actually a river trip!) are the country's most popular tracks, and three of them are on the North Island. Summer can be more crowded on the North Island Great Walks, but less so than on the the incredibly popular Milford and Routeburn tracks in the country's South Island.

All nine Great Walks are described in more detail in Lonely Planet's *Tramping in New Zealand,* and are detailed in pamphlets provided by DOC visitor centres. You will also find a park map handy.

To tramp these tracks you'll need to buy a Great Walk Pass, sold at DOC visitor centres near each walk, before setting out. These track-specific passes cover you for hut accommodation (from $12 to $45 per person per night, depending on the track and the season) and/or camping (free to $15 per person per night). You can camp only at designated camping grounds (note there's no camping on the Milford Track). In the off-peak season (May to September), Backcountry Hut Passes ($90, valid for 12 months) and pay-as-you-go hut tickets can be used instead of a Great Walk Pass in many huts (see p76). Kids under 18 stay in huts and camp for free on Great Walks.

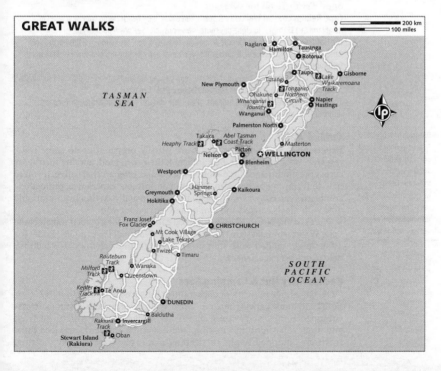

GREAT WALKS

NORTH ISLAND'S 'GREAT WALKS'

Walk	Distance	Duration	Difficulty	Description
Lake Waikaremoana Track (p359)	46km	3-4 days	Easy to medium	Lake views, bush-clad slopes and swimming in Te Urewera National Park
Tongariro Northern Circuit (p291)	41km	3-4 days	Medium to hard	Through the active volcanic landscape of Tongariro National Park; see also Tongariro Alpine Crossing (p292)
Whanganui Journey (p262)	145km	5 days	Easy	Canoe or kayak down the Whanganui River in Whanganui National Park

DOC has introduced a booking system for the most popular of the Great Walks, to avoid overcrowding and protect the environment. Trampers must book their chosen hut or campsite and specify dates when they purchase a Great Walk Pass. Bookings are required year-round for the Lake Waikaremoana Track, but are not required for the Whanganui Journey.

Bookings can be made online (www.doc.govt.nz), by email (greatwalks booking@doc.govt.nz), by phone, by fax or in person at DOC offices close to the tracks. For full details see the DOC website. There's no c harge to do a day walk on any track, but you have to pay if you're staying overnight.

Other Tracks

Of course, there are a lot more walks in the North Island than just the Great ones! Try these on for size:

Cape Reinga Coastal Walkway A 50km, three-day, easy beach tramp (camping only) in Northland. A 132km six- to eight-day route is also possible. See www.doc.govt.nz.

Mt Holdsworth – Jumbo Circuit A medium-to-hard, three-day tramp in Holdsworth Forest Park, out of Masterton. The walk passes through forest and over the top of alpine Mt Holdsworth. See www.doc.govt.nz.

Pouakai Circuit A 25km, two- to three-day loop passing lowland rainforest, cliffs and subalpine forest at the foot of Mt Taranaki in Egmont National Park. See p246.

Tongariro Alpine Crossing A brilliant, 18km, one-day, medium tramp through Tongariro National Park. See p292.

Guided Walks

Due to open in late 2010, Te Araroa (www.teararoa. org.nz) is ambitious: a 3000km walking trail from Cape Reinga in NZ's north to Bluff in the south, linking existing trails and adding new sections. Stay tuned…

Experienced, independent hikers are usually prepared to do some track research, book hut tickets, buy and cook their own food, and lug their tents across the mountains of NZ – but guided walks offer an alternative. If you're new to tramping or just want a more comfortable experience, quite a few companies can escort you through the wilds, usually staying in comfortable huts with meals cooked and equipment carried for you.

Places on the North Island where you can sign up for a guided walk include Lake Waikaremoana (p361) and Tongariro National Park (p288). Prices for a four-night guided walk start around $1500, and rise towards $2000 for deluxe guided experiences.

Backcountry Hut & Camping Fees

DOC has a huge network of backcountry huts (more than 950) in NZ's national and forest parks. There are 'Great Walk category huts' (with mattress-equipped bunks or sleeping platforms, water supply, toilets, heating, and often solar lighting, cooking facilities and a warden); 'serviced huts' (mattress-equipped bunks or sleeping platforms, water supply, heating,

RESPONSIBLE TRAMPING

To help preserve the ecology and beauty of NZ, have a scan through the following tramping tips. If you went straight from the cradle into a pair of hiking boots, some of these will seem ridiculously obvious; others you mightn't have considered. Online, www.lnt.org is a great resource for low-impact hiking, and the DOC site www.camping.org.nz has plenty more responsible camping tips. When in doubt, ask DOC or i-SITE staff.

The ridiculously obvious:

- If you can, time your tramp to avoid peak season: less people = less stress on the environment and fewer snorers in the huts.

- Carry out *all* your rubbish (including unglamorous items like condoms, tampons and toilet paper). Burying rubbish disturbs soil and vegetation, encourages erosion, and animals will probably dig up what you bury anyway.

- Don't use detergents, shampoo or toothpaste in or near watercourses, even if the products are biodegradable.

- Don't depend on open fires for cooking. Instead, use lightweight kerosene, alcohol or Shellite (white gas) stoves; avoid cookers powered by disposable butane gas canisters.

- Where there's a toilet, use it. Where there isn't one, dig a hole and bury your by-product (at least 15cm deep, 100m from any watercourse). Cover it up with soil and a rock. In snow, dig down until you're into the dirt.

- If a track passes through a muddy patch, just plough straight on through – skirting around the outside increases the size of the bog.

- Always seek permission to camp on private land.

You mightn't have considered:

- Wash your dishes 50m from watercourses; use a scourer, sand or snow instead of detergent.

- If you *really* need to scrub your bod, use biodegradable soap and a bucket, at least 50m from any watercourse. Spread the waste water around widely to help the soil filter it.

- If open fires are allowed, use only dead, fallen wood in existing fireplaces (collecting firewood around campsites strips the forest bare in quick time). Don't surround fires with rocks, and leave any extra wood for the next happy camper.

- Keep food-storage bags out of reach of scavengers by tying them to rafters or trees.

- Feeding wildlife can lead to unbalanced populations, diseases and animals becoming dependent on handouts. Keep your dried apricots to yourself.

- If you're bunking down in local accommodation near trailheads, consider environmentally savvy places; for some great sustainable accommodation choices see p474

toilets and sometimes cooking facilities); 'standard huts' (no cooking equipment or heating); and 'basic huts' (just a shed!). Details about the services in every hut can be found on the DOC website. Backcountry hut fees per adult per night range from free to $45, with tickets bought in advance at DOC visitor centres. Children under 10 can use huts free of charge; 11- to 17-year-olds are charged half-price. If you do a lot of tramping, DOC sells an annual **Backcountry Hut Pass** (adult/child $90/45), applicable to most huts except those identified in the DOC Backcountry Huts brochure – which includes many Great Walk huts in summer (for which you'll need a Great Walk Pass – see p75). Backcountry hut tickets and passes can be used to procure a bunk or campsite on some Great Walks in low season (May to September; see p75).

Depending on the hut category, a night's stay may use one or two tickets. When you arrive at a hut, date your tickets and put them in the box provided. Accommodation is on a first-come, first-served basis.

DOC also manages 250 vehicle-accessible 'Conservation Campsites'. The most basic of these ('basic' sites) are free; 'standard' and 'serviced' grounds cost between $3 and $14 per adult per night. Serviced grounds have full facilities (flush toilets, tap water, showers and picnic tables); they may also have barbecues, a kitchen and a laundry. Standard grounds have toilets and water supply and perhaps barbecues and picnic tables.

Getting There & Away

Getting to and from trailheads can be a problem, except for popular trails serviced by public and dedicated trampers' transport. Having a vehicle only helps with getting to one end of the track (you still have to collect your car afterwards). If the track starts or ends down a dead-end road, hitching will be difficult.

It's a good idea to arrange private transport, either with a friend or by chartering a vehicle to drop you at one end then pick you up at the other. If you intend to leave a vehicle at a trailhead and return for it later, don't leave anything valuable inside – theft from cars in isolated areas is a significant problem.

EXTREME ADVENTURE

Bungy jumping was made famous by Kiwi AJ Hackett's 1986 plunge from the Eiffel Tower, after which he teamed up with champion NZ skier Henry

---

TOP GEAR

Here are the best places to fix a fractured tent pole or buy a warmer sleeping bag:

- Auckland: **Kathmandu** (Map p92; ☎ 09-377 7560; www.kathmandu.co.nz; 200 Victoria St; ⏲ 9am-5.30pm Mon-Thu, 9am-7pm Fri, 9am-5pm Sat, 10am-4.30pm Sun)
- Hamilton: **Bivouac Outdoor** (Map p210; ☎ 07-839 4206; www.bivouac.co.nz; 611 Victoria St; ⏲ 9.30am-5.30pm Mon-Fri, 10am-4pm Sat, 10am-3pm Sun)
- Napier: **Kathmandu** (Map p363; ☎ 06-835 5859; www.kathmandu.co.nz; 8 Dickens St; ⏲ 9am-5.30pm Mon-Thu, 9am-6pm Fri, 9am-4pm Sat, 10am-4pm Sun)
- New Plymouth: **Kiwi Outdoors** (Map p238; ☎ 06-758 4152; www.kiwioutdoorsstores.co.nz; 18 Ariki St; ⏲ 8.30am-5pm Mon-Fri, 9am-2.30pm Sat, 10am-2pm Sun)
- Palmerston North: **Bivouac Outdoor** (Map p266; ☎ 06-359 2162; www.bivouac.co.nz; 400 Ferguson St; ⏲ 9am-5.30pm Mon-Thu, 9am-6pm Fri, 9am-4pm Sat, 10am-4pm Sun)
- Rotorua: **Outdoorsman Headquarters** (Map p319; ☎ 07-345 9333; www.outdoorsman.co.nz; 6 Tarawera Rd; ⏲ 9am-5.30pm)
- Taupo: **Outdoor Attitude** (Map p282; ☎ 06-378 6628; www.outdoorattitude.co.nz; 37 Tuwharetoa St; ⏲ 9am-5pm Mon-Fri, 9am-4pm Sat, 10am-3pm Sun)
- Tauranga: **Bivouac Outdoor** (Map p323; ☎ 07-579 5127; www.bivouac.co.nz; 131 Willow St; ⏲ 9am-5pm Mon-Fri, 9am-4pm Sat, 10am-3pm Sun)
- Wellington: **Bivouac Outdoor** (Map p384; ☎ 04-473 2587; www.bivouac.co.nz; 39 Mercer St; ⏲ 9am-5.30pm Mon-Thu, 9am-7pm Fri, 10am-5pm Sat, 11am-5pm Sun)
- Whanganui: **Kathmandu** (Map p256; ☎ 06-348 2262; www.kathmandu.co.nz; 128 Victoria Ave; ⏲ 9am-5pm Mon-Fri, 10am-4pm Sat)
- Whangarei: **Kathmandu** (Map p148; ☎ 09-438 7193; www.kathmandu.co.nz; 22 James St; ⏲ 9am-5.30pm Mon-Fri, 9am-4pm Sat, 10am-3pm Sun)

van Asch to turn the endeavour into a profitable enterprise. The fact that a pant-wetting, illogical activity like bungy jumping is now an everyday pursuit in NZ says much about how 'extreme sports' have evolved here. Bungy, skydiving, jetboating, paragliding and kiteboarding are all well established, but keep an eye out for weird-and-wonderful activities like zorbing (rolling down a hill inside a transparent plastic ball), quad-biking, cave rafting, river sledging (white-water body boarding) and blokarting (windsurfing on wheels). Auckland's Sky Jump (p101) and Sky Screamer (p101) are variations on the extreme theme – all against the laws of nature, and all great fun!

Bungy Jumping

Bungy jumping (hurtling earthwards from bridges with nothing between you and eternity but a gigantic rubber band strapped to your ankles) has plenty of daredevil panache.

On the North Island, you can bungy bounce to your heart's content in Taupo, Auckland, Rotorua, and from Mokai Bridge over the Rangitikei River.

Skydiving

Ejecting yourself from a plane at high altitude is big business in NZ. There are plenty of professional operators, and at most drop zones the views on the way up (not to mention the way down) are sublime.

Some operators and clubs offer static-line jumps and Accelerated Free Fall courses, but for most first-timers a tandem skydive is the way to go. After bonding with a fully qualified instructor, you get to experience up to 45 seconds of high-speed free fall before the chute opens. The thrill is worth every dollar (specifically as much as $250/330/430 for a 9000/12,000/15,000ft jump). You'll pay extra for a video/DVD/photograph of your exploits.

Try tandem skydiving in Auckland, Matamata, Tauranga, the Bay of Islands, Taupo and Rotorua.

Jetboating

The jetboat is a local invention, dreamed up by CWF Hamilton in 1957. An inboard engine sucks water into a tube in the bottom of the boat, and an impeller driven by the engine blows it out of a nozzle at the stern in a high-speed stream. The boat is steered simply by directing the jet stream. Jetboats make short work of shallow and white water because there are no propellers to damage, there's better clearance under the boat and the jet can be reversed instantly for quick braking. The jet's instant response enables these craft to execute passenger-drenching 360-degree spins almost within the length of the boat.

The Whanganui, Motu, Rangitaiki and Waikato Rivers are excellent for jetboating, and there are sprint jets at the Agrodome in Rotorua. Jetboating around the Bay of Islands in Northland is also de rigueur, particularly the trip to the Hole in the Rock.

The rather literally named New Zealand Parachute Federation (www.nzpf.org) is the governing body for skydiving in NZ. Check the website for info and operator listings.

Paragliding & Kiteboarding

Paragliding is perhaps the easiest way for humans to achieve assisted flight. The sport involves taking to the skies in what is basically a parachute that's been modified so it glides through the air. After a half-day of instruction you should be able to do limited solo flights, and before you know it you could be soaring through the sky, 300m high. The **New Zealand Hang Gliding & Paragliding Association** (www.nzhgpa.org.nz) rules the roost. Tandem flights, where you are strapped to an experienced paraglider, are offered all over the country.

Kiteboarding (aka kitesurfing), where a mini parachute drags you across the ocean on a mini surfboard, is pretty 'extreme', and can be attempted at Paihia, Tauranga, Mt Maunganui, Raglan and Wellington. You can tee up lessons at most of these places, too. Karikari Peninsula near Cape Reinga on NZ's northern tip is a kiteboarding mecca.

SKIING & SNOWBOARDING

Global warming is triggering a worldwide melt, but NZ remains an essential southern-hemisphere destination for snow bunnies, with downhill, cross-country and ski mountaineering all passionately pursued. Heliskiing, where choppers lift skiers to the top of long, isolated stretches of virgin snow, also has its fans. The NZ ski season is generally June to October, though it varies considerably from one ski area to another, and can run as late as November.

Unlike Europe, America or even Australia, NZ's commercial ski areas aren't generally set up as 'resorts' with chalets, lodges or hotels. Rather, accommodation and après-ski carousing are often in surrounding towns that connect with the slopes via daily shuttles.

For a range of snowboarding and skiing tours in the North Island, go to www.newzealandsnowtours.com.

In the North Island, the key wintersports area is on Mt Ruapehu in the Tongariro National Park, with the compact settlements at National Park and Ohakune offering accommodation and nightlife (definitely with a small 'n' compared to Queenstown). There are small club-operated fields on Mt Ruapehu and southwest on Mt Taranaki. Many club areas have lodges you can stay at, subject to availability – winter holidays and weekends will be fully booked, but midweek you'll be OK.

Visitor information centres in NZ, and the New Zealand Tourism Board (NZTB) internationally, have brochures on the various ski areas and packages, and can make bookings. Lift passes can cost anywhere from $35 to $90 a day (roughly half that for children and two-thirds for students). Lesson-and-lift packages are available at most areas. Ski-equipment rental (skis, boots and poles) starts at around $40 a day; snowboard-and-boots hire starts at around $45. Prices decrease for multiday hire. Try to rent equipment close to where you'll be skiing, so you can exchange gear if there's a problem with the fit.

The North Island is dominated by volcanic-cone skiing. Rumbling Mt Ruapehu in Tongariro National Park is the premier ski zone.

Tongariro National Park

On either side of Mt Ruapehu (a near neighbour of Mt Ngaruhoe, aka Mt Doom from *Lord of the Rings*), the twin resorts **Whakapapa** and **Turoa** (☎ Whakapapa 07-892 3738, snow-phone 08-322 2182, Turoa 06-385 8456, snow-phone 08-322 2180; www.mtruapehu.com; daily lift pass adult/child $83/48) comprise NZ's largest ski area. Lift passes are valid at both resorts. Whakapapa, 6km above Whakapapa Village in Tongariro National Park, has 30 groomed runs. There are plenty of snowboarding possibilities, cross-country, downhill and ski touring, a terrain park and the highest lift access in the country. You can drive yourself up to the slopes or take a shuttle minibus from Whakapapa Village, National Park township, Taupo or Turangi. Smaller Turoa has a beginners' lift, snowboarding, and downhill and cross-country skiing. There's no road toll or parking fee and daily ski-area transport is available from Ohakune 16km away, which has the liveliest post-ski scene in the north.

Club-operated **Tukino** (☎ 0800 885 466, 06-387 6294, snow-phone 08-822 5000; www.tukino.co.nz; daily lift pass adult/child $45/25) is on the eastern side of Mt Ruapehu, 50km from Turangi. It's quite remote, 14km down a gravel road from the sealed Desert Rd (SH1), and you need a 4WD vehicle to get in (or make a prior arrangement to use club transport). Because access is so limited the area is uncrowded, but most runs are beginner or intermediate.

See Tongariro National Park (p288) for more info.

Taranaki
Manganui (☎ 027 280 0860, snow-phone 06-759 1119; www.skitaranaki.co.nz; daily lift pass adult/child $40/25) offers volcano-slope, club-run skiing on the eastern slopes of spectacular Mt Taranaki in the Egmont National Park, 22km from Stratford. You can ski off the summit; when conditions permit, it's a sweaty two-hour climb to the crater, but the exhilarating 1300m descent compensates.

For local info, see Mt Taranaki (p235).

MOUNTAIN BIKING
The North Island is laced with quality mountain-biking opportunities. Mountain bikes can be hired in major towns or adventure-sports centres such as Taupo and Rotorua; both also have repair shops.

Various companies will take you up to the tops of mountains and volcanoes (eg Mt Ruapehu) so you can hurtle down without the grunt-work of getting to the top first. Rotorua's Redwood Grove offers famously good mountain biking, as does the 42 Traverse near National Park township (close to Tongariro National Park). Other North Island options include Woodhill Forest, Waihi, Te Aroha, Te Mata Peak and Makara Peak in Wellington.

Some traditional tramping tracks are open to mountain bikes, but DOC has restricted access in many cases due to track damage and the inconvenience to walkers, especially at busy times. Never cycle on walking tracks in national parks unless it's permissible (check with DOC), or you risk heavy fines and the unfathomable ire of hikers.

CYCLE TOURING
On any given stretch of highway, especially during summer, you'll come across plenty of pannier-laden cyclists with one eye on the scenery and the other looking out for potholes. Not that potholes are really an issue – the roads here are generally solid. Most towns offer touring-bike hire, at either backpacker hostels or specialist bike shops. Bike service and repair shops can be found in big towns; see the regional chapters in this book.

Some excellent cycle-touring books are available, including Lonely Planet's *Cycling New Zealand,* and the *Pedallers' Paradise* booklets by Nigel Rushton (see www.paradise-press.co.nz).

The proposed $50-million **New Zealand Cycle Trail** (www.tourism.govt.nz/our-work/new-zealand-cycle-trail-project) – a national bike path from Kaitaia to Bluff – is still in the developmental stages, with some parts already open: watch this space...

Online, www.cycletour.co.nz has loads of two-wheeled info.

SEA KAYAKING
Highly rated sea kayaking areas in NZ's north include the Hauraki Gulf (particularly off Waiheke and Great Barrier Islands), the Bay of Islands and Coromandel Peninsula. Also try the Waitemata Harbour, Hahei, Raglan and East Cape. The **Kiwi Association of Sea Kayakers** (KASK; www.kask.org.nz) is the main NZ organisation.

CANOEING
Canoeing is so popular on the North Island's Whanganui River that it's been designated one of NZ's 'Great Walks'! You can also dip your paddle into northern lakes like Lake Taupo and Lake Rotorua.

Websites such as www.snow.co.nz, www.chillout.co.nz and www.nzski.com provide ski reports, employment opportunities, webcams and virtual tours across NZ.

Classic New Zealand Mountain Bike Rides details short and long rides all over NZ (see www.kennett.co.nz). *New Zealand Mountain Biker* (www.nzmtbr.co.nz) mag comes out every two months.

For wannabe paddlers, the Sea Kayak Operators Association of New Zealand (www.skoanz.org.nz) website has a map of NZ paddling destinations and links to operators working in each area.

Many backpacker hostels close to canoe-friendly waters have Canadian canoes and kayaks for hire or free use, and loads of commercial guided trips (for those without equipment or experience) are offered on rivers and lakes throughout the country.

WHITE-WATER RAFTING & KAYAKING

Check the Whitewater
NZ (www.rivers.org.
nz) website for rainfall
and river-flow updates
around the country.

There are almost as many white-water rafting possibilities as there are rivers in the country, and there's no shortage of companies to get you into the rapids. **Whitewater NZ** (www.rivers.org.nz) covers all things white-water.

There are plenty of raft-worthy rivers to try, including the Rangitaiki, Wairoa, Motu, Mokau, Mohaka, Waitomo, Tongariro and Rangitikei. There are also the Kaituna Cascades near Rotorua, the highlight of which is the 7m drop at Okere Falls.

Rivers are graded from I to VI, with VI meaning 'unraftable'. The grading of the Shotover canyon varies from III to V+, depending on the time of year. The Kawarau River is rated IV; the Rangitata River has everything from I to V. On the rougher stretches there's usually a minimum age limit of 12 or 13 years. Safety equipment is supplied by operators. The **New Zealand Rafting Association** (NZRA; www.nz-rafting.co.nz) has an online river guide, and lists registered operators.

HORSE RIDING

Horse riding is commonplace in NZ. Unlike in some other parts of the world where beginners get led by the nose around a paddock, here you can

---

SURFING IN NEW ZEALAND *Josh Kronfeld*

As a surfer I feel particularly guilty in letting the reader in on a local secret – NZ has a sensational mix of quality waves perfect for beginners and experienced surfers. As long as you're willing to travel off the beaten track, you can score some great, uncrowded waves. The islands of NZ are hit with swells from all points of the compass throughout the year. So, with a little weather knowledge and a little effort, numerous options present themselves. Point breaks, reefs, rocky shelves and hollow sandy beach breaks can all be found – take your pick!

Surfing has become increasingly popular in NZ and today there are surf schools up and running at most premier surf beaches. It's worth doing a bit of research before you arrive: **Surfing New Zealand** (www.surfingnz.co.nz) recommends a number of surf schools on its website. If you're on a surf holiday in NZ, consider purchasing a copy of the *New Zealand Surfing Guide*, by Mike Bhana.

Surf.co.nz (www.surf.co.nz) provides information on many great surf spots, but most NZ beaches hold good rideable breaks. Some of the North Island ones I particularly enjoy:

- **Waikato** Raglan, NZ's most famous surf break and usually the first stop for overseas surfies
- **Coromandel** Whangamata
- **Bay of Plenty** Mt Maunganui, now with a 250m artificial reef that creates huge waves, and Matakana Island
- **Taranaki** Fitzroy Beach, Stent Rd and Greenmeadows Point all lie along the 'Surf Highway'
- **East Coast** Hicks Bay, Gisborne city beaches and Mahia Peninsula
- **Wellington Region** Beaches such as Lyall Bay, Castlepoint and Tora

NZ water temperatures and climate vary greatly from north to south. For comfort while surfing, wear a wet suit. In summer on the North Island you can get away with a spring suit and boardies, but use a 2-3mm steamer in winter.

Josh is a keen surfer originally hailing from the Hawke's Bay region. While representing the All Blacks (1995–2000) he successfully juggled surfing, pop music and an international rugby career.

really get out into the countryside on a farm, forest or beach. Rides range from one-hour jaunts (from around $50) to week-long, fully catered treks.

Taupo has options for wilderness horse trekking and for rides in the hills overlooking thermal regions. The Coromandel Peninsula, Waitomo, Pakiri, Ninety Mile Beach, Rotorua, the Bay of Plenty and East Cape are top places for an equine encounter.

For equine info online, see the **Auckland SPCA Horse Welfare Auxiliary Inc** (www.horsetalk.co.nz) website. For trek-operator listings see www.truenz.co.nz/horse trekking or www.newzealand.com.

ROCK CLIMBING

Popular rock-climbing areas include the Mt Eden Quarry in Auckland; Whanganui Bay, Kinloch, Kawakawa Bay and Motuoapa near Lake Taupo; Mangatepopo Valley and Whakapapa Gorge on the Central Plateau; Humphries Castle and Warwick Castle on Mt Taranaki; and Piarere near Cambridge. Wharepapa, about 20km southeast of Te Awamutu, is regarded as one of the best places in the country for climbing.

> NZ's premier kayaking magazine is *New Zealand Kayak*, published every two months – look for it in newsagencies.

> The website www.climb.co.nz has the low-down on the hottest rock-climbing spots around NZ, plus access and instruction info.

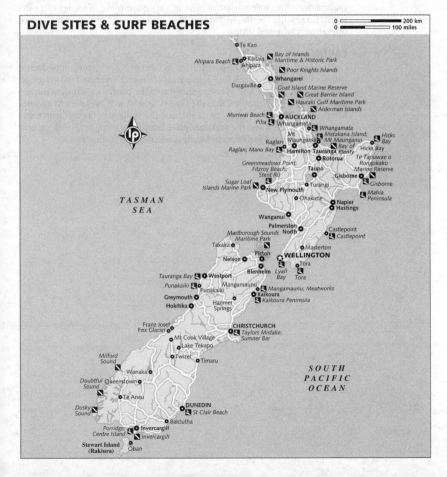

DIVE SITES & SURF BEACHES

SCUBA DIVING

NZ is prime scuba territory, with warm waters up north, brilliant sea-life and plenty of interesting dive sites for beginners and experts.

On (or rather, off) the North Island, get wet at the Bay of Islands Maritime and Historic Park, Hauraki Gulf Maritime Park, the Bay of Plenty, Great Barrier Island, Goat Island Marine Reserve, the Alderman Islands, Te Tapuwae o Rongokako Marine Reserve near Gisborne, and Sugar Loaf Islands Marine Park near New Plymouth. The Poor Knights Islands, off the east coast of the North Island, are reputed to have the best diving in NZ – the late, great Jacques Cousteau rated them among the top 10 diving spots in the world. Nearby is the diveable wreck of the Greenpeace flagship *Rainbow Warrior*.

Expect to pay anywhere from $170 for a short, introductory, pool-based scuba course; and from $495 for a four-day, PADI-approved, ocean dive course. One-off organised boat- and land-based dives start at around $165.

For more on NZ's explorable depths contact the **New Zealand Underwater Association** (☎ 09-623 3252; www.nzunderwater.org.nz) in Auckland. The **Dive New Zealand** (www.divenewzealand.com) website is a treasure-trove of underwater information, with the low-down on dive and wreck sites, plus listings of operators, clubs and shops.

CAVING

Caving (aka spelunking) opportunities abound in NZ's honeycombed karst (limestone) regions. You'll find active local clubs and organised tours around Auckland, Waitomo and Whangarei. One of the most awesome caving experiences is the 100m abseil into the Lost World *tomo* (cave) near Waitomo. Local underground organisations include the **Wellington Caving Group** (www.caving.wellington.net.nz) and the **Auckland Speleo Group** (www.asg.org.nz). For more info see the **New Zealand Speleological Society** (www.caves.org.nz) website.

Auckland Region

Paris may be the city of love, but Auckland is the city of many lovers, according to its Maori name, Tamaki Makaurau. In fact, her lovers so desired this beautiful place that they fought over her for centuries.

It's hard to imagine a more geographically blessed city. Its two magnificent harbours frame a narrow isthmus punctuated by volcanic cones and surrounded by fertile farmland. From any of its numerous vantage points you'll be astounded at how close the Tasman Sea and Pacific Ocean come to kissing and forming a new island.

As a result, water's never far away – whether it's the ruggedly beautiful west-coast surf beaches or the glistening Hauraki Gulf with its myriad islands. The 135,000 pleasure crafts filling Auckland's marinas have lent the city its most durable nickname: the 'City of Sails'.

Within an hour's drive from the high-rise heart of the city are dense tracts of rainforest, thermal springs, deserted beaches, wineries and wildlife reserves. Yet big-city comforts have spread to all corners of the Auckland Region: a decent coffee or chardonnay is usually close at hand.

Yet the rest of the country loves to hate it, tut-tutting about its traffic snarls and the supposed self-obsession of the quarter of the country's population that call it home. With its many riches, Auckland can justifiably respond to its detractors, 'Don't hate me because I'm beautiful'.

HIGHLIGHTS

- Going with the flows, exploring Auckland's fascinating **volcanic field** (p90)
- Getting back to nature on the island sanctuaries of the beautiful **Hauraki Gulf** (p121)
- Being awed by the Maori *taonga* (treasures) of the **Auckland Museum** (p90)
- Going west to the mystical and treacherous black sands of **Karekare** (p134) and **Piha** (p134)
- Swimming with the fish at **Goat Island Marine Reserve** (p142)
- Schlepping around world-class wineries and beaches on **Waiheke Island** (p123)
- Buzzing around the cafes and bars of **Kingsland** (p112) and **Ponsonby** (p112)
- Soaking up the Polynesian vibe at the **Pasifika Festival** (p114), held in March at Western Springs Park

- Telephone code: 09
- www.aucklandnz.com
- www.arc.govt.nz

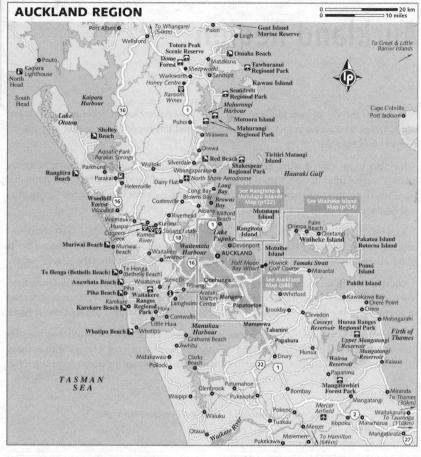

AUCKLAND REGION

MAORI NZ: AUCKLAND REGION

Evidence of Maori occupation is literally carved into Auckland's volcanic cones (p90). The dominant *iwi* (tribe) of the isthmus was Ngati Whatua, but these days there are Maori from almost all NZ's *iwi* living here, sometimes collectively known as Ngati Akarana, or the Auckland Tribe.

For an initial taste of Maori culture, start at Auckland Museum (p90), where there's a wonderful Maori collection, a massive war canoe and a culture show. For a more personalised experience, take either Potiki's Urban Maori tour (p104) or Ngati Whatua's Tamaki Hikoi (p104).

Climate

Auckland has a mild climate, with the occasional frost in winter and high humidity in summer. Summer months have an average of eight days of rain, but the weather is famously fickle, with 'four seasons in one day' possible at any time of the year.

AUCKLAND

pop 1.2 million

Auckland's a city of volcanoes, with the ridges of lava flows forming its main thoroughfares and its many cones providing islands of green within the sea of suburbs. As well as being by far the largest, it's the most multicultural of

NZ's cities. A sizable Asian community rubs shoulders with the biggest Polynesian population of any city in the world.

The traditional Kiwi aspiration for a freestanding house on a quarter-acre section has resulted in a vast, sprawling city. The CBD was long ago abandoned to commerce, and inner-city apartment living has only just started to catch on. While geography has been kind, city planning has been less so. Unbridled and ill-conceived development has left the centre of the city with some architectural embarrassments. To get under Auckland's skin you're best to head for the rows of Victorian and Edwardian villas in its hip inner-city suburbs.

HISTORY

Maori occupation in the Auckland area dates back around 800 years. Initial settlements were concentrated on the coastal regions of the Hauraki Gulf islands, but gradually the fertile isthmus beckoned and land was cleared for growing food.

Over hundreds of years Tamaki's many different tribes wrestled for control of the area, building *pa* (fortified villages) on the numerous volcanic cones. The Ngati Whatua *iwi* (tribe) from the Kaipara Harbour took the upper hand in 1741, occupying the major *pa* sites. During the Musket Wars of the 1820s they were decimated by the northern tribe Ngapuhi, leaving the land all but abandoned.

At the time of the signing of the Treaty of Waitangi in 1840, Governor Hobson had his base at Okiato, near Russell in the Bay of Islands. When Ngati Whatua chief Te Kawau offered 3000 acres of land for sale on the northern edge of the Waitemata Harbour, Hobson decided to create a new capital, naming it after one of his patrons, George Eden (Earl of Auckland).

Beginning with just a few tents on a beach, the settlement quickly grew, and soon the port was kept busy exporting the region's produce, including kauri timber. However, it lost its capital status to Wellington after just 25 years.

Since the beginning of the 20th century Auckland has been NZ's fastest-growing city and its main industrial centre. Political deals may be done in Wellington, but Auckland is the big smoke in the land of the long white cloud.

AUCKLAND REGION FACTS

Eat Multiculturally, at one of the city's numerous food halls (p110)

Drink Waiheke Island rosé on a hot summer's day

Read *Under The Mountain* (1979) – Maurice Gee's teenage tale of slimy things lurking under Auckland's volcanos

Listen to *One Tree Hill* (1987) – U2's elegy to their Kiwi roadie is no less poignant now the tree's gone (see p91)

Watch *Sione's Wedding* (2006), Chris Graham's comedy set in Grey Lynn and central Auckland

Swim at Onetangi (p123)

Festival Pasifika (p21, 105, 114)

Tackiest tourist attraction Sheepworld's fluorescent flock of sheep – New Rave goes too far (p140)

Go green Encounter endangered birds among the regenerated forest of Tiritiri Matangi Island (p127)

ORIENTATION

The Auckland isthmus runs roughly west-east, with Waitemata Harbour lying to the north (feeding into the Hauraki Gulf) and Manukau Harbour to the south (feeding into the Tasman Sea). The Harbour Bridge links the city to the North Shore, with the CBD to its east.

The commercial heart of the city is Queen St, which runs from the waterfront up to Newton's Karangahape Rd (K Rd), a lively, bohemian, sometimes gritty strip of inexpensive restaurants and boisterous bars.

In the early days, the area immediately east of the city tended to be upmarket and Anglican, while the west was more Catholic and working-class. While they're all rather pricey neighbourhoods nowadays, Parnell and Remuera retain vestiges of old-money snobbery while Ponsonby and Grey Lynn are slightly more alternative. Mt Eden sits somewhere between the two, both physically and sociologically.

The airport is 23km south of the city centre.

Maps

Auckland Map Centre (Map p92; ☎ 09-309 7725; www.aucklandmapcentre.co.nz; 209 Queen St; 9am-5pm Mon-Fri, 10am-4pm Sat)

INFORMATION
Bookshops

Unity Books (Map p92; ☎ 09-307 0731; 19 High St; 8.30am-7pm Mon-Thu, 8.30am-9pm Fri, 9am-6pm

AUCKLAND REGION

AUCKLAND

0 ——— 5 km
0 ——— 2.5 miles

To Northland;
Whangarei
(145km)

A **B** **C** **D**

1

Glenfield

12

Milford
Beach

Lake
Pupuke

33

4

37

1

27

Takapuna

Takapuna
Beach

46

St Leonards
Beach

26

Rangitoto
(260m)

Lava
Caves

Rangitoto
Island

Rangitoto
Channel

See Rangitoto & Motutapu Islands Map (p122)

2

Onewa Rd

Shoal
Bay

Bayswater

Northcote
Central

Birkenhead

35

34

Ngataringa
Bay

See Devonport
Map (p96)

Devonport

Ferry to Waiheke Island

Kauri
Point

Waitemata
Harbour

Harbour
Bridge

Westhaven
Marina

Motukorea
(Browns Island)

6

14

Kohimarama

Achilles
Point

Mission
Bay

St Heliers
Bay

Ladies Bay

Point
Chevalier

Herne
Bay

Ponsonby

See Central
Auckland
Map
(p92)

See Ponsonby &
Grey Lynn
Map (p102)

City
Centre

See Parnell &
Newmarket
Map (p98)

Okahu
Bay

13

Bastion
Point

15

16

5

St Heliers

5

St Heliers

Mission
Bay

Mission Bay
Reserve

Kohimarama
Rd

3

North Western Mwy

18

41

9

24

38

17

16

Kingsland

Newmarket

Mt Eden
(Maungawhau)
(196m)

30

Orakei

Hobson
Bay

Orakei

20

Meadowbank

Meadowbank

Baldwin Ave

Morningside

See Mt Eden &
Kingsland Map (p100)

31

Mt
Hobson

Remuera

Glen Innes

25

32

Remuera Rd

Mt Albert

39

Mt
Albert

Mt
Albert

Mt
Albert
Rd

Balmoral Rd

Epsom

Alexandra
Park

Greenlane Rd

42

Ellerslie
Racecourse

Mt Wellington

Tamaki

To Titirangi
(6km), Waitakere
Ranges (7km)

Avondale

1

Ellerslie

Ellerslie Panmure Hwy

To Howick
(1.5km)

Lloyd
Elsmore
Park

4

Three
Kings

19

Cornwall
Park

11

Greenlane

Ellerslie

Mt
Wellington

Panmure

22

One Tree
Hill

45

Penrose

Mt
Roskill

28

Mt
Roskill

20

5

Pakuranga Rd

Blockhouse
Bay

Hillsborough

10

Onehunga

36

Mt Smart Rd

Southdown

Pakuranga

Manukau Harbour

Mangere Bridge

Mangere
Inlet

Westfield

Otahuhu

Otahuhu

5

26

Mt Mangere

20

Puketutu
Island

Manukau
Purification
Works

Montgomerie
Rd

20A

Mangere

14

Auckland
Golf Course

Papatoetoe

40

Otara

6

23

29

Ihumatau

Auckland
International
Airport

44

International
Terminal

2

Domestic
Terminal

43

Tom Pearce Dr

Papatoetoe

Puhinui

Puhinui

21

Manukau

To Hamilton (102km);
Coromandel Town (145km);
Rotorua (207km)

8

Sat, 11am-6pm Sun) Excellent independent bookshop with knowledgeable staff.

Whitcoulls (Map p92; ☎ 09-984 5400; 210 Queen St; ⊗ 8am-7pm Mon-Thu, 8am-9pm Fri, 9am-6pm Sat, 10am-6pm Sun) Local chain with good travel and fiction sections.

Women's Bookshop (Map p102; ☎ 09-376 4399; 105 Ponsonby Rd; ⊗ 10am-6pm Mon-Fri, 10am-5pm Sat & Sun) A community resource as well as a good independent bookshop.

Emergency

Ambulance, fire service & police (☎ 111)
Auckland Central police station (Map p92; ☎ 09-302 6400; cnr Vincent & Cook Sts)

Internet Access

Expect to pay around $3 an hour at internet cafes; a few are open 24 hours. Parnell has a free wi-fi zone, which you should be able to access from most cafes along the strip.

Internet Resources

Auckland NZ (www.aucklandnz.com) Official tourist site.
Auckland Regional Council (ARC; www.arc.govt.nz) Information about regional parks and events.
Dine Out (www.dineout.co.nz) Locals' comments on restaurants.
MAXX Regional Transport (www.maxx.co.nz) Public transport timetables and route planner.

Medical Services

Auckland City Hospital (Map p92; ☎ 09-379 0000; Park Rd, Grafton; ⊗ 24hr) The city's main hospital; has an accident and emergency (A&E) section.

Auckland Metro Doctors & Travelcare (Map p92; ☎ 09-373 4621; 17 Emily Place, Auckland Central; ⊗ 9am-5.30pm Mon-Fri, 10am-2pm Sat) Specialises in health care for travellers, such as vaccinations and travel consultations.

Starship Children's Hospital (Map p92; ☎ 09-367 0000; Park Rd, Grafton; ⊗ 24hr) Has its own A&E department.

Media

Metro Glossy monthly magazine covering Auckland issues in depth.
New Zealand Herald (www.nzherald.co.nz) The country's biggest daily newspaper.

Money

There are plenty of moneychangers, banks and ATMs, especially on Queen St. For weekend banking visit the **ASB** (Map p92; cnr Queen & Customs Sts; ⊗ 9am-4.30pm Mon-Fri, 9am-4.30pm Sat, 10am-4pm Sun) in Westfield Downtown.

Post

Wellesley St post office (Map p92; 24 Wellesley St) The place to pick up poste restante mail (ID is required).

Tourist Information

Auckland Domestic Airport i-SITE (Map p88; ☎ 09-256 8480; ⊗ 6am-10pm) In the Air New Zealand section of the domestic airport.
Auckland International Airport i-SITE (Map p88; ☎ 09-275 6467; ⊗ 24hr) Located on your left as you exit the customs hall. You can make free calls to Auckland accommodation providers from here.

AUCKLAND REGION

AUCKLAND IN...

Two Days

Book ahead for tomorrow night's dinner. Breakfast in **Ponsonby** (p112) and take the Link Bus to **Auckland Museum** (below) for the Maori gallery and culture show. Wander through the Domain towards **K Rd** (p111), where you can grab lunch. Follow the walking tour on p103, stopping along the way for at least a quick whiz around the NZ section of the **Auckland Art Gallery** (p95). End with a relaxing drink or meal at the **Viaduct Harbour** (p99).

On day two, grab breakfast in the city before catching the 9.15am ferry to **Rangitoto** (p121). This will give you time to explore the volcanic island before it starts to bake. Catch the 12.45pm ferry to **Devonport** (p96) for lunch. If you've still got energy, check out **North Head** (p97) and then cool off at **Cheltenham Beach** (p97), if the weather and tide permit. Stay on the North Shore for a memorable dinner at the **Engine Room** (p113) or **Eight.Two** (p113).

Four Days

On the third day, head west. Grab breakfast in **Titirangi** (p133) before exploring the **Waitakere Ranges Regional Park** (p133), **Karekare** (p134) and **Piha** (p134). If you don't have a car, book in a day trip with **Potiki Tours** (p104). On the way back, stop in at **Elevation** (p134) for a glass of wine and breathtaking views of the city. Freshen up for a night eating and drinking your way around **Kingsland** (p112).

On day four, breakfast in **Mt Eden** (p112) and then climb **Maungawhau** (opposite). Catch the train back to Britomart for the 11am ferry to **Waiheke Island** (p123). Have lunch and dinner at a winery, and spend the afternoon at the beach (or more wineries if the weather's bad). Don't miss the last ferry back.

Auckland i-SITE (Map p92; ☎ 09-363 7182; www.aucklandnz.com; Sky Tower Atrium, cnr Victoria & Federal Sts; ☼ 8am-8pm)

Automobile Association (AA; Map p92; ☎ 09-966 8919; www.aa.co.nz; 99 Albert St; ☼ 9am-5pm Mon-Fri) Maps and accommodation directories.

Cornwall Park Information Centre (Map p88; ☎ 09-630 8485; www.cornwallpark.co.nz; Huia Lodge; ☼ 10am-4pm)

Devonport i-SITE (Map p96; ☎ 09-446 0677; www.tourismnorthshore.org.nz; 3 Victoria Rd; ☼ 8.30am-5pm) Internet access and information.

DOC information centre (Map p92; ☎ 09-379 6476; www.doc.govt.nz; 137 Quay St; ☼ 9am-5pm Mon-Fri, 10am-3pm Sat)

New Zealand i-SITE (Map p92; ☎ 09-307 0612; 137 Quay St; ☼ 9am-5.30pm May-Oct, 8am-7pm Nov-Apr)

Takapuna i-SITE (Map p88; ☎ 09-486 8670; 49 Hurstmere Rd; ☼ 8.30am-5pm Mon-Fri, 10am-3pm Sat & Sun)

SIGHTS
Auckland Volcanic Field

Some cities think they're tough by living in the shadow of a volcano. Auckland's built on 50 of them and, no, they're not all extinct. The last one to erupt was Rangitoto (p121) about 600 years ago and no one can predict when the next eruption will occur. Auckland's quite literally a hot spot – with a reservoir of magma

100km below waiting to bubble to the surface. But relax: this has only happened 19 times in the last 20,000 years.

Some of Auckland's volcanoes are cones, some are filled with water and some have been completely quarried away. Moves are afoot to register the field as a World Heritage site and protect what remains. Most of the surviving cones show evidence of terracing from when they formed a formidable series of Maori *pa*.

Apart from those mentioned separately in this section, these sites are also worth a visit:

Mt Wellington (Maungarei; Map p88)
Mt Albert (Owairaka; Map p88)
Mt Roskill (Map p88)
Lake Pupuke (Map p88)
Mt Mangere (Map p88)
Mt Hobson (Map p88)

Auckland Museum & Domain

Covering about 80 hectares, the green swathe of the **Auckland Domain** (Map p98) contains sports fields, interesting sculpture, formal gardens, wild corners and the **Wintergarden** (Map p98; admission free; ☼ 9am-5.30pm Mon-Sat, 9am-7.30pm Sun Nov-Mar, 9am-4.30pm Apr-Oct), with its fernery, tropical house, cool house, cute cat statue and neighbouring cafe. The mound in the centre of the park is all that remains of **Pukekaroa** (Map p98), one of Auckland's volcanoes. At its humble peak, a totara surrounded by a palisade honours the first Maori king (see the boxed text, p209).

Dominating it all is the magnificent **Auckland Museum** (Map p98; ☎ 09-309 0443; www. aucklandmuseum.com; adult/child $5/free; ☾ 10am-5pm), an imposing Greek temple with an impressive modern dome. Its comprehensive display of Pacific Island and Maori artefacts on the ground floor deserves to be on your 'must see' list. Highlights include a 25m war canoe and an extant carved meeting house from the Thames area (see p186) that you can enter (remove your shoes first).

Bookings are required for the **museum highlights guided tour** (☎ 09-306 7048; adult/child $10/5; ☾ 10.30am & 2pm). **Maori gallery tours** (same prices) take place at 11.30am and 2pm. Daily **Maori cultural performances** (adult/child $25/13; ☾ 11am, noon & 1.30pm) provide a good (and good-humoured) introduction to things Maori.

Admirers of the male form should check out the Domain's **Grafton Gate** (Map p92; Park Rd), a wonderful art-deco sandstone construction topped with a larger-than-life bronze nude.

Walking here from the city will take about 30 minutes, or you can catch the Link Bus (p120) to the neighbouring hospital.

One Tree Hill (Maungakiekie)

This volcanic cone (Map p88) was the isthmus' key *pa* and the greatest fortress in the country. It's easy to see why: a drive or walk to the top (182m) offers amazing 360-degree views. At the summit is the grave of John Logan Campbell, who gifted the land to the city in 1901, requesting that a memorial (the imposing obelisk and statue above the grave) be built to the Maori people. Nearby is the stump of the last 'one tree' (see the boxed text, below).

Allow a few hours to explore the craters and surrounding **Cornwall Park** (Map p88), with its impressive mature trees and historic cottage. The information centre (opposite) has fascinating interactive displays illustrating what the *pa* would have looked like when 5000 people lived here.

Near the excellent **children's playground**, the **Stardome Observatory** (Map p88; ☎ 09-624 1246; www. stardome.org.nz; adult/child $16/8) offers regular stargazing and planetarium shows that aren't dependent on Auckland's fickle weather (usually 8pm Wednesday to Saturday; phone ahead).

To get here from the city, take bus 328 from Customs St to Manukau Rd (adult/child $4.30/2.40, 21 minutes). By car, take the Greenlane exit of the Southern Motorway and turn right into Green Lane West.

Mt Eden (Maungawhau)

The view from Mt Eden (Map p100), Auckland's highest cone (196m), is superb. The symmetrical crater (50m deep) is known as Te Ipu Kai a Mataaho (the Food Bowl of Mataaho, the god of things hidden in the ground) and is highly *tapu* (sacred); don't enter it, but feel free to explore the remainder of the mountain. The remains of *pa* terraces and storage pits are clearly visible.

On its eastern slopes, **Eden Gardens** (Map p100; ☎ 09-638 8395; 24 Omana Ave, Epsom; adult/child $6/free; ☾ 9am-4pm) is a horticultural showpiece noted for camellias, rhododendrons and azaleas.

Western Springs

Auckland Zoo (Map p88; ☎ 09-360 3800; www.auckland zoo.co.nz; Motions Rd; adult/child $19/9; ☾ 9.30am-5.30pm) is an excellent modern zoo with spacious, natural compounds. The infrared lighting of the nocturnal house offers a rare chance to see

---

ONE TREE TO RULE THEM ALL

Looking at One Tree Hill, your first thought will probably be 'Where's the bloody tree?'. Good question. Up until 2000 a Monterey pine stood at the top of the hill. This was a replacement for a sacred totara that was chopped down by British settlers in 1852. Maori activists first attacked the foreign usurper in 1994, finishing the job in 2000. It's unlikely that another tree will be planted until local land claims have moved closer to resolution, but you can bet your boots that this time around it'll be a native.

Auckland's most beloved landmark achieved international recognition in 1987 when U2 released the song 'One Tree Hill' on their acclaimed *The Joshua Tree* album. It was only released as a single in NZ, where it went to number one.

CENTRAL AUCKLAND

See Ponsonby & Grey Lynn Map (p102)

AUCKLAND REGION

kiwi fossicking about. The big foreigners tend to steal the attention from the timid natives, but if you can wrestle the kids away from the tigers and elephants you'll find tuataras and a large selection of native birds.

Neighbouring **Western Springs Park** (Map p88) centres on a lake formed by a confluence of lava flows. Until 1902 this was Auckland's main water supply; more than four-million litres bubble up daily. Kids come here to be traumatised by pushy, bread-fattened geese and partake of the popular adventure playground. It's a great spot for a picnic and to get acquainted with playful pukeko (swamp hens).

Nothing makes you feel quite as old as seeing your childhood appliances in a museum. That sobering experience is offered at **MOTAT** (Museum of Transport & Technology; Map p88; ☎ 09-815 5800; www.motat.org.nz; 805 Great North Rd; adult/child $14/7; ☉ 10am-5pm), a 19-hectare trainspotter's paradise spreading over two sites. In MOTAT 1 look out for Helen Clark's Honda 50 motorbike and the cutesy pioneer village. MOTAT 2 is an aircraft graveyard, featuring rare military and commercial planes. The two sites are linked by a vintage tram (adult/child $2/1, every 30 minutes, 10am to 4.30pm), which passes the park and zoo. It's a fun kids' ride whether you visit MOTAT or not.

From the city, catch any bus (adult/child $3.20/1.80, 16 minutes) heading west via Great North Rd. By car, take the Western Springs exit from the North Western Motorway.

Auckland Art Gallery

The **Auckland Art Gallery** (Map p92; ☎ 09-379 1349; www.aucklandartgallery.com; admission free; ☼ 10am-5pm) spreads over two neighbouring buildings. The **Main Gallery** (cnr Wellesley & Kitchener Sts), built in French chateau style, isn't terribly big, but it houses important works by Pieter Bruegel the Younger and Guido Reni in the European collection, and an extensive collection of NZ art. It's worth calling in for the intimate 19th-century portraits of tattooed Maori subjects by Charles Goldie and Gottfried Lindauer alone. The **New Gallery** (cnr Wellesley & Lorne Sts) concentrates on contemporary art and temporary exhibitions (with varying admission charges). Ten commercial galleries can be found in the immediate vicinity.

If you're reading this before April 2011, the Main Gallery is closed for a major renovation. You'll find the highlights of the permanent collection housed in the New Gallery.

Sky Tower

The impossible-to-miss **Sky Tower** (Map p92; ☎ 09-363 6000; www.skycityauckland.co.nz; cnr Federal & Victoria Sts; adult/child $25/8; ☼ 8.30am-10.30pm Sun-Thu, 8.30am-11.30pm Fri & Sat) looks like a giant hypodermic giving a fix to the heavens. Spectacular lighting renders it even more space-age at night. The colours change for special events and shooting fireworks make it even more phallic on New Year's Eve.

The tower is the best part of the SkyCity complex, a tacky 24-hour casino with restaurants, cafes, bars and a hotel. At 328m it is the tallest structure in the southern hemisphere. A lift takes you up to the observation decks in 40 stomach-lurching seconds; look down through the glass floor panels if you're after an extra kick. It costs $3 extra to catch the skyway lift to the ultimate viewing level. Late afternoon is a good time to go up: you can sip a beverage in the Sky Lounge as the sun sets. See p101 for crazy stuff you can do while you're up here.

Kelly Tarlton's Antarctic Encounter & Underwater World

Housed in old stormwater and sewage holding tanks is this unique **aquarium** (Map p88; ☎ 09-531 5065; www.kellytarltons.co.nz; 23 Tamaki Dr, Orakei; adult/child $32/16; ☼ 9.30am-5.30pm). A transparent tunnel runs along the centre of the tank, through which you travel on a conveyor belt, with the fish, including sharks and stingrays, swimming around you. You can step off at any time to take a closer look.

The big attraction, however, is the permanent winter wonderland known as Antarctic Encounter. It includes a walk through a replica of Scott's 1911 Antarctic hut, and a ride aboard a heated Snow Cat through a frozen environment where a colony of king and gentoo penguins lives at sub-zero temperatures. Displays include an Antarctic scientific base of the future and exhibits on the history of Antarctica. Needless to say, this whole experience is a fantastic adventure for adults travelling with children.

Less fantastic are the entry queues at busy times of the year. Book online for a shorter wait.

Buses numbered 745 to 769 head here from Britomart. There's also a free shark-shaped shuttle bus that departs 172 Quay St (opposite the ferry terminal) on the hour between 9am and 4pm (except 2pm) and SkyCity's atrium 10 minutes later (departing Kelly Tarlton's 40 minutes later).

Tamaki Drive

This scenic, pohutukawa-lined road heads east from the city, hugging the waterfront. In summer it's a jogging/cycling/rollerblading blur offering plenty of eye candy.

Just past Kelly Tarlton's, Hapimana St heads up to Bastion Point (see the boxed text, p97) and the **Michael Joseph Savage Memorial** (Map p88). Savage (1872–1940) was the country's first Labour prime minister and widely considered one of its best. His socialist reforms left him adored by the populace, as this elaborate cliff-top garden mausoleum demonstrates. Follow the lawn to a WWII gun embankment – one of many that line the harbour.

Below the headland is **Mission Bay**, a popular beach with an iconic fountain, historic mission house, restaurants and bars. Safe swimming beaches **Kohimarama** and **St Heliers** follow. Further east along Cliff Rd, the **Achilles Point lookout** (Map p88) offers panoramic views. At its base is **Ladies Bay**, where nudists put up with mud and shells for the sake of seclusion.

Buses 745 to 769 from Britomart follow this route.

Albert Park & Auckland University

Hugging the hill on the city's eastern flank, **Albert Park** (Map p92) is a charming Victorian formal garden overrun by students during term time, the more radical of whom periodically deface the statues of Governor Grey and Queen Victoria. Auckland University campus stretches over several streets and incorporates a row of stately **Victorian merchant houses** (Map p92; Princes St) and **Old Government House** (Map p92; Waterloo Quadrant). The latter was the colony's seat of power from 1856 until 1865, when Wellington became the capital.

The **University Clock Tower** (Map p92; 22 Princes St) is Auckland's architectural triumph. The stately 'ivory' tower (1926) tips its hat towards art nouveau (the incorporation of NZ flora and fauna into the decoration) and the Chicago School (the way it's rooted into the earth). It's usually open, so wander inside.

At the centre of the campus is a wall of the **Albert Barracks** (1847; Map p92), a fortification that enclosed nine hectares, including Albert Park, during the New Zealand Wars.

Devonport

Located at the bottom of the North Shore, Devonport makes a pleasant day trip by ferry from the city. Quaint without being sickeningly twee, it retains a village atmosphere,

DEVONPORT

0   500 m
0   0.25 miles

WHAT BECAME OF NGATI WHATUA?

By the end of the 1840s Maori were already a minority in the Auckland area, and eventually the Ngati Whatua o Orakei *hapu* (subtribe) was reduced to a small block of land in the vicinity of Okahu Bay and Bastion Point. In 1886 Bastion Point was confiscated by the government for military use, and then in 1908 more land was taken to build a sewage pipe that pumped raw effluent into the water in front of the *hapu*'s last remaining village at Okahu Bay. All but the cemetery was confiscated in 1951, with the people dragged out of their homes and the village destroyed to 'clean up' the area before the royal visit of Queen Elizabeth II.

When the government decided to sell the prime real estate on Bastion Point in 1977, the *hapu* staged a peaceful occupation that lasted for 507 days before they were once again dragged into custody. It was a seminal moment in the Maori protest movement. During the next decade the government apologised and returned the land where the *marae* now stands. At the time of research, further negotiations between the government and *hapu* were progressing, with several of the volcanic cones likely to be part of the final settlement. The former railway land on which the Vector Arena now sits has already been returned.

with many well-preserved Victorian and Edwardian buildings and loads of cafes. If your interests are less genteel, there are two volcanic cones and easy access to the first of the North Shore's beaches.

The navy is based here, its history on display at the **Navy Museum** (Map p96; ☎ 09-445 5186; www.navymuseum.mil.nz; King Edward Pde; admission by donation; ☷ 10am-4.30pm). Its civilian neighbours have theirs preserved in the **Devonport Museum** (Map p96; ☎ 09-445 2661; www.devonportmuseum.org.nz; 33a Vauxhall Rd; admission free; ☷ 2-4pm Sat & Sun).

Mt Victoria (Takarunga; Map p96; Victoria Rd) and **North Head** (Maungauika; Map p96; Takarunga Rd; ☷ 6am-10pm) were Maori *pa* and are both still fortresses of sorts, with the navy maintaining a presence. Both have gun embankments and North Head is riddled with tunnels. Started at the end of the 19th century in response to the Russian threat, they were extended during WWI and WWII. The gates are locked at night, but that's never stopped teenagers from jumping the fence and terrifying themselves in the tunnels. Devonport Museum stands on the remains of a third cone that was largely quarried away.

For a self-guided tour of historic buildings, pick up the *Old Devonport Walk* pamphlet from the i-SITE (p90).

Ferries to Devonport (adult/child $10/5 return, 12 minutes) depart from the Auckland Ferry Building every 30 minutes (hourly after 7pm) from 6.15am to 11pm (until 1am Friday and Saturday), and from 7.15am to 10pm on Sundays and public holidays. Some Waiheke Island and Rangitoto ferries also stop here.

North Shore Beaches

A succession of fine swimming beaches stretches from North Head to Long Bay. The gulf islands provide a picturesque backdrop and shelter them from strong surf, making them safe for supervised children. Aim for high tide unless you fancy a lengthy walk to waist-deep water. **Cheltenham Beach** (Map p96) is a short walk from Devonport. **Takapuna Beach** (Map p88), closest to the Harbour Bridge, is Auckland's answer to Bondi and the most built up. Nearby **St Leonards Beach** (Map p88), popular with gay men, requires clambering over rocks at high tide.

Parnell & Newmarket

Parnell likes to think of itself as a village, although the only tractors to be seen are the SUVs driven by the affluent suburb's soccer mums. Inexplicably, it has an excellent selection of budget accommodation, although it's doubtful that backpackers will be frequenting the pricey eateries of the main strip. Neighbouring Newmarket is a busy shopping precinct, known for its boutiques.

This is one of Auckland's oldest areas and has retained several heritage buildings. **Highwic** (Map p98; ☎ 09-524 5729; www.historic.org.nz; 40 Gillies Ave; adult/child $7.50/free; ☷ 10.30am-noon & 1-4.30pm Wed-Sun) is a marvellous example of a Carpenter Gothic house (1862), sitting amid lush, landscaped grounds. **Ewelme Cottage** (Map p98; ☎ 09-379 0202; www.historic.org.nz; 14 Ayr St; adult/child $7.50/free; ☷ 10.30am-noon & 1-4.30pm Fri-Sun) is a storybook affair that was built for a clergyman in 1864 and has been left in startlingly good condition.

PARNELL & NEWMARKET

| 0 | 500 m |
| 0 | 0.25 miles |

SIGHTS & ACTIVITIES

Auckland Domain	**1**	A4
Auckland Museum	**2**	B4
Ewelme Cottage	**3**	C4
Highwic	**4**	A6
Holy Trinity Cathedral	**5**	C3
Kinder House	**6**	C4
Olympic Pools & Fitness Centre	**7**	B5
Parnell Baths	**8**	D1
Parnell Rose Gardens	**9**	C1
Pukekaroa	**10**	A4
St Mary's Church	**11**	C3
St Stephen's Chapel	**12**	D1
Wintergarden	**13**	A4

SLEEPING

Auckland International Backpackers	**14**	B1
City Garden Lodge	**15**	C3
Kingsgate Hotel	**16**	C1
Lantana Lodge	**17**	B2
Parnell City Lodge	**18**	C3
Parnell Inn	**19**	B3
Quality Hotel Barrycourt	**20**	C3

EATING

Baci Lounge	(see 26)	
Kokako	**21**	B4
La Cigale	**22**	C2
Non Solo Pizza	**23**	B3
Rosehip Cafe	**24**	C2
Urban Cafe	**25**	B5

ENTERTAINMENT

Rialto Cinemas	**26**	B5
Windsor Castle & Juice Bar	**27**	B2

SHOPPING

Karen Walker	**28**	B6
Zambesi	**29**	B6

Close to Ewelme Cottage is the simply restored **Kinder House** (Map p98; ☎ 09-379 4008; 2 Ayr St; adult/child $4/2; ☺ 11am-3pm Tue-Sun), built of volcanic stone (1857). Designed by Frederick Thatcher, it displays the subtle but skilful watercolours and memorabilia of the Reverend Dr John Kinder (1819–1903), who was the headmaster of the Church of England Grammar School. Enthusiastic and informative guided tours are provided.

Holy Trinity Cathedral (Map p98; ☎ 09-303 9500; www.holy-trinity.org.nz; Parnell Rd; ☺ 10am-3pm Mon-Sat, 11am-3pm Sun) is worth visiting for its modern stained-glass windows. Its blue-coloured rose window, designed by English artist Carl Edwards, is particularly striking above the simple kauri altar. Next door is **St Mary's** (Map p98), a wonderful wooden Gothic Revival church (1886), with a burnished wooden interior and lovely stained-glass windows.

The **Parnell Rose Gardens** (Map p98; Gladstone Rd) are blooming excellent from November to March. A pleasant stroll leads to peaceful **Judges Bay** and tiny **St Stephen's Chapel** (Map p98; Judge St), built for the signing of the constitution of NZ's Anglican Church (1857).

Civic Theatre

Opening its doors in 1929, the mighty **Civic** (Map p92; ☎ 09-357 3355; www.civictheatre.co.nz; cnr Queen & Wellesley Sts) is one of seven 'atmospheric theatres' remaining in the world and a fine survivor from cinema's Golden Age. The auditorium has lavish Moorish decoration and a starlit southern-hemisphere sky in the ceiling, complete with cloud projections. The foyer is an Indian indulgence, with elephants and monkeys hanging from every conceivable fixture. Buddhas were planned to decorate the street frontage but were considered too risqué at the time – they chose neoclassical naked boys instead!

If at all possible, try to attend a performance here. It's mainly used for touring musicals, big premieres and Film Festival screenings (see p105).

Viaduct Harbour

Once a busy commercial port, the Viaduct Harbour was given a major makeover leading up to the 1999/2000 and 2003 America's Cup tournaments. It's now a fancy dining and boozing precinct for the boat-shoes brigade, and guaranteed to have at least a slight buzz any night of the week. Historical plaques, interesting sculpture and the chance to gawk at millionaires' yachts make it a pleasant place for a stroll.

The well-presented **Voyager – New Zealand Maritime Museum** (Map p92; ☎ 09-373 0800; www.nzmaritime.org; cnr Quay & Hobson Sts; adult/child $16/8; ☺ 9am-5pm) traces NZ's seafaring history from Maori voyaging canoes to the America's Cup. Recreations include a tilting 19th-century steerage-class cabin and a fab 1950s-era bach (holiday home). Its newest showcase, *Blue Water Black Magic*, is a tribute to Sir Peter Blake, the Whitbread-Round-The-World and America's Cup-winning yachtsman who was murdered in 2001 while on an environmental monitoring trip on the Amazon. Check the website for details of semiregular historic steamboat and sailing-ship cruises.

St Patrick's Cathedral

Auckland's Catholic **cathedral** (Map p92; ☎ 09-303 4509; www.stpatricks.org.nz; 43 Wyndham St; ☺ 7am-7pm) is one of its loveliest buildings. Polished wood and Belgian stained glass lend warmth to the interior of this majestic Gothic Revival church (1907). There's a historical display in the old confessional on the left-hand side.

Alberton

A classic colonial mansion (1863), **Alberton** (Map p88; ☎ 09-846 7367; www.historic.org.nz; 100 Mt Albert Rd; adult/child $8/free; ☺ 10.30am-4pm Wed-Sun) offers tours and was used as a location for some scenes in *The Piano*. Bring a picnic lunch and enjoy the grounds.

Auckland Botanical Gardens

The 64-hectare **Auckland Botanical Gardens** (Map p88; ☎ 09-267 1457; Hill Rd, Manurewa; admission free; ☺ 8am-6pm) has dozens of themed gardens, threatened plants, and a hell of a lot of brides and grooms. By car, take the Southern Motorway, exit at Manurewa and follow the signs. Otherwise take the train to Manurewa ($5.70, 40 minutes) and then walk along Hill Rd (1.5km) or catch bus 466 ($1.60, 15 minutes).

ACTIVITIES

Trading on the country's action-packed reputation, Auckland has sprouted its own set of insanely frightening activities. Look around for backpacker reductions or special offers before booking anything.

MT EDEN & KINGSLAND

| 0 | 500 m |
| 0 | 0.25 miles |

Spiderman Activities

The wise men of bungy, **AJ Hackett Bungy & Bridge Climb** (Map p88; ☎ 09-361 2000; www.ajhack ett.com/nz; Westhaven Reserve, Curran St) offer the chance to climb up or jump off the Auckland Harbour Bridge. Both the 40m bungy leap and the 1½-hour guided tour along the arch (with a harness attached to a static line) cost $120.

Not to be outdone, the Sky Tower (p95) offers an ever-expanding selection of pant-wetting activities. If you thought the observation deck was for pussies, **Sky Walk** (Map p92; ☎ 0800 759 925; www.skywalk.co.nz; adult/child $135/100; ☼ 10am-5.30pm) involves circling the 192m-high, 1.2m-wide outside halo of the tower without rails or a balcony – but with a safety harness (they're not completely crazy). **Sky Jump** (Map p92; ☎ 0800 759 586; www.skyjump.co.nz; adult/child $195/145; ☼ 10am-5.30pm) is an 11-second, 85km/h base wire jump from the observation deck. It's more like a parachute jump than a bungy and it's a rush and a half. You can combine both in the Look 'n Leap package ($260).

Sky Screamer (Map p92; ☎ 09-377 1328; www.reverse-bungy.com; cnr Albert & Victoria Sts; ride $40; ☼ 10.30am-10pm Sun-Thu, 10am-2am Fri & Sat) involves being strapped into a seat and reverse-bungied 60m up in the air. Should you hurl, rest assured – you can get a video of it.

Cruises

Getting out on the water is an intrinsic part of the Auckland experience. If you can't afford a cruise or yacht, take a ferry instead; details are listed in each destination section.

Fullers (Map p92; ☎ 09-367 9111; www.fullers.co.nz; Ferry Bldg, 99 Quay St) operates ferry services (Birkenhead, Northcote Point, Devonport, Rangitoto, Waiheke Island, Great Barrier Island) and daily harbour cruises (adult/child $35/18, 1½ hours, 10.30am and 1.30pm), which include a stop on Rangitoto, a complimentary cuppa and a free return ticket to Devonport.

360 Discovery (Map p92; ☎ 09-307 8005; www.360discovery.co.nz; Pier 4 kiosk, Quay St) also runs ferries (Gulf Harbour, Motuihe, Tiritiri Matangi, Coromandel Town) along with the Harbour Discovery cruise (adult/child $29/15, 1½ hours), departing at 10am, noon and 2.30pm, which stops at Devonport, Rangitoto, Motuihe and Orakei Wharf (for Kelly Tarlton's Antarctic Encounter).

Sailing

Hey, this is the 'City of Sails' and nothing gets you closer to the heart and soul of Auckland than sailing on the gulf.

Sail NZ (Map p92; ☎ 0800 397 567; www.sailnewzea land.co.nz; Viaduct Harbour) heads out on genuine America's Cup yachts (adult/child $150/110, two hours). This experienced and highly regarded outfit also offers daily Whale and Dolphin Safaris (adult/child $150/100); dolphins are spotted 90% of the time and whales 75%. Its *Pride of Auckland* fleet of glamorous large yachts offers tours ranging from the 90-minute Coffee Cruise (adult/child $70/37) to the full-day Sailing Adventure (adult/child $135/110).

Gulfwind Sailing Academy (Map p88; ☎ 09-521 1564; www.gulfwind.co.nz; Westhaven Marina) provides cruises (half-/full-day $395/795 for up to six people), as well as personalised tuition and flexible small-group sailing courses; a two-day RYA Start Yachting course costs $545.

Penny Whiting Sailing School (Map p88; ☎ 09-376 1322; www.pennywhiting.com; Westhaven Marina) runs courses that consist of five three-hour practical sailing lessons ($650).

Tramping

Visitors centres, DOC offices and public libraries have pamphlets on walks in and around Auckland. The city council's *Auckland City's Walkways* pamphlet has a good selection of urban walks, including the **Coast to Coast Walkway** (Map p88; 16km, four hours). Heading clear across the country, from Waitemata Harbour to Manukau Harbour, the walk encompasses Albert Park, the University, the Domain, Mt Eden (Maungawhau) and One Tree Hill (Maungakiekie), keeping as much as possible to reserves rather than city streets. Starting from the Viaduct Basin and heading south, it's marked by yellow markers and milestones; heading north from Onehunga there are blue markers. To get back to the city, take bus 328, 334, 348 or 354 from Onehunga Mall ($5.40, 50 minutes).

Hang Gliding & Skydiving

Active Sky Hang Gliding (☎ 021 170 3646; www.active skyhanggliding.co.nz) lets you fly like a kahu (native hawk – NZ doesn't have eagles) in a tandem flight ($175) off the cliffs at Kariotahi beach, southwest of Auckland.

NZ Skydive (☎ 09-373 5778; www.nzskydive.co.nz) offers an exhilarating tandem skydive from

12,000ft (including a 7000ft free fall) for $299; capture your excitement/terror on DVD for $165. It all takes place at Mercer airfield, 55km south of Auckland.

Swimming

When the weather conspires to keep you off the beaches, Auckland offers excellent alternatives:

Olympic Pools & Fitness Centre (Map p98; ☎ 09-522 4414; www.theolympic.co.nz; 77 Broadway; adult/child $7/4.50; ⏱ 5.45am-10pm Mon-Fri, 7am-8pm Sat & Sun) Pools, gym, sauna, steam room and crèche.

Parnell Baths (Map p98; ☎ 09-373 3561; www.parnellbaths.co.nz; Judges Bay Rd; adult/child $5.70/3.90; ⏱ 6am-8pm Mon-Fri, 8am-8pm Sat & Sun Nov-Apr)

Outdoor saltwater pools with an awesome 1950s mural and popular sunbathing areas.

Other Activities

Fergs Kayaks (Map p88; ☎ 09-529 2230; www.fergskayaks.co.nz; 12 Tamaki Dr, Okahu Bay; ⏱ 9am-6pm Mon-Fri, 8am-6pm Sat & Sun) hires out kayaks ($15 to $40 per hour or $50 to $120 per day), bikes (per hour/day $20/120) and inline skates (per hour/day $15/30). Day and night guided kayak trips are available to Devonport (8km, three hours, $95) or Rangitoto Island (13km, six hours, $120).

NZ Surf Tours (☎ 09-828 0426; www.newzealandsurftours.com) runs day-long surfing courses ($120) that include transport, equipment and two lessons. A five-day small-group course ($799,

PONSONBY & GREY LYNN

0 — 500 m
0 — 0.25 miles

To Harbour Bridge (200m)

St Marys Bay

Northern Mwy

INFORMATION
Women's Bookshop.....................1 D3

SLEEPING
23 Hepburn.................................2 D3
Abaco on Jervois.........................3 C1
Brown Kiwi..................................4 C2
Great Ponsonby Arthotel.............5 C2
Henry's.......................................6 A4
Ponsonby Backpackers................7 C3
Red Monkey................................8 C4
Uenuku Lodge.............................9 C3
Verandahs.................................10 D4

EATING
Delicious...................................11 A4
Dizengoff..................................12 C2
Harvest Wholefoods..................13 A4
Landreth & Co...........................14 C2
Murder Burger...........................15 D4
Ponsonby Road Bistro................16 D3
Ponsonby Village Food Court.....17 D4
Prego..18 C3
Queenie....................................19 D2
Richmond Road Cafe.................20 A3
Soto..21 C2
SPQR...22 D3

DRINKING
Dida's Wine Lounge & Tapas
Bar...23 C2
Gypsy Tea Room........................24 A4
Ponsonby Social Club................25 D3

SHOPPING
Karen Walker.............................26 C3
Marvel......................................27 D3
Zambesi....................................28 D3

Herne Bay
Hamilton Rd
Jervois Rd
Curran St
Shelly Beach Rd
Seymour Rd
Melford Rd
Dedwood St
St Marys Rd
New St
Beaumont St

Sheehan St
College Hill
Pompallier Tce
Renall St
Wood St
Costley St
Georgia St
England St
Ireland St
Spring St
Clarence St
Prosford St
Cowan St
Arthur St
Ryle St
Ponsonby
Ponsonby Tce
Tole St
Gunson St
O'Neill St
Summer St
Wellington St
Franklin Rd
Freemans Bay
Angelsea St
Collingwood St
Vermont St
Ponsonby Rd
Lincoln St
Hepburn St
Norfolk St
Douglas St
Picton St
Brown St
Richmond Rd
Western Park
Peel St
Grey Lynn
Hopetoun St
Crummer Rd
Arch Hill

See Central Auckland Map (p92)

October to May) heads to Ahipara (p174) and includes accommodation, transport and food.

Both the **Dive Centre** (Map p88; ☎ 09-444 7698; www.divecentre.co.nz; 97 Wairau Rd, Takapuna; PADI Open Water $499) and **Orakei Scuba Centre** (Map p88; ☎ 09-524 2117; www.orakeidive.co.nz; 234 Orakei Rd, Remuera; PADI Open Water $399-599) have dive shops and run courses.

Balloon Expeditions (☎ 09-416 8590; www.balloon expeditions.co.nz; flight $320) and **Balloon Safaris** (☎ 09-415 8289; www.balloonsafaris.co.nz; flight $330) offers early-morning hot-air balloon flights that take about four hours (one hour in the air), with breakfast and a bottle of bubbles.

Rainbow's End Adventure Park (Map p88; ☎ 09-262 2030; www.rainbowsend.co.nz; 2 Clist Cres, Manukau; superpass adult/child $45/35; ⊗ 10am-5pm) has enough rides (including a corkscrew roller coaster and the 'Power Surge'), shows and interactive entertainment to keep the kids happy all day, plus plenty of sugary snacks to fuel it all. Superpasses allow unlimited rides.

WALKING TOUR

Auckland's CBD can seem grim and generic, so this walk aims to show you some interesting hidden nooks and architectural treats.

Start among the funky second-hand boutiques of **St Kevin's Arcade (1)** and take the stairs down to Myers Park. Look out for the reproduction of **Michelangelo's Moses (2)** to the right at the bottom of the stairs. Continue through the park, taking the stairs on the right just before the overpass to head up to street level.

Heading down Queen St, you'll pass the **Auckland Town Hall (3**; p116) and **Aotea Square (4)**, the civic heart of the city. On the next corner is the wonderful **Civic Theatre (5**; p99). Turn right on Wellesley St and then left onto Lorne St. Immediately to your right is the **New Gallery (6**; p103) and a pretty little square with tiling celebrating the suffragettes who won NZ women the vote before anywhere else in the world. Head up the stairs and cross the road to the **Main Gallery (7**; p95).

Take the stairs up into **Albert Park (8**; p96) and cross through to the **University Clock Tower (9**; p96). Head onto campus, taking the path to the right of the building, and you'll come out on a grassy quadrant and the remains of the **Albert Barracks (10**; p96). Cut through the centre of the university, following the signs to **Old Government House (11**; p96).

Head back to Princes St, where there's an interesting row of Victorian merchants'

WALKING TOUR

WALK FACTS

Start St Kevin's Arcade, Karangahape Rd
Finish Viaduct Harbour
Distance 4km
Duration Around two hours

houses and, on the corner, the **former synagogue (12)**. Take Bowen Ave and cut through the park to the **Chancery precinct (13)**, an upmarket area of designer stores and cafes. A small square leads to **High St (14)**, Auckland's main fashion strip. Take a left onto **Vulcan Lane (15)**, lined with historic pubs. Turn right onto Queen St and follow it down to the **Britomart Train Station (16)**, housed in the grand former Central Post Office. You're now standing on reclaimed land – the original shoreline was at Fort St.

Turn left on Quay St and head to **Viaduct Harbour (17**; p99), where you can explore along the waterline or just grab a beverage.

AUCKLAND FOR CHILDREN

Auckland has plenty to keep kids entertained, whatever the weather. All of the east coast beaches (St Heliers, Kohimarama, Mission Bay, Okahu Bay, Cheltenham, Narrow Neck, Takapuna, Milford, Long Bay) are safe for supervised kids, while Rainbow's End Adventure Park (p103), Kelly Tarlton's Antarctic Encounter & Underwater World (p95) and Auckland Zoo (p91) are other favourites. Parnell Baths (p102) has a children's pool and is open year-round. On a wintry day, head to the thermal pools at Parakai (p137) or Waiwera (p139).

TOURS

Three-hour bus tours will typically take you around the city centre, over the Harbour Bridge and out along Tamaki Dr, including stops at Mt Eden, the Auckland Museum and Parnell, for about $67. **Gray Line** (☎ 09-307 7880; www.graylinetours.co.nz) and **Great Sights** (☎ 09-583 5790; www.greatsights.co.nz) both offer this service.

Potiki Tours (☎ 09-845 5932; www.potikitours. com) runs an excellent Urban Maori day tour (adult/child $195/100) for small groups. They leave Mt Eden to the buses, and head to One Tree Hill (Maungakiekie) instead, pointing out features of the mountain *pa* site. After a quick lunch it's off to the west-coast beaches, where bush and beach walks are peppered with Maori creation stories, *karakia* (incantations) and explanations of the traditional uses of plants. More personalised tours can be tailored to your interests, such as visits with local artists.

Another recommended Maori-led tour is Ngati Whatua's **Tamaki Hikoi** (☎ 0800 282 552; www.tamakihikoi.co.nz; adult/child $80/40), which includes transfers up Mt Eden (Maungawhau) and a three-hour guided walk pointing out features of significance, from the mountain down to the harbour.

The hop-on, hop-off **Explorer Bus** (☎ 0800 439 756; www.explorerbus.co.nz; adult/child $35/15) departs from the Ferry Building every hour from 10am to 3pm (more frequently in summer), heading to 14 tourist sites around the central city.

Other options:

Auckland Adventures (☎ 09-379 4545; www.auck landadventures.co.nz; afternoon/day tours $85/120) The afternoon tour (12.45pm to 5pm) includes Muriwai gannet colony, an orchard, wineries and Mt Eden; day tours (9am to 5pm) can include a hike or mountain-biking experience.

Auckland Ghost Tours (☎ 09-630 5721; www. aucklandghosttours.com; adult/child $50/25) Stories about Auckland's scary side – and we don't just mean the

architecture – shared on a two-hour walking tour of the central city.

Bush & Beach (☎ 0800 423 224; www.bushandbeach. co.nz; 5hr/7hr walks $135/205) Guided walks in the Waitakere Ranges, black-sand beaches and the central city.

Fine Wine Tours (☎ 09-529 5227; www.insidertouring. co.nz) Tours the West Auckland wineries, including lunch: four-hour tour ($149), with cheese ($169); six-hour tour including Muriwai Beach and a microbrewery ($269); food and wine tour with stops at city providores ($199).

Great Taste Tours (☎ 09-424 1741; www.greattaste tours.co.nz; tours $115-245) Food, wine and art tours in either Matakana or Kumeu.

Hiking NZ (☎ 0800 697 232; www.hikingnewzealand. com) Runs 'hiking safaris' leaving from Auckland: Volcanic Plateau ($745, five days); Far North ($795, six days); and Volcanoes & Rainforest ($1550, 10 days).

Ports of Auckland Tours (☎ 0800 360 3472; www.360discovery.co.nz; ✆ tours Tue fortnightly) Free hour-long boat tours around the ports; bookings essential.

TIME Unlimited (☎ 09-446 6677; www.newzealand tours.travel) To Integrate Maori Experiences (TIME) is the motto. A hefty set of cultural, fishing, kayaking, trekking and sightseeing tours are outlined on its website, including excellent kayak-fishing excursions (day/overnight $290/590).

Wine Trail Tours (☎ 09-630 1540; www.winetrail tours.co.nz) Small-group tours around West Auckland wineries and the Waitakere Ranges (half-/full-day $105/215); further afield to Matakana ($235); or a combo of the two ($235).

FESTIVALS & EVENTS

Check www.aucklandnz.com for full details of what's on in the city.

January

ASB Classic (www.asbclassic.co.nz) Watch some leading women tennis players warm up for the Aussie Open; held early January at the ASB Tennis Centre.

Heineken Open (www.heinekenopen.co.nz) The men's equivalent; held mid-January.

Big Day Out (www.bigdayout.com) Australasia's biggest music festival, attracting big-name alternative bands and lots of Kiwi up-and-comers to Mt Smart Stadium in mid-January.

Auckland Anniversary Day Regatta (www.regatta. org.nz) The 'City of Sails' lives up to its name; Monday of last weekend in January.

Music In Parks A series of free gigs and movies in parks around the city; runs until March.

February

Waitangi Day Festival Maori culture, food and a free concert, held at Okahu Bay on February 6.

Devonport Food & Wine Festival (www.devonport winefestival.co.nz) Sip and sup with the smart set at this two-day festival in mid-February.

Big Gay Out (www.biggayout.co.nz) The big event on the gay and lesbian calendar; 12,000 people descend on Coyle Park, Pt Chevalier for a free festival.

Mission Bay Jazz & Blues Streetfest (www.jazz andbluesstreetfest.com) New Orleans comes to the Bay as jazz and blues bands line both sides of the street as the sun sets; held late February.

Lantern Festival (www.asianz.org.nz) Three days of Asian food and culture in Albert Park to welcome the lunar New Year.

Starlight Symphony The Auckland Philharmonic entertains picnickers in the Domain; late February.

March

Auckland Cup Week (www.aucklandcupweek.co.nz) Try to spot the winner at the biggest horse race of the year; at Ellerslie Racecourse, early March.

Auckland Festival (www.aucklandfestival.co.nz) Held in odd-numbered years, this is Auckland's biggest celebration of the arts.

Pasifika Festival Western Springs Park hosts this excellent (and giant) Polynesian party with music, dancing and food; held in early to mid-March.

Polyfest (www.asbpolyfest.co.nz) Auckland secondary schools' Maori and Pacific Islands cultural festival – the biggest Pacific Islander (PI) cultural festival in the world.

Royal Easter Show (www.royaleastershow.co.nz) Fun for all the family, with an agricultural flavour.

April/May

NZ International Comedy Festival (www.comedy festival.co.nz) Three-week laughfest with local and international comedians; held mid-April to early May.

NZ Boat Show (www.boatshow.co.nz) One of the world's best yachting nations shows off its wares – find something to float your boat; held mid-May.

Auckland Art Fair (www.aucklandartfair.co.nz) Held in May in odd-numbered years at the Viaduct Harbour.

Out Takes (www.outtakes.org.nz) Gay and lesbian film festival, running from late May to early June.

July

New Zealand International Film Festival (www. nzff.telecom.co.nz) Auckland goes crazy for art-house films from mid- to late July.

September

Air New Zealand Fashion Week (www.nzfashion week.com) Is any country better qualified to show what you can do with merino wool and a sense of imagination? Find the next Karen Walker or Kate Sylvester here. Held in mid- to late September.

Heritage Festival Two weeks of fabulous (mainly free) tours of Auckland's neighbourhoods and historic buildings.

October

Diwali Festival Of Lights (www.asianz.org.nz/diwali) Auckland's Indian community light up the Viaduct with an explosion of colour, music and dance; held in mid-October.

November

Queen of the Whole Universe (www.queenwhole universe.com) A fundraising drag-fest (queens not cars) held at the Aotea Centre in mid-November.

December

Christmas in the Park (www.christmasinthepark.co.nz) A party so big it has to be held in the Auckland Domain.

SLEEPING

Our accommodation listings for Auckland fall into the following categories:

- Budget – doubles under $100
- Midrange – cheapest doubles from $100 to $200
- Top End – doubles more than $200

Budget

Invariably the backpackers who leave with a bad impression of Auckland have stayed in crummy, noisy hostels in the city centre. Not all of the cheap city accommodation is bad – the ones we've listed are all perfectly acceptable – but you're better off grabbing a bed in the surrounding suburbs. Parnell is relatively pricey but it has some excellent hostels. Mt Eden and Ponsonby have some good options, but the otherwise backpacker-friendly suburbs of Kingsland and Grey Lynn are poorly served.

CENTRAL AUCKLAND

Nomads Auckland (Map p92; ☎ 09-300 9999; www.no madsauckland.com; 16 Fort St; dm $22-30, r $80-90; 🖳 🛜) Bustling is an understatement for this large backpackers with a cafe, bar, nightclub, reading room, travel agency, female-only floor and a roof deck with sauna and spa. All of the dorms have lockers and the private rooms have TVs but not necessarily windows.

Frienz.com (Map p92; ☎ 09-307 6437; www.frienz.com; 27-31 Victoria St; dm $23-28, d $72; 🖳 🛜) Raising the bar for this part of town, Frienz has actually put an effort into its decor (crazy wallpaper and bright colours) and into organising regular social events (free barbecue nights, poker tournaments etc). Add to that free internet access, fridges in the private rooms and a terrific rooftop terrace and you get the inner city's best hostel.

City Groove (Map p92; ☎ 09-303 4768; www.city groove.co.nz; 6 Constitution Hill; dm $24-26, tw/d $60/65; P ⬛) Nestled in a forgotten strip of inner-city houses edging a steep park near the university, this homely hostel has only seven rooms and a great backyard.

Base Auckland (Map p92; ☎ 09-358 4877; www. stayatbase.com; 229 Queen St; dm $27-29, d $74-92, q $130; ⬛ ⬤) With more than 500 beds and a network of sightseeing and job-seeking contacts, this is the place where many young visitors get their bearings. If you don't like a hive of activity (or stained carpets and ceiling panels), then you'll need to go elsewhere, as this place hums with questions about where the cheapest places to eat can be found, who's got work where, whether bungy jumping's worth it and where the cute guys/girls are. There's a bar to aid this last search.

City Lodge (Map p92; ☎ 09-379 6183; www.citylodge. co.nz; 150 Vincent St; s/tr $68/118, d $88-98; P ⬛ ⬤) City Lodge is a very well-run, purpose-built tower for the budget market. The bright, tiny rooms and stamp-sized bathrooms may be plain, but they make a perfectly comfortable, clean and secure resting place. There's a fantastic industrial-style kitchen, cleaned daily by housekeepers, and a comfy, modern lounge and TV room.

Aspen House (Map p92; ☎ 09-379 6633; www.aspen house.co.nz; 62 Emily Pl; s $69, d $89-129, tr $99-149, q $219; P ⬛ ⬤) Located on a sweet, steep street a stone's throw from one of Auckland's most intriguing little parks, the Aspen is split into a renovated wing (high ceilings, en suites) and an older wing (lumpy beds, two toilets between 12 rooms). It's worth paying more for the former. The excellent communal spaces, friendly staff and tucked-away location make this the best of the inner-city hostels.

Hotel Formule 1 (Map p92; ☎ 09-308 9140; www. formule1.co.nz; 20 Wyndham St; r $75; ⬛) You'll feel like a giant in the minirooms with teensy TVs, stereos, ironing boards and kitchenettes, but they're clean and stocked with everything you need. The building itself is spectacularly skinny.

NEWTON
Auckland City YHA (Map p92; ☎ 09-309 2802; www.yha. co.nz; 18 Liverpool St; dm $24-41, s/d/tr $69/82/94; ⬛ ⬤) Struggle up one of the city's steepest streets to

this big, impersonal tower block near the K Rd party strip. The rooms are clean and well kept, and some have views and terraces.

Auckland International YHA (Map p92; ☎ 09-302 8200; www.yha.co.nz; 5 Turner St; dm $26-31, d $88-124, tr $118; P ⬛) Clean and brightly painted, this 170-bed YHA has a friendly vibe, good security, a games room and lots of lockers. In short, it's your typical, well-run YHA.

BK Hostel (Map p92; ☎ 09-307 0052; www.bkhostel. co.nz; 3 Mercury Lane; s $40-45, d $50-58, tr $81; ⬛ ⬤) Prices are cheaper for windowless rooms, but if you're planning to be partying in the neighbourhood's all-night clubs, that might be an advantage. The hostel is housed in a cool 1910 building with high ceilings and decent security.

PARNELL
Auckland International Backpackers (Map p98; ☎ 09-358 4584; www.aucklandinternationalbp.com; 2 Churton St; dm $23-25, s $48, d $62-72; ⬛) Eat in the sunroom, in the large dining room or out in the small garden at this backstreet backpackers. Linen and towels cost extra for dorm dwellers.

Lantana Lodge (Map p98; ☎ 09-373 4546; www.lantana lodge.co.nz; 60 St Georges Bay Rd; dm/s/d/tr $26/65/70/90; P ⬛) There are only eight rooms available in this cosy villa, on a quiet street with an instantly welcoming, social vibe. It's not flash by any means, but it's clean enough to be homely.

City Garden Lodge (Map p98; ☎ 09-302 0880; www. citygardenlodge.co.nz; 25 St Georges Bay Rd; dm $28-30, s/d $52/68, tw $58-68; P ⬛ ⬤) Housed within a character-filled, two-storey house built for Tongan royalty, this friendly and well-run backpackers has a lovely garden and high-ceilinged rooms with solid period features. If you need privacy a cute double room will do the trick, and if you need to unwind, indulge in some yoga on the front lawn.

Quality Hotel Barrycourt (Map p98; ☎ 09-303 3789; www.barrycourt.co.nz; 20 Gladstone Rd; r $95-165, units $120-199; ⬛ ⬤) A mixed bag of more than 100 motel rooms and units are available in this large, well-maintained complex with friendly multilingual staff. The older south wing is spacious but dated, while the north wing has some fantastic harbour views. Simple, cheaper rooms with kitchenette in the south wing are a good deal.

Parnell Inn (Map p98; ☎ 09-358 0642; www.parnell inn.co.nz; 320 Parnell Rd; d $99-120, tw $130, tr $145-155, q $170; P ⬛ ⬤) You'll get a chipper welcome at this revamped, good-looking motel, with new-look furniture and local photography on the walls. Smaller studios are on your right as you walk down the hall from reception; larger, sunnier rooms are on your left. Rooms 3 and 4 have great harbour views.

MT EDEN
Oaklands Lodge (Map p100; ☎ 09-638 6545; www. oaklands.co.nz; 5a Oaklands Rd; dm $23-25, s $43, d $60-66; 🖳 🛜) Situated in one of Mt Eden's loveliest quiet suburban streets, this bright, well-kept hostel is close to Mt Eden village and city buses. The communal facilities are in good knick.

Bamber House (Map p100; ☎ 09-623 4267; www. hostelbackpacker.com; 22 View Rd; dm $25-28, d $66-86; 🖳 🛜) The original house here is a mansion of sorts, with some nicely maintained period trimmings. The new prefab cabins have less character but come with en suites. There's plenty of space for its 60-odd guests to stretch out on the lawns and there's a playground for the kids. All in all, an excellent choice.

Pentlands Backpackers Hostel (Map p100; ☎ 09-638 7031; www.pentlands.co.nz; 22 Pentland Ave; dm $26-28, s $42, d $64; 🖳 🛜) Down a peaceful tree-lined cul-de-sac, Pentlands offers a homely environment, small dorms, a sunny deck and quiet tables on the lawn.

PONSONBY & HERNE BAY
Uenuku Lodge (Map p102; ☎ 09-378 8990; www.uenuku lodge.co.nz; 217 Ponsonby Rd; dm $24-28, s $49, d $58-78, tr/q $93/112; 🅿 🖳 🛜) This gay-friendly hostel is well located and some of the rooms afford city views. There's a decent lounge, a large kitchen, good security and an attractive outdoor area.

Ponsonby Backpackers (Map p102; ☎ 09-360 1311; www.ponsonby-backpackers.co.nz; 2 Franklin Rd; dm $25-27, s/d $42/60; 🖳 🛜) The interiors don't live up to the imposing exterior of this turreted wooden villa, commanding a corner site on tree-lined Franklin Rd. Yet it's kept reasonably clean and the staff are charming.

Brown Kiwi (Map p102; ☎ 09-378 0191; www.brown kiwi.co.nz; 7 Prosford St; dm $26-28, d/tr $68/84; 🅿 🖳 🛜) As unassuming as its namesake, this two-storey hostel is tucked away in a busy-by-day commercial strip, a stone's throw from all the good shopping and grazing opportunities. Dorms have four or eight beds, and the triple rooms are set in the small, verdant garden courtyard.

our pick Verandahs (Map p102; ☎ 09-360 4180; www.verandahs.co.nz; 6 Hopetoun St; dm $26-28, s $53, d $70-88, tr $90; 🖳 🛜) Ponsonby Rd, K Rd and the city are an easy walk from this grand hostel, housed in two neighbouring villas overlooking the mature trees of Western Park. The bunkless dorms sleep a maximum of five people.

Red Monkey (Map p102; ☎ 09-360 7977; www. theredmonkey.co.nz; 49 Richmond Rd; weekly s/d/apt $185/230/260; 🖳) If you're planning to stay for a week or longer, make this renovated villa your home away from home. There are lamps, bedside tables and built-in wardrobes in all the smartly decorated rooms, including three in the quiet back garden. It's well worth booking ahead.

Abaco on Jervois (Map p102; ☎ 09-360 6850; www. abaco.co.nz; 57 Jervois Rd; r $75-269; 🅿) The upstairs rooms at this motel have been transformed into a stylish, neutral-toned escape. Furnishings are modern and comfortable, with plenty of fluffy white towels for spa lovers, and slick stainless-steel kitchenettes (which include dish drawers and proper ovens). Downstairs the darker, unrenovated rooms are a good deal, especially if you're planning on spending all your time at the cafes across the road.

NORTH SHORE
Takapuna Beach Holiday Park (Map p88; ☎ 09-489 7909; www.takapunabeachholidaypark.co.nz; 22 The Promenade, Takapuna; campsites $32, cabins $65, caravans $65-80, units $115; 🖳 🛜) Superbly positioned looking onto one of Auckland's most popular beaches, this little park is a smart proposition. The clean, new cabins have decks.

Auckland North Shore Motels & Holiday Park (Map p88; ☎ 09-418 2578; www.nsmotels.co.nz; 52 Northcote Rd, Takapuna; sites per 2 people $35, dm $38, units $48-145; 🅿 🖳 🛜 🐾) An indoor pool, spa and 24-hour check-in are all available at this oddly located holiday park and motel complex near the motorway, 4km north of the Harbour Bridge. Despite the position it's surprisingly peaceful.

OTHER AREAS
Ambury Regional Park campsite (Map p88; ☎ 09-366 2000; www.arc.govt.nz; Ambury Rd, Mangere; sites per adult/child $10/5) A slice of country in the middle of suburbia, this regional park is also a working farm. Facilities are limited (a vault toilet, warm showers and not much shade) but it's handy to the airport, right on the water and dirt cheap.

Duke's Midway Lodge (Map p88; ☎ 09-625 4399; www.dukes.co.nz; 4 Vagus Pl, Royal Oak; d $95-110, tr/q $125/165; �) Duke's brings a touch of Las Vegas to suburban Auckland's Vagus Pl, thanks to its rather eye-catching swimming pool which takes the shape of a guitar. In every other respect, Duke's is a well-priced run-of-the-mill motor lodge. Rooms are comfortable, with OK beds, cable TV and decent bathrooms, while the quiet location (off busy Pah Rd, midway to the airport) means you'll sleep soundly.

Midrange

Most motels (of which there are plenty) and B&Bs fall into this category. There are few options in the city centre, where accommodation swings from hostels to luxury hotels. Devonport has masses of beautiful Edwardian B&Bs within a relaxing ferry ride of the CBD.

CENTRAL AUCKLAND & NEWTON

Quadrant (Map p92; ☎ 09-984 6000; www.thequadrant.com; 10 Waterloo Quadrant; apt $123-400;) Slick, central and full of all the whiz-bang gadgets, this apartment-style complex in the nicest part of the city is an excellent option. The only catch is that the apartments are tiny and the bathrooms beyond small.

Elliott Hotel (Map p92; ☎ 09-308 9334; www.theelliotthotel.com; cnr Elliott & Wellesley Sts; apt $139-209;) Housed in one of the city's grandest historic buildings (1880s), this apartment-style hotel is much plusher than the price implies. Rooms may not be huge but the high ceilings will let your spirits rise.

Langham (Map p92; ☎ 09-379 5132; www.auckland.langhamhotels.co.nz; 83 Symonds St; r $190-370, ste $470-2420;) The Langham may be five-star, but the glamour of the giant chandelier in the reception dissipates somewhat once you reach the low-ceilinged guest floors. Perhaps that's why you can often nab a special and take advantage of the faultless service and heavenly beds at a midrange price.

Other options:

Auckland City Hotel (Map p92; ☎ 09-925 0777; www.achhobson.co.nz; 157 Hobson St; r $120-130, ste $270;) The heritage frontage opens onto a modern block with smart, spacious apartments at very reasonable prices.

CityLife (Map p92; ☎ 09-379 9222; www.heritagehotels.co.nz/citylife-auckland; Durham St; r $165-483, ste $185-1890;) A worthy tower-block hotel offering hundreds of rooms over dozens of floors.

PARNELL & NEWMARKET

Parnell City Lodge (Map p98; ☎ 09-377 1463; www.parnellcitylodge.co.nz; 2 St Stephens Ave; apt $105-170;) Old and newer sections are available in this motel, where every unit is different, some have a bit of character and all have a kitchenette. It's on a busy intersection though, so traffic noise might be a nuisance if you're a light sleeper.

Off Broadway Motel (Map p88; ☎ 09-529 3550; www.offbroadway.co.nz; 11 Alpers Ave; units $139-255;) The Off Broadway is a dandy little performer in Auckland's accommodation scene and deserves a few stage-door Johnnies singing its praises. The three small studios are a little dark but the larger studios are a great deal as they have a balcony and bathtub. Executive suites have separate bedrooms and represent very good value.

Kingsgate Hotel (Map p98; ☎ 0800 782 548, 09-377 3619; www.millenniumhotels.co.nz; 92 Gladstone Rd; r $140-199, tr $155-229;) Opposite the Parnell Rose Gardens, this large hotel has generic rooms clustered in landscaped 'Tudor' or 'Colonial' blocks (although they look the same to us), together with a restaurant, pool, spa and plenty of parking. It's popular with tour groups.

MT EDEN

Bavaria B&B (Map p100; ☎ 09-638 9641; www.bavariabandbhotel.co.nz; 83 Valley Rd; s $105-115, d $149-165;) This clean, long-running B&B in a spacious villa has been freshened up with new carpets and a coat of paint. The rooms are big and airy, and there's a decent TV lounge, dining room and deck where guests can mix and mingle.

Eden Park B&B (Map p100; ☎ 09-630 5721; www.bedandbreakfastnz.com; 22 Bellwood Ave; s $135-155, d $200-225;) If you know any rugby fans who require chandeliers in their bathrooms, send them here. The hallowed turf of Auckland's legendary rugby ground is only a block away and while the rooms aren't overly large for the prices, they mirror the Edwardian elegance of this fine wooden villa.

PONSONBY & GREY LYNN

23 Hepburn (Map p102; ☎ 09-376 0622; www.23hepburn.co.nz; 23 Hepburn St; r $185-205;) The three boutique rooms are a symphony in muted whites and creams, inducing the pleasant sensation of waking up inside an extremely chic pavlova. You can sleep in as long as you like as the continental breakfast is self-service –

left in your in-room fridge the previous evening.

our pick **Henry's** (Map p102; ☎ 09-360 2700; www.henrysonpeel.co.nz; 33 Peel St; r/apt $200/240; ☉ ☒) These beautiful wooden villas are what Auckland's inner suburbs are all about. Henry's has been stylishly renovated, adding en suites to the downstairs rooms and a self-contained harbour-view apartment above.

NORTH SHORE

Parituhu (Map p96; ☎ 09-445 6559; www.parituhu.co.nz; 3 King Edward Pde, Devonport; r $100-150) This gay-friendly accommodation consists of just one double bedroom with a private bathroom in the owners' waterfront bungalow. It's a homely, relaxing and welcoming place.

Jasmine Cottage (Map p96; ☎ 09-445 8825; www.photoalbum.co.nz/jasmine; 20 Buchanan St, Devonport; r $120) Scrupulously maintained and cute as a button, this little courtyard garden hut behind the owner's house has its own kitchenette.

Devonport Sea Cottage (Map p96; ☎ 09-445 7117; www.homestaysnz.co.nz/listings/46; 3a Cambridge Tce, Devonport; r $130) Head up the path to your own self-contained cottage, which holds everything you'll need for a relaxing stay near the sea (including a set of French doors opening onto a garden). Excellent weekly rates are on offer in winter.

Devonport Motel (Map p96; ☎ 09-445 1010; www.devonportmotel.co.nz; 11 Buchanan St, Devonport; r $130) This minimotel has just two simple units in the back garden, but they're modern, clean, self-contained and in a nice quiet location that's still close to Devonport's action (such as it may be).

Number Nine B&B (Map p96; ☎ 09-445 3059; tainui@xtra.co.nz; 9 Tainui Rd, Devonport; r $170) You'll get a warm welcome from Christine and Pari at this cosy home that has two attractive rooms for guests, one with a claw-foot tub. If you fancy a game of golf at the nearby club, you can borrow clubs here and have a round organised.

Emerald Inn (Map p88; ☎ 09-488 3500; www.emerald-inn.co.nz; 16 The Promenade, Takapuna; units $171-297, villa/cottage $450/675; ☐ ☉ ☒) No, it's not an Irish pub. This leafy complex has lush gardens, smart furnishings and the beach at the end of the road. The luxury self-contained holiday homes have views to Rangitoto.

OTHER AREAS

Nautical Nook (Map p88; ☎ 09-521 2544; www.nauticalnook.com; 23b Watene Cres, Orakei; s/d $97/157) If you're a sailing buff you'll find a kindred spirit in Keith, who runs this cosy homestay with his wife Trish. The lounge and terrace have views over the harbour, and Okahu Bay is close at hand.

Jet Park (Map p88; ☎ 09-275 4100; www.jetpark.co.nz; 63 Westney Rd, Mangere; r $135-165, ste $240-275; ☐ ☒) Friendly Jet Park has a decent vibe, even though many of its rooms follow the 'could be anywhere' design ethos that seems to be compulsory if you want to sleep near an airport. There are arrival/departure screens in the lobby and free airport shuttles. Kick back by the pool, which resembles something from an episode of *Hawaii 5-0*.

Omahu Lodge (Map p88; ☎ 09-524 5648; www.omahulodge.co.nz; 33 Omahu Rd, Remuera; s $160-200, d $195-240, ste $295; ☉ ☒) Art and family photos cover the walls at this cheerful, deluxe B&B. The three en-suite rooms in the main house all have neighbourhood views, but the spacious suite opens straight onto the enticing solar-heated pool. Free gifts of wine, beer and snacks are a nice touch.

Top End

Auckland has plenty of luxury hotels, with many of the big chains taking up inner-city real estate.

CENTRAL AUCKLAND

our pick **Hotel de Brett** (Map p92; ☎ 09-925 9000; www.hoteldebrett.com; 2 High St; r $290-590; ☐ ☉) Supremely hip, this lavishly refurbished historic hotel has been zooshed up with supercool stripey carpets and clever designer touches in every nook of the extremely comfortable rooms. Prices include breakfast, free broadband and a pre-dinner drink.

Westin (Map p92; ☎ 09-909 9000; www.westin.com/auckland; 21 Viaduct Harbour Ave; r $435-710; ☐ ☐ ☒) Auckland's Westin has outdone itself with simple, exquisite design, Maori art and sumptuous furnishings (we love the 250-thread-count sheets and goose-down pillows). There's water everywhere you look – in the form of the harbour or tinkling water features – which is very restful, as long as it doesn't induce a constant need to pee.

PONSONBY

Great Ponsonby Arthotel (Map p102; ☎ 09-376 5989; www.greatpons.co.nz; 30 Ponsonby Tce; r $235-400; ☐ ☐) Not as slick as the others in this bracket but this deceptively spacious Victorian villa has gregarious hosts, impressive sustainability practices, great breakfasts and it's located a stone's throw from cool Ponsonby Rd in a quiet cul-de-sac. Studio apartments open onto an attractive rear courtyard.

NORTH SHORE

Esplanade Hotel (Map p96; ☎ 09-445 1291; www.es planadehotel.co.nz; 1 Victoria Rd, Devonport; r $200-375, ste $350-750) This beautiful boutique hotel takes pride of place on the corner in a 1903 heritage building. It features lovingly tended period details such as supremely high ceilings, and has much more style than many of the luxury hotels in the city centre. It's perfectly located and achingly romantic, with sumptuous rooms that steadfastly refuse to fall into cookie-cutter territory when it comes to decor.

Hampton Beach House (Map p96; ☎ 09-445 1358; www.hamptonbeachhouse.co.nz; 4 King Edward Pde, Devonport; r $205-280; 🖳 🛜) One of a fine strip of waterside mansions, this upmarket, gay-friendly, Edwardian B&B has rooms with views and others opening onto the rear garden. It's all very tastefully done; expect quality linen and gourmet breakfasts.

Peace & Plenty Inn (Map p96; ☎ 09-445 2925; www. peaceandplenty.co.nz; 6 Flagstaff Tce, Devonport; s $195-265, d $265-350; 🅿 🖳) This perfectly located, wonderful five-star period house is stocked with antique furnishings and a thousand conversation pieces – the charming Judith can tell you the provenance of each and every one of them. The romantic, luxurious rooms have en suite, TV, flowers, free sherry/port and local chocolates. A delight, and truly exceptional.

REMUERA

Aachen House (Map p88; ☎ 09-520 2329; www.aachen house.co.nz; 39 Market Rd; r $390-590; 🛜) An exceptional boutique B&B, Aachen House is a grand old dame that's still looking mighty fine. The attention to painstaking detail is impressive: fresh flowers, hair turbans, shell-shaped soap and complementary port. Come breakfast time, the chef cooks up a gourmet storm.

EATING

Because of its size and ethnic diversity, Auckland tops the country when it comes to dining options and quality. Lively eateries have sprung up to cater to the numerous Asian students, offering inexpensive Japanese, Chinese and Korean staples. If you're on a budget, you'll fall in love with the city's food halls.

Aucklanders love a good coffee, so you never have to walk too far to find a decent cafe. Suburbs such as Ponsonby, Grey Lynn, Kingsland, Mt Eden, Parnell and Devonport are teeming with them. Some double as wine bars or have gourmet aspirations, while others are content to fill their counters with fresh, reasonably priced snacks.

Ponsonby attracts a hip, young crowd who come to drink and dine before heading out to party. The upmarket Princes Wharf and Viaduct Basin waterfront area is where some of the buzziest and busiest restaurants have sprung up. This area is popular with suits and tourists, and can be especially heaving on Friday and Saturday evenings. Two petite enclaves that have recently established themselves as foodie favourites are Kingsland and the West Lynn shops on Richmond Rd, Grey Lynn.

Central Auckland

MacGregor Brothers (Map p92; ☎ 09-309 9924; 17 Wellesley St; snacks $5-7; ⏱ 6.30am-3pm Mon-Fri) The wonderful internal features of this petite art-deco shopfront have survived, making this a great spot for a quality coffee and cake served on fine china.

Reslau (Map p92; ☎ 09-309 5039; 39 Elliott St; snacks $5-10; ⏱ 7am-8.30pm Mon-Sat) Spilling into the laneway, this tiny cafe-wine bar literally has a trolley-load of delicious snacks and light meals.

Ima (Map p92; ☎ 09-300 7252; 57 Fort St; breakfast $5-18, lunch $13-22, dinner $18-32; ⏱ breakfast & lunch Mon-Sat, dinner Wed-Sat) Named after the Hebrew word for mother, the menu is a harmonious blend of Israeli, Palestinian, Yemenite and Lebanese dishes. Excellent coffee, too.

Raw Power (Map p92; ☎ 09-303 3724; Level 1, 10 Vulcan Lane; mains $7-17; ⏱ 7am-4pm Mon-Fri, 11am-4pm Sat; 🅥) Vegetable-shaped salt-and-pepper shakers, superbright walls and the freshest ingredients entice punters to this upstairs eatery, popular with visiting vegetarian/vegan rock royalty. Grab a window seat if you can.

Euro (Map p92; ☎ 09-309 9866; Shed 22, Princes Wharf; mains $23-80; ⏱ lunch & dinner) Euro is a thoroughly slick package of imaginative Mod-NZ cuisine, good-looking wait staff and sexy surrounds. The harbour views aren't the greatest, but the dishes are always pretty as a picture.

O'Connell St Bistro (Map p92; ☎ 09-377 1884; 3 O'Connell St; lunch $28-32, dinner $29-45; ☻ lunch Tue-Fri, dinner Mon-Sat) Delightful O'Connell St is a grown-up treat, with elegant decor and truly wonderful food and wine, satisfying lunch-time powerbrokers and dinnertime daters. The menu leans heavily on the duck, salmon and lamb side of things.

our pick **Grove** (Map p92; ☎ 09-368 4129; St Patrick's Sq, Wyndham St; mains $32-48; ☻ lunch Mon-Fri, dinner Mon-Sat) Romantic fine dining at its best: the room is cosy and moodily lit, the menu encourages sensual experimentation and the service is effortless. If you can't find anything to break the ice from the extensive wine list, give it up mate – it's never going to happen.

Clooney (Map p92; ☎ 09-358 1702; 33 Sale St; mains $36-44; ☻ lunch Fri, dinner Mon-Sat) Like the Hollywood actor of the same name, Clooney is suave, stylish and extremely sophisticated. While the taste combinations are complex (venison with cocoa *millefeuille*, preserved cherries, black pudding and licorice jus, for example) the outcomes are faultless.

For quick eats, head to **Revive** (Map p92; ☎ 09-307 1586; 16 Fort St; mains $8-14; ☻ 11am-8pm Mon-Thu, 11am-3pm Fri; **V**), a vegetarian heaven that has an enticing salad bar and extremely economi-cal daily meal deals. Fast food that's healthy? Healthy food that's cheap and tasty? How can this be?

For authentic Asian fare, you can't beat the large, no-frills **Food Alley** (Map p92; ☎ 09-373 4917; 9 Albert St; mains $9-17; ☻ 10.30am-10pm) food court, where nearly every meal comes in under $12. Choose between Chinese, Indian, Thai, Vietnamese, Turkish, Malaysian, Korean, Japanese and Indonesian.

Newton

K Rd is known for its late-night clubs, but cafes and plenty of inexpensive ethnic restau-rants are mixed in with the fashion boutiques, tattooists and adult shops.

Rasoi (Map p92; ☎ 09-377 7780; 211 K Rd; mains $6-17; ☻ lunch & dinner Mon-Sat; **V**) Lip-smackingly good (and delightfully cheap) vegetarian thali and South Indian food can be found here, together with lassi and Indian sweets.

Alleluya (Map p92; ☎ 09-377 8424; St Kevin's Arcade, K Rd; mains $10-19; ☻ breakfast & lunch) Alleluya is a very cool little cafe-cum-bar in the city's hip-pest arcade. It has moreish cakes and lots of vegetarian options.

Satya (Map p92; ☎ 09-377 0007; 271 K Rd; mains $11-26; ☻ lunch Mon-Sat, dinner daily; **V**) Hugely popu-lar, this humble-looking and humbly priced eatery has the best *dahi puri* (an entrée of chickpea, potato and yoghurt on a pappadam) and masala dosa (a crepe filled with potato-and-onion curry) in town.

O'Sarracino (Map p92; ☎ 09-309 3740; 3 Mt Eden Rd; mains $16-38; ☻ dinner Tue-Sat) A delicious re-minder that Neapolitan cuisine offers so much more than pizza, this excellent restaurant serves generous antipasti, light and simple pasta, and delectable seafood *secondi*. The somewhat grand surroundings were once the chapel of a funeral parlour.

French Cafe (Map p92; ☎ 09-377 1911; 210 Symonds St; mains $40; ☻ lunch Fri, dinner Tue-Sat) The legen-dary French Cafe has been rated as one of Auckland's top restaurants for around 20 years now and it still continues to excel. The cuisine is (unsurprisingly) French, but chef Simon Wright manages to sneak in some Pacific Rim touches. Book well ahead if you want to snag a table.

Parnell

Kokako (Map p98; ☎ 09-366 4464; 492 Parnell Rd; mains $8-17; ☻ breakfast & lunch; **V**) Kokako offers vegetar-ian, fair trade and organic delights in a smart cafe atmosphere that won't unduly strain the bank balance – a feat nearly as rare as the native bird it's named after. There's a good selection of counter food as well as delicious cooked breakfasts.

Rosehip Cafe (Map p98; ☎ 09-369 1182; 82 Gladstone Rd; mains $13-25; ☻ 7am-4pm) The name fits: it's near the Rose Gardens and it's pretty hip. It's a tad pricey but the food's delicious, particularly the buttermilk pancakes and the Vietnamese-style squid.

Non Solo Pizza (Map p98; ☎ 09-379 5358; 259 Parnell Rd; mains $23-39; ☻ lunch & dinner) Like the name says, there's not only pizza on offer here – deli-cious though that is. NSP has a bewilderingly large menu of classic Italian antipasto, pasta and grills and a cool street-facing bar with a chandelier made of Peroni bottles. *Bellissimo*.

Newmarket

Urban Cafe (Map p98; ☎ 09-966 6977; 139 Carlton Gore Rd; mains $7-18; ☻ breakfast & lunch) Its urbanity high-lighted by an industrial aesthetic, this chic cafe serves spicy Baghdad baked eggs (with lentils and Turkish bread), daily pasta dishes and enticing sweet stuff.

Baci Lounge (Map p98; ☎ 09-529 4360; Level 1, Rialto Centre, Broadway; mains $9; ⏰ 9.30am-10.30pm) Round padded booths are nestled among the shelves at this very appealing bookshop-cafe. Devour delicious counter food (salads, paninis, fancy pies, gluten-free slices) and literary greats all at the same time.

Mt Eden

CAC Bar & Eatery (Map p100; ☎ 09-630 5790; 26 Normanby Rd; tapas $8-19; ⏰ lunch & dinner) The terrible name references the Colonial Ammunition Company, who was responsible for erecting the very sturdy bluestone walls of this stylishly renovated warehouse. Cannonballs have since given way to risotto balls and the only danger is from taste explosions emanating from the tapas menu – particularly from the 12-hour lamb.

Gala (Map p100; ☎ 09-623 1572; Zone 23, Edwin St; mains $9-20; ⏰ breakfast & lunch) Mixing modern architecture and antique silver tea services, this bright cafe brings sophistication to the prison precinct. The whiteboard menu is crammed with interesting options: try My Mother-in-law's North Indian Eggs for a fragrant version of eggs on toast.

Molten (Map p100; ☎ 09-638 7236; 422 Mt Eden Rd; mains $29-35; ⏰ lunch Tue-Sat, dinner Mon-Sat) Under the volcano's shadow, Molten oozes neighbourhood charm. The consistently excellent seasonal menu fuses Pacific Rim tastes into a delicious whole.

Merediths (Map p100; ☎ 09-623 3140; 385 Dominion Rd; mains $38, degustation $100; ⏰ lunch Thu & Fri, dinner Tue-Sat) Dining at Merediths is the culinary equivalent of black-water rafting – tastes surprise you at every turn, you never know what's coming next and you're left with a sense of breathless exhilaration. You'll need to book well in advance to secure a table for the weekend degustation-only sittings; this is one of NZ's best restaurants.

Kingsland

Fridge (Map p100; ☎ 09-845 5321; 507 New North Rd; mains $8-18; ⏰ breakfast & lunch; Ⓥ) Serves excellent coffee, gourmet pies, healthy salads and wraps, and drool-inducing cakes.

Shaky Isles (Map p100; ☎ 09-815 3591; 492 New North Rd; mains $8-19; ⏰ breakfast & lunch; 📶) Kingsland's coolest cafe has cute cartoons on the wall and free wi-fi. They do excellent breakfasts and super-food salads, but it's hard to go past 'good stuff in a bun', the good stuff being mushrooms, avocado, feta, pesto and mayonnaise.

Mekong Neua (Map p100; ☎ 09-846 0323; 483 New North Rd; mains $17-24; ⏰ dinner; Ⓥ) Plundering the cuisine of Northeast Thailand and Laos, this welcoming restaurant will fill your head with delicious fragrances and dreams of rice paddies.

Winehot (Map p100; ☎ 09-815 9463; 605 New North Rd; mains $19-26; ⏰ dinner Tue-Sat) Behind an unlikely-looking doorway, this tiny black-painted and chandelier-festooned hideaway serves up hearty French cuisine and an extensive wine list.

Tabou (Map p100; ☎ 09-846 3474; 462 New North Rd; mains $28-32; ⏰ lunch Tue-Fri, dinner Tue-Sun) Elegant and refined but informal and friendly, Tabou is the French restaurant you wish was in your neighbourhood. It doubles as a bar later in the evening.

Ponsonby

Auckland's busiest restaurant-cafe-bar strip is so damn cool it has its own website (www.ponsonbyroad.co.nz).

Dizengoff (Map p102; ☎ 09-360 0108; 256 Ponsonby Rd; mains $5-18; ⏰ 7am-5pm) This superstylish shoebox crams in a mixed crowd of corporate and fashion types, gay guys, Jewish families, Ponsonby denizens and visitors. Mouthwatering scrambled eggs, tempting counter food, heart-starting coffee, plus a great stack of reading material if you tire of eavesdropping and people-watching.

Queenie (Map p102; ☎ 09-378 8977; 24 Spring St, Freemans Bay; breakfast $7-17, lunch $12-21; ⏰ breakfast & lunch Mon-Sat) Kiwiana reigns supreme at this eccentric corner cafe with one wall devoted to a 1950s paint-by-numbers Maori maiden mural. The food is a step up from standard cafe fare, with a short, adventurous menu justifying the prices.

Landreth & Co (Map p102; ☎ 09-360 7440; 272 Ponsonby Rd; mains $12-23; ⏰ 7am-4pm) A popular brunch spot with an old-Ponsonby feel and a sunny rear courtyard. For something a bit different, try the kedgeree (kippers, rice and egg).

Prego (Map p102; ☎ 09-376 3095; 226 Ponsonby Rd; mains $22-35; ⏰ noon-midnight) This friendly and stylish Italian restaurant covers all the bases, with a fireplace in winter and a courtyard in summer. And on the subject of bases, the pizza is pretty damn fine, as are the inventive Italian mains.

Ponsonby Road Bistro (Map p102; ☎ 09-360 1611; 165 Ponsonby Rd; mains $26-34; ⏰ lunch Mon-Fri, dinner Mon-Sat) Portions are massive at this modern, upmarket restaurant with an Italian/French sensibility and first-rate service. Pick at a charcuterie platter over a glass of wine on the street tables.

SPQR (Map p102; ☎ 09-360 1710; 150 Ponsonby Rd; mains $26-40; ⏰ lunch & dinner) This ivy-covered Ponsonby Rd hot spot is well known for good Roman-style, thin, crusty pizzas and excellent Italian-influenced mains. The surrounds are a stylish blend of the industrial and the chic, the lights *low* (bring your reading glasses!), the buzz constant and the staff smooth and camp all at the same time.

Soto (Map p102; ☎ 09-360 0021; 13 St Marys Rd; mains $29-31; ⏰ lunch Tue-Fri, dinner Tue-Sat) Auckland has a surfeit of excellent Japanese restaurants but this is the best. The staff glide by in kimonos leaving a trail of exquisitely presented dishes in their wake – including sushi, sashimi and *zensai* (Japanese tapas).

For quick eats, try **Murder Burger** (Map p102; ☎ 09-550 5500; 128a Ponsonby Rd; burgers $8-17; ⏰ lunch & dinner), where there is no gilding the lily: the staff wear Meat Is Murder T-shirts, the logo features a diabolically carnivorous-looking kitty and the burgers are full of free-range, organic dead stuff: eye fillet, Angus sirloin, chicken, wild boar, venison, ostrich and fish.

The city's best food hall is **Ponsonby Village Food Court** (Map p102; 106 Ponsonby Rd; mains $8-18; ⏰ 10am-10pm; Ⓥ). Choose between Italian, Japanese, Malaysian, Chinese, Turkish, Thai, Lao, Indian, Mexican and the best Vietnamese in the central city.

Grey Lynn

Richmond Road Cafe (Map p102; ☎ 09-360 5559; 318 Richmond Rd; mains $13-29; ⏰ 7am-4pm) Auckland's current 'it' cafe, and with good reason. The service is impeccable and the menu is full of well-priced and interesting cafe fare. If it doesn't have a cardamom-cream or lavender-syrup twist it's too boring for this place. Try the spiced banana and rum porridge with fresh coconut.

Delicious (Map p102; ☎ 09-360 7590; 472 Richmond Rd; mains $26-29; ⏰ lunch Wed-Fri, dinner Tue-Sat) The name doesn't lie. Foodies flock to this neighbourhood eatery for simple but first-rate pasta at reasonable prices. They don't take bookings so expect to wait – it's always busy.

North Shore

Stone Oven (Map p96; ☎ 09-445 3185; 5 Clarence St, Devonport; mains $5-19; ⏰ 6.30am-4.30pm; 🖵) On weekends you'll want to get in early or get ready to queue for the breads, pastries, cakes and baked goods. Perfect for scoffing *in situ*, or away from the madding crowd.

Takapuna Beach Cafe (Map p88; ☎ 09-484 0002; The Promenade, Takapuna; mains $13-25; ⏰ 7am-6pm) With a menu that reads like a travel magazine (Moroccan eggs, Tunisian eggplant, French-style terrine, chorizo, pancetta…) and absolute beach views, it's no wonder this modern cafe is constantly buzzing. If you can't snaffle a table you can always grab an award-winning ice cream or snack from the attached shop.

Engine Room (Map p88; ☎ 09-480 9502; 115 Queen St, Northcote; meals $31-34; ⏰ dinner Tue-Sat) A strong contender for Auckland's best restaurant, this informal eatery serves up lighter-than-air goat's cheese soufflés, inventive whiteboard mains and oh-my-God chocolate truffles. It's worth booking ahead and catching the ferry.

Eight.Two (Map p88; ☎ 09-419 9082; 82 Hinemoa St, Birkenhead; mains $35-37; ⏰ dinner Tue-Sat) Hollowed out of an old villa, this dazzlingly white dining room offers a similarly modern menu and a great wine list. Catch the Birkenhead ferry from the city for a memorable night out.

Self-catering

You'll find large supermarkets (Countdown, Foodtown, New World, Pak N Save, Woolworths) in most neighbourhoods. As well as the places listed here, self-caterers should consider the Otara Market and Avondale Sunday Market for cheap, fresh vegetables; see p118.

No self-respecting city with a position like this should be without a fish market. **Auckland Fish Market** (Map p92; ☎ 09-379 1490; www.auckland fishmarket.co.nz; cnr Jellicoe & Daldy Sts; ⏰ 7am-6.30pm) not only has a boisterous early-morning auction, but also a market, eateries and a seafood-cooking school.

City Farmers Market (Map p92; ☎ 09-232 7933; www. cityfarmersmarket.co.nz; cnr Gore & Galway Sts; ⏰ 8.30am-12.30pm Sat) stocks fresh seasonal produce and fancy treats.

our pick La Cigale (Map p98; ☎ 09-366 9361; 69 St Georges Bay Rd; ⏰ market 8am-1pm Sat, 9am-2pm Sun) caters to Francophiles and homesick Gauls, stocking all manner of French produce (wine, cheese, tinned snails etc), and the in-house cafe (mains $7.50 to $17.50) serves delicious

---

PASIFIKA

There are nearly 180,000 Pacific Islanders (PI) living in Auckland, making it the world's principal Polynesian city. Samoans are by far the largest group, followed by Cook Islanders, Tongans, Niueans, Fijians, Tokelauans and Tuvaluans. The biggest PI communities can be found in South Auckland and pockets of West and Central Auckland.

Like the Maori renaissance of recent decades, Pasifika has become a hot commodity for Auckland hipsters. You'll find PI motifs everywhere: in art, architecture, fashion, homewares and especially in music. Movies *Sione's Wedding* and *No. 2* have put PI Auckland on the big screen, while *bro'Town* is NZ's answer to *South Park*. Ironically, as Pakeha Aucklanders look to the Pacific, PI teenagers turn to Black America for inspiration. Hip-hop culture is massive in Auckland, with home-grown rap at an all-time high.

The annual Pasifika Festival (p105) is one of the city's best events. Thousands descend on Western Springs Park to load up on island food, hang out in the sun and catch cultural performances. If you miss it, you can get a taste of the Pacific vibe at the Otara and Avondale markets (p118) or at any hip-hop night in the city's clubs. Check out Pauanesia (p118) for interesting gifts and art.

---

delicatessen platters ($18). Yet it's during the weekend farmers markets that this *cigale* (cicada) really chirps. Lose yourself among stalls laden with produce, home-made jam, honey and all manner of tasty snacks.

Auckland's legendary organics store **Harvest Wholefoods** (Map p102; ☎ 09-376 3107; 405 Richmond Rd; ☺ 9am-7pm Mon-Fri, 9am-5pm Sat, 10am-5pm Sun; Ⓥ), stocks planet-friendly fresh produce, grocery items and cosmetics. It's a meat-free zone, but there's an organic butchery across the road.

DRINKING

Auckland's nightlife tends to be quiet during the week and positively funereal on Sunday, but wakes up late on Friday and Saturday, when most pubs and bars are open until 1am or later. If in doubt head to Ponsonby, K Rd or the bottom end of the city.

Central Auckland

Agents & Merchants/Racket (Map p92; ☎ 09-309 5852; 46-50 Customs St) Tucked into their own covered laneway with an outdoor fireplace and sofas, this duo conjures an old-world yet thoroughly modern atmosphere. A&M serves excellent tapas and wine while Racket kicks off a little later with DJs on duty.

Bluestone Room (Map p92; ☎ 09-302 0930; 9 Durham Lane; ☺ 11am-late Mon-Fri, 4pm-late Sat) There's no shortage of character in this 1861 stone building, secreted down a dingy alley in the old part of town (a glassed-over well in the floor dates to 1841). The Rolling Stones played here in the '60s and live blues and rock are still a feature on the weekends.

Chambers Bar (Map p92; ☎ 09-309 8151; 6 O'Connell St; ☺ 4pm-late Tue-Sat) Sneak down the stairs to a glamorous world of sparkling chandeliers, leather couches and artful cocktails.

Hotel de Brett (Map p92; ☎ 09-925 9000; 2 High St; ☺ noon-late) Grab a cocktail in the chic art-deco Housebar or nab a spot by the fire in the Atrium, an interesting covered space fashioned from the alleyway between the old buildings.

Lenin Bar (Map p92; ☎ 09-377 0040; Princes Wharf; ☺ 3pm-late) This Russian-themed affair boasts numerous vodkas and DJs from Thursday to Saturday. A window looks into Minus 5° Bar, giving you a glimpse of the icy world without the chills (or prices).

Minus 5° Bar (Map p92; ☎ 09-377 6702; Princes Wharf; before/after 6pm $25/30; ☺ noon-1am Sun-Wed, noon-2am Thu-Sat) Everything from the seats to your glass is made of ice. Put on special clothing (including gloves and shoes) and sip a complimentary vodka-based cocktail. You can only stay inside the shimmering ice world for 30 minutes, making it a quick way to blow your cold hard cash.

Mo's (Map p92; ☎ 09-366 6066; cnr Wolfe & Federal Sts; ☺ 4pm-3am Mon-Fri, 8pm-3am Sat) There's something about this tiny corner bar that makes you want to invent problems just so the bar-person can solve them with soothing words and an expertly poured martini.

Northern Steamship Co. (Map p92; ☎ 09-374 3952; 122 Quay St) Standard lamps hang upside-down from the ceiling while the bar mural dreams of NZ summer holidays in this cool big pub by the train station.

Occidental Belgian Beer Cafe (Map p92; ☎ 09-300 6226; 6 Vulcan Lane; ✆ 7am-late Mon-Fri, 9am-late Sat & Sun) Belgian beer, Belgian food (plenty of *moules* and *frites* – mussels and chips) and live music are on offer at this historic (1870) pub.

Pasha (Map p92; ☎ 09-355 0077; Princes Wharf; ✆ 4pm-late) Awesome cocktails and Moorish exoticism combine in this impressive Viaduct bar.

Shakespeare (Map p92; ☎ 09-373 5396; 61 Albert St; ✆ 24hr) An old-fashioned corner pub with a sunny terrace and an in-house microbrewery.

Newton

Galbraith's Alehouse (Map p92; ☎ 09-379 3557; 2 Mt Eden Rd; ✆ noon-11pm Mon-Sat, noon-10pm Sun) Brewing up real ales and lagers on-site, this English-style pub offers bliss on tap. The backdoor beer garden trumps the brightly lit bar.

Wine Cellar (Map p92; ☎ 09-337 8293; St Kevin's Arcade, K Rd; ✆ 5pm-midnight Mon-Thu, 5pm-2am Fri & Sat) Secreted down some stairs in an arcade, this is the kind of bar that Buffy the Vampire Slayer would have hung out in on Auckland-based assignments. It's dark, grungy and very cool, with regular live music in the neighbouring Whammy Bar.

Kingsland

Neighbourhood Brewbar (Map p100; ☎ 09-529 9178; 498 New North Rd; ✆ 11am-late Mon-Fri, noon-late Sat & Sun) With picture windows overlooking Eden Park and a front terrace that's already pick-up central after dark, this upmarket pub is guaranteed to be the place-to-be during the Rugby World Cup.

Ponsonby & Grey Lynn

Along Ponsonby Rd, the line between cafe, restaurant, bar and club gets blurred. A lot of food places also have live music or become clubs later on.

Gypsy Tea Room (Map p102; ☎ 09-361 6970; 455 Richmond Rd; ✆ 4-11.30pm Sun-Thu, 3pm-2am Fri & Sat) No one comes here for tea. This cute wine/cocktail bar has dishevelled charm in bucketloads.

Dida's Wine Lounge & Tapas Bar (Map p102; ☎ 09-376 2813; 54 Jervois Rd; ✆ 11am-late) Great food and an even better wine list attract a grown-up crowd. Easy, cougar.

Ponsonby Social Club (Map p102; ☎ 09-361 2320; 152 Ponsonby Rd; ✆ 5pm-late) Half-and-half alleyway and bar, the back end of this long, narrow

space heaves on the weekends when the DJs crank out classic funk and hip-hop.

ENTERTAINMENT

The *NZ Herald* has an in-depth run-down of the coming week's happenings in its *Time Out* magazine on Thursday and again in its Saturday edition. If you're planning a big night along K Rd, then visit www.kroad.co.nz for a detailed list of bars and clubs.

Tickets for most major events can be bought from:

Ticketek (☎ 09-307 5000; www.ticketek.co.nz) Outlets include Aotea Centre and SkyCity Atrium.

Ticketmaster (☎ 09-970 9700; www.ticketmaster. co.nz) Outlets at Real Groovy (p118), Vector Arena (p124) and Britomart station.

Live Music

Dogs Bollix (Map p92; ☎ 09-376 4600; www.dogsbollix .co.nz; cnr K & Newton Rds) This Irish pub is a live-music venue from Tuesday to Sunday but doesn't only play Irish music. Spot local musos here when they're off-duty.

Thirsty Dog (Map p92; ☎ 09-377 9190; www.thirsty dog.co.nz; 469 K Rd; ✆ 11am-late) This Dog's both thirsty and noisy, with a decent sound system and a regular roster of local bands.

Kings Arms Tavern (Map p92; ☎ 09-373 3240; www. kingsarms.co.nz; 59 France St; ✆ 11am-late) One of Auckland's leading small venues for live (and local) rock bands, which play most nights. A rite of passage if you want to get into the local scene.

AN AUCKLAND PLAYLIST

Download these Auckland songs to your MP3 player for cruising the city's streets:

- *Chains* – Che Fu and DLT
- *Kare Kare* – Crowded House
- *Hopetoun Bridge* – Dave Dobbyn
- *Andy* – The Front Lawn
- *Auckland CBD Part Two* – Lawrence Arabia
- *Dominion Rd* – The Mutton Birds
- *A Brief Reflection* – Nesian Mystik
- *We Are the OMC* – Otara Millionaires Club
- *Haul Away* – Split Enz
- *One Tree Hill* – U2

Windsor Castle & Juice Bar (Map p98; ☎ 09-356 3650; www.thewindsor.co.nz; 144 Parnell Rd) Established in 1847, this once grungy boozer was at the heart of Auckland's pub-rock scene of the 1970s and '80s. In 2009 it reopened its doors, completely zooshed up, but committed to re-establishing itself as the city's pre-eminent live rock pub.

For big international and major local bands, the main venues in Auckland include the following:

Mt Smart Stadium & Supertop (Map p88; ☎ 09-571 1603; www.mtsmartstadium.co.nz; Maurice Rd, Penrose)

North Shore Events Centre (Map p88; ☎ 09-443 8199; www.nseventscenter.zes.zeald.com; Argus Pl, Glenfield)

Vector Arena (Map p92; ☎ 09-358 1250; www.vectorarena.co.nz; Mahuhu Cres, City)

Western Springs Stadium (Map p88; ☎ 09-849 3807; Great North Rd, Western Springs)

Nightclubs

The Viaduct and K Rd are the main places to find late-night clubs, but there are also a few around Fort St and Ponsonby Rd. Some clubs have a cover charge, depending on the night and the event.

Cassette Number Nine (Map p92; ☎ 09-366 0196; www.cassettenine.com; 9 Vulcan Lane; entry Fri & Sat $10; ☙ 5pm-late) Auckland's most out-there hipsters gravitate to this eccentric bar/club where swishy nouvelle New Romantic clones rub shoulders with girls in very short dresses and the music ranges from live indie to international DJ sets.

Ink & Coherent (Map p92; ☎ 09-358 5103; www.inkcoherent.co.nz; 268 & 262 K Rd; entry free–$45) Neighbouring clubs for serious dance aficionados, sometimes hosting big name DJs.

Rising Sun & 4:20 (Map p92; ☎ 09-358 5643; www.420.co.nz; 373 K Rd) Downstairs is a straight-out nightclub hosting different nights (particularly hip-hop, but also electro, crunk, reggaetron etc), while upstairs is a large room with a view and another small dance floor.

Khuja Lounge (Map p92; ☎ 09-377 3711; 536 Queen St; ☙ 8pm-3am Wed-Sat) Above the Westpac building, this laid-back venue offers DJs and jazz/soul/hip-hop bands.

Boogie Wonderland (Map p92; ☎ 09-361 6093; www.boogiewonderland.co.nz; cnr Galway & Queen Sts; ☙ 9pm-late Thu-Sat) As trashy and fun as it sounds, the disco never ended in this basement club that's popular with women of a certain age.

Sport

Eden Park (Map p100; ☎ 09-815 5551; www.edenpark.co.nz; Reimers Ave, Kingsland) This is the stadium for top rugby (winter) and cricket (summer) matches, and at the time of research it was well in the throes of its Rugby World Cup 2011 makeover. The All Blacks, the Black Caps and the Auckland Blues all play here. To get there, take the train from Britomart to Kingsland station.

Mt Smart Stadium Hosts soccer, rugby league (Warriors) and *really* big-name concerts (see left).

ASB Tennis Centre (Map p92; ☎ 09-373 3623; 72 Stanley St) In January the women's ASB Classic is followed by the men's Heineken Open. Some famous tennis names show up to battle it out at this venue.

Theatre, Classical Music & Comedy

Aotea Sq and the buildings that surround it comprise Auckland's main arts and entertainment complex, branded the **Edge** (☎ 09-357 3355; www.the-edge.co.nz), comprising the Town Hall, Civic Theatre and Aotea Centre.

Auckland Town Hall (Map p92; 305 Queen St) This elegant Edwardian venue (1911) hosts concert performances by the likes of the NZ Symphony Orchestra (www.nzso.co.nz) and Auckland Philharmonia (www.apo.co.nz).

Aotea Centre (Map p92; 50 Mayoral Dr) Auckland's main venue for theatre, dance, ballet and opera, with two main stages: the cavernous ASB Auditorium and the tiny Herald Theatre. Auckland Theatre Company (www.atc.co.nz), Silo Theatre (www.silotheatre.co.nz) and NZ Opera (www.nzopera.com) all regularly perform here.

Civic Theatre (Map p92; cnr Queen & Wellesley Sts) This restored grand dame of a theatre (p99) is used by major touring productions, including opera, musicals and live theatre, as well as by the Auckland International Film Festival (p421).

Classic Comedy Club (Map p92; ☎ 09-373 4321; www.comedy.co.nz; 321 Queen St; tickets $5-27) Auckland's top venue for comedy, with performances most nights. There are late shows on Friday and Saturday.

Other theatres:

Maidment Theatre (Map p92; ☎ 09-308 2383; www.maidment.auckland.ac.nz; Auckland University, 8 Alfred St)

SkyCity Theatre (Map p92; ☎ 09-363 6000; www.skycity.co.nz; cnr Victoria & Federal Sts)

GAY & LESBIAN AUCKLAND

One of Auckland's nicknames is the Queen City, so it's fitting that it has the country's biggest gay population. While the bright lights attract gays and lesbians from all over the country, the even brighter lights of Sydney eventually steal many of the 30- to 40-somethings, leaving a gap in the demographic. There are a handful of gay venues, but they're not as buzzy as you might expect.

To find out what's going on, grab a copy of the fortnightly newspaper *Express* (available from gay venues) or log on to www.gaynz.com. The big events on the calendar are the Big Gay Out (p422), Out Takes film festival (p105) and Queen of the Whole Universe (p105).

Venues change with alarming regularity, but these ones, along with straight-friendly SPQR (113), are the stayers:

- **Family** (Map p92; ☎ 09-309 0213; www.familybar.co.nz; 270 K Rd) Trashy, brash and young, but this bar can be a lot of fun.

- **Naval & Family** (Map p92; ☎ 09-373 3409; cnr K Rd & Pitt St) Family's sister bar, directly across the road, has more of a pub feel.

- **Urge** (Map p92; ☎ 09-307 2155; www.urgebar.co.nz; 490 K Rd; ☷ 9pm-late Thu-Sat) Older and hairier than Family, this is the country's longest-running gay bar, with DJs Friday and Saturday nights, raunchy parties and lots of cruising.

- **Dot's** (Map p92; ☎ 09-379 7335; www.dotsbar.com; 223 Symonds St; ☷ 3pm-late Tue-Sun) Camp as they come, with drag shows every Friday and Saturday.

- **Centurian** (Map p92; ☎ 09-377 5571; 18 Beresford St; admission before/after 3pm $21/26; ☷ noon-2am Sun-Thu, 11am-6am Fri & Sat) Gay men's sauna.

Cinemas

Most cinemas offer cheaper rates on weekdays before 5pm; Tuesday is usually bargain day.

SkyCity Queen St (Map p92; ☎ 09-979 2401; www.skycitycinemas.co.nz; Level 3, 291 Queen St; adult $10-15.50, child $8-9.50) Part of SkyCity Metro, a modernistic mall that includes Borders bookshop, bars and a food court.

Academy Cinemas (Map p92; ☎ 09-373 2761; www.academycinemas.co.nz; 44 Lorne St; adult/concession $15/11) In the basement of the Central City Library is the Academy, which shows independent foreign and art-house films.

Rialto Cinemas (Map p98; ☎ 09-529 2218; www.rialto.co.nz; 167 Broadway, Newmarket; adult $10-16, child $8-10) Screens art-house and international, plus some mainstream fare.

NZ Film Archives (Map p92; ☎ 09-379 0688; www.filmarchive.org.nz; 300 K Rd; ☷ 11am-5pm Mon-Fri, 11am-4pm Sat) A wonderful resource of more than 1000 Kiwi feature films and documentaries dating from 1905, which you can watch for free on a TV screen. See p21 for some recommended Kiwi feature films.

SHOPPING

Followers of fashion should head to High St, Chancery Lane, Newmarket, Ponsonby Rd and K Rd. An official All Black rugby shirt costs around $180. The central city area (especially Queen St) has lots of stores selling outdoor clothes and equipment.

Clothing & Accessories

Karen Walker City (Map p92; ☎ 09-309 6299; 15 O'Connell St); Newmarket (Map p98; ☎ 09-522 4286; 6 Balm St); Ponsonby (Map p102; ☎ 09-361 6723; 171 Ponsonby Rd) Join Madonna and Björk in wearing Walker's cool (but pricey) threads.

Marvel (Map p102; ☎ 09-376 4204; 143 Ponsonby Rd) Smart, tailored shirts and trousers in interesting fabrics and quirky partywear are the mainstays of this excellent local menswear designer.

Royal Jewellery Studio (Map p100; ☎ 09-846 0200; 486 New North Rd) Displaying interesting work by local artisans, including some beautiful Maori designs, this is a great place to pick up authentic *pounamu* (greenstone) jewellery.

Zambesi City (Map p92; ☎ 09-303 1701; cnr Vulcan Lane & O'Connell St); Newmarket (Map p98; ☎ 09-523 1000; 38 Osborne St); Ponsonby (Map p102; ☎ 09-360 7391; 169 Ponsonby Rd) Hands-down, the most interesting and influential fashion label to come out of the country, and much sought after by local and international celebs.

Gifts & Souvenirs

Pauanesia (Map p92; ☎ 09-366 7782; 35 High St) A colourful treasure-trove of Polynesian craft and gifts.

Native Agent (Map p100; ☎ 09-845 3289; 507b New North Rd) There's a strong Maori bent to the jewellery, clothing and knick-knacks on offer here, and it's all NZ-made.

O'Kai Oceanikart (Map p92; ☎ 09-379 9051; 65 K Rd) Pan-Pacific art, from well-known artists like Fatu Feu'u to exciting up-and-comers.

Markets

Otara Market (Map p88; ☎ 09-274 0830; Newbury St; ☒ 6am-noon Sat) Held in the car park between the Manukau Polytech and the Otara town centre, this market has a real Polynesian atmosphere, and you can buy South Pacific food, music and fashions. Take bus 497 from Britomart ($5.40, 50 minutes).

Avondale Sunday Market (Map p88; ☎ 09-818 4931; Avondale Racecourse, Ash St; ☒ 6am-noon Sun) A similar vibe to the Otara Market; take the train to Avondale station.

Music

Real Groovy (Map p92; ☎ 09-302 3940; 438 Queen St) A music-lovers' nirvana, this huge store has masses of new, second-hand and rare releases, as well as concert tickets, giant posters, DVDs, books, magazines and clothing.

GETTING THERE & AWAY
Air

Auckland International Airport (Map p88; ☎ 09-275 0789; www.auckland-airport.co.nz) is 21km south of the city centre. It has an international terminal and a domestic terminal, each with a tourist information centre. A free shuttle service operates every 20 minutes (6am to 10.30pm) between the terminals and there's also a signposted footpath (about a 1km walk).

At the international terminal there's a free phone for accommodation bookings. Both terminals have left-luggage facilities, ATMs and car-rental desks, although you get better rates from companies in town.

Auckland is the major gateway to NZ, and a hub for domestic flights. See p432 for information on international flights.

Domestic airlines operating to and from Auckland and the destinations they serve:

Air New Zealand (Map p92; ☎ 09-336 2400; www. airnewzealand.co.nz; cnr Customs & Queen Sts) Kaitaia, Kerikeri, Whangarei, Hamilton, Tauranga, Whakatane, Gis-

---

> ### PLANE DELAYED? TIME FOR A TIPPLE!
>
> Clearly the roar of jets doesn't bother grapes, as NZ's most awarded winery is just 4km from the airport. The parklike grounds of **Villa Maria Estate** (Map p88; ☎ 09-255 0666; 118 Montgomerie Rd; ☒ 9am-6pm Mon-Fri, 10am-5pm Sat & Sun) are a green oasis in the encircling industrial zone. Short tours ($5) take place at 11am and 3pm. There's a charge for tastings ($5), but lingering over wine and antipasto on the terrace sure beats hanging around the departure lounge.

---

borne, Rotorua, Taupo, New Plymouth, Napier, Whanganui, Palmerston North, Masterton, Wellington, Nelson, Blenheim, Christchurch, Queenstown and Dunedin.

Fly My Sky (☎ 09-256 7025; www.flymysky.co.nz) Great Barrier Island.

Great Barrier Airlines (☎ 09-275 9120; www. greatbarrierairlines.co.nz) Great Barrier Island.

Jetstar (☎ 0800 800 995; www.jetstar.com) Wellington, Christchurch and Queenstown.

Pacific Blue (☎ 0800 670 000; www.pacificblue.co.nz) Wellington, Christchurch, Queenstown and Dunedin.

Bus

The main long-distance bus company in Auckland, as for the rest of NZ, is **InterCity** (☎ 09-583 5780; www.intercity.co.nz) and its travel and sightseeing arm **Newmans Coach Lines** (www. newmanscoach.co.nz). Its buses go to almost all bigger towns and the main tourist areas. Services leave from the **SkyCity Coach Terminal** (Map p92; ☎ 09-913 6220; 102 Hobson St).

Naked Bus (www.nakedbus.com) buses travel along SH1 as far as Paihia (four hours) and Wellington (12 hours), as well as heading to Waitomo Caves (3¾ hours) Whitianga (3¾ hours), Tauranga (3½ hours), Gisborne (nine hours) and Napier (12 hours). Fares start from $1. **Dalroy Express** (☎ 0508 465 622; www.dalroytours.co.nz) operates a daily service between Auckland and New Plymouth ($59, 5½ hours). **Main Coachline** (☎ 09-278 8070; www.main coachline.co.nz) runs six buses per week between Auckland and Dargaville ($48, three hours). All of these buses stop on Quay St, opposite the Ferry Building (Map p92).

Go Kiwi (☎ 07-866 0336; www.go-kiwi.co.nz) has daily door-to-door shuttle services to/from Auckland, Thames and Whitianga along with seasonal services to Tauranga and Rotorua.

Car
HIRING A CAR
Auckland has countless car-hire operators and is the best city in which to hire (or buy) a vehicle for touring NZ or the city itself. Some good deals can be had for long-term hire, but be warned that cheapest is not necessarily the best.

A swag of car-rental companies can be found conveniently grouped together along Beach Rd and Stanley St close to the city centre. The major companies (Avis, Budget, Hertz and Thrifty) are reliable, offer full insurance and have offices at the airport and all over the country. They are more expensive, but rates are often negotiable for longer hires or off-season.

If you are prepared to take limited insurance and risk losing an excess of around $750, then the cheaper operators offer some pretty good deals. Prices vary with the season, the age of the car and length of hire. Ignore prices quoted in brochures and shop around by phone. Always read the hire agreement thoroughly before you sign.

Some of the more reputable car-hire companies (which may also hire out sleeper vans and campervans):

A2B (Map p92; ☎ 0800 222 929, 09-377 0824; www.a2b-car-rental.co.nz; 11 Stanley St) Cheap older cars with no visible hire-car branding, making them less of a thief-magnet.

Britz (Map p88; ☎ 0800 831 900, 09-275 9090; www.britz.co.nz; 36 Richard Pearse Dr, Mangere)

Budget (Map p92; ☎ 0800 283 438, 09-529 7788; www.budget.co.nz; 163 Beach Rd)

Escape (Map p92; ☎ 0800 216 171, 021 288 8372; www.escaperentals.co.nz; 7 Gore St) Eccentrically painted campervans.

Explore More (Map p88; ☎ 0800 447 363, 09-255 0620; www.exploremore.co.nz; 36 Richard Pearse Dr, Mangere)

Go Rentals (Map p88; ☎ 0508 246 684, 09-525 7321; www.gorentals.co.nz; 688 Great South Rd, Penrose)

Hertz (Map p92; ☎ 0800 654 321, 09-367 6350; www.hertz.co.nz; 154 Victoria St)

Jucy (Map p92; ☎ 0800 399 736, 09-374 4360; www.jucy.co.nz; 2-16 The Strand)

Maui (Map p88; ☎ 0800 651 080, 09-255 3910; www.maui.co.nz; 36 Richard Pearse Dr, Mangere)

Omega (Map p92; ☎ 0800 525 210, 09-377 5573; www.omegarentals.com; 75 Beach Rd)

Thrifty (Map p92; ☎ 0800 737 070, 09-309 0111; www.thrifty.co.nz; 150 Khyber Pass Rd)

BUYING A CAR
For stays of two months or more, many people look at buying a car. You can buy through dealers on the buy-back scheme, at car fairs or auctions, or through ads at backpacker hostels. Before buying a car you must check that it is mechanically sound, has not been stolen, and does not have money owing on it to a finance company or bank.

Buy-backs, where the dealer agrees to buy back your car for an agreed price (often 50% of what you pay), are not a good deal, but offer a safety net if you have trouble selling the car.

A popular way to buy a car is at the car fairs where people bring their own cars to sell them. Arrive between 8.30am and 9.30am for the best choice; car fairs are over by about noon. For a credit check quote chassis and licence-plate numbers. Mechanical inspection services, credit agencies and Auto Check details are on hand at the following car fairs:

Auckland Car Fair (Map p88; ☎ 09-529 2233; www.carfair.co.nz; Ellerslie Racecourse, Green Lane East; ☉ 9am-noon Sun) It's the largest car fair and it costs $30 to display your vehicle.

City Car Fair (Map p92; ☎ 09-837 7817; cnr Halsey & Gaunt Sts; ☉ 9am-1pm Sat) It costs $20 to display your car.

Motorcycle
NZ Motorcycle Rentals (Map p88; ☎ 09-486 2472; www.nzbike.com; 72 Barrys Point Rd, Takapuna) offers motorbike hire for $105 to $400 a day (insurance excess is $1500 and upwards). Guided tours are also available.

Train
Overlander (☎ 0800 872 467; www.tranzscenic.co.nz) trains arrive at and depart from **Britomart station** (Map p92; Queen St), the largest underground diesel train station in the world. They depart from Auckland at 7.25am (daily late September to April, Friday to Sunday otherwise) and arrive in Wellington at 7.25pm (the return train from Wellington departs and arrives at the same time). Useful stops include Hamilton (2½ hours), Otorohanga (three hours), Te Kuiti (3¼ hours), Taumarunui (4½ hours), National Park (5½ hours), Ohakune (6½ hours), Palmerston North (9½ hours) and Paraparaumu (11 hours). A standard fare to Wellington is $118, but a limited number of *Go Anywhere* discounted seats are available for each journey at $49, $69 and $89 (first-in, first-served).

GETTING AROUND

To/From the Airport

The **Airbus Express** (☎ 09-366 6400; www.airbus. co.nz; one way/return adult $16/23, backpacker $14/21, child $6/12) runs every 15 minutes from 7am to 7.30pm and every 30 minutes from 7.30pm to 7am, between the terminals and the city. Stops include Mt Eden Rd (as requested), Symonds St, Queen St and the Ferry Terminal. Reservations are not required and you buy a ticket from the driver. The trip takes less than an hour each way (longer during rush hour).

The convenient door-to-door **Super Shuttle** (☎ 0800 748 885; www.supershuttle.co.nz) will charge about $25 for one person heading between the airport and a city hotel. You'll save money per head if there's a group of you. The price increases if you want to go to an outlying suburb.

A taxi between the airport and the city costs around $70.

Bicycle

Adventure Cycles (Map p88; ☎ 09-940 2453; www.adventure -auckland.co.nz/adventurecycles; 9 Premier Ave, Western Springs; hire per day $20-40, per week $90-150, per month $200-300; ◷ 7.30am-7pm Thu-Mon) hires out road, mountain and long-term touring bikes, runs a buy-back scheme and does repairs.

Maxx Regional Transport (☎ 09-366 6400; www. maxx.co.nz) publishes free cycle maps, available from public buildings such as stations, libraries and i-SITEs. Bikes can be taken on ferries (free) and trains ($1), but only folding bikes are allowed on buses.

Boat

Fullers and 360 Discovery both run ferries from Quay St in the city. See p101 for destinations.

Car & Motorcycle

Auckland's motorways jam up badly at peak times, particularly the Northern and Southern. It's best to avoid them between 7am and 9am, and from 5pm to 7pm. Things also get tight around 3pm during term time, which is the end of the school day.

Expect to pay for parking in central Auckland during the day, from Monday to Saturday. Most parking meters (from $1 an hour) are pay-and-display; follow the instructions, collect your ticket and display it inside your windscreen. You usually don't have to pay between 6pm and 8am or on Sunday – check the meters and parking signs carefully.

Prices can be steep at parking buildings. Better value are the council-run open-air parks near the train station, Beach Rd ($7 per day) and on Ngaoho Pl, off The Strand ($5 per day).

Public Transport

Due to rampant privatisation during the 1980s, Auckland's public transport system is run by a hodgepodge of different operators, none of which seem to co-operate. As a result there are few integrated public transport passes. The Auckland Regional Council is trying to sort out the mess and runs the excellent **Maxx** (☎ 09-366 6400; www.maxx.co.nz) information service, covering buses, trains and ferries. The website has an excellent trip-planning feature.

BUS

Bus routes spread their tentacles throughout the city. Many services terminate around Britomart station (Map p92). Bus stops often have electronic displays, giving an estimate of waiting times. Be warned: they lie.

Single-ride fares in the inner city are 50c for an adult and 30c for a child (you pay the driver when you board), but if you're travelling further afield there are fare stages from $1.60/1 (adult/child) to $9.70/5.80. A one-day pass (which includes the North Shore ferries) costs $11, while a weekly pass costs $45 ($40 from an agent) – there's no reduction for children.

The environmentally friendly Link Bus ($1.60, every 10 to 15 minutes, 6am to 11.30pm) is a very handy service that travels clockwise and anticlockwise around a loop that includes Queen St, SkyCity, Victoria Park Market, Ponsonby Rd, K Rd, Newmarket, Parnell and Britomart station.

The red City Circuit bus (every 10 minutes, 8am to 6pm) provides free transport around the inner city from Britomart station, up Queen St, past Albert Park to Auckland University, across to the Sky Tower and back to Britomart.

TRAIN

Auckland's train service is excellent but a bit limited. Trains are generally clean, cheap and (usually) on time – although any hiccup on the lines can bring down the entire network. You will need to refer to a timetable, as they aren't particularly frequent.

Impressive Britomart station (Map p92) has food retailers, foreign-exchange facilities and a ticket office. Downstairs are plush toilets and left-luggage lockers.

There are just three train routes: one runs west to Waitakere, while two run south to Pukekohe. Services are at least hourly and run from around 6am to 8pm (later on the weekends). A $13 Discovery Pass allows a day's travel on most bus, train and North Shore ferry services. Otherwise, pay the conductor on the train (one stage $1.40); they'll come to you. All trains have wheel-chair ramps.

Taxi

Auckland's many taxis usually operate from ranks, but they also cruise popular areas. **Auckland Co-op Taxis** (☎ 09-300 3000) is one of the biggest companies. Flagfall is $3, then it's $2.40 to $2.60 per kilometre. There's a sur-charge for transport to and from the airport and cruise ships.

HAURAKI GULF ISLANDS

The Hauraki Gulf, stretching between Auckland and the Coromandel Peninsula, is dotted with *motu* (islands) and gives the Bay of Islands some rather stiff competition in the beauty stakes. Some are only min-utes from the city and make excellent day trips: wine-soaked Waiheke and volcanic Rangitoto really shouldn't be missed. Great Barrier requires more effort (and cash) to get to, but provides an idyllic escape from modern life.

There are 47 islands in the Hauraki Gulf Maritime Park, administered by DOC. Some are good-sized islands, others are no more than rocks jutting out of the sea. They're loosely put into two categories: recreation and conservation. The recreation islands can easily be visited and their harbours are dotted with yachts in summer. The conservation islands, however, have restricted access. Permits are required to visit some, while others are closed refuges for the preservation of rare plants and animals, especially birds.

The gulf is a busy highway for marine mammals. Sei, minke and Bryde's whales are regularly seen in its outer reaches, along with orcas and bottlenose dolphins. You might even spy a passing humpback.

Information

The DOC information centre (p90) and the New Zealand i-SITE (p90), both on the Auckland waterfront, are good sources of information, maps and walking pamphlets.

Getting There & Around

Most island ferries leave from the Auckland waterfront, but some depart from Devonport, Half Moon Bay (East Auckland), Gulf Harbour (Whangaparaoa Peninsula) and Sandspit (near Warkworth). If you miss the last ferry, **Auckland Water Taxis** (☎ 0800 890 007; www.watertaxis.co.nz) operates a 24-hour water-taxi service (Auckland to Waiheke has a mini-mum charge of $210; to Rangitoto, $100). See also p101 for cruises and p101 for sailing trips.

RANGITOTO & MOTUTAPU
pop 75

Sloping elegantly from the waters of the gulf, 260m **Rangitoto** (www.rangitoto.org), the largest and youngest of Auckland's volcanic cones, provides a picturesque backdrop to all of the city's activities. As recently as 600 years ago it erupted from the sea and was probably active for several years before settling down. Maori living on Motutapu (Sacred Island), to which Rangitoto is now joined by a causeway, cer-tainly witnessed the eruptions, as footprints have been found embedded in ash and oral history details several generations living here before the eruption.

The island makes for a great day trip. Its harsh scoria slopes hold a surprising amount of flora and there are excellent walks, but you'll need sturdy shoes and plenty of water. Although it looks steep, up close it's more like an egg sizzling in a pan. The walk to the summit only takes an hour and is rewarded with sublime views. At the top a loop walk goes around the crater's rim. A walk to lava caves branches off the summit walk and takes 30 minutes return. There's an information board with walk maps at the wharf.

Motutapu (www.motutapu.org.nz), in contrast to Rangitoto, is mainly covered in grass-land, which is grazed by sheep and cattle. Archaeologically, this is a very significant island, with the traces of centuries of con-tinuous human habitation etched into its landscape.

A **DOC campsite** (☎ 09-372 7348; www.doc.govt.nz; Home Bay; adult/child $5/2.50) has basic facilities, with only a water tap and flush toilet provided.

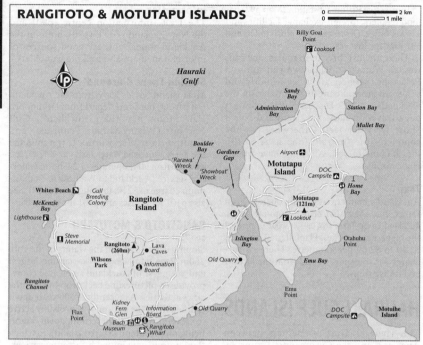

RANGITOTO & MOTUTAPU ISLANDS

Bring cooking equipment, as open fires are for-bidden. It's a three-hour walk from Rangitoto wharf; Fullers run a weekend-only service to Home Bay in the summer months.

Fullers (☎ 09-367 9111; www.fullers.co.nz; adult/child return $25/13) has 20-minute ferry services to Rangitoto from Auckland's Ferry Building (three daily on weekdays, four on weekends) and Devonport (two daily). Fullers also offers the **Volcanic Explorer** (adult/child $55/28), a guided tour around the island in a canopied 'road train', to a 900m boardwalk leading to the summit. Prices include the ferry.

Reubens (☎ 0800 111 616; www.reubens.co.nz; return $64) operates a shuttle service to Islington Bay on Wednesday, Friday, Saturday and Sunday (also Mondays from November to March).

MOTUIHE ISLAND

Between Waiheke and Rangitoto Islands, 176-hectare Motuihe Island has a lovely white-sand beach and a fascinating his-tory. There are three *pa* sites, last occupied by the Ngati Paoa tribe. The island was sold in 1840 (for a heifer, blankets, frocks, gar-den tools, pots and pans) and from 1872 to

1941 served as a quarantine station. During WWI the dashing swashbuckler Count von Luckner launched a daring escape from the island (where he was interned with other German and Austrian nationals), making it 1000km to the Kermadec Islands before being recaptured.

Motuihe has been rendered pest-free and is now subject to a vigorous reforestation project by enthusiastic volunteers. As a result, endan-gered birds have started to return, including the loquacious tieke (saddleback). Contact the **Motuihe Trust** (☎ 0800 668 844; www.motuihe.org.nz) if you want to get involved.

Apart from the trust's headquarters, the only accommodation on the island is a basic **DOC campsite** (Map p122; ☎ 09-379 6476; www.doc.govt. nz; adult/child $5/2.50); only toilets and water are provided. There are no shops or permanent residents.

360 Discovery (☎ 0800 888 006; www.360discovery. co.nz; adult/child return $24/15) runs three daily fer-ries to/from Auckland. On the weekends you can choose between heritage- and restoration-themed guided tours ($7.50, summer only). **Reubens** (☎ 0800 111 616; www.reubens.co.nz; adult/child return $34/17) operates a shuttle service four to five days a week.

WAIHEKE ISLAND
pop 7700

Waiheke is 93 sq km of island bliss only a 35-minute ferry ride from the CBD. Once they could hardly give land away here; nowadays multimillionaires rub shoulders with the old-time hippies and bohemian artists who gave the island its green repute. Auckland office workers fantasise about swapping the daily motorway crawl for a watery commute and a warm, dry microclimate.

On Waiheke's city side, emerald waters lap at rocky bays, while its ocean flank has some of the region's best sandy beaches. While beaches are the big drawcard, wine is a close second. There are 17 boutique wineries to visit, many with swanky restaurants and breathtaking city views. On top of that, the island boasts dozens of galleries and craft stores.

Waiheke has been inhabited since at least the 14th century, most recently by Ngati Paoa, and there are more than 40 *pa* sites scattered around the island. Europeans arrived with the missionary Samuel Marsden in the early 1800s and the island was soon stripped of its kauri forest.

Orientation & Information

Nearly 2km from Matiatia wharf is Oneroa, the main village, with a sandy beach. The eastern half of the island (locals call it the bottom end) is lightly populated and well worth exploring. There are petrol stations in Oneroa and Onetangi, ATMs in Oneroa and a supermarket in Ostend.

The **Waiheke Island i-SITE** (☎ 09-372 1234; 2 Korora Rd; www.waihekenz.com; ❨ 9am-5pm) and library (with free internet access) are in the Artworks complex. They also have a (usually unstaffed) counter in the ferry terminal at Matiatia Wharf.

Sights & Activities
ART & CULTURE

The **Artworks complex** (☎ 09-379 2020; 2 Korora Rd) houses a **community theatre** (☎ 09-372 2941; www.artworkstheatre.org.nz), an art-house **cinema** (☎ 09-372 4240; www.wicc.co.nz) and an attention-grabbing **art gallery** (☎ 09-372 9907; www.waihekeart gallery.org.nz; admission free; ❨ 10am-4pm). Also part of the complex is **Whittaker's Musical Museum** (☎ 09-372 5573; www.musical-museum.org; admission by donation; ❨ 1-4pm), a collection of antique concert instruments.

The **Waiheke Island Historic Village** (☎ 09-372 2970; www.waihekemuseum.org.nz; 165 Onetangi Rd; admission by donation; ❨ noon-4pm Wed, Sat & Sun) displays Islander artefacts in six restored buildings.

Connells Bay (☎ 09-372 8957; www.connellsbay.co.nz; Cowes Bay Rd; adult/child $30/15; ❨ by appointment, late Oct to late Apr) is a pricey but excellent private sculpture park featuring a stellar roster of NZ artists. Admission is by way of guided tour.

Another jealousy-inducing private property open to visitors is **Te Whau Garden** (☎ 09-372 6748; www.tewhaugarden.co.nz; 31 Vintage Lane; admission $10; ❨ 9am-5pm), giving you the opportunity to wander steep pathways through rainforest, wetlands and gardens scattered with sculpture.

The *Waiheke Art Map* brochure, free from the i-SITE, lists 37 galleries and craft stores.

BEACHES

Waiheke's two best beaches are **Onetangi**, a long stretch of white sand at the centre of the island, and **Palm Beach**, a pretty little horseshoe

---

BATTLE OF THE BACHES

During the 1920s a dinky set of simple baches started to sprout on Rangitoto on land leased from the council, forming a thriving community of holiday-makers. In the 1930s prison labour was used to construct roads, public toilets, tennis courts and a swimming pool out of the scoria. It was back-breaking work, but the men weren't locked up and by all accounts enjoyed island life. The threat of fire was, and is, a constant danger for the bach-holders – the baking scoria keeping the leaf litter tinder-dry.

During the 1970s and '80s the bach community itself came under threat – a significant number of houses were removed when their leases expired, with the plan to remove them all. Following a public outcry, the remaining communities were listed as Historic Areas by the Historic Places Trust in 1997. Just left of the wharf, a 1929 bach has been fully restored and opened as a **Bach Museum** (admission by donation; ❨ 9.30am-3.30pm Sat & Sun summer only).

WAIHEKE ISLAND

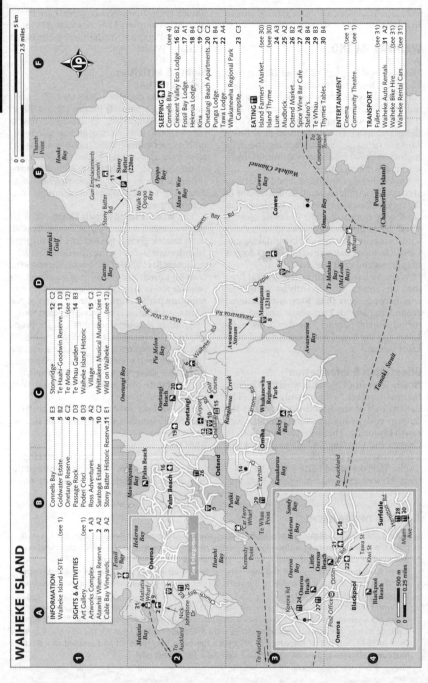

INFORMATION

Waiheke Island i-SITE	(see 1)

SIGHTS & ACTIVITIES

Art Gallery	(see 1)
Artworks Complex	1 A3
Atawhai Whenua Reserve	2 A2
Cable Bay Vineyards	3 A2
Connells Bay	4 E3
Goldwater Estate	5 B2
Onetangi Reserve	6 C2
Passage Rock	7 D3
Poderi Crisci	8 D3
Ross Adventures	9 A2
Saratoga Estate	10 C2
Stony Batter Historic Reserve	11 E1
Stonyridge	12 C2
Te Haahi-Goodwin Reserve	13 D3
Te Motu	(see 12)
Te Whau Garden	14 B3
Waiheke Island Historic Village	15 C2
Whittakers Musical Museum	(see 1)
Wild on Waiheke	(see 12)

SLEEPING

Connells Bay	(see 4)
Crescent Valley Eco Lodge	16 B2
Fossil Bay Lodge	17 A1
Hekerua Lodge	18 B4
Kina	19 C2
Onetangi Beach Apartments	20 C2
Punga Lodge	21 B4
Tawa Lodge	22 A4
Whakanewha Regional Park Campsite	23 C3

EATING

Island Farmers' Market	(see 30)
Island Thyme	(see 30)
Lure	24 A3
Mudbrick	25 A2
Ostend Market	26 B2
Spice Wine Bar Cafe	27 A3
Stefano's	28 B4
Te Whau	29 B3
Thymes Tables	30 B4

ENTERTAINMENT

Cinema	(see 31)
Community Theatre	(see 1)

TRANSPORT

Fullers	(see 31)
Waiheke Auto Rentals	31 A2
Waiheke Bike Hire	(see 31)
Waiheke Rental Cars	(see 31)

bay between Oneroa and Onetangi. Both have nudist sections; head west just past some rocks in both cases. **Oneroa** and neighbouring **Little Oneroa** are also excellent.

WINERIES
Waiheke's hot, dry microclimate has proved excellent for Bordeaux reds, syrah and some superb rosés. Because of an emphasis on quality rather than quantity, the premium wine produced here is relatively expensive. It's also NZ's only wine region where all the wineries charge for tastings (from $3 to $10; sometimes free if you make a purchase). Some are spectacularly located and worth a visit for that reason alone. Over summer many extend their hours, some even sprouting temporary restaurants.

Goldwater Estate (☎ 09-372 7493; www.goldwater wine.com; 18 Causeway Rd; ☿ noon-4pm Wed-Sun Mar-Nov, daily Dec-Feb) Waiheke's wine pioneers, Goldwater has been producing wine from these 21 acres for over 30 years.

Passage Rock (☎ 09-372 7257; www.passagerock wines.co.nz; 438 Orapiu Rd; ☿ noon-4pm) Excellent pizza among the vines.

Poderi Crisci (☎ 09-372 2148; www.podericrisci.co.nz; 205 Awaawaroa Rd; ☿ 11am-4.30pm Thu-Sun) Recently purchased by the Italian-born patriarch behind Non Solo Pizza (p111), we expect great things from the soon-to-come cafe. Italian varietals (Montepulciano, Nebbiolo) and olives have been planted alongside the existing pinot grigio and merlot.

Saratoga Estate (☎ 09-372 6450; www.saratoga estate.com; 72 Onetangi Rd; ☿ 11am-4pm) With a cafe and microbrewery on-site.

Stonyridge (☎ 09-372 8822; www.stonyridge.co.nz; 80 Onetangi Rd; ☿ 11.30am-5pm) Famous organic reds, an atmospheric cafe, tours ($10, 35 minutes, 11.30am Saturday and Sunday) and the occasional dance party.

Te Motu (☎ 09-372 6884; www.temotu.co.nz; 76 Onetangi Rd; ☿ 11am-4pm Wed-Sun) Shares the same driveway as Stonyridge and also has a restaurant.

Wild On Waiheke (☎ 09-372 3434; www.wildon waiheke.co.nz; 82 Onetangi Rd; ☿ 11am-4pm Thu-Sun, daily in summer) If you like to shoot stuff after a few drinks, this winery and microbrewery offers tastings, archery, clay shooting, *pétanque* and a giant chess board.

See also Te Whau, Cable Bay and Mudbrick (p127). Pick up the *Waiheke Island of Wine* map for a complete list.

TRAMPING
The *Explore Waiheke Island's Walkways* pamphlet has detailed maps and descriptions of eight excellent coastal hikes that take from one to three hours. Some head to the Royal Forest & Bird Protection Society's three reserves: **Onetangi** (Waiheke Rd), **Te Haahi-Goodwin** (Orapiu Rd) and **Atawhai Whenua** (Ocean View Rd). Other tracks traverse the **Whakanewha Regional Park**, a haven for rare coastal birds.

At the bottom end of the island, the **Stony Batter Historic Reserve** (www.fortstonybatter.org.nz; Stony Batter Rd; admission/tour $8/15; ☿ 10am-3.30pm) has WWII tunnels and gun emplacements that were built in 1941 to defend Auckland's harbour. The walk leads through private farmland, and derives its name from the boulder-strewn fields. Bring a torch.

KAYAKING
It's the fervently held opinion of Ross of **Ross Adventures** (☎ 09-372 5550; www.kayakwaiheke.co.nz; Matiatia beach; 2hr/4hr/day trips $55/85/145, per hr hire from $25) that Waiheke offers kayaking every bit as good as the legendary Abel Tasman National Park. He should know – Ross has been offering guided kayak trips for over 20 years. Experienced sea kayakers can comfortably circumnavigate the island in four days, exploring hidden coves and sand spits inaccessible by land.

Tours
Ananda Tours (☎ 09-372 7530; www.ananda.co.nz) Offers a food and wine tour ($95) and a Wine Connoisseur's Tour ($190). Small-group, informal tours can be customised, including visits to artists' studios.

Fullers (☎ 09-367 9111; www.fullers.co.nz; Matiatia Wharf) Runs a Wine On Waiheke Tour (adult $115, 4¾ hours, departs Auckland 1pm) that visits three of the island's top wineries and includes a platter of nibbles. Taste Of Waiheke (adult $112, 5½ hours, departs Auckland 11am) also includes three wineries plus an olive grove and light lunch. There's also a 1½-hour Explorer Tour of the island (adult/child $48/24, departs Auckland 10am, 11am and noon). All prices include the ferry and an all-day bus pass.

Waiheke Executive Transport (☎ 0800 372 200; www.waiheketransport.co.nz) Short tours (from $15), wine tours (half-day/day/premium $55/71/95), arts and crafts tours ($71) and walking tours (from $25).

Waiheke Island Adventures (☎ 09-372 6127; www.waihekeislandadventures.com) Scenic tours ($25), vineyard tours ($25), or Stony Batter tours ($35) in a 15-seater bus. Art and beach tours also available.

Festivals & Events
Sculpture on the Gulf (www.sculptureonthegulf.co.nz) A wacky 2km cliff-top sculpture walk, held every second January (odd-numbered years).

Waiheke Food & Wine Festival (www.whatson waiheke.co.nz; admission $60) Sometimes shifts but currently on Waitangi Day (6 February).

Sleeping

Waiheke is so popular in the summer holidays that many locals rent out their houses for exorbitant rates and bugger off elsewhere. You'll need to book ahead and even then there are very few bargains. Prices drop considerably in winter, especially midweek.

BUDGET

Whakanewha Regional Park campsite (☎ 09-366 2000; www.arc.govt.nz; Gordons Rd; sites per adult/child $10/5) A pretty but basic campsite with toilets, cold showers, gas barbecues and drinking water. Phone ahead for the code to unlock the gate.

Hekerua Lodge (☎ 09-372 8990; www.hekerualodge. co.nz; 11 Hekerua Rd, Oneroa; sites per person $17, dm $36, s/tr $53/108, d $80-110, cabin $270; 🖥 🐾) This secluded hostel is surrounded by native bush and has a barbecue, stone-tiled pool, sunny deck, casual lounge area and its own walking track. It's far from luxurious, but it has a laid-back feel, no doubt assisted by the serene images of Buddha and the Tibetan prayer flags flapping about.

Fossil Bay Lodge (☎ 09-372 8371; www.fossil bay.webs.com; 58 Korora Rd, Oneroa; sites per person $18, s $35-45, d $67; 🛜) Three cutesy cabins open onto a courtyard facing the main building, which houses the toilets, a large communal kitchen and living area and, on the other side, a Steiner kindergarten. Apart from the occasional squawking duck (or toddler), it's a peaceful place.

Kina (☎ 09-372 8971; www.kinabackpackers.co.nz; 419 Seaview Rd, Onetangi; dm/s/tw $24/45/56, d $65-75; 🛜) This scuffed but well-positioned hostel has a large garden overlooking Onetangi Beach. The dorms are a little cell-like but have only two bunk beds, and linen is provided. Mountain bikes can be hired.

MIDRANGE & TOP END

our pick Tawa Lodge (☎ 09-372 9434; www.pungalodge. co.nz; 15 Tawa St, Oneroa; r $110, apt $165-200) Between the self-contained cottage at the front and the apartment at the rear are three reasonably priced loft rooms sharing a small kitchen and bathroom. On a hot day there's a wonderfully languid vibe as guests spill out onto the deck.

Punga Lodge (☎ 09-372 6675; www.pungalodge. co.nz; 223 Ocean View Rd, Oneroa; r $140-160, apt $135-200; 🖥) Both the colourful en-suite rooms in the house and the self-contained garden units have access to decks looking onto a lush tropical garden. There's a spa, and prices include home-made breakfast, afternoon tea and wharf transfers.

Crescent Valley Eco Lodge (☎ 09-372 4321; www. waihekeecolodge.co.nz; 50 Crescent Rd East, Ostend; r $145) Surrounded by bush and peaceful gardens this little ecoretreat has only two tidy rooms, affable hosts and a spa pool under the stars. Bathrooms are private but not en suite.

Onetangi Beach Apartments (☎ 09-372 0003; www.onetangi.co.nz; 27 The Strand, Onetangi; apt $185-400; 🛜) Three different blocks of townhouses are clumped together, all offering smart, modern, perfectly located, well-managed accommodation, along with a spa and sauna. Best (and priciest) are the Strand Apartments, with large decks overlooking the sea.

Connells Bay (☎ 09-372 8957; www.connellsbay. co.nz; Cowes Bay Rd; cottage $350-450) Fancy your own private art-filled retreat that combines the best of the country and the seaside and is luxurious without being glitzy? Descend to this extraordinary property via a perilously steep driveway to the sculpture garden. The century-old weatherboard two-bedroom cottage is comfortable and chic, with kauri floors, a smart kitchen, veranda, garden and absolute water frontage.

Eating

Priding itself on the finer things in life, Waiheke has some excellent eateries, and if you're lucky the views will be enough to distract from the hole being bored into your hip pocket. The island's isolation is an excuse for overcharging yet simultaneously limits the capacity to find good staff. Consequently you may find yourself paying exorbitantly for meals served by clueless local teenagers.

Spice Wine Bar Cafe (☎ 09-372 7659; 153 Ocean View Rd, Oneroa; mains $7-14; �'Y breakfast & lunch) A snappy little place with tables on the street, excellent coffee and delectable lemon tarts.

Lure (☎ 09-372 9035; 29 Waikare Rd, Oneroa; mains $8-18; �'Y breakfast & lunch) Enjoy beach views, great coffee, enticing counter food and a short focused menu. The chicken Caesar salad is superb.

Stefano's (☎ 09-372 5309; 18 Hamilton Rd, Surfdale; mains $16-27; �'Y 5.30-9.30pm Wed-Mon) Stefano's is the best-smelling joint on Waiheke, serving pasta staples and wonderful pizzas in the presence of a dodgy mural. It also does takeaways.

Thymes Tables (☎ 09-372 3400; 8 Miami Ave, Surfdale; mains $31; ⊙ dinner Tue-Sat) Fussy eaters should look elsewhere as this excellent French-style eatery offers only one or two dishes per evening, which change daily. The food is as elegant as the white-walled dining room, and the island's best deli is downstairs.

Te Whau (☎ 09-372 7191; 218 Te Whau Dr; mains $33-40; ⊙ lunch Wed-Mon, dinner Sat) Perched on the end of Te Whau peninsula, this winery restaurant has exceptional views, food and service, and one of the finest wine lists you'll see in the country (1982 Chateau Mouton Rothschild, $3000). Try its impressive Bordeaux blends, merlot and rosé for $3 per taste (11am to 5pm).

Cable Bay Vineyards (☎ 09-372 5889; www.cable bayvineyards.co.nz; 12 Nick Johnstone Dr; mains $36-49; ⊙ lunch & dinner) Impressive ubermodern architecture, sculpture and beautiful views set the scene for this acclaimed restaurant. The food is sublime but the service isn't always. If the budget won't stretch to a meal, stop in for a wine tasting ($5) or a drink on the terrace.

Mudbrick (☎ 09-372 9050; 126 Church Bay Rd; mains $38-42; ⊙ lunch & dinner) Auckland and the gulf are at their glistening best when viewed from Mudbrick's picturesque veranda. The adventurous menu is crammed with quality ingredients, well put together. This venue also offers tours and wine tasting ($5 to $10, 11am to 5pm).

For fresh local produce head to the bustling **Ostend market** (Ostend Hall, Belgium St; ⊙ 8am-1pm Sat) or the **Island Farmers Market** (8 Belgium St; ⊙ 11am-2pm Sun). For prepackaged gourmet meals, deli goodies, tempting pastries and excellent coffee, clock in on Island Thyme (see Thymes Tables, above). There's a supermarket in Ostend.

Drinking

Apart from the wineries, you'll find some swanky bars in Oneroa, local pubs in Surfdale and Ostend, and nice spots for an afternoon drink on the waterfront in Onetangi.

Getting There & Away

Fullers (☎ 09-367 9111; www.fullers.co.nz; adult/child return $32/16; ⊙ 5.20am-11.45pm Mon-Fri, 6.25am-11.45pm Sat, 7am-9.30pm Sun) has frequent ferries from Auckland to Matiatia Wharf (on the hour from 9am to 5pm), some via Devonport.

Sealink (☎ 09-300 5900; www.sealink.co.nz; adult/child/car/motorcycle return $30/17/130/48; ⊙ 4.30am-6.30pm Mon-Thu, 4.30am-8pm Fri, 6am-6.30pm Sat, 8am-6.30pm Sun) runs car ferries to Kennedy Point, mainly from Half Moon Bay (East Auckland) but some leave from the city. The ferry runs at least every two hours and takes 45 minutes; bookings are essential.

You can pick up the **360 Discovery** (☎ 0800 888 006; www.360discovery.co.nz) tourist ferry at Orapiu on its journey between Auckland and Coromandel Town (see p192).

Getting Around
BUS

The island has regular bus services, starting from Matiatia Wharf and heading through Oneroa (adult/child $1.40/80c, 3 minutes) on their way to all the main settlements, as far west as Onetangi (adult/child $4/2.20, 30 minutes). Enquire through **MAXX** (☎ 09-366 6400; www.maxx.co.nz). A day pass (adult/child $8/5) is available from the Fullers counter at Matiatia Wharf.

CAR & BICYCLE

The island has 12km-, 25km- and 70km-loop bicycle routes, but prepare for a lot of hills. Mountain bikes (half-/full day $20/30) can be hired at **Waiheke Bike Hire** (☎ 09-372 7937; Matiatia Wharf; ⊙ 9am-5pm), or you can cheat on the inclines with electric bikes. The i-SITE also rents mountain bikes (half-/full day $20/30) and scooters (day/overnight $50/60).

Waiheke Auto Rentals (☎ 09-372 8998; www. waihekerentals.co.nz; Matiatia Wharf; car/scooter/motorbike/4WD from $50/55/75/80) and **Waiheke Rental Cars** (☎ 09-372 8635; www.waihekerentalcars. co.nz; Matiatia Wharf; car/4WD from $50/80) offer rentals, but you must be over 21 and pay 65c a kilometre for cars or 4WDs. The insurance excess (deposit) is $1000.

TAXI

Try **Waiheke Taxi Co-op** (☎ 09-372 8038), **Waiheke Taxis** (☎ 09-372 3000) or **Waiheke Independent Taxis** (☎ 0800 300 372).

TIRITIRI MATANGI ISLAND

This magical, 220-hectare, predator-free **island** (www.tiritirimatangi.co.nz) is home to the tuatara (NZ's pint-sized dinosaur) and lots of endangered native birds, including the very rare and colourful takahe. Other birds that can be seen here include the bell bird,

OTHER ISLANDS

Little Barrier Island, located 25km north-east of Kawau Island, is NZ's ark: a predator-free refuge for endangered birds, reptiles and plants. Access to the island is highly restricted, and a DOC permit is required for landing on this closely guarded sanctuary. The steep volcanic cliffs help keep out intruders.

Motuora Island, halfway between Kawau and Tiritiri Matangi, has 80 predator-free hectares and is used as a kiwi 'crèche'. There's a wharf on the west coast of the island, but you'll need your own boat to get here. The **DOC campsite** (☎ 027 492 8586; www.doc.govt. nz; adult/child $6/3) requires bookings and provides toilets, cold showers and water. It also rents a **bach** ($55) that sleeps five; bring your own linen and food.

stitch bird, saddleback, whitehead, kakariki, kokako, little spotted kiwi, brown teal, NZ robin, fernbird and penguins; 78 different species have been sighted in total. The saddleback was once close to extinction with just 150 left, but now there are more than 600 on Tiritiri alone. To experience the dawn chorus in full flight, stay overnight at the **DOC bunkhouse** (☎ 09-425 7812; www.doc.govt.nz; adult/child $24/18); book well ahead.

Ngati Paoa were the last tribe to live here. The land was sold to the Crown in 1841, deforested and farmed until the 1970s. Since 1984 hundreds of volunteers have planted 250,000 native trees and the forest cover has regenerated. An 1864 lighthouse stands on the eastern end of the island.

From Wednesday to Sunday, **360 Discovery** (☎ 0800 888 006; www.360discovery.co.nz; return Auckland/ Gulf Harbour $66/39) has ferries to the island, leaving Auckland at 9am and Gulf Harbour (on the Whangaparaoa Peninsula) at 9.50am (check-in 30 minutes prior). They arrive back in Gulf Harbour at 4pm and Auckland at 4.50pm. A guided walk on the island is a good deal at $5/2.50 per adult/child.

KAWAU ISLAND
pop 300

Kawau Island lies 50km north of Auckland off the Mahurangi Peninsula. There are no proper roads through the island, the residents relying totally on boats. The main attraction

is **Mansion House** (☎ 09-422 8882; adult/child $4/2; ☺ noon-2pm Mon-Fri, noon-3.30pm Sat & Sun), an impressive wooden manor extended from an 1845 structure by Governor George Grey, who purchased the island in 1862. It houses a fine collection of Victoriana, including some of Grey's effects, and is surrounded by the original exotic gardens. A set of short walks (10 minutes to two hours) are signposted from Mansion House, leading to beaches, the old copper mine and a lookout; download DOC's *Kawau Island Historic Reserve map* (www. doc.govt.nz).

Kawau Lodge (☎ 09-422 8831; www.kawaulodge. co.nz; North Cove; s $160, d $195-220) is an ecoconscious boutique hotel with its own jetty, wraparound decks and views. Meals ($10 to $60) can be arranged, as can excursions on the 42ft yacht or power catamaran.

In the north of the island, on Kawau's only sandy beach, the upmarket **Beach House Resort** (☎ 09-422 8850; www.kawauresort.co.nz; Vivian Bay; ste $320-440) has rooms facing the beach, facing a large paved courtyard or in a cottage set back in the bush. All meals are included in the rate, as is equipment for fishing, snorkelling, kayaking and sailing.

If you haven't packed a picnic, the idyllically situated **Mansion House Cafe Restaurant** (☎ 09-422 8903; lunch $12-18, dinner $18-28; ☺ hours vary) will be a welcome relief, serving all-day breakfasts, sandwiches and hearty evening meals. It's also your only option for stocking up on bread, milk, ice and pre-ordered newspapers.

Reubens (☎ 0508 282 552; www.aucklandescape. co.nz) is based at Sandspit (p141) and operates daily cruises to Kawau (adult/child return $47/25; departs 10.30pm daily and 2.30pm weekends and summer holidays; returns 2.30pm and 5pm). The Super Cruise (adult/child $65/28, barbecue lunch $22/10) departs Sandspit at 10.30am and circles the island, delivering the post to 75 different wharves. It also runs a water-taxi service (minimum charge $125).

GREAT BARRIER ISLAND
pop 900

Great Barrier (Aotea) is the largest island in the gulf (285 sq km) and NZ's fourth-largest behind North, South and Stewart Islands. It's rugged and scenic, resembling the Coromandel Peninsula to which it was once joined. Named by Captain James Cook,

Great Barrier Island later became a whaling, mining and logging centre, but all these industries have had their day. Most of the island is publicly owned and managed by DOC.

Great Barrier has unspoilt beaches, hot springs, old kauri dams, a forest sanctuary and a network of tramping tracks. Because there are no possums on the island, the native bush is lush. The west coast has safe sandy beaches, while the east coast beaches are good for surfing. Mountain biking, swimming, fishing, diving, boating, kayaking and just relaxing are other popular activities.

Although only 88km from Auckland, Great Barrier seems a world – and a good many years – away. The island has no supermarket, no electricity supply (only private generators) and no main drainage (only septic tanks); many roads are unsealed; and petrol costs are high. Mobile-phone reception is very limited and there are no banks, ATMs or street lights. It's a wild, untamed and very special place with its own rules, and is a definite breath of fresh air.

From around mid-December to mid-January is the peak season, so make sure you book transport, accommodation and activities well in advance.

Orientation

Tryphena is the main settlement, 4km from the ferry wharf at Shoal Bay. Strung out along several kilometres of coastal road, it consists of a few dozen houses, a primary school and a handful of shops and accommodation places. From the wharf it's 3km to Mulberry Grove, and then another 1km over the headland to Pa Beach and the Stonewall Store.

The airport is at Claris, a small settlement with a general store, bottle shop, laundrette, vehicle-repair garage, pharmacy, adventure centre and cafe, 10km north of Tryphena. Whangaparapara is an old timber town and the site of the island's 19th-century whaling activities. Port Fitzroy is the other main harbour on the west coast, a one-hour drive from Tryphena. Only these four main settlements have petrol and diesel available.

Information

The free *This Is Great Barrier Island* (www. greatbarriernz.com) pamphlet has a handy map and is full of useful information, as is the *Great Barrier Island Visitor Information Guide* booklet (www.thebarrier.co.nz). There's an information kiosk at the GBI Rent-A-Car office in Claris (p133). Claris Texas Cafe (p132) has internet access and you'll find post offices in Tryphena and Claris.

Aotea Health Centre (☎ 09-429 0356; Hector Sanderson Rd, Claris; ☺ 9am-4pm Mon-Fri)

DOC office (☎ 09-429 0044; www.doc.govt.nz; Port Fitzroy; ☺ 8am-4.30pm Mon-Fri) Call in for brochures, maps, weather information and to sign the intentions book for longer walks.

Visitor information centre (☎ 09-429 0848; Port Fitzroy; ☺ 9.30am-3pm Mon-Sat)

Activities
SWIMMING & SURFING

Beaches on the west coast are safe, but care needs to be taken on the surf-pounded eastern beaches. **Medlands Beach**, with its wide sweep of white sand, is one of the best beaches on the island and is easily accessible from Tryphena. Remote **Whangapoua** in the northeast requires more effort to get to, while **Kaitoke**, **Awana Bay** and **Harataonga** on the east coast are also worth a visit.

Okiwi Bar has an excellent right-hand break, while Awana has both left- and right-hand breaks. Tryphena's bay, lined with pohutukawa, has sheltered beaches.

OTHER WATER SPORTS

There's pinnacle diving, shipwreck diving, lots of fish and more than 33m visibility at some times of the year.

Hooked on Barrier (☎ 09-429 0740; info@greatbarrier lodge.co.nz; 89 Hector-Sanderson Rd, Claris) sells and hires out diving, snorkelling, fishing, surfing and kayak (both from $35 per hour) gear. You can dive from a beach or charter a boat through **Tryphena Charters** (☎ 09-429 0596).

Aotea Sea Kayaks (☎ 09-429 0664; www.greatbarrier kayaks.co.nz; Mulberry Grove, Tryphena) runs harbour ($50, two hours), sunset ($60, two hours), snorkelling ($90, four hours) and phosphorescent night paddles ($90). Kayaks (per day $40 to $60) and snorkelling equipment (per day $25) can be hired, as well as sea kayaks kitted out with lines and tackle for fishing (per day $80).

MOUNTAIN BIKING

With rugged scenery and little traffic on the roads, mountain biking is a popular activity here. There's a designated 20km mountain bike trail through the forest from Whangaparapara Rd towards Port Fitzroy.

GREAT BARRIER ISLAND

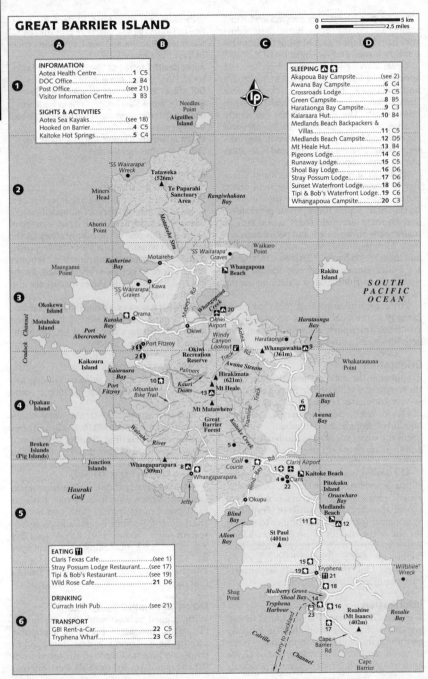

INFORMATION
Aotea Health Centre................1 C5
DOC Office..........................2 B4
Post Office.....................(see 21)
Visitor Information Centre.........3 B3

SIGHTS & ACTIVITIES
Aotea Sea Kayaks...............(see 18)
Hooked on Barrier.................4 C5
Kaitoke Hot Springs...............5 C4

SLEEPING
Akapoua Bay Campsite............(see 2)
Awana Bay Campsite...............6 C4
Crossroads Lodge.................7 C5
Green Campsite...................8 B5
Haratonga Bay Campsite...........9 C3
Kaiaraara Hut....................10 B4
Medlands Beach Backpackers &
  Villas.........................11 C5
Medlands Beach Campsite..........12 D5
Mt Heale Hut.....................13 B4
Pigeons Lodge....................14 C6
Runaway Lodge....................15 C5
Shoal Bay Lodge..................16 D6
Stray Possum Lodge...............17 D6
Sunset Waterfront Lodge..........18 D6
Tipi & Bob's Waterfront Lodge...19 C6
Whangapoua Campsite..............20 C3

EATING
Claris Texas Cafe...............(see 1)
Stray Possum Lodge Restaurant...(see 17)
Tipi & Bob's Restaurant.........(see 19)
Wild Rose Cafe...................21 D6

DRINKING
Currach Irish Pub..............(see 21)

TRANSPORT
GBI Rent-a-Car...................22 C5
Tryphena Wharf...................23 C6

Cycling on other DOC walking tracks is prohibited.

You can hire a bike from GBI-Rent-A-Car (p133) for $30 per day.

WALKING

Many people come here for the walks, but be aware that trails are not always well signposted, although they are regularly upgraded. Be properly equipped with water and food, and be prepared for bad weather. The best tramping trails are in the Great Barrier Forest north of Whangaparapara, where there has been a great deal of reforestation.

The most spectacular short walk is from Windy Canyon to Hirakimata (Mt Hobson). **Windy Canyon**, which is only a 15-minute walk from the main Port Fitzroy–Harataonga (Aotea) road, has spectacular rock outcrops and affords great views of the island. From Windy Canyon, an excellent trail continues for another 1½ hours through scrubby forest to **Hirakimata** (621m), the highest point on the island, with views across to the Coromandel and Auckland on a fine day. Near the top of the mountain are lush forests and a few mature kauri trees that survived the logging days. From Hirakimata it's two hours through forest to the hut closest to Port Fitzroy and then 45 minutes to Port Fitzroy itself.

Another very popular walk is the **Kaitoke Hot Springs Track**. The natural hot pools in a bush stream can be reached from Whangaparapara Rd (45 minutes).

A more challenging tramp is the **Tramline Track** (five hours), which starts on Aotea Rd and follows old logging tramlines to Whangaparapara Harbour. The track is hilly and in some parts the clay becomes slippery after rain. Of a similar length but flatter is the 11km **Harataonga Coastal Walk** (five hours) which heads from Harataonga Bay to Whangapoua.

Many other trails traverse the forest, taking between 30 minutes and five hours. Pick up a copy of DOC's fold-out *Great Barrier Island* hiking brochure ($2), which has a detailed map and short descriptions of 23 hikes. It's available from the DOC office and the various accommodation places.

There is a good trampers' bus service that will drop you at the start of a trail and pick you up at the other end; see Getting Around, p133 for details.

Sleeping

There are half a dozen campsites and backpacker hostels, and more than 50 lodges, cottages and B&Bs spread around the island. Some places cater for a range of visitors, from backpackers and campers to luxury-seeking honeymooners, and also run restaurants and bars that are open to nonguests. Prices are generally quite steep but what's offered but drop in the off-season; summer prices are quoted here. **Island Accommodation** (☎ 09-429 0995; www.islandaccommodation.co.nz) offers a booking service, which is particularly handy for finding self-contained cottages for longer stays.

BUDGET

DOC campsites (www.doc.govt.nz; adult/child $9/4.50) There are campsites at Haratonga Bay, Medlands Beach, Akapoua Bay, Whangapoua, The Green (Whangaparapara) and Awana Bay. All have basic facilities, including water, cold showers (none at The Green), chemical toilets and a food preparation area. You need to bring your own gas cooking stove as open fires are prohibited. Book in advance online as the sites are not staffed.

Kaiaraara & Mt Heale Huts (www.doc.govt.nz; per adult/child $15/5) These DOC huts in the Great Barrier Forest sleep between 24 and 28 people in bunk-rooms. Facilities include cold water, chemical toilets and a kitchen with a wood stove. Bring your own sleeping bag and cooking equipment. Book online.

Stray Possum Lodge (☎ 09-4290109; www.straypossum .co.nz; 64 Cape Barrier Rd; sites per person $12, dm/d/tr/q $23/70/85/100, chalets $135-195) Nestled in the bush south of Tryphena is this popular place with its own bar and restaurant. A stray possum wouldn't stand a chance against the two resident German shepherds, which are a little unnerving as a welcome party. The chalets are self-contained and sleep up to six. In the dorms you'll be charged $5 extra for linen.

Runaway Lodge (☎ 09-429 0628; www.runaway lodge.co.nz; 41 Medlands Rd, Tryphena; dm $25, d $90-130, tr $125-150, q $145-170) A well-tended sunny garden surrounds this small, tidy block of mezzanine units, perched on the hill just above Tryphena. One has been set up as a six-sleeper dorm (linen $10 extra) but even this has an en suite and cooking facilities.

Medlands Beach Backpackers & Villas (☎ 09-429 0320; www.medlandsbeach.com; 9 Mason Rd; dm/d $25/70, villas $120-200) Buddhas meditate in the garden of this chilled-out house on the hill, overlooking beautiful Medlands Beach. The backpackers area is simple but tidy and there's a little double cabin for romantic budgeteers at a slight remove from the rest. The self-contained villas sleep up to six.

Crossroads Lodge (☎ 09-429 0889; www.xroadslodge. com; 1 Blind Bay Rd, Claris; dm/s/d $30/45/70; ▣) This comfy, low-key backpackers is 2km from the airfield and close to the forest walks and hot springs. Mountain bikes can be hired, and golf clubs can be borrowed to play on the nearby nine-hole golf course.

MIDRANGE & TOP END

Shoal Bay Lodge (☎ 09-429 0890; www.shoalbaylodge. co.nz; 145 Shoal Bay Rd, Tryphena; apt $110-240) Hidden among the trees these comfy self-contained apartments offer sea views, bird song, solar power, environmentally friendly cleaning products and cruelty-free toiletries. Best is the three-bedroom lodge with its sunset-guzzling deck.

ourpick Pigeons Lodge (☎ 09-429 0437; www.pigeons lodge.co.nz; 179 Shoal Bay Rd; apt/d $145/175) Above the beach, south of Tryphena, this lovely lodge has a 2.5-acre bush setting, friendly management and good breakfasts (free for B&B guests, $15 for apartment dwellers).

Tipi & Bob's Waterfront Lodge (☎ 09-429 0550; www.waterfrontlodge.co.nz; Puriri Bay Rd, Tryphena; units $195-320) West of Tryphena, these smart but pricey motel-style units have some wonderful sea views. The complex includes a restaurant and bar (see right).

Sunset Waterfront Lodge (☎ 09-429 0051; www. sunsetlodge.co.nz; Mulberry Grove, Tryphena; apt $189-234) Gaze across the lawn to the sea from the attractive studio units, or fight over who's going to get the pointy room in the two-bedroom A-frame villas. There's a small shop and cafe next door.

Eating & Drinking

In summer, most places are open daily but for the rest of the year the hours are sporadic. There's a monthly guide as to what's open when posted on www.thebarrier.co.nz but it still pays to call ahead for an evening meal.

Wild Rose Cafe (☎ 09-429 0905; Blackwell Dr, Tryphena; mains $5-18; ⏱ 9am-3pm) Wild Rose does the best impersonation of an Auckland cafe on the island, albeit with the addition of local crowd-pleasers such as toasted sandwiches and burgers. It uses free-range, organic and local produce whenever possible.

Claris Texas Cafe (☎ 09-429 0811; 129 Hector-Sanderson Rd, Claris; mains $7.50-15; ⏱ 8am-4pm; ▣ ▣) While it doesn't live up to the promise of its quirky name, this is the best gap-filler in the centre of the island, serving pretty good nachos, salads and pies.

Currach Irish Pub (☎ 09-429 0211; Blackwell Dr, Tryphena; mains $14-28; ⏱ from 4pm) This lively and child-friendly pub has a changing menu of seafood, steak and burgers, and is the island's social centre. Rub shoulders with local musos on Thursday jam nights.

Stray Possum Lodge Restaurant (☎ 09-429 0109; 64 Cape Barrier Rd; mains $14-30; ⏱ dinner) Offers pizzas and a varied menu in a convivial atmosphere (especially in summer), and is fully licensed. Ring ahead as opening hours aren't set in stone.

Tipi & Bob's Restaurant (☎ 09-429 0550; www. waterfrontlodge.co.nz; Puriri Bay Rd, Tryphena; mains $26-30; ⏱ breakfast & dinner) Serving simple but satisfying meals in large portions, this popular haunt has an inviting deck overlooking the harbour. There's a cheaper bistro menu in the bar.

Self-caterers will find small stores in Tryphena, Claris, Whangaparapara and Port Fitzroy.

Getting There & Away

AIR

Great Barrier Airlines (☎ 09-275 9120; www.greatbarrier airlines.co.nz; one-way standard/advance $109/89) flies from Auckland Domestic Airport (at least three daily), North Shore Aerodrome (Map p86; south of Orewa, at least two daily) and Whangarei (one-way $129; twice weekly). All flights take about 30 minutes and stop at both Claris and Okiwa. The fly/boat deal ($169) is a cheaper return option, with one leg by ferry to/from Auckland.

Fly My Sky (☎ 09-256 7025; www.flymysky.co.nz; one-way standard/advance $109/89, fly/boat deal adult/child $169/110) flies at least three times a day from Auckland. Cheaper flights are available if you travel to the island on a Sunday or leave on a Friday ($66).

BOAT

Sealink (☎ 09-300 5900; www.sealink.co.nz; return adult/child/car/motorcycle $120/80/350/95) is the main provider, running car ferries from three to six days a week from Wynyard Wharf in Auckland to Tryphena's Shoal Bay (4½ hours).

Fullers (☎ 09-367 9111; www.fullers.co.nz; adult/child one way $69/39) runs faster services (2½ hours) from Auckland's Ferry Building to Tryphena's Shoal Bay (some continue to Port Fitzroy) from mid-December to the end of January, as well as on the Labour Day and Easter long weekends. Look out for early bird specials.

Getting Around

Most roads are narrow and windy but even small hire cars can handle the unsealed sections.

Great Barrier Travel (☎ 0800 426 832; www.great barriertravel.co.nz) runs shuttles all around the island and an excellent trampers' service, which can drop you off at any of the main trailheads and pick you up at the other end. Call for specific prices (Tryphena to Claris is $15, for example) or purchase a multi-use pass (day/weekend/three-day $50/75/99). The associated **Aotea Car Rentals** (☎ 0800 426 832; www.aoteacarrentals.co.nz) hires out cars (from $55), 4WDs (from $75) and vans (from $99). Rentals clients get to use the trampers' shuttles for free.

GBI Rent-A-Car (☎ 09-429 0062; www.greatbarrier island.co.nz; 67 Hector-Sanderson Rd, Claris) has a somewhat battered fleet of cars starting at $55 and 4WDs from $85. It also operates shuttles; from Claris to Tryphena ($20), Medlands ($15), Whangaparapara ($30) and Port Fitzroy ($30, minimum four passengers).

Many of the accommodation places will pick you up from the airport or wharf if notified in advance.

WEST OF AUCKLAND

West Auckland epitomises rugged: wild black-sand beaches, bush-shrouded ranges, and mullet-haired and black-T-shirt-wearing 'Westies'. The latter is just one of several stereotypes of the area's denizens. Others include the back-to-nature hippie, the eccentric bohemian artist and the dope-smoking surfer dude, all attracted to a simple life at the edge of the bush.

Add to the mix Croatian immigrants, earning the fertile fields at the base of the Waitakere Ranges the nickname 'Daly Valley' after the Dalmatian coast where many hailed from. These pioneering families planted grapes and made wine, unwittingly founding one of NZ's major industries.

TITIRANGI

pop 3200

This little village marks the end of Auckland's suburban sprawl and is a good place to spot all of the stereotypes mentioned above over a caffe latte, fine wine or cold beer. Once home to NZ's greatest modern painter, Colin McCahon, there remains an artsy feel to the place. Titirangi means 'Fringe of Heaven' – an apt name for the gateway to the Waitakere Ranges, or indeed a hair salon. This is the last stop for petrol and ATMs on your way west.

Lopdell House Gallery (☎ 09-817 8087; www.lopdell. org.nz; 418 Titirangi Rd; admission free; ☸ 10am-4.30pm) is an excellent modern art gallery housed in the former Hotel Titirangi (1930) at the edge of the village.

It's a mark of the esteem in which Colin McCahon is held that the house he lived and painted in during the 1950s has been opened to the public as a minimuseum, **McCahon House** (www.mccahonhouse.org.nz; 67 Otitori Bay Rd, French Bay; admission $5; ☸ 10am-2pm Wed, Sat & Sun). The swish pad next door is home to the artist lucky enough to win the McCahon Arts Residency. Look for the signposts pointing down Park Rd, just before you reach Titirangi village.

Surrounded by native bush, the Frank Lloyd Wright-inspired **Fringe of Heaven** (☎ 09-817 8682; www.fringeofheaven.com; 4 Otitori Bay Rd; d $185-220, tr $225-260; ℗) offers glorious views over Manukau Harbour, an outdoor bath, glow-worms in the garden and a songbird choir – all within 20 minutes of the city centre. The 'bed' and 'breakfast' parts of the equation are pretty special too.

Great for Westie watching, the popular licensed **Hardware Café** (☎ 09-817 5059; 404 Titirangi Rd; mains $5-31; ☸ 8am-5pm Mon & Tue, 8am-10pm Wed-Sun) serves delicious and reasonably priced cooked breakfasts and lunches along with a tempting array of counter food. More substantial evening meals start from $22.

WAITAKERE RANGES

This 16,000-hectare wilderness was covered in kauri until the mid-19th century, when logging claimed most of the giant trees. A few stands of ancient kauri and other mature natives survive amid the dense bush of the regenerating rainforest, which is now protected inside the **Waitakere Ranges Regional Park**. Bordered to the west by the wildly beautiful beaches on the Tasman Sea, the park's rugged terrain makes an excellent day trip from Auckland.

Scenic Drive winds its way 28km from Titirangi to Swanson, passing waterfalls and lookouts. The **Arataki visitors centre** (☎ 09-817 0077; www.arc.govt.nz; Scenic Dr; ☺ 9am-5pm daily Sep-Apr, 10am-4pm Mon-Fri, 9am-5pm Sat & Sun May-Aug) is 6km west of Titirangi and is a brilliant starting point for exploring the ranges. As well as providing information on the 250km of trails in the area, this impressive, child-friendly centre, with its Maori carvings (some prodigiously well-hung) and spectacular views, is an attraction in its own right. The giant carving that greets visitors at the entrance depicts the ancestors of the Kawerau *iwi*. You can also book here for several basic **campsites** (☎ 09-366 2000; adult/child $5/3) within the park – toilets are provided but there's nothing much else.

A 1.6km nature trail opposite the centre leads visitors past labelled native species, including mature kauri. This is also the starting point for the 70km **Hillary Trail**, opened in 2010 to honour NZ's most famous son, Everest-conqueror Sir Edmund Hillary. It can be tackled in stages or in its four-day entirety, staying at campsites along the way. Walkers head to the coast at Huia then tick off all the iconic Westie beaches: Whatipu, Karekare, Piha and, Sir Ed's favourite, remote Anawhata. From here you can continue up the coast through Bethells Beach to Muriwai or head through bush to the Cascades Kauri area to end at Swanson train station.

Other noted walks in the park, all taking in impressive waterfalls, include the Kitekite Track (1.8km, 45 minutes one way), the Fairy Falls Track (5.7km, three-hour loop) and the Auckland City Walk (1.5km, one-hour loop).

AWOL Canyoning (☎ 09-834 0501; www.awol adventures.co.nz; half-/full day $135/165) offers plenty of slippery, slidey, wet fun in Piha Canyon. Pick-up from Auckland (if required), lunch and snacks are included in the price. Night trips ($155) provide plenty of glowworm action. **Canyonz** (☎ 0800 422 696; www.canyonz.co.nz; trips $175) runs canyoning trips from Auckland to the Blue Canyon, which has a series of 18 waterfalls ranging from 2m to 25m in height.

There are a couple of miniature train rides through the ranges; both must be booked in advance. The **Rain Forest Express** (☎ 09-302 8028; www.watercare.co.nz; 280 Scenic Dr; 2½hr trip adult/child $25/12) departs from Jacobsons' Depot and follows an old logging track through several tunnels deep into the bush. You'll need to book well ahead; check the website for the schedule. Less regular are the 3½-hour brunch or twilight trips (adult/child $28/14), the latter offering glimpses of glowworms and cave weta. On the other side of the park the **Waitakere Tramline Society** (☎ 09-818 4946; www.waitakeretram line.org.nz; adult/child $10/5) runs four scenic trips every Sunday that pass through a glowworm tunnel en route to the Waitakere Falls and Dam. Trips start from the end of Christian Rd, which runs south of Swanson station.

In a city not short on great views, **Elevation** (☎ 09-814 1919; 473 Scenic Dr; mains $16-29; ☺ lunch & dinner Wed-Sun) has the best of them. Perched on a slope 350m above Auckland, this restaurant even looks down on the Sky Tower. Apart from being the only half-decent eatery between Titirangi and Piha, it has excellent pizzas.

KAREKARE

Few stretches of sand have more personality than Karekare. Those prone to metaphysical musings inevitably settle on descriptions such as 'spiritual' and 'brooding'. Perhaps history has left its imprint: in 1825 it was the site of a ruthless massacre of the local Kawerau *iwi* by Ngapuhi invaders. Wild and gorgeously undeveloped, this famous beach has been the setting for onscreen moments both high- and lowbrow, from Oscar-winner *The Piano* to *Xena, Warrior Princess*.

From the car park the quickest route to the black-sand beach involves wading through an ankle-deep stream. Karekare rates as one of the most dangerous beaches in the country, with strong surf and ever-present rips, so don't even think about swimming unless the beach is being patrolled by lifeguards (usually only in summer). Pearl Jam singer Eddie Vedder nearly drowned here while visiting Neil Finn's Karekare pad.

Follow the road over the bridge and uphill along Lone Kauri Rd for 100m. A short track begins on the left, leading to the impressive **Karekare Falls**. This leafy picnic spot is the start of several walking tracks.

Karekare has no shops of any description and no public transport. To get here take Scenic Dr and Piha Rd until you reach the well-signposted turn-off to Karekare Rd.

PIHA

If you notice an Auckland surfer dude with a faraway look, chances are they're daydreaming about Piha…or just stoned. This beautifully rugged, iron-sand beach has long been a favourite for refugees from the city's stresses – whether for day trips, weekend teenage parties or holidays.

Although Piha is popular, it's also incredibly dangerous, with wild surf and strong undercurrents; so much so that it's spawned its own popular reality TV show, *Piha Rescue*. If you don't want to inadvertently star in it, always swim between the flags, where lifeguards can provide help if you get into trouble.

Piha may be bigger and more populated than Karekare, but there's still no supermarket, liquor shop, bank or petrol station, although there is a small general store that doubles as a cafe, takeaway shop and post office.

There's no public transport, but **NZ Surf'n'Snow Tours** (☎ 09-828 0426; www.newzealand surftours.com) provides shuttles when the surf's up ($25 one way).

Sights & Activities

The view of the coast as you drive down Piha Rd is spectacular. Perched on its haunches near the centre of the beach is **Lion Rock** (101m), whose 'mane' glows golden in the evening light. It's actually the eroded core of an ancient volcano and a Maori *pa* site. A path at the south end of the beach takes you to some great lookouts. At low tide you can walk south along the beach and watch the surf shooting through a ravine in another large rock known as the **Camel**. A little further along, the waves crash through the **Gap** and form a safe swimming hole. A small colony of blue penguins nests at the beach's north end.

Surfboards (three hours/day $25/35), wet suits ($8/15) and boogie boards ($15/25) can be hired from Piha Surf Shop & Crafts (right). Private surfing lessons can also be arranged.

Sleeping & Eating

Piha Domain Motor Camp (☎ 09-812 8815; pihacamp@ xtra.co.nz; 21 Seaview Rd; sites per adult/child $10/6, cabins s/d/tr $50/60/85) Smack-bang on the beach, this well-kept campsite doesn't have a lot of shelter from the elements but it's cheap as chips. The cabins are tiny but clean.

Piha Surf Accommodation (☎ 09-812 8723; www. pihasurf.co.nz; 122 Seaview Rd; caravans & cabins per person $24-40) Each basic but charmingly tatty caravan has its own linen, TV, fridge, cooker, long-

drop toilet and shares a very simple shower. The private cabins have the same rudimentary bathroom arrangement but are a more comfortable option.

our pick **Piha Beachstay** (☎ 09-812 8381; www. pihabeachstay.co.nz; 38 Glenesk Rd; dm/s $30/70, d $80-140; 🖳 🛜) Attractive and ecofriendly, just like the surf lifesaver who runs it, this wood-and-glass lodge has extremely smart facilities. It's 1km from the beach but there's a little stream at the bottom of the property and bushwalks nearby. In winter an open fire warms the wonderful large communal lounge.

Black Sands Lodge (☎ 021 969 924; www.pihabeach. co.nz/Black-Sands-Lodge.htm; Beach Valley Rd; cabin $130, apt $210-260; 🖳 🛜) With said sands only steps away, these two modern apartments with private decks match their prime location with attractive touches such as stereos, DVD players, good firm beds with natty bed linen and polished floorboards. The cabin is kitted out in a 1950s Kiwiana bach style and shares a bathroom with the main house. Bikes and wi-fi are free for guests, and in-room massage and lavish catered dinners can be arranged on request. It's gay-friendly too.

Piha Cafe (☎ 09-812 8808; www.thepihacafe.co.nz; 20 Seaview Rd; mains $10-24; ⏰ 7.30am-5pm, extended in summer) Amid a storm (in a teacup) of controversy, this attractive ecofriendly cafe (solar energy, worm farm, own bore water) opened for business in 2010. Fears that hordes of cafe-society types would destroy Piha's sand-between-toes crustiness have dissipated and now at least you can enjoy a decent meal and coffee between surfs.

Piha Store (☎ 09-812 8844; Seaview Rd; ⏰ 8am-5.30pm Mon-Fri, 8am-6pm Sat & Sun) has groceries, ice cream and home baking.

Shopping

West Coast Gallery (☎ 09-812 8029; www.westcoast gallery.co.nz; Seaview Rd; ⏰ 10am-5pm Thu-Sun) The work of more than 180 local artists is sold from this small not-for-profit gallery next to the Piha fire station.

Piha Surf Shop & Crafts (☎ 09-812 8723; www.piha surf.co.nz; 122 Seaview Rd; ⏰ 8am-5pm) A family-run venture, with well-known surfboard designer Mike Jolly selling his wares downstairs and wife Pam selling crafts and coffee upstairs.

TE HENGA (BETHELLS BEACH)

Breathtaking Bethells Beach is reached by taking Te Henga Rd at the northern end of Scenic

Dr. It's another raw, black-sand beach with surf, windswept dunes and bush walks, such as the popular one over giant sand dunes to Lake Wainamu (starting near the bridge on the approach to the beach).

Bethells Beach Cottages (☎ 09-810 9581; www. bethellsbeach.com; 267 Bethells Rd; cottages $335-620) has two charming, self-contained cottages and an apartment, all in a hillside setting with sea and sunset views. Meals can be arranged which generate as much admiration as the accommodation.

KUMEU & AROUND

West Auckland's main wine-producing area still has some vineyards that are owned by the original Croatian families who kick-started NZ's wine industry. Unlike on Waiheke Island, most cellars here offer free tastings. It's only about 30km from central Auckland; take the Northwestern Motorway (SH16) and follow the signs. For internet access, try **Kumeu Library** (298 Main Rd).

Still owned by the Brajkovich family, **Kumeu River** (Map p86; ☎ 09-412 8415; 550 SH16, Kumeu; ☺ 9am-5pm Mon-Fri, 11am-5pm Sat) produces wonderful chardonnay and pinot gris. Another Croat-Kiwi family vineyard, **Soljans Estate** (Map p86; ☎ 09-412 2680; 366 SH16, Kumeu; ☺ 9am-5.30pm) also boasts a wonderful **cafe** (mains $16-33; ☺ 11am-3.30pm Mon-Fri, 9am-3.30pm Sat & Sun) offering exceptionally tasty brunch dishes, Dalmatian-style squid and Vintner's platters crammed with Mediterranean treats. At **Coopers Creek** (Map p86; ☎ 09-412 8560; 601 SH16, Huapai; ☺ 9am-5.30pm Mon-Fri, 10.30am-5.30pm Sat & Sun) you can buy a bottle, spread out a picnic in the attractive gardens and, from January to Easter, enjoy Sunday afternoon jazz sessions.

If you'd rather hit the hops, **Hallertau** (☎ 09-412 5555; www.hallertau.co.nz; 1171 Coatesville-Riverhead Hwy; lunch $11-22, dinner $24-33; ☺ 11am-late) offers tasting paddles of five of its microbrews ($12), served on the vine-covered terrace edging its bar and restaurant.

Architecturally impressive, **Bees Online** (☎ 09-411 7953; 791 SH16, Waimauku; mains $14-27; ☺ 11am-4pm Mon-Fri, 9am-5pm Sat & Sun) allows you to watch the busy bees at work from safely behind glass, and then taste the results in the store. The wonderful cafe showcases not only honey but also native bush ingredients. Mum and dad might even get a coffee in peace while the kids play spot-the-queen in the hive.

Buses 54, 55, 66 and 67 head here from Lower Albert St in Central Auckland.

MURIWAI BEACH

Yet another rugged black-sand surf beach, stretching 60km, Muriwai Beach's main claim to fame is the **Takapu Refuge gannet colony**, spread over the southern headland and outlying rock stacks. Viewing platforms get you close enough to watch (and smell) these fascinating seabirds. Every August hundreds of adult birds return to this spot to hook up with their regular partners and get busy – expect lots of outrageously cute neck-rubbing, bill-touching and general snuggling. The net result is a single chick per season; December and January are the best times to see the little fellas testing their wings before embarking on an impressive odyssey (see the boxed text, below).

Nearby, a couple of short tracks will take you through beautiful native bush to a lookout that offers views along the length of the beach. Wild surf and treacherous rips mean that swimming is safe only when the beach is patrolled (swim between the flags). Apart from surfing, Muriwai Beach is a popular spot for hang gliding, parapunting, kiteboarding and horse riding. There are also tennis courts, a golf course and a cafe that doubles as a takeaway chippie.

Muriwai Beach Motor Camp (☎ 09-411 9262; www. muriwaimotorcamp.co.nz; Muriwai Beach; sites per adult/child $12/5) is a sheltered campsite under the shade of pines right by the beach, with a communal kitchen and coin-operated laundry.

KIWIS OR GANNETS?

After honing their flying skills, young gannets get the ultimate chance to test them – a 2000km journey to Australia. They usually hang out there for several years before returning home, never to attempt the journey again. Once back in the homeland they spend a few years waiting for a piece of waterfront property to become available in the colony, before settling down with a regular partner to nest – returning to the same patch of dirt every year.

In that regard, perhaps the gannet's a more fitting symbol for many young Aucklanders than the kiwi.

HELENSVILLE
pop 2500

A smattering of historical buildings, antique shops and cafes makes village-like Helensville a good whistle-stop for those taking SH16 north. The **visitor information centre** (☎ 09-420 8060; www.helensville.co.nz; 87 Commercial Rd; ☉ 10am-4.30pm) has details on the area, including free brochures detailing the *Helensville Heritage Trail* and *Helensville Riverside Walkway*. **Helensville Library** (Commercial Rd) has free internet access.

Aquatic Park Parakai Springs (Map p86; ☎ 09-420 8998; www.parakaisprings.co.nz; 150 Parkhurst Rd; adult/child $16/8; ☉ 10am-9pm), 2km northwest of Helensville, has large hot-spring swimming pools, private spas ($6 per hour) and a couple of hydroslides. Aucklanders bring their bored children here on wet wintry days as a cheaper alternative to Waiwera (p139). If you stay at the **camping ground** (sites per adult/child $10/8), next door, you can enter the hot pools for half price.

Woodhill Mountain Bike Park (☎ 027-278 0949; www.bikepark.co.nz; adult/child $6/4, bike hire per hr $25-30; ☉ 10am-5pm Mon, Tue, Thu & Fri, 10am-10pm Wed, 8am-5pm Sat & Sun) has many challenging tracks (including jumps and beams) around Woodhill Forest, 14km south of Helensville. Its neighbour is **Tree Adventures** (☎ 0800 827 926; www.treeadventures.co.nz; price per 1/4/8/9 courses $15/37/42/62; ☉ 9.30am-5.30pm), a set of nine high-ropes courses consisting of swinging logs, nets, balance beams, Tarzan swings and a flying fox. Also heading through the forest is **4 Track Adventures** (☎ 09-420 8104; www.4trackadventures.co.nz; 1/2/3hr tours $155/215/255), this time on quad bikes. A beach ride is included on the two- and three-hour tours. Pick-up from Auckland is $50 per person.

Extreme 4WD Adventures (☎ 0800 493 238; www.extreme4wd.co.nz; 606 Peak Rd; 1-2 people $180) offers the chance to charge around a special two-hour adventure trail in a 4WD.

Malolo House B&B (☎ 09-420 7262; www.helensville.co.nz/malolo.htm; 110 Commercial Rd; dm $30-35, d $65-120) is a wonderful kauri villa that served for a time as the town's hospital. Beautifully refurbished, it offers a range of restful accommodation, including two luxury en-suite doubles, cheaper ones with shared bathrooms and a small dorm. There's also a spa and a guest lounge with views.

Buses 66 and 67 head from near Britomart (Lower Albert St) to Parakai and Helensville ($9.70, 1½ hours).

NORTH OF AUCKLAND

The Auckland region sprawls 90km north of the CBD to just past the point where SH16 and SH1 converge at Wellsford. Beaches, regional parks, tramping trails, quaint villages, wine, kayaking and snorkelling are the main drawcards.

LONG BAY REGIONAL PARK

The northernmost of Auckland's East Coast Bays, Long Bay is a popular family picnic and swimming spot, attracting over a million visitors a year. A three-hour-return coastal walk heads north from the sandy beach to the Okura River, taking in secluded Grannys Bay and Pohutukawa Bay (which attracts nude bathers).

Regular buses head to Long Bay (adult/child $6.50/3.80, one hour) from Albert St in the city. The $11 day pass is the best option; enquire through **Maxx** (☎ 09-366 6400; www.maxx.co.nz). If you're driving, leave the Northern Motorway at the Oteha Valley Rd exit, heading towards Browns Bay, and follow the signs.

SHAKESPEAR REGIONAL PARK

Shooting out eastward just before Orewa, the Whangaparaoa Peninsula is a heavily developed spit of land with a sizable South African expat community. At its tip is the gorgeous 376-hectare **Shakespear Regional Park**. Sheep, cows, peacocks and pukeko ramble over the grassy headland, while pohutukawa-lined **Te Haruhi Bay** provides great views of the gulf islands and the city. Walking tracks take between 40 minutes and two hours, exploring native forest, WWII gun embankments, Maori sites and lookouts. If you can't bear to leave, there's an idyllic beachfront **campsite** (☎ 09-366 2000; www.arc.govt.nz; adult/child $10/5) with flush toilets and cold showers.

It's possible to get here via a torturous bus trip (about two hours; routes 896, 898 and 899) from Auckland's Britomart station; enquire via **Maxx** (☎ 09-366 6400; www.maxx.co.nz). The one-way fare is $9.70, so it's best to buy an $11 day pass. An alternative is to take the **360 Discovery** (☎ 09-424 5510; www.360discovery.co.nz) ferry service to Gulf Harbour (adult/child $13.40/8), a Noddy-town development of matching townhouses, a marina, country club and golf course. Enquire at the ferry office about picking up a bus or taxi from here. Alternatively, walk or cycle the remaining 3km to the park. The ferry is a good option for cyclists wanting to skip the boring road trip out of Auckland; carry-on bikes are free.

OREWA
pop 7300

Locals have fears that Orewa is turning into NZ's equivalent of Queensland's Gold Coast, but until they start exporting retirees and replacing them with bikini-clad parking wardens that's unlikely to happen. It is, however, very built-up and high-rise apartment towers have begun to sprout.

Information
Hibiscus Coast i-SITE (☎ 09-426 0076; 214a Hibiscus Coast Hwy (HCH)); ⏰ 9am-5pm Mon-Fri, 10am-4pm Sat & Sun) Information and internet access.
Post office (Hillary Sq)

Sights & Activities
The 3km-long sheltered and sandy beach is patrolled by lifeguards in the peak season.

The **Alice Eaves Scenic Reserve** (Old North Rd), to the north of the town, is 10 hectares of native bush with labelled trees, a *pa* site, a lookout and easy short walks. The 8km **Millennium Walkway** starts from South Bridge, looping through this and other parks before returning along the beach; follow the blue route markers.

Snowplanet (☎ 09-427 0044; www.snowplanet.co.nz; 91 Small Rd, Silverdale; day pass adult/child from $54/42; ⏰ 10am-10pm) is a winter wonderland that allows every day to be a snowy one, with indoor skiing, tobogganing and snowboarding. It's just off SH1, 8km south of Orewa.

Sleeping
Orewa Beach Top 10 Holiday Park (☎ 0800 673 921; www.orewabeachtop10.co.nz; 265 HCH; sites per adult/child $21/9, cabins $52-89, flats $98-114; 🖳) Taking up a large chunk of the beach's south end, this well-kept park has excellent facilities. The prefab 'tourist flats' even have art on the walls and bedside lamps. Road noise can be a problem.

Marco Polo Backpackers Lodge (☎ 09-426 8455; www.marcopolo.co.nz; 2d Hammond Ave, Hatfields Beach; sites per person $19, dm $26-28, s/d $48/66) The lush garden lends a tropical vibe to this hillside complex, a few kilometres north of Orewa. The rooms are simple and there's no TV to spoil the peace.

Pillows Travellers Lodge (☎ 09-426 6338; www.pillows.co.nz; 412 HCH; dm $20, r $49-65) Eleven rooms open onto a pleasant garden at this well-located backpackers. There are separate male and female dorms, a spa pool, a relaxing lounge, free tea and coffee, a piano and TVs in the private rooms.

Orewa Motor Lodge (☎ 09-426 4027; www.orewa motorlodge.co.nz; 290 HCH; units $135-185; 🖳) One of a string of motels that line Orewa's main road, this complex has scrupulously clean wooden units that are prettied up with hanging flower baskets. There's also a spa pool.

Waves (☎ 09-427 0888; www.waves.co.nz; cnr HCH & Kohu St; units $176-293) Like a motel only much flasher, this complex offers spacious, self-contained, modern units with double glazing, wall-mounted CD players and smart furnishings. The downstairs units have gardens and most have spa baths. Best of all, it's only a few metres from the beach.

Eating
Plantation (☎ 09-426 5083; 226 Hibiscus Coast Hwy; mains $4-21; ⏰ 7.30am-8pm) Any Auckland kid who's ever headed north has pestered their parents to stop here for an ice cream. It also has pies, takeaway food, cooked meals and a nice selection of counter food.

Asahi (☎ 09-426 0065; 6 Bakehouse Lane; mains $12-22; ⏰ 9am-3pm Mon, 9am-9pm Tue-Sat) Asahi is a handy little option for a Japanese fix. The *bento* boxes ($21.50) are recommended.

There's also a big branch of the **New World** (11 Moana Ave; ⏰ 7am-10pm) supermarket chain for snacks and self-catering.

Getting There & Away

Direct buses run between Orewa and Albert St in the city (adult/child $9.70/5.80, 75 minutes), as well as Shakespear Regional Park (adult/child $3.20/1.80, 40 minutes) and Waiwera (adult/child $1.60/1, 10 minutes). **Maxx** (☎ 09-366 6400; www.maxx.co.nz) handles all bus enquiries.

WAIWERA

This pleasant river-mouth village has a great beach, but it's the *wai wera* (hot waters) that people come here for. Warm mineral water bubbles up from 1500m below the surface to fill the 19 pools of the **Waiwera Infinity Thermal Spa Resort** (☎ 09-427 8800; www.waiwera.co.nz; 21 Main Rd; adult/child $25/15; ◷ 9am-9pm Sun-Thu, 9am-10pm Fri & Sat). There's a movie pool, 10 big slides, barbecues, private tubs ($40) and a health spa. If you can't face driving afterwards, luxuriously appointed modern houses have been built nearby (doubles $215 to $245); enquire about indulgence packages.

For those with simpler needs, the **Holiday Park** (☎ 09-426 5270; www.waiweraholidaypark.co.nz; 37 Waiwera Pl; sites per adult/child $18/9, cabins $65; ▨) has a great possie, right by the water, and friendly management.

Squeezed between the Waiwera and Puhoi Rivers, the exquisite 134-hectare **Wenderholm Regional Park** has a diverse ecology, abundant bird life, beaches and walks (30 minutes to 2½ hours). **Couldrey House** (☎ 09-528 3713; adult/child $3/free; ◷ 1-4pm Sat & Sun, daily Boxing Day-Easter), the original homestead (1860s), is now a museum. A **campsite** (☎ 09-366 2000; adult/child $10/5) provides tap water and long-drop toilets only.

Bus 895 from Auckland's Albert St heads to Waiwera (adult/child $9.70/5.80, one hour) via Orewa; enquire through **Maxx** (☎ 09-366 6400; www.maxx.co.nz).

PUHOI
pop 450

Forget dingy cafes and earnest poets – this quaint village is a slice of the real Bohemia. In 1863 around 200 immigrants from the present-day Czech Republic settled in what was then dense bush. The **Bohemian Museum** (www.puhoihistoricalsociety.org.nz; Puhoi Rd; adult/child $3/free; ◷ 1-4pm Sat & Sun, daily Christmas-Easter) tells their story of hardship and perseverance. Next door is the village's pretty **Catholic Church** (1881), with an interesting tabernacle painting, stained glass and statues.

Puhoi River Canoe Hire (☎ 09-422 0891; www. puhoirivercanoes.co.nz; 84 Puhoi Rd) hires kayaks and Canadian canoes, either by the hour (single/double kayak $20/40) or for an excellent 8km downstream journey from the village to Wenderholm Regional Park (single/double kayak $40/80, including return transport). Bookings are essential.

In the 1879 **Puhoi Hotel** (☎ 09-422 0812; cnr Saleyards & Puhoi Rds; ◷ 10am-10pm) there's character and then some, with bar walls completely covered in old photos, animal heads and vintage household goods.

Puhoi Cottage Tea Rooms (☎ 09-422 0604; 50 Ahuroa Rd; ◷ 9.30am-5pm Thu-Tue), 500m beyond the village, is well known for its Devonshire teas ($10). Just 3km further on is the **Art of Cheese Cafe** (☎ 09-422 0670; 275 Ahuroa Rd; platters $19-22; ◷ 9am-5pm), where the people understand that any balanced diet consists of about 90% cheese. Watch cheese being made, buy a big hunk of yellow happiness or dine on very good platters in the licensed cafe. There's also a kids' menu and playground.

Puhoi is a kilometre west of SH1; the turn-off is 2km past the Johnstone Hills tunnel.

MAHURANGI & SCANDRETT REGIONAL PARKS

Straddling the head of Mahurangi Harbour, this boaties' paradise has three distinct 'fingers': Mahurangi West, accessed from a turn-off 3km north of Puhoi; Scott Point on the eastern side, with road access 16km southeast of Warkworth; and isolated Mahurangi East, which can only be reached by boat. The park incorporates areas of coastal forest, *pa* sites and a historic homestead and cemetery. Its sheltered beaches offer prime sandy spots for a dip or picnic and there are loop walks ranging from 1½ to 2½ hours. **Accommodation** (☎ 09-366 2000; www.arc.govt.nz; sites per person $5-10, baches $100-120) is available in four basic campsites and four baches sleeping six to eight.

On the way to Mahurangi West you'll pass **Zealandia Sculpture Garden** (☎ 09-422 0099; www.zealandiasculpturegarden.co.nz; 138 Mahurangi West Rd; admission $10; ◷ 10am-4pm Sat & Sun Nov-Dec & Feb-Mar, 10am-4pm daily Jan), where the work of Terry Stringer is showcased within impressive architecture and grounds. There are guided tours at 11am and 2pm.

On the ocean side of the Mahurangi Peninsula, **Scandrett Regional Park** has a sandy beach, walking tracks, patches of regenerating forest, another historic homestead, more *pa* sites and great views towards Kawau Island. Three **ARC baches** (☎ 09-366 2000; www.arc.govt.nz; baches $120) are available for rent.

WARKWORTH
pop 3300

River-hugging Warkworth makes for a pleasant pit stop, its dinky main street retaining a village atmosphere. Grab a free *Heritage Trail* brochure from the **Warkworth i-SITE** (☎ 09-425 9081; www.warkworthnz.com; 1 Baxter St; ☽ 8.30am-5pm Mon-Fri, 9am-4.30pm Sat, 9am-3pm Sun; ☐ ☎) if you've got some time to kill.

Just south of town, the 8.5-hectare **Parry Kauri Park** has short walks and a couple of giant kauri trees, including the 800-year-old McKinney kauri (girth 7.6m). Also at the park, the small **Warkworth & District Museum** (☎ 09-425 7093; www.wwmuseum.orcon.net.nz; Tudor Collins Dr; adult/child $6/1; ☽ 9am-3.30pm) features pioneer-era exhibits.

About 5km south of Warkworth, the **Honey Centre** (Map p86; ☎ 09-425 8003; www.honeycentre.co.nz; cnr SH1 & Perry Rd; ☽ 8.30am-5pm) has a cafe, free honey tasting and glass-fronted hives. The shop sells all sorts of bee-related products, from candles to mead.

Nearby, **Ransom Wines** (Map p86; ☎ 09-425 8862; www.ransomwines.co.nz; Valerie Close; tasting free with purchase, otherwise $5 donation to Tawharanui Open Sanctuary; ☽ 10am-5pm Tue-Sun) produces great food wines and showcases them with matching tapas ($16 for five) and tasting platters ($18).

Sheepworld (Map p86; ☎ 09-425 7444; www.sheepworldfarm.co.nz; SH1; adult/child $14/7, incl sheep & dog show $24/8; ☽ 9am-5pm), 4km north of Warkworth, offers farm experiences for city slickers (kids' pony rides, lamb feeding) and the ubiquitous sheep and dog show, including a shearing demonstration (showtimes 11am and 2pm). The **Black Sheep Café** (mains $8-16) serves home-baked goods and coffee. In late September Sheepworld hosts the eccentric two-week **Warkworth Scarecrow Festival**.

Two kilometres further north, a walkway leads from SH1 through the regenerating **Dome Forest** to the Dome summit (336m). On a fine day you can see the Sky Tower from a lookout near the top. The summit walk takes about 1½ hours return, or you can continue for a gruelling seven-hour one-way tramp through the **Totora Peak Scenic Reserve**, exiting on Govan Wilson Rd.

Bridge House Lodge & Shark Bar (☎ 09-425 8351; www.bridgehouse.co.nz; 16 Elizabeth St; tw $75, d $85-100, tr $125) has a riverside location and a mixed bag of rooms – some newer and nicer than others but all clean enough. The refurbished bar (open 11am to 1am) is downright swanky, dishing up fancy pub grub including chorizo burgers and pizzas (mains $15 to $30).

InterCity (☎ 09-583 5780; www.intercity.co.nz) and associated daily buses stop here heading to/from Auckland ($27, one hour), Orewa ($18, 24 minutes), Whangarei ($31, two hours), Paihia ($42, three hours) and Kerikeri ($44, 3½ hours). **Naked Bus** (☎ 0900 625 33 per min $1.80; www.nakedbus.com) heads to Auckland and as far north as Paihia, with limited advance fares starting from $1.

MATAKANA & AROUND

Matakana suffers from reverse alcoholism – the more wine gets poured into it, the more genteel it becomes. A few years ago it was a nondescript rural village with a handful of heritage buildings and an old-fashioned country pub. Now the locals watch bemused as Auckland's chattering classes idle away the hours in stylish wine bars and cafes. The most striking symbol of the transition is the fantastical **Matakana Cinemas** (☎ 09-422 9833; www.matakanacinemas.co.nz; 2 Matakana Valley Rd; adult/child $15/8) complex, its domed roof reminiscent of an Ottoman bathhouse. The humble **Farmers Market** (☽ 8am-1pm Sat) is held in its shadow – or should that be Farmers Upmarket?

The reason for this epicurean ecstasy is the success of the area's boutique wineries. They're developing a name for pinot gris, merlot, syrah and a host of obscure varietals. Local vineyards are detailed in the free *Matakana Coast Wine Country* (www.matakanacoast.com) and *Matakana Wine Trail* (www.matakanawine.com) brochures. Both are available from the **Matakana Information Centre** (☎ 09-422 7433; www.matakanavillage.co.nz; ☽ 10am-1pm) in the foyer of the cinema. In the same building, the **Vintry** (☎ 09-423 0251; tastings from $8.50; ☽ 10am-10pm) is a wine bar that serves as a one-stop cellar door for all the producers.

Vineyards open for regular tastings include: **Ascension Wine Estate** (☎ 09-422 9601; www.ascensionwine.co.nz; 480 Matakana Rd; tasting $3-5, refundable with purchase; ☽ 11am-4pm Mon-Fri, 10am-5pm Sat & Sun) Has an acclaimed restaurant (mains $17 to $34).

Hyperion Wines (☎ 09-422 9375; www.hyperion-wines.co.nz; 188 Tongue Farm Rd; ✆ 10am-5pm Sat & Sun)
Omaha Bay Vineyard (☎ 09-423 0022; www.omahabay.co.nz; 189 Takatu Rd; tastings $5, refundable on purchase; ✆ 11am-5pm Wed-Sun)

Brick Bay Wines is the home of the **Brick Bay Sculpture Trail** (☎ 09-425 4690; www.brickbaysculpture.co.nz; Arabella Lane; adult/child $10/8; ✆ 10am-5pm), an hour-long artistic ramble through the wonderfully sculpted grounds. Tastings and snacks are available at the chic cafe.

Morris & James (☎ 09-422 7116; www.morrisandjames.co.nz; 48 Tongue Farm Rd; ✆ 8am-4.30pm Mon-Fri, 9am-5pm Sat & Sun) has creative, colourful ceramics for sale and a lovely courtyard cafe. There are free weekday tours at 11.30am.

The nearest swimming beach is **Omaha**, 7km east, with a long stretch of white sand, good surf and holiday homes. Shortly after the Omaha turn-off, the partly unsealed Takatu Rd leads to the 588-hectare **Tawharanui Regional Park** at the end of the peninsula. This special place is an open sanctuary for native birds, protected by a pest-proof fence, while the northern coast is a marine park (bring a snorkel). There are plenty of walking tracks (1½ to four hours) but the main attraction is Anchor Bay, one of the region's finest white-sand beaches. **Camping** (☎ 09-366 2000; www.arc.govt.nz; sites per adult/child $10/5) is allowed at a basic site near the beach and the ARC also has a six-person bach for hire ($120).

Sleeping

Sandspit Holiday Park (☎ 09-425 8610; www.sandspitholidaypark.co.nz; 1334 Sandspit Rd, Sandspit; sites per adult/child $15/8, cabins $50-160; 🖳 🛜) A campsite masquerading as a pioneer village, this wonderful place incorporates historic buildings and faux shopfronts into its facilities. The self-contained waterside cottages are excellent. It's right by the water at Sandspit, 8km from Matakana village.

Matakana House Motel (☎ 09-422 7497; www.matakanahouse.co.nz; 975 Matakana Rd; apt $110-360) Right in the middle of the village but far enough back from the pub to avoid the noise, this motel is more like a set of terraced townhouses. Ranging from studios to two-bedroom apartments, they're a smart proposition.

Eating & Drinking

Brookview Teahouse (☎ 09-423 0390; 1335 Leigh Rd; Devonshire tea $12; ✆ 10am-4pm Wed-Mon) Devoted to

the pursuit of the perfect cuppa, this delightful bungalow surrounded by boxed gardens serves traditional morning and afternoon teas (scones, lamingtons and club sandwiches), and light lunches.

Tapiano (☎ 09-423 0383; mains $29-36; ✆ lunch Fri-Sun, dinner Tue-Sun) Snagging the stream frontage of the cinema complex (opposite), Matakana's flashest restaurant's menu meanders around the Mediterranean – from hearty French classics to tagines and tapas ($9 to $15) – along with tempting brunch standards ($10 to $17) during the day.

Matakana House (☎ 09-422 9770; 11 Matakana Valley Rd; ✆ 3pm-late Mon-Fri, noon-late Sat & Sun) A real local pub, this 1903 wooden hotel has taxidermied animals everywhere, a beer garden out front and occasional live music and DJs. It's an affectation-free zone.

Getting There & Away

Matakana village is a 10km drive northeast of Warkworth along Matakana Rd; there's no public transport. Ferries for Kawau Island leave from Sandspit, 8km east of Warkworth along Sandspit Rd.

LEIGH
pop 390

Appealing little Leigh (www.leighbythesea.co.nz) has a picturesque harbour dotted with fishing boats, and a decent swimming beach at Matheson Bay. Its two main drawcards are its proximity to Goat Island (p142) and the legendary Leigh Sawmill live-music venue.

Goat Island Dive (☎ 0800 348 369, 09-422 6925; www.goatislanddive.co.nz; 142a Pakiri Rd; ✆ 9am-5pm) has a shop in Leigh and a boat that can take you diving anywhere in the Hauraki Gulf, including wreck dives, at any time of year. Snorkel, fin and mask hire is $18. Gear for a two-tank dive costs $100, dive trips are $80 to $140, and a shore dive with instruction is $250. PADI courses ($500), including Advanced and Rescue, are offered.

Leigh Sawmill Café, Micro Brewery & Accommodation (☎ 09-422 6019; www.sawmillcafe.co.nz; 142 Pakiri Rd; brunch $9-26, dinner $25-31; ✆ 10am-late daily late Dec–mid-Feb, 5-9pm Thu & 10am-1am Fri-Sun mid-Feb–late Dec) is a spunky little venue that's a regular stop on the summer rock circuit, sometimes attracting surprisingly big names. The pizzas are thin and crunchy like they should be, and best enjoyed in the garden on a lazy summer's evening. If you imbibe too much at the on-site microbrewery (☼ 1-5pm Fri-Sun), there's accommodation inside an old sawmill shed, including backpacker rooms ($25, $40 with linen) and massive doubles with en suites ($125). Alternatively, you can hire the Cosy Sawmill Family Cottage (from $300, sleeps 10).

Leigh Rd heads northeast from Matakana village; there's no public transport.

GOAT ISLAND MARINE RESERVE

Quick, grab the highlighter for this one. Only 3km from Leigh, this 547-hectare area was established in 1975 as the country's first marine reserve. In a scant 30 years the sea has reverted to a giant aquarium, giving an impression of what it was like before humans arrived. You only need step knee-deep into the water to see snapper (the big fish with blue dots and fins), blue maomao and stripy parore swimming around. You can snorkel or scuba dive from the beach, and there are dive areas all round Goat Island, just offshore. You can see colourful sponges, forests of brown seaweed, boarfish, crayfish, stingrays and, if you're very lucky, orcas and bottle-nosed dolphins. Visibility is claimed to be at least 10m, 75% of the time.

Excellent interpretive panels explain the area's Maori significance (it was the landing place of one of the ancestral canoes) and provide pictures of the species you're likely to encounter.

A **glass-bottomed boat** (☎ 09-422 6334; www.glassbottomboat.co.nz; adult/child $25/13) provides a great all-year on-the-hour trip around Goat Island to see the underwater life. Trips last 45 minutes and run from the beach. When the sea is too rough the boat doesn't operate; ring to check.

Beach Hire (☎ 09-422 6663) rents kayaks and snorkelling gear either from the beach or from a neighbouring house. Snorkelling gear ($14),

wetsuits ($16 to $18) and underwater cameras ($35) can be hired at **Seafriends** (☎ 09-422 6212; www.seafriends.org.nz; 7 Goat Island Rd; ☼ 9am-7pm), 1km before Goat Island beach. You can hire a mask with a lens if you are short-sighted or a buoyant wetsuit if you are a poor swimmer. Seafriends also runs a saltwater aquarium, marine education centre and cafe.

If one day's snorkelling isn't enough, **Goat Island Camping** (☎ 09-422 6185; www.goatislandcamping.co.nz; Goat Island Rd; sites per adult/child $18/8, caravans & cabins $60-100, units $150-190) occupies view-greedy farmland above the beach. Pitch a tent, snaffle a hippy caravan or splash out on the self-contained unit with spa. It's just a shame that the bathroom facilities are so limited.

PAKIRI

Stunning Pakiri Beach, 12km past Goat Island (4km of the road is unsealed), is an unspoilt expanse of white sand and rolling surf. In 2005 the Auckland Regional Council purchased a 52-hectare chunk from champion boxer David Tua, creating Auckland's 25th regional park. No doubt the ARC will in time develop walking tracks and campsites to its usual high standards, preserving this magical location for future generations.

Pakiri Beach Holiday Park (☎ 09-422 6199; www.pakiriholidaypark.co.nz; 261 Pakiri River Rd; sites per adult/child $15/8, dm $25-30, cabins $80-170, units $130-310) has a shop and good units in a secure beachfront setting.

Just 6km from Pakiri is **Pakiri Horse Riding** (☎ 09-422 6275; www.horseride-nz.co.nz; Rahuikiri Rd), which has more than 80 horses for superb bush-and-beach rides ranging from one hour ($55) to all day ($250) or longer 'safaris'. **Accommodation** (dm/cabin/4-bedroom house $30/150/500) is provided in basic but spectacularly situated beachside cabins or a comfortable house secluded among the dunes.

Northland & the Bay of Islands

For many New Zealanders, the phrase 'up north' conjures up sepia-toned images of family fun in the sun, pohutukawa in bloom and dolphins frolicking in pretty bays. It's uttered in almost hallowed tones, as if describing a mythical place. From school playgrounds to work cafeterias, owning a bach (holiday house) 'up north' is a passport to popularity.

Beaches are the main drawcard and they're present in profusion. Take your pick from surfy or sheltered, massive or minuscule, fashionable or forgotten, and from sand that's golden, grey, pink or blindingly white. There are beaches suited to all sorts of aquatic pursuits imaginable, including splashing about in the nuddy. Visitors from more crowded countries are flummoxed to wander onto beaches without a scrap of development or another human being in sight.

Northland's reserves shelter the most spectacular remnants of the ancient kauri forests that once blanketed the top of the country. The remaining giant trees are an awe-inspiring sight and one of the nation's treasures.

It's not just natural attractions that are on offer: history hangs heavily here as well. The country was colonised from the top down by successive migrations from Polynesia and a strong Maori presence remains to this day, adding an extra dimension to any visit. The Bay of Islands was also the site of the first permanent European settlement, as well as the signing of the Declaration of the Independence of New Zealand (NZ) by local chiefs in 1835 and the Treaty of Waitangi five years later. Northland is unquestionably the birthplace of the nation.

HIGHLIGHTS

- Leaving footprints in the sand anywhere along **Bream Bay** (p154)
- Watching oceans collide while souls depart at **Cape Reinga** (p172)
- Paying homage to the ancient giants of the **Waipoua Kauri Forest** (p179)
- Diving at one of the world's top spots, the **Poor Knights Islands** (p151)
- Claiming your own island paradise among the many in the **Bay of Islands** (p153)
- Surfing the sand dunes at **Ninety Mile Beach** (p172) or Hokianga's **North Head** (p178)
- Delving into history and culture at the **Waitangi Treaty Grounds** (p160)

★ Cape Reinga

★ Ninety Mile Beach

★ Bay of Islands

Waitangi ★

North Head ★

Waipoua ★ Kauri Forest

★ Poor Knights Islands

★ Bream Bay

- Telephone code: 09
- www.northlandnz.com
- www.kauricoast.co.nz

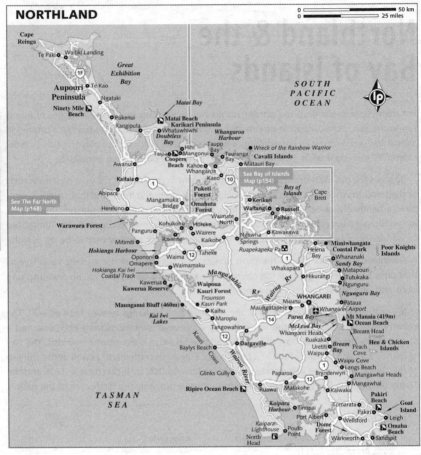

Climate

The 'winterless north' averages seven rainy days per month in summer but 16 in winter. Temperatures are often a degree or two warmer than Auckland, especially on the east coast.

Getting There & Around

There are two main routes heading north: SH1 on the east coast, and SH12, which branches off at Brynderwyn and follows the west coast to the Hokianga before rejoining SH1 near Kaikohe. This chapter roughly follows an anticlockwise loop, starting with the east coast, but you should choose your direction based on your interests and the prevailing weather.

Whangarei, Kerikeri and Kaitaia all have domestic airports, connecting through Auckland to international flights. Northland has no passenger train service, but **InterCity** (☎ 09-583 5780; www.intercity.co.nz) and associated buses ply SH1 from Auckland to Kaitaia. **Naked Bus** (☎ 0900 625 33, per min $1.80; www.nakedbus. com; advance fares from $1) covers the same route but only as far as Paihia. Other areas are poorly served, with only **Main Coachline** (☎ 09-278 8070; www.maincoachline.co.nz) heading from Auckland along SH12 as far as Dargaville (six services per week).

Only tourist buses head to Cape Reinga, the Hokianga and Waipoua Kauri Forest. The **Magic Travellers Network** (☎ 09-358 5600; www. magicbus.co.nz) has a useful service from Paihia

---

NORTHLAND & THE BAY OF ISLANDS FACTS

Eat Kumara, Dargaville's knobbly purple claim to fame (p189)

Drink Orange juice, Kerikeri's signature squeeze (p164)

Read *The House of Strife* (1993), Maurice Shadbolt's novel set during the Northland War

Listen to *Treaty* (1998) by Moana & the Moahunters

Watch *The Strength of Water* (2009), small-town Hokianga life on the big screen

Swim at Mermaid Pool, Matapouri (p151)

Festival Waitangi Day (p160)

Tackiest tourist attraction Ancient Kauri Kingdom (p173)

Go green Sing to the trees with Footprints Waipoua (p178)

---

to Auckland (in that direction only) via the Hokianga and Kauri Coast on SH12. The fixed fare ($69, four buses weekly) allows you to stop anywhere along the route, as often as you like.

See the end of each town section for detailed bus options. For details on backpacker discounts, passes and hop-on, hop-off tourist services, see p437.

WHANGAREI DISTRICT

To truly experience this area you have to be prepared to get wet. Beach after clear-watered beach offers munificent opportunities for swimming, surfing, splashing about or just wading in the shallows. Consequently the hot spots heave with Kiwi holidaymakers at peak times, but even then it's possible to

find isolated stretches of sand where your footprints are the only ones.

If you're reading this and you're a diving fanatic, drop everything and head to Tutukaka immediately. The neighbouring Poor Knights Islands are considered one of the world's top diving spots.

MANGAWHAI
pop 1200

Magical Mangawhai – that's what the official road sign says, and such signs don't tend to lie. Leave SH1 at Kaiwaka and drive 13km east (there's no bus) to snug Mangawhai village at the base of a horseshoe harbour. But it's at Mangawhai Heads, 5km further on, that the enchantment really takes hold.

A narrow spit of powdery white sand stretches for kilometres to form the south head, sheltering a seabird sanctuary. Across the water sits an uncomplicated holiday town with a surf beach at its northern tip. Life-savers patrol on weekends in summer and daily during school holidays, but despite the rollers it's not especially dangerous. The **Mangawhai Cliffs Walkway** (three hours return) starts here, affording extensive views of sea and land.

Various Maori tribes inhabited the area before the 1660s, when Ngati Whatua became dominant. In 1807 Ngati Whatua defeated Ngapuhi from the north in a major battle, letting the survivors escape. One of them was Hongi Hika, who in 1825 returned, armed with muskets obtained from Europeans. The ensuing bloodbath all but annihilated Ngati Whatua and the district became *tapu* (sacred, taboo). British squatters moved in and were rewarded with land titles by the government in the 1850s. Ceremonies were only performed to lift the *tapu* in the 1990s.

MAORI NZ: NORTHLAND & THE BAY OF ISLANDS

The Northland region, known to Maori as Te Tai Tokerau, has a long and proud Maori history and today has one of the country's highest percentages of Maori people. Along with the East Coast, it's a place where you might hear Maori being spoken. In mythology the region is known as the tail of the fish of Maui.

Maori sites of particular significance include the Waitangi Treaty Grounds (p168), Cape Reinga (p172) and Tane Mahuta (p179).

Maori cultural experiences are offered by Footprints Waipoua (p178), Sandtrails Hokianga (p177), Terenga Paraoa (p149), Waka Tai-a-Mai (p162) and Culture North (p162). Many businesses catering to travellers are owned or run by Maori individuals or *hapu* (subtribal) groups. **Tai Tokerau Tourism** (www.taitokerau.co.nz) lists dozens of them on its website, and many of them are reviewed in this chapter.

Mangawhai Heads has a part-time **information centre** (☎ 09-431 5090; www.mangawhai.co.nz; Molesworth Dr; ☻ 2-5pm Fri, 11am-5pm Sat, 10am-1pm Sun) next to full-time information panels.

In Mangawhai village, the **Mangawhai District Museum** (Moir St; adult/child $2/1; ☻ 10.30am-1pm Sat) has a tiny display of settler and Maori artefacts. Combine it with a trip to the **farmers market** (☻ 9am-1pm Sat), next door in the library hall, and stock up on local organic produce including wine and olive oil.

Smashed Pipi Cafe, Bar, Restaurant & Gallery (☎ 09-431 4848; www.smashedpipi.co.nz; 40 Moir St; mains $9-18; ☻ breakfast & lunch daily, dinner Thu-Sat) is a funky combination, with occasional live music in the bar, vibrant ceramics and glassware in the gallery (open 9am to 5.30pm), and counter food and a blackboard menu in the cafe.

Rural France comes to the village in the form of **Bennetts** (☎ 09-431 5072; www.bennettsofmangawhai.com; 52 Moir St; mains $30-32; ☻ shop 9am-4.30pm, cafe breakfast & lunch Tue-Sun, dinner Fri & Sat), a chocolaterie and cafe where you can sit by the fountain in the courtyard listening to Edith Piaf while pigging out on *macarons*, gateaux and delectable truffles.

Mangawhai Heads is where you'll want to stay. **Coastal Cow Backpackers** (☎ 09-431 5444; www.mangawhaibackpackers.com; 299 Molesworth Dr; dm/d/tr/q $23/56/76/96) is a homely hostel with cow-themed decorative touches. The rooms are clean and simple.

The boutique **Mangawhai Lodge B&B** (☎ 09-431 5311; www.seaviewlodge.co.nz; 4 Heather St; s $150-185, d $175-230; ☐ ☏) has a commanding position and great views. The comfortable, smartly furnished rooms have access to the picture-perfect wraparound veranda.

Milestone Cottages (☎ 09-431 4018; www.milestonecottages.co.nz; 27 Moir Pt Rd; cottages $200-320; ☒) conjure a Pasifika paradise with its lush tropical gardens and self-contained cottages (sleeping up to five). Free videos, kayaks, croquet and *pétanque* are available.

Sail Rock Cafe (☎ 09-431 4051; 12a Wood St; mains $12-28; ☻ 9.30am-late) takes justified pride in its salt-and-pepper squid, a dish that provokes an almost-religious experience in many a diner. At the tail end of a day's surfing this is the place to chat about the break that got away over an ice-cold beer.

On the last Sunday of the month it's the Heads' turn for the **farmers market** (Wood St; ☻ 9am-1pm).

WAIPU & BREAM BAY
pop 1980

Generations of Kiwi kids have giggled over the name 'Waipu'; the makers of Imodium missed a golden opportunity by failing to adopt it as their product's brand name for the NZ market. Be that as it may, Waipu and neighbouring **Waipu Cove** are bonny wee places.

The original 934 British settlers came from Scotland via Nova Scotia (Canada) between 1853 and 1860. These dour Scots at least had the good sense to eschew frigid Otago, where so many of their kindred settled, for sunnier northern climes. Their story comes to life through holograms, a short film and interactive displays at the **Waipu Museum** (☎ 09-432 0746; 36 The Centre; adult/child $8/3; ☻ 9.30am-4.30pm; ☐). Only 10% of current residents are direct descendants, but there's a big get-together on 1 January every year, when the **Highland Games** (☎ 09-432 1514; www.waipugames.co.nz; adult/child $15/5), established in 1871, take place in Caledonian Park.

Bream Bay has miles of blissfully deserted beach, blighted only slightly by a giant oil refinery at the north end. At **Uretiti**, a stretch of beach near a **Department of Conservation (DOC) campsite** (SH1; sites per adult/child $7/3.50) is unofficially considered 'clothing optional'. Over New Year the crowd is evenly split between Kiwi families, hardcore European nudists and gay guys.

Information

Tourist information and internet access are available at the museum.

Sleeping

Camp Waipu Cove (☎ 09-432 0410; www.campwaipucove.com; Cove Rd; sites per s/d/tr $20/30/45, cabins $50-105) Taking up a fair chunk of beach, this is a large and comfortable camping ground with spotless facilities.

Stonehouse (☎ 09-432 0432; www.stonehousewaipu.co.nz; 641 Cove Rd; dm/s/d/tr/q $20/110/120/150/180) On the main road between Waipu Cove and Waipu is this unique Cornish-style house built of huge stone slabs. Guests are accommodated in separate units and can use a kayak or rowing boat to cross the saltwater lagoon and get to the ocean beach. The backpackers' loft is a cutesy attic, but you'll have to brave an outhouse toilet.

Waipu Wanderers Backpackers (☎ 09-432 0532; www.wanderers@xtra.co.nz; 25 St Marys Rd; dm/s/d $30/45/60;

(☏) There are only three rooms at this bright and friendly backpackers in Waipu township – a real home away from home – with free fruit in season.

Dragon Tree Lodge (☎ 09-946 0899; www.dragontree. co.nz; 239 Massey Rd; r $180-230; ☐ ☏) Sometime between our last edition and this one, this hilltop retreat changed from a women's only B&B run by a charming lesbian couple to a men's only B&B run by a charming gay couple – which no doubt caused confusion to many of our readers. It offers a rural ambience, stylish furnishings and superb views over Bream Bay from the rooms and the outdoor spa.

Eating

Waipu Cafe/Deli (☎ 09-432 0990; 29 The Centre; mains $10-20; ☽ 9am-4pm) Self-caterers and coffee hounds should check out this cute little deli with 'serious fudge brownies'.

Pizza Barn (☎ 09-432 1011; 2 Cove Rd; mains $11-24; ☽ 11.30am-late Wed-Sun Apr-Nov, daily Dec-Mar) In Waipu even the pizza has a tartan logo. It also has popular platters, light fare and hunger-assuaging pizzas that go well with cold beer as this cool place morphs into a bar.

Beach House (☎ 09-432 0877; 891 Cove Rd; mains $20-35; ☽ lunch Sun, dinner Wed-Sun) With a reputation as one of Northland's best, this little restaurant offers hearty meals in a distinctive courtyard enclosed by *ponga* (tree fern) logs.

Getting There & Away

Waipu Cove can be reached by a particularly scenic route heading from Mangawhai Heads through Langs Beach. Otherwise turn off SH1, which skirts Waipu, 38km south of Whangarei.

InterCity (☎ 09-583 5780; www.intercity.co.nz) and associated daily buses stop here on the way from Auckland ($36, 2½ hours) to Whangarei ($22, 30 minutes), Paihia ($32, two hours) and Kerikeri ($33, 2½ hours) via Warkworth ($23, 1¼ hours).

Naked Bus (☎ 0900 625 33, per min $1.80; www. nakedbus.com; advance fares from $1) heads daily to Auckland (two hours), Warkworth (one hour), Whangarei (40 minutes) and Paihia (two hours).

WHANGAREI

pop 45,800

On the pretty-to-ugly continuum Whangarei sits somewhere in the middle. But beauty is never far away and there are plenty of attrac-

tive natural and artistic things to keep you distracted in Northland's gateway. You may be pleasantly surprised by the interesting choice of eateries and the general 'going off-ness of the bars on a Saturday night. The city centre has an inordinate number of hairdressers and parking lots – although the standard of coiffure or car isn't noticeably different from the Kiwi average.

Information

Automobile Association (AA; ☎ 09-438 4848; 17 James St; ☽ 8.30am-5pm Mon-Fri)
DOC office (☎ 09-470 3300; www.doc.govt.nz; 149 Bank St; ☽ 8.30am-4pm Mon-Fri)
Post office (16-20 Rathbone St) Offers poste restante.
Quay Info (Town Basin; ☽ 9am-5pm) Housed in Clapham's Clocks; internet access.
Whangarei i-SITE (☎ 09-438 1079; www.whangarei nz.com; 92 Otaika Rd/SH1; ☽ 8.30am-5pm Mon-Fri, 9am-4.30pm Sat & Sun) Information, cafe, toilets and internet access ($6 per hour).

Sights & Activities

The budget traveller's answer to Waitomo, **Abbey Caves** (Abbey Caves Rd; admission free) is an undeveloped network of three caverns full of glowworms and limestone formations, 4km east of town. Grab a torch, strong shoes and a mate (you wouldn't want to be stuck down here alone if things go pear-shaped) and prepare to get wet. The surrounding reserve is a forest of crazily shaped rock extrusions. If you're staying at neighbouring Little Earth Lodge (p149), you can borrow helmets and hire head torches.

The 26m-high **Whangarei Falls** (Otuihau; Ngunguru Rd) are the Paris Hilton of NZ waterfalls – not the most impressive but reputedly the most photographed. Short walks provide views of the water cascading over the edge of an old basalt lava flow. The falls can be reached on the Tikipunga bus ($3, Monday to Saturday only), leaving from Rose St in the city.

The free *Whangarei Walks* brochure, available from the i-SITE, has maps and detailed descriptions of some excellent local tracks. The **Hatea River Walk** follows the river from the Town Basin to the falls (three hours return). Along the way you'll pass the **AH Reed Memorial Kauri Park** (Whareora Rd), where you can take a 35-minute detour that includes a cleverly designed boardwalk high up in the treetops.

WHANGAREI

To Quarry Gardens (1.2km); Whangarei Views B&B (2km); Hikurangi (8km)

To à Deco (1km); AH Reed Kauri Park (3km); Whangarei Falls (5km); Tutukaka (25km); Paihia (71km)

To Pilgrim Planet (500m); Whangarei Top 10 Holiday Park (1km)

To Pohutukawa Lodge (200m); Lodge Bordeaux (200m)

To Stumpy's (600m); Waimahanga Walkway (3km); Abbey Caves (4km); Little Earth Lodge (4km); Whangarei Airport (5km); Whangarei Heads (35km)

To Museum & Kiwi House (5km); Native Bird Recovery Centre (5km); Dargaville (56km)

To Bunkdown Lodge (700m); Whangarei i-SITE (700m)

INFORMATION	
Automobile Association (AA)	**1** B2
DOC office	**2** B1
Post Office	**3** B2
Quay Info	(see 5)

SIGHTS & ACTIVITIES	
Botanica	**4** A2
Clapham's Clocks	**5** C2
Old Library Arts Centre	**6** B2
Pou	**7** B2
Pupurangi Hire & Tour	**8** C2
Quarry Arts Centre	**9** A1
Terenga Paraoa Departure Point	**10** C2
Whangarei Art Museum	**11** A2

SLEEPING	
Punga Lodge B&B	**12** D2
YHA Manaakitanga	**13** D2

EATING	
Bob	**14** B2
Caffeine	**15** B2
Deluca Cafe	**16** B2
Fresh	**17** B2
Nectar	**18** B2
Pak N Save	**19** C2
Pimarn Thai	**20** B2
Salut Bar & Brasserie	**21** B2

DRINKING	
Brauhaus Frings	**22** C2
Butter Factory & Butterbank	**23** B2
Danger! Danger!	**24** B2
McMorrissey's	**25** B2

SHOPPING	
Classics	**26** B2
Kathmandu	**27** B2
Tuatara	**28** B2

TRANSPORT	
Local Bus Stop	**29** B3
Northland Coach & Travel Centre	**30** B3

Longer tracks head through **Parihaka Reserve**, encompassing the remnants of a volcanic cone (241m) and a major *pa* (fortified village) site. The city is spread out for inspection from the lookout at the top, which is equally accessible by car. Southeast of Whangarei, the **Waimahanga Walkway** in Onerahi is an easy 1½-hour tramp through mangroves, along an old railway embankment.

Other tracks head through **Coronation Scenic Reserve**, an expanse of bush just west of the centre that includes two *pa* sites and abandoned quarries that have been converted into inspiring community projects. Green-fingered volunteers have transformed **Quarry Gardens** (☎ 09-437 7210; www.whangareiquarrygardens.org.nz; Russell Rd; admission by donation; ☺ 8am-5pm) into a blissful park with a lake, waterfalls, pungent floral aromas, wild bits, orderly bits and lots of positive energy. On the other side of the reserve, the **Quarry Arts Centre** (☎ 09-438 1215; www.quarryarts.org; 21 Selwyn Ave; admission free; ☺ 9.30am-4.30pm) is an eccentric village of artists' studios and co-operative galleries.

The **Old Library Arts Centre** (☎ 09-430 6432; www.apt.org.nz; 7 Rust Ave; ☺ 10am-4pm Tue-Fri, 9am-noon Sat) exhibits local artists in a wonderful art-deco building. Between this and the library is **Pou**, an intriguing sculpture consisting of 10 large poles carved with Maori, Polynesian, Celtic and Korean motifs. Grab an interpretive pamphlet from the library. The newest addition is a brightly painted Croatian gumdigger with a gum-seeking stake in one hand and his heart

NORTHLAND & THE BAY OF ISLANDS

on fire for his woman back home – portrayed upside down and balanced on his head (see the boxed text, p174).

The **Whangarei Art Museum** (☎ 09-430 4240; www. whangareiartmuseum.co.nz; admission by donation; ☺ 10am-4pm Tue-Fri, noon-4pm Sat & Sun) is an interesting little gallery with changing displays in cute **Cafler Park**, which spans Waiarohia Stream.

Nearby, **Botanica** (☎ 09-430 4200; First Ave; admission free; ☺ 10am-4pm) displays native ferns, tropical plants and cacti, although the 'restful' music might have you murderously agitated.

Clapham's Clocks (☎ 09-438 3993; Town Basin; adult/child $8/4; ☺ 9am-5pm) is far more interesting than it sounds. This collection of 1400 ticking, gonging and cuckoo-ing timepieces constitutes the National Clock Museum.

West of Whangarei, 5km down the road to Dargaville at Maunu, is the **Museum & Kiwi House** (☎ 09-438 9630; www.whangareimuseum.co.nz; SH14; adult/child $10/5; ☺ 10am-4pm). The complex includes a veritable village of 19th-century buildings and an impressive collection of Maori artefacts. It also offers a rare chance to see a North Island brown kiwi, although he's a bit shy and doesn't always feel the need to face his adoring public. Beside the museum is the **Native Bird Recovery Centre** (☎ 09-438 1457; www.whangareinativebirdrecovery.org.nz; admission by donation; ☺ 10.30am-4.30pm Tue-Thu, noon-4.30pm Mon & Fri), which nurses sick and injured birds back to health. Say hi to Woof Woof, the talking tui.

Skydive Ballistic Blondes (☎ 0800 695 867; www.skydiveballisticblondes.co.nz; 12,000ft tandem $380) is not only the oddest-named skydiving outfit in the country, but also the only one licensed to land on the beach (Ruakaka, Ocean Beach or Paihia).

Tours

Pupurangi Hire & Tour (☎ 09-438 8117; www.hirentour.co.nz; Jetty 1, Riverside Dr) Offers hour-long waterfall abseils in the Kauri Park ($35), hour-long bike tours of the town ($35), six-person *waka* (canoe) trips on the river ($35) or 2½-hour combos of the above ($85). It also hires kayaks (per hour $15), *waka* ($20), aquacycles ($15), bikes ($15) and rollerblades ($10).

Terenga Paraoa (☎ 09-430 3083; www.tours.maori.nz; departs Town Basin; adult/child $50/30; ☺ 9.30am & 1pm) Guided 2½-hour Maori cultural tour taking in Parihaka Pa, Whangarei Falls and the Kauri Park.

Sleeping

BUDGET

our pick **Little Earth Lodge** (☎ 09-430 6562; www.littleearthlodge.co.nz; 85 Abbey Caves Rd; sites per person/

dm/s/d/tr $15/28/54/64/84; ☐ ☎) One of the very best hostels, Little Earth might spoil you for all the rest. Set on a farm 4km from town and right next to Abbey Caves (p147), the place is brimming with art and Balinese furnishings. Forget dorm rooms crammed with nasty spongy bunks: settle down in a proper cosy bed with nice linen and a maximum of two roommates. Resident critters include miniature horses Tom and Jerry, and the lovable pooch Muttley.

Whangarei Top 10 Holiday Park (☎ 09-437 6856; www.whangareitop10.co.nz; 24 Mair St; sites per person $17, units $50-121; ☐ ☎) This holiday park has friendly owners, a better-than-average set of units and supershiny stainless-steel surfaces.

Bunkdown Lodge (☎ 09-438 8886; www.bunkdownlodge.co.nz; 23 Otaika Rd; dm $25-26, s/tw/d $53/53/55; ☐) There's a homely atmosphere to this lovely old villa, which is a short walk from the town centre. Two large lounges well equipped with board games encourage socialising.

YHA Manaakitanga (☎ 09-438 8954; www.yha.co.nz; 52 Punga Grove Ave; dm/r $25/63; ☐ ☎) This small, easy-going hostel has only a handful of rooms on a quiet hillside overlooking the river. It has a covered deck and barbecue area, and a short walk leads through the bush to glowworms.

Punga Lodge B&B (☎ /fax 09-438 3879; 9 Punga Grove Ave; s/d $55/75) Just down from the YHA, this well-kept B&B is a regular suburban home, but the guest rooms have a sense of privacy and space. Request the one with the balcony and views.

MIDRANGE & TOP END

Whangarei Views B&B (☎ 09-437 6238; www.whangareiviews.co.nz; 5 Kensington Heights Rise; s/d/tr/q $99/160/200/240; ☎) The name clearly articulates its prime proposition: views over the city and then some. Modern and peaceful, it has a self-contained two-bedroom flat downstairs and a B&B room in the main part of the house.

Pilgrim Planet (☎ 09-459 1099; www.pilgrimplanet.co.nz; 63 Hatea Dr; r $110-130; ☐ ☎) Upmarket rooms open onto a shared kitchen and lounge, giving this smart place the sociability of a hostel but without the German teenagers living off rice and canned corn (not that there's anything wrong with that!).

Pohutukawa Lodge (☎ 09-4308634; www.pohutukawalodge.co.nz; 362 Western Hills Dr; units $115-150; ☐ ☎) Just west of town, this straightforward, nicely furnished motel has 14 units with well-kept facilities and ample parking.

Lodge Bordeaux (☎ 09-438 0404; www.lodgebordeaux.co.nz; 361 Western Hills Dr; units $190-300; 🖵 🕽) Sitting somewhere between a superschmick motel and an apartment hotel, Lodge Bordeaux has tasteful units with stellar kitchens and bathrooms, private balconies and excellent wines available.

Eating

Bob (☎ 09-438 0881; 29 Bank St; breakfast $6-16, lunch $15-17; 🕑 breakfast & lunch) Hey Bob, nice coffee. How would you describe yourself? Deli? Cafe? All that fancy produce spices up the standards – like the kransky sausages in the big breakfast. Nice one, Bob.

Caffeine (☎ 09-438 6925; 4 Water St; meals $6-17; 🕑 7am-2.30pm Mon-Fri, 7am-1.30pm Sat & Sun) There's no prize for guessing what the regular junkies are here for. Nice brekkies and cafe snacks too.

Deluca Cafe (☎ 09-438 7154; 6 Rust Ave; mains $7-19; 🕑 breakfast & lunch Mon-Sat) Sink into one of the moulded white-plastic chairs at this stylish yet relatively reasonably priced cafe and order something delectable from the cabinet.

Nectar (☎ 09-438 8084; 88 Bank St; mains $9-24; 🕑 breakfast & lunch Mon-Sat, dinner Tue-Sat) Oozing boho cool, Nectar has strong fair-trade coffee, hip staff, chilled-out grooves and urban views from the back of a fabulous old building. Breakfast couldn't be sweeter than the passionfruit muesli sundae.

Fresh (☎ 09-438 2921; 12 James St; mains $10-20; 🕑 8am-4pm Mon-Fri, 8am-2pm Sat) Fresh as a daisy with white walls and supersized flower photography, this chic cafe serves up great coffee and interesting breakfasts.

Pimarn Thai (☎ 09-430 0718; 12 Rathbone St; mains $16-22; 🕑 lunch & dinner Mon-Sat; Ⓥ) As gaudy as every good Thai restaurant should be – there's plenty of gold and glass bling on the walls and around the necks of the serving staff. The lengthy menu features all Thailand's blockbuster dishes, including a tasty *pad thai*.

Salut Bar & Brasserie (☎ 09-430 8080; 69 Bank St; lunch $20, dinner $26-32; 🕑 lunch & dinner) A grand setting for a boozy lunch. Grab one of the booths scooped out of dark chocolate leather and settle in for delicious fresh dishes such as the tuna carpaccio salad.

ourpick à Deco (☎ 09-459 4957; 70 Kamo Rd, Kensington; mains $34-36; 🕑 lunch Wed-Fri, dinner Tue-Sat) Northland's best restaurant, with an inventive menu that prominently features local produce: Northland scallops, Tutukaka tuna, Waimate mushrooms, Kaipara flounder, Dargaville kumara (sweet potato) and the native flavours of horopito and manuka. Art-deco fans will adore the setting – a wonderfully curvaceous marine-style villa with original fixtures.

For quick eats or self-catering, consider the following:

Stumpy's (☎ 09-438 1775; 121 Riverside Dr; meals $4-18; 🕑 10am-7pm Mon-Thu, 10am-8pm Fri-Sun) A legendary chippie with a seafood basket ($12) that could leave you stumped.

Pak N Save (☎ 09-438 1488; Carruth St; 🕑 8am-9pm Mon-Fri, 8am-8pm Sat & Sun) The big, budget supermarket.

Drinking & Entertainment

Brauhaus Frings (☎ 09-438 4664; 104 Dent St; 🕑 10am-late) This popular microbrewery has a range of great chemical-free beers, a terrace, board games and live music on Wednesday and Friday nights.

McMorrissey's (☎ 09-430 8081; 7 Vine St; 🕑 noon-late) A better-than-average Irish pub with cosy old-world decor and live music (trad Irish, rock and jam sessions).

ourpick Butter Factory & Butterbank (☎ 09-430 0044; 8 Butter Factory Lane & 84 Bank St; 🕑 4pm-late Wed-Sat) Tucked away in a back lane, Butter Factory is an atmospheric wine bar with stone walls, exposed beams and so-cool-it-hurts staff. As the hours dissolve, DJs kick in and the crowd spills outside. It's proved so popular that it's taken over the old bank upstairs and converted it into a nearly-as-cool tapas and cocktail bar.

Danger! Danger! (☎ 09-459 7461; 37 Vine St; 🕑 10.30am-very late) Be very afraid: you may find yourself screaming along as the covers band belts out 'Living on a Prayer' to the packed-out scrum of booze hags and hogs at this popular and populist wood-clad barn.

Shopping

Kathmandu (☎ 09-438 7193; 22 James St; 🕑 9am-5.30pm Mon-Fri, 9am-4pm Sat, 10am-3pm Sun) A branch of the excellent outdoor and travel supplies chain, selling everything from tents to plug adapters.

Classics (☎ 09-430 8867; 41 Bank St) Interesting eclectica, from Rubik's cubes to literature.

Tuatara (☎ 09-430 0121; 29 Bank St) A primo spot for funky Maori and Pasifika design, art and craft.

Getting There & Around

AIR

Whangarei Airport (WRE; ☎ 09-436 0047; www.whangarei airport.co.nz; Handforth St) is at Onerahi, 6km east of the centre. Taxis into town cost around $25. A city bus stops 400m away on Church St ($3, 19 buses on weekdays, six on Saturday).

Air New Zealand (☎ 0800 737 000; www.airnz.co.nz) Flies to Auckland (35 minutes, seven to nine daily) and Wellington (1½ hours, weekdays).

Great Barrier Airlines (☎ 09-275 9120; www. greatbarrierairlines.co.nz) Flies to Great Barrier Island (30 minutes, one-way $129, twice weekly).

Salt Air Xpress (☎ 09-402 8338; www.saltair.co.nz) Flies to Kerikeri and Auckland's North Shore ($139, 30 minutes), every day except Saturday.

BUS

Buses stop outside the **Northland Coach & Travel Centre** (☎ 09-438 3206; 3 Bank St; ☺ 8am-5pm Mon-Fri, 8.30am-2.30pm Sat & Sun). There's a left-luggage service here.

InterCity (☎ 09-583 5780; www.intercity.co.nz) and associated daily buses head to Auckland ($40, three hours), Orewa ($34, 2¼ hours), Waipu ($22, 30 minutes), Paihia ($27, 80 minutes) and Kerikeri ($24, 1¾ hours).

Naked Bus (☎ 0900 625 33, per min $1.80; www. nakedbus.com; advance fares from $1) heads daily to Auckland (2¼ hours), Warkworth (90 minutes), Waipu (40 minutes) and Paihia (1¼ hours).

A private operator runs a **Whangarei-to-Dargaville Shuttle** (☎ 021 380 187; fare $10) on weekdays.

Local buses leave from across the square on Rose St. Useful routes head to Whangarei Falls and the airport. In summer there are special services to Ocean Beach and Waipu Cove.

TAXI

A1 Cabs (☎ 0800 438 3377)
Kiwi Carlton Cabs (☎ 09-470 2299)

WHANGAREI HEADS

Whangarei Heads Rd winds 35km along the northern reaches of the harbour to its entrance, passing mangroves and picturesque pohutukawa-lined bays. Holiday homes, B&Bs and galleries are dotted around the water-hugging small settlements. There are great views from the top of **Mt Manaia** (419m), a sheer rock outcrop above McLeod Bay, but prepare for a lung- and leg-busting 1½-hour climb.

Bream Head caps off the finger of land. A five-hour one-way walking track from Urquharts Bay to Ocean Beach passes through the Bream Head Scenic Reserve and lovely Smugglers Bay and Peach Cove. DOC's *Whangarei District Walks* brochure gives options that break this into smaller legs.

Magnificent **Ocean Beach** stretches for miles on the other side of the peninsula. There's decent surfing to be had and lifeguards patrol the beach in summer. A detour from Parua Bay takes you to glorious **Pataua**, a small settlement that lies on a shallow inlet linked to a surf beach by a footbridge.

At McLeod Bay, take the long leafy drive down to **Breakaway Retreat** (☎ 09-434 0711; www. breakawayretreat.co.nz; 1856 Whangarei Heads Rd; house $290-380), a semidetached two-bedroom house where the lawn terminates at a secluded slice of beachfront paradise. There are warmly wooden interiors, a spa bath and free kayaks.

A magical spot on a summer's day, **Parua Bay Tavern** (☎ 09-436 5856; 1034 Whangarei Heads Rd; ☺ 11.30am-late) is a friendly pub set on a thumb-shaped peninsula, with a sole pohutukawa blazing red against the green water. Grab a seat on the deck, a cold beverage and a decent pub meal.

Whangarei's regular buses don't venture beyond Onerahi, but in summer there are special services to Ocean Beach.

TUTUKAKA COAST & THE POOR KNIGHTS ISLANDS

If Goat Island Marine Reserve (p142) whetted your appetite, diving at the Poor Knights is the feast followed by a wafer-thin mint that might cause your stomach to explode. Apart from the natural underwater scenery (see the boxed text, p152), two decommissioned navy ships have been sunk nearby for divers to explore.

Following the road northeast of Whangarei for 26km, you'll first come to the sweet village of **Ngunguru** near the mouth of a broad river. **Tutukaka** is a kilometre further on, its marina bustling with yachts, dive crews and game-fishing boats.

From Tutukaka the road heads slightly inland, popping out 10km later at the golden sands of **Matapouri**. At the beach's north end a sign points through the long grass to **Mermaid Pool**, a deep natural rock pool with crystal-clear water flushed out by the tide. It's an effort to reach but well worth it; follow the track through an unlikely looking hole in the rock, turn right and clamber along the rocks for about 10 minutes.

Continuing north from Matapouri, the wide expanse of **Sandy Bay**, one of Northland's premier surf beaches, comes into view. Longboarding competitions are held here in summer. The road then loops back to join SH1 at Hikurangi. A branch leading off from this road doubles back north to the coast at **Whananaki**, where there are more glorious beaches and the Otamure Bay **DOC campsite** (sites per adult/child $7/3.50).

Activities

Dive trips leave from Tutukaka and cater for first-timers and experts.

Dive! Tutukaka (☎ 0800 288 882; www.diving.co.nz; Marina Rd; ☺ 7am-7pm) is deservedly the main operator, winning an array of tourism, business and environmental awards. It offers a variety of dive courses and excursions, including a five-day PADI open-water course ($695). Perhaps the jewel in its crown is the much-raved-about Perfect Day Ocean Cruise ($129), which includes a commentary, lunch and snacks, snorkelling from a platform in the middle of the marine reserve, kayaking through caves and arches, and sightings of dolphins and rare seabirds (usually), and occasionally whales, orcas and fur seals. Cruises depart at 11am, returning at 4.15pm.

Yukon Dive (☎ 09-434 4506; www.yukon.co.nz; full day $125) is a small operator that takes groups of four to eight.

If you've got the bushy bushy blond hairdo and baggy boardies but need credibility to pull off the look, **Tutukaka Surf Co** (☎ 09-434 4135; www.tutukakasurf.co.nz; Marina Dr, Tutukaka; 2hr lesson $75) runs regular surf lessons at 9am most days in summer and on the weekends otherwise,

operating from whichever beach has the best beginner breaks that day. If you've already got the skills, you can hire or buy a board here.

Sleeping

Tutukaka Holiday Park (☎ 09-434 3938; www.tutukaka-holidaypark.co.nz; Matapouri Rd, Tutukaka; sites per adult/child $15/7, dm $25, cabins $70-180) Look for the giant marlin at the gate of this well-kept complex, not far from the marina. Facilities are clean and bright, and communal areas are in good condition.

Bellmain House (☎ 09-434 3898; www.bellmainhouse.co.nz; 2049 Ngunguru Rd, Ngunguru; s $70, d $115-120, cottage $140-180; 🖳) Share this homely house with the welcoming hosts or nab the self-contained cottage in the garden (sleeps four).

Lupton Lodge (☎ 09-437 2989; www.luptonlodge.co.nz; 555 Ngunguru Rd, Glenbervie; s $125-160, d $160-200, tr $225; 🐆) The rooms are spacious, luxurious and full of character in this historic homestead (1896), peacefully positioned in farmland halfway between Whangarei and Ngunguru. Wander the orchard, splash around the pool or shoot some snooker in the guest lounge.

Eating & Drinking

Schnappa Rock (☎ 09-434 3774; breakfast/lunch $6-20, dinner $26-33; ☺ breakfast, lunch & dinner) Filled with expectant divers in the morning and those capping off their Perfect Days in the evening, this cafe-restaurant-bar is often buzzing – not least because of the excellent coffee. Top NZ bands play on summer weekends.

Whangarei Deep Sea Anglers Club (☎ 09-434 3249; mains $9-23; ☺ 4-8pm Tue-Thu & Sun, 4-10pm Fri & Sat) This venue plays host to the nicely named Moocha's, where standard eats (burgers, fish and chips, ham steaks) and a good children's

---

MARINE RICHES AT THE POOR KNIGHTS

Established in 1981, this marine reserve is rated as one of the world's top-10 diving spots. The islands are bathed in a subtropical current from the Coral Sea, so varieties of tropical and subtropical fish not seen in other NZ waters are observed here. The waters are clear, with no sediment or pollution problems. The 40m to 60m underwater cliffs drop steeply to the sandy bottom and are a labyrinth of archways, caves, tunnels and fissures that attract a wide variety of sponges and colourful underwater vegetation. Manta rays are common.

The two main volcanic islands, Tawhiti Rahi and Aorangi, were home to the Ngai Wai tribe, but since a raiding-party massacre in the early 1800s the islands have been *tapu* (forbidden). Even today the public is banned from the islands, in order to protect their pristine environment. Not only do tuatara and Butler's shearwater breed here, but there are unique species of flora, such as the Poor Knights red lily.

menu mingle with mounted fish and garrulous locals.

Marina Pizzeria (☎ 09-434 3166; pizzas $13-24; ☾ lunch & dinner Thu-Sun) Everything is homemade at this excellent takeaway and restaurant – the bread, the pasta, the pizza and the ice cream.

Getting There & Away

In summer there are buses from Whangarei (enquire at the i-SITE, p147). **Tutukaka Shuttles** (☎ 021-901 408) depart Whangarei at 7.10am and 3pm, and Tutukaka at 8.15am and 4.30pm ($15). Dive! Tutukaka has free daily shuttles from Whangarei for its customers.

RUSSELL RD

The quickest route to Russell takes SH1 to Opua and then crosses by ferry. The old Russell Rd is a snaking scenic route that adds about half an hour to the trip.

The turn-off is easy to miss, 6km north of Hikurangi at Whakapara. It's worth a stop after 14km at the **Gallery & Cafe** (☎ 09-433 9616; mains $9-17; ☾ 10am-5pm) high above Helena Bay for excellent organic fair-trade coffee, scrummy cake, amazing views and a gander at some interesting Kiwiana art and craft. Is there anything that corrugated iron can't do?

At **Helena Bay** an unsealed detour leads 8km to **Mimiwhangata Coastal Park**, a gorgeous part of the coastline with sand dunes, pohutukawa trees, jutting headlands and picturesque beaches. **DOC** (☎ 09-433 6554; www.doc. govt.nz) manages a range of accommodation in the reserve, including a well-appointed lodge ($500 to $2000 per week) and a simpler but comfortable cottage and beach house (both $350 to $1500 per week); each sleeps seven to eight people. Basic camping (per adult/child $8/4) is available at secluded Waikahoa Bay.

Back on Russell Rd, you'll find the **Farm** (☎ 09-433 6894; www.thefarm.co.nz; 3632 Russell Rd, Tutaematai; sites per person/dm/s $12/20/30, d $60-80), a chilled-out backpackers rambling through various buildings, including an old woolshed fitted out with a mirror ball. Best of all, you can arrange a horse trek or motorbike ride through the 1000-acre working farm. The dorms are basic but the cabins and en-suite rooms are much more comfortable.

At an intersection shortly after the Farm, Russell Rd branches off to the left for an unsealed, winding section traversing the **Ngaiotonga Scenic Reserve**. Unless you're planning to explore the forest (there are two short

walks: the 20-minute **Kauri Grove Nature Walk** and the 10-minute **Twin Bole Kauri Walk**) you're better off veering right onto the sealed Rawhiti Rd. After 2.6km, a side road leads to the **Whangaruru North Head Scenic Reserve**, which has beaches, another **DOC campsite** (☎ 09-433 6160; sites per adult/child $7/3.50), walks and fine coastal scenery.

If you want to head directly to Russell, continue along Rawhiti Rd for another 7km before veering left onto Manawaora Rd, which skirts a succession of idyllic tiny bays before reconnecting with Russell Rd. At Jacks Bay, **Russell B&B** (☎ 09-403 7887; www.russellbedandbreak fast.co.nz; 24 Kingfisher Rd; d $125-135, bach $130) has a quiet bush location overlooking the water. Choose between a room in the house and a self-contained bach (sleeping three). From here it's a further 16km to Russell.

Otherwise take a detour to isolated **Rawhiti**, a small Ngapuhi settlement where life still revolves around the *marae*. Rawhiti is the starting point for the tramp to **Cape Brett** (www.capebrett walks.co.nz), a tiring eight-hour, 16.3km walk to the top of the peninsula where overnight stays are possible in DOC's **Cape Brett Hut** (sites per adult/child $12/6). An access fee is charged for crossing private land (full track adult/child $30/15, day walkers adult/child $10/5), which you can pay at the Russell Booking & Information Centre (p158). Another option is to take a water taxi (p164) to Cape Brett lighthouse from Russell, Paihia or Rawhiti and walk back.

A shorter one-hour walk leads through Maori land and the **Whangamumu Scenic Reserve** to Whangamumu Harbour. There are more than 40 ancient Maori sites on the peninsula and the remains of an unusual whaling station. A net fastened between the mainland and Net Rock was used to ensnare or slow down whales so the harpooners could get an easy shot in.

BAY OF ISLANDS

Undeniably pretty, the Bay of Islands ranks as one of NZ's top tourist drawcards. The footage that made you want to come to NZ in the first place no doubt featured lingering shots of lazy, sun-filled days on a yacht floating atop these turquoise waters punctuated by around 150 undeveloped islands. The reality is that NZ has many beautiful spots and this bay, while wonderful, could be a teensy bit overhyped.

What sets it apart from the rest is its fascinating history and substantial tourist infrastructure. Paihia has one of the best selections of budget accommodation of anywhere in the country. After that the budget goes out the window as a bewildering array of boat trips clamour to wrestle money out of your wallet. There's no point coming here if you don't head out on the water, so be prepared to fork out.

The Bay of Islands is a place of enormous historical significance. Maori knew it as Pewhairangi and settled here early in their migrations. As the site of NZ's first permanent English settlement (at Russell), it is the birthplace of European colonisation. It was here that the Treaty of Waitangi was drawn up and first signed in 1840; the treaty remains the linchpin of race relations in NZ today (see p31).

Activities
SCUBA DIVING
The Bay of Islands offers some fine subtropical diving, made even better by the sinking of the 113m navy frigate HMNZS *Canterbury* in Deep Water Cove near Cape Brett. Local operators also head to the wreck of the *Rainbow Warrior* off the Cavalli Islands, about an hour from Paihia by boat.

Dive HQ (Map p161; ☎ 09-402 7551; www.divenz.com; Williams Rd, Paihia; reef & wreck $215) offers combined reef and wreck trips to either the *Canterbury* or the *Rainbow Warrior*. Various PADI courses are available and gear can be hired.

Dive North (☎ 09-402 5369; www.divenorth.co.nz; reef & wreck $235) heads to the *Rainbow Warrior* and other sites, and offers lunch and free pick-ups from Paihia.

SEA KAYAKING
There are plenty of opportunities for kayaking around the bay, either on a guided tour or by renting and going it alone.

Coastal Kayakers (Map p161; ☎ 09-402 8105; www.coastalkayakers.co.nz; Te Karuwha Pde, Paihia) Runs guided tours (half-/full-/two-day tours $60/80/130); minimum two people. Kayaks can also be rented (half-/full day $30/40).

Island Kayaks (Map p161; ☎ 09-402 6078; www.baybeachhire.co.nz; Marsden Rd, Paihia; half-/full-day tour $55/90) Operates from Bay Beach Hire.

BAY OF ISLANDS

SKYDIVING

NZ Skydive (☎ 0800 427 593; www.nzskydive.com)
Operates from Haruru Falls or Kerikeri Airfields, offering
12,000ft tandem skydives ($299).

Skydive Zone (☎ 09-407 7057; www.skydivezoneboi.
co.nz) From Kerikeri Airfield; 12,000/15,000ft tandem
$290/355.

OTHER ACTIVITIES

Bay Beach Hire (Map p161; ☎ 09-402 6078; www.
baybeachhire.co.nz; Marsden Rd, Paihia; ⏰ 9am-5.30pm)
Hires kayaks (from $10 per hour), small sailing catamarans
($50 first hour, $25 per additional), small motor boats ($65
first hour, $25 per additional), mountain bikes ($20 per
day), boogie boards ($25 per day), fishing rods ($10 per
day), wet suits and snorkelling gear ($15 per day).

Flying Kiwi Parasail (☎ 0800 359 691; www.parasail
-nz.co.nz) One-hour parasailing trips ($79 to $89), leaving
from Paihia's wharf hourly during summer.

Salt Air (☎ 09-402 8338; www.saltair.co.nz) Has scenic
flights including a five-hour flight-and-4WD tour to Cape
Reinga and Ninety Mile Beach ($395). Helicopter flights out
to the Hole in the Rock cost $215.

Tours

Where do you start? First by praying for
good weather, as torrential rain or choppy
seas could literally put a dampener on some
options. The information centre at Paihia is
extremely helpful and can book tours. Some
of the hostels can arrange cheap deals and
several of the main operators offer backpacker
specials.

BOAT TRIPS

You can't leave the Bay of Islands without
taking some sort of cruise and there are plenty
of vessels keen to get you on board, including sailing boats, jetboats and large launches.

Boats leave from either Paihia or Russell, calling into the other town as their first stop.

Fullers (☎ 0800 653 339; www.dolphincruises.co.nz)
runs full-day (adult/child $99/50) and half-
day ($89/45) tours, taking in the Hole in the
Rock off Cape Brett (passing through it if
conditions are right) and stopping on an island. The full day 'Cream Trip' follows the
old supply and mail route around the islands
and includes dolphin swimming and boom
netting (where you can get close to the critters while being dragged through the water
in a net).

Overnight Cruises

The cheapest way to spend a night on the
water is aboard the **MV Souvenir** (☎ 0800 773 569;
dm/4-person cabin $125/400), an unglamorous but
sturdy 40-ton boat that stops at various DOC
reserves before finding a remote anchorage.
You'll need to bring your own lunch for the
first day and any booze or snacks.

You just need to roll up to the **Rock** (☎ 0800
762 527; www.rocktheboat.co.nz; 22hr cruise $178), a former
vehicle ferry that's now a floating hostel, with
four-bed dorms, twin and double rooms, and
(of course) a bar. A private room costs an extra
$20 per person. The cruise departs at 5pm
and includes a barbecue and seafood dinner
with live music, then a full day spent island-
hopping, fishing, kayaking, snorkelling and
swimming.

A more glamorous option is Fullers' launch
Ipipiri (☎ 0800 653 339; www.overnightcruise.co.nz; s/d
$642/732), where the accommodation is by way
of en-suite state rooms, all meals are included,
and if you get sick of lazing around the bar
on the sundeck, you can partake in kayaking,
snorkelling or island walks.

DETOUR: TOILET, TRAIN & GLOWING GRUBS

Kawakawa is just an ordinary Kiwi town, located on SH1 south of Paihia, but the public toilets (60
Gillies St) were designed by Austrian-born artist and ecoarchitect Friedensreich Hundertwasser. He
lived near Kawakawa in an isolated house without electricity from 1973 until his death in 2000.
The most photographed toilets in NZ are typical Hundertwasser – lots of wavy lines decorated
with ceramic mosaics and brightly coloured bottles, and with grass and plants on the roof. Other
examples of his work can be seen in Vienna and Osaka.

Kawakawa's other claim to fame is the railway line running through the centre of the main
street, on which you can take a 40-minute spin on **Gabriel the steam engine** (☎ 021 171 2697;
www.bayofislandsvintagerailway.org.nz; adult/child $10/3; ⏰ 11am, noon, 1pm, 2pm Fri-Sun).

South of town, a signpost from SH1 points to **Kawiti Glowworm Caves** (☎ 09-404 0583; adult/
child $15/7.50; ⏰ 8.30am-4.30pm). Explore the insect-illuminated caverns with a 30-minute subter-
ranean tour.

Ecocruz (☎ 0800 432 627; www.ecocruz.co.nz; cruises dm/d $595/1350) is a highly recommended three-day/two-night sailing cruise aboard the 72ft ocean-going yacht *Manawanui*, with an emphasis on the marine environment. Prices include accommodation, food, fishing, kayaking and snorkelling.

Sailing
The best way to explore the bay is under sail. In most cases you can either help crew the boat (no experience required), or just spend the afternoon island-hopping, sunbathing, swimming, snorkelling, kayaking and fishing. Recommended boats offering day trips:

Carino (☎ 09-402 8040; www.sailingdolphins.co.nz; adult/child $99/60) A 50ft catamaran offering swimming with dolphins and a barbecue lunch ($6).

Gungha II (☎ 0800 478 900; www.bayofislands sailing.co.nz; trips $85) A beautiful 65ft ocean yacht with a friendly crew offering freshly made sandwiches.

On the Edge (☎ 09-402 8234; www.explorenz.co.nz; adult/child $120/79) NZ's fastest commercial catamaran, capable of speeds over 30 knots. It also has a licensed bar.

Phantom (☎ 0800 224 421; www.yachtphantom.com; adult/child $99/50) A fast 50ft racing sloop, known for its wonderful food (10 people maximum, BYO allowed).

R Tucker Thompson (☎ 09-402 8430; www.tucker.co.nz; adult/child $120/60) A majestic tall ship with daily tours that include a barbecue lunch. Run by a charitable trust with an education focus, it partners with the Historic Places Trust and DOC for special sailings.

She's a Lady (☎ 0800 724 584; www.bay-of-islands. com; trips $90) Try your hand at snorkelling or paddling about in a see-through-bottomed kayak.

If you're interested in learning to sail, **Great Escape Yacht Charters** (☎ 09-402 7143; www.great escape.co.nz; yacht hire per day $160-390) offers sailing lessons, including a two-day course ($345), which can be combined with an additional three-day yacht hire ($590).

Dolphin Swimming
These trips operate all year and you get to cruise around the islands as well as watch or swim with dolphins. They have a high success rate and operators generally offer a free trip if dolphins are not sighted. Dolphin swims are subject to weather and sea conditions, with restrictions if the dolphins have young. As well as encountering bottlenose and common dolphins, you may see orcas, other whales and penguins. With all operators a portion of the cost goes towards marine research, via DOC.

Dolphin Discoveries (☎ 09-402 8234; www.ex plorenz.co.nz; adult/child $89/45) was the first to offer dolphin-swimming trips in the bay. The price includes a four-hour trip, with an additional $30 payable if you choose to swim.

As well as the Cream Trip, Fullers offers a three-hour dolphin-swimming cruise (adult/child $89/45, $30 extra for swim). The only yacht to be licensed for dolphin swims is *Carino*.

Jetboating
Fasten your seatbelt for a high-speed Hole in the Rock trip on board a jetboat – good fun and handy if you're short on time. **Mack Attack** (☎ 0800 622 528; www.mackattack.co.nz; adult/child $85/40) and Fuller's **Excitor** (☎ 09-402 7421; www.awesomenz. com; adult/child $89/45) have daily 1½-hour trips.

CAPE REINGA TOURS
It's cheaper and quicker to do trips to Cape Reinga from Ahipara, Kaitaia or Doubtless Bay (see p173). But if you're short on time, several long day trips (10 to 12 hours) leave from the Bay of Islands. They all drive one way along Ninety Mile Beach, stopping to sandboard on the dunes and at Ancient Kauri Kingdom.

Fullers (☎ 0800 653 339; www.dolphincruises.co.nz) runs regular bus tours and backpacker-oriented versions, both stopping at Puketi Forest. Its standard, child-friendly version (adult/child $115/58) includes an optional barbecue lunch at Houhora ($23). Otherwise there's **Awesome NZ** (☎ 0800 653 339; www.awe somenz.com; tour $99), with louder music, more time sandboarding and stops to chuck a Frisbee around at Taputaputa Beach and devour fish and chips at Mangonui.

Dune Rider (☎ 09-402 8234; www.explorenz.co.nz; adult/child $139/109) tours also sample Mangonui's feted fish and chips and includes a stop at Gumdiggers Park.

HOKIANGA & WAIPOUA FOREST TOURS
Transport options to these west-coast destinations are limited, so a day trip makes sense if you don't have your own car or if you're time starved. **Crossings Hokianga** (☎ 0800 653 339; www. dolphincruises.co.nz; adult/child $93/47) leaves Paihia at 8.30am and heads to the forest for a one-hour tour with a Footprints Waipoua guide (p178). Then it's back to Opononi, where there's a choice of a crayfish lunch ($65) or a picnic ($17). Rawene and Kohukohu follow, heading

back to Paihia by 4pm. The tours run according to demand, but you can enquire about stopping off overnight and picking up the rest of the tour at a later date.

Festivals & Events

Tall Ship Race Held in Russell on the first Saturday of January.

Waitangi Day Various ceremonial events at Waitangi on 6 February.

Country Rock Festival (www.country-rock.co.nz) Second weekend in May.

Russell Birdman Where a bunch of lunatics with flying contraptions jump off the wharf into the frigid (July) waters to the amusement of all.

Jazz & Blues Festival (www.jazz-blues.co.nz) Second weekend in August.

Weekend Coastal Classic (www.coastalclassic.co.nz) NZ's largest yacht race, from Auckland to the Bay of Islands, held on Labour Weekend in October.

RUSSELL

pop 820

Although it was once known prosaically as 'the hellhole of the Pacific', those coming to Russell for debauchery will be sadly disappointed: they've missed the orgies on the beach by 170 years. Instead they'll find a sweetly historic town that is a bastion of cafes, gift shops and B&Bs.

Before it was known as a hellhole, or even as Russell, it was Kororareka (Sweet Penguin), a fortified Ngapuhi village. In the early 19th century the tribe permitted it to become Aotearoa's first European settlement. It quickly became a magnet for rough elements such as fleeing convicts, whalers and drunken sailors. By the 1830s dozens of whaling ships at a time were anchored in the harbour. Charles Darwin described it in 1835 as full of 'the refuse of society'.

In 1830 the settlement was the scene of the so-called Girls' War, when two pairs of Maori women were vying for the attention of a whaling captain called Brind. A chance meeting between the rivals on the beach led to verbal abuse and fighting. This minor conflict quickly escalated as family members rallied around to avenge the insult and harm done to their respective relatives. Hundreds were killed and injured over a two-week period before missionaries managed to broker a peace agreement.

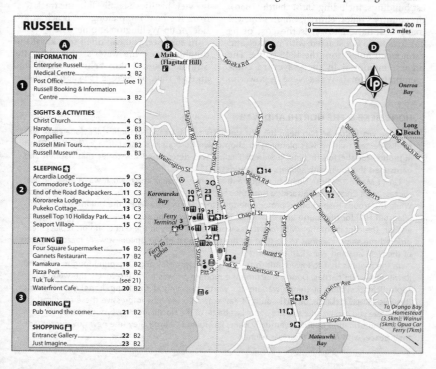

After the signing of the Treaty of Waitangi in 1840, Okiato (where the car ferry now leaves from) was the residence of the governor and the temporary capital. The capital was officially moved to Auckland in 1841 and Okiato, which was by then known as Russell, was eventually abandoned. The name Russell ultimately passed to Kororareka – a marginally better choice than Bruce or Barry.

Information

Enterprise Russell (Traders Mall; 🛜) Internet access.
Medical Centre (☎ 09-403 7690; Church St)
Post office (Traders Mall)
Russell Booking & Information Centre (☎ 09-403 8020; www.russellinfo.co.nz; 🕙 8.30am-4.30pm Apr-Sep, 8am-7pm Oct-Mar) On the pier.

Sights & Activities

The small but modern **Russell Museum** (☎ 09-403 7701; www.russellmuseum.org.nz; 2 York St; adult/child $7.50/2; 🕙 10am-4pm) has a well-presented Maori section, a large 1:5-scale model of Captain Cook's *Endeavour* and a 10-minute video on the town's history.

Russell lays claim to some of NZ's oldest buildings, including **Christ Church** (1836), the country's oldest church. Charles Darwin made a donation towards the cost of its construction. It's scarred with musket and cannonball holes from the 1845 battle. The biggest memorial in the graveyard commemorates Tamati Waka Nene, a powerful

Ngapuhi chief from the Hokianga who sided against Hone Heke in the Northland War.

Pompallier (☎ 09-403 9015; www.pompallier.co.nz; The Strand; tours adult/child $7.50/free; 🕙 10am-4pm) is a rammed-earth building constructed in 1842 to house the Roman Catholic mission's printing press, which printed a staggering 40,000 books in Maori. In the 1870s it was converted into a private home but it has been restored to its original state, complete with tannery and printing workshop. On the excellent guided tour you get to play with the tools and learn how to 'skive off' and become a 'dab hand'. It's the last remaining building of the Catholic mission in the Western Pacific.

Run by the local *marae* society, the recently opened **Haratu** (☎ 09-403 7212; cnr The Strand & Pitt St; 🕙 10am-5pm) brings authentic Maori art and craft to the Russell waterfront, most of which is available for purchase. There are also audiovisual displays and information boards.

Overlooking Russell is **Maiki** (Flagstaff Hill; Flagstaff Rd), where Hone Heke chopped down the flagpole four times. You can drive up but the view justifies a climb. Take the track west from the boat ramp along the beach at low tide, or up Wellington St otherwise.

In summer, you can often rent kayaks or dinghies from the water's edge along the Strand. About 1.5km behind Russell and an easy walk or cycle is **Long Beach** (Oneroa

---

HONE HEKE & THE NORTHLAND WAR

Just five years after he had been the first signatory to the treaty, Ngapuhi chief Hone Heke was so disaffected that he was planning to chop down Kororareka's flagstaff, a symbol of British authority, for the fourth time. Governor FitzRoy was determined not to let that happen and garrisoned the town with soldiers and marines.

On 11 March 1845 the Ngapuhi staged a diversionary siege of the town. It was a great tactical success, with Chief Kawiti attacking from the south and another party attacking from Long Beach. While the troops rushed off to protect the township, Hone Heke felled the Union Jack on Maiki (Flagstaff Hill) for the fourth and final time. The British were forced to evacuate to ships lying at anchor. The captain of the HMS *Hazard* was wounded severely in the battle and his replacement ordered the ships' cannons to be fired on the town; most of the buildings were razed. The first of the New Zealand Wars had begun.

In the months that followed, British troops (united with Hokianga Ngapuhi) fought Heke and Kawiti in several battles. During this time the modern *pa* was born, effectively the world's first sophisticated system of trench warfare. It's worth stopping at the **Ruapekapeka Pa Historic Reserve** (Ruapekapeka Rd), off SH1 south of Kawakawa, to see how impressive these fortifications were. Here you can wander the site of the last battle of the Northland War, brought to life through detailed information boards. Eventually Heke, Kawiti and George Grey (the new governor) made their peace, with no side the clear winner.

Bay Beach). Turn left (facing the sea) to visit Donkey Bay, a small cove that is an unofficial nudist beach.

Tours

Russell Mini Tours (☎ 09-403 7866; cnr The Strand & Cass St; adult/child $25/10; ⏰ 11am, noon, 1pm & 2pm May-Sep, plus 10am, 3pm & 4pm Oct-Apr) Minibus tour with commentary.

See p155 for other tours around the bay.

Sleeping

Being a tourist trap, Russell has few decent midrange options. There are several tiny budget lodges, but you'll need to book ahead at busy times. If budget's not a consideration, Russell does luxury very well.

BUDGET

Pukeko Cottage (☎ 09-403 8498; www.pukekocottage backpackers.co.nz; 14 Brind Rd; s/d $25/50) More like staying at a mate's place than a hostel, this homely house has just two bedrooms for rent and a caravan in the back garden. It's certainly not dirty, but the cleanliness is bloke-standard. Barry, the artist owner, is always up for a chat.

End of the Road Backpackers (☎ 09-403 8827; 13 Brind Rd; dm/d $30/60; **P**) Another tiddler, this basic bach sleeps only four people in two bedrooms (a double and a twin). It's a quiet spot with views over the marina.

ourpick Wainui (☎ 09-403 8278; stocken@xtra.co.nz; 92d Te Wahapu Rd; dm/d/tr $30/60/90) Hard to find but well worth the effort, this modern bush retreat with direct beach access has only two rooms sharing a pleasant communal space. It's 5km from Russell on the way to the car ferry. Take Te Wahapu Rd and then turn right into Waiaruhe Way.

Seaport Village (☎ 09-403 7833; www.seaport village.co.nz; 10 Chapel St; dm $30, d $130-195, apt $150-390) This central 'village' spans all price brackets, with comfortable B&B rooms with polished wooden floors and self-contained multiroom apartments. The two linked dorms have proper mattresses, an en suite and a kitchen – and they're just over the fence from the local pub.

Russell Top 10 Holiday Park (☎ 09-403 7826; www. russelltop10.co.nz; 1 James St; sites per 2 people $39, units $80-230; 🖳) This leafy park has a small store, good facilities, wonderful hydrangeas, tidy cabins and nice units. Showers are clean, but metered.

MIDRANGE & TOP END

Kororareka Lodge (☎ 09-403 8494; www.kororareka.com; 22 Oneroa Rd; r $125-148) A solid option, sitting on the hill between the township and the beach. The front rooms have views, while the cheaper ones at the back only have small windows and share bathrooms. A communal lounge and deck compensate.

Commodore's Lodge (☎ 09-403 7899; www.commo doreslodgemotel.co.nz; 28 The Strand; units $150-650; 🖳) Being the envy of every passer-by makes up for the lack of privacy in the front apartments facing the waterfront promenade. Spacious, nicely presented units are the order of the day here, along with a really nice pool and free kayaks, dinghies and bikes.

Arcadia Lodge (☎ 09-403 7756; www.arcadialodge. co.nz; 10 Florance Ave; d $190-295) The stylish, characterful rooms of this 1890 hillside house are decked out with interesting antiques and fine linen, while the breakfast is probably the best you'll eat in town – it's not only organic, it's delicious. Enjoy the homemade muesli and Kerikeri orange juice while taking in a tranquil bay view.

Orongo Bay Homestead (☎ 09-403 7527; www. thehomestead.co.nz; Aucks Rd; s/d $400/650; 🛜) This wooden homestead (c 1860) was NZ's first American consulate, located a discreet 4km from Russell's rabble. It now contains four stylishly plush rooms, two in the house and two in the converted barn facing a chocolate-box lake. When one of the charming hosts is an acclaimed food critic, you can be assured that the breakfast will be memorable (dinners by arrangement).

Eating & Drinking

For a country so hooked on cafe culture and a town so touristy, it's disappointing that Russell doesn't have more on offer.

Pizza Port (☎ 09-403 8869; Cass St; pizza $11-20; ⏰ 5-9pm Mon-Wed, noon-9pm Thu-Sun) There are a couple of tables, but you're better off grabbing one of the gourmet wood-fired pizzas and battling the seagulls at the beach.

Waterfront Cafe (☎ 09-403 7589; 23d The Strand; mains $12-18; ⏰ breakfast & lunch) It's a sausage-roll-and-custard-square kind of place, but it's Russell's best weekday breakfast option.

Tuk Tuk (☎ 09-403 7111; 19 York St; mains $15-24; ⏰ 10am-11pm; **V**) Thai fabrics adorn the tables and Thai favourites fill the menu. In clement weather grab a table out front and watch Russell's little world go by.

Gannets Restaurant (☎ 09-403 7990; cnr York & Chapel Sts; mains $15-31; ☽ dinner Tue-Sat) This funky eatery has an emphasis on seafood that would put a smile on any gannet's beak.

our pick **Kamakura** (☎ 09-403 7771; 29 The Strand; lunch $15-30, dinner $29-33; ☽ breakfast Sat & Sun, lunch & dinner daily) The flashest option in Russell by a long way, this restaurant has a breezy beachhouse feel. The Pacific Rim menu gainfully plunders Asian and French styles to produce beautifully presented, delicious meals. In summer it hosts a monthly artisan market (www.artisanmarket.co.nz).

Pub 'round the corner (☎ 09-403 7831; 19 York St; ☽ noon-10pm Sun & Mon, noon-midnight Tue-Sat) A cool, cosy tavern with a beer garden and pool tables, in the same complex as Tuk Tuk.

There's a **Four Square supermarket** (The Strand) on the waterfront.

Shopping

Entrance Gallery (☎ 09-403 7716; 13 York St) A genuinely local gallery, where Russell's artists have been selling their wares for over 22 years.

Just Imagine… (☎ 09-403 8360; 25 York St) Full of gorgeous glassware and paintings, this gallery also offers art junkies a caffeine fix.

Getting There & Away

The quickest way to reach Russell by car is via the car ferry (car and driver $10, motorcycle and rider $5, passenger adult/child $1/50c), which runs every 10 minutes from Opua (5km from Paihia) to Okiato (8km from Russell), between 6.50am and 10pm. Buy your tickets on board. If you're travelling from the south, a scenic alternative is Russell Rd (p153).

On foot, the quickest and easiest way to reach Russell is on the regular passenger ferry (adult/child one way $6/3, return $10/5) from Paihia. It runs from 7am to 7pm (until 10pm October to May), generally every 20 minutes but hourly in the evenings. Buy your tickets on board or at the i-SITE in Paihia.

PAIHIA & WAITANGI
pop 1800 & 800

The birthplace of NZ (as opposed to Aotearoa), Waitangi inhabits a special, somewhat complex place in the national psyche – aptly demonstrated by the mixture of celebration, commemoration, protest and apathy that accompanies the nation's birthday (Waitangi Day, 6 February).

It was here that the long-neglected and much-contested Treaty of Waitangi was first signed between Maori chiefs and the British Crown, establishing British sovereignty or something a bit like it, depending on whether you're reading the English or Maori version of the document. If you're interested in coming to grips with NZ's history and race relations, this is the place to start.

Joined to Waitangi by a bridge, Paihia would be a fairly nondescript coastal town if it wasn't the main entry point to the Bay of Islands.

Information

Bay of Islands i-SITE (☎ 09-402 7345; www.visit northland.co.nz; Marsden Rd; ☽ 8am-5pm Mar–mid-Dec, 8am-8pm mid-Dec–Feb; ☐ �wi) Information and internet access ($4 per hour).

Maritime Building (Marsden Rd) Tour operators and internet access ($4 per hour); buses stop outside.

Medical services (☎ 09-402 8407; Selwyn Rd; ☽ 8.30am-5pm Mon-Fri)

Post office (2 Williams Rd) Offers poste restante service.

Sights & Activities
WAITANGI TREATY GROUNDS

A visit to the **Waitangi Treaty Grounds** (☎ 09-402 7437; www.waitangi.net.nz; 1 Tau Henare Dr; adult/child $20/10; ☽ 9am-5pm mid-Apr–Oct, 9am-7pm Nov–mid-Apr) is a must for every itinerary. It's full of cultural icons – the colonial-style Treaty House with its manicured garden and lawns, the surrounding bush full of native birds, the spiritual *whare* and the warlike *waka*, the three flags (UK, NZ and Maori) and the hillside views of a still-beautiful land.

The **Treaty House** has special significance in NZ's history. Built in 1832 as the four-room home of British resident James Busby, eight years later it was the setting for the signing of the Treaty of Waitangi. The house, with its gardens and lawn running down to the bay, was restored in 1989 and is preserved as a memorial and museum. Inside are photographs and displays, including a facsimile copy of the treaty.

Just across the lawn, the magnificently detailed **whare runanga** (meeting house) was completed in 1940 to mark the centenary of the treaty. The fine carvings represent the major Maori tribes.

Near the cove is the 35m **waka taua** (war canoe) *Ngatokimatawhaorua*. It too was built for the centenary, and a photographic exhibit

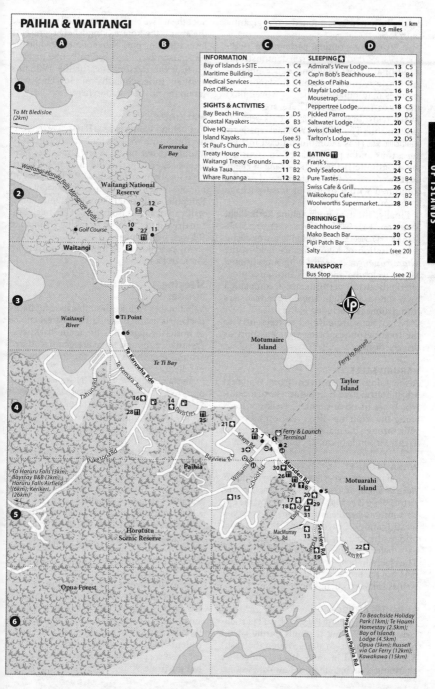

PAIHIA & WAITANGI

NORTHLAND & THE BAY OF ISLANDS

INFORMATION
Bay of Islands i-SITE	**1** C4
Maritime Building	**2** C4
Medical Services	**3** C4
Post Office	**4** C4

SIGHTS & ACTIVITIES
Bay Beach Hire	**5** D5
Coastal Kayakers	**6** B3
Dive HQ	**7** C4
Island Kayaks	(see 5)
St Paul's Church	**8** C5
Treaty House	**9** B2
Waitangi Treaty Grounds	**10** B2
Waka Taua	**11** B2
Whare Runanga	**12** B2

SLEEPING
Admiral's View Lodge	**13** C5
Cap'n Bob's Beachhouse	**14** B4
Decks of Paihia	**15** C5
Mayfair Lodge	**16** B4
Mousetrap	**17** C5
Peppertree Lodge	**18** C5
Pickled Parrot	**19** D5
Saltwater Lodge	**20** C5
Swiss Chalet	**21** C4
Tarlton's Lodge	**22** D5

EATING
Frank's	**23** C4
Only Seafood	**24** C5
Pure Tastes	**25** B4
Swiss Cafe & Grill	**26** C5
Waikokopu Cafe	**27** B2
Woolworths Supermarket	**28** B4

DRINKING
Beachhouse	**29** C5
Mako Beach Bar	**30** C5
Pipi Patch Bar	**31** C5
Salty	(see 20)

TRANSPORT
Bus Stop	(see 2)

details how it was fashioned from gigantic kauri logs.

A 30-minute **cultural performance** (adult/child $15/8; ☺ check website or call) demonstrates traditional Maori song and dance, including *poi* (a women's formation dance that involves manipulating a ball of woven flax) and *haka* (war dance). There are various **guided tours** (adult/child $15/8; ☺ check website or call) available. The **Ultimate Waitangi Experience** (adult/child $25/14) is a combined ticket including a tour and a performance. In summer, the 45-minute twilight show **Land of Plenty** (adult/child $25/8; ☺ 6pm) is staged and can be combined with a drinks or meal package at the cafe.

Finally, the two-hour **Culture North Night Show** (☎ 09-402 5990; www.culturenorth.co.nz; admission $60; ☺ 7.30pm Mon-Sat Oct-Apr) is a wonderful dramatisation of Maori history held in the *whare runanga*. It begins with a traditional Maori welcome and heads into an atmospheric theatrical performance accompanied by a sound-and-light show. Free transfers from Paihia are included in the price.

NZ citizens are entitled to free entry to the treaty grounds; bring your passport or drivers' license.

HARURU FALLS

A few kilometres upstream from Waitangi are the attractive horseshoe Haruru Falls, which are lit up at night. A walkway leads along the Waitangi River and on a boardwalk through the mangroves from here to the Treaty Grounds (6km, 2½ hours one-way).

WAKA JOURNEY

For a hands-on experience of Maori culture, **Waka Tai-a-Mai** (☎ 09-405 9990; www.taiamaitours.co.nz; 2hr trip $75; ☺ 10am & 1pm Oct-Apr) gives you the opportunity to paddle a traditional 50ft carved *waka* (canoe). Leaving from the Waitangi bridge, the journey heads up to the Haruru Falls before visiting a replica Maori village. The Ngapuhi hosts wear traditional garb and perform the proper *karakia* (incantations), as well as some excellent storytelling.

ST PAUL'S CHURCH

Paihia's **St Paul's Church** (Marsden Rd) isn't particularly old (1925), but it stands on the site of NZ's first church – a simple raupo (bulrush) hut constructed in 1823. It's an altogether charming church, built from Kawakawa stone.

Spot the native birds in the stained glass above the altar – the kotare (kingfisher) represents Jesus (the king plus 'fisher of men'), while the tui (parson bird) and kereru (wood pigeon) portray the personalities of the Williams brothers (one scholarly, one forceful) who set up the mission station here.

WALKING

Just behind Paihia is **Opua Forest**, a regenerating forest with walking trails ranging from 10 minutes to five hours. A few large trees have escaped axe and fire, including some big kauri. If you walk up from School Rd for about 30 minutes, you'll find a couple of good lookouts. Pamphlets with details on all the Opua Forest walks are available from the i-SITE (free). You can drive into the forest by taking Oromahoe Rd west from Opua.

An easy 5km track follows the coast from Opua to Paihia.

Sleeping
BUDGET

What makes Paihia a desirable base for backpackers is the high standard and great choice of hostels. Kings Rd is the main 'backpackers' row', although there are gems scattered around elsewhere. All of the following are excellent.

Mayfair Lodge (☎ 09-402 7471; www.mayfairlodge.co.nz; 7 Puketona Rd; sites per person $15, dm/s/tw/d/q $25/55/62/65/108; ▢) Set apart from the rest but handy for the supermarket, Mayfair has colourful fish on the walls and resin toilet seats inset with shellfish.

Pickled Parrot (☎ 09-402 6222; www.pickledparrot.co.nz; Greys Lane; sites per person $18, dm $25-27, s/d $58/64; ▢ ☏) Surrounded by tropical plants, this friendly, well-maintained backpackers' stalwart has cute cabins, free bikes, free breakfast, a good vibe and, of course, a pet parrot.

Beachside Holiday Park (☎ 09-402 7678; www.beachsideholiday.co.nz; 1290 SH11; sites per person $20, units $70-230; ▢) Wake up at the water's edge at this sheltered camping ground, south of the township. The angular lemon cabins have 1970s charm, and there are kayaks for hire.

Mousetrap (☎ 09-402 8182; www.mousetrap.co.nz; 11 Kings Rd; dm $23-26, r $62; ▢) There are plenty of small chill-out areas in this friendly nautical-themed (which is much better than being rodent-themed) hostel. It has a variety of nice rooms, plus bikes, barbecues and boules out the front.

Peppertree Lodge (☎ 09-402 6122; www.peppertree. co.nz; 15 Kings Rd; dm $25-28, r $68-78; ☐ ☎) Simple, tidy rooms with high ceilings are on offer, plus there's a stash of bikes, racquets, kayaks and two barbecues for guests' use, making this a sociable choice.

Cap'n Bob's Beachhouse (☎ 09-402 8668; www. capnbobs.co.nz; 44 Davis Cres; dm/s $26/50, d $62-88; ☐) This small backpackers is a home-away-from-home, with hard-working owners, sea views from the veranda and more than a touch of charm. It's popular, so book ahead.

Saltwater Lodge (☎ 09-402 7075; www.saltwater lodge.co.nz; 14 Kings Rd; dm $27-33, d/tr/q $115/135/155; ☐ ☎) Even the dorms at this excellent, large, purpose-built backpackers have attached bathrooms, bedding and lockers. Cow-print and red-leather couches make for a cool communal lounge. There are large balconies, a bar and free bicycles, movies and racquets.

MIDRANGE & TOP END

Admiral's View Lodge (☎ 09-402 6236; www.admi ralsviewlodge.co.nz; 2 MacMurray Rd; apt $110-270; ☐) This hillside lodge offers natty units with balconies just begging for a relaxed sunset gin and tonic. Some have spa baths and bay views.

Baystay B&B (☎ 09-402 7511; www.baystay.co.nz; 93a Yorke Rd, Haruru Falls; r $115-145; ☐ ☎) Probably the only accommodation in NZ to have a Johnny Mnemonic pinball machine in the lounge room, this isn't your average B&B. Enjoy valley views from the spa pool of this slick, gay-friendly establishment.

Te Haumi Homestay (☎ 09-402 6818; joshlefi@xtra. co.nz; 41b Te Haumi Dr; s/d $125/140) A proper homestay, at Te Haumi you'll join the hospitable hosts for breakfast in the morning and wine and nibbles in the evening – yet once you're in your comfy downstairs room you'll have all the privacy you'll need. The house backs on to a nature reserve and has bay views. Listen for kiwi at night.

our pick **Tarlton's Lodge** (☎ 09-402 6711; www. tarltonslodge.co.nz; 11 Sullivans Rd; r incl breakfast $150-240) Striking architecture combines with up-to-the-minute decor in this hilltop B&B with expansive bay views. Of the three luxurious suites in the main building, two have their own outdoor spa. The mid-priced rooms are in an older building across the lane but they share the same aesthetic, pleasing panoramas and breakfast.

Swiss Chalet (☎ 09-402 7615; www.swisschalet.co.nz; 3 Bayview Rd; units $165-460) This motel has a spa, barbecue, Sky TV and a wide range of good clean rooms with balconies. There's a slight (Swiss) cheese factor but you can't accuse it of looking anonymous.

Decks of Paihia (☎ 09-402 6146; www.decksofpaihia. com; 69 School Rd; d $195-245; ☐ ☎) Architecturally impressive, this place offers light, modern bedrooms, granite bathrooms and a big deck with bay views. The elegant pool, set between house and bush, is irresistible.

Bay of Islands Lodge (☎ 09-402 6075; www.bayof islandslodge.co.nz; SH11, Port Opua; d $580; ☎) This luxurious, private retreat affords glorious views and has a chic little pool with an infinity lip. A wheelchair-accessible room is available.

Eating

our pick **Waikokopu Cafe** (☎ 09-402 6275; Waitangi Treaty Grounds; mains $14-20; ☉ 9am-5pm) The setting is a cracking start – by a pond, backed by bush and overlooking the Treaty Grounds. The locale is matched by Kiwi icons on the menu – the ever popular 'fush and chips' and the Rainbow Warrior, 'French toast sunk in maple syrup, bacon and banana'.

Frank's (☎ 09-402 7590; 68 Marsden Rd; mains $14-22; ☉ breakfast, lunch & dinner) While it moonlights as a cafe and a bar, it's as a pizza parlour that Frank's really shines. Share a large pizza for a well-priced carbo load.

Swiss Cafe & Grill (☎ 09-402 6701; 48 Marsden Rd; mains $17-29; ☉ dinner) Unpretentious but excellent, this waterfront restaurant has a wide-ranging and eclectic menu, which includes pizza, nicely prepared fish dishes and Swiss comfort food such as schnitzel and home-made strudel.

Only Seafood (☎ 09-402 6066; 40 Marsden Rd; mains $29-33; ☉ dinner) A superb place for local seafood, with dishes ranging from the simple (catch-of-the-day with lemon and parsley) to all manner of creamy, spicy concoctions. The fat Pacific oysters served with soy, wasabi and pickled ginger are sublime.

Pure Tastes (☎ 09-402 0003; 116 Marsden Rd; breakfast $16-19, mains $31-34; ☉ breakfast, lunch & dinner) Occupying a small canvas-and-glass corner of the Paihia Beach Resort, this first-rate restaurant serves interesting, beautifully presented Pacific fusion food using mainly Northland ingredients.

Self-caterers can buy supplies at **Woolworths supermarket** (6 Puketona Rd; ☉ 7am-10pm).

Drinking & Entertainment

God bless backpackers: they certainly keep the bars buzzing. There are plenty of places along Kings Rd and in the town centre to explore, so don't feel hemmed in by our list.

Pipi Patch Bar (☎ 09-402 7111; 18 Kings Rd; ❤ 4pm-late) The party hostel has the party bar: a funky spot with large video screens and a decent terrace. You'll be shuffled inside at midnight to keep the neighbours happy – although most of them are backpackers who'll be here anyway.

Salty (☎ 09-402 6080; 14 Kings Rd; ❤ 4.30pm-1am) Attached to Saltwater Lodge, this bar serves OK pizzas and has karaoke, games and quizzes.

Beachhouse (☎ 09-402 7479; 16 Kings Rd; ❤ 8am-midnight) There's live music Thursday through Sunday nights at this lively place, decorated with leis and a trippy surfie/Pasifika-fantasy mural.

Mako Beach Bar (☎ 09-402 8952; 50 Marsden Rd; ❤ noon-late) If you get sick of hanging around with other travellers, head to this locals' hangout where you might catch some live music on the weekends.

Getting There & Around

All buses serving Paihia stop at the Maritime Building by the wharf. **InterCity** (☎ 09-583 5780; www.intercity.co.nz) and associated buses head daily to Auckland ($25, four hours), Whangarei ($23, 70 minutes), Kerikeri ($17, 25 minutes), Mangonui ($30, 80 minutes) and Kaitaia ($37, two hours). **Naked Bus** (☎ 0900 625 33 per min $1.80; www.nakedbus.com; advance fares from $1) departs at 7.20am for Whangarei (95 minutes) and Auckland (four hours), carrying on to Rotorua (8½ hours), Taupo (10 hours) and Napier (12 hours).

Various daily tours head to Cape Reinga (see p156), while the Crossings Hokianga tour is based on demand. Another Opononi option is to purchase the Paihia-Auckland leg of the **Magic Travellers Network** (☎ 09-358 5600; www.magicbus.co.nz) hop-on, hop-off service. The fare ($69, four buses weekly) includes unlimited stops and pick-ups anywhere along the route, including the Waipoua Forest and Dargaville.

Ferries depart regularly for Russell. If you've more money to spend and less time to wait, **Ocean Blue Water Taxis** (☎ 021 273 1655; fishcatcher@xtra.co.nz) and **Paihia Island Shuttle** (☎ 0800 387 892; www.islandshuttle.co.nz) will take you anywhere.

For bikes, visit **Bay Beach Hire** (☎ 09-402 6078; www.baybeachhire.co.nz; Marsden Rd; ❤ 9am-5.30pm).

URUPUKAPUKA ISLAND

The largest of the bay islands, Urupukapuka is the only one with a regular ferry service and a choice of accommodation. The **Urupukapuka Island Archaeological Walk** takes five hours and visits Ngare Raumati *pa* sites dating back to the 16th century – a DOC pamphlet is available. Ngare Raumati were defeated by Ngapuhi in 1829.

There are **DOC campsites** (sites per adult/child $8/4) at Cable, Sunset and Urupukapuka Bays. They have water supplies, cold showers (except Sunset Bay) and composting toilets; bring food, a stove and fuel. Idyllically positioned **Zane Grey Resort** (☎ 09-402 5207; www.zanegrey.co.nz; Otehei Bay; dm/d/cottage $30/85/125) has a restaurant and bar and hires kayaks.

Explore NZ (☎ 09-402 8234; www.explorenz.co.nz) runs a ferry service departing from Paihia ($40 return).

KERIKERI
pop 5900

Kerikeri means 'dig dig', and a lot of digging goes on in the surrounding fertile farmland. Famous for its oranges, Kerikeri also produces plenty of kiwifruit (don't call them kiwis unless you want to offend Kiwis), vegetables and, increasingly, wine. If you're looking for some back-breaking, poorly paid work that Kiwis (the people, as opposed to kiwifruit) aren't keen to do, your working holiday starts here.

Information

Post office (6 Hobson Ave) Has poste restante service.
Procter Library (☎ 09-407 0773; www.kerikeri.co.nz; Cobham Rd; ❤ 8am-5pm Mon-Fri, 9am-2pm Sat, 9am-1pm Sun; ❤) The library has tourist information and free internet access.

Sights & Activities
KERIKERI BASIN

A snapshot of early Maori and Pakeha interaction is offered by a cluster of historic sites centred on this picturesque river basin. In 1819 the powerful Ngapuhi chief Hongi Hika allowed Rev Samuel Marsden to start a mission under the shadow of his **Kororipo Pa**.

The **Mission House** is the country's oldest wooden building (1822) and contains some original fittings and chattels. Its neighbour,

KERIKERI

To SH10 (5km)

Waipapa Rd

To Aroha Island (10km)

Kendall Rd

Mission Rd

Landing Rd

Selwyn Pl

Rainbow Falls Rd

Rainbow Falls

Kerikeri River Track

Kerikeri River Scenic Reserve

Wharepoke Falls

Kerikeri River

Kerikeri Track

Basin Recreation Reserve

Kemp Rd

6

5

7

17

Kerikeri Basin

4

Kerikeri Inlet

Heritage Bypass

Peacock Gardens Dr

Fairy Pools

9

8

Kerikeri Gr

Hongi Hika Recreation Reserve

12

Pa Rd

Golfview Rd

Kerikeri Golf Course

King Rd

Support St

Stella Dr

Wairoa Stream

Fairway Dr

Homestead St

Kerikeri Rd

Oak Rd

Wendover L'a

Jacaranda Pl

10

SLEEPING

Bed of Roses..............................8 B2
Colonial House Lodge
    Motel....................................9 B2
Hone Heke Lodge.....................10 C3
Kerikeri Top 10 Holiday
    Park.....................................11 A3
Pagoda Lodge.........................12 C2

16

14

Cobblestone Mall

18

2

Kerikeri Domain

15

1

3

19

Butler Rd

11

Aranga Rd

Cannon Dr

Hobson Ave

13

Norfolk Pl

Mill La

Cobham Rd

Hone Heke Rd

To Makana Confections (2km);
Get Fudged (2.5km); Cafe Blue (2.6km)
Kerikeri Farm Hostel (4km); SH10 (5km);
Kerikeri Airport (8km); Paihia (26km)

INFORMATION

Post Office.................................1 A3
Procter Library...........................2 B3

SIGHTS & ACTIVITIES

Bay of Islands Farmers'
    Market...................................3 A3
Kororipo Pa...............................4 D2
Mission House............................5 C2
Rewa's Village............................6 C2
St James Anglican Church...........7 C2
Stone Store..........................(see 5)

EATING

Black Olive...............................13 A4
Cafe Jerusalem........................14 B3
Cafe Zest.................................15 A3
Fishbone.................................16 A3
Pear Tree................................17 C2

DRINKING

Rocksalt..................................18 A3

TRANSPORT

Bus Stop..................................19 B3

NORTHLAND & THE BAY OF ISLANDS

---

the **Stone Store** (☎ 09-407 9236; 246 Kerikeri Rd; ☒ 10am-5pm Nov-Apr, 10am-4pm May-Oct), is the oldest stone building in NZ (1836). It sells interesting gifts as well as the type of goods that used to be sold in the store – although these days you'll have a hard time bartering pigs for muskets. Tours ($10) of the Mission House depart from here and include entry to the displays on the 1st floor of the store.

Just up the hill is a marked historical walk, which leads to the *pa* site. Huge war parties led by Hika once departed from here, terrorising much of the North Island and slaughtering thousands during the Musket Wars (see p28). The role of missionaries in arming Ngapuhi remains controversial. The walk emerges near the cute wooden **St James Anglican Church** (1878).

There's an ongoing campaign to have the area including the store, house and neighbouring *pa* recognised as a Unesco World Heritage Site.

If you had a hard time imagining the *pa* in its original state, take the footbridge across the river to **Rewa's Village** (☎ 09-407 6454; Landing Rd; adult/child $5/1; ☒ 9.30am-4.30pm), a fascinating mock-up of a traditional Maori fishing village.

Starting from the neighbouring scenic reserve the 4km-long Kerikeri Walkway leads to the 27m **Rainbow Falls**, passing by the Wharepoke Falls and the Fairy Pools. Alternatively, you can reach the Rainbow Falls from Rainbow Falls Rd, in which case it's only a 10-minute walk.

FOOD & WINE

Everyone in Kerikeri seems to be involved in some cottage industry or other, as the bombardment of craft shops on the way into town attests. If you're a recovering sugar junkie, you may need to drive into town with your eyes closed to avoid the boutique chocolate factory **Makana Confections** (☎ 09-407 6800; www.makana. co.nz; 504 Kerikeri Rd; ☒ 9am-5.30pm) and **Get Fudged** (☎ 09-407 1111; www.getfudged.co.nz; 560 Kerikeri Rd; ☒ 8.30am-5pm).

The **Bay of Islands Farmers Market** (www.boifm.org. nz; Hobson Ave; ☒ 8.30am-noon Sun) is a good place to sample a range of what the region has to offer, from sausages to *limoncello*.

The little-known red grape chambourcin has proved particularly suited to the region's subtropical humidity, along with pinotage and syrah, so while Northland isn't known for its wine, four vineyards near Kerikeri are doing their best to change this:

Ake Ake (Map p154; ☎ 09-407 8230; www.akeake vineyard.co.nz; 165 Waimate North Rd; ☒ 10am-6pm Tue-Sun) Has a swanky restaurant (lunch $14 to $26, dinner $26 to $31; open lunch Tuesday to Sunday, dinner Tuesday to Saturday), a *pétanque* court, and offers vineyard tours ($5, 11.30am Saturday and Sunday) and tastings ($3, free if dining).

Cottle Hill Winery (Map p154; ☎ 09-407 5203; www. cottlehill.co.nz; Cottle Hill Dr; ☒ 10am-5pm Nov-Mar, 10am-5pm Wed-Sun Apr-Oct) Tastings $5; free with purchase.

Fat Pig Vineyard (Map p154; ☎ 09-407 3113; www. fatpig.co.nz; 177 Puketotara Rd; ☒ 11am-6pm)

Marsden Estate Winery (Map p154; ☎ 09-407 9398; www.marsdenestate.co.nz; Wiroa Rd; ☒ 10am-5pm Sep-Jun, 10am-4pm Tue-Sun Jul & Aug) Offers meals and platters on its deck.

Total Tours (☎ 0800 264 868; www.totaltours.co.nz) has full-day food, wine and craft tours ($99), half-day wine tours ($75) and evening *Wine & Dine* tours ($120), departing from Paihia's Maritime Building.

AROHA ISLAND

Aroha Island Ecological Centre (☎ 09-407 5243; www. arohaisland.co.nz; Rangitane Rd; admission free; ☒ 9.30am-5.30pm Thu-Tue) is located on a tiny 5-hectare island (Map p154), 10km northeast of Kerikeri, reached via a permanent causeway through mangroves. The island provides a haven for the North Island brown kiwi and other native birds, as well as an excellent picnic spot for their nonfeathered admirers. There's a visitor centre, and kayaks can be rented ($25 for four hours).

Sleeping

Aroha Island (☎ 09-407 5243; www.arohaisland.co.nz; Rangitane Rd; sites per adult/child $15/7.50, dm/s $20/65, d $90-120, tr $110-140, q $130-160) Kip among the kiwi on the eco island of love (*aroha*). There's a wide range of reasonably priced options, from the peaceful campsites by the shelly beach to an extremely comfortable lodge gazing over the water.

Kerikeri Top 10 Holiday Park (☎ 09-407 9326; www. kerikeritop10.co.nz; Aranga Rd; sites per adult/child $15/11, units $78-245; ☒ 🛜) This large, attractive, riverside camping ground with good facilities is within walking distance of the town centre. Avoid the joyless attached backpackers.

Kerikeri Farm Hostel (☎ 09-407 6989; http://kkfarm hostel.blogspot.com; 1574 SH10; dm/s/d $25/43/58; ☒ 🛜) Less a farm, more an orange grove, this spot 4km out of town features a quiet rural cottage that sleeps only 12. It's a homely place, with a sole chandelier adding a bit of bling to the cosy lounge.

Hone Heke Lodge (☎ 09-407 8170; www.honeheke. co.nz; 65 Hone Heke Rd; dm $25, s $43-63, d $58-80; ☒ 🛜) Hone Heke has a row of single-storey rooms with their own fridges, a small kitchen and a sociable covered courtyard. Weekly rates are available and recreation areas (TV lounge, pool tables, ping pong, barbecues) are good.

Pagoda Lodge (☎ 09-407 8617; www.pagoda.co.nz; 81 Pa Rd; d $85-160, tr $130-270, q $190-390) Built in the 1930s by an oddball Scotsman with an Asian fetish, this lodge features pagoda-shaped roofs grafted onto weatherboard cottages. The property descends to the river and is dotted with Buddhas and two- to three-'room' tents with proper beds ($65 to $140). The Jade House – built to hold a collection that now resides in the British Museum – is a smartly decorated studio cottage.

Colonial House Lodge Motel (☎ 09-407 9106; www. colonialhousemotel.co.nz; 178 Kerikeri Rd; units $100-195; 🛜 🎬) The Colonial has restful rooms opening onto a tropical garden. It may be getting on a bit, but it has freshened itself up with wi-fi and DVD players.

Bed of Roses (☎ 09-407 4666; www.bedofroses.co.nz; 165 Kerikeri Rd; d $225-325; ☒) Much more comfortable than an actual bed of roses, this stylish B&B is furnished with French antiques, luxe linens and comfy beds. The interesting building has an art-deco ambience and awesome views.

Eating & Drinking

Fishbone (☎ 09-407 6065; 88 Kerikeri Rd; mains $6-17; ❤ breakfast & lunch) Stylish Fishbone does a great coffee and serves imaginative food; Dr Seuss fans should try the green (pesto) eggs and ham.

Cafe Zest (☎ 09-407 7164; 73 Kerikeri Rd; mains $7-17; ❤ breakfast & lunch) Bathed in Kerikeri's orange glow, cute little Zest serves up a tempting array of counter food with plenty of vegetarian options.

Cafe Blue (☎ 09-407 5150; 582 Kerikeri Rd; mains $9-18; ❤ 9am-3pm) It may be on the main road into town but this garden cafe is a peaceful oasis, serving sandwiches, salads, renowned Cornish pasties and sub-$20 grills.

Black Olive (☎ 09-407 9693; 308 Kerikeri Rd; mains $11-32; ❤ dinner Tue-Sun) Call in for popular pasta and pizza takeaways, or grab a seat in the restaurant or garden.

Pear Tree (☎ 09-407 8479; 215 Kerikeri Rd; mains $15-30; ❤ lunch & dinner) Lovely views of the basin from this homestead are this restaurant's big drawcard, ably matched by the food.

Cafe Jerusalem (☎ 09-407 1001; Cobblestone Mall, Kerikeri Rd; mains $16-19; ❤ 11am-late) Northland's best falafels, served with a smile and a social vibe.

Rocksalt (☎ 09-407 1050; Kerikeri Rd; ❤ 11am-9pm Mon-Tue, 11am-11pm Wed-Thu, 11am-2am Fri & Sat) The most popular nightspot in town, this smart bar has a beer garden and an orange-neon radiance.

See Food & Wine, opposite, for some self-catering options.

Getting There & Away

AIR

Bay of Islands (Kerikeri) Airport (Map p154; ☎ 09-407 7147; www.bayofislandsairport.co.nz; 218 Wiroa Rd) is 8km southwest of town. **Air New Zealand** (☎ 0800 737 000; www.airnz.co.nz) operates three to five flights daily (except Sunday) from Auckland (40 minutes); see its website for prices and discounts. **Salt Air Xpress** (☎ 09-402 8338; www.saltair.co.nz) flies to Whangarei and Auckland's North Shore ($169, 30 minutes), every day except Saturday.

BUS

InterCity (☎ 09-583 5780; www.intercity.co.nz) and partner buses leave from a stop on Cobham Rd, opposite the library. Daily services head to Auckland ($55, five hours), Whangarei ($24, 1¾ hours), Paihia ($17, 25 minutes), Mangonui ($24, 54 minutes) and Kaitaia ($33, 1½ hours).

THE FAR NORTH

If it sounds remote, that's because it is. The far-flung Far North is always playing second fiddle to the Bay of Islands for attention and funding, yet the subtropical tip of the North Island has more breathtaking coastline per square kilometre than anywhere but the offshore islands. Parts of the Far North are noticeably economically depressed and in places could best be described as gritty. While the 'winterless north' may be a popular misnomer, summers here are long and leisurely. Here's your chance to get off the beaten track, although that often means unsealed roads.

MATAURI & TAURANGA BAYS

It's a short detour from SH10, but the loop route leading inland to these awesome beaches is a world away from the glitzy face presented for tourists in the Bay of Islands.

Matauri Bay is a long sandy surf beach, 18km off SH10, with the 17 Cavalli Islands scattered offshore. **Matauri Bay Holiday Park** (☎ 09-405 0525; www.matauribay.co.nz; sites per adult/child $18/8, cabins $100-130) takes up the north end of the beach and has a shop (which sells booze) and petrol station. On top of the headland above the park is a monument to the *Rainbow Warrior* (see the boxed text, p169); the Greenpeace ship's underwater resting place among the Cavalli Islands is a popular dive site (see p154).

DOC maintains a 12-person **hut** (☎ 09-407 0300; www.doc.govt.nz; sites per adult/child $12/6) on Motukawanui Island, but you'll need a boat or kayak to reach it and you'll need to book ahead. Only water, mattresses and a composting toilet are provided; bring everything else.

Back on the main road the route heads west, passing through pleasant Te Ngaere village and a succession of little bays before the turnoff to Tauranga Bay, a smaller beach where the sand is a peachy pink colour. **Tauranga Bay Holiday Park** (☎ 09-405 0436; www.taurangabay.co.nz; sites per person $15, cabins $60-160; 🖳 🛜) has well-maintained accommodation on the picturesque beachfront, but it lacks trees and bears the brunt of the weather. A minimum $50

NORTHLAND & THE BAY OF ISLANDS

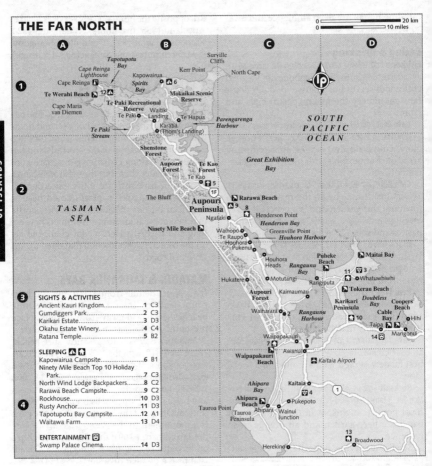

THE FAR NORTH

charge per night for campsites and a seven-night minimum stay apply in January.

Down a private road leading from Tauranga Bay, **Northland Sea Kayaking** (☎ 09-405 0381; www.northlandseakayaking.co.nz; half-/full day tours $65/85) leads kayak explorations of this magical coastline of coves, sea caves and islands. Accommodation is available in conjunction with tours for $20 extra per person.

There's no public transport to these parts or to neighbouring Whangaroa.

WHANGAROA HARBOUR

Just around the headland from Tauranga Bay is the narrow entrance to Whangaroa Harbour. The small fishing village of Whangaroa is 6km from SH10 and calls

itself the 'Marlin Capital of NZ', meaning it's a popular place to dislocate your shoulder while trying to land a Lee Marvin–sized monster. **Boyd Gallery** (☎ 09-405 0230; Whangaroa Rd; 8am-7pm) is the general store but also acts as a tourist information office.

There are plenty of charter boats for **gamefishing** (December to April). Prices start at around $1200 a day. If you're planning to hook a marlin, insist on it being released once caught – striped marlin is one of NZ's least-sustainable species (see the boxed text, p170).

The 15m yacht **Sea Eagle** (☎ 09-405 1963; www.seaeaglecharters.com; per person $110, minimum 2) makes day trips to the Cavalli Islands, where there are excellent beaches, diving spots, snorkelling opportunities and walks. Longer charters can also be arranged.

An excellent 20-minute hike starts from the car park at the end of Old Hospital Rd and goes up **St Paul's Rock** (213m), which dominates the village. At the top you have to use a wire cable to pull yourself up, but the views make it worth the effort.

The **Wairakau Stream Track** north to Pekapeka Bay begins near the church hall on Campbell Rd in Totara North on the other side of the bay. The two-hour hike passes through farmland, hills and shoreline before arriving at DOC's **Lane Cove Cottage** (☎ 09-407 8474; sole occupancy $160), which has 16 beds and composting toilets. Bring everything else and book ahead. **Duke's Nose Track** (45 minutes each way) starts behind the cottage and leads up Kairara Rocks; look for the Duke of Wellington's aquiline profile in the rock face.

On the other side of the harbour's north head is **Taupo Bay**, a surf beach that attracts a loyal Kiwi contingent in summer. It's reached by an 11km, partly unsealed road signposted from SH10.

Sleeping & Eating

Sunseeker Lodge (☎ 09-405 0496; www.sunseekerlodge.co.nz; Old Hospital Rd; sites per person $15, dm/s $25/50, d $50-86, units $150-250; 🖳) Up the hill in Whangaroa, this friendly lodge has a sublime spa with a jaw-dropping view, hires out kayaks and motor boats, and will pick you up from Kaeo on SH10.

ourpick Kahoe Farms Hostel (☎ 09-405 1804; www.kahoefarms.co.nz; dm/s $25/53, d $68-88) On SH10, 10km north of the turn-off to Whangaroa, this hostel has a deservedly great reputation – for its comfortable accommodation, for its bucolic setting, for its home-cooked Italian food, but mostly for its welcoming young owners. The backpackers' villa is great but there's an even more atmospheric cottage slightly up the hill with excellent value en-suite rooms. There are bushwalks on the property to old kauri dams and swimming holes, and you can hire a kayak to tackle the harbour.

Marlin (☎ 09-405 0347; Whangaroa Rd; mains $12-25; 🕑 lunch & dinner) A friendly local pub with good honest tucker served from the attached cafe.

THE BOMBING OF THE RAINBOW WARRIOR

On the morning of 10 July 1985, New Zealanders awoke to news reporting that a terrorist attack had killed a man in Auckland Harbour. The Greenpeace flagship *Rainbow Warrior* had been sunk at its anchorage at Marsden Wharf, where it was preparing to sail to Moruroa Atoll near Tahiti to protest against French nuclear testing.

It took some time to find out exactly what had happened, but a tip-off from a Neighbourhood Watch group lead to the arrest of two French foreign intelligence service (DGSE) agents, posing as tourists. The agents had detonated two mines on the boat in staggered explosions – the first designed to cause the crew to evacuate and the second to sink her. However, after the initial evacuation, some of the crew returned to the vessel to investigate and document the attack. Greenpeace photographer Fernando Pereira was drowned below decks following the second explosion.

The arrested agents pleaded guilty to manslaughter and were sentenced to 10 years' imprisonment. In response, the French government threatened to embargo NZ goods from entering the European Economic Community – which would have crippled NZ's economy. A deal was struck whereby France paid $13 million to NZ and apologised, in return for the agents being delivered into French custody on a South Pacific atoll for three years. France eventually paid over $8 million to Greenpeace in reparation – and the bombers were quietly freed before their sentence was served.

Initially French President Mitterrand denied any government involvement in the attack, but following an inquiry he eventually sacked his Defence Minister and the head of the DGSE, Admiral Pierre Lacoste. On the 20th anniversary of the attack, Le Monde newspaper published a report from Lacoste dating from 1986 declaring that the president had personally authorised the operation.

The bombing left a lasting impact on NZ, and French nuclear testing at Moruroa ceased for good in 1996. The wreck of the *Rainbow Warrior* was re-sunk near Northland's Cavalli Islands, where it can be explored by divers. The masts were bought by the Dargaville Museum and overlook the town. The memory of Fernando Pereira endures in a peaceful bird hide in Thames. A memorial to the boat sits atop a Maori *pa* site at Matauri Bay, north of the Bay of Islands.

DOUBTLESS BAY
pop 6030

The bay gets its unusual name from an entry in Cook's logbook, where he wrote that the body of water was 'doubtless a bay'. No kidding, Cap'n. It's a bloody big bay at that, with a string of pretty swimming beaches heading towards the Karikari Peninsula.

The main centre, **Mangonui** (meaning 'Big Shark'), retains a fishing-port feel, despite cafes and gift shops now infesting its well-labelled line of historical waterfront buildings. They were constructed in the days when Mangonui was a centre of the whaling industry (1792–1850) and exported flax, kauri wood and gum.

The popular holiday settlements of **Coopers Beach**, **Cable Bay** and **Taipa** are restful pockets of beachside gentrification.

Information
Doubtless Bay visitor information centre (☎ 09-406 2046; www.doubtlessbay.co.nz; 118 Waterfront Rd, Mangonui; 🕙 10am-4pm Mon-Sat; 🖳)
Post office (Beach Rd, Mangonui)

Sights & Activities
Grab the free **Heritage Trail** brochure from the information centre for a 3km self-guided walk taking in 22 historic sites. Other walks lead to attractive **Mill Bay**, west of Mangonui, and **Rangikapiti Pa Historic Reserve**, with ancient Maori terracing and a spectacular view of Doubtless Bay – particularly at sunrise and sunset. A walkway runs from Mill Bay to the top of the *pa*, but you can drive nearly to the top if you're not feeling energetic.

You can sample and purchase the best of the region's wines at the **Far North Wine Centre** (☎ 09-406 2485; www.farnorthwinecentre.co.nz; 60 Waterfront Dr, Mangonui; 🕙 11am-4pm Wed-Mon) and then pick up some Pasifika knick-knacks at nearby **Flax Bush** (☎ 09-406 1510; www.flaxbush.co.nz; 50 Waterfront Dr).

At Hihi, 15km northeast of Mangonui, is **Butler Point**, where you can take a guided tour around the small **Whaling Museum** (☎ 09-406 0006; www.butlerpoint.co.nz; Marchant Rd; adult/child $12/2; 🕙 by appointment), housed in a Victorian homestead (1843) with lovely gardens. Its first owner, Captain Butler, left Dorset when he was 14 and at 24 was captain of a whaling ship. He settled here in 1839, had 13 children and became a trader, farmer, magistrate and Member of Parliament.

FISH FOR THE FUTURE

While NZ's fisheries are more tightly controlled than most, conservation groups are quick to point out that most fishing is still unsustainable at present levels. The **Royal Forest & Bird Protection Society** (☎ 0800 200 064; www.forestandbird.org.nz) publishes an annual *Best Fish Guide*, which is downloadable from its website. The following are the best and worst choices if you're hankering for a seafood chow-down.

■ **Ten best** Kina, anchovy, pilchard, sprats, skipjack tuna, garfish, yellow-eyed mullet, cockles, kahawai, blue cod

■ **Ten worst** Orange roughy, bluefin tuna, oreos (deepwater dory), shark (lemonfish/rig), snapper, bluenose, jack mackerel, squid, skate, striped marlin

---

Sleeping
There's plenty of accommodation around the bay but most is horribly overpriced in summer – the following recommendations being noble exceptions. Outside the peak months things settle down considerably.

our pick **Puketiti Lodge** (☎ 09-406 0369; www.puketiti lodge.co.nz; 10 Puketiti Dr; dm/s/d/tr $40/90/130/150; 🖳) If this is what they mean by flashpacking, bring it on. For $40 you get a comfy bunk in a spacious six-person dorm opening on to a large deck with awesome views, a locker big enough for the burliest backpack and, most surprisingly, breakfast. The private en-suite rooms are much more luxurious than the price implies. Turn inland at Midgley Rd, 6km south of Mangonui village, just after the Hihi turn-off.

Rosie's B&B (☎ 09-406 1443; www.rosiesbandb.co.nz; 136 SH10; r $80) Informal Rosie's offers two unremarkable but reasonably priced en-suite rooms in a Coopers Beach house. Try for the upstairs one; it's small but has a balcony with sea views.

Doubtless Bay Lodge (☎ 09-406 1661; www.doubt lessbaylodge.co.nz; 33 Cable Bay Block Rd; s/d $80/120) A 10-minute walk from Coopers Beach, this hillside lodge offers motel-style privacy coupled with B&B-style friendliness and food. Rooms have cable TV and facilities for making a nice cuppa. It was on the market when we visited, so we hope the new owners maintain the high standards.

Old Oak (☎ 09-406 1250; www.theoldoak.co.nz; 66 Waterfront Dr, Mangonui; s $125, d $175-225, ste $295) When we visited, the paint was still drying on this atmospheric 1861 kauri inn, which was in the throes of being completely reborn as an elegant boutique hotel. The Old Oak oozes character, not least because the building is reputedly haunted.

Mangonui Waterfront Motel (☎ 09-406 0347; www.mangonuiwaterfront.co.nz; Waterfront Dr; apt $155-245) Sleeping two to eight people, these historic apartments on the Mangonui waterfront have loads of character, each one different but all with balconies, a sense of space and its own barbecue. Try to book 100-year-old Tahi.

Eating

There are a few cafes, takeaways and stores scattered around the other beaches, but Mangonui has the best eating options – and they're actually pretty great.

Mangonui Fish Shop (☎ 09-406 0478; Waterfront Dr; mains $5-25; ☻ 10am-8pm) You can eat outdoors over the water in this licensed and deservedly famous fish-and-chip shop, which also sells smoked fish and seafood salads. Grab a crayfish salad and a cold beer, and all will be right with the world.

Waterfront Cafe & Bar (☎ 09-406 0850; Waterfront Dr; brunch $7-21, dinner $14-29; ☻ 8.30am-late) The best cafe in the Far North, Waterfront has an inventive menu, water views, friendly service and old-world charm. For breakfast try the market fish on spinach with citrus hollandaise.

ourpick Thai Chef (☎ 09-406 1220; 80 Waterfront Dr; mains $18-26; ☻ dinner Tue-Sun) While we're on the superlatives, this is quite simply the best Thai restaurant we've found in the upper North Island, Auckland included. Dishes have names such as *3 Alcoholics* and *Bananas with Hairy Legs*. The *Sexy Little Duck* is irresistible.

There's also a **Four Square supermarket** (Waterfront Rd) next to the post office.

Entertainment

Swamp Palace Cinema (☎ 09-408 7040; Oruru Rd) This tiny cinema is quite the experience, often offering a verbal prelude to the screenings. It's 7km inland from Taipa.

Getting There & Away

InterCity (☎ 09-583 5780; www.intercity.co.nz) buses stop at the BP service station on Waterfront Dr in Mangonui, travelling to Kaitaia ($21, 40 minutes) and Kerikeri ($24, 54 minutes). The same services stop outside the wholesalers in Coopers Beach, opposite the shop in Cable Bay and outside the Shell station in Taipa.

Busabout Kaitaia (☎ 09-408 1092; www.cbec.co.nz) has services to Kaitaia ($5, one hour).

KARIKARI PENINSULA

The oddly shaped Karikari Peninsula bends into a near-perfect right angle. The result is beaches facing north, south, east and west in close proximity; if the wind's annoying you or you want to catch some surf, a sunrise or a sunset, just swap beaches. Despite its natural assets, the peninsula's blissfully undeveloped, with farmers well outnumbering tourist operators. There's no public transport and you won't find a lot of shops or eateries either.

Sights & Activities

Tokerau Beach is the long, lovely stretch forming the western edge of Doubtless Bay. Neighbouring **Whatuwhiwhi** is smaller and more built-up, facing back across the bay. **Maitai Bay**, with its tiny twin coves, is the loveliest of them all, at the lonely end of the peninsula down an unsealed road. It's a great spot for swimming – sheltered enough for the kids but with enough swell to body surf.

Rangiputa faces west at the elbow of the peninsula; the pure white sand and crystal-clear sheltered waters come straight from a Pacific Island daydream. A turn-off on the road to Rangiputa takes you to remote **Puheke Beach**, a long, windswept stretch of snow-white sand dunes forming Karikari's northern edge.

This unique setup makes Karikari Peninsula one of the world's premium spots for kiteboarding, or at least that's the opinion of the experienced crew at **Airzone Kitesurfing School** (☎ 09-408 7129; www.kitesurfnz.com; 1-/2-day course $175/325). You can chase the wind around the peninsula; learners get to hone their skills on flat water before heading to the surf.

An ominous sign of creeping gentrification is the luxury golf club and winery on the way to Maitai Bay. Impressive **Karikari Estate** (Map p168; ☎ 09-408 7222; www.karikariestate.co.nz; Maitai Bay Rd; tastings $12; ☻ 11am-5pm) produces acclaimed red wines and has a cafe attached (mains $14 to $25).

Sleeping & Eating

DOC campsite (☎ 09-408 6014; www.doc.govt.nz; Maitai Bay; sites per adult/child $8/4) A large camping ground with chemical toilets and cold showers.

Rusty Anchor (Map p168; ☎ 0800 787 892; www.rustyanchor.co.nz; 1 Tokerau Beach Rd; sites per person $10, dm $25, d/tr/q $65/85/105; 🖳) A one-stop backpackers' haven, with an information centre, a bar, takeaways and a laundromat as part of the complex.

Rockhouse (Map p168; ☎ 09-406 7151; rochousian@clear.net.nz; Inland Rd; s/d/tr $30/50/75) Fred Flintstone meets Hundertwasser at this guest house, just 1km off of SH10, which has unusual but comfortable en-suite accommodation.

Whatuwhiwhi Top 10 Holiday Park (☎ 09-408 7202; www.whatuwhiwhitop10.co.nz; 17 Whatuwhiwhi Rd; sites per 2 people $40, units $96-375; 🖳) This camping ground has good facilities, kayaks for hire and a great location – sheltered by hills and overlooking the beach.

White Sands Apartments (☎ 09-408 7080; www.whitesands.co.nz; Rangiputa Beach; units $125-185) Seventies style imbues these comfortable wooden units. There's a shop downstairs and within a few steps your feet will find the white sand.

CAPE REINGA & NINETY MILE BEACH

Maori consider Cape Reinga (Te Rerenga-Wairua) the jumping-off point for souls as they depart on the journey to their spiritual homeland. That makes the Aupouri Peninsula a giant diving board, and it certainly resembles one – long and thin, it reaches 108km to form NZ's northern extremity. On its west coast Ninety Mile Beach (Ninety Kilometre Beach would be more accurate) is a continuous stretch lined with high sand dunes, flanked by the Aupouri Forest.

Sights

Standing at windswept **Cape Reinga lighthouse** and looking out over the ocean gives a real end-of-the-world feeling. This is where the waters of the Tasman Sea and Pacific Ocean meet, breaking together into waves up to 10m high in stormy weather. Little tufts of cloud often cling to the ridges, giving sudden spooky chills even on hot days. Visible on a promontory slightly to the east is a spiritually significant 800-year-old **pohutukawa tree**; souls are believed to slide down its roots. Out of respect to the most sacred site in Maoridom,

don't go near the tree and refrain from eating or drinking anywhere in the area.

Contrary to expectation, Cape Reinga isn't actually the northernmost point of the country; that honour belongs to Surville Cliffs further to the east. A walk along Te Werahi Beach to **Cape Maria van Diemen** (five hours loop) takes you to the westernmost point. This is one of many sections of the three- to four-day, 53km **Cape Reinga Coastal Walkway** (from Kapowairua to Te Paki Stream) that can be tackled individually. Beautiful **Tapotupotu Bay** is a two-hour walk east of Cape Reinga, via Sandy Bay and the cliffs. From Tapotupotu Bay it's an eight-hour walk to the eastern end of **Kapowairua** (Spirits Bay). Both bays are also accessible by road.

A large chunk of the land around Cape Reinga is part of the **Te Paki Recreation Reserve** managed by DOC. It's public land with free access; leave the gates as you found them and don't disturb the animals. There are 7 sq km of giant sand dunes on either side of the mouth of Te Paki Stream. Clamber up to take flying leaps off the dunes or toboggan down them.

On the east coast, **Great Exhibition Bay** has dazzling snow-white silica dunes. There's no public road access, but some tours pay a *koha* (donation) to cross Maori farmland or approach the sand by kayak from Parengarenga Harbour.

Beside the highway at Te Kao, 46km south of Cape Reinga, stands a **Ratana temple** (Map p168; 6576 Far North Rd) known as Nga-Tapuwae-Ote-Mangai (the Sacred Steps of the Mouthpiece). Ratana is a Maori Christian sect with more than 50,000 adherents, formed in 1925 by Tahupotiki Wiremu Ratana, who was known as 'the mouthpiece of God'. This temple is built on land where Ratana once stood. It resembles a mosque, with its two domed towers (Arepa and Omeka, alpha and omega) and the Ratana emblem of the star and crescent moon.

Kauri forests covered this area for over 100,000 years, leaving ancient logs and the much-prized gum (used for making varnish and linoleum) buried beneath. **Gumdiggers Park** (Map p168; ☎ 09-406 7166; www.gumdiggerspark.co.nz; Heath Rd, Waiharara; adult/child $10/5; ☯ 9am-5pm) covers a major gumdigging site – the region's main industry from the 1870s to the 1920s. In 1900, some 7000 gumdiggers (wearing gumboots – the NZ name for Wellingtons) were digging holes all over Northland. Start with the 15-minute video telling the story of the trees, their mysterious destruction and the gum industry. Rope paths head through the bush, leading past reproductions of gumdiggers' huts, ancient kauri stumps and holes left by the diggers. It was a hard life for the workers, who used jute sacks for their tents, bedding and clothing.

It's tacky and overpriced, but **Ancient Kauri Kingdom** (Map p168; ☎ 09-406 7172; www.ancientkauri. co.nz; 229 Far North Rd, Awanui; ⏰ 8.30am-5pm) is still worth a stop. Here 50,000-year-old kauri stumps, dragged up from swamps, are fashioned into furniture, woodcraft products and a fair bit of tourist tat. The large complex includes a cafe, gift shop and workshop. A huge kauri log has an impressive spiral staircase carved into it that takes you to the mezzanine level.

Tours

Bus tours go to Cape Reinga from Kaitaia, Ahipara, Doubtless Bay and the Bay of Islands (see p156). There's no other public transport up here and many car-rental companies prohibit driving on the sands of Ninety Mile Beach or the partly unsealed road north of Waitiki Landing.

Cape Reinga Adventures (☎ 09-409 8445; www. capereingaadventures.co.nz; half-/full-day 4WD trips $75/135) Real action men who offer 4WD tours (including sunset visits to the cape after the crowds have gone), fishing, kayaking, sand-boarding and dune-surfing as day activities or as overnight camping trips ($150 to $220). They also hire kayaks ($60 for 24 hours) and sandboards ($20).

Far North Outback Adventures (☎ 09-408 0927; www.farnorthtours.co.nz) Flexible, day-long tours from Kaitaia/Ahipara for $600 (one to three people) to $650 (four or five people), including morning tea and lunch. You can visit remote areas such as Great Exhibition Bay ($10 per person access fee).

Harrison's Cape Runner (☎ 0800 227 373; www. harrisonscapereingatours.co.nz; 123 North Rd, Kaitaia; adult/child $45/25) Day bus trips that include sand tobogganing and a picnic lunch.

Paradise 4x4 (☎ 0800 494 392; www.paradisenz.co.nz; for 2 $600, per additional person $50) Operates flexible, exclusive 4WD tours from Doubtless Bay up Ninety Mile Beach to Cape Reinga, including Devonshire tea and gourmet lunch with local wine. Hokianga tours also available.

Sand Safaris (☎ 0800 869 090; www.sandsafaris.co.nz; adult/child $55/30) A family-owned operation running coach trips, including a picnic lunch and a guided tour of Gumdiggers Park.

Sleeping & Eating

Unless you're a happy camper you won't find much decent accommodation north of Pukenui. Literally 'Big Stomach', it's also the best place to fill yours; you'll find a cafe, takeaways and grocery store. The only other options are unremarkable eateries at Ancient Kauri Kingdom (left), Houhora Heads and Waitiki Landing.

DOC campsites (Map p168; sites per adult/child $7.50/3.50) There are stunningly positioned sites at Kapowairua, Tapotupotu Bay and Rarawa Beach. Only water and toilet facilities are provided. Bring a cooker, as fires are not allowed, and plenty of repellent to ward off the evil mosquitoes and sandflies. 'Freedom/Leave No Trace' camping is allowed along the Cape Reinga Coastal Walkway.

Ninety Mile Beach Top 10 Holiday Park (Map p168; ☎ 09-406 7298; www.ninetymilebeach.co.nz; 6 Matai St, Waipapakauri; sites per person $16, cabins $80-110; 🖳) Rows of tidy units line the sunburnt grass at this well-positioned holiday park, within earshot of Ninety Mile Beach's roaring surf.

Pukenui Lodge Motel (☎ 09-409 8837; www.pukenui lodge.co.nz; cnr SH1 & Wharf Rd, Pukenui; dm/r $25/65, units $115-170; 🖳 🐾) This clean, welcoming backpackers occupies a historic villa (1891) filled with mismatched furniture and an ancient TV. It's a more charming prospect than the bog-standard motel units.

North Wind Lodge Backpackers (Map p168; ☎ 09-409 8515; www.northwind.co.nz; 88 Otaipango Rd, Henderson Bay; dm/tw/d/tr $27/58/64/84) Six kilometres down an unsealed road on the peninsula's east side, this unusual turreted house offers a homely environment and plenty of quiet spots on the lawn to sit with a beer and a book.

Getting There & Around

Apart from numerous tours, there's no public transport past Pukenui, which is linked to Kaitaia ($5, 45 minutes) by **Busabout Kaitaia** (☎ 09-408 1092; www.cbec.co.nz).

Far North Rd (SH1F) is sealed as far as Waitiki Landing. The final 7km are currently being sealed, starting from Cape Reinga and heading backwards. This project isn't expected to be completed until 2012; prepare for delays. At the end of the road there's a 1km walk from the car park to the lighthouse.

The other major route is Ninety Mile Beach itself, suited to rugged vehicles. Cars have been known to hit soft sand and be swallowed by the tides – look out for unfortunate vehicles

NGATI TARARA

As you're travelling around the north you might notice the preponderance of road names ending in '-ich'. *Haere mai, dobro došli* and welcome (as the sign leading into Kaitaia proclaims) to one of the more peculiar ethnic conjunctions in the country.

From the end of the 19th century, men from the Dalmatian coast of Croatia started arriving in NZ looking for work. Many ended up in Northland's gum fields. Pakeha society wasn't particularly welcoming to the new immigrants, particularly during WWI – they were considered Austrians. Not so in the small Maori communities of the north. Here they found an echo of Dalmatian village life, with its emphasis on extended family and hospitality, not to mention a shared history of injustice at the hands of colonial powers.

The Maori jokingly named them Tarara, as their rapid conversation in Serbo-Croat sounded like 'ta-ra-ra-ra-ra' to Maori ears. Many Croatian men married local *wahine* (women), founding clans that have left several of today's famous Maori with Croatian surnames, like singer Margaret Urlich and former All Black Frano Botica. You'll find large Tarara communities in the Far North, Dargaville and West Auckland.

poking through the sands. Check tide times before setting out; avoid it 2½ hours either side of high tide. Watch out for 'quicksand' at Te Paki Stream – keep moving. If you get stuck, your hire-car insurance won't cover you. Enquire at Tuatua Tours (opposite) about 4WD hire.

Fill up with petrol before hitting the Aupouri Peninsula. The petrol station at Waitiki Landing has been known to run out.

KAITAIA
pop 5300

Nobody comes to the Far North to hang out in this provincial town, but it's a handy stop if you're after a supermarket, a post office or an ATM. It's also a jumping-off point for tours to Cape Reinga and Ninety Mile Beach (see p173).

The **Far North i-SITE** (☎ 09-408 0879; www.topofnz.co.nz; Jaycee Park, South Rd; ☻ 8.30am-5pm) has internet access and information on the region. Nearby, the **Far North Regional Museum** (☎ 09-408 1403; www.farnorthmuseum.co.nz; 6 South Rd; adult/child $4/1; ☻ 10am-4pm) has an eclectic mix of exhibits focusing on local history, including a massive 1769 anchor.

Just south of Kaitaia, off the road to Ahipara, **Okahu Estate Winery** (Map p168; ☎ 09-408 2066; www.okahuestate.co.nz; cnr Okahu & Awaroa Rds; ☻ noon-4pm Mon-Fri) offers free tastings.

The friendly owners of **Mainstreet Lodge** (☎ 09-408 1275; www.mainstreetlodge.co.nz; 235 Commerce St; dm $26-30, s $55-70, d $62-75, tr $87-99, q $112-128; 💻 🛜) know the area inside-out. Maori carvings abound at this groovy old cottage, which has a modern purpose-built wing facing the rear courtyard.

Beachcomber (☎ 09-408 2010; 222 Commerce St; mains $16-32; ☻ 11am-late Mon-Sat) is easily the best place to eat in town, with a wide range of seafood and meatier fare, all deftly executed, and a well-stocked salad bar.

The airport is 6km north of town, and **Air New Zealand** (☎ 0800 737 000; www.airnz.co.nz) offers daily flights between Kaitaia and Auckland (45 minutes, check website for prices).

Alternatively, **InterCity** (☎ 09-623 1503; www.intercity.co.nz) buses stop at the i-SITE, travelling to Mangonui ($21, 40 minutes) and Kerikeri ($33, 1½ hours). **Busabout Kaitaia** (☎ 09-408 1092; www.cbec.co.nz) has services to Doubtless Bay ($5, one hour), Pukenui ($5, 45 minutes) and Ahipara ($3.50, 15 minutes).

AHIPARA
pop 1200

All good things must come to an end, and Ninety Mile Beach does it at this spunky beach town. A few holiday mansions have snuck in, but mostly it's just the locals keeping it real, rubbing shoulders with visiting surfers. The area is known for its huge sand dunes and massive gum field, where 2000 people once worked. Sand tobogganing and quad-bike rides are popular activities on the dunes above Ahipara and further around the Tauroa Peninsula.

Activities
Ahipara Adventure Centre (☎ 09-409 2055; www.ahiparaadventure.co.nz; 15 Takahe St) hires out sand- and surfboards ($10 per hour), mountain bikes ($25 per hour), kayaks ($25 per hour), blokarts for sand yachting ($60 per hour) and quad bikes ($70 per hour).

Tuatua Tours (☎ 09-409 4875; www.tuatuatours.com; 250 Ahipara Rd; 2hr ride per person $135, 2 people $150) gets great word-of-mouth for its reef- and dune-rider tours and *Ultimate Sand Dune Safaris* (three hours including sand tobogganing, per one/two people $185/200). You can hire a 4WD ($280 per day) to explore Ninety Mile Beach at your own pace without risking the wrath of regular hire companies.

Another option for exploring the beach is on horseback. **Ahipara Treks** (☎ 09-409 4122; ahiparahorsetreks@xtra.co.nz) offers one- to five-hour beach canters ($60 to $150), including some farm and ocean riding (when the surf permits). Surf and ride packages are another option ($180).

Sleeping & Eating

90 Mile Beach Ahipara Holiday Park (☎ 09-409 4864; www.ahiparaholidaypark.co.nz; 168 Takahe St; sites per person $16, dm/r $28/75, cabins $55-90, units $125-145; 🖵) There's a large range of accommodation on offer at this holiday park, including cabins, motel units and a worn but perfectly presentable YHA-affiliated backpackers' lodge. The communal hall has an open fire and colourful murals.

ourpick Endless Summer Lodge (☎ 09-409 4181; www.endlesssummer.co.nz; 245 Foreshore Rd; dm $28, d $68-80; 🖵) Across from the beach, this superb kauri villa (1880) has been beautifully restored and converted into the Far North's best hostel. There's no TV, which encourages bonding around the long table on the vine-covered back terrace. Free boogie boards and sandboards are available, and surfboards can be hired ($20). Book ahead or be very sorry.

Beach Abode (☎ 09-409 4070; www.beachabode.co.nz; 11 Korora St; apt $125-185; 🛜) Wander through the subtropical garden to the beachfront from your self-contained studio or two-bedroom apartment, or just lie in bed and lose yourself in the view.

Beachfront (☎ 09-409 4007; www.beachfront.net.nz; 14 Kotare St; apt $175-360) Who cares if it's a bit bourgeois for Ahipara? These two upmarket, self-contained apartments have stunning views and there's direct access to the beach. Both sleep up to six people.

Bidz Takeaways (☎ 09-409 4727; Takahe St; meals $5-11; 🕐 8.30am-8pm) You'll need a flip-top head to fit Bidz' seafood burger ($11) into your mouth – it's jam-packed with battered oysters, scallops, mussels and fish. Bidz also has a store attached.

Gumdiggers Cafe (☎ 09-409 2012; 3 Ahipara Rd; meals $6-16; 🕐 8am-7pm Easter-Christmas, 7.30am-10pm Christmas-Easter) Good coffee and tasty treats are the hallmarks of this funky little cafe, owned by the people who run Sand Safaris (p173).

Getting There & Around

Busabout Kaitaia (☎ 09-408 1092; www.cbec.co.nz) runs services from Kaitaia ($3.50, 15 minutes).

HOKIANGA

The Hokianga Harbour stretches out its skinny tentacles to become the fourth-biggest in the country. Its ruggedly beautiful landscape is painted in every shade of green and brown. The water itself is rendered the colour of ginger ale by the bush streams that feed it.

Of all the remote parts of Northland, this is the pocket that feels the most removed from the mainstream. Pretension has no place here. Isolated, predominantly Maori communities nestle around the harbour's many inlets as they have done for centuries. Discovered by legendary explorer Kupe, it's been settled by Ngapuhi since the 14th century. Hippies settled in the late 1960s and their legacy is a thriving little artistic scene.

Many of the roads remain unsealed and in poor repair after decades of neglect from government bodies. Tourism dollars are channelled eastward to the Bay of Islands, leaving this truly fascinating corner of the country remarkably undeveloped, which is the way many of the locals like it.

EASTERN HOKIANGA
Puketi & Omahuta Forests

Inland from the eastern reaches of the harbour, the Puketi and Omahuta Forests form a continuous expanse of native bush. Logging in Puketi was stopped in 1951 to protect not only the remaining kauri but also the endangered kokako bird. Keep an eye out for this rare charmer (grey with a blue wattle) on your wanders.

The forests are reached by several entrances and contain a network of walking tracks varying in length from 15 minutes (the wheelchair-accessible Manginangina kauri walk) to two days (the challenging Waipapa River track). You'll find a **DOC campsite** (☎ 09-407 0300; www.doc.govt.nz; Waiare Rd; sites per adult/child $7/3.50), three-person cabins ($20) and

NORTHLAND & THE BAY
OF ISLANDS

NGAWHA SPRINGS

Near Kaikohe, these hot springs have been used by Ngapuhi for their curative powers since the 17th century. Hone Heke brought his injured warriors here during the Northland War.

Unlike many of NZ's thermal resorts, there are no hydroslides or big pools for the kids to splash about in. There aren't even any showers. Here it's all about stewing in the murky water in small pools of varying temperatures. Ngawha has two complexes next to each other, the better of which is **Ngawha Springs Pools** (☎ 09-405 2245; adult/child $4/2; 🕒 9am-9pm).

24-bunk hut (exclusive use $60) at Puketi Recreation Area on the forests' eastern fringe. The hut has hot showers, a kitchen and a flush toilet, while the cabins and campsite make do with cold showers.

See the DOC website for other walk options.

Horeke

Tiny Horeke was NZ's second European settlement after Russell. A Wesleyan mission operated here from 1828 to 1855. In 1840, 3000 Ngapuhi gathered here for what was the single biggest signing of the Treaty of Waitangi.

Completed in 1839, **Mangungu Mission House** (☎ 09-401 9640; www.historic.org.nz; Motukiore Rd; adult/child $3/1; 🕒 noon-4pm Sat & Sun) is a sweet wooden cottage with relics of the missionaries and Horeke's shipbuilding past. In the grounds you'll see a large stone cross and a simple wooden church. You'll find it 1km down the unsealed road leading along the harbour from Horeke village.

Wairere Boulders Nature Park (☎ 09-401 9935; www.waireboulders.co.nz; McDonnell Rd; adult/child $10/5; 🕒 daylight hr) resembles a Jurassic Zen garden. Paths lead around and over massive basalt rock formations that have been eroded into odd fluted shapes by the acidity of ancient kauri forests. The main loop takes about 40 minutes and follows a burbling Coca-Cola–coloured stream. It's a good path, but wear sensible shoes and expect a few ducks and climbs. An additional hour leads through rainforest to a platform at the end of the boulder valley. The park is sign-

posted from SH1 and Horeke; the last 3km are unsealed.

You'll feel like lord of the manor in **Riverhead Guest House** (☎ 09-401 9610; www.hokianga.co.nz/riverheadguesthouse; Main Rd; s/d/tr $75/95/130), an 1871 kauri villa with old-world furnishings literally looking down on Horeke. The cheaper upstairs rooms share a bathroom, but the harbour views more than compensate.

NORTHERN HOKIANGA
Kohukohu
pop 190

Quick, someone slap a preservation order on Kohukohu before it's too late. There can be few places in NZ where a Victorian village full of interesting kauri buildings has been so completely preserved with nary a modern monstrosity to be seen. During the height of the kauri industry it was a busy town with a sawmill, shipyard, two newspapers and banks. These days it's a very quiet backwater on the north side of Hokianga Harbour, 4km from the car ferry (opposite).

our pick **Tree House** (☎ 09-405 5855; www.treehouse.co.nz; 168 West Coast Rd; sites per person $18, dm $30-38, s/d $66/76) is a fantastic place with helpful hosts and brightly painted little cottages set among exotic fruit and nut trees. This quiet retreat is 2km from the ferry terminus (turn sharp left as you come off the ferry). You can sleep in an old school bus ($26 to $40 per person), wander the macadamia orchard or just sink into beanbags in the communal lounge.

Waterline Cafe (☎ 09-405 5552; meals $8-18; 🕒 breakfast & lunch daily, dinner Fri & Sat) serves superb food, including interesting pizzas and burgers, from a building jutting over the water. The chairs look like they've been raided from an old school, and newspaper clippings about the town are imbedded in the tables.

We're assured that the cheese-makers are indeed blessed at **Waitawa Farm** (Map p168; ☎ 09-409 5809; www.farmstaynz.co.nz; 164 Pukemiro Rd, Broadwood; s $60, d $70-80), a working dairy and sheep farm offering accommodation and cheese-making courses (four to six people, $250).

There are no regular bus services, but you might be able to arrange to jump off a Crossings Hokianga (p156) bus from Paihia and continue the tour at a later date; call to enquire. Kohukohu is connected to Rawene by a car ferry (opposite).

Mitimiti

The tiny community at Mitimiti, which consists of only 30 families and not even a shop, has the ruggedly beautiful 20km stretch of coast between the Hokianga and Whangape Harbours all to itself. The 40km drive from Kohukohu via Panguru (14km of it unsealed), is quite an experience: prepare to dodge cows, sheep, potholes and kids.

About halfway along, it's worth a short detour to visit **St Mary's Church** (Motuti Rd), where NZ's first Catholic bishop is buried beneath the altar. Jean Baptiste Pompallier arrived in the Hokianga in 1838, celebrating NZ's first Mass at Totara Point. He was interred here in 2002 after an emotional 14-week pilgrimage full of Maori ceremony brought his remains back from France.

Sandtrails Hokianga (☎ 09-409 5035; wwwsand trailshokianga.co.nz; 32 Paparangi Dr) offers an inside perspective on Mitimiti's tight-knit Maori community, with two-hour Sandscapes dune buggy tours, which head 12km along the beach to the giant dunes that form the harbour's north head (adult/child $135/60), or personally tailored tours staying overnight in the guide's house (adult $395).

Mitimiti Beach House (☎ 09-409 5347; www.beach -house.co.nz; 3881 West Coast Rd; s/d/tr/q $100/130/150/180; 💻) is a self-contained three-bedroom bach, sleeping up to eight ($25 per additional person). It's a comfortable base for exploring the often-deserted beach.

RAWENE
pop 440

Founded shortly after Horeke, Rawene was NZ's third European settlement. There is still a surprising number of historic buildings (including six churches) from a time when the harbour was considerably busier than it is now. There aren't any ATMs or banks, but you can get petrol here.

A heritage trail complete with information boards tours the main sights. **Clendon House** (☎ 09-405 7874; www.historic.org.nz; Clendon Esplanade; adult/child $5/2.50; ⊙ 10am-4pm Sat-Mon Nov-Apr, 10am-4pm Mon & Tue May-Oct) was built in the bustling 1860s by James Clendon, a trader, shipowner and magistrate. After his death, his 34-year-old half-Maori widow Jane was left with a brood of kids and a whopping £5000 debt. She managed to clear the debt and her descendants remained in the house until 1972, when it passed to the Historic Places Trust.

Quirky **Outpost Hokianga** (☎ 09-405 7423; 5 Parnell St) stocks local art, crafts, clothing, music, cosmetics and both second-hand and new books. Across the road **Hokianga Art Gallery** (☎ 09-405 7899; hokiangaartgallery@hotmail.com; 2 Parnell St; ⊙ Wed-Sun 10am-3pm) sells interesting contemporary art, also with a local focus.

Sleeping

Rawene Motor Camp (☎ 09-405 7720; www.rawene motorcamp.co.nz; 1 Marmon St; sites per adult/child $14/7, dm $18, cabins $40-80; 💻 🛁) Sheltered tent sites hide in the bush at this nicely managed caravan park. The cabins are simple, with one converted into a bunkroom for backpackers. Linen is extra.

Postmaster's Lodgings (☎ 09-405 7676; www. thepostmasterslodgings.co.nz; 3 Parnell St; d $100-120, tr $125-145; 🛜) Comfortable high-ceilinged rooms, four-poster beds, rolled-end leather couches and a wraparound veranda are all part of the old-world charm offered in this kauri villa.

Hokianga Blue (☎ 09-405 7675; wicked1s@xtra.co.nz; 49 Parnell St; d/tr $110/135) Offers a studio apartment with harbour views and a kitchenette. It's on the main road leading into town.

Old Lane's Store Homestay (☎ 09-405 7554; 9 Clendon Esplanade; r $120) Right by the harbour, accommodation is offered in a self-contained apartment above the historic store. If you're after a glam cocktail dress, check out the owner's workshop downstairs.

Eating & Drinking

Wardy's (☎ 09-405 7717; 12 Parnell St; ⊙ 11am-6.30pm Mon-Fri, 11am-2pm Sat & Sun) At Wardy's you can stock up on (mainly) organic fruit, vegetables and meat.

Boatshed Cafe (☎ 09-405 7728; 8 Clendon Esplanade; mains $6-17; ⊙ 8.30am-4pm) You can eat overlooking the water at this excellent cafe, a cute place with heart-warming food and a gift shop.

Masonic Hotel (☎ 09-405 7822; 8 Parnell St) The local pub, with occasional live country-and-western music.

Getting There & Away

The **car ferry** (☎ 09-405 2602; car & driver one way/return $14/19, passenger $2/4; ⊙ 7.30am-7.30pm) heads to northern Hokianga, docking near Kohukohu at least hourly. You can buy your ticket for this 15-minute ride on board. It usually leaves Rawene on the half-hour and the north side on the hour. There are no regular bus services, but Magic Travellers Network (p164) and Crossings Hokianga (p156) have tourist buses.

OPONONI & OMAPERE
pop 500

These tranquil settlements near the south head of Hokianga Harbour more or less run into one another. The water's much clearer here and good for swimming. Views are dominated by the mountainous sand dunes across the water at **North Head**.

The **Hokianga i-SITE** (☎ 09-405 8869; hokianga@visitnorthland.co.nz; SH12, Opononi; ☼ 9am-5.30pm) has internet access.

Activities

The **Hokianga Kai Iwi Coastal Track** leads south along the coast from the **Arai-Te-Uru Recreation Reserve** (Signal Station Rd), on the South Head of Hokianga Harbour. It's three hours to Kaikai Beach, six hours to Kawerua and 12 hours to the Kerr Rd exit, or you can tramp the entire 15 hours (allow about three days) to Kai Iwi Lakes. Hikers must carry all their own water and food, and cross the major rivers within two hours either side of low tide. It's usually possible to camp on the beach. DOC advises that you check with them before setting out, particularly to discuss the river crossings.

From Cemetery Rd on the eastern outskirts of Opononi, a half-hour climb leads up **Mt Whiria**, a *pa* site with harbour views.

Two kilometres east of Opononi, Waiotemarama Gorge Rd turns south for 6km to the **Waiotemarama Waterfall Loop Walk**, which passes kauri and a picturesque waterfall. From the top of the loop you can detour on the Hauturu Highpoint Track which climbs Mt Hauturu (679m). It's a five-hour walk to the summit and back again. On the road to the walks you'll pass **Labyrinth Woodworks** (☎ 09-405 4581; 647 Waiotemarama Gorge Rd; www.nzanity.co.nz; maze $4; ☼ 9am-5pm), an Aladdin's cave of handmade puzzles and games. Crack the code in the outdoor maze by collecting letters to form a word.

The **Six Foot Track** at the end of Mountain Rd gives access to many Waima Forest walks.

Tours

Hokianga Express (☎ 09-405 8872; adult/child $25/15) leaves from Opononi Jetty and takes you across the harbour to the large golden sand dunes, where you can sandboard down a 30m

slope and skim over the water. Boats leave on the hour, on demand; board provided.

Sandtrails Hokianga (☎ 09-409 5035; www.sandtrailshokianga.co.nz; 32 Paparangi Dr, Mitimiti) collects you from Opononi for a dune buggy tour to Mitimiti (3¾ hours, adult/child $220/105) or a 70-minute Sandsecrets tour (adult/child $110/55); prices include the Hokianga Express.

Footprints Waipoua (☎ 0800 687 836; www.footprintswaipoua.co.nz; adult/child $95/35) is a four-hour twilight tour led by Maori guides into Waipoua Kauri Forest (opposite). As an introduction to Maori culture, it's fantastic. Tribal history and stories are shared, and mesmerising *karakia* recited before the giant trees. A (child-friendly) shorter version is offered (90 minutes, adult/child $70/35), as well as guided daytime visits, meeting at the Tane Mahuta car park ($25).

Sleeping & Eating

Each of these neighbouring villages has its own superette and takeaways.

OPONONI

Okopako Lodge Farm Hostel (☎ /fax 09-405 8815; 140 Mountain Rd; sites per adult/child $12/5, dm/s/d $25/42/54) High up in the bush 5km east of Opononi and 1.5km down a gravel road, this simple hostel is quiet and suited to hikers (the Six Foot Track starts here). It was for sale at the time of research, so call ahead.

Opononi Hotel (☎ 09-405 8858; www.opononihotel.com; SH12; s $114, d $114-129, tr $134-150, q $172) The old Opononi pub has reinvented itself into elegant accommodation. The rooms aren't huge, but the white-paint and blond-wood makeover has left them quietly stylish. Try to grab one of the front two – they're a bit bigger and have the best views. Otherwise aim for those facing away from the very cool pub (open 9am till late), which also happens to be the best spot to eat down this end (meals $18 to $26).

Opononi Lighthouse Motel (☎ 09-405 8824; www.lighthousemotel.co.nz; SH12; d/tr/q $140/165/195; ☐) Scrupulously clean, this refurbished motel has very comfortable harbour-side units, plus a great communal barbecue, a spa pool, and a cutesy lighthouse and waterfall in the front garden.

OMAPERE

GlobeTrekkers Lodge (☎ 09-405 8183; www.globetrekkerslodge.com; SH12; dm/d $26/60, f $76-96; ☐) This home-style lodge is ideally placed to put you in touch with myriad local activities, or you can just relax and unwind in casual style.

Ti Kouka B&B (☎ 09-405 8622; tikouka@xtra.co.nz; 68 Signal Station Rd; r $100) Look forward to nights in red satin (bedding) in this hilltop house with views straight through the heads. The room opens on to a beautiful garden at the bottom of the house.

Hokianga Haven B&B (☎ 09-405 8285; www.hokiangahaven.co.nz; 226 SH12; r $160) This modern house with original Kiwi art on the walls offers spacious accommodation on the harbour's edge and glorious views of the sand dunes. Alternative healing therapies can be arranged.

Copthorne Hotel & Resort (☎ 09-405 8737; www.omapere.co.nz; SH12; d $169-350, tr $204-385; 🛜 🖳) Despite the original grand Victorian villa being violated by aluminium joinery, this waterside complex remains an attractive spot for a summer's drink or bistro meal ($13 to $30). A modern wing has smart units; the more expensive have terraces and water views.

Getting There & Away

There's no regular public transport to Opononi, but Magic Travellers Network (p164) and Crossings Hokianga (p156) are options.

KAURI COAST

Apart from the odd bluff and river, this coast is basically unbroken and undeveloped for the 110km between the Hokianga and Kaipara harbours. The main reason for coming here is to marvel at the kauri forests, one of the great natural highlights of NZ. This is one for the chubby chasers of the tree-hugging fraternity – you'd need 8m arms to get them around some of the big boys here.

HOKIANGA TO DARGAVILLE

Here's where most of the action lies. If you're planning to stay overnight, bring your own food as there are few stores or restaurants between Opononi and Dargaville, and no ATMs. Trampers should check DOC's website for walks in the area (www.doc.govt.nz); see also Hokianga Kai Iwi Coastal Track (opposite).

Waipoua Kauri Forest

The highlight of Northland's west coast, this superb forest sanctuary – proclaimed in 1952

after much public pressure – is the largest remnant of the once-extensive kauri forests of northern NZ. The forest road (SH12) stretches for 18km and passes some huge trees – a kauri can reach 60m in height and have a trunk 5m in diameter.

Control of the forest has recently been returned to Te Roroa, the local *iwi* (tribe), as part of a settlement for Crown breaches of the Treaty of Waitangi. Te Roroa runs the **Waipoua Forest visitor centre** (☎ 09-439 6445; www.teroroa.iwi.nz; 1 Waipoua River Rd; 🕓 9am-6.30pm summer, 9am-4.30pm winter) and camping ground near the south end of the park.

SIGHTS & ACTIVITIES

Near the north end of the park, not far from the road, stands mighty **Tane Mahuta**, named for the Maori forest god. At 51m, with a 13.8m girth and wood mass of 244.5 cubic metres, he's the largest kauri alive. You don't so much look at Tane Mahuta; it's as if you're granted an audience to his hushed presence. He's been holding court here for somewhere between 1200 and 2000 years.

A little further south a short road leads to the Kauri Walks car park. Theft from cars has been a problem and the car park is often guarded ($2 donation suggested). From here, a 20-minute (each way) walk leads to **Te Matua Ngahere** (the Father of the Forest). Even the most ardent tree-hugger wouldn't consider rushing forward to throw their arms around him and call him 'Daddy', even if there wasn't a fence. At 30m he's shorter than Tane Mahuta, but he has the same noble presence, reinforced by his substantial girth – he's the widest living kauri (16.4m). He presides over a clearing surrounded by mature trees that look like matchsticks in comparison.

Close by are the **Four Sisters**, a graceful stand of four tall trees that have fused together at the base. A 40-minute walk leads to **Yakas**, the seventh-largest kauri.

Near the very south end of the park there's a turn-off to a **forest lookout** that offers spectacular views. The 10-minute **Toatoa viewpoint walk** is 1km further on.

SLEEPING & EATING

Waipoua Forest Campground (☎ 09-439 6445; www.teroroa.iwi.nz; 1 Waipoua River Rd; sites per adult/child $14/7, cabin s/tw/tr/q $15/50/60/80, house $175) Situated next to the Waipoua River and the visitor centre, this peaceful camping ground offers hot showers, flush toilets and a kitchen. The cabins are DOC-style – spartan, with unmade swab beds (bring your own linen or hire it).

Waipoua Lodge B&B (☎ 09-439 0422; www.waipoua lodge.co.nz; SH12; r incl breakfast $570-590; ☎) This fine old villa at the southern edge of the forest has four luxurious, spacious suites, which were originally the stables, the woolshed and the calf-rearing pen! Decadent dinners ($90) are available.

Morrell's Cafe (☎ 09-405 4545; 7235 SH12, Waimamaku; mains $8-14; ☺ 9am-4pm) Perhaps this is where Hokianga's hippies ended up. This bright-yellow cafe and craft shop serves up tasty snacks in a former cheese factory near the north end of the forest.

Trounson Kauri Park

The 450-hectare Trounson Kauri Park has an easy half-hour loop walk leading from the picnic area by the road. It passes through beautiful forest with streams, some fine kauri stands, a couple of fallen trees and another Four Sisters – two pairs of trees with conjoined trunks. DOC operates a **campsite** (sites per adult/child $10/5) at the edge of the park, which has a communal kitchen and hot showers.

Just 2km from SH12, **Kauri Coast Top 10 Holiday Park** (☎ 09-439 0621; www.kauricoasttop10. co.nz; Trounson Park Rd; sites per person $25, units $70-180; ▣) is an attractive riverside camping ground with good facilities and a small shop. It also organises night-time **nature walks** (adult/child $20/12), which explain the flora and nocturnal wildlife that thrives here. This is a rare chance to see a kiwi in the wild. Trounson has a predator-eradication program and has become a mainland refuge for threatened native bird species, so you should at least hear a morepork (a native owl) or a brown kiwi.

If you're approaching from the north it's easier to take the second turn-off to the park, near Kaihu, which avoids a rough unsealed road.

Kai Iwi Lakes

These three trout-filled freshwater lakes nestle near the coast, 12km off SH12. The largest, Taharoa, has blue water fringed with sandy patches and pine trees. Lake Waikere is popular with water-skiers, while Lake Kai Iwi is relatively untouched. A half-hour walk leads from the lakes to the coast and it's another two hours to reach the base of volcanic Maunganui Bluff (460m); the hike up and down it takes five hours.

Camping (☎ 09-439 0986; lakes@kaipara.govt.nz; adult/child $10/5) is permitted among the pines at the side of Lake Taharoa; cold showers, drinking water and flush toilets are provided.

Baylys Beach

A village of brightly coloured baches and a few new holiday mansions, Baylys Beach is 12km from Dargaville, off SH12. It lies on 100km-long Ripiro Ocean Beach, a surf-pounded stretch of coast that has been the site of many shipwrecks. The beach is a gazetted highway: you can drive along its hard sand at low tide, although it is primarily for 4WDs. Despite being NZ's longest drivable beach, it's less well known and hence less travelled than Ninety Mile Beach. Ask locals about conditions and check your hire-car agreement before venturing onto the sand. Quad bikes can be hired at the holiday park.

It's pretty kooky, but **Skydome Observatory** (☎ 09-439 1856; www.skydome.org.nz; 28 Seaview Rd; stargazing $20-40) is a massive, technologically advanced telescope and it's located on the front lawn of someone's house. Call ahead for bookings.

A midsized camping ground, **Baylys Beach Holiday Park** (☎ 09-439 6349; www.baylysbeach.co.nz; 24 Seaview Rd; sites per adult/child $15/8, cabins $50-110, units $90-180; ▣) has good management and facilities, and quad bikes for hire ($75 to $95 per hour).

If gin-in-hand sunset-gazing is your thing, **Sunset View Lodge** (☎ 09-439 4342; www.sunsetview lodge.co.nz; Alcemene Lane; r $150-175; ▣ ▣), a large, modern B&B, fits the bill. The upstairs rooms have terrific sea views and there's a self-service bar with an honesty box in the guest lounge.

At **Sharky's** (☎ 09-439 4549; 1 Seaview Rd; meals $6-17; ☺ breakfast, lunch & dinner), a handy combination of bottle shop, general store, bar and takeaway, quick snacks and all-day breakfasts are the order of the day.

Brightly decorated with murals and mosaics **Funky Fish** (☎ 09-439 8883; 34 Seaview Rd; lunch $11-16, dinner $18-30; ☺ 11am-late Tue-Sun) is a highly popular restaurant, cafe and bar with a wide-ranging menu, although the fish dishes are the standouts. Bookings are advisable in summer.

A taxi to Baylys Beach from Dargaville should cost around $25.

DARGAVILLE

pop 4500

When a town proclaims itself the 'kumara capital of NZ' (it produces two-thirds of the country's sweet potatoes), you should know not to expect too much. Founded in 1872 by timber merchant Joseph Dargaville, this once-important river port thrived on the export of kauri timber and gum. As the forests were decimated, it declined and today is a quiet backwater servicing the agricultural Northern Wairoa area.

Information

DOC Kauri Coast Area Office (☎ 09-439 3450; 150 Colville Rd; 8am-4.30pm Mon-Fri)

Post office (80 Victoria St)

Visitor information centre (☎ 09-439 8360; www.kauriinfocentre.co.nz; 4 Murdoch St; 9am-6pm;) Operates out of the interesting Woodturners Kauri Gallery & Working Studio. Books accommodation and tours.

Sights & Activities

Perched on top of a hill, the **Dargaville Museum** (☎ 09-439 7555; www.dargavillemuseum.co.nz; adult/child $10/2; 9am-4pm) is more interesting than most. There's a large gumdigging display, plus maritime, Maori and musical-instrument sections and a neat model railway. Outside, the masts of the *Rainbow Warrior* (see the boxed text, p169) are mounted at a lookout near a *pa* site.

In the centre of town, **Taha Awa Riverside Gardens** has cool stuff for the kids, including a playground shaped like a tall ship and a whale jawbone. You'll also find a fernery, and swamp, coastal and scented gardens. The 5km **Historic River Walk** starts its loop here; pick up a brochure from the information centre and follow the yellow signs up to the museum.

If you want to learn more about the district's knobbly purple claim-to-fame, catch Kumara Ernie's show at the **Kumara Box** (☎ 09-439 1813; www.kumarabox.co.nz; 503 Pouto Rd; tours $15, bookings essential) – it's surprisingly entertaining.

Sleeping & Eating

Greenhouse Backpackers (☎ 09-439 6342; greenhouse backpackers@ihug.co.nz; 15 Gordon St; dm/d $23/56;) This converted 1921 schoolhouse has classrooms partitioned into large dorms, cosy units in the back garden and colourful, school-like murals.

McLeans B&B (☎ 09-439 5915; mcleans@igrin.co.nz; 136 Hokianga Rd; s/d $50/90) Guests share a large upstairs lounge in this spacious 1934 house,

decorated with antique plates and lacy bedspreads. The affable hosts provide breakfast, tea-making facilities and yummy biscuits.

Blah, Blah, Blah... (☎ 09-439 6300; 101 Victoria St; breakfast $6-20, lunch $8-28, dinner $20-28; breakfast & lunch daily, dinner Tue-Sat) The number-one eatery in Dargaville (admittedly that's not saying much) has a garden area, hip music, deli-style snacks, a global menu (dukkha, nachos, steak) and cocktails.

Self-caterers should head to **Woolworths supermarket** (129 Victoria St; 7am-9pm). Pop into the **Central Hotel** (☎ 09-439 8034; cnr Victoria & Edward Sts) if you feel like a handle of something cold in a straight-up NZ pub.

Getting There & Away

The main bus stop is in Kapia St. **Main Coachline** (☎ 09-278 8070; www.maincoachline.co.nz) runs six buses per week to and from Auckland ($48, three hours) via Matakohe ($18, 35 minutes). A private operator runs a **Whangarei-to-Dargaville Shuttle** (☎ 021 380 187; trip $10) on weekdays. Magic Travellers Network (p164) is an option if you're coming from Paihia, Rawene or Opononi and continuing on to Matakohe or Auckland.

POUTO POINT

A narrow spit descends south of Dargaville, bordered by the Tasman Sea and Wairoa River, and comes to an abrupt halt at the entrance of Kaipara Harbour, NZ's biggest. It's an incredibly remote headland, punctuated by dozens of petite dune lakes and the lonely **Kaipara Lighthouse** (built from kauri in 1884). Less than 10km separates Kaipara Harbour's north and south heads, but if you were to drive between the two you'd cover 267km.

A 4WD can be put to its proper use on the ocean-hugging 71km stretch of beach from Dargaville to **Pouto Point**. DOC's *Pouto Hidden Treasures* pamphlet has a helpful guide for motorists, with tips for protecting both your car and the fragile ecosystem. The inland road is a similar distance but it's winding and partly unsealed. If you'd rather not risk getting stuck, **Taylor Made Tours** (☎ 09-439 1576; www.taylormade tours.co.nz; tour $95) run guided excursions.

Lighthouse Lodge B&B (☎ 09-439 5150; www.light house-lodge.co.nz; 6577 Pouto Rd; d $250, ste $350-450;) is a contemporary building in a remote spot, with bright, stylish rooms with verandas and sea views. Meals and tours can be arranged on request.

NORTHLAND & THE BAY OF ISLANDS

MATAKOHE
pop 400

Matakohe's a sweet village on one of the Kaipara's many inlets. Apart from its rural charms, the reason for visiting is the superb **Kauri Museum** (☎ 09-431 7417; www.kaurimuseum.com; 5 Church Rd; adult/child $15/3; ☼ 9am-5pm). The giant cross-sections of trees are astounding in themselves, but the entire industry is brought to light through life-sized reproductions of a pioneer sawmill, boarding house, gumdigger's hut and Victorian home – along with photos, artefacts, and fabulous furniture and marquetry. The Gum Room holds a weird and wonderful collection of kauri gum, the amber substance that can be carved, sculpted and polished to a jewel-like quality. The museum shop stocks mementoes crafted from kauri wood and gum.

Facing the museum is the tiny kauri-built **Matakohe Pioneer Church** (1867), which served both Methodists and Anglicans, and acted as the community's hall and school. Nearby, you can wander through a historic **school house** (1878) and **post office/telephone exchange** (1909).

Sleeping & Eating

Matakohe Top 10 Holiday Park (☎ 09-431 6431; www.matakohetop10.co.nz; Church Rd; sites per person $19, cabins $50-87, units $105-145; ☐) With perhaps the cosiest lounge you'll find in a camping ground,

this little park has modern amenities, plenty of space and good views of Kaipara Harbour.

Petite Provence (☎ 09-431 7552; www.petiteprovence.co.nz; 703c Tinopai Rd; s/d $110/150) This attractive, French-influenced B&B is a popular weekender for Aucklanders, so it pays to book ahead. Excellent dinners can be arranged for a bargain $45 per person.

Matakohe House (☎ 09-431 7091; www.matakohehouse.co.nz; 24 Church Rd; s/d $135/160; ☐) A short walk from the museum, this B&B occupies a pretty villa with a cafe attached (mains $29 to $32). The simply furnished rooms open out onto a veranda and offer winning touches like complimentary port and chocolates.

Sahara (☎ 09-431 6833; cnr Franklin & Paparoa Valley Rds, Paparoa; brunch $10-15, mains $18-33; ☼ brunch, lunch & dinner Thu-Sun) Nothing about the cuisine or fit-out screams North African desert, but the incongruity of the name is nothing on the surprise of finding such a stylish restaurant in little Paparoa, 6km east of Matakohe. Housed in a lovingly restored bank building, Sahara offers a small but stellar menu with a focus on local produce.

Getting There & Away

Main Coachline (☎ 09-278 8070; www.maincoachline.co.nz) runs six buses per week to/from Auckland ($40, 2½ hours) and Dargaville ($18, 35 minutes). See p164 for details of the Magic Travellers Network service.

Coromandel Region

Looking a bit like the side view of a hand with its middle finger raised, the Coromandel Peninsula juts defiantly into the Pacific east of Auckland and forms the eastern edge of the Hauraki Gulf. Its dramatic, mountainous spine bisects it into two very distinct parts.

The eastern edge has some of the North Island's best white-sand beaches. When Auckland shuts up shop for Christmas/New Year this is where it heads. Marinas and cafes cater to the chattering set in the wealthier enclaves, while sandy toes and board shorts are the norm elsewhere. The cutesy historic gold-mining towns on the west side escape the worst of the influx, their muddy wetlands and stony bays holding less appeal for the masses. This coast has long been a refuge for alternative lifestylers – although the hippy communes have gradually given way to organic farms and Buddhist retreats.

Down the middle, the mountains are crisscrossed with walking tracks, allowing trampers to lose themselves (hopefully only figuratively) among large tracts of untamed bush where kauri trees once towered and are starting to do so again. At the base of the peninsula the Hauraki Plains were once massive swampy wetlands, rich with bird life. Pockets remain, with Miranda being the premier holiday spot for feathered jetsetters and their admirers.

Although relatively close to Auckland, the Coromandel offers easy access to splendid isolation. Some of the more remote communities in these parts are still accessed by gravel roads, and an aura of rugged individualism hangs like mist over this compact and special region.

COROMANDEL REGION

HIGHLIGHTS

- Travelling remote gravel roads under a crimson canopy of ancient pohutukawa trees in **Far North Coromandel** (p192)
- Staking out your own patch of footprint-free sand at **Opoutere Beach** (p200), **Otama Beach** (p194) or **Opito Beach** (p194)
- Exploring hidden islands, caves and bays by kayak from **Whitianga** (p194), **Hahei** (p197) or **Coromandel Town** (p190)
- Burning your butt in a freshly dug thermal pool in the sands of **Hot Water Beach** (p198)
- Pigging out on smoked mussels in **Coromandel Town** (p192)
- Penetrating the mystical depths of the dense bush of **Coromandel Forest Park** (p189) and **Karangahake Gorge** (p203)

★ Far North Coromandel
★ Otama Beach
★ Coromandel Town
★ Opito Beach
★ Whitianga ★ Hahei
★ Hot Water Beach
★ Coromandel Forest Park
★ Opoutere Beach
★ Karangahake Gorge

Telephone code: 07	www.thecoromandel.com	www.ew.govt.nz

COROMANDEL REGION

0 ——————— 20 km
0 ——————— 10 miles

INFORMATION
DOC Kauaeranga Visitor Centre...1 B4

SIGHTS & ACTIVITIES
Broken Hills Gold-Mine Workings.2 C4
Butterfly & Orchid Garden.......(see 19)
Highzone.................................3 B3
Karangahake Gorge Historic
Walkway..............................4 B6
Kauri Grove...........................5 B3

Miranda Hot Springs..................6 A5
Miranda Shorebird Centre..........7 A5
Ohinemuri Estate Winery..........8 C6
Purangi Estate........................9 C3
Rapaura Water Gardens...........10 B4
Twin Oaks Riding Ranch...........11 C3
Waterlily Gardens...................12 C6
Waterworks.........................13 B3

SLEEPING
Billygoat Basin Campsite...........14 B4
Broken Hills Campsite.............(see 2)
Coastal Motor Lodge...............15 B4
Colville Farm........................16 B2
Copsefield B&B.....................17 C5
Dickey's Flat Campsite.............18 C6
Dickson Holiday Park...............19 B4
Fantail Bay Campsite................20 A1
Fletcher Bay Backpackers..........21 A1
Fletcher Bay Campsite.............22 A1
Huia Lodge...........................23 B4
Jacaranda Lodge....................24 B2
Kuaotunu Bay Lodge...............25 C2
Mahamudra Centre.................26 A2
Manawa Ridge......................27 C6
Miranda Holiday Park.............(see 6)
Moss Creek Campsite...............28 B4
Pinnacles Campsite.................(see 29)
Pinnacles Hut........................29 C4
Port Jackson Campsite..............30 A1
Stony Bay Campsite................31 A1
Tangiaro Kiwi Retreat..............32 A1
Waikawau Bay Campsite...........33 B1
Waterlily Gardens..................(see 12)
Wentworth Valley Campsite......34 C5

EATING
Colenso Country Shop & Cafe...35 C3
Matatoki Farm Cheese.............36 B5

History

This whole area, including the peninsula, the islands and both sides of the gulf, was known to Maori as Hauraki. Various *iwi* (tribes) held claim to pockets of it, including the Pare Hauraki branch of the Tainui tribes and others descended from Te Arawa and earlier migrations. Polynesian artefacts and evidence of moa-hunting have been found, pointing to around 1000 years of continuous occupation.

The Hauraki *iwi* were some of the first to be exposed to European traders. The region's proximity to Auckland, safe anchorages and ready supply of valuable timber initially lead to a booming economy. Kauri logging was big business on the peninsula. Allied to the timber trade was shipbuilding, which took off in 1832 when a mill was established at Mercury Bay. Things got tougher once the kauri around the coast became scarce and the loggers had to penetrate deeper into the bush for timber. Kauri dams, which used water power to propel the huge logs to the coast, were built. By the 1930s virtually no kauri remained and the industry died.

Gold was first discovered in New Zealand (NZ) near Coromandel Town in 1852. Although this first rush was short-lived, more gold was discovered around Thames in 1867 and later in other places. The peninsula is also rich in semiprecious gemstones, such as quartz, agate, amethyst and jasper. A fossick on any west-coast beach can be rewarding.

Despite successful interactions with Europeans for decades, the Hauraki *iwi* were some of the hardest hit by colonisation. Unscrupulous dealings by settlers and government to gain access to valuable resources resulted in Maori losing most of their lands by the 1880s. Even today there is a much lower Maori presence on the peninsula than in neighbouring districts.

Climate

Being mountainous, the region attracts more rainfall (3000mm or even 4500mm a year) than elsewhere on the east coast.

Getting There & Around

Car is the only option for accessing some of the more remote areas, but be careful to check hire agreements as there are plenty of gravel roads and a few streams to ford. Most of them are in good nick and even a small car can cope unless the weather's been particularly wet.

MAORI NZ: COROMANDEL REGION

Although it has a long and rich Maori history, the Coromandel doesn't offer many opportunities to engage with the culture. Pioneer pursuits such as gold-mining and kauri logging have been given much more attention, although this is starting to change.

Historic *pa* sites are dotted around, with the most accessible being Paku (p199). There are others at Opito Beach (p194), Hahei (p197) and Hot Water Beach (p198).

Daily buses on the Auckland-to-Tauranga route pass through Thames and Waihi, while others loop through Coromandel Town, Whitianga and Tairua.

It's definitely worth considering the beautiful ferry ride from Auckland via Waiheke Island to Coromandel Town (see p192).

MIRANDA

It's a pretty name for a settlement on the swampy Firth of Thames, just an hour's drive from Auckland. The two reasons to come here are splashing around the thermal pools and birdwatching – but doing both at the same time might be considered impolite.

This is one of the most accessible spots for studying waders or shore birds all year round. The vast mud flat is teeming with aquatic worms and crustaceans, which attract thousands of Arctic-nesting shore birds over the winter – 43 species of wader have been spotted here. The two main species are the bar-tailed godwit and the lesser or red knot, but it isn't unusual to see turnstones, sandpipers and the odd vagrant red-necked stint. One godwit tagged here was tracked making an 11,570km nonstop flight from Alaska. Short-haul travellers include the pied oystercatcher and the threatened wrybill from the South Island, and banded dotterels and pied stilts.

The **Miranda Shorebird Centre** (Map p184; ☎ 09-232 2781; www.miranda-shorebird.org.nz; 283 East Coast Rd; ☪ 9am-5pm) has bird-life displays, hires out binoculars and sells useful birdwatching pamphlets ($2). Nearby are a hide and several walks (30 minutes to two hours). The centre offers clean bunk-style accommodation (dorm beds/double rooms $20/60) with a kitchen.

COROMANDEL REGION

COROMANDEL REGION FACTS

Eat Buckets of bivalves at Whitianga's Scallop Festival (p195)

Drink Boiled water from a mountain campsite

Read *The Penguin History of New Zealand* (2003) by the late Michael King, an Opoutere resident

Listen to Top kiwi bands at the Coromandel Gold New Year's Eve festival (p195)

Watch The birds in the Firth of Thames (p185)

Swim at Any of the peninsula's beautiful east coast beaches

Festival The peninsula-wide Pohutukawa Festival (www.pohutukawafestival.co.nz)

Tackiest tourist attraction Scallop-headed marching band at Whitianga's Scallop Festival (p195)

Go green Witness forest regeneration at Driving Creek Railway (p191)

Miranda Hot Springs (Map p184; ☎ 07-867 3055; Front Miranda Rd; adult/child $13/6; ☽ 9am-9.30pm), 5km south, has a large thermal swimming pool (reputedly the largest in the Southern Hemisphere), a toasty sauna pool and private spas ($10 extra).

Next door is **Miranda Holiday Park** (Map p184; ☎ 07-867 3205; www.mirandaholidaypark.co.nz; sites per adult/child $21/11, dm $33, units $139-305; ▢ ⑀ ⑂), which has excellent sparkling-clean units and facilities, its own hot-spring pool and a flood-lit tennis court.

THAMES
pop 10,000

Thames dates from a time when gold-digging had a much different connotation to what it does today. Dinky 19th-century wooden buildings still dominate the town centre, but grizzly prospectors have been replaced by alternative lifestylers. If you're a vegetarian ecowarrior you'll feel right at home. It's a good base for tramping or canyoning in the nearby Kauaeranga Valley.

Captain Cook arrived here in 1769, naming the Waihou River 'Thames' 'on account of its bearing some resemblance to that river in England'. This area belonged to the Ngati Maru, a tribe of Tainui descent. Their spectacular meeting house, Hotunui (1878), holds pride of place in the Auckland Museum (p90).

After opening Thames to gold-miners in 1867, the Ngati Maru were swamped by 10,000 European settlers within a year. When the initial boom turned to bust, a dubious system of government advances resulted in Maori debt and forced land sales.

Information

Post office (517 Pollen St) Offers poste restante service.

Thames i-SITE (☎ 07-868 7284; www.thamesinfo.co.nz; 206 Pollen St; ☽ 8.30am-5pm Mon-Fri, 9am-4pm Sat & Sun) Information and internet access.

Sights

The i-SITE stocks free Historic Places Trust self-tour pamphlets of Thames' significant buildings. The Trust also runs tours of the interesting **School of Mines & Mineral Museum** (☎ 07-868 6227; 101 Cochrane St; adult/child $5/2; ☽ 11am-3pm Wed-Sun), which has an extensive collection of NZ rocks, minerals and fossils. The oldest section (1868) was part of a Methodist Sunday school, situated on a Maori burial ground.

The **Goldmine Experience** (☎ 07-868 8514; www.goldmine-experience.co.nz; cnr Moanataiari Rd & SH25; adult/child $15/5; ☽ 10am-4pm Jan-Mar, 10am-1pm Apr-Sep) allows you to walk through a gold-mine tunnel, watch a stamper battery crush rock, learn about the history of the Cornish miners and try your hand at panning for gold ($2 extra).

The **historical museum** (☎ 07-868 8509; cnr Cochrane & Pollen Sts; adult/child $5/2; ☽ 1-4pm) houses pioneer relics, rocks and old photographs of the town.

Kids (little or large) with a fairy complex will adore the **Butterfly & Orchid Garden** (Map p184; ☎ 07-868 8080; Victoria St; adult/child $9.50/5; ☽ 10am-4pm), north of town within the Dickson Holiday Park. It's an enclosed jungle full of hundreds of exotic flappers.

Activities

Bird lovers can take advantage of the **Karaka Bird Hide**. Built with compensation funds from the *Rainbow Warrior* bombing, it's reached by a boardwalk through the mangroves just off Brown St. Nearby, young 'uns can ride on the cute-as-a-button 900m **Thames Small Gauge Railway** (☎ 07-868 6803; tickets $2; ☽ 11am-3pm Sun).

Eyez Open (☎ 07-868 9018; www.eyezopen.co.nz; per day $30, 1- to 4-day tours $110-750) rents out bikes and organises small-group cycling tours of the peninsula (minimum four to six people).

Canyonz (☎ 0800 422 696; www.canyonz.co.nz; trips $235) runs canyoning trips to the Sleeping God Canyon in the Kauaeranga Valley. Expect a vertical descent of over 300m, requiring

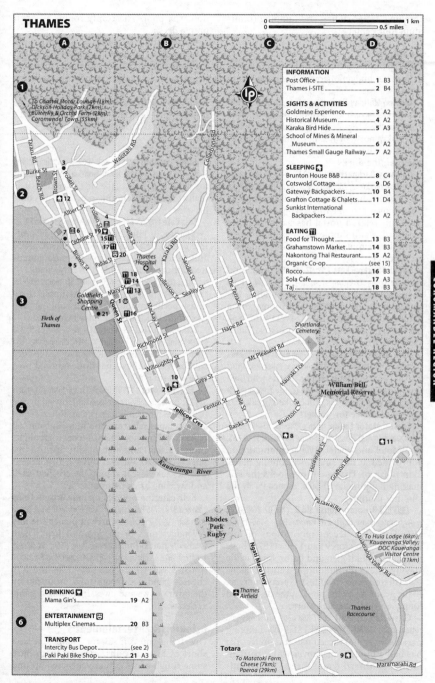

THAMES

0 _____ 1 km
0 _____ 0.5 miles

INFORMATION
Post Office **1** B3
Thames i-SITE **2** B4

SIGHTS & ACTIVITIES
Goldmine Experience **3** A2
Historical Museum **4** A2
Karaka Bird Hide **5** A3
School of Mines & Mineral
   Museum **6** A2
Thames Small Gauge Railway **7** A2

SLEEPING
Brunton House B&B **8** C4
Cotswold Cottage **9** D6
Gateway Backpackers **10** B4
Grafton Cottage & Chalets **11** D4
Sunkist International
   Backpackers **12** A2

EATING
Food for Thought **13** B3
Grahamstown Market **14** B3
Nakontong Thai Restaurant **15** A2
Organic Co-op .... (see 15)
Rocco **16** B3
Sola Cafe **17** A3
Taj **18** B3

To Coastal Motor Lounge (1km);
Dickson Holiday Park (2km);
Butterfly & Orchid Farm (2km);
Coromandel Town (55km)

Firth of
Thames

Goldfields
Shopping
Centre

Thames
Hospital

Shortland
Cemetery

William Bell
Memorial Reserve

Rhodes
Park
Rugby

To Hula Lodge (6km);
Kauaeranga Valley;
DOC Kauaeranga
Visitor Centre
(11km)

Thames
Airfield

Thames
Racecourse

Totara
To Matatoki Farm
Cheese (7km);
Paeroa (29km)

Maramarahi Rd

DRINKING
Mama Gin's **19** A2

ENTERTAINMENT
Multiplex Cinemas **20** B3

TRANSPORT
Intercity Bus Depot .... (see 2)
Paki Paki Bike Shop **21** A3

COROMANDEL REGION

abseiling, water-sliding and jumping (minimum four people).

Sleeping

Thames has a good crop of B&B accommodation, but budget operators are more thinly spread.

Dickson Holiday Park (Map p184; ☎ 07-868 7308; www.dicksonpark.co.nz; sites per person $16, dm $25, cabins $55-109, units $99-120; ☐ ☎ ☎) Tucked away in a valley 3km north of Thames, this aging camping ground has a shop, free bikes, bush walks and roaming ducks.

Gateway Backpackers (☎ 07-868 6339; www.gate waybackpackers.co.nz; 209 Mackay St; dm $23-26, s $45, d $58-72; ☐) Generations of Kiwis grew up in state houses just like this, giving it a homely feel. This relaxed hostel has basic rooms, a nice garden and simple facilities. Bathrooms are in short supply but free laundry and bikes are on offer.

Sunkist Backpackers (☎ 07-868 8808; www.sunkist backpackers.com; 506 Brown St; dm $24-28, r $64; ☐) This character-filled 1860s heritage building has spacious dorms, spotless bathrooms and a garden. It offers free bikes, 4WD hire ($65 per day) and shuttles to the Kauaeranga Valley ($35 return).

Huia Lodge (Map p184; ☎ 07-868 6557; www.thames -info.co.nz/HuiaLodge; 589 Kauaeranga Valley Rd; s/d/tr $75/110/150) The affable empty-nesters who own this homely farmhouse close to the forest park provide decent rooms, full cooked breakfasts and good advice for walkers.

Coastal Motor Lodge (Map p184; ☎ 07-868 6843; www.stayatcoastal.co.nz; 608 Tararu Rd; units $140-185; ☎) Motel and chalet-style accommodation is provided at this smart, welcoming place, 2km north of Thames. It overlooks the sea, making it a popular choice, especially in the summer months.

ourpick **Brunton House B&B** (☎ 07-868 5160; www.bruntonhouse.co.nz; 210 Parawai Rd; r $160-180, tr $195; ☐ ☎ ☎) Recent renovations of this impressive two-storey kauri villa (1875) have upgraded the kitchen and bathrooms, while staying true to the building's historic credentials (there are no en suites). Guests can relax in the grounds, by the pool, in the designated lounge or on the upstairs terrace.

Cotswold Cottage (☎ 07-868 6306; www.cotswold cottage.co.nz; 36 Maramarahi Rd; r $165-200) Looking over the river and racecourse, this pretty villa has had a modern makeover with luxuriant linen (225-thread-count sheets) and an out-door spa pool. The comfy rooms all open onto a deck.

Grafton Cottage & Chalets (☎ 07-868 9971; www. graftoncottage.co.nz; 304 Grafton Rd; units $165-210; ☐ ☎) Perched on a hill, most of these attractive wooden chalets have decks with awesome views and are self-contained. The hospitable hosts provide free internet access and breakfast, as well as use of the pool, spa and three barbecue areas.

Eating

Food for Thought (☎ 07-868 6065; 574 Pollen St; pies $1.80-4; ☺ breakfast & lunch Mon-Sat) You might toy with a panini, cake or coffee, but it is really the award-winning pies that you come here for.

Sola Cafe (☎ 07-868 8781; 720b Pollen St; mains $9-13; ☺ 8am-4pm; ☑) Bright and friendly, this meat-free cafe is first rate. Expect excellent coffee and a range of vegan, dairy-free and gluten-free options that include heavenly salads.

Taj (☎ 07-868 8122; 620 Pollen St; mains $11-16; ☺ lunch Wed-Fri, dinner daily; ☑) A simple curry house perhaps, but Taj does a sublime *saag paneer* and all the other spicy favourites.

Nakontong Thai Restaurant (☎ 07-868 6821; 730 Pollen St; mains $16-21; ☺ lunch Mon-Fri, dinner daily; ☑) Although the bright lighting may not induce romance, the tangy Thai dishes should provide a warm glow.

ourpick **Rocco** (☎ 07-868 8641; 109 Sealey St; mains $24-25; ☺ lunch daily, dinner Tue-Sun) Housed in one of Thames' gorgeous kauri villas, Rocco serves a lively tapas selection and more substantial mains, making good use of local ingredients (mussels, fish) and high-quality Spanish imports (chorizo, cheese, olives). In clement weather take a seat among the crushed-shell and swirling brick paths outside.

Self-catering options include **Organic Co-op** (☎ 868 8797; 736 Pollen St; ☺ 9am-5pm Mon-Fri, 8.30am-noon Sat; ☑), a good source of planet-friendly vegetables, nuts, bread, eggs and meat. There is also **Matatoki Farm Cheese** (Map p184; ☎ 07-868 1284; cnr SH26 & Wainui Rd; ☺ 8am-4.30pm Mon-Fri, 10am-4pm Sat & Sun), where you can taste and buy cheeses handmade from milk produced by the farm's cows and ewes, including organic varieties.

Drinking & Entertainment

One thing you can say for Thames, it isn't short of historic pubs. Most of them have some rough edges and are clustered around

Pollen St. You won't need us to plot your pub crawl.

Mama Gin's (☎ 07-868 6994; 746 Pollen St; ☽ 7pm-late Wed-Sat) The cutest little bar in the 'Mandel, with art-deco chandeliers, zany wallpaper and regular live music. It's the sort of place where a solo traveller of any gender can chill out over a glass of wine.

Multiplex Cinemas (☎ 07-868 6602; www.cinema thames.co.nz; 708 Pollen St; adult/child $12/8) Screening recent blockbusters in poorly sound-insulated cinemas.

Shopping

Pollen St has a good selection of gift and homeware stores selling local art and craft. On Saturday mornings the **Grahamstown Market** (Pollen St; ☽ 9am-noon Sat) fills the street with organic produce and handicrafts.

Getting There & Around

Thames is the transport hub of the Coromandel. **InterCity** (☎ 09-583 5780; www.inter city.co.nz) and its associates have daily buses to/from Auckland ($28, two hours), Coromandel Town ($16, 72 minutes), Whitianga ($34, 90 minutes), Tairua ($17, 44 minutes), Waihi ($20, 45 minutes), Hamilton ($24, 1¾ hours) and Tauranga ($28, 1¾ hours), stopping outside the i-SITE and Sunkist Backpackers.

Naked Bus (www.nakedbus.com) operates in conjunction with **Tairua Bus Company** (☎ 07-864 7770; www.tairuabus.co.nz) for daily services between Thames and Tairua (from $1, 50 minutes), stopping at Ngatea for connections to Auckland, Tauranga and Rotorua.

Go Kiwi (☎ 0800 446 549; www.go-kiwi.co.nz) has daily shuttles to/from Auckland ($42, two hours), Auckland Airport ($54, 90 minutes), Whitianga ($36, 1¾ hours), Tairua ($26, 70 minutes) and Whangamata ($64, 75 minutes).

Paki Paki Bike Shop (☎ 07-867 9026; www.pakipaki bikeshop.co.nz; Goldfields Shopping Centre) rents out bikes for $25 a day and performs repairs.

COROMANDEL FOREST PARK

More than 30 walks crisscross the Coromandel Forest Park, spread over several major blocks throughout the centre of the peninsula. The most popular hike is the challenging six- to eight-hour return journey up to the **Pinnacles** (759m) in the Kauaeranga Valley behind Thames. Other outstanding tramps include

the **Coromandel Coastal Walkway** from Fletcher Bay to Stony Bay (see p193) and the **Puketui Valley** walk to abandoned gold mines (see p200).

The **Department of Conservation (DOC) Kauaeranga Visitor Centre** (Map p184; ☎ 07-867 9080; Kauaeranga Valley Rd; ☽ 9am-4pm daily Oct-Apr, 9am-3pm Wed-Sun May-Sep) is a flash new complex with interesting displays about the kauri forest and its history. Its staff sell maps ($1 to $2), dispense advice and take bookings for the Pinnacles hut. The centre is 14km off SH25; it's a further 9km along a gravel road to the start of the trails. Enquire at the Thames hostels about shuttles.

The DOC **Pinnacles hut** (Map p184; adult/child $15/7.50) has 80 beds, gas cookers, heaters, toilets and cold showers, and must be pre-booked. There are also three basic **backcountry campsites** (Map p184; adult/child $5/2) in this part of the park: one near the hut and others at Moss Creek and Billygoat Basin. Expect only a toilet and running water. A further eight **conservation campsites** (adult/child $9/2) are accessible from the forest road and, at the time of research, there was talk of building a second hut.

Other campsites in other parts of the park are mentioned later in this chapter.

THAMES TO COROMANDEL TOWN

Narrow SH25 snakes along the coast past pretty little bays and rocky beaches. Sea birds are plentiful, and you can fish, dig for shellfish and fossick for quartz, jasper and even gold-bearing rocks on the beaches. The landscape turns crimson when the pohutukawa (often referred to as the 'NZ Christmas tree') blooms in December. At Wilsons Bay the road heads away from the coast and climbs over several hills and valleys before dropping down to Coromandel Town, 55km from Thames. The view looking towards the island-studded Coromandel Harbour is exquisite.

A handful of stores, motels, B&Bs and camping grounds are scattered around the tiny settlements that front the picturesque bays. At Tapu it's worth turning inland for a mainly sealed 6km drive to the **Rapaura Water Gardens** (Map p184; ☎ 07-868 4821; www.rapaura.com; 586 Tapu-Coroglen Rd; adult/child $12/5; ☽ 9am-5pm), a marriage of water, greenery, sculpture and platitudes. There's also accommodation (cottage/lodge $165/275) and a decent cafe.

COROMANDEL TOWN

pop 1620

Even more crammed with heritage buildings than Thames, Coromandel Town is a thoroughly quaint little place. Its natty cafes, interesting art stores, excellent sleeping options and delicious smoked mussels could keep you here longer than you expected.

Gold was discovered at Driving Creek in 1852. Initially the local Patukirikiri *iwi* kept control of the land and received money from digging licences. After initial financial success the same fate befell them as the Ngati Maru in Thames (see p186). By 1871, debt had forced them to sell all but 778 mountainous acres of their land. Today fewer than 100 people remain who identify as part of this *iwi*.

Information

Coromandel Town i-SITE (☎ 07-866 8598; www.coromandeltown.co.nz; 355 Kapanga Rd; ☻ 9am-5pm Mon-Fri, 9am-4pm Sat & Sun Apr-Oct, 9am-5pm daily Nov-Mar) Has internet access ($6 per hour) and maps of local walks ($1).

Police station (☎ 07-866 1190; 405 Kapanga Rd)

Post office (Kapanga Rd)

Sights

Heritage buffs can tour around 28 historic sites featured in the Historic Places Trust's Coromandel Town pamphlet (free from the i-SITE).

The **Coromandel Goldfield Centre & Stamper Battery** (☎ 07-866 7933; 410 Buffalo Rd; adult/child $10/5; ☻ tours 2pm & 3pm Tue, Thu, Sat & Sun) is an

COROMANDEL TOWN

INFORMATION
Coromandel Town i-SITE 1 C3
Police Station 2 C3
Post Office 3 C3

SIGHTS & ACTIVITIES
Coromandel Goldfield
  Centre & Stamper
  Battery 4 C1
Coromandel Mining &
  Historic Museum 5 C2
Driving Creek Railway &
  Pottery 6 C1

SLEEPING
Anchor Lodge 7 B3
Coromandel Court Motel 8 C3
Coromandel Holiday Park 9 C3
Driving Creek Villas 10 C1
Lion's Den 11 C2
Little Farm 12 C4
Tui Lodge 13 D3

EATING
Coromandel Smoking
  Company 14 C3
Driving Creek Cafe 15 C1
Peppertree Restaurant &
  Bar 16 C3
Umu 17 B3

DRINKING
Star & Garter Hotel 18 B3

TRANSPORT
InterCity Bus Stop 19 C3

1899 rock-crushing plant with informative one-hour tours. You can also try panning for gold ($5). Outside of the tours it's worth stopping for a gander at NZ's largest working water wheel.

The small **Coromandel Mining & Historic Museum** (☎ 07-866 7251; 841 Rings Rd; adult/child $3/50c; ☽ 10am-1pm Sat & Sun Feb–mid-Dec, 10am-4pm daily mid-Dec–late Jan) provides a glimpse of pioneer life.

Activities

The amazing **Driving Creek Railway & Potteries** (☎ 07-866 8703; www.drivingcreekrailway.co.nz; 380 Driving Creek Rd; adult/child $20/11; ☽ departures 10.15am & 2pm) is 3km north of Coromandel Town. The unique train runs up steep grades, across four trestle bridges, along two spirals and a double switch-back, and through two tunnels, finishing at the 'Eye-full Tower'. The hour-long trip passes artworks and regenerating native forest – more than 17,000 natives have been planted, including 9000 kauri. It's worth lingering for the video about the extraordinary guy behind it all, well-known potter Barry Brickell.

Megan from **Mussel Barge** (☎ 07-866 7667; adult/child $50/25) offers fishing trips with a uniquely local flavour and lots of laughs. Her father runs **Argo Tours** (3hr trips $150), exploring native bush and old gold workings in a mini 8WD. If you can muster a posse (up to five people), prices drop as low as $40 per person.

Coromandel Kayak Adventures (☎ 07-866 7466; www.kayakadventures.co.nz) offers paddle-powered tours ranging from half-day ecotours (for 1/2/3/4/5/6 paddlers, $200/200/267/356/425/474) to fishing trips (half-/full day $195/375).

Tri Sail Charters (☎ 0800 024 874; www.trisailcharters. co.nz; half/full day $50/100) will have you and your mates (a minimum of four) exploring the Coromandel Harbour on an 11.2m trimaran (three-hulled yacht).

Sleeping

Coromandel Town is spoilt for accommodation choice, with much better budget options than Thames.

ourpick **Tui Lodge** (☎ 07-866 8237; www.coromandeltuilodge.co.nz; 60 Whangapoua Rd; sites per person $12, dm $25, r $55-75; ▫) Pleasantly rural, this cheery backpackers has plenty of trees, a sauna ($5), free bikes, fruit (in season) and straight-up rooms. The pricier ones have en suites.

Coromandel Holiday Park (☎ 07-866 8830; www. coromandelholidaypark.co.nz; 636 Rings Rd; sites per person

$20, dm $30, cabins $77-137, units $137-177; ▫ ☎ ▣) Well-kept and welcoming, with nicely painted cabins and manicured lawns, this large park includes the semi-separate Coromandel Town Backpackers. It gets busy in summer, so book ahead.

Lions' Den (☎ 07-866 8157; www.lionsdenhostel. co.nz; 126 Te Tiki St; dm/r $24/55; ☎) Chill out to the hippy vibe in this magical place. A tranquil garden with fish pond, fairy lights and wisteria vines, and a relaxed collection of comfy rooms (dotted with African and North American bits and bobs) make for a soothing spot to rest your bones. There are no locks on the doors, but we suspect the right spells have been set to protect your materialistic trappings. Hey, who really owns anything anyway?

Anchor Lodge (☎ 07-866 7992; www.anchorlodge coromandel.co.nz; 448 Wharf Rd; dm $25, d $60-65, units $125-275; ☎ ▣) Not many places can boast its own goldmine and glowworm cave, but this upmarket backpacker/motel combo has them and a heated swimming pool and spa to boot. The 2nd-floor units look over the nikau palms and agaves to the harbour.

Jacaranda Lodge (Map p184; ☎ 07-866 8002; www. jacarandalodge.co.nz; 3195 Tiki Rd; s $75, d $120-160; ☎) Jacaranda is a two-storey cottage located among six hectares of bucolic farmland and rose gardens. Some rooms share bathrooms, but expect fluffy towels and personalised soap in mini *kete* (woven flax bags). Kosher facilities available and Hebrew spoken.

Little Farm (☎ 07-866 8427; www.thelittlefarm coromandel.co.nz; 750 Tiki Rd; r $100-120) Positioned overlooking a private wetland reserve at the rear of a fair dinkum farm, these three comfortable units offer plenty of peace and quiet. The largest has a full kitchen and superb sunset views.

Coromandel Court Motel (☎ 07-866 8402; www. coromandelcourtmotel.co.nz; 365 Kapanga Rd; units $145-215; ☎) These spick-and-span units are spotless, smart and ideally located, just behind the information centre. The owners clearly love their lot.

Driving Creek Villas (☎ 07-866 7755; www.driving creekvillas.com; 21a Colville Rd; villas $275-415; ☎) This is the posh, grown-up's choice – two spacious, self-contained, modern wooden villas, with plenty of privacy. The interior design is slick (with a Polynesian bent), the appliances first-rate and the bush setting, complete with bubbling creek, sublime.

Eating

our pick **Driving Creek Cafe** (☎ 07-866 7066; 180 Driving Creek Rd; mains $8-16; ✎ 9.30am-5pm; 🖥 V) A large selection of vegetarian, vegan, gluten-free, organic and fair-trade delights awaits at this funky mud-brick cafe. The food is wonderful – beautifully presented, fresh and healthy. Once sated, the kids can play in the sandpit while the adults check their email ($6 per hour).

Umu (☎ 07-866 8618; 22 Wharf Rd; breakfast $9-16, lunch $9-24, dinner $14-32; ✎ breakfast, lunch & dinner daily; 🛜) Umu serves up classy cafe fare, including excellent pizza, mouth-watering counter food (tarts and quiches around $7), superb coffee and tummy-taming breakfasts.

Pepper Tree Restaurant & Bar (☎ 07-866 8211; 31 Kapanga Rd; lunch $17-25, dinner $23-33; ✎ lunch & dinner daily; 🛜) C-Town's most upmarket option, Pepper Tree dishes up generously proportioned French-style cooking with a particular emphasis on local seafood. On a summer's evening, the courtyard tables under the shady tree are the place to be.

For a delicious snack or cooking supplies, **Coromandel Smoking Co** (☎ 07-866 8793; 70 Tiki Rd; ✎ 9am-5pm Sun-Thu, 9am-5.30pm Fri & Sat) has a wonderful range of smoked fish and seafood. You can't leave town without trying the extremely addictive smoked mussels.

If you prefer your bivalves au naturel, the roadside **Coromandel Oyster Company** (☎ 07-866 8028; 1611 Tiki Rd; ✎ 7.30am-6.30pm) is the place for newly landed mussels, scallops, cooked crayfish and, of course, oysters.

Drinking

Coromandel doesn't have the same volume of pubs as Thames, but there are still several choices on the main street.

Star & Garter Hotel (☎ 07-866 8503; 5 Kapanga Rd; 🛜) Making the most of the simple kauri interior of an 1873 building, this smart pub has pool tables, decent sounds and a roster of live music and DJs on the weekends. The beer garden is awesome, smartly styled in corrugated iron.

Getting There & Away

By far the nicest way to travel from Auckland is by ferry. Operator **360 Discovery** (☎ 0800 888 006; www.360discovery.co.nz) has five boats weekly to/from Auckland (one way/return $49/79, two hours) via Orapiu on Waiheke Island (one way/return $39/69, 70 minutes). It makes

---

SENSIBLE CYCLISTS' LEAPFROG

There's no charge for carrying your bike on a 360 Discovery ferry. Touring cyclists can avoid Auckland's traffic fumes and treacherous roads completely by catching the ferry at Gulf Harbour (p137) to Auckland's ferry terminal, and then leapfrogging directly to Coromandel Town.

---

a great day trip, and there's a guided-tour option (adult/child $136/78) that includes Driving Creek Railway and the Goldfield Centre. The boats dock at Hannafords Wharf, Te Kouma, where free buses shuttle passengers the 10km into town.

InterCity (☎ 09-583 5780; www.intercity.co.nz) and its partners have daily buses to/from Whitianga ($18, 80 minutes), Thames ($16, 72 minutes), Te Aroha ($20, 2¾ hours) and Hamilton ($40, 3¾ hours).

Naked Bus (www.nakedbus.com) operates in conjunction with **Tairua Bus Company** (☎ 07-864 7770; www.tairuabus.co.nz; advance fares from $1) for daily services to Tairua (two hours), via Whitianga (one hour), Hahei (90 minutes) and Hot Water Beach (95 minutes).

Go Kiwi (☎ 0800 446 549; www.go-kiwi.co.nz) runs shuttles from late October to Easter to/from Auckland ($50, 3¾ hours), Auckland Airport ($66, 3¼ hours) and Whitianga ($23, 50 minutes).

FAR NORTH COROMANDEL

Supremely isolated and gobsmackingly beautiful, the rugged tip of the Coromandel Peninsula is well worth the effort required to reach it. The best time to visit is summer, when the metal roads are dry, the pohutukawa are in their crimson glory and camping's an option (there isn't a lot of accommodation up here).

The 1260-hectare **Colville Farm** (Map p184; ☎ 07-866 6820; www.colvillefarmholidays.co.nz; 2140 Colville Rd; sites per person $12, dm/s/d $23/38/62, units $70-158; 🖥) has a range of interesting accommodation, including bare-basics bush lodges and self-contained houses. Guests can try their hands at farm work (including milking) or go on horse treks ($30 to $120, one to five hours).

The nearby **Mahamudra Centre** (Map p184; ☎ 07-866 6851; www.mahamudra.org.nz; sites per person $12, dm $20, s $40-75, tw/d $60/85) is a serene Tibetan Buddhist retreat that has a stupa, meditation hall and regular meditation courses. It offers simple accommodation in a parklike setting.

Another kilometre brings you to the tiny settlement of **Colville** (25km north of Coromandel Town). It's a remote rural community by a muddy bay and a magnet for alternative lifestylers. There's not much here except for **Colville Café** (07-866 6690; 2312 Colville Rd; mains $5-19; 11am-4pm Mon-Wed, 8am-4pm Thu-Sun), which has extended hours in summer, and the quaint **Colville General Store** (07-866 6805; Colville Rd; 8.30am-5pm), selling just about everything from organic food to petrol (warning: this is your last option for either).

Three kilometres north of Colville the seal stops and the road splits to straddle each side of the peninsula. Following the west coast, ancient pohutukawa spread overhead as you pass turquoise waters and stony beaches. The small DOC-run **Fantail Bay campsite** (Map p184; adult/child $9/2), 23km north of Colville, has running water and a couple of long-drop toilets under the shade of puriri trees. Another 7km brings you to the **Port Jackson campsite** (Map p184; adult/child $9/2), a larger DOC site right on the beach.

There's a spectacular lookout about 4km further on, where a metal dish identifies the various islands on the horizon. Great Barrier Island (p128) is only 20km away, looking every part the extension of the Coromandel Peninsula that it once was.

The road stops at **Fletcher Bay** – a magical land's end. Although it's only 37km from Colville, allow an hour for the drive. There's another DOC **campsite** (Map p184; adult/child $9/2) here, as well as **Fletcher Bay Backpackers** (Map p184; 07-866 6685; www.fletcherbay.co.nz; dm $25) – a simple affair that has four rooms with four bunks in each. Bring sheets and food.

The **Coromandel Coastal Walkway** is a scenic, three-hour one-way hike between Fletcher Bay and **Stony Bay**. It's a relatively easy walk with great coastal views and an ambling section across farmland. If you're not keen on walking all the way back, **Coromandel Discovery** (0800 668 175; www.coromandeldiscovery.co.nz; adult/child $95/55) will drive you from Coromandel Town up to Fletcher Bay and pick you up from Stony Bay four hours later.

There's another DOC **campsite** (Map p184; adult/child $9/2) at Stony Bay, where the east-coast road terminates. Heading south you pass a couple of nice beaches peppered with baches (holiday homes) on your way to the slightly larger settlement of **Port Charles**.

Tangiaro Kiwi Retreat (Map p184; 07-866 6614; www.kiwiretreat.co.nz; 1299 Port Charles Rd; units $225-350;) offers eight brand-new one- or two-bedroom self-contained wooden cottages, each pair sharing a barbecue. There's a bush-fringed spa, an in-house masseuse (per hour $70) and, in summer, a cafe and licensed restaurant.

Another 8km brings you to the turn-off leading back to Colville, or you can continue south to **Waikawau Bay**, where there's a large DOC **campsite** (Map p184; 07-866 1106; adult/child $9/2, bookings required Dec-Jan) which has internet access (per hour $10) and a summer-only store. The road then winds its way south past **Kennedy Bay** before cutting back to come out near the Driving Creek Railway.

COROMANDEL TOWN TO WHITIANGA

There are two routes from Coromandel Town southeast to Whitianga. The main road is the slightly longer but quicker SH25, which follows the coast, enjoys sea views and has short detours to pristine sandy beaches. The other is the less-travelled but legendary 309 Rd, an unsealed, untamed route through deep bush.

State Highway 25

SH25 starts by climbing sharply to an incredible lookout before heading steeply down with craggy Castle Rock (526m) in the distance. The turn-off at Te Rerenga follows the harbour to Whangapoua. There's not much here but generic holiday homes, but you can walk along the rocky foreshore to the often-deserted **New Chum's Beach** (30 minutes).

Continuing east you soon reach **Kuaotunu**, a more interesting holiday town on a beautiful stretch of white-sand beach, with a cafe-gallery, store and ancient petrol pump. **Black Jack Backpackers** (07-866 2988; www.black-jack.co.nz; 201 SH25; dm/tw $25/70, d $80-90) has a prime position directly across from the beach. It's a lovely little hostel with smart facilities and bikes and kayaks for hire. The owners sometimes shut up shop in the off-season.

For a touch more luxury, head back along the beach and up the hill to **Kuaotunu Bay Lodge** (Map p184; 07-866 4396; www.kuaotunubay.co.nz; SH25; s $180-225, d $250-275), an elegant B&B set among manicured gardens, offering a small set of spacious sea-gazing rooms.

Heading off the highway at Kuaotunu takes you (via an unsealed road) to one of Coromandel's best-kept secrets. First the long stretch of **Otama Beach** comes into view – deserted but for a few houses and farms. There's extremely basic camping (think long-drop toilet in a corrugated shack) in a farmer's field at **Otama Beach Camp** (☎ 07-866 2362; www.otamabeachcamp.co.nz; 400 Blackjack Rd; sites per adult/child $10/5, cottage $220-260). Down by the beach they've recently built a self-contained, ecofriendly cottage (sleeping six), with solar power, a composting waste water system and ocean views.

Continue along the road and you'll be in for a shock. Just when you think you're about to fall off the end of the earth, the seal starts again and you reach **Opito** – a hidden-away enclave of 250 flash properties (too smart to be called baches), of which only 16 have permanent residents. It's more than a little weird, but it is a magical beach. You can walk to a Ngati Hei *pa* (fortified village) site at the far end.

One of the 'real' residences houses the de-lightful folks of **Leighton Lodge** (☎ 07-866 0756; www.leightonlodge.co.nz; 17 Stewart Pl; s/d/tr $125/160/195; 🖳). This smart B&B has an upstairs room with a view-hungry balcony and a self-contained flat downstairs.

309 Road

Starting 3km south of Coromandel Town, the 309 cuts through the ranges for 21km (14km of which is unsealed but well maintained), rejoining SH25 7km south of Whitianga. The **Waterworks** (Map p184; ☎ 07-866 7191; www.thewater works.co.nz; 471 309 Rd; adult/child $15/10; 🕙 9am-6pm Nov-Apr, 10am-4pm May-Oct), 5km from SH25, is a wonderfully bizarre park filled with whimsi-cal water-powered amusements made from old kitchen knives, washing machines, bikes and toilets.

Two kilometres later there's a two-minute walk through a pretty patch of bush to the 10m-high **Waiau Falls**. Stop again after another 500m for an easy 10-minute walk through peaceful native bush to an amazing **kauri grove** (Map p184). This stand of 13 600-year-old giants escaped the carnage of the 19th cen-tury, giving a majestic reminder of what the peninsula once looked like. The biggest has a 6m circumference.

If you're carless or unwilling to risk the metal road, Coromandel Discovery (p193) has a **309 Road and Coromandel Highlights Tour** (adult/child $150/90), taking the 309 from Coromandel Town, stopping at the Waterworks, kauri

grove, Cathedral Cove and Hot Water Beach (or Whitianga's Lost Spring spa if the tides aren't right) before looping back on SH25.

WHITIANGA
pop 3800

If you come to Whitianga you'd better want to get wet. The big attractions are the sandy beaches of Mercury Bay and the diving, boat-ing and kayaking opportunities afforded by the craggy coast and nearby Te Whanganui-A-Hei Marine Reserve. If you've a lust for the luxe, a number of upmarket eateries and accommodation options have sprung up, catering to the boatie set who constantly breeze into the pretty harbour. Most of the restaurants are overpriced and not particu-larly interesting.

A genuine nautical hero, the legendary Polynesian explorer and seafarer Kupe, is believed to have landed near here in around 950AD. The name Whitianga is a contraction of Te Whitianga a Kupe (the Crossing Place of Kupe). Nearby are two famous and fantastic natural attractions, Cathedral Cove and Hot Water Beach.

Information
Medical Centre (☎ 07-866 5911; 87 Albert St; 🕙 8.30am-5pm Mon-Fri, 9-11am Sat)
Post office (72 Albert St)
Whitianga i-SITE (☎ 07-866 5555; www.whitianga. co.nz; 66 Albert St; 🕙 9am-5pm Mon-Fri, 9am-4pm Sat & Sun, extended in summer) Information and internet access ($9 per hour).

Sights & Activities
Buffalo Beach stretches along Mercury Bay, north of the harbour. A five-minute **passen-ger ferry ride** (adult/child/bicycle $2/1/50c; 🕙 7.30am-2.15am Christmas-Jan, 7.30am-6.30pm & 7.30-8.30pm & 9.30-11pm Feb-Christmas) will take you across the harbour to **Whitianga Rock Scenic & Historical Reserve**, **Flaxmill Bay**, **Shakespeare's Lookout**, **Captain Cook's Memorial**, **Lonely Bay** and **Cooks Bay**, all within walking distance. Further afield are Cathedral Cove (p197; 15km), Hahei (p197; 13km) and Hot Water Beach (p198; 18km, one hour by bike). On the way to Hahei, **Purangi Estate** (Map p184; ☎ 07-866 3724; www.purangi.co.nz; 501 Purangi Rd; 🕙 9am-5pm) has a cafe and free tastings of fruit wines and liqueurs.

The **Lost Spring** (☎ 07-866 0456; www.thelostspring. co.nz; 121a Cook Dr; hr/day $25/50) is an intriguing

Disney-meets-Rotorua thermal complex, involving a series of hot pools in a lush junglelike setting, complete with an erupting volcano. Yet this is an adult's indulgence (children under 14 not permitted), leaving the grown-ups to marinate themselves in tranquillity, cocktail in hand. There's also a day spa (treatments $20 to $320) and an excellent restaurant.

Mercury Bay Museum (☎ 07-866 0730; 11a The Esplanade; adult/child $5/50c; ✆ 10am-4pm) is small but interesting, focusing on local history – especially Whitianga's most famous visitors, Kupe and Cook.

Dive HQ (☎ 07-867 1580; www.divethecoromandel. co.nz; 7 Blacksmith Lane; trips $120-225) is a PADI five-star accredited dive facility offering a range of shore, kayak and boat dives. Come November, it also organises a **dive festival** (www.divefestival. co.nz).

If you're more interested in catching fish than admiring them, the Whitianga marina is a well-known base for **game-fishing** (particularly marlin and tuna) between January and March. There are numerous charters on offer, starting at around $500 and heading into the thousands. Enquire at the i-SITE or around the marina. See p170, for a guide to sustainable fishing.

Seafari Windsurfing (☎ 07-866 0677; Brophy's Beach), 4km north of Whitianga, hires out sailboards (from $25 per hour) and kayaks (from $15 per hour), and provides windsurfing lessons (from $40 including gear).

Another option for watery fun is a bright-yellow, motorised **Banana Boat** (☎ 07-866 5617; www.whitianga.co.nz/bananaboat; rides $10-30), but these only operate between Boxing Day and the end of January.

Twin Oaks Riding Ranch (Map p184; ☎ 07-866 5388; www.twinoaksridingranch.co.nz; SH25; 2hr trek $50) will take you horse-trekking over farmland and through bush 9km north of Whitianga.

Highzone (Map p184; ☎ 07-866 2113; www.highzone. co.nz; 49 Kaimarama Rd; activities $10-70) offers high adventure on a ropes course, including a trapeze leap and flying fox. It's located 7km south of Whitianga, just off the main road. Call for opening hours.

Tours

There are a baffling number of tours to **Te Whanganui-A-Hei Marine Reserve**, where you'll see amazing rock formations and, if you're lucky, dolphins, fur seals, penguins and orcas.

Some are straight cruises while others offer optional swims and snorkels. Try one of these tour companies:

Cave Cruzer (☎ 0800 427 893; www.cavecruzer.co.nz; 1-2½hr tour $50-75) A rigid-hull inflatable.

Glass Bottom Boat (☎ 07-867 1962; www.glassbottom boatwhitianga.co.nz; 2hr tour adult/child $85/50)

Whitianga Adventures (☎ 0800 806 060; www. whitianga-adventures.co.nz; 1½hr tour adult/child $55/35) Offers a two-hour Sea Cave Adventure in an inflatable (adult/child $65/40) and four-hour trips to the Mercury Islands in a 14m launch (adult/child $125/70).

Windborne (☎ 07-866 4607; www.windborne.co.nz; per person $80) Day sails in a 19m 1928 schooner.

Festivals & Events

In August, the **Scallop Festival** (www.scallopfestival. co.nz) provides a week of sublime food and entertainment. The inaugural 2009/2010 New Year's Eve **Coromandel Gold Festival** (www.coromandel gold.co.nz; Ohuka Farm, Buffalo Beach Rd; tickets $88) got a big thumb's up from punters, showcasing top NZ bands.

Sleeping

Mercury Bay Holiday Park (☎ 07-866 5579; www.mercury bayholidaypark.co.nz; 121 Albert St; sites per adult/child $22/8, cabins & units $100-268; 🖥 🛜 🐾) Strangely planted in a suburban neighbourhood, this small camp is comfortable and clean, with playgrounds, trampoline, swimming pool and pool table.

Cat's Pyjamas (☎ 07-866 4663; www.cats-pyjamas. co.nz; 12 Albert St; dm $23, d $55-65; 🖥 🛜) Good communal facilities make this place not just the cat's pyjamas but also the bee's knees. It's perfectly positioned between the pubs and the beach.

On the Beach Backpackers Lodge (☎ 07-866 5380; www.coromandelbackpackers.com; 46 Buffalo Beach Rd; dm $24-26, s $49-53, d $66-96; 🖥) Brightly painted, beachside and brilliant, this well-run YHA has a large choice of sleeping options, including some with sea views and en suites. It provides free kayaks, boogie boards and spades (for Hot Water Beach).

Cosy Cat Cottage B&B (☎ 07-866 4488; www.cosycat. co.nz; 41 South Hwy; s/d/tr/q $85/105/120/160) Kooky in the extreme, this long-running B&B is crawling with feline images, including a human-sized one in the front garden. Not all rooms have en suites, but they're comfortable enough.

our pick **Pipi Dune B&B** (☎ 07-869 5375; www. pipidune.co.nz; 5 Pipi Dune; s/d $85/125; 🛜) You'll be

WHITIANGA & AROUND

as snug as a pipi in its shell in this attractive B&B in a quiet cul-de-sac, and you'll have a lot more room to move: pipi shells don't tend to come with guest lounges with kitchenettes, laundries and free wi-fi.

Albert Number 6 (☎ 07-866 0036; www.albertnumber6.co.nz; 6 Albert St; r $95-140; 🖳) Close to the beach and shops, these bright and sunny units are like motel rooms without kitchenettes. The hosts provide a light breakfast.

Within the Bays (☎ 07-866 2848; www.withinthebays.co.nz; 49 Tarapatiki Dr; r $360; 🖳) Modern European design couples with incredible views at this hilltop B&B. It's extremely well set up for guests with restricted mobility – there's even a wheelchair-accessible bush track on the property.

Eating

Tuatua (☎ 07-866 0952; 45 Albert St; tapas $5-14, mains $25-37; 🕙 10am-5pm Mon-Thu, noon-late Fri & Sat) The tapas craze has made it to Whitianga, but with a local flavour – try the Madrid-style Coromandel mussels.

Cog (☎ 07-866 0592; 10 Coghill St; mains $8-18; 🕙 7am-5pm) Get an early start on the sunny terrace of this side-street cafe, where the counter food beckons enticingly and the toasted sandwiches have gourmet aspirations.

Cafe Nina (☎ 07-866 5440; 20 Victoria St; mains $8-18; 🕙 breakfast & lunch) Barbecue for breakfast? Why the hell not. Too cool to be constricted to four walls, the kitchen grills bacon and eggs on an outdoor hotplate while the punters spill out onto tables in the park.

Sangam Indian Cuisine (☎ 07-867 1983; 13/1 Blacksmith Lane; mains $15-22; ☾ dinner; Ⓥ) North India comes to Whitianga via this large, up-market restaurant with exotic light fittings. If the kids aren't spice-friendly there's a fish-and-chips lifeline.

our pick **18sixtyfive** (☎ 07-866 0456; 121a Cook Dr; lunch $14-17, dinner $32-35; ☾ lunch & dinner) A fitting indulgence after a hot-water soak, the Lost Spring's restaurant offers smart fusion dining in the elegant surrounds of a converted 1865 schoolhouse.

Self-catering foodies should head to **Monk St Market** (☎ 07-866 4500; 1 Monk St; ☾ 10am-6pm Mon-Sat) for deli goods, imported chocolate and organic produce.

Entertainment

Mercury Twin Cinemas (☎ 07-867 1001; Lee St) Offers latest-release mainstream and independent films as an alternative to getting wet.

Getting There & Around

InterCity (☎ 0508 353 947; www.intercity.co.nz) has a daily bus to/from Thames ($34, 90 minutes)

via Tairua ($17, 44 minutes), stopping at the i-SITE, Cat's Pyjamas and On the Beach.

Naked Bus (www.nakedbus.com) partners with **Tairua Bus Company** (☎ 07-864 7770; www.tairuabus. co.nz; advance fares from $1) for daily services to Coromandel Town (one hour), Hahei (30 minutes), Hot Water Beach (40 minutes) and Tairua (one hour).

Go Kiwi (☎ 0800 446 549; www.go-kiwi.co.nz) shuttles head to Tairua ($24, one hour), Thames ($36, 1¾ hours) and Auckland ($65, four hours) daily, with services to Waihi ($42, 2¼ hours) and Tauranga ($60, three hours) from December to Easter.

HAHEI

pop 270 (7000 in summer)

A legendary Kiwi beach town, little Hahei balloons to bursting in summer but is nearly abandoned otherwise – apart from the bus-loads of tourists doing the obligatory stop-off at Cathedral Cove. It's a charming spot, and a great place to unwind for a few days, especially in the quieter months. It takes its name from Hei, the eponymous ancestor of the Ngati Hei people, who arrived in the 14th century on the *Te Arawa* canoe.

Sights & Activities

Beautiful **Cathedral Cove**, with its famous gigantic stone arch and natural waterfall shower, is best enjoyed early or late in the day – avoiding the worst of the hordes. At the car park, a kilometre north of Hahei, the signs suggest that the walk to the cove will take 45 minutes, but anyone who's not on a ventilator will do it in 30. On the way there's rocky **Gemstone Bay** (which has a snorkelling trail where you're likely to see big snapper, crayfish and stingrays) and sandy **Stingray Bay**.

It's a 70-minute walk from Cathedral Cove to **Hahei Beach**. From the southern end of Hahei Beach, it's a 15-minute walk up to **Te Pare**, a *pa* site with splendid coastal views.

Cathedral Cove Sea Kayaking (☎ 07-866 3877; www.seakayaktours.co.nz; 88 Hahei Beach Rd; half/full day $85/145) runs guided kayaking trips around the rock arches, caves and islands in the Cathedral Cove area. The Remote Coast Tour heads the other way when conditions permit, visiting caves, blowholes and a long tunnel.

If that sounds too much like hard work, you can tour the coast in an hour-long jet boat ride with **Hahei Explorer** (☎ 07-866 3910; www. haheiexplorer.co.nz; adult/child $65/40).

Cathedral Cove Dive & Snorkel (☎ 07-866 3955; www.hahei.co.nz/diving; Hahei Beach Rd; dives $69-105) takes daily dive trips and rents out scuba gear ($60), snorkelling gear ($20), bikes ($20) and boogie boards ($20). A Discover Scuba half-day beginners' course costs $160 including all the gear.

Sleeping & Eating

Hahei really does have a 'gone fishing' feel in the off-season. The local store remains open and the eateries take it in turns so that there's usually one option every evening. For more choice, catch the ferry over to Whitianga.

our pick Tatahi Lodge (☎ 07-866 3992; www.tatahilodge.co.nz; Grange Rd; dm/d $30/80; units $140-310; 🖳 🛜) A wonderful place where backpackers are treated with at least as much care and respect as the lush bromeliad-filled garden. The dorm rooms and excellent communal facilities are just as attractive as the pricier self-contained units. Gifts of free fruit in season provide much-needed vitamin replenishment to those hardcore bag-of-rice-a-week types.

Church (☎ 07-866 3533; www.thechurchhahei.co.nz; 87 Hahei Beach Rd; cottages $130-220; 🖳) These beautifully kitted-out, rustic timber cottages have stylish, modern interiors in a photogenic garden setting. Housed in the ultracharming wooden church at the top of the drive is Hahei's swankiest eatery (mains $30 to $37).

Getting There & Around

Tairua Bus Company (☎ 07-864 7770; www.tairuabus.co.nz; advance fares from $1), in association with **Naked Bus** (www.nakedbus.com), has daily services to Coromandel Town (90 minutes) via Whitianga (30 minutes) and Tairua (30 minutes) via Hot Water Beach (10 minutes).

From Boxing Day to Waitangi Day the council runs a bus service from the Cooks Beach side of the Ferry Landing to Hot Water Beach, stopping at Hahei (adult/child $2/1).

HOT WATER BEACH

Justifiably famous, Hot Water Beach is quite extraordinary. For two hours either side of low tide, you can access an area of sand in front of a rocky outcrop at the middle of the beach where hot water oozes up from beneath the surface. Bring a spade, dig a hole and voila, you've got a personal spa pool. Surfers stop off before the main beach to access some decent breaks. The headland between the two beaches still has traces of a Ngati Hei *pa*.

> **GETTING YOURSELF INTO HOT WATER...**
>
> Hot Water Beach has dangerous rips, especially directly in front of the main thermal section. It's one of the four most dangerous beaches in NZ in terms of drowning numbers, although this may be skewed by the huge number of tourists that flock here. Regardless, swimming here is *not* safe, so restrict your activities to burning your bum – unless the beach is patrolled.

Spades ($5) can be hired from the **Hot Water Beach Store** (☎ 07-866 3006; Pye Pl; ☽ 9am-7pm summer, low tide winter), which has a cafe attached. The wonderful **Hot Waves Café** (☎ 07-866 3887; 8 Pye Pl; meals $10-17; ☽ 8.30am-4pm) also hires spades ($5) and serves excellent food in cool surroundings. In summer there are queues out the door.

Near the beach, **Moko** (☎ 07-866 3367; www.moko.co.nz; 24 Pye Pl; ☽ 10am-5pm) is full of beautiful things – art, sculpture, jewellery – with a modern Pasifika/Maori bent.

Bordered by bamboo and gum trees **Hot Water Beach Holiday Park** (☎ 07-866 3116; www.hotwaterbeachholidaypark.com; 790 Hot Water Beach Rd; sites per person/dm $20/35; 🖳) is a smallish, newish camping ground with a modern shower and toilet block and four bunk-room cabins.

Auntie Dawn's Place (☎ 07-866 3707; www.auntiedawn.co.nz; 15 Radar Rd; dm $25, units $120-135) is a comfortable, spacious and homely house with a big garden that includes ancient pohutukawa trees. Backpacker beds are available in garden huts in summer.

A nice hillside pad, **Hot Water Beach B&B** (☎ 07-866 3991; www.hotwaterbedandbreakfast.co.nz; 48 Pye Pl; r $250) has priceless views, a spa bath on the deck and attractive living quarters.

The Hahei bus services also stop here, but only on prebooked requests.

COROGLEN & AROUND

Coroglen is a blink-and-you'll-miss-it village on SH25, south of Whitianga and west of Hot Water Beach. The legendary **Coroglen Tavern** (☎ 07-866 3809; www.coroglentavern.com; 1937 SH25) is the archetypal middle-of-nowhere country pub that attracts big-name Kiwi bands in summer.

Coroglen Farmers Market (☎ 07-866 3315; SH25; ☽ 9am-1pm Sun) sells a bit of everything produced in the local area, from vegetables to compost.

Nearby, the folks at **Rangihau Ranch** (☎ 07-866 3875; www.rangihauranch.co.nz; Rangihau Rd; 1/2hr trek $40/60) will lead you on horseback up a historic packhorse track, through beautiful bush to spectacular views.

Colenso Country Shop & Cafe (Map p184; ☎ 07-866 3725; Whenuakite; mains $7-17; ☷ 10am-5pm) has excellent fair-trade coffee, scones, cakes and light snacks, and a sweet atmosphere.

TAIRUA

pop 1269

Tairua and its twin town Pauanui sit either side of a river estuary that's perfect for windsurfing or for little kids to splash about in. Both have decent surf beaches (Pauanui's is probably a shade better), but that's where the similarity stops. Where Tairua is a functioning residential town (with shops, ATMs and a choice of eateries), Pauanui is an upmarket refugee camp for over-wealthy Aucklanders – the kind who jet in and park their private planes by their grandiose beach houses before knocking out a round of golf. Friendly Tairua knows how to keep it real. Both are ridiculously popular in the summertime.

Information

Tairua Information Centre (☎ 07-864 7575; www.tairua.info; 223 Main Rd; ☷ 9am-5pm Mon-Fri, 9am-4pm Sat & Sun)

Sights & Activities

Forming the north head of the harbour is craggy **Paku**, which around seven million years ago was a volcanic island. More recently it was a Ngati Hei *pa*, before being invaded by Ngati Maru in the 17th century. It's a steep 15-minute walk to the summit from the top of Paku Dr, with the payoff being amazing views over Tairua, Pauanui and the Alderman Islands. Plaques along the way detail Tairua's colonial history, with only one rather dismissive one devoted to its long Maori occupation.

Tairua Dive & Fishinn (☎ 07-864 8054; www.divetairua.co.nz; The Esplanade; ☷ 8am-5pm Wed-Sun, daily summer) hires out kayaks (some with glass bottoms), plus scuba, snorkel and fishing gear. The company also runs fishing charters, dive trips out to the Alderman Islands (dive and full gear $220, trip only $130, snorkelling $95) and PADI courses ($595).

Various operators offer fishing charters and sightseeing trips, including **Waipae Magic** (☎ 07-864 9415; dewy@slingshot.co.nz), **Taranui Charters**

(☎ 07-864 8511; www.tairua.info/taranui), **Pauanui Charters** (☎ 07-864 9262; www.pauanuicharters.co.nz) and **Epic Adventures** (☎ 07-864 8193; www.epicadventures.co.nz). For a much cheaper option, the Tairua–Pauanui ferry (p200) offers two- to three-hour evening fishing trips for $25 (minimum four people).

Sleeping

Tairua Beach Villa Backpackers (☎ 07-864 8345; tairuabackpackers@xtra.co.nz; 200 Main Rd; sites per person $22, dm $25-28, s $50-55, d $60-64, tr/q $90/116; 🖳) Rooms are homey and casual at this estuary-edge hostel in a converted house, and the dorm scores great views. Guests can help themselves to avocados, feijoas, eggs, fishing rods, kayaks, sailboards and bikes, and windsurfing lessons cost a paltry $20.

Pinnacles Backpackers (☎ 07-864 8448; www.pinnaclesbakpak.co.nz; 305 Main Rd; dm $25-28, d $56; 🖳 ☎) A more than life-sized Obelix cartoon welcomes you to this midsized hostel, north of the town centre. A recent renovation has left new carpets and paintwork in its wake and there's a balcony, a free pool table and bikes for hire.

Pacific Harbour Lodge (☎ 07-864 8581; www.pacificharbour.co.nz; 223 Main Rd; chalets $189-259; 🖳 ☎) This 'island-style' resort in the town centre has spacious self-contained chalets, with natural wood and Gauguin decor inside and a South Seas garden outside. Discount packages are usually available.

Dell Cote (☎ 07-864 8142; www.dellcote.com; Rewarewa Valley Rd; s/d $210/240) Nontoxic mud bricks and macrocarpa timber give this place an organic feel, and the swooping gardens add a dose of tranquillity. The loft room is particularly lovely.

Eating & Drinking

Out of the Blue Cafe (☎ 07-864 8987; 227 Main Rd; meals $8-18; ☷ 7am-4pm) This popular meeting place serves decent coffee, breakfast, counter snacks and light meals such as salads and sandwiches.

Old Mill Cafe (☎ 07-864 9390; 1 The Esplanade; mains $8-19; ☷ 8.30am-4.30pm Thu-Sun) There's nothing run-of-the-mill about this old dear. Zooshed up with bright pink feature walls and elegant veranda furniture, it serves delights such as buttermilk-and-blueberry pancakes, *croque monsieurs*, New England chowder and perfectly gooey chocolate tarts.

Punters Bar & Grill (☎ 07-864 9370; Main Rd; mains $10-30; ☷ 11am-late Tue-Sun) Punters is primarily a pub, but it also serves decent snacks (such as crunchy panini slices with dips) and giant burgers with a choice of scotch fillet or fish instead of the usual random meat patty.

Manaia Cafe & Bar (☎ 07-864 9050; 228 Main Rd; brunch $12-17, dinner $18-27; ☯ breakfast, lunch & dinner Tue-Sun) With courtyard seating for lazy summer brunches and a burnished copper bar to prop up later in the night, Manaia is a slick addition to the Tairua strip. The dinner menu features bistro faves with some artful twists.

Getting There & Around

InterCity (☎ 0508 353 947; www.intercity.co.nz) has daily buses to/from Thames ($17, 44 minutes) and Whitianga ($17, 44 minutes). **Tairua Bus Company** (☎ 07-864 7770; www.tairuabus. co.nz; advance fares from $1), in conjunction with **Naked Bus** (www.nakedbus.com), has daily services to Thames (50 minutes) and to Coromandel Town (two hours) via Hot Water Beach (25 minutes), Hahei (30 minutes) and Whitianga (one hour).

Go Kiwi (☎ 0800 446 549; www.go-kiwi.co.nz) door-to-door shuttles head to Whitianga ($24, one hour), Thames ($26, 70 minutes) and Auckland ($66, 2¼ hours) daily, with services to Waihi ($30, 1½ hours) and Tauranga ($48, 2¼ hours) from December to Easter.

Tairua and Pauanui are connected by a passenger **ferry** (☎ 027-497 0316; one way/return $3/5; ☯ Sat & Sun Mar-Nov, daily Dec-Feb), which departs every two hours from 9am to 5pm, running more frequently and for longer hours in summer.

AROUND TAIRUA
Puketui Valley

Located 12km south of Tairua is the turn-off to Puketui Valley and the historic **Broken Hills gold-mine workings** (Map p184), which are 8km from the main road along a mainly gravel road. There are short walks up to the sites of stamper batteries, but the best hike is through the 500m-long Collins Drive mine tunnel. After the tunnel, look out for the short 'lookout' side trail which affords panoramic views. It takes about three hours return; remember to take a torch and a jacket with you.

You can stay at the basic DOC **campsite** (Map p184; adult/child $9/2), located in a pretty spot by the river. This is a wilderness area so take care and be properly prepared. Water from the river should be boiled before drinking.

Slipper Island

The privately owned **Slipper Island** (☎ 07-864 7560; www.slipper.co.nz) has campsites (adult/child $20/15) in South Bay and chalet accommodation (self-contained units $250 to $750) in Home Bay. You'll need to call ahead to arrange transfers by charter boat ($65 per person, minimum four), light plane or helicopter.

OPOUTERE

File this one under best-kept secrets. Maybe it's a local conspiracy to keep at bay the hordes of Aucklanders who seasonally invade Pauanui and Whangamata, as this unspoilt long sandy expanse has been kept very quiet. Apart from a cluster of houses there's nothing for miles around. Swimming can be dangerous, especially near Hikinui Islet, which is close to the beach. On the sand spit is the **Wharekawa Wildlife Refuge**, a breeding ground for the endangered NZ dotterel.

One of the guardians of the secret is **Opoutere Coastal Camping** (☎ 07-865 9152; www.opouterebeach.co.nz; 460 Ohui Rd; sites per adult/child $13/8, cabins $75-145) – its motto is 'remote and untouched, just the way we like it'. Numbers are strictly limited, so book ahead for this summer-only camping ground, offering flat, sheltered tent sites and a few cabins.

our pick Opoutere YHA (☎ 07-865 9072; www.yha. co.nz; 389 Opoutere Rd; sites per person $17, dm $27-30, d $76-106; 💻 🛜) is a wonderful get-away-from-it-all hostel with plenty of birdsong. Kayaks, hot-water bottles, alarm clocks, stilts and hula hoops can all be borrowed. The largest dorm is housed in what was once Opoutere Native School. You can harvest shellfish from the beach but you'll need to bring other food with you.

A peaceful country-style villa with kind hosts and en-suite rooms, **Copsefield B&B** (Map p184; ☎ 07-865 9555; www.copsefield.co.nz; 1055 SH25; r $140-200) is set in attractive, lush gardens with a spa and a riverside swimming hole. There's a guest lounge with complimentary hot beverages, which you can sip on the jasmine-scented decks.

Go Kiwi (☎ 0800 446 549; www.go-kiwi.co.nz) runs shuttles between Opoutere and Whangamata ($11, 10 minutes); call for dates and times.

WHANGAMATA
pop 3600

While Auckland's socially ambitious flock to Pauanui, the city's young and horny head to Whangamata to surf, get stoned and hook up.

It can be a raucous spot over New Year, when the population swells to over 40,000. A true summer holiday town, in the off-season there may as well be tumbleweeds rolling down the main street.

Information

Bartley Internet & Graphics (☎ 07-865 8832; 706 Port Rd) Internet access.

Whangamata i-SITE (☎ 07-865 8340; www.whanga matainfo.co.nz; 616 Port Rd; ☒ 9am-5pm Mon-Fri, 10am-4.30pm, 10am-2pm Sun)

Activities

Besides fishing (game-fishing runs from January to April), snorkelling near Hauturu (Clarke) Island, surfing, kayaking, orienteering and mountain biking, there are excellent walks. The **Wentworth Falls walk** (end of Wentworth Valley Rd) takes two hours one way; it starts 3km south of the town and 4km down a good gravel road. A further 3km south of Wentworth Valley Rd is the turn-off to the **Wharekirauponga walk** (end of Parakiwai Quarry Rd), a sometimes muddy 10km return track (allow four hours) to a mining camp, battery and waterfall that passes unusual hexagonal lava columns and loquacious birdlife.

A local version of Crocodile Dundee, Doug Johansen offers informative one- to 14-day wilderness walks under the name **Kiwi Dundee Adventures** (☎ 07-865 8809; www.kiwidundee. co.nz).

Sleeping

Wentworth Valley campsite (Map p184; ☎ 07-865 7032; adult/child $9/2) More upmarket than most DOC camping grounds, it's accessed from the Wentworth Falls walk, and has toilets, hot showers ($1) and gas barbecues.

Southpacific Accommodation (☎ 07-865 9580; www.thesouthpacific.co.nz; 249 Port Rd; dm $27-29, s $46, d $68-74, units $138-153; ☐ ☜) This hard-to-miss, corner-hogging complex consists of a big barn for backpackers and self-contained motel units. Facilities are clean and modern; bikes and kayaks are available for hire.

Gabry's Place (☎ 07-865 6295; livio@xtra.co.nz; 103 Mark St; unit $80) If you feel like you missed out by not having Italian grandparents, come and stay here. The very sweet hosts will fuss around a bit, make sure you're set up with milk and cookies, and then leave you to enjoy this large, scrupulously clean, self-contained unit.

Marine Reserved (☎ 07-865 9096; www.marine reservedapartments.co.nz; cnr Ocean Rd & Lowe St; units $250; ☜) It's a peculiar name but the other strange thing about this excellent townhouse complex is that up to six of you can stay here in considerable comfort for $250. Each has secure ground floor parking, a full modern kitchen and barbecues on the decks. Try for the three-level apartments fronting Ocean Rd – they're larger, and the extra height ensures sea views.

Eating & Drinking

Craig's Traditional Fish & Chips (☎ 07-865 8717; 701 Port Rd; meals $4-10; ☒ lunch & dinner Wed-Mon) All you could ask for in a chippie, Craig's cooks up pieces of grilled fresh fish and fat, salted chips. The service is friendly, and there's a TV and a stack of trashy mags to speed up the wait.

Lazy Lizard (☎ 07-865 7340; 427 Port Rd; mains $6-14; ☒ 7.30am-3.30pm Tue-Sun) Winning points for bizarre hand-shaped stools, this funky lizard does delicious counter food, cooked breakfasts, bagels and salads. The fair-trade organic coffee is first rate.

Soul Burger (☎ 07-865 8194; 441 Port Rd; burgers $7-11; ☒ dinner Thu-Sun winter, daily summer) It's hard to argue with the 'Eat, Love, Live' motto or the audacious burgers of this hip corner joint. Try a Coromandel Ninja (beef, wasabi, pickled ginger, salad) or a Vegan Vibe.

The monster-sized **New World** (☎ 07-865 0400; 300 Aickin St; ☒ 7.30am-6.30pm) will take care of your grocery needs.

Getting There & Away

Go Kiwi (☎ 0800 446 549; www.go-kiwi.co.nz) has shuttles to Thames ($64, 70 minutes), Auckland ($82, 2¼ hours) and Hamilton ($70, 3½ hours), with services to Waihi ($25, 35 minutes) and Tauranga ($40, 90 minutes) from December to Easter.

WAIHI
pop 4500

Where most towns have hole-in-the-wall ATMs for people to access their riches, Waihi's main street has a giant open-cast gold mine. They've been dragging gold and silver out of Martha Mine, NZ's richest, since 1878. The town formed quickly and blinged itself up with grand buildings and a show-offy avenue of phoenix palms, now magnificently mature.

After closing down in 1952, open-cast mining restarted in 1988. The mine is still productive, but only just – it takes a tonne

COROMANDEL REGION

of rock to yield 3g to 6g of gold. It's expected to run out soon, and when it does, plans are afoot to convert the town's gaping wound into a major tourist attraction. Watch this space.

Information

Post office (21 Rosemont Rd) Has poste restante service.
Waihi visitor centre (☎ 07-863 6715; www.waihi.org. nz; 126 Seddon St; ☑ 9am-5pm) Offers internet access.

Sights & Activities

The main drag, Seddon St, has interesting sculptures, information panels about Waihi's golden past and roundabouts that look like squashed daleks. The *Historic Hauraki Gold Towns* pamphlet (free from the visitor centre) outlines walking tours of both Waihi and Paeroa's town centres.

Opposite the visitor centre, the skeleton of a derelict **Cornish Pumphouse** (1904) is the town's main landmark, atmospherically lit at night. From here the **Pit Rim Walkway** has fascinating views into the 250m-deep Martha Mine. If you want to get down into it, the mining company runs 1½-hour **Waihi Gold Mine Tours** (☎ 07-863 9015; tours adult/child $25/13; ☑ 10am & 12.30pm Mon-Sat).

Goldfields Railway (☎ 07-863 8251; www.waihirail. co.nz; 30 Wrigley St; adult/child return $15/8; ☑ Fri-Mon Apr-Aug, daily Sep-Mar) runs vintage trains to Waikino, leaving Waihi station daily at 10am, 11.45am and 1.45pm; from Waikino it's 11am, 1pm and 2.30pm. The 7km-long scenic journey takes 25 minutes.

The **Waihi Arts Centre & Museum** (☎ 07-863 8386; www.waihimuseum.co.nz; 54 Kenny St; adult/child $5/3; ☑ 11am-3pm Thu-Sun) features displays and models of the region's gold-mining history and a gallery. Prepare to squirm before the collection of miners' chopped-off thumbs preserved in glass jars.

Waterlily Gardens (Map p184; ☎ 07-863 8267; www.waterlily.co.nz; 441 Pukekauri Rd; adult/child $8.50/free; ☑ 10am-4pm Oct-Apr) is 18 acres of ponds, peacocks and pretty things, 7km southwest of Waihi. There's a cafe on-site.

If that sounds a bit too clean and calm, you can hit the slopes on a mutant snowboard/skateboard with **Dirtboard Waihi** (☎ 021-244 1646; www.dirtboard.co.nz; per hr $30) or take an on-/off-road dirt bike tour with **Over The Top Adventures** (☎ 021-205 7266; www.overthetopadventures.co.nz; 1 Surrey St; tours $90-460). The latter also rents mountain bikes (per day $35 to $45), which will be especially handy when the **Hauraki Rail Trail** is completed. At the time of research the gov-

ernment had announced the decision to fast-track this cycle route from Waihi to Paeroa via the Karangahake Gorge, incorporating it into its proposed National Cycleway.

If you'd rather exercise your wallet than your calf muscles, **Artmarket** (☎ 07-863 9010; 65 Seddon St; ☑ 10am-5pm) has a first-rate selection of local arts and crafts.

Sleeping & Eating

Westwind B&B (☎ 07-863 7208; westwindgarden@xtra. co.nz; 58 Adams St; s/d $50/90) Run by a charming couple who are inveterate travellers themselves, this old-fashioned homestay B&B has two comfortable rooms with a shared bathroom. Expect a good chat over breakfast.

Waterlily Gardens (Map p184; ☎ 07-863 8267; www. waterlily.co.nz; 441 Pukekauri Rd; cottages $250) You get the gardens all to yourself after-hours if you're staying in one of the two gorgeous modern cottages. They're beautifully decked out with comfy beds, quality linen, polished concrete floors and interesting art.

Manawa Ridge (Map p184; ☎ 07-863 9400; www. manawaridge.co.nz; 267 Ngatitangata Rd; r $650) The views from this castlelike ecoretreat, perched on a 310m ridge 6km northeast of Waihi, take in the entire Bay of Plenty. Made entirely of recycled railway timber, mud brick and lime-plastered straw walls, the rooms marry earthiness with sheer luxury.

Ti-tree Cafe (☎ 07-863 8668; 14 Haszard St; brunch $5-17, dinner $17-24; ☑ breakfast & lunch daily, dinner Fri & Sat) Housed in a cute little wooden building with punga-shaded outdoor seating, Ti-tree serves fair-trade organic coffee, cooked breakfasts and wood-fired pizza.

Meeting Place Bar & Restaurant (☎ 07-863 7474; 22 Haszard St; mains $16-28; ☑ lunch Mon-Sat, dinner daily) These grand chambers once belonged to the local council. The cosy bar is more appealing than the cavernous dining room, but servings are massive and the slightly retro fare is surprisingly nice.

Getting There & Away

Waihi is a stop for **InterCity** (☎ 0508 353 947; www. intercity.co.nz) buses heading between Auckland ($36, 2¾ hours) and Tauranga ($20, one hour) via Thames ($20, 45 minutes), Paeroa ($20, 19 minutes) and Waihi Beach ($9, 12 minutes).

Naked Bus (☎ 0900 625 33 per min $1.80; www.naked bus.com; advance fares from $1) also has daily buses on the Auckland–Tauranga route, with connections to Paihia, Rotorua and Gisborne.

Go Kiwi (☎ 0800 446 549; www.go-kiwi.co.nz) offers seasonal shuttles from December to Easter between Whitianga ($42, 2¼ hours) and Mt Maunganui ($28, 80 minutes), also stopping in Tairua ($30, 1½ hours) Whangamata ($25, 35 minutes) and Tauranga ($25, one hour).

WAIHI BEACH
pop 1800
While Waihi is interesting for a brief visit, it's Waihi Beach where you'll want to linger. The two places are as dissimilar as surfing is from mining, separated by 11km of farmland. The long sandy beach stretches 9km to Bowentown, on the northern limits of Tauranga Harbour, where you'll find sheltered harbour beaches such as beautiful Anzac Bay. There's a very popular 45-minute walk north through bush to pristine Orokawa Bay, which has no road access.

Sunshine Surf Coaching (☎ 07-863 4857; www.sunshinesurfcoaching.co.nz; lesson $80) takes advantage of Waihi Beach's relatively gentle breaks to offer all-age surf instruction.

Down the south end, **Bowentown Beach Holiday Park** (☎ 07-863 5381; www.bowentown.co.nz; 510 Seaforth Rd; sites per adult/child $19/11, cabins $65-145, units $105-218; 🖳) has nabbed a stunning stretch of sand. It's impressively maintained and even has a barbecue area with a water feature.

Hugging the harbour is **Athenree Hot Springs & Holiday Park** (☎ 07-863 5600; www.athenreehotsprings.co.nz; Athenree Rd; sites per adult/child $22/11, cabins $60, units $140-150; 🖳 🛜 🐾), with two blissful outdoor thermal pools (adult/child $7/4.50, open 10am to 7.30pm). Entry is free if you stay in the smart accommodation.

The massive, resort-style **Waihi Beach Top 10 Holiday Park** (☎ 07-863 5504; www.waihibeach.com; 15 Beach Rd; sites per adult/child $25/16, cabins $75-175, units $160-250; 🖳 🛜 🐾) is pretty damn flash, with a pool, gym, spa, beautiful kitchen and smorgasbord of sleeping options.

Beachfront B&B (☎ 07-863 5393; www.beachfrontbandb.co.nz; 3 Shaw Rd; d/tr $120/160) is true to its name, with absolute beachfront and spectacular sea views. The comfortable downstairs flat has a TV, fridge and direct access to the surf.

Porch (☎ 07-863 1330; 23 Wilson Rd; brunch $12-19, dinner $26-33; ☾ breakfast & lunch daily, dinner Tue-Sat) is the town's coolest chow-down spot, serving sophisticated, substantial mains.

Funky, licensed and right by the beach, **Flatwhite** (☎ 07-863 1346; 21 Shaw Rd; brunch $13-20, dinner $17-30; ☾ breakfast, lunch & dinner; 🛜) has a lively brunch menu and decent pizzas.

KARANGAHAKE GORGE
The road between Waihi and Paeroa, through the bush-lined ramparts of the Karangahake Gorge, is one of the best short drives in the country. There are interesting walks in the area, taking in old Maori trails, historic mining and rail detritus, and spookily dense bush. In Maori legend the area is said to be protected by a *taniwha*, a supernatural creature. The local *iwi* managed to keep this area closed to miners until 1875, aligning themselves with the militant Te Kooti (see the boxed text, p352).

The very worthwhile 4.5km **Karangahake Gorge Historic Walkway** (Map p184) takes 1½ hours (each way) and starts from the car park, 14km west of Waihi. It follows the disused railway line and the Ohinemuri River to Owharoa Falls and Waikino station, where you can pick up the vintage train to Waihi. **Waikino Station Café** (☎ 07-863 8640; SH2; mains $4-16; ☾ 9.30am-3pm daily, dinner Fri) is a perfect lunch stop before heading back.

There are a range of shorter walks and loop tracks leading from the car park; bring a torch as some head through tunnels. A two-hour tramp will bring you to Dickey's Flat, where there's a free DOC **campsite** (Map p184; Dickey's Flat Rd) and a decent swimming hole. River water will need to be boiled for drinking. You'll find DOC information boards about the walks and the area's history at both the station and the main car park.

Across from the car park, **Golden Owl Backpackers** (☎ 07-862 7994; www.goldenowl.co.nz; 3 Moresby St; dm/d $28/60; 🖳 🛜) is a homely, handy tramping base, sleeping only 12. Allow $5 extra for linen in the dorm rooms.

Further up the same road, **Ohinemuri Estate Winery** (Map p184; ☎ 07-862 8874; www.ohinemuri.co.nz; Moresby St; mains $17-28; ☾ 10am-5pm daily Oct-Apr, 10am-5pm Fri-Sun May-Sep) has Latvian-influenced architecture and serves excellent lunches. The portions are large and the prices extremely reasonable. You'd be right if you thought it was an unusual site for growing grapes – the winery imports fruit from other regions. Tastings are $5, refundable with purchase. If you imbibe too much, snaffle the chalet-style hut and revel in the charming atmosphere of this secluded place (double/triple/quad $110/125/140).

Nearby **Talisman Cafe** (☎ 07-862 8306; SH2; meals $5-21; ✆ 9am-4pm) is more distinguished by its magical new-age decor and kitschy crafts than its coffee and food, but there's plenty to sustain hungry hikers.

PAEROA
pop 4000

If you find yourself scratching your head in Paeroa, don't worry too much about it. The whole town is an elaborate Kiwi in-joke. It's the birthplace of Lemon & Paeroa (L&P), an icon of Kiwiana that markets itself as 'world famous in NZ'. The fact that the beloved fizzy drink is now owned by global monster Coca-Cola Amatil and produced in Auckland only serves to make the ubiquitous L&P branding on every shopfront even more darkly ironic.

Still, generations of Kiwi kids have pestered their parents to take this route just to catch a glimpse of the giant L&P bottles.

The small **museum** (☎ 07-862 8486; 37 Belmont Rd; adult/child $2/1; ✆ 10.30am-3pm Mon-Fri) has a grand selection of Royal Albert porcelain and other pioneer and Maori artefacts – look in the drawers. If pretty crockery is your thing, Paeroa is known for its antique stores.

L&P Cafe & Bar (☎ 07-862 7773; SH2; mains $11-19; ✆ breakfast & lunch daily, dinner Wed-Sun) has a truck-stop ambience, but is as good a place as any to find out what all the fuss is about. You can order L&P fish and chips or an L&P brekkie, along with the lemony lolly water itself. The cafe shares the space with the **information centre** (☎ 07-862 8636; www.paeroa. org.nz; ✆ 9am-4pm).

Waikato & the King Country

If the colour green had a homeland this would be it. Verdant fields give way to rolling hills in the countryside around New Zealand's mightiest river, the Waikato. Visitors from southern England might wonder why they bothered leaving home, especially in quaint towns like Cambridge where every effort has been made to replicate the 'mother country'. It's little wonder that Peter Jackson chose the Waikato as the bucolic Shire in his movie adaptation of *Lord of the Rings*.

But this veneer of conspicuous Englishness only partly disguises another reality. Move over hobbits, this is Tainui country. This powerful coalition of related tribes joined with others to elect a king in the 1850s to resist the loss of their land and sovereignty. Although the fertile Waikato was taken from them by war, they retained control of the limestone crags and forests of what became known as the King Country to within a whisper of the 20th century. The back roads along the coast still contain tiny outposts of Maoridom, echoes of an earlier era.

Today's visitors can experience first-hand the area's genteel/free-wheeling dichotomy. Adrenaline junkies will be drawn to the wild surf of Raglan or rough-and-tumble underground pursuits in the extraordinary Waitomo Caves, while others will warm to the more sedate delights of Te Aroha's Edwardian thermal complex or Hamilton's gardens.

It's the Waikato River that symbolises this best – in places idyllic lakes have been created by harnessing it to hydroelectric projects while elsewhere its *mauri* (life force) flows fast and free.

HIGHLIGHTS

- Seeking subterranean thrills in the **Waitomo Caves** (p226)
- Hanging with the bronzed crowd while hanging-ten at **Raglan** (p214)
- Discovering your own bush-framed black-sand beach on the rugged **west coast** (p230)
- Pigging out on Maori culture at Kawhia **Kai Festival** (p224)
- Soaking up 'the love' in the thermal waters of **Te Aroha** (p223)
- Plotting a pub crawl in surprisingly buzzy **Hamilton** (p212)
- Tramping through an inland island paradise at **Maungatautari** (p219)

★ Te Aroha

★ Raglan ★ Hamilton

★ Kawhia ★ Maungatautari Ecological Island

★ Waitomo Caves

West Coast ★

WAIKATO & THE KING COUNTRY

 Telephone code: 07 www.waikatonz.co.nz www.kingcountry.co.nz

WAIKATO & THE KING COUNTRY

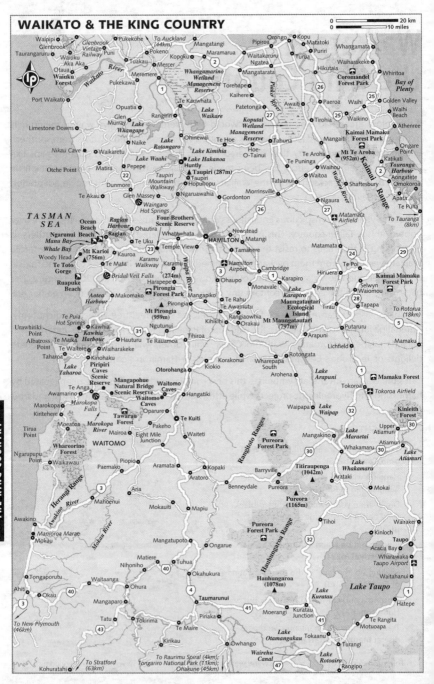

Climate

The southern area around Taumarunui is wetter and colder than the rest of the region, which can suffer summer droughts.

Getting There & Around

Hamilton is the transport hub, with its airport (p213) servicing some international and extensive domestic routes. Buses link the city to everywhere in the North Island. Most inland towns are also well connected on bus routes, but the remote coastal communities (apart from Mokau on SH3) are less well served.

Trains are another option but they are infrequent and surprisingly expensive on short legs. The main trunk-line between Auckland and Wellington stops at Hamilton, Otorohanga, Te Kuiti and Taumarunui.

WAIKATO

History

By the time Europeans started to arrive, this region – stretching as far north as Auckland's Manukau Harbour – had long been the homeland of the Waikato tribes, descended from the Tainui migration (p208). In settling this land they displaced or absorbed tribes from earlier migrations.

Initially European contact was on Maori terms and to the advantage of the local people. Their fertile land, which was already cultivated with kumara and other crops, was well suited to the introduction of new fruits and vegetables. By the 1840s the Waikato economy was booming, with bulk quantities of produce exported to the settlers in Auckland and beyond. Rangiaowhia, near Te Awamutu, became a prosperous farming town – much to the envy of the new arrivals, who coveted the flat fecund Waikato plains.

Relations between the two cultures soured during the 1850s, largely due to the colonists' pressure to purchase Maori land. In response, a confederation of tribes united to elect a king to safeguard their interests, forming what became known as the 'King Movement' (see the boxed text, p209).

In July 1863 Governor Grey sent a huge force to invade the Waikato and exert colonial control. After almost a year of fighting, known as the Waikato War, the Kingites retreated south to what became branded the King

---

WAIKATO & THE KING COUNTRY FACTS

Eat Rotten corn at Kawhia's Kai Festival (p224)

Drink Gut-cleansing soda water in Te Aroha (p223)

Read *Potiki* (1986) by Patricia Grace

Listen to The sacred sounds of Te Awamutu (see the boxed text, p218): Crowded House's 'Mean to Me', Split Enz' 'Kia Kaha', 'Haul Away'

Watch *Black Sheep* (2006) – those Te Kuiti shearers should be very afraid

Swim at Ngarunui Beach near Raglan (p216)

Festival Running of the Sheep, Te Kuiti (p231)

Tackiest tourist attraction The *Big Shearer*, Te Kuiti (p231)

Go green Off-the-grid tepees at Solscape (p216)

Country. Europeans didn't dare to venture there for several decades.

The war resulted in the confiscation of 360,000 hectares of land, much of which was given to colonial soldiers to farm and defend. In 1995 the Waikato tribes received a full Crown apology for the wrongful invasion and confiscation of their lands, as well as a $170 million package, including the return of land that the Crown still held.

NORTH OF HAMILTON

Most people blast along SH1 between Auckland and Hamilton in about 90 minutes, but if you're in the mood to meander, the upper Waikato has some interesting diversions.

Port Waikato

While the name might conjure up images of heavy industry and crusty seadogs, that's far from the reality of this petite village at the mouth of the mighty river. There's little here apart from an old-fashioned collection of baches (holiday homes), a couple of *marae* (meeting house) complexes, a store and a beautiful but treacherous surf beach. Lifeguards are on duty in summer, but only between 10am and 6pm on weekends and school holidays; strong rips render it unsafe for swimming at other times.

Waikatoa Beach Lodge (☎ 09-232 9961; www.sunsetbeach.co.nz; 8 Centreway Rd; dm/s/d from $28/38/64, tw $56-64) spoils visiting beach-bums with smart rooms, decent linen and a welcoming kitchen/lounge area with gas cooking.

MAORI NZ: WAIKATO & THE KING COUNTRY

Despite or perhaps because of its turbulent history (see p207), this area remains one of the strongest pockets of Maori influence in the country. This is the heartland of the Tainui tribes, descended from those who disembarked from the *Tainui waka* (canoe) in Kawhia in the 14th century. Split into four main tribal divisions (Waikato, Hauraki, Ngati Maniapoto and Ngati Raukawa), Tainui are inextricably linked with the Kingitanga (King Movement; opposite), which has its base in Ngaruawahia.

The best opportunities to interact with Maori culture are the Kawhia Kai Festival (p224), and Ngaruawahia's Regatta Day and Koroneihana celebrations (opposite). Interesting *taonga* (treasures) are displayed at museums in Hamilton (opposite) and Te Awamutu (p217). Reminders of the Waikato Land War can be found at Rangiriri (below), Rangiaowhia (p218) and Orakau (p219).

Dozens of *marae* (meeting house) complexes are dotted around the countryside – including Awakino (p232) and Kawhia (p224), where the *Tainui waka* is buried. You won't be able to visit these without permission but you can get decent views from the gates. Some regional tours include an element of Maori culture, including Ruakuri Cave (p227) and Kawhia Harbour Cruises (p224).

To get here, turn off SH1 at Pokeno, 50km south of central Auckland, and head towards Tuakau (which has some decent cafes) until you see the Port Waikato signs. It's a pleasant 35km drive following the ever-widening river with its abundant bird life. Hobbit-hoppers can continue on the coastal road south past Port Waikato for a further 10km, where the limestone bluffs formed Weathertop Hollow – NZ's northernmost *Lord of the Rings* location.

Keep on this road and turn inland on SH22 to reach **Nikau Cave** (☎ 09-233 3199; www.nikaucave.co.nz; 1770 Waikaretu Rd, Waikaretu; adult/child $30/15; ☼ by appointment), where a tour (minimum two people) will take you through tight wet squeezes to glowworms, limestone formations and subterranean streams. There's a cafe here, too.

Rangiriri

As you follow SH1 south you're retracing the route of the colonial army in the spectacular land grab that was the Waikato War. On 20 November 1863, 1500 British troops (some say it was 850 – either way, there was a lot of 'em), backed by gunboats and artillery, attacked the substantial fortifications erected by the Maori king's warriors at Rangiriri. They were repulsed a number of times and lost 49 men, but overnight many of the 500 Maori defenders retreated; the remaining 183 were taken prisoner the next day after the British gained entry to the *pa* (fortified village) by conveniently misunderstanding a flag of truce. It's worth stopping at the **Rangiriri Heritage Centre** (☎ 07-826 3663; www.nzmuseums.

co.nz; 12 Rangiriri Rd; ☼ 8am-4pm) for an interesting short documentary (20 minutes, $2) about the battle, and a thoroughly British cream scone. Across the road the **Maori War & Early Settlers Cemetery** (Rangiriri Rd; admission free; ☼ 24hr) houses the soldiers' graves and a mound covering the mass grave of 36 Maori warriors.

Next to the heritage centre is the historic, elaborately wallpapered **Rangiriri Hotel** (☎ 07-826 3467; Rangiriri St; mains $15-30; ☼ 11am-11pm), a cheery spot for lunch or a beer at sunny outdoor tables.

Ngaruawahia & Around

From Rangiriri the road follows the Waikato River all the way to Hamilton. Along the way is **Huntly** (population 7070), a utilitarian coalmining town with a large power station. The friendly **Huntly i-SITE** (☎ 07-828 6406; SH1; www.huntly.net.nz; ☼ 9am-5pm Mon-Fri, 9am-3pm Sat & Sun) is a good source of information about visiting Taupiri and Ngaruawahia.

The sacred mountain of the Tainui people, **Taupiri** (287m), is a further 8km south on SH1. You'll recognise it by the cemetery on its slopes and the honking of passing car horns – locals saying hi to their loved ones and their mountain as they pass by. In August 2006 tens of thousands gathered here as the much-loved Maori queen, Dame Te Atairangikaahu, was transported upriver by *waka* (canoe) to her final resting place in an unmarked grave among her ancestors at the top of the mountain. Tourists aren't welcome, but those genuinely wishing to pay their respects may enter as long as they follow the correct protocol (no eating, stick to the paths, wash your hands afterwards to remove the *tapu* – see p56).

If you're fit, the **Taupiri Mountain Walkway** (80 minutes return) offers excellent views. It doesn't actually take you on the sacred mountain but treks through part of the **Hakarimata Scenic Reserve**, which has 600-year-old kauri trees. The Huntly i-SITE has maps and information.

A little further south, **Ngaruawahia** (population 4940), 19km north of Hamilton on SH1, is the headquarters of the Maori King movement (see below). The impressive fences of **Turangawaewae Marae** (☎ 07-824 5189; 29 River Rd) maintain the privacy of this important place, but twice a year visitors are welcomed. Ask at the **post office** (☎ 07-824 8661; www.nzpost.co.nz; 3 Jesmond St; ✆ 8am-5pm Mon-Fri, 9am-4pm Sat) for directions. **Regatta Day** is held in mid-March, with *waka* races and all manner of Maori cultural activities. For a week from 15 August the *marae* is open to celebrate **Koroneihana**, the anniversary of the coronation of the current king, Tuheitia. Call ahead to find out about the opening day's flag-raising ceremony and history tours.

HAMILTON
pop 140,700
Landlocked cities in an island nation are never going to have the glamorous appeal of their coastal sisters. Rotorua compensates with boiling mud while Taupo has its lake – but Hamilton and Palmerston North, despite their majestic rivers, are left clutching the short straws.

However, something strange has happened in Hamilton recently. Perhaps it's a sign of the rising fortunes of Waikato farmers that the city's main street has sprouted a sophisticated and vibrant stretch of bars and eateries around Hood and Victoria Sts that – on the weekend at least – leave Auckland's Viaduct Harbour for dead in the boozy fun stakes.

Oddly, the great grey-green greasy Waikato River rolls right through town, but the city's layout ignores its presence almost completely – unless you're driving across a bridge you'll hardly know it's there.

Information
Anglesea Clinic (☎ 07-858 0800; www.anglesea medical.co.nz; cnr Anglesea & Thackeray Sts; ✆ 24hr) For accidents and urgent medical assistance.
Browsers (☎ 07-839 1919; browsers@clear.net.nz; 221 Victoria St; ✆ 9.30am-9.30pm Mon-Fri, 10am-9.30pm Sat & Sun) A jazzy, musty, locally owned secondhand bookshop with a good NZ section, kids' books and fiction.
City Internet (☎ 07-839 0215; 430 Victoria St; ✆ 9am-1am Mon-Thu, 9am-2am Fri & Sat, 9am-midnight Sun)
Department of Conservation (DOC; ☎ 07-858 1000; www.doc.govt.nz; Level 5, 73 Rostrevor St; ✆ 8am-4.30pm Mon-Fri)
Dymocks (☎ 07-957 0440; www.dymocks.co.nz; 49 Bryce St; ✆ 9am-5pm Mon-Sat, 10am-4pm Sun) Specialist books and maps.
Hamilton i-SITE (☎ 07-839 3580; www.visithamilton. co.nz; 5 Garden Pl; ✆ 9am-5.30pm Mon-Fri, 9.30am-3.30pm Sat & Sun)
Post office (36 Bryce St) Currency exchange available.
Waikato Hospital (☎ 07-839 8899; www.waikatodhb. govt.nz; Pembroke St; ✆ 24hr) South of the centre.

Sights
The excellent **Waikato Museum** (☎ 07-838 6606; www.waikatomuseum.co.nz; 1 Grantham St; admission by donation, charge for touring exhibitions; ✆ 10am-4.30pm)

KINGITANGA
The concept of a Maori people is a relatively new one. Until the mid-19th century, NZ was effectively comprised of many independent tribal nations, operating in tandem with the British from 1840.

In 1856, faced with a flood of Brits, the Kingitanga movement formed to unite the tribes to better resist further loss of land and possible cultural annihilation. A gathering of leaders elected Waikato chief Potatau Te Wherowhero as the first Maori king, hoping that his increased *mana* (prestige) could achieve the cohesiveness that the British had under their queen.

Despite the huge losses of the Waikato War (p207) and the eventual opening up of the King Country (p224), the Kingitanga survived – although it has no formal constitutional role. A measure of the strength of the movement was the huge outpouring of grief when Te Arikinui Dame Atairangikaahu, Potatau's great-great-great-granddaughter, died in 2006 after 40 years at the helm. Although it's not a hereditary monarchy (leaders of various tribes vote on a successor), Potatau's line continues to the present day with King Tuheitia Paki.

has five main areas: an art gallery; interactive science galleries; Tainui galleries housing Maori treasures, including the magnificently carved *waka taua* (war canoe) *Te Winika*; a Hamilton history exhibition entitled 'Never a Dull Moment'; and a Waikato River exhibition. The museum also runs a rigorous program of public events.

Stretching over 50 hectares of riverbank southeast of the centre, **Hamilton Gardens** (☎ 07-838 6782; www.hamiltongardens.co.nz; Cobham Dr; admission free; enclosed section ☑ 7.30am-sunset) incorporates a large park, cafe, restaurant and extravagantly themed enclosed gardens. The Paradise Garden Collection has separate Italian Renaissance, Chinese, Japanese, English,

HAMILTON

INFORMATION
Anglesea Clinic	1	C4
Bivouac Outdoor	2	C3
Browsers	3	D1
City Internet	4	C3
DOC	5	B3
Dymocks	6	B3
Hamilton i-SITE	7	C4
Post Office	8	B3

SIGHTS & ACTIVITIES
ArtsPost	9	D1
Cruise Waikato	10	D4
Riff Raff Statue	11	D1
SS Rangiriri	12	D4
Waikato Museum	13	D1

SLEEPING
Anglesea Motel	14	A3
City Centre B&B	15	D5
Eagles Nest Backpackers	16	B2
YHA Hamilton	17	A2
YWCA	18	C5

EATING
Hydro	19	D5
Pak N Save Supermarket	20	A2
Palate	21	D1
River Kitchen	22	C1
Scott's Epicurean	23	D1
Singer HaBARdashery	24	D2

DRINKING
Bank	25	D1
Cook	26	D5
Diggers Bar	27	D2

ENTERTAINMENT
Founders Theatre	28	B3
Shine	29	D1
Skycity Cinemas	30	C3
Victoria Cinema	31	B3

TRANSPORT
Budget	32	B3
Hamilton Transport Centre	33	B3
Rent-a-Dent	34	B3

WAIKATO & THE KING COUNTRY

American and Indian gardens complete with colonnades, pagodas, dovecotes, raked sand and a mini Taj Mahal. Equally interesting is the Productive Garden Collection with its model family-sized sustainable garden, a fragrant herb garden and the precolonisation Maori Te Parapara garden. Look out for the impressive *Nga Uri O Hinetuparimaunga* (Earth Blanket) sculpture at the main roadside gates.

ArtsPost (☎ 07-838 6928; www.artspost.co.nz; 120 Victoria St; admission free; ☺ 10am-4.30pm), near the museum, is a contemporary gallery and gift shop housed in the grand former post office. It focuses on the best of local art: paintings, glass, prints, textiles and photography. Check out the awesome floorboards.

Hamilton Zoo (☎ 07-838 6720; www.hamiltonzoo. co.nz; 183 Brymer Rd; admission adult/child/family $14/7/42; ☺ 9am-5pm, last entry 3.30pm) houses 500-plus species and takes part in conservation breeding projects. The rotating 'Meet the Keeper' program provides interesting information from the critters' caregivers…and it has NZ's only tapir! The zoo is 8km from the city centre: take Norton Rd off Tristram St, then SH23 west towards Raglan, turn right at Newcastle Rd and then left onto Brymer Rd.

One of Hamilton's more unusual public artworks is a life-size statue of *Rocky Horror Picture Show* writer Richard O'Brien in the guise of **Riff Raff** (Victoria St), the time-warping alien from the planet Transsexual. It looks over a small park on the site of the former Embassy Theatre where O'Brien worked as a hairdresser. The Embassy's 'late-night double-feature picture shows' found a place in the ultimate cult classic – although it's hard to imagine 1960s Hamilton inspired the tale of bisexual alien decadence.

Activities

The strong-flowing Waikato River is well worth investigating. **Cruise Waikato** (☎ 0508 426 458; www.cruise-waikato.co.nz; Memorial Park Jetty; cruises from adult/child $20/10) runs a range of cruises, focussed variously on sightseeing, history or your belly (coffee and muffins, sausage sizzles or picnics).

Another river option is the **City Bridges River Tour** (☎ 07-847 5565; www.canoeandkayak.co.nz; 2hr trip adult/child $50/30), a guided kayak ride through the city. **Wiseway Canoe Adventures** (☎ 021 988 335; www.wisewayadventures.com; 2hr trip adult/child $50/20) runs a similar trip, and offers freedom hire.

Bush-covered riverside walkways run along both sides of the Waikato River and provide the city's green belt. Jogging paths continue to the boardwalk circling **Lake Rotoroa**, west of the centre. **Memorial Park** is closer to town, and has the remains of **SS Rangiriri** – an iron-clad, steam-powered gunboat from the Waikato War – embedded in the riverbank (under restoration at the time of research).

Waterworld (☎ 07-958 5860; www.hamiltonpools. co.nz; Garnett Ave; admission adult/child $5/2.50; ☺ 6am-9pm Mon-Fri, 7am-9pm Sat, 9am-9pm Sun) has indoor and outdoor pools, water slides, a gym, spa and crèche.

Kiwi Balloon Company (☎ 07-843 8538, 021 912 679; www.kiwiballooncompany.co.nz; per person $290) provides the best vehicle for gazing down on the lush countryside. The experience takes about four hours and includes a champagne breakfast and an hour's flying time.

Festivals & Events

In April rev-heads and airheads flock to town for the **Hamilton 400** (www.v8supercar.co.nz) V8 supercar street race, and **Balloons over Waikato** (www.balloonsoverwaikato.co.nz), a hot-air balloon festival.

Sleeping

The road into town from Auckland (Ulster St) is lined with dozens of unremarkable, traffic-noisy midrange motels, adequate enough for short stays.

YWCA (☎ 07-838 2219; www.ywcahamilton.org.nz; cnr Pembroke & Clarence Sts; s/d $25/50) You don't have to be young or female to stay at this four-storey apartment block of a hostel. The rooms are cell-like but they're spotless, cheap and private. Each floor has shared bathroom facilities, a kitchen and TV lounge.

Eagles Nest Backpackers (☎ 07-838 2704; www. eaglesbackpackers.co.nz; 937 Victoria St; dm/s/d $25/50/60; ☐) This 1st-floor eyrie has windowless internal rooms (with skylights) but they're clean and mercifully quiet given the hostel's busy position. The communal lounge is a tad 'nursing-home chic', but there's a decent terrace looking over the street. 'No luxuries', says the lady at the desk.

J's Backpackers (☎ 07-856 8934; www.jsbackpackers .co.nz; 8 Grey St; dm/s/d/tr $28/60/66/82; ☐ ☎) A homely hostel occupying a characterful house near Hamilton Gardens, friendly J's offers good security, a smallish kitchen and bright, tidy rooms with new mattresses. There's also a barbecue out the back.

YHA Hamilton (☎ 07-957 1848; www.yha.co.nz; 140 Ulster St; dm/s $29/49, d $59-69; ☐ ☎) Freshly painted, super-clean, quality linen, Sky TV, funky lounge, sauna, laundry, supermarket across the street…what's the catch? Well, the hostel occupies a former 'micro hotel', so the rooms and kitchen are tiny. If you're over 6ft tall you might struggle.

Hamilton City Holiday Park (☎ 07-855 8255; www. hamiltoncityholidaypark.co.nz; 14 Ruakura Rd; unpowered/ powered sites $30/32, cabins $40-55, tourist flats $70-95; ☐ ☎) Good simple cabins and well-maintained communal facilities are the rule at this shady park, 2km east of town.

City Centre B&B (☎ 07-838 1671; www.citycentrebnb. co.nz; 3 Anglesea St; s/d/tr $80/99/130; ☐ ☒) At the quiet riverside end of a central city street (five-minutes walk to the Victoria/Hood St action), this sparkling self-contained apartment opens on to a swimming pool. Self-catering breakfast provided.

Anglesea Motel (☎ 0800 4264 5732, 07834 0010; www.angleseamotel.co.nz; 36 Liverpool St; d/2-bedroom units/3-bedroom units from $135/260/305; ☎ ☒) A far preferable option to anything on Ulster St's 'motel row', the Anglesea has plenty of space, friendly managers, free wi-fi, pool and squash and tennis courts, and not un-stylish decor. Hard to beat.

Eating

River Kitchen (☎ 07-839 2906; 237 Victoria St; mains $7-16; ☺ 7am-4pm Mon-Fri, 8am-4pm Sat & Sun) Heralded as Waikato's 'Best New Cafe' by *Cafe* magazine, hip River Kitchen does things with simple style: cakes, gourmet breakfasts and fresh seasonal lunches (angle for a slice of the Spanish duck pie), and a barista who knows his beans.

Hydro (☎ 07-859 0020; 33 Jellicoe Dr; mains $8-19; ☺ 9am-3pm Mon & Tue, 8am-3.30pm Wed-Fri, 8am-4pm Sat & Sun; ☎ Ⓥ) On the east side of the river (you can walk here along the water's edge), Hydro has converted an old block of neighbourhood shops into a fun cafe with tables spilling onto the pavement. Great for brunch and light meals with novel taste combinations.

our pick Singer HaBARdashery (☎ 07-839 1537; 15 Hood St; brunch $11-19, tapas $9-19; ☺ lunch & dinner) A classy operator on the Hood St strip, Singer is a moody tapas and wine bar occupying the oldest stone building in Hamilton – a former haberdashery. Expect a dizzying selection of wines and beers, great coffee, satisfying brunches and zingy tapas (try the 'Needle': eye fillet, mushroom, scallop, chorizo, and haloumi skewered on a knitting needle).

Scott's Epicurean (☎ 07-839 6680; 181 Victoria St; mains $11-20; ☺ 7am-4pm Mon-Fri, 8.30am-4pm Sat & Sun) This gorgeous joint features swanky leather banquettes, pressed-tin ceilings, great coffee and an interesting and affordable menu: try the sweet orange breakfast couscous or the ever-popular *spaghetti aglio e olio*. Service is friendly, it's fully licensed, and a charming outdoor area beckons in the warmer months.

Palate (☎ 07-834 2921; 170 Victoria St; mains $25-33; ☺ dinner Tue-Sat) Given this restaurant's deserved status as the best in the central North Island, it's surprisingly reasonably priced. Chef/owner Mat McLean delivers an innovative mod-NZ menu and free tasters between courses.

Self-caterers can swing into **Pak N Save** (☎ 07-839 7870; Mill St; ☺ 8am-10pm).

Drinking

The blocks around Victoria and Hood Sts offer a decent bar hop, with weekend live music and DJs. See also Singer HaBARdashery (left).

Diggers Bar (☎ 07-834 2228; 17b Hood St; ☺ 3pm-late Tue-Sun) This funky good-time bar has a wealth of liquid bread on tap and nightly live music in a huge room out the back. Wednesday night's $25 'pizza, fries and two drinks' is a damn good deal.

Cook (☎ 07-856 6088; 7 Cook St; ☺ 9am-late Mon-Fri, 8.30am-late Sat & Sun) Rambling through a noble, burgundy-coloured timber hall (1874), this buzzy cafe-bar dishes up good pub grub (mains $13 to $24), plus live music, poker, comedy and quiz nights.

Bank (☎ 07-839 4740; cnr Victoria & Hood Sts; ☺ 11am-midnight Sun-Thu, to 3am Fri & Sat) Inside this snappily renovated 1878 heritage building are plenty of beers on tap, a good wine selection and lots of screens to catch the big games.

See also Singer HaBARdashery (left) and Shine (below).

Entertainment

Shine (☎ 07-839 3173; www.shinenightclub.co.nz; 161 Victoria St; ☺ 10pm-3am Sat & Sun) It's a measure of Hamilton's increasing sophistication that its main gay-and-lesbian club is now visible to

Victoria St's passing parade. There's a dance floor at the back and an intimate beer garden in front.

Victoria Cinema (☎ 07-838 3036; www.victoriacinema. co.nz; 690 Victoria St; tickets adult/child $15.50/10; ☽ 5pm-late) Watch art-house films while sipping on alcoholic beverages.

Skycity Cinemas (☎ 07-835 0088; www.skycity cinemas.co.nz; Level 2, Centreplace Mall, cnr Ward & Anglesea Sts; tickets adult/child $15/9; ☽ 10am-11pm) A seven-screen mainstream multiplex. Adults pay $10 on Tuesdays.

For live theatre and concerts (anything from Bee Gees tributes to the New Zealand Symphony Orchestra), try **Founders Theatre** (☎ 07-838 6600; www.hamiltontheatres.co.nz; 221 Tristram St; ☽ box office 9am-5pm Mon-Fri).

Getting There & Away
AIR
Air New Zealand (☎ 0800 737 000; www.airnew zealand.co.nz) has regular direct flights from **Hamilton Airport** (☎ 07-848 9027; www.hamilton airport.co.nz; Airport Rd) to Auckland, Christchurch, Gisborne, Napier, New Plymouth, Palmerston North, Rotorua, Tauranga, Wellington and Whakatane.

Internationally, **Pacific Blue** (☎ 0800 670 000; www.pacificblue.com.au) flies from Hamilton to Sydney and Brisbane.

Sunair Aviation Ltd (☎ 07-575 7799; www.sunair. co.nz) offers direct flights to Gisborne, Napier, New Plymouth, Palmerston North and Whakatane.

BUS
All buses arrive and depart from the **Hamilton Transport Centre** (☎ 07-834 3457; cnr Anglesea & Bryce Sts).

Environment Waikato's **Busit!** (☎ 0800 4287 5463; www.busit.co.nz) has numerous services throughout the region, including Ngaruawahia ($3.70, 25 minutes), Cambridge ($6, 40 minutes), Te Awamutu ($6, 30 minutes) and Raglan ($7.30, one hour).

Dalroy Express (☎ 0508 465 622, 06-759 0197; www. dalroytours.co.nz) operates a daily service between Auckland ($22, two hours) and New Plymouth ($40, four hours), stopping at most towns, including Te Kuiti ($18, 1¾ hours) and Te Awamutu ($12, 20 minutes).

Raglan Shuttle Co (☎ 0800 8873 2 7873, 0212 612 563; www.solscape.co.nz/shuttle.html) links Hamilton with Raglan (one-way $60). Auckland connections are also available.

InterCity (☎ 09-583 5780; www.intercity.co.nz) services numerous destinations including:

Destination	Price	Duration	Frequency
Auckland	$21	2hr	10 daily
Cambridge	$19	25min	5 daily
Matamata	$25	1hr	2 daily
Ngaruawahia	$18	20min	10 daily
Rotorua	$34	1½hr	6 daily
Te Aroha	$10	1hr	2 daily
Te Awamutu	$17	25min	3 daily
Wellington	$75	9hr	4 daily

Naked Bus (☎ 0900 625 33; www.nakedbus.com) services run to the following destinations (among many others). Consider booking in advance for big savings.

Destination	Price	Duration	Frequency
Auckland	$21	2¼hr	3-5 daily
Cambridge	$14	30min	3-4 daily
Matamata	$15	1hr	1 daily
Ngaruawahia	$28	30min	3-5 daily
Rotorua	$24	2hr	2-3 daily
Wellington	$49	10hr	1-3 daily

TRAIN
Hamilton is on the **Overlander** (☎ 0800 872 467; www.tranzscenic.co.nz; daily Oct-Apr, Fri-Sun May-Sep) route between Auckland ($53, 2½ hours) and Wellington ($107, 9½ hours) via Otorohanga ($53, 45 minutes). Trains stop at Hamilton's **Frankton train station** (Queens Ave), 1km west of the city centre; there are no ticket sales here.

Getting Around
TO/FROM THE AIRPORT
Hamilton Airport is 12km south of the city. International departure tax is $25 for those 12 years and over; $10 for kids. The **Super Shuttle** (☎ 0800 748 885, 07-843 7778; www.supershuttle.co.nz; one-way $21) offers a door-to-door service into the city. A taxi costs around $40.

BUS
Hamilton's **Busit!** (☎ 0800 4287 5463; www.busit. co.nz; tickets adult/child $2.90/1.30) network services the city-centre and suburbs daily from around 7am to 7.30pm (later on Friday). All buses pass through Hamilton Transport Centre. Busit! also runs a free **CBD shuttle** (☽ 7am-6pm Mon-Fri, 9am-1pm Sat), looping around Victoria, Liverpool, Anglesea and Bridge Sts every 10 minutes.

WAIKATO & THE KING COUNTRY

CAR
Budget (☎ 07-838 3585; www.budget.co.nz; 4 Vialou St; ⏰ 7.30am-5.30pm Mon-Fri, 9am-noon Sat & Sun)
Rent-a-Dent (☎ 07-839 1049; www.rentadent.co.nz; 383 Anglesea St; ⏰ 7.30am-5pm Mon-Fri, 8am-noon Sat)

TAXI
Hamilton Taxis (☎ 07-8477 477)
Red Cabs (☎ 07-839 0500)

RAGLAN
pop 2700

Laid-back Raglan may well be NZ's perfect surfing town. It's small enough to have escaped mass development – perhaps due to a mainstream Kiwi preference for the safer white-sand east-coast beaches – yet it's big enough for a bit of bustle. There are several good eateries and a bar that attracts big-name bands in summer.

The nearby surf spots – Indicators, Whale Bay and Manu Bay – are internationally famous for their point breaks, attracting surfers from around the world. Bruce Brown's classic 1964 wave-chasing film *The Endless Summer* features Manu Bay. Closer to town, the harbour is excellent for kayaking, fishing and swimming. This all serves to attract fit guys and gals from all over the planet; Raglan may also be NZ's best-looking town.

Have a look online at www.raglan.net.nz.

Information
Post office (39 Bow St)
United Video (☎ 07-825 0008; 9a Bow St; ⏰ 10am-9pm) Also has internet access.
Visitor Information Centre (☎ 07-825 0556; www.raglan.org.nz; 2 Wainui Rd; ⏰ 9.30am-5pm Mon-Fri, 10am-5pm Sat, 10am-4pm Sun) DOC brochures plus information about local accommodation and activities. Reduced hours in winter.
West Coast Health Centre (☎ 07-825 0114; 12 Wallis St; ⏰ 9am-5pm Mon-Fri) General medical assistance.

Sights & Activities
A community hub, the **Old School Arts Centre** (☎ 07-825 0023; www.raglanartscentre.co.nz; Stewart St; admission free; ⏰ 10am-2pm Mon & Wed, exhibitions vary) has changing exhibitions and workshops, including weaving, carving, yoga and storytelling. The hippie-organic **Raglan Creative Market** (☎ 07-825 8862; www.raglanmarket.com; ⏰ 9am-2pm 2nd Sun of the month) happens out the front once a month.

The small, musty **Raglan & District Museum** (☎ 07-825 8416; 13 Wainui Rd; admission by donation; ⏰ 1-3.30pm Sat & Sun) explores the stories of local Maori and Pakeha pioneers through artefacts, photos and newspapers.

Te Kopua Recreational Reserve, over the footbridge by the holiday park, is a safe, calm swimming beach popular with families.

The instructors at **Raglan Surf School** (☎ 07-825 7873; www.raglansurfingschool.co.nz; 5b Whaanga Rd, Whale Bay; 3hr lesson incl transport $89) pride themselves on getting 95% of first-timers standing during their first lesson. Experienced wave hounds can rent surfboards (from $15 per hour), boogie boards ($5 per hour) and wet suits ($5 per hour). They're based at Karioi Lodge (p216) in Whale Bay. **Solscape** (☎ 07-825 8268; www.solscape.co.nz; 611 Wainui Rd, Manu Bay; lessons $85) offers 2½-hour lessons, as well as board and wetsuit hire (per half-day $40).

If you'd rather spend more time above the water than in it, **Raglan Kite Surf School** (☎ 07-825 8702, 0212 524 117; lessons per hr $60) runs one-on-one lessons wherever the wind's blowing.

Raglan Harbour is great for kayaking. The gentle Opotoru River is good for learning basic skills, but before too long you'll be wanting to investigate the nooks and crannies of the pancake rocks on the harbour's north edge. Raglan Backpackers (below) has single/double ocean kayaks for hire (per half-day $30/40). Alternatively, see if **Raglan Kayak** (☎ 07-825 8862; www.raglaneco.co.nz) has recovered from the fire that destroyed its premises in April 2010.

Sleeping
It pays to book Raglan accommodation ahead, especially in peak season. See p216 for options at the neighbouring surf beaches.

Raglan Kopua Holiday Park (☎ 07-825 8283; www.raglanholidaypark.co.nz; Marine Pde; sites per adult/child $15/7.50, dm/cabins/units from $23/65/85; 🖥 🔊) A nicely maintained facility on the spit of land across the inlet from town (there's a footbridge, or drive the long way around). Not much shade but there's beach swimming and plenty of room to run amuck.

ourpick **Raglan Backpackers** (☎ 07-825 0515; www.raglanbackpackers.co.nz; 6 Wi Neera St; dm/s $25/52, d $66-76; 🖥) This welcoming, purpose-built hostel has a laid-back holiday-house vibe. It's right on the water's edge, with sea views from some rooms and the rest arranged around a garden courtyard. For small groups there's a

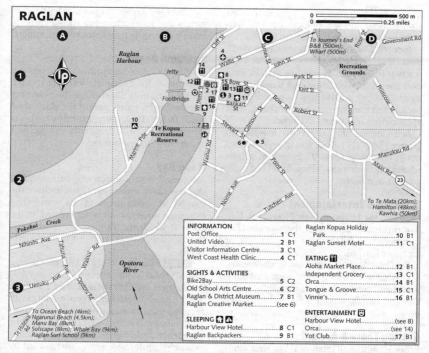

RAGLAN

INFORMATION	
Post Office	1 C1
United Video	2 B1
Visitor Information Centre	3 C1
West Coast Health Clinic	4 C1

SIGHTS & ACTIVITIES	
Bike2Bay	5 C2
Old School Arts Centre	6 C2
Raglan & District Museum	7 B1
Raglan Creative Market	(see 6)

SLEEPING	
Harbour View Hotel	8 C1
Raglan Backpackers	9 B1

Raglan Kopua Holiday Park	10 B1
Raglan Sunset Motel	11 C1

EATING	
Aloha Market Place	12 B1
Independent Grocery	13 C1
Orca	14 B1
Tongue & Groove	15 B1
Vinnie's	16 B1

ENTERTAINMENT	
Harbour View Hotel	(see 8)
Orca	(see 14)
Yot Club	17 B1

separate self-contained wing sleeping up to eight. There are kayaks for hire (from $15), or if that's too strenuous you can take a yoga class, swan about in a hammock, strum a guitar or drip in the sauna. Can we stay another night?

Harbour View Hotel (☎ 07-825 8010; harbourview hotel@paradise.net.nz; 14 Bow St; s/d $60/80, f $95-110) If you think that going to bed before the party finishes is for the faint and feeble, then this two-storey 100-year-old pub (licensed until late), with sunny verandas and kauri trimmings, is for you. The rooms are clean although the beds are saggy and you'll be sharing bathrooms.

Raglan Sunset Motel (☎ 07-825 0500; www.raglan sunsetmotel.co.nz; 7 Bankart St; d $140; ☎) A block or so back from the action, this two-storey motel with faux shutters randomly adhered to the facade is barely seven years old. As you'd expect, everything's in good nick. The owners also have self-contained apartments (doubles from $150) and beach houses (four people from $250) available around town.

Journey's End B&B (☎ 07-825 6727; www.raglan ac commodation.co.nz; 49 Lily St; s/d $90/140, exclusive use per 2/4 people $180/240) No, it's not Mt Doom; quite the opposite, in fact. These two attractive en-suite rooms share a central modern lounge with a kitchenette and a deck overlooking the wharf and harbour.

Eating

Aloha Market Place (☎ 07-825 7440; 5 Bow St; sushi $1.50-2, mains $7.50-12; ☎ 11am-5pm) It's takeaway without the grease, Japanese surfer-style. Grab some delicious rolled-to-order sushi, some udon noodles or a *donburi* rice bowl and head for the harbour. Reduced hours in winter.

Vinnie's (☎ 07-825 7273; 7 Wainui Rd; meals $8-23; ☎ 10am-late Tue-Sun; ☎) Run by a long-lost New Yorker, Vinnie's looks like a truck stop from the outside, but inside it's all Hawaiian prints, reggae tunes and surf movies flickering on the walls. On the food front it's burgers, salads, wraps, cheese-steaks, pizzas and its 'famous' meatloaf. Free wi-fi is available, too.

Tongue & Groove (☎ 07-825 0027; 19 Bow St; mains $9-18; ☎ 8.30am-3pm Mon-Thu, 8.30am-8.30pm Fri & Sat, 8.30am-8pm Sun; Ⓥ) There are plenty of street-side seats and retro couches for wine sipping

WAIKATO & THE KING COUNTRY

in this funky corner cafe, with surf mags strewn about and lots of local art. The delicious vegetarian roti is a bargain ($14).

Orca (☎ 07-825 6543; 2 Wallis St; breakfast $11-17, mains $17-32; ☺ 9am-late Mon-Fri, 8am-late Sat & Sun) A day started at Orca's window seat, looking over the water, with some eggs Benedict and a superb coffee is a day well launched. Come back in the evening for seafood paella, wine appreciation nights and live music.

Self-caterers should try the **Independent Grocery** (☎ 07-825 6533; 37 Bow St; ☺ 9am-5.30pm Mon-Fri, 10am-5pm Sat & Sun; Ⓥ) for organics, bulk wholefood, fresh fruit and veg, bread and really good peanut butter.

Drinking & Entertainment

Orca and the Harbour View Hotel both host live music, especially on the weekends in summer when the Harbour View attracts the cream of Kiwi rock.

Yot Club (☎ 07-825 8702; 9 Bow St; admission free-$25; ☺ 9pm-late) This raucous, nocturnal bar is where everyone goes to dance, with visiting DJs and bands, a pool table and imported beers.

Getting There & Around

From Hamilton, Raglan is 48km west along SH23. Unsealed back roads connect Raglan to Kawhia, 50km south; they're slow, winding and prone to rockslides, but scenic and certainly off the beaten track. Head back towards Hamilton for 7km and take the Te Mata/Kawhia turn-off and follow the signs; allow at least an hour.

Environment Waikato's **Busit!** (☎ 0800 4287 5463; www.busit.co.nz; adult/child $7.30/3.70) heads between Hamilton and Raglan (one hour) three times daily on weekdays and twice daily on weekends.

Raglan Shuttle Co (☎ 0800 8873 2 7873, 0212 612 563; www.solscape.co.nz/shuttle.html) links Raglan with Hamilton (one-way $60) and Auckland ($100).

Bike2Bay (☎ 07-825 0309; www.bike2bay.com; 24b Stewart St; hire per hr/half-/full day $8/22/33; ☺ 9.30am-5pm) has mountain bikes for hire, and does repairs.

If you need a cab call **Raglan Taxi** (☎ 07-825 0506).

SOUTH OF RAGLAN
Ocean Beach

Just 4km southwest of Raglan, down Riria Kereopa Memorial Dr, this beach at the mouth of the harbour is popular with windsurfers and kite surfers, but strong currents make it extremely treacherous for swimmers.

Ngarunui Beach

Less than a kilometre further south, this is a great beach for grommets learning to surf. On the clifftop is the club for the volunteer lifeguards who patrol part of the black-sand beach from late October until April. This is the only beach with lifeguards and the best ocean beach for swimming.

Manu Bay

Another 2.5km journey will bring you to this legendary surfing spot, said to have the longest left-hand break in the world. The elongated uniform waves are created by the angle at which the Tasman Sea swell meets the coastline (it works best in a southwesterly swell).

our pick **Solscape** (☎ 07-825 8268; www.solscape.co.nz; 611 Wainui Rd; sites per person $15, cabooses dm/d $25/60, tepees s/d/q $50/68/136, cottages d $110-180; 🖳 📶) has backpacker accommodation in recycled train carriages with a homely communal lounge/kitchen. The ultimate greenie experience could well be chilling out in a surprisingly comfortable tepee, surrounded by native bush, knowing that you're completely 'off the grid' – while not sacrificing hot showers (solar) and decent toilets (composting). Self-contained sea-view cottages, surf lessons (p214) and massage therapy ($65 per hour) complete the bewildering array of services.

Whale Bay

This renowned surfing spot is a kilometre further west from Manu Bay and is usually less crowded, but from the bottom of Calvert St you do have to clamber 600m over the rocks to get here.

Deep in native bush, **Karioi Lodge** (☎ 07-825 7873; www.karioilodge.co.nz; 5b Whaanga Rd; dm/d $27/69; 🖳) offers a sauna, a flying fox, mountain bikes, bush and beach walks, sustainable gardening, tree planting and the Raglan Surf School (p214). There are no en suites but the rooms are clean and cosy. These friendly folks also run **Sleeping Lady Lodging** (☎ 07-825 7873; www.sleepinglady.co.nz; 5b Whaanga Rd; lodges $125-240), a collection of luxury self-contained lodges nearby. They range from the Sweet As studio apartment to the Lava Lounge, which has a private spa, ocean views and can sleep up to 12.

Indicators Beach House (☎ 07-825 7889; www.indicators .co.nz; Whaanga Rd, d $150-220, extra person $50; ▣) is a two-level affair, bookable as one or as two separate self-contained units. Sleeping up to 12, it's roomy and timber-lined, with a huge deck (those views!) and every modern need met. Kids under 12 stay free. You'll want to move in!

Mt Karioi

In legend, **Mt Karioi** (756m), the Sleeping Lady (check out that profile), is the sister to Mt Pirongia (right). At its base the **Te Toto Gorge** is a steep cleft in the mountainside. Starting from the Te Toto Gorge car park south of Whale Bay, a strenuous but scenic track goes up the western slope. It takes 2½ hours to reach a lookout point, followed by an easier hour up to the summit. From the east side, the Wairake Track is a steeper 2½-hour climb to the summit, where it meets the Te Toto Track.

Ruapuke Beach

Whale Bay marks the end of the sealed road, but a gravel road continues to **Ruapuke Beach**, 28km from Raglan, which is dangerous for swimmers but popular with surf-casting fisherfolk. **Ruapuke Beach Motor Camp** (☎ 07-825 6800; unpowered/powered sites $20/24, cabins from $35) is near the beach and has an end-of-the-world feel. The gravel road continues on round Mt Karioi and rejoins the inland road at Te Mata.

Bridal Veil Falls

Just past Te Mata (a short drive south of the main Raglan–Hamilton road) is the turn-off to the 55m Bridal Veil Falls, 4km from the main road. From the car park, it's an easy 10-minute walk through mossy native bush to the top of the falls. It's a magical place, the effect compounded by the dancing rainbows swirling around the khaki-coloured pool far below. A further 10-minute walk leads down to the bottom. Make sure you lock your car, as theft is a problem here.

Back in Te Mata, **Magic Mountain Horse Treks** (☎ 07-825 6892; www.magicmountain.co.nz; 334 Houtchen Rd; rides ½hr $40/65) runs horse treks around the hills, plus a ride to Bridal Veil Falls ($80).

Four Brothers Scenic Reserve

Halfway between Hamilton and Raglan on SH23, the **Karamu Walkway** wanders through this reserve. A 15-minute hike up a gully covered in native bush leads to a hilltop where cows and sheep enjoy panoramic views.

Pirongia Forest Park

The main attraction of this 17,000-hectare park is **Mt Pirongia** (www.mtpirongia.org.nz), its 959m summit clearly visible from much of the Waikato. The mountain is usually climbed from Corcoran Rd (three to five hours, one-way). Interestingly, NZ's tallest known kahikatea tree (66.5m) grows on the mountainside. There's a six-bunk DOC hut near the summit if you need to spend the night. Maps and information are available from DOC in Hamilton (p209).

TE AWAMUTU
pop 9800

Deep into dairy-farming country, Te Awamutu (which means 'The River Cut Short'; the Waikato beyond this point was unsuitable for large canoes) is a real working town with real working people living in it – agrarian integrity by the bucketload! (a sign on the pub door says 'Please Remove Gumboots'). With a blossom-treed main street and a good museum, 'TA' makes a decent overnighter (Finn fans might need longer – see the boxed text, p218).

Information

The **Te Awamutu i-SITE** (☎ 07-871 3259; www.teawa mutuinfo.com; 1 Gorst Ave; ☺ 9am-4.30pm Mon-Fri, 10am-4pm Sat & Sun) has plenty of local information.

Sights

Te Awamutu Museum (☎ 07-872 0085; www.tamuseum. org.nz; 135 Roche St; admission by donation; ☺ 10am-4pm Mon-Fri, 10am-1pm Sat, 1-4pm Sun), 'where history never repeats', has a *True Colours*–painted shrine to local heroes Tim and Neil Finn. There are gold records, original lyrics and Finn memorabilia and oddities such as Neil's form-two exercise book. There's also a fine collection of Maori *taonga* (treasures), including the revered 'Uenuku', and an excellent display on the Waikato War. A great little museum.

The **Rose Garden** (cnr Gorst Ave & Arawata St; admission free; ☺ 24hr) is next to the i-SITE and has 2000 bushes and 51 varieties with fabulously fruity names like Big Daddy, Disco Dancer, Lady Gay and Sexy Rexy. The roses usually bloom from November to April.

Sleeping

Rosetown Motel (☎ 0800 767 386, 07-871 5779; www.rose townmotel.co.nz; 844 Kihikihi Rd; d $99-110, f $155; 🛜 ▣)

The older-style units at Rosetown (plenty of teak veneer and yellow faux-marble) have kitchens, Sky TV and share a spa, making them a solid choice if you're hankering for straight-up small-town sleeps.

Cloverdale House (☎ 07-872 1702; www.cloverdale house.co.nz; 141 Long Rd; d/q $140/200) Indulge your farmer fantasies at this smart new place in the dairy heartland, 8km east of Cambridge Rd. Two double rooms with en suites share a common lounge and kitchen (breakfast ingredients provided).

Eating & Drinking

Indian Aroma (☎ 07-871 5555; 23 Arawata St; mains $13-17; ☽ lunch Mon-Fri, dinner daily; ⓥ) Brightening up the town with a saffron-yellow glow, this attractive restaurant with orderly glass-topped tables serves all the fragrant favourites.

Redoubt Bar & Eatery (☎ 07-871 4768; cnr Rewi & Alexandra Sts; mains $16-32; ☽ 11am-late) A relaxed little place to eat or drink, with cheap but potent cocktails, old photos on the walls and a decent menu stretching from pasta to curry. Try the chicken bagel.

Entertainment

Regent 3 Cinema (☎ 07-871 6678; www.regent3.itgo. com; Alexandra St; tickets adult/child $15/13; ☽ varies) Built in 1932, this art-deco cinema has five screens and fabulous movie memorabilia in the foyer.

The Redoubt Bar & Eatery (above) has comedy every second Wednesday and live music on Friday nights.

Getting There & Away

Te Awamutu is on SH3, halfway between Hamilton and Otorohanga (29km either way). The regional bus service **Busit!** (☎ 0800 4287 5463; www.busit.co.nz) is the cheapest option for Hamilton (adult/child $6/4, 30 minutes, five daily).

Three daily **InterCity** (☎ 09-583 5780; www.inter city.co.nz) services connect Te Awamutu with Auckland ($43, 2½ hours), Hamilton ($21, 40 minutes) and Otorohanga ($21, 25 minutes).

The **Dalroy Express** (☎ 0508 465 622; www.dalroy tours.co.nz) bus runs daily between Auckland ($28, 2½ hours) and New Plymouth ($39, 3½ hours), leaving from outside the visitor information centre. Stops include Hamilton ($12, 25 minutes) and Otorohanga ($11, 20 minutes).

AROUND TE AWAMUTU
Battle Sites

Before the Waikato invasion, **Rangiaowhia** (5km east of Te Awamutu) was a thriving Maori farming town – with thousands of inhabitants, two churches, a flour mill and a racecourse – exporting wheat, maize, potatoes and fruit to as far afield as Australia. In many ways it was the perfect model of what NZ under the Maori version of the Treaty of Waitangi had desired – two sovereign peoples interacting to mutual advantage.

In February 1864 the settlement was left undefended while King Tawhiao's warriors held fortified positions further north. In a key tactical move, General Cameron outflanked them and took the town, killing women, children and the elderly in the process. This was a turning point in the campaign, demoralising the Maori and drawing the warriors out of their near impregnable *pa* fortifications.

Sadly, all that remains is the cute Anglican **St Paul's Church** (1854) and the Catholic mission's **cemetery**, standing in the midst of rich

---

TE AWAMUTU'S SACRED SOUND

In the opening lines of Crowded House's first single ('Mean to Me'), Neil Finn single-handedly raised his sleepy hometown, Te Awamutu, to international attention. It wasn't the first time it had provided inspiration – Split Enz songs *Haul Away* and *Kia Kaha*, with older brother Tim, include similar references.

Despite NZ's brilliant songwriting brothers being far from the height of their fame, Finn devotees continue to make Te Awamutu pilgrimages – just ask the staff at the i-SITE. They do a brisk trade in Finn T-shirts, Finn stamps and walking-tour brochures of sites from Finn history (their childhood home at 588 Teasdale St, their school, even Neil's piano tutor's house). It's NZ's version of Graceland.

If you're hoping for a close encounter with greatness, it's unlikely: the boys skipped town decades ago.

farming land – confiscated from the Maori and distributed to colonial soldiers.

The war ended further south at **Orakau**, where a roadside obelisk marks the site where 300 Maori led by Rewi Maniapoto repulsed three days of attacks against an unfinished *pa* by 1500 troops, before breaking out and retreating to what is now known as the King Country (losing 70 warriors). Rewi's defiant cry *'Ka whawhai tonu ahau ki a koe, ake, ake, ake'* (We shall fight on forever and ever and ever) is a rallying call for Maori activists to this day. There's a **memorial to Rewi Maniapoto**, who was well respected by both sides, in nearby Kihikihi, 4km south of Te Awamutu on SH3.

Maungatautari

Can a landlocked volcano become an island paradise? Inspired by the success of pest eradication and native species reintroduction in the Hauraki Gulf, a community trust has erected 47km of pest-proof fence around the triple peaks of Maungatautari (797m) to create the impressive **Maungatautari Ecological Island** (☎ 07-823 7455 www.maungatrust.org). This atoll of rainforest dominates the skyline between Te Awamutu and Karapiro and is now home to its first kiwi chicks in 100 years. The shortest route to the peak (an hour and 40 minutes) is from the northern side while the entire north–south walk will take around six hours. Take Maungatautari Rd then Hicks Rd if coming from Karapiro, or Arapuni Rd then Tari Rd from Te Awamutu.

Out In The Styx (☎ 07-872 4505; www.styx.co.nz; 2117 Arapuni Rd, Pukeatua; dm $85, s $130-155, d $260-310), near the south end of the Maungatautari, provides a drop-off service to the northern entrance for guests ($10 per person). The three luxuriously furnished themed rooms (Polynesian, African or Maori) are especially nice, and there's a spa for soothing weary legs. Prices include a four-course dinner and breakfast.

Wharepapa South

A surreal landscape of craggy limestone provides some of the best rock climbing in the North Island. This isn't the best place for wannabe Spidermen (or women) to don their lycra bodysuits for the first time, but if you have the basic skills get ready to let your inner superhero shine.

Bryce's Rockclimbing (☎ 07-872 2533; www.rock climb.co.nz; 1424 Owairaka Valley Rd; dm/d $25/66) is suited

to the serious climber. On site is NZ's largest retail climbing store that sells and hires out a full range of gear and has an indoor bouldering cave (free to those staying out back in the shipshape accommodation) and a licensed cafe (light meals $4 to $10; open for lunch). A day's instruction for one or two people costs $365.

CAMBRIDGE
pop 15,200

The name says it all. Despite the rambunctious Waikato River looking nothing like the Cam, the good burghers of Cambridge have done all they can to assume an air of English gentility. There are village greens, avenues lined with magnificent exotic trees and an indecent number of faux-Tudor houses. Even the public toilet looks like a Victorian cottage.

Famous for the breeding and training of thoroughbred horses, you can almost smell the wealth along the main street, dotted with fine Edwardian and art-deco buildings. Equine references are rife in public sculpture, and plaques boast of Melbourne Cup winners. It's an altogether pleasant place to work on your 'rah-rah' voice and while away a day or two.

Information

The **Cambridge i-SITE** (☎ 07-823 3456; www.cambridge. co.nz; cnr Victoria & Queen Sts; ☽ 9am-5pm Mon-Fri, 10am-4pm Sat & Sun; ▣) has free heritage trail and town maps, and internet access.

Sights & Activities
HERITAGE

Whether you're hip to history or tantalised by trees, the **Heritage & Tree Trail** and **Boutique Trail** cover all the sights, including the **Waikato River** and leafy little **Lake Koutu**. Don't miss the impressive vaulted interior of the 1873 **St Andrew's Anglican Church** (☎ 07-827 6751; www. standrewcambridge.wordpress.com; 85 Hamilton Rd; admission free; ☽ services 8am & 9.30am Sun), the oldest building in Cambridge (look for the Gallipoli window).

Apart from its Spanish Mission **town clock**, **Jubilee Gardens** (Victoria St) is a wholehearted tribute to the 'mother country'. A British lion guards the **cenotaph**, with a plaque that reads 'Tell Britain ye who mark this monument faithful to her we fell and rest content'. Outmoded sentiment or awkward grammar – either way, the soldier statue looks confused.

The quirky old **Cambridge Museum** (☎ 07-827 3319; www.cambridgemuseum.org.nz; 24 Victoria St; admission by donation; ☟ 10am-4pm), housed in the former courthouse, has plenty of pioneer relics, a military history room and a scale model of the local Te Totara Pa before it was wiped out.

HORSEY

Cambridge Thoroughbred Lodge (☎ 07-827 8118; www.cambridgethoroughbredlodge.co.nz; tours adult/child $8/5, shows adult/child $12/5; ☟ tours 10am-3pm by arrangement), 6km south of town on SH1, is a top-notch horse stud. Book ahead for hour-long tours, or 'NZ Horse Magic' shows which take place several times a week.

Stud Tours (☎ 07-827 5910, 027 497 5346; www.barrylee.co.nz; tours $120) offers visits to local stud farms by a bloodstock expert. Prices are for up to four people, which makes this a reasonably priced and unique tour. Bookings should be made in advance.

The very verdant **Cambridge Raceway** (☎ 07-827 5506; www.cambridgeraceway.co.nz; Taylor St; admission $5) is the venue for harness and greyhound racing three times a month. Check the website for dates and times.

LAKE KARAPIRO

Eight kilometres southeast of Cambridge, Karapiro is the furthest downstream of a chain of eight hydroelectric power stations on the Waikato River. It's an impressive sight, especially when driving across the top of the 1947 dam. The 21km-long lake is popular for all kinds of aquatic sports, especially rowing.

The **Boatshed Cafe** (☎ 07-827 8286; www.theboatshed.net.nz; 21 Amber Lane; mains $10-17; ☟ 10am-4pm Wed-Fri, 9.30am-5pm Sat & Sun) on the lakeside (take Gorton Rd from SH1) sells mainly homemade food, some of which is gluten- and dairy-free. The rowing boat of Olympian Rob Waddell is part of the decor – he used to practise here. Basic kayaks can be hired for $20/40 per half-/ full day or better ones for $25/50. You can paddle to a couple of waterfalls in around an hour.

Camjet (☎ 0800 226 538; www.camjet.co.nz; trips adult/child $65/40) can help adrenaline junkies shake off the Cambridge cobwebs with a 45-minute spin to Karapiro on a jetboat (minimum two people).

CYCLING

Winding east from Cambridge, the 100km **Waikato River Trails** (www.waikatorivertrails.com) track has been ascribed 'Quick Start' status as part of the proposed **New Zealand Cycle Trail** (www.tourism.govt.nz/our-work/new-zealand-cycle-trail-project) project. Much of the track is already open; check the websites for updates.

Sleeping

Lake Karapiro Camping & Pursuits Centre (☎ 07-827 4178; www.lakekarapiro.co.nz; 601 Maungatautari Rd; sites per adult/child $12/9, chalets d/tr/q $60/72/96) Geared for rowing events, this lakeside complex 15 minutes from town is serenely peaceful outside of the big fixtures. The trim wooden chalets have bunk beds, en suites, fridges and communal kitchen facilities.

Cambridge Motor Park (☎ 07-827 5649; www.cambridgemotorpark.co.nz; 32 Scott St; sites $28, cabins s/d from $35/45, units d $95; ☏) A quiet, well-maintained camping ground with lots of green, green grass. You'll find it over the skinny Victoria Bridge from Cambridge town centre.

Birches (☎ 07-827 6556; www.birches.co.nz; 263 Maungatautari Rd; s/d $80/120; ☒) There's a pool, spa and tennis court at this picturesque 1930s weatherboard farmhouse, in farmland southeast of Cambridge. Sleep in the main house, or book the self-contained Cherry Tree Cottage. Sheep and daffodils line the driveway.

Lofthouse (☎ 07-827 3693; www.lofthouse.co.nz; 17 Dunning Rd; apt $130) If you're travelling with friends, this self-contained rural retreat is an absolute steal – sleeping four people for the price. Jump in the spa and enjoy the awesome views. It's 3km off SH1, near the top of Karapiro, and 11km from Cambridge.

Cambridge Mews (☎ 07-827 7166; www.cambridgemews.co.nz; 20 Hamilton Rd; units $145-190; ☏) All the spacious units in this chalet-style motel have double spa baths, decent kitchens and are immaculately maintained. The architect did a great job but the interior decorator less so.

Park House (☎ 07-827 6368; www.parkhouse.co.nz; 70 Queen St; d incl breakfast $160-310; ☒) Try to avoid the word 'charming' when describing this centrally located 1918 Tudor impostor, full of antiques, brass beds, quilts and period features. The same word applies to the experienced hosts, who serve an ample breakfast (stewed fruits, farm eggs, sausages etc) in the formal dining room.

Houseboat Holidays (☎ 07-827 2195; www.houseboatescape.co.nz; 2 nights $600) Humming 'Proud Mary' is acceptable as Lake Karapiro is technically still a river, but you're more likely to be relaxing than rolling. Load up this smart houseboat (sleeping seven) with kayaks and fishing gear and sail away for a splashy couple of days.

Emanuel's Lake Karapiro Lodge (☎ 07-823 7414; www.emanuels.co.nz; 1829 SH1; d/ste incl breakfast $400/750; 🛜) Call it rustic grandeur. This modern house with commanding views of Lake Karapiro has high ceilings, moulded cornices and leadlights. If you think the standard rooms are luxurious, check out the sumptuous Versace Suite (gold bathroom fittings) and mammoth Sir Tristram Suite. It's located 20km from Cambridge, high above the road near the Tauranga turn-off.

Eating

our pick Red Cherry (☎ 07-823 1515; cnr SH1 & Forrest Rd; meals $6-17; 🕙 9am-3pm) With happy staff and a cherry-red espresso machine working overtime, barn-like Red Cherry offers coffee roasted on-site, delicious counter food and impressive cooked breakfasts (perhaps oat hotcakes or a breakfast risotto). It's Cambridge's best cafe by a country mile (it's actually a country 4km out of Cambridge on the way to Hamilton). There are a couple of tables outside, too, if you feel like sniffing the bucolic splendour.

Rata (☎ 07-823 0999; 64c Victoria St; meals $6-20; 🕙 8.30am-4pm) Sit in either the funky old shopfront or the courtyard garden for, as the local media described it, 'robust food – nicely cooked and plenty of it'.

Onyx (☎ 07-827 7740; 70 Alpha St; mains $17-24; 🕙 breakfast, lunch & dinner) All-day Onyx occupies a lofty space, with onyx-black furnishings and a warm-toned timber floor. Wood-fired pizzas are the mainstay, plus salads, tortillas, sandwiches, steaks, cakes and good coffee. At night it's almost urbane.

Cafe Oasis (☎ 07-827 8004; 35 Duke St; mains $20-30; 🕙 9am-9pm Mon-Thu, 9am-late Fri & Sat, 10am-9pm Sun; 🅥) It's a strange combo – from the name you'd expect felafels but instead you get blaring FM radio and a menu that's half authentic Thai, half classic European. Fusion be damned.

Getting There & Away

Being on SH1, 22km southeast of Hamilton, Cambridge is well connected by bus. Environment Waikato's **Busit!** (☎ 0800 4287 5463; www.busit.co.nz) heads to Hamilton ($6, 40 minutes) three times each weekday.

InterCity (☎ 09-583 5780; www.intercity.co.nz) services numerous destinations including:

Destination	Price	Duration	Frequency
Auckland	$38	2½hr	10 daily
Hamilton	$21	30min	8 daily
Matamata	$20	30min	1 daily
Rotorua	$28	1¼hr	5 daily
Wellington	$75	8½hr	3 daily

Naked Bus (☎ 0900 625 33; www.nakedbus.com) services to the same destinations are as follows. Consider booking in advance for big savings.

Destination	Price	Duration	Frequency
Auckland	$27	2½hr	5 daily
Hamilton	$14	30min	3 daily
Matamata	$12	40min	2 daily
Rotorua	$15	1½hr	2 daily
Wellington	$45	9½hr	1 daily

TIRAU
pop 730

Cambridge's cosy Anglophilia seems even more exaggerated when you reach the next stop on SH1. Tirau has fallen head-over-heels in love with corrugated iron. The **Tirau i-SITE** (☎ 07-883 1202; www.tirauinfo.co.nz; SH1; 🕙 9am-5pm) is inside a giant corrugated dog, while many other buildings have similarly crinkly oversized sculptures (a wedge of cheese, a shepherd, a tulip…).

Just off SH27, 5km north of Tirau, **Oraka Deer Park** (☎ 07-883 1382; www.oraka-deer.co.nz; 71 Bayly Rd; d $100, cottage $200-260; 🐾) offers a self-contained cottage (easily sleeping five) or an en-suite room in the house. Kids will love the deer, not to mention the pool, spa and tennis court.

MATAMATA
pop 7800

Not as well-heeled as Cambridge but just as horsey, Matamata was just one of those pleasant country towns you drove through until Peter Jackson's epic film trilogy *Lord of the Rings* put it on the map. During filming Matamata was a great place to live if you were short, chubby-cheeked and Hobbit-like – 300 locals got work as extras (hairy feet weren't a prerequisite).

Most tourists who come to Matamata are dedicated hobbit-botherers: for everyone else there's a great cafe, avenues of mature trees and undulating green hills that are pleasantly

Shire-like. And if your souvenir checklist includes a thoroughbred racehorse, this is the place to come.

Information

The super-helpful **Matamata i-SITE** (☎ 07-888 7260; www.matamatanz.co.nz; 45 Broadway; ☺ 9am-5pm Mon-Fri, 9am-3pm Sat & Sun) has free town maps, all the guff on local attractions and extended summer hours. Hobbiton tours leave from here.

Sights & Activities

Hobbiton Movie Set & Farm Tours (☎ 07-888 6838; www.hobbitontours.com; adult/under 5/5-9yr/10-14yr $58/free/5/29; ☺ tours 9.50am, 10.45am, noon, 1.15pm, 2.30pm, 3.45pm) is the country's top attraction for *LOTR*-ites, and pretty interesting even if you haven't seen the movies. Due to copyright, all of the intricately constructed movie sets around the country had to be destroyed, but Hobbiton's owners successfully negotiated to keep the hobbit holes, albeit without their wonderful exteriors. Still, for the devotee (of which there are many), it's an opportunity to let your imagination fly. Also on offer is a hands-on **Sheep Farm Experience** (adult/child $16/8), explaining all things woolly. Free transfers leave from the Matamata i-SITE. Otherwise, head towards Cambridge and turn right into Puketutu Rd and then left into Buckland Rd, stopping at the Shire's Rest cafe.

Skydive Waikato (☎ 07-888 8763; www.freefall.co.nz; 9000-15,000ft tandem $240-290) and **Dropzone** (☎ 027 494 2537; www.dropzonenz.co.nz; 9000ft tandem $220) both offer thrilling gravity-powered plummets from Matamata Airfield, 10km north of Matamata on SH27.

Firth Tower (☎ 07-888 8369; www.frithtower.co.nz; Tower Rd; admission free; ☺ 10am-4pm) was built by Auckland businessman Josiah Firth after acquiring 56,000 acres from his friend Wiremu Tamihana, chief of Ngati Haua. The 18m concrete tower (1882) was a fashionable status symbol rather than for defensive purposes. It's filled with Maori and pioneer artefacts and around it are 10 other historic buildings (closed Tuesday and Wednesday), including a schoolroom, church and jail. It's 3km east of town.

Opal Hot Springs (☎ 07-888 8198; www.opalhotsprings.co.nz; 257 Okauia Springs Rd; admission adult/child $6/3, 30min private spas $8/4; ☺ 9am-9pm) isn't nearly as glamorous as it sounds but it does have three large thermal pools. Turn off just north of Firth Tower and follow the road for 2km.

Carry on past Opal Pools and then follow the Kaimai Ranges north for 9km to visit the spectacular 150m-high **Wairere Falls**. From the car park it's a 45-minute walk through native bush to the lookout or a steep 90-minute climb to the summit.

Sleeping

Broadway Motel & Miro Court Villas (☎ 07-888 8482; www.broadwaymatamata.co.nz, www.mirocourt.co.nz; 128 Broadway; s $70-135, d $85-155; ☐ ☒) This sprawling motel complex has spread from a well-maintained older-style block to progressively newer and flasher blocks set back from the street. The nicest are the chic apartment-style Miro Court villas. There's a fun kids' play area in the centre.

Southern Belle (☎ 07-888 5518; www.southernbelle.co.nz; 101 Firth St; s & d $120, extra person $40; ☜) Taking over the top floor of a grand old house (a transported vision from Savannah or Baton Rouge), this suite has three elegant bedrooms, a comfortable lounge and a kitchenette (just a microwave for cooking, but there's a barbecue downstairs guests can use).

Eating & Drinking

Redoubt Bar & Eatery (☎ 07-888 8585; 48 Broadway; lunch $10-18, dinner $22-31; ☺ breakfast, lunch & dinner Tue-Sun) The sister establishment of Te Awamutu's Redoubt (p218), Matamata's version is just as good: thin-crust pizzas, chowder, steak sandwiches and live music every Friday. Oh, and plenty of Monteiths!

our pick **Workman's Cafe Bar** (☎ 07-888 5498; 52 Broadway; lunch $15-16, dinner $28-32; ☺ breakfast, lunch & dinner) Truly eccentric (one wall is lined with art-deco mirrors while another holds an impressive collection of busts of African women), this funky eatery has built itself a reputation that extends beyond Matamata. The poached salmon Benedict is quite possibly the best in the country.

Getting There & Away

Matamata is on SH27, 20km north of Tirau.

InterCity (☎ 09-583 5780; www.intercity.co.nz) runs one bus daily to Cambridge ($20, 30 minutes), Hamilton ($25, one hour), Rotorua ($26, one hour) and Tauranga ($21, one hour).

Naked Bus (☎ 0900 625 33; www.nakedbus.com) runs once daily to Auckland ($27, 3½ hours), Cambridge ($12, 30 minutes), Hamilton ($15, one hour) and Tauranga ($12, 45 minutes). Book in advance for fares as low as $1.

TE AROHA
pop 3800

Te Aroha has a great vibe. You could even say that it's got 'the love', which is the literal meaning of the name. Tucked under the elbow of the bush-clad Mt Te Aroha (952m), it's a good base for bushwalking or 'taking the waters' in the town's therapeutic thermal springs.

Information

Te Aroha i-SITE (☎ 07-884 8052; www.tearohanz. co.nz; 102 Whitaker St; ⊗ 9.30am-5pm Mon-Fri, 9.30am-4pm Sat & Sun)

Sights & Activities

The town's thermal area is in the quaint Edwardian **Hot Springs Domain**, a park behind the i-SITE, split into separate facilities for soakers and splashers. The **Te Aroha Mineral Spa Bath House** (☎ 07-884 8717; www.tearohapools.co.nz; 30min session per couple $30; ⊗ 10.30am-10pm) offers relaxing private tubs, massage, beauty therapies and aromatherapy. Near the entrance a **drinking fountain** allows you to try the warm soda water – an acquired taste but reputedly good for constipation. Also here is the temperamental **Mokena Geyser** – the world's only known soda geyser – blows its top every 40 minutes or so, shooting water 3m into the air (the most ardent eruptions are between noon and 2pm).

Lower down the domain, the **Leisure Pools** (☎ 07-884 4498; www.tearohapools.co.nz; admission adult/child $5/3; ⊗ 10am-5.45pm Mon-Fri, to 6.45pm Sat & Sun) have outdoor heated freshwater pools for splashing about in.

Just down the hill, the **Te Aroha Museum** (☎ 07-884 4427; www.tearoha-museum.com; admission adult/child $3/1; ⊗ 11am-4pm Nov-Mar, noon-3pm Apr-Oct) is in the ornate former thermal sanatorium. Displays include quirky souvenir ceramics.

Hiking trails up Mt Te Aroha start at the top of the domain. It takes 45 minutes to climb up to the **Bald Spur/Whakapipi Lookout** (350m). Then it's another 2.7km (two hours) climbing to the summit.

Sleeping

Te Aroha Holiday Park (☎ 07-884 9567; www.tearoha holidaypark.co.nz; 217 Stanley Rd; sites per person $10, dm $15, cabins $35-45, units $50-90; ▯ 🛜 🐾 ▣) Wake up to a bird orchestra among the large oaks at this site, equipped with grass tennis court, gym and hot pool, 2km southwest of

town. The owners also speak German and Japanese.

Te Aroha YHA (☎ 07-884 8739; www.yha.co.nz; Miro St; dm/tr $23/56) The Love YHA is a cosy, TV-free, three-bedroom cottage with a homely atmosphere, welcoming management and a well-stocked herb rack. Free mountain bikes are available; a 10km mountain-bike track starts at the back door. Call in advance to make sure they're open (they're closed sometimes in winter).

Te Aroha Motel (☎ 07-884 9417; tearohamotel@ xtra.co.nz; 108 Whitaker St; s/d/tr/q $80/95/115/135; 🛜) Welcome to The Love Motel (with a couple of palm trees out the front, this could almost be Vegas!). Inside are old-fashioned but reasonably priced and tidy units with kitchenettes, right in the centre of town. There's free wi-fi, too.

Aroha Mountain Lodge (☎ 07-884 8134; www. arohamountainlodge.co.nz; 5 Boundary St; s/d/ste/cottage $115/125/145/250) Spread over two *aroha*-ly Edwardian villas on the hillside above town, the Mountain Lodge offers affordable luxury (*sooo* much nicer than a regulation motel) and optional breakfasts ($20 per head). The self-contained Gold Miner's Cottage sleeps six.

Eating & Drinking

Behr Burger (☎ 07-884 9451; 176 Whitaker St; burgers $8-12; ⊗ 4-9pm Mon-Wed, 11am-9pm Thu-Sun) Awesome gourmet hamburgers are the go at this buzzy main-street nook. 'The Chief' (NZ rump steak, honey-smoked bacon, a free-range egg, cheddar cheese, salad and aioli) will plug any hungry gaps.

Berlusconi on Whitaker (☎ 07-884 9307; 149 Whitaker St; brunch $12-18, mains $22-28; ⊗ 5.30pm-late Wed, 10am-late Thu-Sun) We know the Italian PM has fingers in many pies but surely they don't extend to this upmarket wine, tapas and pizza bar in Te Aroha. Mind you, it is suave enough.

Self-caterers should try the **Organic Health Shop** (☎ 07-884 9696; 9 Lawrence Ave; ⊗ 9am-5pm Mon-Fri) for fresh produce, dairy products, cereals and all things gluten-free.

Getting There & Away

Te Aroha is on SH26, 21km south of Paeroa and 55km northeast of Hamilton. Environment Waikato's **Busit!** (☎ 0800 4287 5463; www.busit.co.nz) has three services on weekdays to Hamilton ($7.80, one hour).

THE KING COUNTRY

Holding good claim to the title of NZ's rural heartland, this is the kind of no-nonsense place that raises cattle and All Blacks. A bastion of independent Maoridom, it was never conquered in the war against the King Movement (see the boxed text, p209). The story goes that King Tawhiao placed his hat on a large map of NZ and declared that all the land it covered would remain under his *mana* (authority), and the region was effectively off limits to Europeans until 1883.

At this stage it was still largely covered by *Te Nehe-nehe-nui* (the big forest) and home to Ngati Maniapoto, descended from the Tainui migration. After allowing railway surveyors to assess the land, Maori control was gradually chipped away. An example is the Waitomo Caves, which were taken by the Crown in 1906 and only returned to its rightful owners in 1989.

The caves are the area's major drawcard. An incredible natural phenomenon in themselves, they've been sexed up even more with a smorgasbord of adrenaline-inducing activities on offer.

For more regional info, see www.sacred peaks.com.

KAWHIA
pop 670

Along with resisting cultural annihilation this fishing village ('Think mafia with a K', says a lady on the street) has avoided large-scale development, retaining its sleepy feel despite its considerable natural attractions. It's basically Raglan (p214) and Hot Water Beach (p198) rolled into one, but without the tourists. There's not much here except for the general store/post office, a couple of takeaways and a petrol station. Even Captain Cook blinked and missed the narrow entrance to the large harbour when he sailed past in 1770.

It was in Kawhia that the *Tainui waka* – one of the ancestral canoes that arrived during the 14th century – made its final landing. The two leaders of the expedition – Hoturoa, the chief/captain, and Rakataura, the *tohunga* (priest) – knew that their new home was destined to be on the west coast, searching until they finally recognised the prophesised place. When they landed, they tied the *waka* to a pohutukawa tree on the shore, naming the tree Tangi te Korowhiti. The unlabelled tree still stands on the shoreline between the wharf and Maketu Marae. At the end of its long, epic voyage, the *waka* was dragged up onto a hill and buried. Sacred stones were placed at either end to mark its resting place.

Famed Ngati Toa warrior chief Te Rauparaha, composer of the famous *haka* 'Ka Mate', was born nearby in the 1760s.

Sights & Activities

Kawhia Museum & Gallery (☎ 07-871 0161; www. kawhiaharbour.co.nz; Kawhia Wharf; admission free; ◷ 11am-4pm Wed-Sun) is a modest but cute affair near the wharf, and serves as the information centre.

Kayaks can be hired on the incoming tide from Kawhia Beachside S-Cape (below) for $10 per hour. The skipper of **Kawhia Harbour Cruises** (☎ 07-871 0149; cruises 1hr/2hr $25/35) is well placed to provide a cultural and historical commentary as his family has resided in Kawhia since the arrival of the *Tainui waka*. For fishing trips contact **Dove Charters** (☎ 07-871 5854; www.westcoastfishing.co.nz; full day $100).

Four kilometres west of Kawhia is **Ocean Beach** and its high, black-sand dunes. Swimming can be dangerous, but one to two hours either side of low tide you can find the **Te Puia Hot Springs** in the sand – dig a hole for your own natural hot pool.

From the wharf, a track extends along the coast to **Maketu Marae**, which has an impressively carved meeting house, Auaukiterangi. Through the *marae* grounds and behind the wooden fence, two stones (Hani and Puna) mark the burial place of the *Tainui waka* (see left). This *marae* is private property – don't enter without permission from the Maketu Marae Committee (info@kawhia.maori.nz). Unfortunately you can't see a lot from the road.

Festivals & Events

During the annual **Kai Festival** (www.kawhiaharbour. co.nz/maori-kai-festival.html) in early February, over 10,000 people descend to enjoy traditional Maori *kai* (food) and catch up with *whanau* (relations). Once you've filled up on seafood, *rewana* bread and rotten corn you can settle in to watch the bands and rousing *kapa haka* performances.

Sleeping & Eating

Kawhia Beachside S-Cape (☎ 07-871 0727; www.kawhia beachsidescape.co.nz; 225 Pouewe St; sites from $34, cabins

lonelyplanet.com
THE KING COUNTRY •• Otorohanga **225**

dm/s/d from $30/45/55, cottages $130-180) Perfectly positioned on the water's edge at the entrance to Kawhia, this camping ground has comfortable cottages. There's a new laundry and ablutions block, but the backpackers area is rudimentary at best – camping is a better bet.

Kawhia Motel (☎ 07-871 0865, kawhiamotel@xtra. co.nz; cnr Jervois & Tainui Sts; s $99-155, extra person $20) Six perkily painted, well-kept, old-school motel units right next to the shops.

Annie's Cafe & Restaurant (☎ 07-871 0198; 146 Jervois St; meals $5-25; ☺ 9.30am-4pm, closed Mon & Tue in winter) An old-fashioned licensed eatery in the main street, serving espresso, sandwiches and local specialities such as flounder and whitebait. There's also an internet terminal.

Getting There & Away

This remote outpost doesn't have a bus service. Take SH31 from Otorohanga (58km) or explore the scenic but rough unsealed road to Raglan (see p216).

OTOROHANGA
pop 2700

One of several nondescript North Island towns to adopt a gimmick (we're looking at you Tirau, Paeroa, Katikati, Bulls and Hobbiton, sorry, Matamata), Otorohanga (Oto to his mates) has a main street lined with cherished icons of Kiwiana. You'll learn about sheep, gumboots, jandals, No 8 wire, All Blacks, the beloved Buzzy Bee children's toy and – bravely risking fisticuffs with the Australian Country Women's Association – the pavlova (a creamy meringue dessert). Gimmicks aside, the Kiwi House is well worth a visit.

Information

Otorohanga i-SITE (☎ 07-873 8951; www.otorohanga. co.nz; 21 Maniapoto St; ☺ 9am-5pm Mon-Fri, 10am-2pm Sat & Sun) has internet access and local information.

Sights

The **Otorohanga Kiwi House Native Bird Park** (☎ 07-873 7391; www.kiwihouse.org.nz; 20 Alex Telfer Dr; admission adult/child $16/4; ☺ 9am-5pm Sep-May, 9am-4.30pm Jun-Aug) has a nocturnal enclosure where you can see active kiwi energetically digging with their long beaks, searching for food. This is the only place in NZ where you can see a Great Spotted Kiwi, the biggest of the three kiwi species. Other native birds, such as kaka, kea, falcon, morepork and weka, are also on show.

The small **Otorohanga Museum** (☎ 07-873 8849; Kakamutu Rd; admission free; ☺ 1-5pm Sun) covers local history and has a collection of historic buildings, including a church and a lock-up.

As well as the Kiwiana main street, the **Ed Hillary Walkway** running off Maniapoto St has information panels on the All Blacks, Marmite, NZ competing in the America's Cup, and of course, Sir Ed.

Sleeping

Otorohanga Holiday Park (☎ 07-873 7253; www. kiwiholidaypark.co.nz; 20 Huiputea Dr; unpowered/powered sites $30/34, cabins $52-58, units $75-105; 🖳 🛜) It's not the most attractive locale, backing on to the train tracks, but the owners are quick with a smile and the park's tidy facilities include a fitness centre and sauna. And if you can't find a bed in Waitomo, Otorohanga is only 16km away.

Eating & Drinking

Thirsty Weta (☎ 07-873 6699; 57 Maniapoto St; meals $7-16; ☺ 10am-1am) The top pick in town, with hearty snacks (of the pizza, pasta and quesadilla variety) and the promise of things kicking off after dinner when the wine-bar vibe takes over and the musos plug in.

Origin Coffee Station (☎ 07-873 8550; 7 Wahanui Cres; coffee $3-5; ☺ 8.30am-4.30pm Mon-Fri) It's a long way from Malawi to the old Otorohanga railway station, but the beans don't seem to mind. The folks at Origin are dead serious about coffee, sourcing, importing and roasting it themselves and then delivering it to your table, strong and perfectly formed, and possibly with a slice of cake.

As there's no supermarket at Waitomo Caves, stock up at Oto's **Woolworths** (☎ 07-873 7378; 123 Maniapoto St; ☺ 7am-10pm) on the Waitomo side of town.

Getting There & Away

InterCity (☎ 09-583 5780; www.intercity.co.nz) buses arrive and depart from outside the i-SITE. There are daily buses to Auckland ($50, 3¼ hours, four daily), Te Awamutu ($21, 20 minutes, three daily), Te Kuiti ($17, 20 minutes, three daily) and Rotorua ($52, 2½ hours, one daily).

Naked Bus (☎ 0900 625 33; www.nakedbus.com) runs around five buses weekly to Waitomo Caves ($12, 20 minutes), Hamilton ($13, 50 minutes) and New Plymouth ($37, 3¼ hours). Book in advance for lower fares.

The **Waitomo Shuttle** (☎ 07-873 8279; waikiwi@ ihug.co.nz; one way adult/child $10/5) heads to the caves five times daily, coordinating with bus and train arrivals.

The **Dalroy Express** (☎ 0508 465 622; www.dalroy tours.co.nz) bus runs daily between Auckland ($36, three hours) and New Plymouth ($34, 3¼ hours), stopping at Otorohanga. Other stops include Hamilton ($16, 50 minutes) and Te Awamutu ($11, 25 minutes).

Otorohanga is on the **Overlander** (☎ 0800 872 467; www.tranzscenic.co.nz; daily Oct-Apr, Fri-Sun May-Sep) train route between Auckland ($81, 3¼ hours) and Wellington ($107, nine hours) via Hamilton ($53, 50 minutes) and Te Kuiti ($53, 15 minutes).

WAITOMO CAVES

Even if damp, dark tunnels sound like your idea of hell, take a chill pill and head to Waitomo anyway. These limestone caves with accompanying geological formations and glowing bugs are deservedly one of the premier attractions of the North Island.

Your Waitomo experience can be as claustrophobe-friendly as the electrically lit, cathedral-like and extremely beautiful Glow-worm Cave. But if it's adrenaline-pumping, gut-wrenching, soaking-wet, pitch-black, squeezing, plummeting excitement you're after, Waitomo can take care of that, too.

The name Waitomo comes from *wai* (water) and *tomo* (hole or shaft); dotted throughout the countryside are numerous shafts dropping abruptly into underground cave systems and streams. There are more than 300 mapped caves in the Waitomo area. The three main caves – the Glow-worm Cave, Ruakuri and Aranui – have been bewitching visitors for over 100 years.

History

Ruakuri Cave was discovered by Maori 400 to 500 years ago when a hunter travelling in a war party with Kawhia chief Tane Tinorau was attacked by a pack of dogs living in the cave entrance. The dogs were caught and eaten but the name Ruakuri (Den of Dogs) stuck. Shortly after, Tinorau moved his people into the area and the cave became a *wahi tapu*

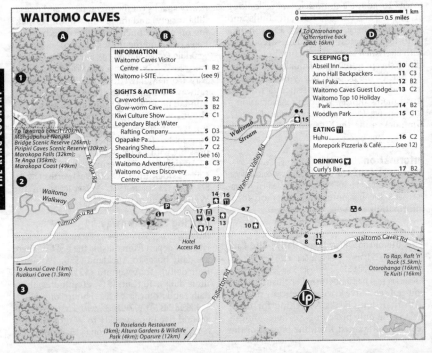

WAITOMO CAVES

0 ____ 1 km
0 ____ 0.5 miles

INFORMATION
Waitomo Caves Visitor Centre 1 B2
Waitomo i-SITE .... (see 9)

SIGHTS & ACTIVITIES
Caveworld 2 B2
Glow-worm Cave 3 B2
Kiwi Culture Show 4 C1
Legendary Black Water Rafting Company 5 D3
Opapake Pa 6 D2
Shearing Shed 7 C2
Spellbound ....(see 16)
Waitomo Adventures 8 C3
Waitomo Caves Discovery Centre 9 B2

SLEEPING
Abseil Inn 10 C2
Juno Hall Backpackers 11 C3
Kiwi Paka 12 B2
Waitomo Caves Guest Lodge 13 C2
Waitomo Top 10 Holiday Park 14 B2
Woodlyn Park 15 C1

EATING
Huhu 16 C2
Morepork Pizzeria & Café .... (see 12)

DRINKING
Curly's Bar 17 B2

To Otorohanga (alternative back road; 16km)

To Tawarau Forest (20km); Mangapohue Natural Bridge Scenic Reserve (26km); Piripiri Caves Scenic Reserve (30km); Marokopa Falls (32km); Te Anga (35km); Marokopa Coast (49km)

Waitomo Walkway

Tumurumu Rd

Te Anga Rd

Waitomo Valley Rd

Waitomo Stream

Fullerton Rd

Hotel Access Rd

To Aranui Cave (1km); Ruakuri Cave (1.5km)

To Roselands Restaurant (3km); Altura Gardens & Wildlife Park (4km); Oparure (12km)

Waitomo Caves Rd

To Rap, Raft 'n' Rock (5.5km); Otorohanga (16km); Te Kuiti (16km) (sacred site), used for burials and for storing important *taonga*. By the 20th century the land had passed into the hands of the Holden family, who own it to this day.

The Glow-worm Cave had long been known to local Maori but they had no desire to explore it. That changed in December 1887 when the local chief, another Tane Tinorau, headed into the cave system, taking English surveyor Fred Mace with him. Mace prepared an account of the expedition, a map was made, photographs given to the government, and before long Tane Tinorau was operating tours of the cave. The tours must have made an impression as the government nationalised the land 19 years later – depriving the local *hapu* (subtribe) of a nice little earner. In 1989 this injustice was corrected and the *hapu* now owns and leases back the land, gets a slice of admission charges and provides much of the workforce.

Information

Waitomo i-SITE (☎ 07-878 7640; www.waitomocaves.com; 21 Waitomo Caves Rd; ☺ 8am-8pm Jan & Feb, 8.45am-5pm Mar-Dec; ▣) has internet access and acts as a post office and booking agent.

Sights

WAITOMO CAVES

The big-three caves are all operated by the same company, based at the new **Waitomo Caves Visitor Centre** (☎ 0800 456 922; www.waitomo. com; Waitomo Caves Rd; ☺ 9am-5pm). Various combo deals are available, including the Triple Cave Combo (adult/child $105/44). Try to avoid the large tour groups, most of which arrive between 10.30am and 2.30pm.

The 45-minute guided tour of the **Glow-worm Cave** (Waitomo Caves Rd; tours adult/child $39/18; ☺ tours every 30min 9am-5pm), which is behind the visitor centre, leads past impressive stalactites and stalagmites into a large cavern known as the Cathedral. The acoustics are so good that Dame Kiri Te Kanawa and the Vienna Boys Choir have given concerts here. The highlight comes at the tour's end when you board a boat and swing off onto the river. As your eyes grow accustomed to the dark you'll see a Milky Way of little lights surrounding you – these are the glowworms. You can see them in lots of other places in NZ, but the ones in this cave are something special. Conditions for their growth are just about perfect so there are a remarkable number of them.

Three kilometres west from the Glow-worm Cave is **Aranui Cave** (Tumutumu Rd; tours adult/child $39/18; ☺ 45min tours 10am, 11am, 1pm, 2pm, 3pm). This cave is dry (hence no glowworms) but compensates with an incredible array of limestone formations. Thousands of tiny 'straw' stalactites hang from the ceiling. It's an hour's walk to the caves, otherwise the visitors centre can arrange transport.

Culturally significant **Ruakuri Cave** (☎ 0800 228 464; Tumutumu Rd; tours adult/child $60/24; ☺ 2hr tours 9am, 10am, 11.30am, 12.30pm, 1.30pm, 2.30pm & 3pm) has an impressive 15m-high spiral staircase, removing the need to trample through the Maori burial site (see History, opposite) at the cave entrance (as tourists did for 84 years). Tours lead through 1.6km of the 7.5km system, taking in vast caverns with glowworms, subterranean streams and waterfalls, and intricate limestone structures. For as long as this cave has been open to the public, people have described it as spiritual – some claim it's haunted. It's customary to wash your hands when leaving to remove the *tapu* (see p56). Tours depart from the Legendary Black Water Rafting Company (see below).

Adjoining the i-SITE, this **Waitomo Caves Discovery Centre** (☎ 07-878 7640; www.waitomo -museum.co.nz; 21 Waitomo Caves Rd; admission adult/child $5/3; ☺ 8am-8pm Jan & Feb, 8.45am-5pm Mar-Dec) has excellent exhibits explaining how caves are formed, the flora and fauna that thrive in them and the history of Waitomo's caves and cave exploration.

ALTURA GARDENS & WILDLIFE PARK

At this privately run five-acre **park** (☎ 07-878 5278; www.alturapark.co.nz; 477 Fullerton Rd; adult/child $12/5; ☺ 9am-5pm) you can chat with a cockatoo, outstare a morepork or pat a blue-tongue lizard. There are 85 species of birds and animals here, but it's not a zoo – expect llamas and sheep rather than lions and giraffes. It also runs leisurely **horse treks** (30/60/90min $50/65/80).

Activities

The array of underground adventures available here is overwhelming, with most operators offering various combo experiences. The i-SITE is the best place for info, but booking ahead can often save you a dollar or twenty.

UNDERGROUND

Legendary Black Water Rafting Company (☎ 0800 228 464; 585 Waitomo Caves Rd; www.waitomo.com) claims to have invented black-water rafting! Its Black Labyrinth tour (three hours, $110, minimum age 12) involves floating in a wetsuit on an inner tube down a river that flows through Ruakuri Cave. The highlight is leaping off a small waterfall and then floating through a long, glowworm-covered passage. The trip ends with showers, soup and bagels in the cafe. The Black Abyss tour (five hours, $215, minimum age 16) is more adventurous and includes a 30m abseil into Ruakuri Cave and more glowworms, tubing and cave climbing.

Spellbound (☎ 0800 773 552, 07-878 7622; www. glow-worm.co.nz; 10 Waitomo Caves Rd; tours adult/child $66/24) is a good option if you don't want to get wet and want to avoid the big groups in the main caves. This three-hour tour and raft-ride departs from the pyramid-like booking office in the middle of town (usually 10am, 11am, 2pm and 3pm, varying seasonally) and goes through parts of the glowworm-filled Mangawhitikau cave system, 12km south of Waitomo.

Waitomo Adventures (☎ 0800 924 866, 07-878 7788; www.waitomo.co.nz; 654 Waitomo Caves Rd) offers five different cave adventures, with discounts for various combos and for advance bookings. The Lost World (four-/seven-hour trip $270/395) trip starts with a 100m abseil down into the cave, then – by a combination of walking, climbing, spider-walking, inching along narrow rock ledges, wading and swimming through a river – you take a three-hour journey through a 30m-high cave to get back out, passing glowworms, amazing rock formations, waterfalls and more. The price includes lunch (underground) and dinner. The shorter version skips the wet stuff and the meals.

Haggas Honking Holes (four hours, $215) includes professional abseiling instruction followed by three abseils, rock climbing and travelling along a subterranean river with waterfalls, traversing narrow passageways and huge caverns. Along the way you see glowworms and a variety of cave formations, including stalactites, stalagmites, columns, flowstone (calcite deposited by a thin sheet of flowing water) and cave coral. The adventure's name derives from a local farmer (Haggas) and characters in a Dr Seuss story (honking holers).

TumuTumu Toobing (four hours, $150) is a walking, wading, swimming and tubing trip. St Benedict's Cavern (three hours, $145) in-cludes abseiling and a subterranean flying fox in an attractive cave with straw stalagmites.

Readers recommend **Green Glow Eco-Adventures** (☎ 0800 476 459; www.greenglow.co.nz; 6hr tours per person $100 for 2-4 people, $200 for 1 person), which runs customised, small-group Waitomo tours, putting a caving, rock-climbing, abseiling, photographic or glowworm spin on your day (or all of the above!). It's based in Te Kuiti, 20 minutes from Waitomo. **Caveworld** (☎ 0800 228 396; www.caveworld.co.nz; cnr Waitomo Caves Rd & Hotel Access Rd) runs the Black Magic (2½ hours, $124) black-water rafting trip through glowworm-filled Te Anaroa. You've also got the choice of a day or (glowworm-illuminated) night abseil down a 45m crevice called The Canyon (two hours, night/day $144/175). Various combo discounts apply.

Rap, Raft 'n' Rock (☎ 0800 228 372, 07-873 9149; www.caveraft.com; 95 Waitomo Caves Rd; trips $135) runs five-hour small-group expeditions. It starts with abseil training, followed by a 27m descent into a natural cave, and then floating along a subterranean river on an inner tube with plenty of glowworms. After some caving, a belayed rock climb up a 20m cliff brings you to the surface.

WALKING

The i-SITE has free pamphlets on walks in the area. The walk from the Aranui Cave to the Ruakuri Cave is an excellent short path. From the Glow-worm Cave ticket office, there's a 10-minute walk to a lookout. Also from here, the 5km, three-hour-return **Waitomo Walkway** takes off through farmland, following Waitomo Stream to the **Ruakuri Scenic Reserve**, where a 30-minute return walk passes by a natural limestone tunnel. There are glowworms here at night – drive to the car park and bring a torch to find your way. Near Juno Hall Backpackers a steep 20-minute walk leads through bush then along farmland to the abandoned **Opapake Pa**, where terraces and kumara pits are visible.

The privately run **Dundle Hill Walk** (☎ 0800 924 866, 07-878 7788; www.waitomowalk.com; adult/child $75/35) is a 27km, two-day/one-night loop walk through bush and farmland, including overnight bunk-house accommodation high up in the bush.

OTHER ACTIVITIES

Kiwi Culture Show (☎ 07-878 6666; www.woodlynpark. co.nz; 1177 Waitomo Valley Rd; admission adult/child $25/13;

GLOWWORM MAGIC

Glowworms are the larvae of the fungus gnat, which looks much like a large mosquito without mouth parts. The larva glowworms have luminescent organs that produce a soft, greenish light. Living in a sort of hammock suspended from an overhang, they weave sticky threads that trail down and catch unwary insects attracted by their lights. When an insect flies towards the light it gets stuck in the threads – the glowworm just has to reel it in for a feed.

The larval stage lasts for six to nine months, depending on how much food the glowworm gets. When it has grown to about the size of a matchstick, it goes into a pupa stage, much like a cocoon. The adult fungus gnat emerges about two weeks later.

The adult insect doesn't live very long because it doesn't have a mouth. It emerges, mates, lays eggs and dies, all within about two or three days. The sticky eggs, laid in groups of 40 or 50, hatch in about three weeks to become larval glowworms.

Glowworms thrive in moist, dark caves but they can survive anywhere if they have the requisites of moisture, an overhang to suspend from and insects to eat. Waitomo is famous for its glowworms but you can see them in many other places around NZ, both in caves and outdoors.

When you come upon glowworms, don't touch their hammocks or hanging threads, try not to make loud noises and don't shine a light right on them. All of these things will cause them to dim their lights. It takes them a few hours to become bright again, during which time the grub will go hungry. The glowworms that shine most brightly are the hungriest.

---

shows 1.30pm) is a rustic theatre where local blokes put on a one-hour farm show that combines history, broad humour, local critters and audience participation.

At the **Shearing Shed** (☎ 07-878 8371; shearing shed@xtra.co.nz; 718 Waitomo Caves Rd; admission free; ✆ 9am-4pm) big, fluffy, surprisingly sociable Angora rabbits are sheared for an audience (12.45pm daily). It's SPCA-approved and the rabbits really don't seem to mind. The store sells Angora products.

Sleeping

Juno Hall Backpackers (☎ 07-878 7649; www.juno waitomo.co.nz; 600 Waitomo Caves Rd; sites per person $15, dm $27, d with/without bathroom $76/66, tr $95/85, q $120; 🖥 🛜 🐾) A slick purpose-built hostel a kilometre from the village with a warm welcome, a warmer wood fire in the woody lounge area, and an outdoor pool and tennis court.

Waitomo Top 10 Holiday Park (☎ 0508 498 666, 07-878 7639; www.waitomopark.co.nz; 12 Waitomo Caves Rd; sites from $20, cabins $65-110, units $130-170; 🖥 🛜 🐾) This superb camping ground in the heart of the village has spotless facilities, beaut new cabins and plenty of outdoor action to keep the kids busy (pool, spa, playground and neighbouring rugby pitch…).

Rap, Raft 'n' Rock Backpackers (☎ 0800 228 372, 07-873 9149; www.caveraft.com; 95 Waitomo Caves Rd; dm/d $28/66; 🖥 🛜) The homeliest of Waitomo's hostels, this basic bunk-house occupies a farm cottage 7km from the village. The brightly painted walls may burn your retinas after a day spent underground.

Kiwi Paka (☎ 07-878 3395; www.kiwipaka.co.nz; Hotel Access Rd; dm/s/d $29/62/66, chalets tw/d/q $95/110/145; 🖥) It's too big to be social but this snazzy, purpose-built, Alpine-style hostel has four-bed dorms, peak-roofed chalets, Morepork restaurant (p230) on-site and super-tidy facilities.

Waitomo Caves Guest Lodge (☎ 07-878 7641; www.waitomocavesguestlodge.co.nz; 7 Waitomo Caves Rd; s $80, d $100-120, extra person $25, all incl breakfast; 🛜) Bags your own cosy little en-suite cabin at this central lodge with a sweet garden setting. The top cabins have valley views. Large continental breakfast and resident dog included.

Abseil Inn (☎ 07-878 7815; www.abseilinn.co.nz; 709 Waitomo Caves Rd; d incl breakfast $135-165; 🛜) A *veeery* steep driveway (abseiling in from a helicopter might be an easier approach) takes you to this delightful B&B with four themed rooms, great breakfasts and witty hosts. The biggest room has a double bath and valley views.

Woodlyn Park (☎ 07-878 6666; www.woodlynpark.co.nz; 1177 Waitomo Valley Rd; d $160-225, extra person $15) Boasting the world's only hobbit motel (set into the ground with round windows and doors), Woodlyn Park's other sleeping options include the cockpit of a combat plane, train carriages and the 'Waitanic' – a converted WWII patrol boat fitted with chandeliers, moulded ceilings and shiny brass portholes.

It's extremely well done and the kids will love you for it.

Eating & Drinking

There isn't a supermarket, ATM or general store in Waitomo: buy provisions in Otorohanga (p225) or Te Kuiti (p232) before you visit.

Morepork Pizzeria & Cafe (☎ 07-878 3395; Kiwi Paka, Hotel Access Rd; breakfast & lunch $7-15, dinner $13-27; ☻ 8am-8pm) At the Kiwi Paka backpackers is this cheery joint, a jack-of-all-trades eatery serving breakfast, lunch and dinner either inside or out on the deck. The 'Caveman' pizza is a winner (the first person to ask for more pork will be shown the door).

ourpick Huhu (☎ 07-878 6674; 10 Waitomo Caves Rd; lunch $12-19, dinner $23-35; ☻ 10.30am-9pm; ☛ Ⓥ) Easily the best choice, you won't be disappointed if you come here twice a day. Slick and modern with charming service, it has great views from the afternoon-tipple-friendly terrace and sublime contemporary NZ food. Graze from a seasonal tapas-style menu (large or small plates) of Kiwi specialities such as *rewana* bread and beetroot-coloured *urenika* potatoes. Free wi-fi, too. Downstairs the Huhu Store sells designer NZ gifts.

Roselands Restaurant (☎ 07-878 7611; 579 Fullerton Rd; buffet per adult/child $27/14; ☻ 11am-2pm) Set amid genteel gardens 3km from Waitomo and popular with the tour-bus set, Roselands runs a generous lunchtime buffet: fresh fish, stir-fries and great-looking steaks.

Curly's Bar (☎ 07-878 8448; Hotel Access Rd; ☻ 11am-2am; ▣) A decent tavern with lots of beers on tap, good-value pub grub (mains $7 to $18), chunky wooden tables, internet access and occasional live music.

Getting There & Away

Naked Bus (☎ 0900 625 33; www.nakedbus.com) runs around five buses weekly to/from Otorohanga ($12, 20 minutes), Hamilton ($29, one hour) and New Plymouth ($39, three hours). Book in advance for fares as low as $1.

Waitomo Shuttle (☎ 07-873 8279; waikiwi@ihug. co.nz; one way adult/child $10/5) heads to the caves five times daily from Otorohanga (15 minutes away), coordinating with bus and train arrivals.

Waitomo Wanderer (☎ 0508 926 337; www.waitomo tours.co.nz; day tours incl Glow-worm Cave entry $119) operates a daily return services from Rotorua or Taupo, with optional caving and tubing

add-ons (packages $188 to $288). Shuttle-only services are $45 each way.

WAITOMO TO AWAKINO

This obscure route, heading west of Waitomo on Te Anga Rd, is the definition of off-the-beaten-track. It's a slow but fascinating alternative to SH3 if Taranaki's your goal. Only 12km of the 111km route remains unsealed, but it's nearly all winding and narrow. Allow around two hours (not including stops) and fill up with petrol.

Walks in the **Tawarau Forest**, 20km west of the caves, are outlined in DOC's *West of Marokopa* pamphlet ($1), including a one-hour track to the Tawarau Falls from the end of Appletree Rd.

The **Mangapohue Natural Bridge Scenic Reserve**, 26km west of Waitomo, is a 5.5-hectare reserve with a giant natural limestone arch. It's a five-minute walk to the arch on a wheelchair-accessible pathway. On the far side, big rocks full of 35-million-year-old oyster fossils jut up from the grass, and at night you'll see glow-worms: allow 15 minutes to loop back to the car park.

About 4km further west is **Piripiri Caves Scenic Reserve**, where a five-minute walk leads to a large cave containing fossils of giant oysters. Bring a torch and be prepared to get muddy after heavy rain. Steps wind down into the gloom…

The impressively tiered **Marokopa Falls** are located 32km west of Waitomo. A short track (15 minutes return) from the road leads to the bottom of the falls.

The falls are near Te Anga, where you can stop for a drink, some pub grub and a game of pool at friendly **Te Anga Tavern** (☎ 07-876 7815; Te Anga Rd; meals $12-13; ☻ noon-1am Tue-Sun), and maybe fire up the jumpin' country jukebox. Just past Te Anga you can turn north to Kawhia (p224), 59km away, or continue southwest to **Marokopa** (population 1560), a small black-sand village on the coast with some scarily big new mansions starting to appear. The whole Te Anga/Marokopa area is riddled with caves.

Marokopa Campground (☎ 07-876 7444; marokopa campground@xtra.co.nz; Rauparaha St; unpowered/powered sites $24/28, dm $18, van d $45) ain't flash but it's in a nice spot, close to the coast. There's a small shop that will cover the catering basics (bread, milk, cheese), as well as a tennis court and tiny library.

The road heads south to Kiritehere where it follows a bubbling stream through idyllic farmland to Moeatoa where it turns right (south) into Mangatoa Rd. Now you're in serious backcountry, heading into the dense **Whareorino Forest**. It would pay not to watch the movie *Deliverance* before tramping in this spectacularly remote tract of native bush. The 16-bunk DOC-run **Leitch's Hut** (www.doc.govt.nz; per adult $5) has a toilet, water and a wood stove; pick up a fact sheet from the DOC office in Hamilton or Te Kuiti.

At Waikawau it's worth taking the 5km detour along the unsealed road to the coast near **Ngarupupu Point**, where a 100m walk through a dank tunnel opens out on an exquisitely isolated stretch of black-sand beach. Think twice about swimming here; if you get caught in a rip you'll be halfway to Melbourne before your friends can reach help (but visit early and the only footprints in the sand will be yours).

The road then continues through another twisty 28km passing lush forest and the occasional farm before joining SH3 east of Awakino (p232).

TE KUITI
pop 4380

Cute little Te Kuiti sits in a valley between picturesque hills. It doesn't so much have a gimmick as an odd claim to fame: welcome to the shearing capital of the world! You won't have any doubt as to the veracity of that statement if you're here for the very sheepish Great New Zealand Muster (see below).

Information

Department of Conservation (DOC; ☎ 07-878 1050; www.doc.govt.nz; 78 Taupiri St; �比 8am-4.30pm Mon-Fri)
i-SITE (☎ 07-878 8077; www.waitomo.govt.nz; Rora St; �比 9am-5pm Mon-Fri, 10am-4pm Sat & Sun; ▢) Internet access and visitor information.

Festivals & Events

The highlight of the **Great New Zealand Muster** (www.waitomo.govt.nz; �比 late Mar/early Apr) is the legendary Running of the Sheep. Pamplona's got nothing on the sight of 2000 woolly demons stampeding down Te Kuiti's main street. The festival includes sheep-shearing championships, a parade, Maori cultural performances, live music, barbecues, *hangi* (feast from an oven in the ground) and lots of market stalls.

Sights & Activities

The most prominent landmark in town is the 7m, 7½-tonne **Big Shearer** statue at the south end of the Rora St shopping strip. Diagonally opposite is the magnificently carved **Te Tokanganui-a-noho Marae**. This was guerrilla leader Te Kooti's grateful gift to his hosts, Ngati Maniapoto, who sheltered him before his pardon in 1883 (see p352). You can't enter without permission, but you can get a good view from the gate.

Further down Rora St, **Te Kuititanga-O-Nga-Whakaaro** (the Gathering of Thoughts and Ideas) is a beautiful pavilion of etched-glass, *tukutuku* (woven flax panels) and wooden carvings that celebrates the town's history.

On the northwestern boundary of Te Kuiti, hill-topped **Brook Park** (Te Kumi Rd) has a 40-minute walk leading up the slope to the site of historic Matakiora Pa, constructed in the 17th century.

South of Te Kuiti, the **Central North Island Rail Trail** has been ascribed 'Quick Start' status as part of the proposed **New Zealand Cycle Trail** (www.tourism.govt.nz/our-work/new-zealand-cycle-trail-project) project. Most of the track will be on DOC-administered land; check the website for updates.

Sleeping

Casara Mesa Backpackers (☎ 07-878 6697; casara@xtra.co.nz; Mangarino Rd; dm/tw $25/55, d with/without bathroom $60/55) Feel the stress ease away as you're collected from town and driven five minutes up the hill to this ramshackle, homespun farmstay with a sublime vista from its quiet veranda.

Simply the Best B&B (☎ 07-878 8191; www.simplythebestbnb.co.nz; 129 Gadsby Rd; s/d incl breakfast $50/100) It's hard to argue with the immodest name when the prices are this reasonable and the hosts this charming. Warning: the spectacular views may illicit involuntary choruses of the Tina Turner anthem.

our pick **Waitomo Lodge Motel** (☎ 07-878 0003; www.waitomo-lodge.co.nz; 62 Te Kumi Rd; d/f from $110/185) If you can't find a bed in Waitomo itself (it happens), then this snappily designed motel at the Waitomo end of Te Kuiti is a brilliant alternative. Twenty spacious, modern rooms clad in plywood feature contemporary art, moody low-voltage lighting, flat-screen TVs and little decks overlooking Mangaokewa Stream in the units at the back. Bosco Cafe (p232) is across the street. Hipness in an un-hip town!

Eating & Drinking

Bosco Cafe (☎ 07-878 3633; 57 Te Kumi Rd; mains $9-20 ⏱ breakfast & lunch; Ⓥ) It's not damning it with faint praise to say that Bosco is the coolest place in Te Kuiti. This excellent industrial-chic cafe offers great coffee, tempting food (try the spinach, feta and pine-nut tart) and sweet service. It comes into its own on a sunny afternoon when the doors swing open onto Brook Park.

Riverside Lodge (☎ 07-878 8027; 1 Riverside Lane; lunch $9-23, dinner $18-35; ⏱ lunch & dinner Tue-Sun) On the riverbank just off King St, this family-friendly bar and bistro serves excellent shellfish, substantial pub meals or mini pizzas for a filling snack ($9). There are a couple of pool tables and the Eagles' 'Lyin' Eyes' on the juke.

Self caterers bound for Waitomo should stock up at **New World** (☎ 07-878 8072; Te Kumi Rd; ⏱ 8am-8pm).

Getting There & Away

InterCity (☎ 09-583 5780; www.intercity.co.nz) buses run daily to the following destinations (among others):

Destination	Price	Duration	Frequency
Auckland	$55	3½hr	4 daily
Mokau	$28	1hr	2 daily
New Plymouth	$28	2½hr	2 daily
Otorohanga	$20	20min	3 daily
Taumarunui	$27	1¼hr	1 daily

Naked Bus (☎ 0900 625 33; www.nakedbus.com) runs around five buses weekly to Auckland ($33, four hours), Hamilton ($20, 1½ hours), New Plymouth ($45, 2¼ hours) and Otorohanga ($13, 40 minutes). Book in advance for lower fares.

The **Dalroy Express** (☎ 0508 465 622; www.dalroy tours.co.nz) bus runs daily between Auckland ($38, 3½ hours) and New Plymouth ($28, 2¼ hours), stopping at Te Kuiti. Other stops include Hamilton ($18, 1½ hours), Mokau ($17, one hour) and Otorohanga ($11, 15 minutes).

Te Kuiti is on the **Overlander** (☎ 0800 872 467; www.tranzscenic.co.nz; daily Oct-Apr, Fri-Sun May-Sep) train route between Auckland ($81, 3½ hours) and Wellington ($107, 8¾ hours) via Hamilton ($53, one hour) and Taumarunui ($53, 50 minutes).

TE KUITI TO MOKAU
☎ 06

From Te Kuiti, SH3 runs southwest to the coast before following the rugged shoreline

PHONE ZONE

If you've been rabidly punching the 07 area code into your phone for weeks across Waikato and the King Country, note that the code changes to 06 from around Awakino heading south into Taranaki.

to New Plymouth. Along this scenic route the sheep stations sprout peculiar limestone formations before giving way to lush native bush as the highway winds along the course of the Awakino River.

The river spills into the Tasman at **Awakino** (population 60), a small settlement where boats shelter in the estuary while locals find refuge at the down-to-earth (or down-to-sea?) **Awakino Hotel** (☎ 06-752 9815; SH3; meals $5-20; ⏱ 11am-11pm Mon-Wed, 11am-midnight Thu-Sat, noon-8pm Sun).

A little further south the impressive **Maniaroa Marae** dominates the cliff above the highway. This important complex houses the anchor stone of the *Tainui waka* which brought this region's original people from their Polynesian homeland. Note the palisade tower and the intimidatingly carved meeting house, Te Kohaarua. You can get a good view from outside the fence – don't cross into the *marae* unless someone invites you.

Five kilometres further south, as the perfect cone of Mt Taranaki starts to take shape on the horizon, is the village of **Mokau** (population 400). It offers a fine stretch of black-sand beach and good surfing and fishing. From August to November the Mokau River (the second longest on the North Island) spawns some of the best whitebait in the North Island – and subsequently swarms of fiercely territorial whitebaiters.

The town's **Tainui Historical Society Museum** (☎ 06-752 9072; mokaumuseum@vodafone.co.nz; SH3; admission by donation; ⏱ 10am-4pm) has an interesting collection of old photographs and artefacts (pianolas, whale bones, dusty photos of the Queen) from the time when this once-isolated outpost was a coal and lumber shipping port for settlements along the river.

Mokau River Cruises (☎ 0800 665 2874, 06-752 9775; www.mokaurivercruises.co.nz; cruises adult/child $40/15) operates a three-hour river cruise with commentary onboard the historic *MV Cygnet*.

Just north of Mokau, **Seaview Holiday Park** (☎ /fax 06-752 9708; SH3; unpowered/powered sites $20/30,

WAIKATO & THE KING COUNTRY

cabins d $50-60, units from $85) is basic but it's right on the beach and the cabins have pastel paint schemes.

On the hill above the village the austere-looking but actually very friendly **Mokau Motel** (☎ 06-752 9725; www.mokaumotels.co.nz; SH3; s/d/tr $80/100/110; 🛜) offers fishing advice, no-nonsense self-contained units and three city-standard luxury studios (what a surprise!).

The **River Run Cafe** (☎ 06-752 9859; SH3; meals $5-23; ☽ 7am-7pm) has whitebait on the menu during the season (mid-August till the end of November), as well as everything from burgers, pies and cooked meals to ice cream and homemade cakes.

TAUMARUNUI
pop 5140

Maybe Taumarunui should get a gimmick, as this little town can feel a bit grim. The main reason to stay here is to kayak on the Whanganui River (see p262) or as a cheaper base for skiing in Tongariro National Park.

Information

Department of Conservation (DOC; ☎ 07-895 8201; www.doc.govt.nz; Cherry Grove Domain; ☽ 8am-5pm Mon-Fri) A field office not always open (call in advance).

Taumarunui i-SITE (☎ 07-895 7494; www.visit ruapehu.com; Hakiaha St; ☽ 9am-5pm) Visitor information and internet access. Pick up the *Ruapehu Chosen Pathways* brochure for regional information.

Sights & Activities

The main drag, Hakiaha St, has a few items of interest. At the eastern end is **Hauaroa Whare**, a beautifully carved house. At the western end **Te Rohe Potae** memorialises King Tawhiao's assertion of his *mana* (authority) over the King Country in a sculpture of a top hat on a large rock (see p224). At the end of Marae St, **Ngapuwaiwaha Marae** has interesting carvings and two historic river *waka* visible from the street. Don't enter the complex without permission.

The 3km **Riverbank Walk** along the Whanganui River runs from Cherry Grove Domain, 1km south of town, to Taumarunui Holiday Park (right). **Te Peka Lookout**, across the Ongarue River on the western edge of town, is a good vantage point.

The **Raurimu Spiral**, 30km south, is a unique feat of railway engineering that was completed in 1908 after 10 years' work. Rail buffs can experience the spiral by taking the train

(see below) to National Park township (return $106).

Taumarunui Jet Tours (☎ 0800 853 886, 07-896 6055; www.taumarunuijettours.co.nz; Cherry Grove Domain; 30min/1hr tour $60/90) runs high-octane jet-boat trips on the Whanganui River.

For details on the **Forgotten World Highway** between Taumarunui and Stratford, see p248.

For details on Whanganui River canoe and kayak operators, see p262.

Sleeping & Eating

Taumarunui Holiday Park (☎ 07-895 9345; www.taum arunuiholidaypark.co.nz; SH4; sites $27, cabins d $45-55, cottage d $65, extra person $15; 🖳) On the banks of the Whanganui River, 3km east of town, this shady camping ground offers safe river swimming and clean facilities.

Twin Rivers Motel (☎ 07-895 8063; www.twin riversinfo.co.nz; 23 Marae St; units $85-185; 🛜) Spick and span and constantly being upgraded (civic pride!). Some of the bigger units sleep up to seven.

Flax (☎ 07-895 6611; 1 Hakiaha St; brunch $9-17, dinner $22-34; ☽ 10am-2pm Tue, 9am-2pm & 5pm-late Wed & Thu, 9am-late Fri-Sun) Some locals say this place ain't what it used to be, but it's still the only place in Taumarunui where you can get a haloumi and semidried tomato tart. There are art-hung walls and an inventive modern menu.

Getting There & Away

Taumarunui is on SH4, 81km south of Te Kuiti and 41km north of National Park township.

InterCity (☎ 0508 353 947; www.intercity.co.nz) buses depart daily from the i-SITE, heading to Auckland ($58, 4½ hours, two daily) via Te Kuiti ($27, one hour, two daily), and Palmerston North ($52, 4¾ hours, one daily) via National Park ($21, 30 minutes, one daily).

Taumarunui is on the **Overlander** (☎ 0800 872 467; www.tranzscenic.co.nz; daily Oct-Apr, Fri-Sun May-Sep) train route between Auckland ($81, 4¾ hours) and Wellington ($107, 7½ hours) via Te Kuiti ($53, 1¼ hours) and National Park ($53, 1¼ hours).

OWHANGO
pop 210

A pint-sized village where all the street names start with 'O', Owhango makes a cosy base for walkers, mountain bikers (the 42 Traverse ends here; see p295) and skiers who can't afford to stay closer to the slopes in Tongariro National Park (p80). Take Omaki Rd for a two-hour loop walk through virgin forest in Ohinetonga Scenic Reserve.

Sleeping

Forest Lodge (☎ 07-895 4773; www.forest-lodge.co.nz; 12 Omaki Rd; dm/s/d $25/45/65, motel & cottage $95-120; 🖳) An excellent, snug backpackers with comfortable, clean rooms and good communal spaces. For privacy junkies there are separate self-contained motel and cottage units next door. It was up for sale when we visited – we hope the new owners don't drop the ball.

Blue Duck Lodge (☎ 07-895 6276; www.blueduck lodge.co.nz; RD2; dm $35, d $80-185, extra adult/child $37/20) Overlooking the Retaruke River 36km southwest of Owhango (take the Kaitieke turn-off 1km south of town), this ecosavvy place is actually three lodges, offering accommodation from dorms in an old shearers' quarters to a self-contained family cottage sleeping eight. The owners are mad-keen conservationists, restoring native bird habitats and historic buildings (you can volunteer and lend a hand).

Fernleaf B&B (☎ 07-895 4847; www.fernleaffarmstay. co.nz; 58 Tunanui Rd; s $85, d $100-120, all incl breakfast) This characterful villa on a third-generation cattle-and-sheep farm has two en-suite rooms with garden outlooks, plus a twin and a separate cottage double which share a bathroom. Generous breakfast and dinners ($30 per person by arrangement) are labours of love. It's just off SH4, 7km north of Owhango.

Eating & Drinking

Out Of The Fog Cafe (☎ 07-895 4800; SH4; meals $9-17; 🕑 breakfast & lunch Sat & Sun) Transport this uber-stylish cafe into any major city and it would get by just fine. The food is delicious and reasonably priced, the coffee is excellent and the electric fire will make you want to linger on cold days. Sadly, it's just open on weekends.

Owhango Hotel (☎ 07-895 4854; SH4; mains $15-24; 🕑 10.30am-late) The country pub doubles as the local store, and dishes up solid fare like lamb shanks and vegetarian pasta.

Getting There & Away

Owhango is 14km south of Taumarunui on SH4. All the **InterCity** (☎ 0508 353 947; www.inter city.co.nz) buses that stop in Taumarunui also stop here.

Taranaki

Halfway between Auckland and Wellington, Taranaki sits out on a limb in more ways than one. Somewhat off the main drag, the region relies upon the fat of the land and the natural riches offshore. Indeed, Taranaki is the Texas of New Zealand, with oil and gas streaming in from the rigs, plumping the region with an enviable affluence and stability. However, it's not only overseas visitors who miss the turn-off to Taranaki; lots of Kiwi travellers do, too.

This is remarkable when you consider what it is that puts the region on the map: the moody and magnetic volcanic cone of Mt Taranaki, standing smack-bang in the middle of Egmont National Park. It demands to be visited.

In the shadow of the mountain are many small towns, mostly sleepy and rural, but friendly to boot. On the eastern boundary of the province you'll find NZ's only republic – Whangamomona – a bushy little settlement, stranded in paradise.

New Plymouth is the hub of the 'naki (as they call it), home to the fabulous Govett-Brewster Art Gallery and an excellent provincial museum. It also has enough decent espresso joints to keep you wide awake.

Taranaki has a glut of black-sand beaches, and the summer months see the region swell as a wave of surfers and holidaymakers hit the coast. As for the rest of the year, there are plenty of things to see and places to visit – as long as you're as laid-back as the locals.

HIGHLIGHTS

- Walking up or around the massive cone of **Mt Taranaki** (p245)
- Riding the big breaks along **Surf Hwy 45** (p249)
- Getting experimental at New Plymouth's **Govett-Brewster Art Gallery** (p238)
- Taking a seal-spotting trip out to the **Sugar Loaf Islands Marine Park** (p239)
- Wandering through the rhododendron blooms at **Pukeiti Rhododendron Trust** (p244)
- Bouncing from bean to bean in **New Plymouth's cafes** (p243)
- Finding the **Forgotten World Hwy** (p248) and crossing the border into the **Republic of Whangamomona** (p248)

- Telephone code: 06
- www.taranaki.co.nz
- www.newplymouthnz.com

TARANAKI

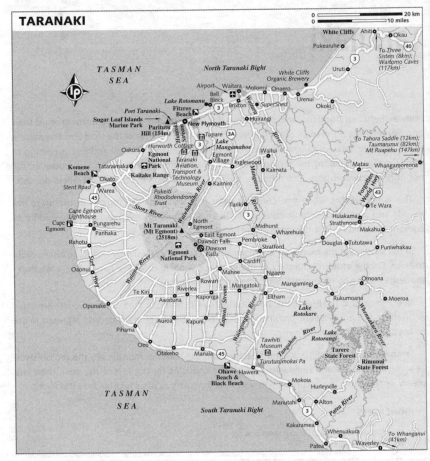

Climate

Mt Taranaki is one of NZ's wettest spots, and frequently cops snowfalls. The moisture-laden winds coming in from the Tasman Sea are the climatic culprits as they are swept up to freezing heights by the mountain. Weather on the mountain can be extremely change-able (see the boxed text, p246) and snow is common even in summer. Ironically, New Plymouth frequently tops the list of most sunshine hours in the North Island, empha-sising the changeability of weather in the region.

November to April are the region's warmer months when temperatures hover around 20°C. From May to August, the temperatures drop to around 5°C to 14°C.

Getting There & Around

Air New Zealand has domestic flights and onward connections to/from New Plymouth. InterCity and Naked Bus run several bus serv-ices connecting to New Plymouth; Dalroy Express and White Star are smaller companies on local routes.

Getting to Mt Taranaki is easy, as many shuttle services (p247) run between the mountain, New Plymouth and other sur-rounding towns.

NEW PLYMOUTH
pop 45,230

Dominated by Mt Taranaki and surrounded by lush farmland, New Plymouth acts as the west coast's only international deep-water port, handling cargo for much of this part of the North Island. The city has a thriving arts scene and an outdoorsy focus, with good beaches both in and around it and Egmont National Park just a short drive away. The town centre supports a heartening number of locally owned businesses (of little architectural merit), and the obligatory small-town convoy of boy-racers – who get to cruise the longest main street in the country.

History

Local Maori *iwi* (tribes) have long contested Taranaki lands. In the 1820s they fled to the Cook Strait region to escape Waikato tribes, who eventually took hold of the area in 1832. Only a small group remained, at Okoki Pa (New Plymouth), where whalers soon joined the fray. When European settlers arrived in 1841, the coast of Taranaki seemed deserted and there was little opposition to land claims. The New Zealand Company bought extensive tracts from the remaining Maori.

When other members of local tribes returned after years of exile, they fiercely objected to the land sale. Their claims were upheld when Governor FitzRoy ruled that the New Zealand Company was only allowed just over 10 sq km of the 250 sq km it had claimed as its own around New Plymouth. The Crown gradually acquired more land from Maori, and European settlers became increasingly greedy for the fertile land around Waitara.

The settlers forced the government to abandon negotiations with Maori, and war erupted in 1860. While Maori engaged in guerrilla warfare and held the rest of the province, the settlers seized Waitara. Taranaki chiefs had refused to sign the Treaty of Waitangi in 1840 and were brutally treated as rebels. By 1870 over 500 hectares of their land had been confiscated with the remainder acquired through dubious transactions.

In a time of relative peace, economic stability was largely founded on dairy farming. The discovery of natural gas and oil in 1959 and the creation of a natural gas field off the South Taranaki Bight have kept the province economically healthy in recent times.

Orientation

Devon St (East and West) is the city's hub and allegedly the longest main street in the country.

TARANAKI FACTS

Eat Anything at Sugar Juice Café (p250)
Drink A bottle of Mike's Mild Ale from White Cliffs Organic Brewery (p245)
Read *The Captive Wife* by Fiona Kidman, the fictionalised account of Betty Guard's largely satisfactory captivity among Taranaki Maori in the whaling days of the 1830s
Listen to Way, way too much Bryan Adams, Shania Twain and Fleetwood Mac on the local radio stations
Watch *The Last Samurai,* starring Tom Cruise (although Mt Taranaki was the real star)
Swim at Black-sand and surf Oakura Beach (p249)
Festival WOMAD (World of Music Arts and Dance) every March at New Plymouth's Bowl of Brooklands (p241)
Tackiest tourist attraction The 'Welcome to Manaia the Bread Capital' sign on Surf Hwy 45
Go green Environmental Products (p248) – every possum product purchased equals one less varmint chomping beautiful native bush

Information

For information about the region, pick up the free guides: *Taranaki: Like No Other, Northern Taranaki* and *South Taranaki.* Online, check out www.newplymouthnz.com and www.windwand.co.nz.

BOOKSHOPS

Benny's Books (☎ 06-759 4350; www.bennysbooks.co.nz; 21 Devon St E; ⏰ 8.30am-5.30pm Mon, Wed & Thu, 9am-5.30pm Tue, 8.30am-6pm Fri, 9am-2pm Sat) New releases, kids' books and mags.

INTERNET ACCESS

Internet access is available at the i-SITE and **Cyber Surf** (11b Devon St E; ⏰ 8.30am-7pm Mon-Fri, 9.30am-7pm Sat & Sun).

MEDICAL SERVICES

Medicross (☎ 06-759 8915; medicross@xtra.co.nz; 8 Egmont St; ⏰ 8am-8pm)
Phoenix Urgent Doctors (☎ 06-759 4295; npdocs@clear.net.nz; 95 Vivian St; ⏰ 8.30am-8pm)
Taranaki Base Hospital (☎ 06-753 6139; www.tdhb.org.nz; David St; ⏰ 24hr)

MONEY

The major banks have outlets and ATMs here. Visit the post office or **TSB Foreign Exchange** (☎ 06-968 3713; www.tsbbank.co.nz; 87 Devon

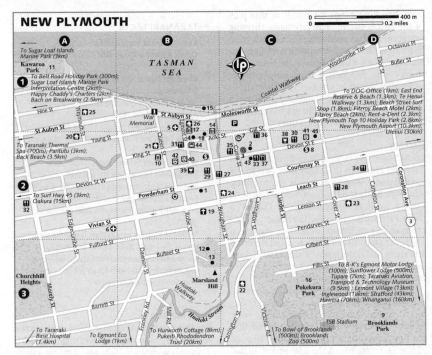

St E; 9am-5pm Mon-Fri, 10am-1pm Sat) for foreign exchange.

POST
Post office (www.nzpost.co.nz; 21 Currie St) Foreign exchange available.

TOURIST INFORMATION
Automobile Association (AA; ☎ 06-759 4010; www. aa.co.nz; 49-55 Powderham St; 8.30am-5pm Mon & Wed-Fri, 9am-5pm Tue)

Department of Conservation (DOC; ☎ 06-759 0350; www.doc.govt.nz; 55a Rimu St; 8am-4.30pm Mon-Fri)

New Plymouth i-SITE (☎ 0800 639 759, 06-759 6060; www.newplymouthnz.com; 1 Ariki St; 9am-6pm Mon, Tue, Thu & Fri, 9am-9pm Wed, 9am-5pm Sat & Sun;) In the Puke Ariki building; internet available.

Sights
PUKE ARIKI
Translating as 'Hill of Chiefs', **Puke Ariki** (☎ 06-759 6060; www.pukeariki.com; 1 Ariki St; admission free; 9am-6pm Mon & Tue, Thu & Fri, 9am-9pm Wed, 9am-5pm Sat & Sun) is home to the i-SITE, a museum, library, a cafe and the fabulous Arborio restaurant (p242). The excellent **museum** has

an extensive collection of Maori artefacts, plus wildlife and colonial exhibits. The regular 'Taranaki Experience' show tells the history of the province while the audience sits in pod-like seats that rumble and glow.

GALLERIES
The **Govett-Brewster Art Gallery** (☎ 06-759 6060; www.govettbrewster.com; 42 Queen St; admission free; 10am-5pm) is arguably the country's best regional art gallery and the crowd-pulling jewel in the town's crown. Presenting contemporary – often experimental – local and international shows, it's most famous for its connection with NZ sculptor, filmmaker and artist Len Lye (1901–80). His work is well represented here, with showings of his 1930s animation as well as super-clever kinetic works. The glass-fronted **Café Govett-Brewster** (meals $5-20; 8am-5pm Mon-Fri, 9am-5pm Sat & Sun) is also here.

To see what local artists have to offer, visit the reconstructed warehouse **Real Tart Gallery** (☎ 06-769 5717; www.real.tart.co.nz; 19 Egmont St; admission free; 10am-5pm Mon-Fri, 11am-4pm Sat & Sun). Exhibitions change regularly and most works are for sale.

PARKS

New Plymouth has several picturesque parks, the pick of which is the superb **Pukekura Park** (☎ 06-758 0370; www.pukekura.org.nz; end of Liardet St; ☺ daylight hr). A 10-minute stroll from the city centre, the park has 49 hectares of gardens, playgrounds, bush walks, streams, waterfalls, ponds and display houses (open 8.30am to 4pm). Next to the main lake (full of arm-sized eels and ducklings), the **Tea House** (snacks $3-8; ☺ 10am-5pm) serves up light meals and cream teas. **Row boats** (per 30min $10) make for lazy meanderings across the water on weekends and summer evenings. The technicoloured Festival of Lights (see p241) here draws the summer crowds, as does the classically English cricket oval, with terrace seating cut into the surrounding hills.

Adjoining Pukekura is **Brooklands Park** (☎ 06-759 6060; www.newplymouthnz.com; Brooklands Park Dr; ☺ daylight hr) home to the **Bowl of Brooklands** (www.bowl.co.nz), a world-class outdoor soundshell, hosting festivals like WOMAD (p241) and old-school rockers like Elton John and Fleetwood Mac. The park itself was once the grounds of a settler's home, destroyed by Maori, though the fireplace and chimney survive today. Highlights include a 2000-year-old puriri tree, a 300-variety rhododendron dell and the farmy **Brooklands Zoo** (admission free; ☺ 9am-5pm).

Along the city waterfront is **Puke Ariki Landing** (St Aubyn St), an historic area studded with sculptures, including the wonderfully eccentric **Wind Wand** (www.windwand.co.nz). Designed by Len Lye – the artist who has put this town

on the map in modern times – this 45m-high kooky kinetic sculpture is a truly beloved icon of bendy poleness.

HISTORIC SITES

The free *Heritage Trail New Plymouth* brochure available from the i-SITE outlines an interesting self-guided tour of around 31 historic sites.

The humble, artefact-filled **Richmond Cottage** (☎ 06-759 6060; www.pukeariki.com; cnr Ariki & Brougham Sts; admission free; ☺ 11am-3.30pm Sat & Sun) was built in 1854 across St Aubyn St, and was moved to its present site in the early 1960s. We think it still qualifies as one of New Plymouth's oldest buildings!

The austere **St Mary's Church** (☎ 06-758 3111; www.stmarys.org.nz; 37 Vivian St; services 8am, 10am & 5pm Sun), built in 1846, is the oldest stone church in NZ. Its graveyard has the headstones of early settlers and soldiers who died during the Taranaki Land Wars (1860–61 and 1865–69). Impressed by their bravery, the British also buried several Maori chiefs here.

SUGAR LOAF ISLANDS MARINE PARK

These rugged islets, a section of Back Beach on the west side of Paritutu and its waters 1km offshore were made into a **marine park** (http://homepages.ihug.co.nz/~lealand) in 1991. The islands, which are eroded volcanic remnants, are a refuge for sea birds and over 400 NZ fur seals. Most seals come here from June to October but some stay all year round. You can learn more about the marine park at the tiny **Interpretation Centre** (Ocean View Pde; admission

TARANAKI

MAORI NZ: TARANAKI

Ever since Mt Taranaki fled here to escape romantic difficulties (p245), the region has had a turbulent history. The region has seen conflicts between local *iwi* (tribes) and invaders from the Waikato, followed by two wars with the government (see the boxed text, p33) – first in 1860–61, when Waikato *iwi*, traditionally an enemy (p208), came to Taranaki's aid; and then again in 1865–69, when local forces were surprisingly successful under the remarkable general, Titikowaru. Following the wars there were massive land confiscations and an extraordinary passive-resistance campaign at Parihaka (see the boxed text, p250).

To further explore the history of local Maori, visit Puke Ariki (p238) in New Plymouth, and Parihaka if you can. Readers should look out for Dick Scott's *Ask That Mountain* or Maurice Shadbolt's very funny *Monday's Warriors*.

---

free; 9am-5pm daily) on the Lee Breakwater promenade.

You can visit the islands with **Happy Chaddy's Charters** (06-758 9133; www.windwand.co.nz/chaddies charters; Ocean View Pde; trips adult/child $30/10). Chaddy is quite the character and offers great value for money: expect at least four laughs a minute on this one-hour bob around on the chop. Departs daily from Lee Breakwater, tide and weather permitting. You can also hire kayaks (single/double $15/30 per hour) and bikes ($10 per 30 minutes) here.

See also Canoe & Kayak Taranaki (opposite).

NEW PLYMOUTH OBSERVATORY
Atop Marsland Hill (great views!) is this wee **observatory** (06-753 2358; http://sites.google.com/site/astronomynp; Marsland Hill, off Robe St; admission $5; 7.30-9.30pm Tue Mar-Oct, 8.30-10pm Tue Nov-Feb). Public nights include a planetarium program and, if the weather is clear, viewing through a 15cm refractor telescope. Also on the hill is the cacophonous 37-bell **Kibby Carillon**, a huge automated glockenspiel-like device which tolls out across the New Plymouth rooftops.

PARITUTU
Above the power station west of town is Paritutu, a steep-sided and craggy **hill** whose name translates appropriately as 'Rising Precipice'. From the summit you can see for miles around: out to the Sugar Loaves, down to the town and back to the mountain beyond. These views have to be earned by a 20-minute scramble to the top. Well worth it.

Activities
SURFING
The black, volcanic-sand beaches of Taranaki are world renowned for surfing and wind-surfing. Close to the eastern edge of town are **Fitzroy Beach** and **East End Beach** (allegedly the cleanest beach in Oceania). There's also decent surf at **Back Beach**, near Paritutu, at the western end of the city. **Oakura** is popular too (p249; reachable by CityLink buses; see p244). In fact there are so many surf beaches along the coast that the road south is now known as Surf Hwy 45 (p249).

Beach Street Surf Shop (06-758 0400; www.taranaki surf.com; 39 Beach St, Fitzroy; 2hr lesson $75; 9am-6pm) offers lessons, gear hire and tours. **Tarawave Surf School** (06-752 7474; tarawave@xtra.co.nz; 1½-hr lesson $65) is based further south at Oakura, while **Taranaki Coastal Surf Charters** (06-751 2483) provides customised guided surf tours.

TRAMPING
The i-SITE stocks the *New Plymouth District Guide to Walkways* leaflet, including coastal, local reserve and park walks. The **Coastal Walkway** (7km) from Lake Rotomanu to Port Taranaki, makes for a scenic orientation of the town. The highly recommended **Te Henui Walkway** (6km), extending from the coast at East End Reserve to the city's southern boundary, is an interesting streamside amble. **Huatoki Walkway** (5km), following Huatoki Stream, makes an attractive walk to the city centre.

OTHER ACTIVITIES
The warm mineral water filling the tanks at **Taranaki Thermal Spa** (06-759 1666; www.windwand.co.nz/mineralpools; 8 Bonithon Ave; treatments $5-245; 9am-5pm Mon & Tue, 9am-9pm Wed-Fri, noon-9pm Sat, noon-8pm Sun) was discovered during the search for oil around 1910. The private baths are filled on arrival, and there's a suite of massage and beauty therapies available. An absolute tonic.

Just west of town in grassy Kawaroa Park is the **Todd Energy Aquatic Centre** (☎ 06-759 6060; www. newplymouthnz.com; Kawaroa Park; admission adult/child $4/3, waterslide $3.50; ⏱ 6am-8.30pm Mon-Fri, 8.30am-7pm Sat & Sun), which has a waterslide, outdoor pool and indoor pool.

See also Canoe & Kayak Taranaki (below).

Tours

See also Scenic Flights (p246), and Happy Chaddy's Charters (opposite).

Canoe & Kayak Taranaki (☎ 06-769 5506; www. canoeandkayak.co.nz; half-day trips incl hire $70) Paddle out to the Sugar Loaf Islands or over the gentle Waitara River rapids.

Taranaki Adventure Tours (☎ 021 183 9044; www. taranakiadventure.com; tours 1-/2-day $249/949) Comprehensive tours of city, mountain and region involving plenty of exercise.

Taranaki Tours (☎ 0800 886 877, 06-757 9888; www. taranakitours.com; tours half-/full day from $80/120) Offers several themed tours, strong on Maori culture and natural history.

Festivals & Events

Festival of Lights (☎ 06-759 6060; www.festivalof lights.co.nz) Complete with costumed characters roaming the undergrowth, this colourful display lights up Pukekura Park from late December to mid-February.

Taranaki Rhododendron & Garden Festival (☎ 06-759 8412; www.rhodo.co.nz) NZ's oldest and most famous garden festival, held late October/early November each year.

WOMAD (World of Music Arts & Dance; ☎ 06-759 8412; www.womad.co.nz) A diverse array of local and international artists perform at the Bowl of Brooklands each March.

Sleeping

BUDGET

Sunflower Lodge (☎ 0800 422 257, 06-759 0050; www. sunflowerlodge.co.nz; 33 Timandra St; dm/d $25/65; 🖵 🛜) Down a steep driveway a few minutes' drive south of town, Sunflower does its best to transcend its mid-'80s rest-home origins, and (with the exception of some relentlessly floral wallpaper) succeeds. Bonuses like quality mattresses, free local calls and a heavy-duty kitchen and laundry help the cause.

Shoestring Backpackers (☎ 06-758 0404; www. shoestring.co.nz; 48 Lemon St; dm/s/d $28/50/70; 🖵 🛜) Inside a labyrinthine 1920s heritage building with a forest full of timber detailing, this isn't the fanciest option but it's well maintained and brimming with character. The upstairs

rooms are the pick: secluded, quiet and catching the morning sun. Out the back is a deck and barbecue. The co-owned Cottage Mews Motel (p242) is next door.

Egmont Eco Lodge (☎ 06-753 5720; www.yha.co.nz; 12 Clawton St; dm/d from $28/70; 🖵) An immaculate YHA in a glade with chirping birds and a chuckling creek. There are mixed dorms in the main lodge, smaller pinewood cabins down below (sleeping up to four), and a tidy (if small) kitchen. It's a bit of a hike uphill from town, but the prospect of free nightly Egmont cake will put a spring in your step.

Seaspray House (☎ 06-759 8934; www.seasprayhouse. co.nz; 13 Weymouth St; dm/s/d $29/45/70; 🖵) A big old house with gloriously high ceilings, Seaspray has had a recent makeover inside but remains relaxed and affordable, with well-chosen retro and antique furniture. Fresh and arty, it's a rare bunk-free backpackers (just 14 beds!). Closed June and July.

Arcadia Lodge (☎ 0508 272 233, 06-769 9100; www.arca dialodge.net; 52 Young St; dm/d/f incl breakfast $35/85/150; 🖵 🛜) A former rest home tacked onto a big old lemon villa (originally built for the local newspaper editor), Arcadia is a homey B&B with a lovely breakfast room, genteel lounge, spa, barbecue, and a superb timber-ceilinged family room upstairs with sea views.

Belt Road Holiday Park (☎ 0800 804 204, 06-758 0228; www.beltroad.co.nz; 2 Belt Rd; sites $32, cabins $65-120; 🖵 🛜) This pohutukawa-covered holiday park isn't the flashest contender, but it sits atop a bluff overlooking the increasingly interesting Lee Breakwater area, about a 10-minute walk from town. Million-dollar views!

New Plymouth Top 10 Holiday Park (☎ 0800 758 256, 06-758 2566; www.nptop10.co.nz; 29 Princes St, Fitzroy; sites/cabins from $38/75, units $85-110, motels $95-180; 🖵 🛜 🐕) Sequestered in Fitzroy, 3.5km east of town and a seven-minute walk to the beach, the Top 10 feels a bit like a school camp, with a dinky little row of blue-and-yellow units. Life-sized chess set, trampoline, laundry and spacious kitchen make a stay here worthwhile.

MIDRANGE & TOP END

Carrington Motel (☎ 06-757 9431; www.newplymouth motel.co.nz; 61 Carrington St; s/d/f $90/105/165) Sixteen old but tidy units close to Pukekura Park and a 10-minute walk to town. It's very family friendly and great value (especially in winter), but noisy when the hoons career up

Carrington St. The showers are like a tsunami from the sky.

Cottage Mews Motel (☎ 06-758 0403; www.cottage mews.net.nz; 50 Lemon St; s/d $95/105; 🛜) A small, modest motel where you'll feel like family, rather than a guest. The well-kept rooms have interesting layouts, there's a lawn out the front instead of a car park, and you can pop next door to the co-owned Shoestring Backpackers (p241) and remember how travelling was before your career took off.

B-K's Egmont Motor Lodge (☎ 0800 115 033, 06-758 5216; www.egmontmotorlodge.co.nz; 115 Coronation Ave; d $115-170; 🖳 🛜) Opposite the racecourse, corporate B-K's has ground-floor units and oceans of parking. Rooms are plain but comfortable and clean, and the manager readily shares a few laughs with the cleaners (a good sign). Free internet and DVDs.

Bella Vista (☎ 0800 235 528, 06-769 5932; www.bella vistamotels.co.nz; cnr King & Queen Sts; d $120-160; 🖳 🛜) A dependable, vaguely Spanish-looking option right in the centre of town. Basic rooms have toast-making facilities only; fancier rooms have full kitchenettes. Bonuses, such as fair-trade plunger coffee and free bicycles and internet abound.

our pick Fitzroy Beach Motel (☎ 06-757 2925; www.fitzroybeachmotel.co.nz; 25 Beach St; s/d $120/130, 2br unit $165; 🛜) Brand-new when we visited, this old-time motel (just 160m from Fitzroy Beach) has been thoroughly redeemed with a major overhaul and extension. Highlights include quality carpets, double glazing, lovely bathrooms, 32in LCD TVs, and an absence of poky studio-style units (all one- or two-bedroom). Winner!

Waterfront (☎ 06-769 5301; www.waterfront.co.nz; 1 Egmont St; r $190-550; 🖳 🛜) Sleek and snazzy, the Waterfront is *the* place to stay, particularly if the boss is paying. The minimalist studios are pretty flash, while the penthouses steal the show with big TVs and little balconies. It's got terrific views from some – but not all – rooms, but certainly from the curvy-fronted bar and restaurant.

Nice Hotel (☎ 06-758 6423; www.nicehotel.co.nz; 71 Brougham St; d/ste from $230/290; 🛜) High-class from top to tail, 'nice' is the understatement of the decade. Seven rooms feature luxury furnishings, designer bathrooms and select *objets d'art*: the ground-floor multiroom suite even has a grand piano! The in-house restaurant, Table, is one for the gourmands (mains $35, open for dinner).

Eating

RESTAURANTS

Frederic's (☎ 06-759 1227; 34 Egmont St; plates $7-18; 🕑 2pm-late Mon-Thu, 11am-late Fri-Sun) Freddy's is a fab new gastro-bar with quirky interior design (rusty medieval chandeliers, peacock-feather wallpaper, religious icon paintings), serving generous share-plates. Order some meatballs with bell-pepper sauce, or some green-lipped mussels with coconut cream, chilli and coriander to go with your beer.

Bach on Breakwater (☎ 06-769 6967; Ocean View Pde; brunch $10-20, dinner $24-34; 🕑 9.30am-10pm Wed-Sun; V) Constructed from weighty recycled timbers, this cool cafe-bistro in the emerging Lee Breakwater precinct looks like an old sea-chest washed up after a storm. Expect plenty of seafood and steak, plus Asian- and Middle Eastern–influenced delights (curries, wontons, felafels) and killer coffee. The seafood chowder is a real winter warmer.

our pick Arborio (☎ 06-759 1241; inside Puke Ariki, 1 Ariki St; brunch $11-13, dinner $16-32; 🕑 breakfast, lunch & dinner) Despite looking like a cheese grater, Arborio is the star of New Plymouth's local food show. It's airy, arty and modern, with sea views and faultless service. The Med-influenced menu ranges from an awesome Moroccan lamb pizza to pastas, risottos and barbecued chilli squid with lychee-and-cucumber noodle salad. Cocktails and NZ wines also available.

IndiaToday (☎ 06-758 4444; 40 Devon St E; mains $16-18; 🕑 lunch Mon-Fri, dinner daily; V) A sumptuous gold-walled room draped with bolts of silk, IndiaToday wafts with spicy aromas and snaky tabla tunes enticing you in off the street. Dapper waiters, subcontinentally perfect in gold tunics and black pants, serve up classic and creative curries.

Portofino (☎ 06-757 8686; 14 Gill St; mains $19-60; 🕑 dinner) This discreet little family-run eatery has been here for years, serving old-fashioned Italian pasta and pizza just like *nonna* used to make. The *rigatoni Portofino* is a knockout (spinach, fetta, garlic and sun-dried tomatoes).

André L'Escargot (☎ 06-758 4812; 37 Brougham St; mains $30-34; 🕑 dinner Mon-Sat, lunch by appointment) If you're looking for the best in town, this is it. Audaciously serving up snails in the 'naki since 1976, we doff our beret to the man who has no doubt raised the bar and kept it there. All classic French fare, indulgent and largely gout-inducing, plus killer cocktails.

CAFES

Chaos (☎ 06-759 8080; 36 Brougham St; snacks $4-6, meals $6-16; ☽ breakfast & lunch; Ⓥ) Not so much chaotic as endearingly scruffy, Chaos is a dependable spot for a coffee and a zingy breakfast. Ricotta-and-blueberry pancakes, background jazz, smiley staff and boho interior design – hard to beat! Plenty of vegetarian and gluten-free options, too.

Empire (☎ 06-758 1148; 112 Devon St W; lunch $6-10; ☽ 7.30am-4.30pm Mon-Fri, 9am-2pm Sat) A perfectly evolved Kiwi tearoom with pretty china plates nailed to the wall and a sunny courtyard out back. Tasty sandwiches, salads, lasagne and filos, plus delectable cakes and biscuits for afters.

Elixir (☎ 06-769 9020; 117 Devon St E; brunch $7-18, dinner $18-22; ☽ 7.30am-4pm Mon, 7.30am-late Tue-Fri, 9am-late Sat, 9am-3pm Sun) Behind a weird louvered wall facing onto Devon St, Elixir fosters an American-diner vibe, serving up everything from coffee, cake, bagels and eggs on toast, through to more innovative evening fare. Below a wall of rock posters, the coffee machine gets a serious work-out.

Petit Paris (☎ 06-759 0398; 34 Currie St; lunch $8-15; ☽ 7.30am-4pm) Ooh-la-la: lashings of buttery treats! Flying the *tricolore* with pride, Petit Paris is a *boulangerie* and patisserie turning out crispy baguettes and *tart au citron* (lemon tart), or an omelette or *croque monsieur* for lunch.

QUICK EATS

Andre's Pies & Patisserie (☎ 06-758 3062; 44 Leach St; snacks $3-7; ☽ 6am-3.30pm Mon-Fri) Expanding waistlines since 1972, this is an easy pull-over off the main road through town. Dive on in for hefty pies and calorific slabs of cake.

Sandwich Extreme (☎ 06-759 6999; 52 Devon St E; meals $7-13; ☽ 8am-4pm Mon-Fri, 8.30am-3pm Sat) Toasties, sandwiches, baked spuds, coffee, salads, bagels and cakes served fresh and fast by friendly staff.

SELF-CATERING

Fresha (☎ 06-758 8284; cnr Devon & Morley Sts; snacks $7-13; ☽ 9am-6pm Mon-Fri, 9am-5pm Sat; Ⓥ) A drool-worthy emporium for picnic-basket essentials: meats, wines, olive oil, relish, fruit and veg, cheeses, jams and prepackaged meals (try the fish pie). There's an excellent cafe here too.

The gargantuan **Pak N Save** (☎ 06-758 1594; 53 Leach St; ☽ 8am-midnight) supermarket is just east of the town centre.

Drinking

Matinee (☎ 06-759 2088; 69 Devon St W; ☽ 9.30am-late Tue-Sat) A good option (one of the only ones, actually) for those who prefer top shelf to Tui, and electronica to '80s rock. Inside a former theatre, the design is all mirrors, silk drapes and art nouveau wallpaper; the tables outside afford puffing and people-watching. Jazz Fridays; DJs Saturdays.

Powder Room (☎ 06-759 2089; 108 Devon St W; ☽ 4pm-late Tue-Sat) With slabs of shagpile carpet stapled to the wall, this slinky red-white-and-black bar serves super-smooth cocktails and wondrous wines. After sipping a few you might feel like sidling onto the dance floor (frequent DJs) to throw a few decorous shapes.

Crowded House (☎ 06-759 4921; 93 Devon St E; ☽ 10am-late) A sporty hive of boozy activity with pool tables (in good nick), restaurant (fries with everything) and big-screen TVs. No sign of Neil Finn…

Entertainment

Basement Bar (☎ 06-758 8561; Basement, cnr Devon St W & Egmont St; admission free-$10; ☽ varies with gigs) Underneath a regulation Irish pub, the grungy Basement Bar is the best place in town to catch up-and-coming live acts, broadly sheltering under a rock, metal and punk umbrella.

TSB Showplace (☎ 06-759 0021; 92 Devon St W; ☽ box office 9am-5pm Mon-Fri, 10am-1pm Sat) Housed in the old opera house, the three-venue Showplace stages a variety of big performances *(Miss Saigon, Swan Lake)*, as does the Bowl of Brooklands (p239), administered by the same people. For bookings go to Ticketek (www.ticketek.co.nz) or Ticket Direct (www.ticketdirect.co.nz).

Top Town Cinema 5 (☎ 06-759 9077; www.skycitycinemas.co.nz; 119 Devon St E; tickets adult/child $12.50/7.50; ☽ 10am-11pm) is a worn cinema complex, the floor a sea of popcorn.

Getting There & Away

You can book tickets for InterCity, Tranz Scenic, Interislander and Bluebridge ferries at the i-SITE inside Puke Ariki.

AIR

Air New Zealand (☎ 0800 737 000, 06-757 3300; www.airnz.co.nz; 12 Devon St E; ☽ 9am-5pm Mon-Wed & Fri, 9.30am-5pm Thu) has daily direct flights to/from Auckland (45 minutes, four daily), Wellington

TARANAKI

(50 minutes, four daily) and Christchurch (1½ hours, one daily), with onward connections.

New Plymouth Airport (☎ 06-755 2250) is 11km east of the centre off SH3. **Scott's Airport Shuttle** (☎ 0800-373 001, 06-769 5974; www.npairportshuttle.co.nz; adult from $22) operates a door-to-door shuttle to/from the airport – you can book online.

BUS
The bus centre is on the corner of Egmont and Ariki Sts.

InterCity (☎ 09-583 5780; www.intercity.co.nz) services numerous destinations including:

Destination	Price	Duration	Frequency
Auckland	$52	6¼hr	4 daily
Hamilton	$45	4hr	2 daily
Palmerston North	$29	4hr	1 daily
Wellington	$39	7hr	1 daily
Whanganui	$29	3hr	1 daily

Naked Bus (☎ 0900 625 33; www.nakedbus.com) services run to the following destinations (among many others). Book in advance for big savings.

Destination	Price	Duration	Frequency
Auckland	$29	6¼hr	1 daily
Hamilton	$26	3½hr	1 daily
Palmerston North	$18	3½hr	1 daily
Wellington	$29	6hr	1 daily
Whanganui	$17	2½hr	1 daily

The **Dalroy Express** (☎ 0508 465 622, 06-759 0197; www.dalroytours.co.nz) bus runs daily to/from Auckland ($59, six hours) via Hamilton ($40, four hours), extending south to Hawera ($18, 45 minutes).

White Star (☎ 0800 465 622, 06-759 0197; www.whitestarbus.co.nz) has two buses each Thursday and Friday and one every other day to/from Whanganui ($27, 2½ hours), Palmerston North ($30, 4¼ hours), Wellington ($47, 6¼ hours) and many small towns in between.

Getting Around
CityLink (☎ 06-758 2799; www.taranakibus.info; adult $3-5) services run Monday to Saturday around town, as well as north to Waitara and south to Oakura on weekdays. Buses depart the bus centre on the corner of Egmont and Ariki Sts.

Cycle Inn Bike Hire (☎ 06-758 7418; www.cycleinn.co.nz; 133 Devon St E; per half-/full day $10/15; 8.30am-5pm Mon-Fri, 9am-3pm Sat, 10.30am-1pm Sun) rents out

bicycles. **Happy Chaddy's Charters** (p240) also rents out bikes.

For cheap car hire, try **Rent-a-Dent** (☎ 06-757 5362; www.newplymouthcarrentals.co.nz; 592 Devon St E), or for a cab call **Energy City Cabs** (☎ 06-757 5580).

For shuttle services to Mt Taranaki, see p247.

AROUND NEW PLYMOUTH
Although Egmont National Park is the pinnacle of the region's attractions, there are plenty of other happy time-wasters around New Plymouth's fringes.

South of Town
PUKEITI RHODODENDRON TRUST
This 4-sq-km **garden** (☎ 06-752 4141; www.pukeiti.org.nz; 2290 Carrington Rd; adult/child $12/free; 9am-5pm Oct-Mar, 10am-3pm Apr-Sep), located 20km south of New Plymouth, is home to a remarkable collection of rhododendrons and azaleas. The flowers generally bloom between September and November, but it's worth a visit any time of year. The scenic journey there passes between the Pouakai and Kaitake Ranges, both part of Egmont National Park (it's a skinny road – keep your wits about you!). The Gatehouse Café (meals $7 to $18; open 10am to 4pm) is here too.

TUPARE
Tupare (☎ 06-765 7127; www.tupare.info; 487 Mangorei Rd; admission free; 9am-5pm, tours 11am Mon-Fri) is a Tudor-style house designed by the renowned architect James Chapman-Taylor. It is a picture, but the highlight of this 7km trip south of town will likely be the stunning 3.6 hectare garden surrounding it. Bluebells, birdsong – a picnicker's dream.

HURWORTH COTTAGE
This 1856 **cottage** (☎ 06-759 2006; www.historic.org.nz; 906 Carrington Rd; adult/child $5/2; 11am-3pm Sat & Sun), about 8km south of New Plymouth, was built by four-time NZ prime minister Harry Atkinson. The cottage is the sole survivor of a settlement abandoned at the start of the Taranaki Land Wars, and as such affords interesting insights into the lives of early settlers.

TARANAKI AVIATION, TRANSPORT & TECHNOLOGY MUSEUM & LAKE MANGAMAHOE
Around 9.5km south of New Plymouth is the **Taranaki Aviation, Transport & Technology Museum** (TATATM; ☎ 06-752 2845; www.nzmuseums.co.nz; cnr SH3

& Kent Rd; adult/child $7/2; 10.30am-4pm Sat & Sun), which takes you on a trip down memory lane with its ramshackle displays of old planes, trains, automobiles and general household miscellany. Ask to see the stuff made by the amazing bee guy (hexagons ahoy!). The duck-filled Lake Mangamahoe (access from 7am to 8.30pm) is across the highway.

North via SH3
Heading north along the coast from New Plymouth is the scenic SH3. This is the way to Waitomo, and one of the roads to Hamilton. Get the free *Northern Taranaki* brochure from the i-SITEs in Otorohanga (p225) or New Plymouth (p238).

Continuing north on SH3 are various seaward turn-offs to high sand dunes and surf beaches. **Urenui**, 16km past Waitara, is a summer hot spot.

About 5km past Urenui you'll find arguably the highlight of North Taranaki – **White Cliffs Organic Brewery** (06-752 3676; www.organicbeer. co.nz; Main Rd Nth; tastings free, tours $5; 10am-6pm) – home of award-winning beers. The brewery offers tours (book in advance), takeaways, tastings of the legendary Mike's Pale Ale (the pilsener and lager are ace, too), and an Oktoberfest party every (you guessed it) October. A little further on is the turn-off to Pukearuhe and **Whitecliffs**, huge precipices that resemble their Dover namesake. From here the **Whitecliffs Walkway** (Oct-Jun) leads to the Tongaporutu River via a tunnel from the beach (check the tides – go when it's low). On clear days the five- to seven-hour walk affords superb views of the coastline and the mountains (Taranaki and Ruapehu).

If you're continuing up to Mokau, it's worth stopping at the **Three Sisters**, signposted just south of the Tongaporutu Bridge – you can walk along the coast at low tide. The beach is quietly dramatic, with the two sisters standing somewhat forlornly off the coast (their other sister sadly collapsed in a heap).

MT TARANAKI (EGMONT NATIONAL PARK)
A classic 2518m volcanic cone dominating the landscape, Mt Taranaki is a magnet to all who catch his eye. Geologically, Taranaki is the youngest of three large volcanoes – Kaitake and Pouakai are the others – which stand along the same fault line. With the last eruption over 350 years ago (you can see lava flows covering the top 1400m), experts say that the mountain is overdue for another go. But don't let that put you off – this mountain is an absolute beauty and the highlight of any visit to the region.

History
According to Maori legend, Taranaki belonged to a tribe of volcanoes in the middle of the North Island. However, he was forced to depart rather hurriedly when he was caught with Pihanga, the beautiful volcano near Lake Taupo and the lover of Mt Tongariro. As he fled south (some say in disgrace; others say to keep the peace), Taranaki gouged out a wide scar in the earth (now the Whanganui River) and finally settled in the west in his current position. He remains here in majestic isolation, hiding his face behind a cloud of tears.

It is said that Maori did not heavily settle the area between Taranaki and Pihanga because they feared the reunification of the lovers in a spectacular eruption. Instead, Maori settlements in this district lined the coast between Mokau and Patea, concentrated around Urenui and Waitara. The mountain itself was supremely sacred, both as a burial site for chiefs and as a hideout in times of danger.

It was Captain Cook who named the mountain Egmont, after the Earl he sought to flatter at that particular moment. Egmont National Park was created in 1900, making it NZ's second oldest. Mt Taranaki eventually reclaimed its name, although the name Egmont has stuck like, well, egg. The mountain starred as Mt Fuji in *The Last Samurai* (2003), the production of which caused near-hysteria in the locals, especially when Tom Cruise came to town.

Information
Dawson Falls visitor centre (027 443 0248; www. doc.govt.nz; Manaia Rd, Kaponga; 9am-4pm Thu-Sun Mar-Nov, daily Dec-Feb) On the southeastern side of the mountain, fronted by an awesome totem pole.
Metphone (0900 999 06) Weather updates.
North Egmont visitor centre (06-756 0990; North Egmont; www.doc.govt.nz; 8am-4.30pm) Current and comprehensive national park info, plus a greasy-spoon cafe (meals $11 to $19).

Activities
TRAMPING
Due to its accessibility, Mt Taranaki ranks as the 'most climbed' mountain in NZ. Nevertheless, tramping on this mountain is dangerous and

should not be undertaken lightly (see the boxed text, below). It's *crucial* to get advice before departing and to leave your intentions with a DOC visitor centre or i-SITE.

Most walks are accessible from North Egmont, Dawson Falls or East Egmont. Check out DOC's pamphlet *Short Walks in Egmont National Park* ($2.50), and the free *Taranaki: A Walker's Guide* booklet for more info.

From North Egmont, the main walk is the scenic **Pouakai Circuit**, a two-day 23km loop through alpine, swamp and tussock areas with awesome mountain views. Short, easy walks from here include the **Ngatoro Loop Track** (one hour), **Veronica Loop** (two hours) and **Connett Loop** (40 minutes return). The **Summit Track** also starts from North Egmont. It's a poled route taking eight to 10 hours (14km) return, and should not be attempted by inexperienced people, especially in icy conditions and snow.

East Egmont has disabled access on **Potaema Track** (30 minutes return) and **East Egmont Lookout** (30 minutes return); a longer walk is the steep **Enchanted Track** (two to three hours return).

At Dawson Falls you can do several short walks including **Wilkies Pools Loop** (one hour return) or the excellent but challenging **Fanthams Peak Return** (five hours return), which is snowed-in during winter. The **Kapuni Loop Track** (1½ hours) runs to the impressive **Dawson Falls** themselves.

The difficult 55km **Around-the-Mountain Circuit** takes three to five days and is for expe-

rienced trampers only. There are a number of huts en route, tickets for which should be purchased in advance (see Sleeping, below).

The **York Loop Track** (three hours), accessible from York Rd north of Stratford, is a fascinating walk following part of a disused railway line.

You can tramp without a guide from February to March when snowfalls are low, but at other times inexperienced climbers can check with DOC for details of local clubs and guides. It costs around $300 per day to hire a guide. Reliable operators include the following:
Adventure Dynamics (☎ 0800 151 589, 06-751 3589; www.adventuredynamics.co.nz)
MacAlpine Guides (☎ 06-765 6234, 027 441 7042; www.macalpineguides.com)
Top Guides (☎ 0800 448 433, 021 838 513; www.topguides.co.nz)

SCENIC FLIGHTS
To get up above the slopes, try the following operators:
Beck Helicopters (☎ 0800 336 644, 06-764 7073; www.heli.co.nz) Scenic mountain flights from $225.
Heliview (☎ 0508 435 484, 06-753 0123; www.heliview.co.nz) Offers a range of sightseeing tours; a 30-minute city-and-mountain flight costs $280.
New Plymouth Aero Club (☎ 06-755 0500; www.airnewplymouth.co.nz) Standard and customised scenic flights from $66.
Precision Helicopters Limited (PHL; ☎ 0800 246 359, 06-752 3291; www.precisionhelicopters.com) A 50-minute mountain flight costs $280.

SKIING
From Stratford take Pembroke Rd up to Stratford Plateau, from where it's a 1.5km walk to the small **Manganui** club ski field (see p80). The Stratford i-SITE has daily weather and snow reports; otherwise you can ring the **snow-phone** (☎ 06-759 1119) or check the webcam at www.skitaranaki.co.nz.

Sleeping
Several DOC huts are scattered about the mountain, accessible by tramping tracks. Most cost $15 per night (Syme and Kahui cost $5); purchase hut tickets in advance from DOC. BYO cooking, eating and sleeping gear, and bookings are not accepted – it's first come, first served. Remember to carry out *all* your rubbish.

Missing Leg (☎ 06-752 2570; missingleg@xtra.co.nz; 1082 Junction Rd, Egmont Village; unpowered/powered sites $15/17, dm/d $25/60; ▣) This eccentric backpacker

---

DECEPTIVE MOUNTAIN

Mt Taranaki may look like an easy climb, but this scenic mountain has claimed more than 60 lives. The principal hazard is the weather, which can change from summery to whiteout conditions unexpectedly and almost in an instant. You may leave New Plymouth in sunshine and find yourself in snowfall up at altitude. There are also precipitous bluffs and steep icy slopes.

There are plenty of short walks, safe for much of the year, but for adventurous trampers January to March is the best time to go. You must take an appropriate map (DOC's detailed *Egmont National Park* map costs $19) and consult a DOC officer for current conditions. You *must* also register your tramping intentions with the DOC visitor centre or i-SITE.

property has a strange lack of natural light – OK for sleeping! Dorm accommodation is up in the loft, plus there's a handful of shabby-chic baches out the back.

Konini Lodge (☎ 06-756 0990; www.doc.govt.nz; Upper Manaia Rd; dm adult/child $20/10) Basic bunkhouse accommodation 100m downhill from the Dawson Falls visitor centre. Dorms feed off a huge communal space.

Eco Inn (☎ 06-752 2765; www.ecoinn.co.nz; 671 Kent Rd; s/tw/d $30/52/60; ⌂) About 6.5km up the road from the turn-off at the Aviation, Transport & Technology Museum (p244), this super ecofriendly place is made from recycled timber and runs on solar, wind and hydropower. There's a spa and pool table, and transport to and from the mountain is available. Good for groups.

Camphouse (☎ 0800 688 272, 06-756 9093; www.mttaranaki.co.nz/retreat/camphouse; North Egmont; dm/d/f $30/70/160) Bunkhouse-style accommodation behind the North Egmont visitor centre in a historic 1850 corrugated-iron building, complete with bullet holes in the walls (from shots fired at settlers by local Maori during the Taranaki Land Wars). Endless horizon views from the porch.

Rahiri Cottage (☎ 06-756-9093; www.mttaranaki.co.nz; Egmont Rd, RD6; d with/without breakfast $160/145) Right on the edge of Egmont National Park on the way to North Egmont, this 1929 clinker-brick cottage was once the park tollgate, and today offers luxury B&B rooms in a bush setting. Upmarket but unpretentious; sleeps five (whole cottage $305).

Anderson's Alpine lodge (☎ 06-765 6620; www.andersonsalpinelodge.co.nz; 922 Pembroke Rd; d incl breakfast $160-190; ⌂) With picture-postcard mountain views, this lovely Swiss-owned lodge is on the Stratford side of the mountain. Inside are three en-suite rooms with lots of timberwork; outside are billions of birds and Lady Hookswood-Smith, a rather obstreperous pig.

Mountain House (☎ 06-765 6100; www.mountainhouse.co.nz; Pembroke Rd; s/d $170/195) This lodge, on the Stratford side of the mountain (15km from the SH3 turn-off and 3km to the Manganui ski area), has recently renovated motel-style rooms and chalets with kitchens. There's a European-style restaurant here too (meals $12 to $42, open for breakfast, lunch and dinner).

Getting There & Away

There are three main entrance roads to Egmont National Park, all of which are well signposted and either pass by or end at a DOC visitor centre. Closest to New Plymouth is North Egmont: turn off SH3 at Egmont Village, 12km south of New Plymouth, and follow the road for 14km. From Stratford, turn off at Pembroke Rd and continue for 15km to East Egmont and the Manganui ski area (p80). From the southeast, Upper Manaia Rd leads up to Dawson Falls, 23km from Stratford.

There are no public buses to the national park but numerous shuttle-bus operators will gladly take you there (one way $30 to $40, return $45 to $50):

Cruise NZ Tours (☎ 0800 688 687; kirkstall@xtra.co.nz) Departs New Plymouth 7.30am for North Egmont; returns 4.30pm. Other pick-ups/drop-offs by arrangement.

Eastern Taranaki Experience (☎ 06-765 7482; www.eastern-taranaki.co.nz) Departs from Stratford; extra charge from New Plymouth.

Kiwi Outdoors (Map p238; ☎ 06-758 4152; www.kiwioutdoorsstores.co.nz; 18 Ariki St, New Plymouth; ⌚ 8.30am-5pm Mon-Fri, 9am-2.30pm Sat, 10am-2pm Sun) Pick-up points and times to suit; gear hire available.

Taranaki Tours (☎ 0800 886 877, 06-757 9888; www.taranakitours.com) Pick-up points and times by arrangement.

AROUND MT TARANAKI

There are two principal highways around the mountain, both linking New Plymouth and Hawera. SH3, on the inland side of the mountain, is the road most travelled; the longer coastal route is SH45, aka Surf Hwy 45 (p249).

Inglewood
pop 3090

Handy to the mountain on SH3, the little main-street town of Inglewood (www.inglewood.co.nz) is an adequate stop for supermarket supplies and a noteworthy stop for a steak-and-egg pie at **Nelsons Bakery** (☎ 06-756 7123; 45 Rata St; pies $3-4; ⌚ 6am-4.30pm Mon-Fri, 7am-4pm Sat). Inglewood's other shining light is the cute **Fun Ho! National Toy Museum** (☎ 06-756 7030; www.funho.com; 25 Rata St; adult/child $6/free; ⌚ 10am-4pm), which shows and sells old-fashioned sand-cast toys of Kiwi yesteryear. It doubles as the local visitor information centre.

On the road into town from New Plymouth, **White Eagle Motel** (☎ 06-756 8252; www.whiteeaglemotel.co.nz; 87b Rata St; s/d from $90/95, extra person $20) is basic but clean and quiet. The two-bedroom units feel bigger than they are.

Inside a fire-engine-red heritage building, jazzy **Macfarlane's Caffe** (☎ 06-756 6665; 1 Kelly St; brunch $9-17, dinner $14-28; ☼ 9am-5pm Sun-Wed, 9am-late Thu-Sat) sells super-sized custard squares and coffee during the day and wild boar sausages at night (among other things). Its venison Taranaki Burger rules.

Funkfish Grill (☎ 06-756 7287; 32 Matai St; mains $24-33; ☼ 4pm-late Tue-Thu, Sat & Sun, 3pm-late Fri) is a hip pizzeria and fish-and-chippery doing eat-in and takeaway meals, and doubles as a bar at night. Try the tempura scallops.

Stratford
pop 5330

Forty kilometres southeast of New Plymouth on SH3, Stratford plays up its namesake of Stratford-upon-Avon, Shakespeare's birth-place, by naming its streets after bardic characters. Stratford also claims NZ's first **glockenspiel** (☼ 10am, 1pm, 3pm & 7pm). Four times daily this clock doth chime out Shakespeare's greatest hits with some fairly wooden performances.

Stratford i-SITE (☎ 0800 765 6708, 06-765 6708; www.stratfordnz.co.nz; Prospero Pl; ☼ 8.30am-5pm Mon-Fri, 10am-3pm Sat & Sun) also houses the **Percy Thomson Gallery** (☎ 06-765 0917; www.percythomsongallery.org.nz; admission free; ☼ 10.30am-4pm Mon-Fri, 10.30am-3pm Sat & Sun), a community gallery displaying eclectic local and touring art shows.

One kilometre south of Stratford on SH3, the **Taranaki Pioneer Village** (☎ 06-765 5399; www.pioneervillage.co.nz; adult/child/family $10/5/20; ☼ 10am-4pm) is a 4-hectare outdoor museum housing 40 historic buildings. It's very bygone-era and more than a little spooky: a visit here will stop you complaining about how hard life is nowadays.

Not far from the Dawson Falls turn-off, 11km from Stratford, is **Environmental Products** (☎ 06-764 6133; www.envirofur.co.nz; 1013 Opunake Rd, Mahoe; ☼ 9am-5pm Mon-Fri, 10am-4pm Sat & Sun), a possum-skin tannery and manufacturer of bags, boots, slippers, hats, rugs and other accessories. Less pesky possums means more native wildlife and vegetation.

Seemingly embalmed in calamine lotion, the pretty-in-pink **Stratford Top Town Holiday Park** (☎ 06-765 6440; www.stratfordtoptownholidaypark.co.nz; 10 Page St; dm from $22, unpowered/powered sites from $28/34, cabins/units from $50/90; ☼) is a trim caravan park offering one-room cabins, motel-style units and backpackers' bunks, plus spa, bar-becue and bike hire.

All stone-clad columns, jaunty roof angles, timber louvres and muted cave-colours, flashy **Amity Court Motel** (☎ 06-765 4496; www.amitycourt motel.co.nz; 35 Broadway N; d/1br/2br $120/140/160; ☼) is the new kid on the Stratford block, upping the town's accommodation standings 100%.

For more accommodation around Stratford, see p246.

Across the street from Stratford i-SITE is the disarmingly retro, trapped-in-a-time-warp tearoom, **Casa Pequena** (☎ 06-765 6680; 280 Broadway; snacks $3-5, meals $12-28; ☼ 6am-4pm Mon-Fri, 7am-1.30pm Sat), serving classics like bangers-and-mash and hot beef-and-gravy sandwiches.

Forgotten World Hwy

The 150km road between Stratford and Taumarunui (SH43) has become known as the Forgotten World Hwy. The drive winds through hilly bush country with 12km of un-sealed road, and along the way passes many historic and heritage sites such as Maori *pa*, abandoned coal mines and memorials to those long gone. Allow four hours and plenty of stops, and fill up with petrol at either end as there are no petrol stations along the route itself. A pamphlet is available from i-SITEs or DOC visitor centres in the area.

The town of **Whangamomona** (population 170) is a highlight. This quirky village became an independent republic after disagreements with local councils (see the boxed text, oppo-site). In the middle of town is the unmissable grand old **Whangamomona Hotel** (☎ 06-762 5823; www.whangamomonahotel.co.nz; 6018 Forgotten World Hwy; meals $12-18; ☼ 11am-late), a pub with accommo-dation ($110 per person including dinner and breakfast), offering 'real country hospitality'.

In the Tahora Saddle, the highest point on the highway, **Kaieto Café** (☎ 06-762 5858; kaieto cafe@quicksilver.net.nz; SH43; meals $7-20; ☼ lunch) has lunches, panoramic views, a four-bed cabin and a campsite (sites/cabin per person $10/35).

Eastern Taranaki Experience (☎ 06-765 7482; www.eastern-taranaki.co.nz) runs tours through the area (day trips per person from $45; four day/three night trips per person $460, minimum four people).

The **Central Taranaki Tourism Network** (☎ 06-765 7180; cttn@xtra.co.nz) runs several regional day trips, including the Forgotten World Discoveries ($189 per person) and Highway 43 Explorer ($99) excursions.

POODLE FOR PRESIDENT!

Whangamomona is New Zealand's only republic, declared so after a disagreement with government authorities. The story goes that in 1989 the local council sought to adjust the town's boundaries, shifting its jurisdiction from Taranaki council to that of Manawatu-Whanganui. The citizens – independent, flinty folk – were not prepared to take this lying down. For starters it meant they'd have to play for a rival rugby team. And so it was that they dumped both councils and became a republic, complete with democratically elected presidents who have included Billy Gumboot the goat (elected after eating all the opposition's votes) and Tai Poutu the poodle (who stepped down after an assassination attempt). The current overlord is Murt 'Murtle the Turtle' Kennard (who is actually a human).

The town celebrates Republic Day in January every two years, with a military themed extravaganza. Visitors (many railed in from Auckland – passports required) can throw a gumboot, crack a whip, bet on the sheep races, skin a possum and engage in all manner of other forgotten world activities.

SURF HWY 45

Sweeping south from New Plymouth to Hawera, the 105km-long SH45 is known as Surf Hwy 45, and although it does indeed have many good beaches dotted along it, don't expect to see waves crashing ashore the whole way. The drive generally just undulates through farmland – be ready to swerve for random tractors and Holden drivers. Pick up the *Surf Highway 45* brochure at visitor centres.

Oakura
pop 1220

From New Plymouth, first cab off the rank is laid-back Oakura, 15km southwest on SH45. Its broad sweep of beach is hailed by waxheads for its right-hander breaks, but it's also great for families (take sandals – that black sand scorches feet). A surf shop on the main road, **Vertigo** (☎ 06-752 7363; vertigosurf@xtra.co.nz; 2hr lessons $75; 9am-5pm Mon-Fri, 10am-4pm Sat) runs surf lessons. See also Tarawave (p240).

SLEEPING & EATING
Wave Haven (☎ 06-752 7800; www.thewavehaven.co.nz; cnr Ahu Ahu Rd & SH45; dm/s/d $20/40/60) A surfy backpackers close to the big breaks, this colonial charmer has a coffee machine, a large deck to chill out on, and surfboards and empty wine bottles strewn about the place.
Oakura Beach Holiday Park (☎ 06-752 7861; www.oakurabeach.com; 2 Jans Tce; unpowered/powered sites $32/36, cabins $65-120;) A classic beachside park catering best to caravans but with basic cabins and well-placed spots to pitch a tent (absolute beachfront!).
Oakura Beach Motel (☎ 06-752 7680; www.oakurabeachmotel.co.nz; 53 Wairau Rd; s/d from $90/100;) A

very quiet, seven-unit motel set back from the main road, just three minutes' walk to the beach. It's a '70s number, but the owners keep things ship-shape, and there are 300 DVDs to choose from!
Ahu Ahu Beach Villas (☎ 06-752 7370; www.ahu.co.nz; 321 Ahu Ahu Rd; s/d/f from $250/250/350;) Pricey, but pretty amazing. Set on a knoll overlooking the big wide ocean, these luxury, architect-designed villas are superbly eccentric, with huge recycled timbers, bottles cast into walls, lichen-covered roofs and polished-concrete floors with inlaid paua. Even rock stars stay here.
Snickerdoodles (☎ 06-752 7227; 1151 SH45; baked goods $4-7; breakfast & lunch Mon-Sat) On the main road this tiny bakery bakes daily. Swing in for a chunky cheese scone, some yummy pumpkin bread or a coffee.
Carriage (☎ 06-752 1007; rear of 1145 SH45; brunch $12-15, dinner $14-28; 5pm-late Mon-Thu, 10am-3pm & 5pm-late Fri-Sun) Housed in a very slow moving railway carriage set back from the main street, this is an unusual stop for good-value burgers, steaks, pasta, spring rolls and curries.

Oakura to Opunake
From Oakura, SH45 veers inland, with detours to sundry beaches along the way. On the highway near Okato the 130-year-old **Stony River Hotel** (☎ 06-752 4253; www.stonyriverhotel.co.nz; 2502 SH45, Okato; s/d/tr incl breakfast $80/122/183) has simple country-style en suite rooms and a straight-up public bar (mains $10 to $28, open for dinner Wednesday to Saturday).

Just after Warea is **Stent Road**, a legendary shallow reef break, suitable for experienced surfers. Newbies will prefer the gentler waves of **Komene Beach**, which at the mouth of Stony River attracts its fair share of interesting bird life, including black swans.

Another coastward turn-off at **Pungarehu** leads 20km to **Cape Egmont Lighthouse** (☎ 06-278 8599; Bayly Rd; ☺ Sat & Sun by appointment), a photogenic cast-iron lighthouse that was shifted here in 1881. The road to Parihaka (see the boxed text, below) leads inland from this stretch of highway.

Opunake
pop 1500

A summer town and the surfie epicentre of the 'naki, Opunake has a sheltered family beach and plenty of challenging waves further out.

The **Opunake i-SITE** (☎ 0800 111 323, 06-761 8663; opunakei@stdc.govt.nz; Tasman St; ☺ 9am-5pm Mon-Fri, 9.30am-1pm Sat; ☐ ☎) is in the local library and has free internet. **Dreamtime Surf Shop** (☎ 06-761 7570; 102 Tasman St; ☺ 9am-5pm) has internet access and surf-gear hire (surfboards/bodyboards/wetsuits per half-day $30/20/10).

Opunake Motel & Backpackers (☎ 06-761 8330; www.opunakemotel.co.nz; 36 Heaphy Rd; dm $25, cottage & units d $85-100) offers a range of options from old-style motels to a funky dorm lodge on the edge of some sleepy fields (a triumph in genuine retro).

An old bank plastered with hyper-coloured surf murals, **Surf Lodge 45** (☎ 06-761 8345; sl45@xtra. co.nz; cnr Tasman & Napier Sts; s/d/f $25/50/75) is much less exciting inside, with low-key, no-frills backpacker rooms upstairs.

Opunake Beach Holiday Park (☎ 0800 758 009, 06-761 7525; www.opunakebeachnz.co.nz; Beach Rd; sites/cabins/cottages $32/60/85; ☐ ☎) is a mellow spot right on the surf beach. The laugh-a-minute host will direct you to your grassy site, the big camp kitchen or the cavernous amenities block.

our pick **Sugar Juice Café** (☎ 06-761 7062; 42 Tasman St; snacks $4-10, mains $25-29; ☺ 9am-4pm Tue & Sun, 9am-10pm Wed-Sat) has the best food on SH45. It is buzzy and brimming with delicious, filling things (try the basil-crusted snapper or cranberry lamb shanks). Terrific coffee, salads, wraps, tarts, cakes and big brekkies too – don't pass it by.

Hawera
pop 11,000

Don't expect much urban virtue from agricultural Hawera, the largest town in South Taranaki. Still, it's a good pit stop for supplies, to stretch your legs, or to bed down for a night. Not quite on the coast, it's 70km south of New Plymouth via SH3 and 90km from Whanganui.

PARIHAKA

From the mid-1860s Parihaka, a small Maori settlement east off Hwy 45 near Pungarehu, became the centre of a peaceful resistance movement, one which involved not only other Taranaki tribes, but Maori from around the country. Its leaders, Te Whiti-o-Rongomai and Tohu Kakahi, were of both Taranaki and Te Ati Awa descent.

After the Land Wars (see the boxed text, p33), confiscation of tribal lands was the central problem faced by Taranaki Maori, and under Te Whiti's leadership a new approach to this issue was developed: resisting European settlement through nonviolent methods.

When the government started surveying confiscated land on the Waimate plain in 1879, unarmed followers of Te Whiti, wearing the movement's iconic white feather in their hair and in good humour, obstructed development by ploughing troughs across roads, erecting random fences and pulling survey pegs. Many were arrested and held without trial on the South Island, but the protests continued and intensified. Finally, in November 1881 the government sent a force of over 1500 troops to Parihaka. Its inhabitants were arrested or driven away, and the village was later demolished. Te Whiti and Tohu were arrested and imprisoned until 1883. In their absence Parihaka was rebuilt and the ploughing campaigns continued into the 1890s. The imprisonment of Parihaka protesters without trial also continued until the late 1890s.

In 2006 the NZ government issued a formal apology and financial compensation to the tribes affected by the invasion and confiscation of Parihaka lands.

Te Whiti's spirit lives on at Parihaka, with annual meetings of his descendants and a public music-and-arts festival held early each year. Parihaka is open to the public on the 18th and 19th of each month. For more information, read Dick Scott's *Ask That Mountain*, Gregory O'Brien and Te Miringa Hohaia's beautiful *Parihaka – The Art of Passive Resistance*, or see www.parihaka.com.

INFORMATION

Automobile Association (AA; ☎ 06-278 5095; www.aa.co.nz; 121 Princes St; �9 8.30am-5pm Mon-Fri)
Hawera i-SITE (☎ 06-278 8599; www.stdc.co.nz; 55 High St; �9 8.30am-5.15pm Mon-Fri, 10am-3pm Sat & Sun, reduced hr in winter)

SIGHTS & ACTIVITIES

The austere **Hawera Water Tower** (adult/child/family $2/1/5; �9 10am-2pm) beside the i-SITE is one of the coolest things in Hawera. Grab the key from the i-SITE, ascend, then scan the horizon for signs of life (you can see the coast and Mt Taranaki on a clear day).

Elvis lives! At least he does at the **Elvis Presley Memorial Record Room** (☎ 027 498 2942; www.digitalus.co.nz/elvis; 51 Argyle St; admission by donation; �9 by appointment only), which houses a collection of the King's records (over 5000), souvenirs and the man's Cadillac. Maybe.

The excellent **Tawhiti Museum** (☎ 06-278 6837; www.tawhitimuseum.co.nz; 401 Ohangai Rd; adult/child $10/2; �9 10am-4pm Fri-Mon Feb-Apr & Sep-Dec, Sun only Jun-Aug, daily Jan) houses a private collection of remarkable exhibits, models and dioramas. The creepily lifelike human figures were modelled on people around the region, while a large collection of tractors pays homage to the province's rural heritage. It's near the corner of Tawhiti Rd, 4km from town.

Try some white-knuckle white-water sledging with **Kaitiaki Adventures** (☎ 06-752 8242; www.damdrop.com; 3hr trip $100), which involves sliding down a 7m dam on a sledge, then sledging a further 5km on the Waingongoro River (Grade II to III). Also included is a journey past an historic *pa* site, birthplace of the Maori prophet Tohu Kakahi. Kaitiaki also run trips from Rotorua (see p310).

Two kilometres north of Hawera, on Turuturu Rd, are the remains of the pre-European **Turuturumokai Pa**. The name translates to 'stakes for dried heads', which were used to ward off potential attackers. Today, all that's left are a few remains of ramparts and storage pits. The reserve is open to the public daily.

Northeast of Hawera is **Lake Rotorangi**, the longest artificial lake in NZ (46km). There are three access roads: Ball Rd, north of Patea, from which you can visit the dam; Tangahoe Rd (largely unsealed); and Mangamingi Rd, where there's a public domain. Freedom camping is allowed at the Patea Ball Rd, Tangahoe and Eltham (Glen Nui) entrances to the lake, where freshwater access and toilet facilities are available. Ask for a detailed map at the Hawera i-SITE or Automobile Association (left).

SLEEPING & EATING

our pick **Wheatly Downs Farmstay** (☎ 06-278 6523; www.mttaranaki.co.nz; 46 Ararata Rd, Hawera; unpowered sites $36, dm/s/tw $30/70/70, d with/without bathroom $115/70) Set in a rural idyll, this heritage building is a classic, with its clunky wooden floors and no-nonsense fittings. Host Gary is an affable bloke, showing you his special pigs and letting you milk his cows. To get there, head past Tawhiti Museum and keep going on the Ararata Rd for 5.5km. Pick-ups by arrangement.

Caniwi Lodge (☎ 06-764 7577; www.caniwilodge.co.nz; 505a Aorere Rd, Lake Rotorangi; d cabins/chalets $50/295) On the shores of Lake Rotorangi, this lodge caters for all with its basic cabins and luxury chalets. Back-to-nature activities to enjoy include kayaking, birdwatching or hanging out with the farm animals. From Eltham follow King Edward St (soon Rawhitiroa Rd) for 15km, turning right into Aorere Rd. It's 5km from there.

Hawera Central Motor Lodge (☎ 06-278 8831; www.haweracentralmotorlodge.co.nz; 53 Princes St, Hawera; d $125-165; 🖳) The pick of the town's motels (better positioned and much quieter than any of those along South Rd), the shiny new Hawera Central does things with style: grey-and-eucalypt colour scheme, frameless-glass showers, big flat-screen TVs, good security, DVD players, free movie library… Nice one!

Indian Zaika (☎ 06-278 3198; 91 Princess St, Hawera; mains $16-19; �9 lunch Mon-Sat, dinner daily) For a fine lunch or dinner, try this spicy-smelling, black-and-white diner, serving decent curries in upbeat surrounds. Takeaways available.

Whanganui & Palmerston North

The Whanganui and Manawatu districts comprise a sizeable chunk of the North Island's south, running from Tongariro National Park in the north down towards Wellington. This is mellow, pastoral country, draped with rounded green hills, gently bent roads, socially significant cities and magical national parks, rivers and gorges.

The history-rich Whanganui River curls through Whanganui National Park down to Whanganui city. Ripe with outdoor opportunities, the splendiferous Whanganui River Rd mimics the river's bows, while Whanganui itself, a 19th-century river port, has aged gracefully, recently reinventing itself as a centre for New Zealand glass art.

Palmerston North, the Manawatu's main city, is a town of two peoples: tough-talkin' country fast-foodies in hotted-up cars and caffeinated Massey University literati, coexisting with none of Cambridge's 'Town vs Gown' sabre-rattling. During the semester the cafes jump and pubs overflow with students.

Beyond the city the Manawatu blends rural grace with yesterday's pace, cut by the dramatic slice of Manawatu Gorge. A meandering Manawatu drive is the perfect antidote to NZ's tourism juggernaut – you might even squeeze in a little laziness!

HIGHLIGHTS

- Watching a glass-blowing demonstration at one of **Whanganui's glass studios** (p255)
- Blowing out the cobwebs with a jetboat ride on the **Whanganui River** (p263)
- Traversing the rainy **Whanganui River Road** (p264) – it's all about the journey, not how fast you get there
- Tramping the Matemateaonga and Mangapurua Tracks in the **Whanganui National Park** (p263)
- Flexing your All Blacks spirit at Palmerston North's **New Zealand Rugby Museum** (p265)
- Recaffeinating on the hip George St cafe strip in **Palmerston North** (p268)
- Connecting life, art and mind at **Te Manawa** (p265) museum in Palmerston North
- Hiking through the awesome **Manawatu Gorge** (p270)

Whanganui
★ National Park

Whanganui
River ★

★ Whanganui
River Road

★ Whanganui

Palmerston North ★   ★ Manawatu
Gorge

- Telephone code: 06
- www.wanganui.com
- www.manawatunz.co.nz

WHANGANUI & PALMERSTON NORTH

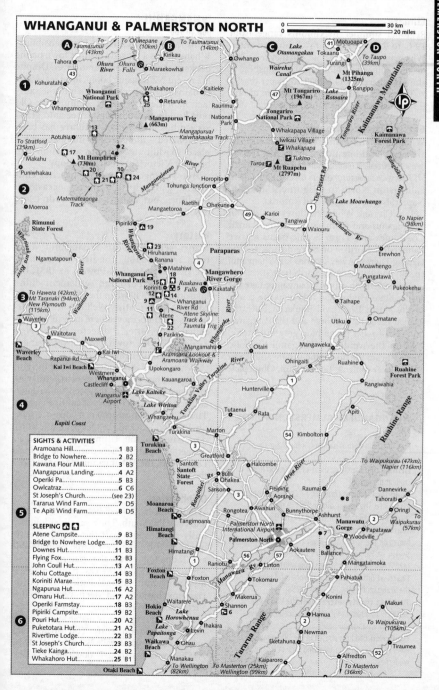

| 0 | | | 30 km |
| 0 | | | 20 miles |

SIGHTS & ACTIVITIES

Climate

Regional summer maximums range from 19°C to 24°C; 10°C to 14°C during winter. Whanganui winters are mild, but they're chillier on the Palmerston North plains. Sunshine is abundant hereabouts – 2000 hours per year!

The region receives around 60mm of rain through summer and 95mm in winter.

Getting There & Around

Whanganui and Palmerston North airports are serviced domestically by **Air New Zealand** (www.airnewzealand.com). **Sunair Aviation Ltd** (☎ 07-575 7799; www.sunair.co.nz) offers direct flights from Palmerston North to Gisborne, Hamilton, Napier, New Plymouth and Rotorua.

InterCity and White Star buses service both Whanganui and Palmerston North. Tranzit Coachlines and Tranz Scenic trains service Palmerston North. For more details, see the Getting There & Away sections for Whanganui (p260) and Palmerston North (p269).

Heading north from Whanganui, take the scenic State Highway 4 (SH4) to the centre of the North Island via Raukawa Falls, the Mangawhero River Gorge and the Paraparas, an area of *papa* (large blue-grey mudstone) hills, or the winding Whanganui River Rd (p264). From the north, the Whanganui River is road-accessible at Taumarunui, Ohinepane and Whakahoro.

WHANGANUI & PALMERSTON NORTH FACTS

Eat Anything from Whanganui's hip main-street eateries (p259)

Drink A cold handle or six at a Palmerston North student bar (p268)

Read The *Wanganui Chronicle*, NZ's oldest newspaper

Listen to The rockin' album *Back to the Burning Wreck* by Whanganui riff-monsters The Have

Watch The colonial epic *River Queen* (2006), filmed on the Whanganui River

Swim at Palmerston North's Lido Aquatic Centre (p265), whistling Boz Scaggs' *Lido* all the while

Festival Tinted, warped and wonderful glass at the Wanganui Festival of Glass (p258)

Tackiest tourist attraction The kitsch pay-per-view fountain at Virginia Lake Scenic Reserve (p256) in Whanganui

Go Green Paddle a stretch of the Whanganui River (p262) – an awe-inspiring slice of NZ wilderness

---

WHANGANUI

pop 40,700

With rafts of casual Huck Finn sensibility, Whanganui is a raggedy historic town on the banks of the wide Whanganui River. Despite the recent NZ housing boom, local real estate remains relatively cheap, much to the satisfaction of the thriving arts community. Old port buildings are being turned into glass-art studios and the town centre has been rejuvenated – there are few more appealing places to while away a sunny afternoon than beneath Victoria Ave's leafy canopy.

But Whanganui isn't all peaches-and-cream: gang violence makes occasional headlines, but visitors really needn't lose any sleep.

History

Maori settlement at Whanganui dates from around 1100. The first European on the river was Andrew Powers in 1831, but Whanganui's European settlement didn't take off until 1840 when the New Zealand Co could no longer satisfy Wellington's land demands – settlers moved here instead. Initially called Petre, after a director of the New Zealand Co, the town's name was changed to Whanganui in 1844.

When the Maori understood that the gifts the Pakeha had given them were in permanent exchange for their land, they were understandably irate, and seven years of conflict ensued. Thousands of government troops occupied the Rutland Stockade in Queens Park, which dominates the hill. Ultimately, the struggle was settled by arbitration; during the Taranaki Land Wars the Whanganui Maoris assisted the Pakeha.

Orientation

Whanganui is midway between Wellington and New Plymouth. The river slides lugubriously north–south past the city, the centre of which is on the west bank. Somme Pde and Taupo Quay trace the western shoreline; Anzac Pde parallels the east bank and leads to Whanganui National Park in the north. Hanging baskets and deep verandas line Victoria Ave, Whanganui's main street.

Free town maps are available at the i-SITE visitor information centre. You can also pick up maps at the **Automobile Association** (AA; ☎ 06-348 9160; www.aatravel.co.nz; 78 Victoria Ave; ✆ 8.30am-5pm Mon-Fri).

MAORI NZ: WHANGANUI & PALMERSTON NORTH

A drive up the Whanganui River Road (p264) takes you deep into traditional Maori territory, passing the Maori villages of Atene, Koriniti, Ranana and Hiruharama along the way. Read up on the area's Maori heritage in the History section on p261, and run your eyes over the amazing indigenous exhibits at the Whanganui Regional Museum (below) in Whanganui itself. Also in Whanganui, Putiki Church (below) is emblazoned with superb Maori carvings.

Over in Palmerston North, Te Manawa (p265) museum has a strong Maori focus, while the New Zealand Rugby Museum (p265) pays homage to Maori All Blacks, without whom the team would never have become a world force. Northeast of Palmerston North, Manawatu Gorge (p270) is steeped in Maori lore – well worth the detour.

Information

Major banks and ATMs line Victoria Ave.

Computer Valet (☎ 06-348 5805; 1 Victoria Ave; ⏱ 8.30am-5pm Mon-Fri, 10am-12.30pm Sat) Internet access.

Department of Conservation (DOC; ☎ 06-349 2100; www.doc.govt.nz; 74 Ingestre St; ⏱ 8.30am-4.30pm Mon-Fri) For tourist information.

Paper Plus (☎ 06-348-0351; www.nzpost.co.nz; Trafalgar Square Shopping Mall, Taupo Quay) Offers postal services.

Post office (☎ 06-345 4103; www.nzpost.co.nz; 226 Victoria Ave; ⏱ 8.30am-5pm Mon-Fri, 9am-noon Sat)

Sacred Peaks (www.sacredpeaks.com) For regional information.

Whanganui Hospital (☎ 06-348 1234; www.wdhb. org.nz; 100 Heads Rd; ⏱ 24hr)

Whanganui i-SITE (☎ 06-349 0508; www.wanganui. com; 101 Guyton St; ⏱ 8.30am-5pm Mon-Fri, 9am-3pm Sat & Sun; 🖳) Tourist information and internet access.

Whanganui police station (☎ 06-349 0600; www. police.govt.nz; 10 Bell St; ⏱ 24hr)

Whitcoulls (☎ 06-345 8747; www.whitcoulls.co.nz; 115 Victoria Ave; ⏱ 8.30am-5.30pm Mon-Fri, 9am-4pm Sat, 10am-4pm Sun) A good selection of books.

Sights & Activities

WHANGANUI RIVERBOAT CENTRE

The **Riverboat Centre** (☎ 0800 783 2637, 06-347 1863; www.riverboats.co.nz; 1a Taupo Quay; admission free; ⏱ 9am-4pm Mon-Sat, 10am-4pm Sun Sep-Jul) has historical displays, but the crowds come for the *Waimarie*, the last of the Whanganui River's paddle steamers. In 1900 the *Waimarie* was shipped in a box from England then reassembled in Whanganui. After paddling the Whanganui for 50 years, she sank ingloriously at her mooring in 1952. Submerged for 41 years, she was finally raised, restored, then relaunched on the first day of the 21st century. See p257 for details of tours on the coal-fired dreamboat.

Next to the Riverboat Centre on Saturday mornings the **River Traders Market** (☎ 06-343 9795; www.therivertraders.co.nz; ⏱ 9am-1pm Sat) is crammed with local crafts and organic produce.

MUSEUMS, GALLERIES & CHURCHES

The **Whanganui Regional Museum** (☎ 06-349 1110; www.wanganui-museum.org.nz; Watt St, Queens Park; adult/child $10/free; ⏱ 10am-4.30pm) is one of NZ's better natural-history museums. Maori exhibits include the carved *Te Mata o Houroa* war canoe and some vicious-looking *mere* (greenstone clubs). The colonial and wildlife installations are first rate, and there's plenty of button-pushing and drawer-opening to keep the kids engaged.

'Historical, Contemporary, Unique' – the elegantly neoclassical **Sarjeant Gallery** (☎ 06-349 0506; www.sarjeant.org.nz; Queens Park; admission free; ⏱ 10.30am-4.30pm) covers all the bases with its extensive permanent art exhibition and frequent special exhibits (including glass from the annual Wanganui Festival of Glass; p258).

The pick of Whanganui's many glass studios is the **Chronicle Glass Studio** (☎ 06-347 1921; www.chronicleglass.co.nz; 2 Rutland St; admission free; ⏱ 9am-5pm Mon-Fri, 10am-4pm Sat & Sun) where you can watch glass-blowers working, check out the gallery, take a weekend glass-blowing course ($375) or a 'Make a Paperweight' lesson ($100), or just hang out and warm up on a chilly afternoon.

By the river's edge is the **Wanganui Community Arts Centre** (☎ 06-345 1551; www.communityartscentre. org.nz; 19 Taupo Quay; admission free; ⏱ 10am-4pm Mon-Sat, 1-4pm Sun), which exhibits mostly local artists and musters up a decidedly South Pacific vibe with glass, ceramics, jewellery, photography and painting.

Across the City Bridge from town and 1km towards the sea is the **Putiki Church**, aka St Paul's Memorial Church. It's nothing out of the ordinary externally but, just like the faithful pew-fillers, it's what's inside that counts.

WHANGANUI

The interior is magnificent, completely covered in Maori carvings and *tukutuku* (wall panels). Unless it's a Sunday (service at 9am) the church will probably be closed, but the caretaker (☎ 06-347 8087) might show you through, or you can pick up the key from the i-SITE ($5 plus $20 deposit).

PARKS, LOOKOUTS & BEACHES

Whanganui has a few grassy, stroll-worthy parks, including **Queens Park** (where the museum and gallery are) and **Cooks Gardens**. The i-SITE stocks a couple of free walk and drive brochures directing visitors around the city.

The **Moutoa Gardens** are considered sacred Maori land and were occupied by Maoris for four months in 1995, in an acrimonious land claim that strained local Maori-Pakeha relations. The city council, abandoned by Wellington, fought the claim in the High Court while angry Pakeha counter-demonstrated under the banner of 'One New Zealand'. Police raids exacerbated the situation. When the claim was dismissed by the courts the country expected violence, but the gardens were peacefully relinquished after a moving night-long meeting addressed by Maori leaders.

The **Virginia Lake Scenic Reserve** (Great North Rd; admission free; ⏰ winter gardens 9am-5pm, aviary 8.30am-5pm), about 1km north from the top end of Victoria Ave, is a rambling reserve with a lake, colourful winter garden, walk-through aviary and the Higginbottom Fountain – possibly the world's only pay-per-view geyser ($1 per 10-minute eruption).

Across City Bridge from the town centre is the **Durie Hill Elevator** (☎/fax 06-345 8525; Anzac Pde; one-way $2; ☺ 8am-6pm Mon-Fri, 10am-5pm Sat & Sun), built with grand visions for Durie Hill's residential future. A tunnel burrows 200m into the hillside, from where the elevator rattles 65m to the top. There are two viewpoints at the summit: one on top of the lift machinery room, the other up the 176 steps of the **War Memorial Tower**. Assess the condition of Whanganui's roof-tiles, or scan the horizon for Mt Taranaki, Mt Ruapehu and even the South Island on a clear day.

Kai Iwi Beach is a wild ocean frontier, strewn with black sand and masses of broken driftwood. To get here follow Great North Rd 4km north of town, then turn left onto Rapanui Rd and head seawards for 10km. If the sea is angry, try the **Splash Centre** (☎ 06-349 0113; www.splashcentre.co.nz; Springvale Park, London St; admission adult/child $4.50/3; ☺ 6am-8pm Mon-Fri, 8am-6pm Sat & Sun) for a safe swim.

Tours

See p262 for Whanganui River canoe, kayak and jetboat tours.

Scenic Flights (☎ 06-345 0914; wanganui.aero.club@xtra.co.nz; Whanganui Airport, Airport Rd; 15min-2hr flight from $45) Mile-high panoramas above Whanganui, Moutoua Island, Mt Ruapehu and Whanganui National Park.

Waimarie Paddle-Steamer Tours (☎ 0800 783 2637, 06-347 1863; www.riverboats.co.nz; 1a Taupo Quay; adult/child/family $45/15/105; ☺ tours 2pm daily Nov-May, 1pm Sat & Sun Jun-Oct, closed Aug) Two-hour tour weekdays; three hours with a one-hour stopover at weekends. Also six-hour trips further upriver on the motorised 1904 *Wairua* (adult/child $50/20).

WHANGANUI OR WANGANUI?

Yeah, we know, it's confusing. Is there an 'h' or isn't there? Either way, the pronunciation is identical: 'wan-ga' not (as in the rest of the country) 'fan-ga'.

Everything was originally spelled Wanganui, because in the local dialect *whanga* (harbour) is pronounced 'wan-ga'. However, in 1991 the New Zealand Geographic Board officially adopted the correct Maori spelling (with an 'h') for the Whanganui River and Whanganui National Park. This was a culturally deferential decision: the Pakeha-dominated town and region retained the old spelling, while the river area – Maori territory – adopted the new.

In 2009 the Board assented that the town and region should also adopt the 'h'. This caused much community consternation, opinions on the decision split almost evenly (outspoken Mayor Michael Laws was particularly anti-'h'). Ultimately, NZ Minister for Land Information Maurice Williamson decreed that either spelling was acceptable, and that adopting the querulous 'h' is up to individual businesses or entities. A good old Kiwi compromise! Whanderful…

Whanganui Tours (☎ 06-347 7534; www.whanganui tours.co.nz) Join the mailman on the Whanganui River Road to Pipiriki (weekday/weekend $55/60; departs 7.30am) with lots of social and historical commentary. You can also take the mail van to Pipiriki then canoe back to Whanganui (single/double $80/115, guide $120) or cycle back (one-/two-day trip $80/120, accommodation $55 to $70). There are optional jetboat trips from Pipiriki to the Bridge to Nowhere ($55).

Festivals & Events

NZ Masters Games (☎ 06-349 1815; www.nzmg. com) The country's biggest multisport event, held in early February every odd-numbered year.

Heritage Weekend (☎ 06-349 0511; www.wanganui heritage.org.nz) Riverboats, architectural adoration and markets in mid-March.

Wanganui Festival of Glass (☎ 06-349 0508; www. wanganuiglass.com) Classy glass fest in September.

Wanganui Literary Festival(☎ 06-349 0511; www. writersfest.co.nz) Words, thoughts, and thoughts about words every September.

Cemetery Circuit Motorcycle Race (☎ 06-349 1815; www.cemeterycircuit.co.nz) Pandemonic Boxing Day bike race.

Sleeping
BUDGET

Tamara Backpackers Lodge (☎ 06-347 6300; www.tam aralodge.com; 24 Somme Pde; dm $25, s $45-55, tw $54-64, d $60-64; ☐) Tamara is a mazelike two-storey heritage house with a wide balcony, kitchen, TV lounge, free bikes and a leafy, hammock-hung back garden. Ask for one of the beaut doubles overlooking the river.

Braemar House YHA (☎ 06-348 2301; www.braemar house.co.nz, www.yha.co.nz; 2 Plymouth St; dm $25, cabin s/d $50/60, guest house incl breakfast s/d $80/100; ☐ ☎) Riverside Braemar brings together an 1895 Victorian B&B guest house and a rambunctious backpackers. Centrally heated guest-house rooms are floral and fancy; airy dorms and no-frills cabins abut limited tent space out the back.

Avro Motel & Caravan Park (☎ 0800 367 287, 06-345 5279; www.wanganuiaccommodation.co.nz; 36 Alma Rd; unpowered & powered sites from $30, units from $80; ☎ ☒) Avro's yellow biplane heralds the closest camping to the city centre, 1.5km west. Both powered and unpowered sites have their own freestanding bathrooms, and the camp kitchen is a wee winner. Standard motel units also available.

our pick Anndion Lodge (☎ 0800 343 056, 06-343 3593; www.anndionlodge.co.nz; 143 Anzac Pde; dm/s $35/65, d $85-135, ste $140; ☐ ☎ ☒) Hell-bent on constantly improving and expanding their business, hosts Ann and Dion (Anndion, get it?) go to enormous lengths to make things homey: stereo systems, big TVs, Playstation, spa, swimming pool, barbecue area, courtesy van etc. It's pricier than your average hostel, but everything's new, clean and thoroughly worth it.

Whanganui River Top 10 Holiday Park (☎ 0800 272 664, 06-343 8402; www.wrivertop10.co.nz; 460 Somme Pde; unpowered & powered sites $38-50, cabins $55-85, units $115-170; ☐ ☎ ☒) This top-notch Top 10 park sits on the Whanganui's west bank 6km north of Dublin Bridge. Facilities (including pool and jumping pillow) are immaculate and prodigious. Kayak hire also available: the owners shuttle you up river then you paddle back to camp. Self-catering or dining in town is your best bet food-wise.

MIDRANGE & TOP END

Grand Hotel (☎ 0800 843 472, 06-345 0955; www.the grandhotel.co.nz; cnr St Hill & Guyton Sts; s/d $75/95, ste $120-150; ☐ ☎) If you can't face another soulless motel room, rooms at this stately old-school Whanganui survivor have a bit more personality. Singles and doubles are basic but good value; suites are spacious. Rosie O'Grady's Irish pub (opposite) and a restaurant are downstairs.

Kembali B&B (☎ 06-347 1727; www.bnb.co.nz/kem bali.html; 26 Taranaki St, St Johns Hill; s/d incl breakfast from $80/110) Up on leafy St Johns Hill on the way to Taranaki, this home-spun B&B has two private upstairs guest rooms sleeping four, available on an exclusive-use basis. It's a sedate place overlooking some wetlands, all achirp with tuis, pukekos and native whistling frogs.

Astral Motel (☎ 0800 509 063, 06-347 9063; www. astralmotel.co.nz; 46 Somme Pde; s/d/f from $85/95/110; ☒) Astrally aligned with the terrestrial Dublin Bridge nearby, rooms here are a bit dated but are well serviced and have 24-hour check-in if you're rolling in off the midnight highway.

Acacia Park Motel (☎ 0800 800 225, 06-343 9093; www.acacia-park-motel.co.nz; 140 Anzac Pde; r $95-120) Acacia's dozen jade-coloured bungalows are dotted among mature trees, the boughs home to roosting doves. The retro rooms have seen better days but you get what you pay for.

Riverview Motel (☎ 0800 102 001; 06-345 2888; www. wanganuimotels.co.nz; 14 Somme Pde; d $95-150; ☎) Take your pick from one of 15 '80s-style kitchenette units in the main block or the five spiffy spa suites out the back. Nothing too flash, but a decent central option.

Siena Motor Lodge (☎ 0800 888 802, 06-345 9009; www.siena.co.nz; 335 Victoria Ave; ste $125-145; 🖥) Aiming for Tuscany but hitting Taranaki, the compact rooms here are five star and spotless. Business travellers enjoy double glazing, a DVD library, heated towel rails, coffee plungers and real coffee.

Rutland Arms Inn (☎ 0800 788 5263, 06-347 7677; www.rutland-arms.co.nz; 48 Ridgway St; ste $130-180; 🖥) Billed as a 'luxury heritage experience', this restored 1849 building has an old-fashioned pub downstairs with colonial-style accommodation above. Rooms have TV, phone, plump pillows and spine-straightening beds. English hunting scenes adorn the bar's beer taps.

Aotea Motor Lodge (☎ 06-345 0303; www.aoteamotorlodge.co.nz; 390 Victoria Ave; d $160-200; 🖥) It gladdens the heart to see a job done well, and the owners of Whanganui's newest motel have done just that. On the upper reaches of Victoria Ave, this flashy, two-storey contemporary motel features roomy suites, lavish linen, dark-timber furniture and plenty of marble and stone –sassy stuff.

Eating

Rapido Espresso House (☎ 06-347 9475; 71 Liverpool St; snacks $3-6; 🕑 7.30am-6pm Mon-Fri, 9am-3pm Sat) If you're hungry, don't expect more than a wedge of cake or some sushi at this raffish, royal blue cafe – what you're here for is the coffee. Organic and fair-trade all the way, the brew here is the best in town.

Red Eye Café (☎ 06-345 5646; 96 Guyton St; meals $5-18; 🕑 7.30am-3.30pm Mon & Tue, to 4pm Wed-Fri, 8am-3pm Sat; 🅥) With inexplicable familiarity (maybe it's the friendly staff), this bohemian urban cafe has colourful local art, tasty light snacks (bagels, salads) as well as more substantial meals (curries, organic chicken sandwiches). Good coffee, too.

Yellow House Café (☎ 06-345 0083; cnr Pitt & Dublin Sts; brunch $5-19, dinner $27-34; 🕑 8am-4pm Sun-Wed, to 9pm Thu-Sat; 🅥) Local art, funky tunes, outdoor tables, buttermilk pancakes and great omelettes. Dinner veers from lamb to lasagne. Actually, it's more of a taupe colour…

Ceramic (☎ 06-348 4449; 51 Victoria Ave; tapas $6-14, mains $27-29; 🕑 3pm-late Tue-Sat; 🖥) In a split-business arrangement with Orange (right), Ceramic takes over for the dinner shift, serving upmarket cafe food and tapas in a low-lit, rust-coloured interior. Occasional DJs ooze

tunes across the tables to cocktail-sipping seducers.

Orange (☎ 06-348 4449; 51 Victoria Ave; meals $8-22; 🕑 7.30am-5pm Mon-Fri, 9am-5pm Sat & Sun; 🖥) Orange is a babbling espresso bar serving gourmet burgers, big breakfasts, muffins, cakes and sandwiches (try the BLT). The outdoor tables go berserk during summer.

Vega (☎ 06-345 9955; 49 Taupo Quay; mains $10-18; 🕑 9.30am-late Mon-Fri, 9am-late Sat & Sun; 🖥) Vega's riverside building has been a merchant store and a brothel, but today it's 100% class. A packed house testifies to the virtuoso menu, professional service and meticulously constructed wine list. There's plenty of seafood for the *poisson*-impassioned, and vegetarian and children's options too. Open 'til the wee smalls, it's a moody spot for a late-night vino or two, too.

Thai Villa (☎ 06-348 9089; 7 Victoria Ave; lunch from $10, dinner $19-25; 🕑 lunch & dinner) There are a few Thai joints along Victoria Ave, but Thai Villa is by far the most authentic. Try the *massaman* beef curry or the *laab* duck washed down with a Singha beer.

ourpick Indigo (☎ 06-348 7459; cnr Majestic Sq & Watt St; lunch $12-19, dinner $18-31; 🕑 10am-4pm Mon & Tue, 10am-late Wed-Fri, 9am-11pm Sat, 9am-4pm Sat) Along with Vega, Indigo dragged Whanganui dining into the new millennium. A decade later and the vibe is still up-to-the-minute snazzy; the lofty interior and outdoor terrace swim with NZ wines, and contemporary meat, pasta and fish dishes are assembled with progressive flair. The lamb pasties are huge.

Stellar (☎ 06-345 7278; 2 Victoria Ave; lunch $15, dinner $20-31; 🕑 10pm-late Mon-Fri, 8.30am-late Sat & Sun; 🖥) Stellar lives up to its name – a cavernous barcum-restaurant with a convivial family atmosphere, it's the town's pride and joy. Reclining contentedly on leather couches, locals and tourists alike sip premium lagers and feast on bar morsels, gourmet pizzas and surf 'n' turf fare. Frequent bands, DJs and quiz nights to boot.

Self-caterers can hit the supermarkets:
Countdown (☎ 06-348 9470; cnr Victoria Ave & Glasgow St; 🕑 6am-midnight)
New World (☎ 06-349 0990; 374 Victoria Ave; 🕑 7am-9pm)

Drinking

Rosie O'Grady's (☎ 06-345 0955; cnr St Hill & Guyton Sts; 🕑 11am-late) Siphoning into NZ's insatiable (and, it has to be said, annoying) passion for Irish pubs, Rosie's, in the Grand Hotel, is as good a spot as any to elbow down a few pints of Guinness on a misty river afternoon. Good pub meals too.

Spirit'd (☎ 0800 737 793; 75 Guyton St; ☽ 10am-late) Pool tables, Jack Daniels, Metallica on the jukebox and local young bucks trying to out-strut each other – just like 1989 minus the cigarettes.

See also Rutland Arms Inn (p259), Stellar (p259) and Ceramic (p259).

Entertainment

Embassy 3 Cinemas (☎ 06-345 7958; www.embassy3.co.nz; 34 Victoria Ave; tickets adult/child/concession $12/9/8; ☽ 11am-midnight) Nightly new-release blockbusters selling out faster than you can say 'bored Whanganui teenagers'. All Tuesday tickets are $7.50.

Getting There & Away
AIR

Whanganui Airport (WAG; ☎ 06-345 5593; www.airport.u.nu/WAG) is 4km south of town, across the river towards the sea. **Air New Zealand** (☎ 06-348 3500; www.airnewzealand.co.nz; 133 Victoria Ave; ☽ 9am-5pm Mon-Fri) has direct flights from Whanganui to Auckland (one hour, one to four daily) and Wellington (35 minutes, one daily) with onward connections.

BUS

InterCity (☎ 09-583 5780; www.intercity.co.nz) buses operate from the **Whanganui Travel Centre** (☎ 06-345 7100; www.tranzit.co.nz; 160 Ridgway St; ☽ 8.15am-5.15pm Mon-Fri). Some destinations:

Destination	Price	Duration	Frequency
Auckland	$80	8hr	2-4 daily
New Plymouth	$29	2½hr	1-2 daily
Palmerston North	$20	1½hr	1-3 daily
Taumarunui	$47	2¾hr	1 daily
Wellington	$39	4hr	1-4 daily

Naked Bus (☎ 0900 625 33; www.nakedbus.co.nz) departs from Whanganui i-SITE to most North Island centres, including the following:

Destination	Price	Duration	Frequency
Auckland	$39	9¼hr	1 daily
Hamilton	$27	6½hr	1 daily
New Plymouth	$17	2½hr	1 daily
Palmerston North	$9	1¼hr	1 daily
Wellington	$19	3½hr	1 daily

Also departing the i-SITE, **White Star** (☎ 0800 465 622, 06-349 0508 www.whitestarbus.co.nz) has two

buses each Thursday and Friday and one every other day to/from Wellington ($30, 3½ hours) via Palmerston North ($20, one hour), and New Plymouth ($27, 2½ hours).

Getting Around
BICYCLE

Bike Shed (☎ 06-345 5500; www.bikeshed.co.nz; cnr Ridgway & St Hill Sts; ☽ 8.30am-5.30pm Mon-Fri, 9am-2pm Sat) hires out mountain bikes from $35 per day, including helmet and lock. Ask them for updates on the **Mountain to Sea** Ohakune-to-Whanganui bike track, which has been ascribed 'Quick Start' status as part of the proposed **New Zealand Cycle Trail** (www.tourism.govt.nz/our-work/new-zealand-cycle-trail-project) project.

BUS

Tranzit City Link (☎ 0508 800 800, 06-345 4433; www.horizons.govt.nz; single trip/day pass $2/6) operates four looped local bus routes departing from the Maria Pl bus stop, including routes 5 and 6 past the Whanganui River Top 10 Holiday Park in Aramoho. Buses run from 7am to 6pm Monday to Friday; 10.30am to 5.30pm Saturday.

CAR

The following car-rental companies have pick-up/drop-off at Whanganui Airport:

Avis (☎ 06-358 7528; www.avis.co.nz)
Budget (☎ 06-345 5122; www.budget.co.nz)
Hertz (☎ 06-348 7624; www.hertz.co.nz)

TAXI

Rivercity Cabs (☎ 0800 345 3333, 06-345 3333)
Wanganui Taxis (☎ 06-343 5555)

WHANGANUI NATIONAL PARK

The Whanganui River – the lifeblood of Whanganui National Park – curls 329km from its source on Mt Tongariro (p290) to the Tasman Sea. It's the longest navigable river in NZ, a fact that's been shaping its destiny for centuries (see History, opposite). The river today conveys canoes, kayaks and jetboats, its waters shifting from deep mirror greens in summer to turbulent winter browns.

The native bush here is thick podocarp broad-leaved forest interspersed with ferns. Occasionally you'll see poplar and other introduced trees along the river, remnants of long-vanished settlements. Traces of Maori settlements also crop up here, with old *pa* (fortified village) and *kainga* (village) sites, and Hauhau *niu* (war and peace) poles at the convergence of the Whanganui and Ohura Rivers at Maraekowhai. The Ratakura, Reinga Kokiri and Te Rerehapa Falls, all near Maraekowhai on the Ohura, are where Maori caught small *tuna riki* (freshwater eels).

The impossibly scenic Whanganui River Road, a mostly unsealed river-hugging road from Whanganui to Pipiriki, makes a fabulous alternative to the faster but less magical SH4.

History

In Maori legend the Whanganui River was formed when Mt Taranaki, after brawling with Mt Tongariro over the lovely Mt Pihanga, fled the central North Island for the sea, leaving a long gouge behind him. He turned west at the coast, finally stopping at his current address. Mt Tongariro sent cool water to heal the gouge – thus the Whanganui River was born.

Kupe, the great Polynesian explorer, is believed to have travelled 20km up the Whanganui around AD 800; Maori lived here by 1100. By the time Europeans put down roots in the late 1830s, Maori settlements lined the river valley. Missionaries sailed upstream and their settlements – at Hiruharama, Ranana, Koriniti and Atene – have survived to this day despite a dwindling river population.

Steamers first tackled the river in the mid-1860s, a dangerous time for Pakeha. Aligned with Taranaki Maoris, some river tribes joined the Hauhau Rebellion – a Maori movement seeking to expel settlers.

In 1886 a Whanganui company established the first commercial steamer transport service. Others soon followed, utilising the river between Whanganui and Taumarunui. Supplying river communities and linking the sea with the interior, the steamers' importance grew, particularly after 1903 when the Auckland railway reached Taumarunui from the north.

New Zealand's contemporary tourism leviathan was seeded here. Internationally advertised trips on the 'Rhine of Maoriland' became so popular that by 1905 12,000 tourists a year were making the trip upriver from Whanganui to Pipiriki or downriver from Taumarunui. The engineering feats and skippering ability required on the river became legendary.

From 1918 land upstream of Pipiriki was granted to returning WWI soldiers. Farming here was a major challenge, with many families struggling for years to make the rugged land productive. Only a few endured into the early 1940s.

The completion of the railway from Auckland to Wellington and the improving roads ultimately signed river transport's death warrant; 1959 saw the last commercial riverboat voyage. Today, just one old-fleet vessel cruises the river – the *Waimarie* (p255).

Orientation & Information

Pipiriki and Taumarunui are the main entry and exit points to the river with the most facilities, though you are also able to access the river from Ohinepane and Whakahoro.

For national park information, try the affable Whanganui i-SITE or DOC Office (p255). There's also **Pipiriki DOC** (☎ 06-385 5022; Owairua Rd; www.doc.govt.co.nz; ☼ 8am-5pm Mon-Fri) and **Taumarunui DOC** (☎ 07-895 8201; Cherry Grove Domain; ☼ 8am-5pm Mon-Fri), though they're both field centres rather than tourist offices and aren't always staffed. Taumarunui's i-SITE is a safer bet (p233).

Check out www.whanganuiriver.co.nz online; otherwise, a more tangible resource is the NZ Recreational Canoeing Association's *Guide to the Whanganui River* ($10). DOC's *In and Around Whanganui National Park* ($3) covers tramping territory, or the Wanganui Tramping Club (☎ 06-346 5597 www.wanganuitramp ingclub.org.nz) puts out the quarterly *Wanganui Tramper* magazine, full of local info.

Sights

The scenery along the **Whanganui River Road** (Map p253) en route to Pipiriki is camera conducive – stark, wet mountain slopes plunge into lazy jade stretches of the Whanganui River. A French Catholic mission led by Suzanne Aubert established the Daughters of Our Lady of Compassion in Jerusalem in 1892. Around a corner in the road, the pictureperfect **St Joseph's Church** (see p264) stands tall on a spur of land above a deep river bend.

Other sights along the road include the restored 1854 **Kawana Flour Mill** near Matahiwi, **Operiki Pa** and other *pa* sites, and **Aramoana Hill**, from where there's a panoramic view. The Maori villages of **Atene**, **Koriniti**, **Ranana** and **Hiruharama** crop up along the way – ask a local before you go sniffing around. Note that the River Road is unsealed between Matahiwi and 3km south of Pipiriki.

Pipiriki (Map p253) is beside the river at the north end of Whanganui River Road. It's a rainy river town without much going on (no shops or petrol), but was once a humming holiday hot spot serviced by river steamers and paddleboats. Seemingly cursed, the old Pipiriki Hotel, formerly a glamorous resort full of international tourists, burned to the ground twice. Recent attempts to rebuild it have stalled due to funding issues; it's been vandalised and stripped of anything of value, leaving a hollow brick husk riddled with potential. Pipiriki is the end point for canoe trips coming down the river and the launching pad for jetboat rides.

Standing in mute testimony to the optimism of the early settlers is the **Bridge to Nowhere** (Map p253), built in 1936. The walking track from Mangapurua Landing (upstream from Pipiriki, accessible by jetboat) to the lonesome bridge was part of a long-lost 4.5m-wide roadway from Raetihi to the river.

Activities
CANOEING & KAYAKING
The most popular stretch of river for canoeing and kayaking is downstream from Taumarunui to Pipiriki. This has been added to the NZ Great Walks system (p73) and is called the 'Whanganui Journey' (despite the fact that there's more sitting down than walking involved). It's a Grade II river – easy enough for the inexperienced, with enough moiling rapids to keep things interesting. See the free DOC leaflet *Whanganui Journey* for information.

Between 1 October and 30 April you'll need a **Great Walks Hut & Campsite Pass** (adult/child $45/free) for boat trips involving overnight stays between Taumarunui and Pipiriki. The rule applies only to this stretch of the river. The pass is valid for four nights and five days; you can stay overnight in the huts, the camps beside the huts or in other campsites along the river. If you're only doing an overnighter from Taumarunui to Whakahoro the pass costs $10; if you exclude Tieke Kainga *marae* (meeting house complexes) the pass costs $50. If you're just paddling and not sleeping anywhere, there's no charge. Bookings are not required for huts of campsites.

Outside the main season you'll only need a **Backcountry Hut Pass** (adult/child 1 year $90/45, 6 months $60/30), or you can pay on a hut-by-hut basis ($15 to $45 per night). All passes and tickets are available at the Whanganui i-SITE and regional DOC offices; some canoe operators also sell them. During summer, hut wardens and conservation officers patrol the river.

Taumarunui to Pipiriki is a five-day/four-night trip, Ohinepane to Pipiriki is a four-day/three-night trip, and Whakahoro to Pipiriki is a three-day/two-night trip. Taumarunui to Whakahoro is a popular overnight trip, especially for weekenders, or you can do a one-day trip from Taumarunui to Ohinepane or Ohinepane to Whakahoro. From Whakahoro to Pipiriki, 88km downstream, there's no road access so you're wed to the river for a few days; this is the trip everyone clamours to do. Most canoeists stop at Pipiriki.

The season for canoe trips is usually from September to Easter. Up to 5000 people make the river trip each year, mostly between Christmas and the end of January. During winter the river is almost deserted – the winter currents run swift and deep, as cold weather and short days deter potential paddlers.

To hire a two-person Canadian canoe for one/three/five days costs around $80/220/300 including transport. A single-person kayak costs about $50 per day not including transport (around $50 per person). Operators provide you with everything you need, including life jackets and waterproof drums (essential if you go bottom-up).

You can also take guided canoe or kayak trips – prices start at around $300/800 per person for a two-/five-day guided trip.

Operators include the following:

Awa Tours (☎ 06-385 8297; www.wakatours.com; Raetihi)

Blazing Paddles (☎ 0800 252 946, 07-895 5261; www.blazingpaddles.co.nz; Taumarunui)

Bridge to Nowhere Tours (see Jetboating, opposite)

Canoe Safaris (☎ 0800 272 335, 06-385.9237; www.canoesafaris.co.nz; Ohakune)

Taumarunui Canoe Hire (☎ 0800 226 6348, 07-895 7483; www.taumarunuicanoehire.co.nz; Taumarunui)

Wades Landing Outdoors (☎ 0800 226 631, 07-895 5995; www.whanganui.co.nz; Whakahoro)

Whanganui Kayak Hire (☎ 0211 336 938; www.kayakhire.co.nz; Whanganui)

Whanganui River Adventures (see Jetboating, opposite)

Whanganui River Guides (☎ 07-896 6727; www.whanganuiriverguides.co.nz; Taumarunui)

Whanganui Tours (☎ 06-347 7534; www.whanganuitours.co.nz; Whanganui)

Yeti Tours (☎ 0800 322 388, 06-385 8197; www.canoe.co.nz; Ohakune)

Whanganui River canoe companies also operate from National Park Village (p295) and Ohakune (p298).

JETBOATING

Hold onto your hats – jetboat trips give you the chance to see parts of the river that would otherwise take you days to paddle through. Jetboats depart from Pipiriki and Whanganui; four-hour tours start at around $105 per person. The following operators can also provide transport to the river ends of the Matemateaonga and Mangapurua Tracks (see Tramping, below):

Bridge to Nowhere Tours (☎ 0800 480 308, 06-385 4622; www.bridgetonowheretours.co.nz; Pipiriki)

Spirit of the River Jet (☎ 0800 538 8687, 06-342 5572; www.spiritoftheriverjet.co.nz; Whanganui)

Whanganui River Adventures (☎ 0800 862 743, 06-385 3246; www.whanganuiriveradventures.co.nz; Pipiriki)

Whanganui Scenic Experience Jet (☎ 0800 945 335, 06-342 5599; www.whanganuiscenicjet.com; Whanganui)

TRAMPING

The most popular track in Whanganui National Park is the 40-minute walk from **Mangapurua Landing** (Map p253) to the Bridge to Nowhere, 30km upstream from Pipiriki by jetboat.

The Matemateaonga and Mangapurua/Kaiwhakauka Tracks are brilliant longer tramps (DOC booklets $1). Both are one-way tracks beginning (or ending) at remote spots on the river, so you have to organise jetboat transport to or from the trailheads – ask any jetboat operator (above). To Pipiriki from the Matemateaonga Track is around $50 per person; from the Mangapurua Track it's around $100.

Three to four days from end to end, the 42km **Matemateaonga Track** gets kudos as one of NZ's best walks. Probably due to its remoteness, it doesn't attract the hordes of trampers that amass on NZ's more famous tracks. Penetrating deep into wild bush and hill country, it traces an old Maori track and a disused settlers' dray road between the Whanganui and Taranaki regions. It follows the crest of the Matemateaonga Range along the route of the Whakaihuwaka Rd, started in 1911 to create a more direct link from Stratford to the railway at Raetihi. WWI interrupted planning and the road was never finished.

On a clear day, a 1½-hour side-trip to the top of Mt Humphries (730m) rewards you with sigh-inducing views all the way to Mt Taranaki and the volcanoes of Tongariro. There's a steep section between the Whanganui River (75m above sea level) and the Puketotara Hut (Map p253; 427m above sea level) but mostly it's easy walking. There are three DOC backcountry huts along the way: Omaru, Pouri and Puketotara (see Map p253); hut tickets cost $15 per person per night.

The **Mangapurua/Kaiwhakauka Track** is a 40km trail between Whakahoro and the Mangapurua Landing, both on the Whanganui River. The track runs along the Mangapurua and Kaiwhakauka Streams (both Whanganui River tributaries). Between these valleys a side track leads to the 663m Mangapurua Trig, the area's highest point, from which cloudless views extend to the Tongariro and Egmont National Park volcanoes. The route passes the Bridge to Nowhere and abandoned farming land cleared by settlers in the 20th century. Unless you're an insane tramping dynamo, walking the track takes 20 hours (three to four days). The Whakahoro Hut (see Map p253) at the Whakahoro end of the track is the only hut, but there's plenty of good camping. There's road access to the track both at the Whakahoro end and from a side track from the end of the Ruatiti Valley–Ohura Rd (from Raetihi).

The DOC booklet *In and Around Whanganui National Park* ($2.50) details a couple of shorter walks branching off the Whanganui River Rd that offers glimpses of wilderness.

The 18km **Atene Skyline Track** begins at Atene on the Whanganui River Rd, 22km north of the SH4 junction. The track takes six to eight hours, showcasing native forest, sandstone bluffs and the **Taumata Trig** (523m), with its broad views as far as Mt Ruapehu, Mt Taranaki and the Tasman Sea. The track ends back on the Whanganui River Rd, 2km downstream from the starting point.

A 1km track cuts through native bush from the Pipiriki DOC field centre to the top of Pukehinau, a hill with great valley vistas.

Sleeping
WHANGANUI NATIONAL PARK

The park has a sprinkling of huts, a lodge and numerous camping grounds (see Map p253). Along the Taumarunui–Pipiriki section are three huts classified as Great Walks Huts during summer and Serviced Huts in the off-season: Whakahoro Hut, John Coull Hut and Tieke Kainga, which has been revived as a *marae*. You can stay at Tieke Kainga, but full *marae* protocol must be observed (see p56). On the lower part of the river, Downes Hut is on the west bank, opposite Atene.

Bridge to Nowhere Lodge (Map p253; ☎ 0800 480 308, 06-385 4622; www.bridgetonowheretours.co.nz; un-powered sites $20, per person self-catering/incl breakfast & dinner $45/125) Across the river from the Tieke Kainga *marae*, this remote lodge lies deep in the national park, 21km upriver from Pipiriki near the Matemateaonga Track. The only way to get here is by jetboat from Pipiriki or on foot. It has a licensed bar, and meals are quality home-cooked affairs. The lodge also runs jetboat tours (p263) and canoe trips (p262).

WHANGANUI RIVER ROAD

Book the following places in advance – no one's going to turn you away, but they appreciate a bit of warning! There's no mobile-phone coverage along the road, and no petrol or shops. There are a couple of takeaway food vans in Pipiriki open during summer. From south to north, accommodation includes the following:

Rivertime Lodge (Map p253; ☎ 06-342 5595; www.rivertimelodge.co.nz; Whanganui River Rd; d self-catering/incl breakfast $110/130) A rural idyll: hills folding down towards the river and the intermittent bleating of sheep. Friendly and farmy, Rivertime is a moss green farmhouse with three bedrooms, a barbecue and no TV!

Flying Fox (Map p253; ☎ 06-342 8160; www.theflyingfox.co.nz; Whanganui River Rd; unpowered sites $20, d $100-200) This place is a superb, eco-attuned getaway on the riverbank across from Koriniti. You can self-cater in the Brewhouse, James K or Glory Cart (self-contained cottages), opt for B&B ($120 per person), or pitch a tent in a secluded bush clearing. Access is by jetboat; otherwise you can park across the river from the accommodation then soar over the river on the flying fox.

Kohu Cottage (Map p253; ☎ 06-342 8178; kohu.cottage @xtra.co.nz; Whanganui River Rd, Koriniti; d $70) A snug little lime green weatherboard cottage (100 years old!) above the road in Koriniti, sleeping three to four bods. There's a basic kitchen and a wood fire for chilly riverside nights.

Koriniti Marae (Map p253; ☎ 06-348 0303, 021 365 176; www.koriniti.com; Koriniti Pa Rd, Koriniti; dm $30) This *marae* on the east bank offers dorm-style beds for prebooked visitors; offer *koha* (a donation) plus the fee. It also runs a 24-hour 'cultural experience' for groups, including a *haka* (war

dance), weaving, storytelling and three meals ($190 per person).

Operiki Farmstay (Map p253; ☎ 06-342 8159; www.whanganuiriver.co.nz; Whanganui River Rd, Operiki; incl breakfast & dinner s/d $55/110) On a steep hillside 1.5km north of Korinити, this is a cheery in-with-the-family farmhouse. There are scenic walks around the property, and macadamia-nut muffins come hot from the oven.

St Joseph's Church (Map p253; ☎ 06-342 8190; www.compassion.org.nz; Whanganui River Rd, Hiruharama; dm $20) Taking in bedraggled travellers and offering 20 dorm-style beds, the sisters at St Joe's await to issue your deliverance – book ahead for the privilege. Moutoa Island, site of an historic 1864 battle, is just downriver.

There's an informal campsite with toilets and cold water at Pipiriki and another one (even less formal) just north of Atene (see Map p253).

Getting There & Away

From the north, there's road access to the Whanganui River at Taumarunui, Ohinepane and Whakahoro, though the latter is a long, remote drive on mostly unsealed roads. Roads to Whakahoro lead off from Owhango and Raurimu, both on SH4. There isn't any further road access to the river until Pipiriki.

From the south, the Whanganui River Rd veers off SH4 14km north of Whanganui, rejoining it at Raetihi, 91km north of Whanganui. It takes about two hours to drive the 79km between Whanganui and Pipiriki. The full circle from Whanganui through Pipiriki and Raetihi and back along SH4 through the Paraparas and Mangawhero River Gorge takes about four hours. The Whanganui River Rd is unsealed between Matahiwi and Mangeatoroa; petrol is available at Raetihi and Upokongaro but nowhere in between.

Alternatively, take a River Road tour from Whanganui (p258).

PALMERSTON NORTH
pop 80,700

The rich sheep- and dairy-farming Manawatu region embraces the districts of Rangitikei to the north and Horowhenua to the south. The hub of it all, on the banks of the Manawatu River, is Palmerston North, with its moderate high-rise attempts reaching up from the plains. Massey University, NZ's largest, informs the town's cultural and social structures. As a result 'Palmy' has an open-minded, rurally bookish vibe.

None of this impressed a visiting John Cleese who scoffed, 'If you ever do want to kill yourself, but lack the courage, I think a visit to Palmerston North will do the trick.' The city exacted revenge by naming a rubbish dump after him.

Orientation

The grassy expanse of the Square is the centre of city life. One block to the west, George St is the main cafe and restaurant strip. Massey University is 3km south of town.

Free town maps are available at the i-SITE visitor information centre. The **Automobile Association** (AA; ☎ 06-357 7039; www.aatravel.co.nz; 185 Broadway Ave; 8.30am-5pm Mon-Fri) also stocks maps.

Information

Banks and ATMs proliferate around the Square and Main St.

Bruce McKenzie Booksellers (☎ 06-356 9922; books@bmbooks.co.nz; 37 George St; 9am-6pm Mon-Thu, to 8pm Fri, to 5pm Sat, 10am-5pm Sun) Palmerston North's only independent bookseller; discount outlet at 16 Coleman Pl.

Department of Conservation (DOC; ☎ 06-350 9700; www.doc.govt.nz; 717 Tremaine Ave; 8am-4.30pm Mon-Fri) Tourist information 3km north of the Square.

i Café (☎ 06-353 7899; 39 Broadway Ave; 9am-11pm Sat-Thu, 24hr Fri) Internet access.

Palmerston North City Portal (www.palmy.net.nz)

Palmerston North Hospital (☎ 06-356 9169; www.midcentraldhb.govt.nz; 50 Ruahine St; 24hr)

Palmerston North i-SITE (☎ 06-350 1922; www.manawatunz.co.nz; the Square; 9am-5pm Mon-Fri, 10am-4pm Sat & Sun) For tourist information.

Palmerston North police station (☎ 06-351 3600; www.police.govt.nz; 400 Church St; 24hr)

Post office (☎ 06-356 9495; www.nzpost.co.nz; cnr Main St & the Square; 8.30am-5.30pm Mon-Fri, 9am-5.30pm Sat)

Radius Medical, The Palms (☎ 06-354 7737; www.radiusmedical.co.nz; 445 Ferguson St; 8am-7pm Mon-Fri, 9am-6pm Sat & Sun) Doctors by appointment, with a pharmacy next door.

Student City Palmerston North (www.studentcity.co.nz)

Sights & Activities

Taking the English village-green concept to a whole new level, the **Square** is Palmy's heart and soul. Seventeen spacey acres, with a clock tower, duck pond, Maori carvings, statues and trees of all seasonal dispositions.

Locals eat lunch on the manicured lawns in the sunshine.

Te Manawa (☎ 06-355 5000; www.temanawa.co.nz; 326 Main St; museum & gallery admission free, science centre adult/child/family $8/5/20; 10am-5pm) has merged a museum, art gallery and science centre into one complex. Vast collections (around 55,000 items) join the dots between 'life, art and mind'. The museum has a strong Maori focus, while the gallery's exhibits change frequently. Kids will get a kick out of the hands-on exhibits at the science centre. The New Zealand Rugby Museum will be relocating here as part of a wholesale redevelopment.

Rugby fans holler about the **New Zealand Rugby Museum** (☎ 06-358 6947; www.rugbymuseum.co.nz; 87 Cuba St; admission adult/child $5/2; 10am-4pm Mon-Sat, 1.30-4pm Sun). This amazing room overflows with rugby paraphernalia, from a 1905 All Blacks jumper to the actual whistle used to start the first game of every Rugby World Cup. After a humiliating exit from the 2007 World Cup in France, NZ is hosting the 2011 event – time to brush up on your *haka*. The museum is planning to relocate to Te Manawa (above) in time for 2011 – look for it there if it's not on Cuba St.

Victoria Esplanade (8am-6pm Apr-Sep, to 9pm Oct-Mar) is a riverbank park. Mooch around the adventure playground, aviary, conservatory, bike trails, walkways, the **Esplanade Scenic Railway** (☎ 06-357 3049; www.esplanaderail.org.nz; per ride $2; 1-4pm Sat & Sun) or just chill out on the lawns. The **Dugald MacKenzie Rose Garden**, once voted among the world's top five loveliest gardens, brings tears of pride to local eyes, and there's a permanent **orienteering course** (☎ 06-357 5288; www.rk.orienteering.org.nz; maps $2) here too. Pick up a map from the park cafe or i-SITE.

When the summer plains bake, dive into the **Lido Aquatic Centre** (☎ 06-357 2684; www.lidoaquaticcentre.co.nz; 50 Park Rd; adult/child $3.50/2.50, hydroslide $5; 6am-8pm Mon-Thu, to 9pm Fri, 8am-8pm Sat & Sun). It's a long way from Lido Beach in Venice, but it has a 50m pool, waterslides, cafe and gym.

Palmy is, as the locals say, 'flat as'. Grab the free *City Heritage Trail* and *City Walkways* booklets from the i-SITE, detailing local pathways. Hire a bike from Crank It Cycles (p270).

Tours

Feilding Saleyard Tours (☎ 06-323 3318; www.feilding.co.nz; 10 Manchester Sq, Feilding; tours $5; tours 11am Fri) Local farmers instruct you in the gentle art of selling livestock at this small town north of the city centre. Farmers market from 9am to 2pm every Friday.

Manawatu Gorge Experience Jet (☎ 0800 945 335, 06-342 5599; www.manawatugorgejet.com; 25min tours per person $65) Manawatu Gorge jetboat tours, departing Woodville Ferry Domain on SH3.

Manawatu Wind Farm & Gorge Tour (☎ 0800 626 292, 06-350 1922; www.manawatunz.co.nz; 3hr tours

per person $55; ☺ tours 2pm Mon-Fri) Visits Te Apiti Windfarm and Manawatu Gorge; bookings/departures at the i-SITE.

Festivals & Events

Festival of Cultures (☎ 0212 715 862; www.foc. co.nz) Multicultural food, crafts, dance and music in late March.

Manawatu Jazz & Blues Festival (☎ 0800 484 253, 06-357 9740; www.manawatunz.co.nz) All things jazzy, bluesy and swingin' in early June, including workshops.

Manawatu Wine & Food Festival (☎ 0800 484 253, 06-357 9740; ww.mwff.co.nz) Mid-June weekend fiesta of culinary creations and the best local drops.

Sleeping
BUDGET

Peppertree Backpackers (☎ 06-355 4054; peppertree hostel@clear.net.nz; 121 Grey St; dm/s/d $26/48/62; 🖳) Inexplicably strewn with green-painted boots, this enduring and endearing hostel is the best budget option in town. Mattresses are thick, the kitchen will never run out of spatulas, and the piano and wood fire make things feel downright homey. Doubles off the kitchen are a bit noisy – angle for one at the back.

Grandma's Place (☎ 06-358 6928; www.grandmas -place.com; 146 Grey St; dm/s/d $26/49/66) Ignore the terrifying spectre of Grandma on the sign out the front – inside are tidy, old-fashioned rooms with floral wallpaper and macramé rugs. There are plenty of beds and a functional kitchen.

Palmerston North Holiday Park (☎ 06-358 0349; www.holidayparks.co.nz; 133 Dittmer Dr; unpowered & powered sites $30, cabins & units $35-75) About 2km from the Square, off Ruha St, this shady park has a wheezy boot-camp feel to it, but it's quiet and right beside Victoria Esplanade.

Café de Paris Inn (☎ 06-355 2130; www.cafedeparisinn. co.nz; 267 Main St; s/d $60/80) It ain't Montmartre, but this friendly, old-fashioned boozer three minutes' walk from the Square has surprisingly decent pub accommodation upstairs, all rooms with TV and en suite. Parking is limited.

Empire Hotel (☎ 06-357 8002; www.empirehotel.co.nz; cnr Princess & Main Sts; s/d/f $80/90/140) With slicker-than-average, colonial-style pub rooms upstairs, the Empire is a solid central option. Beyond a tandem bizarrely suspended in the stairwell, rooms have TV and fridge. The pub downstairs gets raucous – steer for a room far from the beer cheer.

Ann Keith's B&B Hotel (☎ 06-358 6928; www.back packersnbnb.co.nz; 123 Grey St; s/d/tw/f from $80/100/110/140) This B&B has five rooms in an old-fangled house, with TV, tea- and coffee-making facilities and electric blankets for cold Palmy nights. Run by the same folks as Grandma's Place; expect similar servings of chintz plus a generous breakfast.

MIDRANGE & TOP END

Fitzherbert Castle Motel (☎ 0800 115 262, 06-358 3888; www.fitzherbertcastle.co.nz; 124 Fitzherbert Ave; d $110-125; 🛜) It looks unapologetically like a Tudor castle from outside, but inside it's more like an intimate hotel. Fourteen immaculate rooms with cork-tiled bathroom floors and quality carpets, plenty of trees, friendly staff and small kitchens in some units. Free wi-fi is available.

Rose City Motel (☎ 06-356 5388; www.rosecitymotel. co.nz; 120 Fitzherbert Ave; units $125-145; 🛜) One for the postmodern aesthetes, Rose City's townhouse-style units are spacey (especially the split-level ones) and shipshape but stylistically rather '80s. Free DVDs, a squash court and a kids' play area are bonuses.

ourpick Plum Trees Lodge (☎ 06-358 7813; www. plumtreeslodge.co.nz; 97 Russell St; d $135-185; 🖳) In a flat-grid town with more motels than seems plausible, this place comes as sweet relief. Down a leafy driveway on a quiet street, ascend past leadlighting to a secluded lodge. Brilliantly designed using recycled native timbers from demolition sites around Palmerston North, the raked timber ceiling is punctuated with skylights, with the balcony set among swaying boughs. Romantic nights beneath a mosquito net slide lazily into breakfast – a sumptuous hamper of fresh fruit, croissants, jams, eggs, cheese, coffee and juice.

Braemar Motor Lodge (☎ 0800 355 805, 06-355 8053; www.braemarmotorlodge.co.nz; 177 Ruahine St; ste $135-205; 🖳 🛜) It's a bit of a hike into town, but Braemar's studio units have king-size bed, TV, spa, kitchenette, DVD player and stereo, and with 50-plus titles in the DVD library, there should be something up your alley. Units on the street are double-glazed.

Bentleys Motor Inn (☎ 0800 2368 5397, 06-358 7074; www.bentleysmotorinn.co.nz; 67 Linton St; ste $140-300) One of the highest branches on Palmerston North's motel tree, Bentleys' five-star apartments are worth the investment. Inside are new appliances, DVD player, spa, stereo, contemporary furnishings and Sky TV; outside are a full-blown gym, a squash court and a sauna.

Cornwall Motor Lodge (☎ 0800 170 000, 06-354 9010; www.cornwallmotorlodge.co.nz; 101 Fitzherbert Ave; ste $160-240) Cornwall has 27 enormous self-contained apartments on a bleak corner block. But don't let that bother you – rooms have spas, Sky TV, superking-size beds and balconies. Double-glazing culls the Fitzherbert Ave fracas.

Eating

Moxies (☎ 06-355 4238; 67 George St; meals $6-20; 🕒 7am-5pm Mon-Sat, 7.30am-5pm Sun; 🅥) This chipper corner cafe is decked out in primary colours with big windows. Staff members are equally upbeat, the all-day menu is top value (stellar omelettes) and if you've got gluten issues, this is the place for you.

Café Cuba (☎ 06-356 5750; cnr George & Cuba Sts; meals $7-21; 🕒 7am-midnight) Need a sugar shot? Proceed to Café Cuba – the cakes here are for professional chocoholics only. Supreme coffees and traditional cafe fare (risottos, salads, corn fritters) also draw the crowds. Live music Friday nights.

Indian2nite (☎ 06-353 7400; 22 George St; mains $10-20; 🕒 11.30am-2.30pm Wed-Fri, 5pm-late daily; 🅥) A million miles from Bollywood schmaltz, this upmarket place won't break the bank. Behind

George St picture windows, northern Indian curries are served by superpolite waiting staff. Try the *dahl makhani*.

Bella's Café (☎ 06-357 8616; 2 The Square; brunch $10-22, dinner $35; 🕒 7.30am-late Tue-Sat) Romantically candlelit Bella's has been around for a while now, its warm red walls continuing to conjure an inviting atmosphere for a mature crowd. Windows fold open in summer revealing an Italian-Pacific menu – pasta rules at lunchtime, dinners are more agricultural (beef, lamb, chicken and salmon).

Aqaba (☎ 06-357 8922; 186 Broadway Ave; meals $13-20; 🕒 7.30am-late Mon-Fri, 9am-late Sat & Sun) Family-friendly cafe classics (pasta, fish and chips, soups, nachos, steaks and pies) served inside a cavernous former Masonic Hall (no secret handshake required). R&B beats are spun as you dine in the Egyptian interiors.

Stage Door Café (☎ 06-359 2233; 96 King St; mains $16-18; 🕒 7.30am-5pm Mon-Fri, 8am-4pm Sat, 9am-4pm Sun) A low-key affair with mellow tunes, spiky green plants, orange plastic chairs and students on the run from the books. Big on coffee, eggs, curries, salads, wraps, muffins and cakes.

our pick Halikarnas Café (☎ 06-357 5777; 23 Fitzherbert Ave; mains $18-23; 🕒 11am-late) Angling for an *Ali-Baba-and-the-Forty-Thieves* vibe, with magic carpets, brass hookahs and funky trans-Bosphorus beats, Halikarnas plates up generous Turkish delights, from lamb shish kebabs to felafels and kick-arse Turkish coffee. Takeaway kebabs next door.

Aberdeen Steakhouse & Bar (☎ 06-952 5570; 161 Broadway Ave; mains $26-36; 🕒 11am-3pm Tue-Fri, 5pm-late daily) A plush, cow-coloured space studded with photos of prize bulls. Chew into 'The Buster' prime rib, or 'The Contender' Wagyu – the 'granddaddy of marbled steaks'.

For self-caterers:

Countdown (☎ 06-356 6066; cnr Ferguson & Ashley Sts; 🕒 7am-midnight)

Pak N Save (☎ 06-356 4043; 335 Ferguson St; 🕒 8am-midnight)

Drinking

Fish (☎ 06-359 3474; Regent Arcade; admission free; 🕒 4-11pm Wed, to 1am Thu, to 3am Fri & Sat) A progressive, stylish, Pacifically-hewn cocktail bar, the Fish has got its finger firmly on the Palmy pulse. DJs smooth over the week's problems on Friday and Saturday nights as a sexy, urbane crew sips Manhattans and Tamarillo Mules (yes, they kick).

Brewer's Apprentice (☎ 06-358 8888; 324 Church St; admission free; ☼ 11am-late Mon-Fri, 10am-late Sat & Sun) What was once a grungy student pub is now a slick Monteiths-sponsored bar. Business crowds flock for lunch (lunch $10 to $17, dinner $27 to $29), and 20-somethings fill the beer terrace after dark. Live music Friday and Saturday nights.

Mao Bar (☎ 06-354 8410; 64 George St; admission free; ☼ 7am-late) Cool cafe by day, full-scale cocktail bar by night, serving East-meets-West fusion food (lunch $10 to $20, dinner $18 to $32). The interior is aptly bamboo-strewn, with tall screens, red lanterns and dark timbers.

Celtic Inn (☎ 06-357 5571; Regent Arcade; admission free; ☼ 11am-3am Mon-Sat, 4pm-11am Sun) The Celtic expertly offsets the Fish nearby with good old-fashioned pub stuff, labourers, travellers and students bending elbows with a few tasty pints of the black stuff. Friendly staff, live music, red velvet chairs, kids darting around parents' legs – it's all here.

Entertainment

Downtown Cinemas (☎ 06-355 56; www.dtcinemas.co.nz; Downtown Shopping Arcade, Broadway Ave; tickets adult/child $13.50/8.50, Tue all tickets $8.50; ☼ 10am-midnight) The capacious Downtown Cinemas megaplex shows mainstream new-release flicks.

CinemaGold (☎ 06-353 1902; www.cinemagold.co.nz; Downtown Shopping Arcade, Broadway Ave; tickets adult/child $16/11; ☼ 10am-midnight) In the same complex as the Downtown Cinemas, CinemaGold has plush seats and a booze licence to enhance art-house classics and limited-release screenings.

There's a simmering theatre scene in Palmy. Check out what's playing at the following:

Abbey Theatre (☎ 06-355 4165; www.abbeymusical theatre.co.nz; 369 Church St) Quality amateur productions, with a penchant for cheesy musicals.

Centrepoint Theatre (☎ 06-354 5740; www.centre point.co.nz; 280 Church St) Bigger-name professional shows, theatre sports and seasonal plays.

Globe Theatre (☎ 06-351 4409; www.globetheatre. co.nz; cnr Pitt & Main Sts) Large community theatre; home to the Manawatu Theatre Society.

Regent Theatre (☎ 06-350 2100; www.regent. co.nz; 63 Broadway Ave) Divinely detailed theatre hosting big-ticket international acts like the Russian Ballet and the Platters.

Getting There & Away

AIR

Palmerston North International Airport (PMR; ☎ 06-351 4415; www.pnairport.co.nz; Airport Dr) is 4km north of the town centre. **Air New Zealand** (☎ 06-351 8800; www.airnewzealand.co.nz; 382 Church St; ☼ 9am-5pm Mon-Fri) runs daily direct flights to Auckland, Christchurch and Wellington.

Sunair Aviation Ltd (☎ 07-575 7799; www.sun air.co.nz) offers direct flights to Gisborne, Hamilton, Napier, Rotorua, Tauranga and Whakatane.

BUS

InterCity (☎ 09-583 5700; www.intercity.co.nz) buses operate from the **Palmerston North Travel Centre** (☎ 06-355 4955; cnr Main & Pitt Sts; ☼ 8.45am-5pm Mon-Thu, to 7.30pm Fri, to 3.30pm Sat, to 7pm Sun). Destinations include the following:

Destination	Price	Duration	Frequency
Auckland	$81	9hr	2 daily
Napier	$29	2¾hr	2-3 daily
Taupo	$32	4¼hr	3 daily
Wellington	$31	2¼hr	6 daily
Whanganui	$19	1½hr	3 daily

Naked Bus (☎ 0900 625 33; www.nakedbus.co.nz) services also depart the Travel Centre, servicing North Island centres including these:

Destination	Price	Duration	Frequency
Auckland	$36	10¼hr	2-3 daily
Napier	$19	2½hr	1 daily
Taupo	$23	3½hr	1 daily
Wellington	$12	2¼hr	2-3 daily
Whanganui	$11	1¼hr	1 daily

White Star (☎ 0800 465 622, 06-349 0508 www.whitestar bus.co.nz) services also depart the Travel Centre, running two buses each Thursday and Friday and one every other day to/from Wellington ($25, 2¼ hour) and New Plymouth ($30, 4¼ hours) via Whanganui ($20, one hour).

TRAIN

Tranz Scenic (☎ 0800 872 467, 04-495 0775; www. tranzscenic.co.nz) runs long-distance trains between Wellington and Auckland, stopping at the retro-derelict **Palmerston North Train Station** (Mathews Ave), off Tremaine Ave about 2.5km north of the Square. From Palmy to Wellington, take the *Overlander* ($53, 2½ hours, one daily) departing at 5pm (Friday, Saturday and Sunday only May to November); or the *Capital Connection* ($24, two hours, one daily Monday to Friday) departing Palmy at 6.20am. Buy tickets from Tranz Scenic directly (no ticket sales at the station).

Getting Around

TO/FROM THE AIRPORT

There's no public transport between the city and airport, but taxis abound or **Super Shuttle** (☎ 0800 748 885; www.supershuttle.co.nz) can whiz you into town in a minivan ($13; bookings required).

If you're driving into the CBD from the airport, take Ruahine St then turn right onto Main St. If you're heading through to Wellington, Main St becomes SH56 and continues to Wellington via Foxton, or turn left at the Square into Fitzherbert Ave, which leads to SH57 for Wellington via Shannon. It's a two- to three-hour drive either way.

BICYCLE

Crank It Cycles (☎ 06-358 9810; www.crankitcycles.co.nz; 203 Cuba St; ☉ 8am-6pm Mon-Fri, 9am-3pm Sat) hires out mountain bikes from $40 per day, including helmet and lock.

BUS

Tranzit City Link (☎ 0508 800 800, 06-952 2800; www. horizons.govt.nz; ticket $2) runs daytime buses departing from the Main St bus stop on the east side of the Square. Bus 12 goes to Massey University; none go to the airport.

CAR

The following companies have airport offices:
Avis (☎ 06-357 0168, 06-358 7528; www.avis.co.nz)
Budget (☎ 06-356 8565, 06-345 5122; www.budget. co.nz)
Europcar (☎ 06-353 0001; www.europcar.co.nz)
Hertz (☎ 06-357 0921, 06-348 7624; www.hertz. co.nz)
Thrifty (☎ 06-355 4365; www.thrifty.co.nz)

TAXI

A city-to-airport taxi costs around $15.
Gold & Black Taxis (☎ 06-351 2345)
Manawatu Taxis (☎ 06-355 5111)
Taxis Palmerston North (☎ 06-355 5333)

AROUND PALMERSTON NORTH

Just south of 'Student City' in the underrated Horowhenua district, **Shannon** (population 1510) and **Foxton** (population 2000) are sedentary country towns en route to Wellington.

Our fine feathered friends at **Owlcatraz** (Map p253; ☎ 06-362 7872; www.owlcatraz.co.nz; SH57, Shannon; adult/child incl tour $20/7; ☉ 9am-5pm) have obligingly adopted oh-so-droll names like Owlvis Presley and Owl Capone. It's a 30-minute drive south from Palmerston North.

Foxton Beach is one of a string of broad, shallow Tasman Sea beaches along this stretch of coast – brown sand, driftwood and holiday houses proliferate. Other worthy beaches include Himatangi, Hokio and Waikawa.

The town of **Levin** is more sizeable (population 19,550), but suffers from being too close to both Wellington and Palmerston North to warrant the through-traffic making a stop.

Manawatu Gorge & Around

About 15km northeast of Palmerston North, SH2 dips into **Manawatu Gorge** (Map p253). Maori named the gorge Te Apiti (the Narrow Passage), believing the big reddish rock near the centre of the gorge was its guardian spirit. The rock's colour is said to change intensity when a prominent Rangitane tribe member dies or sheds blood. It takes around four hours to walk through the gorge from either end, or you can see it via jetboat (see p266).

On the southwestern edge of the gorge, about 40 minutes drive from Palmerston North, is the **Tararua Wind Farm** (Map p253; ☎ 07-574 4754; www.trustpower.co.nz; Hall Block Rd), allegedly the largest wind farm in the southern hemisphere. From Hall Block Rd there are awesome views of the turbines. Spinning similarly, north of the gorge is **Te Apiti Wind Farm** (Map p253; ☎ 0800 946 463; www.meridianenergy.co.nz; Saddle Rd, Ashhurst). Ask the i-SITE for directions, or take a tour (p266).

Alternatively, flee the city with a visit to **Timeless Horse Treks** (☎ 06-376 6157; www.timeless horsetreks.co.nz; Gorge Rd, Ballance; 1/2hr rides $35/60). Gentle trail rides take in the Manawatu River and surrounding hills, or saddle up for an overnight all-inclusive trek, taking in the Tararua Wind Farm ($175). Palmerston North pick-up/drop-off costs $40 per person.

Taupo & the Central Plateau

Don't think for a minute that this plateau is some boring old 'elevated flat landmass' as per the dictionary definition. For a start, it ain't flat. In the middle of the plateau, at the heart of Tongariro National Park, are three massive peaks: Tongariro, Ruapehu and Ngauruhoe. Then there's New Zealand's largest lake, Taupo: a vast, water-filled crater – the legacy of a volcanic blast that shook up the world and shattered the island more than 26,500 years ago. This is all part of the Taupo Volcanic Zone, a line of geothermal surfacings that stretches to Whakaari/White Island via Rotorua; and the area is still active, with Mt Ruapehu often having a hissy fit, the last blast occurring in 2007.

And the drama doesn't stop there, for this area now rivals Rotorua for back-to-nature activities and daredevil escapades. Perhaps you fancy fly-fishing in the world-class Tongariro River, hooning up to Huka Falls in a jetboat, or bouncing on a bungy over the Waikato River? Or this could be your chance to skydive. If rambling's your thing, there's always Tongariro Northern Circuit, one of NZ's most achievable Great Walks, or the Tongariro Alpine Crossing, touted as one of the world's top one-dayers. Then again, you could wait until winter, when the mountains are dusted with snow: there's top skiing at Turoa and Whakapapa ski fields.

From river deep to mountain high, and out on the luscious lake, New Zealand's diverse geology takes centre stage here and my-oh-my does it get its shimmy on.

HIGHLIGHTS

- Exploring a fascinating volcanic terrain while tramping the **Tongariro Alpine Crossing** (p292)
- Hurtling to earth from 15,000ft at 200km/h strapped to a complete stranger in the world's skydiving capital, **Taupo** (p275)
- Carving fresh powder at **Turoa Ski Area** or **Whakapapa Ski Area** (p293)
- Biking till your bum burns on the **42 Traverse** (p295)
- Paddling **Lake Taupo** (p276) to check out the modern Maori carvings
- Rediscovering the 'lost valley' of **Orakei Korako** (p284)
- Rocketing up the Waikato River to the base of **Huka Falls** (p282) in a jetboat
- Plunging 47m over the **Waikato River** (p276) on the end of a rubber band

- Telephone code: 07
- www.laketauponz.com
- www.visitruapehu.com

Climate

Due to its altitude, the Central Plateau has a generally cool climate, with temperatures ranging from around 3°C in winter up to a maximum of around 24°C in summer. Above 2500m there is a small year-round snowfield, while July to October is the skiing season at Whakapapa and Turoa, and in some places snow can linger on into spring. On the mountains, storms and freezing temperatures can occur at any time.

Getting There & Around

Air New Zealand (www.airnz.co.nz) has regular flights from Taupo to Auckland and Wellington. The **Tranz Scenic Overlander** (www.tranzscenic.co.nz)

train on the Auckland–Wellington line stops at National Park village, Ohakune and Taihape.

InterCity (www.intercity.co.nz) buses travel to all of the region's major towns, connecting with most major destinations around NZ, while **Naked Bus** (www.nakedbus.com) is useful for Taupo and Turangi. However, there are no direct public buses between the State Hwy 1 (SH1) towns (Taupo and Turangi) and the State Hwy 4 (SH4) towns (National Park and Ohakune). Private shuttle-bus services operate around Tongariro National Park, some picking up from Taupo and Turangi.

LAKE TAUPO REGION

NZ's largest lake, Lake Taupo, sits in the caldera of a volcano that began erupting about 300,000 years ago. The caldera was formed by a collapse during the Oruanui eruption about 26,500 years ago, which threw out 750 cu km of ash and pumice, making Krakatoa (8 cu km) look like a pimple. The surrounding area is still volcanically active and, like Rotorua, has fascinating thermal areas.

Today the 606-sq-km lake and its surrounding waterways are serene enough to attract fishing enthusiasts from all around the world. Well positioned by the lake, both Taupo and Turangi are popular tourist centres. Taupo, in particular, has plenty of activities and facilities to cater for families and independent travellers alike.

TAUPO
pop 21,040
The increasingly exciting town of Taupo now rivals Rotorua as the North Island's adrenaline capital, with an abundance of blood-pumping activities. With a postcard-perfect setting on the northeastern shores of the lake, it boasts shimmering views of the snowy peaks of Tongariro National Park. NZ's longest river, the Waikato, originates from Lake Taupo at the township, before crashing its way through the Huka Falls and Aratiatia Rapids and then settling down for a sedate ramble to the west coast, just south of Auckland.

SH1 passes through the middle of Taupo, making the town easily accessible for travellers and packed with transient traffic for much of the high season.

TAUPO & THE CENTRAL PLATEAU FACTS

Eat Trout, preferably smoked. But you'll have to catch it first!
Drink A mouthful of water from the Waikato River as you bungy over it (p276)
Read *Awesome Forces* by Hamish Campbell and Geoff Hicks – the geological story of NZ in explosive detail
Listen to *Ka mate* – the famous haka, written on the shores of Lake Rotoaira
Watch *The Return of the King,* starring Ngauruhoe (p291) as Mt Doom
Swim at Lake Taupo – truly invigorating
Festival Ohakune's Carrot Festival, celebrating all that is orange and pointy (p300)
Tackiest tourist attraction Shawn the Prawn at Huka Prawn Farm (p283)
Go green Explore Tongariro National Park's alpine flora and geological oddities

History
When Maori chief Tamatea-arikinui first visited this area, his footsteps reverberated – making him think the ground was hollow; he therefore dubbed the area Tapuaeharuru (Resounding Footsteps). The modern name, however, originates from the story of Tia. After Tia discovered the lake and slept beside it draped in his cloak, the area became known as Taupo Nui a Tia (The Great Cloak of Tia).

Europeans settled here in force during the East Coast Land War (1868–72), when it was a strategic military base: Colonel JM Roberts built a redoubt in 1869, and a garrison of mounted police remained until the defeat of Te Kooti (see p352) later that year.

In the 20th century the mass ownership of the motorcar saw Taupo grow from a lakeside village of about 750 people to a large resort town, easily accessible from most points of the North Island. Today the population still grows considerably at peak holiday times, when New Zealanders and international visitors alike flock to the lakeshore.

Information
Automobile Association (AA; Map p274; ☎ 07-378 6000; 3 Tamamutu St)
Cybershed (Map p274; 115 Tongariro St; ☺ 9am-10pm) Offers IT services and internet access and sells British treats to the homesick.

TAUPO & THE CENTRAL PLATEAU

CENTRAL TAUPO

Experience Taupo (Map p274; ☎ 07-377 0704; www.experiencetaupo.com; 29 Tongariro St) Books most local traveller services and has internet access.
Global Gossip (Map p274; 11 Tuwharetoa St) Internet access.
Post office (46 Horomatangi St) Offers poste restante service.
Taupo i-SITE (Map p274; ☎ 07-376 0027; www.laketauponz.com; Tongariro St; ⏰ 8.30am-5pm) Handles bookings for accommodation, transport and activities; has a free town map as well as Department of Conservation (DOC) maps and information.

Sights

Taupo's main attraction is the lake and all the things you can do in, on and around it. The water is famously chilly, but in several places (such as **Hot Water Beach**, Map p282, immediately south of the centre) there are thermal springs just below the surface. You can swim right at the township, but **Acacia Bay** (Map p272), 5km west, is a particularly pleasant spot.

The **Taupo Museum & Art Gallery** (Map p274; ☎ 07-376 0414; www.taupomuseum.co.nz; Story Pl; adult/child $5/free; ⏰ 10am-4.30pm) has historical displays covering the local forestry, nautical and trout-fishing industries, a mock-up of a 19th-century shop and a moa skeleton. There are regular visiting art exhibitions, too. The centrepiece of the collection is a Maori meeting house, Te Aroha o Rongoheikume, adorned with elaborate carvings. Situated in a courtyard, the Ora Garden of Wellbeing is a re-creation of NZ's gold-medal-winning entry into the 2004 Chelsea Flower Show. It's quite small, but features more than 1000 native plants and a steamy lizard scene.

There are 10m-high **Maori carvings**, accessible only by boat, at the lake's Mine Bay (Map p272; see Fishing & Cruising, p276, and Water Sports, p276, for boat-charter operators). They were carved by master carver Matahi Whakataka-Brightwell in the late 1970s, and depict Ngatoro-i-rangi, the visionary Maori navigator who guided the Tuwharetoa and Te Arawa tribes to the Taupo area over a thousand years ago. There are also two smaller Matahi figures here, both of Celtic design, which depict the south wind and a mermaid.

Activities

Adrenaline addicts should look out for special deals that combine several activities for a reduced price.

SKYDIVING

More than 30,000 jumps a year are made from Taupo, which makes it the skydiving capital of the world. It's certainly a terrific spot to do it: all those beautiful places you see from ground level are patchworked together in a brilliant blanket of natural colour, the highlights of which are the deep blue lake and the brilliant white of the snowcapped peaks. The following operators sit alongside each other at the airport and offer some of the best rates in NZ. They offer similar packages, which can include town pick-ups, video, photos and T-shirts.
Skydive Taupo (☎ 0800 586 766; www.skydivetaupo.co.nz; 12,000ft/15,000ft $250/340)
Taupo Tandem Skydiving (☎ 07-377 0428; www.tts.net.nz; 12,000ft/15,000ft $249/339)

MAORI NZ: CENTRAL PLATEAU

The North Island's central region is home to a group of mountains that feature in several Maori legends of lust and betrayal, which end with a few mountains fleeing to other parts of the island (see Mt Taranaki's sad tale, p245).

Long after all that action was over, the chief Ngatoro-i-rangi (see the boxed text, p291), fresh off the boat from Hawaiki, explored this region and named the mountains that remained. The most sacred was Tongariro, consisting of at least 12 volcanic cones, seen as the leader of all the other mountains.

The major *iwi* (tribe) of the region is **Tuwharetoa** (www.tuwharetoa.co.nz), one of the few *iwi* in NZ that has retained an undisputed *ariki* (high chief). The current *ariki* is Tumu Te Heuhu Tukino VIII, whose great-great-grandfather, Te Heuhu Tukino IV (a descendent of Ngatoro-i-rangi), gifted the mountains of Tongariro to NZ in 1887.

To discover the stories of local Maori and their ancestors, visit the meeting house at Taupo Museum (above), the carved cliff faces at Mine Bay (above), Wairakei Terraces (p283), or take a Nature-Culture Walk with pureORAwalks (p278).

BUNGY JUMPING

The picturesque **Taupo Bungy** (Map p282; ☎ 07-377 1135; www.taupobungy.co.nz; jump $109; ☽ 8.30am-5pm) site is the most popular on the North Island. It sits on a cliff edge over the mighty Waikato River, with plenty of vantage points if you're too chicken to jump. Nonchickens will be led onto a platform jutting 20m out over a cliff (the world's first cantilever jump, for engineering boffins) and convinced, with masterly skill, to throw themselves off the edge. A heart-stopping 47m hurtle and a few bounces back and it's safely into the boat. You can also opt for a slight dunk in the river, or strap yourself to a friend and leap off together. Alternatively, try the giant swing.

FISHING & CRUISING

Anglers are in the right place because this region is justifiably world famous for trout. Fly-fishing is the only fishing permitted on all rivers flowing into the lake and within a 300m radius of the river mouths. Spin fishing is allowed only on the Waikato River (flowing *out* of the lake) and, on the other side of the lake, on the Tokaanu tailrace, flowing into the lake from the Tokaanu Power Station. A licence is required for lake and river fishing. Make sure you always carry it with you, as there are hefty fines for violations. Licences cost $16/36/85 per day/week/season and are available from the places listed below, as well as via the i-SITE (p273).

There are numerous fishing guides around Taupo and Turangi (see p285); most are happy to negotiate a price depending on the trip ($250 for a half-day is a rough ballpark, and will include equipment and licence).

You can arrange guided trips or get gear and licences for independent trips at **Greenstone Fishing** (Map p274; ☎ 07-378 3714; www.greenstonefishing.co.nz; 147 Tongariro St; gear hire from $10; ☽ 8.30am-5.30pm Mon-Fri, to 4.30pm Sat & Sun) and **Taupo Rod & Tackle** (Map p274; ☎ 07-378 5337; www.tauporodandtackle.co.nz; 7 Tongariro St; gear hire $15-45; ☽ 8.30am-6pm Mon-Sat, 9.30am-5pm Sun).

There are plenty of boat-charter operators offering both lake fishing trips and cruises. Most will take you to the see the Maori carvings at Mine Bay (p275) and take between one and 2½ hours. The 1926 50ft yacht **Barbary** (☎ 07-378 3444; adult/child $40/10; ☽ 10.30am, 2pm & 5pm) is a popular option. For something with a little more zip on calm days, take the **Cruise Cat** (Map p274; ☎ 07-378 0623; www.chrisjolly.co.nz; adult/child $40/16; ☽ 10.30am & 1.30pm), a large, modern launch. Sunday brunch trips ($58) are especially worthwhile.

The best place to book trips – whether fishing or cruising – is through the **launch office** (Lake Taupo Charter Office; Map p274; ☎ 07-378 3444; www.fishcruisetaupo.co.nz; Marina; ☽ 9am-5pm Dec-Mar, 9.30am-3pm Apr-Nov), which books for around 20 boats, catering to individuals or groups.

SWIMMING & BATHING

The **AC Baths** (Map p282; ☎ 07-376 0350; www.taupovenues.co.nz; AC Baths Ave; adult/child $6.50/2.50, slides $4; ☽ 6am-9pm) at the Taupo Events Centre, about 2km east of town, has a big, heated pool with a waterslide, an indoor kids pool, private mineral pools and a sauna. There's also a **climbing wall** (adult/child $13/9; ☽ hours vary).

Twenty minutes' walk from town you'll find the Huka Falls Walkway **hot springs** (Map p282), a pleasant and well-worn spot under a bridge, where you can take a dip for free in natural surrounds.

Taupo Hot Springs Spa (Map p282; ☎ 07-377 6502; www.taupohotsprings.com; SH5; adult/child $15/4; ☽ 8.30am-9.30pm) has a variety of mineral-rich indoor and outdoor thermal pools, freshwater pools and a giant dragon waterslide for the young ones. Adults can enjoy a wide choice of treatments, such as massage and body scrubs. There's a health-food cafe on-site as well as picnic and barbecue facilities.

WATER SPORTS

With the big lake in the middle and the Waikato and Tongariro Rivers at either end (plus the wild Rangitaiki and Wairoa Rivers not far away), there's plenty of opportunity to get wet and wild around Taupo. Kayaking is popular on the lake and rivers, and there are raft trips available on both white-water rapids and gentle river sections. Locals offer rentals and tuition, so there's absolutely no excuse to not get your boat afloat.

Big Sky Parasail (☎ 0800 724 475; www.bigskyparasail.co.nz; Lake Tce; ☽ 8am-6pm summer only) Runs lake parasailing (400ft/800ft $75/85) from the lakefront.

Canoe & Kayak (Map p274; ☎ 07-378 1003; www.canoeandkayak.co.nz; 77 Spa Rd; ☽ 9am-5pm Mon-Sat) Instruction and boat hire (from the lake's edge in high summer), as well as guided tours: two-hour trip on the Waikato River ($45) or a half-day to the Maori carvings ($90).

Chris Jolly Outdoors (Map p274; ☎ 07-378 5596; www.chrisjolly.co.nz; Marina; ☽ 9am-5.30pm) Can sort

out all sorts of water sports, including kayak hire (single/
double per hour $20/30) and self-drive boats ($70 to $85
per hour). Also organises helicopter tours and books other
activities.

Kiwi River Safaris (☎ 07-377 6597; www.krs.co.nz)
Two-hour white-water rafting trips on the Rangitaiki
($110), Wairoa ($115) and Tongariro Rivers ($110), includ-
ing free pick-up from Taupo and lunch. Also runs kayak
tours down the Waikato River (adult/child $45/25).

Rapid Sensations/Kayaking Kiwi (Map p282; ☎ 07-
378 7902; www.rapids.co.nz, www.kayakingkiwi.com; 413
Huka Falls Rd) Kayak trips to the Maori carvings (4½ hours,
$108) and a gentle paddle along the Waikato (two hours,
$45). Also runs six-hour white-water rafting trips on the
Tongariro River ($135) and shorter trips along a calmer
section (2½ hours, $115).

Sailing Centre (Map p282; ☎ 0274 967 350; www.sail
ingcentre.co.nz; Lake Tce; ☼ 8.30am-8.30pm) Hires out
kayaks ($25), canoes ($35), windsurfers ($35), catamarans
($65) and sailboats ($60) in summer. Rates are per hour.

Wilderness Escapes (☎ 07-378 3413; www.wilderness
escapes.co.nz) Half-day to multiple-day kayaking trips,
including Maori carvings (half-day $85) and a sunset
paddle on the lake ($85). Also offers kayak hire ($60 per
day). Packages combine kayaking with a helicopter ride,
boat cruise or tramp.

CYCLING & MOUNTAIN BIKING

Exploring Taupo on two wheels is fun and
easy, with dedicated cycle lanes along Lake
Tce and Heu Heu St, and shared paths elsewhere. There are blue bike racks throughout
town. Lake Taupo is also the location of two of
NZ's biggest annual cycling events: the 160km
Lake Taupo Cycle Challenge (www.cyclechallenge.org.nz),
held on the last Saturday in November, and
September's 12-hour **Day-Night Thriller** (www.
daynightthriller.co.nz), regularly attracting more
than 3000 mountain bikers.

There are good mountain-bike tracks just
out of town in the Wairakei and Pureora
Forests and along the Waikato River. You
can download maps for these from www.bike
taupo.org.nz.

Rapid Sensations (above) runs guided
three-hour rides in the Wairakei Forest
(guided trips $75, bike hire half-/full day
$45/55). Rainbow Lodge (p279) and **Life
Cycles** (Map p274; ☎ 07-378 6117; 16 Oruanui St; per day
$40; ☼ 8.30am-5pm Mon-Fri) also rent bikes. For
luxury rough riding, **Heli-Biking** (☎ 07-384 2816;
www.kaimanawahelibiking.co.nz; 4hr ride $395) will pick
you up in a helicopter and drop you on top of
the highest point in the Kaimanawas, allowing
you to bike all the way down.

TRAMPING

There are some great walks in and around
Taupo, ranging from sedate ambles to more
gnarly all-dayers. A good place to start is
DOC's leaflet *Lake Taupo – A Guide to Walks
and Hikes* ($2.50).

The **Huka Falls Walkway** is an enjoyable, easy
walk from Taupo to the falls along the east
bank of the Waikato River, crossing a hot
stream en route. The falls are about a 1½-hour
walk from the centre. To reach the walkway
from town, head up Spa Rd, passing the Taupo
Bungy site; turn left at County Ave and continue through Spa Thermal Park to the street's
end. The path heads off to the left of the end
car park, up over a hill and down to the hot
springs by the river.

Carrying on from the falls is the **Huka Falls
to Aratiatia Rapids Walking Track**. The rapids are
7km away (another two-plus hours). There
are good views of the river, Huka Falls and
the power station across the river. To just
walk this part, drive out to the falls car park
and cross the bridge.

Another walk goes to **Mt Tauhara** (Map
p282), from the top of which there are magnificent views. Take the Taupo–Napier Hwy
(SH5) turn-off, 2km south of Taupo town
centre; about 6km along SH5, turn left into
Mountain Rd. The start of the track is signposted on the right-hand side. It will take
about two hours to the top, walking slowly.

The pleasant **Great Lake Walkway** follows
the Taupo lakefront south to Five Mile Bay
(8km). It's a flat, easy walk along public-access
beaches.

Taupo can also serve as a base from which to
walk the Tongariro Alpine Crossing (see p292).

GOLF

Taupo Golf Club (Map p282; ☎ 07-378 6933; www.
taupogolf.co.nz; 32 Centennial Dr; 9/18 holes $35/60) Has
two good 18-hole courses; one is a park course and the
other an inland links.

Wairakei International Golf Course (Map p282;
☎ 07-374 8152; www.wairakeigolfcourse.co.nz; SH1,
Wairakei; 18 holes $100-200) 8km north of Taupo; a chal-
lenging course set in 150 hectares of beautiful countryside,
rated within the top 100 courses worldwide. In late 2009 a
2m-high, 5km-long pest-proof fence was erected, turning
the whole course into a native bird sanctuary.

Wairakei Resort (Map p282; ☎ 07-374 8021; www.
wairakei.co.nz; SH1, Wairakei; adult/child $12/$8) Nine-
hole course set in similarly verdant surroundings 1km up
the road from the international course.

HORSE TREKKING

Moehiwa Horse Ventures (Map p282; ☎ 07-378 3727; http://moehiwa.tripod.com; 73 Poihipi Rd; 1-2hr rides $45-80) Treks through pasture, pine forest and riverbeds.

Taupo Horse Treks (Map p282; ☎ 07-378 0356; www. taupohorsetreks.co.nz; Karapiti Rd; per hr $60) Conducts treks through some fine forest with good views over the Craters of the Moon (p283).

SKIING

Taupo is tantalisingly close to the ski fields, being 1¼ hours drive to Whakapapa, and two hours to Turoa (see p293). There's gear hire all around and up the mountain, and also at **Pointons Ski Shop** (Map p274; ☎ 07-377 0087; 57 Tongariro St; ski/snowboard hire $30/40; ☺ 7am-7pm Apr-Sep, 8.30am-5.30pm Mon-Fri, 8.30am-4pm Sat, 10am-3pm Sun Oct-Mar).

OTHER ACTIVITIES

Thrill seekers with petrol-head tendencies should head to the **Taupo Motorsport Park** (off Map p282; ☎ 07-376 5033; www.tauporacetrack.co.nz; Broadlands Rd). This state-of-the-art 3.5km racetrack and drag circuit has staged the A1 Grand Prix. There's often something to watch here, from sidecar races to 'drifters' and, on occasion, the police testing their skills. You can get out on the track in a V8 or Formula Challenge Race Car with **Formula Challenge** (☎ 07-377 0338; www.fcr.co.nz; 1-3 sessions of laps $290-695), or superfast rides with a pro in the driver's seat and driving tuition can be organised through **Track Drive** (☎ 027 288 9037; www.trackdrive.co.nz).

Taupo Quad Adventures (☎ 07-377 6404; www.4x4quads.com; SH1; 1-3hr trips $79-189), 24km north of town opposite the turn-off to Orakei Korako, offers fully guided off-road quad-bike trips.

For a more peaceful activity, **Taupo Gliding Club** (Map p282; ☎ 07-378 5627; www.taupoglidingclub. co.nz; Centennial Dr; flights $120-180) glides daily by appointment (weather permitting) at Centennial Park.

Tours

AERIAL SIGHTSEEING

Air Charter Taupo (☎ 07-378 5467; www.aircharter taupo.co.nz; Taupo Airport; flights $80-250) Scenic flights ranging from 15 minutes to one hour, across Huka Falls, Lake Taupo and Tongariro National Park.

Helipro (☎ 07-377 8805; www.helipro.co.nz; Taupo Airport; flights $95-1695) Specialises in heli-tours, which include alpine and White Island landings, as well as shorter scenic flights over the town, lake and volcanoes (minimum 10 minutes).

Helistar Helicopters (Map p282; ☎ 07-374 8405; www.helistar.co.nz; 415 Huka Falls Rd; flights $99-995) Located about 3km northeast of town, Helistar offers a variety of scenic helicopter flights, from 10 minutes to two hours. Combine a Helistar trip with the Huka Falls Jet in the Huka Star combo (from $193).

Taupo Air Services (☎ 07-378 5325; taupoair@xtra. co.nz; Taupo Airport; flights $90-500) Runs scenic flights, from the 15-minute Local Look to a nearly two-hour trip to White Island.

Taupo's Floatplane (Map p274; ☎ 07-378 7500; www.tauposfloatplane.co.nz; flights $75-590) Located at the entrance to the marina, the floatplane does a variety of trips, including quick flights over the lake and longer ones over Mt Ruapehu or White Island. Packages include the Taupo Trifecta Combo (floatplane trip, followed by a jetboat trip and a walk through Orakei Korako; $385).

OTHER TOURS

Paradise Tours (☎ 07-378 9955; www.paradisetours. co.nz; tours adult/child $99/45) Three-hour tours to the Aratiatia Rapids, Craters of the Moon and Huka Falls. Also offers tours to Tongariro National Park, Orakei Korako, Rotorua, Hawke's Bay and Waitomo Caves.

pureORAwalks (☎ 021-042 2722; www.pureorawalks. com; adult/child $85/62) Four-hour Nature-Culture walks in Pureora Forest Park, Lake Rotopounamu and Whirinaki Forest Park, offering insight into *Maoritanga* (things Maori) – including traditional uses of flora and fauna, local history and legends.

Whirinaki Rainforest Experiences (☎ 07-377 2363; www.rainforest-treks.co.nz) Runs fascinating and educational ecocultural guided walks in the Whirinaki Forest Park (one- to three-day trips $155 to $745). Transport from Taupo, meals and camping necessities are included.

Sleeping

BUDGET

YHA Taupo Action Downunder (Map p274; ☎ 07-378 3311; www.yha.co.nz; 56 Kaimanawa St; campsites/dm/s/tr $16/29/58/97, d $78-88; ☐ ☎) A good hostel with cosy communal areas and a sun-trap deck with barbecues, a barrel spa pool and an extensive DVD library. The kitchen space is a little limited, but they make up for it with guitar hire.

Taupo DeBretts Spa Resort (Map p282; ☎ 07-378 8559; www.taupodebretts.com; SH5; campsites per adult/child $20/10, cabins $60-115, units $130-190; ☐ ☎ ☒) More of an upmarket holiday park than a flashy resort, DeBretts offers everything from tent sites to motel-style units, and has kid-friendly features such as a playground and trampoline in well-tended grounds. It's a five-minute drive from downtown, but is well worth the hop for its peaceful location and the indulgent Taupo Hot Springs that shares its home (see p276). At the time of research the neighbouring Terraces Hotel (1889) was being converted into a Hilton, complete with upmarket restaurants.

our pick Blackcurrant Backpackers (Map p274; ☎ 07-378 9292; www.blackcurrentbp.co.nz; 20 Taniwha St; dm $22-25, s/d/tr $50/70/84) Still with that new-paint-and-carpet smell when we visited, this ageing motel has been fitted out with flash en suites and supercomfy beds. The staff rivals the cartoon blackcurrants in the Ribena ads for chirpiness.

Rainbow Lodge (Map p274; ☎ 07-378 5754; www.rainbowlodge.co.nz; 99 Titiraupenga St; dm $23-26, s $45-55, d $52-64, tr/q $78/104; ☐ ☎) A solid, sociable hostel offering clean rooms, including some with en suite. Bonuses include bike ($20 per day) and fishing-tackle hire, free coffee and a sauna.

Taupo Urban Retreat (Map p274; ☎ 07-378 6124; www.tur.co.nz; 65 Heu Heu St; dm $23-27, d $68; ☐ ☎) A purpose-built hostel with a publike hub, enjoyed by a younger crowd who fit right in with its carefree style. It's refreshingly modern in design, with a beach-house feel, although it's a busy road on your doorstep instead of the ocean.

Lake Taupo Top 10 Holiday Resort (Map p282; ☎ 07-378 6860; www.taupotop10.co.nz; 28 Centennial Dr; campsites per adult/child $23/13, cabins $99-128, units $149-365; ☐ ☎ ☒) The slickest of the local camping grounds, this 20-acre park has all the mod cons, including heated swimming pool, tennis courts and an on-site shop. It's about 2.5km from the i-SITE.

All Seasons Holiday Park (Map p282; ☎ 0800 777 272; www.taupoallseasons.co.nz; 16 Rangatira St; campsites per s/d $25/40, dm $37, cabins $60-129, units $95-212) A pleasant holiday park five minutes' walk to town, with well-established trees and hedgerows between sites. Playground, games room, thermal pool and good kitchen facilities.

Also recommended:

Reid's Farm Recreation Reserve (Map p282; Huka Falls Rd; free for max 7 nights in a 14-day period; ☺ late Oct-early Apr) A beautiful spot for freedom camping beside the Waikato River (summer only). Apart from a handful of portaloos there are no facilities.

Silver Fern Lodge (Map p274; ☎ 07-377 4929; www.silverfernlodge.co.nz; cnr Tamamutu & Kaimanawa Sts; dm $25, r $90-110; ☐) 'Flash-packers' screams the signage, and what's delivered is a shiny custom-built complex trimmed in corrugated aluminium, with pleasant, if lifeless, decor. The spruce rooms range from 10-bed dorms to studio units with en suite, and there's a large communal kitchen and lounge.

Tiki Lodge (Map p274; ☎ 07-377 4545; www.tikilodge.co.nz; 104 Tuwharetoa St; dm $26, d $75-85, tr $84-90, q $112-120; ☐) This slick hostel has great lake and mountain views from the balcony, a spacious kitchen, comfy lounges, lots of Maori artwork and a spa pool out back.

Dunrovin Motel (Map p274; ☎ 07-378 7384; www.dunrovintaupo.co.nz; 140 Heu Heu St; r $90-130; ☐ ☎) A chirpy old bird, recently given a fresh lick of paint. Functional units remain true to the period (built 1962), and are surrounded by pretty gardens with tui often about.

MIDRANGE

Lynwood Lodge (Map p274; ☎ 07-378 4967; 52 Rifle Range Rd; d/tr/q $110/130/150; ☒) Taupo's first motel, built in 1952. So what you get is pebble-dash and concrete and rooms as big as a small house, made up like your granny's in residence. It's all shipshape though, and homey, and a real slice of Kiwi hospitality.

Bella Vista (Map p274; ☎ 07-378 9043; www.bellavistamotels.co.nz; 143 Heu Heu St; d $110-145, tr $145-165, q $185; ☎) One of the growing number of Bella Vista motels nationwide, this one offers personal service by way of dog-loving owners Aaron and Tracey. Rooms are clean and comfortable, if a little bland. The communal barbecue is well located away from the road – good for a sundowner of an evening.

Chelmswood Motel (Map p282; ☎ 07-378 2715; www.chelmswood.co.nz; 250 Lake Tce; r $110-250; ☐ ☒) This unpretentious Tudor-style manor on the south side of town has simple studios and larger family rooms, most with their own mineral pool. There's a heated outdoor pool, a sauna, and a sandpit for the littlies.

Catelli's of Taupo (Map p274; ☎ 0800 88 44 77; www.catellis.co.nz; 23-27 Rifle Range Rd; r $135-145, ste $160-235; ☎) The exterior is all hobbitish '80s curves, sloping roofs and nipple-pink trim, but inside these orderly motel units have a fresh, modern feel. In summer it's worth paying the extra $5 for a garden studio with an outside sitting area.

Suncourt (Map p274; ☎ 07-378 8265; www.suncourt.co.nz; 14 Northcroft St; d $135-170, tr $155-190, q $170-220; ☐ ☎ ☒) This rambling, lake-gazing complex encloses comfortable, well-furnished units with facilities including a spa pool and kids playground. Larger rooms with verandas and full kitchens are ideal for families, though regular conferences can book the place out.

Beechtree (Map p274; ☎ 07-377 0181; www.beech treemotel.co.nz; 56 Rifle Range Rd; d $140-180, tr $170, apt $220-250; 🖳 🛜) The Beechtree, and its sister motel Miro next door, offer classy rooms at a reasonable rate. The neutral-toned decor is fresh and modern, and creates a feeling of light and air, as do the large windows, ground-floor patios and upstairs balconies.

Lake (Map p274; ☎ 07-378 4222; www.thelakeonline. co.nz; 63 Mere Rd; r $150-195) A reminder that 1960s and '70s design wasn't all Austin Powers–style groovaliciousness and bell-bottoms, this unusual boutique motel is crammed with classic furniture from the likes of Saarenin and Mies Van der Rohe. The studio is a tight fit, but the four one-bedroom units all have kitchenettes and dining/living areas.

TOP END

Acacia Cliffs Lodge (off Map p282; ☎ 07-378 1551; http:// acaciacliffslodge.co.nz; 133 Mapara Rd, Acacia Bay; r $650; 🖳 🛜) Pushing the romance switch way past 'rekindle', this luxurious B&B, high in the hills above Acacia Bay, offers four modern suites – three with sumptuous lake views and one that compensates for the lack of them with a curvy bath and a private garden. If you don't want to venture too far from the bedroom, dinners can be arranged.

Huka Lodge (Map p282; ☎ 07-378 5791; www. hukalodge.com; Huka Falls Rd; s/d/tr/cottages from $1095/1460/1905/3060; 🖳 🞉) Welcome to paradise. One of the best hotels in NZ, Huka Lodge basks in accolades and a procession of famous guests, including at least three queens. Surrounded by lush bush and delightful gardens, the main lodge has a homey feel (albeit the home of a wealthy aesthete) and features shared dining and lounge areas, and a library. Individual guest lodges are dotted along the riverside, with views and privacy. Rates include breakfast and a five-course dinner. There are also two entirely self-contained cottages set apart on the grounds.

Eating

Taupo is large enough to offer a good range of options, from burger bars to world-class restaurants.

RESTAURANTS

Lotus Thai (Map p274; ☎ 07-376 9497; 137 Tongariro St; mains $16-21; ⏲ lunch Wed-Fri, dinner Wed-Mon) A warm and inviting restaurant with Siamese trim-

mings throughout, offering standard Thai fare in plentiful portions.

our pick Pimentos (Map p274; ☎ 07-377 4549; 17 Tamamutu St; mains $26-29; ⏲ dinner Wed-Mon) Such a local favourite that you may well need to book to enjoy some of the town's best food in this convivial environment. Its lamb shanks and mash are legendary, but the relatively short menu offers plenty of well-considered experimentation.

Plateau (Map p274; ☎ 07-377 2425; 64 Tuwharetoa St; mains $30-34; ⏲ lunch & dinner) One of a growing number of brewery-branded gastro-pubs, Plateau is a great place for a drink (Monteith's beer being the main poison), but the food is the key. The menu is predominantly modern NZ (think lamb rump and rib-eye), with plenty of fancy fusion twists.

Brantry (Map p274; ☎ 07-378 0484; 45 Rifle Range Rd; mains $32-37; ⏲ dinner) Chef Prue Campbell and sister Felicity continue to run the best and most consistent restaurant in the region at this 1950s town house, a few minutes from the town centre. Dine in intimate, unobtrusive surrounds, inside or out. The menu makes use of some of NZ's finest ingredients, including top-quality cuts of beef and lamb. The set menu (two-/three-courses $40/50) is a gift.

CAFES

Stir Taupo (Map p274; cnr Redoubt St & Ferry Rd; crepes $5-10; ⏲ breakfast & lunch Tue-Sun) Despite operating out of a caravan by the marina, Stir managed to snaffle a 2009 cafe award. The formula's simple: killer coffee and scrumptious sweet and savoury crepes.

Fine Fettle (Map p274; ☎ 07-378 7674; 39 Paora Hape St; mains $6-15; ⏲ breakfast & lunch) An airy cafe on a quieter edge of town, serving wholefood, organic, and GE- and gluten-free options. The healthy, satisfying offerings include quiches and fresh salads, plus juices, smoothies and iced chai.

Replete (Map p274; ☎ 07-378 0606; 45 Heu Heu St; mains $6-16; ⏲ breakfast & lunch) Widely regarded as one of Taupo's best cafes, Replete's counter is packed full of delicatessen delights – running the gamut from sandwiches and salads to sweets. Its pastry selection is particularly commendable. A blackboard menu offers inexpensive and interesting light meals.

Eruption (Map p274; ☎ 027-310 0421; Suncourt Centre, Tamamutu St; mains $7-15; ⏲ breakfast & lunch Mon-Sat) Shelter behind one of the free newspapers while Eruption's espresso machine steams and spurts out black rivers topped with creamy foam. The food selection's limited but tasty.

L'Arté (off Map p282; ☎ 07-378 2962; 255 Mapara Rd, Acacia Bay; mains $10-25; 9am-4pm Wed-Sun, daily Jan) A 10-minute drive from town will reward you with a fantastically artful cafe in an ebullient sculpture garden with a gallery alongside. Lots of mouth-watering treats are made from scratch here, including the pesto that sits on the must-have antipasto platter. The home baking is a triumph.

SELF-CATERING

Pak N Save (Map p274; Taniwha St; 8am-9.30pm)

Beaut Bakery (Map p274; 179 Spa Rd; 5am-3.30pm) Try their award-winning mincemeat-and-gravy pies.

Drinking

Things get lively in the height of summer when the town fills up with travellers. The rest of the year it might pay to take a newspaper to read over your pint.

Bond (Map p274; ☎ 07-377 2434; 40 Tuwharetoa St) Aiming for 007-like sophistication, this is Taupo's most upmarket bar, with European beers, tapas and DJs up late. The drinks cost a pretty Money-Penny, but you may still see a Q at the bar.

Finn MacCuhal's (Map p274; ☎ 07-378 6165; cnr Tongariro & Tuwharetoa Sts) With Irish ephemera nailed to the walls and a backpackers' next door, you can be sure that there will be plenty of craic here; DJs on the weekends.

Jolly Good Fellows (Map p274; ☎ 07-378 0457; 76 Lake Tce) Corr, Guvnor! You ain't seen a pub like this since old Blighty, with lashings of cultural clichés and cheeky humour added to its pub grub, along with Old Speckled Hen, Tetleys and Bulmers cider on tap.

Mulligans (Map p274; ☎ 07-376 9101; 15 Tongariro St) A locals' hang-out, this Irish boozer offers hearty meal-and-drink deals and is a good spot for a quiet Guinness.

Shed (Map p274; ☎ 07-376 5393; 18 Tuwharetoa St) A lively place to sup a beer and catch the big game, sit outside and watch the world go by, or strut your stuff to DJs at the weekends. Food is punter-pleasing pub fare in man-sized portions.

Entertainment

Great Lake Centre (Map p274; ☎ 07-376 0340; Tongariro St) Hosts performances, exhibitions and conventions. Ask at the i-SITE for the current program.

Starlight Cinema Centre (Map p274; ☎ 07-377 1085; Starlight Arcade, off Horomatangi St; adult/child $13/8.50) Screens the latest Hollywood blockbusters.

Getting There & Away

AIR

Taupo Airport (☎ 07-378 7771; www.taupoairport.co.nz; Anzac Memorial Dr) is 8km south of town. **Air New Zealand** (☎ 0800 737 000; www.airnz.co.nz) has daily direct flights to Auckland (45 minutes) and Wellington (one hour), with onward connections.

BUS

The main bus stop is at the **Taupo Travel Centre** (Map p274; ☎ 07-378 9032; 16 Gascoigne St), which operates as a booking office. **InterCity/Newmans** (☎ 09-583 5780; www.intercity.co.nz) runs several daily buses to Turangi ($25, 44 minutes), Auckland ($57, five hours), Hamilton ($51, three hours), Rotorua ($29, one hour), Tauranga ($47, 2¾ hours), Napier ($35, two hours), Palmerston North ($51, 4¼ hours) and Wellington ($61, six hours).

Budget operator **Naked Bus** (☎ 0900 625 33 per min $1.80; www.nakedbus.com) has daily services to the same destinations (excluding Tauranga), with super-early-bird prices starting from $1. Buses stop outside the i-SITE.

Shuttle services operate year-round between Taupo, Turangi and Tongariro National Park. In winter, services run to Whakapapa Ski Area (1½ hours) and can include package deals for lift tickets and ski hire. See p294 for details.

Getting Around

Taupo's Hotbus (Map p274; ☎ 0508 468 287; www.hotbus.co.nz; 1st stop $15, then per stop $5; 9am-4pm Oct-Mar, 10am-3pm Apr-Sep) is a hop-on, hop-off bus that does an hourly circuit of all the major attractions in and around Taupo, from the i-SITE.

Taxi services are provided by **Taupo Taxis** (☎ 07-378 5100) and **Top Cabs** (Map p274; ☎ 07-378 9250; Tuwharetoa St). Expect to pay about $23 for a cab to the airport from the centre of town.

AROUND TAUPO
Wairakei Park

Crossing the river at Tongariro St and heading north from town on SH1, you'll arrive at the Wairakei Park area, also known as the Huka Falls Tourist Loop. Take the first right turn after you cross the river and you'll be on Huka Falls Rd, which runs along the river and arches around to meet SH1 further north. Here you can turn left to pass other interesting spots on your way back to town.

HUKA FALLS

Clearly signposted and with a car park and kiosk alongside, these falls mark the spot where NZ's longest river, the Waikato – which, here, has only just been born from Lake Taupo – is slammed into a narrow chasm, making a dramatic 10m drop into a surging pool. As you cross the footbridge you can see the full force of this torrent that the Maori called Hukanui (Great Body of Spray). On sunny days the water is crystal clear and you can take great photographs

TAUPO & WAIRAKEI

SIGHTS & ACTIVITIES	
AC Baths	1 B3
Craters of the Moon	2 B2
Helistar Helicopters	3 B2
Honey Hive	4 B2
Hot Springs	5 B3
Hot Water Beach	6 B4
Huka Falls River Cruise	7 D1
Huka Prawn Farm	8 C1
Hukafalls Jet	(see 8)
Moehiwa Horse Ventures	9 A3
Rapid Sensations/Kayaking Kiwi	10 B2
Rapids Jet	11 D1
Rock'n Ropes	(see 4)
Sailing Centre	12 B5
Taupo Bungy	13 B3
Taupo Gliding Club	14 D3

Taupo Golf Club	15 C3
Taupo Horse Treks	16 B2
Taupo Hot Springs Spa	17 C4
Volcanic Activity Centre	18 B2
Wairakei International Golf Course	19 B2
Wairakei Resort	20 B2
Wairakei Terraces	21 B1

SLEEPING	
All Seasons Holiday Park	22 B3
Chelmswood Motel	23 B4
Huka Lodge	24 B3
Lake Taupo Top 10 Holiday Resort	25 B3
Reid's Farm Recreation Reserve	26 B3
Taupo DeBretts Spa Resort	27 C4

from the lookout on the other side of the footbridge. You can also take a few short walks around the area or pick up the longer Huka Falls Walkway back to town, or the Aratiatia Rapids Walking Track to the rapids (see p277).

ROCK'N ROPES & THE HONEY HIVE

Less than a kilometre beyond the Huka Falls turn-off is the **Honey Hive** (Map p282; ☎ 07-374 8553; www.honeyhivetaupo.com; Karetoto Rd; admission free; ☼ 10am-5pm), which has a glass-enclosed viewing hive, honey tastings and all manner of bee products – edible, medicinal and cosmetic – as well as mead. The cafe serves honey ice cream, too.

Right next door is **Rock'n Ropes** (☎ 07-374 8111; www.rocknropes.co.nz; Karetoto Rd; giant swing $20, adrenaline combo $40, half-day $65), a vertiginous and challenging high-ropes course that includes balancing in teetering 'tree-tops', negotiating a tricky two-wire bridge and scaling ropes. The combo includes the swing, high beam and trapeze.

VOLCANIC ACTIVITY CENTRE

What's the story with all the geothermal activity in this area? The **volcanic activity centre** (Map p282; ☎ 07-374 8375; www.volcanoes.co.nz; Karetoto Rd; adult/child $9.50/5; ☼ 9am-5pm Mon-Fri, 10am-4pm Sat & Sun) has all the answers. This observatory monitors volcanic activity in the volatile Taupo Volcanic Zone, and the visitor centre has some excellent, if text-heavy, displays on NZ's geothermal and volcanic activity, including a working seismograph.

A favourite exhibit with kids is the Earthquake Simulator, a little booth you can sit in to experience an earthquake, complete with teeth-chattering shudders and sudden shakes. You can also configure your own tornado then watch it wreak havoc, or see a simulated geyser above and below ground. A small theatre screens footage of the 1995 Ruapehu eruption and the 2007 breach of the crater lake.

HUKAFALLS JET & PRAWN FARM

Further down the Falls loop road is the launching site for **Hukafalls Jet** (Map p282; ☎ 07-374 8572; www.hukafallsjet.com; trips adult/child $99/59). This 30-minute thrill ride takes you up the river to the spray-filled foot of the Huka Falls and down to the Aratiatia Dam, all the while dodging daringly and doing acrobatic 360-degree turns. Trips run all day (prices include transport from Taupo) and you can bundle it in with a helicopter ride (see p278).

Just next door, the **Huka Prawn Farm** (Map p282; ☎ 07-374 8474; www.hukaprawnpark.co.nz; adult/child $24/14; ☼ 9am-3.30pm, longer hours in summer) is one of the world's only geothermally heated freshwater prawn farms. There's a surprising array of activities here, including prawn 'fishing' and Killer Prawn Golf (balls $1 each, $10 for 20), which allows you to shoot balls over the prawn beds. For a more educational experience, tours leave hourly (11am to 4pm; adult/child $15/10). Best of all, though, is the restaurant where you can try prawns all ways, and nonprawn dishes if you wish (mains $13 to $30).

CRATERS OF THE MOON

This lesser-known geothermal area sprang to life as a result of the hydroelectric tinkering of the 1950s that created the power station. When underground water levels fell and pressure shifted, the **Craters of the Moon** (Map p282; www.cratersofthemoon.co.nz; adult/child $6/2.50; ☼ 8.30am-5.30pm) appeared with new steam vents and bubbling mud pools pocking the landscape. The perimeter loop walk takes about 45 minutes and affords great views down to the lake and mountains beyond. There's a kiosk at the entrance, staffed by volunteers who kindly keep an eye on the car park. Craters of the Moon is signposted on SH1, about 5km north of Taupo.

WAIRAKEI TERRACES

Known to Maori as Waiora and latterly as Geyser Valley, this area was once one of the most active thermal areas in the world, with 22 geysers and 240 mud pools and springs. In 1958 the valley was significantly changed by the geothermal power project and today it's the site of **Wairakei Terraces** (Map p282; ☎ 07-378 0913; www.wairakeiterraces.co.nz; adult/child $18/9; ☼ 9am-5pm), artificially made silica terraces, pools and geysers re-creating, on a smaller scale, the famous Pink and White Terraces, which were destroyed by the Tarawera eruption in 1886. There's also a small meeting house, a re-created Maori village and a carving centre. The **Maori Cultural Experience** (adult/child $85/42.50; ☼ 6pm) here – which includes a traditional challenge, welcome and *hangi* meal – gives an insight into Maori life in the geothermal areas.

ARATIATIA RAPIDS

Two kilometres off SH5, the Aratiatia Rapids were a spectacular part of the Waikato River until the government plonked a hydroelectric dam across the waterway, shutting off the flow. But the spectacle hasn't disappeared completely, with the floodgates opened from 1 October to 31 March at 10am, noon, 2pm and 4pm and from April to September at 10am, noon and 2pm. You can see the water crash through the dam from two good vantage points.

Get another perspective from **Rapids Jet** (Map p282; ☎ 07-374 8066; www.rapidsjet.com; Rapids Rd, off SH5; adult/child $90/50), a jetboat that shoots along the lower part of the rapids. It's a sensational 35-minute ride – some say it rivals the Huka Falls trip. The boat departs from the end of the access road to the Aratiatia lookouts. Go down Rapids Rd and look for the signpost to the National Equestrian Centre.

For a less rapid, more photo-friendly ride, try **Huka Falls River Cruise** (Map p282; ☎ 0800 278 336; www.hukafallscruise.co.nz; Aratiatia Dam; adult/child $35/10; ☺ departs 12.30 & 2.30pm year-round, plus 10.30am & 4.30pm in summer), a relaxed jaunt (80 minutes) from Aratiatia Dam to Huka Falls.

Five kilometres further north on SH1 is **Taupo Adventure Park** (off Map p282; ☎ 07-374 8495; www.taupoadventurepark.com; activities $3-40; ☺ 10am-4pm Wed-Sun, school & public holidays), a family-oriented park with minigolf, maze, laser tag, paintball, video games, animal park, quad bikes and go-karts.

Orakei Korako

A bit off the beaten track, **Orakei Korako Cave & Thermal Park** (☎ 07-378 3131; www.orakeikorako.co.nz; adult/child $34/14; ☺ 8am-5.30pm summer, to 5pm winter) gets fewer visitors than other thermal areas. But, since the destruction of the Pink and White Terraces, it is arguably the best thermal area left in NZ. Although three-quarters of it now lies beneath the dam waters of Lake Ohakuri, the remaining quarter is pretty interesting.

A walking track (allow 1½ hours) that's steep in parts largely follows a boardwalk around the colourful silica terraces for which the park is famous, and passes geysers and **Ruatapu Cave**. This impressive natural cave has a jade-green pool, thought to have been used as a mirror by Maori women who prepared for rituals here (Orakei Korako means 'the place of adorning'). Entry includes a boat ride across Lake Ohakuri.

It's about 25 minutes to Orakei Korako from Taupo. Take SH1 towards Hamilton for 23km, and then travel for 14km from the signposted turn-off. From Rotorua the turn-off is on SH5, via Mihi.

Alternatively, **NZ River Jet** (☎ 07-333 7111; www.riverjet.co.nz; SH5, Mihi; 2½hr ride incl entry to Orakei Korako adult/child $145/75) will zip you there in thrilling fashion from Mihi, 20km upstream on the Waikato River. They also offer the Squeeze – a jetboat ride through Tutukau Gorge to a spot where you can disembark in warm water and edge your way through a crevice to a concealed natural hot spring surrounded by native bush ($130).

Another option is **Riverboat Waireka** (☎ 07-333 8845; www.riverboatwaireka.com), which will transport you from the Mihi bridge to Orakei Korako via a leisurely 3½-hour cruise in a 1908 riverboat.

If it was difficult to resist all that enticing but scalding water at Orakei Korako, but you don't fancy a squeeze, a 30km detour will take you to **Butcher's Pool** (admission free), a bedecked but otherwise purely natural thermal spring in the middle of a farmer's paddock. Alongside is a small parking area and changing sheds. To get there, turn left onto SH5 at Mihi (follow the signs to Rotorua). After 4km look out for Homestead Rd on your right. Follow it to the end, turn left and look for a row of trees lining a gravel driveway off to your right about 300m away (the signpost can be difficult to spot as it's pointing from the other side of the road).

Mangakino & Whakamaru

These neighbouring towns, like their respective lakes (Maraetai and Whakamaru), are by-products of hydroelectric schemes on the Waikato River. Mangakino's population is roughly a fifth of its 1959 peak, when the then 14-year-old town heaved with construction workers, engineers and their families. The power stations are still in operation, but the main drawcards today are activities on or around the lakes.

M-I-A Wakeboarding (☎ 021 864 254; www.m-i-a.co.nz; wakeboard or wakeskate/wakesurf $100/75) tears up the water on Mangakino's Lake Maraetai, offering wakeboarding, wakeskating and wakesurfing as well as canoe tours, mountainbiking trips and backpacker accommodation (dorm/double $23/54).

Free camping is permitted close to the **Bus Stop Café** (☎ 027 203 7110; mains $7-12), where local identity Garry Gradwell dishes out burgers and toasties from the back of an old Bedford bus parked on the Maraetai lakefront.

Eventually Mangakino and Whakamaru will be linked by the **Waikato River Trail** (www. waikatorivertrail.com), a proposed 425km route following the river all the way from Lake Taupo to Port Waikato. A 26km section heading upriver from Whakamaru to Atiamuri has been completed.

Pureora Forest Park

Fringing the western edge of Lake Taupo, the 78,000-hectare Pureora Forest is home to NZ's tallest totara tree. Logging was stopped in this forest in the 1980s after a long campaign by conservationists, and the subsequent regeneration is impressive. There are mountain-bike tracks and hiking routes through the park, including tracks to the summits of Mt Pureora (1165m) and the rock pinnacle of Mt Titiraupenga (1042m). A 12m-high tower, a short walk from the Bismarck Rd car park, provides a canopy-level view of the forest for birdwatchers.

To stay overnight in one of three standard DOC huts (adult/child $5/2.50), you'll need to buy backcountry hut tickets in advance. The three campsites (adult/child $8/2) have self-registration boxes. Hut tickets, maps and information on the park are available from the DOC offices in Turangi (below) and Te Kuiti (p231).

TURANGI
pop 3900

Once a service town for the nearby hydroelectric power station, Turangi's claim to fame nowadays is undoubtedly its fish. It proclaims itself 'Trout Fishing Capital of the World'. The Tongariro River, however, can be enjoyed in many other ways, including white-water rafting and swimming. The township also provides ready access to the ski fields and walking tracks of Tongariro National Park.

Information

The **Turangi i-SITE** (☎ 07-386 8999; www.laketauponz. com; Ngawaka Pl; ⏲ 8.30am-5pm) is a good stop for information on Tongariro National Park, Kaimanawa Forest Park, trout fishing, and snow and road conditions. It issues DOC hut tickets (although this may change if hut tickets

become an online-only purchase), ski passes and hunting and fishing licences, and makes bookings for transport, accommodation and activities. It also has internet facilities and a detailed relief model of the national park. The main bus stop is outside.

The Turangi–Taupo **DOC visitors centre** (☎ 07-386 8607; Turanga Pl; ⏲ 8am-4.30pm Mon-Fri) is near the junction of SH41 and Ohuanga Rd.

There are plenty of ATMs in the town centre, along with a post office.

Sights & Activities
TROUT FISHING

Ever since trout were introduced into Lake Taupo in 1898 there have been yarns of fish weighing more than a sack of spuds and measuring the length of a surfboard. The truth is that more than 28,000 brown and rainbow trout of legal size are bagged yearly.

February and March are the best months for brown trout, but rainbow fishing is good year-round on the river. This unique fishery is protected by special conditions, including a bag limit of three fish, no use of bait (except flies) and a minimum size of 40cm, depending on where you fish – this is detailed on your licence, which you must carry at all times while fishing. Licences are available from DOC or the i-SITE.

If you're not sure where to start, a fishing guide can give you some local know-how, as well as transport, gear, licence and meals by arrangement.

Brett Cameron (☎ 07-378 8192; www.cpf.net.nz; half-/full day from $280/580) Also offers boat charters (per hour $100, minimum three hours) and quad-bike adventure fishing in National Park (one/two people $750/850). Licences extra.

Ian Jenkins (☎ 07-386 0840; www.tui-lodge.co.nz/guides.php; half-/full day $350/600)

Brent Pirie (☎ 07-377 8054; www.flyfishtaupo.com; half-/full day $350/685)

John Sommervell (☎ 07-386 5931, www.nymphfish. com; half-/full day from $250/500)

Tightline Charters (☎ 07-386 0033; www.tightline charters.co.nz; per hr $85)

There are several companies in town that hire and sell gear, and handle bookings for guides and charters.

Barry Greig's Sporting World (☎ 07-386 6911; www.greigsport.co.nz; 59 Town Centre; ⏲ 9am-5pm)

Creel Tackle House (☎ 07-386 7929; 183 Taupahi Rd; ⏲ 8am-5pm Mon-Fri, 7.30am-3.30pm Sat & Sun)

TURANGI

esting stops en route, including an underwater viewing chamber, a hatchery, keeping ponds and a picnic area. The **River Walk visitor centre** (☎ 07-386 8085; www.troutcentre.org.nz; adult/child $2/free; ⏰ 10am-3pm), run by volunteers, has polished educational displays, a collection of rods and reels dating back to the 1880s and a theatrette showing a 14-minute film about the river.

TRAMPING
There are several short walks around town, most of which are detailed in DOC's *Lake Taupo – A Guide to Walks and Hikes* ($2.50), along with many others around the district.

A favourite is the **Tongariro River Lookout Track** (one hour loop), a riverside amble affording views of Mt Pihanga. This track joins the **Tongariro River Walkway** (three hours return), which follows the east bank of the river to the Red Hut suspension bridge.

Other good leg-stretchers include **Hinemihi's Track**, near the top of Te Ponanga Saddle, 8km west of Turangi on SH47 (15 minutes return); **Maunganamu Track**, 4km west of Turangi on SH41 (40 minutes return); and **Tauranga-Taupo River Walk** (30 minutes), which starts at Te Rangiita, 12km north of Turangi on SH1.

There is another nice lake stroll at **Lake Rotopounamu** (Greenstone Lake), 11km southwest of Turangi on SH47. A favourite for walkers, swimmers, twitchers and tree huggers alike, it's a 30-minute walk to the lake

Sporting Life (☎ 07-386 8996; www.sportinglife-turangi .co.nz; Town Centre; ⏰ 8am-5.30pm) Its website details the latest fishing conditions.

Fishing trips can also be booked via Taupo's launch office (p276).

Ten kilometres east of Turangi at Motuoapa you can hire aluminium dinghies for lake fishing from **Motuoapa Hire Boats** (☎ 07-386 7000; per hr $39). These can be used in the bay only.

TONGARIRO NATIONAL TROUT CENTRE
About 4km south of Turangi on SH1 is the DOC-managed trout hatchery, which is a pleasant stop even if you're not a fish fanatic. The landscaped walkway makes for a short and gentle stroll, and there are several inter-

from the car park, and two hours around. Ten Minute Beach and Long Beach are ideal for picnics.

TOKAANU THERMAL POOLS

The **Tokaanu Thermal Pools** (☎ 07-386 8575; Mangaroa St; public pools adult/child $6/4, private pools per 20min $9/5; ⏱ 10am-9pm), 5km northwest of Turangi, is an unpretentious facility with hot pools, a trout stream, a picnic area, displays and a shop. A 20-minute stroll along the boardwalk (wheel-chair accessible) showcases mud pools and thermal springs.

OTHER ACTIVITIES

The Tongariro River has some superb Grade III rapids for river rafting, as well as Grade I stretches suitable for beginners in the lower reaches during summer. **Tongariro River Rafting** (☎ 07-386 6409; www.trr.co.nz; Atirau Rd; adult/child $109/99) can start you off with a three-hour trip on Grade II Tongariro rapids or take you on a full day's raft fishing (summer only, price on enquiry). The company also hires out mountain bikes (two hours/half-day/full day/42 Traverse, $25/35/45/65) and runs guided and unguided biking trips on the 42 Traverse (see p295), Tongariro River Track, Moerangi Station, Tree Trunk Gorge and Fishers Track (two hours to full day, $70 to $160).

Rafting NZ (☎ 0800 865 226; www.raftingnew zealand.com; 41 Ngawaka Pl) runs the Whitewater Tongariro trip (Grade III) with an optional waterfall jump (four hours, adult/child $119/109), or the Family Fun raft over more relaxed rapids (Grade II, three hours, adult/child $75/65). Groups of four or more can tackle an overnighter (Grade III+, per person $350), rafting to a riverside campsite and then hitting more rapids the following day.

Wai Maori (☎ 07-386 0315; www.waimaori.com; 203 Puanga St, Tokaanu) offers guided white-water kayaking (November to April, per person $129) or trips accompanied only by trout down the gentle Tokaanu Stream to Lake Taupo, passing boiling mud, hot pools and wetlands on the way (90 minutes/half-day/full day $30/40/65).

Rapid Sensations in Taupo also runs white-water trips on the Tongariro River (see p277).

For indoor fun, head to the **Vertical Assault Climbing Wall** (☎ 07-386 8949; 22 Ngawaka Pl; adult/child $15/11) to scale walls that challenge all skill levels.

Sleeping

Parklands Motor Lodge (☎ 07-386 7515; www.parklands motorlodge.co.nz; 25 Arahori St; campsites per person $16, r $94-140; 🛜 🖥) On SH1 but set back beyond an epic front lawn, this motor lodge serves campers and motel seekers with its small but functional camping area and splay of well-presented units. There's a swimming pool and play area for the kids, while free-ranging ball sports are definitely on out front.

Extreme Backpackers (☎ 07-386 8949; www.extreme backpackers.co.nz; 22 Ngawaka Pl; dm $23-25, s $43-53, d $56-66; 🖥 🛜) Crafted from pine and corrugated iron, this modern backpackers has the bonus of a climbing wall and cafe. Cheaper dorms have eight bunks and skip the carpet, while pricier doubles have en suites, but all rooms are clean and comfy. A lounge with an open fire, a sunny courtyard with hammocks and a barbecue make this a relaxing budget bet.

Riverstone Backpackers (☎ 07-386 7004; www. riverstonebackpackers.com; 222 Tautahanga Rd; dm $25-30, d $61-84; 🖥) Rob's pad is a cleverly refitted old home reborn as a bijou backpackers. Facilities include sports-gear storage, an enviable kitchen and lounge, and a stylish landscaped yard (with pizza oven) of which any Kiwi homeowner would be proud. This is a true home away from home, although Rob is eager to help you get out of the house and into some local activities.

Sportmans Lodge (☎ 07-386 8150; www.sports manslodge.co.nz; 15 Taupahi Rd; r $69, cottage $105-120) Backing on to the river, this motel-style spot with a sweet garden is a hidden bargain for trout-fishing folk. All the rooms share the lounge and well-equipped kitchen. The self-contained cottage sleeps three.

Judges Pool Motel (☎ 07-386 7892; www.judgespool motel.co.nz; 92 Taupahi Rd; s/d/q $90/100/140) This older motel has tidy, spacious rooms with kitchenettes and new bathrooms, and a fish-cleaning area. All one-bedroom units have outdoor decks for relaxing beers, although the nice new barbecue area is the best place to talk about the one that got away.

ourpick Creel Lodge (☎ 07-386 8081; www.creel. co.nz; 183 Taupahi Rd; s $95-130, d $110-150, tr $130-170, q $150-190; 🛜 🖥) Set in green and peaceful grounds, this heavenly hideaway backs onto a fine stretch of the Tongariro River. All the ground-level suites conveniently have their own kitchens and a balcony overlooking attractive gardens.

Anglers Paradise Motel (☎ 07-386 8980; www.anglers paradise.co.nz; cnr Ohuanga Rd & Raukura St; d $115-160, tr $130-160, q $145-160; 🖵 🖭) Looking like something out of Twin Peaks, this place sits in a 1-hectare leafy pocket where privacy prevails. Rooms are trimmed in dark wood and feature big televisions and superking beds. It's geared up for anglers, with guides happily arranged and a smokehouse on-site. The restaurant has a crackling fireplace.

Oreti Village Resort (☎ 07-386 7070; www.oretivillage. com; Mission House Dr, Pukawa Bay; apt $210-270; 🖭) This enclave of luxury self-contained apartments might give you a hankering for 'village' life – which in Oreti's case entails gazing at blissful lake views from the comfort of a rolled-arm leather couch, before wandering up to the excellent bar and restaurant (below) or down to the beach. Take SH41 for 15km, heading northwest of Turangi, and look for the sign.

Eating

our pick **Oreti** (☎ 07-386 7070; Mission House Dr, Pukawa Bay; mains $29-34; 🕑 lunch Thu-Sun, dinner Tue-Sun) It's hard to imagine a more romantic spot to while away a balmy summer's evening than looking over the lake from Oreti's terrace. It's an added bonus that the food matches up – the modern NZ menu doesn't disappoint. As you pick your way through a heavily laden antipasti lunch platter you might have to remind yourself that you're not actually on the Mediterranean.

Tongariro Lodge (☎ 07-386 7946; Grace Rd; mains $35; 🕑 dinner) Some of the world's most famous blokes (Robert Mitchum, Liam Neeson, Larry Hagman, Jimmy Carter, Timothy Dalton) have come to this luxury riverside fishing lodge, set in 9 hectares of parkland, to relax in wood-panelled anonymity. Not surprisingly, the menu's orientated around man-sized slabs of meat but the real squeals of delight come when a lucky lodger is presented with their day's catch, smoked and served to perfection.

There are also cafe-style options around town:

Grand Central Fry (☎ 07-386 5344; 8 Ohuanga Rd; meals $6-9; 🕑 11am-8.30pm) A local legend serving top fish and chips, plus burgers and anything else fryable.

Thyme for Food (☎ 07-386 0552; Town Centre; meals $6-16; 🕑 breakfast & lunch) A popular tearoom, good for fast and simple fare such as pies, all-day brekkie, burgers and milkshakes.

Licorice (☎ 07-386 5551; SH1, Motuoapa; meals $9-17; 🕑 breakfast & lunch Wed-Sun) It's worth holding off

for this pit stop 8km north of Turangi for excellent coffee, cheap, light meals, and lovely home baking.

Self-caterers should head to the big, centrally located **New World** (☎ 07-386-8780; Ohuanga Rd; 🕑 8am-8pm) supermarket.

Getting There & Away

InterCity/Newmans (☎ 09-583 5780; www.intercity. co.nz) services stop outside the i-SITE. The Auckland–Wellington and Tauranga–Rotorua–Wellington buses that travel along the eastern side of the lake all stop at Turangi (from Taupo $16, 45 minutes).

Naked Bus (☎ 0900 625 33 per min $1.80; www. nakedbus.com; advance fares from $1) uses the same stop for their daily services to Auckland (6½ hours) via Taupo (one hour) and Rotorua (two hours). Going south, buses run to Wellington (5½ hours) via all major stops, including Palmerston North (3 hours).

For Tongariro shuttle services, see p294.

TONGARIRO & AROUND

TONGARIRO NATIONAL PARK

Established in 1887, Tongariro was NZ's first and the world's fourth national park, and is one of NZ's three World Heritage Sites. Originally covering the three mountains of the park (Tongariro, Ngauruhoe and Ruapehu), the name Tongariro comes from *tonga* (south wind) and *riro* (carried away). The three peaks were a gift to NZ from the local *iwi* (tribe), who saw the act as the only way to preserve an area of spiritual significance.

With its towering active volcanoes, Tongariro is one of NZ's most spectacular parks, perhaps best known for its cameo as Mordor in Peter Jackson's *Lord of the Rings* trilogy. In summer it offers excellent short walks and longer tramps, most notably the Tongariro Northern Circuit and the Tongariro Alpine Crossing. In winter it's a busy ski area.

Information

The **DOC visitor centre** (Map p290; ☎ 07-892 3729; www.doc.govt.nz; 🕑 8am-6pm Dec-Mar, to 5pm Apr-Nov) is in Whakapapa (pronounced 'fa-ka-pa-pa') Village, on the northwestern side of the park. It has maps and info on all corners of the park, including walks, huts and current skiing, track and weather conditions. It also

TONGARIRO NATIONAL PARK & AROUND

TAUPO & THE
CENTRAL PLATEAU

SIGHTS & ACTIVITIES		
Mountain Air	1	B3
Tukino Ski Area	2	C4
Turoa Ski Area	3	B4
Whakapapa Ski Area	4	B3

SLEEPING		
Blyth Hut	5	B4

Discovery Lodge	6	B3
Ketetahi Hut	7	C2
Mangaehuehu Hut	8	B4
Mangahuia	9	B3
Mangatepopo Hut	10	C2
Mangaturuturu Hut	11	B4
Mangawhero	12	A5
Mountain Heights Lodge	13	A3

Oturere Hut	14	C3
Rangipo Hut	15	C4
Tongariro Holiday Park	16	C2
Waihohonu Hut	17	C3
Whakapapaiti Hut	18	B3

TRANSPORT		
Adventure HQ	(see 16)	

has interesting exhibits on the geological and human history of the area, including an audio visual display, and a small shop: the perfect place for rainy days. The detailed *Tongariro National Park* map ($19) is worth buying before tramping.

Each January, DOC offers an excellent guided-walks program in and around the park; ask at DOC centres for information or book online (www.doc.govt.nz). Further national park information is available from the DOC centre in Turangi (p288) and from the i-SITE in Ohakune (p297) .

Many visitors to NZ come unstuck in the mountains. The weather can change more quickly than you expect, and rescues (and fatalities) are not uncommon. When visiting Tongariro National Park, you must be properly equipped and take safety precautions, including leaving your itinerary with a responsible person. For more on track safety, see p74.

There are plenty of transport operators willing to take you to trail heads and pick you up again (see p294). Make sure you book them in advance.

Sights & Activities
PEAKS
Mt Ruapehu
The long, multipeaked summit of Ruapehu (2797m) is the highest and most active of the park's volcanoes. The upper slopes were sprayed with hot mud during the volcanic hiccups of 1969 and 1975, and in December 1988 the volcano spewed hot rocks. These were just tame precursors to the spectacular 1995 eruptions, when Ruapehu spurted volcanic rock and cloaked the area in clouds of ash and steam. From June to September the following year the mountain rumbled, groaned and thrust ash clouds high into the sky, writing off the 1996 ski season. The latest eruption, accompanied by a small earthquake, came out of the blue in September 2007, seriously injuring a climber sleeping in a hut on the mountain.

Worse events have occurred. In fact, Ruapehu was the cause of one of NZ's deadliest natural disasters. From 1945 the level of Crater Lake rose dramatically as eruptions blocked the overflow. On Christmas Eve 1953 the dam burst and the flood of volcanic mud (known as a lahar) swept down the mountain and took out a railway bridge at Tangiwai (between Ohakune and Waiouru), just moments before a crowded express train arrived. The train was derailed and 153 people lost their lives.

The crater lake was blocked again by the 1995–96 eruption. As the levels rose, it was foreseen that a major lahar could lead to another catastrophe. Alarm systems were set up at the crater lake's edge and in March 2007 they were triggered when a moderate lahar swept down the Whangaehu Valley. No one was injured and there was little damage to infrastructure.

Ruapehu is the centrepiece of the national park, with Whakapapa Village (including the DOC visitor centre) on its slopes, numerous walking tracks and three ski fields.

Mt Tongariro
The Red Crater of Mt Tongariro (1968m) last erupted in 1926. This old but still active volcano has a number of coloured lakes dotting its uneven summit as well as hot springs gushing out of its side at Ketetahi. The Tongariro Alpine Crossing (p292), a magnificent walk, passes beside the lakes, right through several craters, and down through lush native forest.

WHAKAPAPA VILLAGE

Mt Ngauruhoe

Much younger than the other two volcanoes, it is estimated that Ngauruhoe (2290m) formed in the last 2500 years. In contrast to the others, which have multiple vents, Ngauruhoe is a conical, single-vent volcano with perfectly symmetrical slopes – the only one of the three that looks like a stereotypical volcano and the reason why it was chosen to star as Mt Doom in *Lord of the Rings*. It can be climbed in summer, but in winter (under snow) this steep climb is only for experienced mountaineers.

TRAMPING

Scattered around the park's tramping tracks are ten huts (Map p289) that can be used for accommodation. Prices vary according to hut and season, but range from $15 to $25 per person. You can camp beside the huts for $5 to $20 per person. The DOC centres and i-SITEs in Turangi, Whakapaka and Ohakune sell hut tickets and Backcountry Hut Passes.

In the summer season – between Labour Weekend (late October) and Queen's Birthday (early June) – a Great Walks Ticket is required for the popular four Tongariro Northern Circuit huts (Mangatepopo, Ketetahi, Oturere and Waihohonu), and must be bought in advance. This pass is also available from DOC centres, i-SITES or online at www.doc.govt. nz; ordinary hut tickets and the Backcountry Hut Pass cannot be used during these months.

Take note that Ketetahi Hut is the most popular in the park. It has bunks for 24 people, but regularly has 50 to 60 people trying to stay there on Saturday nights and at the busiest times of year (summer and school holidays). As bunks are claimed on a first-come, first-served basis, it's advisable to bring camping gear, just in case. Campers can use all of the hut facilities, which can make the kitchen crowded, especially at peak times.

For more information on tramping, hut accommodation and hut passes, see Active New Zealand (p73).

Tongariro Northern Circuit

Classed as one of NZ's Great Walks, the Northern Circuit circumnavigates Ngauruhoe and affords spectacular views all around, particularly of Mt Tongariro. As a circuit, there

---

HOTHEADS TO THE RESCUE

Maori legend tells of the great chief Ngatoro-i-rangi, who climbed Mt Tongariro in search of more land for his tribe. While acclaimed as a warrior, Ngatoro-i-rangi was only an amateur navigator and as night fell he couldn't find his way back down. He called on the fire gods, Te Pupu and Te Hoata, for help. The gods roared underground from Hawaiki to find Ngatoro-i-rangi, but stuck their heads up firstly at Whakaari (White Island), then exploded out at Rotorua before finally bursting forth in the volcanoes of Tongariro to warm the chief.

Because of this divine intervention, Maori revere these sites and once used the pools around them for rituals as well as cooking, dyes and medicine.

---

are several start and finish points, including Whakapapa Village, Ketetahi Rd, Desert Rd and by continuing the Round the Mountain Track. The walk covers the famous Tongariro Alpine Crossing (p292).

Highlights of the circuit include tramping through or past several volcanic craters, including the **South Crater**, **Central Crater** and **Red Crater**; brilliantly colourful volcanic lakes, including the **Emerald Lakes**, **Blue Lake** and the **Upper** and **Lower Tama Lakes**; the cold **Soda Springs**; and various other volcanic formations, including cones, lava flows and glacial valleys.

There are several possibilities for side trips that take from a few hours to overnight. The most popular side trip from the main track is to Ngauruhoe's summit (three hours return), but it is also possible to climb Tongariro from Red Crater (two hours return) or walk to the cold-water Ohinepango Springs from Waihohonu Hut (one hour return).

The safest and most popular time to walk the track is from December to March. The track is served by four well-maintained huts: **Mangatepopo**, **Ketetahi**, **Oturere** and **Waihohonu** (see Map p289). The huts have mattresses, gas cookers in summer, toilets and water. This track is quite difficult in winter, when it is covered in snow, and becomes a tough alpine trek requiring ice axes and crampons. You may need to factor in significant extra walking time, or not attempt it at all.

Estimated walking times in summer:

Route	Time (hr)
Whakapapa Village to Mangatepopo Hut	3-5
Mangatepopo Hut to Emerald Lakes	3½
Emerald Lakes to Oturere Hut	1½
Oturere Hut to Waihohonu Hut	3
Waihohonu Hut to Whakapapa Village	5½

Tongariro Alpine Crossing

Reputedly the best one-day walk in NZ, the Tongariro Alpine Crossing traverses spectacular volcanic geography, from an active crater to steaming vents and beautiful coloured lakes. And the views aren't bad either. The track passes through vegetation zones ranging from alpine scrub and tussock, to places at higher altitudes where there is no vegetation at all, to the lush podocarp forest as you descend from Ketetahi Hut towards the end of the track. It covers the most spectacular features of the Tongariro Northern Circuit between the Mangatepopo and Ketetahi Huts. (Trampers tackling the Northern Circuit complete this section on their second day, with the extra walk along the Ketetahi track.)

Although achievable in one day, the Crossing is exhausting and shouldn't be taken lightly. Weather can change without warning, so make sure you are adequately equipped.

If you're not in top walking condition you may prefer to do the Crossing in two days, throwing in a few side trips to keep it interesting. Worthwhile side trips from the main track include ascents to the summits of Mts Ngauruhoe and Tongariro. Mt Ngauruhoe can be ascended most easily from the Mangatepopo Saddle, reached near the beginning of the track after the first steep climb. The summit of Tongariro is reached by a poled route from Red Crater.

The Mangatepopo Hut, reached via Mangatepopo Rd, is near the start of the track, and the Ketetahi Hut is a couple of hours before the end. Estimated summer walking times:

Route	Time (hr)
Mangatepopo Rd end to Mangatepopo Hut	¼
Mangatepopo Hut to Mangatepopo Saddle	1½
Mangatepopo Saddle to Mt Ngauruhoe summit (side trip)	2 (return)
Red Crater to Tongariro summit (side trip)	1½ (return)
Mangatepopo Saddle to Emerald Lakes	1½-2
Emerald Lakes to Ketetahi Hut	1½
Ketetahi Hut to road end	1½

The Tongariro Alpine Crossing can be reached from Mangatepopo Rd, off SH47, and from Ketetahi Rd, off SH46. Theft from parked vehicles is a problem at both ends: don't leave valuables in the car and keep everything out of sight.

Because of its popularity, there are plenty of shuttle services to both ends of the track. The shuttles need to be booked and you'll need to complete the track in a reasonable time to be assured of your lift home – they won't wait if you dawdle.

Note: this may be one of the world's great walks, but it's not an experience you'll enjoy if you're badly prepared or the weather is awful. In winter, the colourful lakes are hidden under a blanket of snow and much of the effect is lost. If it's blowing a gale, pelting with rain or if you're wearing unsuitable clothing (jeans and flip-flops aren't alpine-appropriate), you're all but guaranteed to have a miserable, not to mention dangerous, time.

Round the Mountain

This off-the-beaten-track hike is known as being a quieter alternative to the busy Northern Circuit, but it's particularly tough, has some potentially tricky river crossings, and is not recommended for beginners or the unprepared. Looping around Mt Ruapehu, the trail takes in a diversity of country, from glacial rivers to tussocky moors to majestic mountain views. You should allow at least four days to complete the hike, with six days a realistic estimate if you're including side trips to the remote Blyth Hut or Tama Lakes.

You can get to the Round the Mountain trail from Whakapapa Village, the junction near Waihohonu Hut, Ohakune Mountain Rd, or Whakapapaiti Hut. Most trampers start at Whakapapa Village and return there to finish the loop.

The track is safest from December to March when there is little or no snow, and less chance of avalanche. At other times of year, navigation and walking is made difficult by snow, and full alpine gear (ice axe, crampons and specialised clothing) is a requirement. To attempt the track you should prepare thoroughly. Take sufficiently detailed maps, check on the latest conditions, and carry clothing for all climes and more-than-adequate food supplies. Be sure to leave your plans and intended return date with a responsible person and check in when you get back.

This track is served by Waihohonu, **Rangipo, Mangaehuehu, Mangaturuturu** and **Whakapapaiti Huts**, and a side trip can be made to **Blyth Hut** (see Map p289). Estimated summer walking times:

Route	Time (hr)
Whakapapa Village to Waihohonu Hut	5-6
Waihohonu Hut to Rangipo Hut	5
Rangipo Hut to Mangaehuehu Hut	5-6
Mangaehuehu Hut to Mangaturuturu Hut	5
Mangaturuturu Hut to Whakapapaiti Hut	6
Whakapapaiti Hut to Whakapapa Village	2-3
Tama Lakes (side trip)	1½
Blyth Hut (side trip)	1

Other Walks

The DOC and i-SITE visitor centres at Whakapapa, Ohakune and Turangi have maps and information on interesting short and long walks in the park, as well as track and weather conditions.

The walk up to Ruapehu's **Crater Lake** (seven hours return) is a good one, allowing you to see the acidic lake up close, but this walk is strictly off limits when there's volcanic activity. This moderate-to-difficult walk begins at Iwikau Village at the Top of the Bruce Rd. You can cut three hours off it by catching the **chairlift** (adult/child $23/13; ☼ 9am-3.30pm mid-Dec–April) from Whakapapa Ski Area. **Guided walks** (☎ reservations 07-892 3738; adult/child incl lift pass $90/55) to Crater Lake meet daily at 9am at the Vertical store in Iwikau Village. Like most of the walks in Tongariro, you'll need to check conditions before heading out and don't attempt it in winter unless you're a mountaineer.

In addition to those below, several good tracks start from Ohakune Mountain Rd.

A number of fine walks beginning near the Whakapapa visitor centre and from the road leading up to it (see Map p290) are listed in DOC's *Walks in and around Tongariro National Park* ($3), including the following:

Ridge Track A 30-minute return walk that climbs through beech forest to alpine-shrub areas for views of Ruapehu and Ngauruhoe.

Silica Rapids A 2½-hour, 7km loop track to the Silica Rapids, named for the silica mineral deposits formed there by the rapids on Waikare Stream. The track passes interesting alpine features and, in the final 2.5km, passes down Top of the Bruce Rd above Whakapapa Village.

Tama Lakes A 17km track to the Tama Lakes (five to six hours return), on the Tama Saddle between Ruapehu and Ngauruhoe. The upper lake affords fine views of Ngauruhoe and Tongariro (beware of winds on the saddle).

Taranaki Falls A two-hour, 6km loop track to the 20m Taranaki Falls on Wairere Stream.

Whakapapa Nature Walk A 15-minute loop track suitable for wheelchairs, beginning about 200m above the visitor centre and passing through beech forest and gardens typical of the park's vegetation zones.

SKIING

Ruapehu's **Whakapapa Ski Area** (Map p289; ☎ 07-892 3738; www.mtruapehu.com; lift pass per half-day/full day $52/83) and **Turoa Ski Area** (Map p289; ☎ 06-385 8456; website & prices as above) offer similar skiing to suit all levels: around 400 hectares of field each, both taking you up to a maximum altitude of around 2300m. Beginners are well catered for, with gear hire, ski school, good learner areas and some nice easy runs. During the ski season you can tune into SKI FM 93.4, Aerial FM 96.6 or Peak FM 95.8 for updates on the slopes, or ring the **Snowphone** (☎ Turoa 083 222 180, Whakapapa 083 222 182).

You can hire gear in Taupo, National Park, Ohakune, or at Whakapaka at **Edge to Edge** (Map p290; ☎ 0800 800 754; www.edgetoedge.co.nz; Skotel Alpine Resort; 1-day full ski gear $35-43, 1-day snowboard gear $43-50), which also stocks a full range of climbing and alpine gear. The only accommodation at the ski fields is in private lodges, so most skiers stay at Whakapapa Village (see below), National Park village (see p296) or Ohakune (see p299).

The **Tukino Ski Area** (Map p289), on the eastern side of Ruapehu, is only accessible by a 4WD road. See also p80.

Sleeping

There are two basic DOC camping grounds in this area: **Mangahuia** (Map p289; SH47; campsites per person $4), between National Park village and the SH48 turn-off heading to Whakapapa; and **Mangawhero** (Map p289; Ohakune Mountain Rd; campsites per adult/child $4/2), near Ohakune. Both have cold water and pit toilets. See p291 for information on the DOC huts scattered around the park's tramping tracks.

Whakapapa Village has limited accommodation and prices quoted here are for summer; rates are generally much higher during the ski season. National Park village (p296) and Ohakune (p299) offer a greater range of options. National Park has the best selection of budget accommodation while Ohakune is a proper town, with a better array of eateries and shops.

Tongariro Holiday Park (Map p289; ☎ 07-386 8062; www.thp.co.nz; SH47; campsites per person $15-17, cabins $55-80, units $130-140) Located on SH47 halfway between Turangi and National Park (approximately 24km from each), this old Kiwi classic has basic cabins and newer units. Camping is pleasant and the communal facilities are more than adequate. Next door there's a cafe, Adventure HQ (ski hire) and the Tongariro Expeditions' base (below).

Whakapapa Holiday Park (Map p290; ☎ 07-892 3897; www.whakapapa.net.nz; Whakapapa Village; campsites per adult/child $17/10, dm/cabins/units $25/70/99) This well-maintained and popular park in the village has a wide range of accommodation options, including a 32-bed backpackers lodge, campsites perched on the edge of beautiful bushland and self-contained units for couples.

Skotel Alpine Resort (Map p290; ☎ 07-892 3719; www.skotel.co.nz; Whakapapa Village; s/d/tr/cabins $40/55/80/160, r $135-215; ☐ ☎) NZ's highest hotel offers three-bed backpacker rooms, cabins and regular hotel rooms. With timbered decor, the complex has an alpine feel; it also has a few luxuries, including sauna, spa pool, gym, ski shop, games room, licensed restaurant (dinner only; mains $19 to $29) and, most importantly, bar.

Fergusson Villas (Map p290; ☎ 07-892 3809; www.chateau.co.nz; Whakapapa Village; d/q $155/175) These small, self-contained chalets are good for families or small groups, with kitchens and diminutive decks for relaxing on. Booking and check-in is through the Bayview Chateau Tongariro.

Bayview Chateau Tongariro (Map p290; ☎ 07-892 3809; www.chateau.co.nz; Whakapapa Village; d $190-280, ste $350-1000; ☐ ☎) The landmark of the village, the 106-room Chateau harks back to a refined era, with classic European mansion-house grandeur. Opened in 1929, its refurbishments have seen it retain an old-world charm and dramatic snooker-room styling. The hotel boasts a cinema, restaurant, bar and cafe, nine-hole public golf course, tennis court, and, of course, views of mountains out the back and sweeping plateau below.

Eating & Drinking

Fergusson's Cafe (Map p290; mains $5-8; ☀ breakfast & lunch; ☐ ☎) Across the road from the Chateau, Fergusson's is a casual tearoom with outdoor tables, and proffers pies, sandwiches, cakes and coffee.

Lorenz Bar & Cafe (mains $9-23; ☀ breakfast & lunch) Up on the edge of the ski field itself, Lorenz

offers a similarly unassuming standard of grub.

Tussock (Map p290; mains $14-18; ☀ 3pm-late) At the foot of the village, Tussock has a beer garden, views and occasional live entertainment in winter.

Pihanga Cafe (Map p290; mains $19-25; ☀ lunch & dinner) One of the Chateau's two in-house dining options, the Pihanga is a consistent performer with good-value meals along the lines of soup, salads and fancier fare such as osso bucco. Next-door, the T-bar is a cosy spot for a winter warmer or a beer outside in the sunshine.

Ruapehu Room (Map p290; mains $34-39; ☀ dinner) The Chateau's elegant à la carte option.

Whakapapa Camp Store (Map p290) at the Whakapapa Holiday Park sells basic groceries, though you're better off stocking up en route.

Getting There & Around

BUS

There are numerous shuttle services to Whakapapa Village, the Tongariro Alpine Crossing and other key destinations from Taupo, Turangi, National Park and Ohakune. In summer tramping trips are their focus, but in winter most offer ski-field shuttles. Book your bus in advance to avoid unexpected strandings. As well as those listed below, most of the National Park backpackers offer their own shuttles at similar rates (see p299).

Adventure HQ (☎ 07-386 0969; www.adventureheadquarters.co.nz) Runs scheduled Tongariro Alpine Crossing services ($30) from its base at Tongariro Holiday Park. It also sells and hires gear.

Extreme Backpackers (p287) Provides shuttles from Turangi to the Crossing ($35) and Northern Circuit ($40) and, in winter, Whakapapa Ski Area ($40).

Matai Shuttles (p300) Picks up from Ohakune, National Park and Whakapapa for the Crossing (return $35).

Mountain Shuttle (☎ 0800 117 686; mountainman 989@hotmail.com) Runs between Turangi and Whakapapa/Tongariro Alpine Crossing daily ($35).

Tongariro Expeditions (☎ 0800 828 763; www.tongariroexpeditions.com) Runs shuttles from Turangi ($35, 40 mins), Taupo ($55, 1¼ hours), National Park village ($35, 30 minutes) and Whakapapa ($35, 15 mins) for the Crossing and the Northern Circuit.

Turangi Coachlines (☎ 07-386 8226; turangicoachlines@xtra.co.nz) Plys the Turangi–Whakapapa route ($40).

CAR & MOTORCYCLE

Tongariro National Park is bounded by roads: SH1 (called the Desert Rd, despite being sandless) to the east, SH4 to the west, SH46 and SH47 across the northern side and SH49 along the south. The main road up into the park is SH48, which leads to Whakapapa Village and continues further up the mountain to the Whakapapa Ski Area. Ohakune Mountain Rd leads up to the Turoa Ski Area from Ohakune. The Desert Rd is regularly closed when the weather is bad – large signs will direct you to other routes. Likewise, the Ohakune Mountain Rd and Top of the Bruce Rd are subject to closures, and access beyond certain points may be restricted to 4WDs or cars with snow chains.

NATIONAL PARK VILLAGE
pop 460

Named for nearby Tongariro National Park, this tiny outpost lies at the junction of SH4 and SH47, 15km from the hub of Whakapapa Village. In ski season the township is packed, but in summer it's sleepy – despite being a great base for activities in and around the park.

There's little to do in National Park itself, its major enticement being its proximity to the ski fields, national park tramps (p291), the 42 Traverse mountain-bike trail (below) and canoe trips on the Whanganui River. Daily shuttles leave from here to the Tongariro Alpine Crossing and Whakapapa Village in summer, and the ski area in winter.

As you'll discover, it's railway country around here. About 20km south on SH4 at Horopito is a monument to the Last Spike, the spike that marked the completion of the Main Trunk Railway Line between Auckland and Wellington in 1908 (the train chugs on through to this day). Five kilometres north from National Park, at Raurimu, is evidence of the engineering masterpiece that is the 'spiral' (p233). Trainspotters will marvel, while non-trainspotters will probably wonder what the hell they're looking at it (there's not much to see).

Information

There's no i-SITE in National Park, so visit www.nationalpark.co.nz for info. For everything else, go to Gasoline Alley on the main road. It's got fuel, postal services, groceries, gear hire, an ATM and slightly dubious convenience food.

Activities
MOUNTAIN BIKING
This area is most famous for the **42 Traverse**, a three- to six-hour, 45km mountain-bike

trail through the Tongariro Forest, one of the most popular one-dayers on the North Island. The Traverse follows old logging tracks, making for relatively dependable going, although there are plenty of ups and downs – more downs as long as you start from SH47 and head down to Owhango.

The 50km **Fishers Track** is another revered ride. Starting from National Park, the track itself is mainly downhill – for about 21km – and some lightweights choose to get picked up at the nadir near Owhango. Others, however, continue the loop back to National Park via a fairly gruelling grind.

From National Park, Howard's Lodge provides transport and bike hire, while Plateau and Adventure Lodge offer transport only (see p296).

OTHER ACTIVITIES
For details on **skiing** Whakapapa and Turoa, see p293. Gear hire is available from **Eivins** (☎ 07-892 2843; www.nationalpark.co.nz/eivins; Carroll St), **Roy Turner** (☎ 07-892 2757; www.snowzone.co.nz; Buddo St) and **Ski Biz** (☎ 07-892 2717; www.skibiz.co.nz; 10 Carroll St). Most accommodation in town offers packages for lift passes and ski hire, sparing you the steeper prices further up the mountain.

Mountain Air (Map p289; ☎ 0800 922 812; www.mountainair.co.nz; flights $110-195), on SH47 near the turn-off to Whakapapa, offers three standard **scenic flights**, ranging from 15 to 35 minutes, covering the volcanoes and lakes. They also depart from Turangi ($265, 45 minutes) and Taupo ($295, 65 minutes).

Tongariro Forest Conservation Area can be explored with relatively little effort with **Quad Biking NZ** (☎ 07-378 8349; www.quadbikingnz.co.nz; half-/full day $195/295).

Adrift Guided Outdoor Adventures (☎ 07-892 2751; www.adriftnz.co.nz) runs guided **canoe trips** on the Whanganui River (half-day to six days, $130 to $950), as well as freedom canoe hire and necessary transfers. They also offer one- to three-day guided tramps in the national park ($125 to $725).

Wade's Landing Outdoors (☎ 07-895 5995; www.whanganui.co.nz) also offers guided canoe trips on the Whanganui River, along with freedom kayak hire and transfers (one to five days, $80 to $180), jetboat rides ($95 to $150) and jetboat/road transfers to trail heads ($150 to $270).

For those rainy days there's an 8m-high indoor **climbing wall** (☎ 07-892 2870; www.npbp.co.nz;

Finlay St; adult/child $15/10; ⏰ 9am-9pm) at National Park Backpackers. Outdoor climbers with their own gear can find spots near Manataupo Valley and Whakapapa Gorge.

Sleeping

National Park is a town of budget and mid-range accommodation. This makes sense, as you'll probably spend most of your time in the great outdoors. We list summer prices here; be warned they increase somewhat in the ski season when accommodation is tight and bookings are essential.

Discovery Lodge (Map p289; ☎ 07-892 2744; www.discovery.net.nz; campsites per person $14, cabins/d $50/90, units $135-175; 🖳) Handy for skiers, this lodge is on SH47, between National Park and the Whakapapa turn-off. The restaurant has excellent views of Ruapehu, plus there's a bar and comfy lounge. Cabins are basic, but large chalets are great getaways for up to four people.

Howard's Lodge (☎ 07-892 2827; www.howardslodge.co.nz; Carroll St; dm $27, s $60-75, d $68-105, tr $84-120, q $140; 🖳 🛜) Howard's moved on, but he's left his legacy in this large, freshly decorated lodge with spa, two comfortable lounges with supersized TVs, and spotless, well-equipped kitchens. Dorms are relatively roomy, with only three or four bunks. For outdoor action, there are plenty of skis, snowboards, tramping gear and mountain bikes for hire. Howard's also runs shuttle services around the park. Book InterCity buses and interisland ferries here.

Plateau (☎ 07-892 2993; www.plateaulodge.co.nz; Carroll St; dm $28, d $65-85, tr $93-113, q $141, apt $155-235; 🖳 🛜) The sort of schmick backpackers that you don't need to be of college age to enjoy, Plateau has immaculate cosy rooms, some with en suite and TV, and an attractive communal lounge, kitchen and hot tub. The dorms don't get bigger than two sets of bunks and there are two-bedroom apartments (sleeping up to six) available as well.

Adventure Lodge & Motel (☎ 07-892 2991; www.adventurenationalpark.co.nz; Carroll St; lodge dm/s/d/tr/q $30/50/65/90/120, B&B tw/d $130/170, units $130-190; 🖳 🛜) This place caters to Tongariro alpine crossers, offering cosy, comfortable accommodation. You can also get dinner as part of a good-value all-inclusive package (two nights, breakfast, lunch, dinner, T-shirt and transport for $165 to $195). For homebodies, there are good facilities including relaxing lounge, spa

pools and a barbecue. The B&B rooms have en suites.

Park Travellers' Lodge (☎ 07-892 2748; www.the-park.co.nz; Millar St; dm $30-35, d $100-130, apt $150-340; 🖳 🛜) There's no way you can miss this big flashpackers on the main road. Inside it's smart and comfortable, with a laid-back courtyard surrounded by 200 beds' worth of dorms, doubles and self-contained micro-apartments. Conveniences are modern and hardwearing, while the in-house Spiral cafe does dinner à la blackboard for $11 to $23. The railway-inspired house bar is a highlight (and we're not just saying that because of the beer).

Mountain Heights Lodge (Map p289; ☎ 07-892 2833; www.mountainheights.co.nz; units $110-170, d $140-160) This friendly Swiss-chalet-style lodge on SH4, 2km south of National Park, has good-quality, self-contained motel units that sleep up to six people; and B&B in comfortable en suite rooms with TVs and tea-making facilities. Other meals are offered by arrangement, and mountain bikes are available for hire (per two hours/half-day/full day/42 Traverse $20/30/40/60).

our pick Tongariro Crossing Lodge (☎ 07-892 2688; www.tongarirocrossinglodge.com; 37 Carroll St; d $145-164, tr $165-184, q $204; 🖳) As pretty as a picture in white weatherboard with baby-blue trim and rambling blooms in summer. Rooms range from a standard double to larger self-contained rooms that include a full kitchen; the lodge also offers B&B with optional dinner (by arrangement).

Eating & Drinking

In the winter season when town is full, all options will be open most of the time. When the ski fields close, however, plan ahead: options dry up, although there's always food to be had somewhere.

Basekamp (☎ 07-892 2872; Carroll St; mains $17-18; ⏰ dinner Fri-Sun summer, daily winter) Basekamp does wood-fired pizza, tasty gourmet burgers and other tummy-filling grub for hungry ski folk.

National Park Hotel (☎ 07-892 2805; 61 Carroll St; mains $18-25; ⏰ 10am-11pm) The only Kiwi boozer in town, and a good old-fashioned one to boot. Pool tables, mixed grill and chicken Kiev, real live locals having a few quiet ones, and beer by the quart or jug.

Schnapps (☎ 07-892 2788; Finlay St; mains $19-27; ⏰ lunch Sat & Sun, dinner daily) This popular pub does excellent pizzas, generous burgers and better-than-average pub fare. Bands pack the place out on wintry Saturday nights.

our pick **Station** (☎ 07-892 2881; cnr Station & Finlay Sts; mains $24-32; ☺ 10am-11pm) Count your blessings ye who find this little railway station along the line, a lovely old dear lovingly restored and now serving eggy brunch, lunch, coffee and cakes, plus an impressive à la carte evening menu.

Getting There & Away

BUS

InterCity (☎ 09-583 5780; www.intercity.co.nz) buses arrive at, and depart from, outside Ski Haus on Carroll St daily, heading to Auckland ($62, 5½ hours) via Hamilton ($43, 3½ hours), and Palmerston North ($47, four hours) via Whanganui ($37, two hours). Book at Howard's Lodge (opposite).

For local shuttle services, see p294.

TRAIN

The **Tranz Scenic Overlander** (☎ 04-495 0775; www.tranzscenic.co.nz; tickets $49-81) trains on the Auckland–Wellington line stop at National Park (and Ohakune). The service runs in both directions from Friday to Sunday, May to September, and daily October to April. Train tickets are sold from Howard's Lodge, not at the station.

OHAKUNE

pop 1100

Expect to see carrots crop up all over Ohakune, for this is overwhelmingly the country's carrot capital. Not only do they creep into burgers and sneak onto pizzas, they litter the roadside in season. To learn more (and you know you want to), visit during October's annual Carrot Carnival (see the boxed text, p300).

But they needn't mention liver cleansing and eyesight improvement to win us over to the charms of this little town. A pretty retreat in the summer, offering outdoor adventure galore, Ohakune springs to life in winter when the snow drifts down on Turoa Ski Area and the snow bunnies invade (they no doubt love carrots themselves).

There are two ends to the town: the commercial hub strings along the highway, but in winter the northern end around the train station, known as the Junction, is the epicentre of action.

Information

Library (☎ 06-385 8364; Ayr St; ☺ 9am-5pm Mon-Fri) Offers free internet access.
Ruapehu i-SITE (☎ 06-385 8427; 54 Clyde St; ☺ 9am-5pm Mon-Sun) Can make bookings for activities, transport and accommodation; DOC officer on hand from 9am to 3.30pm, Wednesday to Sunday.
Take Note (5 Goldfinch St; ☺ 7am-5pm Mon-Fri, to 4pm Sat) Has a post office.

Activities

SKIING & SNOWBOARDING

Ohakune is all abuzz in winter when the town fills up with skiers, snowboarders, and staff to look after them. Lift passes (half-day/full day $52/83) are available at the ski fields, with equipment available from various places around town, including the following:
Powderhorn Snow Centre (☎ 06-385 9100; www.snowcentre.co.nz; 194 Mangawhero Tce)
Ski Shed (☎ 06-385 9173; www.skished.com; 71 Clyde St)
SLR (☎ 06-385 8018; www.slr.co.nz; 60 Thames St)
TCB (☎ 06-385 8433; www.tcbskiandboard.co.nz; 27 Ayr St)

For more information on skiing and snowboarding, see p80.

TRAMPING

There are several scenic walks near the town, many starting from the Ohakune Mountain Rd, which stretches 17km from Ohakune to the Turoa Ski Area on Mt Ruapehu. The handy DOC brochure *Walks in and around Tongariro National Park* ($3) is a good starting point, available from the i-SITE.

An easy stroll starting near the beginning of Ohakune Mountain Rd is the **Mangawhero Forest Walk** (one hour return, 3km). This takes in native forest and the Mangawhero River. It is well graded and suitable for wheelchairs and pushchairs. Also leaving from Ohakune Mountain Rd are popular and more challenging tracks, including **Waitonga Falls** (1½ hours return, 4km), with magnificent views of Mt Ruapehu and Tongariro's highest waterfall (39m); and **Lake Surprise** (five hours return, 9km).

Tramps in Tongariro National Park (p291), including the Tongariro Alpine Crossing, are easily accessible from Ohakune, and shuttle services are provided by Matai Shuttles (p300). The Round the Mountain track (p292) can be accessed by continuing on the Waitonga Falls track.

OHAKUNE

INFORMATION		
Library	1	D3
Ruapehu i-SITE	2	C4
Take Note	3	C4

SIGHTS & ACTIVITIES		
Big Carrot	4	C4
Powderhorn Snow Centre	(see 13)	
Ski Shed	5	D4
SLR	6	D1
TCB	7	D3

SLEEPING		
Alpine Motel & Lodge	8	D4
Hobbit Motor Lodge	9	C3
Mountain View Motel	10	A4
Ohakune Top 10 Holiday Park	11	A4

Peaks Motor Inn	12	C2
Powderhorn Chateau	13	D1
Rimu Park Lodge	14	D1
Snowhaven	15	B4
Tussock Grove	16	C4

EATING		
Bearing Point	17	D4
Cyprus Tree	18	D3
Matterhorn	(see 13)	
Mountain Kebabs	19	C3
Mountain Rocks	20	C4
New World	21	D3
Powderkeg	(see 13)	
Projection Room	22	D1
Utopia Cafe	23	C4

By the time you read this, the **Old Coach Road** walkway and cycleway should be open. The walk is a community-led restoration of the original coach route from Ohakune to Horopito. Begun in 1886, it was built largely by hand by people who experienced great hardships, living in canvas tents and working in harsh winter conditions. It was gradually upgraded to carry passengers and goods, and used until 1909, when SH49 opened and it fell into disuse. The road has remained largely untouched ever since.

The gently graded walk promises a number of unique engineering features including the historic Hapuawhenua and Toanui viaducts – these are the only two remaining curved viaducts in the southern hemisphere. It passes through ancient forest that survived the Taupo blast, being in the lea of Ruapehu. Giant rimu and totara trees can be seen.

OTHER ACTIVITIES

There are plenty of good **mountain-biking** routes in the area, starting with the 1km descent down the sealed Ohakune Mountain Rd (check those brakes first!). The Old Coach Rd cycleway will eventually form part of a 245km Mountain-to-Sea cycle route, reaching the coast at Whanganui. TCB (p297) is a good source of information and they also rent out bikes (half-day/full day from $30/40).

You can take Whanganui River **kayaking** trips from Ohakune with **Canoe Safaris**

(☎ 06-385 9237; www.canoesafaris.co.nz; guided tours 2-5 days $365-840, freedom hire 2-5 days $140-190), which also runs guided rafting trips on the Mohaka (two to four days, $405 to $895) and the Rangitikei (one to four days, $105 to $765); or **Yeti Tours** (☎ 06-385 8197; www.canoe.co.nz; guided tours 2-6 days $375-795, 2-5 day freedom hire $140-215).

Five minutes out of Ohakune, at Rangataua, **Ruapehu Homestead Horsetrekking** (☎ 06-385 8799; ruapehuhomestead@xtra.co.nz; SH49, Rangataua; 30min-day adult $20-95, child $15-80) runs guided **horse treks** around its paddocks, as well as longer rides along the river and on backcountry trails with views of the mountain.

Sleeping

In summer the Junction is a bit of a ghost town, so stay near SH49. The prices listed here are for summer (October to March); expect to pay up to 50% more in winter and book ahead. Good savings can be made on winter rates by booking midweek.

BUDGET

Ohakune Top 10 Holiday Park (☎ 0800 825 825; www.ohakune.net.nz; 5 Moore St; campsites per adult/child $19/12, s $29-145, d $58-145, tr $75-166, q $97-186; 🖥 🤶) The stream edges this holiday park, which offers spacious communal facilities and several self-catering options. Extras include playground, *pétanque* court, barbecue area and spa bath.

Hobbit Motorlodge (☎ 06-385 8248; www.the-hobbit.co.nz; cnr Goldfinch & Wye Sts; dm $22, units $90-180; 🤶) A leafy and quiet option halfway between the town and the Junction, the Hobbit has a back-packer wing, motel units and fancier suites. The bush-setting hot tub is a real bonus. There's a children's play area, too.

our pick **Rimu Park Lodge** (☎ 06-385 9023; www.rimupark.co.nz; 27 Rimu St; backpackers dm/d $25/60, cabins d/tr/q $60/80/100, carriages $100-120, apt $210-490; 🖥 🤶) This rambling, character-filled complex is close to the Junction and has an option for every budget. Pine Tree Lodge sleeps up to 10 ($180), plus there are cabins, slick self-contained apartments and a 1934 train carriage, popular with families.

Alpine Motel & Lodge (☎ 06-385 8758; www.alpinemotel.co.nz; 7 Miro St; dm $25, d $105-110, tr $115-125, q $130-250; 🖥 🤶) Right in the middle of town, the Alpine offers 40 beds in motor-lodgey rooms and a four-bedroom townhouse next door, great for families or groups. There's also a fairly basic backpackers wing and an in-house restaurant.

Mountain View Motel (☎ 06-385 8675; www.mountain-viewmotel.co.nz; 2 Moore St; d $60-90, tr $90-100, q $110) In this old-style motel the comfortable rooms are clean, quiet and good value, with all other necessary facilities (including spa) on the doorstep.

Peaks Motor Inn (☎ 06-385 9144; www.thepeaks.co.nz; cnr Mangawhero Tce & Shannon St; d $95-109, tr $110-124, q $139; 🖥 🤶) This quadrangular, modern motel offers spacious rooms with good bathrooms. Communal facilities include basic gym, large outdoor spa and sauna.

MIDRANGE & TOP END

Snowhaven (☎ 06-385 9498; www.snowhaven.co.nz; 92 Clyde St; apt/townhouse/r $95/180/190; 🤶) A tasty trio's on offer here: modern studio apartments in a slate-fronted block on the main drag; three self-contained, three-bedroom townhouses by the Junction; or luxury B&B rooms somewhere between the other two. All are top options.

Tussock Grove (☎ 06-385 8771; www.tussockgrove.co.nz; 3 Karo St; r $120-160, tr $175-190, ste $220-250; 🤶) Cooking on holiday? No way, mister. In a town full of motels this boutique hotel fills a gap for those who just want a decent mid-range room, perhaps with a mountain view. Facilities include Sky TV, sauna, spa, *pétanque* and tennis courts.

Powderhorn Chateau (☎ 06-385 8888; www.powderhorn.co.nz; cnr Thames St & Mangawhero Tce; ste/apt $198/750; 🖥 🤶 🛁) Enjoying a long-standing reputation as the hub of activity during the ski season, the Powderhorn has a Swiss-chalet feel with woody interiors and exposed rafters. The grotto-like indoor pool is a relaxing way to recover from the slopes before enjoying revelry in the popular in-house establishments the Powderkeg and the Matterhorn (p300).

Eating & Drinking

The Junction is active during winter with the après-ski crowd, but little is open in summer. Many hotels open their restaurants during the ski season.

our pick **Utopia Cafe** (☎ 06-385 9120; 47 Clyde St; mains $7-20; ⏲ breakfast & lunch) A funky, upbeat and perennially popular destination for locals and visitors alike, with good reason. Great breakfast staples such as eggs Benedict and brioche with bacon and banana, plus a good vegie selection and fresh homemade counter food.

Mountain Kebabs (☎ 06-385 9047; 29 Clyde St; kebabs $9-12; ⊙ lunch & dinner) Any old kebabery can come up with the basic lamb, chicken or felafel varieties – but here camembert, hummus, sprouts and olives are rolled into the mix, too.

Projection Room (☎ 06-385 8664; 4 Thames St; mains $14-30; ⊙ 6pm-late Wed-Sun winter) This funky little spot has occasional films and dancing to DJs, as well as a comfort-food menu featuring burgers, curries, noodles and steak.

Powderkeg & Matterhorn (☎ 06-385 8888; cnr Thames St & Mangawhero Tce; bar menu $16-22, à la carte $21-32; ⊙ lunch & dinner) The Powderkeg is the party bar of the Powderhorn Chateau, with bands in winter and regular dancing on the tables – once the detritus of the burger and pizza meals have been cleared. Upstairs is the swankier Matterhorn, serving cocktails and sophisticated bar snacks as well as relaxed but chic à la carte dining.

Mountain Rocks (☎ 06-385 8295; cnr Clyde & Goldfinch Sts; mains $20-29; ⊙ 8am-late) A log-cabin-like space that feels more like a watering hole than an eatery. However, decent sandwiches, homemade burgers and great cakes are available, as well as substantial evening meals to soak up the alcohol.

Cyprus Tree (☎ 06-385 8857; 19a Goldfinch St; mains $22-30; ⊙ lunch Sat & Sun, dinner Thu-Mon) Distinctly Italian food – pizza, pasta and antipasto – served in a chic yet relaxed space. Thursday 'pizza and pint' nights are great value – especially as the 'pizza' stretches to pasta and the 'pint' to house wine.

Bearing Point (☎ 06-385 9006; Clyde St; mains $23-33; ⊙ lunch Sat & Sun, dinner Tue-Sun) Hearty après-ski fare is offered at this upmarket establishment run by local identities. Warm your cockles

---

CARROT CRAZY

No matter who you ask in NZ, the name Ohakune means carrots; the town produces two-thirds of the North Island's crop. In 1984 the township saluted the town's biggest vegetable crop by erecting the **Big Carrot** (Rangataua Rd), which quickly became one of NZ's most hugged 'Big Things'. Carrots were first grown in the area during the 1920s by Chinese settlers, who cleared land by hand and explosives! Today the **Carrot Carnival** (www.carrotcarnival.org.nz) is celebrated at the beginning of October with a parade and lots of dressing up in orange.

---

with aged eye fillet, maple-glazed salmon, lamb rump or a seafood curry.

Self-caterers should head for **New World** (☎ 06-385 8587; 14 Goldfinch St; ⊙ 7am-7pm), which offers the last chance to stock up before leaving for National Park or Whakapapa.

Getting There & Away

InterCity (☎ 09-583 5780; www.intercity.co.nz) buses stop outside Mountain Kebabs, en route to Auckland ($66, six hours) via Hamilton ($49, four hours), and Palmerston North ($41, three hours) via Whanganui ($31, 1½ hours).

Ohakune is the next stop south of National Park on the Tranz Scenic Overlander route; see p297 for details.

Getting Around

Several operators run services around the area including to and from the ski fields and the national park walks.

Matai Shuttles (☎ 06-385 8724; www.mataishuttles. co.nz) Runs Turoa ski shuttle (return $20) and drop-offs all around the volcanic plateau including the Tongariro Alpine Crossing (return $35). It also run a handy night shuttle around Ohakune's pubs during the ski season ($4).

Snow Express (☎ 06-385 4022; return $20) Offers transport to Turoa.

LAKE ROTOKURA

Rotokura Ecological Reserve is 14km southeast of Ohakune, at Karioi, just off SH49 (*karioi* means 'places to linger'). There are two lakes here: the first is Dry Lake, actually quite wet and perfect for picnicking; the furthest is Rotokura, *tapu* (sacred) to Maori, so eating, fishing and swimming are prohibited. The round-trip walk will take you 45 minutes; longer if you linger to admire the ancient beech trees and waterfowl such as dabchicks and paradise ducks.

WAIOURU
pop 1400

At the junction of SH1 and SH49, 27km east of Ohakune, Waiouru is primarily an army base and a refuelling stop for the 56km-long Desert Rd leading to Turangi. Rangipo Desert isn't a true desert as it receives plenty of rainfall; its stunted scrubby vegetation is due to its high altitude, windswept nature and the Taupo eruption that obliterated the ancient forests, affected the soil quality and caused a mass sterilisation of seeds. The road often closes in winter due to snow.

At the south end of the township in a large, concrete castle is the **National Army Museum** (☎ 0800 369 999; www.armymuseum.co.nz; adult/child $12/7; ⏰ 9am-4.30pm), which preserves the history of the NZ army and its various campaigns, from colonial times to the present. Its moving stories are well told through displays of arms, uniforms, memorabilia and other collections.

Once you're done with playing soldier, head 11km south to **Lazy H Horseback Riding & Adventures** (☎ 06-388 1144; www.lazyh.co.nz; 159 Maukuku Rd; 1½hr/half-day/full day/overnight $110/180/250/410), where you can channel your inner cowboy.

TAIHAPE & AROUND
pop 1800

If you have a penchant for gumboots (Wellingtons), a visit to Taihape, 20km south of Waiouru, is a must. The town has the dubious distinction of being the Gumboot Capital of the World, celebrated with – you guessed it – a giant corrugated gumboot on the main street. It is also the access point for **Gravity Canyon** (☎ 06-388 9109; www.gravitycanyon.co.nz; Mokai; 1-/2-/3-activities $110/175/240), 20km southeast, where adrenaline-junkies can take a 1km, 170m-high flying-fox ride at speeds of up to 160km/h; dive from the North Island's highest bridge bungy (80m); or swing on the world's highest tandem swing.

If you didn't give horseback riding a go in Ohakune or Waiouru, giddy-up to **River Lodge Stables** (☎ 06-388 1444; www.rivervalley.co.nz), 28km northeast of Taihape (follow the signs from Taihape's Gretna Hotel). Enjoy views of Mt Ruapehu, the Ruahine Ranges and the Rangitikei River on two-hour ($105), half-day ($165) or day-long ($215) excursions. On summer evenings the two-hour Sunset Ride ends with a glass of champagne. Break in the littlies with a half-hour hand-led Pony Ride.

Rotorua & the Bay of Plenty

Captain Cook christened the Bay of Plenty as he sailed past in 1769, and plentiful it remains to this day, blessed with buckets of sunshine and a long sandy coastline. The Bay stretches from Waihi Beach in the west to Opotiki in the east, with a sprinkling of seaside towns and the happening hub of Tauranga in between. Nearby Mt Maunganui has been popular with Kiwi holidaymakers for generations.

Further east along the pohutukawa-covered coast is Whakatane, the launch pad for tours to New Zealand's most active volcano, Whakaari (White Island). Volcanic activity defines the landscape from here to the Central Plateau, a constant reminder that under this fertile soil lies a molten core, oozing upwards to the surface.

Nowhere is this subterranean sexiness more obvious than in Rotorua, NZ's most famous tourist destination. Here the daily business of life goes on among steaming hot springs, explosive geysers, bubbling mud pools, and the clouds of sulphurous gas responsible for the town's 'unique' eggy smell.

Rotorua and the Bay remain strongholds of Maori tradition and history, so there are plenty of opportunities to explore the rich culture of the indigenous people of NZ: check out a power-packed concert performance, chow down at a *hangi* or discover the meaning and techniques behind Maori arts and crafts.

HIGHLIGHTS

- Watching Rotorua's famous geyser **Pohutu** (p305) blow its top, then tucking into a Maori **hangi** (p307)
- Checking out kaleidoscopic colours and bubbling mud pools at **Wai-O-Tapu** (p321)
- Mountain biking on tracks from humble to hardcore at the **Redwoods – Whakarewarewa Forest** (p309)
- Surfing NZ's first artificial reef at **Mt Maunganui** (p330)
- Flying or boating out to NZ's only active marine volcano, **Whakaari** (White Island; p339)
- Kicking back for a few days in **Whakatane** (p335) – NZ's most underrated seaside town?
- Swimming with dolphins at **Tauranga** (p324) or **Whakatane** (p335)

- Mt Maunganui
- Tauranga
- Whakaari (White Island)
- Whakatane
- Rotorua
- The Redwoods – Whakarewarewa Forest
- Wai-O-Tapu

| Telephone code: 07 | www.rotoruanz.com | www.bayofplenty.co.nz |

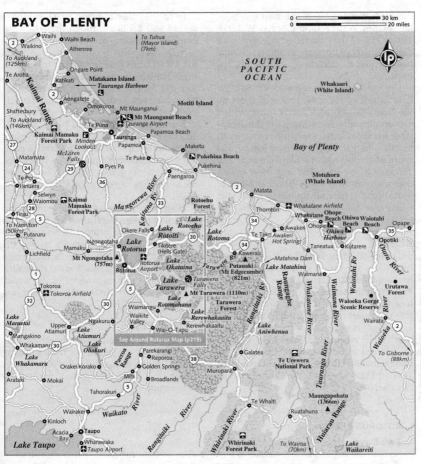

BAY OF PLENTY

Climate

The Bay of Plenty is one of the sunniest regions of NZ, with Whakatane and the Eastern Bay recording the most hours of sunshine (2350 per year on average). In summer, temperatures hover between 20°C and 27°C, while winter sees the mercury fall as low as 5°C, although it's slightly warmer on the coast. Rainfall is heavier inland in places such as Rotorua, which also experiences long dry spells in summer.

Getting There & Around

Air New Zealand has flights from Tauranga and Whakatane to Auckland and Wellington; as well as from Rotorua to Sydney (every Tuesday and Saturday), Auckland, Wellington

and Christchurch. Qantas also links Auckland with Tauranga, Whakatane and Rotorua.

InterCity and Naked Bus services connect Tauranga, Rotorua and Whakatane with most other main cities in NZ. Bay Hopper bus services run between Tauranga, Whakatane and Opotiki. Twin City Express buses link Tauranga and Rotorua.

ROTORUA

pop 70,400

Catch a whiff of Rotorua's sulphur-rich, asthmatic airs and you've already got a taste of NZ's most dynamic thermal area, home to spurting geysers, steaming hot springs and exploding mud pools. The Maori revered this place, naming one of the most spectacular springs Wai-O-Tapu (Sacred Waters). Today 35% of the population is Maori, with their cultural performances and traditional *hangi* as big an attraction as the landscape itself.

Despite the pervasive eggy odour, 'Sulphur City' is one of the most touristed spots on the North Island, with nearly three million visitors annually. Some locals say this steady trade has seduced the town into resting on its laurels, and that socially Rotorua lags behind more progressive towns like Tauranga and Taupo by a long shot. And with more motels than nights in November, the urban fabric of 'RotoVegas' is far from appealing…but still, where else can you see a 30m geothermal geyser!

HISTORY

This area was first settled in the 14th century when the canoe *Te Arawa*, captained by Tamatekapua, arrived from Hawaiki at Maketu in the central Bay of Plenty. Settlers took the tribal name Te Arawa to commemorate the vessel that had brought them here. Tamatekapua's grandson, Ihenga, explored much of the inland forest, naming geographical features as he discovered them. Ihenga unimaginatively dubbed the lake Rotorua (or 'Second Lake') as it was the second lake he came across.

In the next few hundred years, subtribes spread and divided through the area, with conflicts breaking out over limited territory. A flashpoint occurred in 1823 when the Arawa lands were invaded by tribes from the Northland in the so-called Musket Wars (see p31 for more on these conflicts). After heavy losses on both sides, the Northlanders eventually withdrew.

During the Waikato Land War (1863–64) Te Arawa threw in its lot with the government against its traditional Waikato enemies, gaining troop support and preventing East Coast reinforcements getting through to support the Kingitanga movement (see the boxed text, p209).

With peace in the early 1870s, word spread of scenic wonders, miraculous landscapes and watery cures for all manner of diseases. The town boomed. Its main attraction was the fabulous Pink and White Terraces, formed by volcanic silica deposits. Touted at the time as the eighth natural wonder of the world, they were destroyed in the 1886 Mt Tarawera eruption (see p321).

ORIENTATION

Tutanekai St is the central shopping area, part of which is a pedestrian mall. Running parallel is the major through road, Fenton St, which is lined with motels, particularly to the south.

ROTORUA AREA IN…

Two Days

Up with the lark and order breakfast near the lakeside at **Lime Caffeteria** (p316), after which the **Rotorua Museum of Art & History** (p308) will be open. Stroll along the water's edge to **Ohinemutu** (p309) and back to town via steamy **Kuirau Park** (p306). Then head to the **Blue Baths** (p309) for a relaxing soak. In the evening, catch a *hangi* and concert at **Tamaki** (p307) or **Mitai** (p307) Maori villages.

Start the second day with a tour of **Whakarewarewa Thermal Village** (p306) and watch **Pohutu** geyser blow its top. From there, it's a quick hop to **The Redwoods – Whakarewarewa Forest** (p309) for a couple of hours' exploration by mountain bike. Hop across town to ride the gondola, luge and sky swing at **Skyline Skyrides** (p318), but not before catching the falcons at **Wingspan Birds of Prey Trust** (p318).

Four Days

Take the two-day itinerary, then explore further afield starting with **Agroventures** (p320), where you can while away several hours with a farm show, bungy, giant swing and the zany zorb. A compulsory stop en route for nature-lovers is **Rainbow Springs Kiwi Wildlife Park** (p318), where you can take a **Kiwi Encounter** tour. On your last day, head southeast and visit the **Buried Village** (p321), swim in **Lake Tarawera** (p321), or take a long walk on one of the tracks at nearby **Lake Okataina** (p311).

INFORMATION

Bookshops
McLeods Booksellers (Map p306; ☎ 07-348 5388; www.mcleodsbooks.co.nz; 1269 Tutanekai St; ♨ 8.30am-5.30pm Mon-Thu, to 7pm Fri, 9am-4pm Sat, 10am-3pm Sun) Independent bookshop with maps, mags and extensive travel and Maori sections.

Emergency
Ambulance, fire & police (☎ 111)

Internet Access
Cyber World (Map p306; 1174 Haupapa St; ♨ 10am-8pm)
Cybershed (Map p306; 1176 Pukuatua St; ♨ 9.15am-7pm Mon & Fri, to 8.30pm Tue-Thu, 10am-late Sat)

Medical Services
Lakes Care Medical Centre (Map p306; ☎ 07-348 1000; 1165 Tutanekai St; ♨ 8am-11pm) Urgent medical care.
Rotorua Hospital (Map p306; ☎ 07-348 1199; www.lakesdhb.govt.nz; Arawa St; ♨ 24hr)

Money
There's a Travelex at the i-SITE, and most banks offer currency exchange, including Kiwibank at the post office.

Post
Post office (Map p306; www.nzpost.co.nz; 1189 Hinemoa St; ♨ 7.30am-5pm Mon-Fri, 8.30am-2pm Sat)

Tourist Information
Automobile Association (AA; Map p306; ☎ 07-348 3069; www.aatravel.co.nz; 1121 Eruera St; ♨ 8.30am-5pm Mon-Fri) Has maps and other travel information.
Rotorua i-SITE (Map p306; ☎ 0800 768 678, 07-348 5179; www.rotoruanz.com; 1167 Fenton St; ♨ 8am-6pm) The hub for all travel information and bookings including Department of Conservation (DOC) walks. Also has an exchange bureau, cafe, showers and lockers.
Rotorua Sustainable Tourism (www.sustainablenz.com) How to make your Rotorua visit more ecofriendly.

SIGHTS
Geothermal Attractions
Rotorua's main drawcard is **Te Whakarewarewa** (pronounced 'Fa-ka-re-wa-re-wa'), a thermal reserve 3km from the city centre at the south end of Fenton Street. This area's full name is Te Whakarewarewatanga o te Ope Taua a Wahiao, meaning 'The Gathering Together of the War Party of Wahiao', although many people just call it 'Whaka'. Whatever you

---

> **ROTORUA & THE BAY OF PLENTY FACTS**
>
> **Eat** A buttery corncob, pulled out of Rotorua's only genuine thermal *hangi* at Whakarewarewa (p306)
> **Drink** Croucher Brewing Co's microbrewed Pale Ale at Rotorua's Underground Bar (p316)
> **Read** *How to Watch a Bird,* an exposition on the joys of avian observation, written by Mt Maunganui schoolboy Steve Braunias
> **Listen to** *Kora,* the eponymous rootsy album from Whakatane's soulful sons
> **Watch** Maori TV and Te Reo, NZ's two Maori TV stations
> **Swim at** Mount Beach, Mt Maunganui (p330)
> **Festival** The National Jazz Festival in Tauranga (p325)
> **Tackiest tourist attraction** The kiwifruit-shaped viewing tower at Kiwi360 (p333)
> **Go green** Waimarino Adventure Park (p325), where good clean fun means getting wet behind the ears

prefer, the reserve is as famous for its Maori cultural significance as its steam and bubbling mud. There are more than 500 springs here, varying from cold to boiling cauldrons. The most famous spring is **Pohutu** ('Big Splash' or 'Explosion'), a geyser which erupts up to 20 times a day, spurting hot water up to 30m skyward. You'll know when it's about to blow because the **Prince of Wales' Feathers** geyser will start up shortly before.

There are two main tourist operations here: Te Pui and Whakarewarewa Thermal Village. Pohutu and the Prince of Wales' Feathers geyser are part of **Te Puia** (Map p319; ☎ 0800 837 842, 07-348 9047; www.tepuia.com; Hemo Rd; admission incl tour & daytime cultural performance adult/child $50/25, tour & Te Po evening concert & hangi $99/50, combination $130/65; ♨ 8am-6pm summer, to 5pm winter), the most polished of NZ's Maori cultural attractions. Also here is the National Carving & Weaving School, where you can discover the work and methods of traditional Maori weavers and woodcarvers. More of these arts are displayed at Rotowhio Marae, which has a carved meeting house. Also here are a cafe, two museums, a Kiwi reserve and a gift shop that stocks an excellent range of arts and crafts.

Tours of Te Puia take 90 minutes and depart on the hour from 9am (last tour 4pm in winter, 5pm in summer). Daytime cultural performances (lasting 45 minutes) start at

10.15am, 12.15pm and 3.15pm, while nightly **Te Po Indigenous Experience** *hangi* concerts are held in the evenings at 6.15pm.

Whakarewarewa Thermal Village (☎ 07-349 3463; www.whakarewarewa.com; 17 Tryon St; admission incl tours & concerts adult/child/family $28/12.50/68.50; ⏲ 8.30am-5pm, tours 9am-4pm, concerts 11.15am & 2pm), on the eastern side of Te Whakarewarewa, is a living village, where *tangata whenua* (the locals) still reside, as they and their ancestors have for centuries. It's these local villagers who show you around and tell you the stories of their way of life and the significance of the steamy bubbling pools, silica terraces and the geysers that, although inaccessible from the village, are easily viewed from vantage points (the view of Pohutu is just as good from here as it is from Te Puia, and is considerably cheaper).

The village shops sell authentic arts and crafts, and you can learn more about Maori traditions such as flax weaving, carving, and *ta moko* (tattooing). Nearby you can eat tasty, buttery sweetcorn pulled straight out of the hot mineral pool – the only genuine geothermal *hangi* in town. There are cultural performances at 11.15am and 2pm, and guided tours at 9.30am, 10.30am, 11.45am, 12.30pm, 1.30pm and 3.30pm.

Want some cheap geothermal thrills? Close to the centre of Rotorua is **Kuirau Park**, a volcanic area that you can wander around for free. Its most recent eruption in late 2003 covered much of the park (including the trees)

ROTORUA

in mud, drawing crowds of spectators hoping for more displays. It has a crater lake, pools of boiling mud and plenty of huffing steam.

Maori Concerts & Hangi

Maori culture is a major drawcard in Rotorua and, although some find it heavily commercialised, it's a great opportunity to learn more about the indigenous culture of NZ. The two big activities are concerts and *hangi* meals, often packaged together in an evening's entertainment that features the famous *hongi*, *haka*, and *poi* dances.

An established favourite is **Tamaki Maori Village** (Map p306; ☎ 07-349 2999; www.maoriculture.co.nz; booking office 1220 Hinemaru St; admission adult/child $100/58; ☼ tours depart 5pm, 6pm & 7pm summer, 5pm & 7pm winter), which does an excellent twilight tour to a *marae* (meeting house) and Maori village 15km south of Rotorua. Buses collect from the Hinemaru St booking office and also from most accommodation, and feature a briefing on *marae* protocol by a Maori 'entertainer' (aka hilarious bus driver). The concert is followed by a meat-heavy *hangi*.

A similar package is offered by **Mitai Maori Village** (Map p319; ☎ 07-343 9132; www.mitai.co.nz;

196 Fairy Springs Rd; concert & hangi adult/child 5-9yr/child 10-15yr/family $99/19/49/259; ☼ 6.30pm). This family-run outfit offers a popular three-hour evening event of concert performance, *hangi* and glowworm bushwalk, which can be combined with a tour of Rainbow Springs Kiwi Wildlife Park (see p318) next door where you can enjoy the coloured nightlights and walk through the open Kiwi enclosure (four hours total, adult/child under 9/child under 15 $116/31.50/63). Pick-ups are available.

Te Puia (p305) puts on three daytime shows (10.15am, 12.15pm & 3.15pm) and one nightly show (6.15pm), while **Whakarewarewa Thermal Village** (opposite) has two daylight shows (11.15am and 2pm; included with admission), great for busy people.

Many of the big hotels offer Maori concerts and *hangi*, making up for what they lack in ambience with convenience. Some of the main venues:

Kingsgate Hotel (Map p319; ☎ 07-348 0199; www.millenniumhotels.co.nz; Fenton St; concert adult/child $30/15, incl hangi $45/22.50; ☼ 6.45pm)
Millennium Hotel (Map p306; ☎ 07-347 1234; www.millenniumrotorua.co.nz; cnr Eruera & Hinemaru Sts; concert adult/child $20/10, incl hangi $65/32.50; ☼ 6.30pm)

HINEMOA & TUTANEKAI

Hinemoa was a young woman of a *hapu* (subtribe) that lived on the western shore of Lake Rotorua, while Tutanekai was a young man of Mokoia Island *hapu*. The pair met and fell in love during a regular tribal meeting. While both were of high birth, Tutanekai was illegitimate and so, while Hinemoa's family thought he was a fine young man, marriage between the two was forbidden.

Home on Mokoia, the lovesick Tutanekai played his flute for his love, the wind carrying the melody across the water. Hinemoa heard his declaration; her people took to tying up the canoes at night to ensure she wouldn't go to him.

Finally, Tutanekai's music won her over. Hinemoa undressed and swam the long distance from the shore to the island. When she arrived on Mokoia, Hinemoa found herself in a quandary. Shedding her clothing in order to swim, she could hardly walk into the island's settlement naked! She hopped into a hot pool to think about her next move.

Eventually a man came to fetch water from a cold spring beside the hot pool. In a deep man's voice, Hinemoa called out, 'Who is it?' The man replied that he was Tutanekai's slave on a water run. Hinemoa grabbed the slave's calabash and smashed it to pieces. More slaves came, but she smashed their calabashes too, until finally Tutanekai came to the pool and demanded that the interloper identify himself – imagine his surprise when it turned out to be Hinemoa! He secreted her into his hut.

Next morning, after a suspiciously long lie-in, a slave reported that someone was in Tutanekai's bed. The two lovers were rumbled, and when Hinemoa's superhuman efforts to reach Tutanekai had been revealed, their union was celebrated.

Descendants of Hinemoa and Tutanekai still live around Rotorua today.

Novotel Rotorua Lakeside (Map p306; ☎ 07-346 3888; www.novotelrotorua.co.nz; 11 Tutanekai St; concerts adult/child $35/15, incl hangi $65/30; ☼ 6.30pm)

Pohutu Cultural Theatre (Heritage Rotorua) (Map p319; ☎ 0800 108 114, 07-348 1189; www.pohututheatre.co.nz; cnr Froude & Tryon St; concerts & hangi adult/child $65/32.50; ☼ 6.30pm)

Lake Rotorua

Lake Rotorua is the largest of the district's 16 lakes and is – underneath all that water – a spent volcano. Sitting in the lake is **Mokoia Island**, which has for centuries been occupied by various subtribes of the area. The lake can be explored by boat with several operators situated at the lakefront.

Mokoia Island Wai Ora Experiences (Map p306; ☎ 0800 665 642; www.mokoiaisland.co.nz; Lakefront, at Volcanic Air Safaris; Ultimate tour adult/child $120/60, Taste tour $75/38) has exclusive rights to take visitors to Mokoia Island, and offers several tours. The 2½- to three-hour Ultimate Island Experience tour (9.30am, 1pm and 3pm) includes hearing famous tales of the island and takes you to the legendary hot pool of Hinemoa (see the boxed text, above). This is followed by an indigenous food tasting. The shorter 1½- to two-hour Taste of Mokoia tour is similar but with less of a walkabout.

The **Lakeland Queen Paddle Steamer** (Map p306; ☎ 0800 572 784; www.lakelandqueen.com; Lakefront) offers one-hour breakfast (adult/child $40/20), and longer lake cruises (lunch $48/24; Saturday-night summer dinner $60/30).

To explore the lake under your own steam, head for **Mana Adventures** (Map p306; ☎ 0800 333 660; www.manaadventures.co.nz; Lakefront; ☼ 9am-5pm), which offers (weather permitting) rental of pontoon boats (per hour $95), pedal boats (20 minutes per adult/child $8/5) and kayaks (per hour/half day $25/50). It also runs one-hour lake cruises (per adult/child $55/30) and runs trout-fishing charters (see p311).

Speed things up by jetboating with **Kawarau Jet** (☎ 0800 538 7746; www.nzjetboat.co.nz; Lakefront; 30min $69, 2½hr $120), which tears around the lake.

Rotorua Museum of Art & History

This impressive **museum** (Map p306; ☎ 07-350 1814; www.rotoruamuseum.co.nz; Government Gardens; admission adult/child/family $12/5.50/28; ☼ 9am-5pm Apr-Sep, to 8pm Oct-Mar, tours hourly 10am-4pm plus 5pm Dec-Feb) is housed in a grand mock-Tudor building originally constructed as a spa retreat in 1908. Displays in the former shower rooms offer an insight into the eccentric therapies once practised here, including exposure to radium as a cure for gout, and running an electrical current through baths as a treatment for 'nervous exhaustion'.

A gripping 20-minute film on the history of Rotorua, including the Tarawera eruption, runs every 20 minutes from 9am (not for small kids – the seats vibrate and the eruption noises are authentic!). Also here is a collection of *taonga* (treasures) of Te Arawa, featuring woodcarving, flax weaving and jade. Other exhibits relate the stories of the WWII 28 Maori Battalion, a revered military unit formed of local Arawa people (a movie on the battalion runs every 30 minutes from 9.30am). There's also a cool cafe with picturesque garden views, although the best view in town can be had from the viewing platform on the rooftop.

Government Gardens

The English-style **Government Gardens** (Map p306) surrounding the Rotorua Museum of Art & History are pretty-as-a-picture, with roses aplenty and civilized amenities such as croquet lawns and bowling greens, and steaming thermal pools dotted about. If you fancy some **lawn bowls** (☎ 07-348 0385; 30min/1hr $15/20; ⏰ 1-3.30pm Tue & Thu Sep-Apr), reservations are essential. Otherwise there's **Government Gardens Golf** (Map p306; ☎ 07-348 9126; www.governmentgardensgolf.co.nz; Queens Dr; ⏰ 7.30am-8pm) – either the nine-hole course (adult/child $20/14), minigolf ($10/8) or the driving range (80 balls $11). As well there's a **baseball batting cage** where you can attempt to drill a few home runs (35 balls $8).

Also within the gardens are the gorgeous Spanish Mission–style **Blue Baths** (Map p306; (☎ 07-350 2119; www.bluebaths.co.nz; admission adult/child/family $11/6/30; ⏰ noon-6pm Mon-Fri, 10am-6pm Sat & Sun Apr-Nov, 10am-7pm daily Dec-Mar), which opened in 1933 (and, amazingly, were closed from 1982 to 1999). Today you can visit a small museum (open 10am to 5pm) recalling the building's heyday, with recorded anecdotes and displays in the old changing rooms. If it all makes you feel like taking a dip yourself, the heated pool awaits. Ask about occasional dinner-and-cabaret shows (per person from $125).

Also in the gardens is the Polynesian Spa (see p310).

Ohinemutu

Ohinemutu is a charmingly ramshackle lakeside Maori village that traces the fusing of European and Maori cultures. The historic

St Faith's Anglican Church (Map p306; ☎ 07-348 2393; cnr Mataiawhea & Korokai Sts; admission by donation; ⏰ 8am-6pm, services 9am Sun & 10am Wed) is intricately decorated with Maori carvings, *tukutuku* (woven panels), painted scrollwork and stained-glass windows. One window features an image of Christ wearing a Maori cloak as he appears to walk on the waters of Lake Rotorua.

Opposite the church is **Tama-te-kapua Meeting House**, built in 1905 and named for the captain of the *Arawa* canoe. This sacred meeting house for Te Arawa people is not open to visitors but can be admired from the outside.

ACTIVITIES

Note that several of the following operators have teamed up under the banners of **Rotorua Adventure Combos** (☎ 0800 338 786, 07-357 2236; www.rotoruacombos.com) and **Rotorua Hot Deals** (☎ 0800 768 678; www.rotoruahotdeals.com), delivering a slew of good-value skydiving, white-water rafting, sledging, jetboating and helicopter experiences (plus zorbing, gondola rides, mountain biking…).

See also Argoventures (p320) and Skyline Skyrides (p318).

Mountain Biking

On the edge of town is the **Redwoods – Whakarewarewa Forest** (see p320), home to some of the best **mountain-bike trails** in the country. There are close to 100km of tracks to keep bikers of all skill levels happy for days on end. Note that not all tracks in the forest are designated for bikers, so adhere to the signposts. The Redwoods area of the forest has a **visitor centre** where you can get a trail map and learn more about the area.

At the Waipa Mill car park entrance to the forest, the starting point for the bike trails, you can hire bikes from **Planet Bike** (Map p319; ☎ 07-346 1717; 027 280 2817; www.planetbike.co.nz; Waipa State Mill Rd; bikes per 2hr/day $35/55, guided 2hr rides from $65; ⏰ 10am-3pm daily Nov-Apr, Sat & Sun only May-Oct). It can also arrange shuttles to get you to the park.

In Rotorua itself you can hire bikes from **Bike Vegas** (Map p306; ☎ 07-347 1151; www.bikevegas.co.nz; 1275 Fenton St; mountain bikes per half/full day from $40/80; ⏰ 9am-5.30pm Mon, Tue, Thu & Fri, to 4pm Wed, to 3pm Sat, 10am-2pm Sun) and **Lady Jane's Ice Cream Parlour** (Map p306; ☎ 07-347 9340; 1092 Tutanekai St; bikes per hr/day $10/30; ⏰ 10am-late).

Pick up the *Get on Your Bike* Rotorua cycle map and the *Rotorua Mountain Biking*

MAORI NZ: BAY OF PLENTY

The Bay of Plenty's traditional name, Te Rohe o Mataatua, recalls the ancestral *Mataatua* canoe, which arrived here from Hawaiki to make an eventful landfall at Whakatane (see the boxed text, p338). The region's history stretches back further than that, though, with the Polynesian settler Toi setting up what's claimed to be Aotearoa's first settlement in about AD 800.

Major tribal groups in the region are the Ngati Awa (www.ngatiawa.iwi.nz) of the Whakatane area, Whakatohea (www.whakatohea.co.nz) of Opotiki, Ngai Te Rangi (www.ngaiterangi.org.nz) of Tauranga, and Te Arawa (www.tearawa.iwi.nz) of Rotorua. Tribes in this region were involved on both sides of the Land Wars of the late 19th century (see the boxed text, p33), with those fighting against the government suffering considerable land confiscations that have caused legal problems right up to the present day.

There's a significant Maori population in the Bay, and there are many ways for travellers to learn about their culture. Opotiki has Hiona St Stephen's Church (p340) – the death here of government spy Rev Volkner in 1865 inspired the charming eyeball-eating scene in *Utu*. Whakatane has Toi's Pa (p335), perhaps NZ's oldest *pa* site. Rotorua has traditional villages at Te Whakarewarewa (p305) and Ohinemutu (p309), cultural performances and *hangi* meals (p307), and much, *much* more.

---

brochure from the i-SITE (p305) for more info on biking in and around town.

Thermal Pools & Massage

The **Polynesian Spa** (Map p306; ☎ 07-348 1328; www.polynesianspa.co.nz; Government Gardens, off Hinemoa St; main pool adults-only $20, private pools per 30min adult/child $25/4, family pool adult/child/family $13/6/32, spa therapies from $80; ☼ 8am-11pm, spa therapies 9am-8pm) is in the Government Gardens. A bathhouse was opened at these springs in 1882 and people have been swearing by the waters ever since.

There is mineral bathing (36°C to 42°C) in several picturesque pools at the lake's edge, marble-lined terraced pools and a larger, main pool. Also housed in the modern complex are several more commercial activities such as luxury therapies (massage, mud and beauty treatments) as well as a cafe and gift shop.

Beyond the airport, Wai Ora Spa at Hell's Gate (p320) has a full program of massage, mud and spa treatments. If you feel like exploring further, take a dip south of Rotorua at the outdoor Waikite Valley Thermal Pools (p322).

White-water Rafting & Sledging

Thrill seekers can find plenty of white-water action around Rotorua with the chance to take on the Grade V Kaituna River, complete with a startling 7m drop at Okere Falls. Most of these trips take a day, but times are often negotiable. Some companies head further out to the Rangitaiki (Grade III–VI) and Wairoa River (Grade V), raftable only when the dam is opened every second Sunday. Sledging (in

case you didn't know) is zooming downriver on a highly manoeuvrable body board.

Most of the following operators can arrange transport.

Kaitiaki Adventures (☎ 0800 338 736, 07-357 2236; www.kaitiaki.co.nz) Offers white-water rafting trips on the Kaituna ($85) and Wairoa ($99), and sledging on the Kaituna ($99) and Wairoa (one guide per person; $299).

Kaituna Cascades (☎ 0800 524 8862, 07-345 4199; www.kaitunacascades.co.nz) Does rafting on the Kaituna ($82), Rangitaiki ($108) and Wairoa ($98).

Raftabout (☎ 0800 723 822, 07-343 9500; www.raftabout.co.nz) Does rafting on the Kaituna ($89), Rangitaiki ($120) and Wairoa ($120), plus raft-sledge combos on the Kaituna ($175).

River Rats (☎ 0800 333 900, 07-345 6543; www.riverrats.co.nz) Takes on the Wairoa ($110), Kaituna ($90) and Rangitaiki ($120), and runs a scenic trip on the Rangitaiki, good for youngsters (adult/child $120/80). Tongariro trips by arrangement.

Wet 'n' Wild (☎ 0800 462 7238, 07-348 3191; www.wetnwildrafting.co.nz) Runs trips on the Kaituna ($95), Wairoa ($99) and the Mokau ($145), as well as easy-going Rangitaiki trips (adult/child $120/80) and longer, helicopter-access trips to remote parts of the Motu and Mohaka (two to five days $550 to $925).

Kayaking

Three companies can get you paddling on the waterways:

Adventure Kayaking (☎ 027-4997 402; www.adventurekayaking.co.nz; hire per day $40, trips per half/full day from $70/110) Takes trips on Lakes Rotorua, Rotoiti, Tarawera and Okataina; also offers freedom hire.

Kaituna Kayaks (☎ 07-362 4486; www.kaitunakayaks.com; half-day trip $149, lessons half/full day

$149/290) Guided tandem trips and kayaking lessons on the Kaituna.

River Rats (☎ 0800 333 900, 07-345 6543; www.river rats.co.nz; hire per half/full day from $25/45, 2/4hr trip $40/95) Freedom hire plus two-hour self-guided trips down the Ohau Channel and four-hour guided paddles to Manupirua Springs Hot Pools on Lake Rotoiti.

Tramping

There are plenty of opportunities to stretch your legs around Rotorua, with day walks a speciality. The booklet *Walks in the Rotorua Lakes area* ($2.50), available from the i-SITE, showcases town walks, including the popular lakefront stroll (20 minutes).

All the following walks are shown on the map on p319.

The area around **Lake Okataina** offers walks of varying distance and difficulty. One of the most popular – albeit not for beginners – is the **Western Okataina Walkway** (seven hours one way), which takes in lake views and a dry crater known as the 'Bullring'. The track runs from Millar Rd at Lake Okareka to Ruato on Lake Rotoiti with public transport past the Ruato end only.

The **Eastern Okataina Walkway** (three hours one way) goes along the eastern shoreline of Lake Okataina to Lake Tarawera and passes the **Soundshell**, a natural amphitheatre that has *pa* (fortified village) remains, and several swimming spots. The **Northern Tarawera Track** (three hours one way) connects to the Eastern Okataina Walkway, creating a two-day walk from either Lake Okataina or Ruato to Lake Tarawera with an overnight camp at either **Humphries Bay** (sites free) or **Tarawera Outlet** (sites per adult/child $7/2). From Tarawera Outlet you can walk on to **Tarawera Falls** (four hours return; see p340). There's a forestry road into Tarawera Outlet from Kawerau – access costs $4, with permits available from the Kawerau visitor centre (p340).

The **Okere Falls** are about 21km northeast of Rotorua on SH33, with an easy **track** (30 minutes return) past the 7m falls (popular for rafting), through native podocarp forest and along the Kaituna River. Along the way is a lookout over the river at **Hinemoa's Steps**.

Just north of Wai-O-Tapu on SH5 (see p321), the **Rainbow Mountain Track** (1½ hours one way) makes for a strenuous walk up to the summit of the peak known to Maori as Maungakakaramea (Mountain of coloured earth). There are spectacular views from the

summit with a panorama that takes in Lake Taupo, Tongariro National Park and the Paeroa Range.

Fishing

There's always good fishing to be had some-where around the lakes. You can hire guides to fish for trout or go solo, but either way a licence (per day/season $21/105) is essential, available from **O'Keefe's Fishing Specialists** (Map p306; ☎ 07-346 0178; www.okeefesfishing.co.nz; 1113 Eruera St; ⏰ 8am-4.30pm Mon-Fri, to 2pm Sat, 8.30am-12.30pm Sun). You can fish Rotorua's lakefront with a licence, though not all lakes can be fished year-round; check with O'Keefe's or the i-SITE (p305).

Some recommended guides:

Clark Gregor (☎ 07-347 1123; www.troutnz.co.nz; per hr $105) Does fly- and boat fishing.

Gordon Randle (☎ 07-349 2555; www.rotoruatrout. co.nz; half-/full-day charters $350/680) Transport, tuition and equipment included, plus cleaning, smoking and vacuum-packing of your catch.

Mana Adventures (p308) Fishing boat hire (per hour from $95), and trout-fishing trips (boat charter with skipper per three hours from $285).

Silver Hilton Trout Fishing (☎ 07-332 3488; www. troutfly.co.nz; boat/river fishing trips from $285/380, charter per day $760) Boat and fly-fishing with gear and lunch supplied.

Trout Man (☎ 021 951 174; www.waiteti.com; 2hr/day trip from $30/120) Learn to fish and share the passion with experienced angler and fishing correspondent Harvey Clark, from a couple of hours to multiday trips.

Other Activities

Another opportunity to get limbered up is at the **Wall Climbing Gym** (Map p306; ☎ 07-350 1400; www.basementcinema.co.nz; basement, 1140 Hinemoa St; admission incl gear adult/child $16/12; ⏰ noon-10pm Mon-Fri, 10am-10pm Sat & Sun), which has a three-storey climbing wall with overhangs aplenty.

NZONE (☎ 0800 376 796, 07-345 7520; www.nzone. biz; Rotorua Airport; dives $249-399) offers tandem skydives from 9000ft, 12,000ft or 15,000ft, giving you a bird's-eye view of the lakes and volcanoes. Town pick-ups available.

Several companies will help you saddle up for horse treks on idyllic trails around Rotorua. North of Lake Rotorua at the **Farmhouse** (Map p319; ☎ 07-332 3771; www.thefarm house.co.nz; 55 Sunnex Rd, off Central Rd, Ngongotaha; rides 30min/1hr/2hr $25/40/70), take a shorter trip for beginners or a longer trip for experienced riders. The very safe and professional **Paradise**

Valley Ventures (off Map p319; ☎ 07-348 3300; www.
paradisetreks.co.nz; 679 Paradise Valley Rd; rides 1hr/1½hr
$65/90) takes treks for novices and experi-
enced riders through a 700-acre farm north
of Rotorua. Shorter and longer treks also
available.

WALKING TOUR
Start out from **Rotorua Museum of Art & History**
(1; p308); once a bathhouse for the affluent,
it remains the town's most impressive building. Follow the road west through the elegant
Government Gardens (2; p309), which conclude
at Princes Gate Arches. Through the arch
you'll see the grand **Princes Gate Hotel** (3; p315),
moved here in the 1920s from Waihi.

Follow Arawa St west to the roundabout
then turn right down Fenton St towards the
lake. Turn left onto Pukaki St then right onto

Tutaneki St (4; p315), Rotorua's main eat street.
Continue north across War Memorial Park
to **Lake Rotorua** (5; p308) and walk alongside
the glittering waters. The road veers away
from the water onto Memorial Dr, which in
turn takes you to the historic Maori village of
Ohinemutu with its intricately carved Tama-
te-kapua Meeting House and **St Faith's Anglican
Church** (6; p309), which combines Christian
and Maori traditions.

Double back to Lake Rd and head up the
hill to **Kuirau Park** (7; p306), with its steamy
scenes and whiffs of sulphur. Once you're
done exploring, turn left into Pukuatua St,
left into Amohia St and right into Haupapa
St. Head up this street to the old police station, now the **Pig & Whistle** (8; p316) – have you
earned yourself a drink yet?

ROTORUA FOR CHILDREN
Rotorua is bound to be a hit with kids. Many
of the geothermal areas such as Wai-O-Tapu
and Te Puia have pram-able boardwalks,
so bring the stroller for when little legs get
tired. For legs with energy to burn, go to the
Redwoods – Whakarewarewa Forest (p320) for

WALK FACTS
Start Rotorua Museum
Finish Pig & Whistle
Distance 2.8km

a mini mountain-bike ride or walk in the woods.

To climb up high without dragging your feet, take a gondola ride at **Skyline Skyrides** (p318) and luge the afternoon away. See the sights on land and lake with the biofuelled **Rotorua Duck Tours** (p313), or under your own steam by pedal boat from **Mana Adventures** (p308) at the lakefront. There's a brilliant kids' playground at the lakefront too.

Tree-huggers and animal patters have plenty of choice with a plethora of nature parks (p318) not far out of town. And if all else fails you can threaten to strap troublesome teens into a **zorb** (p320) and roll them down the hill.

TOURS

To make sense of it all, or if time is tight, take a tour – book at the i-SITE or via many hostels and hotels.

Elite Adventures (☎ 07-347 8282; www.eliteadven tures.co.nz) Half-day (adult/child from $75/55) and full-day tours (adult/child from $200/110) covering a selection of Rotorua's major cultural and natural attractions.

Geyser Link Tours (☎ 07-343 6764; www.geyser link.co.nz) Tours of some of the major sights, including Wai-O-Tapu (adult/child $58/29, half-day) and Waimangu Volcanic Valley ($58/29, half-day), or both ($98/49, full day). Transport-only options available.

Indigenous Trails (☎ 07-542 1074; www.itrails. co.nz; day trip $338) Full-day Maori-guided tours around Rotorua, with a bungy jump, river cruise, kiwi-meeting, cultural show and *hangi*.

Mt Tarawera New Zealand (☎ 07-349 3714; www. mt-tarawera.co.nz) Guided half-day 4WD tours to the top of Mt Tarawera (adult/child $133/78) as well as a half-day 4WD/helicopter combo (per person $435) and the full-day Volcanic Eco Tour, which combines the 4WD trip with Wai-O-Tapu and Waimangu (adult/child $255/90). Also available are 4WD/mountain bike ($325) and helicopter/mountain bike ($610) combos.

Pure Cruise New Zealand (☎ 0800 272 456, 027 272 4561; www.purecruise.co.nz) Slow-boat catamaran cruises on Lake Rotoiti on an exclusive charter or nonexclusive basis. Call for prices and sailing times.

Rotorua Duck Tours (☎ 07-345 6522; www.rotorua ducktours.co.nz; adult/child/family $62/35/145; ☼ tours 11am, 1pm & 3.30pm summer, 11am & 2.15pm winter) Ninety-minute trips in an amphibious, biofuelled vehicle taking in the major sites around town and heading out onto three lakes (Rotorua, Okareka and Tikitapu).

For a bird's-eye tour of the region, opt for a scenic flight. Just as well there are only window seats…there's plenty to see.

Air Discovery (☎ 0800 247 347, 07-575 7584; www. airdiscovery.co.nz; Rotorua Airport; 1½hr/half-day flights $399/599) Volcanic explorations over White Island and the Taupo region (including Mt Ruapehu, Mt Ngarahoe and Mt Tongariro).

Helipro (☎ 0800 435 4776, 07-357 2512; www.helipro. co.nz; 8min-3½hr trips $89-855) Based at Te Puia, Helipro does a variety of helicopter trips including city flights, and Mt Tarawera and White Island landings.

Volcanic Air Safaris (Map p306; ☎ 07-348 9984; www.volcanicair.co.nz; 6min-3¼hr trips $70-845) Float-plane and helicopter flights from the lakefront, including a combined flight and Mokoia Island experience or combined helicopter flight and guided tour of Hell's Gate. The company also runs a 3¼-hour trip exploring White Island and Mt Tarawera.

SLEEPING
Budget

Rotorua has plenty of holiday parks and an ever-changing backpacker scene offering good options close to the action.

Crank Backpackers (Map p306; ☎ 0508 224 466, 07-348 0852; www.crankbackpackers.com; 1140 Hinemoa St; dm $23-25, d with/without bathroom $69/59; 🖳 🛜) A cavernous newcomer determined to compete with the old stagers, Crank occupies an old shopping mall (you might be sleeping in a florist or a delicatessen). Dorms over the street are sunny, and there are sexy co-ed bathrooms, a free gym and a climbing wall and art-house cinema in the basement.

Cactus Jacks Backpackers (Map p306; ☎ 07-348 3121; www.cactusjackbackpackers.co.nz; 1210 Haupapa St; dm/s/tw/d $24/39/52/57; 🖳) If you're looking for character, pardner, then this Western-themed spot is just your gunfight. Shabby-chic rooms range from Jail (dorms) to Madam Fifi's bordello (two twins). Sociable staff, relaxed lounges, courtyard, and undercover thermal pool make it an ideal spot for weary cowpokes.

our pick **Funky Green Voyager** (Map p306; ☎ 07-346 1754; www.funkygreenvoyager.com; 4 Union St; dm from $24, d with/without bathroom $65/57; 🖳 🛜) Green on the outside and the inside – due to several cans of paint and a dedicated environmental policy – the Funky GV features laid-back tunes and plenty of sociable chat among a spunky bunch of guests and worldly wise owners, who know what you want when you travel. The best doubles have bathroom; dorms are roomy with quality mattresses.

Rotorua Central Backpackers (Map p306; ☎ 07-349 3285; 1076 Pukuatua St; www.bbh.co.nz; dm $24-27, d $58; 🖳 🛜) This heritage hostel was built in 1936 and retains historic features including dark-wood skirting boards and door frames, deep bathtubs and geothermal radiators. Dorms are no more than six beds (and no bunks), plus there's a spa pool and barbecue, all within strolling distance of the museum.

Treks Rotorua YHA (Map p306; ☎ 0508 487 357; www.yha.co.nz; 1278 Haupapa St; dm $24-29, d $68-84; ☐ ☎) Bright and sparkling-clean, this purpose-built and well-maintained hostel is great for those wanting to get outdoors, with staff eager to assist with trip bookings, and storage for bikes and kayaks. Pricier rooms come with bathroom, and there's a barbecue area and deck for hanging out on. Off-street parking a bonus.

Kiwi Paka (Map p306; ☎ 07-347 0931; www.kiwipaka.co.nz; 60 Tarewa Rd; unpowered & powered sites $21, dm $27, chalets with bathroom d/tr/q $80/100/140, lodge s/d $50/60; ☐ ☎ ☒) One kilometre from town, this hostel is away from the action and feels like a school camp, with acceptable amenities and a range of accommodation from campsites to plain four-bed dorms, lodge rooms and pine-clad chalets. The Twisted Pippie cafe is on-site.

Regent Flashpackers (Map p306; ☎ 07-348 3338; www.regentflashpackers.co.nz; 1181 Pukaki St; dm/d from $25/90; ☐ ☎) Angling for a mature, upmarket backpacker market (is there such a thing?), the very decent Regent does things with style: sturdy bunks, cosy kitchen, quality linen, underfloor heating and fill-your-own mineral pools out the back. A bar was being built when we visited, which should help lower the tone a little.

Base Rotorua (Map p306; ☎ 0800 227 369, 07-348 8636; www.stayatbase.co.nz; 1286 Arawa St; dm/s/d from $27/70/70; ☐ ☎ ☒) Another link in the Base chain, this huge hostel is ever-popular with partying backpackers who love the Lava Bar (cheap meals, toga parties, disco nights etc). Rooms can be tight, with up to 12 beds in some dorms, but extras such as girls-only rooms, a large outdoor heated pool and off-street parking compensate.

Waiteti Trout Stream Holiday Park (Map p319; ☎ 07-357 5255; www.waiteti.com; 14 Okona Cres, Ngongotaha; sites $30, dm from $20, d cabins/motels from $45/80; ☐ ☎) This is a great option for folk who like it rustic and don't mind a short 10-minute drive into town. Set in two acres of garden on the banks of a trout-filled stream, this cute old classic has character-filled motel units, compact cabins, a backpackers'

lodge and relaxed camping. Free kayaks and dinghies.

Rotorua Thermal Holiday Park (Map p319; ☎ 07-346 3140; www.rotoruathermal.co.nz; Old Taupo Rd; unpowered/powered sites $30/34, d from $21, d cabins/motels from $54/95; ☐ ☎ ☒) This epic holiday park on the edge of town has a real holiday-resort feel, with rows of cabins and tourist flats, a 100-bed lodge, campsites galore and convenience facilities such as a shop and cafe. There's plenty of room to move with lots of open grassy areas, plus hot mineral pools for the soakers.

Rotorua Top 10 Holiday Park (Map p306; ☎ 07-348 1886; www.rotoruatop10.co.nz; 1495 Pukuatua St; unpowered/powered sites $38/40, d cabins/motels $65/95-130, 2br units $150; ☐ ☎ ☒) A small but perfectly formed holiday park with a continual improvement policy that has seen a nice new pool and various other revamps on the agenda. Cabins are in good nick and have small fridges and microwaves. Plenty of shrubbery and picnic tables.

Midrange

Generic motels crowd Fenton St, but better and often more interesting rooms can be found away from the main drag.

Six on Union (Map p306; ☎ 0800 100 062, 07-347 8062; www.sixonunion.co.nz; 6 Union St; d/f from $95/150; ☎ ☒) Hanging baskets ahoy! This modest place is a budget bonanza with pool, spa and small kitchenettes. Rooms are functional and freshly painted, and the swimming-pool area is in good nick. The location is away from traffic noise, but still an easy walk to the city centre.

Ann's Volcanic Rotorua (Map p306; ☎ 0800 768 683, 07-347 1007; www.rotoruamotel.co.nz; 107 Malfroy Rd; d $99-149, 2br ste & house $159-179; ☎) Ann's is a basic and affordable motel that has family charm and an ever-friendly host with loads of advice on things to see and do. Larger rooms feature courtyard spas and facilities for travellers with disabilities, with a house available for big groups. Rooms close to the street are a tad noisy.

Jack & Di's Troutbeck Lodge (Map p319; ☎ 0800 522 526; www.jackanddis.co.nz; 5 Arnold St, Ngongotaha; d/cottage from $99/450; ☎) A lakeside position in a quiet, secluded spot makes this large lodge a good retreat from central Rotorua. Multiple rooms cater for families or groups up to 11, and high-end facilities such as dishwasher, spa and full kitchen make for pleasant stays. Good winter rates; free kayaks.

Ambassador Thermal Motel (Map p306; ☎ 0800 479 581, 07-347 9581; www.ambassrotorua.co.nz; cnr Whakaue & Hinemaru Sts; d/f from $105/165; 🛜 🖳) Handily located in a quiet corner just a few minutes' walk to town and the lakefront, this mildly kooky motel boasts no fewer than four pools: two indoor mineral pools, an outdoor spa and a large figure-eight swimming pool. Comfortable rooms of various sizes can sleep up to seven, many with full kitchens.

Jack & Di's Lake Road Lodge (Map p306; ☎ 0800 522 526; www.jackanddis.co.nz; 21 Lake Rd; s/d/apt $99/119/250; 🛜) Lakeside views and a central-but-secluded location make this boutique hotel a persuasive option. The upstairs penthouse is ideal for couples, while downstairs is better for families or groups. A spa pool, lazy lounge areas and full kitchens add to the appeal.

Sandi's Bed & Breakfast (Map p319; ☎ 0800 726 3422, 07-348 0884; www.sandisbedandbreakfast.co.nz; 103 Fairy Springs Rd; d/f incl breakfast $120/150; 🛜 🖳) A friendly, family B&B run by the well-humoured Sandi who offers helpful tourist advice and a ready smile. The best bets are the two chalets with TV and plenty of room to move. Thoughtful extras including fresh fruit with brekkie and sun deck ensure rave reviews from former guests. Located a couple of kilometres north of town.

Victoria Lodge (Map p306; ☎ 0800 100 039, 07-348 4039; www.victorialodge.co.nz; 10 Victoria St; d/apt $120/180; 🛜) The friendly Vic is starting to look a bit weary (scuff marks, old carpets, messy gardens), but all the rooms here feel individual, and the studios are particularly attractive with their thermal plunge pools. Fully equipped apartments can squeeze in seven adults, though four would be very comfortable.

Tuscany Villas (Map p319; ☎ 0800 802 050, 07-348 3500; www.tuscanyvillasrotorua.co.nz; 280 Fenton St; d from $140) With its Italian-inspired architecture, this family-owned hotel is a real eye-catcher from the road. It pitches itself perfectly at both the corporate and leisure traveller, both of whom will appreciate the lavish furnishings, multiple TVs, DVD players and huge, deep spa baths.

Top End

Princes Gate Hotel (Map p306; ☎ 07-348 1179; www.princesgate.co.nz; 1057 Arawa St; d/ste from $165/275; 🖵 🛜 🖳) A well-loved and warmly welcoming 19th-century dame with 56 different rooms, such as the richly decorated Marvelly

suite – perhaps too pink for all but Barbara Cartland. Sink into the bottomless bath, however, and all is forgiven. Other amenities include cascading mineral baths, sauna, restaurant and streetside cafe.

Millennium Hotel (Map p306; ☎ 07-347 1234; www.millenniumrotorua.co.nz; cnr Eruera & Hinemaru Sts; d from $340; 🖵 🛜 🖳) The slick Maori-inspired lobby sets the scene for this elegant five-storey motel. Lakefront rooms afford excellent views as does the club room, a laid-back lounge available exclusively to guests. The poolside *hangi* is one of the better ones in town (see p307).

EATING

The lake end of Tutanekai St has a strip of good eating places, but there are plenty of others all over town.

Restaurants

Urbano Bistro (Map p319; ☎ 07-349 3770; cnr Fenton & Grey Sts; breakfast & lunch mains $13-20, dinner $20-38; 🕑 9am-11pm Mon-Sat, to 3pm Sun) This suburban cafe, with mega-checkerboard floor and striking wallpaper, is a bold move by reputable local restaurateurs. Some of the most delicious fare in town (try the beef, pineapple and capsicum curry), rich and well executed. Fine wines and five-star service.

Indian Star (Map p306; ☎ 07-343 6222; 1118 Tutanekai St; mains $14-25; 🕑 lunch & dinner; 🆅) Getting rave reviews from readers, this is one of several Indian eateries around town, elevating itself above the competition with immaculate service and marvellous renditions of subcontinental classics. Generous portions and a good vegetarian selection.

Amazing Thai (Map p306; ☎ 07-343 9494; 1246 Fenton St; mains $15-19; 🕑 lunch & dinner) This large, glass-fronted restaurant dishes up better-than-average, spicy-as-you-like Thai food in generous servings. Obligatory portraits of Thai royals and sundry elephants.

Sabroso (Map p306; ☎ 07-349 0591; 1184 Haupapa St; mains $15-36; 🕑 5-10pm Thu-Tue) What a surprise! This modest Latin American cantina – adorned with sombreros, guitars, hessian tablecloths and salt-and-pepper shakers made from Corona bottles – serves adventurous south-of-the-border fare to spice up bland Kiwi palates. The black bean chilli is a knockout (as are the margaritas).

Bistro 1284 (Map p306; ☎ 07-346 1284; 1284 Eruera St; mains $30-35; 🕑 6pm-late) Definitely one of

RotoVegas' hot dining spots, this intimate place (all chocolate and mushroom colours) serves stylish NZ cuisine with an Asian influence. It's an excellent place to sample great local ingredients, and be sure to leave room for some delectable desserts.

Cafes

Zippy Central Bar & Café (Map p306; ☎ 07-348 8288; 1153 Pukuatua St; snacks $4-10, mains $10-22; ⏲ 7am-7pm) A snappy little cafe with a decidedly retro groove (Laminex tables, an ultracool booth…), Zippy zips up all sorts of tasty food from breakfast, sandwiches, snacks to stir-fries and curries. There are plenty of healthy options, which is probably why this place is popular with cyclists and other wholesome types.

Capers Epicurean (Map p306; ☎ 07-348 8818; 1181 Eruera St; breakfast & lunch mains $6-20, dinner $13-28; ⏲ 7.30am-late; **V**) This slick, barnlike deli is always busy with diners showing up for cabinets crammed full of delicious gourmet sandwiches, pastries, salads and cakes, and an excellent blackboard menu of brekkies and other tasty hot foods (try the carrot, leek and fetta lasagne). There's also a deli section stocked with olive oils, marinades, relish, jams and chocolates.

Relish (Map p306; ☎ 07-343 9195; 1149 Tutanekai St; breakfast $9-22, lunch & dinner mains $19-33; ⏲ 7am-4pm Mon & Tue, to 9pm Wed-Fri, 8am-9pm Sat, to 4pm Sun) A top spot serving all-day breakfast, pizza and the like, with a keen eye on delicate spices, aromatic herbs and wood smoke. A modern and relaxed interior with local artwork on the walls.

Fat Dog Café (Map p306; ☎ 07-347 7586; 1161 Arawa St; breakfast & lunch mains $11-17, dinner $26-30; ⏲ breakfast, lunch & dinner; **V**) With paw prints up the walls and silly poems painted on the chairs, this is the town's friskiest and most child-friendly eatery. During the day it dishes up big bowls of brekkie, nachos, salads and sandwiches; in the evening it's candlelit lamb and venison. The only cafe in NZ brave enough to play *Unskinny Bop* by Poison.

ourpick Lime Caffeteria (Map p306; ☎ 07-350 2033; cnr Fenton & Whakaue Sts; mains $13-24; ⏲ 7.30am-4.30pm; **V**) Sitting on a quiet, leafy corner near the lake, this refreshing cafe is especially good for alfresco breakfasts and dishes with a welcome twist: try the chicken-and-chorizo salad or prawn-and-salmon risotto in lime sauce. It also offers classy counter snacks,

excellent coffee and outdoor tables. 'This is the best lunch I've had in ages', says one happy punter.

Quick Eats

Weilin's Noodle House (Map p306; ☎ 07-343 9998; 1148 Tutanekai St; mains $11-17; ⏲ lunch & dinner Wed-Mon) A neat-and-tidy shop serving trad Chinese dumplings and oodles of noodles in soups and stirfries. Eat in or take away.

Ali Baba's Tunisian Takeaway (Map p306; ☎ 07-348 2983; 1146 Tutanekai St; meals $13-15; ⏲ 11.30am-late; **V**) Follow the belly-dancing music (and your nose) into this neat little eatery serving kebabs and Tunisian-inspired pizzas, salads, pastas and rice meals. Eat in or take away.

Self-catering

Countdown (Map p306; ☎ 07-350 3277; 246 Fenton St; ⏲ 6am-midnight)

Pak N Save (Map p306; ☎ 07-347 8440; cnr Fenton & Amohau Sts; ⏲ 8am-10pm)

DRINKING

There are a few good spots to slake your thirst, with Euro-style pubs well represented.

ourpick Underground Bar (Map p306; ☎ 07-348 3612; www.croucherbrewing.co.nz; basement, 1282 Hinemoa St; ⏲ 4-8pm Wed & Thu, to 11pm Fri & Sat, 2-6pm Sun) 'It's all about the beer' at this crafty underground bunker, run by the lads from Croucher Brewing Co, Rotorua's best microbrewers. Sip down a pint of fruity Pale Ale, aromatic Drunken Hop Bitter or malty Pilsener and wonder how you'll manage a sleep-in tomorrow morning.

Pig & Whistle (Map p306; ☎ 07-347 3025; www.pig andwhistle.co.nz; cnr Haupapa & Tutanekai Sts; ⏲ 11.30am-late) This excellent microbrewery pub in the former police station offers a conducive atmosphere in which to enjoy its Swine lager (big-screen TV, beer garden, live music Thursday to Saturday), while serving up some of the best simple grub in town (mains $19 to $30). Their menu runs the gamut from spare ribs to a gluten-free vegetarian toastie.

Belgian Bar (Map p306; ☎ 07-348 6190; 1151 Arawa St; ⏲ 4pm-late Tue, 11.30am-late Wed-Sun) The best bar in town for lovers of gigs and good beer. Half a dozen Euro-beers on tap and 42 in the bottle make for quality supping while a menu of meatballs, mash and *moules et frites* will allow you to stick around and sup a few more. Regular blues and acoustic acts.

Pheasant Plucker (Map p306; ☎ 07-343 7071; www.thepheasantplucker.co.nz; 1153 Arawa St; ⏰ 4pm-late Mon-Fri, 3pm-late Sat, 11am-late Sun) Another place for a proper pint, but this time á l'Anglais. The Pheasant proffers locally brewed and British beer, along with bangers 'n' mash and nonstop carvery with Yorkshire pud (mains $15 to $36).

ENTERTAINMENT
Several local pubs such as the Pig & Whistle and Chambers regularly host bands. For late-night action, head to **Bar Barella** (Map p306; ☎ 07-347 6776; 1263 Pukuatua St; admission free-$10; ⏰ 11pm-3am Wed, Fri & Sat), where bands and DJs play metal, hip-hop, reggae, rock and dub to a nocturnal crowd.

Princes Gate Hotel (Map p306; ☎ 07-348 1179; www.princesgate.co.nz; 1057 Arawa St; show & meal $85) hosts regular dinners alongside a 1930s-style cabaret show. Cabaret shows also kick up their knickers at the Blue Baths (see p309).

Reading Cinema (Map p306; ☎ 07-3490061; www.reading cinemas.co.nz; 1281 Eruera St; admission adult/child $15/10; ⏰ 10.30am-11pm) shows mainstream movies, while **Basement Cinema** (Map p306; ☎ 07-350 1400; www.basementcinema.co.nz; basement, 1140 Hinemoa St; adult $14; ⏰ vary) shows art-house and foreign films.

SHOPPING
Being the tourist centre of NZ, Rotorua has an abundance of souvenirs. Genuine Maori and other NZ-made arts and crafts will be labelled. **Jade Factory** (Map p306; ☎ 07-349 1828; www.jadefactory.com; 1288 Fenton St; ⏰ 9am-6pm) Specialises in high-end, hand-crafted greenstone jewellery and carvings. **Of Hand & Heart** (Map p306; ☎ 07-348 9505; 1180 Haupapa St; ⏰ 10am-5pm) Gorgeous hand-spun ceramics: watch the potter at work. **Out of New Zealand** (Map p306; ☎ 07-346 2968; 1189 Fenton St; ⏰ 9am-6pm) Stocks predominantly NZ-made craft and gifts including carvings, ceramics and jewellery. Plenty of affordable, packable souvenirs.

To the south of town, Te Puia and Te Whakarewarewa (p305) have excellent selections of genuine Maori-made arts.

GETTING THERE & AWAY
Air
Air New Zealand (Map p306; ☎ 07-343 1100; www.airnewzealand.co.nz; 1103 Hinemoa St; ⏰ 9am-5pm Mon-Fri) offers daily direct flights to Auckland, Christchurch and Wellington, with onward connections to other destinations. Air New Zealand also links Rotorua with Sydney every Tuesday and Saturday.

Bus
All the major bus companies stop outside the i-SITE (see p305), from where you can arrange bookings.

InterCity (☎ 09-583 5780; www.intercity.co.nz) runs buses to destinations such as the following:

Destination	Price	Duration	Frequency
Auckland	$50	4hr	8 daily
Gisborne	$60	4½hr	1 daily
Hamilton	$35	1½hr	6 daily
Napier	$52	3hr	4 daily
Taupo	$32	1hr	5 daily
Tauranga	$25	1½hr	4 daily
Wellington	$57	8hr	4 daily
Whakatane	$33	1½hr	1 daily

Naked Bus (☎ 0900 625 33; www.nakedbus.com) services run to the same destinations, as listed below. Substantial fare savings can be made by booking in advance.

Destination	Price	Duration	Frequency
Auckland	$35	4hr	3 daily
Gisborne	$43	4¾hr	1 daily
Hamilton	$24	1½hr	3 daily
Napier	$29	3hr	1 daily
Taupo	$19	1hr	2 daily
Tauranga	$11	1½-4hr	2-3 daily
Wellington	$39	8hr	1 daily
Whakatane	$21	1½hr	1 daily

Twin City Express (☎ 0800 422 9287; www.baybus.co.nz) buses run twice daily Monday to Friday between Rotorua and Tauranga/Mt Maunganui via Te Puke ($11, 1½ hours).

GETTING AROUND
To/From the Airport
The airport is about 10km out of town to the east. **Super Shuttle** (☎ 0800 748 885, 07-345 7790; www.supershuttle.co.nz) offers a door-to-door airport service for $20 for the first person and $6 for each additional passenger. A taxi from the city centre costs about $25. Cityride (below) runs a daily airport bus service.

Bus
If you're trying to get around local attractions, ask about their shuttle services: many offer courtesy pick-up and drop-off. **Cityride** (☎ 0800 422 9287; www.baybus.co.nz) operates convenient local bus services around town

and Ngongotaha ($2.20), and the airport ($2.50).

Several shuttles run around the town's attractions with pick-ups at most hotels and hostels:

Affordable Adventures (☎ 0508 278 946; www.affordableadventures.co.nz) Runs a small bus wherever you want to go for whatever it costs; good for groups.

Geyser Link Tour Service (☎ 07-343 6764; www.geyserlink.co.nz) Goes to Wai-O-Tapu (return $35) and Paradise Valley Springs (return $25).

Tim's Thermal Shuttle (☎ 027 494 5508) Goes to Wai-O-Tapu (return including entry $50) and the Buried Village on request.

Car

In Rotorua car-rental competition is fierce so there are bargains to be had. Try the following:

Avis (☎ 07-345-6055; www.avis.co.nz; Rotorua Airport; ⏰ 8am-8pm Mon-Fri, 8.30am-3pm Sat, to 4pm Sun)

Budget (Map p306; ☎ 07-348 8127; www.budget.co.nz; 1230 Fenton St; ⏰ 7.30am-5.30pm Mon-Fri, 8am-noon Sat & Sun)

Rent-a-Dent (Map p319; ☎ 0800 736 823, 07-349 3993; www.rotoruacarrentals.co.nz; 316 Te Ngae Rd; ⏰ 8.30am-5.30pm Mon-Fri, 8am-noon Sat)

Taxi

Fast Taxis (☎ 07-348 2444)

Rotorua Taxis (☎ 07-348 1111)

AROUND ROTORUA

NORTH OF ROTORUA
Nature Parks

Surrounding Rotorua are several places devoted to native wildlife.

Rainbow Springs Kiwi Wildlife Park (Map p319; ☎ 0800 724 626, 07-350 0440; www.rainbowsprings.co.nz; 192 Fairy Springs Rd; 24hr pass adult/child/family $26/15/69; ⏰ 8am-10pm) is a must-do for nature-lovers. At the heart of the park are the natural springs, home to wild trout and eels, which you can see from the underwater viewer. There are walkways for wanderings with interpretive displays along the way. Animals abound, both introduced species such as wallabies, emus and rainbow lorikeets, and interesting native birds such as kea, kaka and pukeko.

The highlight of the park is **Kiwi Encounter** (www.kiwiencounter.co.nz; admission adult/child/family $27.50/17.50/75; ⏰ tours hourly 10am-4pm), home to NZ's largest kiwi recovery program – a nationally significant nonprofit conservation project.

It offers visitors a rare peek into the lives of not only these greatly endangered birds, but the people trying to save them from extinction. Be prepared for an emotional roller coaster on the excellent 45-minute tours that have you tiptoeing through the actual incubator and hatchery areas. A combo Kiwi Encounter/Wildlife Park ticket costs adult/child/family $42/23/110.

Rainbow Springs comes alive at night with colourful illuminations and a chance to walk through the outdoor kiwi enclosure. Also offered are special joint four-hour evening tours with the neighbouring Mitai Maori Village (see p307). Rainbow Springs is 3km north of central Rotorua on SH5 towards Hamilton and Auckland.

In Paradise Valley at the foot of Mt Ngongotaha are two wildlife parks. Eight kilometres from town is **Paradise Valley Springs** (off Map p319; ☎ 07-348 9667; 467 Paradise Valley Rd, www.paradisevalleysprings.co.nz; adult/child $26/13; ⏰ 8am-5pm), a six-hectare park with trout springs, big slippery eels, and various land-dwelling animals such as deer, alpaca, possums and a pride of lions (fed at 2.30pm). There's also a coffee shop and a new elevated treetop walkway.

Wingspan Birds of Prey Trust (off Map p319; ☎ 07-357 4469; www.wingspan.co.nz; 1164 Paradise Valley Rd; adult/child $15/5; ⏰ 9am-3pm) is dedicated to conserving three threatened NZ birds: the falcon, hawk and owl. Learn about the birds in the museum display, then take a sneaky peek into the incubation area before walking through the all-weather aviary. Go in time to see the 2pm flying display.

Mamaku Blue

You may find grapes overrated once you've visited this **blueberry winery** (off Map p319; ☎ 07-332 5840; www.mamakublue.co.nz; Maraeroa Rd, Mamaku; tours $20, museum $2; ⏰ 10am-5pm). There are delicious daily tastings, and also on offer are other blueberry delights such as chocolates, chutneys, jams, sauces, vinegars and liqueurs. Take a tour and find out more, and visit the upstairs museum which has a collection of photos documenting the history of the area.

Mamaku Blue is 20km northwest of Rotorua; take SH5 and turn off onto Maraeroa Rd. It's well signposted.

Skyline Skyrides

Swinging up Mt Ngongotaha is **Skyline Skyrides** (Map p319; ☎ 07-347 0027; www.skylineskyrides.co.nz; Fairy

AROUND ROTORUA

0 ――――― 10 km
0 ――――― 5 miles

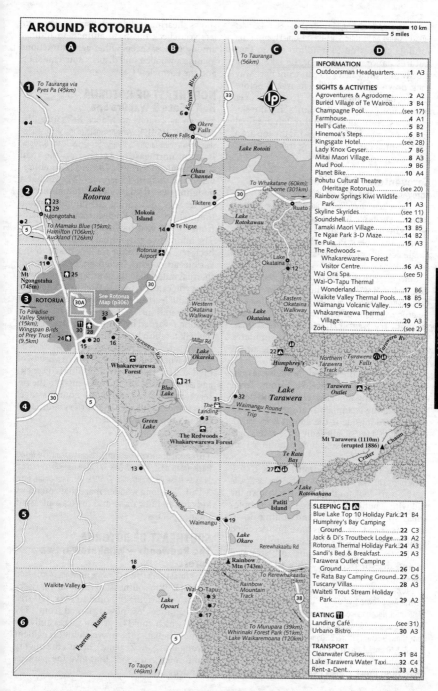

ROTORUA & THE BAY OF PLENTY

Springs Rd; gondola adult/child/family $24/12/60, luge 5 rides $30, sky swing adult/child $30/20; 9am-11pm). This gondola cruises up to a hilltop of fun that features panoramic views of the lake and a speedy luge on which you can scoot part-way back down on three different tracks before coming back up on a chairlift (to do it all over again). For even speedier antics, try the sky swing, a screaming swoosh through the air at speeds of up to 160km/h. Also at the top are a restaurant, a cafe and walking tracks around the mountain.

Agroventures & Agrodome

Agroventures (Map p319; 0800 949 888, 07-357 4747; www.agroventures.co.nz; Western Rd, Ngongotaha; 9am-5pm) is a veritable hive of entertaining activities, 9km north of Rotorua on SH5 (courtesy shuttle available). Prices that follow are for single activities but there are lots of deals for combos.

Start off with the 43m **bungy** (www.rotoruabungy.co.nz; adult/child $95/80) and the **Swoop** (www.swoop.co.nz; adult/child $49/35), a 130km/h swing that can be enjoyed alone or with friends. If that's not enough, try **Freefall Xtreme** (www.freefallxtreme.co.nz; 3min per adult/child $85/49) which simulates skydiving by blasting you 5m into the air on a column of wind.

Also here is the **Shweeb** (www.shweeb.co.nz; adult/child $49/35), a monorail velodrome from which you hang in a clear capsule and pedal yourself along recumbently at speeds of up to 60km/h. Alongside is the **Agrojet** (www.agrojet.co.nz; adult/child $49/35), allegedly NZ's fastest jet-boat, speeding and splashing around a 1km manmade course.

Across the road is the **zorb** (0800 227 474; www.zorb.co.nz; rides from $49; 9am-5pm Apr-Nov, to 7pm Dec-Mar) – look for the grassy track down the hill with what looks like large, clear, people-filled spheres bouncing and rolling down at some speed. Your eyes have not deceived you! There are two courses: 150m straight, or the 180m zigzag. Do your zorb strapped in and dry, or freestyle with a whole lot of water thrown in.

Next door to Agroventures is the educational **Agrodome** (07-357 1050; www.agrodome.co.nz; Western Rd, Ngongotaha; 1hr tour adult/child/family $30/15/78, 1hr show $26/13/75, tour & show $50/25/110; 8.30am-5pm, shows 9.30am, 11am & 2.30pm, tours 10.40am, 12.10pm, 1.30 & 3.40pm). Learn everything you need to know about sheep during a show that parades champion rams, runs a livestock auction, and

shows shearing and doggy displays. The tour lets you check out farm animals including, among others, sheep. Other agro-attractions include a woollen mill display, souvenir shop and the Farmview Café.

NORTHEAST OF ROTORUA
Hell's Gate & Wai Ora Spa

Known as Tikitere to Maori, **Hell's Gate** (Map p319; 07-345 3151; www.hellsgate.co.nz; SH30; admission adult/child/family $30/15/75; 8.30am-8.30pm) is 16km northeast of Rotorua on the road to Whakatane (SH30). Tikitere is an abbreviation of *Taku tiki i tere nei* (My youngest daughter has floated away), remembering the tragedy of a young girl jumping into a thermal pool. The English name originates from a 1934 visit by George Bernard Shaw. The impressive geothermal reserve covers 10 hectares, with a 2.5km walking track to the various attractions, including the largest hot thermal waterfall in the southern hemisphere. Here you can also see a master woodcarver at work, and learn about flax weaving and other Maori traditions.

Long regarded by Maori as a place of healing, Tikitere also houses the **Wai Ora Spa** (mud bath & spa adult/child/family $105/55/265, massage per 30min/1hr $80/130) where you can relax with a variety of mud and spa treatments. The UltiMUD package (adult/child $235/180) includes entry to the reserve, mud bath, spa and one-hour massage, plus some manuka tea. A courtesy shuttle to/from Rotorua is available.

3-D Maze

Three kilometres beyond the airport, **Te Ngae Park** (Map p319; 07-345 5275; 3dmaze@wave.co.nz; 1135 Te Ngae Rd; adult/child $7.50/5; 9am-5pm) is a 3-D, 1.7km-long wooden maze that entertains kids for an hour or so and makes a pleasant picnic spot.

SOUTHEAST OF ROTORUA
The Redwoods – Whakarewarewa Forest

This **forest park** (Map p319; www.redwoods.co.nz; admission free) is 3km southeast of town on Tarawera Rd. It was originally home to over 170 tree species (a few less now), planted from 1899 to see which could be grown successfully for timber. Radiata pine proved a hit (as evident throughout New Zealand), but it's the mighty Californian redwoods that give the park its grandeur today.

ROTORUA & THE BAY OF PLENTY

Clearly signposted walking tracks range from a half-hour wander through the **Redwood Grove** to an enjoyable whole-day route to the Blue and Green Lakes. Most walks start from the **Redwoods Gift Shop & Visitor Centre** (Map p319; ☎ 07-350 0110; Long Mile Rd; ☑ 8.30am-5.30pm Mon-Fri & 10am-5pm Sat & Sun Oct-Mar, 8.30am-4.30pm Mon-Fri & 10am-4pm Sat & Sun Apr-Sep), where you can get maps and view displays about the forest. There's also a shop featuring a good selection of hand-crafted wooden items and nature-inspired gifts.

Aside from walking, the park is great for picnics, and is acclaimed well beyond the town for its enjoyable and accessible mountain biking (see p309).

Buried Village of Te Wairoa

Fifteen kilometres from Rotorua on the Tarawera Rd, which passes the pretty Blue and Green Lakes, is the **buried village** (Map p319; ☎ 07-362 8287; www.buriedvillage.co.nz; Tarawera Rd; admission adult/child/family $30/8/68; ☑ 9am-5pm Nov-Mar, to 4.30pm Apr-Oct), the site of one of the most dramatic natural events to occur in NZ in the last 150 years – the 1886 eruption of Mt Tarawera. Here you can see the buildings submerged by the eruption, creating an odd time capsule of NZ in the 19th century, with highlights such as the Rotomahana Hotel, a blacksmith's shop and several *whare* (houses).

A small museum tells the stories of the eruption and includes an interesting short film. Of particular interest is the story of the *tohunga* (priest) Tuhoto Ariki who, according to some, was blamed for the destruction. His *whare* has been excavated and reconstructed.

There's a short bush walk through the valley to Te Wairoa Falls, where the Wairoa River drops 30m over a series of rocky outcrops. The end of the track is steep, slippery and unsuitable for young children.

Lake Tarawera

Tarawera means 'Burnt Spear', named by a visiting hunter who left his bird spears in a hut and on returning the following season found both the spears and hut had been burnt. The lake is picturesque and good for swimming, fishing, cruises and nature walks.

A good place to access the lake is at The Landing, about 2km past the buried village. Here you'll find **Clearwater Cruises** (☎ 07-362 8590; www.clearwater.co.nz; The Landing, Lake Tarawera; per hr cruise vessel/self-drive runabout $510/125), which runs

scenic cruises for groups and trout-fishing trips aboard a variety of vessels, with self-drive boats available. Also at The Landing is the **Landing Café** (☎ 07-362 8502; mains $26-30; ☑ breakfast & lunch), serving hearty mains like spiced lamb rump, salmon pasta and seafood chowder. Around 2km beyond The Landing is **Lake Tarawera Water Taxi** (☎ 07-362 8080; www.scenictarawera.co.nz; 93 Spencer Rd; lake excursions from $60), which can take you anywhere on the lake, anytime.

There are **DOC campsites** (www.doc.govt.nz) at Hot Water Beach (adult/child $8/4) on Te Rata Bay (boat access only), Tarawera Outlet (adult/child $7/2) and Humphrey's Bay (free). **Blue Lake Top 10 Holiday Park** (☎ 0800 808 292, 07-362 8120; www.bluelaketop10.co.nz; 723 Tarawera Rd; unpowered/powered sites $36/40, cabins $55-229) offers camping next to Blue Lake, 6km before you get to Lake Tarawera. Good facilities, well run and with a handy range of cabins.

SOUTH OF ROTORUA
Waimangu Volcanic Valley

This interesting **thermal area** (Map p319; ☎ 07-366 6137; www.waimangu.com; 587 Waimangu Rd; walking tour adult/child $32.50/10; boat cruise $40/10; ☑ 8.30am-5pm daily, to 6pm Jan) was created during the eruption of Mt Tarawera in 1886, making it young in geological terms. Waimangu (Black Water) refers to the dark, muddy colour of much of the water here.

Taking the easy downhill stroll through the valley you'll pass many spectacular thermal and volcanic features, including Inferno Crater Lake, where overflowing water can reach 80°C, and Frying Pan Lake, the largest hot spring in the world. The walk continues down to Lake Rotomahana (meaning 'Warm Lake'), from where you can either get a lift back up to where you started or take a 45-minute boat trip on the lake, past steaming cliffs and the former site of the Pink and White Terraces.

Waimangu is approximately a 20-minute drive south from Rotorua, 14km along SH5 (towards Taupo) and then 6km from the marked turn-off. Last admission is at 3.45pm (4.45pm in January).

Wai-O-Tapu Thermal Wonderland

Also south of Rotorua, **Wai-O-Tapu** (Map p319; ☎ 07-366 6333; www.waiotapu.co.nz; 201 Loop Rd, off SH5; admission adult/child/family $30/10/75; ☑ 8.30am-5pm), meaning 'Sacred Waters', is one of the most famous of the thermal reserves. It has many interesting features packed into a small area, including the boiling, multi-hued **Champagne Pool**, bubbling **mud pool**, stunning mineral terraces and the **Lady Knox Geyser**, which spouts off (with a little prompting from an organic soap) punctually at 10.15am and gushes up to 20m for about an hour. A fairly commercial attraction, it has a large shopping area and cafe, which makes for a reasonable pit stop.

Wai-O-Tapu is 27km south of Rotorua along SH5 (towards Taupo), and a further 2km from the marked turn-off. Last admission 3.45pm.

Waikite Valley Thermal Pools

Approximately 30km south of Rotorua on SH5 are the open-air **Waikite Valley Thermal Pools** (Map p319; ☎ 07-333 1861; www.hotpools.co.nz; 648 Waikite Valley Rd; public pools adult/child/family $12/6/30, private pools 40min $15; ⏱ 10am-9pm). As well as the four main pools there are two more relaxing, smaller pools and four private spas, all ranging from 35°C to 40°C. There's also a cafe and camping on-site (unpowered/powered sites $32/36; pools free for campers).

To get here turn right off SH5 at the signpost opposite the Wai-O-Tapu turn-off, and continue for 6km.

Whirinaki Forest Park

The exceptional feature of this **forest park** (www.doc.govt.nz, www.whirinakirainforest.info) is some of NZ's finest podocarp (conifer) forest, although there is much more to see here, including canyons, waterfalls, lookouts, and many streams and rivers. The Oriuwaka Ecological Area and Arahaki Lagoon are also here.

You can explore the park via a network of tracks varying in length and difficulty. The best source of information is **DOC Rangitaiki visitor centre** (☎ 07-366 1080; SH38) in Murupara. The DOC booklet *Walks in Whirinaki Forest* ($2.50) gives details about walking and camping in the park.

A good short walk is the **Whirinaki Waterfalls Track** (four hours return), which follows the Whirinaki River, while one of the longer walks is the **Whirinaki Track** (two days, 27km), which can be combined with **Te Hoe Track** (four days). There's also a rampaging 16km **mountain-bike track** here.

There are several easily accessible **camping areas** and 10 **backcountry huts** ($5-15) in the park; pay at the DOC office.

Whirinaki Forest Park is 90km southeast of Rotorua, with access off SH38 on the way to Te Urewera National Park; take the turn-off at Te Whaiti to Minginui. The closest town to the park is Murupara, where there are basic amenities.

WESTERN BAY OF PLENTY

The Western Bay of Plenty stretches along the coast from Waihi Beach to Maketu and inland as far as the Kaimai Range. This is where New Zealanders have come on holiday for generations, lapping up salt-licked activities and lashings of sunshine.

TAURANGA

pop 118,200

Tauranga (pronounced Tao-wronger) has been booming since the 1990s and remains one of NZ's fastest-growing cities. The busy port – with its petrol refineries and mountains of coal and lumber – serves the land for miles around, but it's the migrants (many from Auckland) and holidaymakers who have seen the old workhorse reborn as a show pony. Restaurants and bars line the revamped waterfront, fancy hotels rise high, and the once-sleepy suburbs of Mt Maunganui and Papamoa have woken up to new wealth and homogeny.

Tauranga is the place to fulfil all your watery dreams: with marinas chock-a-block with beautiful boats, sandy surf beaches and water sports aplenty, this is about as Riviera as NZ gets.

Information

Automobile Association (Map p323; AA; ☎ 07-927 7760; www.aa.co.nz; cnr Devonport Rd & First Ave; ⏱ 8.30am-5pm Mon-Fri, 9am-noon Sat) Maps and driving info.

BA Reader (Map p323; ☎ 07-577 0990; www.bareader. co.nz; 26 Wharf St; ⏱ 9.30am-5pm Mon-Fri, 10am-9.30pm Sat, to 4pm Sun) Beachy secondhand reads.

Dymocks (Map p323; ☎ 07-927 7476; www.dymocks. co.nz; 50 Devonport Rd; ⏱ 9am-5pm Mon-Fri, to 4pm Sat, 10am-4pm Sun) For books and maps.

Gateway Cyber Cafe (Map p323; ☎ 07-571 1112; 26 Devonport Rd; ⏱ 9am-10pm) Internet access.

Paper Plus (Map p323; www.nzpost.co.nz; 17 Grey St; ⏱ 8.30am-5.30pm Mon-Fri, 9am-4pm Sat, 10am-3pm Sun) The local NZ Post branch.

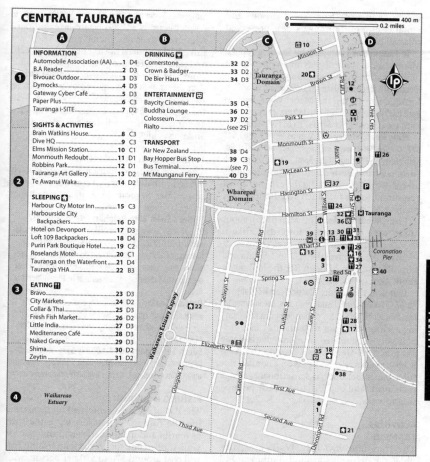

CENTRAL TAURANGA

0 — 400 m
0 — 0.2 miles

Waikareao
Estuary

Waikareao Estuary Expwy

Tauranga
Domain

Wharepai
Domain

Coronation
Pier

ROTORUA & THE BAY OF PLENTY

Tauranga Hospital (Map p326; ☎ 07-579 8000; www.bopdhb.govt.nz; 375 Cameron Rd; ☻ 24hr) A couple of kilometres south of town.

Tauranga i-SITE (Map p323; ☎ 07-578 8103; www.bayofplentynz.com; 95 Willow St; ☻ 8.30am-5.30pm Mon-Fri, 9am-5pm Sat & Sun) Local tourist information, bookings and InterCity bus tickets and DOC maps.

Sights

The **Tauranga Art Gallery** (Map p323; ☎ 07-578 7933; www.artgallery.org.nz; cnr Wharf & Willow Sts; admission by donation; ☻ 10am-4.30pm) presents historic and contemporary art, and houses a permanent collection along with frequently changing local and visiting exhibitions. The building itself is a former bank, although you'd hardly know it – it's an altogether excellent space

with no obvious compromise (cue: applause!). Touring the ground and mezzanine galleries, with a stop to poke your nose into the video cube, will take an hour or so.

Built in 1847, **Elms Mission Station** (Map p323; ☎ 07-577 9772; www.theelms.org.nz; Mission St; admission house adult/child $5/50c, gardens free; ☻ house 2-4pm Wed, Sat & Sun, gardens 9am-5pm daily) is the oldest building in the Bay of Plenty. Furnished in period style, it sits among other well-preserved mission buildings in leafy grounds. The spooky **Mission Cemetery** (Map p326) lies not far away at the intersection of Marsh Street and Dive Crescent – good for a little epitaph-reading.

The demure **Brain Watkins House** (Map p323; ☎ 07-578 1835; www.library.tauranga.govt.nz/localhistory; cnr Elizabeth St & Cameron Rd; admission $2; ☻ 2-4pm Sun) was built in 1881 from kauri (wood) and remains one of Tauranga's best-preserved colonial homes.

Te Awanui Waka (Map p323; The Strand), a replica Maori canoe, is on display in an open-sided building at the top of the Strand. Up the hill, **Monmouth Redoubt** (Map p323; Monmouth St) was a fortified site during the Maori Wars. **Robbins Park** (Map p323; Cliff Rd) is a verdant pocket of roses with excellent views across to Mt Maunganui.

Mills Reef Winery (off Map p326; ☎ 0800 645 577, 07-576 8800; www.millsreef.co.nz; 143 Moffat Rd, Bethlehem; ☼ tastings 10am-5pm), 7km from the town centre at Bethlehem, has tastings of its award-winning wines (dig the cab sav) and a restaurant (open for lunch and dinner daily; mains $24 to $33).

From **Minden Lookout** (off Map p326), about 10km west of Tauranga towards Katikati, there's a superb view back over the Bay of Plenty. To get there, take SH2 to Te Puna and turn off south on Minden Rd; the lookout is about 4km up the road.

Out near the airport, **Classic Flyers NZ** (Map p326; ☎ 07-572 4000; www.classicflyersnz.com; 8 Jean Batten Dr; admission adult/child $10/5; ☼ 10am-4pm) is a fascinating aviation museum with on-site cafe.

If you're interested in *marae*, **Huria Marae** (Map p326; ☎ 07-578 7838; www.teara.govt.nz; Te Kaponga St, Judea; admission free; ☼ varies) is on a nondescript suburban street but has sensational carvings both inside and out. Call to organise permission to visit.

Activities
TRAMPING

The free *Tauranga City Walkways* pamphlet details walks around Tauranga and Mt Maunganui, including the fascinating **Waikareao Estuary Walkway** (9km, two hours), and the popular **Mauao Base Track** (see p330) in Mt Maunganui. History buffs should pick up the free *Historic Tauranga* brochure and stroll around the town's cache of historic sites.

The backdrop to the Western Bay of Plenty is the rugged 70km-long **Kaimai Mamaku Forest Park** (off Map p326), 35km southwest of Tauranga on SH29, with tramps for the intrepid and basic camping (sites free to $5, huts $5 to $10). For more info see DOC's pamphlet *Kaimai Mamaku Forest Park Day Walks* ($1.50).

In the Wairoa River valley, 15km southwest of Tauranga just off SH29, **McLaren Falls Park** (off Map p326; ☎ 07-577 7000; www.tauranga.govt.nz/

mclarenfalls; admission free; ☼ 8am-5.30pm winter, to 7.30pm summer) is a 190-hectare lakeland park with great trees and picnic areas. There are three basic modern hostels here (dorms $20) and campsites ($5 per person). Also accessible from McLaren Falls is **Marshalls Animal Park** (off Map p326; ☎ 07-543 1099; www.marshallsanimalpark.co.nz; admission adult/child/family $10/5/30; ☼ 10am-2pm Wed & Thu, to 4.30pm Sat & Sun) which has family fun such as animal petting, a flying fox, playground and pony rides.

SWIMMING WITH DOLPHINS

The waters around Tauranga are particularly blessed with dolphins and even the odd whale in summer. Several operators offer a chance to see or even swim with them.

Butler's Swim With Dolphins (☎ 0508 288 537, 07-578 3197; www.swimwithdolphins.co.nz; full-day trips adult/child $125/100; ☼ trip leaves Tauranga 9am, Mt Maunganui 9.30am) Even without dolphins, the trips are always entertaining, particularly with Cap'n Butler, a real old salt who protested against nuclear testing at Mururoa Atoll.

Dolphin Seafaris (☎ 0800 326 8747, 07-577 0105; www.nzdolphin.com; half-day trip adult/child $140/90; ☼ 8am) Eco-attuned trips departing Tauranga and Mt Maunganui.

South Sea Vagabond (☎ 07-579 6376; www.southseasailing.com; trips from adult/child $120/85). Runs trips on an 18m catamaran. Kayaks available for nonswimmers.

FISHING & DIVING

The Bay of Plenty is renowned for its marine life and fishing – especially big game such as marlin and mako sharks, and snapper for your suppertime too. A daylong fishing trip will cost around $70 to $90 per person, with several companies offering 24-hour trips for around $120. The i-SITE can assist with bookings.

Bay Fishing Charters (☎ 0800 229 347; www.bayfishingcharters.co.nz) Small-group half- and full-day fishing charters on the good ship *Resolution*.

Blue Ocean Charters (☎ 0800 224 278; www.blueocean.co.nz) Fishing, diving and sightseeing trips (including one to Tuhua Island) on the TS *Ohorere*, MV *Te Kuia* and MV *Ratahi*.

Dive HQ (Map p323; ☎ 07-578 4050; www.divehqtauranga.co.nz; 213 Cameron Rd; courses from $600, trips from $95) PADI-qualifying courses or trips to local wrecks and reefs, plus gear rental.

Earth2ocean (☎ 07-571 5286; www.earth2ocean.co.nz; courses from $500, trips from $100) Runs an extensive range of diving courses and trips.

Fat Boy Charters (☎ 07-575 5986; fatboycharters@xtra.co.nz) Runs small-group fishing and diving trips on a 7m runabout.

Tauranga Marine Charters (☎ 07-552 6283; www.taurangamarinecharters.co.nz) Full-day fishing trips and diving trips once a month, on the MV *Manutere*.

KAYAKING
The Wairoa River is great for kayaking, offering something for paddlers at all levels. **Waimarino Adventure Park** (off Map p326; ☎ 07-576 4233; www.waimarino.com; 36 Taniwha Pl, Bethlehem; kayak tours from $55, park day-pass adult/child $39/30), on the banks of the river, offers freedom kayak hire for leisurely paddles along 12km of flat water, runs self-guided tours further up the river, and sea kayaking trips. Its Glowworm Tour ($120 per person) is a magical after-dark journey at McLaren Falls Park where you slip into a secret glowworm-filled wonderland. Waimarino also has an adventure park with a kayak slide, diving board, ropes course, warm pools and wildlife-spotting – a great place to spend a day, especially if there are children in tow.

WHITE-WATER RAFTING & SLEDGING
White-water rafting is popular around Tauranga, particularly on the Wairoa River, although it's definitely a rafting trip for thrill-seekers. The Wairoa's levels are controlled by a dam, so can only be rafted 26 days of the year: advance bookings are essential. You can find a list of rafting operators on p310.

OTHER ACTIVITIES
If you're new to water sports and want to get safely into the action, contact **Elements Watersports** (☎ 0800 486 729; www.elementsonline.co.nz; lessons per hr from $20). It offers tuition in sailing, windsurfing, powerboating and jetskiing, and has gear for hire.

Landlubbers might also consider jumping out of a plane…or maybe they won't. **Tauranga Tandem Skydiving** (Map p326; ☎ 07-576 7990; www.tandemskydive.co.nz; Tauranga Airport; jumps 8000/10,000/12,000ft $245/275/345) with views of White Island, Mount Ruapehu and the East Cape.

Tours
Adventure Bay of Plenty (☎ 0800 238 267; www.adventurebop.co.nz; 2hr/half-day/full-day tours from $85/125/150) Offers an enticing array of adventure tours by boat, kayak, mountain bike and horse. Matakana Island day tours cost $180.

Mount Classic Tours (☎ 07-574 1779; www.mctours.co.nz; 3-6 day tours $1675-3445) Longer tours around the Bay of Plenty including accommodation and most meals.

No.8 Farm Tours (☎ 07-579 3981; www.no8farmtours.co.nz; tours $210) Half-day 4WD tours of a working NZ farm, featuring shearing, milking, sheep dogs, deer and morning tea.

Tauranga Tasting Tours (☎ 07-544 1383; www.tastingtours.co.nz; tours $130) Whips around a local brewery, Mills Reef and Morton Estate wineries, and back to town for cocktails.

Touring Company (☎ 07-577 0057; www.newzealandadventure.co.nz; tours from $140) Half- and full-day local scenic tours and trips further afield to Waitomo, Rotorua and White Island.

Or take to the sky on one of the following aerial escapades – most departing Tauranga Airport (p326) – book through the i-SITE or directly. Minimum passenger numbers apply.
Aerius Helicopters (☎ 0800 864 354; www.aerius.co.nz; flights from $59) Local flights and excursions as far as Waitomo and White Island.

Air Discovery (☎ 0800 247 347, 07-575 7588; www.airdiscovery.co.nz; flights from $299) Offers one- to two-hour fixed-wing flights over White Island and Mt Tarawera.

Gyrate (☎ 07-575 6583; www.gyrate.co.nz; flights from $95) Flights in a gyroplane (the jetski of the sky), from local, scenic flights to learn-to-fly packages.

M*A*S*H Chopper Scenic Flights (☎ 07-572 4077; www.adventureaviation.co.nz; flights 12/20min $110/150) As seen on TV but without Hot Lips Houlihan. City and surrounds.

Festivals & Events
This town is no cultural desert; events on the calendar include the following:
National Jazz Festival (☎ 07-577 7018; www.jazz.org.nz) An Easter extravaganza of big blowers and scoobee-doobee-doobop, with concerts and food galore.

Tauranga Arts Festival (☎ 07-577 7018; www.taurangafestival.co.nz) Kicking off on Labour weekend in October (in odd-numbered years), showcasing dance, comedy, plays and other things arty.

Sleeping
BUDGET
Tauranga Tourist Park (Map p326; ☎ 07-578 3323; www.taurangatouristpark.co.nz; 9 Mayfair St; unpowered/powered sites $24/28, cabins from $50; 🖳) Located on the harbour edge, this is a good option for tenters and campervans with nice grassed sites and a new TV lounge. The amenities are a bit poky, but it's all well maintained, clean and tidy.

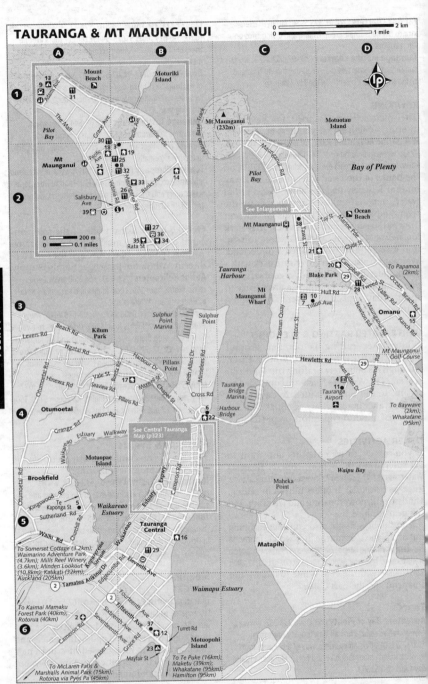

TAURANGA & MT MAUNGANUI

Just the Ducks Nuts Backpackers (Map p326; ☎ 07-576 1366; www.justtheducksnuts.co.nz; 6 Vale St; dm from $24, d with/without bathroom $62/56; 🖴 🛜) Just out of the town centre, this is a friendly place with colourful rooms, a fulsome library, TVs and videos strewn about and quirky touches like flowers planted in a bathtub and duck-themed toilets – like a university share-house minus the parties! Free shuttles to/from the bus stop; self-contained flats also available.

Loft 109 Backpackers (Map p323; ☎ 07-579 5638; www.loft109.co.nz; upstairs, 109 Devonport Rd; dm/d/tr $25/58/80; 🖴) This central spot feels like somebody's flat, with an intimate kitchen and lounge, rooftop balconies in upper rooms, and (oddly) a boat built into the roof. It's bright with plenty of skylights and a gas fire for colder days.

Harbourside City Backpackers (Map p323; ☎ 07-579 4066; www.backpacktauranga.co.nz; upstairs, 105 The Strand; dm/d from $28/72; 🖴 🛜) Enjoy sea views from this sociable hostel, handy to the Strand's bars. Rooms are smallish but clean, and you'll spend more time on the roof terrace anyway. There's no car park, but down the road is a public car park that's empty at the right time.

Tauranga YHA (Map p323; ☎ 07-578 5064; www.yha.co.nz; 171 Elizabeth St; unpowered sites/dm $36/28, d with/without bathroom $80/72; 🖴 🛜) A well-kept, deceptively big YHA with a big grassy backyard and a nearby mangrove swamp boardwalk to explore. Camping spots are spot-on; inviting dorms have individual lockers. There's info available on local coastal-care policies and a noticeboard for all things green.

MIDRANGE

Ambassador Motor Inn (Map p326; ☎ 0800 735 294, 07-578 5665; 9 Fifteenth Ave; www.ambassador-motorinn. co.nz; d/f from $105/165; 🛜 🖴) On one of the main roads into town, this tidy motor inn has noise-reducing glass for peaceful sleeps and family-friendly facilities including a swimming pool and trampoline. Some rooms have spa baths; all have kitchen facilities. The interiors are a bit '90s (not particularly ambassadorial), but spotlessly clean.

Roselands Motel (Map p323; ☎ 07-578 2294; www.roselands.co.nz; 21 Brown St; d/ste from $115/135; 🛜) Tarted up with splashes of orange paint and new linen, this sweet, old-style motel is in a quiet but central location. Expect roomy units (all with kitchens), highchairs for the kids and yoga lessons by arrangement. Don't mess with the resident cat...

Puriri Park Boutique Hotel (Map p323; ☎ 0800 4787 474, 07-577 1480; www.puriri.co.nz; 32 Cameron Rd, ste $130-225; 🖴) With large rooms (all with either terrace or balcony), king-sized beds, spas, swimming pool and secure parking, this upmarket motel is popular with wandering business bods. Picasso the turtle surveys proceedings from the lobby.

Harbour City Motor Inn (Map p323; ☎ 07-571 1435; www.taurangaharbourcity.co.nz; 50 Wharf St; d from $150; 🛜) In the middle of town with plenty of parking, this newish motor inn has all the mod cons such as a spa bath, TV and business desk in every room. Friendly staff offer sound local advice on your itinerary.

Tauranga on the Waterfront (Map p323; ☎ 0800 109 007, 07-578 7079; www.thetauranga.co.nz; 1 Second Ave; d/ste from $150/195; 🖴) This quiet place, only a short walk to the centre, has some excellent harbour-view suites if you're feeling romantic. Some rooms have deluxe spa baths that will get you back into the mood if the architecture fails you.

TOP END

Hotel on Devonport (Map p323; ☎ 07-578 2668; www. hotelondevonport.net.nz; 72 Devonport Rd; d/ste $160/200) City-centre Devonport is top of the town, with bay-view rooms, noise-reducing glass, slick interiors and sassy staff, all of which appeal to business travellers and luxury weekenders.

Sebel Trinty Wharf (Map p326; ☎ 0800 937 373, 07-577 8700; www.mirvachotels.com; 51 Dive Cres; d from $180; 🖵 🛜 🛋) This blocky high-rise is on the water's edge near the harbour bridge. A slick contemporary lobby – all retro white vinyl and trendy plush greys – leads to the in-house restaurant Halo, a key player in the local cuisine scene. Rooms are supersized and luxurious in tones au naturel. Amenities include an underutilised gym and infinity-edge swimming pool.

Eating

Devonport Rd is the place to grab lunch, but places on the Strand excel at dinner and drinks to follow. Tauranga's pubs also do solid meals (see Drinking, right).

Fresh Fish Market (Map p323; ☎ 07-578 1789; 1 Dive Cres; meals from $5; 🕑 lunch & dinner) A local legend serving up fresh fish and chips right on the water's edge.

Naked Grape (Map p323; ☎ 07-579 5555; 97 The Strand; breakfast & lunch $7-21, dinner mains $28-32; 🕑 7am-late) With cheery staff, wine-coloured rugs and lilting jazz, this hip Strand wine bar draws the daytime crowds with pastas, pizzas, salads, good coffee and beaut breakfasts. At night it's moodier, with mains like honey-braised lamb and lemon-marinated chicken breast.

Shima (Map p323; ☎ 07-571 1382; 15 Wharf St; mains $10-21; 🕑 lunch & dinner Mon-Sat) Shima is a simple, unpretentious sushi and sashimi bar, hung with Japanese fans, umbrellas and lanterns. Bento boxes and set-price menus are great bang for your buck.

Mediterraneo Café (Map p323; ☎ 07-577 0487; 62 Devonport Rd; mains $12-19; 🕑 7am-4pm Mon-Fri; 7.30am-4pm Sat, 8am-4pm Sun) A hot spot, reeling with regulars enjoying terrific coffee and scrumptious all-day breakfasts. Order off the blackboard or from the cabinet stuffed with sandwiches, flans and cakes. Lunchtime crowds can be frantic (but the chicken salad is worth it).

Collar & Thai (Map p323; ☎ 07-577 6655; Goddards Centre, 21 Devonport Rd; mains $16-30; 🕑 lunch Mon-Sat, dinner daily) No tie required at this upstairs, upper-end eatery that artfully elaborates on Thai standards and uses plenty of fresh seafood. This place has good-value lunch specials.

Little India (Map p323; ☎ 07-579 0910; 113 The Strand; mains $17-20; 🕑 lunch & dinner; **V**) Part of a consistent nationwide chain, this flavoursome curry house offers the best value on the Strand, especially for lunch specials. Outdoor tables for a hot night and a hot prawn *jhalfrezee*.

Zeytin (Map p323; ☎ 07-579 0099; 83 The Strand; mains $19-27; 🕑 lunch & dinner Tue-Sun) Ask the locals to name their favourite restaurant, and odds-on they'll name Zeytin – a real Turkish delight. Real food, real cheap, with something for everyone along the lines of kebabs, delicious homemade breads, dips and healthy salads, wood-fired pizza and a few exotic surprises.

Bravo (Map p323; ☎ 07-578 4700; Red Sq; mains $23-33; 🕑 breakfast, lunch & dinner; **V**) This trendy, well-regarded restaurant and bar is a pleasant spot for breakfast, flash sandwiches, salads, wood-fired pizza and freshly squeezed juices. There's outside seating on the pedestrianised street and a few good vegetarian options.

Somerset Cottage (off Map p326; ☎ 07-576 6889; 30 Bethlehem Rd, Bethlehem; mains $35; 🕑 lunch Wed-Fri, dinner Tue-Sun) The most awarded restaurant in the Bay, Somerset Cottage is a simple-but-elegant venue for that special treat. The food is highly seasonal, made from the best NZ ingredients, impressively executed without being too fussy. Standout dishes include blue cheese soufflé, duck with coconut kumara and the famous liquorice ice cream.

Self caterers should swing by **Pak N Save** (Map p326; ☎ 07-578 7037, 476 Cameron Rd; 🕑 8am-10pm) or the fruit-and-veg **City Markets** (Map p323; ☎ 07-577 0270; cnr Willow & Hamilton Sts; 🕑 9am-5pm Mon-Fri, to noon Sat).

Drinking

De Bier Haus (Map p323; ☎ 07-928 0833; 109 The Strand; 🕑 11am-late) With a pavement packed with happy punters, this hot Haus features Belgian beers and sophisticated environs. The interior's a classic manly hunting lodge with an antler or two in the midst. Kitchen-work is swift and savvy, turning out Euro-offerings such as German sausage, *brezels, moules, frites* and an excellent squid salad (mains $16 to $30).

Crown & Badger (Map p323; ☎ 07-571 3038; cnr The Strand & Wharf St; admission free; 🕑 9am-late) A particularly convincing Brit boozer that does pukka pints of Tennent's and Guinness, and food (mains $13 to $20) along the lines of bangers and mash. Things get lively at the weekends when live bands play.

Cornerstone (Map p323; ☎ 07-928 1120; 55 The Strand; admission free; ☺ 10am-late) A cheerful watering hole attended by on-the-ball staff and a mature crowd (let's say over 25). A solid no-surprises menu offers whopping meals (mains $12 to $35), while sports fans can watch the game on the big telly and groovers can swing a hip (live music Thursday to Sunday).

Entertainment

Colosseum (Map p323; ☎ 07-571 0718; www.colosseum bar.co.nz; 17 Harington St; admission varies; ☺ 7pm-late Thu, 8pm-3am Fri & Sat) Your first choice for big-screen sports (30 screens!) and live music (Katchafire, dub DJs, Hendrix tribute bands etc).

Buddha Lounge (Map p323; ☎ 07-928 1516; www. thebuddhalounge.co.nz; upstairs, 61b The Strand; entry price varies; ☺ 7pm-late Thu, 8pm-3am Fri & Sat) A cocktail lounge and dance venue hosting local and visiting DJs.

There are two cinemas in town: the art-house **Rialto** (Map p323; ☎ 07-577 0445; www.rialtotau ranga.co.nz; Goddards Centre, 21 Devonport Rd; tickets adult/child $15/9; ☺ vary) and the megaplex **Baycity Cinemas** (Map p323; ☎ 07-577 0800; www.bay citycinemas.co.nz; 45 Elizabeth St; tickets adult/child $15/9; ☺ 10.30am-late).

Getting There & Away

AIR

Air New Zealand (Map p323; ☎ 07-577 7300; www.air newzealand.co.nz; cnr Devonport Rd & Elizabeth St ☺ 9am-5pm Mon-Fri) has daily direct flights to Auckland, Wellington and Christchurch, with connections to other centres.

BUS

InterCity (☎ 09-583 5780; www.intercity.co.nz) tickets and timetables are available at the i-SITE. It runs buses to destinations including the following:

Destination	Price	Duration	Frequency
Auckland	$45	4¼hr	6 daily
Hamilton	$31	2-3hr	5 daily
Rotorua	$25	1½hr	4 daily
Taupo	$40	3hr	4 daily
Wellington	$96	9hr	3 daily

Naked Bus (☎ 0900 625 33; www.nakedbus.com) offers substantial fare savings when you book in advance. Its services connect Tauranga with a number of destinations including those listed below:

Destination	Price	Duration	Frequency
Auckland	$25	4¼hr	2 daily
Hamilton	$22	2hr	2 daily
Napier	$57	12hr	1 daily
Rotorua	$11	1½hr	3 daily
Taupo	$29	6hr	3 daily
Wellington	$41	12½hr	1 daily
Whakatane	$19	1½hr	1 daily

Bay Hopper (☎ 0800 422 928; www.baybus.co.nz) runs the Twin City Express bus twice daily between Tauranga/Mt Maunganui and Rotorua via Te Puke ($11, 1½ hours). Bay Hopper also runs the a Whakatane–Tauranga Link bus from Monday to Saturday, ($12, two hours), with onward connections to Ohope and Opotiki.

Luxury & Coastline Shuttles (☎ 0800 454 678, 07-574 9600; www.coastlineshuttles.co.nz) runs airport transfers to Auckland ($90), Hamilton ($75) and Rotorua ($90), and runs from Tauranga Airport into Central Tauranga ($15).

CAR
If you're heading to Hamilton on route K, don't forget the toll road costs $1.

Getting Around
Tauranga's bright yellow **Bay Hopper** (☎ 0800 4229 287; www.baybus.co.nz) buses run Monday to Saturday to most locations around the area, including Mt Maunganui ($2.50, 15 minutes) and Papamoa ($3, 30 minutes). There's a central stop on Wharf St; timetables available from the i-SITE. The **Mt Maunganui Ferry** (☎ 07-579 1325; www.kiwicoastcruises.co.nz; one-way adult/child $8/5; ☺ Dec-Mar) to/from Mt Maunganui departs the Strand; ask the i-SITE for a schedule.

Numerous car-rental agencies have offices in Tauranga, including **Rent-a-Dent** (Map p326; ☎ 0800 736 823, 07-578 1772; www.rentadent.co.nz; 19 Fifteenth Ave) and **Rite Price Rentals** (Map p326; ☎ 0800 250 251; www.ritepricerentals.co.nz; 25 Totara St, Mt Maunganui).

A taxi from the centre of Tauranga to the airport costs around $18. Local taxi companies:
Citicabs (☎ 07-577 0999)
Tauranga Mount Taxis (☎ 07-578 6086)

MT MAUNGANUI

pop 18,600

Named after the hulking 232m hill that punctuates the sandy peninsula occupied by the township, up-tempo Mt Maunganui is often just called 'the Mount', or Mauao, which translates as 'caught by the light of day'. It's considered part of greater Tauranga, but really is an enclave unto itself, with great cafes and restaurants, hip bars and fab beaches. Sun-seekers flock to the Mount in summer, supplied by an increasing number of 10-storey apartment towers studding the spit.

Information

The friendly **Mt Maunganui i-SITE** (Map p326; ☎ 07-575 5099; www.bayofplentynz.com; Salisbury Ave; ⏱ 9am-5pm) will assist you with information and bookings.

Sights & Activities

The Mount lays claim to being NZ's premier surf city (they teach surfing at high school!). Carve up the waves at **Mount Beach**, which has an 100m artificial surf reef not far offshore, or there's sheltered-beach swimming on the western side of the peninsula. To learn to surf, try the following operators:

Backdoor (Map p326; ☎ 07-575 7831; www.backdoor.co.nz; 24 Pacific Ave; 2hr lesson $66)

Hibiscus (☎ 07-575 3792; www.surfschool.co.nz; 2hr/2-day lesson $80/150) Run by experienced surfer Rebecca Taylor.

Mount Surfshop (Map p326; ☎ 07-575 9133; www.mountsurfshop.co.nz; 96 Maunganui Rd; rental per day wetsuit/surfboard $15/40, 2hr lesson $60)

New Zealand Surf School (☎ 021 477 873; www.nzsurfschools.co.nz; 1/2hr lesson $50/80)

To learn more about surfing in the area (and beyond) visit the excellent **Mount Surf Museum** (Map p326; ☎ 07-927 7234; www.mountsurfshop.co.nz; 139 Totara St; admission free; ⏱ 9am-5pm Mon-Sat, 9.30am-5pm Sun). Don't fancy surfing? Learn kiteboarding with **Assault** (☎ 027 245 7540; www.assault.co.nz; 1hr lesson $100), or try rock climbing at the **Rock House** ((Map p326; ☎ 07-572 4920; www.therockhouse.co.nz; 9 Triton Ave; admission adult/child $14/10; ⏱ noon-late Tue-Fri, 10am-6pm Sun).

Mauao itself can be explored via **walking trails**, winding around it and leading up to the summit. The summit walk takes about an hour and gets steep near the top. You can also climb around the rocks on **Moturiki Island**, which adjoins the peninsula. The island and the base of Mauao also make up the **Mauao Base Track** (3½km, 45 minutes), wandering through magical groves of pohutukawa trees that bloom between November and January. **Mauao Tours** (☎ 027 218 1816, 07-575 6961; www.mauaotours.co.nz; tours from 1hr $30) runs guided walking tours around the Mount and Papamoa with a focus on Maori history.

After all that walking you'll have earned a soak at **Mt Maunganui Hot Saltwater Pools** (Map p326; ☎ 07-575 0868; www.tcal.co.nz; 9 Adams Ave; admission adult/child $9.50/7; ⏱ 6am-10pm Mon-Sat, 8am-10pm Sun) at the foot of the Mount. For traditional swimming-pool action plus a wave pool, hydroslide and aqua aerobics, visit **Baywave** (off Map p326; ☎ 07-575 0276; www.tcal.co.nz; cnr Girven & Gloucester Rds; admission adult/child $6.50/4.50; ⏱ 6am-9pm Mon-Fri, 7am-7pm Sat & Sun).

Sleeping

Mt Maunganui is a hugely popular holiday destination with plenty of accommodation – particularly apartment style – with prices higher than Tauranga.

Pacific Coast Lodge & Backpackers (Map p326; ☎ 0800 666 622; www.pacificcoastlodge.co.nz; 432 Maunganui Rd; dm/d from $24/70; 🖥) Not far from the action, this efficiently run, clean hostel is the pick of the bunch for those who want a good night's sleep, with drinkers encouraged to go into town after 10pm. Purpose-built bunkrooms are roomy and spangled with jungle murals.

Mount Backpackers (Map p326; ☎ 07-575 0860; www.mountbackpackers.co.nz; 87 Maunganui Rd; dm/d from $25/70; 🖥 🛜) A tight but tidy hostel, bolstered by location – close to the beach and a mere stagger from the restaurants and bars – plus extras like a travel desk, job board, cheap weekly rates and deals on activities including surf lessons.

Beachside Holiday Park (Map p326; ☎ 07-575 4471; www.mountbeachside.co.nz; 1 Adams Ave; sites $30-50; 🛜) With three different camping areas all nestled into the base of Mt Maunganui, this community-run park has spectacular camping with all the expected facilities, plus it's handy to the saltwater pools and a strip of good eateries.

Cosy Corner Holiday Park (Map p326; ☎ 07-575 5899; www.cosycorner.co.nz; 40 Ocean Beach Rd; powered sites $40, cabins & flats $75-155; 🖥 🛜 🛜) This spartan camping ground has a sociable feel, with barbecues, trampolines and a games room. Cabins may prove too cosy for some (and look elsewhere if you're allergic to Laminex), but beach convenience compensates.

Mount Maunganui B&B (Map p326; ☎ 07-575 4013; www.mountbednbreakfast.co.nz; 463 Maunganui Rd; s/d incl cooked breakfast from $60/100) This five-room B&B is on the main road into town and cops some traffic noise, but rooms are presentable (if a little tight). Don't expect too much and you'll be fine.

Westhaven Motel (Map p326; ☎ 07-575 4753; www. westhavenmotel.co.nz; 27a The Mall; d from $100; 🛜) The unmolested 1970s architecture here is soooo *Brady Bunch*, with wooden shelving between kitchen and lounge, and funky mirrors to re-tune your afro. Full kitchens are perfect for self-caterers, plus there are free fishing rods and dinghies. The cheapest hotel in miles.

Mission Belle Motel (Map p326; ☎ 0800 202 434; www.missionbellemotel.co.nz; cnr Victoria Rd & Pacific Ave; d/f $120/180; 🛜) With a distinctly Tex-Mex exterior (like something out of an old Clint Eastwood movie), this family-run motel goes all modern inside, with especially good two-storey family rooms with large bathtubs, plus sheltered barbecue and courtyard areas.

Belle Mer (Map p326; ☎ 0800 100 235, 07-575 0011; www.bellemer.co.nz; 53 Marine Pde; apt $190-450; 🛜 🐾) A classy beachside complex of two- and three-bedroom apartments, some with sea-view balconies and others opening onto private courtyards (though you'll more likely head for the resort-style pool terrace). Rooms are taste-fully decorated in warm tones with soft edges, and have everything you need for longer stays, with proper working kitchens and laundries.

Eating

our pick **Providores Urban Food Store** (Map p326; ☎ 07-572 1300; 19a Pacific Ave; meals $5-18; 🕑 7.30am-5pm; Ⓥ) Surf videos set the mood as your eyes peruse fresh-baked breads, buttery croissants, home-smoked meats and cheeses, organic jams and free-range eggs – perfect ingredients for a bang-up breakfast or a hamper-filling picnic on the beach. Superb!

Slow Fish (Map p326; ☎ 07-574 2949; shop 5, Twin Towers, Marine Pde; meals $6-19; 🕑 7am-4.30pm) There's no slacking about in the kitchen of this award-winning, eco-aware cafe, which promotes the art of savouring fine, locally sourced food. It's so popular you'll have to crowbar yourself in the door or pounce on any available alfresco seat, but it's absolutely worth it for its free-range eggs and ham, Greek salads and divine counter selection.

Gusto (Map p326; ☎ 07-575 5675; 200 Maunganui Rd; breakfast $5-15, lunch $12-16; 🕑 7am-4pm) This friendly spot keeps its menu affordable but interesting, with Kiwi standards such as lamb and kumara (sweet potato) given a refreshing treatment. Cool tunes; sassy staff.

Zambezi (Map p326; ☎ 07-575 4202; 108 Maunganui Rd; breakfast $9-16, lunch $13-18; 🕑 9am-4pm) A cheap-and-cheerful cafe serving burgers, panini and nice simple sandwiches. There's eggy brekkies and coffee of course, plus plenty of healthy options such as juices and salads. Licensed too, if you feel like a Mac's or Monteiths.

Astrolabe (Map p326; ☎ 07-574 8155; 82 Maunganui Rd; brunch $12-20, dinner $22-34; 🕑 10am-1am Mon-Sat, 9am-1am Sun) A clever combo of swish, style and Pacifica-rustica, Astrolabe is probably the Mount's best restaurant, catering largely to a deep-pocketed hip crowd who indulge in gourmet goodies like venison, confit duck and oysters. You can also come in for a bou-tique bevvie in the beer garden and a whack of pool.

Kwang Chow (Map p326; ☎ 07-575 5063; 241 Maunganui Rd; lunch/dinner $13/19; 🕑 lunch & dinner) This all-you-can-eat Chinese place is a local favourite with a bargain bite that maintains tasty flavours rather than resorting to a bland melange. Discount dinners from Monday to Wednesday.

Zeytin Café (Map p326; ☎ 07-574 3040; 118 Maunganui Rd; mains $19-27; 🕑 lunch & dinner Tue-Sun) Readers recommend Greco-Moroccan Zeytin for its slow-cooked tagines, spanakopita and mous-saka, plus live jazz or swing on Thursday nights. Stripy cushions and Arabic lanterns adorn the cavelike interior.

Self-caterers will find **New World** (Map p326; ☎ 07-572 7080; cnr Tweed St & Maunganui Rd; 🕑 7am-9pm) south of town.

Drinking

Latitude 37 (Map p326; ☎ 07-572 3037; 181 Maunganui Rd; 🕑 4pm-1am Mon, noon-1am Tue-Fri, 11.30am-1am Sat & Sun; 🛜) A classy, upmarket bar with stone-faced walls, fold-back windows and flaming torches out the front. A lot of folk come here to eat (brunch $14 to $26, dinner $21 to $42), but it's a beaut spot for a cold Heineken after a day in the surf.

Mount Mellick Hotel (Map p326; ☎ 07-574 0047; 317 Maunganui Rd; meals $9-28; 🕑 11am-1am) A blokey Irish pub with hefty meals, regular jam ses-sions and poker and quiz nights, plus live bands on weekends.

Rosie O'Grady's (Map p326; ☎ 07-575 3135; 2 Rata St; meals from $10; ☻ 7am-1am) Rosie's is slightly less blokey than the Mellick, with NZ boutique beers on tap, open-deck DJ nights, big screens and good-value pub grub.

Entertainment
Once the sun goes down, Mt Maunganui's pubs and bars often host live bands and DJs (see Drinking, p331). Go to the movies at **Cinema 4** (Map p326; ☎ 07-572 3311; www.baycitycinemas.co.nz; 249 Maunganui Rd; admission adult/child $15/9).

Getting There & Away
Mt Maunganui is across the harbour bridge from Tauranga, or accessible from the south via Te Maunga on SH2. See p329 for local Bay Hopper bus details. **InterCity** (☎ 09-583 5780; www.intercity.co.nz) and **Naked Bus** (☎ 0900 625 33; www.nakedbus.com) services also stop at Mt Maunganui, with fares similar to those to/from Tauranga (see p329). All buses depart the i-SITE.

The **Tauranga Ferry** (☎ 07-579 1325 www.kiwicoast cruises.co.nz; tickets one-way adult/child $8/5; ☻ Dec-Mar) to/from Tauranga departs Salisbury Wharf; ask the i-SITE for a schedule (see p330).

AROUND TAURANGA
Papamoa
pop 17,500
Papamoa is a fast-growing suburb near the edge of Mt Maunganui, separated now by just a paddock or two also destined for subdivision. Burgeoning with big new houses on pristine streets, parts of Papamoa have the air of a gated community about them. That said, the beaches beyond the sheltering dunes are truly spectacular, so you can't blame folk for moving in.

For speedsters, **Game On Activities** (☎ 07-572 4033; www.gameonactivities.co.nz; 176 Parton Rd, Papamoa; blokarting 15min $15; ☻ by arrangement) has NZ's first purpose-built course for land-based windsurfing on zippy 'blokarts'.

The huge **Papamoa Beach Top 10 Holiday Resort** (☎ 07-572 0816; www.papamoabeach.co.nz; 535 Papamoa Beach Rd; sites from $36, villas & units $120-210; ☐ ☎) is a spotless, modern park that has been primed and priced-up beyond its caravan-park origins, with an array of accommodation options, including self-contained villas.

With its angular corrugated-iron exterior and tasteful caneware furnishings, **Beach House Motel** (☎ 0800 429 999, 07-572 1424; www.beachhousemotel.co.nz; 224 Papamoa Beach Rd; d from $110; ☐ ☎ ☻) offers an upmarket version of the Kiwi bach holiday, relaxed and close to the beach.

Turkish to Go (☎ 07-542 1404; cnr Beach & Domain Rds; kebabs $8-12; ☻ lunch & dinner) wraps up very big small kebabs and even bigger big ones, with free coffee and apple tea.

Bluebiyou (☎ 07-572 2099; 559 Papamoa Beach Rd; mains $15-35; ☻ 11am-late) is a casual, breezy restaurant riding high on the dunes, serving big brunches and seafood specialities.

Tuhua (Mayor Island)
Commonly known as Mayor Island, this dormant volcano is located 35km north of Tauranga. The island is known for its black, glasslike obsidian rock and diverse bird life including a clutch of kiwi, introduced to the predator-free island in 2006. Walking tracks cut through the now-overgrown crater valley, and the northwest corner is a marine reserve. The area is managed by the Tuhua Trust Board and to land here you need permission from **DOC** (☎ 07-578 7677; taurangainfo@doc.govt.nz) with a $5 landing fee.

There's limited **camping and cabin accommodation** (☎ 07-578 7677; unpowered sites $10, dm from $10) on the island; bring your own food and water (there are no fridges). The landing fee is included in accommodation costs. Several boat-charter companies will take you to the island including Blue Ocean Charters (p324).

Matakana Island
Twenty-four kilometres long and forming, more or less, the seaward side of Tauranga harbour, Matakana Island is laced with secluded white-sand surf beaches on its eastern shore (for the experienced only) and enjoys a laid-back island lifestyle. The best way to explore it is on a **tour** with Adventure Bay of Plenty (see p325). Alternatively you can catch the **vehicle ferry** (☎ 0274 927 251; return passenger/car & passenger $8/50; ☻ departures 7.45am, 9am, 2pm & 4pm) from Omokoroa (between Tauranga and Katikati).

Katikati
pop 3580
'Katikat' to the locals, this small town was the only planned Ulster settlement in the world, and celebrates this history with colourful **murals** spangling the town's buildings – the moniker 'Mural Town' seems to have stuck.

The **Mural Town Information Centre** (☎ 07-549 1658; www.katikati.co.nz; 36 Main Rd; 9am-4.30pm Mon-Fri, 9.30am-2pm Sat, 10am-2pm Sun) sells a guide to the various murals for $2.50 (as well as doing other good deeds), but you can also take a small-group **guided tour** (☎ 07-549 0869; per person $4). From the information centre you can also explore the **Haiku Pathway**, rambling along the Uretara River past boulders inscribed with haiku verses.

Katikati Heritage Museum (☎ 07-549 0651; katikati .heritage.museum@xtra.co.nz; cnr SH2 & Wharawhara Rd; admission adult/child $6/4, minigolf adult/child $4/3; 8.30am-4.30pm) traces local history with an engaging mix of Maori artefacts and Ulster history, some moa bones and reputedly the largest bottle collection in the southern hemisphere. There's also a carvery serving roast lunches and dinners.

About 7km south of town, the 10-acre **Katikati Bird Gardens** (☎ 07-549 0912; www.bird gardens.co.nz; Walker Rd East; admission adult/child $9/4; 10am-4.30pm) is all aflap with native birdlife. There's a cafe and gallery here too.

The monastic-looking **Morton Estate** (☎ 07-552 0795; www.mortonestatewines.co.nz; SH2; 9.30am-5pm), one of NZ's bigger wineries, is located on SH2, 8km south of Katikati, and open for tastings and stock-ups. Try the famous chardonnay.

SLEEPING
Wanderlust Backpackers (☎ 07-549 5102; info@ wanderlustbackpackers.com; 5 Main Rd; dm/d $25/50;) Festooned with more than 80 rugby jumpers and 418 toy fire engines (!), Wanderlust is a pleasantly oddball hostel in a converted 1935 barbershop. The owners can help find you farm work (picking flowers, avocados and kiwifruit), and rope you into a poker game just as easily.

Kaimai View Motel (☎ 07-549 0398; www.kaimai view.co.nz; 78 Main Rd; d from $120;) Beyond a funky mural on the streetside wall, this jaunty, modern motel offers neat rooms with CD player, kitchenette and, in larger rooms, spa. Breakfast available on request.

Panorama Country Lodge (☎ 07-549 1882; www. panoramalodge.co.nz; 901 Pacific Coast Hwy; d from $170;) Run by jocular Brits, this neat little B&B is set in a diverse orchard 10km north of town, and lives up to its name with sweeping views of the bay. It's a real farm experience, with quail and alpacas wandering the grounds. Luxury rooms have extras beyond

brass beds and DVDs, including slippers and fresh coffee.

Warm Earth Cottage (☎ 07-549 0962; www. warmearthcottage.co.nz; 202 Thompson's Track; d $200) Reignite your romance or just simmer in simple pleasures at this rural idyll, 5km south of town then 2km west of SH2. Two pretty cottages sit by the Waitekohe River – they're electricity-less, so indulge in wood-fired outdoor baths and candlelit evenings. There's no kitchen either, so fire up the barbecue (generous barbecue packs $80). A big brunch is included in the price, as is the odd dram of moonshine.

EATING
Rustic Pumpkin (☎ 07-549 1924; 603 SH2; lunch $8-17; 8am-4pm; V) It's well worth going the extra 5km north of town for this cracker little cafe on the main road, which serves up generous portions of homemade soups, burgers, quiches, sandwiches and cakes. The cinnamon waffles and kumara curry are showstoppers.

Katz Pyjamas (☎ 07-549 1902; cnr SH2 & Beach Rd; meals $12-22; 8am-4pm Mon-Fri) Royal blue outside, rude orange inside, this arty main-street cafe serves home-made soups, salads, panini and cakes and the best coffee in town.

Talisman Hotel (☎ 07-549 3218; 7 Main Rd; meals $15-36; lunch & dinner) The local pub, with occasional live music and karaoke, and the Landing restaurant serving all-day grub including pizza and steak.

Twickenham Café & Restaurant (☎ 07-549 1383; cnr SH2 & Mulgan St; lunch $13-29, dinner $24-38; 9.30am-3.30pm Tue-Sun; dinner from 5.30pm Tue-Sat) In a century-old villa surrounded by elegant gardens, this restaurant is a bit twee but makes amends with admirable Devonshire teas. Lunch and dinner runs along the lines of panini and rib-eye respectively.

Te Puke
pop 6775
Welcome to the 'Kiwifruit Capital of the World', a busy town during the picking season when there's plenty of work around for willing workers (see the boxed text, p334). The **Te Puke visitor information centre** (☎ 07-573 9172; www.tepuke.co.nz; 130 Jellicoe St; 8am-5pm Mon-Fri, 9am-noon Sat) is located in the same building as the public library (staff will confirm that 'Puke' rhymes with cookie, not fluke).

For the low-down on all things kiwifruit, swing into **Kiwi360** (☎ 0800 549 4360, 07-573 6340; www.kiwi360.com; 35 Young Rd, off SH2; admission adult/child

$20/6; 9am-5pm) at the turn-off for Maketu. Sitting among orchards of nashi pears, citrus, avocados and (you guessed it) kiwifruit, this visitor centre peels off a range of attractions including a 35-minute kiwicart orchard ride, kiwifruit viewing tower and a cafe serving up kiwifruit delights.

After something sweeter? About 10km south of Te Puke, **Comvita** (☎ 0800 493 782, 07-533 1987; www.comvita.com; 23 Wilson Rd South, Paengaroa; admission free; 8.30am-5pm, talks 10am & 2pm) is home to New Zealand's most famous honey- and bee-derived health-care products. There's a gallery, shop, cafe and educational talks twice daily. Grab a pot of vitamin E cream with bee pollen and manuka honey on the way out.

Not far from Comvita, **Spring Loaded** (☎ 0800 867 386, 07-533 1515; www.springloadedfunpark.co.nz; 316 SH33, Paengaroa; adult/child jetboat $95/45, 4WD $75/35, helicopter flights 10min $105; 8.30am-5pm summer, 9am-4.30pm winter) offers various adventures from jet-boat rides on a gorgeous stretch of the Kaituna River, to 'mud bug' 4WD trips, helicopter flights and rafting and sledging trips. There's a cafe and shop on-site.

There aren't many beds in Te Puke town itself, but home- and farmstays dapple the surrounding area: ask the visitor centre for a list. A pretty, private self-contained cottage, **Lazy Daze B&B** (☎ 07-573 8188; www.lazydazecottage. co.nz; 144 Boucher Ave; cottage d with/without breakfast $130/120, house $120) sits out the back of Mel and Sharron's property and has a relaxing deck overlooking its own garden. Delicious breakfast provisions are included and there's also a tidy two-bedroom, self-contained house available next door, sleeping six. Call for directions. Right on the main road of

town, the **Beacon** (☎ 07-573 7825; beacon.motel@ wave.co.nz; 173 Jellicoe St; s/d $99/120;) is an old-style, mustard-coloured motel. It's a bit noisy, but is passable if you're just passing through. There's a string of cheap burger joints and cafes along Jellicoe St. The lime-coloured **Pizza Place** (☎ 07-573 3324; 33 Jellicoe St; mains $9-14; 4.30pm-late) is the pick of them, serving decent discs.

Maketu
pop 1240

Take SH2 through Te Puke and turn left onto Maketu Rd, and you'll find yourself at this historic but rather shabby seaside town.

Maketu played a significant role in NZ's history as the landing site of *Te Arawa* canoe (see p304), which is commemorated with a somewhat underwhelming stone monument on the foreshore. Arguably, though, the town is more famous for **Maketu Pies** (☎ 07-533 2358; www.maketupies.co.nz; 6 Little Waihi Rd; pies from $3; 10am-3pm Mon-Fri), baked fresh daily here and employing a good proportion of the population. Very good pies they are, too.

Beach bums should head for **Newdick's Beach**, reached by following Town Point Rd to a small dirt track. It's on private property, so pay the $3-per-car donation at the gate. From here you can walk to Little Waihi, a few kilometres down the coast towards the estuary. Beachside horse treks can be had with **Briars Seaside Ride** (☎ 07-533 2582, 0274 062 477; www.briarshorsetrek.co.nz; Town Point Rd, 1½/2/3hr rides $70/90/120).

Maketu Beach Holiday Park (☎ 07-533 2165; www. maketubeach.co.nz; 1 Town Point Rd; powered sites $25, d $55-115) is a shabby last-resort resort, with campsites, cabins and motel rooms.

HOT FUZZ

The humble kiwifruit earns NZ over a billion dollars every year, and with the Bay of Plenty in the thick of the action, it's no wonder the locals are fond of this fruit.

The fruit's origins are in China, where it was called the monkey peach because they were considered ripe when the monkeys munched them. As they migrated to NZ, they were renamed the Chinese gooseberry – they were a lot smaller then, but canny Kiwis engineered them to more generous sizes and began exporting them in the 1950s. The fruit was then sexily rebranded the Zespri. Today the Zesprians grow two types of kiwifruit: the common fuzzy-covered green fruit, and the gold fruit with its smooth complexion. To learn more about the kiwifruit, visit Kiwi360 (see p333).

For visitors after a dollar or two, there's always kiwifruit work around the area – most of it during harvest (May and June) and odd jobs at other times. Enquire at Wanderlust backpackers in Katikati (p333), at regional i-SITEs, or check online at www.picknz.co.nz.

EASTERN BAY OF PLENTY

Stretching from Maketu to Opotiki, the Eastern Bay of Plenty's main drawcard is long stretches of sandy beaches with a backdrop of cliffs covered in majestic pohutukawa trees. It's beautiful country, and often overlooked, which is absolutely integral to its charm.

WHAKATANE
pop 17,700

A true pohutukawa paradise, the town of Whakatane (pronounced Fokka-tar-nay) sits in a natural harbour at the mouth of the river of the same name. It's the hub of the Rangitaiki agricultural district, but there's much more to Whakatane than farming – blissful beaches, a sunny main-street vibe and volcanic Whakaari (White Island) for starters. And (despite Nelson's protestations) it's officially the sunniest city in NZ!

Information

Whakatane Hospital (07-306 0999; www.bopdhb.govt. nz; cnr Stewart & Garaway Sts; 24hr) For emergency medical treatment.

Post office (www.nzpost.co.nz; 4 Commerce St) Also has foreign exchange.

Whakatane i-SITE (0800 942 528, 07-308 6058; www.whakatane.com; Quay St; 8am-5pm Mon-Fri, 10am-4pm Sat & Sun;) Free internet access (including 24-hour wi-fi on the terrace outside the building), tour bookings, accommodation and general enquiries for DOC.

Sights

Whakatane Museum & Gallery (07-306 0505; www. whakatanemuseum.org.nz; 11 Boon St; admission by donation; 10am-4.30pm Mon-Fri, 11am-3pm Sat & Sun) is an impressive regional museum with artfully presented displays on early Maori and European settlers. Of particular interest are the *taonga* of local Maori tracing their lineage back to the *Mataatua waka* (see the boxed text, p338), while the art gallery presents a varied program of NZ and international exhibitions.

Beside the roundabout is **Pohaturoa** (cnr The Strand & Commerce St), a large *tapu* (sacred) rock outcrop, where baptism, death, war and *moko* (tattoo) rites were performed. The Treaty of Waitangi was also signed here by Ngati Awa chiefs in 1840 and there's a monument to the Ngati Awa chief Te Hurinui Apanui. Another Maori site is the partially collapsed **Muriwai's Cave** (Te Ano o Muriwa), which once extended 122m into the hillside and sheltered 60 people, including Muriwai, Wairaka's aunt and famous seer. Two exquisitely carved **ceremonial waka** are displayed opposite the cave.

On the clifftops behind the town are two ancient Ngati Awa *pa* sites – **Te Papaka** and **Puketapu** – both of which offer sensational (and very defendable) outlooks over Whakatane. Tumbling down the cliffs, **Wairere Falls** (Te Wairere) occupies a deliciously damp nook, and once powered flax and flour mills and supplied Whakatane's drinking water.

Activities

MARINE MAMMAL–WATCHING, DIVING & FISHING

The sea along the Whakatane coast is alive with marine mammals including dolphins (25,000 of them!), fur seals, orca, pilot and minke whales; as well as bird life such as gannets and little blue penguins. The area is also renowned for diving and big-game fishing. Several operators can get you out among it, including swimming with the dolphins.

Whale & Dolphin Watch (0800 354 7737, 07-308 2001; www.whalesanddolphinwatch.co.nz; 96 The Strand; view adult/child $110/80, swim $150/130; 7.15am, 8.30am & 1pm) runs dolphin-viewing and swimming trips year-round.

Run by White Island Tours (see p339), **Dolphin & Whale Nature Rush** (0800 733 529, 07-308 9588; www.dolphinandwhale.co.nz; 15 The Strand; trips adult/ child $80/50; 10am daily Jan-Mar) offers a two-hour trip out to Motuhora (Whale Island), with plenty of critter-spotting in the sea and sky.

Diveworks Charters (0800 308 5896, 07-308 5896; www.whaleislandtours.com; tours per person $85) runs two-hour ecotrips out to Motuhora, plus longer trips where you can swim with dolphins and seals (adult/child $150/125), and fishing and diving trips.

See also Dive White Island (p339).

TRAMPING

The i-SITE sells *Discover the Walks Around Whakatane* ($2), a booklet detailing walks ranging from 30 minutes to half a day. Most walks are part of the **Nga Tapuwae o Toi Track** (Footsteps of Toi; 13 hours, 18km), a large loop that takes in Ohope Beach and several historic sites along the way. A flatter option is the **River Walk** (two to three hours), following the Whakatane River past the

ROTORUA & THE BAY OF PLENTY

WHAKATANE

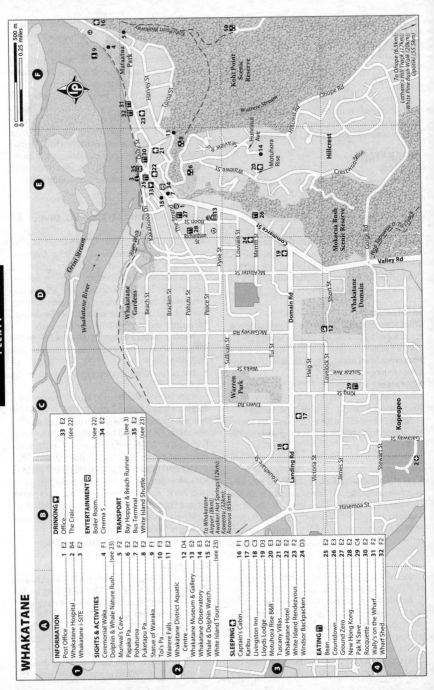

Botanical Gardens, Muruwai's Cave and on to Wairaka's statue.

Another popular stroll is **Kohi Point Walkway** (four hours, 5.5km), which extends through the Kohi Point Scenic Reserve, passing lookouts and **Toi's Pa** (Kapua te Rangi), reputedly the oldest *pa* site in NZ. Other walkways include **Latham's Hill Track** (1½ to two hours), starting 17km south of town on SH30, and **White Pine Bush Walk** (30 minutes), accessible by wheelchair and pram and starting 20km south of Whakatane.

OTHER ACTIVITIES
Whakatane District Aquatic Centre (☎ 07-308 4192; www.tlc.net.nz; 28 Short St; admission adult/child $3.60/1.80; ☺ 6am-8pm Mon-Fri, 7am-6pm Sat & Sun) has indoor and outdoor pools, spa pools and a waterslide.

Whakatane Observatory (☎ 07-308 6495; www. skyofplenty.com; Hurinui Ave, Hillcrest; adult/child/family $10/4/15; ☺ dusk Tue & Fri) offers a great chance to star-spot when the sky is clear.

Tours
For boat and helicopter tours out to the explosive Whakaari (White Island), see p339.

Matata Eco Tours (☎ 0800 628 282, 07-322 2102; www.matataecotours.co.nz; tours per person half/full day $75/135) runs tours of the Tarawera Valley where you can learn about the native flora, fauna, and cultural heritage of the area.

Sleeping
Whakatane Hotel (☎ 07-307 1670; whakatanehotel@ newzealandhotelgroup.co.nz; 79 The Strand; dm/s $20/40, d $50-65) This art-deco classic has basic rooms to suit lively backpackers – those who love to be in the thick of it or those who carry earplugs to muffle weekend band noise.

Windsor Backpackers (☎ 07-308 8040; www.windsor lodge-backpackers.co.nz; 10 Merritt St; dm/s $25/35, d $50-80; 🖳 🛜) Whakatane's best backpackers occupies a converted funeral parlour, so expect a restful sleep. Excellent rooms range from dorms to motel-standard doubles, and the communal kitchen, lounge area and barbecue courtyard are spacious and tidy.

Karibu (☎ 07-307 8276; www.karibubackpackers.co.nz; 13 Landing Rd; sites $28, dm $25-27, s/tw $35/60, 2br units $80-150; 🖳) This converted house a wee walk from town has basic dorms, two-bed units, and a garden out the back with a few tent sites. Barbecues and free bikes available.

Lloyds Lodge (☎ 07-307 8005; www.lloydslodge. co.nz; 10 Domain Rd; dm $27; 🖳) In an old house plastered with grandma-style floral wallpaper on every available surface, Lloyds is an intimate, friendly option, with just 16 beds and a homey kitchen-dining area. The manager runs a podiatry clinic in the front room if you've stubbed your toe.

Captain's Cabin (☎ 07-308 5719; www.captainscabin. co.nz; 23 Muriwai Dr; r $115) In a serene part of town with breathtaking views of the harbour entrance, this homely self-contained unit is the perfect spot for those hanging round for a few days. A cosy living area cleverly combines bedroom, lounge, kitchen and dining, with a second smaller room and bijou bathroom – all sweetly decorated along nautical lines.

Livingston Inn (☎ 0800 770 777, 07-308 5665; www. livingston.co.nz; 42 Landing Rd; d/f $125/210; 🛜) The ranch-style Livingston remains one of the better motels in town, with spacious, well-kept units that are popular with the motor-inn crowd. Large spas in executive suites are a great fringe benefit.

White Island Rendezvous (☎ 0800 242 299; www. whiteisland.co.nz; The Strand; d/f from $130/150, 2br apt per 4 people $260; 🛜) An immaculate 26-room complex run by the on-the-ball White Island Tour people. Lots of balcony and deck space for enjoying the sea air, with interiors decked out in timber floors for a beach cottage vibe. Deluxe rooms come with spas and there are facilities for travellers with disabilities.

Tuscany Villas (☎ 0800 801 040, 07-308 2244; www.tuscanyvillas.co.nz; 57 The Strand; d $140-200; 🛜) This modern model may be a long way from Florence, but still offers a few rays of Italian sunshine with interesting architecture, wraparound balcony and attractive floral plantings wherever there is room. Rooms are luxurious and comfy, with spa pools and superking beds.

Motuhora Rise B&B (☎ 07-307 0224; www.motu horarise.com; 2 Motuhora Rise; s/d incl breakfast $200/215; 🛜) At the top of the town in both senses (the driveway is steep!), this hilltop spot affords a distant glimpse of Whale Island. You can expect a gourmet cheeseboard on arrival, along with other extras such as a DVD home-theatre suite, outdoor spa pool on decking, and fishing rods and golf clubs.

Eating
Bean (☎ 07-307 0494; 72 The Strand; bagels & soup $5-12; ☺ 8.30am-4pm Mon-Fri, Sat 9.30am-1.30pm) The loungiest spot in town to get good coffee (roasted on the premises). Pull up a chair,

WAKA LIKE A MAN

Whakatane's name originated some eight centuries ago, 200 years after the original Maori settlers arrived here. The warrior Toroa and his family sailed into the estuary in a huge ocean-going *waka* (canoe), the *Mataatua*. As the men went ashore to greet local leaders, the tide turned, and the *waka* – with all the women on board – drifted out to sea. Toroa's daughter, Wairaka, cried out *'E! Kia whakatane au i ahau!'* (Let me act as a man!) and, breaking the traditional *tapu* on women steering a *waka*, she took up the paddle and brought the boat safely ashore. A whimsical **statue of Wairaka** stands proudly atop a rock in Whakatane's harbour in commemoration of her brave deed.

and get yourself going with a quick fix and a freshly baked biscuit or bagel.

Wally's on the Wharf (☎ 07-307 1100; The Wharf, The Strand; meals $6-18; ⏲ 11am-8pm) Wally sure knows a thing or two about fish and chips. Hoki, snapper, flounder, john dory and tarakihi – done in the deep fry, on the grill or in a burger. Whitebait fritters in season, and chips that score well on the crispometer.

New Hong Kong (☎ 07-308 6864; 32 Richardson St; mains $6-23; ⏲ lunch Tue-Fri, dinner Tue-Sun) This no-fuss Chinese restaurant does Sino-Kiwi grub such as chop suey, chow mein and, of course, chips. Lunch deals ($6) are a good bet, as is the two-hour $10-dish 'happy hour' from 5.30pm.

Ground Zero (☎ 07-308 8548; 163 The Strand; meals $7-17; ⏲ 8am-4.30pm) It's a good sign when the staff can share a laugh with the boss! Ground Zero's chipper vibe is infectious, bolstered by cafe delights like Jamaican chicken burgers, veggie stacks with hummus and garlic aioli, Moroccan wraps, and serious coffee and cakes. Sunny outdoor tables, too.

Wharf Shed (☎ 07-308 5698; The Wharf, The Strand; lunch $11-21, dinner $27-45; ⏲ lunch & dinner) An award winner for beef and lamb but famous for its fish dishes, which include locally bagged crayfish, corpulent mussels and fresh Pacific Oysters. Right on the waterside with alfresco dining on balmy evenings.

Rocquette (☎ 07-307 0722; 23 Quay St; lunch $14-30, dinner $18-35; ⏲ 10am-late Mon-Sat) A modern waterside restaurant on the ground floor of one of the town's big new apartment blocks, sunny Rocquette serves up refreshing Mediterranean-influenced fare with lots of summery salads, risotto and fish dishes. Laid-back tunes, good coffee and sexy staff to boot.

For self-caterers:

Countdown (☎ 07-306 0014; 105 Commerce St; ⏲ 7am-10pm)

Pak N Save (☎ 07-308-0388; King St; ⏲ 8am-9pm)

Drinking & Entertainment

There aren't many nocturnal options here – the handsome **Whakatane Hotel** (☎ 07-307 1670; 79 The Strand; ⏲ 11am-late) is home to two of them. The Craic is a busy locals' pub of the Irish ilk, good for a pint or two, or a cup of hot chocolate if you're feeling sub-par. Next door, the Boiler Room is a cavernous space with pool tables, Friday-night DJs and live bands on Saturdays.

Across the road is the more upmarket **Office** (☎ 07-307 0123; 82 The Strand; ⏲ 10am-late), doing what it does well: beer, big meals with chips and salad all over, and live bands on Friday nights.

Cinema 5 (☎ 07-308 7623; 100 The Strand; admission adult/child $13/8; ⏲ 10am-10pm) screens new-release movies.

Getting There & Around

Air New Zealand (☎ 0800 737 000, 07-308 8397; www.airnewzealand.com) has daily flights linking Whakatane to Auckland, with connections to other centres.

Sunair Aviation Ltd (☎ 07-575 7799; www.sunair.co.nz) offers direct flights to Gisborne, Hamilton, Napier, New Plymouth and Palmerston North.

InterCity (☎ 09-583 5780; www.intercity.co.nz) buses stop outside the i-SITE and connect Whakatane with Rotorua ($33, 1½ hours, one daily) and Gisborne ($44, three hours, one daily), with onward connections. Gisborne buses travel via Opotiki.

Naked Bus (☎ 0900 625 33; www.nakedbus.com) services run to the following destinations. Book in advance for big savings.

Destination	Price	Duration	Frequency
Auckland	$54	6½hr	1 daily
Gisborne	$24	3¼hr	1 daily
Hamilton	$37	3hr	1 daily
Rotorua	$24	1½hr	1 daily
Tauranga	$18	1½hr	1 daily
Wellington	$55	10hr	1 daily

ROTORUA & THE BAY OF PLENTY

Local **Bay Hopper and Beach Runner** (☎ 0800 422 928; www.baybus.co.nz) buses run to Ohope ($3, 30 minutes, four to six daily), Opotiki ($7.50, one hour, one daily Monday and Wednesday) and Tauranga ($12, two hours, one daily Monday to Saturday).

GKM Shuttles (☎ 0800 007 005, 07-308 9906) to/from the airport cost $20 per adult for the first adult, with discounted prices per additional passenger. Taxi services are available from **Dial a Cab** (☎ 0800 342 522, 07-308 0222).

White Island Shuttle (☎ 0800 733 529; return adult/child $60/35; ☑ Mon-Sat) runs a Rotorua–Whakatane tour shuttle that can be used by nontour people. The shuttle departs Rotorua from pre-arranged pick-up points between 7am and 7.30am, and returns between 4pm and 5pm.

WHAKAARI (WHITE ISLAND)

New Zealand's most active volcano (it last erupted in 2000) lies 49km off the Whakatane coast. The small island was originally formed by three separate volcanic cones of different ages. The two oldest have been eroded, while the younger cone has risen up between them. Mt Gisborne is the highest point on the island at 321m. Geologically, Whakaari is related to Motuhora (Whale Island) and Putauaki (Mt Edgecumbe), as all lie along Taupo Volcanic Zone.

The island is dramatic, with hot water hissing and steaming from vents over most of the crater floor. Temperatures of 600°C to 800°C have been recorded.

The island is privately owned so you can only visit it with a licensed tour operator. Fixed-wing air operators run flyover tours only, while boat and helicopter tours will usually include a walking tour around the island including a visit to the ruins of the sulphur-mining factory – an interesting story in itself.

Numerous helicopter and fixed-wing operators run trips out of Rotorua (see p313) and Tauranga (see p325), while local operators include the following:

Dive White Island (☎ 0800 348 394, 07-307 0714; www.divewhite.co.nz; snorkelling/diving trips per person $180/325) Full-day snorkelling and diving trips with lunch and gear provided.

Vulcan Helicopters (☎ 0800 804 354, 07-308 4188; www.vulcanheli.co.nz; per person from $455) A 2½-hour trip to Whakaari that includes a one-hour guided walk on the volcano.

White Island Tours (Map p336; ☎ 0800 733 529; www.whiteisland.co.nz; 15 The Strand; 6hr tours adult/child $185/120; ☑ departures btwn 7am-9.15am, plus 12.30pm summer)The only official boat trip to Whakaari, with dolphin-spotting en route and 90-minute tour of the island.

MOTUHORA (WHALE ISLAND)

Nine kilometres off Whakatane is Motuhora, or Whale Island – so-called because of its leviathan shape. This island is yet another volcano along the Taupo Volcanic Zone but is much less active, although there are hot springs along its shore. The summit is 353m high and the island has several historic sites, including an ancient *pa* site, quarry and camp.

Whale Island was originally home to a Maori settlement. In 1829, Maori massacred sailors from the trading vessel *Haweis* while it was anchored at Sulphur Bay. In the 1840s the island passed into European ownership and remains privately owned, although since 1965 it has been a DOC-protected wildlife refuge for sea and shore birds.

The island's protected status means landing is restricted, with tours running only from January to March. Operators include Dolphin & Whale Nature Rush (see p335), Diveworks Charters (see p335) and KG Kayaks (below).

OHOPE
pop 3010

Just 7km over the hill from Whakatane, Ohope has great beaches, perfect for lazing or surfing, and is backed by sleepy **Ohiwa Harbour**. Just beyond the harbour is the small Sandspit Wildlife Refuge. You can explore the harbour with **KG Kayaks** (☎ 07-315 4005; www.kgkayaks.co.nz; tours $70-135, 2hr hire s/d $40/60), which runs a 2½-hour guided tour, plus kayak trips to Whale Island and freedom hire.

If you want to take on the surf, get some lessons from Beaver at **By Salt Surf School** (☎ 07-312 4909, 0211 491 972; beaver@e3.net.nz; 2hr lesson $90), which provides all gear and offers discounts for groups.

There's plenty of accommodation around the town including **Ohope Beach Top 10 Holiday Park** (☎ 0800 264 673, 07-312 4460; www.ohopebeach.co.nz; 367 Harbour Rd; unpowered/powered sites $42/44, cabins $70-130, units $90-195, apts $170-285; ▯ �🛜 🖳), a family-friendly caravan park with sports courts, minigolf, pool and apartments peeking over the dunes at the Bay of Plenty. For a quieter, motel-style option, try **Aquarius Motor Lodge** (☎ 07-312 4550; www.aquariusmotorlodge.co.nz; 103 Harbour Rd; d from $75, 1/2br from $110/120; 🛜) a basic complex with various options, all with kitchens and just 100m from the beach.

Hungry? The cavernous **Ohope Chartered Club** (☎ 07-312 5008; Bluett Rd; mains $11-16; ☽ dinner) – at which you must sign in as a guest – is the place to meet locals, drink some cheap beers and chow down on pub grub. Upstairs, a quieter dining option is **C'Vue** (☎ 07-312 5808; mains $20-35; ☽ dinner Wed-Sun).

Not far from the holiday park, **Sea Thai** (☎ 07-312 4005; Pier 5, Fisherman's Wharf, Harbour Rd; mains $19-27; ☽ lunch Sat & Sun, dinner Tue-Sun; Ⓥ) is a beaut spot overlooking bobbing boats on the harbour. On the highway to Opotiki is **Ohiwa Oyster Farm** (☎ 07-312 4565; Wainui Rd; meals $6-16; ☽ 9am-8pm), perfect for a fish-and-chip (and oyster) picnic.

WHAKATANE TO ROTORUA

Sixteen kilometres from Whakatane to Rotorua along SH30 you'll come to the immaculate **Awakeri Hot Springs** (☎ 07-304 9117; www.awakerisprings.co.nz; SH30; sites $30, d cabins/flats/units $70/80/95), complete with **springs** (admission adult/child $5/3; ☽ 8am-9.30pm), picnic areas and a bed for every budget.

Eighteen kilometres beyond Awakeri is the grim timber town **Kawerau**, the highlight of which is **Aotearoa Breweries** (☎ 07-323 8370; www.mata.net.nz; 57 Onslow St; ☽ vary), brewing Mata, 'a beer from the edge' (of civilisation?). Call ahead if you want to visit. Kawerau's **visitor centre** (☎ 07-323 7550; www.kawerau.co.nz; Plunkett St bus terminal; ☽ 9am-4pm) has details on local accommodation and sells permits to access walks and camping at Tarawera Outlet and Tarawera Falls (see p311).

Dominating Kawerau is **Putauaki (Mt Edgecumbe)**, a volcanic cone with panoramic views of the entire Bay of Plenty (often closed in summer due to high fire risk). Access permits are $4, available from **Maori Investments** (☎ 07-323 8146) located on the road up. It's closed at the weekends so you need to obtain a permit in advance for weekend tramps.

Close to Kawerau, **Tui Glen Farm** (☎ 07-323 6457; www.tuiglen.net.nz; Kawerau Loop Rd; rides adult/child from $40/30) offers horse treks through bush and farm for beginners and the adventurous. Dorm accommodation also available ($20).

OPOTIKI
pop 9200

The Opotiki area was settled from at least 1150, some 200 years before the larger 14th-century Maori migration. Maori traditions are well preserved here, with the work of master carvers lining the main street and the occasional facial *moko* passing by. The town acts as a gateway to the East Coast, and has excellent beaches – Ohiwa and Waiotahi – and an engaging museum.

Information

The **Opotiki i-SITE** (☎ 07-315 3031; www.opotikinz.com; cnr St John & Elliott Sts; ☽ 9am-5pm summer, reduced hr in winter) and **DOC** (☎ 07-315 1001; www.doc.govt.nz; ☽ 8am-2.30pm) are in the same building. The i-SITE takes bookings for activities and stocks the indispensable free East Coast booklet *Pacific Coast Highway*. Internet access is available at **Opotiki Internet Café** (97 Church St; ☽ 7am-5pm Mon-Sat, 2-5pm Sun).

The **post office** (www.nzpost.co.nz; 106 Church St) is on the main drag.

Sights & Activities

Pick up the *Historic Opotiki* brochure from the i-SITE for the low-down on the town's heritage buildings.

The excellent **Opotiki Museum** (☎ 07-315 5169; ohas@xtra.co.nz; 123 Church St; admission adult/child/family $5/2.50/10; ☽ 10am-4pm Mon-Fri, to 2pm Sat) offers a chance to learn more about the rich history of the area. Run by volunteers, the museum has interesting heritage displays including Maori *taonga* and militaria, and agricultural items including a horse-drawn wagon. Just down the road is the adjunct **Shalfoon & Francis Museum** (129 Church St), Opotiki's original general store born again, with shelves piled high with old grocery and hardware products – you name it, they had it.

Known by the local Whakatohea tribe to have acted as a government spy, Rev Carl Volkner was murdered in 1865 in the **Hiona St Stephen's Church** (☎ 07-315 8319; 126 Church St; admission free; ☽ services 8am & 9.30am Sun, 10am Thu) on the main street.

Around 8km south of the town centre is **Hukutaia Domain** (☎ 07-315 6167; Woodlands Rd; admission free; ☽ daily), home to one of the finest collections of native plants in NZ. In the centre is Taketakerau, a 23m puriri tree estimated to be more than 2000 years old and a burial place for the distinguished dead of the Upokorere *hapu* (subtribe) of Whakatohea. The remains have been since been reinterred elsewhere.

In the middle of the town's shopping street is **Tangata Whenua Gallery** (☎ 07-315 5558; 106 Church St, ☽ 9am-5pm Mon-Fri, to 2pm Sat & Sun), stocking

OPOTIKI

INFORMATION	
DOC Office	(see 1) D1
Opotiki i-SITE	**1** D1
Opotiki Internet Café	**2** D2
Post Office	**3** D1

SIGHTS & ACTIVITIES	
Hiona St Stephen's Church	**4** D1
Opotiki Museum	**5** D1
Shalfoon & Francis Museum	**6** D1
Tangata Whenua Gallery	**7** D1

SLEEPING	
Central Oasis Backpackers	**8** D2
Eastland Pacific Motor Lodge	**9** D3

EATING	
Hunters Bar & Restaurant	**10** D2
New World	**11** B3
Two Fish	**12** D2
Welcome India	**13** D1

ENTERTAINMENT	
De Luxe Cinema	**14** D1

TRANSPORT	
Bus Stop	**15** D3
Travel Shop	**16** D2

Maori- and New Zealand–themed arts and crafts, including *kete* (baskets) and *pounamu* jewellery.

Motu River Jet Boat Tours (☎ 07-325 2735; www. motujet.co.nz; trips per person from $85) has as many as three 1½-hour trips daily on the Motu River.

Wet 'n' Wild (☎ 0800 462 7238, 07-348 3191; www. wetnwildrafting.co.nz; trips from $795) offers two- to four-day rafting and camping adventures on the Motu.

Waioeka River Kayaks (☎ 07-315 5553; www. newzealandsbestspot.co.nz; trips adult/child 1hr $40/30, 2hr $60/40) runs one- and two-hour kayaking trips down the scenic and easy Waioeka River.

Come December, don a cowboy hat for the annual **Opotiki Rodeo** (www.opotikirodeo.co.nz).

Sleeping

Central Oasis Backpackers (☎ 07-315 5165; www.central oasispackpackers.co.nz; 30 King St; dm/d $20/48; 💻) Inside a late-1800s house, this central backpackers is a snug spot with spacious rooms, a crackling fire and a big front yard to hang out in. The pet rabbit keeps the grass down.

our pick **Opotiki Beach House Backpackers** (☎ 07-315 5117; www.opotikibeachhouse.co.nz; 7 Appleton Rd; dm/d $28/66) A cruisy, shoe-free beachside pad with a sunny, hammock-hung deck, sea views and plenty of opportunities to get in the water with free kayaks and body boards. Beyond the dorms and breezy lounge are attractive doubles and a quirky caravan alongside for those who want a real slice of the Kiwi summer holiday.

Kukumoa Lodge (☎ 07-315 8545; www.kukumoa lodge.co.nz; 19a Bairds Rd; d $90-110, f $300; 📶 🛋) This imposing farmhouse is five minutes from town on the way to Ohope, and sports a spacious double and a family area sleeping up to six. There's a games room for the kids, a pool and spa, and a large balcony and patio for lounging around in the sunshine.

Eastland Pacific Motor Lodge (☎ 0800 103 003, 07-315 5524; www.eastlandpacific.co.nz; cnr Bridge & St John Sts; d/2br units from $100/140; 📶) Bright, clean Eastland is a well-kept motel with new carpets, spa baths as standard, and a shipshape rose garden in the car park. The two-bedroom units are top value.

Capeview Cottage (☎ 0800 227 384, 07-315 7877; www.capeview.co.nz; 167 Tablelands Rd; d $145; 📶) Set amid chirruping birds and kiwifruit orchards,

ROTORUA & THE BAY OF PLENTY

this serene, self-contained cottage has two bedrooms, barbecue and a brilliant outdoor spa from which you can soak up some rather astonishing coastal views. Weekly rates available.

Eating

Two Fish (☎ 07-315 5548; 102 Church St; snacks $4-8, mains $9-19; ☽ 8am-4pm Mon-Fri, 9am-2pm Sat) Undoubtedly the best bet for cafe-fare and a coffee fix, serving up hefty burgers, chowder, toasties and salads plus a jumbo selection in the cabinet. Retro-groovy interior and courtyard; happy staff.

Hunters Bar & Restaurant (☎ 07-315 5760; cnr Church & King Sts; mains $12-25; ☽ 5.30-10pm) On the ground floor of the old Royal Hotel is this reasonably stylish wine bar, serving upmarket pub grub (you can still get steak and eggs). There are kooky record covers on the walls and occasional wine-appreciation nights.

Welcome India (☎ 07-315 5879; 120 Church St; mains $13-18; ☽ lunch & dinner Mon-Sat) Beyond the mandatory Taj Mahal pic in the window, casual Welcome India serves reliable standards with $10 curries on Monday and Tuesday.

Self-caterers should make a beeline for **New World** (☎ 07-315 6723; 19 Bridge St; ☽ 8am-8pm).

Entertainment

The beguiling old **De Luxe Cinema** (☎ 07-315 6110; 127 Church St; tickets adult/child 8/5; ☽ varies) shows the occasional movie and brass-band concert. Check the window for upcoming events, including the annual **Silent Film Festival** (www.silentfilmfest.org.nz) in September

Getting There & Away

Travelling east from Opotiki there are two routes: SH2, crossing the spectacular Waioeka Gorge, or the SH35 around East Cape (see the East Coast chapter for this route). The SH2 route offers some day walks in the **Waioeka Gorge Scenic Reserve**, with the gorge getting steeper and narrower as you travel inland, before the route crosses typically green, rolling hills, dotted with sheep, on the descent to Gisborne.

Buses pick up/drop off at the Hot Bread Shop on the corner of Bridge and St John Streets, though tickets and bookings are through the **Travel Shop** (☎ 07-315 8881; 104 Church St; ☽ 9am-5pm Mon-Fri, to noon Sat).

InterCity (☎ 09-583 5780; www.intercity.co.nz) has daily buses connecting Opotiki with Whakatane ($21, 45 minutes, one daily), Rotorua ($33, 2½ hours, one daily) and Auckland ($68, seven hours, one daily). Heading south, buses connect Opotiki with Gisborne ($33, two hours, one daily).

Naked Bus (☎ 0900 625 33; www.nakedbus.com) runs a daily service to the following destinations. Book in advance for big savings.

Destination	Price	Duration
Auckland	$57	6hr
Gisborne	$23	2¼hr
Rotorua	$29	2hr
Tauranga	$36	3hr
Wellington	$64	10½hr

The local **Bay Hopper** (☎ 0800 422 928; www.baybus.co.nz) bus runs to Whakatane ($7.50, one hour, one daily Monday and Wednesday).

The East Coast

New Zealand is known for its mix of wildly divergent landscapes, but in this region it's the sociological contours that are most pronounced. From the remote settlements of the East Cape to Havelock North's prosperous, wine-soaked streets, the East Coast displays a spectrum of authentic Kiwi experiences that anyone with a passion for *Maoritanga* (things Maori) will find fascinating.

Maori culture is never more visible than on the East Coast. Exquisitely carved *marae* (meeting house complexes) dot the landscape, and while the locals may not be wearing flax skirts and swinging *poi* (flax balls on strings) like they do for the tourists in Rotorua, you can be assured that *te reo* and *tikanga* (the language and customs) are alive and well.

Intrepid types will have no trouble losing the tourist hordes – along the Pacific Coast Hwy, through the rural back roads, on remote beaches, or in the mystical wilderness of Te Urewera National Park.

When the call of the wild gives way to caffeine withdrawal, a fix will quickly be found in the urban centres of Gisborne and Napier. You'll also find plenty of wine, as the region strains under the weight of grapes. From *kaimoana* (seafood) to berry fruit and beyond, there are riches here for everyone.

HIGHLIGHTS

- Time-warping to the 1930s amid the art-deco delights of **Napier** (p362)
- Avoiding being the designated driver as you embark on a grand wine-tasting tour of **Gisborne** (p353) or **Hawke's Bay** (p372)
- Meeting with Maori culture in the hidden nooks of **East Cape** (p345) and **Te Urewera National Park** (p358)
- Beach-hopping between secluded gems such as **Maraehako Bay** (p347), **Tokomaru Bay** (p348), **Anaura Bay** (p349), **Waimarama** (p370), **Mangakuri** and **Aramoana** (p376)
- Searching for wood nymphs among the magical forest paths of **Eastwoodhill Arboretum** (p352)

★ Maraehako Bay ★ East Cape

★ Tokomaru Bay
★ Anaura Bay

Eastwoodhill
Arboretum
★ ★ Gisborne

★
Te Urewera
National Park

Napier
★
Hawke's Bay

★ Waimarama
★ Mangakuri
★ Aramoana

THE EAST COAST

Telephone code: 07 & 06 | www.hawkesbaynz.com | www.gisbornenz.com

THE EAST COAST

Climate

The East Coast basks in a warm, dry climate. Summer temperatures around Napier and Gisborne nudge 25°C, rarely dipping below 8°C in winter. The Hawke's Bay region also suns itself in mild, dry grape-growing conditions, with an average annual rainfall of 800mm. Heavy downpours sometimes wash out sections of the Pacific Coast Hwy (SH35) around the Cape.

Getting There & Around

The region's only airports are in Gisborne and Napier. Air New Zealand flies to both from Auckland and Wellington, and also to Napier from Christchurch. Sunair Aviation connects Gisborne and Napier to Hamilton, Palmerston North, Rotorua, Tauranga and Whakatane.

Regular bus services ply SH2 and SH5, connecting Gisborne, Wairoa, Napier, Hastings and Waipukurau with all the main centres. Transport is much more limited around East Cape (below) and Te Urewera National Park (p361).

EAST CAPE

The East Cape is quite unlike any other part of NZ. Maori life is at the forefront here, in sleepy villages centred upon the many *marae* that dot the beautiful bays. Housed in close communities, drawing much of their livelihoods off the sea and the land, the *tangata whenua* (local people) of the Cape offer a fascinating insight into what might have been had they not been so vigorously divested of their land in the 19th century.

Everyone seems to know everyone here, with community ties built on rural enterprise and a shared passion for the ocean. The pace is slow and the people are wound down. Horseback commuters, tractors on the beach, fresh fish for tea…its all part of daily life around these parts.

Inland, the wild Raukumara Range forms the Cape's jagged spine. Near the edge of the sea, the Pacific Coast Hwy (SH35) runs from Opotiki to Gisborne, and stupendous views can be had along much of its 323km length. Lonely shores lie strewn with driftwood, while picture-postcard sandy bays lure in modest numbers of visitors. On sunny days the sea is a shimmering turquoise; at other times clouds brood and the surf crashes into the craggy shore in shades of deep green and thick white foam. The summer months see the seaside drive flanked with the crimson blooms of the old, gnarled pohutukawa.

Getting Around

Unless you're behind the wheel, transport around East Cape can be tricky, especially on weekends, but couriers regularly link Opotiki with Gisborne via Hicks Bay.

Coastal View Couriers (☎ 027-249 4200) runs from Tuesday to Friday between Opotiki ($45, three hours, 1.15pm and 2.30pm) and Hicks Bay ($45, three hours, 6.30am). **Polly's Passenger Couriers** (☎ 06-864 4728) continues

---

> **THE EAST COAST FACTS**
>
> **Eat** Fresh *kaimoana* (seafood) whenever you get the chance
> **Read** Judith Binney's *Encircled Lands: Te Urewera, 1820–1921* (2009) – 680 fresh pages of fascinating Maori history
> **Listen to** Uawa FM (88.5, 99.3 FM) in Tolaga Bay (p349)
> **Watch** *Whale Rider* (2002), then take the tour (p354)
> **Swim at** Anaura Bay (p349)
> **Festival** Art Deco Weekend in Napier and Hastings (p365)
> **Tackiest tourist attraction** The statue of the mystery man at Cook's Plaza on Titirangi, Gisborne (p364)
> **Go green** Millton vineyard (p353) – organic, biodynamic and delicious to boot

from here to Gisborne Monday to Friday from Hick's Bay ($40, 3½ hours, 6.30am), and from Gisborne ($40, 3½ hours, 1pm). **Cook's Couriers** (☎ 021-371 364) covers the same route Monday to Friday from Te Araroa ($40, 3½ hours, 7.15am) and from Gisborne (2pm, 1pm Saturday).

An alternative is **Kiwi Experience** (☎ 09-366 9830; www.kiwiexperience.com; per person $395), which runs the four-day 'East As' backpacker bus leaving from Taupo or Rotorua.

PACIFIC COAST HWY

NZ's not short on awesome drives, and SH35 is up with the best of them. You're not going to get anywhere quickly on this route but that's hardly the point. While you can shoot the gap in a solid six hours, lingering along the way will pay rich dividends. If you haven't got time to enjoy the entire coastal road this time around, don't despair. The shorter route between Opotiki and Gisborne (144km) follows SH2 through the bushy Waioeka Gorge before spilling out into picturesque orchards and vineyards.

Before you hit the road, collect the free *Pacific Coast Highway* booklet from the

---

> **TELEPHONE CODES**
>
> The telephone area code from Opotiki east to Hicks Bay, just before East Cape itself, is ☎ 07. The rest of the region is ☎ 06.

MAORI NZ: THE EAST COAST

The main *iwi* (tribes) in the region are Te Whanau-a-Apanui (west side of East Cape), Ngati Porou (east side of East Cape), Ngati Kahungunu (the coast from Hawke's Bay down) and Tuhoe (inland in Te Urewera).

Ngati Porou and Ngati Kahungunu are the country's second- and third-biggest *iwi*. In the late 19th century they produced the great leaders James Carroll (the first Maori cabinet minister) and Apirana Ngata (who was briefly acting Prime Minister). Ngata, whose face adorns the $50 bill, worked tirelessly in parliament to orchestrate a cultural revival within Maoridom. The region's magnificent carved meeting houses are part of his legacy.

There are opportunities to interact with Maori while you're in the region. For accommodation with a distinctly Maori flavour, consider Te Kaha Homestead Lodge (below), Maraehako Bay Retreat (opposite), Mel's Place (p348) and Eastender Backpackers (p348).

For an intimate introduction to *Maoritanga* (things Maori), consider a guided tour. Ask about climbing Mt Hikurangi at the Ngati Porou Visitors Centre (p348), or look out for Motu River AAA Jet Boating (below), Tipuna Tours' Whale Rider tour (p354), Long Island Tours (p371) or Te Hakakino (p371). Te Aute College (p376) welcomes visitors but you'll need to call ahead.

Te Urewera has a long and proud history of resistance to colonisation: start your explorations at Aniwaniwa (p359) and if you have time, visit the unique communities at Ruatahuna and Maungapohatu (p358).

For a more passive brush with the culture, visit Gisborne's Tairawhiti Museum (p352), the Hawke's Bay Museum & Art Gallery (p364), Otatara Pa (p364), and Tikitiki's St Mary's Church (p348). Throughout the text we've listed *marae* that can be admired from the road.

Opotiki or Gisborne i-SITE. Set off with a full petrol tank, and stock up on snacks and groceries – shops and petrol stations are in short supply. Sleeping and eating options are pretty spread out, so we've listed them in the order you'll find them.

Opotiki to Te Kaha

The first leg offers hazy views across to Whakaari (White Island; p339), a chain-smoking active volcano. The desolate beaches at **Torere**, **Hawai** and **Omaio** are steeply shelved and littered with flotsam. Check out the magnificent *whakairo* (carving) on the Torere school gateway. Hawai marks the boundary of the Whanau-a-Apanui tribe whose *rohe* (traditional area) extends to Cape Runaway.

About 42km east of Opotiki the road crosses the broad pebbly expanse of the **Motu River**, the first river in NZ to be designated as a protected wilderness area. Action seekers head here for back-to-nature rafting and jet-boating adventures. **Wet 'n' Wild Rafting** (☎ 0800 462 7238; www.wetnwildrafting.co.nz; 2-5 days $795-925) offers multiday excursions, with the longest taking you 100km down the river. The river is so remote that the two-day tour requires you to be helicoptered in, therefore costing almost as much as the five-day trip. **Motu River AAA Jet Boating** (☎ 027-686 6489; 1hr trip for 2 people $130)

includes an ecological and historical commentary from a Maori perspective (departs near Motu Bridge daily 1 December to 30 April, weather permitting).

Twenty-five kilometres further along, the fishing town of **Te Kaha** once sounded the death knell for passing whales. From the roadside you get a decent view of the sublimely carved Tukaki *marae*. There's a shop here, a modern waterside hotel with an uncertain future (at time of print) and several accommodation options.

The remote **Maungaroa Station** (☎ 07-325 2727; www.maungaroa.co.nz; Maungaroa Access Rd; campsites $10, dm $20) is a Raukumara Range lodge that requires a 45-minute drive up a scenic, gravel road (off Copenhagen Rd) and two river crossings to reach it. Bunk down in the self-contained cottage (sleeps 12 in four bedrooms) or camp outside; dunk yourself in the Kereu River, hug a tree or saddle-up for a horse trek ($35 to $65, one to four hours).

Located on the waterfront, **Te Kaha Homestead Lodge** (☎ 07-325 2194; fax 07-325 2193; SH35; campsites per person $10, dm/s/tw/d $30/40/60/80; 🖳) is a friendly hostel that sits among old pohutukawa trees with spa views to White Island. Rooms are basic, but the rambunctious owner organises fishing trips and bursts into choruses of 'Welcome to the Homestead at Te

THE EAST COAST

Kaha' (to the tune of *Hotel California*) given the slightest provocation.

Tui Lodge (☎ 07-325 2922; www.tuilodge.co.nz; Copenhagen Rd, Te Kaha; s/d incl breakfast $125/150; 🖳) is a capacious, modern guest house that sits on groomed three-acre gardens, irresistible to tui and many other birds. Delicious meals are available by arrangement. Horse trekking, fishing and diving trips can be organised for you.

Te Kaha to Cape Runaway

A succession of sleepy bays follows. At **Papatea Bay** stop to admire the gateway of **Hinemahuru marae**, carved with images of WWI Maori Battalion soldiers. Nearby **Christ Church Raukokore** (1894) is an immaculately maintained beacon of belief on a lonely promontory. **Waihau Bay** has an all-in-one petrol station–post office–store-takeaway at its western end, alongside the pub. There's another store-takeaway attached to the holiday park in the centre of the beach. **Cape Runaway**, where kumara was first introduced to NZ, can only be reached on foot. There are few accommodation options in these parts, and what you will find will be small and personal.

Run by the same *hapu* (subtribe) as the retreat next door is **Maraehako Camping Ground** (☎ 07-325 2901; SH35; campsites per adult/child $12/8). Little more is offered than clean toilets (BYO paper), water (needs boiling) and beachfront nirvana. Toddlers will adore splashing about in the clear stream.

Nestled among ancient pohutukawa trees, the waterfront **Maraehako Bay Retreat** (☎ 07-325 2648; www.maraehako.co.nz; SH35; dm/s/d $28/43/63; 🖳) is a hostel that looks like it was cobbled together from flotsam and jetsam washed up in the craggy cove. It's rustic, but unique, for what it lacks in crossed t's and dotted i's it more than makes up for in *manaakitanga* (hospitality). Enjoy a spa under the stars ($5), kayak hire, as well as fishing charters, marae

tours, guided walks, horse treks and more, at reasonable prices.

Towards Whanarua Bay, the magical **Waikawa B&B** (☎ 07-325 2070; www.waikawa.net; 7541 SH35; d $100-130; 🖳) sits in a private rocky cove with views of the sunset and White Island. The artful buildings blend weathered timber, corrugated iron and paua inlay to great effect. There are two double B&B rooms, and a two-bedroom self-contained bach ($130 to $200), perfect for two to four people.

There are plenty of beds at **Oceanside Apartments** (☎ 07-325 3699; www.waihaubay.co.nz; 10932 SH35; d $110-130; 🖝), between two nicely kept apartments and a next-door bach. (Add $30 per extra bod beyond the double price.) Meals and picnic lunches are available by arrangement. Bookings can be made for kayak hire and local activities.

Heaven is a tub of homemade macadamia and honey ice cream at **Pacific Coast Macadamias** (☎ 07-325 2960; SH35, Whanarua Bay; snacks $2-9; ⏲ 10am-3pm), accompanied by views along one of the most spectacular parts of the coast. Toasted sandwiches and nutty sweet treats make this a great lunch stop.

Cape Runaway to East Cape

The road heads inland from Whangaparaoa, crossing into Ngati Porou territory before hitting the coast at **Hicks Bay**, a real middle-of-nowhere settlement with a grand beach.

Nearly 10km further is **Te Araroa**, a lone-dog village with a shop, petrol station, take away and beautifully carved *marae*. The geology changes here from igneous outcrops to sandstone cliffs. More than 350 years old, 20m high and 40m wide, Te-Waha-O-Rerekohu, allegedly NZ's largest pohutukawa tree, stands in Te Araroa schoolyard. The progressive **East Cape Manuka Company** (☎ 0508 626 852; www.east capemanuka.co.nz; 4464 Te Araroa Rd; ⏲ 9am-4pm daily Nov-Mar, Mon-Fri Apr-Oct) is also here, selling soaps, oils, creams and honey made from potent East Cape manuka. Stop for coffee and *kai* (food).

THE EAST COAST

FREEDOM TO CAMP

Gisborne District Council (GDC) is one of the few authorities to permit Freedom Camping (extremely cheap informal camping), but only at a handful of designated sites from the end of September to April. You can apply for a permit online (www.gdc.govt.nz/freedom-camping-permit-request) for two, 10 or 28 consecutive nights at a cost of $10, $25 and $60 respectively. Freedom camping is a privilege, so please follow the requirements in the GDC *Freedom Camping* leaflet, available online or at visitor centres. Your own gas cooker, chemical toilet and water supply are obligatory.

From Te Araroa, drive out to see the **East Cape Lighthouse**, the easterly tip of mainland NZ. It's 21km (30 minutes) east of town along a mainly unsealed road, with a 25-minute climb to the lighthouse. Set your alarm and get up there for sunrise.

It's a long way between drinks (or anything else) on this leg. **Mel's Place** (☎ 06-864 4694; www.eastcape.co.nz; 89 Onepoto Beach Rd, Hicks Bay; campsites per person $20, dm $30) is located on an ancestral *pa* (fortified village) site. Mel and Joe manage this hostel with aplomb, sharing with their guests a wealth of local Maori history. As well as a homely dorm there are campsites with wicked bay views (bring your own cooking gear), a supercute double cabin ($125) and smart self-contained caravan by the beach ($75). If you like dogs, you'll get plenty of tail-wags from the family pets.

Brilliant views distract from the barrack ambience at the sprawling **Hicks Bay Motel Lodge** (☎ 06-864 4880; www.hicksbaymotel.co.nz; 5198 SH35; dm $25, d $75-145; 🖩 🕿) above Hicks Bay. The old-fashioned rooms are nothing flash, although the restaurant, shop, pool and glowworm grotto offer some compensation.

East Cape to Tokomaru Bay

Heading through farmland south of Te Araroa, the first town you come to is **Tikitiki**. If you've been itching to get on to a *marae*, you'll get a fair idea of what you're missing out on by visiting the extraordinary **St Mary's Church** (1924). It's nothing special from the outside but step inside for a sensory overload. There are woven *tukutuku* (flax panels) on the walls, geometrically patterned stained-glass windows, painted beams and amazing carvings – check out the little guys holding up the pulpit. A stained-glass crucifixion scene behind the pulpit depicts WWI Maori Battalion soldiers in attendance.

Mt Hikurangi (1752m), jutting out of the Raukumara Range, is the highest non-volcanic peak in the North Island and the first spot on the planet to be touched by the sun each day. According to local tradition it was the first piece of land dragged up when Maui snagged the North Island (p52). The Ngati Porou version of the Maui story has his canoe and earthly remains resting here on their sacred mountain. The **Maui Whakairo**, nine massive wooden carvings, has been erected 1000m up on Hikurangi's shoulder to honour their ancestor.

Hikurangi is not a tramp for the inexperienced but hardy walkers can access the mountain by turning off SH35 at Tapuaeroa Valley Rd, 3km north of Ruatoria, and heading towards Pakihiroa Station. From here it's a four-hour tramp to the hut ($15; book at the Ngati Porou Visitors Centre) and then a further two hours to the summit.

A few kilometres off SH35 and 20km south of Tikitiki, **Ruatoria** is the Ngati Porou's biggest town. It's a slow-mo place with a mini-market, petrol station, pub and a couple of cafes. The welcoming **Ngati Porou Visitors Centre** (☎ 06-864 8660; www.ngatiporou.com; 144 Waiomatatini Rd; ☼ 8.30am-5pm Mon-Fri) has authentic local art for sale, but more importantly offers tailored cultural tours, including trips to Hikurangi. Standard options are a 4WD guided tour to Maui Whakairo (four hours), a sunrise tour (departs 4.30am), and guided tours to the summit (eight-hour/overnight). Prices run from $165 to $500 but vary greatly according to numbers. It also runs a pick-up/drop-off service to the mountain (each way $20 to $50), and can arrange *marae* stays, fishing, diving, horse trekking, surfing and kayaking.

About 26km south is **Te Puia Springs**, a blink-and-you'll-miss-it hot-springs village with a handy petrol station–store. The actual thermal pools are in an old shed (with no changing facilities) at the back of the **Te Puia Hot Springs Hotel** (☎ 06-864 6755; 4689 SH35; pools $5). It's an informal set-up; ask at the hotel for access to the small pool of milky water, which reputedly has the highest mineral content of any in the world. Don't splash about as there's a risk of amoebic meningitis. Nearby **Waipiro Bay** is a knockout.

A further 11km south is **Tokomaru Bay**, perhaps the most beautiful spot on the entire route, with its broad beach framed by sweeping cliffs. This romantically crumbling town has weathered hard times since the local freezing works closed in the 1950s. The big attractions here are the famous surf break, Toko Point and the town's great pub. You'll also find a petrol station, a small supermarket and post office, a couple of takeaways and a summer-only cafe.

As far removed from the grim London soap opera as imaginable, the cheery sit-around-the-campfire **Eastender Backpackers** (☎ 06-864 3033; www.eastenderhorsetreks.co.nz; 836 Rangitukia Rd; campsites per person $10, dm $23, d $50-60; 🖩) is a farmstay that has clean rooms and snappy communal areas. The beach is dicey for swimming, but there's a safe waterhole nearby. Horse treks (two hours, $85) and bone-carving lessons (from $35) are offered and you might even get to try a *hangi* (Maori feast; $14).

Just a block from the beach, **Footprints in the Sand** (☎ 06-864 5858; www.footprintsinthesand.co.nz; 13 Potae St, Tokomaru Bay; campsites per person $15, dm/d/tr $20/60/80) is a most amenable host that offers a squeaky-clean, comfortable dorm along with a cabin and pleasant camping. Ace alfresco dining area, kayak and bike hire. Look out for continuous improvements.

Up on the hill, **Brian's Place** (☎ 06-864 5870; www.briansplace.co.nz; 21 Potae St, Tokomaru Bay; campsites per person $15, dm/s/d $25/43/60) scores the awards for views and eco-loos. The bunkhouse has tricky loft rooms (stay sober), a couple of rustic tent pitches on the knoll, and desirable cabins.

Experience local hospitality at **Te Puka Tavern** (☎ 06-864 5466; Beach Rd, Tokomaru Bay; meals $5-20; 🕑 2.30pm-late Tue, 11am-late Wed-Sun), a friendly pub with cracker views and respectable burgers.

Tokomaru Bay to Gisborne

After a bucolic 22km of highway and further 7km to the coast, it's a definite 'wow' moment when isolated **Anaura Bay** springs into view far below. A plaque near the centre of the bay commemorates Captain Cook's arrival in 1769 when he commented on the 'profound peace' in which the people were living and their 'truly astonishing' cultivations. **Anaura Bay Walkway** is a 3.5km ramble through native forest and grassland, starting at the northern end of the bay. There's a basic free Department of Conservation (DOC) campsite here (your own toilet is required).

East Cape's largest community is **Tolaga Bay**, 14km further south. There's an **information centre** (☎ 06-862 6862; 55 Cook St; 🕑 6am-6pm Mon-Fri) in the foyer of the local radio station (Uawa 88.5, 99.3FM). Just off the main street, **Tolaga Bay Cashmere Company** (☎ 06-862 6746; www.cashmere.co.nz; 31 Solander St; 🕑 10am-4pm Mon-Sat) inhabits the art-deco former council building. You can watch the knitters at work and then purchase one of their delicate, pricey handiworks; the seconds are sold at a discount.

Tolaga is defined by the remarkable **historic wharf** (1929) – the longest in the southern hemisphere at 660m – which is slowly surrendering to the sea (although locals are fundraising to preserve it). Take the time to walk its length. Nearby is **Cooks Cove Walkway** (2½ hours, 5.8km, closed August to October), an easy loop through farmland and native bush to another cove where the captain landed. At the northern end of the beach is the **Tatarahake Cliffs Lookout**, a sharp 10-minute walk to an excellent vantage point.

Te Tapuwae o Rongokako Marine Reserve is a 2450-hectare haven for many species of marine life including fur seals, dolphins and whales – and heaven for snorkellers and divers.

Dive Tatapouri (☎ 06-686 6139; www.divetatapouri.com; SH35, Tatapouri Beach) offers an array of watery activities including dive trips, snorkel hire, a reef ecology tour, shark-cage diving and even stingray feeding.

Campers are catered for best around these parts, although a few B&Bs come and go in the midst. **Anaura Bay Motor Camp** (☎ 06-862 6380; Anaura Bay Rd; unpowered/powered sites adult $12/14, child $6/8) is all about the location – right on the beachfront by the little stream where James Cook once stocked up with water. There's a decent kitchen and perfectly acceptable toilets.

Tolaga Bay Holiday Park (☎ 06-862 6716; www.tolagabayholidaypark.co.nz; 167 Wharf Rd; unpowered/powered sites $12/14, cabins $60-75) There's little here except the dear old wharf, but this is a place where absence becomes substance. The stiff ocean breeze tousles Norfolk Island pines as open lawns bask in the sunshine – who needs anything more?

There's a shabby charm to the 1930s faux-Tudor **Tolaga Inn** (☎ 06-862 6856; hutchroy@xtra.co.nz; 12 Cook St; dm/s/d $25/50/75) with basic but clean rooms. Downstairs is a respectable cafe (meals $8 to $27) with bonzer biscuits and tables in the sunshine.

Freedom Camping (p347) is available at the north end of Tolaga Bay, Waihau Bay and at Pouawa Beach, just off SH35 on the edge of the marine reserve.

GISBORNE
pop 32,700

Gizzy to her friends, Gisborne's a pretty thing and increasingly self-confident. Squeezed between surf beaches and a sea of chardonnay, most Kiwis would describe the lifestyle here as 'not bad' – meaning, of course, bloody brilliant.

It proudly claims to be the first city on earth to see the sun and once it does it hogs it and heads to the beach. Poverty Bay starts here, hooking south to Young Nick's Head.

Perhaps it's the isolated location that's helped Gisborne maintain its small-town charm and interesting main street. Grand Edwardian buildings sit alongside modernist 1950s, five-storey 'skyscrapers' and the odd slice of audacious art deco.

It's a good place to put your feet up for a few days, hit the beaches and sip heavenly wine.

History

The Gisborne region has been settled for over 700 years. A pact between two migratory *waka* (canoe) skippers, Paoa of the *Horouta* and Kiwa of the *Takitimu*, led to the founding of Turanganui a Kiwa (now Gisborne). Kumara flourished in the fertile soil and the settlement blossomed.

In 1769 this was the first part of NZ sighted by Cook's expedition. Eager to replenish supplies and explore the land, they set ashore, much to the amazement of the local people. Setting an unfortunate benchmark for Maori/Pakeha (non-Maori) relations, the crew opened fire when the local men performed their traditional blood-curdling challenge, killing six of them.

The *Endeavour* quickly set sail up the coast without the provisions they were seeking. Cook, perhaps in a fit of petulance, named the area Poverty Bay as 'it did not afford a single item we wanted'. The name stuck, and Cook and crew made a much better impression at their next landfall, Tolaga Bay.

European settlement didn't begin until 1831. Motivated self-starter John Williams Harris established a whaling base on the Turanganui River's west bank and a farm near Manutuke. Whaling boomed and missionaries followed. More Europeans moved to the area but Maori resistance to land sales limited settlement.

In the 1860s battles between settlers and Maori erupted. Beginning in Taranaki, the Hauhau insurrection spread to the East Coast, culminating in the battle of Waerenga a Hika in 1865. The following year the government crushed all opposition and transported survivors, including Te Kooti (p352), to the Chatham Islands.

To discover Gisborne's historical spots on foot, pick up a copy of the trail booklet, *Gisborne: A Historic Walk*, available from the i-SITE (by donation).

Orientation

Known as 'the city of bridges', Gisborne presides over the confluence of the Waimata and Taruheru Rivers, below which the Turanganui River runs to the sea. The main street is Gladstone Rd and Waikanae Beach is immediately south of the town centre. Free town maps are available at Gisborne's i-SITE (below).

Information

The major banks are located along Gladstone Rd.

Ambulance, fire service & police (☎ 111)

DOC (☎ 06-869 0460; www.doc.govt.co.nz; 63 Carnarvon St; ◷ 8am-4.35pm Mon-Fri) Tourist information.

Gisborne Hospital (☎ 06-869 0500; Ormond Rd)

Gisborne i-SITE (☎ 06-868 6139; www.gisbornenz. com; 209 Grey St; ◷ 8.30am-5pm Mon-Fri, 9am-5pm Sat, 10am-4pm Sun) Beside a doozy of a Canadian totem pole, this helpful centre stocks the thorough (and free) *Eastland Region* and *Pacific Coast Hwy* booklets. It also has internet access, toilets and a minigolf course ($3).

Muirs Bookshop (☎ 06-869 0651; www.muirsbook shop.co.nz; 62 Gladstone Rd; ◷ 8.30am-4pm Mon-Fri, 9am-3pm Sat) The best bookshop in Gisborne (and probably the whole East Coast), established in 1905.

Police station (☎ 06-869 0200; Peel St)

Post office (cnr Gladstone Rd & Bright St)

Sights

HISTORIC SITES & MONUMENTS

Gisborne deifies Captain Cook. In a park by the river mouth there's a **statue of Young Nick** (Nicholas Young), Cook's cabin boy, whose eagle eyes were the first to spot NZ (the white cliffs at Young Nick's Head). There's a **Captain Cook statue** here too, erected on a globe etched with his roaming routes.

Across the river at the foot of Titirangi (Kaiti Hill) is the spot where Cook first got NZ dirt on his boots (9 October 1769 according to Cook's journal, but actually the 8th). The **Cook National Historic Reserve** and **Cook monument** is a grim obelisk facing the end of the wharves. This scrappy site is made even more significant by being the landing point of the Horouta *waka*.

Tucked away on the other side of Titirangi is **Te Poho o Rawiri Marae** (☎ 06-868 5364; cnr Ranfurly St & Queens Dr; admission by invitation) with its elaborately carved meeting house. You can get a decent view from the gates but you'll need to call ahead to ask for permission to view the decorated interior.

GISBORNE

EATING 🍴
Bookshop Café.............................(see 4)
Café 1874....................................26 E3
Café Ruba....................................27 E3
Fettucine Brothers.......................28 E3
Just Thai Cuisine..........................29 E3
Pak N Save..................................30 D2
USSCO Bar & Bistro...................(see 27)
Zest...(see 28)

DRINKING 🍷
Kingfisher...................................31 E3
Smash Palace..............................32 B3
Soho Bar....................................33 E3

ENTERTAINMENT 🎭
Odeon Multiplex Theatres.............34 E3
Poverty Bay Club.......................(see 26)

TRANSPORT
Air New Zealand..........................35 D2
InterCity..................................(see 3)

INFORMATION
Automobile Association (AA).........1 D2
DOC Office.................................2 D2
Gisborne i-SITE...........................3 D3
Muirs Bookshop..........................4 E3
Police Station..............................5 D3
Post Office..................................6 D3

SIGHTS & ACTIVITIES
Captain Cook Statue.....................7 D4
Cidery..8 D3
Cook National Historic
  Reserve & Cook Monument.........9 D4
Cook Observatory.......................10 E4
Cook's Plaza..............................11 E4
Gisborne Botanic Gardens...........12 D1
Olympic Pool..............................13 B3
Statue of Young Nick..................14 D4
Sunshine Brewing Company..........15 C2
Tairawhiti Museum.......................16 E2
Te Moana Maritime Museum......(see 16)
Te Poho o Rawiri Marae...............17 F4
Te Tauihu Turanga......................18 E3
Whakamana................................18 E4

SLEEPING 🛏️
Cook's Quarters B&B...................19 E3
Emerald Hotel............................20 E3
Flying Nun Backpackers...............21 C2
Gisborne YHA.............................22 E3
Pacific Harbour Motor Inn.........(see 23)
Senator Motor Inn.......................23 E3
Te Kura B&B..............................24 E2
Waikanae Beach Holiday
  Park..25 D3

THE EAST COAST

Titirangi has magical city views. It was once a *pa* (fortified village); look out for the remnants of terracing and kumara pits on the steep track to the top, which starts near the Cook Monument. If you can handle the disdain of sweaty joggers, you can cheat and drive. Near the summit is yet another Cook edifice, **Cook's Plaza**. Due to a cock-up of historic proportions, the Cook statue here isn't garbed in British naval uniform, nor does it bear any facial resemblance to Captain Jim. A plaque proclaims, 'Who was he? We have no idea!' Further on is the **Cook Observatory** (☎ 06-867 7901; public viewing $2; ☺ viewing 8.30pm Tue), the world's easternmost star-gazing facility.

Adding some balance to all the Cook hoopla, **Te Tauihu Turanga Whakamana** (The Canoe Prow; cnr Gladstone Rd & Customhouse Rd) is a large modern Maori sculpture incorporating the images of two men killed during Cook's first interaction with the locals.

Matawhero is 7km west of Gisborne along SH2. The historic **Presbyterian Church** (☎ 868 5573; Church Ln) is the only building in the village to have survived Te Kooti's 1868 raid. It's a sweetly simple affair with lovingly tended gardens.

GARDENS

Arboreal nirvana, **Eastwoodhill Arboretum** (Map p344; ☎ 06-863 9003; www.eastwoodhill.org.nz; 2392 Wharekopae Rd, Ngatapa; adult/child $10/free; ☺ 9am-5pm) is 35km northwest of Gisborne. Staggeringly beautiful, you could easily lose a day wandering around the 25km of themed tracks in this pine-scented paradise. It's the country's largest collection of imported trees and shrubs, but the birds love it just the same.

The less ambitious **Gisborne Botanic Gardens** (Aberdeen Rd) is beside the Taruheru River.

MUSEUMS

The **Tairawhiti Museum** (☎ 06-867 3832; www.tairawhitimuseum.org.nz; 18 Stout St; adult/under 12 $5/free; Mon free; ☺ 10am-4pm Mon-Sat, 1.30-4pm Sun) focuses on East Coast Maori and colonial history. Its gallery is Gisborne's arts hub, with rotating exhibits, and the permanent display of 'Shutterbug Jack's' photographs is not to be missed. There's a tearoom-style cafe overlooking Kelvin Park, and outside is the reconstructed Wyllie Cottage (1872), Gisborne's oldest house.

Te Moana Maritime Museum occupies a wing of the Tairawhiti complex. When the *Star*

THE EAST COAST

TE KOOTI

Maori history is littered with mystics, prophets and warriors – often combined in the same person. A particularly fascinating example is Te Kooti (rhymes with naughty, not booty).

In 1865 he fought with the government against the Hauhau (adherents of the Pai Marire faith, founded by another warrior-prophet) but was accused of being a spy and imprisoned on the Chatham Islands without trial. His protestations of innocence and demands for justice were foolishly ignored.

While on the Chathams, Te Kooti studied the Bible and claimed to receive visions from the archangel Michael. His charismatic preaching and 'miracles' – including producing flames from his hands (his captors claimed he used phosphorus from the head of matches) – helped win over the Pai Marire to his distinctly Maori take on Christianity.

In 1867 Te Kooti led an astounding, almost bloodless escape from the Chathams, hijacking a supply ship and sailing to Poverty Bay with 200 followers. En route he threw a doubter overboard as a sacrifice. Upon their safe arrival Te Kooti's disciples raised their right hands in homage to God rather than bowing submissively; *ringa tu* (upraised hand) became the name of his church.

Te Kooti requested a dialogue with the colonial government but was once again rebuffed, with magistrate Reginald Biggs demanding his immediate surrender. Unimpressed by Pakeha justice, Te Kooti commenced a particularly effective guerrilla campaign – starting by killing Biggs and around 50 others (including women and children, Maori and Pakeha) at Matawhero.

A merry four-year chase ensued. Eventually Te Kooti took refuge in the area known as King Country, the Maori king's vast dominion where government troops feared to tread.

Proving the pointlessness of the government's approach to the whole affair, Te Kooti was officially pardoned in 1883. By this time his reputation as a prophet and healer had spread and his Ringatu Church was firmly established – at the most recent census it boasted over 16,000 adherents.

of Canada foundered on a Gisborne reef in 1912, the ship's bridge and captain's cabin were salvaged, installed in a local home, then later moved here for restoration. Displays on *waka*, whaling and Cook's Poverty Bay visit pale before the sensational vintage surfboard collection.

The **East Coast Museum of Technology & Transport** (SH2, Makaraka; adult/child $5/2; 10am-4.30pm) is an improbable collation of rusty tractors, lawn mowers, engines, spanners, ploughs, ovens, chainsaws, trucks, pumps, harvesters, motorbikes and so on – a shrine to peoples' inventive capacity or their ability to horde junk?

WINERIES

Gisborne is a major wine-producing area, traditionally famous for its chardonnay (producing just under a third of the country's output) but increasingly being noticed for other white varietals, particularly gewürztraminer and pinot gris. Most of the local vineyards offer free tastings, although some will charge a nominal fee which is subsequently deducted from purchases. The *Winery Guide* (free from the i-SITE) has a map and the latest opening hours for most vineyards. The following all have set public tasting hours; many open longer in summer.

Bushmere Estate (06-868 9317; www.bushmere. com; 166 Main Rd, Matawhero; 11am-6pm Fri-Sun). Great chardonnay, gewürztraminer and cafe-style lunches.

KEW (06-862 7722; www.kew.co.nz; 569 Wharekopae Rd, Patutahi; 11am-4pm) Lovely wines across the board from this award-winning winery committed to sustainable winegrowing. Call ahead in winter or for guided tours and antipasto platters.

Matawhero (06-867 6140; www.matawhero.co.nz; Riverpoint Rd, Matawhero; 2-5pm Thu, Fri & Mon, 1-5pm Sat & Sun) Home of a particularly buttery chardy. Enjoy your picnic in a lovely setting, accompanied by a tasting tray ($10, redeemable against purchase).

Millton (06-862 8680; www.millton.co.nz; 119 Papatu Rd, Manutuke; 10am-5pm Mon-Sat) Sustainable, organic and biodynamic to boot. Linger for a picnic in the beautiful gardens.

BREWERIES

Sunshine Brewing Company (Map p351; 06-867 7777; www.gisbornegold.co.nz; 109 Disraeli St; 9am-6pm Mon-Sat), Gisborne's own natural brewery, offers four quality beers including the famous Gisborne Gold and its big brother Green. Free tours and tastings by arrangement.

The **Cidery** (Map p351; 06-868 8300; www.harvest cider.co.nz; 91 Customhouse St; 9am-4.30pm Mon-Fri) is the apple-hued producer of Bulmers Original, Scrumpy, Harvest and pear ciders, with free tastings and factory viewings on offer.

Activities
SURFING & KITEBOARDING

Surfing is mainstream in Gisborne, with the male teenage population looking appropriately shaggy. **Waikanae Beach** is good for learners and young ones; experienced surfers get tubed south of town at the **Pipe**, or east at **Sponge Bay** and **Tuamotu Island**. Further east along SH35, **Wainui** (Map p344) and **Makorori** (Map p344) beaches also have quality breaks.
Surfing with Frank (06-867 0823; www.surfingwith frank.com; 58 Murphy Rd, Wainui Beach) offers lessons ($50 to $75) as well as tours of the best local (and North Island) breaks.

Freestyle NZ (06-868 8840; www.freestylenz. com; 1hr $50, kayak hire per hr $20) offers kitesurfing lessons and gear hire, as well as customised kayak tours and freedom hire.

SWIMMING

Pick your way through the driftwood to swim safely between the flags at Waikanae and Midway beaches; the detritus is cleared in time for summer. If the ocean is chilly, **Olympic Pool** (06-867 6220; Centennial Marine Pde, Midway Beach; adult/child $3.50/2.50; 6am-8pm) is a tepid 50m indoor/outdoor pool with a 98m wormlike waterslide ($3.50) and aquafitness classes ($6.50).

OTHER ACTIVITIES

There are stacks of walks to tackle in the area, starting with a gentle stroll along the river. The i-SITE can provide you with brochures for the **Arts & Crafts Trail** and **Historic Walk**. Winding its way through farmland and forest with commanding views, the **Te Kuri Walkway** (two hours, 5.6km, closed August to October) starts 4km north of town at the end of Shelley Rd.

For free skull-endangering things to do in NZ you can't beat the **Rere Rockslide** (Map p344). This natural phenomenon occurs in a section of the Rere River 50km northwest of Gisborne along the Wharekopae Rd. Grab a tyre tube or boogie board to cushion the worst of the bruises and slide down the 60m-long rocky run into the pool at the bottom. Three kilometres downriver, the **Rere Falls** (Map p344)

send a 30m-wide curtain of water over a 10m
drop; you can walk behind it if you don't mind
getting wet. Both can be combined with a visit
to Eastwoodhill Arboretum (p352).

Further awaken your sense of mortality
with a shark-cage dive from **Surfit Charters**
(☎ 06-867 2970; www.surfit.co.nz; per person $300).
Tamer fishing and snorkelling trips can also
be arranged.

Tours

After *Whale Rider* was released, the sleepy
Maori village at Whangara, 21km north of
Gisborne, was swamped with sightseers –
some of whom treated the *marae* and private
homes as if they were movie sets. That's why
you won't find any signs pointing to this mystical place from SH35. Your best bet for an
introduction to Whangara and meaningful
insights into Maori culture is to take a tour
with **Tipuna Tours** (☎ 06-862 6118; www.tipunatours.
com). Tailored, small-group tours are offered,
including the **Whale Rider Tour** (two hours,
$50 to $70) and trips around the sights of
Gisborne and around the Pacific Coast Hwy
to Opotiki.

Paradise Leisure Tours (☎ 027 223 9440; grant
sue.hughes@ihug.co.nz; tours $25-150) runs a wide
range of whole and half-day tours around
local hot spots including the wineries,
Eastwoodhill Arboretum, Morere Hot Springs
and Lake Waikaremoana ($150, nine hours).
Book at the i-SITE.

Festivals & Events

On October's Labour weekend, local winemakers and foodies pool talents for the
Gisborne Food & Wine Festival (☎ 0800 447 267;
www.gisbornewine.co.nz/festival; tickets $60), culminat-
ing in the main shindig on the Sunday – the
price includes buses between the vineyards
and tastings. Don't miss Saturday's free street
party and the Wine Waiters' Relay.

The huge event on the music calendar is
Rhythm & Vines (www.rhythmandvines.co.nz; Waiohika
Estate; tickets $95-215), a three-day festival leading
up to New Year's Eve that attracts big-name
local bands and international headliners.
You'll be scrambling to find accommodation
anywhere near Gisborne at this time.

Sleeping

Gisborne's speciality is midrange motor
lodges and unflashy beachside motels, although it tacks on a couple of reasonable

budget options and top-enders around the
edges.

BUDGET

Flying Nun Backpackers (☎ 06-868 0461; yager@xtra.
co.nz; 147 Roebuck Rd; campsites per person $15, dm/d $23/56;
🖥 🛜) It was probably a little more prim and
proper when it was a convent, but this grungy
old place has plenty of character and tight
security.

Gisborne YHA (☎ 06-867 3269; www.yha.co.nz; 32
Harris St; dm/s/d $26/40/62; 🖥 🛜) A short stroll
across the river from town, this well-kept hostel fills a rambling mansion with colour and
transience. The rooms are large and comfortable, but you'll need to head outside for the
bathrooms.

Eastwoodhill Arboretum (Map p344; ☎ 06-863 9003;
www.eastwoodhill.org.nz; 2392 Wharekopae Rd, Ngatapa;
dm/tw $25/80) The bunks and private rooms are
basic and you'll still need to pay the admission
on the first day, but once you're here, endless
woody delights can fill your days and nights.
There's a decent kitchen but bring food as
there's nothing for miles around.

Waikanae Beach Holiday Park (☎ 06-867 5634;
www.gisborneholidaypark.co.nz; Grey St; unpowered sites $26-
28, powered sites $32-35, d $40-62, ste $72-94; 🖥 🛜)
Right by the beach and minutes from town,
this is a useful spot to pitch a tent. Colourful
art doesn't stop the self-contained units from
looking like pensioner flats, but along with the
'ranch' cabins they're excellent value.

MIDRANGE & TOP END

Te Kura B&B (☎ 06-863 3497; www.tekura.co.nz; 14
Cheeseman Rd; r $90-140; 🖥 🛜 🛁) Play lord of the
manor at this lovely 1920s Arts and Crafts-
style riverside home. Two guest rooms (one
with clawfoot-bath en suite) share a stately
lounge and a bright breakfast room opening
on to the river, pool and spa.

Cook's Quarters B&B (☎ 06-863 3708; Cooks
-Quarters@hotmail.com; 66 Wainui Rd; d $120) A ship-
shape faux-Tudor guest house decked out
in a stylish maritime fashion. There are two
pleasantly furnished en-suite rooms, comfortable lounge and pretty garden.

Pacific Harbour Motor Inn (☎ 06-867 8847; www.
pacific-harbour.co.nz; 24 Reads Quay; r $130, ste $130-190;
🖥 🛜) This apartment-style inn overlooks
the harbour, and offers clean and well-kept
units with dated decor. Free wi-fi is available.

Senator Motor Inn (☎ 06-868 8877; www.senator
motorinn.co.nz; 2 Childers Rd; s/d/tr/q $140/140/160/180;

□ ⚹) Next door to the Pacific Harbour, the Senator offers superior views from its private balconies – the perfect place for sipping your chardonnay. The upstairs rooms have more privacy.

Emerald Hotel (☎ 06-868 8055; www.emeraldhotel. co.nz; cnr Reads Quay & Gladstone Rd; r $130-280; □ ⚹ ⚹) Opened in 2006, the Emerald is all about the swimming pool and patio area, which makes a good fist of looking like a foxy international. Surrounding it are 48 luxury suites running along epic corridors connecting the various wings. There's a gym, day spa, and the Grill Room restaurant (mains $22 to $36).

Knapdale Eco Lodge (☎ 06-862 5444; www.knapdale. co.nz; 114 Snowsill Rd, Waihirere; s/tw incl breakfast $200/300, d incl breakfast $362-418; □ ⚹) Indulge and relax at this tranquil, green idyll complete with lake, farm animals and home-grown produce. The stunning modern lodge is filled with international artwork, its glassy frontage flowing out to an expansive patio area, with brazier, barbecue, and pizza oven. Five-course dinner by arrangement ($85).

Eating
Bookshop Café (☎ 06-867 9742; 62 Gladstone Rd; meals $4-14; ⏰ 8.30am-4pm Mon-Fri, 9am-3pm Sat) Situated above Muirs Bookshop in a heritage building, this place has stripped-brick walls, exposed rafters, lovely leadlights, and a veranda over the street, along with a small but sweet selection of counter food and excellent salads. Fans of Supreme coffee and literature may need to be forcibly removed.

Café Ruba (☎ 06-868 6516; 14 Childers Rd; meals $5-19; ⏰ 7am-3pm Tue-Fri, 8.30am-3pm Sat & Sun; Ⓥ) Urbane Ruba is Gizzy's most stylish daytime stop, offering substantial breakfasts, sandwiches to order (on homemade bread) and adventurous lunches. Finish with strong coffee or an afternoon tipple.

Zest (☎ 06-867 5787; 22 Peel St; meals $7-19; ⏰ 7am-4pm Mon-Sat) Zealously zesty with its lime green frontage, this popular cafe serves good coffee, and a range of sweets, sandwiches, salads and blackboard specials using seasonal and organic produce where possible.

Café 1874 (☎ 06-863 2006; 38 Childers Rd; meals $8-19; ⏰ 7am-3pm) The creaky old grandeur of the Poverty Bay gentleman's club (1874) is reason enough to visit. This cafe within it certainly adds impetus: appealing counter food, all-day brunch, blackboard specials, reasonable prices and a pleasant garden.

Just Thai Cuisine (☎ 06-867 8028; 2 Lowe St; mains $11-17; ⏰ lunch & dinner Mon-Sat, dinner Sun; Ⓥ). A reliable purveyor of traditional Thai classics, housed in a refreshingly simple street-corner room overlooking the Taruheru River. Worthy espresso and fine teas.

Fettuccine Brothers (☎ 06-868 5700; 12 Peel St; mains $24-33; ⏰ dinner Mon-Sat) A highly polished yet relaxed affair with separate bar (live music Wednesday to Friday). The menu runs the gamut from garlic bread and antipasto, through to pasta and mammoth steaks. We give the spaghetti marinara the big thumbs up.

our pick USSCO Bar & Bistro (☎ 06-868 3246; 16 Childers Rd; mains $26-39; ⏰ dinner) Housed in the restored Union Steam Ship Company building (hence the name), this place is all class. The talented chef-owner demonstrates silky kitchen skills through a varied and exciting menu featuring the likes of roast duck with coconut sauce, crispy polenta and braised red cabbage. Devilishly good desserts and a drinks list sporting plenty of local wines and NZ beers. Live piano Tuesday to Saturday.

Self-caterers can fill the trolley at **Pak N Save** (☎ 06-868 9029; 274 Gladstone Rd; ⏰ 7am-9pm).

Drinking & Entertainment
Kingfisher (☎ 06-868 8787; 33 Gladstone Rd; ⏰ 11.30am-late Wed-Sun, 3pm-late Tue) This relative newcomer has set up in a grand old banking chamber. Attentive staff, music that's not *too* loud, pool table and proper crispy pizza served from the joint next door.

Soho Bar (☎ 06-868 3888; www.sohobar.co.nz; 2 Crawford Rd; ⏰ 11am-late Wed-Sun) This hip joint morphs from reputable restaurant to *the* place to boogie late at night. Local and occasional big-name DJs at weekends.

Smash Palace (☎ 06-867 7769; 24 Banks St; 3pm-late Mon-Fri, noon-late Sat, 2pm-late Sun) Get juiced at the junkyard. Iconic drinking den full to the gunwales with ephemera and its very own DC3 crash-landed in the garden bar. Live music most weekends.

Poverty Bay Club (☎ 06-863 2006; 38 Childers Rd; ⏰ enquire at cafe) Look out for the special occasions when this club at Café 1874 (left) is opened up to live bands and DJs. The **Dome Cinema** (www.domecinema.co.nz) shares the club rooms, showing decent films three times a week.

Odeon Multiplex Theatres (☎ 06-867 3339; 79 Gladstone Rd) New-release movies screen throughout the day.

THE EAST COAST

DAME KIRI TE KANAWA

New Zealand's most famous daughter was born in Gisborne in 1944. A true megastar of the operatic world, Te Kanawa has played leading lady in some of the world's most renowned opera houses alongside the top leading men of the age. Along the way she's picked up a Grammy and a knighthood, and sung to an audience of 600 million people at the wedding of Prince Charles and Princess Diana.

In 2005 she pulled out of a concert with Aussie pop crooner John Farnham after watching a video of him performing. No, it's wasn't his cheesy soft-rock balladeering that put her off, but rather the footage of women throwing their undies at him on stage. For a high-brow performer whose idea of a risqué show is to slip the odd show tune in among the arias, the risk of a misfired panty hurl was too much too bear.

None too pleased with her withdrawal, the concert promoters took out a lawsuit, which they lost.

Getting There & Around

AIR

Gisborne Airport (☎ 06-868 7951; www.eastland.co.nz/airport; Aerodrome Rd) is 3km west of the city. **Air New Zealand** (☎ 06-868 2700; www.airnewzealand.co.nz; 37 Bright St) flies to/from Auckland (one hour, six daily) and Wellington (70 minutes, four daily), with onward connections. Check the website for fares and special offers.

Sunair Aviation (☎ 0800 786 247; www.sunair.co.nz) offers flights on weekdays to Hamilton ($380, 75 minutes) and Napier ($280, 45 minutes) and onward to New Plymouth, Palmerston North, Rotorua, Tauranga and Whakatane ($280 to $380).

BUS

InterCity (☎ 06-868 6139; www.intercity.co.nz) buses depart daily from the i-SITE for Napier ($44, four hours) via Wairoa ($27, 90 minutes), and Auckland ($81, 9½ hours) via Opotiki ($33, two hours) and Rotorua ($60, 4½ hours).

Organised penny-pinchers can take advantage of limited $1 advance fares on **Naked Bus** (www.nakedbus.com) to Auckland via Opotiki and Rotorua.

For courier services from Gisborne to Opotiki travelling via East Cape's scenic SH35, see p345.

CAR HIRE

The following have counters at the airport:
Avis (☎ 06-868 9084; www.avis.co.nz)
Budget (☎ 06-867 9794; www.budget.co.nz)
Hertz (☎ 06-867 9348; www.hertz.co.nz)
Thrifty (☎ 06-867 4543; www.thrifty.co.nz)

TAXI

A city-to-airport taxi fare costs about $15.
Eastland Taxis (☎ 0800 868 294, 06-867 6767)
Gisborne Taxis (☎ 0800 505 555, 06-867 2222)

GISBORNE TO HAWKE'S BAY

Heading south towards Napier you're confronted with a choice: follow SH2 along the coast or take SH36 inland via Tiniroto. Either way you'll end up in Wairoa.

The coastal route is the better choice, but SH36 is also a pleasant drive. **Doneraille Park**, 49km from Gisborne, is a peaceful bush reserve with a frigid mountain river to jump into. Freedom Camping is permitted (p347). The snow white cascades of **Te Reinga Falls**, 18km further south, are worth a short detour.

South of Gisborne, SH2 runs a few kilometres inland from the coast before entering the Wharerata State Forest. Just out of the woods, 55km from Gisborne, **Morere Hot Springs** (☎ 06-837 8856; www.morerehotsprings.co.nz; SH2; adult/child $6/3; ☺ 10am-5pm, to 9pm summer) burble up from a fault line in the beautiful **Morere Springs Scenic Reserve**. You might want to tackle the bushwalks (20 minutes to two hours) before taking the plunge. The main swimming pool is near the entrance, but a five-minute streamside walk through virgin rainforest leads to the bush setting of Nikau Baths. It's actually ancient seawater that bubbles to the surface here at around 50°C, cooling by 10°C before being pumped into the small stainless-steel baths.

Opposite the springs are the **Morere Tearooms & Camping Ground** (☎ 06-837 8792; SH2; campsites $30, d $60-90). The campsites are located alongside the babbling Tunanui Stream, with basic facilities available, while the cafe makes a respectable toasted sandwich and stocks basic provisions.

Moonlight Lodge (☎ 06-837 8824; www.morerehotsprings.co.nz; SH2, Morere; s/d/tr/q $60/75/95/120) is a peaceful, grassy enclave comprised of a 1917 farmhouse, a cottage, and two cute cabins just off the highway. Graceful trees shelter this small rural idyll, with a stream, sheep, and Molly, the very sweet dog.

As you continue along SH2 keep an eye out for the unusually brightly painted **Taane-nui-a-Rangi Marae**. You can get a decent view from the road; don't enter unless invited.

SH2 continues south to Nuhaka at the northern end of Hawke Bay. From here it's west to Wairoa or east to the salty Mahia Peninsula. Not far from the Nuhaka round-about is **Kahungunu Marae** (Ihaka St). From the street you can note the carving at the house's apex of a standing warrior holding a *taiaha* (spear). It's less stylised than most traditional carving, opting for simple realism.

HAWKE'S BAY

Hawke Bay, the name given to the body of water that stretches from the sunburnt Mahia Peninsula to Cape Kidnappers, looks like it's been bitten out of the North Island's eastern flank. Add an apostrophe and an 's' and you've got a region that stretches south and inland to include fertile farmland, surf beaches, mountainous ranges and wild forests.

The southern edge of the bay is a cable-TV lifestyle channel come to life – food, wine and architecture are the shared obsessions. It's smugly comfortable but thoroughly appealing, and is best viewed through a rosé-tinted wineglass. If the weather's putting a dampener on your beach holiday plans, it's a great place to head.

MAHIA PENINSULA

The Mahia Peninsula's eroded hills, sandy beaches and vivid blue sea make it a mini-ringer of the Coromandel, but without the flash tourists and fancy subdivisions, and with the bonus of dramatic Dover-ish cliffs. It's an enduring holiday spot for the locals, who come to fish, dive, surf, birdwatch, and toast their noses. Mahia has several small settlements, a scenic reserve, and the bird-filled Maungawhio Lagoon, all of which you'll need your own transport to explore.

Cappamore Lodge (☎ 06-837 5523; oconnell capamore@clear.net.nz; 435 East Coast Rd; s/d/tr/q $80/120/140/160) is an oddball self-contained Scandinavian-style log house, crafted by Margaret and Bill. It's huge (comfortably sleeping six) with two living areas and great views from the doorstep.

Seashore B&B (☎ 06-837 5525; www.mahianz.com; 182 Newcastle St, Taylors Bay; s/tw/tr $80/140/180; ☐) is indeed right on the seashore. This modern home has friendly hosts, two bright en-suite rooms, a bunkroom sleeping five and guest lounge. Kayaks are available.

On the east coast, **Café Mahia** (☎ 06-837 5094; 476 East Coast Rd; meals $14-20; ☺ 10am-4pm Thu-Sun, 10am-4pm daily in summer, dinner Thu & Sat; ☐) sells a surprising array of preserves and doubles as the local post office and bread shop. It also has grandmotherly food, dubious coffee, and lovely deck from which you can drink in the view. Book ahead for dinner.

Sunset Point Sports Bar & Bistro (☎ 06-837 5071; cnr Newcastle & Ratau Sts; mains $20-30; ☺ 10am-late) is the (only) place in town to grab a beer and meet the locals. Pool table, darts, (fresh) fish and chips, a quality garden bar and surprisingly tuneful live music most weekends.

WAIROA
pop 5228

Poor little Wairoa is trying really hard to shirk its rough-edged reputation. A new **Wairoa Township River Walkway** takes in sites of interest along the main street, including the old solid kauri **Portland Island Lighthouse** (1877), which once stood off the Mahia Peninsula and now flashes proudly at the entrance to the town centre.

Like many small towns, economic depression seems to have spared heritage buildings from the wrecking ball. As we write there is talk of reopening the restored 1931 **Gaiety Theatre** (252 Marine Pde), so stroll by and take a look. **Wairoa Museum** (☎ 06-838 3108; wairoa museum@xtra.co.nz; 142 Marine Pde; admission by donation; ☺ 10am-4pm Mon-Fri, to 1pm Sat) has an Italianate facade from its former life as a bank.

Bird fanciers should explore **Whakamahi Lagoon**, at the river mouth, and **Whakaki Lagoon**, 10km east of town.

The enthusiastic staff at **Wairoa i-SITE** (☎ 06-838 7440; www.wairoadc.govt.nz; cnr SH2 & Queen St; ☺ 9am-4.45pm Mon-Fri, 10am-11am & 3.15-4pm Sat & Sun; ☐) have information on the wider area along with maps, internet access ($3 per 15 minutes), fishing licenses and DOC passes.

Sleeping & Eating

OUR PICK Riverside Motor Camp (☎ 06-838 6301; www. riversidemotorcamp.co.nz; 19 Marine Pde; campsites $30, dm/d/tr $20/60/80; ☐) Perky owners and the prettiest facilities block you ever did see make this

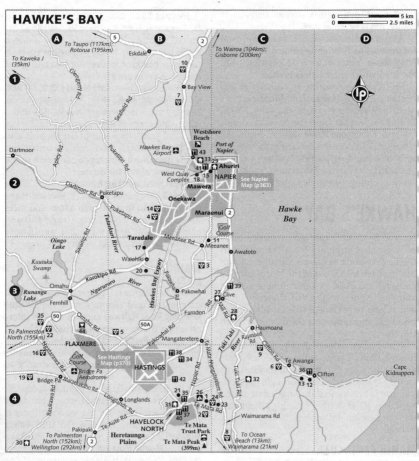

HAWKE'S BAY

place a winner. There's pleasant camping and cute cabins, while the backpacker dorm takes the form of a large room with bunks and TV.

Oslers Bakery & Café (☎ 06-838 8299; 116 Marine Pde; meals $5-15; ⏰ 8am-4pm Mon-Fri, to 3pm Sat & Sun) Call in for an award-winning pie ($3 to $4), sweet treats, decent coffee and cooked breakfast (but maybe not all at once).

East End Café (☎ 06-838 6070; 250 Marine Pde; meals $8-18; ⏰ 7.30am-4pm Tue-Fri, 8.30am-late Sat, 8.30-4pm Sun) In the same building as the Gaiety Theatre, the East End is a breath of fresh air with its spacious interior, toasted sandwiches ($6), fabulous friands, and a concise blackboard ranging from morning eggs to pizza and seafood chowder. Great coffee and juices, too.

Getting There & Away

All **InterCity** (☎ 06-838 7440; www.intercity.co.nz) buses that travel between Gisborne and Napier pass through Wairoa.

TE UREWERA NATIONAL PARK

Shrouded in mist and mysticism, Te Urewera National Park is the North Island's largest, encompassing 212,673 hectares of virgin forest cut with lakes and rivers. The highlight is Lake Waikaremoana (Sea of Rippling Waters), a deep crucible of water encircled by the Lake Waikaremoana Track, one of NZ's Great Walks. Rugged bluffs drop away to reedy inlets, the lake's mirror surface disturbed only by mountain zephyrs and the occasional waterbird taking to the skies.

The name Te Urewera still has the capacity to make Pakeha New Zealanders feel slightly uneasy – and not just because it translates as 'The Burnt Penis'. There's something primal and untamed about this wild woodland, with its rich history of Maori resistance.

The local Tuhoe people – prosaically known as the 'Children of the Mist' – never signed the Treaty of Waitangi and fought with Rewi Maniapoto at Orakau (p218) during the Waikato Wars. The army of Te Kooti (p352) took refuge here during running battles with government troops. The claimant of Te Kooti's spiritual mantle, Rua Kenana, led a thriving community beneath the sacred mountain Maungapohatu (1366m) from 1905 until his politically inspired 1916 arrest. This effectively erased the last bastion of Maori independence in the country. Maungapohatu never recovered, and only a small settlement remains. Nearby, Ruatahuna's extraordinary Mataatua Marae celebrates Te Kooti's exploits.

Tuhoe remain proud of their identity and traditions, with around 40% still speaking *te reo* (the language) on a regular basis. Te Urewera's immense and remote wilderness of seemingly endless forested ridges and pristine waters is a magical place to learn about their culture.

Information

Te Urewera National Park visitor centre (☎ 06-837 3803; www.doc.govt.nz; SH38; ☒ 8am-4.45pm) at Aniwaniwa is currently limited to one small room in a mouldering building (the future of which was undecided at the time of research).

Get your weather forecasts, accommodation information and hut or camping-ground passes for the Lake Waikaremoana Track here.

Activities

LAKE WAIKAREMOANA TRACK

The 46km track scales the spectacular Panekiri Bluff, with open panoramas interspersed with fern groves and forest. The walk is rated as moderate with the only difficult section being the Panekiri ascent. During summer it can get busy so it pays to book ahead.

Although it's a year-round track, winter rain deters many more people and makes conditions much more challenging. At this altitude (580m above sea level), temperatures can drop quickly, even in summer. Walkers should take portable stoves and fuel as there are no cooking facilities en route.

There are five huts (adult/child $25/free) and campsites (per night adult/child $12/free) spaced along the track, all of which must be prebooked through DOC as far ahead as possible, regardless of the season. Book at the Aniwaniwa, Gisborne, Wairoa, Whakatane or Napier DOC offices, i-SITEs or online at www.doc.govt.nz.

If you have a car, it is safest to leave it at the Lake Waikaremoana Motor Camp (p361) or Big Bush Holiday Park (p361) then take a water taxi (p361) to the trail heads.

Propel yourself onto the trail either clockwise from just outside Onepoto in the south or anticlockwise from Hopuruahine Bridge in the north. From Onepoto, all the steep climbing

THE EAST COAST

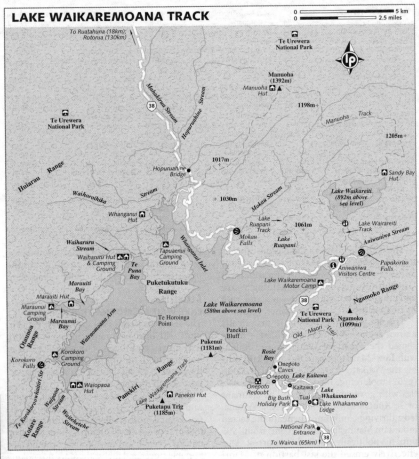

LAKE WAIKAREMOANA TRACK

happens in the first few hours. Water on this section of the track is limited so fill your bottles before heading off.

Estimated walking times:

Route	Time
Onepoto to Panekiri Hut	5hr
Panekiri Hut to Waiopaoa Hut	3-4hr
Waiopaoa Hut to Marauiti Hut	4½hr
Marauiti Hut to Waiharuru Hut	2hr
Waiharuru Hut to Whanganui Hut	2½hr
Whanganui Hut to Hopuruahine Bridge	2hr

OTHER WALKS

There are dozens of walks within the park's vast boundaries, some of which are outlined in DOC's *Lake Waikaremoana Walks* and *Recreation in Northern Te Urewera* pamphlets ($2.50).

Three- to five-day adventures for intrepid and experienced trampers can be had in the **Whakatane River** area starting near Ruatahuna. Be aware that this is serious backcountry and that there are no transport services.

The **Manuoha–Waikareiti Track** is a tough three-day walk, starting near Hopuruahine and heading up to Manuoha Hut, the park's highest point (1392m). It then follows a ridge down to Lake Waikareiti via Sandy Bay Hut, finishing at Aniwaniwa.

Shorter walks and day walks include the **Old Maori Trail** (four hours return) from Rosie Bay to Lake Kaitawa; the **Lake Waikareiti Track** (two hours return, four hours to Sandy Bay Hut one way) through beech and rimu forest; and the **Lake Ruapani Track** (six hours) including wetland wanderings.

Lake Waikareiti (892m), with its untouched islands, is an enchanting place. A fittingly fabulous way to explore it is in a rowboat (you can pick up a boatshed key from the DOC visitor centre for a small charge). You may also be lured in for a skinny dip.

Walking Legends (☎ 0800 925 569; www.walking legends.com) is an enthusiastic and experienced company running three- to four-day guided walks around Lake Waikaremoana and through Te Urewera (from $1080/880 adult/child all-inclusive).

Sleeping & Eating

DOC has over 30 huts and campsites within the park, most of which are very basic (p359).

Lake Waikaremoana Motor Camp (☎ 06-837 3826; www.lake.co.nz; SH38; campsites per adult/child $12/5, cabins $45, units $78-140) Right on the shore, this place has Swiss-looking chalets, fisherman's cabins and campsites, most with watery views. The on-site shop is full of essentials such as hot pies, chocolate and a swarm of fishing flies. The camp can also hook you up with water taxis and petrol.

Big Bush Holiday Park (☎ 0800 525 392; www.lake waikaremoana.co.nz; SH38; campsites per person $12-15, dm/d $25/80) Located 4km from the Onepoto trail head, Big Bush offers tent sites, trim cabins and acceptable backpacker rooms. Pick-ups, water taxis/scenic charters and storage are available.

Lake Whakamarino Lodge (☎ 06-837 3876; www. lakelodge.co.nz; Esplanade, Tuai; s/d/ste $57/69/100) While the lake's name might provoke sheep jokes, trout is the passion here. Originally workers' housing for the local power station, it's now a comfortable *iwi*-run fishing lodge with home-cooked meals by request.

Getting There & Around

Approximately 95km of State Highway 38 between Wairoa and Rotorua remains un-sealed and it'll take around four bone-rattling hours to do the entire journey (Wairoa to Aniwaniwa 61km, Aniwaniwa to Rotorua 139km).

Big Bush Water Taxi (☎ 0800 525 392; www. lakewaikaremoana.co.nz) will ship you to either Onepoto or Hopuruahine trail head ($30 return), with hut-to-hut pack transfers for the less gung-ho. It also runs shuttles to and from Wairoa ($30 one way).

Home Bay Water Taxi & Cruises (☎ 06-837 3826; www.waikaremoana.com) operates from Lake Waikaremoana Motor Camp (left) to either trail head ($35 return) and also offers lake cruises ($30). **Waikaremoana Guided Tours** (☎ 06-837 3729; www.waikaremoanawatertaxi.co.nz) provide a similar service, plus kayak/dinghy hire and guided trips.

WAIROA TO NAPIER

This stretch thrusts through verdant farmland for much of its 117km. Most of it follows a railway line that is currently only used for freight – you'll see what a travesty that is when you pass under the **Mohaka viaduct** (1937), the highest rail viaduct in Australasia (97m).

Occupied by early Maori, **Lake Tutira** has walkways and a bird sanctuary. At Tutira village, just north of the lake, Pohokura Rd leads to the wonderful **Boundary Stream Reserve**, a major conservation area. Three loop tracks start from the road, ranging in length from 40 minutes to three hours. Also along this road you'll find the **Opouahi** and **Bellbird Bush Scenic Reserves**, which all offer rewarding walks.

Off Waipatiki Rd, 34km outside Napier, is the 64-hectare **Waipatiki Scenic Reserve**, echoing with tui and kereru calls while the **White Pine Bush Scenic Reserve**, 29km from Napier on SH2, bristles with kahikatea and nikau palms. **Tangoio Falls Scenic Reserve**, 27km north of Napier, has Te Ana Falls, stands of wheki-ponga (tree ferns) and native orchids. Between White Pine and Tangoio Reserves the **Tangoio Walkway** (three hours return) follows Kareaara Stream.

The highway surfs the coast for the last 25km, with impressive views towards Napier. Hawke's Bay wine country starts in earnest at the mouth of the Esk River. Even the driver should safely be able to stop for a restrained tasting at one of the excellent vineyards just off SH2 (or both if you're spitting).

Esk Valley Estate (Map p358; ☎ 06-872 7430; www.esk valley.co.nz; 745 Main Rd, Bay View; tastings free; ☷ 10am-5pm) is a lovely spot to bring your picnic and enjoy some great reds. With its relaxed, rustic feel, **Crab Farm Winery** (Map p358; ☎ 06-836 6678; www.crabfarmwinery.co.nz; 511 Main Rd, Bay View; tastings free; ☷ 10am-5pm Thu-Mon, cafe 12-3pm Thu-Mon, dinner Fri) is a good stop for lunch and a glass of rosé (among others). See p372 for the full rundown on Hawke's Bay wineries.

THE EAST COAST

NAPIER

pop 55,000

You don't have to be particularly cultured to enjoy Napier but you might find its passion for architecture and fine wine surprisingly contagious. Before long you'll be blathering on about the Chicago School, Mayan decorative devices and 'hints of passionfruit on the palate' with the best of them.

The Napier of today is the silver lining of the dark cloud that was NZ's worst natural disaster. Rebuilt after the deadly 1931 earthquake in the popular styles of the time, the city retains a unique concentration of art-deco buildings. Architecture obsessives flock here from all over the world and the town milks it for all it's worth. Don't expect the Chrysler Building – Napier's art deco is resolutely low-rise – but you will find intact 1930s streetscapes, which can provoke a *Great Gatsby* swagger in the least romantic soul.

For the layperson it's a charismatic, sunny, composed city with the air of an affluent English seaside resort about it.

History

The area has been settled since around the 12th century and was known to Maori as Ahuriri. By the time James Cook eyeballed it in October 1769, Ngati Kahungunu was the dominant tribe, controlling the coast to Wellington.

In the 1830s whalers malingered around Ahuriri, establishing a trading base in 1839. By the 1850s the Crown had purchased – by often dubious means – 1.4 million acres of Hawke's Bay land, leaving Ngati Kahungunu with less than 4000 acres. The town of Napier was planned in 1854 and obsequiously named after the British general and colonial administrator Charles Napier.

At 10.46am on 3 February 1931, the city was levelled by a catastrophic earthquake (7.9 on the Richter scale). Fatalities in Napier and nearby Hastings numbered 258. Napier suddenly found itself 40 sq km larger, as the earthquake heaved sections of what was once a lagoon 2m above sea level (Napier Airport was once more 'port', less 'air'). The government claimed the extra land, also taking (without compensation) six former Ngati Kahungunu islands. A fevered rebuilding program ensued, constructing one of the world's most uniformly art-deco cities.

Orientation

Bluff Hill looms at the northern end of town dividing the CBD and Ahuriri, with its cosmopolitan bar and restaurant strip. Murmuring with economic hubbub, Hastings and Emerson Sts are the prime thoroughfares, with Emerson St evolving into a semipedestrian zone.

Free town maps are available at Napier's i-SITE (below). Road maps are available at the **Automobile Association** (AA; ☎ 06-834 2590; www.aatravel.co.nz; 87 Dickens St)

Information

The big banks cluster around the corner of Hastings and Emerson Sts, with ATMs scattered throughout the centre. Internet access is available at the i-SITE and several cafes in the city.

Beattie & Forbes (☎ 06-835 8968; 70 Tennyson St) A good selection of books.

DOC (☎ 06-834 3111; www.doc.govt.co.nz; 59 Marine Pde; ☻ 9am-4.15pm Mon-Fri) Tourist information.

Napier Health Centre (☎ 06-878 8109; 76 Wellesley Rd; ☻ 24hr)

Napier i-SITE (☎ 06-834 1911; www.visitus.co.nz; 100 Marine Pde; ☻ 9am-5pm; ☐) Tourist information.

Napier police station (☎ 06-831 0700; Station St; ☻ 24hr)

Napier post office (151 Hastings St)

Sights
ARCHITECTURE

The 1931 quake demolished most of Napier's brick buildings. Frantic reconstruction between 1931 and 1933 caught architects in the throes of global art-deco mania. Art deco, along with Spanish Mission and Stripped Classical, was cheap (debts were high), safe (falling stone columns and balconies had killed many during the earthquake) and contemporary (residents wanted to make a fresh start). A cohesive architectural vision grew from the ruins, giving Napier a new *raison d'être*.

The art-deco architectural style first made headlines at the 1925 Paris International Exposition of Modern Decorative and Industrial Arts. The deco is in the detail: zigzags, lightning bolts, sunbursts, fountains, ziggurats, speed lines, streamline shapes and ancient motifs (Mayan, Egyptian and, occasionally, Maori). Soft pastel colours (think *Miami Vice*) are another deco giveaway. Spanish Mission imitates mud-brick adobes,

NAPIER

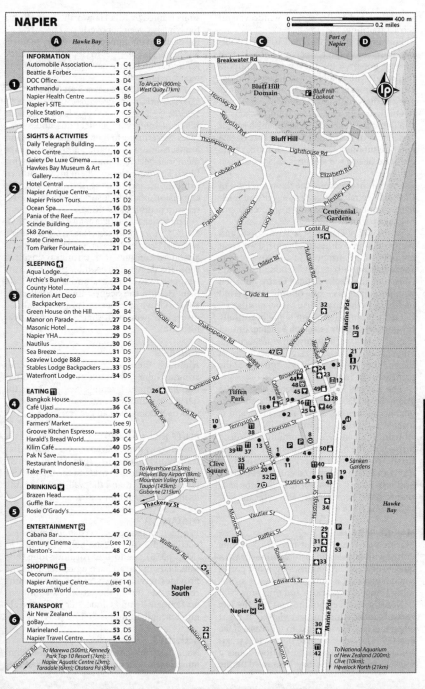

0 — 400 m
0 — 0.2 miles

INFORMATION
Automobile Association	1	C4
Beattie & Forbes	2	C4
DOC Office	3	D4
Kathmandu	4	C4
Napier Health Centre	5	B6
Napier i-SITE	6	D4
Police Station	7	C5
Post Office	8	C4

SIGHTS & ACTIVITIES
Daily Telegraph Building	9	C4
Deco Centre	10	C4
Gaiety De Luxe Cinema	11	C5
Hawkes Bay Museum & Art Gallery	12	D4
Hotel Central	13	C4
Napier Antique Centre	14	C4
Napier Prison Tours	15	D2
Ocean Spa	16	D3
Pania of the Reef	17	D4
Scinde Building	18	C4
Sk8 Zone	19	D5
State Cinema	20	C5
Tom Parker Fountain	21	D4

SLEEPING
Aqua Lodge	22	B6
Archie's Bunker	23	D4
County Hotel	24	D4
Criterion Art Deco Backpackers	25	C4
Green House on the Hill	26	B4
Manor on Parade	27	D5
Masonic Hotel	28	D4
Napier YHA	29	D5
Nautilus	30	D6
Sea Breeze	31	D5
Seaview Lodge B&B	32	D3
Stables Lodge Backpackers	33	D5
Waterfront Lodge	34	D5

EATING
Bangkok House	35	C5
Café Ujazi	36	C4
Cappadona	37	C4
Farmers' Market	(see 9)	
Groove Kitchen Espresso	38	C4
Harald's Bread World	39	C4
Kilim Café	40	D5
Pak N Save	41	C5
Restaurant Indonesia	42	D6
Take Five	43	D5

DRINKING
Brazen Head	44	C4
Guffle Bar	45	C4
Rosie O'Grady's	46	D4

ENTERTAINMENT
Cabana Bar	47	C4
Century Cinema	(see 12)	
Harston's	48	C4

SHOPPING
Decorum	49	D4
Napier Antique Centre	(see 14)	
Opossum World	50	D4

TRANSPORT
Air New Zealand	51	D5
goBay	52	C5
Marineland	53	D5
Napier Travel Centre	54	C6

THE EAST COAST

with plastered walls, arched windows and terracotta tiling.

For guided and self-guided art-deco walking tours of Napier, see opposite. If you haven't got time for that, a few highlights follow herewith (and if you can, take a wander around Napier at night when many buildings are strikingly highlighted in neon).

On the south side of town on Dickens St you'll find the deluxe Moorish-Spanish spirals and stucco of the former **Gaiety de Luxe Cinema** and fine sunburst window decorations of the old **State Cinema** – a fine mix of Spanish and art deco.

On Dalton St admire the flamingo hues of the **Hotel Central**, all zigzag swagger and leadlight complexity – it's now a strip club and massage parlour.

At the end of Dalton St is Tennyson St and many striking architectural gems. Two great examples of the Stripped Classical style are the **Scinde Building** with its Mayan botanical flourishes and the **Napier Antique Centre** adorned with *koru* patterns – one of only four period buildings in the city to use Maori motifs.

Further along Tennyson is the beautifully proportioned **Daily Telegraph Building,** one of Napier's stars, with its superb zigzags, fountain shapes and central ziggurat aesthetic. If the building is open, nip inside and ogle at the painstakingly restored foyer.

The **National Tobacco Company Building** (Map p358; cnr Bridge & Ossian Sts; 9am-5pm Mon-Fri) is arguably the region's deco masterpiece and is located a short ride from the city centre in Ahuriri. Built in 1933, it combines art-deco forms with the natural motifs of art nouveau. Roses, raupo (bulrushes) and grapevines frame the elegantly curved entrance. During business hours it's possible to pull on the leaf-shaped brass door handles and enter the first two rooms.

MARINE PARADE

Marine Pde is an elegant tree-lined avenue dotted with motels and restored timber earthquake survivors. Along its length are parks, sunken gardens, a minigolf course, a swimming complex, aquarium and museum.

Near the north end of the parade is the **Tom Parker Fountain** which is best viewed at night when it is lavishly lit. Next to it is **Pania of the Reef** (1954), Napier's iconic statue. This tragi-romantic figure from local folklore looks a little Maori and a lot Disney, her forced toothy smile framed by Rita Hayworth's hair. With a tiki lying between her overly pert breasts she's the perfect embodiment of the dusky maiden. She has her similarities to Copenhagen's *Little Mermaid,* including having been stolen and recovered in 2005.

The **Hawke's Bay Museum & Art Gallery** (06-835 7781; www.hbmag.co.nz; 9 Herschell St; adult/child/family $10/5/20; 10am-6pm) is a repository for a wide range of interesting collections and showcases these in permanent displays of Maori artefacts and a fascinating 1931 earthquake memorial gallery (do watch the deeply moving film). There are also excellent locally curated exhibitions and touring shows. Watch for expansion-related closures from late 2010; revamp plans look exciting.

The **National Aquarium of New Zealand** (06-834 1404; www.nationalaquarium.co.nz; 546 Marine Pde; adult/child $16/8; 9am-5pm, feedings 10am & 2pm) is a modern complex with a stingray-inspired roof. Inside are a crocodile, piranhas, turtles, eels, kiwi, tuatara and a whole lotta fish. 'Behind the Scenes' tours (adult/child $31/16) leave at 9am and 1pm and qualified divers can swim with sharks (dive $68, gear hire $36).

WINERIES

Although there are a handful of wineries around Napier, the bulk of the Bay's offerings are around Hastings. See p372 for the full winery rundown, and Tours, opposite, for tour operators who can get you there.

BLUFF HILL LOOKOUT

There are expansive views over Hawke Bay from Bluff Hill (102m). Open during daylight hours, the circuitous route to the top makes a pleasant wander, and the well-loved lookout itself is a nice spot for a picnic.

OTATARA PA

Wooden palisades, carved *pou* (memorial posts) and a carved gate help bring this *pa* (Map p358) site to life. An hour-long loop walk takes in the archaeological remains and provides terrific views of the surrounding countryside. From the city head southwest on Taradale Rd and Gloucester St. Turn right into Springfield Rd just before the river.

Activities

Napier's pebbly city beach isn't safe for swimming; locals head north of the city to **Westshore**

(Map p358) or to the surf beaches south of Cape Kidnappers (p375). Otherwise head to **Ocean Spa** (☎ 06-835 8553; 42 Marine Pde; adult/child $8/6; ☺ 6am-10pm Mon-Sat, 8am-10pm Sun), a spiffy waterfront pool complex that includes a beauty spa, gym and cafe.

To the south of town **Napier Aquatic Centre** (☎ 06-834 4150; www.napieraquatic.co.nz; Maadi Rd, Onekawa; adult/child $4.20/3.10, waterslides unlimited rides $4.20; ☺ 6am-9pm Mon-Fri, 11am-6pm Sat & Sun) has a 50m pool, waterslides, spas and a kids' pool.

Skaters should head to **Sk8 Zone** (☎ 06-835 6003; Marine Pde; incl skate hire adult/child $11/9; ☺ 3.30-5.30pm Mon-Fri, 10am-5pm Sat & Sun), where there's an outdoor and indoor skating rink complete with ramps. If you fancy a spin along Marine Pde they also hire rollerblades (adult/child $10/8).

Pandora Kayaks (Map p358); ☎ 06-835 0684; www.pandorakayaks.co.nz; 53 Pandora Rd; kayaks per hr from $14, bikes per day $30; ☺ daily) hire kayaks, windsurfers, surfboards, small yachts and bikes.

See if you're any closer to challenging Spiderman on the climbing wall at **Kiwi Adventure Co** (Map p358; ☎ 06-834 3500; www.kiwi-adventure.co.nz; 58 West Quay, Ahuriri; adult/child $15/12; ☺ 3-9pm Tue & Thu, 10am-6pm Sat & Sun). It also organises caving and kayaking trips.

Sixty kilometres north of Napier on SH5 is **Mountain Valley** (☎ 06-834 9756; www.mountainvalley.co.nz; McVicar Rd, Te Pohue), which offers horse trekking, white-water rafting and kayaking ($25 to $150). There's also accommodation on-site.

Hawke's Bay Wine Country Cat (Map p358; ☎ 0800 946 3228; www.hbwinecountrycat.com; West Quay, Ahuriri; cruises $25-65) schmoozes out onto Hawke Bay on a flexible schedule. It also runs the **Hawke's Bay Wine Country Duck** (☎ 0800 946 338; www.hbwinecountryduck.com; departs i-SITE; 1hr tour adult/child $40/25; ☺ tours 10.30am, 1.30pm & 3pm), an amphibious vehicle that heads in and out of the water on a (groan) 'Art Ducko' tour.

Tours

The majority of tours around Napier are focused on architecture, or wineries.

Napier's Art Deco Trust promotes and protects the city's architectural heritage. Its one-hour guided deco walk ($14) departs the i-SITE daily at 10am; the two-hour version ($20) leaves the **Deco Centre** (☎ 06-835 0022; www.artdeconapier.com; 163 Tennyson St; ☺ 9am-5pm) at 2pm daily. These excellent walks include an introductory spiel, DVD screening and

refreshments. The Deco Centre stocks assorted paraphernalia, including brochures for the excellent self-guided *Art Deco Walk* ($5), *Art Deco Scenic Drive* ($5) and *Marewa Meander* ($3). Marewa is a suburb southwest of Napier's city centre, and deco through-and-through.

Numerous operators offer tours of the deco delights and excursions around the local area: **Absolute de Tours** (☎ 06-844 8699; www.absolutedetours.co.nz) Runs the 'Deco Tour' of the city, Marewa and Bluff Hill ($38, 75 minutes) in conjunction with the Deco Centre, as well as half-day tours of Napier and Hastings ($60).

Deco Affair Tours (☎ 06-835 4492; www.decoaffair.com; tours $20-90) Trips the light fantastic in a cherry red 1934 Buick hosted by the endearingly eccentric Bertie, clad in full period regalia.

Ferg's Fantastic Tours (☎ 0800 428 687; www.fairwaytours.co.nz; half/full day $65/149) Explores Napier and surrounding areas.

Packard Promenade (☎ 06-835 1455; www.packardpromenades.co.nz; tours $130-600) Offers deco and wine tours, in a 1939 Packard Six.

Self-guided bicycle tours are offered by **Takaro Trails** (☎ 06-836 5385; www.takarotrails.co.nz; half- to 5-day tours $55-799) with gear, baggage moving, and back-up supplied. Ask about mountain-bike adventures in Eskdale Mountain Bike Park.

If you fancy going to jail, **Napier Prison Tours** (☎ 06-835 9933; www.napierprison.com; 55 Coote Rd; tours $20) offers fascinating self-guided audio tours (9am to 9pm) and hosted tours (9.30am and 3pm).

For listings of Hawke's Bay winery tours, see p371.

Festivals & Events

In the third week of February, Napier and Hastings co-host the sensational **Art Deco Weekend** (☎ 06-835 0022; www.artdeconapier.com). Dinners, dances, drinks, balls, bands and Gatsby-esque fancy dress fill the week with shenanigans. Bertie, Napier's art-deco ambassador (above), is omnipresent.

In mid-February, Mission Estate (p372) holds the popular open-air **Mission Concert** (☎ 06-845 9350; www.missionconcert.co.nz; tickets $105-205), importing a golden-oldie superstar (Tom Jones, Jimmy Barnes, the Four Tops etc) to belt out some classics.

Not to be outdone, Church Road (p372) hosts **Church Road Jazz** (tickets $45) as part of Harvest Hawke's Bay (p371) in early February.

Sleeping

BUDGET

Aqua Lodge (Map p363; ☎ 06-835 4523; aquaback@inhb.co.nz; 53 Nelson Cres; campsites per person $17, dm $25, d $60-74; 🖳 🛜 🏊) Aqua Lodge sprawls between neighbouring houses on a quiet suburban street, with campsites on the back lawn. It's a fun place – even if 'sex and peeing' are banned from the pool.

Kennedy Park Top 10 Resort (☎ 06-843 9126; www.kennedypark.co.nz; Storkey St, Marewa; campsites per person $19-21, units $107-150; 🖳 🏊) Less a camping ground and more an entire suburb of holidaymakers, this Top 10 park is top dog on the Napier camping scene and winner of the bay's 2009 Sustainable Business Award. It's the closest camping ground to town (2.5km out) and has every facility imaginable, although a larger kitchen would be nice.

ourpick Criterion Art Deco Backpackers (Map p363; ☎ 06-835 2059; www.criterionartdeco.co.nz; 48 Emerson St; dm $20, s $40-75, d $55-80, tr/q $78/87 all incl continental breakfast; 🖳 🛜) If it's interesting architecture and a central location you're after, here you have it. The vast communal area showcases the impressive internal features of what is Napier's best Spanish Mission specimen. There are special deals for guests in the bar-restaurant downstairs.

Waterfront Lodge (Map p363; ☎ 06-835 3429; www.napierwaterfront.co.nz; 217 Marine Pde; dm $21-24, s/d $42/62; 🖳 🛜) The affable hosts work hard to create a communal good-time atmosphere at this well-maintained hostel. It's a great choice if you're looking for seasonal work – they actively vet potential employers, weeding out the dodgy ones.

Stables Lodge Backpackers (Map p363; ☎ 06-835 6242; www.stableslodge.co.nz; 370 Hastings St; dm $22-26, d $58; 🖳 🛜) Formerly an actual stables; if you fill one of the small dorm rooms with blokes it'll probably smell that way again by morning. There's a barbecue courtyard, murals, hammocks, a resident cat and free internet.

Archie's Bunker (Map p363; ☎ 06-833 7990; www.archiesbunker.co.nz; 14 Herschell St; dm/s $23/35, d $56-60; 🖳 🛜) One street back from the foreshore, Archie's is a shipshape modern hostel in an old office building. A few of the rooms are windowless, but on the whole this is a well-ventilated, quiet and secure arrangement with friendly owners and bike hire.

Napier YHA (Map p363; ☎ 06-835 7039; www.yha.co.nz; 277 Marine Pde; dm $29-33, s/d $40/68; 🖳 🛜) Napier's friendly YHA is housed in a beach-front earthquake-survivor with a seemingly endless ramble of rooms; try to book one back from the street. There's a fabulous overhanging reading nook and a sunny rear courtyard.

MIDRANGE

Masonic Hotel (Map p363; ☎ 06-835 8689; www.masonic.co.nz; cnr Herschell & Tennyson Sts; s/d/tr $85/105/130) Trading on its deco heritage, the Masonic is right in the heart of town. In fact, it may well *be* the heart of town, with its accommodation, restaurants and pub taking up most of a city block. The old-fashioned rooms have period charm but the worn furnishings certainly don't add to it.

Sea Breeze (Map p363; ☎ 06-835 8067; seabreeze.napier@xtra.co.nz; 281 Marine Pde; s $95, d $110-130) Inside this Victorian seafront villa are three richly coloured themed rooms (Chinese, Indian and Turkish), decorated with a cornucopia of artefacts and exotic flair.

Green House on the Hill (Map p363; ☎ 06-835 4475; www.the-green-house.co.nz; 18b Milton Oaks, Milton Rd; s/d $110/135; 🖳 🛜) This meat-free B&B is up a steep hill and rewards with leafy surrounds and city views. The guest floor has one en suite room and one with its own bathroom. Home-baked goodies and fine herbal teas are likely to make an appearance.

Rocks Motorlodge (Map p358; ☎ 06-835 9626; www.therocksmotel.co.nz; 27 Meeanee Quay, Westshore; units $110-180; 🖳 🛜) Located just 80m from the beach, the Rocks has corrugated stylings and woodcarving that have raised the bar on Westshore's motel row. Interiors are plush with a colour-splash, and some have a spa bath, others a clawfoot. Free internet, free gym, and laundry.

Seaview Lodge B&B (Map p363; ☎ 06-835 0202; cvulodge@xtra.co.nz; 5 Seaview Tce; s $120-130, d $150-170) This grand Victorian villa (1890) is queen of all she surveys – which is most of the town and a fair bit of ocean. The elegant rooms have tasteful period elements and either bathroom or en suite. It's hard to resist a sunset tipple on the veranda, which opens off the swanky guest lounge.

Manor on Parade (Map p363; ☎ 06-834 3885; manoronparade@xtra.co.nz; 283 Marine Pde; d $140-180) Comfortable and friendly, this two-storey wooden villa on the waterfront has proved itself a solid option, having survived the earthquake and in its latter-day incarnation as a B&B.

TOP END

Crown Hotel (Map p358; ☎ 06-833 8300; www.thecrown napier.co.nz; cnr Bridge St & Hardinge Rd, Ahuriri; apt $150-600; 🖳 🛜) The conversion of this 1932 pub into a ritzy apartment-style hotel must have broken a few fishermen's hearts. The new wing may be generically modern but it offers superb ocean views. There's also a gym.

Nautilus (Map p363; ☎ 06-974 6550; www.nautilus napier.co.nz; 387 Marine Pde; studio/ste $175-300; 🖳 🛜) Napier's newest hotel, and a relatively good bit of architecture it is, too. Views from every room, decor with spunk, spa baths, private balconies and an in-house restaurant.

County Hotel (Map p363; ☎ 06-835 7800; www. countyhotel.co.nz; 12 Browning St; r/ste $350/488; 🖳 🛜) There's luxury infused between the masonry at this elegantly restored Edwardian building (a rare brick earthquake survivor). Chambers restaurant breathes refined formality at dinner (mains $30 to $42) while Winston's portrait gazes victoriously over Churchill's Champagne and Snug Bar.

Eating

RESTAURANTS

Provedore (Map p358; ☎ 06-834 0189; 60 West Quay; tapas $6-15, mains $27-35; ☽ 5pm-late Tue-Fri, 10am-late Sat & Sun) A chic little number, from the deco facade in. Partake in some of the best food in Napier, from tapas, to mains, dessert and cheese. With a clutch of good NZ beers and fine wines, Provedore lures the sophisticated barfly, too.

Kilim Café (Map p363; ☎ 06-835 9100; 193 Hastings St; mains $15-19; ☽ 11am-late; **V**) Authentic Turkish cuisine in a rather smart cafe environment, adorned with suitably Ottoman cushions and wall hangings. Kebabs, felafel, hummus, dolmas, pide and meze – all fresh and every one tasty. Eat in or take away.

Bangkok House (Map p363; ☎ 06-835 5335; 205 Dickens St; mains $16-25; ☽ lunch Tue-Sat, dinner Tue-Sun; **V**) Cheery Thai restaurant with an expansive menu of Siam favourites. Fresh, spicy and good value, too. Deservedly popular with locals.

Restaurant Indonesia (Map p363; ☎ 06-835 8303; 409 Marine Pde; mains $25-29; ☽ dinner Wed-Sun; **V**) Crammed with Indonesian curios, this intimate space oozes authenticity. Lip-smacking Indo-Dutch *rijsttafel* smorgasbords are the house speciality (14 dishes, $35).

CAFES

our pick **Cappadona** (Map p363; ☎ 06-835 3368; 189 Emerson St; snacks $2-9, mains $9-16; ☽ 7am-5pm) In a town of good cafes, this is a standout, both for its modern, upbeat ambience, and a packed cabinet of downright foxy food. Besides an alluring row of biscuit jars, iced muffins and cakes, there are fresh sandwiches, salads and pastries. The hot menu has brunchy, lunchy dishes.

Westshore Fish Café (Map p358; ☎ 06-834 0227; 112a Charles St; takeaway $4-7, meals $14-26; ☽ lunch Wed-Sun, dinner Tue-Sun) If you're the type who needs cutlery, proper sit-down meals are served here. Otherwise grab some of the acclaimed fish and chips and contend with the gulls on the beach.

Café Ujazi (Map p363; ☎ 06-835 1490; 28 Tennyson St; snacks $4-9, meals $10-19; ☽ 8am-5pm; **V**) Ujazi folds back its windows and lets the alternative vibe spill out onto the street. The superb coffee, substantial breakfasts and sparkly staff are a great hangover remedy. Try the *rewana* special – a big breakfast on traditional Maori bread.

Hep Set Mooch (Map p358; ☎ 06-833 6332; 58 West Quay; mains $9-17; ☽ 9am-3pm) A good place if you like a marina view, supersize brunch, fresh baking and good coffee. Not so good if you have an aversion to bright yellow and green walls and dubious artwork.

Groove Kitchen Espresso (Map p363; ☎ 06-835 8530; 112 Tennyson St; breakfast & lunch $8-19, dinner $24-27; ☽ breakfast & lunch Mon-Sun, dinner Fri & Sat) A fitting name for a one of Napier's newer eateries. The sophisticated cafe fare, understated decor and cool tunes give it the X-factor. There's occasional late-night grooving to be had here, too.

Take Five (Map p363; ☎ 06-835 4050; 189 Marine Pde; mains $28-35; ☽ 6pm-late) 'Wine-food-jazz-art-ambience' – that works for us. Live weekend jazz is accompanied by organic, free-range suppers and indulgent desserts.

QUICK EATS & SELF-CATERING

Harald's Bread World (Map p363; ☎ 06-833 6246; 205 Emerson St; lunch $3-7; ☽ 8am-3pm Tue-Fri, to 1pm Sat) A cheap, good stop for lovers of European-style baking, with strong breads, croissants, hefty sandwiches and patisserie.

The weekly **Farmers Market** (Map p363; 49 Tennyson St; ☽ 8.30am-12.30pm Sat) is held behind the Daily Telegraph building and sells an array of local edibles.

Pak N Save (Map p363; ☎ 06-834 3450; 25 Munroe St; ☽ 8am-midnight) is a five-minute walk from the centre of town.

Drinking

If you're looking for late-night action, your best bet is Ahuriri (Map p358), the main feather on Napier's fascinator. This strip of newish restaurant-cum-bars offers a perfunctory array of food (with the exception of the classy Provedore, p367), the focus firmly on emptying the wallets of weekend boozers who flock in, particularly in high summer. Expect barnlike interiors, big screens, nautical themes, open fire, outdoor seating (a highlight) and boring beer options. DJs or live music are a feature, as is the spectacle of the locals breaking out their best dance moves – there's nothing like a bit of '70s twang-rock to bring folk out of their shell. Ahuriri's best is arguably the **Thirsty Whale** (☎ 06-835 8815), followed by **Shed 2** (☎ 06-835 2202) and the **Gintrap** (☎ 06-835 0199). Oh, hang on a minute: that's just about all of them...

Napier town's options for drinking and dancing have a bit more character, and are pretty much centred around Hastings St:

Brazen Head (☎ 06-834 3587; 21 Hastings St) Poker machines compromise the vibe at this Irish bar, but the beer's cold and the outdoor deck is a brazen spot to get through a few.

Guffle Bar (29a Hastings St) Cool tunes, nice drinks and genial pros behind the bar. Ingredients that woo the town's sophisticates through the doors.

Rosie O'Grady's (☎ 06-835 8689; 68 Hastings St) Part of the Masonic megaplex, Rosie's predictable Irishness fills in the gaps between dimly lit corners, pints of Guinness and intermittent live music.

Entertainment

Cabana Bar (☎ 06-835 1102; 11 Shakespeare Rd) This legendary music venue of the '70s, '80s and '90s died in 1997, but thanks to some forward-thinking, toe-tapping folk, it's risen from the grave. Visit its website (www.cabana.net.nz) to see who's on, then get down there and shake your thang.

Harstons (☎ 06-834 1209; 35 Hastings St) The place for live music and DJs. Housed in a former piano showroom which has converted surprisingly well into a music venue (good acoustics, nice dance floor), Harstons brings national and occasionally international artists to town to entertain the late-niters. A great attempt at big-city sophistication in a city that quite possibly doesn't appreciate it.

Century Cinema (☎ 06-835 7781; www.centurycinema.co.nz; 65 Marine Pde; adult/child tickets $13/9) Part of the Hawke's Bay Museum complex, this cinema screens art-house and international films and hosts plays and classical concerts.

Shopping

If deco devotees survive the Deco Centre (p365) with spare cash, they can go completely bonkers in Napier's numerous antique stores including **Decorum** (☎ 06-835 8951; cnr Tennyson & Herschell Sts) and **Napier Antique Centre** (☎ 06-835 9865; cnr Tennyson St & Cathedral Ln).

Those looking for something warm and woolly should try **Opossum World** (☎ 06-835 7697; 157 Marine Pde; ☼ 9am-5pm) or **Classic Sheepskins** (Map p358; ☎ 06-835 9662; 22 Thames St; ☼ 7.30am-5pm Mon-Fri, 9am-4pm Sat & Sun).

Getting There & Away

AIR

Hawke's Bay Airport (☎ 06-835 3427; www.hawkesbay-airport.co.nz) is 8km north of the city.

Air New Zealand (☎ 06-833 5400; www.airnewzealand.co.nz; cnr Hastings & Station Sts) Daily direct flights to Auckland (55 minutes), Wellington (50 minutes) and Christchurch (1 hour 40 minutes); check website for prices and discount fares.

Sunair Aviation (☎ 0800 786 247; www.sunair.co.nz) Offers direct flights on weekdays to Gisborne ($280, 45 minutes), Hamilton ($380, one hour) and onward to New Plymouth, Palmerston North, Rotorua, Tauranga and Whakatane ($280 to $380).

BUS

InterCity (www.intercity.co.nz) operates from the **Napier Travel Centre** (☎ 06-834 2720; Munroe St; ☼ 8am-5pm Mon-Fri, 8-11.30am & 12.30-1.30pm Sat & Sun). Buses depart daily for Auckland ($89, seven hours) via Taupo ($35, two hours), Gisborne ($44, four hours) via Wairoa ($31, 2½ hours), and Wellington ($37, 5½ hours) via Hastings ($16 to $20, 25 minutes) and Waipukurau ($12 to $27, one hour).

If you're superorganised you can take advantage of $1 advance fares on **Naked Bus** (www.nakedbus.com) on the Auckland–Wellington route via Hastings and Taupo.

Bay Xpress (☎ 0800 422 997; www.bayxpress.co.nz) has a daily service to/from Wellington ($40, five hours) via Waipukurau ($10, one hour).

Getting Around

BUS

goBay (☎ 06-878 9250; www.hbrc.govt.nz) runs the local bus service, covering Napier, Hastings, Havelock North and thereabouts. There are ample services between the main centres

Monday to Friday, including three different routes between Napier and Hastings taking between 30 minutes (express) and 55 minutes (all stops). Buses depart from Dalton St near the corner of Station St (Map p363). On Saturdays there are only five all-stop buses (adult/child $4.50/2.50), between 9am and 5pm; signal the driver and pay on the bus.

BICYCLE
Bikes (including tandems and children's) can be hired from **Marineland** (☎ 06-834 4027; 290 Marine Pde; per hr/half-day/full day $10/20/30; ☀ 8am-5pm).

CAR
The following offices are at Napier Airport:
Avis (☎ 06-835 1828; www.avis.co.nz)
Hertz (☎ 06-835 6169; www.hertz.co.nz)
Rent-a-Dent (☎ 06-834 0688; www.napiercarrentals.co.nz)

TAXI
A city-to-airport taxi ride will cost you around $15.
Napier Taxis (☎ 06-835 7777)
Super Shuttle (☎ 0800 748 885; www.supershuttle.co.nz)

HASTINGS & AROUND
pop 67,443
Positioned at the centre of the Hawke's Bay fruit bowl, Hastings is the commercial hub of the region, 20km south of Napier. Similarly devastated by the 1931 earthquake, its fine collation of art-deco and Spanish Mission buildings also emerged in the aftermath. But apart from the architecture, Hastings itself isn't especially enthralling. It's in the surrounding district that epicurean dreams come true.

A few kilometres of orchards still separate Havelock North from Hastings, although these days it's effectively Hastings' ritziest suburb. SUVs and BMWs cruise the streets as bleached-blonde 50-something women sip lattes in a prosperous village atmosphere. The towering backdrop of Te Mata Peak keeps things in perspective.

Orientation
Hastings' flat grid centres on the railway line, with Heretaunga Sts East and West the main commercial strips on either side of the tracks. SH2 heads northeast to Napier, passing through Clive as it nears the coast. Havelock North is southwest of Hastings.

Information
Hastings i-SITE (Map p370; ☎ 06-873 0080; www.hastings.co.nz; cnr Russell St & Heretanga St E; ☀ 8.30am-5pm Mon-Fri, 9am-4pm Sat, to 3pm Sun) Internet access, free maps, trail brochures and bookings.
Havelock North visitor information centre (☎ 06-877 9600; www.villageinfo.co.nz; The Roundabout; ☀ 10am-4pm Mon-Fri, to 2pm Sat & Sun)
Hawke's Bay Hospital (☎ 06-878 8109; Omahu Rd)
Police station (Map p370; ☎ 06-873 0500; Railway Rd, Hastings)
Post office (Map p370; cnr Market St & Heretaunga St W, Hastings)

Sights
ARCHITECTURE & ART
While art deco abounds, Spanish Mission has the upper hand here. Cream of the crop is the **Hawke's Bay Opera House** (Map p370; ☎ 06-873 8962; www.hawkesbayoperahouse.co.nz; Hastings St S, Hastings). Although you wouldn't guess from the sturdy Spanish-Mission exterior, its lavish art-nouveau heart betrays it as an earthquake survivor. Built in 1910, it's recently had a multimillion-dollar refit and a modern plaza and foyer added. Tours take place during Art Deco Weekend (p365).

A close second in the glamorous edifice stakes is the **Westerman's Building** (Map p370; cnr Russell & Heretaunga St E, Hastings). Pop into the i-SITE for a closer look at its intricate leadlight shopfront with intact terrazzo floors. The **Spanish Mission Hastings walking tour** (☎ 0800 427 846; $10; ☀ tours 11am-12.15pm Sat) starts here; book at the i-SITE.

The **Hastings City Art Gallery** (Map p370; ☎ 06-871 5095; www.hastingscityartgallery.co.nz; 201 Eastbourne St E, Hastings; admission free; ☀ 10am-4.30pm) presents contemporary New Zealand art in a pleasant, purpose-built space.

TE MATA PEAK
Spiking melodramatically from the Heretaunga Plains, **Te Mata Peak** (Map p358), 16km south of Havelock North, is part of the 98-hectare Te Mata Trust Park. The road to the 399m summit passes sheep trails, rickety fences and vertigo-inducing stone escarpments cowled in a bleak, lunar-meets-Scottish-Highland atmosphere.

The lookout at the top could do with a makeover by the Rotarians, but it's really all about the views which – on a clear day – fall away to Hawke Bay, Mahia Peninsula and distant Mt Ruapehu.

THE EAST COAST

The view *of* Te Mata is also extraordinary. To local Maori this is the sleeping giant *Te Mata O Rongokako*. From the fields around Havelock North, a little imagination will conjure up the giant, lying on his back with his head to the right.

The park's network of trails offers up walks from 30 minutes to two hours. Our pick is the Peak Trail for views, but all are detailed in the *Te Mata Trust Park* brochure available from local visitor centres.

Activities
FOOD AND WINE

The Hastings area appears to exist solely for the satisfaction of our appetites (for proof, see the *Hawke's Bay Food Trail* brochure, available

from the i-SITE). Beyond a great big bunch of wineries (p372), there is a plethora of boutique food producers:

Arataki Honey (Map p358; ☎ 06-877 7300; www.arataki honey.co.nz; 66 Arataki Rd, Havelock North; ⏰ 9am-5pm) Stock up on buzzy by-products for your toast or your skin. There are kid-conducive hands-on displays outlining the whole sticky cycle from flower to jar.

Filter Room (Map p358; ☎ 06-845 4084; Awatoto Rd; ⏰ 10am-5pm) Surrounded by orchards, these folk offer a large range of beers and ciders, all brewed on-site, plus a $12 tasting tray and tummy-filling food.

Hohepa Organic Cheeses (Map p358; ☎ 06-870 0426; www.hohepa.com; 363 Main Rd, Clive; ⏰ 9am-5pm Mon-Fri, 9.30am-2.30pm Sat) Part of a Steiner-based community of people with intellectual disabilities, this shop sells local produce, including delicious cheese (made

HASTINGS

0 _____ 400 m
0 _____ 0.2 miles

0 ___ 50 m

INFORMATION
Hastings i-SITE.................................(see 6)
Police Station......................................**1** D1
Post Office...**2** D1

SIGHTS & ACTIVITIES
Hastings City Art Gallery....................**3** C3
Hawkes Bay Opera House...................**4** C3
Vidal..**5** D4
Westerman's Building.........................**6** D1

SLEEPING
A1 Backpackers...................................**7** A1
Gloucester House Motel.....................**8** B2
Rotten Apple..**9** D1
Sleeping Giant...................................**10** A2

EATING
New World..**11** C3
Opera Kitchen....................................**12** C3
Rush Munro's.....................................**13** B2

ENTERTAINMENT
Reading Cinemas...............................**14** D1

TRANSPORT
Air New Zealand................................**15** D1
goBay Bus Stop..................................**16** C3
InterCity Bus Stop.............................**17** D1

on-site), biodynamic fruit and vegetables, candles and clothing.

Rush Munro's (Map p370; ☎ 06-878 9634; 704 Heretaunga St W; ice cream $3-8; ☼ noon-5pm Mon-Fri, 11am-5pm Sat & Sun) Rush Munro's is a Hastings icon, serving up locally made ice cream since 1926.

Silky Oak Chocolate Company (Map p358; ☎ 06-845 0908; 1131 Links Rd, Waiohiki; ☼ 9am-5pm Mon-Thu, to 4pm Fri, 10am-4pm Sat & Sun) Watch the chocolatiers at work while deliberating over mouth-watering truffles and chocolate rugby balls. The museum (adult/child $8/5) offers a chocolate-drenched history and the odd ancient Mayan artefact. There's a cafe next door.

Strawberry Patch (Map p358; ☎ 06-877 1350; Havelock Rd; ice creams $3-4; ☼ 9am-5.30pm Mon-Sat, 8.30am-5pm Sun) A berry farm with more to offer than luscious red fruit – fruity ice cream, fresh local produce and espresso.

Telegraph Hill (Map p358; ☎ 06-878 4460; www.telegraphhill.co.nz; 1279 Howard St, Hastings; ☼ 9am-5pm Mon-Fri, 10am-3pm Sat) A small producer of olives, oils and all sorts of Mediterranean-influenced gourmet treats. Four-person picnic baskets ($30) available for on-site indulgence.

Te Mata Cheese Company (Map p358; ☎ 06-875 8282; 393 Te Mata Rd, Havelock North; ☼ 10am-3.30pm) Watch the cheesemakers through the window, have a platter and a glass of vino in the garden, then gather up some picnic supplies to go.

OTHER ACTIVITIES

South of Cape Kidnappers are Ocean Beach and Waimarama, famous for their **surf**. Hastings' massive **Splash Planet** (☎ 06-873 8033; www.splashplanet.co.nz; Grove Rd, Hastings; adult/child $25/18; ☼ 10am-5.30pm Nov-Feb) is the next best thing, with plenty of pools, slides and aquatic excitement.

Early Morning Balloons (☎ 06-879 4229; www.hotair.co.nz; adult/child $325) provides inflated views over grapey Hawke's Bay.

Te Mata is a **paragliding** hotspot, with voluminous updraughts offering exhilarating whooshes through the air. **Airplay Paragliding** (☎ 06-845 1977; www.airplay.co.nz) has tandem paragliding ($140) and full-day beginners' courses ($180).

Tours

Long Island Tours (☎ 0800 875 021; www.longislandtoursnz.com) offers customised tours across a wide range of interests including Maori culture, bush walks, kayaking, horse riding and, inevitably, food and wine.

Te Hakakino (☎ 06-879 9302; www.waimaramaori.com; 2½hr tour adult/child $50/25) hosts guided tours of a historic hill fortress revealing history, archaeological remains and cultural insights en route.

See also Absolute de Tours (p365) and the Spanish Mission Hastings walking tour (p369).

WINE TOURS

The majority of tours in this part of the world are focused on wine. Tours are usually by minibus, lasting around four hours and starting at $55 per person, with four or five wineries on the agenda. Numerous operators offer various (often customised) tour options:

Bay Tours & Charters (☎ 06-844 0601; www.baytours.co.nz)

Friendly Kiwi Tours (☎ 021 229 6223; www.friendlykiwi.co.nz)

Grape Escape (☎ 0800 100 489; www.grapeescape.net.nz)

Odyssey NZ (☎ 0508 639 773; www.odysseynz.com)

Prinsy's (☎ 06-845 3703; www.prinsyexperience.co.nz)

Vince's World Of Wine (☎ 06-836 6705; www.vincestours.co.nz)

BIKE TOURS

Costing between $35 and $50 for a full day, a self-guided bicycle tour will temper your viticulture with a little exercise. The following folk will equip you with a bike, map, helmet, water bottle, backpack and mobile phone (in case you get lost/tired/woozy):

Bike About Tours (☎ 06-845 4836; www.bikeabouttours.co.nz)

Bike D'Vine (☎ 06-833 6697; www.bikedevine.com)

On Yer Bike (☎ 06-879 8735; www.onyerbikehb.co.nz)

Festivals & Events

Harvest Hawke's Bay (☎ 0800 442 9463; www.harvesthawkesbay.co.nz; entry $45, bus from Napier, Hastings or Havelock North $20) is the region's premier wine, food and entertainment festival, held in late January at Roy's Hill near Hastings.

Hastings and Napier co-host the Art Deco Weekend (p365) in mid-February. The **Hastings Blossom Festival** (☎ 06-878 9447; www.blossomfestival.co.nz), a petalled spring fling, happens in the second half of September, with parades, arts, crafts and visiting artists.

Sleeping

Much of the superior accommodation lies outside the city's confines. As for Hastings'

THE EAST COAST

HAWKE'S BAY WINERIES

Once upon a time this district was most famous for its orchards. Today it's vines that have top billing, with Hawke's Bay now New Zealand's second-largest wine-producing region. Elaborate modern edifices have sprung up to house restaurants and tasting rooms, but some of the best vineyards still have an authentic horticultural feel. The stony area just to the west of Flaxmere that is ill-suited to fruit trees is fast becoming recognised as its own subappellation, Gimblett Gravels, and has been producing excellent Bordeaux-style reds, syrah and chardonnay.

The following wineries are all open for tastings throughout the summer and most in winter. Tastings are generally free, but there's a small charge at some (refundable on purchase). The *Hawke's Bay Winery Guide* details all the region's wineries and has a useful map, but you might also like to check out the *Classic New Zealand Wine Trail* (www.classicwinetrail.co.nz) – a useful tool for joining the dots throughout the Hawke's Bay, Wairarapa and Marlborough wine regions. See p371 for wine tours.

- **Black Barn Vineyards** (Map p358; ☎ 06-877 7985; www.blackbarn.com; Black Barn Rd; ✆ 10am-5pm) Bistro gallery, Saturday growers market and an amphitheatre.
- **Brookfields** (Map p358; ☎ 06-834 4615; www.brookfieldsvineyards.co.nz; 376 Brookfields Rd; ✆ 11am-4.30pm) Excellent reds and a restaurant among the roses.
- **Church Road** (Map p358; ☎ 06-844 2053; www.churchroad.co.nz; 150 Church Rd; ✆ 10am-5pm). Winery and museum tours (11am and 2pm).
- **C J Pask** (Map p358; ☎ 06-879 7906; www.cjpaskwinery.co.nz; 1133 Omahu Rd; ✆ 10am-5pm Mon-Sat, 11am-4pm Sun) One of the original Hawke's Bay wineries, dedicated to producing great reds.
- **Clearview Estate Winery** (Map p358; ☎ 06-875 0150; www.clearviewestate.co.nz; 194 Clifton Rd, Te Awanga; ✆ 10am-5pm) Award-winning wines and a decent restaurant. Friendly, rustic and ideal for families.
- **Crab Farm** (Map p358; ☎ 06-836 6678; www.crabfarmwinery.co.nz; 511 Main Rd, Bay View; ✆ 10am-5pm Thu-Mon) Decent, reasonably priced wines and a great cafe (p361).
- **Craggy Range** (Map p358; ☎ 06-873 0141; www.craggyrange.com; 253 Waimarama Rd; ✆ 10am-5pm) Definitely one of the flashest wineries – wonderful wines, excellent restaurant (p374) and accommodation.
- **Elephant Hill** (Map p358; ☎ 06-873 0400; www.elephanthill.co.nz; 86 Clifton Rd, Te Awanga; ✆ 11am-5pm) Ubermodern winery and restaurant with sea views (p374).
- **Esk Valley** (Map p358; ☎ 06-872 7430; www.eskvalley.co.nz; 745 Main Rd, Bay View; ✆ 10am-5pm). Excellent Bordeaux-style reds, chardonnay and riesling. See also p361.
- **Mission Estate** (Map p358; ☎ 06-845 9350; www.missionestate.co.nz; 198 Church Rd, Napier; ✆ 9am-5pm Mon-Sat, 10am-4.30pm Sun) NZ's oldest winery with beautiful grounds, and restaurant housed within a restored, historic seminary.
- **Ngatarawa** (Map p358; ☎ 06-879 7603; www.ngatarawa.co.nz; 305 Ngatarawa Rd; ✆ 10am-5pm) An 1890 farmstead with great picnicking opportunities.
- **Sileni Estates** (Map p358; ☎ 06-879 8768; www.sileni.co.nz; 2016 Maraekakaho Rd; ✆ 10am-5pm) Looks like it's been beamed in from space. Tasting room and gourmet food store.
- **Te Awa** (Map p358; ☎ 06-879 7602; www.teawa.com; 2375 SH50; ✆ 10am-4pm) Casually stylish winery with an excellent restaurant (p374) – a must-do lunch where the kids can come too.
- **Te Mata Estate** (Map p358; ☎ 06-877 4399; www.temata.co.nz; 349 Te Mata Rd; ✆ 9am-5pm Mon-Fri, 10am-5pm Sat, 11am-4pm Sun) Producer of the legendary Coleraine red and Elston chardonnay.
- **Trinity Hill** (Map p358; ☎ 06-879 7778; www.trinityhill.com; 2396 SH50; ✆ 10am-5pm) Serious reds and top-ranking chardonnay.
- **Vidal** (Map p370; ☎ 06-872 7440; www.vidal.co.nz; 913 St Aubyn St E, Hastings; ✆ 10am-5pm) One of the Bay's oldest wineries. Quality wines and restaurant.

THE EAST COAST

hostels, you'll have to fight for your bed with hordes of seasonal workers.

BUDGET

Arataki Holiday Park (Map p358; ☎ 06-877 7479; arataki. motel.holiday.park@xtra.co.nz; 139 Arataki Rd, Havelock North; campsites per person $16, caravan from $55, cabins $60, units from $125; ☒) Judging by its faded minigolf course and museum-piece ovens, this small camping ground has seen plenty of summers. On the upside, it's cheap, pleasantly rural and handy to local attractions.

Sleeping Giant (Map p370; ☎ 06-878 5393; sleeping giant@xtra.co.nz; 109 Davis St; dm/tw $20/50; ☒ ☎) A comfy backpackers in a suburban street, 10 minutes' walk to town. A posse of tanned, wiry agricultural workers ensures an atmosphere of laid-back sociability, in the fairly close communal confines of lounge and courtyard where the odd barbeque takes place. Off-street parking is available.

Rotten Apple (Map p370; ☎ 06-878 4363; www.rotten apple.co.nz; 114 Heretaunga St, Hastings; dm $22-26, s/d $40/70; ☒) The central city option and a fairly nondescript affair save for a fresh lick of paint, pleasant TV lounge and a bit of balcony here and there. The Apple is home to a bunch of fruit-pickers; keen weekly rates encourage them to settle in. There's even handy free evening parking.

A1 Backpackers (Map p370; ☎ 06-873 4285; a1back packers@xtra.co.nz; 122 Stortford St, Hastings; dm/s/d $23/33/56; ☒) Proving that Hawke's Bay hostels during the fruit-picking season don't need to resemble indentured labour camps, this converted suburban house is cheerful and attractive, with leadlight windows, polished wooden floors and a homely garden.

Hastings Top 10 Holiday Park (☎ 06-878 6692; www. hastingstop10.co.nz; 610 Windsor Ave; campsites $30, units $55-155; ☒ ☎) Putting the 'park' back into holiday park, within its leafy confines are sycamore hedges, a topiary 'welcome' sign, stream, duck pond, aviary and plenty of serenity.

Clive Chalets (Map p358; ☎ 06-870 0609; 31 Farndon Rd, Clive; s/d $55/65) Chalet is a fancy name for the kind of basic cabins and units usually found in a motor camp. Perhaps it's the miniforest of Christmas-tree pines that gives it alpine delusions. There's a semidetached campsite with lots of long-termers next door (per person $15).

MIDRANGE & TOP END

Gloucester House Motel (Map p370; ☎ 06-876 3741; www.gloucesterhousemotel.co.nz; 404 Avenue Rd; units $135-190; ☒ ☒) Picket fences and colourful roses welcome you to this spick-and-span motel, five minutes' walk from the centre of town. The 11 units are spotlessly clean and spacious, with kitchen facilities and separate lounge-dining areas. Cool off with a dip in the saltwater pool.

Havelock North Motor Lodge (Map p358; ☎ 06-877 8627; www.havelocknorthmotorlodge.co.nz; 7 Havelock Rd; units $135-190) Smack-bang in the middle of Havelock North, this modern motel is a cut above the rest. Tidy one- and two-bedroom units feature spas, Sky TV and cooking facilities.

our pick Clive Colonial Cottages (Map p358; ☎ 06-870 1018; m.jstones@xtra.co.nz; 198 School Rd, Clive; d from $150) Two minutes walk from the beach and almost equidistant from Hastings, Napier and Havelock, these four purpose-built character cottages sit around a pretty scented garden on two-acre woodland property. Pleasant communal areas include barbecue, games room and *pétanque* court. Bike hire is also available.

Millar Road (Map p358; ☎ 06-875 1977; www.millar road.co.nz; 83 Millar Rd; d $400-500; ☒) Set above a young vineyard in the Tuki Tuki Hills, Millar Road is architecturally heaven-sent. Two seriously plush self-contained cottages (separated by a swimming pool and bar) burgeon with NZ-made furniture and local artworks. Each comfortably sleeps two couples in separate en-suite rooms. Stylish, uncomplicated, perfect.

Greenhill Lodge (Map p358; ☎ 06-879 9944; www. greenhill.co.nz; 103 Greenhill Rd; s $690-920, d $980, ste $1240; ☒ ☎ ☒) Siting proudly on a secluded hilltop, this 1895 Victorian mansion is a well-preserved beauty, offering guests a positively alluring combination of luxury rooms, sumptuous meals, billiard room, barbecue patio, swimming pool, spa, gardens and a gorgeous veranda overlooking the green hills themselves.

Eating

Provincial New Zealand is pretty dependable for high quality coffee, cafe fare and bakeries, and the Hastings area is by no means an exception. However, it is the wineries and artisan food producers we have to thank for the area's culinary highlights, which include some particularly fine Bordeaux-style reds (enjoyed best at numerous winery restaurants), ice cream, lovely cheese, and a perplexing amount

THE EAST COAST

of pickle. See p372 for wineries and p370 for just some of the many visitor-friendly local food producers.

RESTAURANTS

Diva (Map p358; ☎ 06-877 5149; Napier Rd, Havelock North; lunch $15-20, dinner $28-33; ☻ dinner) The most happening place in Havelock, Diva offers good value lunch (from fish and chips to Caesar salad) and a bistro-style menu featuring fresh seafood and seasonal specialities. Designed to within an inch of its life, the interior is divided into flash dining room and groovy bar (snacks from $5), plus lively pavement tables.

our pick **Pipi** (Map p358; ☎ 06-877 8993; 16 Joll Rd, Havelock North; mains $16-30; ☻ 4-10pm Wed-Sun; **V**) Shockingly pink with candy stripes and mismatched furniture, Pipi cheekily thumbs its nose at small-town conventionality. The food focus is on simple pasta dishes and Roman-style thin-crusted pizza.

Elephant Hill (Map p358; ☎ 06-873 6060; 86 Clifton Rd, Te Awanga; mains $21-34; ☻ 11am-10pm) Modern winery with edgy architecture, and food, wine and service to match the stunning sea views.

Te Awa (Map p358; ☎ 06-879 7602; 2375 SH50; mains $24-35; ☻ lunch) The raw-wood-beamed conservatory looking onto the vines is a wonderful locale for a lazy lunch, as is the pretty garden. The menu is packed with fresh, seasonal flavour (lovely salads), chocolate fondant and cheese, which you'd do well to match up with Te Awa's 'wine flight' ($20).

Terrôir at Craggy Range (Map p358; ☎ 06-873 0143; 253 Waimarama Rd, Havelock North; mains $27-35; ☻ lunch Mon-Sun, dinner Mon-Sat) A surprisingly rustic dining room, housed in the cathedral-like 'wine barrel' of the Craggy complex, provides one of the region's most consistent fine-dining experiences. The views of Te Mata peak from the terrace are almost as impressive as the wine list.

CAFES

Jackson's Bakery & Café (Map p358; ☎ 06-877 5708; 15 Middle Rd, Havelock North; pies $3-6; ☻ 6am-5pm Mon-Fri, to 4pm Sat, 7am-4pm Sun) Baking so good it causes pavement snarl-ups on weekends. Blame it on the pies.

Bay Espresso (Map p358; ☎ 06-876 5682; 141 Karamu Rd; snacks/lunch $4-16; ☻ 7am-4pm Mon-Fri, 8am-4pm Sat & Sun) An easy pit stop on the main road, this enduringly popular cafe serves up house-roasted organic coffee as well as handsome counter food and reasonable brunch, best enjoyed in the sunny courtyard out back.

our pick **Opera Kitchen** (Map p370; ☎ 06-870 6020; 312 Eastbourne St E; snacks $5-7, breakfast & lunch $10-22; ☻ breakfast & lunch Mon-Sat) This modern and stylish cafe has an interesting menu including healthy brekkie options, such as strawberries with passionfruit-curd yoghurt. For the less calorie conscious the full breakfast is a real winner, too. Heavenly counter food, great coffee and friendly staff round things out nicely. Eat in or outside in the suntrap courtyard.

SELF-CATERING

Fingers crossed you're here for the weekend so you can visit either the **Hawke's Bay Farmers Market** (Map p358; ☎ 06-974 3931; Hawke's Bay Showgrounds, Kenilworth Rd, Hastings; ☻ 8.30am-12.30pm Sun) or **Black Barn Market** (Map p358; ☎ 06-877 7985; www.blackbarn.com; Black Barn Rd; ☻ 9am-noon Sat Nov-Apr).

Picnickers should head for **Bellatino's** (Map p358; ☎ 06-875 8103; 9 Napier Rd, Havelock North; ☻ 8am-7pm Mon-Fri, to 5.30pm Sat & Sun), which stocks gourmet ingredients from the bay and abroad, along with coffee and cakes to eat in or take away.

Hastings and Havelock North have several supermarkets including **New World** (Map p370; ☎ 06-876 9881; 400 Heretaunga E St; ☻ 7am-10pm).

Drinking

There are not a whole lot of options beyond the winery gates.

Roosters Brewhouse (Map p358; ☎ 06-879 4127; 1470 Omahu Rd; ☻ 10am-7pm Mon-Sat) Roosters produces a range of naturally brewed beers 'made with passion and a great disregard of sensible accounting practices'. Five regular beers plus a seasonal special; tasting room, tours and a sunny courtyard for supping.

Rose & Shamrock (☎ 06-877 2999; cnr Napier Rd & Porter Dr, Havelock North; ☻ 10.30am-late) A carpeted, dark-wood, British-style boozer complete with a few Pommy drops on tap and hearty pub grub ($14 to $26). There's live music on Saturday nights.

Loading Ramp (☎ 06-877 6820; 6 Treachers Lane, Havelock North; ☻ 3pm-late) This lofty timber space pulls a mixed crowd of young 'uns up to high jinks, especially on the weekends when the queue can stretch well down the road. Also offers pub-style meals.

See also Diva (left).

THE EAST COAST

Entertainment

Hawke's Bay Opera House (p369) offers a regular program of music and theatre. There's a ticket office on-site.

Reading Cinemas (Map p370; ☎ 06-873 0345; www.readingcinemas.co.nz; 124 Heretaunga St E; tickets adult/child $14.50/10.50) Big-screen blockbusters.

Getting There & Away

Napier's Hawke's Bay Airport (p368) is a 20-minute drive away. Air New Zealand has an office in central Hastings.

InterCity (www.intercity.co.nz), **Bay Xpress** (www.bayxpress.co.nz) and **Naked Bus** (www.nakedbus.com) buses service Napier (p368).

Getting Around

goBay (☎ 06-878 9250; www.hbrc.govt.nz) runs the local bus service, covering Napier, Hastings, Havelock North and thereabouts. There are ample services between the main centres Monday to Friday, including three different routes between Napier and Hastings taking between 30 minutes (express) and 55 minutes (all stops). Buses depart from the Civic Square bus stop (Map p370). On Saturdays there are only five all-stop buses (adult/child $4.50/2.50), between 9am and 5pm. Services between Hastings and Havelock North run from Monday to Friday (adult/child $3/2, 35 minutes, hourly). Signal the driver and pay on the bus.

Hastings Taxis (☎ 06-878 5055) is the local cab service.

CAPE KIDNAPPERS

From mid-September to late April, Cape Kidnappers (named when local Maori tried to kidnap Cook's Tahitian servant boy) erupts with squawking gannets (p136). These big birds usually nest on remote islands but here they settle for the mainland, completely unfazed by human spectators.

The birds nest up as soon as they arrive, and eggs take about six weeks to hatch with chicks arriving in early November. In March the gannets start their migration; by May they're gone.

Early November to late February is the best time to visit. Take a tour (right) or the **walkway**: it's about five hours return from the Clifton Reserve car park (parking $2), located at the Clifton Motor Camp (right). You'll find interesting cliff formations, rock pools, a shelter-picnic spot, and the birds themselves. The walk is tide dependent. Leave no earlier than three hours after high tide; start back no later than 1½ hours after low tide.

No regular buses go to Clifton, but **Kiwi Shuttle** (☎ 027-459 3669; per person one-way $30) goes on demand, with discounts offered for groups.

Tours

All trips depart according to tide times; the region's i-SITEs and individual operators have schedules.

Gannet Beach Adventures (Map p358; ☎ 0800 426 638; www.gannets.com; adult/child/family $38/23/105) Ride along the beach on a tractor-pulled trailer before wandering out on the Cape for 90 minutes. A great, guided return trip of four hours, departing from Clifton Reserve.

Gannet Safaris (Map p358; ☎ 0800 427 232; www.gannetsafaris.co.nz; Summerlee Station, Clifton; adult/child $60/30) Overland 4WD trips across farmland into the gannet colony. Three-hour tours depart at 9.30am and 1.30pm. Enquire also about small-group Wilderness Safaris (www.kidnapperssafaris.co.nz) heading behind the vermin-proof fence into the conservation zone.

Sleeping & Eating

Clifton Motor Camp (Map p358; ☎ 06-875 0263; fax 06-875 0265; Clifton Rd; campsites $11-25, cabins from $50) is a quaint, end-of-the-world kind of place at the start of the gannet trail. Enjoy absolute beachfront sites or those sheltered by rows of static caravans. The friendly owners engender an old-fashioned Kiwiana vibe throughout the well-kept facilities.

Clifton Bay Café (Map p358; ☎ 06-875 0096; 468 Clifton Rd; meals $9-30; ☺ 10am-4pm) is an airy, civilised place for a meal before or after you run the gannet gauntlet.

CENTRAL HAWKE'S BAY

Grassy farmland stretches south from Hastings, dotted with the grand homesteads of Victorian pastoralists. It's an untouristed area, rich in history and deserted beaches. Waipukurau (aka 'Wai-puk'), the main town, isn't exactly thrilling but it's worth calling in to the extremely helpful **Central Hawke's Bay Information Centre** (☎ 06-858 6488; www.centralhawkesbay.co.nz; Railway Esp; ☺ 9am-5pm Mon-Fri, to 1pm Sat) in the old railway station. It can sort you out with the comprehensive *Experience Central Hawke's Bay* brochure and pamphlets outlining heritage trails and DOC reserves and walkways.

THE EAST COAST

Sights

There are no less than six windswept and interesting beaches along the coast here – **Kairakau, Mangakuri, Pourerere, Aramoana, Blackhead** and **Porangahau**. The first five are good for swimming, and between the lot they offer a range of sandy, salty activities including surfing, fishing, and driftwoody, rockpooly adventures. Between Aramoana and Blackhead Beach lies the **Te Angiangi Marine Reserve** – bring your snorkel.

The prestigious **Te Aute College** (☎ 06-856 8016; SH2, Pukehou) schooled many Maori leaders including James Carroll and Apirana Ngata. Call ahead if you want to visit the wonderful carved meeting house and church. Across the road next to a *marae* is little **Christ Church** (1859), the district's oldest.

The **Central Hawke's Bay Settler's Museum** (☎ 06-857 7288; High St, Waipawa; entry by donation; ☽ 10am-4pm) has pioneer artefacts, informative 'homestead' displays and a good specimen of a river *waka*.

Ongaonga is a historic village 16km west of Waipawa with interesting Victorian and Edwardian buildings. Pick up a pamphlet for a self-guided walking tour from the information centre in Waipukurau. The next town east is **Tikokino**, once a timber town but now known for its lovely private gardens, open to visitors during spring and early summer. Again, the information centre can help you with details.

It's a nondescript hill in the middle of nowhere, but the place with the world's longest name is good for a photo op. Believe it or not, **Taumatawhakatangihangakoauauo tamateaturipukakapikimaungahoronukupokai whenuakitanatahu** is the abbreviated form of 'The Brow of a Hill Where Tamatea, the Man with the Big Knees, Who Slid, Climbed, and Swallowed Mountains, Known as Land Eater, Played his Flute to his Brother'. Tamatea Pokaiwhenua (Land Eater) was so famous for his epic North Island travels, people said he consumed the land with his strides. After his brother's demise in the Matanui battle, Tamatea sat on this hill with his flute and played a lament to his fallen sibling. To get there, fuel-up in Waipukurau and drive 40km to the Mangaorapa junction on route 52. Turn left and go 4km towards Porangahau. At the intersection with the signposts, turn right and continue 4.3km to the sign.

Sleeping & Eating

Lochlea Backpacker Farmstay (☎ 06-855 4816; www.lochleafarm.co.nz; 344 Lake Rd, Wanstead; campsites per person $23, dm/s $28/37, d $56-60, cottage $125; ☐) As far removed from urban stress as possible, this idyllic farm has breezy stands of trees on grazing slopes. Rooms are simple but the communal lounge is cosy. There's a pool, tennis court and endless paddocks to wander.

Gwavas Garden Homestead (☎ 06-856 5810; www.gwavasgarden.co.nz; 5740 SH50, Tikokino; d incl breakfast $265-345) Six kilometres from Tikokino, this grand old 1890 homestead is enjoying a faithful room-by-room renovation with pretty floral wallpaper, period furnishings and divine linens. Enjoy breakfast on the veranda before a spot of lawn tennis or a wander through the internationally renowned 9-hectare 'Cornish' garden – widely considered one of the best private tree collections in the land.

Paper Mulberry Café (☎ 06-856 8688; SH2, Pukehou; meals $8-17; ☽ 7am-4pm Thu-Mon) Directly opposite Te Aute College, this hip cafe hands out fluffy toys instead of table numbers and serves excellent Havana coffee and great home-style food.

our pick **Misty River Café** (☎ 06-857 8911; 12 High Street, Waipawa; mains $14-18; ☽ 9am-4pm Wed-Sun) A little bit of continental chic on the functional high street, this darling little cafe makes a lip-smacking waldorf salad as well fresh ham, pasta, nachos and other global favourites. Drop-dead-gorgeous baking. All made from scratch, and to order (enquire about the chicken-salad sandwich).

Oruawharo (☎ 06-855 8274; www.oruawharo.com; 379 Oruawharo Rd; morning and afternoon tea $14, lunch $20) One of the area's rural mansions, Oruawharo (1879) is a grand setting for high tea or lunch served on fine bone china. Call ahead for sittings.

Getting There & Away

Bay Xpress (☎ 0800 422 997; www.bayxpress.co.nz) buses stop at Waipawa and Waipukurau along the route that runs between Wellington ($36, four hours) and Napier ($10, one hour) via Palmerston North ($22, 90 minutes). **InterCity** (www.intercity.co.nz) runs the same Wellington–Napier route but is considerably more expensive. Early birds might be able to take advantage of limited $1 advance fares on **Naked Bus** (www.nakedbus.com).

KAWEKA & RUAHINE RANGES

The remote Kaweka and Ruahine ranges separate Hawke's Bay from the Central Plateau. These forested wildernesses offer some of the North Island's best tramping. See the DOC pamphlets *Kaweka Forest Park & Puketitiri Reserves* and *Eastern Ruahine Forest Park* for details of tracks and huts.

An ancient Maori track, now a road, runs inland from Omahu near Hastings to Taihape,

via Otamauri and Kuripapango (where there is a basic but charming DOC campground, $5). The route is scenic but partially unsealed and takes around three hours.

Kaweka J, the highest point of the range (1724m), can be reached by a three-to-five-hour walk from the end of Kaweka Rd; from Napier take Puketitiri Rd then Whittle Rd. The drive is worthwhile in itself; it's partly unsealed and takes three hours return.

Wellington Region

If your New Zealand travels thus far have been all about the great outdoors and sleepy rural towns, this is the city that'll blow the cobwebs away. Art-house cinemas, funky boutiques, hip bars, live-music venues and lashings of restaurants – it's all in 'Windy Welly'.

Wellingtonians lay passionate claim to the crown of 'cultural capital', and the mantle is surely theirs. Suited-up civil servants there are, but the city also supports a significant population of creative types who foster an admirably active and accessible arts scene. It's a proud, tight-knit town, where the citizenry are convinced they're living in the world's best-kept secret.

As the crossing point between the North and South Islands, travellers have long been passing through these parts. Te Papa and Zealandia now have visitors stopping in their tracks, and even a couple of days' pause will reveal its myriad other attractions – a beautiful harbour and walkable shoreline, hillsides clad in pretty weatherboard houses, ample inner-city surprises, and some of the freshest city air on the planet.

Less than an hour away to the north, the Kapiti Coast offers more settled weather and a beachy vibe, with the Kapiti Island nature reserve a highlight. On a different tangent, but still only an hour away over the Rimutaka Range, lies the Wairarapa. Here you'll find farming country dotted with cute towns and famed wineries, and a wild, windswept coastline.

HIGHLIGHTS

- Getting interactive at NZ's finest museum, Wellington's **Te Papa** (p387)
- Scaling the lighthouse steps on wild and remote **Cape Palliser** (p410)
- Sampling the great coffee and quality beer that Wellingtonians demand at the city's slick **bars** (p396) and bohemian **cafes** (p395)
- Exploring **Kapiti Island** (p405) and saying hi to the takahe, one of NZ's rarest birds
- Maintaining a straight line on your bicycle as you tour the picturesque **Martinborough wineries** (p408)
- Riding the ratchety **cable car** (p386) from Lambton Quay to the leafy **Wellington Botanic Gardens** (p385)
- Ripping up the trails at **Makara Peak Mountain Bike Park** (p388)

Kapiti Island ★

★ Martinborough

★ Wellington

★ Cape Palliser

▪ Telephone code: 04	▪ www.wellingtonnz.com	▪ www.wairarapanz.com

WELLINGTON REGION

WELLINGTON REGION

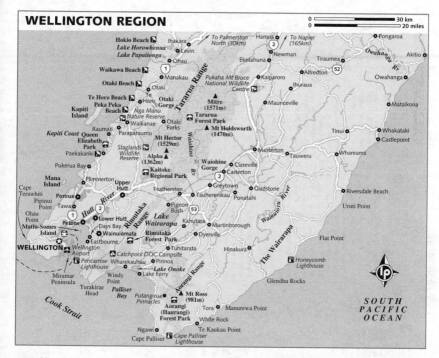

Climate

When Wellington's weather turns bad, it can be *truly* foul: lacerating winds and sheets of freezing rain coming in sideways. It ain't called 'Windy Wellington' for nothing…

November to April are the warmer months and the best months to visit, with average maximums hovering around 20°C. From May to August it's colder and wetter – daily temperatures lurk around 12°C.

Getting There & Around

Wellington is a major transport hub, being the North Island port for the interisland ferries. Wellington Airport is serviced by international and domestic airlines.

Easy train and bus connections make commuting into Wellington a viable option – many people travel to work (or to party) in Wellington from the hinterland. Approaching the city from the north, you'll pass through either the Kapiti Coast to the west via State Highway 1 (SH1), or the Wairarapa and heavily populated Hutt Valley to the east via State Highway 2 (SH2).

InterCity (www.intercity.co.nz) is the main North Island bus company, travelling just about everywhere. Commuter trains run from Wellington to the Kapiti Coast and the Wairarapa; long-distance **Tranz Scenic** (www.tranzscenic.co.nz) trains run from Wellington to Auckland via Palmerston North. See p399 for details on getting to/from Wellington.

WELLINGTON

pop 164,000 (city), 424,000 (region)

A small city with a relatively big reputation, Wellington is most famous for being NZ's capital. It is *infamous* for its weather, particularly the gale-force winds wont to barrel through, wrecking umbrellas and obliterating hairdos. It also lies on a major fault line. And negotiating the inner-city one-way system is like the Krypton Factor on acid.

But don't be deterred. 'Welly' is a brilliant city, as those who spend any more than a couple of days there will attest. For a starter it's lovely to look at, scattered around bushy hillsides encircling a magnificent harbour. There are super lookouts on hilltops, golden sand on the prom, and spectacular craggy shores along the South Coast. Downtown,

WELLINGTON REGION

GREATER WELLINGTON

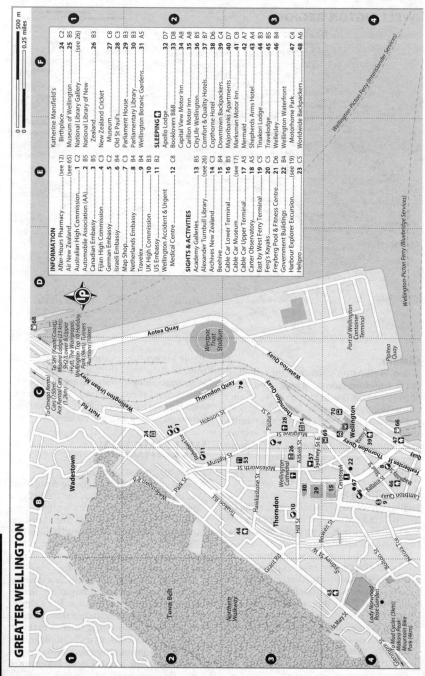

0 .... 500 m
0 .... 0.25 miles

Aotea Quay

Westpac
Trust
Stadium

Port of Wellington
Container
Terminal

Pipitea
Quay

Wellington-Picton Ferry (Interislander Services)

Wellington-Picton Ferry (Bluebridge Services)

To Omega Rental
Cars (750m);
Ace Rental Cars
(1.2km)

To SH1 (Kapiti Coast);
Moana Lodge (23km);
SH2 (Lower & Upper
Hutt, The Wairarapa);
Wellington Top 10 Holiday
Park (9km); Turners
Auctions (0km)

Hutt Rd

Wellington Urban Mwy

Thorndon Quay

Hobson St

Waterloo Quay

Thorndon Quay

Wadestown

Wadestown Rd

Town Belt

Northern
Walkway

Park St

Tinakori Rd

Murphy St

Pipitea St

Mulgrave St

Aitken St

Molesworth St

Sydney St E

Hawkestone St

Hill St

Grant Rd

Bowen St

Thorndon

Wellington
Cathedral

Cenotaph

Wellington

Lambton Quay

Bunny St

Featherston St

Thorndon Quay

Mulgrave St

Ballance St

Stout St

Whitmore St

Sydney St W

Bowen St

Tinakori Rd

St Mary St

Aurora Tce

Bolton St

Lady Norwood
Rose Garden

To Mud Cycles (3km);
Makara Peak
Mountain Bike
Park (4km)

the city is compact and vibrant, buoyed by a surprising number of museums, theatres, galleries and shops. A cocktail- and caffeine-fuelled hospitality scene fizzes and pops among the throng.

Brace yourself for a roller coaster of emotions: 'You can't beat Wellington on a good day', they say, but on a bad day this city's a heartbreaker.

HISTORY

Maori legend has it that the explorer Kupe was first to discover Wellington harbour. Wellington's original Maori name was Te Whanganui-a-Tara (great harbour of Tara), named after the son of a chief named Whatonga who had settled on the Hawke's Bay coast. Whatonga sent Tara and his half-brother to explore the southern part of the North Island. When they returned over a year later, their reports were so favourable that Whatonga's followers moved there, founding the Ngati Tara tribe.

The first European settlers arrived in the New Zealand Company's ship *Aurora* on 22 January 1840, not long after Colonel William Wakefield arrived to buy land from the Maori. The idea was to build two cities: one would be a commercial centre by the harbour (Port Nicholson) and the other, further north, would be the agricultural hub.

However, Maori denied they had sold the land at Port Nicholson, or Poneke, as they called it, as it was founded on hasty and illegal buying by the New Zealand Company. Land rights struggles ensued – they were to plague the country for years, and still affect it today.

By 1850 Wellington was a thriving settlement of around 5500 people; however, there was very little flat land. Originally the waterfront was along Lambton Quay, but reclamation of parts of the harbour began in 1852. In 1855 an earthquake raised part of Hutt Rd and the area from Te Aro flat to the Basin Reserve, which initiated the first major land reclamation.

In 1865 the seat of government was moved from Auckland to Wellington, due to its central location in the country.

One blustery day back in 1968 the wind blew so hard it pushed the almost-new Wellington–Christchurch ferry *Wahine* onto Barrett Reef at the harbour entrance. The disabled ship dragged its anchors, drifted into the harbour and slowly sank – 51 people perished. The Museum of Wellington (p384) has a moving exhibit commemorating this tragedy.

ORIENTATION

The city congregates in the western corner of Wellington harbour, with the city suburbs clinging to the steep valleys and hills on all sides. Lambton Quay, the city's major business thoroughfare, runs more or less parallel to the seafront (which it once was). The central business district stretches from the train station, at the northern end of Lambton Quay, southeast to Cambridge and Kent Tces.

Parliament clusters around the north end of the city, on the cusp of historic Thorndon where various embassies can be found. The waterfront along Jervois Quay, Cable St and Oriental Pde is an increasingly revitalised area and houses Te Papa museum, Waitangi Park and a man-made beach. The historic sheds of Queens Wharf have been reborn as a museum, galleries, restaurants and a coffee roaster, and joined by a couple of new buildings.

Cuba St (literate, arty types) and Courtenay Pl (young larrikins) are the main nightlife hot spots, while Willis St, Queens Wharf and Lambton Quay are peppered with eating, drinking and shopping opportunities.

The airport is 8km southeast of the city centre.

WELLINGTON REGION FACTS

Eat Yourself silly: Wellington has a gut-busting number of great cafes and restaurants; bring trousers with an elasticised waistband

Drink Aro, Emporio, Fuel, Havana, Immigrant's Son, L'Affare, Mojo, Peoples, Revive and Supreme – that's pretty much every locally roasted coffee bean

Read *Big Weather: Poems of Wellington* (Mallinson Rendel, 2000), billet-doux to a hard-to-love city

Listen to *Happy Ending*, by this author's favourite Welly band, the Phoenix Foundation

Watch 'Golden Days' – the rousing short film screened on rotation at Te Papa

Swim at Oriental Bay: it's not nearly as cold as it looks

Festival Summer City (p390) – brilliant, free fun in the sun (or not...)

Tackiest tourist attraction Cuba St's bucket fountain: tacky, a bit slimy, and often malicious

Go green Check out rare NZ wildlife at Zealandia (p386), Wellington's mainland 'conservation island'

Maps

Wellington's i-SITE visitor centre has free city maps.

The **Map Shop** (Map p380; ☎ 04-385 1462; www.mapshop.co.nz; 121 Thorndon Quay; ☼ 8.30am-5.30pm Mon-Fri, 10am-1pm Sat) carries a range of NZ city and regional maps, plus topographic maps and GPS for trampers.

INFORMATION
Bookshops

Arty Bees Books (Map p384; ☎ 04-384 5339; www.artybees.co.nz; The Oaks, Manners St; ☼ 9am-9pm Mon-Thu, to 10pm Fri, 10am-10pm Sat, 11am-9pm Sun) Quality secondhand reads.

Unity Books (Map p384; ☎ 04-499 4245; www.unitybooks.co.nz; 57 Willis St; ☼ 9am-6pm Mon-Fri, 10am-5pm Sat, 11am-5pm Sun) A Wellington institution, with an excellent fiction section specialising in NZ literature.

Emergency

Ambulance, fire service & police (☎ 111)
Wellington police station (Map p384; ☎ 04-381 2000; www.police.govt.nz; cnr Victoria & Harris Sts; ☼ 24hr)

Internet Access

Internet access rooms are plentiful; expect to pay around $3 per hour.

Cybernomad (Map p384; 43 Courtenay Pl; ☼ 9am-11pm Mon-Fri, 10am-11pm Sat & Sun)
Cyber City (Map p384; 97-99 Courtenay Pl; ☼ 9am-11pm)
iPlay (Map p384; 1st fl, 49 Manners Mall; ☼ 24hr)
Wellington i-SITE (Map p384; www.wellingtonnz.com; Civic Sq, cnr Wakefield & Victoria Sts; ☼ 8.30am-5pm Mon-Fri, 9.30am-4.30pm Sat & Sun)

Internet Resources

Feeling Great (www.feelinggreat.co.nz) Events, activities, courses and classes; run by the city council.
Positively Wellington Tourism (www.wellingtonnz.com) Official tourism website for the city.
View Wellington (www.viewwellington.co.nz) Restaurant and bar reviews, activities and special offers.
Word on the Street (www.wordonthestreet.nz) Reader-friendly, entertaining, nonadvertorial site dedicated to the best of the inner city's what, when, where and who.
Wotzon.com (www.wotzon.com) Arts and events listings in Wellington and surrounds.

Media

Capital Times (www.capitaltimes.co.nz) Free weekly newspaper with local news, gossip and gig listings.
Stuff (www.stuff.co.nz) Online news service incorporating Wellington's newspaper, the *Dominion Post*.

Medical Services

Wellington Accident & Urgent Medical Centre (Map p380; ☎ 04-384 4944; 17 Adelaide Rd, Newtown; ☼ 8am-11pm) No appointment necessary; also home to the after-hours Pharmacy (open from 8am to 11pm).
Wellington Hospital (off Map p380; ☎ 04-385 5999; www.ccdhb.org.nz; Riddiford St, Newtown; ☼ 24hr) One kilometre south of the city centre.

Money

Major banks have branches on Courtenay Pl, Willis St and Lambton Quay. Moneychangers include the following:

City Stop (Map p384; ☎ 04-801 8669; 107 Manners St; ☼ 24hr) Convenience store that exchanges travellers cheques.

Travelex (Map p380; ☎ 04-472 8346; www.travelex.com/nz; 120 Lambton Quay; ☼ 8.30am-5.30pm Mon-Fri, 9am-4pm Sat) Foreign-exchange office. Also has a branch at the airport.

Post

Post office (Map p384; www.nzpost.co.nz; 2 Manners St) In the centre of town, with post restante.

Tourist Information

Automobile Association (AA; Map p380; ☎ 04-931 9999; www.aa.co.nz; 1st fl, 42-352 Lambton Quay; ☼ 8.30am-5pm Mon-Fri, 9am-1pm Sat)
DOC visitor centre (Department of Conservation; Map p384; ☎ 04-384 7770; www.doc.govt.nz; 18 Manners St; ☼ 9am-5pm Mon-Fri, 10am-3.30pm Sat) Bookings,

---

MAORI NZ: WELLINGTON REGION

In legend the mouth of Maui's Fish (see p52), and traditionally known as Te Whanganui-a-Tara, the Wellington area became known to Maori in the mid-19th century as 'Poneke' (a transliteration of Port Nicholas, its European name at the time).

The major *iwi* (tribes) of the region in traditional times were Te Ati Awa and Ngati Toa. Ngati Toa was the *iwi* of Te Rauparaha, who composed the now famous *Ka Mate haka* (see p55). Like most urban areas the city is now home to Maori from many *iwi*, sometimes collectively known as Ngati Poneke.

New Zealand's national museum, Te Papa (p403), presents excellent displays on Maori culture, traditional and modern, as well as a colourful *marae*. History buffs can also see the Treaty of Waitangi at the Archives New Zealand (p385).

CENTRAL WELLINGTON

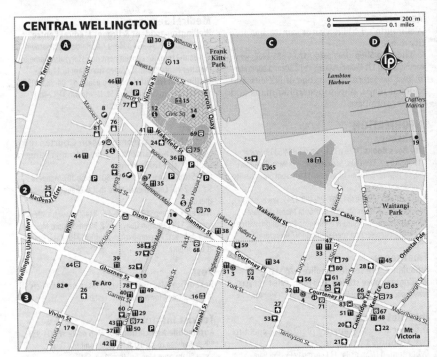

passes and information for national and local walks, parks, huts and camping, plus permits for Kapiti Island.

Wellington Airport Information (☎ 04-385 5104; www.wellington-airport.co.nz; Main Terminal; ⏱ 24hr) Touch-screen information stations.

Wellington i-SITE (Map p384; ☎ 04-802 4860; www.wellingtonnz.com; Civic Sq, cnr Wakefield & Victoria Sts; ⏱ 8.30am-5pm Mon-Fri, 9.30am-4.30pm Sat & Sun; 🖳) Staff book almost everything, and cheerfully distribute the *Official Visitor Guide to Wellington*. Internet access and cafe.

Travel Agencies

Air New Zealand (Map p380; ☎ 0800 737 000, 04-474 8950 or 04-388 9900; www.airnewzealand.co.nz; cnr Lambton Quay & Grey St; ⏱ 9am-5pm Mon-Fri, 10am-1pm Sat)

STA Travel (Map p384; ☎ 04-385 0561; www.statravel.co.nz; cnr Cuba & Ghuznee Sts; ⏱ 9am-5.30pm Mon-Fri, 11am-5pm Sat)

SIGHTS
Museums & Galleries

For an imaginative, interactive experience of Wellington's social and salty maritime history, swing into the **Museum of Wellington** (Map p380; ☎ 04-472 8904; www.museumofwellington.co.nz; Queens Wharf; admission free; ⏱ 10am-5pm). Highlights include a moving documentary about the tragedy of the *Wahine* (see p382), and ancient Maori legends dramatically told using tiny hologram actors and special effects. The building itself is an old Bond Store dating from 1892.

The much-loved **City Gallery** (Map p384; ☎ 04-801 3021; www.citygallery.org.nz; Civic Sq, Wakefield St; admission by donation, charges may apply for major exhibits; ⏱ 10am-5pm) reopened late in 2009 after renovations and the addition of a new wing. Expect surprises: the gallery's a little cracker that secures acclaimed contemporary international artists as well as unearthing and supporting those at the forefront of New Zealand's scene. Excellent Nikau Gallery Cafe on-site.

The **New Zealand Film Archive** (Map p384; ☎ 04-384 7647, film info line 04-499 3456; www.filmarchive.org.nz; cnr Taranaki & Ghuznee Sts; admission free, movies $8; ⏱ from 9am Mon-Fri, from noon Sat) was established in 1981 to protect New Zealand's moving-image history. Collections date from 1895 and represent every genre of filmmaking. The library has more than 30,000 titles you can watch for free and a big-screen program four nights a week. Combined with a cafe and gallery, it's a great place to while away the hours (or days).

Part of the New Zealand Academy of Fine Arts, **Academy Galleries** (Map p380; ☎ 04-499 8807; www.nzafa.com; 1 Queens Wharf; admission free; ⏰ 10am-5pm) features works by New Zealand artists.

The muscular grey concrete of the **National Library of New Zealand** (Map p380; ☎ 04-474 3000; www.natlib.govt.nz; cnr Molesworth & Aitken Sts; admission free; ⏰ 9am-5pm Mon-Fri, to 1pm Sat) is a haven to varied collections of national importance. It encompasses the **Alexander Turnbull Library**, which holds historical photographs, drawings, prints, maps and the like. Regular events are held in the **National Library Gallery** (admission free; ⏰ 9am-5pm Mon-Fri, to 4.30pm Sat, 1-4.30pm Sun), which has changing exhibits. Watch for renovation-induced disruptions.

One block away, the **Archives New Zealand** (Map p380; ☎ 04-499 5595, www.archives.govt.nz; 10 Mulgrave St; admission free; ⏰ 9am-5pm Mon-Fri, to 1pm Sat) is the official guardian of NZ's heritage documents. Inside are gallery displays of significant national treasures, including

the original Treaty of Waitangi (p31), NZ's founding document.

Cricket boffins will be bowled over by the historical memorabilia at the **New Zealand Cricket Museum** (Map p380; ☎ 04-385 6602; www.nzcricket.co.nz; Old Grandstand, Basin Reserve; adult/child $5/2; ⏰ 10.30am-3.30pm daily Nov-Apr, Sat & Sun May-Oct). Comprehensive displays cover the history and development of NZ cricket, including the sport's arrival in the colonies and NZ's first test match in 1894. The original 1743 Addington bat is a showstopper.

Gardens & Lookouts

The expansive, hilltop **Wellington Botanic Gardens** (Map p380; ☎ 04-499 1400; www.wellington.govt.nz; admission free; ⏰ dawn-dusk; P) can be conveniently visited via a cable-car ride (nice bit of planning, eh?). The hilly 25-hectare gardens boast a tract of original native forest along with varied collections including a beaut rose garden and international plant collections. Add in fountains, a cheerful playground, sculptures, duck pond, cafe, magical city views and much more, and you've got a grand day

WELLINGTON REGION

WELLINGTON REGION IN...

Two Days

To get a feel for the lie of the land, drive up **Mt Victoria** (below), or ride the **cable car** (below) up to the **Wellington Botanic Gardens** (p385). After lunch on cool **Cuba St** (p394), immerse yourself in all things Kiwi at **Te Papa** (opposite) or the **Museum of Wellington** (p384). Drink beer by the jug at **Mighty Mighty** (p396).

The next day, fuel-up with coffee and eggs at **Cafe L'Affare** (p395) then head to **Zealandia** (below) to meet the birds and learn about New Zealand conservation, or take a snoop around the **Beehive** (opposite). For dinner try **Chow** (p394) or **Pravda** (p394), then spend your evenings **bar-hopping** (p396) along Courtenay Pl. Nocturnal entertainment could involve live music, a movie at the gloriously restored **Embassy Theatre** (p399), or a midnight snack at a late-closing cafe – or all three.

Four Days

Shake and bake the two-day itinerary, then decorate with the following: hightail it out of Wellington for some wine-tasting around **Martinborough** (p408), followed by a seal-spotting safari along the wild **Cape Palliser** (p409). The next day, take a picnic to **Paekakariki** (p404), have a swim, and then a wander around **Queen Elizabeth Park** (p404) next door.

out. The gardens are also accessible from the Centennial Entrance on Tinakori Rd (Karori bus 3).

One of Wellington's most famous attractions is the little red **cable car** (Map p380; ☎ 04-472 2199; www.wellingtoncablecar.co.nz; one-way adult/child $3/1, return $5/2; ☺ departs every 10min, 7am-10pm Mon-Fri, 8.30am-10pm Sat, 9am-10pm Sun) that clanks up the steep slope from Lambton Quay to Kelburn. At the top are a cafe, the Wellington Botanic Gardens, an observatory and the small-but-nifty **Cable Car Museum** (Map p380; ☎ 04-475 3578; www.cablecarmuseum.co.nz; admission free; ☺ 9.30am-5.30pm Nov-Apr, 10am-5pm May-Oct), which tells the cable car's story since it was built in 1902 to open up hilly Kelburn for development. Take the cable car back down the hill, or ramble down through the Botanic Gardens (a 30- to 60-minute walk, depending on your wend).

At the top of the Botanic Gardens, the **Carter Observatory** (Map p380; ☎ 04-910 3140; www.carterobservatory.org; ☺ 10am-5pm) has re-emerged after a major renovation. New features include a full-dome planetarium in which you can take a simulated trip through the universe; a multimedia display of Polynesian navigation, Maori cosmology, and European explorers; and some of New Zealand's finest telescopes and astronomical artefacts. If your lucky stars are with you, you might be able to safely see our closest star, the Sun, through the Thomas Cooke telescope's solar filter. Check the website for evening stargazing times.

For the best view of the city, harbour and surrounds, venture up to the lookout atop the 196m **Mt Victoria** (Map p380), east of the city centre. You can take bus 20 (Monday to Friday) most of the way up, or if you're feeling energetic sweat it out on the walk. If you've got your own wheels, take Oriental Pde along the waterfront and then scoot up Carlton Gore Rd.

About 3km west of the city is **Otari-Wilton's Bush** (off Map p380; ☎ 04-475 3245; www.wellington.govt.nz; 160 Wilton Rd; admission free; ☺ dawn-dusk; P), the only botanic gardens in NZ specialising in native flora. Expect to see and hear plenty of birds along the 11km of walking trails. Bus 14 from the city passes the gates.

If you have a car, take a long and winding drive around Wellington's **bays and beaches** (see www.greatharbourway.org.nz) – cruise out of town along Oriental Pde and just keep going, keeping the sea on your left. Along the largely craggy shoreline are pretty inlets, million-dollar houses and the odd cafe. You'll end up at Owhiro Bay, from where you can take Happy Valley Rd back into town. The whole loop is about 30km.

Wildlife

The groundbreaking wildlife sanctuary **Zealandia** (off Map p380; ☎ 04-920 9200; www.visitzealandia.com; Waiapu Rd; adult/child/family $15/7/37; ☺ 9am-5pm, last entry 4pm; P) is tucked in the hills about 2km west of town (buses 3, 18, 21, 22 and 23 trundle nearby). The fenced mainland 'conservation island' is home to more than 30 native bird species including kiwi, kaka, saddleback and hihi, as well as the most accessible wild population of tuatara. There are more than 30km of attractive walking tracks and a range of guided tours available. A major new exhibition centre showcases New Zealand's natural history and its world-renowned conservation story.

Wellington Zoo (off Map p380; ☎ 04-381 6755; www.wellingtonzoo.com; 200 Daniell St; adult/concession/child $15/10/7.50; ☻ 9.30am-5pm, last entry 4.15pm; P) has a commitment to conservation and research. There's a plethora of native and non-native wildlife here, including the residents of the outdoor lion and chimpanzee parks; and the nocturnal kiwi house, which also houses tuatara. Check the website for info on 'close encounters', which allow you to meet the big cats, red pandas and giraffes (for a fee). The zoo is 4km south of the city; catch bus 10 or 23.

Notable Buildings

Three Bowen St buildings comprise NZ's seat of parliamentary power. Office workers buzz around the unmissable modernist **Beehive** (Map p380; Bowen St), which looks exactly like its name. It was designed by British architect Sir Basil Spence and built between 1969 and 1980. Controversy dogged its construction and, love it or loathe it, it's become the architectural symbol of the city.

Adjacent to the Beehive is the austere grey-and-cream **Parliament House** (Map p380; ☎ 04-471 9503; www.parliament.nz; Bowen St; tours free; ☻ tours on the hour 10am-4pm Mon-Fri, to 3pm Sat, 11am-3pm Sun),

completed in 1922. Free, one-hour tours depart from the ground-floor foyer (arrive 15 minutes prior). Next door is the 1899 neo-Gothic **Parliamentary Library** (Map p380) building.

Opposite the Beehive are the gorgeous 1876 **Government Buildings** (Map p380), some of the world's largest wooden buildings. With their chunky corner quoins and slab wooden planking, you have to look twice to realise that they aren't made of stone (knock your knuckles on a wall if you don't believe us).

The last lick of paint was splashed on **Old St Paul's** (Map p380; ☎ 04-473 6722; www.oldsaintpauls.co.nz; 34 Mulgrave St; admission by donation; ☻ 10am-5pm) in 1866, and it still looks good-as-new from the outside. The striking interior is a stellar example of early English Gothic timberwork, with magnificent stained-glass windows and displays on Wellington's early history.

Harbour Ferries

Locals have been jumping on the cross-harbour ferry for a swim at Days Bay for decades. Book a seat on the **East by West Ferry** (Map p380; ☎ 04-499 1282; www.eastbywest.co.nz; Queens Wharf; one-way adult/child $10/5; ☻ 6.25am-7pm Mon-Fri, 10am-5pm Sat & Sun), departing from Queens Wharf 16 times daily on weekdays, and eight times daily on weekends. It's a 30- to 40-minute chug over to **Days Bay**, where there are beaches, a park and a boatshed with canoes and rowboats for hire. A 10-minute walk from Days Bay leads to **Eastbourne**, a beachy township with cafes and other diversions.

East by West ferries also stop at **Matiu-Somes Island** (return fare adult/child $21/11), a wildlife

---

TREASURES OF TE PAPA

Te Papa (Map p384; ☎ 04-381 7000; www.tepapa.govt.nz; 55 Cable St; admission free; ☻ 10am-6pm Mon-Wed & Fri-Sun, to 9pm Thu; P), the 'Museum of New Zealand', is an inspiring, interactive repository of historical and cultural artefacts. 'Te Papa Tongarewa' loosely translates as 'treasure box'. The building dominates the Wellington waterfront and has become a national icon – an innovative celebration of the essence of NZ.

Among Te Papa's treasures is a huge Maori collection; its own *marae;* dedicated hands-on 'discovery centres' for children; natural history and environment exhibitions; Pacific and New Zealand history galleries; and traditional and contemporary art and culture. Exhibitions occupy impressive gallery spaces with a touch of high-tech (eg motion-simulator rides and a house shaking through an earthquake). Big-name, temporary exhibitions incur an admission fee.

You could spend a day exploring Te Papa's six floors but still not see it all. To target your areas of interest head to the information desk on level two. To get your bearings, the one-hour 'Introducing Te Papa' tour ($12) is a good idea; tours leave from the info desk at 10.15am and 2pm daily in winter, more frequently in summer. Two cafes and two gift shops round out the Te Papa experience.

WELLINGTON REGION

reserve managed by the Department of Conservation (DOC) where you might see weta, tuatara, kakariki and little blue penguins, among other critters. The island is rich in history, having once been a prisoner-of-war camp and quarantine station. Take a picnic lunch, although the eager can camp overnight (adult/child $10/5) or in a DOC house – book online at www.doc.govt.nz or at Wellington's DOC visitor centre (see p383).

On weekends you can also catch the **Harbour Explorer Excursion**, which runs between Queens Wharf and Days Bay via Somes Island, Petone and Seatoun (return fare adult/child $20/10, three daily Saturday and Sunday).

ACTIVITIES
Cycling & Mountain Biking
Wellington's good for cycling, if you don't mind hills. The excellent **Makara Peak Mountain Bike Park** (off Map p380; www.makarapeak.org.nz) in the hills of Karori is 4km west of the city centre. The main entrance is on South Karori Rd – catch bus 3 or 18. Laced through the 200-hectare park are 24km of bike tracks ranging from beginner to expert. **Mud Cycles** (off Map p380; ☎ 04-476 4961; www.mudcycles.co.nz; 338 Karori Rd, Karori; half-/full-day/weekend bike hire $30/45/70; ⏱ 9.30am-6pm Mon-Fri) has mountain bikes for hire, is close to the park, and also runs guided tours catering for all levels.

On Yer Bike (Map p384; ☎ 04-384 8480; www.onyer bikeavantiplus.co.nz; 181 Vivian St; half-day/full-day/week bike hire $30/40/150; ⏱ 8.30am-5.30pm Mon-Fri, 9am-5pm Sat)

stocks a good range of bicycles for sale and hire, and can help with info on local clubs and trails.

Walking
Wellington will be much enjoyed by walkers. It takes only an hour to amble from one end of the city centre to the other, and there is plenty of good wandering in the immediate surrounds (such as Mt Victoria, Aro Valley and Thorndon), and along one of five walkways around the city fringes (the City to Sea, the Skyline, the Southern, Northern, and Eastern – all accessible by foot or bus). The city council produces excellent 'Explore' walking maps for both inner-city heritage trails and the walkways (available from the i-SITE or at www.feelinggreat.co.nz). See Tours (p390) to connect with a walking guide.

The wild-and-woolly **Red Rocks Coastal Walk** (off Map p380; two to three hours, 8km return), 7km south of the city, follows the tumultuous volcanic coast from Owhiro Bay through Te Kopahou Reserve to Red Rocks and Sinclair Head, where there's a seal colony. Take bus 4 to Owhiro Bay Pde, then it's 1km to the quarry gate where the walk starts.

Other Activities
With all this wind and water, Wellington was made for **sailboarding** and **kiteboarding**, and there are plenty of good launching points within 30 minutes' drive of the city. **Wild Winds** (Map p384; ☎ 04-384 1010; www.wildwinds.co.nz;

KATHERINE MANSFIELD
Often compared to Chekhov and Maupassant, Katherine Mansfield is NZ's most distinguished author, known throughout the world for her short stories.

Born Kathleen Mansfield Beauchamp in 1888, at age 14 she left for Europe, where she spent most of the remainder of her short adult life. She mixed with Europe's most famous writers (DH Lawrence, TS Eliot, Virginia Woolf), and married the literary critic and author John Middleton Murry in 1918. In 1923, aged 34, she died of tuberculosis at Fontainebleau in France. It was not until 1945 that her five books of short stories (In a German Pension, Bliss, The Garden Party, The Dove's Nest and Something Childish) were combined into a single volume, Collected Stories of Katherine Mansfield.

She spent five years of her childhood at 25 Tinakori Rd in Wellington; it's mentioned in her stories Prelude and A Birthday (a fictionalised account of her own birth). The house now opens its doors as **Katherine Mansfield's Birthplace** (Map p380; ☎ 04-473 7268; www.katherinemansfield.com; 25 Tinakori Rd; adult/child $5.50/2; ⏱ 10am-4pm Tue-Sun), and is lovingly restored and maintained with a restful heritage garden. The excellent video A Portrait of Katherine Mansfield screens here and the 'Sense of Living' exhibition displays photographs of the period alongside excerpts from her writing. A doll's house has been constructed from details in the short story of the same name. Wilton bus 14 stops nearby.

Chaffers Marina, Oriental Bay; 10am-6pm Mon-Fri, to 3pm Sat, 11am-3pm Sun) runs two-hour windsurfing lessons for beginners ($110), and three-hour kiteboarding lessons from $195. Prices include equipment but not transport.

At the long-running **Ferg's Kayaks** (Map p380; 04-449 8898; www.fergskayaks.co.nz; Shed 6, Queens Wharf; 10am-8pm Mon-Fri, 9am-6pm Sat & Sun) you can punish your tendons with indoor rock climbing (adult/child $15/9), cruise the waterfront on a pair of inline skates ($15 for two hours) or paddle around the harbour in a kayak (from $15 for one hour). There's also bike hire (one hour from $20) and guided kayaking trips.

Gnarly surf rolls in from the ocean at **Lyall Bay** (off Map p380) near the airport (though it's often too choppy or too small), **Palliser Bay** (p409) and the Wainuiomata Coast, southeast of Wellington. The i-SITE can help with fishing and diving charter info.

Freyberg Pool & Fitness Centre (Map p380; 04-801 4530; www.wellingtonwaterfront.co.nz; 139 Oriental Pde; adult/child $4/2; 6am-9pm) has a heated indoor lap pool, plus a spa, sauna and gym (casual fitness classes $9.50).

WALKING TOUR

Kick-start your Wellington wander by admiring (or deploring, depending on your aesthetics) the modernist **Beehive** (1; p387), then head east along Bowen St and cross Lambton Quay to the **Government Buildings** (2; p387) – yes indeedy, they're timber, not stone.

Truck south along Lambton Quay, aka the 'Golden Mile', for all its retail revelry. Browse elegant **Kirkcaldie & Stains** (3; p399), the city's only department store. If you haven't done it yet, detour up Cable Car Lane and clank up the hillside on the **cable car** (4; p386), or continue along Lambton Quay and splash some cash at the Edwardian **Old Bank Shopping Arcade** (5; p399). Turn right onto Willis St then left at Mercer St. Civic Sq is straight ahead. Book some theatre tickets at the **Wellington i-SITE** (6; p384), duck into the **City Gallery** (7; p384) or, if you've got the kids in tow, see what's cookin' at **Capital E** (8; right).

From Civic Sq, head south for a cruise up and down **Cuba St** (9): bars, boutiques and coffee shops in the hip heart of the city. Back at Civic Sq take the City to Sea footbridge to the waterfront and stroll past the boatsheds to **Mac's Brewery Bar** (10; p396) for a quick pint of Sassy Red and a bowl of fries. Suitably

refreshed, it's time to tackle **Te Papa** (11; p387). Once you've reached your museum maximum, pull up a patch of grass at **Waitangi Park** (12) or hurl yourself into the evening fray on **Courtenay Pl** (13).

WELLINGTON FOR CHILDREN

With ankle biters in tow, your best bet is a visit to colourful **Capital E** (Map p384; 04-913 3720; www.capitale.org.nz; Civic Sq; events free-$12; 9am-5pm), an educational entertainment complex designed especially for kids. Expect interactive rotating exhibitions, children's theatre and TV, readings, workshops and courses. Call or check the website for the events calendar and prices.

Te Papa (p387) is fantastic for children. The Discovery Centres are loaded with interactive activities, and StoryPlace is designed for children five and under. See the dedicated Kids page on the website for more details. Along the waterfront on either side of Te Papa are **Frank Kitts Park** and **Waitangi Park**, both with playgrounds perfect for expending pent-up energy.

A ride up the **cable car** (p386) and a lap around the **Wellington Botanic Gardens** (p385) will pump plenty of fresh air into young lungs, and when darkness descends head to the **Carter Observatory** (p386) where kids can gaze at galaxies far, far away. On a more terrestrial bent, check out some living dinosaurs (aka tuatara) at the **Wellington Zoo** (p387) or **Zealandia** (p386).

For online ideas, have a look at www.feelinggreat.co.nz, operated by the city council, and follow the Young People link for a rundown on events and courses targeted at young 'uns.

TOURS

Flat Earth (☎ 0800 775 805, 04-977 5805; www.flatearth.co.nz; full-day tours $120-220) An array of themed small-group tours (city highlights, Maori treasures, food, arts and Middle-Earth filming locations).

Hammonds Scenic Tours (☎ 04-472 0869; www.wellingtonsightseeingtours.com; city tour adult/child $55/27.50, Kapiti Coast $95/47.50, Wairarapa $200/100; ☺ city tours depart 10am & 2pm, Kapiti 9am & 1.30pm, Martinborough & Wairarapa 8.30am) Runs a 2½-hour city highlights tour, four-hour tour of the Kapiti Coast, and a full-day Wairarapa experience including Cape Palliser. Dedicated Martinborough trip available ($230/115).

Helipro (Map p380; ☎ 04-472 1550; www.helipro.co.nz; Shed 1, Queens Wharf; 10/15/25/35min flights per person $95/185/225/370) Scenic helicopter flights and heli-lunch trips to the Wairarapa, Marlborough Sounds or Wellington's South Coast.

Walk Wellington (☎ 04-802 4860; www.walk.wellington.net.nz; adult/child $20/10; ☺ tours 10am daily, plus 5.30pm Mon, Wed & Fri Nov-Mar) Informative two-hour walking tours focusing on the city and waterfront, departing the i-SITE. Book online or just turn up.

Wellington Movie Tours (☎ 027 419 3077; www.movietours.co.nz; tours from adult/child $40/30) Four- to 8½-hour tours for real movie fiends – more props, clips, film sets and *Lord of the Rings (LOTR)* than you can point a lens at. Confirm pick-up locations when booking.

Wellington Rover (☎ 0800 426 211, 04-471 0044; www.wellingtonrover.co.nz; adult/child $40/25; ☺ departs i-SITE 9am, 11.30am & 2.30pm) The 2½-hour Explorer Tour with a hop-on/hop-off option visits places that are tricky to reach without a car (Mt Victoria, South Coast beaches, Red Rocks seal colony). Customised tours and half- and full-day *LOTR* trips ($90 and $150) complete with hobbit ears.

Wellington Sights (☎ 0800 775 805, 04-977 5805; www.wellingtonsights.co.nz; 2-3hr tours per adult/child $65/40) Two tours – *LOTR* and Snapshot.

Wild About Wellington (☎ 0274 419 010; www.wildaboutwellington.co.nz; tours from $95) Small-group walking and public-transport tours including City of Style, Sights & Bites, Wild About Chocolate or Boutique Beer Tasting. From a few hours to a full day.

Zest Food Tours (☎ 04-801 9198; www.zestfoodtours.co.nz; tours from $125) Runs 2½- to four-hour small-group city sightseeing tours; longer tours include lunch with matched wines at a top restaurant. Also Wairarapa food and wine tours (from $230).

FESTIVALS & EVENTS

Check at the Wellington i-SITE or visit www.wellingtonnz.com/event for comprehensive festival listings; most tickets can be booked through Ticketek (p398).

January/February

Summer City (☎ 04-499 4444; www.feelinggreat.co.nz) A two-month celebration commencing New Year's Eve; includes countless free outdoor events.

February

Cuba St Carnival (☎ 04-801 9390; www.cubacarnival.org.nz) NZ's largest street carnival, where the locals get uncharacteristically colourful. Biennial (odd years).

New Zealand International Sevens (☎ 04-389 0020; www.nzisevens.co.nz) The world's top seven-a-side rugby teams compete, but it's the crowd that plays up.

February/March

International Jazz Festival (☎ 04-473 0149; www.jazzfestival.co.nz) A week-long shoobedoobop featuring local and international artists. Biennial (odd years).

March

Fringe NZ (☎ 04-382 8015; www.fringe.org.nz) More than three weeks of way-out-there experimental visual arts, music, dance and theatre.

New Zealand International Arts Festival (☎ 04-473 0149; www.nzfestival.nzpost.co.nz) A month-long biennial spectacular (even years) of theatre, dance, music, visual arts and literature. International acts aplenty.

April

New Zealand Comedy Festival (www.comedyfestival.co.nz) Three weeks of hysterics. World-famous-in-New-Zealand comedians, and some truly world famous, too.

June

Matariki (www.tepapa.govt.nz) Celebrating the Maori New Year with a free festival of dance, music and other events at Te Papa.

July/August

International Film Festival (☎ 04-384 3840; www.nzff.co.nz) Two-week indie film fest screening the best of NZ and international cinema.

September

World of WearableArt (WOW; ☎ 0800 4969 746; www.worldofwearableart.com) A two-week run of the spectacular nightly extravaganza of amazing garments.

November

Toast Martinborough (☎ 06-306 9183; www.toastmartinborough.co.nz) A day of hedonism around the Martinborough vineyards.

SLEEPING

Wellington accommodation is generally more expensive than in regional areas. Our price listings for the city fall into the following categories: Budget – doubles (with or without bathroom) for under $100; Midrange – doubles (with bathroom) between $101 and $200; Top End – over $201. Accommodation standards are reasonably high, and there are plenty of options right in or within easy walking distance of the city centre. One hassle is the lack of parking; if you have your own wheels, ask about car parking when you book (and be aware you'll probably have to pay for it). Sleeping reviews in this chapter feature a Ⓟ symbol if on-site parking is available.

Wellington's budget accommodation largely takes the form of multistorey hostel megaliths. There's no 'motel alley' in Wellington, but motels are scattered around the city fringe. Being the hub of government and business, self-contained apartments are popular, and bargains can often be found at the weekends.

During the peak season (December to February), or during major festivals, book your bed well in advance.

Budget
HOSTELS

Downtown Backpackers (Map p380; ☎ 0800 225 725, 04-473 8482; www.downtownbackpackers.co.nz; 1 Bunny St; dm $23, s $62-70, d $60-92; 🖥 🛜) An old charmer at the railway end of town, housed in a grand art-deco building. Downtown has clean, bright rooms and plenty of character-filled communal areas (be sure to check out the carved fireplace in the bar). Budget meals in the cafe morning and night.

Base Backpackers (Map p384; ☎ 0800 227 369, 04-801 5666; www.basebackpackers.com; 21-23 Cambridge Tce; dm $25-28, d & tr with bathroom from $87; Ⓟ 🖥 🛜) A slick chain hostel aimed squarely at the young 'uns. Party-perfect location (metres from Courtenay Pl), modern rooms, and the female-only floor will come as a relief to some. Bag yourself a bunkmate at the Basement Bar downstairs. The only gripe: the kitchen and lounge are tiny given the hostel's 200-plus beds. Limited parking $10 per day.

Nomads Capital (Map p384; ☎ 0508 666 237, 04-978 7800; www.nomadscapital.com; 118 Wakefield St; dm $25-31, d with bathroom from $89; 🖥 🛜) Smack-bang in the middle of town Nomads has good security, spick-and-span rooms, an on-site cafe-bar (free modest nightly meals) and discounts for longer stays. Kitchen and lounge spaces are short on elbow room, but heritage features (such as the amazing stairwell) stop you dwelling on the negatives.

Rosemere Backpackers (Map p384; ☎ 04-384 3041; www.backpackerswellington.co.nz; 6 MacDonald Cres; dm/s/tw/d incl breakfast $27/50/62/66; 🖥) A colour-spangled former brothel a short (steep!) walk uphill from the city centre. Free internet and linen, and a couple of tent sites on the tiny lawn out front. Happy vibe.

Wellywood Backpackers (Map p384; ☎ 0508 005 858, 04-381 3899; www.wellywoodbackpackers.co.nz; 58 Tory St; dm $27, s $50, d with/without bathroom $80/70; 🖥 🛜) You'd have to be a zookeeper not to be impressed by this huge zebra-striped building off Courtenay Pl. Rooms are spacious, with weathered retro furniture dotted throughout the place, and unisex bathroom basins in the corridors – very social! Rock music wails over the speakers in communal areas (except the reading room).

Worldwide Backpackers (Map p380; ☎ 0508 888 555, 04-802 5590; www.worldwidenz.co.nz; 291 The Terrace; dm/d incl breakfast $27/66; 🖥) In a 110-year-old house, Worldwide is the most appealing small hostel in town. Clean and homely, with winning features such as free internet, regular barbecues, and nautical reading lamps. It's youthful, down-to-earth and chilled out.

Moana Lodge (off Map p380; ☎ 04-233 2010; www.moanalodge.co.nz; 49 Moana Rd, Plimmerton; dm $29-32, d $60-90; 🖥 🛜) Just off SH1 and only a short train ride or drive from Wellington (25km), this exceptional backpackers right on the beach is immaculate and inviting, with friendly owners superkeen to infuse you with their local knowledge. Kayaks and golf clubs available; occasional boat trips to Mana Island. From Wellington catch the Tranz Metro Paraparaumu train to Plimmerton.

ourpick **YHA Wellington City** (Map p384; ☎ 04-801 7280; www.yha.co.nz; cnr Cambridge Tce & Wakefield St; dm $30-33, d with/without bathroom $108/88; ▯ ☎) YHA Welly wins points for the biggest and best communal areas: superior kitchens, cavernous dining areas (group dinner nights are a blast), games room, reading room and dedicated movie room with high-tech projector. Sustainable initiatives (recycling, composting and energy-efficient hot water) impress, and there's a comprehensive booking service at reception.

HOTELS & MOTELS
Cambridge Hotel (Map p384; ☎ 0800 375 021, 04-385 8829; www.cambridgehotel.co.nz; 28 Cambridge Tce; dm $23-25, s/d/tw without bathroom $61/80/85, s/d/tw/tr/f $90/99/109/130/140; ▯ ☎) Top-quality pub accommodation at affordable prices in a heritage hotel. En suite rooms have Sky TV, phone and fridge (try for a room at the back if you're a light sleeper). The backpacker wing has a well-stocked kitchen, flash bathrooms and dorms with no natural light but sky-high ceilings. Cheap bar meals are a plus.

Shepherds Arms Hotel (Map p380; ☎ 0800 393 782, 04-472 1320; www.shepherds.co.nz; 285 Tinakori Rd; s without bathroom $65-85, d with bathroom $99-169; ℗) With wall-to-wall heritage buildings and close to the Botanic Gardens, Thorndon makes a great home base. This well-preserved hotel serves its patrons in fitting style, with a restaurant and bar, and charming rooms upstairs. Shell out a few extra dollars for a larger room.

Carillon Motor Inn (Map p380; ☎ 04-384 8795; www.carillon.co.nz; 33 Thompson St; s/d/tw/tr $80/90/110/139; ℗) Wow, what a relic! Carillon is a rickety old Victorian mansion that's somehow evaded the wrecking ball, developers' ambitions and renovators' brush strokes. Endearing, old-fashioned and chaotic in a *Fawlty Towers* kind of way, it's clean, central and supercheap.

Halswell Lodge (Map p384; ☎ 04-385 0196; www.halswell.co.nz; 21 Kent Tce; hotel r $90, units $135-160; ℗ ☎) Doggone handy to all the central sights without being too noisy, Tudor-esque Halswell offers a range of options, including small, affordable hotel rooms with TV, fridge and bathroom. The upmarket lodge suites with spa are a better option if you're in the next price bracket; families pile into the two-bedroom motel units.

CAMPING
Campsites are as rare as bad coffee in Wellington. Rosemere Backpackers (see p391) can accommodate a few tents, or head to the Hutt Valley (p403). Motorhomers, however, can now enjoy the brand new and unbelievably convenient **Wellington Waterfront Motorhome Park** (Map p380; ☎ 04-384 4511; www.wwmp.co.nz; 12 Waterloo Quay; powered sites $50; ☎); park during the day (for modest hourly rates) or stay overnight, and make use of the nice new ablution block and power supply.

Midrange
GUEST HOUSES & B&BS
Mermaid (Map p380; ☎ 04-384 4511; www.mermaid.co.nz; 1 Epuni St; s $90-150, d $100-145; ☎) In the ubercool Aro Valley 'hood, Mermaid is a small women-only guest house in a colourfully restored villa. Each room is individually themed with artistic flair (one with private bathroom, three with shared facilities). The lounge, kitchen and deck are homely and laid-back. Great cafe, bakery and deli on your doorstep.

Tinakori Lodge (Map p380; ☎ 0800 939 347, 04-939 3478; www.tinakorilodge.co.nz; 182 Tinakori Rd; s $99-120, d $140-170 all incl breakfast; ℗ ☎) Built in 1868 from native timbers, this lodge is in the thick of historic Thorndon, but a bit too close to the motorway for utter tranquillity. It's still a good option, with its rooms (five with bathroom; four with shared facilities) decorated in refined, motherly style. Free street-parking permits for guests.

Booklovers B&B (Map p380; ☎ 04-384 2714; www.booklovers.co.nz; 123 Pirie St; s/d from $150/180; ℗ ▯ ☎) Booklovers is a gracious B&B run by award-winning author Jane Tolerton (her books are among the thousands shelved around the house). Four guest rooms have TV, CDs and CD/DVD player; three have en suites, one has a private bathroom. Bus 2 runs from the front gate to Courtenay Pl and the train station, and the city's 'green belt' begins right next door. Free wireless internet and limited parking.

HOTELS

Comfort & Quality Hotels (Map p380; ☎ 0800 873 553, 04-385 2156; www.hotelwellington.co.nz; 223 Cuba St; d $100-170; 🖳 🖳) Two hotels in one: the sympathetically renovated historic Trekkers building with its smaller, cheaper rooms (Comfort); and the recently built, snazzier high-rise Quality with modern styling and a swimming pool. Both share in-house bar and dining room (meals available, $14 to $28). Two solid options in the heart of Cuba.

Travelodge (Map p380; ☎ 0800 101 100, 04-499 9911; www.travelodge.co.nz; 2-6 Gilmer Tce; d $105-270; 🅿 🖳 🛜) The zillion-dollar refit is as charmless as a blancmange, but you can't argue with the location and price. An epic 132 smallish rooms, with microwaves, fridges and personal safes. In-house bar and restaurant (mains $25 to $30) will be working pretty hard to win you over with some of Welly's best on your doorstep. Parking $20 per day.

Copthorne Hotel (Map p380; ☎ 0800 782 548, 04-385 0279; www.millenniumhotels.co.nz/copthorneoriental bay; 100 Oriental Pde; d $160-290; 🅿 🖳 🛜 🖳) A tasteful refurb has this upmarket operation on ritzy Oriental Pde looking as good as gold, from the polished reception, through a seemingly endless maze of corridors, to the fancy bar and dining room. Handsome rooms are spread over two wings: the Bay wing has larger rooms with harbour views, the Roxburgh has smaller rooms, some with harbour views and some without. Parking $20 per day.

MOTELS

Apollo Lodge (Map p380; ☎ 0800 361 645, 04-385 1849; www.apollolodge.co.nz; 49 Majoribanks St; d $125-175; 🅿 🛜) Within staggering distance of Courtenay Pl, Apollo Lodge is a loose collation of 35 motel units (one and two bedrooms), ranging from old-school self-contained studios to airy suites.

Victoria Court (Map p384; ☎ 04-472 4297; www.vict oriacourt.co.nz; 201 Victoria St; r $145-200; 🅿 🛜) Our top motel choice, right in the city centre, with plenty of parking. The affable owners offer spotless, stylish studios and apartments with spas, cooking facilities, suede couches, slick blond-wood joinery and new TVs. Two disabled-access units; larger units sleep six.

Other options:

Capital View Motor Inn (Map p380; ☎ 0800 438 505, 04-385 0515; www.capitalview.co.nz; 12 Thompson St; d $120-155; 🅿 🛜) A dependable option close to Cuba St,

many rooms do indeed enjoy capital views. Undergoing gradual renovation, so ask for options.

Marksman Motor Inn (Map p380; ☎ 0800 627 574, 04-385 2499; www.marksmanmotel.co.nz; 40-44 Sussex St; units $125-275; 🅿 🛜) Clean, comfortable studios and apartments across from the Basin Reserve. Can be a tad noisy, but handy for airport runs (or the cricket).

Majoribanks Apartments (Map p380; ☎ 0800 361 645, 04-385 1849; www.apollolodge.co.nz; 38 Majoribanks St; apt for 6 per week $800; 🅿 🛜) Run by the Apollo Lodge folk.

Top End

Museum Hotel (Map p384; ☎ 0800 994 335, 04-802 8900; www.museumhotel.co.nz; 90 Cable St; r & apt Mon-Thu $190-325, Fri-Sun $150-325; 🅿 🖳 🛜 🖳) Sometimes called 'Museum Hotel de Wheels' (to make way for Te Papa, it was rolled here from its original location 120m away), the Museum is a quirky, boutique affair. Eclectic decor (chandeliers, edgy modern art), sassy staff, a decent restaurant and groovy tunes piped into the lobby make a refreshing change from homogenised business hotels. Tasty weekend/weekly rates.

CityLife Wellington (Map p380; ☎ 0800 368 888, 04-922 2800; www.heritagehotels.co.nz; 300 Lambton Quay; d Mon-Thu from $200, Fri-Sun from $169; 🅿 🖳 🛜) Luxurious serviced apartments in the city centre, ranging from studios to three-bedroom arrangements, some with a harbour glimpse. Features include full kitchen, CD/DVD player, and in-room laundry facilities. Weekend rates are great bang for your buck. The vehicle entrance is from Gilmer Tce, off Boulcott St (parking $15 per day).

Wellesley (Map p380; ☎ 04-474 1308; www.wellesley boutiquehotel.co.nz; 2-8 Maginnity St; d $180-300) A stately central choice with buckets of old-world charm and impeccable service. Formerly a gentlemen's club, the Wellesley retains a refined vibe that makes you want to spark up a cigar. The 13 rooms are decked out with original art, antiques and the odd claw-foot bath. On-site Maginnity's restaurant and bar does everything from high tea to top shelf.

EATING

Wellington is an exciting place to eat. Considering its size, there's a bewildering array of restaurants, cafes and food-focused bars, and keen competition keeps standards high and prices reasonable. Excellent options for contemporary NZ fine dining are nicely complemented by numerous budget eateries, including oodles of noodles.

Restaurants

KK Malaysian Cafe (Map p384; ☎ 04-385 6698; 54 Ghuznee St; mains $8-14; ☽ 11.30am-2.30pm Mon-Sat, 5-9.30pm daily; **V**) Decked out like a dirty protest, tiny KK is one of Wellington's most popular cheap Malaysians in a city obsessed with Southeast Asian cuisine. Satay to die for and *rendang* to put a smile on your face, accompanied by the ubiquitous roti, of course. Unlicensed.

Aunty Mena's (Map p384; ☎ 04-382 8288; 167 Cuba St; meals $9-14; ☽ 5.30-9.30pm Sun & Mon, 11.30am-9.30pm Tue & Wed, to 10pm Thu-Sat; **V**) One of many Cuba St noodle houses, cheap 'n' cheerful Aunty Mena's cranks out yummy veggie/vegan Malaysian and Chinese dishes to a diverse clientele. Easy-clean, over-lit interior. Unlicensed.

Sweet Mother's Kitchen (Map p384; ☎ 04-385 444; 5 Courtenay Pl; mains $10-26; ☽ 8am-late; **V**) Perpetually full, predominantly with young cool cats, Sweet Mother's serves dubious takes on the Deep South, such as burritos, nachos, the po' boys and the New Orleans muffaletta. Key lime pie is about as authentic as it gets, but we don't care. It's cheap, cute, has great cakes and gets good sun.

our pick **Scopa** (Map p384; ☎ 04-384 6020; cnr Cuba & Ghuznee Sts; mains $14-30; ☽ 9am-late Mon-Sun) Perfect pizza, proper pasta and other authentic Italian treats. Opened in 2006, this modern *cucina* is already a Wellington institution. Slick, friendly service and consistently good food make it deservedly so. Watch the groovy 'Cubans' from a seat in the window. Lunchtime specials; sexy evenings complete with cocktails.

Great India (Map p384; ☎ 04-384 5755; 141 Manners St; mains $15-26; ☽ noon-2pm Mon-Fri, to 3pm Sat & Sun, 5pm-late Mon-Fri; **V**) This is not your average curry house. While a tad more expensive than its competitors, this place consistently earns its moniker. With any luck you'll be served by Rakesh, one of the capital's smoothest maître d's.

Miyabi Sushi (Map p384; ☎ 04-801 9688; Willis St Village, 142 Willis St; mains $15-27; ☽ 11.30am-late Mon-Fri, 5.30pm-late Sat) A steady stream of customers is testament to the satisfying food served at this low-key Japanese cafe hidden away off the main street. The smiling Mr Chuck prepares superfresh sushi, noodles, soups and set meals including teriyaki (chicken, beef or fish) with

miso soup, rice and salad – delicious and great value. The *gyoza* (pot-sticker dumplings) are hard to pass up.

Osteria del Toro (Map p384; ☎ 04-381 2299; 60 Tory St; mains $18-28; ☽ 11.30am-late Sun-Fri, 5pm-late Sat) Flamboyantly decorated in a baroque style with influences from all around the Mediterranean. The menu plucks popular classics from the region in a similar fashion. Pastas, pizzas and paella sit happily alongside souvlaki, tagine and tapas. Moreish food in Moorish surrounds; this restaurant, however, doesn't charge like a wounded bull.

Chow (Map p384; ☎ 04-382 8585; level 1, 45 Tory St; meals $18-30; ☽ noon-midnight) Home of the legendary blue cheese and peanut wonton, Chow is a stylish pan-Asian restaurant-cum-bar: a must visit for people who love exciting food, interesting decor, and the odd cocktail. The perfect place to share food and conversation. The hip Motel bar is adjacent.

Flying Burrito Brothers (Map p384; ☎ 04-385 8811; cnr Cuba & Vivian Sts; mains $18-32; ☽ 4.30pm-late) Let it all hang out at this lively Tex-Mex cantina. Quesadillas, tortillas, tacos and tostadas laced with avocado and chilli, plus *bocaditos* (small bites, like tapas) and a kids menu, too. The extensive (and informative) tequila menu and premium margaritas will give you lift-off.

Capitol (Map p384; ☎ 04-384 2855; cnr Kent Tce & Majoribanks St; mains $20-30; ☽ lunch & dinner Mon-Fri, brunch, lunch & dinner Sat & Sun) Simple, seasonal food using premium local ingredients, lovingly prepared with a nod to the classic Italian style. The dining room is elegant and intimate with large windows looking out onto busy Courtenay precinct. No dinner bookings are taken, but it's well worth waiting with an aperitif at the tiny bar.

Le Métropolitain (Map p384; ☎ 04-801 8007; cnr Garrett & Cuba Sts; mains $25-29; ☽ noon-2.30pm & 5-10pm Tue-Sat) Prepare to be transported to the heart of France by your charming hosts. Expect unpretentious bistro fare in a suitably Gallic environment. Classics are well covered and include *moules*, onion soup, *steak frites*, coq au vin and escargot (yum). Cheese or scrumptious tart and a sticky wine for dessert, anyone?

Pravda (Map p380; ☎ 04-499 5570; 107 Customhouse Quay; mains $25-35; ☽ 7.30am-late Mon-Fri, 9am-late Sat) A classy downtown cafe (more chic restaurant by Wellington standards), scoring well with readers and folks that hand out culinary excellence awards. The opulent split-level space (styled in quasi-USSR mode) is a formal backdrop for enjoying well-assembled duck, chicken, fish and NZ lamb mains. Fantastic desserts and coffee.

Martin Bosley's (Map p380; ☎ 04-920 8302; 103 Oriental Pde; mains $28-47; ☽ lunch Mon-Fri, dinner Tue-Sun) Swish fish from one of the country's best chefs, in an elegant restaurant with panoramic harbour views. The degustation menu is an excellent way to sample the skills of the kitchen and is $100 very well spent. For an extra $70, you'll get wines selected to match each delicious dish. Top notch.

Logan-Brown (Map p384; ☎ 04-801 5114; 192 Cuba St; mains $39-48; ☽ noon-2pm Mon-Fri, from 5.30pm nightly) Located in a 1920s banking chamber, Logan-Brown oozes class without being pretentious or overly formal. This is seriously good food brought to you by the 2009 Wellingtonians of the Year, in their award-winning restaurant. Believe the hype, sample the paua ravioli – it's been on the menu forever and a day – and peruse the epic wine list. Bookings recommended.

Cafes

Deluxe (Map p384; ☎ 04-801 5455; 10 Kent Tce; snacks $5-8; ☽ 7am-late Mon-Fri, 8am-late Sat & Sun; V) A stalwart of the late-night cafe scene, with off-beat, oft-changing local art adorning the walls. Teeny wee space next to the Embassy Cinema (p399) somehow serves more than 500 coffees a day and mainly vegetarian/vegan counter food and pizza slices to loyal customers.

Lido (Map p384; ☎ 04-499 6666; cnr Victoria & Wakefield Sts; brunch & lunch $5-18, dinner $16-26; ☽ 7.30am-3pm Mon, to late Tue-Fri, 9am-late Sat & Sun) Swing into Lido, at the bottom of a funky old office block, for a wide selection of consistent and reasonably priced Med-inspired food. Pancakes and pasta sit happily alongside, fish, burgers, antipasto and salad. Great coffee and sweet treats, too. Live jazz Saturday and Sunday evenings.

Felix (Map p384; ☎ 04-499 5523; cnr Wakefield & Cuba Sts; brunch $5-22, dinner $10-24; ☽ 7.30am-9pm Mon-Fri, 8.30am-8pm Sat, to 5.30pm Sun) Despite some hard edges in this modern-industrial space, Felix is still a comfortable and attractive cafe that dishes out honest food morning, noon and night. The big windows keep things bright, as do the cheery staff. Great burger and heavenly chips.

Midnight Espresso (Map p384; ☎ 04-384 7014; 178 Cuba St; meals $6-16; ☽ 7.30am-3am Mon-Fri, 8am-3am Sat & Sun; V) The city's original late-night cafe, with food that's hearty, tasty and inexpensive – heavy on the wholesome and vegetarian. Sit in the window with Havana coffee and cake, it's the quintessential Wellington cafe experience.

Cafe L'Affare (Map p380; ☎ 04-385 9748; 27 College St; meals $6-18; ☽ 8am-4pm) Cafe L'Affare is the centre of a small empire, from which its own beans are roasted and distributed. Its Professor Brainstorm–emporium interior is a hive of activity, with speedy baristas, crowded communal tables and a disco ball. At weekends, kids aplenty add to the cacophony, but everyone adds their cheery thanks to snappy service and wicked brekkies of eggie excellence.

Fidel's (Map p380; ☎ 04-801 6868; 234 Cuba St; meals $6-18; ☽ 7.30am-midnight Mon-Fri, 9am-midnight Sat & Sun; V) A Cuba St institution for caffeine-craving, upbeat left-wing subversives. Eggs any-which-way, pizza and amazing salads are pumped out of the itsy kitchen, along with Welly's best milkshakes. Revolutionary memorabilia adorn the walls of the funky interior; decent outdoor areas too. A superbusy crew copes with the chaos admirably.

Nikau Gallery Cafe (Map p384; ☎ 04-801 4168; Civic Sq; lunch $11-24; ☽ 7am-4pm Mon-Fri, 8am-4pm Sat; V) City Gallery (p384): home to fine contemporary art and its culinary equivalent served up at Nikau. Efficient service, a stylish interior and some of the best cafe fare in town make this an obvious lunch-stop while checking out the abundant artworks. Legendary kedgeree and sunny courtyard.

Quick Eats

Pandoro Panetteria (Map p384; ☎ 04-385 4478; 2 Allen St; items $3-6; ☽ 7am-5pm Mon-Fri, to 4pm Sat & Sun; V) A fabulous Italian bakery with smooth coffee, sweet and savoury muffins, stuffed breads, scrolls, cakes and tarts.

Trisha's Pies (Map p380; ☎ 04-801 5515; 32 Cambridge Tce; pies $4-5; ☽ 8am-3.30pm Mon-Fri) Superchunky traditional pies (peppered steak, beef and mushroom) or something different (chicken, apricot and brie). Veggie and fruit options too.

Sushi of Japan (Map p384; ☎ 04-385 0290; 189 Cuba St; meals $5-9; ☽ 8.30am-6pm; V) Superfresh, ready-to-run sushi slices that are cheap and tasty.

Crêpes a Go-Go (Map p384; 57 Manners Mall; crepes $5-9; ☽ 9am-9pm; V) From a tiny yellow stall in the Manners Mall, a Breton batter-master whips up cheap crêpes with your choice of sweet or savoury fillings.

Burger Fuel (Map p384; ☎ 04-801 9222; 101 Courtenay Pl; burgers $5-12; ⏱ 11am-10pm Sun-Thu, to 4am Fri & Sat; **V**) Fast food how it should be. Tasty burgers of all description made with fresh, natural ingredients, beating the pants off Ronald and the Colonel.

Wellington Trawling Sea Market (Map p380; ☎ 04-384 8461; 220 Cuba St; meals $6-14; ⏱ lunch-9pm) Locals' favourite fresh-off-the-boat fish and chips, plus oysters, scallops and whitebait in season. Burgers, too.

Phoenician Falafel (Map p384; ☎ 04-385 9997; 10 Kent Tce; meals $8-15; ⏱ 11.30am-9.30pm Sun-Wed, to 11pm Thu-Sat; **V**) Authentic falafel, shish and *shawarma* (kebab) served up by cheery Lebanese owners. The best kebabs in town.

Good-value (and very worldly) food courts:

BNZ Centre (Map p384; ☎ 04-499 9300; Willis St; meals $4-10; ⏱ 8am-8pm Mon-Fri, 10am-4pm Sat)

Courtenay Central (Map p384; ☎ 04-382 9526; Courtenay Pl; meals $5-10; ⏱ 10am-10pm)

Self-Catering

Two excellent produce markets run on Sunday mornings – next to Te Papa (Wakefield St) and on the corner of Victoria and Vivian Sts.

Commonsense Organics (Map p384; ☎ 04-384 3314; 260 Wakefield St; ⏱ 9am-7pm Mon-Fri, to 6pm Sat & Sun) Organic produce (wine, fruit, veg, nuts, tea, herbs etc), and food for the intolerant.

New World Metro (Map p384; ☎ 04-417 6580; 70 Willis St; ⏱ 7am-11pm Mon-Fri, 8am-11pm Sat, to 10pm Sun); Chaffers (Map p384; ☎ 04-384 8054; 279 Wakefield St; ⏱ 7am-midnight); Thorndon (Map p380; ☎ 04-499 9041; Molesworth St; ⏱ 7am-11pm)

Moore Wilson Fresh (Map p380; ☎ 04-384 9906; cnr College & Tory Sts; ⏱ 7.30am-7pm Mon-Fri, to 6pm Sat, 9am-5pm Sun) An unsurpassed array of (predominantly NZ) produce, baking, mountains of cheese... just endless goodies. Go.

DRINKING

Wellingtonians love a late night, and it's common to see the masses heading into town at a time when normal folk would be boiling the kettle for cocoa. The city's bars and music venues ensure things keep cranking – there are a high number of reputable establishments, with plenty of live music, dance parties, quiz nights and suchlike. You'll also find a raft of great cocktails, fine wines and microbrews, as well as some impressive bar food. Indeed, many places listed below could

easily fit under Eating as well as Drinking (the legendary Matterhorn and Hummingbird, for starters).

Most of the action clusters around two hubs: Courtenay Pl – bustling, brassy, and positively let-your-hair-down; and Cuba St – edgy, groovy and sometimes too cool for school.

our pick Mighty Mighty (Map p384; ☎ 04-384 9085; 104 Cuba St; ⏱ 4pm-late Wed-Sat) Possibly the hippest of the capital's drinking establishments and music venues. Inside-a-pinball-machine decor, pink velvet curtains, kitsch gewgaws and Wellington's best barmaid make this an essential port of call for those wanting to experience the best of New Zealand's bar scene. Get dancing.

Matterhorn (Map p384; ☎ 04-384 3359; 106 Cuba St; ⏱ 10am-late) Perennially popular bar, with a clientele as interesting as its drinks list. Worthy winner of numerous accolades including New Zealand's best bar and restaurant. Slick and ultracool, with great attention to detail. Occasional live music provided by some of Aotearoa's freshest bands and musicians.

Malthouse (Map p384; ☎ 04-802 5484; 48 Courtenay Pl; ⏱ lunch-late Mon-Sat) Beervana. An immense array of beers (both local and international) that would make even the most fervent of hopheads quiver at the knees. New Zealand *does* brew great beer, and this is the place to quaff them. Check out the *Forty Licks*–style toilets in the gents.

Vivo (Map p384; ☎ 04-384 6400; 19 Edward St; ⏱ 3pm-late Mon-Fri, 5pm-late Sat) A tomelike list of approximately 700 wines from around the world, with more than 50 available by the glass. Exposed bricks and timber beams give Vivo an earthy cellarlike feel while the fairy lights look like stars set against the dark ceiling. A vinophile's delight with some decent food too.

Southern Cross (Map p380; ☎ 04-384 9085; 35 Abel Smith St; ⏱ 9am-late) Welly's most stylish crowd-pleasing pub combines a laid-back restaurant, lively bar, pool table, dance floor and the best garden bar in town. Independent beer on tap and a good bowl of chips.

Mac's Brewery Bar (Map p384; ☎ 04-381 2282; cnr Taranaki & Cable Sts; ⏱ 10.30am-late) Occupying a renovated warehouse on a prime waterfront site, this microbrewery does a great job of looking seriously committed to the craft. Author's favourite: Sassy Red, enjoyed in the sun while watching the skateboarders sprain

GAY & LESBIAN WELLINGTON

Wellington is open-minded and sophisticated, so G&L people fit right in almost everywhere they go. The G&L scene is small, but friendly and inclusive, as proven by one of only two gay bars in the city, **Scotty & Mal's** (Map p384; ☎ 04-802 5335; 176 Cuba St; 5pm-late). This is a stylish, welcoming bar and dance lounge where you can enjoy cocktails, small talk and quiz nights upstairs, or strut your stuff and play some pool in the sultry basement bar (DJ's Friday and Saturday).

Larger newsagents will stock the fortnightly magazine **express** (www.gayexpress.co.nz; $3), featuring the latest news, reviews and events. Useful online resources include www.gaynz.com, which has comprehensive national coverage of all things queer; and the Wellington-specific www.gayline.gen.nz, www.gaywellington.org and www.wellington.lesbian.net.nz. See www.gaystay.co.nz for G&L-hosted accommodation around town. For phone information, or just to talk, contact **Wellington Gay Welfare Group** (☎ 04-473 7878; helpline@gaywellington.org; 7.30-9.30pm).

See also Gay & Lesbian Travellers, p422.

themselves on the promenade. Excellent fish and chips.

Leuven (Map p380; ☎ 04-499 2939; 135 Featherston St; 7am-late Mon-Fri, 9am-late Sat & Sun) The menu at this beer cafe is an ode to Belgium's best: mussels come 10 different ways, the *frites* (chips) are cooked to perfection, and the big brewing guns line up at the bar (Hoegaarden, Leffe, Chimay). Popular breakfast specials (waffle, anyone?).

Hummingbird (Map p384; ☎ 04-801 6336; 22 Courtenay Pl; 9am-late) Popular with the sophisticated set, Hummingbird is usually packed – both inside in the intimate, stylish dining room and bar, and outside on streetside tables. Croony music (with regular live jazz), exciting brunch-to-supper menus, and impressive drinks including fine wines and cocktails.

Backbencher (Map p380; ☎ 04-472 3065; 34 Molesworth St; 11am-late) You might spot the odd parliamentarian on the turps at the Backbencher, a pub opposite the Beehive where rubbery puppets of NZ pollies are mounted trophy-style on the walls (David Lange is a beauty). Good weekend brunches.

Good Luck (Map p384; ☎ 04-801 9950; basement, 126 Cuba St; 5pm-late Tue-Sun) Cuba St's Chinese opium den, without the opium. This is a slickly run, sultry basement bar playing fresh hip-hop and electronica. It also brings you the thing no one else could: a middle-of-the-mall alfresco lounge – great for watching the Cuba-cade.

Molly Malone's (Map p384; ☎ 04-384 2896; cnr Courtenay Pl & Taranaki St; 11am-late) A highly polished Irish bar, complete with Guinness, live music, well-priced pub grub and a bottle store.

Upstairs, the Red Head restaurant has fancier food and a balcony with rare afternoon sun.

The hip, late-night bar scene down Courtenay Place may surprise you with its density and variety. Here are just a few of the many best visited late on a Thursday, Friday or Saturday.

Betty's (Map p384; ☎ 04-803 3766; 32 Blair St) Brassy joint with apothecary theme and wraparound digital screen covering three walls.

Hawthorn Lounge (Map p384; ☎ 04-890 3724; 82 Tory St) Akin to a 1920s gentlemen's club. Play poker, drink cocktails and listen to big-band medleys.

Library (Map p384; ☎ 04-382 8593; 1/53 Courtenay Pl) Velveteen booths, books, booze and beats. Regular live music.

Vespa Lounge (Map p384; ☎ 04-385 2438; 7/21 Allen St) When everyone else is safely tucked up in bed, the Vespa crowd just keeps rolling.

ENTERTAINMENT

Wellington's entertainment scene is a bit like the Tardis: it looks small from the outside, but inside it holds big surprises. Not only does it boast its own vibrant theatres and an inordinate number of local musicians, plenty of high-quality performers visit from around New Zealand and abroad too. Hungry, appreciative crowds help things along.

Event and gig listings can be found in the *Capital Times* – the free weekly rag found all over town. Look out, also, for the *Groove Guide* (www.grooveguide.co.nz), which has a gig guide and pertinent articles.

Live Music & Clubs

Entry to most gigs and club nights can be gained via a door sale. Popular gigs, however, may well sell out, so it pays to buy advance tickets from advertised outlets – often **Real Groovy** (Map p380; ☎ 04-385 2020; www.realgroovy. conz; cnr Cuba & Abel Smith Sts), or **Under the Radar** (www.undertheradar.co.nz). Admission prices vary depending on whom, where and when, but generally range from $5 to $70.

San Francisco Bath House (Map p384; ☎ 04-801 6797; www.sfbh.co.nz; 171 Cuba St; ☽ 5pm-late Wed-Fri, 8pm-late Sat) Wellington's best midsized live-music venue, playing host to the cream of NZ artists, as well as quality acts from abroad (Fleet Foxes, Gomez...). Somewhat debauched balcony action, five deep at the bar, but otherwise well run and usually lots of fun.

Bodega (Map p384; ☎ 04-384 8212; www.bodega.co.nz; 101 Ghuznee St; ☽ 4pm-late) A trailblazer of the city's modern live-music scene, and still considered an institution despite its move from a derelict heritage building to a concrete cavern. 'The Bodge' offers a full and varied program of gigs in a pleasant space with a respectable dance floor and filler-up food.

Garden Club (Map p384; ☎ 04-381 2341; www. thegardenclub.co.nz; 13b Dixon St; ☽ 5pm-late Wed-Sat) Three floors of dance-music-fuelled mayhem aimed primarily at a younger crowd. Level one houses the club proper with regular live acts and DJs, while the top floor is home to Welly's other gay bar. In between is a noxious den that pushes NZ's smoking laws to the limit. Well run and definitely fun.

Happy (Map p380; ☎ 04-970 1741; www.myspace. com/happybar; cnr Tory & Vivian Sts) A basement bar that picks up all the cool, stray acts (small and large) that don't seem to fit in anywhere else: spoken word, jazz fusion, acoustic singer-songwriters, electronica, short films and experimental theatre. Open performance nights only.

Sandwiches (Map p384; ☎ 04-385 7698; www. sandwiches.co.nz; 8 Kent Tce; ☽ 4pm-late Tue-Sat) Get yourself a slice of NZ's electronic artists and DJs, regular multiflavoured international acts and the capital's best sound system. Throw shapes in the edgy main room or enjoy cocktails and pizza in the sultry bar. Great club run by a dedicated team that isn't just in it for the bread.

Theatres

Wellington's accessible performing-arts scene sustains a laudable number of professional and amateur companies. Tickets for many events can be purchased from the **Ticketek box**

offices (☎ 04-384 3840; www.ticketek.co.nz; ☽ 9am-5.30pm Mon-Fri, 10am-2pm Sat) at St James Theatre (Map p384) or the Michael Fowler Centre (Map p384). Discount same-day tickets for some productions are often available at the i-SITE.

BATS (Map p384; ☎ 04-802 4175; www.bats.co.nz; 1 Kent Tce; tickets $15-20; ☽ box office open 2hr before each show) Wildly alternative BATS presents cutting-edge and experimental NZ theatre – varied, cheap, and intimate.

Downstage (Map p384; ☎ 04-801 6946; www. downstage.co.nz; cnr Courtenay Pl & Cambridge Tce; tickets $25-45; ☽ box office 9am-5.30pm Mon, to show time Tue-Sat) NZ's most enduring professional theatre company with a strong presence in Wellington (established 1964). Original NZ plays, dance, comedy and musicals in a 250-seat auditorium.

Circa (Map p384; ☎ 04-801 7992; www.circa.co.nz; 1 Taranaki St; tickets adult/stand-by $35/18; ☽ box office 10am-4pm Mon-Sat) Circa's main auditorium seats 240 people, its studio 100. Cheap tickets are available for preview shows (the night before opening night), and there are stand-by tickets available an hour before the show (anything from pantomimes to international comedy).

There are four other significant venues for touring shows and one-off programs:

Michael Fowler Centre (Map p384; ☎ 04-801 4231; www.wellingtonconventioncentre.com; 111 Wakefield St) Home to the New Zealand Symphony Orchestra. The Town Hall next door hosts the occasional concert and special events.

St James Theatre (Map p384; ☎ 04-802 4060; www. stjames.co.nz; 77 Courtenay Pl) A grand old heritage auditorium hosting big productions such as the ballet and opera (www.nzballet.org.nz; www.nzopera.com).

Opera House (Map p384; 111-113 Manners St) Another heritage theatre, with heart-stopping gods, hosting sit-down concerts, touring plays and the odd musical.

TSB Bank Arena (Map p380; www.wellingtonconvention centre.com; Jervois Quay) A hangar-sized venue in which the supersized shows are held.

Cinemas

Movie times are listed in the local newspapers and at www.film.wellington.net.nz. Most cinemas have a discount day early in the week (Monday or Tuesday).

Real film buffs may want to check out the **Weta Cave** (off Map p380; ☎ 04-380 9361; www.wetanz. com; cnr Camperdown Rd & Weka St, Miramar; admission free; ☽ 11am-6pm Mon-Fri, to 4pm Sat), the minimuseum

WELCOME TO WELLYWOOD

In recent years Wellington has stamped its place firmly on the world map as the home of NZ's dynamic film industry, earning itself the nickname 'Wellywood'. Acclaimed director Peter Jackson still calls Wellington home; the success of his *Lord of the Rings* (*LOTR*) films and subsequent productions such as *King Kong* have made him a powerful Hollywood player, and have bolstered Wellington's reputation. *LOTR* fans and movie buffs can experience some local movie magic by visiting the Weta Cave (p398), or one of many film locations around the region (see p390 & p402).

of the Academy Award–winning company that brought *LOTR*, *King Kong*, and *Narnia* to life.

Embassy Theatre (Map p384; ☎ 04-384 7656; www.deluxe.co.nz; 10 Kent Tce; tickets adult/child $15/9; ☺ 11am-midnight) Wellywood's cinema mothership: built in the 1920s, restored in 2003. Screens mainstream films; bar and cafe on-site.

Paramount (Map p384; ☎ 04-384 4080; www.paramount.co.nz; 25 Courtenay Pl; tickets adult/child $14.50/9; ☺ noon-midnight) A lovely old complex screening largely art-house, documentary and foreign flicks.

Reading Cinemas (Map p384; ☎ 04-801 4600; www.readingcinemas.co.nz; Courtenay Central, Courtenay Pl; tickets adult/child $16/10.50; ☺ 9.30am-midnight) Mainstream new-release fodder.

Penthouse Cinema (off Map p380; ☎ 04-384 3157; www.penthousecinema.co.nz; 205 Ohiro Rd, Brooklyn; tickets adult/child $15/11; ☺ 9am-11pm) Art-deco charmer screening a smart range of films. Nice cafe too. Well worth the bus ride – take bus 7 or 8 from town.

Empire Cinema (off Map p380; ☎ 04-939 7557; www.empirecinema.co.nz; cnr Parade & Mersey St, Island Bay; tickets adult/child $16/12; ☺ 10am-midnight) A cracker indie cinema screening everything from Hollywood to Harbicht. Take bus 1 from town.

SHOPPING

Lambton Quay is known as the 'Golden Mile' for the array of flash money pits into which to pour your hard-earned dollars. To 'Buy Kiwi Made', head straight to Cuba St to score a good hit rate.

The fanciest department store in town is **Kirkcaldie & Stains** (Map p380; ☎ 04-472 5899; 165-177 Lambton Quay; ☺ 9.30am-5.30pm Mon-Thu, to 7pm Fri, 10am-5pm Sat, to 4pm Sun), NZ's answer to

Bloomingdale's or Harrods, which has been running since 1863. Nearby is the **Old Bank Shopping Arcade** (Map p380; ☎ 04-922 0600; cnr Lambton Quay & Willis St; ☺ 9am-6pm Mon-Thu, to 7pm Fri, 10am-4pm Sat, 11am-3pm Sun), a dear old building home to some lovely boutique shopping (clothing, accessories and gifts).

Wellington is packed with independent designer stores and boutiques. These are a teeny tip of the iceberg:

Aquamerino (Map p384; ☎ 04-384 9290; 97 Willis St) From the sheep's back to the showroom. Hard wearing, stylish woollens of all shapes and sizes.

Hunters & Collectors (Map p384; ☎ 04-384 8948; 134 Cuba St) Off-the-rack and preloved leather (punk, skate and mod), plus shoes and accessories. Best window displays in New Zealand.

Starfish (Map p384; ☎ 04-385 3722; 128 Willis St) The fashionable Wellingtonian's favourite treat. Beautiful clothing, sustainably made.

If you're looking for something uniquely NZ, try the gift shop at Te Papa museum (p387), or these tried-and-true options:

Kura (Map p384; ☎ 04-802 4934; 19 Allen St) Contemporary indigenous art: painting, ceramics, jewellery and sculpture.

Ora Design Gallery (Map p384; ☎ 04-384 4157; 23 Allen St) The latest in Pacific and Maori art: beautiful sculpture, weaving and jewellery.

Vault (Map p380; ☎ 04-471 1404; 2 Plimmer Steps) Jewellery, clothing, bags, ceramics, cosmetics – a beautiful store with beautiful things.

Several outdoor shops gather around Mercer St, the best of which is **Bivouac Outdoor** (Map p384; ☎ 04-473 2587; 39 Mercer St; ☺ 9am-5.30pm Mon-Thu, to 7pm Fri, 10am-5pm Sat, 11am-5pm Sun).

GETTING THERE & AWAY
Air

Wellington is an international gateway to NZ. See p432 for information on international flights. **Wellington Airport** (WLG; ☎ 04-385 5100; www.wellington-airport.co.nz; ☺ 4am-1.30am) has touch-screen information kiosks in the luggage hall. There's also currency exchange, ATMs, car-rental desks, cafes, shops etc. If you're in transit or have an early flight, you can't linger overnight inside the terminal. Departure tax on international flights is adult/child $25/10.

Air New Zealand (Map p380; ☎ 0800 737 000, 04-474 8950 or 04-388 9900; www.airnewzealand.co.nz; cnr Lambton Quay & Grey St; ☺ 9am-5pm Mon-Fri, 9am-1pm Sat) offers flights between Wellington and most domestic centres, including the following:

Destination	Price	Frequency
Auckland	from $49	up to 20 daily
Christchurch	from $49	up to 14 daily
Dunedin	from $120	up to 6 daily
Queenstown	from $116	1 daily
Rotorua	from $95	up to 3 daily
Westport	from $84	2 daily

Jetstar (☎ 0800 800 995; www.jetstar.com) flies between Wellington and Auckland (from $49, three daily), and Christchurch (from $50, one daily). **Pacific Blue** (☎ 0800 670 000; www.pacificblue.co.nz) flies between Wellington and Auckland (from $65, three daily), and Christchurch (from $50, two daily).

Soundsair (☎ 0800 505 005, 03-520 3080; www.soundsair.com) flies between Wellington and Picton (from $79, up to eight daily), Nelson (from $90, up to three daily) and Blenheim (from $79, one daily).

Air2there (☎ 0800 777 000; www.air2there.com) flies between Wellington and Blenheim ($99, up to four daily), with other local destinations serviced from Paraparaumu airport, 40 minutes up the coast by car or train.

Boat

On a clear day, sailing into Wellington Harbour or through the Marlborough Sounds is magical. Cook Strait is notoriously rough, but the big ferries handle it well, and sport lounges, cafes, bars, information desks, cinemas but no pool tables. There are two options for crossing the strait between Wellington and Picton (timetables subject to change):

Bluebridge Ferries (Map p380; ☎ 0800 844 844, 04-471 6188; www.bluebridge.co.nz; adult/child $50/25) Crossing takes three hours, 20 minutes. Departs Wellington at 3am, 8am, 1pm and 9pm daily (no 3am or 9pm services Saturday). Departs Picton at 2am, 8am, 2pm & 7pm daily (no 8am service Saturday; no 2am service Sunday). Cars and campervans up to 4m long from $110; campervans under 5.5m from $150; motorbikes $50; bicycles $10.

Interislander (Map p380; ☎ 0800 802 802, 04-498 3302; www.interislander.co.nz; adult/child from $46/23) Crossing takes three hours, 10 minutes. Departs Wellington at 2.25am, 8.25am, 2.05pm and 6.25pm; departs Picton at 6.25am, 10.05am, 1.10pm, 6.05pm and 10.25pm. From November through to April there's an extra 10.25am sailing from Wellington and an extra 2.25pm sailing from

Picton. Cars are priced from $101; campervans (up to 5.5m) from $126; motorbikes $46; bicycles $15.

Book ferries at hotels, by phone, online, at travel agents and with operators directly (online is the cheapest option). Bluebridge is based at Waterloo Quay, opposite the Wellington train station. The Interislander terminal is about 2km northeast of the city centre; a shuttle bus ($2) runs to the Interislander from platform 9 at Wellington train station (where long-distance buses also depart) at 7.35am, 9.35am (peak season only), 1.15pm and 5.35pm. It also meets arriving ferries, returning passengers to platform 9. There's also a taxi stand at the terminal.

Car-hire companies allow you to pick-up/drop-off vehicles at ferry terminals. If you arrive outside business hours, arrangements can be made to collect your vehicle from the terminal car park.

Bus

Wellington is a bus-travel hub, with connections north to Auckland and all major towns in between. **InterCity** (☎ 04-385 0520; www.intercity.co.nz) and **Newmans** (☎ 04-385 0521; www.newmanscoach.co.nz) buses depart from platform 9 at the train station. Tickets are sold at the Intercity/Newmans ticket window in the train station. Typical fares include Auckland (from $30, 11 hours, three daily), Palmerston North (from $13, 2¼ hours, six daily), Rotorua (from $30, 7½ hours, twice daily). There are good savings when booked online.

White Star Express (☎ 0800 465 622, 04-478 4734; www.whitestarbus.co.nz) departs once daily (twice on Thursday and Friday) from Bunny St, outside the train station, running to Palmerston North ($23, 2¼ hours), Whanganui ($30, four hours) and New Plymouth ($47, 6½ hours). Connect at Palmerston North for services to Masterton, Hastings, Napier and Gisborne. Call for ticket info or visit **Freeman's Lotto & Cafe** (Map p380; 23 Lambton Quay) or the i-SITE.

Bay Xpress (☎ 0800 422 997; www.bayxpress.co.nz) has a daily service connecting Wellington with Palmerston North ($25, 2¼ hours) continuing to Hastings ($40, 4¾ hours) and Napier ($40, five hours).

Naked Bus (☎ 0900 625 33; www.nakedbus.com) runs north from Wellington to all major North Island destinations, including Palmerston North ($1 to $22, 2½ hours, two daily), Napier ($1 to $35, five hours, four times a week), Taupo (from $1 to $43, 6½ hours, one daily) and Auckland (from $1 to $34, 12 hours, one daily), with myriad stops en route. You can buy bus tickets on the ferry to Picton, connecting to the Naked Bus South Island Network. Buses depart from the Bunny St bus stop. Book online or at Wellington i-SITE; get in early for the cheapest fares.

Train
Wellington train station has four **ticket windows** (☎ 04-498 3000, ext 44324; ⏱ 6.30am-8pm Mon-Thu, to 1pm Fri & Sat, to 3pm Sun), one selling tickets for Tranz Scenic trains, Interislander ferries and InterCity and Newmans coaches; the other three ticketing local/regional Tranz Metro trains (Johnsonville, Melling, Hutt Valley, Paraparaumu and Wairarapa lines).

Long-haul **Tranz Scenic** (☎ 0800 872 467; www.tranzscenic.co.nz) routes include the *Overlander* between Wellington and Auckland (from $49, 12 hours, one daily) departing Wellington at 7.25am (Friday, Saturday and Sunday only May to September); and the *Capital Connection* between Wellington and Palmerston North ($24, 2¼ hours, one daily Monday to Friday) departing Wellington at 5.17pm.

GETTING AROUND
Metlink (☎ 0800 801 700; www.metlink.org.nz) is the one-stop shop for Wellington's regional bus, train and harbour ferry networks all detailed below.

To/From the Airport
Super Shuttle (☎ 0800 748 885; www.supershuttle.co.nz; 1/2 passengers $15/21; ⏱ 24hr) provides a door-to-door minibus service between the city and airport, 8km southeast of the city. It's cheaper if two or more passengers are travelling to the same destination. Shuttles meet all arriving flights.

The **Airport Flyer** (☎ 0800 801 700; www.metlink.co.nz; airport-city per adult/child $8/4.50) bus runs between the airport, Wellington and Lower Hutt (reduced service to Upper Hutt), calling at major stops. Buses run from the city to the airport between 5.50am and 8.50pm; and from the airport, between 6.30am and 9.30pm.

A taxi between the city centre and airport costs around $30.

Bus
Frequent and efficient Go Wellington, Valley Flyer, Newlands Coach Services and Mana Coach Services buses run from 7am to 11.30pm on most suburban routes. Buses depart Wellington train station, or the main bus stop on Courtenay Pl near the Cambridge Tce intersection. Colour-coded route maps and timetables are available at the i-SITE and convenience stores around town. Fares are determined by zones: there are 14 zones, and the cheapest fare is $1 for rides in the city zone, $3 for zones 1 and 2 (maximum fare $15). The Go Wellington Daytripper ticket (zones 1 to 3) costs $6, allowing unlimited bus travel for one day. The Metlink Explorer ticket ($18) gives unlimited travel off-peak and weekends on most services.

After Midnight (☎ 0800 801 700; www.metlink.org.nz) bus services depart the central entertainment strips (Courtenay Pl and Cuba St) between midnight and 4.30am Saturday and Sunday on a number of routes to the outer suburbs. Fares range from $5 to $10, depending on how far away your bed is.

Car
There are a lot of one-way streets in Wellington, the traffic is surprisingly snarly and parking can be a royal (and expensive) pain in the rump. If you've got a car or a caravan, park on the outskirts and walk or take public transport into the city centre.

Aside from the major international rental companies (see p440), Wellington has several operators that will negotiate cheap deals, especially for longer-term rental of two weeks or more, but rates generally aren't as competitive as in Auckland. Rack rates range from around $40 to $85 per day; cars are usually a few years old and in pretty good condition. Operators include the following:

Ace Rental Cars (off Map p380; ☎ 0800 535 500, 04-471 1176; www.acerentalcars.co.nz; 126 Hutt Rd; ⏱ 8am-5pm)

Apex Car Rental (Map p384; ☎ 0800 300 110, 04-385 2163; www.apexrentals.co.nz; 186 Victoria St; ⏱ 8am-5pm)

Omega Rental Cars (off Map p380; ☎ 0800 667 722, 04-472 8465; www.omegarentals.com; 96 Hutt Rd; ⏱ 8am-5pm)

If you plan on exploring both North and South Islands, most companies suggest you leave your car at Wellington and pick up another one in Picton after crossing Cook Strait. This is a common (and more affordable) practice, and car-hire companies make it a painless exercise.

There are often cheap deals on car relocation from Wellington to Auckland (most renters travel in the opposite direction). A few companies offer heavy discounts on this route, with the catch being that you may only have 24 or 48 hours to make the journey.

Turners Auctions (off Map p380; ☎ 04-587 1400; www.turners.co.nz; 120 Hutt Park Rd, Lower Hutt; ⏰ 8am-5.30pm Mon-Wed & Fri, to 8pm Thu, 9am-3pm Sat), not far from the Wellington Top 10 Holiday Park (opposite), buys and sells used cars by auction. Also check noticeboards at backpackers for cheap deals.

Taxi

Popular ranks, packed with cabs, can be found on Courtenay Place, at the corner of Dixon and Victoria Sts, on Featherston St, and outside the railway station. Some operators:

Green Cabs (☎ 0508 447 336)
Wellington City Cabs (☎ 0800 388 8000)
Wellington Combined Taxis (☎ 0800 384 444)

Train

Tranz Metro (☎ 0800 801 700; www.tranzmetro.co.nz) operates four train routes running through Wellington's suburbs to regional destinations. Trains run frequently from around 6am to 11pm, departing Wellington train station. The routes: Johnsonville, via Ngaio and Khandallah; Paraparaumu, via Porirua, Plimmerton and Paekakariki; Melling, via Petone; the Hutt Valley via Waterloo to Upper Hutt. A train service also connects with the Wairarapa, calling at Featherston, Carterton and Masterton. Timetables are available from convenience stores, the train station, Wellington i-SITE and online. Standard fares from Wellington to the ends of the five lines range from $4 to $15. A Day Rover ticket ($10) allows unlimited off-peak and weekend travel on all lines except Wairarapa.

HUTT VALLEY

pop 110,000

The Hutt Valley is home to two of Wellington's dormitory cities – imaginatively named Upper Hutt and Lower Hutt – spread out upon the terraces of the Hutt River. Dotted with a number of town centres and shopping hubs largely functional in form, the main attractions of the Hutt are its forest parks, camping options and the odd museum.

The Hutt Valley begins at the foot of the Tararua Ranges. Upper Hutt lies at the upper end (40km from Wellington city), with Lower Hutt, 15km further downstream, reaching its boundary at Petone, the historic settlement on Wellington Harbour. Visit the **Hutt City i-SITE** (☎ 04-560 4715; www.huttvalleynz.com; 25 Laings Rd, Lower Hutt; ⏰ 9am-5pm Mon-Fri, to 4pm Sat & Sun) for the local low-down.

SIGHTS & ACTIVITIES

The shell-strewn Petone foreshore is home to the art-deco **Petone Settlers Museum** (☎ 04-568 8373; www.petonesettlers.org.nz; The Esplanade; admission by donation; ⏰ noon-4pm Tue-Fri, 1-5pm Sat & Sun), which recalls local migration and settlement, and presents varying exhibitions. **Jackson Street**, running parallel to the Esplanade a couple of blocks inland, is well worth a wander down for lunching and shopping. A short drive south of the Petone, **Days Bay** and **Eastbourne** make a laid-back afternoon detour via road or ferry (see p387).

Just over the hill from Lower Hutt is Wainuiomata, 14km south of which is Catchpool Valley, the main entrance to **Rimutaka Forest Park** (45 minutes' drive from Wellington). Here there's a creek-side **campsite** (adult/child $10/5) and six sole-occupancy bush huts (sleeping eight to 18) – great bases for short and long walks into the forest and gorgeous Orongorongo River valley. Book at Wellington's DOC visitor centre (see p383) or online (www.doc.govt.nz).

Lower Hutt's **NewDowse** (☎ 04-570 6500; www.newdowse.org.nz; 45 Laings Rd, Lower Hutt; admission free; ⏰ 10am-4.30pm Mon-Fri, to 5pm Sat & Sun) is worth visiting for its architecture alone (the pink is positively audacious). It's also a friendly, accessible art museum showcasing NZ art, craft and design. Nice cafe.

The drive from Upper Hutt to Waikanae (on the Kapiti Coast) along the windy, scenic Akatarawa Rd passes the 10-hectare **Staglands Wildlife Reserve** (☎ 04-526 7529; www.staglands.co.nz; Akatarawa Valley; adult/child $16/8; ⏰ 10am-5pm) which helps to conserve native NZ birds and animals, such as the blue duck (whio). It's 16km from SH2, 20km from SH1.

Kaitoke Regional Park, 16km north of Upper Hutt on SH2, has a pleasant **campsite** (adult/child

$5/2$), swimming, picnicking and walks ranging from 15 minutes to six hours long. *LOTR* fans make the pilgrimage here to size-up the fabled site of Rivendell.

SLEEPING

Harcourt Holiday Park (☎ 04-526 7400; www.harcourtholidaypark.co.nz; 45 Akatarawa Rd, Upper Hutt; unpowered/powered sites $30/32, cabins & tourist flats $45-90, motels $110; ⬜) Veritably verdant park 35km northeast of Wellington (35-minute drive), just off SH2, set in parkland by the trout-filled Hutt River. Facilities aren't as numerous as the Wellington Top 10 Holiday Park, but the location is more appealing.

Wellington Top 10 Holiday Park (off Map p380; ☎ 0800 488 872, 04-568 5913; www.wellingtontop10. co.nz; 95 Hutt Park Rd, Seaview, Lower Hutt; sites $40, cabins $55-75, units $105-135, motels $120-160; ⬜) Utilitarian park 13km northeast of Wellington. Family-friendly facilities include three communal kitchens, games room, jumping pillow and a playground, but its industrial location detracts. It's a 15-minute drive from the ferry (follow the signs off SH2 for Petone and Seaview), or take Eastbourne bus 81 or 83.

KAPITI COAST

With wide, people-free beaches, the Kapiti Coast acts as a summer playground and suburban extension for Wellingtonians. The region takes its moniker from Kapiti Island, a bird and marine sanctuary 5km offshore from Paraparaumu.

In the Tararua Range, Tararua Forest Park forms a dramatic backdrop along the length of the coastline and has some accessible day walks and longer tramps.

The Kapiti Coast makes an easy day trip from Wellington, but if you're after a few restful days or are heading further north, there's some quality accommodation here. Pick up a copy of the *Kapiti Coast Arts Guide* from the local visitor information centres if you're interested in the region's abundant galleries, artists and studios.

Orientation & Information

The Kapiti Coast stretches 30km along the North Island's west coast from Paekakariki (41km north of Wellington) to Otaki. Most towns are a tale of two settlements: one along the highway (banks, petrol, hamburger joints) and another by the water (cafes, motels and houses). Paraparaumu is the biggest town here, but still runs at a beachy pace.

The most comprehensive visitor information centres are at Paraparaumu (p404) and Otaki (p406). Online, check out www.naturecoast.co.nz.

Getting There & Around

Getting here from Wellington is a breeze: just track north on SH1. By car, it's about a 45-minute drive to Paraparaumu, and an hour to Otaki, much of it by motorway.

AIR

Plans are underway to upgrade and expand Paraparaumu airport. In the meantime, **Air2there** (☎ 0800 777 000; www.air2there.com) has regular daily flights departing from the current airstrip, connecting the Kapiti Coast with Blenheim and Nelson.

BUS

InterCity (☎ 04-385 0520; www.intercitycoach.co.nz) has buses between Wellington and Palmerston North ($29 to $36, 2¼ hours, seven daily), stopping at Paekakariki ($20, 40 minutes), Paraparaumu ($22, 45 minutes) and Otaki ($29, 1¼ hours).

The daily services into/out of Wellington run by White Star Express, Naked Bus and Bay Express (see p400) also stop in major Kapiti Coast towns.

From SH1 in Paraparaumu, local buses 260, 261 and 262 run to the beach. Bus 290 heads to Otaki, and 280 and 285 to Waikanae, calling at highway settlements and the beach.

TRAIN

Tranz Metro (☎ 0800 801 700; www.tranzmetro.co.nz) commuter trains between Wellington and the coast are easier and more frequent than buses. Services run from Wellington to Paraparaumu ($10, 55 minutes, generally half-hourly off-peak between 6am and 11pm, with more services at peak times), stopping en route in Paekakariki ($9). Weekday off-peak fares (9am to 3pm) are up to $2.50 cheaper.

Tranz Scenic (☎ 0800 872 467; www.tranzscenic. co.nz) has long-distance *Overlander* trains connecting Wellington and Auckland stopping at Paraparaumu, while the weekday-only, peak-hour *Capital Connection* travelling to Wellington in the morning and back to Palmerston North in the evening, stops at

Paraparaumu, Waikanae and Otaki. See p401 for details of these services.

PAEKAKARIKI
pop 1730

Paekakariki is a little seaside village stretched along a black-sand beach, serviced by a train station and passed by the highway. Almost within spitting distance of Wellington (41km to the south), it's an unhurried place to escape for a few days.

Sights & Activities

Queen Elizabeth Park (☎ 04-292 8625; qepranger@ gw.govt.nz; admission free; ☯ 8am-8pm) is a rambling 650-hectare dune-scape park behind the beach, with plenty of opportunities for swimming, walking, cycling and picnicking. There are three entrances: off Wellington Rd in Paekakariki, at MacKays Crossing on SH1, and off the Esplanade in Raumati to the north.

About 5km north of Paekakariki, just off SH1, the **Tramway Museum** (☎ 04-292 8361; www. wellingtontrams.org.nz; Queen Elizabeth Park, MacKay's Crossing; admission adult/child $5/3, with tram ride adult/ child/family $9.50/4/24; ☯ museum 10am-4.30pm daily, trams 11am-4.30pm Sat & Sun, daily 26 Dec-late Jan) has restored wooden trams that ran in Wellington until 1964. A 2km track curls from the museum through Queen Elizabeth Park down to the beach.

Stables on the Park (☎ 06-364 3336; www.stables onthepark.co.nz; Queen Elizabeth Park, MacKay's Crossing; half- /1-/1½hr ride $35/55/75; ☯ daily by arrangement) runs coastal horse riding from its base behind the Tramway Museum. The 1½-hour ride will see you trot along the beach with views of Kapiti Island before heading inland on park tracks. Beginners are welcome.

Sleeping & Eating

Paekakariki Holiday Park (☎ 04-292 8292; www. paekakarikiholidaypark.co.nz; 180 Wellington Rd; sites per adult $13, cabins & flats $65-85) A pleasant, large, leafy park approximately 1.5km north of the township at the southern entrance to Queen Elizabeth Park. Just a hop, skip and a jump from the beach.

Paekakariki Backpackers (☎ 04-902 5967; www. wellingtonbeachbackpackers.co.nz; 11 Wellington Rd; dm $28, d with/without bathroom $76/66; 🖳) Atop a steep hill covered with dense gardens, two houses combine to offer an array of rooms, many with sea and sunset views. Ask about the double with flash new en suite – positively

luxurious. Or maybe you'll prefer the yurt in the front yard. Lie in bed looking out to the sunset, and be lured to sleep by the ocean's crashing waves.

our pick **Beach Road Deli** (☎ 04-902 9029; 5 Beach Rd; snacks $3-8, pizza $9-21; ☯ 7am-8pm Wed-Sun) Bijou deli and pizzeria, packed with home-baked bread and patisserie, cheese, charcuterie and assorted imported goodies. Heaven-sent for the highway traveller, picnic provisioner, or those looking for a sausage to fry and a bun to put it in. Fresh juices and ace coffee.

Finn's (☎ 04-292 8081; www.kapiticoasthotel.co.nz; 2 Beach Rd; mains $15-23; ☯ 10am-3pm Tue-Fri, 9am-3pm Sat & Sun, 6pm-8.30pm Tue-Sun) Opened in 2007, Finn's is the flashy, beige suit of the cutesy railway village, but redeems itself with spacious rooms (doubles $125 to $135), good-value meals, and independent beer on tap. The hush glass keeps the highway at bay.

PARAPARAUMU
pop 6840

Lower-than-low-key Paraparaumu is the principal town on the Kapiti Coast, and a suburban satellite of Wellington. The rough-and-tumble beach is the coast's most developed, sustaining plenty of cafes, motels and takeaway joints. Boat trips to Kapiti Island set sail from here (see opposite).

The correct pronunciation is 'Pah-ra-pah-ra-oo-moo', meaning 'scraps from an oven', which is said to have originated when a Maori war party attacked the settlement and found only scraps of food remaining. It's a bit of a mouthful to pronounce; locals usually just corrupt it into 'Para-par-am'.

Orientation & Information

Coastlands Shoppingtown, the hub of Paraparaumu's highway settlement, is on the left as you head into town from Wellington. Three kilometres west along Kapiti Rd (just past Coastlands) is Paraparaumu Beach; Seaview Rd is the main road here. Sleeping and eating options are most atmospheric (and plentiful) by the beach.

Coastlands has all the services you'll need: banks, ATMs, post office, supermarkets and cinema. The **Paraparaumu visitor information centre** (☎ 04-298 8195; www.naturecoast.co.nz; Coastlands car park, SH1; ☯ 9am-5pm Mon-Fri, 10am-3pm Sat & Sun) is slap-bang in the middle of the Coastlands car park. Pick up the *Nature Coast* brochure while you're here.

Sights & Activities

Paraparaumu Beach, with its beachside park, decent swimming and other watery activities, is the town's raison d'être.

Paraparaumu Beach Golf Club (☎ 04-902 8200; www.paraparaumubeachgolfclub.co.nz; 376 Kapiti Rd; 9/18 holes $55/130; ☼ 7.30am-dusk) is a challenging and beautiful links course that is ranked among NZ's best. It's hosted the NZ Open 12 times and tamed Tiger in 2002. Visitors are welcome: call for tee times, or book online. Clubs, carts and shoes can be hired.

Another kilometre north, just off SH1 in a voluminous hangar, the **Southward Car Museum** (☎ 04-297 1221; www.southward.org.nz; Otaihanga Rd; adult/child $10/3; ☼ 9am-4.30pm) has one of Australasia's largest collections of antique and unusual cars. Check out the DeLorean and the 1950 gangster Cadillac.

Sleeping

Barnacles Seaside Inn (☎ 0800 555 856, 04-902 5856; www.seasideyha.co.nz; 3 Marine Pde; dm/s/f $28/50/90, d $62-80; ☒) Opposite Paraparaumu Beach, Barnacles is a creaky, old-style YHA hostel in a 1920s heritage building. Snug rooms are individually decorated with antique dressers and have sinks and heaters; some have electric blankets and sea views.

Wrights by the Sea (☎ 0508 902 760, 04-902 7600; www.wrightsmotel.co.nz; 387 Kapiti Rd; units $100-150; ☒ ☎) Not quite by the sea, but near enough and even closer to the golf course. A modern motel complex in the conservative style with light, airy rooms, Sky TV and off-road parking. Some with full kitchen.

Eating

Fed Up Fast Foods (☎ 04-902 6686; 40 Marine Pde; meals $5-15; ☼ 10am-9pm Mon-Thu, 9.30am-9.30pm Fri-Sun) A takeaway chippy with the usual battery of fries as well as doner kebabs and fancy burgers. Unfathomably good-value dinner deals, eggy brekkies, espresso and Kapiti ice cream. Clean-as-a-whistle dinette, plus alfresco tables with views to the blue yonder.

Mediterranean Food Warehouse (☎ 0800 334 477, 04-892 0010; Coastlands car park, SH1; meals $13-18; ☼ 9am-9pm) A handy highway pit stop, with excellent wood-fired pizza, luscious cakes, gelato, and a minimarket for picnic supplies. Food so good you'll forget you're in the middle of a car park.

Ambience Café (☎ 04-298 9898; 10 Seaview Rd; lunch $14-18, dinner $20-29; ☼ 8am-4pm Sun-Thu, to late Fri & Sat; Ⓥ) A very 'Wellington' cafe, with both light

and substantial meals made with relish, such as fish cakes, the BLT, and colourful veggie options. Cake cabinet at full capacity, and great coffee (of course).

Soprano Ristorante (☎ 04-298 8892; 7 Seaview Rd; mains $21-28; ☼ 6pm-late Mon-Sat) A welcoming family-run joint with the liveliest evening atmosphere at the beach township. Pizzas, pastas and other Italian classics such as saltimbocca. Sweet treats include the ubiquitous tiramisu and delicious homemade *limoncello* (lemon liqueur). No-nonsense, affordable food and wine in a homely environment – *bella*!

KAPITI ISLAND

Kapiti Island is the coastline's dominant feature, a 10km by 2km slice which since 1897 has been a protected reserve. It's predator-free – many bird species that are now rare or extinct on the mainland still thrive on the island. **Kapiti Island Alive** (☎ 06-362 6606; www.kapiti islandalive.co.nz; walks $20) runs one-hour guided walks and offers homestay accommodation.

The island is open to visitors, limited to around 68 people per day, and it's essential that you book and obtain a permit (adult/child $11/5) at Wellington's DOC visitor centre (p383) – in person, by phone or via email (kapiti.island@doc.govt.nz). During summer it pays to book in advance, especially on weekends. DOC also publishes the detailed *Visiting Kapiti Island* brochure.

Transport is booked separately from the permit (arrange your permit before your boat trip). Two commercial operators are licensed to take visitors to the island, both running to/from Paraparaumu Beach (which can be reached by train, see p403). Departures are between 9am and 9.30am daily, returning between 3pm and 4pm; call in the morning to confirm departure (sailings are weather dependent). All visitors receive an introductory talk; BYO lunch.

Kapiti Marine Charter (☎ 0800 433 779, 04-297 2585; www.kapitimarinecharter.co.nz; adult/child $55/30)

Kapiti Tours (☎ 0800 527 484, 04-237 7965; www. kapititours.co.nz; adult/child $55/30)

WAIKANAE
pop 6930

With a particularly nice stretch of beach, New Zealand's 2008 'Top Town' (and retirees' favourite) is a viable option as your Kapiti Coast rest stop.

About 5km north of Paraparaumu at Waikanae is the turn-off to **Nga Manu Nature Reserve** (☎ 04-293 4131; www.ngamanu.co.nz; 281 Ngarara Rd; adult/child/family $12/4/24; ☺ 10am-5pm), a 15-hectare bird sanctuary dotted with picnic areas, bush walks, aviaries and a nocturnal house with kiwi, owls and tuatara. The eels are fed at 2pm daily, and guided tours run at weekends at 1.30pm (Sunday only in winter). To get here, turn seawards from SH1 onto Te Moana Rd and then right down Ngarara Rd and follow the signs; the sanctuary is 3.5km from the turn-off.

Old but well-maintained **Waikanae Beach Motel** (☎ 0800 486 533, 04-293 6199; www.kapitimotel. co.nz; 95 Te Moana Rd, d $110, f $140; ☐ ☎) has spacious units with full kitchen facilities, about 1km from the beach. All rooms open out onto or overlook the courtyard garden and picturesque golf course beyond. The swimming pool and playground make it an ideal spot for families.

Front Room (☎ 04-905 4142; 42 Tutere St; meals $6-25; ☺ 9am-4pm Mon-Fri, 6-9pm Fri & Sat, 5-9pm Sun) has a stylish, pared-back interior and is home to food a tad more sophisticated that your average cafe. Keep an eye out for the Waikanae crab, a regional speciality. The pleasant garden out back sports a fireplace, welcome on cool evenings.

OTAKI
pop 5650
Unremarkable Otaki is primarily a gateway to the Tararua Range. It has a strong Maori history and presence: the little town has nine *marae* and a Maori college. The historic Rangiatea Church, built under the guidance of Ngati Toa chief Te Rauparaha nearly 150 years ago, tragically burnt to the ground in 1995 but has been rebuilt. This was the original burial site of Te Rauparaha.

Orientation & Information
Most services, including the train station where buses also stop, are on SH1. The main centre of Otaki, with the post office and shops, is 2km seawards on Tasman Rd. Three kilometres further on the same road brings you to Otaki's windswept beach. Note that the telephone area code in Otaki is ☎ 06, not ☎ 04 like most of the rest of the Kapiti Coast.

The **Otaki i-SITE** (☎ 06-364 7620; www.naturecoast. co.nz; Centennial Park, SH1; ☺ 9am-5pm Mon-Fri, 10am-3pm Sat & Sun) is just south of the main roundabout in an 1891 courthouse.

Activities
Two kilometres south of Otaki, scenic Otaki Gorge Rd trucks inland from SH1 and leads 19km (5km unsealed) to **Otaki Forks**, the main western entrance to **Tararua Forest Park**. Otaki Forks has picnic areas, swimming and **camp-sites** (unpowered sites per adult/child $6/2), plus bush walks from 30 minutes to 3½ hours in the immediate area; longer tracks lead to huts. The i-SITE sells detailed maps and knowledgeable staff proffer information and advice about the walks. Ask at DOC in Wellington (p383) for advice on longer tracks in the park. You can tramp in the Tararua Ranges, but you must bring adequate clothing and equipment, and be well prepared for wild weather.

Sleeping & Eating
Byron's Resort (☎ 0800 800 122, 06-364 8119; www. byronsresort.co.nz; 20 Tasman Rd; unpowered/powered sites $31/35, units & motels $100-150; ☐ ☎) A traditional, family-fuelled resort by the beach. The Scuttlebutt restaurant and garden bar (meals $19 to $27; open Tuesday to Sunday) is a welcome haven after a day spent at the pool, spa, sauna, tennis court and playground.

Red House Café (☎ 06-364 3022; 885 Main Rd, SH1, Te Horo; lunch $10-17, dinner $22-29; ☺ 9am-late Mon-Fri, 8.30pm-late Sat & Sun) One of the best highway pit stops round these parts is this fire-engine red cafe 5km south of Otaki. Inside it's all warm polished wood, all-day breakfasts, excellent baking and an extensive blackboard menu. Bargain two-course roast and pudding special on Sunday.

THE WAIRARAPA

The Wairarapa is the large slab of land east and northeast of Wellington, beyond the craggy Tararua and Rimutaka Ranges. Named after Lake Wairarapa (Shimmering Waters), a shallow 8000-hectare lake, the region has traditionally been a frenzied hotbed of sheep farming. More recently, wineries have sprung up – around Martinborough, most famously – which has turned the region into a decadent weekend retreat. A vigorous foodie culture has evolved alongside the wineries and restored B&B cottages.

WELLINGTON REGION

See www.wairarapanz.com for regional info, but also check out the **Classic New Zealand Wine Trail** (www.classicwinetrail.co.nz) – a useful tool for joining the dots throughout the Wairarapa and its neighbouring wine regions of Hawke's Bay and Marlborough.

Note that the telephone area code over here is ☎ 06, not ☎ 04 like most of the rest of the Wellington region.

Getting There & Around
From Wellington, **Tranz Metro** (☎ 0800 801 700; www.tranzmetro.co.nz) commuter trains run to Masterton ($15, 1½ hours, five or six daily on weekdays, two daily on weekends), calling at seven stations including Featherston and Carterton. For other Wairarapa towns, connect with the local bus services.

Tranzit Coachlines (☎ 0800 471 227, 06-370 6600; www.tranzit.co.nz; 316 Queen St, Masterton) has a bus between Masterton and Palmerston North (one-way $21, 1¾ hours, one daily), plus local daily services (bus 200) between Martinborough and Masterton ($4) via Featherston, Greytown and Carterton.

Wairarapa Coach Lines (☎ 0800 666 355, 06-308 9352; www.waicoach.co.nz) runs between Masterton and Martinborough ($6, 1¼ hours, three daily) and meets every Featherston train for a run through to Martinborough ($4, 20 minutes, four to five daily).

MARTINBOROUGH
pop 1360
The most popular visitor spot in the Wairarapa, Martinborough is a pretty town with a leafy town square and some charming old buildings, surrounded by a patchwork of pasture and a pinstripe of grapevines. It is famed for its wineries, which draw in visitors to nose the pinot, avail themselves of its excellent eateries, and snooze it off at boutique accommodation. The best time for an overnight visit is midweek, when accommodation is cheaper (although many restaurants shut up shop on Monday and Tuesday).

Orientation & Information
Martinborough is arrowed off the SH2 from both Featherston and Greytown; it's about 20km from either town. Settler and town planner John Martin designed Martinborough's classic grid, a Union Jack street pattern centred upon a leafy square. The **Martinborough i-SITE** (☎ 06-306 5010; www.wairarapanz.com; 18 Kitchener St; 🕙 9am-5pm Mon-Fri, 10am-4pm Sat & Sun) is full of brochures and information.

Sights & Activities
With so many **wineries** scattered around town, there are no points for guessing what is the town's main attraction. This is closely followed by the excellent food that goes with it – Martinborough punches well above its weight when it comes to food cafes and restaurants.

The town's cultural hub is arguably **Circus** (see p409), a stylish art-house cinema where you can watch the cream of contemporary movies as well as eat and drink in the convivial dining room or sunny courtyard.

About 3km from town off Oxford St is **Olivo** (☎ 06-306 9074; www.olivo.co.nz; Hinakura Rd; admission free; 🕙 10am-5pm Mon-Fri), a welcoming olive grove where you can meet the owners, take a tour and tasting, and buy your oil to go.

Patuna Farm Adventures (☎ 06-306 9966; www.patunafarm.co.nz; Ruakokoputuna Rd) offers horse treks (from $40), a challenging pole-to-pole rope course (from $20), and a four-hour self-guided walk through native bush and a limestone chasm (adult/child $15/10). The chasm is open late October until Easter; other activities operate year-round.

Sleeping
A list of local B&Bs, self-contained weekend-away cottages and farmstays can be found on www.wairarapanz.com; the i-SITE can help with bookings. Expect to pay around $160 per night for two people.

ourpick **Martinborough Village Camping** (☎ 06-306 8946; www.martinboroughcamping.com; cnr Princess & Dublin Sts; unpowered sites $30, cabins s/d $45/60; 🖳 🛜) An appealing camping ground with grapevine views, just five minutes' walk to town. It has shady trees and the town pool over the back fence, making it a cooling oasis on sticky days. Cabins are basic but great value, freeing up your dollars for the cellar door. Bike hire available for $35 per day.

Kate's Place (☎ 06-306 9935; www.katesplace.co.nz; 7 Cologne St; dm $30, d $80; 🖳) An unpretentious home stay–backpackers with a welcoming owner and a laid-back vibe, just a hop and a skip from the Square. The two dorms have solid bunks with extrawide mattresses. Mull over your day's misdemeanours on the front porch.

Claremont (☎ 0800 809 162, 06-306 9162; www.theclaremont.co.nz; 38 Regent St; d $125-160, 4-person apt

WAIRARAPA WINE COUNTRY

Wairarapa's winemakers enjoy an impressive international reputation, but this world-renowned industry was nearly crushed in infancy. The region's first vines were planted in 1883, but the prohibition movement in 1908 soon put a cap on that corker idea. It wasn't until the 1980s that winemaking was revived, after Martinborough's *terroir* was discovered to be similar to Burgundy in France. A few vineyards soon sprang up, but the number has now ballooned to nearly 50 regionwide. Martinborough is the undisputed hub of the action, renowned for its gravels which produce particularly remarkable pinot noir and distinctive whites.

For a good introduction to Wairarapa's wines, visit Martinborough's stylish cinema, **Circus** (☎ 06-306 9442; www.circus.net.nz; 34 Jellicoe St; ☺ screenings 3pm daily; additional screenings peak season), which screens **Vintners' Choice** (www.vintnerschoice.co.nz), a 40-minute documentary with a real-live wine tasting.

The town also plays host to New Zealand's best wine, food and music festival – **Toast Martinborough** (☎ 06-306 9183; www.toastmartinborough.co.nz; tickets $60), held annually on the third Sunday in November. Enjoyable on many levels (standing up and quite possibly lying on the grass), this is a hugely popular event and you'll have to be quick on the draw to get a ticket.

The **Wairarapa Wines Harvest Festival** (☎ 027 477 4717; www.wairarapawines.co.nz; tickets $25-35) celebrates the beginning of the harvest with an extravaganza of wine, food and family fun. It's held at a remote riverbank setting 10 minutes from Carterton on a Saturday in mid-March.

Wairarapa's wineries thrive on visitors; Martinborough's 30-odd are particularly welcoming with well-oiled cellar doors, and noteworthy food served in some gorgeous gardens and courtyards. The *Wairarapa Wine Trail Map* (available from the i-SITE and many other locations) will aid your navigations. Read all about it at www.winesfrommartinborough.com.

You can sample and purchase many wines under one gabled roof at the **Martinborough Wine Centre** (☎ 06-306 9040; www.martinboroughwinecentre.co.nz; 6 Kitchener St; tastings available; ☺ 10am-5pm), which also sells olive oils, books, clothing and art.

Recommended Wineries

Ata Rangi (☎ 06-306 9570; www.atarangi.co.nz; Puruatanga Rd) One of the region's pioneering winemakers. Great drops across the board and cute cellar door.

$275; 💻) A classy accommodation enclave off Jellicoe St, the Claremont has two-storey, self-contained units in great nick, modern studios with spa baths, and sparkling two-bedroom apartments, all at reasonable rates (even cheaper in winter and/or midweek). Attractive gardens, barbecue areas and bike hire.

Peppers Martinborough Hotel (☎ 06-306 9350; www.martinboroughhotel.co.nz; The Square; d incl breakfast $300-385; 💻 🛜) Grand old hotel on the main square that's been magnificently restored, with 16 spacious, luxury rooms, each individually decorated with pizzazz. All open onto either a wide veranda or courtyard garden. Downstairs the Settlers Bar (mains $12 to $20) serves sophisticated pub nosh and local wines by the glass.

Eating & Drinking

Eating and drinking is what Martinborough's all about, with award-winning restaurants and cafes, delicatessens and food shops. Peppers Martinborough Hotel and the no-nonsense pub over the road are the best places to join the locals for a drink.

Café Medici (☎ 06-306 9965; 9 Kitchener St; breakfast & lunch $7-19, dinner $22-30; ☺ 8.30am-4pm Wed-Mon, plus evenings summer) A perennial favourite among townsfolk and regular visitors, this airy cafe has a Florentine/Kiwiana interior and courtyard offering honest home-cooked food. Choose from the tasty counter selection including muffins, pies, quiche and famous scones. The blackboard menu is short but varied with plenty of salad options. Great coffee, too.

Trio Café at Coney Winery (☎ 06-306 8345; Dry River Rd; snacks $10, mains $24-25; ☺ noon-3pm Sat & Sun) Wine and dine in a courtyard featuring gorgeous white roses or in the light and airy tasting room. The great-value food is sophisticated, fresh and delicious, and all made from scratch. The atmosphere is relaxed and fun, a

WELLINGTON REGION

Coney (☎ 06-306 8345; www.coneywines.co.nz; Dry River Rd) Friendly tastings and lovely restaurant (p424). Winery tours by arrangement.

Margrain (☎ 06-306 9292; www.margrainvineyard.co.nz; cnr Princess St & Huangarua Rd) Pretty winery and site of the Old Winery Cafe, a good pit stop overlooking the vines.

Vynfields (☎ 06-306 9901; www.vynfields.com; 22 Omarere Rd) Five-star, spicy pinot noir and a lush lawn on which to enjoy a platter. Organic/biodynamic wines.

Tours

If you have the time and physical ability, the best and most carbon-friendly way to explore the Wairarapa's wines is by bicycle as the flat landscape makes for puff-free cruising.

From Masterton, **March Hare** (☎ 021 668 970; www.march-hare.co.nz; tours incl all gear & a picnic $65) runs self-guided bike tours of the Opaki winegrowing area.

There are three options in Martinborough:

Christina Estate Vineyard (☎ 06-306 8920; christinaestate@xtra.co.nz; 28 Puruatanga Rd; ⏲ 8.30am-6pm) Per hour/day $15/25. Tandems for the coordinated.

Martinborough Village Camping (☎ 06-306 8946; www.martinboroughcamping.com; cnr Princess & Dublin St) Per day $35.

Martinborough Wine Centre (☎ 06-306 9040; www.martinboroughwinecentre.co.nz; 6 Kitchener St) Half-/full day $25/35.

Numerous operators run bus tours around Martinborough and the region:

Dynamic Tours (☎ 04-478 8533; www.dynamictours.co.nz; from $225) Customised wine tours, run from Wellington.

Hammond's Scenic Tours (☎ 04-472 0869; www.wellingtonsightseeingtours.com; full-day tour adult/child $195/97.50) Full-day winery tours including gourmet lunch.

Tranzit Coachlines (☎ 0800 471 227, 06-370 6600; www.tranzit.co.nz; 316 Queen St, Masterton) Two daily tours depart from Wellington or the main Wairarapa towns. The Gourmet Wine Escape ($161) visits Martinborough vineyards and includes tastings and lunch. The Garden Gourmet Escape (adult/child $182/115) takes in two gardens, lunch at the Gladstone Country Inn, and wine tasting.

Zest Food Tours (☎ 04-801 9198; www.zestfoodtours.co.nz; tours incl lunch & wines from $230) Small-group food and wine tours (2½ to five hours) in Greytown and Martinborough.

testament to your host Tim Coney, an affable and knowledgeable character who may sing at random.

Circus (☎ 06-306 9442; www.circus.net.nz; 34 Jellicoe St; mains $18-28, tickets adult/child $14/10; ⏲ 2.30pm-late Wed-Mon) A modern microsized movie complex with two comfy studio theatres. The stylish foyer and cafe, opening out on to a rather Zen garden, offer some of the most sociable surroundings in town. Reasonably priced seasonal food includes bar snacks, pizza, mains with plenty of fresh veg, and a short list of sweet delights.

French Bistro (☎ 06-306 8863; 3 Kitchener St; mains $36-40; ⏲ 6pm-late Wed-Sun) Wendy Campbell's provincial cooking in this tiny but smart family-run bistro has garnered praise both at home and abroad. Francophiles will delight at her dishes using ingredients from the region and beyond. The decor is eclectic as is the carefully selected wine list offering a variety of mainly local vintages.

CAPE PALLISER

The Wairarapa coast south of Martinborough around Palliser Bay and Cape Palliser is remote and sparsely populated. The bendy road to Cape Palliser is utterly scenic: a big ocean and black-sand beaches on one side; barren hills and sheer cliffs on the other. Look for hints of the South Island, visible on a clear day.

Standing like giant organ pipes in the Putangirua Scenic Reserve are the **Putangirua Pinnacles**, formed by rain washing silt and sand away and exposing the underlying bedrock. Accessible by a track near the car park on Cape Palliser Rd, it's an easy three-hour return walk along a streambed to the pinnacles, or take the 3½-hour loop track past hills and coastal viewpoints. For some rugged Wairarapa tramping nearby, head to **Aorangi (Haurangi) Forest Park**. For maps and access info contact DOC in Wellington (p383).

Further south is the wind-worn fishing village **Ngawi**. The first things you'll notice here are the rusty bulldozers on the beach, used to drag fishing boats ashore. Next stop is the malodorous **seal colony**, the North Island's largest breeding area. Whatever you do in your quest for a photo, don't get between the seals and the sea. If you block their escape route they're likely to have a go at you!

Get your thighs thumping on the steep, 250-step (or is it 249?) climb to **Cape Palliser Lighthouse**, from where there are yet more amazing coastal views, as far as the South Island if it's not hazy.

On the way there or back, take the short detour to the wind-blown settlement of **Lake Ferry**, overlooking **Lake Onoke**, where there's birdwatching to be enjoyed. This area is also good for exploration – discover the lake edge, the wild and woolly coastline (prime for surfing), and the cliffs behind. You'll also find the **Lake Ferry Hotel** (☎ 06-307 7831; ✆ from 11am) with its retro fitout (check out the formica), which has great views and fish and chips.

Martinborough i-SITE (p407) can help with accommodation options in the Lake Ferry and Cape Palliser area, which include camping grounds and holiday homes for rent.

GREYTOWN
pop 2000

The most popular of several small towns along SH2, Greytown has spruced itself up over recent years and is now full of Wellingtonians on the weekend. It has plenty of accommodation, some decent food, three high-street pubs, and some swanky shopping. Check out www.greytown.co.nz for more information.

Sights

Greytown was the country's first planned inland town: intact Victorian architectural specimens line the main street. The quaint **Cobblestones Village Museum** (☎ 06-304 9687; www.cobblestonesmuseum.org.nz; 169 Main St; adult/child/family $2.50/1/6; ✆ 10am-4pm) is an enclave of period buildings and various historic objects, dotted around pretty grounds inviting a lie-down on a picnic blanket. No picnic? No worries. Visit **Schoc Chocolate** (☎ 06-304 8960; www.chocolatetherapy.com; 177 Main St; ✆ 10am-5pm Mon-Fri, 10.30am-5pm Sat & Sun) in a 1920s cottage that shares the grounds. Sublime flavours, worth every single penny of 10 bucks a tablet. Truffles, rocky road and peanut brittle, too. Free tastings.

About 10km southeast of Carterton is **Stonehenge Aotearoa** (☎ 06-377 1600; www.

stonehenge-aotearoa.com; tours adult $15, child $6-10; ✆ 10am-4pm Wed-Sun, tours 2pm Sat & Sun, public holidays & by appointment). Explore the southern sky – even in daylight – at this full-scale adaptation of the UK Stonehenge, orientated for its location on a grassy knoll overlooking the Wairarapa Plain. The pretour talk and audiovisual presentation are excellent, and the henge itself a pretty surreal sight, day or night, especially when interpreted by one of its tour guides who are consummate storytellers. Self-guided tours are also available for $5.

Sleeping & Eating

Greytown Camping Ground (☎ 06-304 9837; Kuratawhiti St; unpowered/powered sites $30/36) A basic camping option (with equally basic facilities) scenically spread through Greytown Park, 500m from town.

Greytown Hotel (☎ 06-304 9138; www.greytownhotel.co.nz; 33 Main St; s/d $50/80; ▯) A serious contender for 'oldest hotel in New Zealand', the Top Pub (as it's known) is looking great for her age, having just had a major facelift. Upstairs rooms are small and basic but comfortable, with no-frills furnishings and shared bathrooms. Downstairs is a chic new dining room (classic meals $22 to $29), ol' faithful lounge-bar and popular garden-courtyard.

Oak Estate Motor Lodge (☎ 0800 843 625, 06-304 8188; www.oakestate.co.nz; cnr Main St & Hospital Rd; r $125-185) A stand of gracious roadside oaks and pretty gardens shield a smart complex of self-contained units: studios, one- and two-bedroom options.

French Baker (☎ 06-304 8873; 81 Main St; snacks $4-7, mains $13-19; ✆ 7.30am-3pm Mon, Thu & Fri, to 4pm Fri & Sat) Buttery croissants, tempting tarts and authentic breads; artisan baker Moïse Cerson is le real McCoy. Great coffee too and a compact menu of suitably Gallic offerings, such as Roquefort salad and French toast.

Cuckoo Pizza (☎ 06-304 8992; 128 Main St; mains $15-24; ✆ 11am-8.30pm Wed-Sun) Refreshingly unruly pizza joint littered with mismatched retro furniture in an old house on the main street. Try the 'moa' pizza (pepperoni, mushrooms, anchovies, olives and chilli), or pasta specials. Good coffee too.

MASTERTON & AROUND
pop 19,500

Masterton is the Wairarapa's utilitarian hub, an unselfconscious town getting on with its business. Its main claim to immortality is the 50-year-old sheep-shearing competition, the international Golden Shears (right).

Orientation & Information
State Highway 2 runs through the centre of town. From the south SH2 is named High St, which then becomes Chapel St. Queen St runs parallel to High/Chapel St, one block east. The town's prime attractions are another block east on Dixon St where you will find the **Masterton i-SITE** (☎ 06-370 0900; www.wairarapanz. com; cnr Dixon & Bruce Sts; ✆ 9am-5pm Mon-Fri, 10am-4pm Sat & Sun).

Sights & Activities
Stretch your car-cramped legs in the 32-hectare **Queen Elizabeth Park** (Dixon St; ✆ 24hr), with its aviaries, duck lake, children's playground, minigolf and cricket oval. Opposite the park is **Aratoi Wairarapa Museum of Art & History** (☎ 06-370 0001; www.aratoi.co.nz; cnr Bruce & Dixon Sts; admission by donation; ✆ 10am-4.30pm), documenting the art and cultural heritage of the region, both Maori and Pakeha.

Occupying two historic woolsheds next to Aratoi is **Shear Discovery** (☎ 06-378 8008; www. sheardiscovery.co.nz; Dixon St; adult/child/family $5/2/10; ✆ 10am-4pm), a baaaa-loody marvellous little museum dedicated to NZ's sheep-shearing and wool-production industries.

Castlepoint, on the coast 68km east of Masterton, is an awesome, end-of-the-world place, with a reef, the lofty 162m-high Castle Rock, protected swimming and walking tracks. There's an easy (but sometimes ludicrously windy) 30-minute return walk across the reef to the lighthouse, where 70-plus shell species are fossilised in the cliffs. Another one-hour return walk runs to a huge limestone cave (take a torch), or take the 1½-hour return track from Deliverance Cove to Castle Rock. Keep well away from the lower reef when there are heavy seas. Ask the staff at Masterton i-SITE (above) about accommodation here.

Pukaha Mt Bruce National Wildlife Centre (☎ 06-375 8004; www.mtbruce.org.nz; adult/child/family $15/4/38; ✆ 9am-4.30pm) is not only an important sanctuary for native NZ wildlife (mostly birds), it's also the most readily accessible bush experience off the highway. The visitor centre has various exhibits, while outside there are aviaries, a kiwi house, virgin forest and a scenic one-hour loop track taking in some great views. Slippery eels, tuatara and other creatures also reside here. Take a walk with the ranger (10.30am and 2pm Saturday and Sunday; adult/child $25/12.50) or take the Lookout Lunch Tour (11am Sunday; adult/child $50/25 including lunch). There's a cafe on-site; it's 30km north of Masterton on SH2.

The turn-off to the main eastern entrance of the **Tararua Forest Park** is just south of Masterton on SH2; follow Norfolk Rd about 15km to the gates. Mountain streams dart through virgin forest in this reserve, known as 'Holdsworth'. At the park entrance are swimming holes, picnic areas and **campsites** (unpowered sites adult/child $6/2). Walks include short, easy family tramps, excellent one- or two-day tramps, and longer, challenging tramps for experienced bush-bods (west through to Otaki Forks). The resident caretaker (☎ 06-377 0022) has maps and hut accommodation info. Check weather and track updates before setting off, and be prepared to be baked, battered and buffeted by fickle conditions.

Festivals & Events
For wine and food related events, see p408.
Golden Shears (www.goldenshears.co.nz) Held annually in the first week of March.
Wings over Wairarapa (☎ 06-370 0900; www.wings. org.nz) An exciting three-day air show (biennial; odd years) featuring more than 70 aircraft – from the war birds through to gliders, gyros, jets and batty aerobatics.

Sleeping & Eating
Empire Lodge (☎ 06-377 1902; www.empirelodge. co.nz; 94 Queen St; backpackers dm/s/d $25/30/55, hotel s/d $80/90; 🖥) An 1870s budget hotel and backpackers, well worn and badly colour coordinated. Down its long hallways you'll discover a communal kitchen, TV room, and other surprises. Views of the Tararua Range from the rear deck. Cheap sleep in a handy location.

Copthorne Solway Park (☎ 0800 808 228, 06-370 0500; www.solway.co.nz; High St; d $130-345; 🖥 🔲 ♨) A megabuck refurb has restored this 1970s resort to glory, from its sunken bar and reputable restaurant, to its two swimming pools, tennis court and the driving range which takes up just some of its 24-hectare grounds. Lots of room options, all with classy fit-outs featuring some particularly stylish textiles.

our pick **Ten O'Clock Cookie** (☎ 06-377 4551; 180 Queen St; snacks $3-15; ✆ 7am-4.30pm Mon-Fri,

8am-2.30pm Sat) Loosen that belt and get ready to indulge. Heavenly baking, scrumptious pies, simple sandwiches and cookies of course. Take away or sit down and enjoy your treat with a decent cup of coffee or tea. Relaxed and great value, it's deserving of its many awards.

Lounge Wine Bar (☎ 06-379 6065; 78-81 Main St, Carterton; snacks & meals $5-18; ☙ 3.30pm-late Wed-Sun; Ⓥ) A local hero saves the town of Carterton (indeed, the region) with a steady stream of live music (Friday and Saturday), local wines, independent beers and Spanish food. All this and more lapped up in a groovy 'thrift-shop' interior.

Café Cecille (☎ 06-370 1166; Queen Elizabeth Park; brunch $9-18, dinner $15-30; ☙ 10am-3pm daily, 5-8pm Fri & Sat) In the middle of Queen Elizabeth Park is the century-old Coronation Hall, home to Café Cecille. Its wraparound veranda and simple but wholesome food make it hard to beat on a sunny day. Divine homemade chips.

Gladstone Inn (☎ 06-372 7866; 51 Gladstone Rd, Gladstone; lunch $12-28, dinner $18-30; ☙ 11am-late) Gladstone, 18km south of Masterton, is less a town, more a state of mind. There's very little here except this proud inn, haven of thirsty locals, motorbike enthusiasts, Sunday drivers and lazy-afternoon shandy sippers who hog the tables in the glorious garden bar.

Directory

CONTENTS

BOOK YOUR STAY ONLINE

For more accommodation reviews and recommendations by Lonely Planet authors, check out the online booking service at www.lonelyplanet.com/hotels. You'll find the true, insider low-down on the best places to stay. Reviews are thorough and independent. Best of all, you can book online.

ACCOMMODATION

Across the North Island, you can bed down at night in guest houses that creak with history; in facility-laden hotels; comfortably uniform motel units; beautifully situated campsites; and hostels that range in character from clean-living and relaxed to tirelessly party-prone.

Accommodation listings in this guidebook are ordered by budget from cheapest to most expensive. We generally designate a place as budget accommodation if it charges up to $100 per double. Accommodation qualifies as midrange if it costs roughly $100 to $160 per double, while we've given the top-end tag to double rooms costing over $160. Price ranges generally increase by 20% to 25% in Auckland and Wellington. Here you can still find budget accommodation at up to $100 per double, but midrange stretches from $100 to $200, with top-end rooms more than $200.

If you're travelling during peak tourist seasons, book your bed well in advance. Accommodation is most in demand (and at its priciest) during the summer holidays from Christmas to late January, at Easter, and during winter in snowy towns such as Ohakune. At other times, weekday rates may be cheaper than weekend rates (except in business-style hotels in larger cities, where the reverse applies), and you'll certainly discover that low-season rates abound. When they're not run off their feet, accommodation operators often offer walk-in rates that are significantly below advertised rates – ask late in the day. Also see the big-name global accommodation websites (www.wotif.co.nz, www.lastminute.co.nz, www.hotels.co.nz etc) for last-minute deals.

Visitor information centres provide reams of local accommodation information, often in the form of folders detailing facilities and up-to-date prices; many can also make bookings on your behalf. Alternatively, flick through one of NZ's free, widely available accommodation directories, including the annual *New Zealand Accommodation Guide* published by the **Automobile Association** (AA; www.aatravel.co.nz), as well as the *Holiday Parks & Campgrounds* and *Motels, Motor Lodges & Apartments* directories produced by **Jasons** (www.jasons.com).

B&Bs & Guest Houses

Bed and breakfast (B&B) accommodation in private homes is a growth industry in NZ, popping up in the middle of cities, in rural hamlets and on stretches of isolated coastline, with rooms on offer in everything from

DIRECTORY

suburban bungalows to stately manors owned by one family for generations.

Guest houses are usually spartan, cheap, 'private' (unlicensed) hotels, mostly low-key places patronised by people who eschew the impersonal atmosphere of many motels. Some guest houses are reasonably fancy and offer self-contained rooms.

Although breakfast is included at genuine B&Bs, it may or may not feature at guest houses. Your morning meal may be 'continental' (cereal, toast and tea or coffee), 'hearty continental' (add yoghurt, fruit, home-baked bread or muffins), or a stomach-loading cooked meal including eggs, bacon and sausages. Some B&B hosts, especially in isolated locations or within the smaller towns where restaurants are limited, may cook dinner for guests and advertise dinner, bed and breakfast (DB&B) packages.

Tariffs are typically in the $120 to $180 bracket (per double), though some places charge upwards of $300 per double. Some hosts continue to be cheeky-as-a-Kea, charging hefty prices for what is, in essence, a bedroom in their home. Many upmarket B&Bs demand bookings and deposits at least a month in advance, and enforce strict and expensive cancellation policies – ie cancel within a week of your arrival date and you'll forfeit your deposit plus the balance of the room rate. Check conditions before you book.

New Zealand's *Bed and Breakfast Directory* (www.bed-and-breakfast.co.nz) and *Bed & Breakfast Book* (www.bnb.co.nz) are available online, and at bookshops and visitor information centres.

Camping & Campervan Parks

Campers and campervan drivers alike converge upon NZ's hugely popular 'holiday parks', slumbering peacefully in powered and unpowered sites, cheap bunk rooms (dorm rooms), cabins and self-contained units that are often called motels or tourist flats. Well-equipped communal kitchens, dining areas and games and TV rooms often feature. In cities holiday parks are usually a fair way from the action, but in smaller towns they can be impressively central or near lakes, beaches, rivers and forests.

The nightly cost of holiday-park camping is usually between $15 and $18 per adult, with children charged half-price; powered sites are a couple of dollars more. Cabin/unit accommodation normally ranges from $60 to $120 per double. Unless noted otherwise, the prices we've listed for campsites, campervan sites, huts and cabins are for two people.

If you'll gladly swap facilities for wilder, less-developed locations such as national parks, head for one of the 250-plus, vehicle-accessible camping grounds managed by the **Department of Conservation** (DOC; www.doc.govt.nz). DOC also looks after hundreds of backcountry huts, most of which can only be reached on foot. For more information, see Tramping (p76).

There are plenty of places where 'freedom camping' is permitted in NZ, but you should never just *assume* it's OK to camp somewhere. Always ask a local first. Check at the local i-SITE or DOC office, or even with local commercial camping grounds. See www.camping.org.nz for more tips on freedom camping.

PRACTICALITIES

- For weights and measures, NZ uses the metric system.

- DVDs and videos viewed in NZ are based on the PAL system – the same system used in Australia, the UK and most of Europe.

- Use a three-pin adaptor (the same as in Australia; different to British three-pin adaptors) to plug yourself into the electricity supply (230V AC, 50Hz).

- For news, leaf through Auckland's *New Zealand Herald* or Wellington's *Dominion Post*, or check out www.stuff.co.nz.

- Tune in to Radio National for current affairs and Concert FM for classical and jazz (see www.radionz.co.nz for frequencies). Kiwi FM (www.kiwifm.co.nz) plays 100% NZ music; Radio Hauraki (www.hauraki.co.nz) cranks out classic rock (too much Split Enz is barely enough…).

- Watch one of the national government-owned TV stations (TV One, TV2, TVNZ 6, TVNZ 7, Maori TV and the 100% Maori language Te Reo) or the subscriber-only Sky TV (www.skytv.co.nz).

WWOOFING

If you don't mind getting your hands dirty, an economical way of travelling around NZ involves doing some voluntary work as a member of **Willing Workers on Organic Farms** (WWOOF; ☎ 03-544 9890; www.wwoof.co.nz). Membership of this popular, well-established international organisation (which has representatives in Africa, Asia, North America, Europe and Australia) scores you access to many hundreds of organic and permaculture farms, market gardens and other environmentally sound cottage industries across the country. Down on the farm, in exchange for a hard day's work, owners provide food, accommodation and some hands-on organic farming experience. Contact farm owners a week or two beforehand to arrange your stay, as you would for a hotel or hostel – don't turn up unannounced!

A one-year online membership costs $40 (for one person, or two people travelling together); or $50 for online membership and to have a farm-listing book mailed to you. You should be part of a Working Holiday Scheme (p429) when you visit NZ, as the immigration department considers WWOOFers to be working.

One word of caution: it seems that some hostels have started employing travellers under the name of WWOOFing, without requiring membership or providing any of the benefits (not to mention the lack of an organic farm). It's a vague kind of exploitation, and probably harmless, but it's a definite misnomer.

Farmstays

Farmstays open the door on the agricultural side of NZ life, with visitors encouraged to get some dirt beneath their fingernails at orchards, and dairy, sheep and cattle farms. Costs can vary widely, with B&B generally ranging from $80 to $120. Some farms have separate cottages where you can fix your own food, while others offer low-cost, shared, backpacker-style accommodation.

Farm Helpers in NZ (FHINZ; www.fhinz.co.nz) produces a booklet ($25) that lists around 190 farms throughout NZ providing lodging in exchange for four- to six-hours work per day. **Rural Holidays NZ** (☎ 03-355 6218; www.ruralholidays.co.nz) lists farmstays and homestays throughout the country on its website. See also the WWOOFing boxed text above.

Hostels

The North Island is packed to the rafters with backpacker hostels, ranging from small, homestay-style affairs with a handful of beds to refurbished hotels with scuffed facades, and the towering modern structures you'll find in the big cities. Hostel bed prices listed throughout this book are the non-membership rates.

If you're a Kiwi travelling in your own country, be warned that some hostels only admit overseas travellers, typically inner-city places. If you encounter such discrimination, either try another hostel or insist that you're a genuine traveller and not a bedless neighbour.

HOSTEL ORGANISATIONS

NZ's biggest hostel group is **Budget Backpacker Hostels** (BBH; ☎ 03-379 3014; www.bbh.co.nz), which has around 320 hostels on its books, including homestays and farmstays. Membership costs $45, including a $20 phonecard, and entitles you to stay at member hostels at a cost no greater than the rates advertised in the annual (free) *BBH Backpacker Accommodation* booklet. Non-members pay an extra $3 per night, though not all hostel owners charge the difference. Pick up a membership card from any member hostel, or have one mailed to you overseas for $50 (including postage; see the website for details). BBH rates each hostel according to traveller feedback, using a percentage figure that supposedly tells you how good (or at least how popular) each hostel is.

NZ's **Youth Hostels Association** (YHA; ☎ 0800 278 299, 03-379 9970; www.yha.co.nz) has been around for more than 75 years and has hostels in 54 prime NZ locations. The YHA is part of the **Hostelling International** (HI; www.hihostels.com) network. If you're already an HI member in your own country, your membership entitles you to use NZ hostels. If you don't already have a membership card from home, you can buy one at major NZ YHA hostels for $40 for 12 months, or book online and have your card mailed to you overseas for $50. Nightly charges are usually between $20 and $40 per person for members; hostels also take non-YHA members for an extra $3 per night.

DIRECTORY

YHA hostels provide reliable, basic accommodation for individuals, families and groups in dorms (bunk rooms, usually with four to six beds) and most also have a supply of single, twin and double rooms, sometimes with bathrooms. They have 24-hour access, cooking facilities, a communal area with a TV, laundry facilities and, in larger hostels, travel offices. There's often a maximum-stay period (usually five to seven days). NZ YHA hostels supply all bed linen so you don't need to bring a sleeping bag. The annual *YHA New Zealand Hostel & Discount Guide* booklet details all Kiwi hostels and member discounts (transport, activities etc). Stuff their *Backpacker Map* in your pocket for on-the-road reference.

VIP Backpackers (www.vip.co.nz) run around 70 NZ hostels, mainly in the cities and major tourist spots. VIP is an international organisation with a large network of hostels in nearby Fiji, Australia, southern Africa, Europe and America. For around $52 ($60 including postage) you'll receive a 12-month membership entitling you to a $1 discount on accommodation. You can join online (www.vipbackpackers.com), at VIP hostels or at larger agencies dealing in backpacker travel.

Nomads Backpackers (www.nomadsworld.com) has a handful of franchisees throughout NZ: in Auckland, Paihia, Taupo, Wellington and Rotorua. Membership costs A$35 for 12 months and like VIP offers NZ$1 off the cost of nightly accommodation. You can join at participating hostels, backpacker travel agencies or online.

Base Backpackers (www.stayatbase.com) is a chain with five hostels around the North Island. Expect clean dorms, girls-only areas and party opportunities aplenty.

INDEPENDENT HOSTELS

NZ is an incubator for independent hostels, hatching them across both islands at an impressive rate. Owners try hard to differentiate their properties from their clubby competitors: some promote low-key ambience, lazy gardens, personable management and avoidance of noisy bus groups of backpackers while others bury you in extras such as free breakfasts, free DVDs, spa pools, use of bikes and kayaks, shuttle buses, theme nights and tour bookings. This is usually a successful formula, but with individuality comes risk: if possible, check out your accommodation before handing over the cash to ensure the atmosphere

and facilities correspond with your expectations. If travelling with your family, note that a number of hostels designate themselves 'unsuitable for children'.

Independent backpacker establishments typically charge $20 to $30 for a dorm bed, $40 to $50 for a single and $50 to $80 for a twin or double room (usually with shared bathroom facilities). Some also have space for a few tents.

Hotels & Motels

The least expensive form of North Island hotel accommodation is the humble pub. As is often the case elsewhere, some old pubs are full of character and local characters, while others are grotty, ramshackle places that are best avoided, especially by women travelling solo. If you're renting a room above a pub towards the end of the week, check whether there's a band cranking out the tunes that night – you could be in for some sleeplessness. In the cheapest pubs, singles/doubles might cost as little as $30/50 (with a shared bathroom down the hall), though $50/70 is more common.

At the other end of the hotel scale are five-star international chains, resort complexes and architecturally splendorous boutique hotels, all of which charge a hefty premium for their mod cons, snappy service and/or historic opulence. We quote 'rack rates' (official advertised rates) for such places throughout this book, but discounts and special deals often mean you won't have to pay these prices.

The North Island's towns have a glut of nondescript, low-rise motels and 'motor lodges', charging between $80 and $160 for double rooms. These tend to be squat structures congregating just outside CBDs, or skulking by highways on the edge of towns. Most are modernish (though decor is often mired in the '80s) and have similar facilities (tea- and coffee-making, fridge, TV) – prices vary with standard. Some Kiwis refer to the actual room as a 'motel', rather than the collective complex of rooms – so you might hear, 'Sorry, our motels are full tonight', as opposed to, 'Sorry, our motel is full tonight'.

Rental Accommodation

The basic Kiwi holiday home is called a 'bach' (short for 'bachelor' as they were often used by single men as hunting and fishing hideouts). These are simple self-contained cottages that can be rented in rural and coastal areas, often in isolated locations. They can be handy for longer stays in a region, although some are only available for one or two nights at a time. Prices are typically $80 to $130 per night, which isn't bad for a whole house or self-contained bungalow.

For more upmarket holiday houses, the current trend is to throw rusticity to the wind and erect luxurious cottages on beautiful nature-surrounded plots. Expect to pay anything from $120 to $400 a double.

Good websites to help you find a bach or holiday house include www.holidayhomes.co.nz and the AA's www.bookabach.co.nz; for swanky self-contained apartments try www.newzealand-apartments.co.nz. If it's a longer stay you're thinking about, check out www.nzflats.co.nz.

ACTIVITIES

See the Active North Island chapter (p73) for more info on NZ's outdoor-activity smorgasbord.

Aerial Sightseeing

Small planes and helicopters circle the skies on sightseeing trips (called 'flightseeing' by the locals) all over NZ, operating from local aerodromes. It's a great (but not particularly environmentally friendly) way to absorb the country's contrasting landscapes, soaring mountains and seldom-viewed terrain deep within national parks. On the North Island, some of the most photo-worthy trips take place over the Bay of Islands (p155), the Bay of Plenty (especially Whakaari Island; p325), Tongariro National Park (from Taupo; p278) and Mt Taranaki (p246).

A far more sedate approach is to jump in a hot-air balloon, with balloon trips operating from Auckland, Hamilton, Hastings and Masterton.

Fishing

Thanks to the introduction of trout, salmon, perch and char (among other species), NZ has become one of the world's great recreational fisheries. The central North Island's lakes and rivers are famous for trout fishing, especially around Lake Taupo – the town of Turangi is trout central.

In the warm North Island seas, surfcasting and boat fishing can land grey mullet, trevally, mao mao, porae, John Dory, snapper, gurnard, flounder, mackerel, hapuku (groper), tarakihi,

moki and kahawai. Ninety Mile Beach (Northland) and the Hauraki Gulf beaches are good for surfcasting. The Bay of Islands, Whangaroa, Tutukaka near Whangarei (all in Northland), Whitianga in the Coromandel and Tuhua (Mayor Island) in the Bay of Plenty are big-time big-game fishing areas.

You can hire fishing gear in towns like Taupo and Rotorua and at sports stores in larger towns. If you bring your own rods and tackle they may have to be treated by NZ quarantine officials, especially if they're made with natural materials such as cane or feathers.

A fishing permit is required to fish in inland waters. Sold at sport shops, permits cover particular regions and are valid for a day, month or season. Consult local visitor information centres or DOC offices (p428) for details. Other fishy business is covered at www.fishing.net.nz, a huge website covering recreational fishing in NZ. If you're interested in guided fishing trips, see the **New Zealand Professional Fishing Guides' Association** (www.nzpfga.com) website.

See the boxed text on p170 for some tips on sustainable fishing.

Golf

NZ has more golf courses per capita than any other country, and among over 400 courses there are some magnificently situated fairways and greens. In its 2009 rankings of the world's top 100 courses, *Golf Magazine* gave gongs to two NZ courses: **Cape Kidnappers** (www.capekidnappers.com) in Hawke's Bay (ranked 36th) and **Kauri Cliffs** (www.kauricliffs.com) in the Bay of Islands (ranked 78th). **Paraparaumu Beach** (www.paraparaumubeachgolfclub.co.nz) near Wellington, has made it into such rankings in the past and is regarded as one of the country's best courses. Another popular North Island course is Wairakei near Taupo.

The average green fee for an 18-hole course usually ranges from $30 to $50, though private resorts can charge a substantial amount more – at Cape Kidnappers you'll pay a hefty $300 to $400 for the privilege; Paraparaumu Beach's green fees are a more manageable $110.

For more information check out www.nzgolf.org.nz.

Sailing

Surrounded by sea, NZ has a habit of producing some of the world's best mariners. There's also a good reason why Auckland is called the 'City of Sails'. If you're keen on yacht racing, try visiting the country's various sailing clubs and ask if you can help crew in local competitions. Otherwise, there are plenty of sailing operators who allow you to just laze around on deck or play a more hands-on role.

The Bay of Islands (and Whangaroa to the north) and Auckland are good places to get some wind in your sails.

Go to www.yachtingnz.org.nz for more details.

BUSINESS HOURS

Most shops and businesses open their doors at 9am and close at 5.30pm Monday to Friday, and either 12.30pm or 5pm on Saturday. Late-night shopping (until 9pm) happens in the larger cities on Thursday and/or Friday nights; Sunday trading is the norm in most big towns and cities. Supermarkets are usually open from 8am until at least 7pm, often until 9pm or later in cities. Dairies (corner stores) and superettes (small supermarkets) close later than most shops.

Banks normally open from 9.30am to 4.30pm Monday to Friday (some city branches also open on Saturday mornings). Post offices are open 8.30am to 5pm Monday to Friday, with main branches also open 9.30am to 1pm Saturday; postal desks in newsagencies (Take Note, Paperplus) often open later.

Restaurants typically take orders until at least 9pm, but often serve food until 11pm or later on Friday and Saturday nights; the main restaurant strips in large cities keep longer hours throughout the week. Cafes sometimes open as early as 7am and close around 5pm, though cafe-bar hybrids push the envelope well into the night. Pubs usually serve food from noon to 2pm and from 6pm to 8pm. Pubs and bars generally start pouring drinks at noon and stay open until late, particularly from Thursday to Saturday.

Don't count on many attractions being open on Christmas Day or Good Friday.

CHILDREN

For helpful general tips, see Lonely Planet's *Travel with Children*. All cities and most major towns have centrally located public rooms where mothers (and sometimes fathers) can go to nurse a baby or change a nappy (diaper); check with the local visitor information centre or city council, or ask a local – Kiwis are a friendly bunch!

Practicalities

Many motels and holiday parks have playgrounds, games and DVD players, and occasionally fenced swimming pools and trampolines. Cots, highchairs and baby baths aren't always easy to find at budget and midrange accommodation, but top-end hotels are usually able to supply them and the plushest places have child-minding services. B&Bs are not usually amenable to families – many of these businesses promote themselves as grown-up getaways where peace and quiet are valued above all else. Hostels focussing on the young backpacker demographic don't welcome kids either, but there are plenty of other hostels (including YHA hostels) that do.

There are plenty of so-called family restaurants in NZ, where toddlers' highchairs are provided and kids can choose from their own menu. Pubs often serve kids' meals and most cafes and restaurants (with the exception of upmarket eateries) can handle the idea of child-sized portions.

For specialised childcare, look under 'babysitters' and 'child care centres' in the *Yellow Pages* directory or contact the local council.

Child concessions (and family rates) are often available for accommodation, tours, attraction entry fees, and air, bus and train transport, with discounts of as much as 50% off the adult rate. Do note, however, that the definition of 'child' can vary from under 12 to under 18 years; toddlers (under four years old) usually get free admission and transport.

NZ's medical services and facilities are world-class, with goods like formula and disposable nappies widely available in urban centres. Some smaller car-hire companies struggle with the concept of baby seats – double-check that the company you choose can supply the right size of seat for your child, and that the seat will be properly fitted. Some companies may legally require you to fit the seat yourself.

Sights & Activities

Fabulous kids' playgrounds (with slides, swings, see-saws etc) proliferate across NZ. Some regions produce free information booklets geared towards sights and activities for kids; one example is *Kidz Go!* (www.kidzgo.co.nz), which details child-friendly activities and restaurants in the larger urban centres. Ask at local visitor information centres. Other handy websites for families include www.

kidspot.co.nz, with lots of kid-centric info from pregnancy through to school-age, and www.kidsnewzealand.com, which has plenty of activity suggestions. Finally, www.kids friendlynz.com has extensive links to various facets of kiddy-culture.

CLIMATE CHARTS

NZ sits smack-bang in the Roaring Forties, which means it gets 'freshened' (some say blasted) by cool, damp winds blowing in from the Tasman Sea and is consistently slapped by the winds howling through Cook Strait.

On the North Island, the western sides of the high volcanoes attract a lot more rain than eastern slopes, but the rain shadow isn't as pronounced as in the south – the barrier here isn't as formidable as the Alps. North Island rainfall averages around 1300mm annually.

See p19 for further seasonal instruction.

CUSTOMS REGULATIONS

For the low-down on what you can and can't bring into NZ, see the **New Zealand Customs Service** (www.customs.govt.nz) website.

When entering NZ you can bring most articles in free of duty provided customs is satisfied they're for personal use and that you'll be taking them with you when you leave. There's a per person duty-free allowance of 1125mL of spirits or liqueur, 4.5L of wine or beer, 200 cigarettes (or 50 cigars or 250g of tobacco) and dutiable goods up to the value of $700.

Customs officers are obviously fussy about drugs, so declare all medicines. Bio-security is another customs buzzword – authorities are serious about keeping out any diseases that may harm NZ's agricultural industry. Tramping gear such as boots and tents will be checked and may need to be cleaned before being allowed in; ditto golf clubs and bicycles. You must declare any plant or animal products (including anything made of wood), and food of any kind. You'll also come under greater scrutiny if you've arrived via Africa, southeast Asia or South America. Weapons and firearms are either prohibited or require a permit and safety testing.

DANGERS & ANNOYANCES

Although it's no more dangerous than other developed countries, violent crime does happen in NZ, so it's worth taking sensible precautions on the streets at night or if staying in remote areas. Gang culture permeates some

parts of the country; give any black-jacketed, insignia-wearing groups a wide berth.

Theft, primarily from cars, is a *major* problem around NZ, and travellers are viewed as easy marks. Avoid leaving valuables in vehicles, no matter where it's parked; the worst places to tempt fate are tourist parking areas and the car parks at trailheads. If the crown jewels simply must be left behind, pack them out of sight in the boot (trunk) of the car – but carry your passport with you, just in case.

Don't underestimate the dangers posed by NZ's unpredictable, ever-changing climate, especially in high-altitude areas; see p for information.

NZ has thankfully been spared from the proliferation of venomous creatures found in neighbouring Australia (spiders, snakes, jellyfish etc). Sharks hang out in NZ waters, but are well fed by the abundant marine life and rarely nibble on humans; that said, attacks on humans do occasionally occur. Much greater hazards in the ocean, however, are the rips and undertows that plague some beaches and can quickly drag swimmers out to sea. Take notice of local warnings when swimming, surfing or diving.

The island's roads are often made hazardous by speeding locals, wide-cornering campervans and livestock. Set yourself a reasonable itinerary instead of careening around the country at top speed and keep your eyes on the road no matter how

SANDFLIES *Sir Ian McKellen*

As an unpaid but enthusiastic proselytiser on behalf of all things Kiwi, including the New Zealand tourist industry, I hesitate to mention the well-kept secret of sandflies. I first met them en masse at the glorious Milford Sound, where visitors (after the most beautiful drive in the world) are met, at least during the summer, by crowds of the little buggers. There are patent unctions that cope, and tobacco repels them too, but I would hope that travellers find them an insignificant pest compared with the glory of their habitat.

Oddly, when actually filming scenes for *Lord of the Rings*, I don't recall being bothered by sandflies at all. Honestly. Had there been, we would have set the orcs on them.

Sir Ian McKellen is a UK-based actor who spent several years in NZ filming and has become something of an unofficial ambassador for NZ tourism.

photogenic the scenery may be. If you're cycling, take care – motorists can't always overtake easily on skinny roads.

In the annoyances category, NZ's sandflies are a royal pain (see above). Lather yourself with insect repellent in coastal areas.

DISCOUNT CARDS

The **International Student Travel Confederation** (ISTC; www.istc.org) is an international collective of specialist student travel organisations and the body behind the internationally recognised International Student Identity Card (ISIC). The card is issued to full-time students aged 12 years and over and provides red-hot discounts on accommodation, transport and admission to attractions. The ISTC also produces the International Youth Travel Card (IYTC), available to folks between 12 and 26 who are not full-time students, and gives equivalent benefits to the ISIC. A similar ISTC brainchild is the International Teacher Identity Card (ITIC), available to teaching professionals. All three cards (NZ$25 each) are available online at www.isiccard.co.nz, or from student travel companies like **STA Travel** (www.statravel.co.nz).

Another option is the **New Zealand Card** (www. newzealandcard.com), a $35 discount pass that'll score you between 5% and 50% off a range of accommodation, tours, sights and activities.

Senior and disabled travellers who live overseas will find that the cards issued by their respective countries are not always 'officially' recognised in NZ, but that many places still acknowledge such cards and grant concessions where applicable.

EMBASSIES & CONSULATES

Most principal diplomatic representations to NZ are in Wellington, with a few in Auckland.

Embassies, consulates and high commissions include:

Australia (Map p380; ☎ 04-473 6411; www.australia. org.nz; 72-76 Hobson St, Thorndon, Wellington)

Canada (Map p380; ☎ 04-473 9577; www.newzealand. gc.ca; L11, 125 The Terrace, Wellington)

Fiji (Map p380; ☎ 04-473 5401; www.fiji.org.nz; 31 Pipitea St, Thorndon, Wellington)

France (Map p384; ☎ 04-384 2555; www.ambafrance -nz.org; 34-42 Manners St, Wellington)

Germany (Map p380; ☎ 04-473 6063; www.wellington. diplo.de; 90-92 Hobson St, Thorndon, Wellington)

Ireland (Map p92; ☎ 09-977 2252; www.ireland.co.nz; L7, Citigroup Bldg, 23 Customs St E, Auckland)

Israel (Map p380; ☎ 04-471 0079; L13, Greenock House, 102 Lambton Quay, Wellington)

Japan (Map p384; ☎ 04-473 1540; www.nz.emb-japan. go.jp; L18 & L19, The Majestic Centre, 100 Willis St, Wellington)

Netherlands (Map p380; ☎ 04-471 6390; www. netherlandsembassy.co.nz; L10, Investment House, cnr Featherston & Ballance Sts, Wellington)

UK (Map p380; ☎ 04-924 2888; www.britain.org.nz; 44 Hill St, Thorndon, Wellington)

USA (Map p380; ☎ 04-462 6000; http://wellington. usembassy.gov; 29 Fitzherbert Tce, Thorndon, Wellington)

It's important to know what your national embassy can and can't do to help you if you get into trouble. Generally speaking, embassies won't be much help in emergencies if the fix you're in is self-induced. While in NZ you're bound by NZ laws – your embassy will not be sympathetic if you end up in jail after committing a crime locally, even if such actions are legal in your own country.

In genuine emergencies you might get some assistance, but only if other channels have been exhausted. For example, if you need to get home urgently, a free ticket is exceedingly unlikely – the embassy would expect you to have insurance. If you have all your money and documents stolen, your embassy may assist with getting a new passport, but a loan for onward travel is out of the question.

FESTIVALS & EVENTS

Want to plan your travels around the various food and wine, sporting or arts festivals staged throughout the country? Check out the **Tourism New Zealand** (www.newzealand.com/travel) website – click on Sights, Activities & Events, then Events Calendar. See also www.nzlive.com and www.eventfinder.co.nz.

Details of North Island festivals and events are provided throughout destination chapters in this book. A handful of highlights:

Arts & Cultural Festivals

Te Matatini National Kapa Haka Festival (www.tematatini.org.nz) Maori *haka* competition in February in odd-numbered years; much gesticulation, eye-bulging and tongue extension. Venues vary.

New Zealand International Arts Festival (www.nzfestival.nzpost.co.nz) Month-long biennial spectacular held in February/March every even-numbered year in Wellington. Theatre, dance, music and visual arts.

New Zealand International Comedy Festival (www.comedyfestival.co.nz) Three-week laugh-fest in May with venues across Auckland, Wellington and various regional centres.

Matariki (Maori New Year; www.taitokerau.co.nz/matariki.htm) Remembrance, education and tree planting; in June mainly around Auckland and Northland.

New Zealand International Film Festivals (www.enzedff.co.nz) After separate film festivals in Wellington and Auckland, a selection of flicks hits the road for screenings in regional towns from July to November.

World of Wearable Art Award Show (WOW; www.worldofwearableart.com) Bizarre (in the best possible way) two-week Wellington event in September featuring amazing garments.

Food & Wine Festivals

Harvest Hawke's Bay (www.harvesthawkesbay.co.nz) Indulgent wine and food celebration in February, with participating wineries around Napier and Hastings.

Auckland Wine & Food Festival (www.aucklandwineandfoodfestival.com) Auckland swills itself silly with the best of Kiwi food and drink in March/April.

Toast Martinborough (www.toastmartinborough.co.nz) Wine-willing Wellingtonians head to Martinborough for a day of indulgence in November.

Music Festivals

Rhythm & Vines (www.rhythmandvines.co.nz) Wine, music and song (all the good things) in sunny Gisborne on New Year's Eve. Top DJs, hip-hop acts, bands and singer-songwriters.

Big Day Out (www.bigdayout.com) Much moshing at this international rock extravaganza in Auckland in January.

Splore (www.splore.net) Cutting-edge outdoor summer festival in February at Tapapakanga Regional Park on the Coromandel Peninsula. Contemporary live music, performance, visual arts and safe swimming!

WOMAD (World of Music Arts & Dance; www.womad.co.nz) Local and international arts performances at the Brooklands Bowl in New Plymouth in March.

National Jazz Festival (www.jazz.org.nz) Every Easter Tauranga hosts the longest-running jazz fest in the southern hemisphere.

Sporting Events

New Zealand International Sevens (NZI Sevens; www.nzisevens.co.nz) The world's top seven-a-side rugby teams crack heads in Wellington in February.

Auckland International Boat Show (www.aucklandinternationalboatshow.com) Auckland harbour blooms with sails and churns with outboard motors in March.

Rugby World Cup (www.rugbyworldcup.com) NZ hosts the greatest rugby show on Earth in September/October 2011 (go All Blacks!).

FOOD & DRINK

The NZ foodie scene once slavishly reflected Anglo-Saxon stodge, but nowadays the country's restaurants and cafes are adept at throwing together trad staples (lamb, beef, venison, green-lipped mussels) with Asian, European and pan-Pacific flair.

Eateries themselves range from fry-'em-up fish-and-chip shops and pub bistros; to cafes drowned in faux-European, grungy or retro stylings; restaurant-bars with full à la carte service; and fine-dining establishments with linen is so crisp you're afraid to prop your elbows on it. For online listings, see www.dineout.co.nz and www.menus.co.nz.

Most North Island urban centres have at least one dedicated vegetarian cafe or restaurant. See the **New Zealand Vegetarian Society** (www.vegsoc.org.nz) restaurant guide for listings.

On the liquid front, NZ wine is world class (especially sauvignon blanc and pinot noir), and you'll be hard-pressed to find a NZ town of any size without decent espresso. NZ microbrewed beers have also become mainstream.

Eating recommendations in this book are in budget order, from cheapest to most expensive. Cafes are often the best value, with bang-up meals in casual surrounds for under

$20. Some city pubs label themselves 'gastro-pubs', offering classy restaurant-style fare, but most pubs serve standard bistro meals, usually under $20. Midrange restaurants can charge as much as $30 for a main course, but don't be surprised to see mains priced from $35 to $45 at trendy top-end restaurants.

Smoking is banned in all restaurants, pubs and bars. Tipping in restaurants and cafes is not expected.

For more information, see the Food & Drink chapter (p58).

GAY & LESBIAN TRAVELLERS

The G&L tourism industry in NZ isn't as high-profile as in neighbouring Australia, but homosexual communities are prominent in Auckland and Wellington, with myriad support organisations across the country. NZ has relatively progressive laws protecting the rights of gays and lesbians; the legal minimum age for sex between consenting persons is 16. Generally speaking Kiwis are fairly relaxed and accepting about homosexuality, but that's not to say that homophobia doesn't exist.

There are loads of websites dedicated to gay and lesbian travellers. **Gay Tourism New Zealand** (www.gaytourismnewzealand.com) is a good starting point, with links to various sites. Other worthwhile queer websites include www.gaynz.com, www.gaynz.net.nz and www.lesbian.net.nz. For accommodation listings see www.gaystay.co.nz.

Check out nationwide magazines like *express* (www.gayexpress.co.nz) every second Wednesday and *Out!* (www.out.co.nz) published every two months for the latest happenings, reviews and listings on the NZ gay scene.

Big Gay Out (www.biggayout.co.nz) enlivens Auckland in late February with performances and concerts, and **Out Takes** (www.outtakes.org.nz) is a G&L film festival staged in Auckland, Wellington and Christchurch in June.

For more info, see Gay & Lesbian Auckland (p117) and Gay & Lesbian Wellington (p397).

HOLIDAYS
Public Holidays
NZ's main public holidays:
New Year 1 & 2 January
Waitangi Day 6 February
Easter Good Friday & Easter Monday; March/April
Anzac Day 25 April
Queen's Birthday 1st Monday in June
Labour Day 4th Monday in October
Christmas Day 25 December

Boxing Day 26 December

In addition, each NZ province has its own anniversary-day holiday. The dates of these provincial holidays vary – when these holidays fall between Friday and Sunday, they're usually observed the following Monday; if they fall between Tuesday and Thursday, they're held on the preceding Monday – the great Kiwi tradition of the 'long weekend' continues.

North Island provincial anniversary holidays include:
Wellington 22 January
Auckland 29 January
Waikato 29 January
Northland 29 January
Taranaki 31 March
Hawke's Bay 1 November

School Holidays
The Christmas holiday season, from mid-December to late January, is part of the summer school vacation. It's the time you'll most likely find transport and accommodation booked out, and long, grumpy queues at tourist attractions. There are three shorter school-holiday periods during the year: from mid- to late April, early to mid-July, and mid-September to early October. For exact dates see the **Ministry of Education** (www.minedu.govt.nz) website.

INSURANCE
A watertight travel insurance policy covering theft, loss and medical problems is essential; nothing will ruin your holiday more quickly than an accident or having your duty-free digital camera pilfered. There are plenty of policies to choose from – compare the fine print and shop around.

Some policies specifically exclude designated 'dangerous activities' such as scuba diving, parasailing, bungy jumping, whitewater rafting, motorcycling, skiing, and even bushwalking. If you plan on doing any of these things, make sure the policy you choose covers you fully.

You may prefer a policy that pays doctors or hospitals directly rather than you having to pay on the spot and claim later. If you have to claim later make sure you keep all documentation. Some policies ask you to call back (reverse charges) to a centre in your home country where an immediate assessment of your problem is made. Check that the policy covers ambulances and emergency medical evacuations by air.

It's worth mentioning that under NZ law, you cannot sue for personal injury (other than exemplary damages). Instead, the country's **Accident Compensation Corporation** (ACC; www.acc. co.nz) administers an accident compensation scheme that provides accident insurance for NZ residents and visitors to the country, regardless of fault.

While some people cry foul of this arrangement, others point to the hugely expensive litigation 'industries' in other countries and raise a cheer. This scheme, however, does not cancel out the necessity for your own comprehensive travel insurance policy, as it doesn't cover you for such things as loss of income or treatment in your home country or ongoing illness.

See also p445 for notes on medical insurance. For car insurance information see p441.

Worldwide cover for travellers from over 44 countries is available online at www.lonely planet.com/bookings/insurance.do.

INTERNET ACCESS

Getting online in NZ is easy in all but the most remote locales. If you don't already have one, it's worth setting up a travelling address with one of the many free email services (www. yahoo.com, www.hotmail.com, www.gmail. com etc).

The internet icon (🖳) in accommodation, eating and drinking listings in this book indicates internet access is available (a kiosk or dedicated guest computer); the wi-fi icon (🛜) denotes wireless access.

For a list of useful NZ websites, see p22.

Internet Cafes

Internet cafes in the bigger urban centres or tourist areas are usually brimming with high-speed terminals. Obnoxious teens often swamp the machines in the after-school hours – time your visit anytime other than 4pm to 6pm! Facilities are a lot more haphazard in small, out-of-the-way towns, where a so-called internet cafe could turn out to be a single terminal in the corner of a video store.

Most hostels make an effort to hook you up, with internet access sometimes free for guests. Many public libraries have free internet access too, but there can be a limited number of terminals – head for an internet cafe first.

Internet access at cafes ranges anywhere from \$4 to \$6 per hour – the lowest rates can be found in cities where competition and traveller numbers generate dirt-cheap prices. There's often a minimum period of access, usually 10 or 15 minutes.

Wireless Access & Internet Service Providers

Increasingly, you'll be able to find wi-fi access around the country, from hotel rooms to pub beer gardens to hostel dining rooms. Usually you have to be a guest or customer to access the internet at these locations – you'll be issued with a code, a wink and a secret handshake to enable you to get online. Sometimes it's free; sometimes there's a charge.

The country's main telecommunications company is **Telecom New Zealand** (www.telecom. co.nz), which has wireless hotspots around the country. If you have a wi-fi-enabled device, you can purchase a Telecom wireless prepaid card from participating hotspots. Alternatively, you can purchase a prepaid number from the login page and any wireless hotspot using your credit card. See the website for hotspot listings.

If you've brought your palmtop or notebook computer and want to get connected to a local internet service provider (ISP), there are plenty of options, though some limit their dial-up areas to major cities or particular regions. Major ISPs:

Clearnet (☎ 0508 888 800; www.clearnet.co.nz)
Earthlight (☎ 03-479 0303; www.earthlight.co.nz) Has a page on its website detailing prepaid internet access for travellers to NZ.
Slingshot (☎ 0800 892 000; www.slingshot.co.nz)
Xtra (☎ 0800 003 040; www.xtra.co.nz/products)

Wireless is more common, but if you're planning on manually plugging in, NZ uses British BT431A and RJ-11 jacks, but neither are universal; local electronics shops should be able to help. A lot of midrange accommodation and nearly all top-end hotels have wall sockets, but you'll be hit with expensive call charges. In most cheaper places you'll probably find that phones are hardwired into the wall.

Keep in mind that your PC-card modem may not work in NZ. The safest option is to buy a reputable 'global' modem before you leave home or buy a local PC-card modem once you get to NZ.

DIRECTORY

LEGAL MATTERS

Marijuana (aka 'New Zealand Green', 'electric puha' or 'dac') is widely indulged in but illegal, and anyone caught carrying this or other illicit drugs will have the book thrown at them. Even if the amount of drugs is small and the fine minimal, a conviction will still be recorded against you, which may affect your visa status.

Always carry your licence when driving; for more info, see p439. Drink-driving is a serious offence and remains a significant problem in NZ despite widespread campaigns and severe penalties. The legal blood alcohol limit is 0.08% for drivers over 20, and 0.03% for those under 20.

If you are arrested, it's your right to consult a lawyer before any formal questioning begins.

MAPS

Top-notch maps are widely available throughout NZ – from detailed street maps and atlases to topographic masterpieces.

The **Automobile Association** (AA; www.aa.co.nz) produces excellent city, town, regional, island and highway maps, available from their local offices; members of affiliated overseas automobile associations can obtain free maps and discounts on presentation of a membership card. The AA also produces a detailed *New Zealand Road Atlas*. Other reliable countrywide atlases, available from visitor information centres and bookshops, are published by Hema, KiwiMaps and Wises.

Land Information New Zealand (www.linz.govt.nz) publishes several exhaustive map series, including street, country and holiday maps, national and forest park maps, and topographical trampers' maps. Scan the larger bookshops, or try the nearest DOC office or visitor information centre for topo maps.

Online, log onto **AA SmartMap** (www.aamaps.co.nz) or the **Yellow Maps** (maps.yellowpages.co.nz) to pinpoint exact addresses in NZ cities and towns.

MONEY

See the Quick Reference section on the inside front cover for a list of exchange rates.

ATMs & Eftpos

Branches of the country's major banks, including the Bank of New Zealand, ANZ, Westpac and ASB, have 24-hour ATMs that accept cards from other banks and provide access to overseas accounts. You won't find ATMs everywhere, but they're widespread across both islands.

Many NZ businesses use electronic funds transfer at point of sale (Eftpos), a convenient service that allows you to use your bank card (credit or debit) to pay directly for services or purchases, and often withdraw cash as well. Eftpos is available practically everywhere, even in places where it's a long way between banks. Just like an ATM, you need to know your personal identification number (PIN) to use it.

Bank Accounts

We've heard mixed reports on how easy it is for nonresidents to open a bank account in NZ. Some sources say it's as simple as flashing a few pieces of ID, providing a temporary postal address (or your permanent address) and then waiting a few days while your request is processed. Other sources say that many banks won't allow visitors to open an account with them unless they're planning to stay in NZ for at least six months, or unless the application is accompanied by some proof of employment. Bank websites are also rather vague on the services offered to short-term visitors. If you think you'll need to open an account, do your homework before you arrive in the country and be prepared to shop around to get the best deal.

Credit & Debit Cards

Perhaps the safest place to keep your NZ travelling money is inside a plastic card! The most flexible option is to carry both a credit and a debit card.

Credit cards (Visa, MasterCard etc) are widely accepted for everything from a hostel bed to a bungy jump. Credit cards are pretty much essential if you want to hire a car. They can also be used for over-the-counter cash advances at banks and from ATMs, depending on the card, but be aware that such transactions incur charges. Charge cards such as Diners Club and Amex are not as widely accepted.

Apart from losing them, the obvious danger with credit cards is maxing out your limit and going home to a steaming pile of debt. A safer option is a debit card with which you can draw money directly from your home bank account using ATMs, banks or Eftpos machines. Any card connected to the international banking network (Cirrus, Maestro, Visa Plus and Eurocard) should work, provided you know your PIN. Fees for using your card at a foreign bank or ATM vary depending on your home bank; ask before you leave. Companies such as Travelex offer debit cards (Travelex calls them Cash Passport cards) with set withdrawal fees and a balance you can top-up from your personal bank account while on the road – nice one!

Currency

NZ's currency is the NZ dollar, comprising 100 cents. There are 10c, 20c, 50c, $1 and $2 coins, and $5, $10, $20, $50 and $100 notes. Prices are often still marked in single cents and then rounded to the nearest 10c when you hand over your money.

Unless otherwise noted, all prices quoted in this book are in NZ dollars. For an idea of the costs associated with travelling around the country, see p20.

There are no notable restrictions on importing or exporting travellers cheques. Though not prohibited, cash amounts equal to or in excess of the equivalent of NZ$10,000 (in any currency) must be declared on arrival or departure – you'll need to fill out a Border Cash Report.

Money changers

Changing foreign currency or travellers cheques is usually no problem at banks throughout NZ or at licensed money changers such as Travelex (formerly Thomas Cook) in the major cities. Money changers can be found in all major tourist areas, cities and airports, and conveniently tend to stay open beyond normal business hours during the week (often until 9pm).

Taxes & Refunds

The Goods and Services Tax (GST) is a flat 12.5% tax on all domestic goods and services. Prices in this book include GST, but look out for any small print announcing that the price is GST-exclusive. There's no GST refund available when you leave NZ.

Tipping

Tipping is completely optional in NZ, and staff do not depend on tips for income – the total at the bottom of a restaurant bill is all you need to pay (note that sometimes there's an additional service charge). That said, it's totally acceptable to reward good service and the tip you leave depends entirely on your satisfaction – between 5% and 10% of the bill is the norm.

Travellers Cheques

The ubiquity of debit- and credit-card access in NZ can make travellers cheques seem rather old-hat. Nevertheless, Amex, Travelex and other international brands of travellers cheques are easily exchanged. You need to present your passport for identification when cashing them. Fees per transaction for changing foreign-currency travellers cheques vary from bank to bank, while Amex or Travelex perform the task commission-free if you use their cheques. Private moneychangers found in the larger cities are sometimes commission free, but shop around for the best rates.

POST

The services offered by **New Zealand Post** (☎ 0800 501 501; www.nzpost.co.nz) are reliable and reasonably inexpensive. Within NZ standard post costs 50c for standard letters and postcards, and $1 for larger letters.

International destinations are divided into two zones: Australia and the South Pacific, and the rest of the world. Standard rates (express services also available):

Item	Aust & South Pacific	Rest of World
Postcard	$1.80	$1.80
Letter	$1.80	$2.30
Large letter	$2.30	$2.80
Oversize letter	$3.50	$5
Approx delivery (work days)	3-10	6-10

International parcel zones are the same as for letters; pricing depends on weight and whether you send the parcel 'economy' (three to five weeks), 'air' (one to two weeks) or 'express' (within a matter of days). To send parcels by 'air' is roughly 20% more expensive; by 'express' at least 50% more. Check out the incredibly precise calculator on the website.

Many NZ post offices are called 'PostShops' these days, as most have been removed from their traditional old buildings and set up in modern shop-style premises, but we still stubbornly refer to them as post offices throughout this guidebook. For standard post office opening hours, see p418. Stamps can

DIRECTORY

usually also be purchased at supermarkets and bookshops.

You can have mail addressed to you care of 'Poste Restante, Main PostShop' in whichever town you require. Mail is usually held for 30 days and you need to provide some form of identification (such as a passport) to collect it.

SHOPPING

NZ isn't one of those countries where it's necessary to buy a T-shirt to help you remember your visit; the spectacular landscapes are mementoes in themselves, to be plucked later from the depths of memory or the innards of your camera. But there are numerous locally crafted items you can purchase for their own unique qualities.

Clothing

The main cities of Auckland (p117) and Wellington (p399) boast fashion-conscious boutiques ablaze with the sartorial flair of young and well-established NZ designers. Check out www.fashionz.co.nz for up-to-date information on the hottest designers and labels and where to find them. Keep an eye out for labels such as Zambesi, Kate Sylvester, Karen Walker, Trelise Cooper, NOM D and Little Brother.

In Auckland, head to places like Newmarket, Ponsonby Rd and High St; Wellington offers retro mix-and-match boutiques on Cuba St and high fashion along Lambton Quay. To see just how far New Zealanders are prepared to push the boundaries of fashionable creativity, attend the namesake festival in Wellington (p391).

From the backs of NZ sheep come sheepskin products such as footwear (including the much-loved ugg boot) and beautiful woollen jumpers (jerseys or sweaters) made from hand-spun, hand-dyed wool. Other knitted knick-knacks include hats, gloves and scarves. Look for garments made from a lovely soft yarn that's a combination of merino wool and possum fur.

Long woollen Swanndri jackets, shirts and pullovers are so ridiculously practical, they're practically the national garment in country areas. Most common are the red-and-black or blue-and-black plaid ones; pick up 'Swannies' in outdoor-gear shops.

Crafts

Fine NZ craft products can be purchased in most sizable towns. Few (if any) places in the country are devoid of someone who's been inspired to hand-shape items for sale to passing visitors. The Auckland suburb of Parnell has many shops and galleries selling locally designed and crafted jewellery, ceramics, glassware and accessories. Within striking distance of downtown Auckland, Devonport (p96) is also replete with galleries.

Maori Arts

For some brilliant examples of Maori *whakairo rakau* (woodcarving), check out the efforts of artisans at Te Whakarewarewa cultural area (p305) in Rotorua, then browse the town's Maori craft shops; in some cases you may be able to buy directly from the artist. Carvers produce intricate forms like leaping dolphins, as well as highly detailed traditional Maori carvings. You'll pay a premium for high-quality work; avoid buying poor examples of the craft that lines the souvenir shops in Auckland.

Maori bone carvings are undergoing something of a renaissance around NZ. Maori artisans have always made bone carvings in the shape of humans and animals, but nowadays they cater to the tourist industry. Bone fish-hook pendants, carved in traditional Maori and modernised styles, are most common, worn on a leather string around the neck.

To confirm the authenticity of any Maorimade piece, see if it's accompanied by the trademark **toi iho** (www.toiiho.com), a symbol created by a Maori arts board to identify the output of individual artists or groups of artists of Maori descent. There are also modified versions of the trademark, identifying items produced by groups of 'mainly Maori' artists and via 'co-productions' between Maori and non-Maori artists. Do note that not all Maori artists are registered with this scheme.

Paua

Abalone shell, called paua in NZ, is carved into some beautiful ornaments and jewellery and is often used as an inlay in Maori carvings. Lovers of kitsch and general tackiness will find that it's also incorporated into generic souvenirs, often in delightfully unattractive ways. Shells are used as ashtrays in places where paua is plentiful. Be aware that it's illegal to take natural paua shells out of the country – only processed ornaments can be taken with you.

Pounamu

Maoris consider *pounamu* (greenstone, or jade or nephrite) to be a culturally invaluable raw material. It's found predominantly on the west coast of the South Island – Maoris called the island Te Wahi Pounamu (The Place of Greenstone) or Te Wai Pounamu (The Water of Greenstone).

You're unlikely to come across any *mere* (war clubs) in *pounamu* studios or souvenir shops, but you will find lots of stony green incarnations of Maori motifs. One of the most popular is the *hei tiki,* the name of which literally means 'hanging human form' – in Maori legend, Tiki was the first man created and *hei* is 'to hang'. They are tiny, stylised Maori figures, usually depicted with their tongue stuck out in warlike repose, worn on a leather string or chain around the neck. They've got great *mana* (power), but they also serve as fertility symbols. Other popular motifs are the *taniwha* (monster) and the *marakihau* (sea monster).

On the North Island, the best place to buy *pounamu* is Rotorua (p317) also has its fair share of *pounamu* crafts. To see impressive collections both ancient and modern, visit Te Papa museum (p387) in Wellington and Auckland Museum (p90).

Traditionally, *pounamu* is bought as a gift for another person, not for yourself. Ask a few questions to ensure you're buying from a local operator who crafts local stone, not an offshore company selling imported (usually Chinese or European) jade.

TELEPHONE

Telecom New Zealand (www.telecom.co.nz) is the country's key domestic player and also has a stake in the local mobile (cell) market. Another mobile network option is **Vodafone** (www.vodafone.co.nz).

Local & International Calls

INFORMATION & TOLL-FREE CALLS

Numbers starting with ☎ 0900 are usually re-corded information services, charging upwards of $1 per minute (more from mobiles); these numbers cannot be dialled from payphones.

Toll-free numbers in NZ have the prefix ☎ 0800 or ☎ 0508 and can be called free of charge from anywhere in the country, though they may not be accessible from certain areas or from mobile phones. Telephone numbers beginning with ☎ 0508, ☎ 0800 or ☎ 0900 cannot be dialled from outside NZ.

INTERNATIONAL CALLS

Payphones allow international calls but the cost and international dialling code for calls will vary depending on the provider. International calls from NZ are relatively inexpensive and subject to specials that reduce the rates even more, so it's worth shopping around – consult the *Yellow Pages* for a list of providers.

The toll-free Country Direct service connects callers in NZ with overseas operators to make reverse-charge (collect) or credit-card calls. Country Direct numbers and other details are listed in the front of telephone directories or are available from the NZ international operator. The access number varies, depending on the number of phone companies in the country you call, but is usually ☎ 000-9 (followed by the country code).

To make international calls from NZ you need to dial the international access code (☎ 00), the country code, and the area code (without the initial 0). So for a London number you'd dial ☎ 00-44-20, then the number. Certain operators will have you dial a special code to access their service.

If dialling NZ from overseas, the country code is ☎ 64, followed by the appropriate area code minus the initial zero.

LOCAL CALLS

Local calls from private phones are free! Local calls from payphones cost 50c, though coin-operated payphones are scarce – you'll need a phonecard (see p428). Both involve unlimited talk time. Calls to mobile phones attract higher rates and are timed.

LONG-DISTANCE CALLS & AREA CODES

NZ uses regional area codes for long-distance calls, which can be made from any payphone.

If you're making a local call (ie to someone else in the same town), you don't need to dial the area code. But if you're dialling within a region (even if it's to a nearby town) you do have to dial the area code, regardless of the fact that the place you're calling has the same code as the place you're dialling from. All the numbers in this book are listed with their relevant area codes.

Mobile Phones

Local mobile phone numbers are preceded by the prefix ☎ 021, ☎ 025 or ☎ 027. Mobile phone coverage is good in cities and towns and most parts of the North Island.

If you want to bring your own phone and use a prepaid service with a local SIM card, **Vodafone** (www.vodafone.co.nz) is a practical option. Any Vodafone shop (found in most major towns) will set you up with a SIM card and phone number (about $35, including $10 worth of calls); top-ups can be purchased at newsagencies, post offices and shops practically anywhere.

Alternatively, if you don't bring your own phone from home, you can rent one from **Vodafone Rental** (www.vodarent.co.nz) priced from $6/25 per day/week, with pick-up and drop-off outlets at NZ's major airports. You can also rent a SIM card for $2.50 per day (minimum charge $10) or $40 per month. You can arrange this in advance via the website. We've also had some positive feedback on **Phone Hire New Zealand** (www.phonehirenz.com), who hire out mobile phones, SIM cards, modems and GPS systems.

Phonecards

NZ has a wide range of phonecards available, which can be bought at hostels, newsagencies and post offices for a fixed dollar value (usually $5, $10, $20 and $50). These can be used with any public or private phone by dialling a toll-free access number and then the PIN number on the card. It's worth shopping around – call rates vary from company to company.

TIME

Being close to the international date line, NZ is one of the first places in the world to start the new day (Pitt Island in the Chatham Islands sees the first sunrise each new year). NZ is 12 hours ahead of GMT/UTC and two hours ahead of Australian Eastern Standard Time.

In summer, NZ observes daylight-saving time, where clocks are wound forward by one hour on the last Sunday in September; clocks are wound back on the first Sunday of the following April.

So (excluding the duration of daylight saving), when it's noon in NZ it's 10am in Sydney, 8am in Singapore, midnight in London and 5pm the previous day in San Francisco. The Chathams are 45 minutes ahead of NZ's main islands.

TOURIST INFORMATION

Even before the success of recent international marketing campaigns and the country's cult status as a pseudo-Middle-earth, NZ had a highly developed tourism infrastructure that busily generated mountains of brochures and booklets, plus information-packed Internet pages.

Local Tourist Offices

Almost every Kiwi city or town – whether it has any worthwhile attractions or not – seems to have a visitor information centre. The bigger centres stand united within the outstanding **i-SITE** (www.newzealand.com/travel/i-sites) network, which is affiliated with Tourism New Zealand (the official national tourism body), and have trained staff, abundant information on local activities and attractions, and free brochures and maps. Staff also act as travel agents, booking activities, transport and accommodation. Not to be outdone, staff at smaller centres are often overwhelmingly helpful.

Bear in mind that many information centres only promote accommodation and tour operators who are paying members of the local tourist association, while others are ironically hamstrung by the demands of local operators that they be represented equally. In other words, sometimes information centre staff aren't supposed to recommend one activity or accommodation provider over another, a curious situation that exists in highly competitive environments.

There's also a network of **Department Of Conservation** (DOC; www.doc.govt.nz) visitor centres to help you plan your recreation activities and make bookings. Visitor centres usually have displays and info on local lore, and NZ's unique flora and fauna and biodiversity challenges. DOC visitor centres are found in national parks, major regional centres and in each of the major cities. It's important to check local weather conditions at the nearest visitor centre before you set out. Collect the DOC visitor centres brochure from the website or at visitor centres.

In this book, contact details for local visitor information centres or offices are listed under Information headings in relevant city and town sections.

Tourist Offices Abroad

Tourism New Zealand (☎ 04-917 5400; www.newzealand.com) has representatives in various countries around the world. A good place for pretrip research is the official website (emblazoned with the hugely successful 100% Pure

New Zealand branding), which has information in several languages (including German and Japanese). Overseas offices:

Australia (☎ 02-8299 4800; L12, 61 York St, Sydney)
UK & Europe (☎ 020-7930 1662; New Zealand House, 80 Haymarket, London, UK)
USA & Canada (☎ 310-395 7480; 501 Santa Monica Blvd, Santa Monica, USA)

TRAVELLERS WITH DISABILITIES

Kiwi accommodation generally caters fairly well for travellers with disabilities, with a significant number of hostels, hotels, motels and B&Bs equipped with wheelchair-accessible rooms. Many tourist attractions similarly provide wheelchair access, with wheelchairs often available at key attractions with advance notice.

Tour operators with accessible vehicles operate from most major centres. Key cities are also serviced by kneeling buses(buses that hydraulically stoop down to kerb level to allow easy access); taxi companies offer wheelchair-accessible vans. Large car-hire firms (Avis, Hertz etc) provide cars with hand controls at no extra charge; advance notice is required. Mobility parking permits are available from branches of **CCS Disability Action** (☎ 0800 227 200, 04-384 5677; www.ccsdisabilityaction.org.nz) in the main centres.

For good general information, see NZ's **disability information website** (www.weka.net. nz). Click on Living with a Disability, then categories including Transport, Holiday Accommodation, and Travel and Tourism. The latter lists NZ tour operators catering specifically to travellers with disabilities.

Travellers with disabilities need not miss out on NZ's great outdoors. If you'd like to tackle a wilderness pathway, pick up a copy of *Accessible Walks* by Anna and Andrew Jameson ($26), which offers first-hand descriptions of more than 100 South Island walks. It's available online at www.accessible walks.co.nz. If cold-weather activity is more your thing, see the **Disabled Snowsports New Zealand** (www.disabledsnowsports.org.nz) website.

VISAS

Visa application forms are available from NZ diplomatic missions overseas, travel agents or through **Immigration New Zealand** (☎ 0508 558 855, 09-914 4100; www.immigration.govt.nz). Immigration New Zealand has over a dozen offices overseas; consult the website.

Visitor's Visa

Citizens of Australia don't need a visa to visit NZ and can stay indefinitely (provided they have no criminal convictions). UK citizens don't need a visa either and can stay in the country for up to six months.

Citizens of another 56 countries that have visa-waiver agreements with NZ don't need a visa for stays of up to three months, provided they have an onward ticket, sufficient funds to support their stay (NZ$1000 per month, or NZ$400 per month if accommodation has been prepaid) and a passport valid for three months beyond the date of their planned departure from NZ. Nations in this group include Canada, France, Germany, Ireland, Japan, the Netherlands and the USA.

Citizens of other countries must obtain a visa before entering NZ.Visas come with three months' standard validity and cost NZ$100 if processed in Australia or certain South Pacific countries (eg Samoa, Fiji), or NZ$130 if processed elsewhere in the world.

Visitors' visas can be extended for stays of up to nine months within one 18-month period, or to a maximum of 12 months in the country. Applications are assessed on a case-by-case basis; visitors will need to meet criteria such as proof of ongoing financial self-support. Apply for extensions at any Immigration New Zealand office – see the website for locations.

Work Visa & Working Holiday Scheme

It's illegal for foreign nationals to work in NZ on a visitor's visa, except for Australians who can legally gain work without a visa or permit. If you're visiting NZ to find work, or you already have an employment offer, you'll need to apply for a work visa, which translates into a work permit once you arrive and is valid for up to three years. You can apply for a work permit after you're in NZ, but it's validity will be backdated to when you entered the country. The fee for a work visa ranges from NZ$180 to NZ$280 depending on where it's processed and the type of application.

Eligible travellers who are only interested in short-term employment to supplement their travels can take part in one of NZ's working holiday schemes (WHS). Under these schemes citizens aged 18 to 30 years from 31 countries – including Canada, France, Germany, Ireland, Japan, Malaysia, the Netherlands, Scandinavian countries, the UK and the USA – can apply for a visa. For most nationalities the visa is valid for 12 months. It's only issued to those seeking a genuine working holiday, not permanent work, so you're not supposed to work for one employer for more than three months.

Most WHS-eligible nationals must apply for this visa from within their own country; residents of some countries can apply online. Applicants must have an onward ticket, a passport valid for at least three months from the date they will leave NZ and evidence of at least NZ$4200 in accessible funds. The application fee is NZ$120 regardless of where you apply, and isn't refunded if your application is declined.

The rules vary for different nationalities, so make sure you read up on the specifics of your country's agreement with NZ at www.immigration.govt.nz/migrant/stream/work/workingholiday. See also p430.

WOMEN TRAVELLERS

NZ is generally a very safe place for women travellers, although the usual sensible precautions apply. It's best to avoid walking alone late at night in any of the major cities and towns, and never hitchhike alone. If you're out on the town, always keep enough money aside for a taxi back to your accommodation. The same applies in rural towns where there may be a lot of unlit, semideserted streets between you and your bed. Lone women should also be wary of staying in basic pub accommodation unless it looks safe and well managed.

Sexual harassment is not a widely reported problem in NZ, but of course it does happen.

See www.womentravel.co.nz for more information.

WORK

If you arrive in NZ on a visitor's visa you're not allowed to work for pay. If you're caught breaching this (or any other) visa condition, you could be booted back to where you came from.

If you have been approved for a WHS visa (see p429), look into the possibilities for temporary employment. There's plenty of casual work around, mainly in agriculture (fruit picking, farming), hospitality or ski resorts. Office-based work can be found in IT, banking, finance and telemarketing. Register with a local office-work agency to get started.

Seasonal fruit picking, pruning and harvesting is prime short-term work for visitors. More than 30,000 hectares of apples, kiwi fruit and other fruit and veg are harvested from summer to early autumn. As an optimist once said, 'The pay is bad, but the work is difficult'. Rates are around $10 to $15 an hour for physically taxing toil – turnover of workers is high. You're usually paid by how much you pick (per bin, bucket or kilogram). The picking season is from December to May. Prime North Island picking locations include the Bay of Islands (Kerikeri and Paihia), rural Auckland, Tauranga, Gisborne and Hawke's Bay (Napier and Hastings). Approach prospective employers directly, otherwise local hostels or holiday parks often help travellers to find work. Other agricultural work is available year-round.

Winter work at ski resorts and their service towns includes bartending, waiting, cleaning, ski-tow operation and, if you're properly qualified, ski or snowboard instructing. Check resort websites (p79) for opportunities.

Information

Backpacker publications, hostel managers and other travellers are the best sources of info on local work possibilities.

Kiwi Careers (www.kiwicareers.govt.nz) lists opportunities in various fields (agriculture, creative, health, teaching, volunteer work and recruitment agencies), while **Seek** (www.seek.co.nz) is one of the biggest NZ job-search networks with thousands of jobs listed.

Seasonal Work NZ (www.seasonalwork.co.nz) has a database of thousands of casual jobs, including region-specific 'Harvest Trail' jobs in fruit-picking and agriculture. It gives the contact details of employers looking for workers, rates of pay and nearby accommodation. **Pick NZ** (www.picknz.co.nz) provides a similar service, focusing on seasonal horticultural work.

Base Backpackers (www.stayatbase.com/work) runs an employment service via its website, while the Networking link on **Budget Backpacker Hostels** (BBH; www.bbh.co.nz) lists job vacancies in BBH hostels and a few other possibilities.

Income Tax

There is no escaping it! For the vast majority of travellers, any Kiwi dollars earned in NZ will be subject to income tax, deducted from payments by employers – a process called Pay As You Earn (PAYE). Standard NZ income tax rates are 12.5% for annual salaries up to $17,500, then 21% up to $40,000, 33% up to

$75,000, then 39% for higher incomes. A NZ Accident Compensation Corporation (ACC) scheme levy (1.7%) will also be deducted from your pay packet. At the time of writing, these rates were set to change slightly from April 2011.

If you visit NZ and work for a short time (eg on a working holiday scheme), you may qualify for a tax refund when you leave. Complete a Refund Application – People Leaving New Zealand (document no IR50) form and submit it with your tax return, along with proof of departure (eg air ticket copies) to the Inland Revenue Department (IRD). For more info see the IRD website, or contact the **Inland Revenue Non-Resident Centre** (☎ 03-467 7020; nonres@ird.govt.nz; Private Bag 1932, Dunedin).

IRD Number

Travellers undertaking paid work in NZ must obtain an IRD number. Download the application form from the **Inland Revenue Department** (www.ird.govt.nz) website – use the search function to find document no IR595. An IRD number normally takes eight to 10 working days to be issued.

Transport

TRANSPORT

CONTENTS

New Zealand's isolated location in a distant patch of the South Pacific is a major drawcard, but it also means that unless you travel from Australia, you have to contend with a long-haul flight to get there. As NZ is serviced by good airline and bus networks, travelling around the country is a much less taxing endeavour.

Flights, tours and rail tickets can be booked online at www.lonelyplanet.com/bookings.

GETTING THERE & AWAY

ENTERING THE COUNTRY

Disembarkation in NZ is generally a straightforward affair, with only the usual customs declarations to endure (see Customs, p419) and the uncool scramble to get to the luggage carousel first. Recent global instability has resulted in increased security in NZ airports, in both domestic and international terminals, and you may find customs procedures more time-consuming. One procedure has the Orwellian title Advance Passenger Screening, a system whereby documents that used to be checked after you touched down in NZ (passport, visa etc) are now checked before you board your flight – make sure all your documentation is in order so your check-in is stress-free.

Passport

There are no restrictions when it comes to foreign citizens entering NZ. If you have a current passport and visa (or don't require one; see p429), you should be fine.

AIR

There is a number of competing airlines servicing New Zealand and a wide variety of fares to choose from if you are flying in from Asia, Europe or North America, though ultimately you will still pay a lot for a flight unless you jet in from Australia. NZ's inordinate popularity and abundance of year-round activities mean that almost any time of year airports can be swarming with inbound tourists – if you want to fly at a particularly popular time of year (eg Christmas), book well in advance.

The high season for flights into NZ is during summer (December to February), with slightly less of a premium on fares over the shoulder months (October/November and March/April). The low season generally tallies with the winter months (June to August), though this is still a busy time for airlines ferrying ski bunnies and powder hounds around the country.

Airports & Airlines

Seven NZ airports handle international flights, with Auckland receiving most traffic:
Auckland (AKL; ☎ 0800 247 767, 09-275 0789; www.aucklandairport.co.nz)
Christchurch (CHC; ☎ 03-358 5029; www.christchurchairport.co.nz)

THINGS CHANGE...

The information in this chapter is particularly vulnerable to change. Check directly with the airline or a travel agent to make sure you understand how a fare (and ticket you may buy) works and be aware of the security requirements for international travel. Shop carefully. The details given in this chapter should be regarded as pointers and are not a substitute for your own careful, up-to-date research.

Dunedin (DUD; ☎ 03-486 2879; www.dnairport.co.nz)
Hamilton (HLZ; ☎ 07-848 9027; www.hamiltonairport.co.nz)
Palmerston North (PMR; ☎ 06-351 4415; www.pnairport.co.nz)
Queenstown (ZQN; ☎ 03-450 9031; www.queenstownairport.co.nz)
Wellington (WLG; ☎ 04-385 5100; www.wellingtonairport.co.nz)

AIRLINES FLYING TO & FROM NEW ZEALAND

NZ's own overseas carrier is Air New Zealand, which flies to runways across Europe, North America, eastern Asia and the Pacific. Airlines that connect NZ with international destinations include the following (note that 0800 and 0508 phone numbers mentioned here are for dialling from within NZ only):

Aerolineas Argentinas (airline code AR; ☎ 09-379 3675; www.aerolineas.com.ar)
Air New Zealand (NZ; ☎ 0800 737 000, 09-357 3000; www.airnewzealand.co.nz)
Air Pacific (FJ; ☎ 0800 800 178, 09-379 2404; www.airpacific.com)
Air Vanuatu (NF; ☎ 09-373 3435; www.airvanuatu.com)
Cathay Pacific (CX; ☎ 0800 800 454, 09-379 0861; www.cathaypacific.com)
Emirates (EK; ☎ 0508 364 728, 09-968 2208; www.emirates.com)
Garuda Indonesia (GA; ☎ 09-366 1862; www.garuda-indonesia.com)
Jetstar (JQ; ☎ 0800 800 995; www.jetstar.com)
Korean Air (KE; ☎ 09-914 2000; www.koreanair.com)
Malaysia Airlines (MH; ☎ 0800 777 747, 09-379 3743; www.malaysiaairlines.com)
Pacific Blue (DJ; ☎ 0800 670 000; www.flypacificblue.com)
Polynesian Blue (DJ; ☎ 0800 670 000; www.polynesianblue.com)
Qantas (QF; ☎ 0800 808 767, 09-357 8900; www.qantas.com.au)
Royal Brunei Airlines (BI; ☎ 09-977 2209; www.bruneiair.com)
Singapore Airlines (SQ; ☎ 0800 808 909, 09-379 3209; www.singaporeair.com)
Thai Airways International (TG; ☎ 09-256 8518; www.thaiairways.com)
Virgin Blue (DJ; ☎ 0800 670 000; www.virginblue.com)

Tickets

Automated online ticket sales work well if you're doing a simple one-way or return trip

> ### DEPARTURE TAX
>
> An international departure tax of NZ$25 applies when leaving NZ at all airports except Auckland, payable by anyone aged 12 and over (NZ$10 for children aged two to 11, free for those under two years of age). The tax is not included in the price of airline tickets, but must be paid separately at the airport before you board your flight. Pay via credit card or cash.

on specified dates, but are no substitute for a travel agent with the low-down on special deals, strategies for avoiding layovers and other useful advice.

INTERCONTINENTAL (RTW) TICKETS

If you're flying to NZ from the other side of the world, round-the-world (RTW) tickets can be real bargains. They're generally put together by the three biggest airline alliances, **Star Alliance** (www.staralliance.com), **Oneworld** (www.oneworldalliance.com) and **Skyteam** (www.skyteam.com), and give you a limited period (usually a year) in which to loop the planet. You can go anywhere the participating airlines go, as long as you stay within the prescribed kilometre extents or number of stops and don't backtrack when flying between continents. Backtracking is generally permitted within a single continent, though with certain restrictions; see the websites for details.

An alternative type of RTW ticket is one put together by a travel agent or RTW–specialist websites (see p434 for some listings). These are often more expensive than airline RTW fares but allow you to devise your own itinerary.

Bargain RTW tickets start from around UK£600 ex-UK, US$1500 ex-USA.

CIRCLE PACIFIC TICKETS

A Circle Pacific ticket is similar to a RTW ticket but covers a more limited region, using a combination of airlines to connect Australia, NZ, North America and Asia, with stopover options in the Pacific islands. As with RTW tickets, there are restrictions on how many stopovers you can take.

ONLINE TICKET SITES

For online ticket bookings, including RTW fares, start with the following websites:

TRANSPORT

TRANSPORT

CLIMATE CHANGE & TRAVEL

Climate change is a serious threat to the ecosystems that humans rely upon, and air travel is the fastest-growing contributor to the problem. Lonely Planet regards travel, overall, as a global benefit, but believes we all have a responsibility to limit our personal impact on global warming.

Flying & Climate Change

Pretty much every form of motor travel generates CO_2 (the main cause of human-induced climate change) but planes are far and away the worst offenders, not just because of the sheer distances they allow us to travel, but because they release greenhouse gases high into the atmosphere. The statistics are frightening: two people taking a return flight between Europe and the US will contribute as much to climate change as an average household's gas and electricity consumption over a whole year.

Carbon Offset Schemes

Climatecare.org and other websites use 'carbon calculators' that allow jetsetters to offset the greenhouse gases they are responsible for with contributions to energy-saving projects and other climate-friendly initiatives in the developing world – including projects in India, Honduras, Kazakhstan and Uganda.

Lonely Planet, together with Rough Guides and other concerned partners in the travel industry, supports the carbon offset scheme run by climatecare.org. Lonely Planet offsets all of its staff and author travel.

For more information check out our website: lonelyplanet.com.

Air Brokers (www.airbrokers.com) This US company specialises in cheaper tickets. To fly LA-Tahiti-Auckland-Sydney-Bangkok-Hong Kong-LA costs around US$2200 (excluding taxes).

Cheap Flights (www.cheapflights.com) Informative site with specials, destination information and flight searches from the USA.

Cheapest Flights (www.cheapestflights.co.uk) Cheap worldwide flights from the UK; get in early for the bargains.

Expedia (www.expedia.com) Microsoft's travel site; good for USA-related flights.

Flight Centre International (www.flightcentre.com) Respected operator handling direct flights, with sites for NZ, Australia, the UK, the USA, Canada and South Africa.

Flights.com (www.flights.com) International site for flights; cheap fares and an easy-to-search database.

Roundtheworldflights.com (www.roundtheworldflights.com) This excellent site allows you to build your own trip from the UK with up to six stops. A six-stop trip including Asia, Australia, NZ and the USA costs from UK£550 in the NZ winter.

STA Travel (www.statravel.com) Prominent in international student travel (but you don't have to be a student). Linked to worldwide STA sites.

Travel Online (www.travelonline.co.nz) Good place to check worldwide flights from NZ.

Travel.com.au (www.travel.com.au) Good Australian site; look up fares and flights to/from the country.

Travelocity (www.travelocity.com) US site that allows you to search fares (in US dollars) from/to practically anywhere.

Asia

Most Asian countries offer fairly competitive air-fare deals, with Bangkok, Singapore and Hong Kong being the best places to shop around for discount tickets.

Common one-way fares to Auckland cost approximately US$750 from Singapore, US$850 from Kuala Lumpur, Bangkok and Hong Kong, and US$775 from Tokyo. Going the other way, return fares from Auckland to Singapore cost around NZ$1800, and around NZ$2100 to Kuala Lumpur, Bangkok, Hong Kong and Tokyo, depending on which airline you travel with.

Hong Kong's travel market can be unpredictable, but excellent bargains are sometimes available. **Phoenix Services** (☎ 2722 7378) is recommended.

STA Travel (Bangkok ☎ 02-236 0262; www.statravel.co.th; Singapore ☎ 6737 7188; www.statravel.com.sg; Tokyo ☎ 03-5391 2922; www.statravel.co.jp) has offices in major Asian cities.

Australia

Air New Zealand and Qantas operate a network of flights linking key NZ cities with most major Australian gateway cities, while quite a few other international airlines include NZ and Australia on their Asia-Pacific routes.

Cohorts Pacific Blue, Virgin Blue and Polynesian Blue offer direct flights between Auckland and Wellington and Australian east-coast capitals, with connections on the domestic Virgin Blue network to many other Australian cities.

Qantas' budget subsidiary, Jetstar, flies between Auckland and Sydney, Cairns and the Gold Coast.

If you book early, shop around and have the gods smiling upon you, you may pay under AU$180 for a one-way fare on a budget carrier from either Sydney or Melbourne to Auckland, Christchurch or Wellington. More common prices are from AU$200 to AU$250 one way. If you are visiting the South Island, you can fly into Auckland and out of Christchurch to save backtracking, but you may not get the cheapest fares with this itinerary.

From key NZ cities, you'll pay between NZ$240 and NZ$280 for a one-way ticket to an Australian east-coast city. There's usually not a significant difference in price between seasons, as this is a popular route year-round. The intense competition, however, inevitably results in some tasty discounting.

For some reasonably priced fares, try an Australian capital-city branch of **STA Travel** (☎ 134 782; www.statravel.com.au). Another good option, also with dozens of offices strewn around the country, is **Flight Centre** (☎ 133 133; www.flightcentre.com.au).

Canada

The air routes flown from Canada are similar to those from mainland USA, with most Toronto and Vancouver flights stopping in a US city such as Los Angeles or Honolulu before continuing to NZ. Air New Zealand has direct flights between Auckland and Vancouver year-round.

The air fares sold by Canadian discount air-ticket sellers (consolidators) tend to be about 10% higher than those sold in the USA. **Travel CUTS** (☎ 866 246 9762; www.travelcuts.com) is Canada's national student travel agency and has offices in all major cities.

Return fares from Vancouver to Auckland cost between C$1800 and C$2100 via the US west coast. From Toronto, fares cost around

C$2000. One-way fares from NZ start at around NZ$1800 to Toronto and NZ$1500 to Vancouver.

Continental Europe

Frankfurt and London are the major arrival and departure points for flights to and from NZ, both with extensive connections to other European cities. From these two launching pads, most flights to NZ travel via one of the Asian capitals. Return air fares from NZ to key European hubs such as Paris and Frankfurt usually cost between NZ$2100 and NZ$2600.

A solid option in the Dutch travel industry is **Holland International** (www.hollandinternational.nl). From Amsterdam, return fares start at around €1400.

In Germany, good travel agencies include the Berlin branch of **STA Travel** (☎ 069-7430 3292; www.statravel.de). Return fares from Frankfurt start at around €1400.

In France, return fares from Paris start from €1200. Recommended companies include the following:

Nouvelles Frontières (☎ 0149 206 400; www.nouvelles-frontieres.fr/nf)

Odysia (☎ 0825 082 525; www.odysia.fr)

Voyageurs du Monde (☎ 0892 235 656; www.vdm.com/vdm)

UK & Ireland

Depending on which airline you travel with from the UK, flights to NZ go via Asia or the USA. If you fly via Asia you can often make stopovers in countries such as India, Thailand, Singapore and Australia; in the other direction, stopover possibilities include New York, Los Angeles, Honolulu and sundry Pacific islands.

Discount air travel is big business in London. Advertisements for many travel agencies appear in the travel pages of the weekend broadsheet newspapers, in *Time Out*, in the *Evening Standard* and in the free magazine *TNT*.

Typical one-way/return fares from London to Auckland start at around £550/750; note that June, July and mid-December fares can go up by as much as 30%. From NZ you can expect to pay between NZ$2500 and NZ$3000 for return fares to London.

Popular agencies in the UK:

Flight Centre (☎ 0800 587 0058; www.flightcentre.co.uk)

STA Travel (☎ 0871 230 0040; www.statravel.co.uk)
Trailfinders (☎ 0845 058 5858; www.trailfinders.co.uk)

USA

Most flights between the North American mainland and NZ are to/from west-coast USA, with the bulk routed through Los Angeles but some going through San Francisco. Some airlines offer flights via various Pacific islands (Hawaii, Tahiti, Cook Islands).

San Francisco is the ticket consolidator capital of America, although some good deals can be found in Los Angeles, New York and other big cities. **STA Travel** (☎ 800 781 4040; www.statravel.com) has offices all over the USA.

Return tickets to NZ from the US west coast start around US$1100/1350 in the NZ winter/summer; fares from the east coast start at US$1850 in both seasons. Return fares from NZ to the US west coast are around NZ$2200; to New York NZ$2800.

SEA

It is possible (though by no means easy or safe) to make your way between New Zealand and Australia, and some smaller Pacific islands, by hitching rides or crewing on yachts. Try asking around at harbours, marinas, and yacht and sailing clubs. Popular yachting harbours in NZ include the Bay of Islands and Whangarei (both located in Northland), Auckland and Wellington. March and April are the best months to look for boats heading to Australia. From Fiji, October to November is a peak departure season as cyclones are starting to spin in that neck of the woods.

There are no passenger liners operating to/from NZ and finding a berth on a cargo ship (much less enjoying the experience) is no easy task.

GETTING AROUND

AIR

Those who have limited time to get between NZ's attractions can make the most of a widespread network of intra- and inter-island flights.

Airlines in New Zealand

The country's major domestic carrier, Air New Zealand, has an aerial network covering most of the country. Australia-based Jetstar also flies between main urban areas.

Several small-scale regional operators provide essential transport services to the small outlying islands such as Great Barrier Island in the Hauraki Gulf. Regional operators in the North Island include the following:

Air New Zealand (☎ 0800 737 000, 09-357 3000; www.airnewzealand.co.nz) Offers flights between 26 domestic destinations.

Air2there.com (☎ 0800 777 000, 04-904 5130; www.air2there.com) Connects destinations across Cook Strait, including Blenheim, Napier, Nelson and Wellington.

Fly My Sky (☎ 09-256 7025; www.flymysky.co.nz) At least three flights daily from Auckland to Great Barrier Island.

Golden Bay Air (☎ 0800 588 885, 03-525 8725; www.capitalair.co.nz) Flies regularly between Wellington and Takaka in Golden Bay.

Great Barrier Airlines (☎ 0800 900 600, 09-275 9120; www.greatbarrierairlines.co.nz) Plies the skies over Great Barrier Island, Auckland and Whangarei.

Jetstar (☎ 0800 800 995; www.jetstar.com) Joins the dots between key tourism centres.

Salt Air Xpress (☎ 09-402 8338; www.saltair.co.nz) Flies to Kerikeri from Whangarei and Auckland's North Shore.

Air Passes

With discounting being the norm these days, and a number of budget airlines now serving the trans-Tasman route as well as the Pacific islands, the value of air passes isn't as red-hot as in the past.

Air New Zealand offers the **South Pacific Airpass** (☎ 1800 262 1234; www.airnewzealand.com), valid for selected journeys within NZ, and between NZ, Australia and a number of Pacific islands. The pass is only available to nonresidents of these countries, and must be issued outside NZ. Passes are issued in conjunction with an international ticket (with any airline) and are valid for the life of that ticket.

The pass involves purchasing coupons for domestic flights (one-way from NZ$99 to NZ$378, depending on distance), or flights to/from major Australian cities or Pacific islands including Fiji, New Caledonia and Tonga, and as far afield as the Cook Islands and Samoa (one-way from NZ$231 to NZ$855).

BICYCLE

Touring cyclists proliferate in NZ, particularly over summer – the roads and trails run thick with fluoro-clad creatures with aero-dynamic heads. The country is popular with cyclists because it's clean, green and relatively uncrowded, and has lots of cheap accommodation (including camping) and easily accessible freshwater. The roads are generally in good nick, and the climate generally not too hot or too cold (except on the South Island's rain-soaked West Coast). The many hills make for hard going at times, but there are expansive flats and lows to accompany the highs. As in any country, road traffic is the biggest danger, and you'll hear numerous cyclists' tales about inconsiderate or unsafe behaviour from drivers. Trucks overtaking too close to the cyclist are a particular threat. Take care!

Bikes and cycling gear (to rent or buy) are readily available in the main centres, as are bicycle repair shops. A major nationwide project has been in motion since late 2009, expanding and improving NZ's network of bike trails. See the Ministry of Tourism's website for updates (www.tourism.govt.nz).

By law all cyclists must wear an approved safety helmet (or risk a fine); it's also vital to have good reflective gear, so that you can be easily seen by cars or trucks overtaking from behind. Cyclists who use public transport will find that major bus lines and trains only take bicycles on a 'space available' basis (meaning bikes may not be allowed on) and charge up to $10. Some of the smaller shuttle bus companies, on the other hand, make sure they have storage space for bikes, which they carry for a surcharge.

If importing your own bike or transporting it by plane within NZ, check with the relevant airline for costs and the degree of dismantling and packing required.

Hire

Rates offered by most outfits for renting road or mountain bikes – not including the discounted fees or freebies offered by accommodation places to their guests – are anywhere from $10 to $20 per hour and $30 to $50 per day.

Purchase

Bicycles can be readily bought in the North Island's larger cities, but prices for newer models can be quite high. For a decent hybrid bike or rigid mountain bike you'll pay anywhere from $700 to $1600, though

you can get a cheap one for around $400 to $500 – however, then you still need to get panniers, a helmet and other essential touring gear, and the cost quickly climbs. Arguably you are better off buying a used bike (assuming you can't bring your own over), but finding something that is in good enough shape for a long road trip isn't always as easy as it sounds. Other options include the post-Christmas sales and midyear stocktakes, when newish cycles can be heavily discounted.

BOAT

NZ may be an island nation but there's minimal long-distance water transport around the country. Obvious exceptions include the boat services between Auckland and various islands in the Hauraki Gulf (see p121) and the inter-island ferries that chug across Cook Strait between Wellington and Picton (see p400).

BUS

Bus travel in NZ is relatively easy and well organised, with services transporting you to the far reaches of the North Island (including the start/end of various walking tracks), but it can be expensive, tedious and time-consuming. The bus 'terminals' in smaller places usually comprise a parking spot outside a prominent local business.

The dominant bus company is **InterCity** (☎ Auckland 09-583 5780, Wellington 04-385 0520, Christchurch 03-365 1113, Dunedin 03-471 7143; www.intercity.co.nz), which also has an extra-comfort travel and sightseeing arm called **Newmans Coach Lines** (☎ 09-623 1504; www.newmanscoach.co.nz). InterCity can drive you to just about anywhere on the North Island.

Smaller regional operators running key routes or covering a lot of ground on the North Island include:

Alpine Scenic Tours (☎ 07-378 7412; www.alpine scenictours.co.nz) Has services around Taupo and into Tongariro National Park, plus the ski fields around Mt Ruapehu and Mt Tongariro.

Bay Xpress (☎ 0800 422 997, 06-873 4984; www.bayxpress.co.nz) Connects Wellington with Hastings and Napier via Palmerston North.

Dalroy Express (☎ 0508 465 622, 06-759-0197; www.dalroytours.co.nz) Operates a daily service between Auckland and Hawera via New Plymouth and Hamilton. Also runs from Auckland to Pahia, and from Hamilton to Rotorua and Taupo.

Go Kiwi Shuttles (☎ 07-866 0336; www.go-kiwi. co.nz) Links places like Auckland, Rotorua and Hamilton with various towns across the Coromandel Peninsula.

Magic Travellers Network (☎ 09-358 5600; www. magicbus.co.nz) Has a useful collection of passes available, covering both islands or each individually.

Naked Bus (☎ 0900 625 33; www.nakedbus.com) Low-cost routes across the North (and South) Island, from Auckland to Wellington and most places in between.

Waitomo Wanderer (☎ 0508 926 337, 03-477 9083; www.waitomotours.co.nz) Does a loop from Rotorua to Waitomo.

White Star City to City (☎ 06-759 0197; www.white starbus.co.nz) Shuttles between Wellington, Palmerston North, Wanganui and New Plymouth.

InterCity Bus Passes

InterCity (www.intercity.co.nz; ☎ Auckland 09-583 5780, Wellington 04-385 0520) offers bus passes for the North Island. If you are planning to cover a lot of ground, passes can be cheaper than paying as you go, but they lock you into using InterCity buses (rather than, say, the convenient shuttle buses that cover much of the country). There's a 15% discount for YHA, BBH and VIP backpacker members; there may be an additional reservation charge ($3 per sector, depending on the agent).

NORTH ISLAND PASSES

There are seven InterCity North Island passes:

Thermal Explorer ($39; 1-day minimum travel) Rotorua to Taupo return.

Bay Escape ($106; 1-day minimum travel) Auckland to Paihia and back, via Whangarei.

Eastern Wanderer ($119; 3-day minimum travel) Rotorua to Napier circuit via Whakatane, Gisborne, Taupo.

Maui's Catch ($169; 3-day minimum travel) Auckland to Wellington via Waitomo, Rotorua, Taupo, Napier and Palmerston North. Available in both directions.

Volcanic Explorer ($184; 2-day minimum travel) Auckland to Rotorua loop via Tauranga, Taupo and Waitomo.

Northland Explorer ($205; 3-day minimum travel) Auckland to Paihia return via Whangarei, with a daytrip to Cape Reinga.

North Island Discovery ($243; 4-day minimum travel) Auckland to Wellington return via Waitomo, Rotorua, Taupo, Napier, Palmerston North and Hamilton. Available in both directions.

NATIONWIDE PASSES

InterCity's pan-NZ **Travelpass** (☎ 0800 339 966; www.travelpass.co.nz) combines bus travel with a

Cook Strait ferry crossing. There are three hop-on/hop-off passes available, each valid for a year. Adult and child prices are the same:

Kia Ora New Zealand ($579; 7-day minimum travel) A one-way trip between Auckland and Christchurch via Rotorua, Wellington, Dunedin, Queenstown and Milford Sound. Available in both directions.

Kiwi Explorer ($623; 9-day minimum travel) A one-way trip between Auckland and Christchurch via Rotorua, Napier, Wellington, the West Coast, Milford Sound and Queenstown. Available in both directions.

Aotearoa Adventurer ($1283; 14-day minimum travel) A monster loop from Auckland to Milford Sound and back, via Northland, Rotorua, Wellington, Christchurch, Queenstown, the West Coast and Napier.

The appropriately named **Flexi-Pass** (☎ 0800 222 146; www.flexipass.co.nz) is valid for one year and allows you to travel pretty much anywhere (and in any direction) on the InterCity network; you can get on and off wherever you like and can change bookings up to two hours before departure without penalty.

The Flexi-Pass is purchased in five-hour blocks of travel time, from a minimum of 15 hours ($169) up to a maximum of 60 hours ($605) – the average cost of each block becomes cheaper the more hours you buy. You can also top up the pass if you need more time.

Seat Classes

There are no allocated economy or luxury classes on New Zealand buses, and smoking is a no-no.

Reservations

Over the summer, school holidays and public holidays, book well ahead on the more popular routes. At other times you should have few problems accessing your preferred service, but if your long-term travel plans rely on catching a particular bus, book at least a day or two ahead just to make sure you get a seat.

InterCity fares vary widely depending on availability and how the tickets are booked (online or via an agent). The best prices are generally available online, booked a few weeks in advance.

CAR & MOTORCYCLE

The best way to explore the country in depth is to have your own transport, which allows you to create your own leisurely, flexible itinerary. Good-value car- and campervan-hire rates are not hard to track down; alternatively, consider buying your own set of wheels.

Automobile Association (AA)

New Zealand's **Automobile Association** (AA; ☎ 24hr road service 0800 500 222; www.aa.co.nz) provides emergency breakdown services, has excellent touring maps and detailed guides to accommodation (from holiday parks to motels and B&Bs).

Members of foreign automobile associations should bring their membership cards as many of these bodies have reciprocal agreements with NZ's AA.

Driving Licence

International visitors to New Zealand can use their home country's driving licence – if your licence isn't in English, it's a good idea to carry a certified translation with you.

Alternatively, use an International Driving Permit (IDP), which will usually be issued on the spot (valid for 12 months) by your home country's automobile association.

Fuel

Fuel is available from service stations with the well-known international brand names. LPG (gas) is not always stocked by rural suppliers; if you're on gas it's safer to have dual fuel capability. Prices vary from place to place, but basically petrol (gasoline) isn't pumped cheaply in NZ, with per-litre costs at the time of research averaging around $1.65. More remote destinations may charge a small fortune to fill your tank and you're better off getting fuel in a bigger centre before you reach them.

Hire

CAMPERVAN

Check your rear-view mirror on any far-flung NZ road and you'll likely see a shiny white campervan (aka mobile home, motor home, RV) packed with liberated travellers, mountain bikes and portable barbecues cruising along behind you.

Campervanning around New Zealand is big business. It's flexible and affordable, and you can leave the trampled tourist trails behind and crank up the AC/DC as loud as

NORTH ISLAND ROAD DISTANCES (km)

Distances are approximate only

	Auckland	Cape Reinga	Dargaville	Gisborne	Hamilton	Hicks Bay	Kaitaia	Napier	New Plymouth	Paihia	Palmerston North	Rotorua	Taupo	Tauranga	Thames	Waitomo Caves	Whanganui	Wellington	Whakatane
Cape Reinga	430																		
Dargaville	175	280																	
Gisborne	490	920	675																
Hamilton	125	555	300	390															
Hicks Bay	510	945	690	180	400														
Kaitaia	325	115	170	820	440	800													
Napier	420	860	590	215	300	395	735												
New Plymouth	360	790	530	570	240	580	680	410											
Paihia	225	220	130	720	340	720	120	645	590										
Palmerston North	520	950	690	395	400	570	840	180	230	750									
Rotorua	235	670	405	295	110	285	550	220	300	460	325								
Taupo	280	720	450	330	155	365	600	140	300	505	250	80							
Tauranga	210	635	385	290	110	290	525	300	330	435	400	85	155						
Thames	115	540	280	410	110	400	430	360	340	345	470	170	210	115					
Waitomo Caves	200	620	360	440	75	440	515	300	180	420	340	165	170	150	175				
Whanganui	455	880	615	465	330	645	770	250	160	670	75	310	225	375	430	270			
Wellington	640	1080	805	530	520	730	960	320	350	860	140	450	375	530	590	460	190		
Whakatane	300	740	470	200	190	204	620	300	380	525	410	85	160	95	210	240	380	540	
Whangarei	160	280	55	640	280	650	165	580	515	70	680	390	430	350	265	345	600	790	450

TRANSPORT

TRANSPORT

BACKPACKER VAN RENTALS

There are several budget players in the campervan industry, offering slick deals and funky, well-kitted-out vehicles to attract young, independent travellers (the kind who would shun the larger, more traditional box-on-wheels). All companies offer living, sleeping and cooking equipment, 24-hour roadside assistance, and maps and travel tips. Rates are competitive (from $35 per day May to September; from $70 per day December to February). Check out the following:

- **Backpacker Sleeper Vans** (☎ 0800 325 939, 03-359 4731; www.sleepervans.co.nz) Low-cost family-run business.
- **Escape Rentals** (☎ 0800 216 171; www.escaperentals.co.nz) 'The freedom to sleep around' – loud, original artwork on van exteriors, pitched squarely at young travellers after something different. DVDs, TVs and outdoor barbecues available for rent.
- **Jucy** (☎ 0800 399 736, 09-374 4360; www.jucy.co.nz) The flashpacker's vehicle of choice.
- **Spaceships** (☎ 0800 772 237, 09-526 2130; www.spaceshipsrentals.co.nz) The customised 'Swiss Army Knife of campervans', with extras including DVD and CD players, roof racks and solar showers.
- **Wicked Campers** (☎ 0800 246 870; www.wicked-campers.co.nz) Spray-painted vans bedecked with everything/everyone from Mr Spock to Sly Stone.

hell! Most towns of any size have a camping ground or campervan park with powered sites for around $35 per night. There are also places where 'freedom camping' is permitted, but you should never just *assume* it's OK to camp somewhere. Always ask a local first. Check at the local i-SITE or DOC office, or even with local commercial camping grounds. If you are freedom camping, please treat the area with respect – if your van doesn't have toilet facilities, find a public loo.

Visit www.camping.org.nz for more information and tips on freedom camping.

You can hire campervans from assorted companies, prices varying with time of year, how big you want your home-on-wheels to be, and the length of the rental. Major operators:

Britz (☎ 0800 831 900, 09-255 3910; www.britz.co.nz)
Kea Campers (☎ 0800 520 052, 09-441 7833; www.keacampers.com)
Maui (☎ 0800 651 080, 09-255 3910; www.maui.co.nz)

A small van for two people typically has a mini-kitchen and fold-out dining table, the latter transforming into a double bed when dinner is done 'n' dusted. Larger 'superior' two-berth vans include shower and toilet. Four- to six-berth campervans are the size of trucks (and similarly sluggish) and, besides

the extra space, usually contain a toilet and shower.

Over summer, rates offered by the main rental firms for two-/four-/six-berth vans start at around $160/290/320 per day, dropping to as low as $50/80/95 in winter for month-long rentals; industry infighting often sees even lower rates.

CAR

Competition between car-rental companies in NZ is torrid – rates tend to be variable and lots of special deals come and go (we've heard of discounted rates as low as $15 per day, so shop around). Car rental is most competitive in the cities. The main thing to remember when assessing your options is distance – if you want to travel far, you need unlimited kilometres. Some (but not all) companies require drivers to be at least 21 years old – ask around.

Sizable multinational companies, with offices or agents in most major cities, towns and larger airports:

Avis (☎ 0800 655 111, 09-526-2847; www.avis.co.nz)
Budget (☎ 0800 283 438, 09-529 7784; www.budget.co.nz)
Europcar (☎ 0800 800 115, 03-357 0920; www.europcar.co.nz)
Hertz (☎ 0800 654 321, 03-520 3044; www.hertz.co.nz)
Thrifty (☎ 0800 737 070, 03-359 2720; www.thrifty.co.nz)

Local rental firms and firms with limited locations can also be found in the *Yellow Pages;* see the regional chapters in this guide. These are almost always cheaper than the big boys – sometimes half the price – but the cheap rates may come with serious restrictions, vehicles are often older, and with less formality sometimes comes less protective legal structure for renters.

Affordable, independent operators with national networks:

Ace Rental Cars (☎ 0800 502 277, 09-303 3112; www.acerentalcars.co.nz)

Apex Rentals (☎ 0800 939 597, 03-379 6897; www.apexrentals.co.nz)

Ezy Rentals (☎ 0800 399 736, 09-374 4360; www.ezy.co.nz)

Go Rentals (☎ 0800 467 368, 09-525 7321; www.gorentals.co.nz)

Omega Rental Cars (☎ 0800 525 210, 09-377 5573; www.omegarentalcars.com)

Pegasus Rental Cars (☎ 0800 803 580, 03-548 2852; www.rentalcars.co.nz)

The big firms sometimes offer one-way rentals (eg collect a car in Auckland, leave it in Wellington), but there are a variety of restrictions, and a one-way drop-off fee may apply. However, for rentals of a month or more, one-way fees are often waived. On the other hand, an operator in Wellington may need to get a vehicle back to Auckland and will offer an amazing one-way deal (sometimes for free!).

If you are also travelling to the South Island, car-hire firms suggest (some will insist) that you don't take their vehicles between islands on the Cook Strait ferries. Instead, you leave your car at either the Wellington or Picton terminal and pick up another hire car once you have crossed the strait. This saves you paying to transport a vehicle on the ferries, and is a pain-free exercise.

The major car-rental companies offer a choice of either unlimited kilometres, or 100km (or thereabouts) per day free, plus so many cents per subsequent kilometre. Daily rates in the main cities typically start at around $40 per day for a compact, late-model, Japanese car, and around $75 for medium-sized cars (including GST, unlimited kilometres and insurance). Local firms start at around $30 per day for the smallest vehicle option.

It's obviously cheaper if you rent for a week or more and there are often low-season and weekend discounts. Credit cards are the usual payment method.

MOTORCYCLE

Born to be wild? NZ has great terrain for motorcycle touring, despite the fickle weather in some regions. If you're tempted to bring your own motorcycle into NZ, be aware that this will entail an expensive shipping exercise, valid registration in the country of origin and a *Carnet de Passages en Douanes* (a customs document that identifies your motor vehicle).

Most of the North Island's motorcycle-hire shops are located in Auckland, where you can hire anything from a little 50cc moped (aka nifty-fifty) for zipping around town, to a throbbing 750cc touring motorcycle and beyond. **New Zealand Motorcycle Rentals & Tours** (☎ 09-634 9118; www.nzbike.com) has Yamahas, BMWs, Hondas and Harleys from $120 to $395 per day. Rates vary with the size of the bike, the length of the rental and the season.

Insurance

When it comes to renting a vehicle, you should know exactly what your liability is in the event of an accident. Rather than risk paying out a large amount of cash if you do have an accident (minor collisions are common in NZ), you can take out your own comprehensive insurance policy, or (the usual option) pay an additional daily amount to the rental company for an 'insurance excess reduction' policy. This brings the amount of excess you must pay in the event of an accident down from around $1500 or $2000 to around $150 or $200. Smaller operators offering cheap rates often have a compulsory insurance excess, taken as a credit-card bond, of around $900.

Most insurance agreements won't cover the cost of damage to glass (including the windscreen) or tyres, and insurance coverage is often invalidated on beaches and certain rough (4WD) unsealed roads – always read the fine print.

For information on the country's no-fault Accident Compensation Corporation scheme, see p423.

Purchase

For longer stays and/or for groups, buying a car and then selling it at the end of your travels can be one of the cheapest and best ways to see New Zealand. You can often pick up a car as cheap as (or cheaper than) a one- or two-month rental, and you should be able to get back most of your money when you sell it. The danger, of course, is that you could buy a lemon that breaks down every five minutes.

Auckland is the easiest place for travellers to buy a car. An easy option for a cheap car is to scour the notice boards of backpacker places, where other travellers sell their cars before moving on; sometimes you can pick up an old car for just a few hundred dollars. Some backpackers specials are so cheap it may be worth taking the risk that they may expire on you. Besides, these vehicles often come complete with water containers, tools, road maps and someimes even camping gear.

Car markets and car auctions are also worth investigating – check out information on car markets in the Auckland section (p119). At auctions you can pick up cheap cars from around $1000 to $6000 – **Turners Auctions** (☎ 09-580 9360; www.turners.co.nz) is the country's largest such outfit, with 10 locations.

Make sure that any car you buy has a Warrant of Fitness (WoF) and that the registration lasts for a reasonable period. A WoF certificate, proving that the car is roadworthy, is valid for six months but must be less than 28 days old when you buy a car. To transfer registration, both you and the seller are legally required to independently notify **Land Transport New Zealand** (www.landtransport.govt.nz) of the change of ownership within seven days. To do so, fill out a *Notice of Change of Ownership of Motor Vehicle* form (MR 13 or MR 13B), which can be filed at any AA office or post office. Papers are sent to you by mail within 10 days (you'll need an address!). If needed, registration can be purchased for six months ($268) or for a year ($388).

Car buyers should also take out third-party insurance, covering the cost of repairs to another vehicle in an accident that is your fault: try the **Automobile Association** (AA; ☎ 0800 500 231; www.aainsurance.co.nz). The no-fault Accident Compensation Corporation scheme (p423) covers personal injury, but make sure you have travel insurance as well (p422).

Car inspections are highly recommended as they will protect you against any dodgy WoFs (such scams have been reported in the past) and may save you a lot of grief and repair bills later on. Various car-inspection companies will check a car you intend to buy for less than $150; you'll find them at car auctions for on-the-spot inspections, or they will come to you. Try **Vehicle Inspection New Zealand** (VINZ; ☎ 0800 468 469; www.vinz.co.nz).

The AA also offers a mobile inspection service – it is slightly cheaper if you bring the car to an AA-approved mechanic. AA checks are thorough, but most regular garages will inspect a car for less.

Before you a vehicle, buy it's wise to confirm the ownership of the vehicle, and find out if there's anything dodgy about the car in question (eg any outstanding debts on it). A number of companies offer this service, including the AA's **LemonCheck** (☎ 04-233 8590; www.lemoncheck.co.nz). A search costs $25 and is done using the Vehicle Identification Number (VIN; found on a plate near the engine block) or licence-plate number.

BUY-BACK DEALS

One way of getting around the hassles of buying and selling a vehicle privately is to enter into a buy-back arrangement with a car or motorcycle dealer. However, dealers may find ways of knocking down the price when you return the vehicle (even if it was agreed to in writing), often by pointing out expensive repairs that allegedly will be required to gain the WoF certificate needed to transfer the registration.

The buy-back amount varies, but may be 50% less than the purchase price – in a strictly financial sense, hiring or buying and selling the vehicle yourself (if you have the time) is usually a much better idea.

Road Hazards

The full spectrum of drivers and driving habits occurs on NZ roads, from the no-fuss motorist who doesn't mind pulling over to let you past, to back-road tailgaters who believe they know a particular stretch of bitumen so well they can go as fast as they like, despite narrow, twisting roads.

Traffic is usually pretty light, but it's easy to get stuck behind a slow-moving truck or campervan on uphill climbs – pack plenty of patience. There are also lots of gravel or dirt roads to explore, which require a more cautious driving approach than for sealed roads. And watch out for sheep!

Road Rules

Kiwis drive on the left-hand side of the road and all cars are right-hand drive. A 'give way to the right' rule applies and is interpreted to a rather strange extreme here – if you're turning left and an oncoming vehicle is turning right into the same street, you have to give way to it.

Speed limits on the open road are generally 100km/h; in built-up areas the limit is usually 50km/h. An 'LSZ' (Limited Speed Zone) sign on the open road means that the speed limit is reduced from 100km/h to 50km/h in certain conditions – this applies when conditions are unsafe due to bad weather, limited visibility, pedestrians, cyclists or animals on the road, excessive traffic, or lousy road conditions. Speed cameras and radars are used extensively.

At single-lane bridges (of which there are a surprisingly large number), a smaller red arrow pointing in your direction of travel means that *you* give way, so slow down as you approach and pull a little to the side if you see a car approaching the other end of the bridge.

All new cars in New Zealand have seat belts back and front and it's the law to wear them – you are risking a fine if you don't. Small children must be belted into an approved safety seat.

Drivers might want to buy a copy of the *New Zealand Road Code,* which will tell you all you need to know about life on the road. Versions applicable to both cars and motorcycles are available at AA offices and bookshops, or you can check the online rundown of road rules on the **Land Transport New Zealand** (www.landtransport.govt.nz/roadcode) website.

HITCHING

Until quite recently it was quite fair and logical to think, 'If there's anywhere in the world where I can still hitch a ride, NZ is it.' However, a few unsavoury incidents in recent years suggest that the country is no longer immune from the perils of solo hitching (especially for women). Those who decide to hitchhike should understand that they are taking a small but potentially serious risk. Prospective hitchers will be safer if they travel in pairs and let someone know where they are planning to go. That said, it's not unusual to see hitchhikers by the side of country roads (signalling with a thumbs-up or a downward-pointed finger), although extensive bus networks and cheap car-rental rates mean that hitching a ride isn't as common among travellers as it once was.

People looking for travelling companions for car journeys around the country often leave notices on boards in backpacker accommodation. The website www.carshare.co.nz is an excellent resource for people seeking or offering a lift.

LOCAL TRANSPORT
Bus, Train & Tram

Most of NZ's urban buses have been privatised. Larger cities have fairly extensive bus services but, with a few honourable exceptions, they are mainly daytime, weekday operations; on weekends, particularly on Sunday, bus services can be hard to find or may cease altogether. Negotiating the inner-city area in Auckland is made easier by the Link and City Circuit buses.

The only city with a decent train service is Wellington, which has five suburban routes.

Taxi

The main cities have plenty of taxis and even small towns may have a local service. Taxis cruise the busy areas in Auckland and Wellington, but elsewhere you usually have to either phone for one or find a taxi rank.

TRAIN

In NZ you definitely travel on the train for the journey, not just to get somewhere. **Tranz Scenic** (☎ 0800 872 467; www.tranzscenic.co.nz) operates the visually stunning *Overlander* route between Auckland and Wellington, and the weekday *Capital Connection* commuter service between Palmerston North and Wellington.

Reservations can be made through Tranz Scenic directly, or at most train stations (notably *not* at Palmerston North or Hamilton), travel agents and visitor information centres, where you can also pick up booklets detailing timetables. Ask about discount fares – reductions apply for children (50% off standard fares), seniors and students (30% off), and holders of backpackers cards (20% off). Discounts don't apply on the *Overlander* or *Capital Connection* services. See regional chapters for fare and timetable info.

Train Passes

Given NZ's limited rail network, buying a train pass isn't particularly good value, even if you're considering extending your travel to the South Island.

Tranz Scenic's **Scenic Rail Pass** (www.tranzscenic. co.nz) allows unlimited travel on all of its rail services (with the exception of the *Capital Connection*), with the option of including passage on the Interislander ferry between Wellington and Picton. A pass (with ferry trip) lasting two weeks costs $517/394 per adult/child.

Health Dr David Millar

New Zealand is one of the healthiest countries in the world in which to travel. The risk of diseases such as malaria and typhoid is unheard of, and thanks to NZ's quarantine standards, even some animal diseases such as rabies have yet to be recorded. The absence of poisonous snakes or other dangerous animals makes this a very safe region to get off the beaten track and out into the beautiful countryside.

BEFORE YOU GO

Since most vaccines don't produce immunity until at least two weeks after they're given, visit a physician four to eight weeks before departure. Ask your doctor for an International Certificate of Vaccination (or 'the yellow booklet'), which will list all the vaccinations you've received. This is mandatory for countries that require proof of yellow-fever vaccination upon entry, but it's a good idea to carry it wherever you travel.

Bring medications in their original, clearly labelled containers. A signed and dated letter from your physician describing your medical conditions and medications, including generic names, is also a good idea. If carrying syringes or needles, be sure to have a physician's letter documenting their medical necessity.

INSURANCE

If your current health insurance doesn't cover you for medical expenses incurred overseas, you should think about getting extra insurance – check out www.lonelyplanet.com for more information. Find out in advance if your insurance plan will make payments directly to providers or reimburse you at a later date for overseas health expenditures. (In many countries doctors expect payment in cash.)

RECOMMENDED VACCINATIONS

NZ has no vaccination requirements for any traveller. The World Health Organization recommends that all travellers should be covered for diphtheria, tetanus, measles, mumps, rubella, chickenpox and polio, as well as hepatitis B, regardless of their destination. Planning to travel abroad is an ideal time to ensure that all routine vaccination cover is complete. The consequences of these diseases can be severe and while NZ has high levels of childhood vaccination coverage, outbreaks of these diseases do occur.

INTERNET RESOURCES

You'll find that there's a wealth of travel health advice available on the internet. For further information on health, **Lonely Planet** (www.lonelyplanet.com) is a good place to start. The **World Health Organization** (www.who.int/ith/) publishes an excellent book called *International Travel and Health,* which is revised annually and is available online at no cost. Another good website of general interest is **MD Travel Health** (www.mdtravelhealth.com), which provides complete travel health recommendations for every country and is updated daily.

IN TRANSIT

DEEP VEIN THROMBOSIS (DVT)

Blood clots may form in the legs during plane flights, chiefly because of a prolonged period of immobility. The longer the flight, the greater the risk. The chief symptom of deep vein thrombosis (DVT) is swelling or pain of the foot, ankle or calf, usually – but not always – on just one side. When a blood clot travels to the lungs, it may result in chest pain and difficulty breathing. Travellers with any of these symptoms should seek medical attention immediately.

To prevent the development of DVT on long flights, you should walk about the cabin, perform compressions of the leg muscles (ie flex the leg muscles while sitting), drink plenty of fluids and avoid alcohol and tobacco.

JET LAG & MOTION SICKNESS

Jet lag is common when crossing more than five time zones, resulting in insomnia, fatigue, malaise and/or nausea. To avoid the effects of jet lag, try drinking plenty of nonalcoholic fluids and eating light meals. Upon arrival at your destination, get exposure to natural sunlight and readjust your schedule (for meals, sleep etc) as soon as possible.

Antihistamines such as dimenhydrinate (Dramamine) and meclizine (Antivert, Bonine) are usually the preferred choice for treating motion sickness. Their main side effect is drowsiness. A herbal alternative is ginger, which works like a charm for some people.

IN NEW ZEALAND

AVAILABILITY & COST OF HEALTH CARE

Health insurance is essential for all travellers. While health care in NZ is of a high standard and not overly expensive by international standards, considerable costs can be built up and repatriation can be extremely expensive. See p445 for insurance information.

Health Care in New Zealand

NZ does not have a government-funded system of public hospitals. All travellers are, however, covered for medical care resulting from accidents that occur while in NZ (eg motor-vehicle accidents, adventure-activity accidents) by the Accident Compensation Corporation (ACC). Costs incurred by treatment of a medical illness that occurs while in NZ will only be covered by travel insurance. For more details see www.moh.govt.nz and www.acc.co.nz.

NZ has excellent specialised public health facilities for women and children in the major centres. No specific health concerns exist for women but greater care for children is recommended to avoid environmental hazards such as heat, sunburn, cold and marine hazards.

The 24-hour, free-call **Healthline** (☎ 0800 611 116) offers health advice throughout NZ.

Self-care in New Zealand

In NZ it is possible to find yourself in a remote location where, in the event of a serious accident or illness, there may well be a significant delay in emergency services getting to you. This is usually the result of weather and rugged terrain, particularly on the South Island. Therefore, an increased level of self-reliance and preparation is essential. Consider taking a wilderness first-aid course (such as the one from the Wilderness Medicine Institute). In addition, you should carry a comprehensive first-aid kit that is appropriate for the activities planned. To be really safe, ensure that you

have adequate means of communication – NZ has extensive mobile-phone coverage, but additional radio communication equipment is important for remote areas, and can usually be hired from Department of Conservation visitor centres in popular tramping areas.

Pharmaceutical Supplies

Over-the-counter medications are widely available in NZ through private chemists. These include painkillers, antihistamines for allergies, and skin care products.

Some medications that are available over the counter in other countries are only available by a prescription obtained from a general practitioner. These include the oral contraceptive pill, most medications for asthma and all antibiotics. If you take a medication on a regular basis, bring an adequate supply and ensure you have details of the generic name, as brand names differ between countries. The majority of medications in use outside of the region are available.

INFECTIOUS DISEASES
Amoebic Meningitis

There is a small risk of developing amoebic meningitis as a result of bathing or swimming in geothermal pools in NZ – mostly in regions such as Rotorua and Taupo. In such pools, keeping the head above water to prevent movement of the organism up the nasal passage reduces the risk (which is pretty low to start with). Symptoms usually start three to seven days after swimming in a geothermal pool and early symptoms of this serious disease include headache, fever and vomiting. Urgent medical care is essential to differentiate the disease from other causes of meningitis and for appropriate treatment.

Giardiasis

The giardia parasite is widespread in the waterways of NZ. Drinking untreated water from streams and lakes is not recommended. Using water filters and boiling or treating water with iodine are effective ways of preventing the disease. Symptoms consist of intermittent bad-smelling diarrhoea, abdominal bloating and wind. Effective treatment is available (tinidazole or metronidazole).

Hepatitis C

This disease is a growing problem among intravenous drug users. Blood-transfusion services fully screen all blood before use.

HIV

The country's HIV rates have stabilised after major media campaigns, and levels are similar to other Western countries. Clean needles and syringes are widely available.

Meningococcal Disease

This occurs worldwide and is a risk with prolonged dormitory-style accommodation. A vaccine exists for some types of the disease (meningococcal A, C, Y and W).

Sexually Transmitted Diseases (STDs)

In NZ, STDs (including herpes, gonorrhoea and chlamydia) occur at rates similar to most Western countries. The most common symptoms are pain on passing urine and a discharge. Infection can be present without symptoms, so seek medical screening after any unprotected sex with a new partner. Sexual health clinics are run as part of major hospitals.

TRAVELLER'S DIARRHOEA

If you develop diarrhoea, be sure to drink plenty of fluids, preferably an oral rehydration solution containing lots of salt and sugar. A few loose stools don't require treatment but if you start having more than four or five stools a day, you should start taking an antibiotic (usually a quinolone drug) and an antidiarrhoeal agent (such as loperamide). If diarrhoea is bloody, persists for more than 72 hours and/or is accompanied by fever, shaking chills or severe abdominal pain you should seek medical attention.

ENVIRONMENTAL HAZARDS

Hypothermia

This is a significant risk, especially during the winter months or year-round in the mountains of the North Island and all of the South Island. Mountain ranges and/or strong winds produce a high chill factor which can result in hypothermia, even in moderately cool temperatures. Early signs include the inability to perform fine movements (such as doing up buttons), shivering and a bad case of the 'umbles' (fumbles, mumbles, grumbles, stumbles). The key elements of treatment are changing the environment to one where heat loss is minimised, changing out of any wet clothing, adding dry clothes with wind- and waterproof layers, adding insulation and providing fuel (water and carbohydrate) to allow shivering to build the internal temperature. In severe hypothermia, shivering actually stops; this is a medical emergency requiring rapid evacuation in addition to the above measures.

Spider Bites

NZ has two poisonous spiders, the native katipo (not very poisonous and uncommon to the point of being endangered) and the introduced (thanks, Australia) white-tailed spider (also uncommon). White-tailed spider bites have been known to cause ulcers that are very difficult to heal. Clean the wound thoroughly and seek medical assistance if an ulcer develops.

Surf Beaches & Drowning

NZ has exceptional surf beaches, particularly on the western, southern and eastern coasts. The power of the surf can fluctuate as a result of the varying slope of the seabed at many beaches. Check with local surf life-saving organisations before entering the surf and be aware of your own limitations and expertise.

Ultraviolet Light Exposure

NZ has one of the highest rates of skin cancer in the world, so you should monitor UV exposure closely. UV exposure is greatest between 10am and 4pm – avoid skin exposure during these times. Always use SPF30+ sunscreen, making sure you apply it 30 minutes before exposure and that you reapply regularly to minimise sun damage.

Water

Tap water is universally safe in NZ. Increasing numbers of streams, rivers and lakes, however, are being contaminated by bugs that cause diarrhoea, making water purification when tramping essential. The simplest way of purifying water is to boil it thoroughly. You should also consider purchasing a water filter. It's very important when buying a filter to read the specifications so that you know exactly what it removes from the water and what it doesn't. Simple filtering will not remove all dangerous organisms, so if you cannot boil water it should be treated chemically. Chlorine tablets will kill many pathogens, but not parasites such as giardia or amoebic cysts. Iodine is more effective in purifying water. Follow the directions carefully and remember that too much iodine can be harmful.

HEALTH

Language

New Zealand has two official languages: English and Maori. English is what you'll usually hear, but Maori has been making a comeback. You can use English to speak to anyone in NZ, but there are some occasions when knowing a small amount of Maori is useful, such as when visiting a *marae*, where often only Maori is spoken. Maori is also useful to know since many places in NZ have Maori names.

KIWI ENGLISH

Like the people of other English-speaking countries in the world, New Zealanders have a unique way of speaking the language. The flattening of vowels is the most distinctive feature of Kiwi pronunciation. The NZ treatment of 'fish and chips' – 'fush and chups' – is an endless source of delight for Australians in particular. On the North Island sentences often have 'eh!' attached to the end. In the far south a rolled 'r' is common, a holdover from that region's Scottish heritage – it's especially noticeable in Southland. See the Glossary on p551 for an explanation of some Kiwi English words and expressions.

A Personal Kiwi-Yankee Dictionary by Louis S Leland Jr is an often hilarious book of translations, and explains some of the quirks that distinguish Kiwi and American ways of speaking English.

MAORI

The Maori have a vividly chronicled history, recorded in songs and chants that dramatically recall the migration to NZ from Polynesian Hawaiki as well as other important events. Early missionaries were the first to record the language in a written form, and achieved this with only 15 letters of the English alphabet.

Maori is closely related to other Polynesian languages such as Hawaiian, Tahitian and Cook Islands Maori. In fact, NZ Maori and Hawaiian are quite similar, even though over 7000km separates Honolulu and Auckland.

The Maori language was never dead – it was always used in Maori ceremonies – but over time familiarity with it was definitely on the decline. Fortunately, recent years have seen a revival of interest in it, and this forms an integral part of the renaissance of *Maoritanga* (Maori culture). Many Maori people who had heard the language spoken on the *marae* for years but had not used it in their day-to-day lives, are now studying it and speaking it fluently. Maori is taught in schools throughout NZ, some TV programs and news reports are broadcast in it, and many English place names are being renamed in Maori. Even government departments have been given Maori names: for example the Inland Revenue Department is also known as Te Tari Taake (the last word is actually *take*, which means 'levy', but the department has chosen to stress the long 'a' by spelling it 'aa').

In many places, Maori have come together to provide instruction in their language and culture to young children; the idea is for them to grow up speaking both Maori and English, and to develop a familiarity with Maori tradition. It's a matter of some pride to have fluency in the language. On some *marae* only Maori can be spoken.

PRONUNCIATION

Maori is a fluid, poetic language and surprisingly easy to pronounce once you remember to split each word (some can be amazingly long) into separate syllables.

Most consonants in Maori – **h, k, m, n, p, t** and **w** – are pronounced much the same as in English. The Maori **r** is a flapped sound (not rolled) with the tongue near the front of the mouth. It's closer to the English 'l' in pronunciation.

The **ng** is pronounced as in the English words 'singing' or 'running', and can be used at the beginning of words as well as at the end. To practise, just say 'ing' over and over, then isolate the 'ng' part of it.

The **wh** is generally pronounced as a soft English 'f'. This pronunciation is used in

MAORI GEOGRAPHICAL TERMS

The following words form part of many place names in NZ:

a – of
ana – cave
ara – way, path or road
awa – river or valley
heke – descend
hiku – end; tail
hine – girl; daughter
ika – fish
iti – small
kahurangi – treasured possession; special greenstone
kai – food
kainga – village
kaka – parrot
kare – rippling
kati – shut or close
koura – crayfish
makariri – cold
manga – stream or tributary
manu – bird
maunga – mountain
moana – sea or lake
moko – tattoo
motu – island
mutu – finished; ended; over
nga – the (plural)
noa – ordinary; not *tapu*
nui – big or great
nuku – distance
o – of, place of . . .
one – beach, sand or mud
pa – fortified village
papa – large blue-grey mudstone
pipi – common edible bivalve
pohatu – stone
poto – short

pouri – sad; dark; gloomy
puke – hill
puna – spring; hole; fountain
rangi – sky; heavens
raro – north
rei – cherished possession
roa – long
roto – lake
rua – hole in the ground; two
runga – above
tahuna – beach; sandbank
tane – man
tangata – people
tapu – sacred, forbidden or taboo
tata – close to; dash against; twin islands
tawaha – entrance or opening
tawahi – the other side (of a river or lake)
te – the (singular)
tonga – south
ure – male genitals
uru – west
waha – broken
wahine – woman
wai – water
waingaro – lost; waters that disappear in certain seasons
waka – canoe
wera – burnt or warm; floating
wero – challenge
whaka. . . – to act as . . .
whanau – family
whanga – harbour, bay or inlet
whare – house
whenua – land or country
whiti – east

Knowledge of just a few such words can help you make sense of many Maori place names. For example: Waikaremoana is the Sea *(moana)* of Rippling *(kare)* Waters *(wai)*; Rotorua means the Second *(rua)* Lake *(roto)*; and Taumatawhakatangihangakoauauotamateaturipukakapikimaunga-horonukupokaiwhenuakitanatahu means. . . well, perhaps you'd better see p392 for that translation. Some easier place names composed of words in this list:

Aramoana – Sea *(moana)* Path *(ara)*
Awaroa – Long *(roa)* River *(awa)*
Kaitangata – Eat *(kai)* People *(tangata)*
Maunganui – Great *(nui)* Mountain *(maunga)*
Opouri – Place of *(o)* Sadness *(pouri)*
Te Araroa – The *(te)* Long *(roa)* Path *(ara)*

Te Puke – The *(te)* Hill *(puke)*
Urewera – Burnt *(wera)* Penis *(ure)*
Waimakariri – Cold *(makariri)* Water *(wai)*
Wainui – Great *(nui)* Waters *(wai)*
Whakatane – To Act *(whaka)* as a Man *(tane)*
Whangarei – Cherished *(rei)* Harbour *(whanga)*

(Note that the adjective comes after the noun in Maori constructions. Thus 'cold water' is *wai makariri* not *makariri wai*.)

many place names in NZ, such as Whakatane, Whangaroa and Whakapapa (all pronounced as if they begin with a soft 'f'). There is some local variation: in the region around the Whanganui River, for example, the **wh** is pronounced as in the English words 'when' and 'why'.

The correct pronunciation of the vowels is very important. The examples below are a rough guideline – it helps to listen carefully to someone who speaks the language well. Each vowel has both a long and a short sound with long vowels often denoted by a macron (a line over the letter) or a double vowel. We have not indicated long/short vowel forms in this book.

VOWELS

a	as in 'large', with no 'r' sound
e	as in 'get'
i	as in 'marine'
o	as in 'pork'
u	as the 'oo' in 'moon'

VOWEL COMBINATIONS

ae, ai	as the 'y' in 'sky'
ao, au	as the 'ow' in 'how'
ea	as in 'bear'
ei	as in 'vein'
eo	as 'eh-oh'
eu	as 'eh-oo'
ia	as in the name 'Ian'
ie	as the 'ye' in 'yet'
io	as the 'ye o' in 'ye old'
iu	as the 'ue' in 'cue'
oa	as in 'roar'
oe	as in 'toe'
oi	as in 'toil'
ou	as the 'ow' in 'how'
ua	as the 'ewe' in 'fewer'

Each syllable ends in a vowel and there is never more than one vowel in a syllable. There are no silent letters.

There are many Maori phrasebooks, grammar books and Maori–English dic-tionaries if you want to take a closer look at the language. The *Collins Maori Phrase Book* by Patricia Tauroa is an ideal book for starting to speak the language, with sections on every-day conversation and using the language in a cultural context. Lonely Planet's *South Pacific Phrasebook* has a section on the Maori language and several other Pacific languages that you may hear spoken around Wellington or South Auckland.

Other good references include the *English–Maori Maori–English Dictionary* by Bruce Biggs, and the *Reed Dictionary of Modern Maori* by PM Ryan, which is one of the most authoritative.

Learning a few basic greetings will enrich your travels, especially if you plan to go onto a *marae*.

GREETINGS & SMALL TALK

Maori greetings are finding increased popularity; don't be surprised if you're greeted with *Kia ora*.

Haere mai!	Welcome!
Kia ora.	Hello./Good luck./ Good health.
Tena koe.	Hello. (to one person)
Tena korua.	Hello. (to two people)
Tena koutou.	Hello. (to three or more people)
E noho ra.	Goodbye. (to person staying)
Haere ra.	Goodbye. (to person leaving)

Kei te pehea koe?
How are you? (to one person)
Kei te pehea korua?
How are you? (to two people)
Kei te pehea koutou?
How are you? (to three or more)
Kei te pai.
Very well, thanks./That's fine.

Glossary

This glossary is a list of abbreviations, 'Kiwi English', Maori, and slang terms and phrases you may come across in New Zealand. Also see the Maori Geographical Terms boxed text (p449) in the Language chapter for Maori words that pop up again and again in NZ place names.

AA – New Zealand's Automobile Association; provides road information and roadside assistance
across the ditch – referring to Australia, across the Tasman Sea
afghan – popular homemade chocolate biscuit (origin of recipe unknown, but unlikely to be Afghanistan)
All Blacks – NZ's revered national rugby union team (the name comes from 'All Backs', which is what the press called the NZ rugby team on an early visit to England); this moniker has started a trend for many national sporting teams to be similarly nicknamed (including the Tall Blacks for the basketball team, the Black Caps for the cricket team and, briefly before being dropped, the Black Cocks for the badminton team!)
ANZAC – Australia and New Zealand Army Corps
Aoraki – Maori name for Mt Cook, meaning 'Cloud Piercer'
Aotearoa – Maori name for NZ, most often translated as 'Land of the Long White Cloud'
ariki – chief
aroha – love
atua – spirits or gods
awa – river

B&B – 'bed and breakfast' accommodation
bach – holiday home, usually a wooden cottage (pronounced 'batch'); see also *crib*
Barrier, the – local name for Great Barrier Island in the Hauraki Gulf
BBH – Budget Backpacker Hostels; a popular hostelry affiliation
Beehive – Parliament House in Wellington, so-called because of its distinctive shape
black-water rafting – rafting or tubing underground in a cave or *tomo*
blokarting – sand sailing
bogan – see *Westie*
boozer – public bar
bro – literally 'brother'; usually meaning mate, as in 'just off to see the *bros*'
BYO – 'bring your own' (usually applies to alcohol at a restaurant or cafe)
BYOW – 'bring your own wine', implying you can't bring beer or any other alcoholic beverages

cervena – farmed deer
chardy – chardonnay
chillie bin – cooler; esky; large insulated box for keeping food and drinks cold
choice/chur – fantastic; great
ciggies – cigarettes
cuzzie, cuz – cousin; relative or mate, most often used by Maori to refer to fellow Maori; see also *bro*
cuzzie bro – an emphasised version of both *cuzzie* and *bro*

dairy – small corner store that sells milk, bread, newspapers, ice cream and pretty much everything else
daggy – uncool; from the dags that hang off sheep's bottoms
DB&B – 'dinner, bed and breakfast' accommodation
DOC – Department of Conservation (or *Te Papa Atawhai*); government department that administers national parks and thus all tracks and huts
domain – open grassed area in a town or city, often the focus of recreational activities or civic amenities such as gardens, picnic areas and bowling clubs (and sometimes camping grounds)
Dorkland – derogatory reference to the big city
dropkick – a certain method of kicking a rugby ball; a personal insult

eh – roughly translates as 'don't you agree?' and is commonly added to the end of many *Kiwi* sentences, usually followed by *bro* (as in *'Choice jandals, eh bro?'*)

farmstay – accommodation on a *Kiwi* farm where you're encouraged to join in the typical day-to-day activities
football – rugby, either union or league; occasionally soccer
freezing works – slaughterhouse or abattoir for sheep and/or cattle

Godzone – New Zealand (from Richard Seddon who referred to NZ as 'God's own country')
good as gold, good as – very good; no problem
Great Walks – a set of nine popular tramping tracks within NZ
greenstone – jade; *pounamu*
gumboots – rubber boots or Wellingtons; originated from diggers on the gum-fields

haka – any dance, but usually refers to the traditional challenge; war dance
hakari – feast
handle – beer glass with a handle

hangi – oven made by digging a hole and steaming food in baskets over embers in the hole; a feast of Maori food

hapu – subtribe or smaller tribal grouping

hard case – hilarious, unusual or strong-willed character

Hawaiki – Polynesian homeland from where the Maori tribes migrated by canoe (probably Ra'iatea in the Society Islands); also a name for the Afterworld

hei tiki – carved, stylised human figure worn around the neck representing the first human and supposed to bring good luck; also called a *tiki*

hikoi – march, walk, sometimes a protest march or pilgrimage

hoa – friend; usually pronounced 'e hoa'

hokey pokey – delicious variety of vanilla ice cream with butterscotch chips

hoki – type of fish common in fish and chip shops

homestay – accommodation in a family house where you're treated as one of the family

hongi – Maori greeting; the pressing of foreheads and noses, and sharing of life breath

hui – gathering; meeting

Interislander – large ferries crossing Cook Strait between Wellington and Picton

i-SITE – information centre

'Is it what!' – strong affirmation or agreement; 'Yes, isn't it!'

Islander – Pacific Islander; see also *'Nesian, PI* and *Poly*

iwi – large tribal grouping with common lineage back to the original migration from *Hawaiki;* people; tribe

JAFA – Just Another Fucking Aucklander

jandals – a contraction of Japanese sandals; flip-flops; thongs; usually rubber footwear

jersey – jumper, usually woollen; the shirt worn by rugby players

jiff – short measurement of time (as in 'I'll be back in a *jiff*'); see also *two ticks*

judder bars – bumps in the road to make you drive slowly; speed humps

K Rd – Karangahape Rd in Auckland

ka kite (ano) – see you again; goodbye

ka pai – good; excellent

kai – food; almost any word with *kai* in it has a connection with food

kainga – village; pre-European unfortified Maori village

kapa haka – traditional Maori group singing and dancing

karakia – prayer, incantation

kaumatua – highly respected members of a tribe; the people you would ask for permission to enter a *marae*

kauri – native pine

kina – sea urchins, a Maori delicacy

Kiwi – A New Zealander; an adjective to mean anything relating to NZ

kiwi – the flightless, nocturnal brown bird with a long beak that is the national symbol

Kiwiana – the collective term for anything uniquely connected to NZ life and culture, especially from years gone by, and likely to bring on waves of nostalgia in any expat *Kiwi* (examples include *hokey pokey, jandals* and *pavlova*)

kiwifruit – small, succulent fruit with fuzzy brown skin and juicy green flesh; a Chinese gooseberry; never called a *kiwi*

koha – donation

kohanga reo – schools where Maori language and culture are at the forefront of the education process; also called language nest schools

korero – to talk

kumara – Polynesian sweet potato, a Maori staple food

kunekune – type of wild pig introduced by Chinese gold diggers in the 19th century

Kupe – early Polynesian navigator from *Hawaiki,* credited with the discovery of the islands that are now NZ

L&P – Lemon & Paeroa; lemon-flavoured fizzy drink

laters – 'see you later'

league – rugby league football

lounge bar – more upmarket bar than a public bar; called a 'ladies bar' in some countries

mana – spiritual quality of a person or object; prestige; authority of a chief or priest

manaia – traditional carving design; literally means 'bird-headed man'

'Mandel, the – the Coromandel Peninsula

manuhiri – visitor; guest

Maori – indigenous people of NZ

Maoritanga – Maori culture

marae – literally refers to the sacred ground in front of the Maori meeting house, more commonly used to refer to the entire complex of buildings

marakihau – sea monster

Maui – a figure in Maori (Polynesian) mythology

maunga – mountain

mauri – life force/principle

mere – a *patu* made of *greenstone*

metal/metalled road – gravel (unsealed) road

MMP – Mixed Member Proportional; the electoral system used in NZ and Germany; a form of proportional voting

moa – large, extinct flightless bird

moe – sleep

moko – tattoo; usually refers to facial tattoos

Moriori – isolated Polynesian group, inhabitants of the Chatham Islands

motorway – freeway or expressway

marnis – something or someone shameful

munted – damaged, destroyed

munter – see *Westie*

naiad – rigid-hull inflatable boat (used for dolphin swimming, whale watching etc)

'Naki, the – Taranaki

'Nesian – Pacific Islander; see also *Islander*, *PI* and *Poly*

nga – the (plural); see also *te*

ngai/ngati – literally, 'the people of' or 'the descendants of'; tribe

NZ – the universal term for New Zealand; pronounced 'en zed'

OE – Overseas Experience; a working holiday abroad, traditionally to the UK (the young *Kiwi's* near-mandatory 'tour of duty')

pa – fortified Maori village, usually on a hilltop

Pacific Rim – term used to describe modern NZ cuisine; cuisine with an innovative use of local produce, especially seafood, with imported styles

Pakeha – Maori for a white or European person

papa – large blue-grey mudstones; the word comes from the Maori for Earth Mother

parapenting – paragliding

Pasifika – Pacific Island culture

patch – gang logo worn on clothing

patu – flat war club made of wood, bone or greenstone

paua – abalone; tough shellfish pounded, minced, then made into patties (fritters), which are available in almost every NZ fish-and-chip shop; the beautiful, iridescent *paua* shell is often used in decoration and jewellery

pavlova – meringue cake, usually topped with cream and *kiwifruit;* the quintessential *Kiwi* dessert

PI – Pacific Islander; see also *Islander*, *Poly* and *'Nesian*

pig islander – derogatory term used by a person from one island for someone from the other island

pillocking – 'surfing' across mud flats on a rubbish-bin lid

pipi – common edible bivalve

piss – urine; urinate; alcohol, as in 'get on the piss'

poi – ball of woven flax

poi dance – women's formation dance that involves singing and manipulating a *poi*

polly – politician

Poly – Pacific Islander; see also *Islander*, *PI* and *'Nesian*

pou – wooden post, sometimes carved

ponga – the *silver fern;* called a bungy (pronounced 'bungee', with a soft 'g', in parts of the South Island)

pounamu – Maori name for *greenstone*

powhiri – traditional Maori welcome onto a *marae*

quad bikes – four-wheel farm bikes

rap jump – face-down abseil

'rattle your dags' – move quickly; from the dags that hang off sheep's bottoms

raupo – bulrush

Remuera tractor – 4WD, after wealthy suburbanites pointlessly driving them

Rheiny – affectionate term for Rheineck beer

rigger – a refillable half-gallon plastic bottle for holding draught beer

rip – dangerously strong current running away from the shore at a beach

Roaring Forties – the ocean between 40° and 50° south, known for very strong winds

Rotovegas – derogatory term relating to the touristy aspects of Rotorua

rumble – see *scrap*

sav – sauvignon blanc

scrap – a fight

section – small block of land

silver fern – the symbol worn by the *All Blacks* and other national sportsfolk on their jerseys, representative of the underside of a *ponga* leaf; the national netball team is called the Silver Ferns

Steinie – affectionate term for Steinlager beer

superette – grocery store or small supermarket

sweet, sweet as – all-purpose term like *choice;* fantastic, great

taiaha – spear

tall poppy syndrome – NZ tradition of diminishing successful people, as in 'tall poppies get their heads chopped off'

Tamaki Makaurau – Maori name for Auckland

tane – man

tangata – people

tangata whenua – people of the land; local people

taniwha – awe-inspiring water spirit

taonga – something of great value; a treasure

tapu – a strong force in Maori life, with numerous meanings; in its simplest form it means sacred, forbidden, taboo

tatts – tattoos, often of a gang nature; as opposed to *moko*

tauihu – canoe prow

te – the (singular); see also *nga*

Te Papa – literally 'our place', the national museum in Wellington

Te Papa Atawhai – Maori name for *DOC*

te reo – literally 'the language'; the Maori language

tiki – short for *hei tiki*

tiki tour – scenic tour; roundabout way

toheroa – large clam

tohunga – priest; wizard; general expert

toi toi – tall native grass

tomo – hole; entrance to a cave

tramp – bushwalk; trek; hike

tua tua – type of shellfish

tuatara – prehistoric reptile dating back to the age of dinosaurs

tui – native parson bird
tukutuku – Maori wall panels in *marae* and churches
tuna – eel
two ticks – short measurement of time (as in 'I'll be there in *two ticks*'); see also *jiff*

umu – earth oven
urupa – burial site

varsity – university

wahine – woman
wai – water
waiata – song
Waikikamukau – mythical NZ town, far from anywhere (and pronounced along the lines of 'Why-kick-a-moo-cow')
wairua – spirit
Waitangi – short way of referring to the Treaty of Waitangi
waka – canoe
Warriors – NZ's popular rugby league club, affiliated with Australia's NRL

Watties – the NZ food and canning giant; NZ's answer to Heinz (until Heinz took over the company)
Wellywood – Wellington, because of its thriving film industry
Westie – from West Auckland; rough-edged fellow, probably wearing a black T-shirt, drinking beer and listening to AC/DC; see also *bogan, munter*
whakairo rakau – Maori woodcarving
whakapapa – genealogy
whanau – family
where – house
wharepuni – sleeping house
whare runanga – meeting house
whare whakairo – carved meeting house
whenua – land
whitebait – tiny translucent fish that is scooped up in nets and eaten whole (head, eyes and all!) or made into patties
wopwops – remote; 'out in the *wopwops*' is out in the middle of nowhere

zorbing – rolling down a hill inside an inflatable plastic ball

The Authors

BRETT ATKINSON
Coordinating Author

Rotorua-born, but now a proud Aucklander, Brett has been discovering the North Island for more than 40 years. Early memories include caravanning with his family at the Bay of Islands and Mt Maunganui, but now you're more likely to find him exploring the cafes of Wellington and the vineyards of Martinborough or Hawke's Bay with his wife Carol. Brett has contributed to Lonely Planet guidebooks covering four of the planet's continents, and has covered more than 40 countries as a freelance travel writer. See www. brett-atkinson.net for his latest work, and www.viewauckland.co.nz for his reviews of the bars and restaurants of his hometown.

SARAH BENNETT
The East Coast, Wellington Region

Raised among the cherry trees of Marlborough, Sarah migrated to Wellington at 16 and has lived there ever since, except for various travels and a stint in London working in Lonely Planet's UK office. An arguably flawed guidebook writer due to eternal optimism and irrepressible nationalism ('New Zealand... what's not to like?'), she has done her best to find fault wherever she can, especially in regard to ill-chosen garnish and inadequate beer selection. Sarah's other books are *The Best of Wellington*, *Let's Go Camping* and *The New Zealand Tramper's Handbook*, all of which she co-authored with her husband, Lee Slater.

PETER DRAGICEVICH
The Culture, Auckland Region, Northland & the Bay of Islands, Coromandel Region, Taupo & the Central Plateau

After nearly a decade working for off-shore publishing companies, Peter's life has come full circle, returning to West Auckland where he was raised. As managing editor of Auckland-based *Express* newspaper he spent much of the 90s writing about the local arts, club and bar scene. He has co-authored more than 17 books for Lonely Planet.

LONELY PLANET AUTHORS

Why is our travel information the best in the world? It's simple: our authors are passionate, dedicated travellers. They don't take freebies in exchange for positive coverage so you can be sure the advice you're given is impartial. They travel widely to all the popular spots, and off the beaten track. They don't research using just the internet or phone. They discover new places not included in any other guidebook. They personally visit thousands of hotels, restaurants, palaces, trails, galleries, temples and more. They speak with dozens of locals every day to make sure you get the kind of insider knowledge only a local could tell you. They take pride in getting all the details right, and in telling it how it is. Think you can do it? Find out how at **lonelyplanet.com**.

CHARLES RAWLINGS-WAY

Waikato & the King Country, Taranaki, Whanganui & Palmerston North, Rotorua & the Bay of Plenty

English by birth, Australian by chance, All Blacks fan by choice: Charles considers himself a worldly lad, but his early understanding of Aotearoa was less than comprehensive. He realised there was more to NZ when a wandering uncle returned with a faux-jade *tiki* in 1981. He wore it with pride until he saw the NZ cricket team's beige uniforms in 1982... Mt Taranaki's summit, Raglan's breaks and Whanganui's charm have helped him forgive: he's once again smitten with the country's landscapes, locals, and determination to sculpt its own political and indigenous destiny. Roll on Rugby World Cup 2011!

CONTRIBUTING AUTHORS

Professor James Belich wrote the History chapter (p27). James is one of NZ's pre-eminent historians and the award-winning author of *The New Zealand Wars, Making Peoples* and *Paradise Reforged*. He has also worked in TV – *New Zealand Wars* was screened in NZ in 1998.

Tony Horwitz wrote the Captain James Cook boxed text (p30) in the History chapter. Tony is a Pulitzer-winning reporter and nonfiction author. His fascination with James Cook, and with travel, took him around NZ, Australia and the Pacific while researching *Blue Latitudes* (alternatively titled *Into the Blue*), part biography of Cook and part travelogue.

John Huria (Ngai Tahu, Muaupoko) wrote the Maori Culture chapter (p51). John has an editorial, research and writing background with a focus on Maori culture. He was senior editor for Maori publishing company Huia (NZ) and now runs an editorial and publishing services company, Ahi Text Solutions Ltd (www.ahitextsolutions.co.nz).

Lauraine Jacobs wrote the Food & Drink chapter (p58). Lauraine is an award-winning food writer, and food editor of *Cuisine* magazine. Passionate about NZ's wine and food, she travels the country extensively in her quest to seek out the best culinary experiences.

Josh Kronfeld wrote the Surfing in New Zealand boxed text (p82) in the Active New Zealand chapter. Josh is an ex–All Black flanker, whose passion for surfing NZ's beaches is legendary and who found travelling for rugby a way to surf other great breaks around the world.

Dr David Millar wrote the Health chapter (p445). David is a travel-medicine specialist, diving doctor and lecturer in wilderness medicine.

Gareth Shute wrote the Music section of the Culture chapter (p47). Gareth is the author of four books, including *Hip Hop Music in Aotearoa* and *NZ Rock 1987-2007*. He is also a musician and has toured the UK, Europe and Australia as a member of The Ruby Suns. He now plays in The Conjurors, The Investigations and The Cosbys.

Nandor Tanczos wrote the Environmental Issues in Aotearoa New Zealand boxed text (p66). NZ's first Rastafarian Member of Parliament (NZ Greens Party), and the first to enter parliament in dreadlocks and a hemp suit, he was also the Greens' spokesperson on constitutional issues and the environment from 1999 to 2008.

Vaughan Yarwood wrote the Environment chapter (p65). Vaughan is an Auckland-based writer whose most recent book is *The History Makers: Adventures in New Zealand Biography*. Earlier work includes *The Best of New Zealand, a Collection of Essays on NZ Life and Culture by Prominent Kiwis*, which he edited, and the regional history *Between Coasts: from Kaipara to Kawau*. He has written widely for NZ and international publications and is the former associate editor of *New Zealand Geographic,* for which he continues to write.

Thanks to: Sir Ian McKellen (Sandflies boxed text, p420); Grace Hoet for her contribution to the Maori Culture chapter; and all the New Zealand regional tourism organisations, for their help with pre-research briefings.

Behind the Scenes

THIS BOOK

Lonely Planet's first New Zealand guide came out way back in 1977, when Tony Wheeler, clad in corduroy flares and wide-collared shirt, trawled the length of the island nation to research the book. More than 30 years later, this 1st-edition, stand-alone guide to NZ's North Island was researched and written by the equally snappily dressed Brett Atkinson, Sarah Bennett, Peter Dragicevich and Charles Rawlings-Way. Contributing authors include historian Professor James Belich, journo Tony Horwitz, Maori publisher John Huria, food-award judge Lauraine Jacobs, surfer Josh Kronfeld, health expert Dr David Millar, musician/author Gareth Shute, environmental activist Nandor Tanczos, and author Vaughan Yarwood. The guidebook was commissioned in Lonely Planet's Melbourne office, and produced by the following:

Commissioning Editor Errol Hunt
Coordinating Editor Chris Girdler
Coordinating Cartographer Hunor Csutoros
Coordinating Layout Designer Kerrianne Southway
Managing Editor Liz Heynes
Managing Cartographer David Connolly, Corey Hutchison
Managing Layout Designer Indra Kilfoyle

Assisting Editors Elisa Arduca, Jackey Coyle, Kate Evans, Anne Mulvaney, Alison Ridgway, Dianne Schallmeiner, Elizabeth Swan, Angela Tinson, Simon Williamson
Assisting Cartographer Alex Leung
Cover researcher Naomi Parker, lonelyplanetimages.com
Image researcher Jane Hart, lonelyplanetimages.com
Language Content Laura Crawford
Thanks to Imogen Bannister, Sarah Ewing, Lisa Knights, Daniel Moore, Susan Paterson, Averil Robertson, Suzannah Shwer, Jane Thompson, Maui Tikitiki a Taranga, Saralinda Turner, Chris Zeiher

THANKS
BRETT ATKINSON

Firstly thanks to my Mum and Dad for instilling in me a sense of exploration on our occasional summer jaunts around the North Island, even if the caravan was sometimes a tad small for all four of us. In more contemporary times, thanks to Carol as a supportive and always up-for-it partner in NZ and international travel. Thanks to Errol Hunt at Lonely Planet for his support, and to the whizzbang team of authors and inhouse Lonely Planet folk who made my coordinating role very straightforward. Final thanks to Galbraith's Ale House for sustenance after long days in front of my Apple Mac.

THE LONELY PLANET STORY

Fresh from an epic journey across Europe, Asia and Australia in 1972, Tony and Maureen Wheeler sat at their kitchen table stapling together notes. The first Lonely Planet guidebook, *Across Asia on the Cheap,* was born.

Travellers snapped up the guides. Inspired by their success, the Wheelers began publishing books to Southeast Asia, India and beyond. Demand was prodigious, and the Wheelers expanded the business rapidly to keep up. Over the years, Lonely Planet extended its coverage to every country and into the virtual world via lonelyplanet.com and the Thorn Tree message board.

As Lonely Planet became a globally loved brand, Tony and Maureen received several offers for the company. But it wasn't until 2007 that they found a partner whom they trusted to remain true to the company's principles of travelling widely, treading lightly and giving sustainably. In October of that year, BBC Worldwide acquired a 75% share in the company, pledging to uphold Lonely Planet's commitment to independent travel, trustworthy advice and editorial independence.

Today, Lonely Planet has offices in Melbourne, London and Oakland, with over 500 staff members and 300 authors. Tony and Maureen are still actively involved with Lonely Planet. They're traveling more often than ever, and they're devoting their spare time to charitable projects. And the company is still driven by the philosophy of *Across Asia on the Cheap*: 'All you've got to do is decide to go and the hardest part is over. So go!'

SEND US YOUR FEEDBACK

We love to hear from travellers – your comments keep us on our toes and help make our books better. Our well-travelled team reads every word on what you loved or loathed about this book. Although we cannot reply individually to postal submissions, we always guarantee that your feedback goes straight to the appropriate authors, in time for the next edition. Each person who sends us information is thanked in the next edition and the most useful submissions are rewarded with a free book.

To send us your updates – and find out about Lonely Planet events, newsletters and travelnews–visitouraward-winningwebsite: **lonelyplanet.com/contact**.

Note: we may edit, reproduce and incorporate your comments in Lonely Planet products such as guidebooks, websites and digital products, so let us know if you don't want your comments reproduced or your name acknowledged. For a copy of our privacy policy visit lonelyplanet.com/privacy.

SARAH BENNETT

First up, thanks to helpful pals Betzy Iannuzzi, Bonita Marshall, Jenny Allan, Reece Miller, Trecia Smith, Maria Grau, Fritz Kuckuck, Tricia and Stewart Macpherson, the Wellington posse, and the Bennett clan. Thanks, too, to the many i-SITE and RTO people who shared their time and insight, especially Tina Narsey, Rebecca Mitchell, Chris Barber, Gaylene Sanderson, Astrid Fisher, Amy Chandler, Rachael Brown, Tracy Johnston, Brent Matthews, Vicky Roebuck, Barbara Hyde, and winery experts Lucy Chambers and Julia Hill. I wish to acknowledge the contribution of all the friendly folks who helped me out on the road, and my fellow authors and editors who supported me through the ether. As ever, my deepest gratitude to Lee – you make every day a flight in a microlight.

PETER DRAGICEVICH

If I were to thank everyone who helped me eat and drink my way around the upper North Island it would be a very long list indeed. Particular thanks must go to Phillippa Steel and Scott Judson, Sally Burgess, Bob Dragicevich, Jack Dragicevich, Shenita and Carlos Palmer, Alison Curtis, Miranda Playfair, Mark and Amy Todd, Adrienne and Ben Preston, Tania Wong, Lesley Mensah and Tracey Hand. The i-SITE staff in Paihia, Whangarei, Coromandel Town, Tairua, Turangi and Ohakune are among the nicest in the country. And special thanks to the excellent New Zealand authors – particularly Scott for accompanying me to Matakana and snapping my On the Road shot – you're all bloody brilliant.

CHARLES RAWLINGS-WAY

Thanks to the many generous, knowledgable and quietly self-assured Kiwis I met on the road, especially the staff at the Palmerston North, Matamata, Waitomo Caves and New Plymouth i-SITEs who flew through my questions with the greatest of ease. Thanks to Errol Hunt for signing me up, and the in-house Lonely Planet staff who schmoozed this book through production. Humongous gratitude to my tireless, witty and professional co-authors – Sarah, Peter, Brett and Scott – who infused this book with local low-down. Thanks also to Eloise Jones for the buttered date loaf and tea. Most of all, thank you Meg and Ione, my two (very patient) road-trippin' sweethearts.

OUR READERS

Many thanks to the travellers who used the last edition and wrote to us with helpful hints, useful advice and interesting anecdotes:

A Elisabeth Nordeng Aanes, John Adam, Nikki Annand **B** Heike Baars, Selina Barlet, Rebecca Barnshaw, Bridget Beal, Neil Beaumont, Chris Beek, Nicolas Berger, Insa Beuse, Ben Blee, Jason Borthwick, Judy Bounds, Euan Brown, Catherine Bruckner, Anna Bucholz, Wilco Burghout, Lee Burrows **C** Geoff Caflisch, Sue Cebulko, Laura Claassen, Tiere Clynich, Brendan Connolly, Nicola Coombe, Georgie Curtis, Jonathan Cutler **D** Matthew Dalton, Stuart & Pamela Davis, Annelies De Bruijne, Jan Dependahl, Jo Drew, Tarne Duffield, Angela Dunlop, Alison Dye **E** Alec Edwards, Bernadette Ekberg, Rowan Enright, Jo Evans **F** Robin Falvey, Mutiara Förster, Nick Fowler **G** Franck Gally, Juliane Gansert, Eleanor Gee, Tanya Genthe, Bob Gilchrist, Katherine Golding, Sharine Gordon, Ed Groves, Peter Gush, Stuart Guy **H** Steven Hankey, Bernie Healy, Glenda Heywood, Jo Hibbert, Dave Hill, Leah Holloway, Libby Howard-Blood, Barbara Huijgen **I** Jaki Ilbery **K** Robert Kennedy, Huia Kirk, Rolf Knütter **L** Barry Landesman, Steve Lavezzo, Carol Lee, Robert Levy, Ann Lewis, Brian & Lorna Lewis, Beate Lippold **M** Michael MacBroom, Jerome Magisson, John Mandeville, Hanna Manski, Jane Manson, Stephen Marais, Lou McCarthy, Gail

McConnell, Gillian McIlroy, Jan McVerry, Lisa Moeller, Chris Monson, Melanie Morcom, Bruce Morris, Hugh & Eileen Morton, Alastair Moulton **N** Patrick Näf, Greg Napp, Surasak Netraprajag, Nick Newman, David Nicola, Alexandra Nisbeck, Ronald Noordstrand, Graeme Nye **O** Andrea O'Connor, Michael Ortiz, Jenny Owen, Maurice Owen **P** Benoît Panizzon, Natasha Parker-Coughlin, Marie Parton, Lindsay Petrie, Daniela Petroni, Rochelle Pincini, Katerina Poddana, Neville Pulver, Kerrie Purrington **R** Barbara Rausch, Jim Revell, John Rieley, Christine Rikihana, Valentina Baez Rizzi, Jeffrey Robinson, Louise Rothols, Alba Rull, Jenna Russell **S** Kane Salanoa, Nathan Sandland-Jones, Miriam Schaefer, Miriam Scherpenzeel, Sybil Schlesinger, Lukas Schomann, Armand Schumer, Jonathan Sims, Frank Sinclair, Ray Sinniger, Maren Skrinjar, Afke Smolders, Raina Reva Snyder, Julie Stapleton, Sue Stone, Mona Strandberg, Anne Street **T** David Taylor, Sarah Taylor, Steve Taylor, Monique Teggelove, Britta Thiel, Cathelijne Thiel, Petra Joho Thomma, Kay Toon, Steve Tritt **W** Amanda Watson, Arthur Watts, Kim Whitty, Jackie Whyte, Sven Wiechert, Hanneke Wijkamp, Lynda Willow, Carol Wilson, Tim Wilson, David Wilson-Howarth **Y** Holly Yelf, Kit Yoon **Z** Cosetta Zanobetti-Lawlor

ACKNOWLEDGMENTS

Many thanks to the following for the use of their content:

Globe on title page ©Mountain High Maps 1993 Digital Wisdom, Inc.

Index

000 Map pages
000 Photograph pages

INDEX

GreenDex

GOING GREEN

As Kermit the Frog asserts, it's not easy being green, but in tourism these days everyone wants to be 'eco'. But how can you know which businesses are legitimately ecofriendly and which are just jumping on the sustainable bandwagon?

The following listings have been selected by Lonely Planet authors because they demonstrate active sustainable-tourism policies. Some are involved in conservation or environmental education; many are owned and operated by local and indigenous operators, thus preserving local identity and culture. Some are also accredited by **Qualmark Green** (www.qualmark.co.nz) or listed by **Organic Explorer** (www.organicexplorer.co.nz).

All national parks and reserves (see the main index) and DOC–controlled areas (marked on maps) preserve native bush and fauna, and are by their very nature 'green'.

If you think we've omitted someone or you disagree with our choices, email us at talk2us@ lonelyplanet.com.au and set us straight. For more information about sustainable tourism and Lonely Planet, see www.lonelyplanet.com/responsibletravel.

MAP LEGEND

LONELY PLANET OFFICES

Australia (Head Office)
Locked Bag 1, Footscray, Victoria 3011
☎ 03 8379 8000, fax 03 8379 8111
talk2us@lonelyplanet.com.au

USA
150 Linden St, Oakland, CA 94607
☎ 510 250 6400, toll free 800 275 8555
fax 510 893 8572
info@lonelyplanet.com

UK
2nd fl, 186 City Rd,
London EC1V 2NT
☎ 020 7106 2100, fax 020 7106 2101
go@lonelyplanet.co.uk

Published by Lonely Planet Publications Pty Ltd
ABN 36 005 607 983

© Lonely Planet 2010

© photographers as indicated 2010

Cover photograph: Cathedral Cove, Coromandel Peninsula, Michael Gebicki/Lonely Planet Images. Many of the images in this guide are available for licensing from Lonely Planet Images: lonely planetimages.com.

Printed by Toppan Security Printing Pte. Ltd.
Printed in Singapore

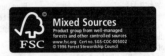

3 1170 00845 9343